Walkin' the Talk

An Anthology of African American Studies

Edited by

Bill Lyne

and

Vernon Damani Johnson

Foreword by

Adolph Reed, Jr.

Prentice
Hall

Upper Saddle River, NJ 07458

Library of Congress Cataloging-in-Publication Data
Walkin' the talk : an anthology of African American studies / edited by
Bill Lyne and Vernon D. Johnson.
    p. cm.
  Includes bibliographical references and index.
  ISBN 0-13-042016-6
    1. African Americans—Politics and government—Sources.   2. African
Americans—Social conditions—Sources.   3. African Americans—Literary collections.
4. American literature—African American authors.   5. Rhetoric—Political aspects—
United States.   6. American literature—Political aspects.   7. Politics in literature.
I. Title: Walking the talk.   II. Lyne, Bill, date   III. Johnson, Vernon Damani.

E184.6 .W35 2002
305.896′073—dc21

                                                                2002276247

Editor-in-Chief: **Leah Jewell**
Sr. Acquisition Editor: **Carrie Brandon**
Editorial Assistant: **Jennifer Migueis**
Production Liaison: **Fran Russello**
Project Manager: **Patty Donovan, Karen Berry/Pine Tree Composition**
Prepress and Manufacturing Buyer: **Sherry Lewis**
Cover Designer: **Robert Farrar-Wagner**
Cover Art: **Diane Kosup/Amana America/Photonica**
Permission Specialist: **Mary Dalton-Hoffman**
Marketing Manager: **Rachel Falk**

This book was set in 10.5/12 Goudy by Pine Tree Composition, Inc., and was printed
and bound by Courier Companies, Inc. The cover was printed by Phoenix Color Corp.

© 2003 by Pearson Education, Inc.
Upper Saddle River, New Jersey 07458

Printed in the United States of America
10 9 8 7 6 5 4 3 2 1

ISBN 0-13-042016-6

Pearson Education Ltd., *London*
Pearson Education Australia Pty, Limited, *Sydney*
Pearson Education Singapore, Pte. Ltd.
Pearson Education North Asia Ltd., *Hong Kong*
Pearson Education Canada, Ltd., *Toronto*
Pearson Educación de Mexico, S.A. de C.V.
Pearson Education—Japan, *Toyko*
Pearson Education Malaysia, Pte. Ltd.
Pearson Education, *Upper Saddle River, New Jersey*

*This book is dedicated to our parents, Vernon Johnson,
Marjorie Johnson, Henry Lyne, and Elaine Lyne,
who always walked their talk.*

Contents

Part Three—Reconstruction   219

13th, 14th, and 15th Amendments to the Constitution of the United States   220

Part Four—The Jim Crow Era   241

Part Five—Civil Rights and Black Power

Preface

The aim of this anthology is to provide a single affordable textbook that can be used for a variety of courses in African American Studies. It was invented out of necessity. In 1999, we found ourselves team teaching an introductory African American Studies course. In order to provide our students with all of the material that we wanted them to read, we had to order several expensive books and provide a packet of (mostly legal) copies. Despite the availability of an excellent array of single author introductory texts, mammoth literature anthologies, and all sorts of topical collections, we could find no single book that attempted to collect a sweep of primary texts and critical commentary that would allow us to survey the experience of Africans in America from the eighteenth century to the present. Once the class had ended, and at the suggestion of Carrie Brandon at Prentice Hall, we set out to create the anthology that would allow us to teach our course without having to cobble together bits and pieces from a variety of disciplines and centuries. The result is *Walkin' the Talk*.

The book is grounded in the idea that African American history, politics, and culture are inseparable. As much as possible, we have tried to blur disciplinary boundaries, making no attempts to categorize our selections. We hope that this allows an instructor, rather than a book, to shape the direction and scope of a course. Our primary goal has been to create a book that can provide a rich context for each of its texts. We do not attempt to present Frederick Douglass as strictly a literary author, Angela Davis as strictly a political thinker, or Langston Hughes as only a poet. Rather, we try to show how all of the writers in this anthology are contributors to the large and ongoing discussion that is African American discourse. And we hope that the book always encourages both students and instructors to recognize that this discourse doesn't end at the parlor or the classroom door, that the talk is never far from the walk. At the same time, we have tried to include a variety of discourses (such as the series of white supremacist tracts by eighteenth century philosophers) that help to illuminate the world context from which African American experiences emerge.

In selecting the texts for this anthology, we have also set out to correct what we see as a glaring omission in African American Studies. We have tried to represent and highlight the vibrant and rich tradition of African American radicalism. The dominant discourses of liberal integrationism and conservative nationalism are accounted for in most African American Studies textbooks, but African American radical and socialist thought rarely receive more than a brief mention. This attempt to be inclusive and to represent what is in fact a major tradition has led us to collect both texts by authors not usually anthologized, and not usually anthologized texts by always anthologized authors. In *Walkin' the Talk* readers will encounter the usually neglected voices of Nat Turner, A. Philip Randolph, Angela Davis, and Manning Marable. They will also find texts by W. E. B. Du Bois beyond *The Souls of Black Folk*, Langston Hughes's radical poetry, portions of Richard Wright's *White Man, Listen!*, and Amiri Baraka's extremely important but usually neglected work since 1975.

Our claims and goals are large ones, but if we have come even close to meeting them, we think this book will be useful in a variety of contexts. *Walkin' the Talk* should be ideal for interdisciplinary and introductory African American studies courses. It should also be a useful text for African American literature, history, and politics courses, especially those courses that want to create a larger context for their disciplinary discussions.

A lot of people have contributed to the making of this and deserve more than just the thanks we can offer here. We should begin by thanking the students in American Cultural Studies 204, especially Kim Morrison and Emily Thuma. The Bureau for Faculty Research at Western Washington University delivered timely funds. Christian Lee provided invaluable assistance along the way. The original readers of the proposal, Terry Kershaw, Virginia Tech; Kasey Morrison, University of Missouri–Columbia; Earl Smith, Wake Forest University; and Peter Ukpokodu, University of Kansas, all came through with important advice. We are extremely grateful for the counsel and insight of our friends and colleagues: Doug Park, Carol Guess, Donna Qualley, Adolph Reed, Jr., Bill Smith, Rick Emmerson, Christine Park, Mona Lyne, Hans von Rautenfeld, Jim Giffen, David Giffen, and June Hopkins. John Purdy and Laura Laffrado deserve special mention for their wonderful support. Ed Bereal's artistic insight and general grace have sustained us at key moments. The extremely patient and intelligent editing of Carrie Brandon is evident throughout the book. Tom DeMarco, Patty Donovan, and Karen Berry were both kind and helpful.

All thanks must always go to our families: Allison Giffen, Nicholas Lyne, Rebecca Johnson, Cedric Johnson, and Elizabeth Johnson.

Introduction

All the hip white boys scream for Bird. . . . And they sit there talking about the tortured genius of Charlie Parker. Bird would've played not a note of music if he just walked up to East Sixty-seventh Street and killed the first ten white people he saw. Not a note!

Clay, just before he is killed
in LeRoi Jones's play *Dutchman*

It is easy to forget the political beginnings of African American Studies. In the late 1960s and early 1970s, at universities such as Yale, Cornell, Howard, and San Francisco State, sit-ins, demonstrations, and student organizing were more instrumental than university administrators and faculty committees for making African American Studies a part of the curriculum. These academic programs were a byproduct of the social and political upheaval surrounding the Civil Rights and Black Power movements and thus presented a challenge to traditional academic notions of detachment and objectivity. As professors in established disciplines argued shrilly that African American Studies (and Womens Studies and Chicano Studies, etc.) was too politically engaged, too much about "empowerment" or "self-help" and not enough about "objective" scholarship, the early incarnations of African American and Black Studies tried hard to remain true to the experience of Africans in America, by making sure that there was never too much distance between the classroom and the street. Since the arrival of the first slave ships in the Americas, African American history, politics, and culture have intertwined in the story of a subjugated people, and early African American Studies programs were not just about describing that subjugation, but also about undoing it.

This anthology is driven by two premises. The first is the idea that the historical and political fate of Africans in America and African American cultural and scholarly production are inseparable. Canonized literary forms such as slave narratives, blues lyrics, social protest fiction, and twentieth-century African American poetry all grow out of the social and political dynamics of race relations in the United States. There is a call and response between those texts that have been categorized (usually by white cultural elites) as "literary," and those that have been read as strictly political or polemical. The second premise of the text is that the growth of African American studies over the last generation has increasingly ignored this symbiotic relationship.

At the beginning of the twenty-first century, political engagement has been subjugated in African American Studies. The discipline is thriving in a secure institutional setting, but it has moved a long way away from its activist beginnings. Most major U.S. universities have departments or programs of African American Studies, and it is the rare history, English, political science, or sociology department that does not have at least one faculty specialist and a couple of courses in African American Studies. The study of African American literature grew especially popular in the 1980s and 1990s. But this growth in departments, programs, graduate studies, and chaired professorships came at a time when real social and economic conditions for the majority of African Americans grew steadily worse. The ironic result of the recent celebration of diversity and multiculturalism is that it has led primarily to the darkening of the curricula in classrooms that remained the playgrounds of the white upper and middle classes. The classroom space that the *Brown vs. Board of Education* Supreme Court decision in 1954 had earmarked for Black bodies was filled with Black texts in the 1990s. While African American Studies was growing to the point where reactionary commentators felt compelled to warn that reading Zora Neale Hurston or Toni Morrison instead of Shakespeare or Dickens could only mean the death of Western Civilization, a young black man in the United States was three times more likely to end up as a cog in the U.S. prison industrial complex than as a student in college. With very few exceptions, the African American Studies that has survived and thrived in the last twenty-five years has lost its connection to any radical or politically activist beginnings.

Walkin' the Talk is an anthology that deliberately attempts to place African American Studies in the social, political, and economic context of Africans in the United States. It tries to do so with little reverence for disciplinary boundaries or critical orthodoxy. We feel that there is an indivisible and symbiotic relationship between African American politics and culture and thus have made no attempt to assign texts to artificially bounded subjects like history, literature, or sociology. We have tried not to impose limiting labels such as "The Harlem Renaissance" or "The Black Arts Movement". In the organization of the anthology, we have been especially careful not to abstract African American "literature" from its social and political contexts. It is important to acknowledge and celebrate the formal and linguistic beauty of African American literature, but it is misleading to divide African American writing into binary categories like Art and Protest, or Literature and Propaganda. As only a glance at the passionate work of Ida B. Wells-Barnet, W. E. B. Du Bois, or Sonia Sanchez shows, making these kinds of false distinctions only distorts the tradition. We feel it is insufficient to read Olaudah Equiano's *Interesting Narrative* or Phillis Wheatley's poems without Thomas Jefferson's and Immanuel Kant's white supremacist writings. Frederick Douglass's 1845 *Narrative* is rightly considered a masterpiece of American literature, but it is only part of the nineteenth-century story that is also told by texts like *The Confessions of Nat Turner* or William Wells Brown's account of the John Brown Raid. As LeRoi Jones points out in the epigraph from *Dutchman*, it has been easy for white

America to celebrate Black culture while ignoring the bitter history that created that culture.

Walkin' the Talk is grounded in the idea that white supremacy and Euro-American industrial capitalism provide the structural framework in which the political, economic, and cultural life of Africans in the United States have unfolded over the last 380 years. Emerging from the superexploitation characterizing U.S. slavery, and moving through the brief moment of Reconstruction, the grinding misery of Jim Crow, and the hope, possibility, and disappointment of the Civil Rights era, the African American experience has been one of unflagging struggle for economic survival and human dignity. This struggle has taken a rich variety of social, political, and cultural forms that have operated both from within and outside of mainstream U.S. institutions. Over the centuries, African Americans have moved within, between, and around the Gramscian strategies of war of maneuver (in which the subaltern is denied formal-legal rights in the civil society) and war of position (in which the subaltern achieves some level of rights and "positionality" in civil society) in a variety of ways. And, while it is important to recognize the obvious truth that African American consciousness and discourse is not only or strictly determined by the material fact of oppression, it is perhaps even more important to never abstract African American Studies too far from that history of oppression.

African American responses to the brutal facts of life in the United States can be arranged generally into three categories: Liberalism, Nationalism, and Socialism. Most African American expressions of aspirations for dignity and equality fall into one of these three very broad categories. The universalizing liberalism that has been the centerpiece of mainstream U.S. ideology has, obviously enough, been the most accepted form of African American liberation politics. The liberal approach emphasizes individualism and integration. It tends to see slavery as a moral mistake rather than an integral part of early U.S. capitalism. Liberal doctrine dreams of a "colorblind" society, where African Americans are fully integrated into bourgeois democratic institutions based on the content of their character rather than the color of their skin. It is easily the most prominent ideology in the African American discourse that has been most celebrated in the U.S. mainstream, from Phillis Wheatley through the early Frederick Douglass and the NAACP to the early work of Martin Luther King, Jr.

Black Nationalism has been a very powerful force in African American history and takes a variety of forms, with important contributions to African American discourse in the writings of people like David Walker, Marcus Garvey, and Sonia Sanchez. It even shows up as a strain in some liberal integrationist discourse. Nationalism recognizes African Americans as a colonized nation within the United States and emphasizes race as a distinguishing characteristic, often in essentialist and Afro-centric ways. Black Nationalist ideology usually gives rise to separatist strategies, which have from time to time led to strange but ultimately logical alliances between some Black Nationalists and equally essentialist white supremacists (such as that between Malcolm X and the Ku Klux Klan in the early 1960s). Quite often very socially and economically conservative forms of Black Nationalism (such as that of the Nation of Islam) have been held up in mainstream U.S. discourse as foils to liberal integrationist strategies. While these Nationalisms are derided as negative and "racist", they are ultimately safe for mainstream consumption because they seek to create all-black societies that are still patriarchal and capitalist, thus posing no real threat to mainstream U.S. ideological assumptions. As Amiri Baraka put it in a radio interview in 1984:

> As long as it was a bourgeois nationalist, reactionary nationalist kind of trend—a "hate whitey" kind of thing, during that period of the movement, they didn't really have any problem with that. They might get officially excited. . . .
>
> That is, if you say that the enemy is "all whites" without making a class analysis and showing that there's only a handful of super-billionaire vampires that actually control the society, the ruling class. When you do that and start making an analysis with your art in a forceful way, then they don't see that as a charming commodity that they need like they might need some tiger teeth around their neck.

The "good" liberal-integrationist versus "bad" nationalist-separatist paradigm has been the orthodox description of African American history in both scholarly and popular discussions. The poles in this division are usually represented in mainstream history in such easy patriarchal oppositions as W. E. B. Du Bois versus Marcus Garvey, Ralph Ellison versus Richard Wright, or Jesse Jackson versus Louis Farrakhan. The pinnacle of this formulation comes with the 1960s media opposition of Martin Luther King, Jr. as eloquent liberal integrationist and Malcolm X as scary racist Black Nationalist. The African American discourse and strategy that gets scant attention is the one that both Malcolm and King were turning toward at the end of their lives. At the times they were shot, both Malcolm X's and King's political positions had evolved beyond the race-based integrationist and separatist analyses that had brought them to prominence and toward more economically and internationally inflected critiques. The last years of Malcolm's life were what George Breitman calls "the evolution of a revolutionary," as he moved from the religious black nationalism of the Nation of Islam to the more international and socialist positions of the Organization for Afro-American Unity. Similarly, the night King died he delivered a speech to striking garbage workers in Memphis and he had expanded his civil rights program to include the Poor People's March on Washington, a proposal for a guaranteed annual income, and a denunciation of U.S. imperialism in Vietnam.

Malcolm X and King, like many African American thinkers before them, had, through real activist experience, found liberal integrationist and nationalist separatist strategies insufficient and thus turned to a more socialist approach that began to see the connections between white supremacy and capitalism. Far from being a departure from traditional African American thought, this turn echoes the ideas we find in the mature work of such figures as W. E. B. Du

Bois, Paul Robeson, James Baldwin, Amiri Baraka, The Black Panthers, Angela Davis, and Audre Lorde. On the basis of their early work, these writers have usually been canonized and categorized as either integrationists or separatists, in a way that has effectively shrouded a rich and vibrant African American socialist tradition. In the twentieth century, as African American thinkers have metamorphosed from either liberal integrationists or nationalist separatists into socialists, they have been harassed and exiled (Du Bois, Robeson, Davis), reviled and critically dismissed (the later Baldwin, Baraka, and Lorde) or murdered (the Panthers, Martin Luther King, and Malcolm X). This has led to a suppressed and misunderstood African American radical tradition.

Perhaps as a subset of the general U.S. antipathy and violence toward radicalism, African Americans expressing socialist sentiments have often been seen as being under the spell of external influences. From 1960s southern sheriffs lamenting "yankee agitators" corrupting their "good nigras" to academic commentators relentlessly pointing out how some prominent African American writers (especially Richard Wright and Ralph Ellison) grew disillusioned with the U.S. Communist Party, mainstream discourse has tended to dismiss African American socialism as something European and imposed, and not as authentically or indigenously African American as integrationist blues or separatist anger. But a revolutionary African American impulse dates back to at least the Nat Turner rebellion, and there is a historical materialist tradition running from David Walker to Sanyika Shakur that reaches the conclusions of Marxism without the benefit of Marx.

The categories of liberalism, nationalism, and socialism are very broad and the lines between them are not indelible. Individual careers and even individual texts often partake of more than one kind of response. *Walkin' the Talk* tries to capture the full range of African American discourse, avoiding static binaries and trying to show a rich and evolving dialectical tradition. Rather than present the dominant liberal-integrationist ideology seasoned with dashes of nationalism and socialism, we try to give all three strategies their due, highlighting the socialist tradition in an effort to show its previously unacknowledged centrality to African American discourse. This approach has led us to choose both texts by neglected or obscure writers, and less canonized works by celebrated authors. *Walkin' the Talk* will expose students to Ottobah Cugoano, Anne Spencer, A. Philip Randolph, Angela Davis, and Bobby Seale, authors not automatically considered a part of mainstream African American discourse. Readers will also encounter relatively unfamiliar texts by such familiar writers as William Wells Brown, W. E. B. Du Bois, Langston Hughes, and Audre Lorde.

Walkin' the Talk is an interdisciplinary anthology intended for use in a variety of classes. We want to emphasize the overlap and connection between politics, economics and culture, so we have made no attempt to classify or categorize texts. This allows instructors in beginning and upper division African American Studies courses to create thematic links and highlight issues across time periods. We also hope that *Walkin' the Talk* will be just as useful in a political science class that attempts to show the way that political debate imbues social and cultural discourse, as it is in a literature course that reads the aesthetic traditions of blues and signifying as coming out of specific economic and social contexts.

The book is organized chronologically into periods that mark epochal shifts in African American political and social status: New World Slavery, Black Resistance and Abolition, Reconstruction, Jim Crow, Civil Rights and Black Power, and The Post-Industrial, Post-Civil Rights Era. The Reconstruction section is very brief, as was Reconstruction itself. Within the sections we have tried to represent as many ideological points of view as possible, as we hope the selection of the texts shows. There are a few features that might seem unexpected in an "African American" anthology. Each section contains texts produced during the period as well as texts produced during other periods that provide background and commentary on the period in question. So, for example, the twentieth-century work on slavery by scholars like Vincent Harding and David Brion Davis is included in Part One—New World Slavery. There is a sprinkling of selections by white writers, both progressive and racist. In order to talk about the historical trajectory of ideologies and movements for change in a racist-capitalist society, it is necessary to hear the voice not only of the oppressed group, but also of the perpetrators of that oppression. We have also included selections by writers from beyond the United States, such as Quobna Ottabah Cugoano and C. L. R. James, whose work we feel has direct relevance to the African American situation.

Walkin' the Talk is of course not anything like a comprehensive anthology. We could easily fill ten books with important texts and still not cover everything. But we hope that the book opens up the field for the twenty-first century in a way that reconnects African American studies to African America.

Foreword

African-American Studies emerged as a field of study on the crest of the activism of the 1960s, both on campus and off. Two facts about this aspect of the field's history are especially significant for making sense of its subsequent development. First, black studies as an academic institution took shape within mainstream academic institutions. The earliest programs and departments were established, as this volume's editors indicate in their introduction, mainly at predominantly white colleges and universities. Howard University was atypical among historically black institutions in launching a black studies program. In fact, on historically black campuses the black studies movement generally took a different direction. Proponents on black campuses of the race-conscious sensibility that spawned black studies were more likely to eschew establishment of separate black studies curricula or programs on the grounds that the regular curriculum should be oriented to reflect black race-conscious concerns and sensibilities.

Second, the impetus shaping black studies derived from political demands articulated within the context of the black power movement and academic institutions' responses to those demands. Early programs emerged from campus struggles at Cornell and San Francisco State universities, which erupted into dramatic expressions that became hallmarks of the generation. Many other black studies initiatives originated in comparable, if less intense or visible protests and confrontations. In the context of the time, the demand for black studies programs was usually linked to claims regarding the need for higher education to be relevant to the concerns and to reflect the perspectives of black people. The range of these concerns extended to both academic and non-academic matters, as the spirit of the time supported calls for more populist understandings of the functions of the university and its relation to the communities it served. This was not a view advocated only by radicals; it was propounded, though with a different notion of the community to be served, by liberal education experts and university administrators well before the black power explosion. However, the argument that black studies programs' justification lay at least partly outside conventional academic criteria was a powerful element in the demand for them, and one that had consequences for how many black studies initiatives defined their mission and structured their programs.

Black studies' emergence on predominantly white campuses exerted an institutional pressure to formalize the field within academic departments or degree-awarding programs and also linked the status of the field's subject matter immediately to the project of hiring and retaining black faculty. This is

hardly an unnatural linkage; those who study the black experience are disproportionately likely to be black, just as those who work in the women's studies
area are disproportionately women. In both instances, therefore, it is reasonable
that the objectives of democratizing or diversifying faculties and consolidating
or advancing the field of study usually are pursued simultaneously. But the two
objectives are not identical. At the same time, the familiar rhetorical justification of black studies on nonacademic grounds encourages treating the personnel and programmatic objectives as though they are isomorphic.

That rhetoric also supports a tendency to claim for black studies a political
mission that may be too much to ask of an academic field. The retreat in the
1980s from a politicized notion of black studies' mission was largely driven by
conservative or narrowly professionalistic currents that swept into the academy
from the elite political consensus outside. Yet, black studies as an intellectual
enterprise was often vulnerable to charges that the field had subordinated intellectual rigor to political posturing.

It is useful to pause to reflect on the impact of the institutional consolidation of black studies on the study of the black American experience. Before
black studies there was the Negro History movement, which was animated
mainly by the scholarly project of setting the record straight about black people, race and the realities of American history. The Negro History movement
dated at least from the late 1910s, when Carter G. Woodson created the Association for the Study of Negro Life and History. The ASNLH (now ASALH)
had a dual mission: deepening and broadening knowledge of the black experience and countering the scurrilously racist propaganda that passed for informed
understanding of race and black people.

As James Weldon Johnson noted in his 1928 article, "The Dilemma of the
Negro Author", these two objectives were not always compatible. Countering
racist propaganda required assuming an audience that did not know much
about blacks; inquiry that would advance knowledge required assuming a more
sophisticated audience, one that did not need to be shown that blacks were
equal members of the human species. This tension haunted engaged black intellectual life for generations. It gave rise to much useful reflection on the state
of black intellectual discourse and debate. During the 1930s and 1940s in particular, these lively critiques appeared frequently in the *Journal of Negro
History*, the *Journal of Negro Education* and *Phylon*, among other organs. The
ranks of significant participants in this critically reflective discourse include
scholars such as William T. Fontaine, Lawrence Reddick, Joseph Bailey, John
S. Lash, and Joseph Sandy Himes, as well as those whose names are more familiar to contemporary readers, such as Sterling Brown, E. Franklin Frazier, Abram
Harris, Ralph Bunche, or Oliver C. Cox.

By the end of the 1950s this lively culture of black intellectual debate had
become a distant memory even among scholars. The momentum of civil rights
protest undermined critical reflection by focusing intellectual activity on assisting what seemed to be the urgent practical objectives of the protest movement.
The victory of the Myrdalian consensus in race relations provided a frame of

reference that supported that pragmatic orientation by reducing the goal of racial justice to struggles against prejudice and exclusion. Moreover, the triumph of McCarthyism considerably raised the potential costs of engaging in more thorough-going political or theoretical critique.

An ironic entailment of the black studies movement's birth on predominantly white campuses is that it was born outside and ignorant of the history of that culture of critical debate. This ignorance stemmed partly from the fact that then, as now, only those scholars who themselves actually work on black subject matter typically pay attention to such literature. Partly also it stemmed from the fact that several of the most visible participants in the earlier discursive community who remained active into the 1970s—for instance, Bunche and Cox—were critics of the Black Power sensibility from which the black studies movement sprang. In addition, as a youth-inspired movement, one of the black studies movement's animating tropes was the notion that a new knowledge had to be produced for the new black consciousness. The movement's populist predilections reinforced that tendency to undervalue building on recent intellectual tradition.

It was in this context that black studies developed primarily in response to intellectual and, more consequentially, institutional imperatives extrinsic to the field. As extramural political mobilization receded during the 1970s and 1980s, the political claims for black studies lost force. Thus the 1980s saw the emergence of a tendency, also discussed by this volume's editors, to purify black studies by stripping it of its political commitments or pretensions. This technicistic tendency, which culminated in the reformation of the Harvard program under the leadership of Henry Louis Gates, is contradictory, however. The claim to transcendence of political aspirations, once empowered, has, in the Harvard case at least, become quite the opposite: Gates, William J. Wilson and Cornel West routinely pontificate on public affairs and advise and consort with elite politicians. This fuels suspicion that the program of intellectual purification of black studies was directed only toward unconventional political commitments.

In any event, the present collection presents a welcome intervention into the canonical world of black studies. The reach and breadth of the selections included in this volume help to reconnect the intellectual enterprise on which black studies rests with the important, intellectually autonomous discourse of the 1930s and 1940s. This collection also underscores the crucial reality that making sense of the black American experience is impossible without situating it in the context of contemporaneous American ideas, debates and social and ideological currents. The authors are to be commended for their service and accomplishment in making these readings available.

Adolph Reed, Jr.
Professor, Graduate Faculty of Political & Social Science
New School for Social Research

Part One—New World Slavery

Olaudah Equiano

from *The Interesting Narrative of the Life of Olaudah Equiano, or Gustavus Vassa, the African*

CHAPTER I

The author's account of his country, and their manners and customs—Administration of justice—Embrenche—Marriage ceremony, and public entertainments—Mode of living—Dress—Manufactures—Buildings—Commerce—Agriculture—War and religion—Superstition of the natives—Funeral ceremonies of the priests or magicians—Curious mode of discovering poison—Some hints concerning the origin of the author's countrymen, with the opinions of different writers on that subject.

I believe it is difficult for those who publish their own memoirs to escape the imputation of vanity; nor is this the only disadvantage under which they labor: it is also their misfortune that what is uncommon is rarely, if ever, believed, and what is obvious we are apt to turn from with disgust, and to charge the writer with impertinence. People generally think those memoirs only worthy to be read or remembered which abound in great or striking events, those, in short, which in a high degree excite either admiration or pity; all others they consign to contempt and oblivion. It is therefore, I confess, not a little hazardous in a private and obscure individual, and a stranger too, thus to solicit the indulgent attention of the public, especially when I own I offer here the history of neither a saint, a hero, nor a tyrant. I believe there are few events in my life which have not happened to many; it is true the incidents of it are numerous, and, did I consider myself an European, I might say my sufferings were great; but when I compare my lot with that of most of my countrymen, I regard myself as a *particular favorite of heaven*, and acknowledge the mercies of Providence in every occurrence of my life. If, then, the following narrative does not appear sufficiently interesting to engage general attention, let my motive be some excuse for its publication. I am not so foolishly vain as to expect from it either immortality or literary reputation. If it affords any satisfaction to my numerous friends, at whose request it has been written, or in the smallest degree promotes the interests of humanity, the ends for which it was undertaken will be fully attained, and every wish of my heart gratified. Let it therefore be remembered, that, in wishing to avoid censure, I do not aspire to praise.

That part of Africa, known by the name of Guinea, to which the trade for slaves is carried on, extends along the coast above 3400 miles, from Senegal to Angola, and includes a variety of kingdoms. Of these the most considerable is the kingdom of Benin, both as to extent and wealth, the richness and cultivation of the soil, the power of its king, and the number and warlike disposition of the inhabitants. It is situated nearly under the line, and extends along the coast about 170 miles, but runs back into the interior part of Africa to a distance hitherto, I believe, unexplored by any traveller, and seems only terminated at length by the empire of Abyssinia, near 1500 miles from its beginning. This kingdom is divided into many provinces or districts, in one of the most remote and fertile of which, I was born, in the year 1745, situated in a charming fruitful vale, named Essaka. The distance of this province from the capital of Benin and the sea coast must be very considerable, for I had never heard of white men or Europeans, nor of the sea; and our subjection to the king of Benin was little more than nominal, for every transaction of the government, as far as my slender observation extended, was conducted by the chief or elders of the place. The manners and government of a people who have little commerce with other countries are generally very simple, and the history of what passes in one family or village may serve as a specimen of the whole nation.

My father was one of those elders or chiefs I have spoken of, and was styled Embrenche, a term, as I remember, importing the highest distinction, and signifying in our language a *mark* of grandeur. This mark is conferred on the person entitled to it, by cutting the skin across at the top of the forehead, and drawing it down to the eyebrows; and while it is in this situation applying a warm hand, and rubbing it until it shrinks up into a thick *weal* across the lower part of the forehead. Most of the judges and senators were thus marked; my father had long borne it; I had seen it conferred on one of my brothers, and I also was *destined* to receive it by my parents. Those Embrenche, or chief men, decided disputes and punished crimes, for which purpose they always assembled together. The proceedings were generally short, and in most cases the law of retaliation prevailed.

I remember a man was brought before my father, and the other judges, for kidnapping a boy; and, although he was the son of a chief or senator, he was condemned to make recompense by a man or woman slave. Adultery, however, was sometimes punished with slavery or death, a punishment which I believe is inflicted on it throughout most of the nations of Africa, so sacred among them is the honor of the marriage bed, and so jealous are they of the fidelity of their wives. Of this I recollect an instance—a woman was convicted before the judges of adultery, and delivered over, as the custom was, to her husband, to be punished. Accordingly he determined to put her to death; but it being found, just before her execution, that she had an infant at her breast, and no woman being prevailed on to perform the part of a nurse, she was spared on account of the child. The men, however, do not preserve the same constancy to their wives which they expect from them; for they indulge in a plurality, though seldom in more than two.

Their mode of marriage is thus—both parties are usually betrothed when young by their parents (though I have known the males to betroth themselves). On this occasion a feast is prepared, and the bride and bridegroom stand up in the midst of all their friends, who are assembled for the purpose, while he declares she is henceforth to be looked upon as his wife, and that no other person is to pay any addresses to her. This is also immediately proclaimed in the vicinity, on which the bride retires from the assembly. Some time after, she is brought home to her husband, and then another feast is made, to which the relations of both parties are invited; her parents then deliver her to the bridegroom, accompanied with a number of blessings, and at the same time they tie round her waist a cotton string of the thickness of a goose-quill, which none but married women are permitted to wear; she is now considered as completely his wife; and at this time the dowry is given to the new married pair, which generally consists of portions of land, slaves, and cattle, household goods, and implements of husbandry. These are offered by the friends of both parties; besides which the parents of the bridegroom present gifts to those of the bride, whose property she is looked upon before marriage; but after it she is esteemed the sole property of her husband. The ceremony being now ended, the festival begins, which is celebrated with bonfires and loud acclamations of joy, accompanied with music and dancing.

We are almost a nation of dancers, musicians, and poets. Thus every great event, such as a triumphant return from battle or other cause of public rejoicing, is celebrated in public dances, which are accompanied with songs and music suited to the occasion. The assembly is separated into four divisions, which dance either apart or in succession, and each with a character peculiar to itself. The first division contains the married men, who in their dances frequently exhibit feats of arms and the representation of a battle. To these succeed the married women, who dance in the second division. The young men occupy the third, and the maidens the fourth. Each represents some interesting scene of real life, such as a great achievement, domestic employment, a pathetic story, or some rural sport; and as the subject is generally founded on some recent event, it is therefore ever new. This gives our dances a spirit and variety which I have scarcely seen elsewhere.[1] We have many musical instruments, particularly drums of different kinds, a piece of music which resembles a guitar, and another much like a stickado. These last are chiefly used by betrothed virgins, who play on them on all grand festivals.

As our manners are simple, our luxuries are few. The dress of both sexes is nearly the same. It generally consists of a long piece of calico, or muslin, wrapped loosely round the body, somewhat in the form of a highland plaid. This is usually dyed blue, which is our favorite color. It is extracted from a berry, and is brighter and richer than any I have seen in Europe. Besides this, our women of distinction wear golden ornaments, which they dispose with

---

[1]When I was in Smyrna I have frequently seen the Greeks dance after this manner. [Equiano's note.]

some profusion on their arms and legs. When our women are not employed with the men in tillage, their usual occupation is spinning and weaving cotton, which they afterwards dye, and make into garments. They also manufacture earthen vessels, of which we have many kinds. Among the rest, tobacco pipes, made after the same fashion, and used in the same manner, as those in Turkey.

Our manner of living is entirely plain; for as yet the natives are unacquainted with those refinements in cookery which debauch the taste: bullocks, goats, and poultry supply the greatest part of their food. These constitute likewise the principal wealth of the country, and the chief articles of its commerce. The flesh is usually stewed in a pan; to make it savory we sometimes use pepper, and other spices, and we have salt made of wood ashes. Our vegetables are mostly plantains, eadas, yams, beans, and Indian corn. The head of the family usually eats alone; his wives and slaves have also their separate tables. Before we taste food we always wash our hands; indeed, our cleanliness on all occasions is extreme, but on this it is an indispensable ceremony. After washing, libation is made, by pouring out a small portion of the drink on the floor, and tossing a small quantity of the food in a certain place, for the spirits of departed relations, which the natives suppose to preside over their conduct and guard them from evil. They are totally unacquainted with strong or spirituous liquors; and their principal beverage is palm wine. This is got from a tree of that name, by tapping it at the top and fastening a large gourd to it; and sometimes one tree will yield three or four gallons in a night. When just drawn it is of a most delicious sweetness; but in a few days it acquires a tartish and more spirituous flavor, though I never saw anyone intoxicated by it. The same tree also produces nuts and oil. Our principal luxury is in perfumes: one sort of these is an odoriferous wood of delicious fragrance, the other a kind of earth, a small portion of which thrown into the fire diffuses a most powerful odor.[2] We beat this wood into powder, and mix it with palm oil, with which both men and women perfume themselves.

In our buildings we study convenience rather than ornament. Each master of a family has a large square piece of ground, surrounded with a moat or fence, or enclosed with a wall made of red earth tempered, which, when dry, is as hard as brick. Within this, are his houses to accommodate his family and slaves, which, if numerous, frequently present the appearance of a village. In the middle, stands the principal building, appropriated to the sole use of the master and consisting of two apartments; in one of which he sits in the day with his family, the other is left apart for the reception of his friends. He has besides these a distinct apartment in which he sleeps, together with his male children. On each side are the apartments of his wives, who have also their separate day and night houses. The habitations of the slaves and their families are distributed throughout the rest of the enclosure. These houses never exceed one story in height;

[2]When I was in Smyrna I saw the same kind of earth, and brought some of it with me to England; it resembles musk in strength, but is more delicious in scent, and is not unlike the smell of a rose. [Equiano's note.]

they are always built of wood, or stakes driven into the ground, crossed with wattles, and neatly plastered within and without. The roof is thatched with reeds. Our day houses are left open at the sides; but those in which we sleep are always covered, and plastered in the inside, with a composition mixed with cow-dung, to keep off the different insects which annoy us during the night. The walls and floors also of these are generally covered with mats. Our beds consist of a platform, raised three or four feet from the ground, on which are laid skins, and different parts of a spongy tree, called plantain. Our covering is calico or muslin, the same as our dress. The usual seats are a few logs of wood; but we have benches, which are generally perfumed to accommodate strangers: these compose the greater part of our household furniture. Houses so constructed and furnished require but little skill to erect them. Every man is a sufficient architect for the purpose. The whole neighborhood afford their unanimous assistance in building them, and in return receive and expect no other recompense than a feast.

As we live in a country where nature is prodigal of her favors, our wants are few and easily supplied; of course we have few manufactures. They consist for the most part of calicoes, earthen ware, ornaments, and instruments of war and husbandry. But these make no part of our commerce, the principal articles of which, as I have observed, are provisions. In such a state, money is of little use; however, we have some small pieces of coin, if I may call them such. They are made something like an anchor, but I do not remember either their value or denomination. We have also markets, at which I have been frequently with my mother. These are sometimes visited by stout mahogany-colored men from the south-west of us: we call them *Oye-Eboe*, which term signifies red men living at a distance. They generally bring us fire-arms, gun-powder, hats, beads, and dried fish. The last we esteemed a great rarity, as our waters were only brooks and springs. These articles they barter with us for odoriferous woods and earth, and our salt of wood ashes. They always carry slaves through our land; but the strictest account is exacted of their manner of procuring them before they are suffered to pass. Sometimes, indeed, we sold slaves to them, but they were only prisoners of war, or such among us as had been convicted of kidnapping, or adultery, and some other crimes, which we esteemed heinous. This practice of kidnapping induces me to think, that, notwithstanding all our strictness, their principal business among us was to trepan our people. I remember too, they carried great sacks along with them, which not long after, I had an opportunity of fatally seeing applied to that infamous purpose.

Our land is uncommonly rich and fruitful, and produces all kinds of vegetables in great abundance. We have plenty of Indian corn, and vast quantities of cotton and tobacco. Our pineapples grow without culture; they are about the size of the largest sugar-loaf, and finely flavored. We have also spices of different kinds, particularly pepper, and a variety of delicious fruits which I have never seen in Europe, together with gums of various kinds, and honey in abundance. All our industry is exerted to improve these blessings of nature. Agriculture is our chief employment; and everyone, even the children and women, are engaged in it. Thus we are all habituated to labor from our earliest years. Every-one contributes something to the common stock; and, as we are unacquainted with idleness, we have no beggars. The benefits of such a mode of living are ob-vious. The West India planters prefer the slaves of Benin or Eboe to those of any other part of Guinea, for their hardiness, intelligence, integrity, and zeal. Those benefits are felt by us in the general healthiness of the people, and in their vigor and activity; I might have added, too, in their comeliness. Defor-mity is indeed unknown amongst us, I mean that of shape. Numbers of the na-tives of Eboe now in London might be brought in support of this assertion: for, in regard to complexion, ideas of beauty are wholly relative. I remember while in Africa to have seen three Negro children who were tawny, and another quite white, who were universally regarded by myself, and the natives in gen-eral, as far as related to their complexions, as deformed. Our women, too, were, in my eye at least, uncommonly graceful, alert, and modest to a degree of bash-fulness; nor do I remember to have heard of an instance of incontinence amongst them before marriage. They are also remarkably cheerful. Indeed, cheerfulness and affability are two of the leading characteristics of our nation.

Our tillage is exercised in a large plain or common, some hour's walk from our dwellings, and all the neighbors resort thither in a body. They use no beasts of husbandry; and their only instruments are hoes, axes, shovels, and beaks, or pointed iron, to dig with. Sometimes we are visited by locusts, which come in large clouds, so as to darken the air, and destroy our harvest. This, however, happens rarely, but when it does, a famine is produced by it. I remember an in-stance or two wherein this happened. This common is often the theatre of war; and therefore when our people go out to till their land, they not only go in a body, but generally take their arms with them for fear of a surprise; and when they apprehend an invasion, they guard the avenues to their dwellings, by driving sticks into the ground, which are so sharp at one end as to pierce the foot, and are generally dipt in poison. From what I can recollect of these bat-tles, they appear to have been irruptions of one little state or district on the other, to obtain prisoners or booty. Perhaps they were incited to this by those traders who brought the European goods I mentioned, amongst us. Such a mode of obtaining slaves in Africa is common; and I believe more are procured this way, and by kidnapping, than any other.[3] When a trader wants slaves, he applies to a chief for them, and tempts him with his wares. It is not extraordi-nary, if on this occasion he yields to the temptation with as little firmness, and accepts the price of his fellow creature's liberty, with as little reluctance as the enlightened merchant. Accordingly he falls on his neighbors, and a desperate battle ensues. If he prevails and takes prisoners, he gratifies his avarice by sell-ing them; but, if his party be vanquished, and he falls into the hands of the enemy, he is put to death; for, as he has been known to foment their quarrels, it is thought dangerous to let him survive, and no ransom can save him, though all other prisoners may be redeemed. We have fire-arms, bows and arrows,

[3]See Benezet's "Account of Guinea," throughout. [Equiano's note.]

broad two-edged swords and javelins; we have shields also which cover a man from head to foot. All are taught the use of these weapons; even our women are warriors, and march boldly out to fight along with the men. Our whole district is a kind of militia: on a certain signal given, such as the firing of a gun at night, they all rise in arms and rush upon their enemy. It is perhaps something remarkable, that when our people march to the field a red flag or banner is borne before them.

I was once a witness to a battle in our common. We had been all at work in it one day as usual, when our people were suddenly attacked. I climbed a tree at some distance, from which I beheld the fight. There were many women as well as men on both sides; among others my mother was there, and armed with a broad sword. After fighting for a considerable time with great fury, and many had been killed, our people obtained the victory, and took their enemy's Chief a prisoner. He was carried off in great triumph, and, though he offered a large ransom for his life, he was put to death. A virgin of note among our enemies had been slain in the battle, and her arm was exposed in our marketplace, where our trophies were always exhibited. The spoils were divided according to the merit of the warriors. Those prisoners which were not sold or redeemed, we kept as slaves; but how different was their condition from that of the slaves in the West Indies! With us, they do no more work than other members of the community, even their master; their food, clothing, and lodging were nearly the same as theirs (except that they were not permitted to eat with those who were free-born); and there was scarce any other difference between them, than a superior degree of importance which the head of a family possesses in our state, and that authority which, as such, he exercises over every part of his household. Some of these slaves have even slaves under them as their own property, and for their own use.

As to religion, the natives believe that there is one Creator of all things, and that he lives in the sun, and is girted round with a belt; that he may never eat or drink, but, according to some, he smokes a pipe, which is our own favorite luxury. They believe he governs events, especially our deaths or captivity; but, as for the doctrine of eternity, I do not remember to have ever heard of it; some, however, believe in the transmigration of souls in a certain degree. Those spirits which were not transmigrated, such as their dear friends or relations, they believe always attend them, and guard them from the bad spirits or their foes. For this reason they always, before eating, as I have observed, put some small portion of the meat, and pour some of their drink, on the ground for them; and they often make oblations of the blood of beasts or fowls at their graves. I was very fond of my mother, and almost constantly with her. When she went to make these oblations at her mother's tomb, which was a kind of small solitary thatched house, I sometimes attended her. There she made her libations, and spent most of the night in cries and lamentations. I have been often extremely terrified on these occasions. The loneliness of the place, the darkness of the night, and the ceremony of libation, naturally awful and gloomy, were heightened by my mother's lamentations; and these concurring with the doleful cries of birds, by which these places were frequented, gave an inexpressible terror to the scene.

We compute the year from the day on which the sun crosses the line, and on its setting that evening, there is a general shout throughout the land; at least, I can speak from my own knowledge, throughout our vicinity. The people at the same time make a great noise with rattles, not unlike the basket rattles used by children here, though much larger, and hold up their hands to heaven for a blessing. It is then the greatest offerings are made; and those children whom our wise men foretell will be fortunate are then presented to different people. I remember many used to come to see me, and I was carried about to others for that purpose. They have many offerings, particularly at full moons; generally two, at harvest, before the fruits are taken out of the ground; and when any young animals are killed, sometimes they offer up part of them as a sacrifice. These offerings, when made by one of the heads of a family, serve for the whole. I remember we often had them at my father's and my uncle's, and their families have been present. Some of our offerings are eaten with bitter herbs. We had a saying among us to anyone of a cross temper, "That if they were to be eaten, they should be eaten with bitter herbs."

We practised circumcision like the Jews, and made offerings and feasts on that occasion, in the same manner as they did. Like them also, our children were named from some event, some circumstance, or fancied foreboding, at the time of their birth. I was named *Olaudah*, which in our language signifies vicissitude, or fortunate; also, one favored, and having a loud voice and well spoken. I remember we never polluted the name of the object of our adoration; on the contrary, it was always mentioned with the greatest reverence; and we were totally unacquainted with swearing, and all those terms of abuse and reproach which find their way so readily and copiously into the language of more civilized people. The only expressions of that kind I remember were, "May you rot, or may you swell, or may a beast take you."

I have before remarked that the natives of this part of Africa are extremely cleanly. This necessary habit of decency was with us a part of religion, and therefore we had many purifications and washings; indeed almost as many, and used on the same occasions, if my recollection does not fail me, as the Jews. Those that touched the dead at any time were obliged to wash and purify themselves before they could enter a dwelling-house. Every woman, too, at certain times was forbidden to come into a dwelling-house, or touch any person, or anything we eat. I was so fond of my mother I could not keep from her, or avoid touching her at some of those periods, in consequence of which I was obliged to be kept out with her, in a little house made for that purpose, till offering was made, and then we were purified.

Though we had no places of public worship, we had priests and magicians, or wise men. I do not remember whether they had different offices, or whether they were united in the same persons, but they were held in great reverence by the people. They calculated our time, and foretold events, as their name imported, for we called them *Ah-affoe-way-cah*, which signifies calculators or yearly men, our year being called *Ah-affoe*. They wore their beards, and when they died, they were succeeded by their sons. Most of their implements and things of value were interred along with them. Pipes and tobacco were also put into the grave with the corpse, which was always perfumed and ornamented, and animals were offered in sacrifice to them. None accompanied their funerals, but those of the same profession or tribe. They buried them after sunset, and always returned from the grave by a different way from that which they went.

These magicians were also our doctors or physicians. They practised bleeding by cupping, and were very successful in healing wounds and expelling poisons. They had likewise some extraordinary method of discovering jealousy, theft, poisoning, the success of which, no doubt, they derived from the unbounded influence over the credulity and superstition of the people. I do not remember what those methods were, except that as to poisoning; I recollect an instance or two, which I hope it will not be deemed impertinent here to insert, as it may serve as a kind of specimen of the rest, as is still used by the Negroes in the West Indies. A young woman had been poisoned, but it was not known by whom; the doctors ordered the corpse to be taken up by some persons, and carried to the grave. As soon as the bearers had raised it on their shoulders, they seemed seized with some sudden impulse, and ran to and fro, unable to stop themselves. At last, after having passed through a number of thorns and prickly bushes unhurt, the corpse fell from them close to a house, and defaced it in the fall; and the owner being taken up, he immediately confessed the poisoning.[4]

The natives are extremely cautious about poison. When they buy any eatables, the seller kisses it all round before the buyer, to shew him it is not poisoned; and the same is done when any meat or drink is presented, particularly to a stranger. We have serpents of different kinds, some of which are esteemed ominous when they appear in our houses, and these we never molest. I remember two of those ominous snakes, each of which was as thick as the calf of a man's leg, and in color resembling a dolphin in the water, crept at different times into my mother's night house, where I always lay with her, and coiled themselves into folds, and each time they crowed like a cock. I was desired by some of our wise men to touch these, that I might be interested in the good

---

[4]An instance of this kind happened at Montserrat, in the West Indies, in the year 1763. I then belonged to the *Charming Sally*, Capt. Doran. The chief mate, Mr. Mansfield, and some of the crew being one day on shore, were present at the burying of a poisoned Negro girl. Though they had often heard of the circumstance of the running in such cases, and had even seen it, they imagined it to be a trick of the corpse bearers. The mate therefore desired two of the sailors to take up the coffin, and carry it to the grave. The sailors, who were all of the same opinion, readily obeyed, but they had scarcely raised it to their shoulders before they began to run furiously about, quite unable to direct themselves, till at last, without intention, they came to the hut of him who had poisoned the girl. The coffin then immediately fell from their shoulders against the hut, and damaged part of the wall. The owner of the hut was taken into custody on this, and confessed the poisoning. I give this story as it was related by the mate and crew on their return to the ship. The credit which is due to it, I leave with the reader. [Equiano's note.]

omens, which I did, for they were quite harmless, and would tamely suffer themselves to be handled; and then they were put into a large earthen pan, and set on one side of the highway. Some of our snakes, however, were poisonous; one of them crossed the road one day as I was standing on it, and passed between my feet without offering to touch me, to the great surprise of many who saw it; and these incidents were accounted by the wise men, and likewise by my mother and the rest of the people, as remarkable omens in my favor.

Such is the imperfect sketch my memory has furnished me with, of the manners and customs of a people among whom I first drew my breath. And here I cannot forbear suggesting what has long struck me very forcibly, namely, the strong analogy which even by this sketch, imperfect as it is, appears to prevail in the manners and customs of my countrymen and those of the Jews, before they reached the land of promise, and particularly the patriarchs while they were yet in that pastoral state which is described in Genesis—an analogy, which alone would induce me to think that the one people had sprung from the other. Indeed, this is the opinion of Dr. Gill, who, in his commentary on Genesis, very ably deduces the pedigree of the Africans from Afer and Afra, the descendents of Abraham by Keturah his wife and concubine (for both these titles are applied to her). It is also conformable to the sentiments of Dr. John Clarke, formerly Dean of Sarum, in his truth of the Christian religion; both these authors concur in ascribing to us this original. The reasonings of those gentlemen are still further confirmed by the scripture chronology; and if any further corroboration were required, this resemblance in so many respects, is a strong evidence in support of the opinion. Like the Israelites in their primitive state, our government was conducted by our chiefs or judges, our wise men and elders; and the head of a family with us enjoyed a similar authority over his household, with that which is ascribed to Abraham and the other patriarchs. The law of retaliation obtained almost universally with us as with them: and even their religion appeared to have shed upon us a ray of its glory, though broken and spent in its passage, or eclipsed by the cloud with which time, tradition, and ignorance might have enveloped it; for we had our circumcision (a rule, I believe, peculiar to that people), we had also our sacrifices and burnt-offerings, our washings and purifications, and on the same occasions as they did.

As to the difference of color between the Eboan Africans and the modern Jews, I shall not presume to account for it. It is a subject which has engaged the pens of men of both genius and learning, and is far above my strength. The most able and Reverend Mr. T. Clarkson, however, in his much admired *Essay on the Slavery and Commerce of the Human Species,* has ascertained the cause in a manner that at once solves every objection on that account, and, on my mind at least, has produced the fullest conviction. I shall therefore refer to that performance for the theory,[5] contenting myself with extracting a fact as related by Dr. Mitchel.[6] "The Spaniards, who have inhabited America, under the torrid

---

[5]Pages 178 to 216. [Equiano's note.]

[6]Philos. Trans. No. 476, Sec. 4, cited by Mr. Clarkson, p. 205. [Equiano's note.]

zone, for any time, are become as dark colored as our native Indians of Virginia; of which *I myself have been a witness.*" There is also another instance[7] of a Portuguese settlement at Mitomba, a river in Sierra Leone, where the inhabitants are bred from a mixture of the first Portuguese discoverers with the natives, and are now become in their complexion, and in the woolly quality of their hair, *perfect Negroes*, retaining however a smattering of the Portuguese language.

These instances, and a great many more which might be adduced, while they show how the complexions of the same persons vary in different climates, it is hoped may tend also to remove the prejudice that some conceive against the natives of Africa on account of their color. Surely the minds of the Spaniards did not change with their complexions! Are there not causes enough to which the apparent inferiority of an African may be ascribed, without limiting the goodness of God, and supposing he forebore to stamp understanding on certainly his own image, because "carved in ebony." Might it not naturally be ascribed to their situation? When they come among Europeans, they are ignorant of their language, religion, manners, and customs. Are any pains taken to teach them these? Are they treated as men? Does not slavery itself depress the mind, and extinguish all its fire and every noble sentiment? But, above all, what advantages do not a refined people possess, over those who are rude and uncultivated? Let the polished and haughty European recollect that his ancestors were once, like the Africans, uncivilized, and even barbarous. Did Nature make *them* inferior to their sons? and should *they too* have been made slaves? Every rational mind answers, No. Let such reflections as these melt the pride of their superiority into sympathy for the wants and miseries of their sable brethren, and compel them to acknowledge that understanding is not confined to feature or color. If, when they look round the world, they feel exultation, let it be tempered with benevolence to others, and gratitude to God, "who hath made of one blood all nations of men for to dwell on all the face of the earth";[8] "and whose wisdom is not our wisdom, neither are our ways his ways."

CHAPTER 9

The author arrives at Martinique—Meets with new difficulties—Gets to Moniserrat, where he takes leave of his old master, and sails for England—Meets Capt. Pascal—Learns the French horn—Hires himself with Doctor Irving, where he learns to freshen sea water—Leaves the Doctor, and goes a voyage to Turkey and Portugal; and afterwards goes a voyage to Grenada, and another to Jamaica—Returns to the Doctor, and they embark together on a voyage to the North Pole, with the Hon. Captain Phipps—Some account of that voyage, and the dangers the author was in—He returns to England.

[7]Same page. [Equiano's note.]
[8]Acts 17:26. [Equiano's note.]

I thus took a final leave of Georgia, for the treatment I had received in it disgusted me very much against the place; and when I left it and sailed for Martinique I determined never more to revisit it. My new captain conducted his vessel safer than any former one; and, after an agreeable voyage, we got safe to our intended port. While I was on this island I went about a good deal, and found it very pleasant; in particular, I admired the town of St. Pierre, which is the principal one in the island, and built more like an European town than any I had seen in the West Indies. In general also, slaves were better treated, had more holidays, and looked better than those in the English islands. After we had done our business here, I wanted my discharge, which was necessary; for it was then the month of May, and I wished much to be at Montserrat to bid farewell to Mr. King, and all my other friends there, in time to sail for Old England in the July fleet. But, alas! I had put a great stumbling block in my own way, by which I was near losing my passage that season to England.

I had lent my captain some money which I now wanted to enable me to prosecute my intentions. This I told him; but when I applied for it, though I urged the necessity of my occasion, I met with so much shuffling from him, that I began at last to be afraid of losing my money, as I could not recover it by law; for I have already mentioned that throughout the West Indies no black man's testimony is admitted, on any occasion, against any white person whatever, and therefore my own oath would have been of no use. I was obliged, therefore, to remain with him till he might be disposed to return it to me. Thus we sailed from Martinique for the Grenadas, I frequently pressing the captain for my money to no purpose; and to render my condition worse, when we got there, the captain and his owners quarrelled, so that my situation became daily more irksome: for besides that, we on board had little or no victuals allowed us, and I could not get my money nor wages, as I could then have gotten my passage free to Montserrat had I been able to accept it. The worst of all was, that it was growing late in July, and the ships in the islands must sail by the 26th of that month. At last, however, with a great many entreaties, I got my money from the captain, and took the first vessel I could meet with for St. Eustatius. From thence I went in another to Basse Terre in St. Kitts, where I arrived on the 19th of July.

On the 22d, having met with a vessel bound to Montserrat, I wanted to go in her; but the captain and others would not take me on board until I should advertise myself, and give notice of my going off the island. I told them of my haste to be in Montserrat, and that the time then would not admit of advertising, it being late in the evening, and the vessel about to sail; but he insisted it was necessary, and otherwise he said he would not take me. This reduced me to great perplexity; for if I should be compelled to submit to this degrading necessity, which every black freeman is under, of advertising himself like a slave, when he leaves an island, and which I thought a gross imposition upon any freeman, I feared I should miss that opportunity of going to Montserrat, and then I could not get to England that year. The vessel was just going off, and no time could be lost; I immediately therefore set about with a heavy heart, to try who I could get to befriend me in complying with the demands of the captain. Luckily I found in a few minutes, some gentlemen of Montserrat whom I knew; and having told them my situation, I requested their friendly assistance in help-ing me off the island. Some of them, on this, went with me to the captain, and satisfied him of my freedom; and, to my very great joy, he desired me to go on board.

We then set sail, and the next day, 23d, I arrived at the wished-for place, after an absence of six months, in which I had more than once experienced the delivering hand of Providence, when all human means of escaping destruction seemed hopeless. I saw my friends with a gladness of heart which was increased by my absence and the dangers I had escaped, and I was received with great friendship by them all, but particularly by Mr. King, to whom I related the fate of his sloop, the *Nancy*, and the causes of her being wrecked. I now learned with extreme sorrow that his house was washed away during my absence, by the bursting of the pond at the top of a mountain that was opposite the town of Plymouth. It swept great part of the town away, and Mr. King lost a great deal of property from the inundation, and nearly his life. When I told him I in-tended to go to London that season, and that I had come to visit him before my departure, the good man expressed a great deal of affection for me, and sorrow that I should leave him, and warmly advised me to stay there, insisting, as I was much respected by all the gentlemen in the place, that I might do very well, and in a short time have land and slaves of my own. I thanked him for this in-stance of his friendship; but, as I wished very much to be in London, I declined remaining any longer there, and begged he would excuse me. I then requested he would be kind enough to give me a certificate of my behavior while in his service, which he very readily complied with, and gave me the following:

MONTSERRAT, JULY 26, 1767.

The bearer hereof, Gustavus Vassa, was my slave for upwards of three years, during which he has always behaved himself well, and discharged his duty with honesty and assiduity.

ROBERT KING

TO ALL WHOM THIS MAY CONCERN.

Having obtained this, I parted from my kind master, after many sincere professions of gratitude and regard, and prepared for my departure for London.

I immediately agreed to go with one Capt. John Hamer, for seven guineas (the passage to London) on board a ship called the *Andromache*; and on the 24th and 25th, I had free dances, as they are called, with some of my country-men, previous to my setting off; after which I took leave of all my friends, and on the 26th I embarked for London, exceedingly glad to see myself once more on board of a ship; and still more so, in steering the course I had long wished for. With a light heart I bade Montserrat farewell, and have never had my feet on it since; and with it I bade adieu to the sound of the cruel whip, and all other dreadful instruments of torture; adieu to the offensive sight of the violated chastity of the sable females, which has too often accosted my eyes; adieu to oppressions (although to me less severe than most of my countrymen); and adieu to the angry, howling, dashing surfs. I wished for a grateful and thankful heart to praise the Lord God on high for all his mercies! in this ecstasy, I steered the ship all night.

We had a most prosperous voyage, and, at the end of seven weeks, arrived at Cherry Garden stairs. Thus were my longing eyes once more gratified with the sight of London, after having been absent from it above four years. I immediately received my wages, and I never had earned seven guineas so quick in my life before; I had thirty-seven guineas in all, when I got cleared from the ship. I now entered upon a scene quite new to me, but full of hope. In this situation my first thoughts were to look out for some of my former friends, and amongst the first of those were the Miss Guerins. As soon, therefore, as I had regaled myself I went in quest of those kind ladies, whom I was very impatient to see; and with some difficulty and perseverance, I found them at May's-hill, Greenwich. They were most agreeably surprised to see me, and I quite overjoyed at meeting with them. I told them my history, at which they expressed great wonder, and freely acknowledged it did their cousin, Captain Pascal, no honor. He then visited there frequently; and I met him four or five days after in Greenwich park.

When he saw me he appeared a good deal surprised, and asked me how I came back? I answered, "In a ship." To which he replied dryly, "I suppose you did not walk back to London on the water." As I saw, by his manner, that he did not seem to be sorry for his behavior to me, and that I had not much reason to expect any favor from him, I told him that he had used me very ill, after I had been such a faithful servant to him for so many years; on which, without saying any more, he turned about and went away. A few days after this I met Capt. Pascal at Miss Guerin's house, and asked him for my prize money. He said there was none due to me; for, if my prize money had been £10,000 he had a right to it all. I told him I was informed otherwise: on which he bade me defiance; and in a bantering tone, desired me to commence a law-suit against him for it: "There are lawyers enough," said he, "that will take the cause in hand, and you had better try it." I told him then that I would try it, which enraged him very much; however, out of regard to the ladies, I remained still, and never made any farther demand of my right.

Some time afterwards these friendly ladies asked me what I meant to do with myself, and how they could assist me. I thanked them, and said, if they pleased, I would be their servant; but if not, I had thirty-seven guineas, which would support me for some time, I would be much obliged to them to recommend me to some person who would teach me a business whereby I might earn my living. They answered me very politely, that they were sorry it did not suit them to take me as their servant, and asked me what business I should like to learn? I said, hair dressing. They then promised to assist me in this; and soon after they recommended me to a gentleman, whom I had known before, one

Capt. O'Hara, who treated me with much kindness, and procured me a master, a hair dresser, in Coventry court Haymarket, with whom he placed me. I was with this man from September till the February following. In that time we had a neighbor in the same court who taught the French horn. He used to blow it so well that I was charmed with it, and agreed with him to teach me to blow it. Accordingly he took me in hand, and began to instruct me, and I soon learned all the three parts. I took great delight in blowing on this instrument, the evenings being long; and besides that I was fond of it, I did not like to be idle, and it filled up my vacant hours innocently. At this time also I agreed with the Rev. Mr. Gregory, who lived in the same court, where he kept an academy and an evening school, to improve me in arithmetic. This he did as far as barter and alligation; so that all the time I was there I was entirely employed.

In February 1768 I hired myself to Dr. Charles Irving, in Pallmall, so celebrated for his successful experiments in making sea water fresh; and here I had plenty of hair dressing to improve my hand. This gentleman was an excellent master; he was exceedingly kind and good tempered; and allowed me in the evenings to attend my schools, which I esteemed a great blessing; therefore I thanked God and him for it, and used all my diligence to improve the opportunity. This diligence and attention recommended me to the notice and care of my three preceptors, who, on their parts, bestowed a great deal of pains in my instruction, and besides, were all very kind to me. My wages, however, which were by two-thirds less than ever I had in my life (for I had only £12 per annum), I soon found would not be sufficient to defray this extraordinary expense of masters, and my own necessary expenses; my old thirty-seven guineas had by this time worn all away to one. I thought it best, therefore, to try the sea again in quest of more money, as I had been bred to it, and had hitherto found the profession of it successful. I had also a very great desire to see Turkey, and I now determined to gratify it. Accordingly, in the month of May, 1768, I told the doctor my wish to go to sea again, to which he made no opposition; and we parted on friendly terms.

The same day I went into the city in quest of a master. I was extremely fortunate in my inquiry, for I soon heard of a gentleman who had a ship going to Italy and Turkey, and he wanted a man who could dress hair well. I was overjoyed at this and went immediately on board of his ship, as I had been directed, which I found to be fitted up with great taste, and I already foreboded no small pleasure in sailing in her. Not finding the gentleman on board, I was directed to his lodgings, where I met with him the next day, and gave him a specimen of my dressing. He liked it so well that he hired me immediately, so that I was perfectly happy; for the ship, master, and voyage, were entirely to my mind. The ship was called the *Delaware*, and my master's name was John Jolly, a neat, smart, good humored man, just such an one as I wished to serve.

We sailed from England in July following, and our voyage was extremely pleasant. We went to Villa Franca, Nice, and Leghorn; and in all these places I was charmed with the richness and beauty of the countries, and struck with the elegant buildings with which they abound. We had always in them plenty of extraordinary good wines and rich fruits, which I was very fond of; and I had frequent occasions of gratifying both my taste and curiosity; for my captain always lodged on shore in those places, which afforded me opportunities to see the country around. I also learned navigation of the mate, which I was very fond of. When we left Italy we had delightful sailing among the Archipelago islands, and from thence to Smyrna in Turkey. This is a very ancient city; the houses are built of stone, and most of them have graves adjoining to them; so that they sometimes present the appearance of church-yards. Provisions are very plentiful in this city, and good wine less than a penny a pint. The grapes, pomegranates, and many other fruits, were also the richest and largest I ever tasted. The natives are well looking and strong made, and treated me always with great civility. In general I believe they are fond of black people; and several of them gave me pressing invitations to stay amongst them, although they keep the franks, or Christians, separate, and do not suffer them to dwell immediately amongst them. I was astonished in not seeing women in any of their shops, and very rarely any in the streets; and whenever I did they were covered with a veil from head to foot, so that I could not see their faces, except when any of them out of curiosity uncovered them to look at me, which they sometimes did. I was surprised to see how the Greeks are, in some measure, kept under by the Turks, as the Negroes are in the West Indies by the white people. The less refined Greeks, as I have already hinted, dance here in the same manner as we do in our nation.

On the whole, during our stay here, which was about five months, I liked the place and the Turks extremely well. I could not help observing one very remarkable circumstance there: the tails of the sheep are flat and so very large that I have known the tail even of a lamb to weigh from eleven to thirteen pounds. The fat of them is very white and rich, and is excellent in puddings, for which it is much used. Our ship being at length richly loaded with silk and other articles, we sailed for England.

In May 1769, soon after our return from Turkey, our ship made a delightful voyage to Oporto, in Portugal, where we arrived at the time of the carnival. On our arrival, there were sent on board of us thirty-six articles to observe with very heavy penalties if we should break any of them; and none of us even dared to go on board any other vessel or on shore, till the Inquisition had sent on board and searched for everything illegal, especially Bibles. Such as were produced, and certain other things, were sent on shore till the ships were going away; and any person, in whose custody a Bible was found concealed, was to be imprisoned and flogged, and sent into slavery for ten years. I saw here many very magnificent sights, particularly the garden of Eden, where many of the clergy and laity went in procession in their several orders with the host, and sung Te Deum. I had a great curiosity to go into some of their churches, but could not gain admittance, without using the necessary sprinkling of holy water at my entrance. From curiosity, and a wish to be holy, I therefore complied with this ceremony, but its virtues were lost upon me, for I found myself nothing the better for it. This place abounds with plenty of all kinds of provisions.

The town is well built and pretty, and commands a fine prospect. Our ship having taken in a load of wine, and other commodities, we sailed for London, and arrived in July following.

Our next voyage was to the Mediterranean. The ship was again got ready, and we sailed in September for Genoa. This is one of the finest cities I ever saw; some of the edifices were of beautiful marble, and made a most noble appearance; and many had very curious fountains before them. The churches were rich and magnificent, and curiously adorned, both in the inside and out. But all this grandeur was, in my eyes, disgraced by the galley slaves, whose condition, both there and in other parts of Italy, is truly piteous and wretched. After we had stayed there some weeks, during which we bought many different things we wanted, and got them very cheap, we sailed to Naples, a charming city, and remarkably clean. The bay is the most beautiful I ever saw; the moles for shipping are excellent. I thought it extraordinary to see grand operas acted here on Sunday nights, and even attended by their majesties. I too, like these great ones, went to those sights, and vainly served God in the day, while I thus served mammon effectually at night. While we remained here, there happened an eruption of Mount Vesuvius, of which I had a perfect view. It was extremely awful; and we were so near that the ashes from it, used to be thick on our deck. After we had transacted our business at Naples, we sailed with a fair wind, once more for Smyrna, where we arrived in December. A seraskier, or officer, took a liking to me here, and wanted me to stay, and offered me two wives; however, I refused the temptation, thinking one was as much as some could manage, and more than others would venture on. The merchants here travel in caravans or large companies. I have seen many caravans from India, with some hundreds of camels, laden with different goods. The people of these caravans are quite brown. Among other articles, they brought with them a great quantity of locusts, which are a kind of pulse, sweet and pleasant to the palate, and in shape resembling French beans, but longer. Each kind of goods is sold in a street by itself, and I always found the Turks very honest in their dealings. They let no Christians into their mosques or churches, for which I was very sorry; as I was always fond of going to see the different modes of worship of the people wherever I went. The plague broke out while we were in Smyrna, and we stopped taking goods into the ship till it was over. She was then richly laden, and we sailed in about March 1770 for England. One day in our passage, we met with an accident, which was near burning the ship. A black cook, in melting some fat, overset the pan into the fire under the deck, which immediately began to blaze, and the flame went up very high under the foretop. With the fright, the poor cook became almost white, and altogether speechless. Happily, however, we got the fire out, without doing much mischief. After various delays in this passage, which was tedious, we arrived in Standgate creek in July; and, at the latter end of the year, some new event occurred, so that my noble captain, the ship, and I, all separated.

In April 1771, I shipped myself as steward, with Captain William Robertson, of the ship *Grenada Planter*, once more to try my fortune in the West Indies; and we sailed from London for Madeira, Barbadoes, and the Grenadas. When we were at this last place, having some goods to sell, I met once more with my former kind of West India customers.

A white man, an islander, bought some goods of me, to the amount of some pounds, and made me many fair promises as usual, but without any intention of paying me. He had likewise bought goods from some more of our people, whom he intended to serve in the same manner; but he still amused us with promises. However, when our ship was loaded, and near sailing, this honest buyer discovered no intention or sign of paying for anything he had bought of us; but on the contrary, when I asked him for my money, he threatened me and another black man he had bought goods of, so that we found we were like to get more blows than payment. On this, we went to complain to one Mr. M'Intosh, a justice of the peace; we told his worship of the man's villainous tricks, and begged that he would be kind enough to see us redressed; but being Negroes, although free, we could not get any remedy; and our ship being then just upon the point of sailing, we knew not how to help ourselves, though we thought it hard to lose our property in this manner. Luckily for us, however, this man was also indebted to three white sailors, who could not get a farthing from him; they therefore readily joined us, and we all went together in search of him. When we found where he was, I took him out of a house and threatened him with vengeance; on which, finding he was likely to be handled roughly, the rogue offered each of us some small allowance, but nothing near our demands. This exasperated us much more; and some were for cutting his ears off; but he begged hard for mercy, which was at last granted him, after we had entirely stripped him. We then let him go, for which he thanked us, glad to get off so easily, and ran into the bushes, after having wished us a good voyage. We then repaired on board, and shortly after set sail for England. I cannot help remarking here, a very narrow escape we had from being blown up, owing to a piece of negligence of mine. Just as our ship was under sail, I went down under the cabin, to do some business, and had a lighted candle in my hand, which, in my hurry, without thinking, I held in a barrel of gunpowder. It remained in the powder until it was near catching fire, when fortunately, I observed it, and snatched it out in time, and providentially no harm happened; but I was so overcome with terror that I immediately fainted at this deliverance.

In twenty-eight days' time, we arrived in England, and I got clear of this ship. But, being still of a roving disposition, and desirous of seeing as many different parts of the world as I could, I shipped myself soon after, in the same year, as steward on board of a fine large ship, called the *Jamaica*, Capt. David Watt; and we sailed from England in December 1771, for Nevis and Jamaica. I found Jamaica to be a very fine, large island, well peopled, and the most considerable of the West India islands. There was a vast number of Negroes here, whom I found as usual, exceedingly imposed upon by the white people, and the slaves punished as in the other islands. There are Negroes whose business is to flog slaves; they go about to different people for employment, and the usual pay is from one to four bits. I saw many cruel punishments inflicted on the slaves, in the short time I stayed here. In particular, I was present when a poor fellow was tied up and kept hanging by the wrists, at some distance from the ground, and then some half hundred weights were fixed to his ankles, in which posture he was flogged unmercifully. There was also, as I heard, two different masters noted for cruelty on the island, who had staked up two Negroes naked, and in two hours the vermin stung them to death. I heard a gentleman, I well knew, tell my captain, that he passed sentence on a Negro man to be burnt alive for attempting to poison an overseer.

I pass over numerous other instances, in order to relieve the reader, by a milder scene of roguery. Before I had been long on the island, one Mr. Smith, at Port Morant, bought goods of me to the amount of twenty-five pounds sterling; but when I demanded payment from him, he was going each time to beat me, and threatened that he would put me in jail. One time he would say I was going to set his house on fire; at another, he would swear I was going to run away with his slaves. I was astonished at this usage, from a person who was in the situation of a gentleman, but I had no alternative, and was, therefore, obliged to submit.

When I came to Kingston, I was surprised to see the number of Africans who were assembled together on Sundays, particularly at a large commodious place, called Spring Path. Here each different nation of Africa meet and dance after the manner of their own country. They still retain most of their native customs; they bury their dead, and put victuals, pipes, and tobacco, and other things, in the grave with the corpse, in the same manner as in Africa.

Our ship having got her loading, we sailed for London, where we arrived in the August following. On my return to London, I waited on my old and good master, Dr. Irving, who made me an offer of his service again. Being now tired of the sea, I gladly accepted it. I was very happy in living with this gentleman once more, during which time we were daily employed in reducing old Neptune's dominions, by purifying the briny element and making it fresh. Thus I went on till May 1773, when I was roused by the sound of fame, to seek new adventures, and find, towards the North Pole, what our Creator never intended we should, a passage to India.

An expedition was now fitting out to explore a north-east passage, conducted by the Honorable Constantine John Phipps, since Lord Mulgrave, in his Majesty's sloop-of-war, the *Race Horse*. My master being anxious for the reputation of this adventure, we therefore prepared everything for our voyage, and I attended him on board the *Race Horse*, the 24th day of May, 1773. We proceeded to Sheerness, where we were joined by his Majesty's sloop, the *Carcass*, commanded by Captain Lutwidge. On the 4th of June, we sailed towards our destined place, the Pole; and on the 15th of the same month, we were off Shetland.

On this day I had a great and unexpected deliverance, from an accident which was near blowing up the ship and destroying the crew, which made me ever after, during the voyage, uncommonly cautious. The ship was so filled that there was very little room on board for anyone, which placed me in a very awkward situation. I had resolved to keep a journal of this singular and interesting voyage; and I had no other place for this purpose but a little cabin, or the doctor's store-room, where I slept. This little place was stuffed with all manner of combustibles, particularly with tow and aquafortis, and many other dangerous things. Unfortunately, it happened in the evening, as I was writing my journal, that I had occasion to take the candle out of the lanthorn, and a spark having touched a single thread of the tow, all the rest caught the flame, and immediately the whole was in a blaze. I saw nothing but present death before me, and expected to be the first to perish in the flames. In a moment the alarm was spread, and many people who were near, ran to assist in putting out the fire. All this time, I was in the very midst of the flames; my shirt and the handkerchief on my neck, were burnt, and I was almost smothered with the smoke. However, through God's mercy, as I was nearly giving up all hopes, some people brought blankets and mattresses, and threw them on the flames, by which means in a short time the fire was put out. I was severely reprimanded and menaced by such of the officers who knew it, and strictly charged never more to go there with a light; and, indeed, even my own fears made me give heed to this command for a little time; but at last, not being able to write my journal in any other part of the ship, I was tempted again to venture by stealth, with a light in the same cabin, though not without considerable fear and dread on my mind.

On the 20th of June, we began to use Dr. Irving's apparatus for making salt water fresh; I used to attend the distillery: I frequently purified from twenty-six to forty gallons a day. The water thus distilled was perfectly pure, well tasted, and free from salt, and was used on various occasions on board the ship. On the 28th of June, being in latitude 78, we made Greenland, where I was surprised to see the sun did not set. The weather now became extremely cold; and as we sailed between north and east, which was our course, we saw many very high and curious mountains of ice; and also a great number of very large whales, which used to come close to our ship, and blow the water up to a very great height in the air. One morning we had vast quantities of sea horses about the ship, which neighed exactly like any other horses. We fired some harpoon guns amongst them, in order to take some, but we could not get any. The 30th, the captain of a Greenland ship came on board, and told us of three ships that were lost in the ice; however, we still held on our course, till July the 11th, when we were stopt by one compact and impenetrable body of ice. We ran along it from east to west about ten degrees; and on the 27th, we got as far north as 80°37′; and in 19 or 20 degrees, east longitude from London.

On the 29th and 30th of July, we saw one continued plain of smooth, unbroken ice, bounded only by the horizon; and we fastened to a piece of ice that was eight yards eleven inches thick. We had generally sunshine, and constant daylight; which gave cheerfulness and novelty to the whole of this striking, grand, and uncommon scene; and, to heighten it still more, the reflection of the sun from the ice gave the clouds a most beautiful appearance. We killed many different animals at this time, and among the rest nine bears. Though they had nothing in their paunches but water, yet they were all very fat. We used to decoy them to the ship sometimes by burning feathers or skins. I thought them coarse eating, but some of the ship's company relished them very much. Some of our people, once in the boat, fired at and wounded a sea horse, which dived immediately, and in a little time after, brought up with it a number of others. They all joined in an attack upon the boat, and were with difficulty prevented from staving or oversetting her; but a boat from the *Carcass* having come to assist ours, and joined it, they dispersed, after having wrested an oar from one of the men. One of the ship's boats had before been attacked in the same manner, but happily no harm was done. Though we wounded several of these animals we never got but one.

We remained hereabouts until the 1st of August, when the two ships got completely fastened in the ice, occasioned by the loose ice that set in from the sea. This made our situation very dreadful and alarming; so that on the 7th day, we were in very great apprehension of having the ships squeezed to pieces. The officers now held a council to know what was best for us to do in order to save our lives; and it was determined that we should endeavor to escape by dragging our boats along the ice towards the sea, which, however, was farther off than any of us thought. This determination filled us with extreme dejection, and confounded us with despair, for we had very little prospect of escaping with life. However, we sawed some of the ice about the ships, to keep it from hurting them, and thus kept them in a kind of pond. We then began to drag the boats as well as we could towards the sea; but, after two or three days' labor, we made very little progress, so that some of our hearts totally failed us; and I really began to give up myself for lost, when I saw our surrounding calamities. While we were at this hard labor, I once fell into a pond we had made amongst some loose ice, and was very near being drowned; but providentially some people were near who gave me immediate assistance, and thereby I escaped drowning.

Our deplorable condition, which kept up the constant apprehension of our perishing in the ice, brought me gradually to think of eternity, in such a manner as I never had done before. I had the fears of death hourly upon me, and shuddered at the thoughts of meeting the grim king of terrors in the natural state I then was in, and was exceedingly doubtful of a happy eternity if I should die in it. I had no hopes of my life being prolonged for any time; for we saw that our existence could not be long on the ice after leaving the ships, which were now out of sight, and some miles from the boats. Our appearance now became truly lamentable; pale dejection seized every countenance; many, who had been before blasphemers, in this our distress, began to call on the good God of Heaven for his help; and in the time of our utter need he heard us, and against hope or human probability, delivered us! It was the eleventh day of the ships' being thus fastened, and the fourth of our drawing the boats in this manner, that the wind changed to the E. N. E. The weather immediately became mild, and the ice broke towards the sea, which was to the S. W. of us. Many of us on this got on board again, and with all our might we hove the ships into every open water we could find, and made all the sail on them in our power; and now, having a prospect of success, we made signals for the boats, and the remainder of the people.

This seemed to us like a reprieve from death, and happy was the man who could first get on board of any ship, or the first boat he could meet. We then proceeded in this manner, till we got into the open water again, which we accomplished in about thirty hours, to our infinite joy and gladness of heart. As soon as we were out of danger, we came to anchor and refitted; and on the 19th of August, we sailed from this uninhabited extremity of the world, where the inhospitable climate affords neither food nor shelter, and not a tree or a shrub of any kind grows amongst its barren rocks; but all is one desolate and expanded waste of ice, which even the constant beams of the sun for six months in the year cannot penetrate or dissolve.

The sun now being on the decline, the days shortened as we sailed to the southward; and, on the 28th, in latitude 73, it was dark by ten o'clock at night. September 10th, in latitude 58, 59, we met a very severe gale of wind and high seas, and shipped a great deal of water in the space of ten hours. This made us work exceedingly hard at all our pumps a whole day; and one sea, which struck the ship with more force than anything I ever met with of the kind before, laid her under water for some time, so that we thought she would have gone down. Two boats were washed from the booms, and the long-boat from the chucks; all other moveable things on the decks were also washed away, among which were many curious things, of different kinds, which we had brought from Greenland; and we were obliged, in order to lighten the ship, to toss some of our guns overboard. We saw a ship at the same time, in very great distress, and her masts were gone; but we were unable to assist her. We now lost sight of the *Carcass*, till the 26th, when we saw land about Orfordness, of which place she joined us. From thence we sailed for London, and on the 30th came up to Deptford.

And thus ended our Arctic voyage, to the no small joy of all on board, after having been absent four months, in which time, at the imminent hazard of our lives, we explored nearly as far towards the Pole as 81 degrees north, and 20 degrees east longitude; being much farther, by all accounts, than any navigator had ever ventured before; in which we fully proved the impracticability of finding a passage that way to India.

Quobna Ottobah Cugoano
from *Thoughts and Sentiments on the Evil of Slavery*

But such is the insensibility of men, when their own craft of gain is advanced by the slavery and oppression of others, that after all the laudable exertions of the truly virtuous and humane, towards extending the beneficence of liberty and freedom to the much degraded and unfortunate Africans, which is the common right and privilege of all men, in every thing that is just, lawful and consistent, we find the principles of justice and equity, not only opposed, and every duty in religion and humanity left unregarded; but that unlawful traffic of dealing with our fellow-creatures, as with the beasts of the earth, still carried on with as great assiduity as ever; and that the insidious piracy of procuring and holding slaves is countenanced and supported by the government of sundry Christian nations. This seems to be the fashionable way of getting riches, but very dishonourable; in doing this, the slave-holders are meaner and baser than the African slaves, for while they subject and reduce them to a degree with brutes, they seduce themselves to a degree with devils.

"Some pretend that the Africans, in general, are a set of poor, ignorant, dispersed, unsociable people; and that they think it no crime to sell one another, and even their own wives and children; therefore they bring them away to a situation where many of them may arrive to a better state than ever they could obtain in their own native country." This specious pretence is without any shadow of justice and truth, and, if the argument was even true, it could afford no just and warrantable matter for any society of men to hold slaves. But the argument is false; there can be no ignorance, dispersion, or unsociableness so found among them, which can be made better by bringing them away to a state of a degree equal to that of a cow or a horse.

But let their ignorance in some things (in which the Europeans have greatly the advantage of them) be what it will, it is not the intention of those who bring them away to make them better by it; nor is the design of slave-holders of any other intention, but that they may serve them as a kind of engines and beasts of burden; that their own ease and profit may be advanced, by a set of poor helpless men and women, whom they despise and rank with brutes, and keep them in perpetual slavery, both themselves and children, and merciful death is the only release from their toil. By the benevolence of some, a few may get their liberty, and by their own industry and ingenuity, may acquire some learning, mechanical trades, or useful business; and some may be brought away by different gentlemen to free countries, where they get their liberty, but no thanks to slave-holders for it. But amongst those who get their liberty, like all other ignorant men, are generally more corrupt in their morals, than they possibly could have been amongst their own people in Africa; for, being mostly amongst the wicked and apostate Christians, they sooner learn their oaths and blasphemies, and their evil ways, than any thing else. Some few, indeed, may eventually arrive at some knowledge of the Christian religion, and the great advantages of it. Such was the case of Ukawsaw Groniosaw, an African prince, who lived in England. He was a long time in a state of great poverty and distress, and must have died at one time for want, if a good and charitable attorney had not supported him. He was long after in a very poor state, but he would not have given his faith in the Christian religion, in exchange for all the kingdoms of Africa, if they could have been given to him, in place of his poverty, for it. And such was A. Morrant in America. When a boy, he could stroll away into a desart, and prefer the society of wild beasts to the absurd Christianity of his mother's house. He was conducted to the king of the Cherokees, who, in a miraculous manner, was induced by him to embrace the Christian faith. This Morrant was in the British service last war, and his royal convert, the king of the Cherokee Indians, accompanied General Clinton at the siege of Charles Town.

These, and all such, I hope thousands, as meet with the knowledge and grace of the Divine clemency, are brought forth quite contrary to the end and intention of all slavery, and, in general, of all slave holders too. And should it please the Divine goodness to visit some of the poor dark Africans, even in the brutal stall of slavery, and from thence to instal them among the princes of his grace, and to invest them with a robe of honor that will hang about their necks for ever; but who can then suppose, that it will be well pleasing unto him to find them subjected there in that dejected state? Or can the slave-holders think that the Universal Father and Sovereign of Mankind will be well pleased with them, for the brutal transgression of his law, in bowing down the necks of those to the yoke of their cruel bondage? Sovereign goodness may eventually visit some men even in a state of slavery, but their slavery is not a cause of that event and benignity; and therefore, should some event of good ever happen to some men subjected to slavery, that can plead nothing for men to do evil that good may come; and should it apparently happen from thence, it is neither sought for nor designed by the enslavers of men. But the whole business of slavery is an evil of the first magnitude, and a most horrible iniquity to traffic with slaves and souls of men; and an evil. [S]orry I am, that it still subsists, and more astonishing to think, that it is an iniquity committed amongst Christians, and contrary to all the genuine principles of Christianity, and yet carried on by men denominated thereby.

In a Christian aera, in a land where Christianity is planted, where every one might expect to behold the flourishing growth of every virtue, extending their harmonious branches with universal philanthropy wherever they came; but, on the contrary, almost nothing else is to be seen abroad but the bramble of ruffians, barbarians and slave-holders, grown up to a powerful luxuriance in wickedness. I cannot but wish, for the honor of Christianity, that the bramble grown up amongst them, was known to the heathen nations by a different name, for sure the depredators, robbers and ensnarers of men can never be Christians, but ought to be held as the abhorrence of all men, and the abomination of all mankind, whether Christians or heathens. Every man of any sensibility, whether he be a Christian or an heathen, if he has any discernment at all, must think, that for any man, or any class of men, to deal with their fellow-creatures as with the beasts of the field; or to account them as such, however ignorant they may be, and in whatever situation, or wherever they may find them, and whatever country or complexion they may be of, that those men, that are the procurers and holders of slaves, are the greatest villains in the world. And surely those men must be lost to all sensibility themselves, who can think that the stealing, robbing, enslaving, and murdering of men can be no crimes; but the holders of men in slavery are at the head of all these oppressions and crimes. And, therefore, however unsensible they may be of it now, and however long they may laugh at the calamity of others, if they do not repent of their evil way, and the wickedness of their doings by keeping and holding their fellow-creatures in slavery, and trafficking with them as with the brute creation, and to give up and surrender that evil traffic, with an awful abhorrence of it, that this may be averred, if they do not, and if they can think, they must and cannot otherwise but expect in one day at last, to meet with the full stroke of the long suspended vengeance of heaven, when death will cut them down to a state as mean as that of the most abjected slave, and to a very eminent danger of a more dreadful fate hereafter, when they have the just reward of their iniquities to meet with.

And now, as to the Africans being dispersed and unsociable, if it was so, that could be no warrant for the Europeans to enslave them; and even though they may have many different feuds and bad practices among them, the continent of Africa is of vast extent, and the numerous inhabitants are divided into several kingdoms and principalities, which are governed by their respective kings and princes, and those are absolutely maintained by their free subjects. Very few nations make slaves of any of those under their government; but such as are taken prisoners of war from their neighbours, are generally kept in that state, until they can exchange and dispose of them otherwise; and towards the west coast they are generally procured for the European market, and sold. They have a great aversion to murder, or even in taking away the lives of those which they judge guilty of crimes; and, therefore, they prefer disposing of them otherwise better than killing them. This gives their merchants and procurers of slaves a power to travel a great way into the interior parts of the country to buy such as are wanted to be disposed of. These slave-procurers are a set of as great villains as any in the world. They often steal and kidnap many more than they buy at first, if they can meet with them by the way; and they have only their certain boundaries to go to, and sell them from one to another; so that if they are sought after and detected, the thieves are seldom found, and the others only plead that they bought them so and so. These kid-nappers and slave-procurers, called merchants, are a species of African villains, which are greatly corrupted, and even viciated by their intercourse with the Europeans; but, wicked and barbarous as they certainly are, I can hardly think, if they knew what horrible barbarity they were sending their fellow-creatures to, that they would do it. But the artful Europeans have so deceived them, that they are bought by their inventions of merchandize, and beguiled into it by their artifice; for the Europeans, at their factories, in some various manner, have always kept some as servants to them, and with gaudy cloaths, in a gay manner, as decoy ducks to deceive others, and to tell them that they want many more to go over the sea, and be as they are. So in that respect, wherein it may be said that they will sell one another, they are only ensnared and enlisted to be servants, kept like some of those which they see at the factories, which, for some gewgaws, as presents given to themselves and friends, they are thereby enticed to go; and something after the same manner that East-India soldiers are procured in Britain; and the inhabitants here, just as much sell themselves, and one another, as they do; and the kid-nappers here, and the slave-procurers in Africa, are much alike. But many other barbarous methods are made use of by the vile instigators, procurers and ensnarers of men; and some of the wicked and profligate princes and chiefs of Africa accept of presents, from the Europeans, to procure a certain number of slaves; and thereby they are wickedly instigated to go to war with one another on purpose to get them, which produces many terrible depredations; and sometimes when those engagements are entered into, and they find themselves defeated of their purpose, it has happened that some of their own people have fallen a sacrifice to their avarice and cruelty. And it may be said of the Europeans, that they have made use of every insidious method to procure slaves whenever they can, and in whatever manner they can lay hold of them, and that their forts and factories are the avowed dens of thieves for robbers, plunderers and depredators.

But again, as to the Africans selling their own wives and children, nothing can be more opposite to every thing they hold dear and valuable; and nothing can distress them more, than to part with any of their relations and friends. Such are the tender feelings of parents for their children, that, for the loss of a child, they seldom can be rendered happy, even with the intercourse and enjoyment of their friends, for years. For any man to think that it should be otherwise, when he may see a thousand instances of a natural instinct, even in the brute creation, where they have a sympathetic feeling for their offspring; it must be great want of consideration not to think, that much more than meerly what is natural to animals, should in a higher degree be implanted in the breast of every part of the rational creation of man. And what man of feeling can help lamenting the loss of parents, friends, liberty, and perhaps property and other valuable and dear connections. Those people annually brought away from Guinea, are born as free, and are brought up with as great a predilection for their own country, freedom and liberty, as the sons and daughters of fair Britain. Their free subjects are trained up to a kind of military service, not so much by the desire of the chief, as by their own voluntary inclination. It is looked upon as the greatest respect they can shew, to their king, to stand up for his and their own defence in time of need. Their different chieftains, which bear a reliance on the great chief, or king, exercise a kind of government some-thing like that feudal institution which prevailed some time in Scotland. In this respect, though the common people are free, they often suffer by the vil-lainy of their different chieftains, and by the wars and feuds which happen among them. Nevertheless their freedom and rights are as dear to them, as those privileges are to other people. And it may be said that freedom, and the liberty of enjoying their own privileges, burns with as much zeal and fervour in the breast of an Æthiopian, as in the breast of any inhabitant on the globe.

But the supporters and favourers of slavery make other things a pretence and an excuse in their own defence; such as, that they find that it was admitted under the Divine institution by Moses, as well as the long continued practice of different nations for ages; and that the Africans are peculiarly marked out by some signal prediction in nature and complexion for that purpose.

This seems to be the greatest bulwark of defence which the advocates and favourers of slavery can advance, and what is generally talked of in their favour by those who do not understand it. I shall consider it in that view, whereby it will appear, that they deceive themselves and mislead others. Men are never more liable to be drawn into error, than when truth is made use of in a guileful manner to seduce them. Those who do not believe the scriptures to be a Divine revelation, cannot, consistently with themselves, make the law of Moses, or any mark or prediction they can find respecting any particular set of men, as found in the sacred writings, any reason that one class of men should enslave another. In that respect, all that they have to enquire into should be whether it be right, or wrong, that any part of the human species should enslave another; and when that is the case, the Africans, though not so learned, are just as wise as the Europeans; and when the matter is left to human wisdom, they are both liable to err. But what the light of nature, and the dictates of reason, when rightly considered, teach, is, that no man ought to enslave another; and some, who have been rightly guided thereby, have made noble defences for the uni-versal natural rights and privileges of all men. But in this case, when the learned take neither revelation nor reason for their guide, they fall into as great, and worse errors, than the unlearned; for they only make use of that sys-tem of Divine wisdom, which should guide them into truth, when they can find or pick out any thing that will suit their purpose, or that they can pervert to such—the very means of leading themselves and others into error. And, in consequence thereof, the pretences that some men make use of for holding of slaves, must be evidently the grossest perversion of reason, as well as an incon-sistent and diabolical use of the sacred writings. For it must be a strange perver-sion of reason, and a wrong use or disbelief of the sacred writings, when any thing found there is so perverted by them, and set up as a precedent and rule for men to commit wickedness. They had better have no reason, and no belief in the scriptures, and make no use of them at all, than only to believe, and make use of that which leads them into the most abominable evil and wickedness of dealing unjustly with their fellow men.

But this will appear evident to all men that believe the scriptures, that every reason necessary is given that they should be believed; and, in this case, that they afford us this information: "That all mankind did spring from one original, and that there are no different species among men. For God who made the world, hath made of one blood all the nations of men that dwell on all the face of the earth." Wherefore we may justly infer, as there are no inferior species, but all of one blood and of one nature, that there does not an inferiority subsist, or depend, on their colour, features or form, whereby some men make a pretence to enslave others; and consequently, as they have all one creator, one original, made of one blood, and all brethren descended from one father, it never could be lawful and just for any nation, or people, to oppress and enslave another.

And again, as all the present inhabitants of the world sprang from the family of Noah, and were then all of one complexion, there is no doubt, but the difference which we now find, took its rise very rapidly after they became dispersed and settled on the different parts of the globe. There seems to be a tendency to this, in many instances, among children of the same parents, having different colour of hair and features from one another. And God alone who established the course of nature, can bring about and establish what variety he pleases; and it is not in the power of man to make one hair white or black. But among the variety which it hath pleased God to establish and caused to take place, we may meet with some analogy in nature, that as the bodies of men are tempered with a different degree to enable them to endure the respective climates of their habitations, so their colours vary, in some degree, in a regular gradation from the equator towards either of the poles. However, there are other incidental causes arising from time and place, which constitute the most distinguishing variety of colour, form, appearance and features, as peculiar to the inhabitants of one tract of country, and differing in something from those in another, even in the same latitudes, as well as from those in different climates. Long custom and the different way of living among the several inhabitants of the different parts of the earth, has a very great effect in distinguishing them by a difference of features and complexion. These effects are easy to be seen; as to the causes, it is sufficient for us to know, that all is the work of an Almighty hand. Therefore, as we find the distribution of the human species inhabiting the barren, as well as the most fruitful parts of the earth, and the cold as well as the most hot, differing from one another in complexion according to their situation; it may be reasonably, as well as religiously, inferred, that He who placed them in their various situations, hath extended equally his care and protection to all; and from thence, that it becometh unlawful to counteract his benignity, by reducing others of different complexions to undeserved bondage.

According, as we find that the difference of colour among men is only incidental, and equally natural to all, and agreeable to the place of their habitation; and that if nothing else be different or contrary among them, but that of features and complexion, in that respect, they are all equally alike entitled to the enjoyment of every mercy and blessing of God. But there are some men of that complexion, because they are not black, whose ignorance and insolence leads them to think, that those who are black, were marked out in that manner by some signal interdiction or curse, as originally descending from their progenitors. To those I must say, that the only mark which we read of, as generally alluded to, and by them applied wrongfully, is that mark or sign which God gave to Cain, to assure him that he should not be destroyed. Cain understood by the nature of the crime he had committed, that the law required death, or cutting off, as the punishment thereof. But God in his providence doth not always punish the wicked in this life according to their enormous crimes, (we are told, by a sacred poet, that he saw the wicked flourishing like a green bay tree) though he generally marks them out by some signal token of his vengeance; and that is a sure token of it, when men become long hardened in their wickedness. The denunciation that passed upon Cain was, that he should be a fugitive and a vagabond on the earth, bearing the curse and reproach of his iniquity; and the rest of men were prohibited as much from meddling with him, or defiling their hands by him, as it naturally is, not to pull down the dead carcase of an atrocious criminal, hung up in chains by the laws of his country. But allow the mark set upon Cain to have consisted in a black skin, still no conclusion can be drawn at all, that any of the black people are of that descent, as the whole posterity of Cain were destroyed in the universal deluge. . . .

The law of God forbids all manner of covetousness and theft: but when any thing is taken away by stealth, it is not like those injuries which cannot be restored, as the cutting off or wounding any of the members of the body; but it admits of a possible restoration, whether the violators can restore it or not as the law requires, so if a man owes a just debt it is not the less due by him if he has got nothing to pay it with; such transgressors ought to be punished according to their trespasses, but not with death: for the law of God is, "If a thief be found breaking up, and he be smitten that he die, if it was in the night there shall be no blood shed for him; but if the sun be risen upon him, there was blood required for him if he was killed; for saith the law it required only he should make full restitution; and if he had nothing, then he should be sold for his theft. And if any manner of theft be found in a man's hand, the law requires a retaliation and restoration; that is, that he should restore double; but if it be sold or made away with, it was then to be four-fold, and, in some cases, five, six or seven times as much." According to this law, when the property of others is taken away, either by stealth, fraud, or violence, the aggressors should be subjected to such bondage and hard labour, (and especially when the trespass is great, and they have nothing to pay) as would be requisite to make restitution to the injured, and to bring about a reformation to themselves. And if they have committed violence either by threats or force, they ought to suffer bodily punishment, and the severity of it according to their crimes, and the stubbornness of their obduracy; and all such punishments as are necessary should be inflicted upon them without pitying or sparing them, though perhaps not to be continued forever in the brutal manner that the West-India slaves suffer for almost no crimes.

But whereas the robbing of others in any manner of their property is often attended with such cruelty and violence, and a severe loss to the sufferers, it may, in some cases, be thought that the law of God sufficiently warrants the taking away the lives of the aggressors; for the taking away of a man's property in general may be considered as taking away his life, or at least the means of his support, and then the punishing the aggressors with death can only in that case be reckoned a constructive murder. Wherefore the transgressors ought to be punished severely; but never with any laws of civilization where death is concerned, without regard to the law of God. And when the law of God admits of a forbearance, and a kind of forgiveness in many things, it ought to be the grand law of civilization to seek out such rules of punishment as are best calculated to prevent injuries of every kind, and to reclaim the transgressors; and it is best, if it can be done, to punish with a less degree of severity than their crimes deserve. But all the laws of civilization must jar greatly when the law of God is screwed up in the greatest severity to punish men for their crimes on the one hand, and on the other to be totally disregarded. When the Divine law points out a theft, where the thief should make restitution for his trespass, the laws of civilization say, he must die for his crime: and when the law tells us, that he who stealeth or maketh merchandize of men, that such a thief shall surely die, the laws of civilization say, in many cases, that it is no crime. In this the ways of men are not equal; but let the wise and just determine whether the laws of God or the laws of men are right.

Amongst some of the greatest transgressors of the laws of civilization, those that defraud the public by forgery, or by substituting or falsifying any of the current specie, ought to have their lives or their liberties taken away; for although they may not do any personal injury, they commit the greatest robbery and theft, both to individuals and the whole community. But even in the suppression of those, men have no right to add or diminish any thing to the law of God, with respect to taking away their lives. Wherefore, if the law of God does not so clearly warrant, that they should die for their theft, it, at least, fully warrants that they should be sold into slavery for their crimes; and the laws of civilization may justly bind them, and hold them in perpetual bondage, because they have sold themselves to work iniquity; but not that they should be sold to the heathen, or to such as would not instruct them: for there might be hope, that if good instruction was properly administered unto them, there might be a possible reformation wrought upon some of them. Some, by their ingenious assiduity, have tamed the most savage wild beasts; it is certainly more laudable to tame the most brutish and savage men, and, in time, there might be some Onesimus's found amongst them, that would become useful to reclaim others. Those that break the laws of civilization, in any flagrant manner, are the only species of men that others have a right to enslave; and such ought to be sold to the community, with every thing that can be found belonging to them, to make a commutation of restitution as far as could be; and they should be kept at some useful and labourious employment, and it might be at some embanka-tion, or recovering of waste ground, as there might be land recovered on rivers and shores, worth all the expence, for the benefit of the community they be-longed to. The continuance of that criminal slavery and bondage, ought to be according to the nature of their crimes, with a reference to their good behav-iour, either to be continued or protracted. Such as were condemned for life, when their crimes were great, and themselves stubborn, might be so marked as to render their getting away impossible without being discovered, and that the very sight of one of them might deter others from committing their crimes, as much as hanging perhaps a dozen of them; and it might be made so severe unto them, that it would render their own society in bondage, almost the only preferable one that they could enjoy among men. The manner of confining them would not be so impracticable as some may be apt to think; and all these severities come under the laws of men to punish others for their crimes, but they should not go beyond the just law of God; and neither should his laws be suspended, where greater trespasses are committed.

In this sense every free community might keep slaves, or criminal prisoners in bondage; and should they be sold to any other, it should not be to strangers, nor without their own consent; and if any were sold for a term of years, they would naturally become free as soon as their purchase could be paid. But if any man should buy another man without his own consent, and compel him to his service and slavery without any agreement of that man to serve him, the en-slaver is a robber, and a defrauder of that man every day. Wherefore it is as much the duty of a man who is robbed in that manner to get out of the hands of his enslaver, as it is for an honest community of men to get out of the hands of rogues and villains. And however much is required of men to forgive one an-other their trespasses in one respect, it is also manifest, and what we are com-manded, as noble, to resist evil in another, in order to prevent others doing evil, and to keep ourselves from harm. Therefore, if there was no other way to deliver a man from slavery, but by enslaving his master, it would be lawful for him to do so if he was able, for this would be doing justice to himself, and be justice as the law requires, to chastise his master for enslaving of him wrongfully.

Thence this general and grand duty should be observed by every man, not to follow the multitude to do evil, neither to recompence evil for evil; and yet, so that a man may lawfully defend himself, and endeavour to secure himself, and others, as far as he can, from injuries of every kind. Wherefore all along, in the history of mankind, the various depredations committed in the world, by enslaving, extirpating and destroying men, were always contrary to the laws of God, and what he had strictly forbidden and commanded not to be done. But insolent, proud, wicked men, in all ages, and in all places, are alike; they disre-gard the laws of the Most High, and stop at no evil in their power, that they can contrive with any pretence of consistency in doing mischief to others, so as it may tend to promote their own profit and ambition. Such are all the depredators, kidnappers, merchandizers and enslavers of men; they do not care, nor consider, how much they injure others, if they can make any advantage to themselves by it. But whenever these things were committed by wicked men, a retaliation was sought after, as the only way of deliverance; for he who leadeth into captivity, should be carried captive; and he which destroyeth with the sword, should die with the sword. And as it became necessary to punish those that wronged others, when the punishers went beyond the bounds of a just retaliation, and fell into the same crimes of the oppressors, not to prevent themselves from harm, and to deliver the oppressed and the captive, but to oppress and enslave others, as much as they before them had done, the consequence is plain, that an impending overthrow must still fall upon them likewise. In that respect, so far as conquerors are permitted to become a judgment and a scourge to others, for their enormous transgressions, they are themselves not a bit more safe, for what they do, they often do wickedly for their own purpose; and when the purpose of Divine Providence, who raised them up, is fulfilled by them, in the punishment of others for their crimes; the next wave thereof will be to visit them also according to their wickedness with some dreadful overthrow, and to swallow them up in the sea of destruction and oblivion.

History affords us many examples of severe retaliations, revolutions and dreadful overthrows; and of many crying under the heavy load of subjection and oppression, seeking for deliverance. And methinks I hear now, many of my countrymen, in complexion, crying and groaning under the heavy yoke of slavery and bondage, and praying to be delivered; and the word of the Lord is thus speaking for them, while they are bemoaning themselves under the grievous bonds of their misery and woe, saying, *Woe is me! alas Africa! for I am as the last gleanings of the summer fruit, as the grape gleanings of the vintage, where no cluster is to eat. The good are perished out of the earth, and there is none upright among men; they all lie in wait for blood; they hunt every man his brother with a net. That they may do evil with both hands earnestly, the prince asketh, and the judge asketh for a reward; and the great man he uttereth his mischievous desire: so they wrap it up.* Among *the best* in Africa, we have found them *sharp as a briar;* among *the most upright,* we have found them *sharper than a thorn-hedge* in the West-Indies. Yet, O Africa! yet, poor slave! *The day of thy watchmen cometh, and thy visitation draweth nigh, that shall be their perplexity. Therefore I will look unto the Lord; I will wait for the God of my salvation; my God will hear me. Rejoice not against me, O mine enemy; though I be fallen, I shall yet arise; though I sit in darkness, the Lord shall yet be a light unto me. I will bear the indignation of the Lord, because I have sinned against him, until he plead my cause, and execute judgment for me, and I shall behold his righteousness. Then mine enemies shall see it, and shame shall cover them which said unto me, Where is the Lord thy God,* that regardeth thee: *Mine eyes shall behold them trodden down as the mire of the streets. In that day that thy walls of deliverance are to be built, in that day shall the decree* of slavery *be far removed.*

What revolution the end of that predominant evil of slavery and oppression may produce, whether the wise and considerate will surrender and give it up, and make restitution for the injuries that they have already done, as far as they can; or whether the force of their wickedness, and the iniquity of their power, will lead them on until some universal calamity burst forth against the abandoned carriers of it on, and against the criminal nations in confederacy with them, is not for me to determine? But this must appear evident, that for any man to carry on a traffic in the merchandize of slaves, and to keep them in slavery; or for any nation to oppress, extirpate and destroy others; that these are crimes of the greatest magnitude, and a most daring violation of the laws and commandments of the Most High, and which, at last, will be evidenced in the destruction and overthrow of all the transgressors. And nothing else can be expected for such violations of taking away the natural rights and liberties of men, but that those who are the doers of it will meet with some awful visitation of the righteous judgment of God, and in such a manner as it cannot be thought that his just vengeance for their iniquity will be the less tremendous because his judgments are long delayed.

None but men of the most brutish and depraved nature, led on by the invidious influence of infernal wickedness, could have made their settlements in the different parts of the world discovered by them, and have treated the various Indian nations, in the manner that the barbarous inhuman Europeans have done; and their establishing and carrying on that most dishonest, unjust and diabolical traffic of buying and selling, and of enslaving men, is such a monstrous, audacious and unparalleled wickedness, that the very idea of it is shocking, and the whole nature of it is horrible and infernal. It may be said with confidence as a certain general fact, that all their foreign settlements and colonies were founded on murders and devastations, and that they have continued their depredations in cruel slavery and oppression to this day: for where such predominant wickedness as the African slave-trade, and the West Indian slavery, is admitted, tolerated and supported by them, and carried on in their colonies, the nations and people who are the supporters and encouragers thereof must be not only guilty themselves of that shameful and abandoned evil and wickedness, so very disgraceful to human nature, but even partakers in those crimes of the most vile combinations of various pirates, kidnappers, robbers and thieves, the ruffians and stealers of men, that ever made their appearance in the world.

Soon after Columbus had discovered America, that great navigator was himself greatly embarrassed and treated unjustly, and his best designs counteracted by the wicked baseness of those whom he led to that discovery. The infernal conduct of his Spanish competitors, whose leading motives were covetousness, avarice and fanaticism, soon made their appearance, and became cruel and dreadful. At Hispaniola the base perfidy and bloody treachery of the Spaniards, led on by the perfidious Ovando, in seizing the peaceable Queen Anacoana and her attendants, burning her palace, putting all to destruction, and the innocent Queen and her people to a cruel death, is truly horrible and lamentable. And led on by the treacherous Cortes, the fate of the great Montezuma was dreadful and shocking; how that American monarch was treated, betrayed and destroyed, and his vast extensive empire of the Mexicans brought to ruin and devastation, no man of sensibility and feeling can read the history without pity and resentment. And looking over another page of that history, sensibility would kindle into horror and indignation, to see the base treacherous bastard Pizarra at the head of the Spanish banditti of miscreant depredators, leading them on, and overturning one of the most extensive empires in the world. To recite a little of this as a specimen of the rest: It seems Pizarra, with his company of depredators, had artfully penetrated into the Peruvian empire, and pretended an embassy of peace from a great monarch, and demanded an audience of the noble Atahualpa, the great Inca or Lord of that empire, that the terms of their embassy might be explained, and the reason of their coming into the territories of that monarch. Atahualpa fearing the menaces of those terrible invaders, and thinking to appease them by complying with their request, relied on Pizzara's feigned pretensions of friendship; accordingly the day was appointed, and Atahualpa made his appearance with the greatest decency and splendor he could, to meet such superior beings as the Americans conceived their invaders to be, with four hundred men in an uniform dress, as harbingers to clear the way before him, and himself sitting on a throne or couch, adorned with plumes of various colours, and almost covered with plates of gold and silver, enriched with precious stones, and was carried on the shoulders of his principal attendants. As he approached near the Spanish quarters the arch fanatic Father Vincent Valverde, chaplain to the expedition, advanced with a crucifix in one hand and a breviary in the other, and began with a long discourse, pretending to explain some of the general doctrines of Christianity, together with the fabulous notion of St. Peter's viceregency, and the transmission of his apostolic power continued in the succession of the Popes; and that the then Pope, Alexander, by donation, had invested their master as the sole Monarch of all the New World. In consequence of this, Atahualpa was instantly required to embrace the Christian religion, acknowledge the jurisdiction of the Pope, and submit to the Great Monarch of Castile; but if he should refuse an immediate compliance with these requisitions, they were to declare war against him, and that he might expect the dreadful effects of their vengeance. This strange harangue, unfolding deep mysteries, and alluding to such unknown facts, of which no power of eloquence could translate, and convey, at once, a distinct idea to an American, that its general tenor was altogether incomprehensible to Atahualpa. Some parts in it, as more obvious that the rest, filled him with astonishment and indignation. His reply, however, was temperate, and as suitable as could be well expected. He observed that he was Lord of the domains over which he reigned by hereditary succession; and, said, that he could not conceive how a foreign priest should pretend to dispose of territories which did not belong to him, and that if such a preposterous grant had been made, he, who was the rightful possessor, refused to confirm it; that he had no inclination to renounce the religious institutions established by his ancestors; nor would he forsake the service of the Sun, the immortal divinity whom he and his people revered, in order to worship the God of the Spaniards, who was subject to death; and that with respect to other matters, he had never heard of them before, and did not then understand their meaning. And he desired to know where Valverde had learned things so extraordinary. In this book, replied the fanatic Monk, reaching out his breviary. The Inca opened it eagerly, and turning over the leaves, lifted it to his ear: This, says he, is silent; it tells me nothing; and threw it with disdain to the ground. The enraged father of ruffians, turning towards his countrymen, the assassinators, cried out, To arms, Christians, to arms; the word of God is insulted; avenge this profanation on these impious dogs.

Phillis Wheatley
On Being Brought from Africa to America

'Twas mercy brought me from my *Pagan* land,
Taught my benighted soul to understand
That there's a God, that there's a *Saviour* too:
Once I redemption neither sought nor knew.
Some view our sable race with scornful eye,
"Their colour is a diabolic die."
Remember, *Christians*, *Negros*, black as *Cain*,
May be refin'd, and join th' angelic train.

To the University of Cambridge, in New-England

While an intrinsic ardor prompts to write,
The muses promise to assist my pen;
'Twas not long since I left my native shore
The land of errors, and *Egyptian* gloom:
Father of mercy, 'twas thy gracious hand
Brought me in safety from those dark abodes.

   Students, to you 'tis giv'n to scan the heights
Above, to traverse the ethereal space,
And mark the systems of revolving worlds.
Still more, ye sons of science ye receive
The blissful news by messengers from heav'n,
How *Jesus*' blood for your redemption flows.
See him with hands out-stretcht upon the cross;
Immense compassion in his bosom glows;
He hears revilers, nor resents their scorn:
What matchless mercy in the Son of God!
When the whole human race by sin had fall'n,
He deign'd to die that they might rise again,
And share with him in the sublimest skies,
Life without death, and glory without end.

Improve your privileges while they stay,
Ye pupils, and each hour redeem, that bears
Or good or bad report of you to heav'n.
Let sin, that baneful evil to the soul,
By you be shunn'd, nor once remit your guard;
Suppress the deadly serpent in its egg.
Ye blooming plants of human race devine,
An *Ethiop* tells you 'tis your greatest foe;
Its transient sweetness turns to endless pain,
And in immense perdition sinks the soul.

To His Excellency General Washington

Sir,

I have taken the freedom to address your Excellency in the enclosed poem,
and entreat your acceptance, though I am not insensible of its inaccuracies. Your
being appointed by the Grand Continental Congress to be Generalissimo of the
armies of North America, together with the fame of your virtues, excite sensations not easy to suppress. Your generosity, therefore, I presume, will pardon the
attempt. Wishing your Excellency all possible success in the great cause you are
so generously engaged in. I am,

Your Excellency's most obedient humble servant,
Phillis Wheatley
1776

Celestial choir! enthron'd in realms of light,
  Columbia's scenes of glorious toils I write.
While freedom's cause her anxious breast alarms,
She flashes dreadful in refulgent arms.
See mother earth her offspring's fate bemoan,
And nations gaze at scenes before unknown!
See the bright beams of heaven's revolving light
Involved in sorrows and veil of night!

  The goddess comes, she moves divinely fair,
Olive and laurel bind her golden hair:
Wherever shines this native of the skies,
Unnumber'd charms and recent graces rise.

  Muse! bow propitious while my pen relates
How pour her armies through a thousand gates,
As when Eolus heaven's fair face deforms,

Enwrapp'd in tempest and a night of storms;
Astonish'd ocean feels the wild uproar,
The refluent surges beat the sounding shore;
Or thick as leaves in Autumn's golden reign,
Such, and so many, moves the warrior's train.
In bright array they seek the work of war,
Where high unfurl'd the ensign waves in air.
Shall I to Washington their praise recite?
Enough thou know'st them in the fields of fight.
Thee, first in peace and honours,—we demand
The grace and glory of thy martial band.
Fam'd for thy valour, for thy virtues more,
Hear every tongue thy guardian aid implore!

 One century scarce perform'd its destined round,
When Gallic powers Columbia's fury found;
And so may you, whoever dares disgrace
The land of freedom's heaven-defended race!
Fix'd are the eyes of nations on the scales,
For in their hopes Columbia's arm prevails.
Anon Britannia droops the pensive head,
While round increase the rising hills of dead.
Ah! cruel blindness to Columbia's state!
Lament thy thirst of boundless power too late.

 Proceed, great chief, with virtue on thy side,
Thy ev'ry action let the goddess guide.
A crown, a mansion, and a throne that shine,
With gold unfading, WASHINGTON! be thine.

1776

Benjamin Banneker
Letter to Thomas Jefferson

Maryland, Baltimore County
Near Ellicotts' Lower Mills, August 19th, 1791

Thomas Jefferson, Secretary of State.

Sir:—I am fully sensible of the greatness of that freedom, which I take with you on the present occasion, a liberty which seemed to me scarcely allowable, when I reflected on that distinguished and dignified station in which you stand, and the almost general prejudice and prepossession which is so prevalent in the world against those of my complexion.

I suppose it is a truth too well attested to you, to need a proof here, that we are a race of beings who have long laboured under the abuse and censure of the world, that we have long been considered rather as brutish than human, and scarcely capable of mental endowments.

Sir, I hope I may safely admit, in consequence of that report which hath reached me, that you are a man far less inflexible in sentiments of this nature than many others, that you are measurably friendly and well disposed towards us, and that you are willing and ready to lend your aid and assistance to our relief, from those many distresses and numerous calamities, to which we are reduced.

Now, sir, if this is founded in truth, I apprehend you will readily embrace every opportunity to eradicate that train of absurd and false ideas and opinions, which so generally prevails with respect to us, and that your sentiments are concurrent with mine, which are that one universal Father hath given Being to us all, and that he hath not only made us all of one flesh, but that he hath also without partiality afforded us all the same sensations, and endued us all with the same faculties, and that however variable we may be in society or religion, however diversified in situation or colour, we are all of the same family, and stand in the same relation to him.

Sir, if these are sentiments of which you are fully persuaded, I hope you cannot but acknowledge, that it is the indispensable duty of those who maintain for themselves the rights of human nature, and who profess the obligations of christianity, to extend their power and influence to the relief of every part of the human race, from whatever burden or oppression they may unjustly labour under, and this I apprehend a full conviction of the truth and obligation of these principles should lead all to.

Sir, I have long been convinced that if your love for yourselves and for those inesteemable laws, which preserve to you the rights of human nature, was found on sincerity, you could not but be solicitous that every individual of whatever rank or distinction, might with you equally enjoy the blessings thereof, neither could you rest satisfied, short of the most active diffusion of your exertions in order to their promotions from any state of degradation to which the unjustifiable cruelty and barbarism of men have reduced them.

Sir, I freely and cheerfully acknowledge that I am of the African race, and in that colour which is natural to them of the deepest dye, and it is under a sense of the most profound gratitude to the Supreme Ruler of the universe that I now confess to you that I am not under that state of tyrannical thraldom and inhuman captivity to which too many of my brethren are doomed; but that I have abundantly tasted of the fruition of those blessings which proceed from that free and unequalled liberty with which you are favoured and which, I hope you will willingly allow you have received from the immediate hand of that Being, from whom proceedeth every good and perfect gift.

Sir, suffer me to recall to your mind that time in which the arms and tyranny of the British Crown were exerted with every powerful effort in order to reduce you to a State of Servitude, look back I entreat you on the variety of dangers to which you were exposed; reflect on that time in which every human aid appeared unavailable, and in which even hope and fortitude wore the aspect of inability to the conflict and you cannot but be led to a serious and grateful sense of your miraculous and providential preservation; you cannot but acknowledge that the present freedom and tranquility which you enjoy you have mercifully received and that it is the pecular blessing of Heaven.

This sir, was a time in which you clearly saw into the injustice of a state of slavery and in which you had just apprehensions of the horrors of its condition, it was now, sir, that your abhorrence thereof was so excited, that you publickly held forth this true and valuable doctrine, which is worthy to be recorded and remembered in all succeeding ages. "We hold these truths to be self-evident, that all men are created equal, and that they are endowed by their creator with certain unalienable rights, that among these are life, liberty and the pursuit of happiness."

Here, sir, was a time in which your tender feelings for yourselves had engaged you thus to declare, you were then impressed with proper ideas of the great valuation of liberty and the free possession of those blessings to which you were entitled by nature; but, sir, how pitiable is it to reflect that although you were so fully convinced of the benevolence of the Father of mankind and of his equal and impartial distribution of those rights and privileges which he had conferred upon them, that you should at the same time counteract his mercies in detaining by fraud and violence so numerous a part of my brethren under groaning captivity and cruel oppression, that you should at the same time be found guilty of that most criminal act which you professedly detested in others with respect to yourselves.

Sir, I suppose that your knowledge of the situation of my brethren is too extensive to need a recital here; neither shall I presume to prescribe methods by which they may be relieved, otherwise than by recommending to you and all others to wean yourselves from those narrow prejudices which you have imbibed with respect to them and as Job proposed to his friends, "put your souls in their souls stead," thus shall your hearts be enlarged with kindness and benevolence towards them, and thus shall you need neither the direction of myself or others, in what manner to proceed herein.

And now, sir, although my sympathy and affection for my brethren hath caused my enlargement thus far, I ardently hope that your candour and generosity will plead with you in my behalf when I make known to you that it was not originally my design; but that having taken up my pen in order to direct to you as a present, a copy of an almanac, which I have calculated for the succeeding year, I was unexpectedly and unavoidably led thereto.

This calculation, sir, is the production of my arduous study in this my advanced stage of life; for having long had unbounded desires to become acquainted with the secrets of nature, I have had to gratify my curiosity herein through my own assiduous application to astronomical study, in which I need not to recount to you the many difficulties and disadvantages which I have had to encounter.

And although I had almost declined to make my calculation for the ensuing year, in consequence of that time which I had allotted therefor being taken up at the Federal Territory by the request of Mr. Andrew Ellicott, yet finding myself under several engagements to printers of this state, to whom I had communicated my design, on my return to my place of residence I industriously applied myself thereto which I hope I have accomplished with correctness and accuracy, a copy of which I have taken the liberty to direct to you and which I humbly request you will favorably receive. Although you may have the opportunity of perusing it after its publication yet I chose to send it to you in manuscript previous thereto that you might not only have an earlier inspection but that you might also view it in my own hand-writing.

And now, sir, I shall conclude and subscribe myself, with the most profound respect, your most obedient humble servant,

B. BANNEKER

Thomas Jefferson
from *Notes on the State of Virginia*

FROM QUERY XIV LAWS

...Many of the laws which were in force during the monarchy being relative merely to that form of government, or inculcating principles inconsistent with republicanism, the first assembly which met after the establishment of the commonwealth appointed a committee to revise the whole code, to reduce it into proper form and volume, and report it to the assembly.... The following are the most remarkable alterations proposed:

To change the rules of descent, so as that the lands of any person dying intestate shall be divisible equally among all his children, or other representatives, in equal degree.

To make slaves distributable among the next of kin, as other moveables.

To have all public expences, whether of the general treasury, or of a parish or county, (as for the maintenance of the poor, building bridges, court-houses, &c.) supplied by assessments on the citizens, in proportion to their property.

To hire undertakers for keeping the public roads in repair, and indemnify individuals through whose lands new roads shall be opened.

To define with precision the rules whereby aliens should become citizens, and citizens make themselves aliens.

To establish religious freedom on the broadest bottom.

To emancipate all slaves born after passing the act. The bill reported by the revisors does not itself contain this proposition; but an amendment containing it was prepared, to be offered to the legislature whenever the bill should be taken up, and further directing, that they should continue with their parents to a certain age, then be brought up, at the public expence, to tillage, arts or sciences, according to their geniusses, till the females should be eighteen, and the males twenty-one years of age, when they should be colonized to such place as the circumstances of the time should render most proper, sending them out with arms, implements of houshold and of the handicraft arts, feeds, pairs of the useful domestic animals, &c. to declare them a free and independant people, and extend to them our alliance and protection, till they shall have acquired strength; and to send vessels at the same time to other parts of the world for an equal number of white inhabitants; to induce whom to migrate hither, proper encouragements were to be proposed. It will probably be asked, Why not retain and incorporate the blacks into the state, and thus save the expence of supplying, by importation of white settlers, the vacancies they will leave? Deep rooted prejudices entertained by the whites; ten thousand recollections, by the blacks, of the injuries they have sustained; new provocations; the real distinctions which nature has made; and many other circumstances, will divide us into parties, and produce convulsions which will probably never end but in the extermination of the one or the other race.—To these objections, which are political, may be added others, which are physical and moral. The first difference which strikes us is that of colour. Whether the black of the negro resides in the reticular membrane between the skin and scarf-skin, or in the scarf-skin itself; whether it proceeds from the colour of the blood, the colour of the bile, or from that of some other secretion, the difference is fixed in nature, and is as real as if its seat and cause were better known to us. And is this difference of no importance? Is it not the foundation of a greater or less share of beauty in the two races? Are not the fine mixtures of red and white, the expressions of every passion by greater or less suffusions of colour in the one, preferable to that eternal monotony, which reigns in the countenances, that immoveable veil of black which covers all the emotions of the other race? Add to these, flowing hair, a more elegant symmetry of form, their own judgment in favour of the whites, declared by their preference of them, as uniformly as is the preference of the Oranootan for the black women over those of his own species. The circumstance of superior beauty, is thought worthy attention in the propagation of our horses, dogs, and other domestic animals; why not in that of man? Besides those of colour, figure, and hair, there are other physical distinctions proving a difference of race. They have less hair on the face and body. They secrete less by the kidnies, and more by the glands of the skin, which gives them a very strong and disagreeable odour. This greater degree of transpiration renders them more tolerant of heat, and less so of cold, than the whites. Perhaps too a difference of structure in the pulmonary apparatus, which a late ingenious experimentalist has discovered to be the principal regulator of animal heat, may have disabled them from extricating, in the act of inspiration, so much of that fluid from the outer air, or obliged them in expiration, to part with more of it. They seem to require less sleep. A black, after hard labour through the day, will be induced by the slightest amusements to sit up till midnight, or later, though knowing he must be out with the first dawn of the morning. They are at least as brave, and more adventuresome. But this may perhaps proceed from a want of forethought, which prevents their seeing a danger till it be present. When present, they do not go through it with more coolness or steadiness than the whites. They are more ardent after their female: but love seems with them to be more an eager desire, than a tender delicate mixture of sentiment and sensation. Their griefs are transient. Those numberless afflictions, which render it doubtful whether heaven has given life to us in mercy or in wrath, are less felt, and sooner forgotten with them. In general, their existence appears to participate more of sensation than reflection. To this must be ascribed their disposition to sleep when abstracted from their diversions, and unemployed in labour. An animal whose body is at rest, and who does not reflect, must be disposed to sleep of course. Comparing them by their faculties of memory, reason, and imagination, it appears to me, that in memory they are equal to the whites; in reason much inferior, as I think one could scarcely be found capable of tracing and comprehending the investigations of Euclid; and that in imagination they are dull, tasteless, and anomalous. It would be unfair to follow them to Africa for this investigation. We will consider them here, on the same stage with the whites, and where the facts are not apocryphal on which a judgment is to be formed. It will be right to make great allowances for the difference of condition, of education, of conversation, of the sphere in which they move. Many millions of them have been brought to, and born in America. Most of them indeed have been confined to tillage, to their own homes, and their own society: yet many have been so situated, that they might have availed themselves of the conversation of their masters; many have been brought up to the handicraft arts, and from that circumstance have always been associated with the whites. Some have been liberally educated, and all have lived in countries where the arts and sciences are cultivated to a considerable degree, and have had before their eyes samples of the best works from abroad. The Indians, with no advantages of this kind, will often carve figures on their pipes not destitute of design and merit. They will crayon out an animal, a plant, or a country, so as to prove the existence of a germ in their minds which only wants cultivation. They astonish you with strokes of the most sublime oratory; such as prove their reason and sentiment strong, their imagination glowing and elevated. But never yet could I find that a black had uttered a thought above the level of plain narration; never see even an elementary trait of painting or sculpture. In music they are more generally gifted than the whites with accurate ears for tune and time, and they have been found capable of imagining a small catch.[1] Whether they will be equal to the composition of a more extensive run of melody, or of complicated harmony, is yet to be proved. Misery is often the parent of the most affecting touches in poetry.—Among the blacks is misery enough, God knows, but no poetry. Love is the peculiar œstrum of the poet. Their love is ardent, but it kindles the senses only, not the imagination. Religion indeed has produced a Phyllis Whately; but it could not produce a poet. The compositions published under her name are below the dignity of criticism. The heroes of the Dunciad are to her, as Hercules to the author of that poem. Ignatius Sancho has approached nearer to merit in composition; yet his letters do more honour to the heart than the head. They breathe the purest effusions of friendship and general philanthropy, and shew how great a degree of the latter may be compounded with strong religious zeal. He is often happy in the turn of his compliments, and his stile is easy and familiar, except when he affects a Shandean fabrication of words. But his imagination is wild and extravagant, escapes incessantly from every restraint of reason and taste, and, in the course of its vagaries, leaves a tract of thought as incoherent and eccentric, as is the course of

---

[1]The instrument proper to them is the Banjar, which they brought hither from Africa, and which is the original of the guitar, its chords being precisely the four lower chords of the guitar.

a meteor through the sky. His subjects should often have led him to a process of sober reasoning: yet we find him always substituting sentiment for demonstration. Upon the whole, though we admit him to the first place among those of his own colour who have presented themselves to the public judgment, yet when we compare him with the writers of the race among whom he lived, and particularly with the epistolary class, in which he has taken his own stand, we are compelled to enroll him at the bottom of the column. This criticism supposes the letters published under his name to be genuine, and to have received amendment from no other hand; points which would not be of easy investigation. The improvement of the blacks in body and mind, in the first instance of their mixture with the whites, has been observed by every one, and proves that their inferiority is not the effect merely of their condition of life. We know that among the Romans, about the Augustan age especially, the condition of their slaves was much more deplorable than that of the blacks on the continent of America. The two sexes were confined in separate apartments, because to raise a child cost the master more than to buy one. Cato, for a very restricted indulgence to his slaves in this particular, took from them a certain price. But in this country the slaves multiply as fast as the free inhabitants. Their situation and manners place the commerce between the two sexes almost without restraint.—The same Cato, on a principle of œconomy, always sold his sick and superannuated slaves. He gives it as a standing precept to a master visiting his farm, to sell his old oxen, old waggons, old tools, old and diseased servants, and every thing else become useless. 'Vendat boves vetulos, plaustrum vetus, ferramenta vetera, servum senem, servum morbosum, & si quid aliud supersit vendat.' Cato de re rusticâ. c. 2. The American slaves cannot enumerate this among the injuries and insults they receive. It was the common practice to expose in the island of Æsculapius, in the Tyber, diseased slaves, whose cure was like to become tedious. The Emperor Claudius, by an edict, gave freedom to such of them as should recover, and first declared, that if any person chose to kill rather than to expose them, it should be deemed homicide. The exposing them is a crime of which no instance has existed with us; and were it to be followed by death, it would be punished capitally. We are told of a certain Vedius Pollio, who, in the presence of Augustus, would have given a slave as food to his fish, for having broken a glass. With the Romans, the regular method of taking the evidence of their slaves was under torture. Here it has been thought better never to resort to their evidence. When a master was murdered, all his slaves, in the same house, or within hearing, were condemned to death. Here punishment falls on the guilty only, and as precise proof is required against him as against a freeman. Yet notwithstanding these and other discouraging circumstances among the Romans, their slaves were often their rarest artists. They excelled too in science, insomuch as to be usually employed as tutors to their master's children. Epictetus, Terence, and Phædrus, were slaves. But they were of the race of whites. It is not their condition then, but nature, which has produced the distinction.—Whether further observation will or will not verify the conjecture, that nature has been less bountiful to them in the endowments of the head, I believe that in those of the heart she will be found to have done them justice. That disposition to theft with which they have been branded, must be ascribed to their situation, and not to any depravity of the moral sense. The man, in whose favour no laws of property exist, probably feels himself less bound to respect those made in favour of others. When arguing for ourselves, we lay it down as a fundamental, that laws, to be just, must give a reciprocation of right: that, without this, they are mere arbitrary rules of conduct, founded in force, and not in conscience: and it is a problem which I give to the master to solve, whether the religious precepts against the violation of property were not framed for him as well as his slave? And whether the slave may not as justifiably take a little from one, who has taken all from him, as he may slay one who would slay him? That a change in the relations in which a man is placed should change his ideas of moral right and wrong, is neither new, nor peculiar to the colour of the blacks. Homer tells us it was so 2600 years ago.

Ἥμισυ, γαξ τ' ἀρετῆς ἀποαίνυ|αι εὐρύθπα Ζεὺς
Ἀνερος, ευτ' ἄν μιν κατὰ δόλιον ἥμαξ ἕλησιν.

Od. 17.323.

Jove fix'd it certain, that whatever day

Makes man a slave, takes half his worth away.

But the slaves of which Homer speaks were whites. Notwithstanding these considerations which must weaken their respect for the laws of property, we find among them numerous instances of the most rigid integrity, and as many as among their better instructed masters, of benevolence, gratitude, and unshaken fidelity.—The opinion, that they are inferior in the faculties of reason and imagination, must be hazarded with great diffidence. To justify a general conclusion, requires many observations, even where the subject may be submitted to the Anatomical knife, to Optical glasses, to analysis by fire, or by solvents. How much more then where it is a faculty, not a substance, we are examining; where it eludes the research of all the senses; where the conditions of its existence are various and variously combined; where the effects of those which are present or absent bid defiance to calculation; let me add too, as a circumstance of great tenderness, where our conclusion would degrade a whole race of men from the rank in the scale of beings which their Creator may perhaps have given them. To our reproach it must be said, that though for a century and a half we have had under our eyes the races of black and of red men, they have never yet been viewed by us as subjects of natural history. I advance it therefore as a suspicion only, that the blacks, whether originally a distinct race, or made distinct by time and circumstances, are inferior to the whites in the endowments both of body and mind. It is not against experience to suppose, that different species of the same genus, or varieties of the same species, may possess different qualifications. Will not a lover of natural history then, one who views the gradations in all the races of animals with the eye of philosophy, excuse an effort to keep those in the department of man as distinct as nature has formed them? This unfortunate difference of colour, and perhaps of faculty, is a powerful obstacle to the emancipation of these people. Many of their advocates, while they wish to vindicate the liberty of human nature, are anxious also to preserve its dignity and beauty. Some of these, embarrassed by the question 'What further is to be done with them?' join themselves in opposition with those who are actuated by sordid avarice only. Among the Romans emancipation required but one effort. The slave, when made free, might mix with, without staining the blood of his master. But with us a second is necessary, unknown to history. When freed, he is to be removed beyond the reach of mixture.

David Hume
Of National Characters

The vulgar are apt to carry all national characters to extremes; and having once established it as a principle, that any people are knavish, or cowardly, or ignorant, they will admit of no exception, but comprehend every individual under the same censure. Men of sense condemn these undistinguishing judgments; though at the same time, they allow that each nation has a peculiar set of manners, and that some particular qualities are more frequently to be met with among one people than among their neighbours. The common people in Switzerland have probably more honesty than those of the same rank in Ireland; and every prudent man will, from that circumstance alone, make a difference in the trust which he reposes in each . . .

Different reasons are assigned for these national characters; while some account for them from moral, others from physical causes. By moral causes, I mean all circumstances, which are fitted to work on the mind as motives or reasons, and which render a peculiar set of manners habitual to us. Of this kind are, the nature of the government, the revolutions of public affairs, the plenty or penury in which the people live, the situation of the nation with regard to its neighbours, and such like circumstances. By physical causes I mean those qualities of the air and climate, which are supposed to work insensibly on the temper, by altering the tone and habit of the body, and giving a particular complexion, which, though reflection and reason may sometimes overcome it, will yet prevail among the generality of mankind, and have an influence on their manners.

That the character of a nation will much depend on moral causes, must be evident to the most superficial observer; since a nation is nothing but a collection of individuals, and the manners of individuals are frequently determined by these causes. As poverty and hard labour debase the minds of the common people, and render them unfit for any science and ingenious profession; so where any government becomes very oppressive to all its subjects, it must have a proportional effect on their temper and genius, and must banish all the liberal arts from among them . . .

As to physical causes, I am inclined to doubt altogether of their operation in this particular; nor do I think, that men owe anything of their temper or genius to the air, food, or climate. I confess, that the contrary opinion may justly, at first sight, seem probable; since we find, that these circumstances have an influence over every other animal, and even those creatures, which are fitted to live in all climates, such as dogs, horses, etc. do not attain the same perfection in all. The courage of bull-dogs and game-cocks seems peculiar to England. Flanders is remarkable for large and heavy horses: Spain for horses light, and of good mettle. And any breed of these creatures, transplanted from one country to another, will soon lose the qualities, which they derived from their native climate. It may be asked, why not the same with men?

There are few questions more curious than this, or which will more often occur in our inquiries concerning human affairs; and therefore it may be proper to give it a full examination.

The human mind is of a very imitative nature; nor is it possible for any set of men to converse often together, without acquiring a similitude of manners, and communicating to each other their vices as well as virtues. The propensity to company and society is strong in all rational creatures; and the same disposition, which gives us this propensity, makes us enter deeply into each other's sentiments, and causes like passions and inclinations to run, as it were, by contagion, through that whole club or knot of companions. Where a number of men are united into one political body, the occasions of their intercourse must be so frequent, for defense, commerce and government, that, together with the same speech or language, they must acquire a resemblance in their manners, and have a common or national character, as well as a personal one, peculiar to each individual. Now though nature produces all kinds of temper and understanding in great abundance, it does not follow, that she always produces them in like proportions and that in every society the ingredients of industry and indolence, valour and cowardice, humanity and brutality, wisdom and folly, will be mixed after the same manner. In the infancy of society, if any of these dispositions be found in greater abundance than the rest, it will naturally prevail in the compositions and give a tincture to the national character ...

If the characters of men depended on the air and climate, the degrees of heat and cold should naturally be expected to have a mighty influence; since nothing has a greater effect on all plants and irrational animals. And indeed there is some reason to think, that all the nations, which live beyond the polar circles or between the tropics, are inferior to the rest of the species, and are incapable of all the higher attainments of the human mind. The poverty and misery of the northern inhabitants of the globe, and the indolence of the southern from their few necessities, may, perhaps, account for this remarkable difference, without our having recourse to physical causes. This however is certain, that the characters of nations are very promiscuous in the temperate climates, and that almost all the general observations, which have been formed of the more southern or more northern people in these climates, are found to be uncertain and fallacious. [In a footnote:] I am apt to suspect the negroes and in general all other species of men (for there are four or five different kinds) to be naturally inferior to the whites. There never was a civilized nation of any other complexion than white, nor even any individual eminent either in action or speculation. No ingenious manufactures amongst them, no arts, no sciences. On the other hand, the most rude and barbarous of the whites, such as the ancient

Germans, the present Tartars, have still something eminent about them, in their valour, form of government, or some other particular. Such a uniform and constant difference could not happen, in so many countries and ages if nature had not made an original distinction between these breeds of men. Not to mention our colonies, there are negroe slaves dispersed all over Europe, of whom none ever discovered any symptoms of ingenuity; though low people without education will start up amongst us and distinguish themselves in every profession. In Jamaica, indeed, they talk of one negroe as a man of parts and learning; but it is likely he is admired for slender accomplishments, like a parrot who speaks a few words plainly [end of footnote] . . .

Lord BACON has observed, that the inhabitants of the south are, in general, more ingenious than those of the north; but that, where the native of a cold climate has genius, he rises to a higher pitch than can be reached by the southern wits. This observation a later writer confirms, by comparing the southern wits to cucumbers, which are commonly all good in their kind; but at best are an insipid fruit; while the northern geniuses are like melons, of which not one in fifty is good; but when it is so, it has an exquisite relish. I believe this remark may be allowed just, when confined to the European nations . . .

Immanuel Kant
On National Characteristics

The Negroes of Africa have by nature no feeling that rises above the trifling. Mr Hume challenges anyone to cite a single example in which a Negro has shown talents, and asserts that among the hundreds of thousands of blacks who are transported elsewhere from their countries, although many of them have even been set free, still not a single one was ever found who presented anything great in art or science or any other praise-worthy quality, even though among the whites some continually rise aloft from the lowest rabble, and through superior gifts earn respect in the world. So fundamental is the difference between these two races of man, and it appears to be as great in regard to mental capacities as in color. The religion of fetishes so wide-spread among them is perhaps a sort of idolatry that sinks as deeply into the trifling as appears to be possible to human nature. A bird feather, a cow's horn, a conch shell, or any other common object, as soon as it becomes consecrated by a few words, is an object of veneration and of invocation in swearing oaths. The blacks are very vain but in the Negro's way, and so talkative that they must be driven apart from each other with thrashings.

Among all savages there is no nation that displays so sublime a mental character as those of North America. They have a strong feeling for honor, and as in quest of it they seek wild adventures hundreds of miles abroad, they are still extremely careful to avert the least injury to it when their equally harsh enemy, upon capturing them, seeks by cruel pain to extort cowardly groans from them. The Canadian savage, moreover, is truthful and honest. The friendship he establishes is just as adventurous and enthusiastic as anything of that kind reported from the most ancient and fabled times. He is extremely proud, feels the whole worth of freedom, and even in his education suffers no encounter that would let him feel a low subservience. Lycurgus probably gave statutes to just such savages; and if a lawgiver arose among the Six Nations, one would see a Spartan republic rise in the New World; for the undertaking of the Argonauts is little different from the war parties of these Indians, and Jason excels Attakakullakulla in nothing but the honor of a Greek name. All these savages have little feeling for the beautiful in moral understanding, and the generous forgiveness of an injury, which is at once noble and beautiful, is completely unknown as a virtue among the savages, but rather is disdained as a miserable cowardice. Valor is the greatest merit of the savage and revenge his sweetest bliss. The remaining natives of this part of the world show few traces of a mental character disposed to the finer feelings, and an extraordinary apathy constitutes the mark of this type of race.

If we examine the relation of the sexes in these parts of the world, we find that the European alone has found the secret of decorating with so many flowers the sensual charm of a mighty inclination and of interlacing it with so much morality that he has not only extremely elevated its agreeableness but has also made it very decorous. The inhabitant of the Orient is of a very false taste in this respect. Since he has no concept of the morally beautiful which can be united with this impulse, he loses even the worth of the sensuous enjoyment, and his harem is a constant source of unrest. He thrives on all sorts of amorous grotesqueries, among which the imaginary jewel is only the foremost, which he seeks to safeguard above all else, whose whole worth consists only in smashing it, and of which one in our part of the world generally entertains much malicious doubt—and yet to whose preservation he makes use of very unjust and often loathsome means. Hence there a woman is always in a prison, whether she may be a maid, or have a barbaric, good-for-nothing and always suspicious husband. In the lands of the black, what better can one expect than what is found prevailing, namely the feminine sex in the deepest slavery? A despairing man is always a strict master over anyone weaker, just as with us that man is always a tyrant in the kitchen who outside his own house hardly dares to look anyone in the face. Of course, Father Labat reports that a Negro carpenter, whom he reproached for haughty treatment toward his wives, answered: "You whites are indeed fools, for first you make great concessions to your wives, and afterward you complain when they drive you mad." And it might be that there were something in this which perhaps deserved to be considered; but in short, this fellow was quite black from head to foot, a clear proof that what he said was stupid. Among all savages there are none by whom the feminine sex is held in greater actual regard than by those of Canada. In this they surpass perhaps even our civilized part of the world. It is not as if they paid the women humble respects; those would be mere compliments. No, they actually exercise authority. They assemble and deliberate upon the most important regulations of the nation, even upon the question of war or peace. They thereupon send their deputies to the men's council and generally it is their voice that determines the decision. But they purchase this privilege dearly enough. They are burdened with all the domestic concerns, and furthermore share all the hardships of the men.

Georges Leopold Cuvier
Varieties of the Human Species

Although the promiscuous intercourse of the human species, which produces individuals capable of propagation, would seem to demonstrate its unity, certain hereditary peculiarities of conformation are observed which constitute what are termed *races*.

Three of them in particular appear very distinct: the *Caucasian* or white, the *Mongolian* or yellow, and *Ethiopian* or negro.

The Caucasian, to which we belong, is distinguished by the beauty of the oval formed by its head, varying in complexion and the colour of the hair. To this variety, the most highly civilized nations, and those which have generally held all others in subjection, are indebted for their origin.

The Mongolian is known by his high cheek bones, flat visage, narrow and oblique eyes, straight black hair, scanty beard and olive complexion. Great empires have been established by this race in China and Japan, and their conquests have been extended to this side of the Great Desert. In civilization, however, it has always remained stationary.

The Negro race is confined to the south of Mount Atlas; it is marked by a black complexion, crisped or woolly hair, compressed cranium, and a flat nose. The projection of the lower parts of the face, and the thick lips, evidently approximate it to the monkey tribe; the hordes of which it consists have always remained in the most complete state of utter barbarism.

The race from which we are descended has been called *Caucasian*, because tradition and the filiation of nations seem to refer its origin to that group of mountains situated between the Caspian and Black Seas, whence, as from a centre, it has been extended like the radii of a circle. Various nations in the vicinity of Caucasus, the Georgians and Circassians, are still considered the handsomest on earth. The principal ramifications of this race may be distinguished by the analogies of language. The Armenian or Syrian branch, stretching to the south, produced the Assyrians, the Chaldeans, the hitherto untamable Arabs, who, after Mahomet were near becoming masters of the world; the Phoenicians, Jews and Abyssinians, which were Arabian colonies; and most probably the Egyptians. It is from this branch, always inclined to mysticism, that have sprung the most widely extended forms of religion; the arts and literature have sometimes flourished among its nations, but always enveloped in a strange disguise and figurative style.

The Indian, German, and Pelasgic branch is much more extended, and was much earlier divided: notwithstanding which, the most numerous affinities may be observed between its four principal languages: the Sanscrit, the present sacred language of the Hindoos, and the parent of the greater number of the dialects of Hindostan; the ancient language of the Pelasgi, common mother of the Greek, Latin, many tongues that are extinct, and of all those of the south of Europe; the Gothic or Teutonic, from which are derived the languages of the north and north-west of Europe, such as the German, Dutch, English, Danish, Swedish, and other dialects; and finally, the Sclavonian, from which spring those of the north-east, the Russian, Polish, Bohemian, etc.

It is by this great and venerable branch of the Caucasian stock, that philosophy, the arts, and the sciences have been carried to the greatest perfection, and remained in the keeping of the nations which compose it for more than three thousand years.

It was preceded in Europe by the Celts, who came from the north, whose tribes, once very numerous, are now confined to its most eastern extremity, and by the Cantabrians, who passed from Africa into Spain, now confounded with the many nations whose posterity have intermingled in that peninsula.

The ancient Persians originate from the same source as the Indians, and their descendants to the present hour bear great marks of resemblance to the people of Europe.

The predatory tribes of the Scythian and Tartar branch, extending at first to the north and north-east, always wandering over the immense plains of those countries, returned only to devastate the happier abodes of their more civilized brethren. The Scythians, who, at so remote a period, made irruptions into upper Asia; the Parthians, who there destroyed the Greek and Roman domination; the Turks, who there subverted that of the Arabs, and subjugated in Europe the unfortunate remnant of the Grecian people, all swarmed from this prolific branch. The Finlanders and Hungarians are tribes of the same division, which have strayed among the Sclavonic and Teutonic nations. Their original country, to the north and north-east of the Caspian Sea still contains inhabitants who have the same origin, and speak similar languages, but mingled with other petty nations, variously descended, and of different languages. The Tartars remained unmixed longer than the others in the country included between the mouth of the Danube to beyond the Irtisch, from which they so long menaced Russia, and where they have finally been subjugated by her. The Mongoles, however, have mingled their blood with that of those they conquered, many traces of which may still be found among the inhabitants of lesser Tartary.

It is to the east of this Tartar branch of the Caucasian race that the Mongolian race begins, when it extends to the eastern ocean. Its branches, the Calmucs, etc., still wandering shepherds, are constantly traversing the desert. Thrice did their ancestors under Attila, Genghis, and Tamerlane, spread far the terror of their name. The Chinese are the earliest and most civilized branch not only of this race, to which they belong, but of all the nations upon earth. A third branch, the Mantchures, recently conquered, and still govern China. The Japanese, Coreans, and nearly all the hordes which extend to the north-east of Siberia, subject to Russia, are also to be considered, in a great measure, as originating from this race and such also is esteemed the fact, with regard to the original inhabitants of various islands of that Archipelago. With the exception of a few Chinese literati, the different nations of the Mongoles are universally addicted to Buddhism or the religion of Fo [sic].

The origin of this great race appears to have been in the mountains of Altai, but it is impossible to trace the filiation of its different branches with the same certainty as we have done those of the Caucasian. The history of these wandering nations is as fugitive as their establishments, and that of the Chinese, confined exclusively to their own empire, gives us nothing satisfactory with respect to their neighbours. The affinities of their languages are also too little known to direct us in this labyrinth.

The languages of the north of the peninsula beyond the Ganges, as well as that of Thibet, are somewhat allied to the Chinese, at least in their monosyllabic structure, and the people who speak them have features somewhat resembling other Mongoles. The south of this peninsula, however, is inhabited by Malays, whose forms approximate them much nearer to the Indians, whose race and language are extended over all the coasts of the islands of the Indian Archipelago. The innumerable little islands of the southern ocean are also peopled by a handsome race, nearly allied to the Indians, whose language is very similar to the Malay; in the interior of the largest of these islands, particularly in the wilder portions of it, is another race of men with black complexions, crisped hair, and Negro faces, called Alfourous. On the coast of New Guinea, and in the neighbouring islands, we find other Negroes, nearly similar to those of the eastern coast of Africa, named Papuas; to the latter, are generally referred the people of Van Diemen's land, and those of New Holland to the Alfourous.

These Malays, and these Papuas are not easily referable to either of the three great races of which we have been speaking, but can the former be clearly distinguished from their neighbours, the Caucasian Hindoos and the Mongolian Chinese? As for us, we confess we cannot discover any sufficient characteristics in them for that purpose. Are the Papuas Negroes, which may formerly have strayed into the Indian Ocean? We possess neither figures nor descriptions sufficiently precise to enable us to answer this question.

The northern inhabitants of both continents, the Samoiëdes, the Laplanders, and the Esquimaux spring, according to some, from the Mongolian race, while others assert that they are mere degenerate offsets from the Scythian and Tartar branch of the Caucasian stock . . .

We have not yet been able to refer the Americans to any of the races of the eastern continent; still, they have no precise nor constant character which can entitle them to be considered as a particular one. Their copper-coloured complexion is not sufficient; their generally black hair and scanty beard would induce us to refer them to the Mongoles, if their defined features, projecting nose, large and open eye, did not oppose such a theory, and correspond with the feature of the European. Their languages are as numberless as their tribes, and no demonstrative analogy has as yet been obtained, either with each other, or with those of the old world.

David Brion Davis

from *The Problem of Slavery in the Age of Revolution, 1770–1823*

WAR AND EMANCIPATION

The wars of the Age of Revolution necessarily shattered the fragile security of many slaveholding societies. Armies moved and fought through regions heavily populated with slaves, some of whom took up arms on opposing sides, while others seized the opportunity to escape. When the French Revolution spread to the Caribbean, it ignited a racial war that fulfilled the darkest prophecies of the preceding century, feeding slaveholders' nightmares for a century to come. Other West Indian colonies were seldom free from threat of invasion or insurrection. Even on the coast of West Africa the British found their position weakened by the American War of Independence; in 1806 traditional slaving patterns were further disrupted when an Ashanti army near Cape Coast annihilated England's Fanti allies.[1]

Many historians have understandably been captivated by the romantic notion of slaves liberating themselves by force of arms. The frequency of insurrection has commonly been taken as a reassuring index of slave discontent, as if no more subtle evidence were available, and as if the main result of such occurrences was not always an increase in mass executions of blacks. The subject of slave accommodation and resistance has recently been studied in considerable depth, and need not concern us here.[2] But it is important to discuss the ways in which a military crisis could affect opportunities for emancipation.

In April, 1775, Lord Dunmore, the royal governor of Virginia, threatened that he would proclaim liberty to the slaves and reduce Williamsburg to ashes if

---

[1] W. E. F. Ward, *A History of Ghana* (rev. 2nd ed., London, 1958), pp. 146–55. Unfortunately, the question of the effects of war on slavery has not received the detailed study it deserves, and has too often been omitted from discussions of slave insurrection. I can only touch on the question here.

[2] There is a large and recent literature on slave "docility and rebelliousness," much of it, provoked by Stanley M. Elkins's seminal study, *Slavery: A Problem in American Institutional and Intellectual Life* (Chicago, 1959). An excellent guide to the shifting terms of the debate can be found in the special issue of *Civil War History*, XIII (Dec., 1967). However, it seems likely that the starting point for all future discussion will be Eugene Genovese's *Roll, Jordan, Roll*, which brilliantly treats accommodation and resistance as parts of a subtle dialectical process.

the colonists resorted to force against British authority. In November, after Dunmore and his small armed force had sought refuge on board warships in Norfolk harbor, he promised freedom to all Negroes "appertaining to Rebels" if they were able and willing to join "His Majesty's Troops ... for the more speedily reducing the Colony to a proper sense of their duty, to His Majesty's crown and dignity." Several hundred Negroes succeeded in joining Dunmore's small army, but their forays along the coast were generally unsuccessful. The fleet finally sailed off to more promising war theaters.[3]

In June, 1793, Léger-Félicité Sonthonax, one of the commissioners sent to St. Domingue by the French Legislative Assembly, found himself in a position somewhat similar to that of Lord Dunmore. The whites of Le Cap, the capital city of the North Province, refused to accept the commissioners' authority. Over one thousand white sailors became involved in a race riot against the free mulattoes, whose rights the commissioners had defended. Sonthonax and his party retired from the city under heavy fire and seemed to face extermination, until Sonthonax called for support from the rebellious slaves in the countryside. Some ten thousand blacks then stormed down upon Le Cap, and it was the pro-planter governor, accompanied by most of the surviving white residents, who fled by sea. Sonthonax soon issued a general emancipation proclamation, which was later validated by the French Convention.[4]

One can quickly think of reasons that help to account for the striking contrast. In 1775, Virginia had not undergone four years of revolutionary turmoil. The white population did not constitute a tiny minority, nor was white supremacy challenged by a powerful group of mulattoes of almost equal numbers. Above all, the slaves of Virginia had not been in armed rebellion for nearly two years. Nor had officials in London begun to conclude that preservation of the empire would depend on free blacks and mulattoes. It would be hazardous, however, to draw hasty conclusions from these two incidents, which were parts of larger and more complex sets of events. In 1793 the French government had no more intention of turning slaves against their masters than the English government had in 1775. Who can say what might have happened if the British, anticipating Abraham Lincoln, had issued a decree emancipating all slaves in rebel hands? Or if the Americans had followed Silas Deane's suggestion of in-

[3]Peter Force, comp., *American Archives: Consisting of a Collection of Authentick Records, State Papers, Debates, and Letters and Other Notices of Publick Affairs* ... (4th ser., Washington, 1840), III, 1385–87; IV 184–85; Gerald W. Mullin, *Flight and Rebellion: Slave Resistance in Eighteenth-Century Virginia* (New York, 1972), pp. 131–32; Benjamin Quarles, *The Negro in the American Revolution* (Chapel Hill, 1961), pp. 19–32.

[4]C. L. R. James, *The Black Jacobins: Toussaint L'Ouverture and the San Domingo Revolution* (2nd rev. ed., New York, 1963), pp. 126–29; James G. Leyburn, *The Haitian People* (New Haven, 1941), *passim*; Theodore Lothrop Stoddard, *The French Revolution in San Domingo* (Boston, 1914), *passim*; J. Saintoyant, *La Colonisation française pendant la révolution*, *passim*. For the politics of French emancipation, see Chapters Two and Three below.

citing insurrections in Jamaica, where in 1776 a massive uprising in Hanover and St. James parishes resulted in more than thirty executions?[5]

Slaveholding colonists universally deplored the practice of arming blacks, whether slave or free, and often hoped that a sense of common peril would give force to an understood taboo. Yet throughout colonial history slaves frequently won their freedom by military service, without weakening the foundations of the institution. The precedents were firmest in the Caribbean and in seventeenth-century Brazil, where the whites were so few in number and the settlements so vulnerable that slaves held the key to military security as well as to disaster. During the Portuguese struggles against Dutch and French encroachments in Brazil, all the combatants enlisted large numbers of slaves. In 1772, when racial war broke out in Surinam, and when Paramaribo was terrorized by armies of fugitives from the surrounding jungle, the Dutch finally armed some three hundred slaves, with promises of freedom, in order to save the colony from annihilation. Similarly, the Jamaicans used black troops to crush the rebellious Maroons of the interior, although the Maroons of Jamaica and other colonies sometimes collaborated with the whites in returning fugitives or suppressing slave revolts. When French warships roamed the Caribbean during the American Revolution, British colonists fearfully armed their more trusted slaves, after first mobilizing them as "pioneers" for work on fortifications.[6]

Even in North America some Negro slaves won their freedom by serving in the various imperial wars between England and France. But in North America the local laws forbidding this practice were more strictly enforced than in Brazil and the Caribbean. The difference, as Carl Degler has pointed out, had nothing to do with attitudes toward slavery but arose from the simple availability of white manpower. Prior to the American Revolution, the arming of slaves was never more than a question of military expedience, always undertaken with reluctance and with the aim of preserving the slave system. If black soldiers fought with the expectation of freedom, they also knew that if they were captured, they would not be treated as prisoners of war.

---

[5]Ragatz, Fall of the Planter Class, p. 145; Patterson, Sociology of Slavery, p. 272. In 1760 over one thousand Jamaican slaves had become involved in a revolt aimed at "a total massacre of the whites and to make the island a Negro colony" (Patterson, p. 271). Ironically, in St. Domingue, unlike Jamaica, there had been few slave revolts prior to 1791.

[6]Henry G. Dalton, The History of British Guiana (London, 1855), I, 197–217; Louise Collis, Soldier in Paradise: The Life of Captain John Stedman, 1744–1797 (New York, 1965), pp. 107–08; Ragatz, Fall of the Planter Class, pp. 32–33, 220–22, and passim; Goveia, Slave Society in the British Leeward Islands, p. 148; Journals of the Assembly of Jamaica (Jamaica, 1805), IX, 28, 248, 420–26; Pares, War and Trade in the West Indies, pp. 252–56. In 1795 the English government urged that slaves be enlisted in a special black corps for the defense of the British Caribbean, a proposal which outraged the white colonists. But by 1795 the French revolutionary army had employed former slaves for the reconquest of Guadeloupe and St. Lucia, and had also begun to incite the slaves and Carib Indians of St. Vincent and Grenada, resulting in brutal civil warfare that nearly overthrew British dominion. Accordingly, the British colonists reluctantly began to arm slaves for local defense, and also deported some five thousand Caribs, ultimately to Ruatan, an island in Honduras Bay.

Moreover, the rules of war were firmer when it came to inciting foreign slaves against their masters. In 1759, for example, the British overruled Commodore John Moore's plan of proclaiming freedom to any slaves in Guadeloupe who would desert or turn against the French. By 1791, French planters themselves were quick to forget traditional rivalries and appeal to Jamaicans as fellow slaveholders who would share a similar fate if St. Domingue were lost. Pleading for troops and money from Jamaica, the governor reported that two hundred plantations had been burned and that over 100,000 slaves were in revolt. In September, 1793, former St. Domingue officials accompanied a British expeditionary force from Jamaica that was welcomed by many of the remaining white colonists, notwithstanding the state of war between Britain and France.[7]

But revolution, and revolutionary ideology, transformed the question of arming slaves. At the outset of the American Revolution, blacks in the northern colonies petitioned the local legislatures, appealing to the principles of natural and inalienable rights. Some of Lord Dunmore's armed fugitives wore the emblem, "Liberty to Slaves." The thousands of blacks in the South who sought refuge behind British or French lines knew that a new era had dawned, that some deliverer might be at hand. In the Caribbean, British slaves sometimes imagined that their masters were resisting and suppressing the king's efforts to free them; in 1790 this conviction sparked a revolt in Tortola. It was said that slaves leading the great St. Domingue uprising carried royalist banners and fought to the cry of God and king. Many had also heard heated discussion of the rights of man. The vague and often confused idea of revolution continued to spread. In 1823 a group of slaves in Honduras addressed a memorial to the Constituent Assembly of Central America, asserting that human bondage was inconsistent with political liberty. The blacks of Boston had made the same point fifty years before.[8]

Obviously "revolution" meant something very different in the United States, in St. Domingue, and in Spanish America. Even an edict of emancipation meant one thing in a context of social fluidity and relative freedom of opportunity, and something very different in a society that took some form of mass serfdom or peonage for granted.

In Mexico, for example, most of the population consisted of Indians and mestizos who were oppressed by the ancient tributes and restrictions of the colonial regime. In 1810, at the time of the Hidalgo revolt, there were fewer Negro slaves in Mexico than in the state of New York. The ideals of the En-

[7]Carl Degler, *Neither Black Nor White: Slavery and Race Relations in Brazil and the United States* (New York, 1971), pp. 75–82; Pares, *War and Trade in the West Indies*, pp. 252–53; *Journals of the Assembly of Jamaica*, IX, 51–52.

[8]Goveia, *Slave Society in the British Leeward Islands*, p. 334; Harold A. Bierck, Jr., "The Struggle for Abolition in Gran Colombia," *Hispanic American Historical Review*, XXXIII (1953), 366; Gaston Martin, *Histoire de l'esclavage*, pp. 210–23; James, *Black Jacobins*, p. 95; Quarles, *Negro in the American Revolution*, pp. 28, 44; *Collections* of the Massachusetts Historical Society, 5th ser., III, 382ff, 432–37; "La libertad de los esclavos," *Boletin del archivo general del gobierno* [Guatemala], III (No. 2, Jan., 1938), 277–78.

lightenment had won some favor, despite rigid censorship, among the educated native-born, or *criollos*, who often resented the privileges of the Spanish governing elite. But Hidalgo, a parish priest who had once been a professor and who knew French, came to envision a social revolution that went far beyond the aims of Thomas Jefferson. Hidalgo's goals shifted, partly because of his immediate need to mobilize an army of peasants, miners, and urban laborers, once his conspiracy had been divulged. In addition to proclaiming the end of tribute for Indian *castas*, lower taxes on liquor, and other popular reforms, he announced that the glorious moment had arrived when his brave American nation could throw off the yoke of three centuries of oppression. He thus ordered all masters to free their slaves within ten days, upon pain of death. In another decree, before his rampaging mob sacked Guanajuato, Hidalgo declared that freed slaves should have full equality with Spaniards. After Hidalgo had been crushed, his successor, José María Morelos, also appealed for mass support through an edict of emancipation. But while many conservative *criollos* could share the rebels' hostility toward European dominion, especially toward a mother country that had become the supine mistress of France, they united to stamp out a movement that threatened to abolish not only the vestiges of Negro slavery but the traditional relations between labor, property, and wealth.[9]

The leaders of the American Revolution were, in their own way, conservative *criollos*, which helps to explain why, for all the natural rights philosophy embellishing the first state constitutions, only that of Vermont moved from a ringing statement that "all men are born equally free and independent, and have certain natural, inherent and inalienable rights," to a "therefore" that specifically prohibited slavery. It is true that the Revolution elicited other official antislavery pronouncements in areas where a zeal for liberty coincided with a small proportion of Negroes. Even the loyalists of Upper Canada finally proclaimed that it was unjust for a people who enjoyed freedom by law (unlike their rebellious brethren to the south) to encourage the introduction of slaves.

The crucial question, however, was whether the emergencies of war would require the arming of slaves. Negroes served with valor in the colonial militia at the battles of Lexington and Bunker Hill. But by November, 1775, Congress and the leading officers of the army had decided to exclude even free blacks from future enlistment, and to rely, as soon as possible, on an all-white army. This restrictive policy arose from a sensitivity to southern opinion, from a fear of British retaliation, and from a desire to make the rebellious forces as "respectable" as possible. It is conceivable that sensitivities would have been less acute in an ordinary war, fought for somewhat less exalted purposes, when blacks would have been less likely to echo all the fine phrases about the rights

[9]Hugh M. Hamill, Jr., *The Hidalgo Revolt: Prelude to Mexican Independence* (Gainsville; Fla., 1966), *passim*; Miguel León-Portilla, *et al.*, eds., *Historia documental de México* (México, D.F., 1964), II, 49, 55–56; Juan N. Chávarri, *Historia de la guerra de independencia de 1810 a 1821* (México, D.F., 1960), pp. 73–75.

of man. In any event, General Washington soon became fearful that the black troops, "very much dissatisfied at being discarded," might seek employment in the British army. The news of Lord Dunmore's proclamation gave bite to the message. Accordingly, Congress decided to allow the re-enlistment of free Negroes who had served in the army at Cambridge.[10]

By 1778 a shortage of manpower had brought a remarkable shift in sentiment, at least in the North, where various states encouraged the emancipation of slaves for military service. Some blacks served as substitutes for their masters, others as mercenaries hired by committees charged with meeting local quotas. In contrast to St. Domingue and Spanish America, the relative availability of white manpower precluded the necessity of exploiting emancipation as an emergency war measure. Yet it would appear—and much research still needs to be done on the subject—that the pressures of war did much to undermine slavery in the northern states. Not only did Tories appeal to slave unrest, feeding rumors that spread panic among slaveholders in areas like the Hudson valley, but the disruptions of civil war and British occupation gave blacks plentiful opportunities for escape. Many slaves posed as freedmen when offering to enlist; others reaped multiple bounties through desertion and re-enlistment. As far south as Virginia, the law required masters to free any slave who had served as a substitute.[11]

But the major challenge arose when the British occupied Savannah, at the end of 1778, and when the theatre of war shifted to the Deep South. Even earlier, John Laurens, a young and idealistic South Carolinian, and an aide-de-camp to Washington, had dreamed of leading a corps of emancipated blacks in the defense of liberty. He and his father, Henry Laurens, finally helped to persuade Congress to approve, unanimously, a plan for recruiting an army of three thousand slave troops in South Carolina and Georgia. The federal government would fully compensate the slaves' owners, and each black, upon the end of the war, would be emancipated and receive a sum of fifty dollars. The plan won the full support of generals of the southern army, such as Benjamin Lincoln and Nathaniel Greene. It did not, however, win the necessary support from the

---

[10]*Vermont State Papers: Being a Collection of Records and Documents, Connected with the Assumption and Establishment of Government by the People of Vermont*...(Middlebury, Vt., 1823), p. 244; Quarles, *Negro in the American Revolution, passim*; Pete Maslowski, "National Policy toward the Use of Black Troops in the Revolution," *South Carolina Historical Magazine*, LXXIII (Jan., 1972), 1–17; William Renwick Riddell, "Slavery in Canada," *Journal of Negro History*, V. (July, 1920), 319. In Commonwealth v. Jennison (1783), Chief Justice William Cushing shied away from interpreting the "free and equal" clause in the Massachusetts constitution as an implicit abolition of slavery, but said that in his judgment slavery was "as effectively abolished as it can be by the granting of rights and privileges wholly incompatible and repugnant to its existence" (see John D. Cushing, "The Cushing Court and the Abolition of Slavery in Massachusetts: More Notes on the Quock Walker Case," *American Journal of Legal History*, V [1961], 118–44). In 1802, long after Pennsylvania had adopted a gradual emancipation act, the state's highest court ruled that slavery *was* compatible with the declaration of rights in the constitution.

[11]McManus, *Black Bondage in the North*, pp. 143–59; Donald L. Robinson, *Slavery in the Structure of American Politics, 1765–1820* (New York, 1971), pp. 98–130.

South Carolina legislature, despite John Laurens's eloquent pleas. One can debate whether a slight change in circumstance, or in military fortune, might have led to a different outcome. In the world of might-have-beens, the implications of arming thousands of slaves in the Deep South, in a Revolutionary war, are incalculable. As a result of the war, many southern slaves were in fact impressed into service as laborers, engineers, and teamsters; thousands were freed and evacuated with the British and French armies. Yet the war brought no major weakening of the slave system, except in the North. The legislators of South Carolina and Georgia, who had not yet heard of Toussaint L'Ouverture, understood the potentialities of revolution.

It might have been otherwise if the British government had approved Dunmore's proposal to conquer the South with an army of ten thousand blacks. In South America the Spanish royalist forces later showed similar reluctance, but discovered that black troops were indispensable for crushing the first independence movements. In response, as early as 1813, Juan del Corral saw that the patriots' cause would require the manumission of slaves; the following year, as temporary dictator, he secured a law for gradual emancipation in Antioquia. In Venezuela, Francisco Miranda promised freedom in 1812 to any slave who would fight the Spaniards for ten years. Similarly, when the Viceroy of Peru invaded Chile in 1814 to suppress rebellion, José Miguel Carrera decreed freedom for slaves joining in the resistance and tried to coerce support from both Negroes and their owners.[12]

With the example of Haiti before them, the Spanish rebels and royalists were if anything more fearful of arming slaves than their Anglo-American counterparts had been a generation before. Yet the struggles for independence were much more prolonged than the American Revolution, the rebels had smaller resources of free manpower, and no ally like France intervened to reinforce the patriot armies and limit the mother country's ability to send soldiers and supplies. For a time the rebels hoped to appeal to the English, as fellow slaveholders, to send troops to suppress "the bandits, and fugitive slaves who carry pillage, death, and desolation to many of the best settlements and haciendas." But by 1816 Simón Bolívar had found an ally in Haiti, and had concluded that slave emancipation provided the key to independence.[13]

Bolívar soon discovered, however, that few slaves yearned to die for the cause of their *criollo* masters, and that Venezuelan masters were no more eager than South Carolinians to see field hands transformed into soldiers. Fearing a second and perhaps bloodier St. Domingue, even the Liberator assured slaveholders that his policy arose from military necessity and should not be confused with a general emancipation. During 1819 and 1820 the patriot army in west-

[12]Eduardo Zuleta, "Movimiento antiesclavista en Antioquia," *Boletín de historia y antigüedades*, X (No. 109, May, 1915), 35–37; Feliú Cruz, *La abolición de la esclavitud en Chile*, pp. 73–79; John V. Lombardi, *The Decline and Abolition of Negro Slavery in Venezuela, 1820–1854* (Westport, Conn., 1971), pp. 36–38.

[13]Lombardi, *Decline and Abolition of Negro Slavery in Venezuela, passim.*

ern New Granada enlisted nearly three thousand Negro slaves, but General Francisco de Paula Santander finally put an end to such recruitment and ordered all Negroes not needed by the army to return to the mines.[14]

It is difficult to assess the effects of war on Spanish American emancipation. When compared with the American Revolution, the wars of liberation brought greater social disruption and more directly undermined plantation discipline. Both rebels and royalists found themselves forced to make far greater use of black manpower. By 1821, both in Gran Colombia (including Venezuela and Ecuador) and Peru, republican congresses had committed themselves to a policy of gradual emancipation. Yet the proportion of slaves in the populations of these countries was no greater than in the northern United States at the time of the Revolution. The process of gradual emancipation took approximately as long in Venezuela and Peru as in New York. In various parts of the New World the need for troops brought freedom for thousands of slaves and in some areas helped to weaken the plantation system. But only in St. Domingue did revolution and independence lead to mass emancipation, and only in St. Domingue did blacks wrest power from the hands of whites.

And by 1823, unfortunately, the example of Haiti gave little encouragement to the antislavery cause. Constantly fearing reconquest by France, its independence unrecognized by other nations, the republic had suffered years of domestic turmoil, war, and economic quarantine. If Henri Christophe had brought a degree of recovery to the North Province, his system of regimented labor could not reverse the effects of revolution and counterrevolution, or restore the regime of unchallenged authority on which the plantation economy had depended. The economic disintegration of the South Province—and of the entire nation when reunited under Jean-Pierre Boyer—gave the island's rulers a continuing excuse to substitute coerced labor for the slavery of the past. Yet for American reformers like Benjamin Lundy, Haiti seemed to present the only promising refuge for North American freedmen who faced an unmistakable hardening of racial prejudice and a new rash of discriminatory laws. Even the idealistic Bolívar, envisioning the nightmare of racial war, saw the problem as a "bottomless pit" where reason disappeared on entrance.[15]

[14]*Ibid.*, pp. 41–46; Bierck, "The Struggle for Abolition," pp. 367–70.

[15]Leyburn, *The Haitian People*, pp. 43–64; Bierck, "The Struggle for Abolition," p. 379.

C. L. R. James
from *The Black Jacobins*

I THE PROPERTY

THE SLAVERS scoured the coasts of Guinea. As they devastated an area they moved westward and then south, decade after decade, past the Niger, down the Congo coast, past Loango and Angola, round the Cape of Good Hope, and, by 1789 even as far as Mozambique on the eastern side of Africa. Guinea remained their chief hunting ground. From the coast they organised expeditions far into the interior. They set the simple tribesmen fighting against each other with modern weapons over thousands of square miles. The propagandists of the time claimed that however cruel was the slave traffic, the African slave in America was happier than in his own African civilisation. Ours, too, is an age of propaganda. We excel our ancestors only in system and organisation: they lied as fluently and as brazenly. In the sixteenth century, Central Africa was a territory of peace and happy civilisation.[1] Traders travelled thousands of miles from one side of the continent to another without molestation. The tribal wars from which the European pirates claimed to deliver the people were mere shamfights; it was a great battle when half-a-dozen men were killed. It was on a peasantry in many respects superior to the serfs in large areas of Europe, that the slave-trade fell. Tribal life was broken up and millions of detribalised Africans were let loose upon each other. The unceasing destruction of crops lod to cannibalism; the captive women became concubines and degraded the status of the wife. Tribes had to supply slaves or be sold as slaves themselves. Violence and ferocity became the necessities for survival, and violence and ferocity survived.[2] The stockades of grinning skulls, the human sacrifices, the selling of their own children as slaves, these horrors were the product of an intolerable pressure on the African peoples, which became fiercer through the centuries as the demands of industry increased and the methods of coercion were perfected.

The slaves were collected in the interior, fastened one to the other in columns, loaded with heavy stones of 40 or 50 pounds in weight to prevent attempts at escape, and then marched the long journey to the sea, sometimes hundreds of miles, the weakly and sick dropping to die in the African jungle. Some were brought to the coast by canoe, lying in the bottom of boats for days

---

[1]See the works of Professor Emil Torday, one of the greatest African scholars of his time, particularly a lecture delivered at Geneva in 1931 to a society for the Protection of Children in Africa.

[2]See Professor Torday's lecture mentioned above.

on end, their hands bound, their faces exposed to the tropical sun and the tropical rain, their backs in the water which was never bailed out. At the slave ports they were penned into "trunks" for the inspection of the buyers. Night and day thousands of human beings were packed in these "dens of putrefaction" so that no European could stay in them for longer than a quarter of an hour without fainting. The Africans fainted and recovered or fainted and died, the mortality in the "trunks" being over 20 per cent. Outside in the harbour, waiting to empty the "trunks" as they filled, was the captain of the slave-ship, with so clear a conscience that one of them, in the intervals of waiting to enrich British capitalism with the profits of another valuable cargo, enriched British religion by composing the hymn "How Sweet the Name of Jesus sounds!"

On the ships the slaves were packed in the hold on galleries one above the other. Each was given only four or five feet in length and two or three feet in height, so that they could neither lie at full length nor sit upright. Contrary to the lies that have been spread so pertinaciously about Negro docility, the revolts at the port of embarkation and on board were incessant, so that the slaves had to be chained, right hand to right leg, left hand to left leg, and attached in rows to long iron bars. In this position they lived for the voyage, coming up once a day for exercise and to allow the sailors to "clean the pails." But when the cargo was rebellious or the weather bad, then they stayed below for weeks at a time. The close proximity of so many naked human beings, their bruised and festering flesh, the foetid air, the prevailing dysentery, the accumulation of filth, turned these holds into a hell. During the storms the hatches were battened down, and in the close and loathsome darkness they were hurled from one side to another by the heaving vessel, held in position by the chains on their bleeding flesh. No place on earth, observed one writer of the time, concentrated so much misery as the hold of a slave-ship.

Twice a day, at nine and at four, they received their food. To the slave-traders they were articles of trade and no more. A captain held up by calms or adverse winds was known to have poisoned his cargo.[3] Another killed some of his slaves to feed the others with the flesh. They died not only from the régime but from grief and rage and despair. They undertook vast hunger strikes; undid their chains and hurled themselves on the crew in futile attempts at insurrection. What could these inland tribesmen do on the open sea, in a complicated sailing vessel? To brighten their spirits it became the custom to have them up on the deck once a day and force them to dance. Some took the opportunity to jump overboard, uttering cries of triumph as they cleared the vessel and disappeared below the surface.

Fear of their cargo bred a savage cruelty in the crew. One captain, to strike terror into the rest, killed a slave and dividing heart, liver and entrails into 300 pieces made each of the slaves eat one, threatening those who refused with the

---

[3]See Pierre de Vaissière, *Saint-Domingue* (1629–1789). Paris, 1909. This contains an admirable summary.

same torture.[4] Such incidents were not rare. Given the circumstances such things were (and are) inevitable. Nor did the system spare the slavers. Every year one-fifth of all who took part in the African trade died.

All America and the West Indies took slaves. When the ship reached the harbour, the cargo came up on deck to be bought. The purchasers examined them for defects, looked at the teeth, pinched the skin, sometimes tasted the perspiration to see if the slave's blood was pure and his health as good as his appearance. Some of the women affected a curiosity, the indulgence of which, with a horse, would have caused them to be kicked 20 yards across the deck. But the slave had to stand it. Then in order to restore the dignity which might have been lost by too intimate an examination, the purchaser spat in the face of the slave. Having become the property of his owner, he was branded on both sides of the breast with a hot iron. His duties were explained to him by an interpreter, and a priest instructed him in the first principles of Christianity.[5]

The stranger in San Domingo was awakened by the cracks of the whip, the stifled cries, and the heavy groans of the Negroes who saw the sun rise only to curse it for its renewal of their labours and their pains. Their work began at day-break: at eight they stopped for a short breakfast and worked again till midday. They began again at two o'clock and worked until evening, sometimes till ten or eleven. A Swiss traveller[6] has left a famous description of a gang of slaves at work. "They were about a hundred men and women of different ages, all occupied in digging ditches in a cane-field, the majority of them naked or covered with rags. The sun shone down with full force on their heads. Sweat rolled from all parts of their bodies. Their limbs, weighed down by the heat, fatigued with the weight of their picks and by the resistance of the clayey soil baked hard enough to break their implements, strained themselves to overcome every obstacle. A mournful silence reigned. Exhaustion was stamped on every face, but the hour of rest had not yet come. The pitiless eye of the Manager patrolled the gang and several foremen armed with long whips moved periodically between them, giving stinging blows to all who, worn out by fatigue, were compelled to take a rest—men or women, young or old." This was no isolated picture. The sugar plantations demanded an exacting and ceaseless labour. The tropical earth is baked hard by the sun. Round every "carry" of land intended for cane it was necessary to dig a large ditch to ensure circulation of air. Young canes required attention for the first three or four months and grew to maturity in 14 or 18 months. Cane could be planted and would grow at any time of the year, and the reaping of one crop was the signal for the immediate digging of ditches and the planting of another. Once cut they had to be rushed to the mill lest the juice became acid by fermentation. The extraction of the juice and manufac-

---

[4]De Vaissière, *Saint-Domingue*, p. 162.

[5]This was the beginning and end of his education.

[6]Girod-Chantrans, *Voyage d'un Suisse en différentes colonies*, Neufchâtel, 1785, p. 137.

ture of the raw sugar went on for three weeks a month, 16 or 18 hours a day, for seven or eight months in the year.

Worked like animals, the slaves were housed like animals, in huts built around a square planted with provisions and fruits. These huts were about 20 to 25 feet long, 12 feet wide and about 15 feet in height, divided by partitions into two or three rooms. They were windowless and light entered only by the door. The floor was beaten earth; the bed was of straw, hides or a rude contrivance of cords tied on posts. On these slept indiscriminately mother, father and children. Defenceless against their masters, they struggled with overwork and its usual complement—underfeeding. The Negro Code, Louis XIV's attempt to ensure them humane treatment, ordered that they should be given, every week, two pots and a half of manioc, three cassavas, two pounds of salt beef or three pounds of salted fish—about food enough to last a healthy man for three days. Instead their masters gave them half-a-dozen pints of coarse flour, rice, or pease, and half-a-dozen herrings. Worn out by their labours all through the day and far into the night, many neglected to cook and ate the food raw. The ration was so small and given to them so irregularly that often the last half of the week found them with nothing.

Even the two hours they were given in the middle of the day, and the holidays on Sundays and feast-days, were not for rest, but in order that they might cultivate a small piece of land to supplement their regular rations. Hard-working slaves cultivated vegetables and raised chickens to sell in the towns to make a little in order to buy rum and tobacco; and here and there a Napoleon of finance, by luck and industry, could make enough to purchase his freedom. Their masters encouraged them in this practice of cultivation, for in years of scarcity the Negroes died in thousands, epidemics broke out, the slaves fled into the woods and plantations were ruined.

The difficulty was that though one could trap them like animals, transport them in pens, work them alongside an ass or a horse and beat both with the same stick, stable them and starve them, they remained, despite their black skins and curly hair, quite invincibly human beings; with the intelligence and resentments of human beings. To cow them into the necessary docility and acceptance necessitated a régime of calculated brutality and terrorism, and it is this that explains the unusual spectacle of property-owners apparently careless of preserving their property: they had first to ensure their own safety.

For the least fault the slaves received the harshest punishment. In 1685 the Negro Code authorised whipping, and in 1702 one colonist, a Marquis, thought any punishment which demanded more than 100 blows of the whip was serious enough to be handed over to the authorities. Later the number was fixed at 39, then raised to 50. But the colonists paid no attention to these regulations and slaves were not unfrequently whipped to death. The whip was not always an ordinary cane or woven cord, as the Code demanded. Sometimes it was replaced by the *rigoise* or thick thong of cow-hide, or by the *lianes*—local growths of reeds, supple and pliant like whalebone. The slaves received the whip with more certainty and regularity than they received their food. It was the incentive to work and the guardian of discipline. But there was no ingenuity that fear or a depraved imagination could devise which was not employed to break their spirit and satisfy the lusts and resentment of their owners and guardians—irons on the hands and feet, blocks of wood that the slaves had to drag behind them wherever they went, the tin-plate mask designed to prevent the slaves eating the sugar-cane, the iron collar. Whipping was interrupted in order to pass a piece of hot wood on the buttocks of the victim; salt, pepper, citron, cinders, aloes, and hot ashes were poured on the bleeding wounds. Mutilations were common, limbs, ears, and sometimes the private parts, to deprive them of the pleasures which they could indulge in without expense. Their masters poured burning wax on their arms and hands and shoulders, emptied the boiling cane sugar over their heads, burned them alive, roasted them on slow fires, filled them with gunpowder and blew them up with a match; buried them up to the neck and smeared their heads with sugar that the flies might devour them; fastened them near to nests of ants or wasps; made them eat their excremeat, drink their urine, and lick the saliva of other slaves. One colonist was known in moments of anger to throw himself on his slaves and stick his teeth into their flesh.[7]

Were these tortures, so well authenticated, habitual or were they merely isolated incidents, the extravagances of a few half-crazed colonists? Impossible as it is to substantiate hundreds of cases, yet all the evidence shows that these bestial practices were normal features of slave life. The torture of the whip, for instance, had "a thousand refinements," but there were regular varieties that had special names, so common were they. When the hands and arms were tied to four posts on the ground, the slave was said to undergo "the four post." If the slave was tied to a ladder it was "the torture of the ladder"; if he was suspended by four limbs it was "the hammock," etc. The pregnant woman was not spared her "four-post." A hole was dug in the earth to accommodate the unborn child. The torture of the collar was specially reserved for women who were suspected of abortion, and the collar never left their necks until they had produced a child. The blowing up of a slave had its own name—"to burn a little powder to the arse of a nigger": obviously this was no freak but a recognised practice.

After an exhaustive examination, the best that de Vaissière can say is that there were good masters and there were bad, and his impression, "but only an impression," is that the former were more numerous than the latter.

There are and always will be some who, ashamed of the behaviour of their ancestors, try to prove that slavery was not so bad after all, that its evils and its cruelty were the exaggerations of propagandists and not the habitual lot of the slaves. Men will say (and accept) anything in order to foster national pride or soothe a troubled conscience. Undoubtedly there were kind masters who did not indulge in these refinements of cruelty and whose slaves merely suffered

[7]*Saint-Domingue*, p. 153–194. De Vaissière uses chiefly official reports in the French Colonial archives, and other documents of the period, giving specific references in each case.

over-work, under-nourishment and the whip. But the slaves in San Domingo could not replenish their number by reproduction. After that dreaded journey across the ocean a woman was usually sterile for two years. The life in San Domingo killed them off fast. The planters deliberately worked them to death rather than wait for children to grow up. But the professional white-washers are assisted by the writings of a few contemporary observers who described scenes of idyllic beauty. One of these is Vaublanc, whom we shall meet again, and whose testimony we will understand better when we know more of him. In his memoirs[8] he shows us a plantation on which there were no prisons, no dungeons, no punishments to speak of. If the slaves were naked the climate was such as not to render this an evil, and those who complained forgot the perfectly disgusting rags that were so often seen in France. The slaves were exempt from unhealthy, fatiguing, dangerous work such as was performed by the workers in Europe. They did not have to descend into the bowels of the earth nor dig deep pits; they did not construct subterranean galleries; they did not work in the factories where French workers breathed a deadly and infected air; they did not mount elevated roofs; they did not carry enormous burdens. The slaves, he concluded, had light work to do and were happy to do it. Vaublanc, in San Domingo so sympathetic to the sorrows of labour in France, had to fly from Paris in August, 1792, to escape the wrath of the French workers.

Malouet, who was an official in the colonies and fellow-reactionary of Vaublanc against all change in the colonies, also sought to give some ideas of the privileges of slavery. The first he notes is that the slave, on attaining his majority, begins to enjoy "the pleasures of love," and his master has no interest in preventing the indulgence of his tastes.[9] To such impertinent follies can the defence of property drive even an intelligent man, supposed in his time to be sympathetic towards the blacks.

The majority of the slaves accommodated themselves to this unceasing brutality by a profound fatalism and a wooden stupidity before their masters. "Why do you ill-treat your mule in that way?" asked a colonist of a carter. "But when I do not work, I am beaten, when he does not work, I beat him—he is my Negro." One old Negro, having lost one of his ears and condemned to lose another, begged the Governor to spare it, for if that too was cut off he would have nowhere to put his stump of cigarette. A slave sent by his master into his neighbour's garden to steal, is caught and brought back to the man who had only a few minutes before despatched him on the errand. The master orders him a punishment of 100 lashes to which the slave submits without a murmur. When caught in error they persisted in denial with the same fatalistic stupidity. A slave is accused of stealing a pigeon. He denies it. The pigeon is discovered hidden in his shirt. "Well, well, look at that pigeon. It take my shirt for a nest."

[8]Quoted extensively in de Vaissière, pp. 198–202.
[9]De Vaissière, p. 196.

Through the shirt of another, a master can feel the potatoes which he denies he has stolen. They are not potatoes, he says, they are stones. He is undressed and the potatoes fall to the ground. "Eh! master. The devil is wicked. Put stones, and look, you find potatoes."

On holidays when not working on their private plots, or dancing, they sat for hours in front of their huts giving no sign of life. Wives and husbands, children and parents, were separated at the will of the master, and a father and son would meet after many years and give no greeting or any sign of emotion. Many slaves could never be got to stir at all unless they were whipped.[10] Suicide was a common habit, and such was their disregard for life that they often killed themselves, not for personal reasons, but in order to spite their owner. Life was hard and death, they believed, meant not only release but a return to Africa. Those who wished to believe and to convince the world that the slaves were half-human brutes, fit for nothing else but slavery, could find ample evidence for their faith, and in nothing so much as in this homicidal mania of the slaves.

Poison was their method. A mistress would poison a rival to retain the valuable affections of her inconstant owner. A discarded mistress would poison master, wife, children and slaves. A slave robbed of his wife by one of his masters would poison him, and this was one of the most frequent causes of poisoning.[11] If a planter conceived a passion for a young slave, her mother would poison his wife with the idea of placing her daughter at the head of the household. The slaves would poison the younger children of a master in order to ensure the plantation succeeding to one son. By this means they prevented the plantation being broken up and the gang dispersed. On certain plantations the slaves decimated their number by poison so as to keep the number of slaves small and prevent their masters embarking on larger schemes which would increase the work. For this reason a slave would poison his wife, another would poison his children, and a Negro nurse declared in court that for years she had poisoned every child that she brought into the world. Nurses employed in hospitals poisoned sick soldiers to rid themselves of unpleasant work. The slaves would even poison the property of a master whom they loved. He was going away; they poisoned cows, horses and mules, the plantation was thrown into disorder, and the beloved master was compelled to remain. The most dreadful of all this cold-blooded murder was, however, the jaw-sickness—a disease which attacked children only, in the first few days of their existence. Their jaws were closed to such an extent that it was impossible to open them and to get anything down, with the result that they died of hunger. It was not a nat-

[10]Incredible as this may sound Baron de Wimpffen gives it as the evidence of his own eyes. His record of his visit to San Domingo in 1790 is a standard work. A good selection, with very full notes, is published, under the title, *Saint-Domingue à la veille de la Révolution*, by Albert Savine, Paris, 1911.

[11]See *Kenya* by Dr. Norman Leys, London, 1926, p. 184. "Some rivalry for a native woman is probably the explanation of most crimes of violence committed by Africans against Europeans in Kenya."

ural disease and never attacked children delivered by white women. The Negro midwives alone could cause it, and it is believed that they performed some simple operation on the newly-born child which resulted in the jaw-sickness. Whatever the method this disease caused the death of nearly one-third of the children born on the plantations.

What was the intellectual level of these slaves? The planters, hating them, called them by every opprobious name. "The Negroes," says a memoir published in 1789, "are unjust, cruel, barbarous, half-human, treacherous, deceitful, thieves, drunkards, proud, lazy, unclean, shameless, jealous to fury, and cowards." It was by sentiments such as these that they strove to justify the abominable cruelties they practised. And they took great pains that the Negro should remain the brute beast they wanted him to be. "The safety of the whites demands that we keep the Negroes in the most profound ignorance. I have reached the stage of believing firmly that one must treat the Negroes as one treats beasts." Such is the opinion of the Governor of Martinique in a letter addressed to the Minister and such was the opinion of all colonists. Except for the Jews, who spared no energy in making Israelites of their slaves, the majority of the colonists religiously kept all instruction, religious or otherwise, away from the slaves.

Naturally there were all types of men among them, ranging from native chieftains, as was the father of Toussaint L'Ouverture, to men who had been slaves in their own country. The creole Negro was more docile than the slave who had been born in Africa. Some said he was more intelligent. Others doubted that there was much difference though the creole slave knew the language and was more familiar with his surroundings and his work. Yet those who took the trouble to observe them away from their masters and in their intercourse with each other did not fail to see that remarkable liveliness of intellect and vivacity of spirit which so distinguish their descendants in the West Indies to-day. Father du Tertre, who knew them well, noted their secret pride and feeling of superiority to their masters, the difference between their behaviour before their masters and when they were by themselves. De Wimpffen, an exceptionally observant and able traveller, was also astonished at this dual personality of the slaves. "One has to hear with what warmth and what volubility, and at the same time with what precision of ideas and accuracy of judgment, this creature, heavy and taciturn all day, now squatting before his fire, tells stories, talks, gesticulates, argues, passes opinions, approves or condemns both his master and everyone who surrounds him." It was this intelligence which refused to be crushed, these latent possibilities, that frightened the colonists, as it frightens the whites in Africa to-day. "No species of men has more intelligence," wrote Hilliard d'Auberteuil, a colonist, in 1784, and had his book banned.

But one does not need education or encouragement to cherish a dream of freedom. At their midnight celebrations of Voodoo, their African cult, they danced and sang, usually this favourite song:

Eh ! Eh ! Bomba ! Heu ! Heu !
    Canga, bafio té !
        Canga, mouné de lé !
    Canga, do ki la !
        Canga, li !

"We swear to destroy the whites and all that they possess; let us die rather than fail to keep this vow."

The colonists knew this song and tried to stamp it out, and the Voodoo cult with which it was linked. In vain. For over two hundred years the slaves sang it at their meetings, as the Jews in Babylon sang of Zion, and the Bantu today sing in secret the national anthem of Africa.[12]

[12]Such observations, written in 1938, were intended to use the San Domingo revolution as a forecast of the future of colonial Africa.

Vincent Harding
from *The Other American Revolution*

CHAPTER 3

Laying the Foundations in North America
(Prerevolutionary Years)

I

Resistance and rebellion on the prison ships continued right to the shores of the New World. In some cases, when the Africans sighted the new coastlines, they made their last attempts to take over the vessels. Then, failing that, they leaped overboard into the strange waters of the Western Hemisphere. Of course, most of the captives on most of the ships were landed on shore; and we are told that the struggles of barracoons and the slaveships were immediately renewed on the North American mainland. (Of course it was taken up everywhere in the Americas, but from this point on, our focus will be on those hundreds of thousands of Africans who landed in the territory which would become the United States of America.)

The earliest recorded settlement that included Africans in the North American mainland was in what would eventually become South Carolina. In the fall of 1526 it also became the first clear location of black rebellion. Those Africans who participated struck for their freedom and fled to the surrounding Native Americans in search of safety. This was an understandable move, one repeated many times in the centuries that followed, for the blacks discovered early that there were many grounds for a natural alliance with the original settlers of this land. In fact, on many occasions, that alliance with the Indians became a significant element in the struggle for black freedom.

In spite of the earlier records of black presence in the North American settlements, the year 1619 is often chosen as the commemorative date for the arrival of the Africans at Jamestown, in the British colony of Virginia. Interestingly enough, there is evidence that conflict did not develop immediately. Rather, the earliest Africans who arrived in Virginia and other English colonies seem to have met a surprising level of civility and fairness.

But as the number of blacks increased, changes came with them. Many of the Africans indicated their firm desire for the privileges of freemen. In contrast, many whites began to see more clearly the great profits that could be obtained from permanently unpaid labor. Even in those early days, most of the whites were steeped enough in the poison of racism to find it impossible to give up a source of profits and domination in exchange for the voluntary sharing of the newly plundered land with the children of Africa.

Soon the imported legal system of Anglo-America, with its accompanying military sanctions, was brought to bear on behalf of white domination. In the course of the seventeenth century, the English colonies introduced laws prohibiting intermarriage between whites and Africans, laws against the ownership of property by Africans, laws against all rituals connected with African religious practices, laws against the sanctity of marriage between Africans, laws against the free status of African children born in slavery, and many more. Though they sometimes varied in severity and extent from colony to colony, the basic intent of the laws was the same: to give permanent legal sanction and moral justification to the white economic exploitation and the white political and social domination of the captives from Africa, to set the poorer whites against their black fellow laborers.

II

Under such repressive circumstances, it was inevitable that black resistance and struggle should continue and expand. Black people fought in a variety of ways. Some raised verbal protests, using the laws and the beliefs espoused by the colonists to support their own call for freedom. Petitions of many kinds appeared in the black community, ranging from painfully misspelled, but honorable scrawlings to elegantly executed statements of rights. In certain places, Africans actually tried to go to court against the injustices they faced, and in the earlier periods they won a few cases.

But there were more than words. Black struggle often took the form of individual acts of resistance, from arson and poisoning to suicides and voluntary abortions. And the trail of runaways was continuous, regularly marked by blood. While some of these individuals fled to the Indians, or to Canada, Florida, and elsewhere, many others stood their ground. Soon, a class of what were called "outlyers" (or "maroons") began to develop among those Africans who had broken out from the bonds of slavery, but who then banded together as independent outlaws. Sometimes these became aggressive, guerrilla bands, attacking the plantations and other white possessions.

In addition to these other forms of struggle, there were always cases of significant armed uprisings. They took place in the North as well as in the South, for slavery, racism, and exploitation existed in both sectors of the colonies. For instance, in New York City in 1712, a group of blacks allied with Indians organized a plot that was supposed to "destroy all the whites in the town." Setting fires, killing whites who came to extinguish the blazes, the insurrectionaries succeeded for a short time, but the group was ultimately routed by the colony's military forces. Most of them were executed, but some members of the rebel group took their own lives first, including one husband and wife who made a pact that they would not allow themselves to be captured alive by the forces of white oppression.

III

One of the most striking examples of the open southern struggles took place in 1739 near Stono, South Carolina, a place some twenty miles west of Charleston. There, a group of enslaved Africans planned an uprising, broke into a weapons warehouse, and finally gathered a company of some seventy to eighty men who were determined to march from Stono toward refuge in Florida, then a Spanish possession. For a time they did march, with two drums beating and flags waving and shouts of "liberty" breaking through the air. Part of their struggle was obviously for the repossession of their own identity, for though the world called them slaves, they clearly saw themselves as soldiers of liberty, and they were determined to act on their own vision. But again they finally had to contend with the militia, and after a pitched battle, another hope for freedom was smashed.

Though such hopes were dashed, the black will to struggle could not be destroyed. All through the colonial period, in North and South, in every conceivable form and situation, the struggle for black freedom continued. Almost invariably, the price for open, armed resistance was high. In Louisiana two leaders of a rebellion were "dragged (to the gallows) from the tail of a packhorse with an . . . halter tied to the neck, feet and hands." Another of the rebels was destined to "remain on the gibbet and have his hands cut off and nailed on the public roads." So, even on the public roads, no one could miss the announcement of the price of freedom. Many counted the cost and stood back. Others, many others, continued the struggle, in every possible way.

Part Two—Black Resistance and Abolition

Thomas Gray
The Confessions of Nat Turner

TO THE PUBLIC

The late insurrection in Southampton has greatly excited the public mind, and
led to a thousand idle, exaggerated and mischievous reports. It is the first instance in our history of an open rebellion of the slaves, and attended with such
atrocious circumstances of cruelty and destruction, as could not fail to leave a
deep impression, not only upon the minds of the community where this fearful
tragedy was wrought, but throughout every portion of our country, in which
this population is to be found. Public curiosity has been on the stretch to understand the origin and progress of this dreadful conspiracy, and the motives
which influences its diabolical actors. The insurgent slaves had all been destroyed, or apprehended, tried and executed, (with the exception of the
leader,) without revealing any thing at all satisfactory, as to the motives which
governed them, or the means by which they expected to accomplish their object. Every thing connected with this sad affair was wrapt in mystery, until Nat
Turner, the leader of this ferocious band, whose name has resounded throughout our widely extended empire, was captured. This "great Bandit" was taken
by a single individual, in a cave near the residence of his late owner, on Sunday, the thirtieth of October, without attempting to make the slightest resistance, and on the following day safely lodged in the jail of the County. His
captor was Benjamin Phipps, armed with a shot gun well charged. Nat's only
weapon was a small light sword which he immediately surrendered, and begged
that his life might be spared. Since his confinement, by permission of the jailor,
I have had ready access to him, and finding that he was willing to make a full
and free confession of the origin, progress and consummation of the insurrec-
tory movements of the slaves of which he was the contriver and head; I determined for the gratification of public curiosity to commit his statements to
writing, and publish them, with little or no variation, from his own words. That
this is a faithful record of his confessions, the annexed certificate of the County
Court of Southampton, will attest. They certainly bear one stamp of truth and
sincerity. He makes no attempt (as all the other insurgents who were examined
did,) to exculpate himself, but frankly acknowledges his full participation in all
the guilt of the transaction. He was not only the contriver of the conspiracy,
but gave the first blow towards its execution.

It will thus appear, that whilst every thing upon the surface of society wore a calm and peaceful aspect; whilst not one note of preparation was heard to warn the devoted inhabitants of woe and death, a gloomy fanatic was revolving in the recesses of his own dark, bewildered, and overwrought mind, schemes of indiscriminate massacre to the whites. Schemes too fearfully executed as far as his fiendish band proceeded in their desolating march. No cry for mercy penetrated their flinty bosoms. No acts of remembered kindness made the least impression upon these remorseless murderers. Men, women and children, from hoary age to helpless infancy were involved in the same cruel fate. Never did a band of savages do their work of death more unsparingly. Apprehension for their own personal safety seems to have been the only principle of restraint in the whole course of their bloody proceedings. And it is not the least remarkable feature in this horrid transaction, that a band actuated by such hellish purposes, should have resisted so feebly, when met by the whites in arms. Desperation alone, one would think, might have led to greater efforts. More than twenty of them attacked Dr. Blunt's house on Tuesday morning, a little before day-break, defended by two men and three boys. They fled precipitately at the first fire; and their future plans of mischief, were entirely disconcerted and broken up. Escaping thence, each individual sought his own safety either in concealment, or by returning home, with the hope that his participation might escape detection, and all were shot down in the course of a few days, or captured and brought to trial and punishment. Nat has survived all his followers, and the gallows will speedily close his career. His own account of the conspiracy is submitted to the public, without comment. It reads an awful, and it is hoped, a useful lesson, as to the operations of a mind like his, endeavoring to grapple with things beyond its reach. How it first became bewildered and confounded, and finally corrupted and led to the conception and perpetration of the most atrocious and heart-rending deeds. It is calculated also to demonstrate the policy of our laws in restraint of this class of our population, and to induce all those entrusted with their execution, as well as our citizens generally, to see that they are strictly and rigidly enforced. Each particular community should look to its own safety, whilst the general guardians of the laws, keep a watchful eye over all. If Nat's statements can be relied on, the insurrection in this county was entirely local, and his designs confided but to a few, and these in his immediate vicinity. It was not instigated by motives of revenge or sudden anger, but the results of long deliberation, and a settled purpose of mind. The offspring of gloomy fanaticism, acting upon materials but too well prepared for such impressions. It will be long remembered in the annals of our country, and many a mother as she presses her infant darling to her bosom, will shudder at the recollection of Nat Turner, and his band of ferocious miscreants.

Believing the following narrative, by removing doubts and conjectures from the public mind which otherwise must have remained, would give general satisfaction, it is respectfully submitted to the public by their ob't serv't,

T. R. GRAY.

Jerusalem, Southampton, Va. Nov. 5, 1831.

We the undersigned, members of the Court convened at Jerusalem, on Saturday, the 5th day of Nov. 1831, for the trial of Nat, *alias* Nat Turner, a negro slave, late the property of Putnam Moore, deceased, do hereby certify, that the confessions of Nat, to Thomas R. Gray, was read to him in our presence, and that Nat acknowledged the same to be full, free, and voluntary; and that furthermore, when called upon by the presiding Magistrate of the Court, to state if he had any thing to say, why sentence of death should not be passed upon him, replied he had nothing further than he had communicated to Mr. Gray. Given under our hands and seals at Jerusalem, this 5th day of November, 1831.

JEREMIAH COBB,   [*Seal.*]
THOMAS PRETLOW, [*Seal.*]
JAMES W. PARKER, [*Seal.*]
CARR BOWERS,   [*Seal.*]
SAMUEL B. HINES,   [*Seal.*]
ORRIS A. BROWNE, [*Seal.*]

State of Virginia, Southampton County, to wit:

I, James Rochelle, Clerk of the County Court of Southampton in the State of Virginia, do hereby certify, that Jeremiah Cobb, Thomas Pretlow, James W. Parker, Carr Bowers, Samuel B. Hines, and Orris A. Browne, esqr's are acting Justices of the Peace, in and for the County aforesaid, and were members of the Court which convened at Jerusalem, on Saturday the 5th day of November, 1831, for the trial of Nat *alias* Nat Turner, a negro slave, late the property of Putnam Moore, deceased, who was tried and convicted, as an insurgent in the late insurrection in the county of Southampton aforesaid, and that full faith and credit are due, and ought to be given to their acts as Justices of the peace aforesaid.

In testimony whereof, I have hereunto set my hand and caused the seal of the Court [Seal.]   aforesaid, to be affixed this 5th day of November, 1831.

JAMES ROCHELLE, C. S. C. C.

CONFESSION

Agreeable to his own appointment, on the evening he was committed to prison, with permission of the jailer, I visited NAT on Tuesday the 1st November, when, without being questioned at all, he commenced his narrative in the following words:—

SIR,—You have asked me to give a history of the motives which induced me to undertake the late insurrection, as you call it—To do so I must go back to the days of my infancy, and even before I was born. I was thirty-one years of age the 2d of October last, and born the property of Benj. Turner, of this COUNTY. In my childhood a circumstance occurred which made an indelible impression on my mind, and laid the ground work of that enthusiasm, which has terminated so fatally to many, both white and black, and for which I am about to atone at the gallows. It is here necessary to relate this circumstance—trifling as it may seem, it was the commencement of that belief which has grown with time, and even now, sir, in this dungeon, helpless and forsaken as I am, I cannot divest myself of. Being at play with other children, when three or four years old, I was telling them something, which my mother overhearing, said it had happened before I was born—I stuck to my story, however, and related somethings which went, in her opinion, to confirm it—others being called on were greatly astonished, knowing that these things had happened, and caused them to say in my hearing, I surely would be a prophet, as the Lord had shewn me things that had happened before my birth. And my father and mother strengthened me in this my first impression, saying in my presence, I was intended for some great purpose, which they had always thought from certain marks on my head and breast—[a parcel of excrescences which I believe are not at all uncommon, particularly among negroes, as I have seen several with the same. In this case he has either cut them off or they have nearly disappeared]—My grandmother, who was very religious, and to whom I was much attached—my master, who belonged to the church, and other religious persons who visited the house, and whom I often saw at prayers, noticing the singularity of my manners, I suppose, and my uncommon intelligence for a child, remarked I had too much sense to be raised, and if I was, I would never be of any service to any one as a slave— To a mind like mine, restless, inquisitive and observant of every thing that was passing, it is easy to suppose that religion was the subject to which it would be directed, and although this subject principally occupied my thoughts—there was nothing that I saw or heard of to which my attention was not directed— The manner in which I learned to read and write, not only had great influence on my own mind, as I acquired it with the most perfect ease, so much so, that I have no recollection whatever of learning the alphabet—but to the astonishment of the family, one day, when a book was shewn me to keep me from crying, I began spelling the names of different objects—this was a source of wonder to all in the neighborhood, particularly the blacks—and this learning was constantly improved at all opportunities—when I got large enough to go to work, while employed, I was reflecting on many things that would present themselves to my imagination, and whenever an opportunity occurred of looking at a book, when the school children were getting their lessons, I would find many things that the fertility of my own imagination had depicted to me before; all my time, not devoted to my master's service, was spent either in prayer, or in making experiments in casting different things in moulds made of earth, in attempting to make paper, gunpowder, and many other experiments, that although I could not perfect, yet convinced me of its practicability if I had the means* I was not addicted to stealing in my youth, nor have ever been—Yet

*When questioned as to the manner of manufacturing those different articles, he was found well informed on the subject.

such was the confidence of the negroes in the neighborhood, even at this early period of my life, in my superior judgment, that they would often carry me with them when they were going on any roguery, to plan for them. Growing up among them, with this confidence in my superior judgment, and when this, in their opinions, was perfected by Divine inspiration, from the circumstances already alluded to in my infancy, and which belief was ever afterwards zealously inculcated by the austerity of my life and manners, which became the subject of remark by white and black.—Having soon discovered to be great, I must appear so, and therefore studiously avoided mixing in society, and wrapped myself in mystery, devoting my time to fasting and prayer—By this time, having arrived to man's estate, and hearing the scriptures commented on at meetings, I was struck with that particular passage which says: "Seek ye the kingdom of Heaven and all things shall be added unto you." I reflected much on this passage, and prayed daily for light on this subject—As I was praying one day at my plough, the spirit spoke to me, saying "Seek ye the kingdom of Heaven and all things shall be added unto you.["] *Question*—what do you mean by the Spirit. *Ans.* The Spirit that spoke to the prophets in former days—and I was greatly astonished, and for two years prayed continually, whenever my duty would permit— and then again I had the same revelation, which fully confirmed me in the impression that I was ordained for some great purpose in the hands of the Almighty. Several years rolled round, in which many events occurred to strengthen me in this my belief. At this time I reverted in my mind to the remarks made of me in my childhood, and the things that had been shewn me— and as it had been said of me in my childhood by those by whom I had been taught to pray, both white and black, and in whom I had the greatest confidence, that I had too much sense to be raised, and if I was, I would never be of any use to any one as a slave. Now finding I had arrived to man's estate, and was a slave, and these revelations being made known to me, I began to direct my attention to this great object, to fulfil the purpose for which, by this time, I felt assured I was intended. Knowing the influence I had obtained over the minds of my fellow servants, (not by the means of conjuring and such like tricks—for to them I always spoke of such things with contempt) but by the communion of the Spirit whose revelations I often communicated to them, and they believed and said my wisdom came from God. I now began to prepare them for my purpose, by telling them something was about to happen that would terminate in fulfilling the great promise that had been made to me— About this time I was placed under an overseer, from whom I ran away—and after remaining in the woods thirty days, I returned, to the astonishment of the negroes on the plantation, who thought I had made my escape to some other part of the country, as my father had done before. But the reason of my return was, that the Spirit appeared to me and said I had my wishes directed to the things of this world, and not to the kingdom of Heaven, and that I should return to the service of my earthly master—"For he who knoweth his Master's will, and doeth it not, shall be beaten with many stripes, and thus have I chastened you." And the negroes found fault, and murmured against me, saying that if they had my sense they would not serve any master in the world. And about this time I had a vision—and I saw white spirits and black spirits engaged in battle, and the sun was darkened—the thunder rolled in the Heavens, and blood flowed in streams—and I heard a voice saying, "Such is your luck, such you are called to see, and let it come rough or smooth, you must surely bare it." I now withdrew myself as much as my situation would permit, from the intercourse of my fellow servants, for the avowed purpose of serving the Spirit more fully—and it appeared to me, and reminded me of the things it had already shown me, and that it would then reveal to me the knowledge of the elements, the revolution of the planets, the operation of tides, and changes of the seasons. After this revelation in the year 1825, and the knowledge of the elements being made known to me, I sought more than ever to obtain true holiness before the great day of judgment should appear, and then I began to receive the true knowledge of faith. And from the first steps of righteousness until the last, was I made perfect; and the Holy Ghost was with me, and said, "Behold me as I stand in the Heavens"—and I looked and saw the forms of men in different attitudes—and there were lights in the sky to which the children of darkness gave other names than what they really were—for they were the lights of the Saviour's hands, stretched forth from east to west, even as they were extended on the cross on Calvary for the redemption of sinners. And I wondered greatly at these miracles, and prayed to be informed of a certainty of the meaning thereof—and shortly afterwards, while laboring in the field, I discovered drops of blood on the corn as though it were dew from heaven—and I communicated it to many, both white and black, in the neighborhood—and I then found on the leaves in the woods hieroglyphic characters, and numbers, with the forms of men in different attitudes, portrayed in blood, and representing the figures I had seen before in the heavens. And now the Holy Ghost had revealed itself to me, and made plain the miracles it had shown me—For as the blood of Christ had been shed on this earth, and had ascended to heaven for the salvation of sinners, and was now returning to earth again in the form of dew—and as the leaves on the trees bore the impression of the figures I had seen in the heavens, it was plain to me that the Saviour was about to lay down the yoke he had borne for the sins of men, and the great day of judgment was at hand. About this time I told these things to a white man, (Etheldred T. Brantley) on whom it had a wonderful effect—and he ceased from his wickedness, and was attacked immediately with a cutaneous eruption, and blood ozed from the pores of his skin, and after praying and fasting nine days, he was healed, and the Spirit appeared to me again, and said, as the Saviour had been baptised so should we be also—and when the white people would not let us be baptised by the church, we went down into the water together, in the sight of many who reviled us, and were baptised by the Spirit—After this I rejoiced greatly, and gave thanks to God. And on the 12th of May, 1828, I heard a loud noise in the heavens, and the Spirit instantly appeared to me and said the Serpent was loosened, and

Christ had laid down the yoke he had borne for the sins of men, and that I should take it on and fight against the Serpent, for the time was fast approaching when the first should be last and the last should be first. *Ques.* Do you not find yourself mistaken now? *Ans.* Was not Christ crucified. And by signs in the heavens that it would make known to me when I should commence the great work—and until the first sign appeared, I should conceal it from the knowledge of men—And on the appearance of the sign, (the eclipse of the sun last February) I should arise and prepare myself, and slay my enemies with their own weapons. And immediately on the sign appearing in the heavens, the seal was removed from my lips, and I communicated the great work laid out for me to do, to four in whom I had the greatest confidence. (Henry, Hark, Nelson, and Sam)—It was intended by us to have begun the work of death on the 4th July last—Many were the plans formed and rejected by us, and it affected my mind to such a degree, that I fell sick, and the time passed without our coming to any determination how to commence—Still forming new schemes and rejecting them, when the sign appeared again, which determined me not to wait longer.

Since the commencement of 1830, I had been living with Mr. Joseph Travis, who was to me a kind master, and placed the greatest confidence in me; in fact, I had no cause to complain of his treatment to me. On Saturday evening, the 20th of August, it was agreed between Henry, Hark and myself, to prepare a dinner the next day for the men we expected, and then to concert a plan, as we had not yet determined on any. Hark, on the following morning, brought a pig, and Henry brandy, and being joined by Sam, Nelson, Will and Jack, they prepared in the woods a dinner, where, about three o'clock, I joined them.

Q. Why were you so backward in joining them.

A. The same reason that had caused me not to mix with them for years before.

I saluted them on coming up, and asked Will how came he there, he answered, his life was worth no more than others, and his liberty as dear to him. I asked him if he thought to obtain it? He said he would, or loose his life. This was enough to put him in full confidence. Jack, I knew, was only a tool in the hands of Hark, it was quickly agreed we should commence at home (Mr. J. Travis') on that night, and until we had armed and equipped ourselves, and gathered sufficient force, neither age nor sex was to be spared, (which was invariably adhered to.) We remained at the feast, until about two hours in the night, when we went to the house and found Austin; they all went to the cider press and drank, except myself. On returning to the house, Hark went to the door with an axe, for the purpose of breaking it open, as we knew we were strong enough to murder the family, if they were awaked by the noise; but reflecting that it might create an alarm in the neighborhood, we determined to enter the house secretly, and murder them whilst sleeping. Hark got a ladder and set it against the chimney, on which I ascended, and hoisting a window, entered and came down stairs, unbarred the door, and removed the guns from their places. It was then observed that I must spill the first blood. On which, armed with a hatchet, and accompanied by Will, I entered my master's chamber, it being dark, I could not give a death blow, the hatchet glanced from his head, he sprang from the bed and called his wife, it was his last word, Will laid him dead, with a blow of his axe, and Mrs. Travis shared the same fate, as she lay in bed. The murder of this family, five in number, was the work of a moment, not one of them awoke; there was a little infant sleeping in a cradle, that was forgotten, until we had left the house and gone some distance, when Henry and Will returned and killed it; we got here, four guns that would shoot, and several old muskets, with a pound or two of powder. We remained some time at the barn, where we paraded; I formed them in a line as soldiers, and after carrying them through all the manœuvres I was master of, marched them off to Mr. Salathul Francis', about six hundred yards distant. Sam and Will went to the door and knocked. Mr. Francis asked who was there, Sam replied it was him, and he had a letter for him, on which he got up and came to the door; they immediately seized him, and dragging him out a little from the door, he was dispatched by repeated blows on the head; there was no other white person in the family. We started from there for Mrs. Reese's, maintaining the most perfect silence on our march, where finding the door unlocked, we entered, and murdured Mrs. Reese in her bed, while sleeping; her son awoke, but it was only to sleep the sleep of death, he had only time to say who is that, and he was no more. From Mrs. Reese's we went to Mrs. Turner's, a mile distant, which we reached about sunrise, on Monday morning. Henry, Austin, and Sam, went to the still, where, finding Mr. Peebles, Austin shot him, and the rest of us went to the house; as we approached, the family discovered us, and shut the door. Vain hope! Will, with one stroke of his axe, opened it, and we entered and found Mrs. Turner and Mrs. Newsome in the middle of a room, almost frightened to death. Will immediately killed Mrs. Turner, with one blow of his axe. I took Mrs. Newsome by the hand, and with the sword I had when I was apprehended, I struck her several blows over the head, but not being able to kill her, as the sword was dull. Will turning around and discovering it, despatched her also. A general destruction of property and search for money and ammunition, always succeeded the murders. By this time my company amounted to fifteen, and nine men mounted, who started for Mrs. Whitehead's, (the other six were to go through a by way to Mr. Bryant's, and rejoin us at Mrs. Whitehead's,) as we approached the house we discovered Mr. Richard Whitehead standing in the cotton patch, near the lane fence; we called him over into the lane, and Will, the executioner, was near at hand, with his fatal axe, to send him to an untimely grave. As we pushed on to the house, I discovered some one run round the garden, and thinking it was some of the white family, I pursued them, but finding it was a servant girl belonging to the house, I returned to commence the work of death, but they whom I left, had not been idle; all the family were already murdered, but Mrs. Whitehead and her daughter Margaret. As I came round to the door I saw Will pulling Mrs. Whitehead out of the house, and at the step he nearly severed her head from her body, with his broad axe. Miss Margaret, when I discovered her, had concealed herself in the corner, formed by the projection of the cellar cap from the house; on my approach she fled, but was soon overtaken, and after repeated blows with a sword, I killed her by a blow on the head, with a fence rail. By this time, the six who had gone by Mr. Bryant's, rejoined us, and informed me they had done the work of death assigned them. We again divided, part going to Mr. Richard Porter's, and from thence to Nathaniel Francis', the others to Mr. Howell Harris', and Mr. T. Doyles. On my reaching Mr. Porter's, he had escaped with his family. In understood there, that the alarm had already spread, and I immediately returned to bring up those sent to Mr. Doyles, and Mr. Howell Harris'; the party I left going on to Mr. Francis', having told them I would join them in that neighborhood. I met these sent to Mr. Doyles' and Mr. Harris' returning, having met Mr. Doyle on the road and killed him; and learning from some who joined them, that Mr. Harris was from home, I immediately pursued the course taken by the party gone on before; but knowing they would complete the work of death and pillage, at Mr. Francis' before I could get there, I went to Mr. Peter Edwards', expecting to find them there, but they had been here also. I then went to Mr. John T. Barrow's, they had been here and murdered him. I pursued on their track to Capt. Newit Harris', where I found the greater part mounted, and ready to start; the men now amounting to about forty, shouted and hurraed as I rode up, some were in the yard, loading their guns, others drinking. They said Captain Harris and his family had escaped, the property in the house they destroyed, robbing him of money and other valuables. I ordered them to mount and march instantly, this was about nine or ten o'clock, Monday morning. I proceeded to Mr. Levi Waller's, two or three miles distant. I took my station in the rear, and as it 'twas my object to carry terror and devastation wherever we went, I placed fifteen or twenty of the best armed and most to be relied on, in front, who generally approached the house as fast as their horses could run; this was for two purposes, to prevent their escape and strike terror to the inhabitants—on this account I never got to the houses, after leaving Mrs. Whitehead's, until the murders were committed, except in one case. I sometimes got in sight in time to see the work of death completed, viewed the mangled bodies as they lay, in silent satisfaction, and immediately started in quest of other victims—Having murdered Mrs. Waller and ten children, we started for Mr. William Williams'—having killed him and two little boys that were there; while engaged in this, Mrs. Williams fled and got some distance from the house, but she was pursued, overtaken, and compelled to get up behind one of the company, who brought her back, and after showing her the mangled body of her lifeless husband, she was told to get down and lay by his side, where she was shot dead. I then started for Mr. Jacob Williams, where the family were murdered—Here we found a young man named Drury, who had come on business with Mr. Williams—he was pursued, overtaken and shot. Mrs. Vaughan was the next place we visited—and after murdering the family here, I determined on starting for Jerusalem—Our number amounted now to fifty or sixty, all mounted and armed with guns, axes, swords and clubs—On reaching Mr. James W. Parker's gate, immediately on the road leading to Jerusalem, and about three miles distant, it was proposed to me to call there, but I objected, as I knew he was gone to Jerusalem, and my object was to reach there as soon as possible; but some of the men having relations at Mr. Parker's it was agreed that they might call and get his people. I remained at the gate on the road, with seven or eight; the others going across the field to the house, about half a mile off. After waiting some time for them, I became impatient, and started to the house for them, and on our return we were met by a party of white men, who had pursued our blood-stained track, and who had fired on those at the gate, and dispersed them, which I new nothing of, not having been at that time rejoined by any of them—Immediately on discovering the whites, I ordered my men to halt and form, as they appeared to be alarmed—The white men, eighteen in number, approached us in about one hundred yards, when one of them fired, (this was against the positive orders of Captain Alexander P. Peete, who commanded, and who had directed to men to reserve their fire until within thirty paces). And I discovered about half of them retreating, I then ordered my men to fire and rush on them; the few remaining stood their ground until we approached within fifty yards, when they fired and retreated. We pursued and overtook some of them who we thought we left dead; (they were not killed) after pursuing them about two hundred yards, and rising a little hill, I discovered they were met by another party, and had haulted, and were re-loading their guns, (this was a small party from Jerusalem who knew the negroes were in the field, and had just tied their horses to await their return to the road, knowing that Mr. Parker and family were in Jerusalem, but knew nothing of the party that had gone in with Captain Peete; on hearing the firing they immediately rushed to the spot and arrived just in time to arrest the progress of these barbarous villians, and save the lives of their friends and fellow citizens.) Thinking that those who retreated first, and the party who fired on us at fifty or sixty yards distant, had all only fallen back to meet others with amunition. As I saw them re-loading their guns, and more coming up than I saw at first, and several of my bravest men being wounded, the others became panick struck and squandered over the field; the white men pursued and fired on us several times. Hark had his horse shot under him, and I caught another for him as it was running by me; five or six of my men were wounded, but none left on the field; finding myself defeated here I instantly determined to go through a private way, and cross the Nottoway river at the Cypress Bridge, three miles below Jerusalem, and attack that place in the rear, as I expected they would look for me on the other road, and I had a great desire to get there to procure arms and amunition. After going a short distance in this private way, accompanied by about twenty men, I overtook two or three who told me the others were dispersed in every direction. After tyring [sic] in vain to collect a sufficient force to proceed to Jerusalem, I determined to return, as I was sure they would make back to their old neighborhood, where they would rejoin me, make new recruits, and come down again. On my way back, I called at Mrs. Thomas's, Mrs. Spencer's, and several other places, the white families having fled, we found no more victims to gratify our thirst for blood, we stopped at Majr. Ridley's quarter for the night, and being joined by four of his men, with the recruits made since my defeat, we mustered now about forty strong. After placing out sentinels, I laid down to sleep, but was quickly roused by a great racket; starting up, I found some mounted, and others in great confusion; one of the sentinels having given the alarm that we were about to be attacked, I ordered some to ride round and reconnoitre, and on their return the others being more alarmed, not knowing who they were, fled in different ways, so that I was reduced to about twenty again; with this I determined to attempt to recruit, and proceed on to rally in the neighborhood, I had left. Dr. Blunt's was the nearest house, which we reached just before day; on riding up the yard, Hark fired a gun. We expected Dr. Blunt and his family were at Maj. Ridley's, as I knew there was a company of men there; the gun was fired to ascertain if any of the family were at home; we were immediately fired upon and retreated, leaving several of my men. I do not know what became of them, as I never saw them afterwards. Pursuing our course back and coming in sight of Captain Harris', where we had been the day before, we discovered a party of white men at the house, on which all deserted me but two, (Jacob and Nat,) we concealed ourselves in the woods until near night, when I sent them in search of Henry, Sam, Nelson, and Hark, and directed them to rally all they could, at the place we had had our dinner the Sunday before, where they would find me, and I accordingly returned there as soon as it was dark and remained until Wednesday evening, when discovering white men riding around the place as though they were looking for some one, and none of my men joining me, I concluded Jacob and Nat had been taken, and compelled to betray me. On this I gave up all hope for the present; and on Thursday night after having supplied myself with provisions from Mr. Travis's, I scratched a hole under a pile of fence rails in a field, where I concealed myself for six weeks, never leaving my hiding place but for a few minutes in the dead of night to get water which was very near; thinking by this time I could venture out, I began to go about in the night and eaves drop the houses in the neighborhood; pursuing this course for about a fortnight and gathering little or no intelligence, afraid of speaking to any human being, and returning every morning to my cave before the dawn of day. I know not how long I might have led this life, if accident had not betrayed me, a dog in the neighborhood passing by my hiding place one night while I was out, was attracted by some meat I had in my cave, and crawled in and stole it, and was coming out just as I returned. A few nights after, two negroes having started to go hunting with the same dog, and passed that way, the dog came again to the place, and having just gone out to walk about, discovered me and barked, on which thinking myself discovered, I spoke to them to beg concealment. On making myself known they fled from me. Knowing then they would betray me, I immediately left my hiding place, and was pursued almost incessantly until I was taken a fortnight afterwards by Mr. Benjamin Phipps, in a little hole I had dug out with my sword, for the purpose of concealment, under the top of a fallen tree. On Mr. Phipps' discovering the place of my concealment, he cocked his gun and aimed at me. I requested him not to shoot and I would give up, upon which he demanded my sword. I delivered it to him, and he brought me to prison. During the time I was pursued, I had many hair breadth escapes, which your time will not permit you to relate. I am here loaded with chains, and willing to suffer the fate that awaits me.

I here proceeded to make some inquiries of him, after assuring him of the certain death that awaited him, and that concealment would only bring destruction on the innocent as well as guilty, of his own color, if he knew of any extensive or concerted plan. His answer was, I do not. When I questioned him as to the insurrection in North Carolina happening about the same time, he denied any knowledge of it; and when I looked him in the face as though I would search his inmost thoughts, he replied, "I see sir, you doubt my word; but can you not think the same ideas, and strange appearances about this time in the heaven's might prompt others, as well as myself, to this undertaking." I now had much conversation with and asked him many questions, having forborne to do so previously, except in the cases noted in parenthesis; but during his statement, I had, unnoticed by him, taken notes as to some particular circumstances, and having the advantage of his statement before me in writing, on the evening of the third day that I had been with him, I began a cross examination, and found his statement corroborated by every circumstance coming within my own knowledge or the confessions of others whom had been either killed or executed, and whom he had not seen nor had any knowledge since 22d of August last, he expressed himself fully satisfied as to the impracticability of his attempt. It has been said he was ignorant and cowardly, and that his object was to murder and rob for the purpose of obtaining money to make his escape. It is notorious, that he was never known to have a dollar in his life; to swear an oath, or drink a drop of spirits. As to his ignorance, he certainly never had the advantages of education, but he can read and write, (it was taught him by his parents,) and for natural intelligence and quickness of apprehension, is surpassed by few men I have ever seen. As to his being a coward, his reason as given for not resisting Mr. Phipps, shews the decision of his character. When he saw Mr. Phipps present his gun, he said he knew it was impossible for him to escape as the woods were full of men; he therefore thought it was better to surrender, and trust to fortune for his escape. He is a complete fanatic, or plays his part most admirably. On other subjects he possesses an uncommon share of intelligence, with a mind capable of attaining any thing; but warped and perverted by the influence of early impressions. He is below the ordinary stature, though strong and active, having the true negro face, every feature of which is strongly marked. I shall not attempt to describe the effect of his narrative, as told and commented on by himself, in the condemned hole of the prison. The calm, deliberate composure with which he spoke of his late deeds and intentions, the expression of his fiend-like face when excited by enthusiasm, still bearing the stains of the blood of helpless innocence about him; clothed with rags and covered with chains; yet daring to raise his manacled hands to heaven, with a spirit soaring above the attributes of man; I looked on him and my blood curdled in my veins.

I will not shock the feelings of humanity, nor wound afresh the bosoms of the disconsolate sufferers in this unparalleled and inhuman massacre, by detailing the deeds of their fiend-like barbarity. There were two or three who were in the power of these wretches, had they known it, and who escaped in the most providential manner. There were two whom they thought they left dead on the field at Mr. Parker's, but who were only stunned by the blows of their guns, as they did not take time to re-load when they charged on them. The escape of a little girl who went to school at Mr. Waller's, and where the children were collecting for that purpose, excited general sympathy. As their teacher had not arrived, they were at play in the yard, and seeing the negroes approach, she ran up on a dirt chimney, (such as are common to log houses,) and remained there unnoticed during the massacre of the eleven that were killed at this place. She remained on her hiding place till just before the arrival of a party, who were in pursuit of the murderers, when she came down and fled to a swamp, where, a mere child as she was, with the horrors of the late scene before her, she lay concealed until the next day, when seeing a party go up to the house, she came up, and on being asked how she escaped, replied with the utmost simplicity, "The Lord helped her." She was taken up behind a gentleman of the party, and returned to the arms of her weeping mother. Miss Whitehead concealed herself between the bed and the mat that supported it, while they murdered her sister in the same room, without discovering her. She was afterwards carried off, and concealed for protection by a slave of the family, who gave evidence against several of them on their trial. Mrs. Nathaniel Francis, while concealed in a closet heard their blows, and the shrieks of the victims of these ruthless savages; they then entered the closet where she was concealed, and went out without discovering her. While in this hiding place, she heard two of her women in a quarrel about the division of her clothes. Mr. John T. Baron, discovering them approaching his house, told his wife to make her escape, and scorning to fly, fell fighting on his own threshold. After firing his rifle, he discharged his gun at them, and then broke it over the villain who first approached him, but he was overpowered, and slain. His bravery, however, saved from the hands of these monsters, his lovely and amiable wife, who will long lament a husband so deserving of her love. As directed by him, she attempted to escape through the garden, when she was caught and held by one of her servant girls, but another coming to her rescue, she fled to the woods, and concealed herself. Few indeed, were those who escaped their work of death. But fortunate for society, the hand of retributive justice has overtaken them; and not one that was known to be concerned has escaped.

The Commonwealth, } Charged with making insurrection,
vs. { and plotting to take away the lives of
Nat Turner. } divers free white persons, &c. on the
22d of August, 1831.

The court composed of—, having met for the trial of Nat Turner, the prisoner was brought in and arraigned, and upon his arraignment pleaded *Not guilty;* saying to his counsel, that he did not feel so.

On the part of the Commonwealth, Levi Waller was introduced, who being sworn, deposed as follows: (*agreeably to Nat's own Confession.*) Col. Trezvant* was then introduced, who being sworn, narrated Nat's Confession to him, as follows: (*his Confession as given to Mr. Gray.*) The prisoner introduced no evidence, and the case was submitted without argument to the court, who having found him guilty, Jeremiah Cobb, Esq. Chairman, pronounced the sentence of the court, in the following words: "Nat Turner! Stand up. Have you anything to say why sentence of death should not be pronounced against you?

Ans. I have not. I have made a full confession to Mr. Gray, and I have nothing more to say.

Attend then to the sentence of the Court. You have been arraigned and tried before this court, and convicted of one of the highest crimes in our criminal code. You have been convicted of plotting in cold blood, the indiscriminate destruction of men, of helpless women, and of infant children. The evidence before us leaves not a shadow of doubt, but that your hands were often imbrued in the blood of the innocent; and your own confession tells us that they were stained with the blood of a master; in your own language, "too indulgent." Could I stop here, your crime would be sufficiently aggravated. But the original contriver of a plan, deep and deadly, one that never can be effected, you managed so far to put it into execution, as to deprive us of many of our most valuable citizens; and this was done when they were asleep, and defenceless; under circumstances shocking to humanity. And while upon this part of the subject, I cannot but call your attention to the poor misguided wretches who have gone before you. They are not few in number—they were your bosom associates; and the blood of all cries aloud, and calls upon you, as the author of their misfortune. Yes! You forced them unprepared, from Time to Eternity. Borne down by this load of guilt, your only justification is, that you were led away by fanaticism. If this be true, from my soul I pity you; and while you have my sympathies, I am, nevertheless called upon to pass the sentence of the court. The time between this and your execution, will necessarily be very short; and your only hope must be in another world. The judgment of the court is, that you be taken hence to the jail from whence you came, thence to the place of execution, and on Friday next, between the hours of 10 A. M. and 2 P. M. be hung by the neck until you are dead! dead! dead and may the Lord have mercy upon your soul.

*The committing Magistrate.

A List of Persons Murdered in the Insurrection, on the 21st and 22d of August, 1831.

Joseph Travers and wife and three children, Mrs. Elizabeth Turner, Hartwell Prebles, Sarah Newsome, Mrs. P. Reese and son William, Trajan Doyle, Henry Bryant and wife and child, and wife's mother, Mrs. Catharine Whitehead, son Richard and four daughters and grand-child, Salathiel Francis, Nathaniel Francis' overseer and two children, John T. Barrow, George Vaughan, Mrs. Levi Waller and ten children, William Williams, wife and two boys, Mrs. Caswell Worrell and child, Mrs. Rebecca Vaughan, Ann Eliza Vaughan, and son Arthur, Mrs. John K. Williams and child, Mrs. Jacob Williams and three children, and Edwin Drury—amounting to fifty-five.

A List of Negroes Brought Before the Court of Southampton, with Their Owners' Names, and Sentence.

Daniel,	Richard Porter,	Convicted.
Moses,	J. T. Barrow,	Do.
Tom,	Caty Whitehead,	Discharged.
Jack and Andrew,	Caty Whitehead,	Con. and transported.
Jacob,	Geo. H. Charlton,	Disch'd without trial.
Isaac,	Ditto,	Convi. and transported.
Jack,	Everett Bryant,	Discharged.
Nathan,	Benj. Blunt's estate,	Convicted.
Nathan, Tom, and Davy, (boys,)	Nathaniel Francis,	Convicted and transport.
Davy,	Elizabeth Turner,	Convicted.
Curtis,	Thomas Ridley,	Do.
Stephen,	Do.	Do.
Hardy and Isham,	Benjamin Edwards,	Convicted and transp'd.
Sam,	Nathaniel Francis,	Convicted.
Hark,	Joseph Travis' estate.	Do.
Moses, (a boy,)	Do.	Do. and transported
Davy,	Levi Waller,	Convicted.
Nelson,	Jacob Williams,	Do.
Nat,	Edm'd Turner's estate,	Do.
Jack,	Wm. Reese's estate,	Do.
Dred,	Nathaniel Francis,	Do.
Arnold, Artist, (free,)		Discharged.
Sam,	J. W. Parker,	Acquitted.
Ferry and Archer,	J. W. Parker,	Disch'd without trial.
Jim,	William Vaughan,	Acquitted.
Bob,	Temperance Parker,	Do.
Davy,	Joseph Parker,	
Daniel,	Solomon D. Parker,	Disch'd without trial.
Thomas Haithcock, (free,)		Sent on for further trial.
Joe,	John C. Turner,	Convicted.
Lucy,	John T. Barrow,	Do.
Matt,	Thomas Ridley,	Acquitted.

Jim,.	Richard Porter,	Do.
Exum Artes, (free,).		Sent on for further trial.
Joe,.	Richard P. Briggs,	Disch'd without trial.
Bury Newsome, (free,)		Sent on for further trial.
Stephen,.	James Bell,	Acquitted.
Jim and Isaac,.	Samuel Champion,	Convicted and trans'd.
Proston, ...	Hannah Williamson,	Acquitted.
Frank,.	Solomon D. Parker,	Convi'd and transp'd.
Jack and Shadrach, ...	Nathaniel Simmons,	Acquitted.
Nelson,.	Benj. Blunt's estate,	Do.
Sam,.	Peter Edwards,	Convicted.
Archer,.	Arthur G. Reese,	Acquitted.
Isham Turner, (free,)		Sent on for further trial.
Nat Turner, ...	Putnam Moore, dec'd, ...	Convicted.

David Walker

David Walker's Appeal To the COLORED CITIZENS OF THE WORLD, but in particular, and very expressly, to those of THE UNITED STATES OF AMERICA

ARTICLE I.

Our Wretchedness in Consequence of Slavery.

My beloved brethren:—The Indians of North and of South America—the Greeks—the Irish, subjected under the king of Great Britain—the Jews, that ancient people of the Lord—the inhabitants of the islands of the sea—in fine, all the inhabitants of the earth, (except however, the sons of Africa) are called *men*, and of course are, and ought to be free. But we, (coloured people) and our children are *brutes! !* and of course are, and *ought to be* SLAVES to the American people and their children forever ! ! to dig their mines and work their farms; and thus go on enriching them, from one generation to another with our *blood* and our *tears! ! ! !*

I promised in a preceding page to demonstrate to the satisfaction of the most incredulous, that we, (coloured people of these United States of America) are the *most wretched, degraded* and *abject* set of beings that *ever lived* since the world began, and that the white Americans having reduced us to the wretched state of *slavery,* treat us in that condition *more cruel* (they being an enlightened and Christian people,) than any heathen nation did any people whom it had reduced to our condition. These affirmations are so well confirmed in the minds of all unprejudiced men, who have taken the trouble to read histories, that they need no elucidation from me. But to put them beyond all doubt, I refer you in the first place to the children of Jacob, or of Israel in Egypt, under Pharaoh and his people. Some of my brethren do not know who Pharaoh and the Egyptians were—I know it to be a fact, that some of them take the Egyptians to have been a gang of *devils,* not knowing any better, and that they (Egyptians) having got possession of the Lord's people, treated them *nearly* as cruel as *Christian Americans* do us, at the present day. For the information of such, I would only mention that the Egyptians, were Africans or coloured people, such as we are—some of them yellow and others dark—a mixture of Ethiopians and the natives of Egypt—about the same as you see the coloured people of the United States at the present day.—I say, I call your attention then, to the children of Jacob, while I point out particularly to you his son Joseph, among the rest, in Egypt.

"And Pharaoh, said unto Joseph, ... thou shalt be over my house, and according unto thy word shall all my people be ruled: only in the throne will I be greater than thou.

"And Pharaoh said unto Joseph, see, I have set thee over all the land of Egypt."

"And Pharaoh said unto Joseph, I am Pharaoh, and without thee shall no man lift up his hand or foot in all the land of Egypt."

Now I appeal to heaven and to earth, and particularly to the American people themselves, who cease not to declare that our condition is not *hard*, and that we are comparatively satisfied to rest in wretchedness and misery, under them and their children. Not, indeed, to show me a coloured President, a Governor, a Legislator, a Senator, a Mayor, or an Attorney at the Bar.—But to show me a man of colour, who holds the low office of a Constable, or one who sits in a Juror Box, even on a case of one of his wretched brethren, throughout this great Republic! !—But let us pass Joseph the son of Israel a little farther in review, as he existed with that heathen nation.

"And Pharaoh called Joseph's name Zaphnathpaaneah; and he gave him to wife Asenath the daughter of Potipherah priest of On. And Joseph went out over all the land of Egypt."

Compare the above, with the American institutions. Do they not institute laws to prohibit us from marrying among the whites? I would wish, candidly, however, before the Lord, to be understood, that I would not give a *pinch of snuff* to be married to any white person I ever saw in all the days of my life. And I do say it, that the black man, or man of colour, who will leave his own colour (provided he can get one, who is good for any thing) and marry a white woman, to be a double slave to her, just because she is *white*, ought to be treated by her as he surely will be, viz: as a NIGGER! ! ! ! It is not, indeed, what I care about inter-marriages with the whites, which induced me to pass this subject in review; for the Lord knows, that there is a day coming when they will be glad enough to get into the company of the blacks, notwithstanding, we are, in this generation, levelled by them, almost on a level with the brute creation: and some of us they treat even worse than they do the brutes that perish. I only made this extract to show how much lower we are held, and how much more cruel we are treated by the Americans, than were the children of Jacob, by the Egyptians.—We will notice the sufferings of Israel some further, under *heathen Pharaoh*, compared with ours under the *enlightened Christians of America*.

"And Pharaoh spoke unto Joseph, saying, thy father and thy brethren are come unto thee:

"The land of Egypt is before thee: in the best of the land make thy father and brethren to dwell; in the land of Goshen let them dwell: and if thou knowest any men of activity among them, then make them rulers over my cattle."

I ask those people who treat us so *well*, Oh! I ask them, where is the most barren spot of land which they have given unto us? Israel had the most fertile land in all Egypt. Need I mention the very notorious fact, that I have known a poor man of colour, who laboured night and day, to acquire a little money, and having acquired it, he vested it in a small piece of land, and got him a house erected thereon, and having paid for the whole, he moved his family into it, where he was suffered to remain but nine months, when he was cheated out of his property by a white man, and driven out of door! And is not this the case generally? Can a man of colour buy a piece of land and keep it peaceably? Will not some white man try to get it from him, even if it is in a *mud hole?* I need not comment any farther on a subject, which all, both black and white, will readily admit. But I must, really, observe that in this very city, when a man of colour dies, if he owned any real estate it most generally falls into the hands of some white person. The wife and children of the deceased may weep and lament if they please, but the estate will be kept snug enough by its white possessor.

But to prove farther that the condition of the Israelites was better under the Egyptians than ours is under the whites. I call upon the professing Christians, I call upon the philanthropist, I call upon the very tyrant himself, to show me a page of history, either sacred or profane, on which a verse can be found, which maintains, that the Egyptians heaped the *insupportable insult* upon the children of Israel, by telling them that they were not of the *human family.* Can the whites deny this charge? Have they not, after having reduced us to the deplorable condition of slaves under their feet, held us up as descending originally from the tribes of *Monkeys* or *Orang-Outangs?* O! my God! I appeal to every man of feeling—is not this insupportable? Is it not heaping the most gross insult upon our miseries, because they have got us under their feet and we cannot help ourselves? Oh! pity us we pray thee, Lord Jesus, Master.—Has Mr. Jefferson declared to the world, that we are inferior to the whites, both in the endowments of our bodies and our minds? It is indeed surprising, that a man of such great learning, combined with such excellent natural parts, should speak so of a set of men in chains. I do not know what to compare it to, unless, like putting one wild deer in an iron cage, where it will be secured, and hold another by the side of the same, then let it go, and expect the one in the cage to run as fast as the one at liberty. So far, my brethren, were the Egyptians from heaping these insults upon their slaves, that Pharaoh's daughter took Moses, a son of Israel for her own, as will appear by the following.

"And Pharaoh's daughter said unto her, [Moses' mother] take this child away, and nurse it for me, and I will pay thee thy wages. And the woman took the child [Moses] and nursed it.

"And the child grew, and she brought him unto Pharaoh's daughter and he became her son. And she called his name Moses: and she said because I drew him out of the water."

In all probability, Moses would have become Prince Regent to the throne, and no doubt, in process of time but he would have been seated on the throne of Egypt. But he had rather suffer shame, with the people of God, than to enjoy pleasures with that wicked people for a season. O! that the coloured people were long since of Moses' excellent disposition, instead of courting favour with, and telling news and lies to our *natural enemies*, against each other—aiding them to keep their hellish chains of slavery upon us. Would we not long before this time, have been respectable men, instead of such wretched victims of oppression as we are? Would they be able to drag our mothers, our fathers, our wives, our children and ourselves, around the world in chains and hand-cuffs as they do, to dig up gold and silver for them and theirs? This question, my brethren, I leave for you to digest; and may God Almighty force it home to your hearts. Remember that unless you are united, keeping your tongues within your teeth, you will be afraid to trust your secrets to each other, and thus perpetuate our miseries under the *Christians* ! ! ! ! ☞ADDITION.—Remember, also to lay humble at the feet of our Lord and Master Jesus Christ, with prayers and fastings. Let our enemies go on with their butcheries, and at once fill up their cup. Never make an attempt to gain our freedom or *natural right*, from under our cruel oppressors and murderers, until you see your way clear—when that hour arrives and you move, be not afraid or dismayed; for be you assured that Jesus Christ the King of heaven and of earth who is the God of justice and of armies, will surely go before you. And those enemies who have for hundreds of years stolen our *rights*, and kept us ignorant of Him and His divine worship, he will remove. Millions of whom, are this day, so ignorant and avaricious, that they cannot conceive how God can have an attribute of justice, and show mercy to us because it pleased Him to make us black—which colour, Mr. Jefferson calls unfortunate! ! ! ! ! ! As though we are not as thankful to our God, for having made us as it pleased himself, as they, (the whites,) are for having made them white. They think because they hold us in their infernal chains of slavery, that we wish to be white, or of their color—but they are dreadfully deceived—we wish to be just as it pleased our Creator to have made us, and no avaricious and unmerciful wretches, have any business to make slaves of, or hold us in slavery. How would they like for us to make slaves of, and hold them in cruel slavery, and murder them as they do us?—But is Mr. Jefferson's assertions true? viz. "that it is unfortunate for us that our Creator has been pleased to make us *black.*" We will not take his say so, for the fact. The world will have an opportunity to see whether it is unfortunate for us, that our Creator *has made us* darker than the *whites*.

Fear not the number and education of our *enemies*, against whom we shall have to contend for our lawful right; guaranteed to us by our Maker; for why should we be afraid, when God is, and will continue, (if we continue humble) to be on our side?

The man who would not fight under our Lord and Master Jesus Christ, in the glorious and heavenly cause of freedom and of God—to be delivered from the most wretched, abject and servile slavery, that ever a people was afflicted with since the foundation of the world, to the present day—ought to be kept with all of his children or family, in slavery, or in chains, to be butchered by his *cruel enemies.* ☜

I saw a paragraph, a few years since, in a South Carolina paper, which, speaking of the barbarity of the Turks, it said: "The Turks are the most barbarous people in the world—they treat the Greeks more like *brutes* than human beings." And in the same paper was an advertisement, which said: "Eight well built Virginia and Maryland *Negro fellows* and four *wenches* will positively be *sold* this day, *to the highest bidder!*" And what astonished me still more was, to see in this same *humane* paper! ! the cuts of three men, with clubs and budgets on their backs, and an advertisement offering a considerable sum of money for their apprehension and delivery. I declare, it is really so amusing to hear the Southerners and Westerners of this country talk about *barbarity*, that it is positively, enough to make a man *smile*.

The sufferings of the Helots among the Spartans, were some-what severe, it is true, but to say that theirs, were as severe as ours among the Americans, I do most strenuously deny—for instance, can any man show me an article on a page of ancient history which specifies, that, the Spartans chained, and hand-cuffed the Helots, and dragged them from their wives and children, children from their parents, mothers from their suckling babes, wives from their husbands, driving them from one end of the country to the other? Notice the Spartans were heathens, who lived long before our Divine Master made his appearance in the flesh. Can Christian Americans deny these barbarous cruelties? Have you not, Americans, having subjected us under you, added to these miseries, by insulting us in telling us to our face, because we are helpless, that we are not of the human family? I ask you, O! Americans, I ask you, in the name of the Lord, can you deny these charges? Some perhaps may deny, by saying, that they never thought or said that we were not men. But do not actions speak louder than words?—have they not made provisions for the Greeks, and Irish? Nations who have never done the least thing for them, while *we*, who have enriched their country with our blood and tears—have dug up gold and silver for them and their children, from generation to generation, and are in more miseries than any other people under heaven, are not seen, but by comparatively, a handful of the American people? There are indeed, more ways to kill a dog, besides choking it to death with butter. Further—The Spartans or Lacedaemonians, had some frivolous pretext, for enslaving the Helots, for they (Helots) while being free inhabitants of Sparta, stirred up an intestine commotion, and were, by the Spartans subdued, and made prisoners of war. Consequently they and their children were condemned to perpetual slavery.

I have been for years troubling the pages of historians, to find out what our fathers have done to the *white Christians of America*, to merit such condign punishment as they have inflicted on them, and do continue to inflict on us their children. But I must aver, that my researches have hitherto been to no effect. I have therefore, come to the immoveable conclusion, that they (Americans) have, and do continue to punish us for nothing else, but for enriching them and their country. For I cannot conceive of anything else. Nor will I ever believe otherwise, until the Lord shall convince me.

The world knows, that slavery as it existed among the Romans, (which was the primary cause of their destruction) was, comparatively speaking, no more than a *cypher*, when compared with ours under the Americans. Indeed I should not have noticed the Roman slaves, had not the very learned and penetrating Mr. Jefferson said, "when a master was murdered, all his slaves in the same house, or within hearing, were condemned to death."—Here let me ask Mr. Jefferson, (but he is gone to answer at the bar of God, for the deeds done in his body while living,) I therefore ask the whole American people, had I not rather die, or be put to death, than to be a slave to any tyrant, who takes not only my own, but my wife and children's lives by the inches? Yea, would I meet death with avidity far! far! ! in preference to such *servile submission* to the murderous hands of tyrants. Mr. Jefferson's very severe remarks on us have been so extensively argued upon by men whose attainments in literature, I shall never be able to reach, that I would not have meddled with it, were it not to solicit each of my brethren, who has the spirit of a man, to buy a copy of Mr. Jefferson's "Notes on Virginia," and put it in the hand of his son. For let no one of us suppose that the refutations which have been written by our white friends are enough—they are *whites*—we are *blacks*. We, and the world wish to see the charges of Mr. Jefferson refuted by the blacks *themselves*, according to their chance; for we must remember that what the whites have written respecting this subject, is other men's labours, and did not emanate from the blacks. I know well, that there are some talents and learning among the coloured people of this country, which we have not a chance to develope, in consequence of oppression; but our oppression ought not to hinder us from acquiring all we can. For we will have a chance to develope them by and by. God will not suffer us, always to be oppressed. Our sufferings will come to an *end*, in spite of all the Americans this side of *eternity*. Then we will want all the learning and talents among ourselves, and perhaps more, to govern ourselves.—"Every dog must have its day," the American's is coming to an end.

But let us review Mr. Jefferson's remarks respecting us some further. Comparing our miserable fathers, with the learned philosophers of Greece, he says: "Yet notwithstanding these and other discouraging circumstances among the Romans, their slaves were often their rarest artists. They excelled too, in science, insomuch as to be usually employed as tutors to their master's children; Epictetus, Terence and Phædrus, were slaves,—but they were of the race of whites. It is not their *condition* then, but *nature*, which has produced the distinction." See this, my brethren! ! Do you believe that this assertion is swallowed by millions of the whites? Do you know that Mr. Jefferson was one of as great characters as ever lived among the whites? See his writings for the world, and public labours for the United States of America. Do you believe that the assertions of such a man, will pass away into oblivion unobserved by this people and the world? If you do you are much mistaken—See how the American people treat us—have we souls in our bodies? Are we men who have any spirits at all? I know that there are many *swell-bellied* fellows among us, whose greatest object is to fill their stomachs. Such I do not mean—I am after those who know and feel, that we are MEN, as well as other people; to them, I say, that unless we try to refute Mr. Jefferson's arguments respecting us, we will only establish them.

But the slaves among the Romans. Every body who has read history, knows, that as soon as a slave among the Romans obtained his freedom, he could rise to the greatest eminence in the State, and there was no law instituted to hinder a slave from buying his freedom. Have not the Americans instituted laws to hinder us from obtaining our freedom? Do any deny this charge? Read the laws of Virginia, North Carolina, &c. Further: have not the Americans instituted laws to prohibit a man of colour from obtaining and holding any office whatever, under the government of the United States of America? Now, Mr. Jefferson tells us, that our condition is not so hard, as the slaves were under the Romans! ! ! ! ! !

It is time for me to bring this article to a close. But before I close it, I must observe to my brethren that at the close of the first Revolution in this country, with Great Britain, there were but thirteen States in the Union, now there are twenty-four, most of which are slave-holding States, and the whites are dragging us around in chains and in handcuffs, to their new States and Territories to work their mines and farms, to enrich them and their children—and millions of them believing firmly that we being a little darker than they, were made by our Creator to be an inheritance to them and their children for ever—the same as a parcel of *brutes*.

Are we MEN! !—I ask you, O my brethren! are we MEN? Did our Creator make us to be slaves to dust and ashes like ourselves? Are they not dying worms as well as we? Have they not to make their appearance before the tribunal of Heaven, to answer for the deeds done in the body, as well as we? Have we any other Master but Jesus Christ alone? Is he not their Master as well as ours?—What right then, have we to obey and call any other Master, but Himself? How we could be so *submissive* to a gang of men, whom we cannot tell whether they are *as good* as ourselves or not, I never could conceive. However, this is shut up with the Lord, and we cannot precisely tell—but I declare, we judge men by their works.

The whites have always been an unjust, jealous, unmerciful, avaricious and blood-thirsty set of beings, always seeking after power and authority.—We view them all over the confederacy of Greece, where they were first known to be any thing, (in consequence of education) we see them there, cutting each other's throats—trying to subject each other to wretchedness and misery—to effect which, they used all kinds of deceitful, unfair, and unmerciful means. We view them next in Rome, where the spirit of tyranny and deceit raged still higher. We view them in Gaul, Spain, and in Britain.—In fine, we view them all over Europe, together with what were scattered about in Asia and Africa, as heathens, and we see them acting more like devils than accountable men. But some may ask, did not the blacks of Africa, and the mulattoes of Asia, go on in the same way as did the whites of Europe. I answer, no—they never were half so avaricious, deceitful and unmerciful as the whites, according to their knowledge.

But we will leave the whites or Europeans as heathens, and take a view of them as Christians, in which capacity we see them as cruel, if not more so than ever. In fact, take them as a body, they are ten times more cruel, avaricious and unmerciful than ever they were; for while they were heathens, they were bad enough it is true, but it is positively a fact that they were not quite so audacious as to go and take vessel loads of men, women and children, and in cold blood, and through devilishness, throw them into the sea, and murder them in all kind of ways. While they were heathens, they were too ignorant for such barbarity. But being Christians, enlightened and sensible, they are completely prepared for such hellish cruelties. Now suppose God were to give them more sense, what would they do? If it were possible, would they not *dethrone* Jehovah and seat themselves upon his throne? I therefore, in the name and fear of the Lord God of Heaven and of earth, divested of prejudice either on the side of my colour or that of the whites, advance my suspicion of them, whether they are *as good by nature* as we are or not. Their actions, since they were known as a people, have been the reverse, I do indeed suspect them, but this, as I before observed, is shut up with the Lord, we cannot exactly tell, it will be proved in succeeding generations.—The whites have had the essence of the gospel as it was preached by my master and his apostles—the Ethiopians have not, who are to have it in its meridian splendor—the Lord will give it to them to their satisfaction. I hope and pray my God, that they will make good use of it, that it may be well with them.*

ARTICLE II.

Our Wretchedness in Consequence of Ignorance.

Ignorance, my brethren, is a mist, low down into the very dark and almost impenetrable abyss in which, our fathers for many centuries have been plunged. The Christians, and enlightened of Europe, and some of Asia, seeing the ignorance and consequent degradation of our fathers, instead of trying to enlighten them, by teaching them that religion and light with which God had blessed them, they have plunged them into wretchedness ten thousand times more intolerable, than if they had left them entirely to the Lord, and to add to their

---

*It is my solemn belief, that if ever the world becomes Christianized, (which must certainly take place before long) it will be through the means, under God of the *Blacks*, who are now held in wretchedness, and degradation, by the white *Christians* of the world, who before they learn to do justice to us before our Maker—and be reconciled to us, and reconcile us to them, and by that means have clear consciences before God and man.—Send out Missionaries to convert the Heathens, many of whom after they cease to worship gods, which neither see nor hear, become ten times more the children of Hell, then ever they were, why what is the reason? Why the reason is obvious, they must learn to do justice at home, before they go into distant lands, to display their charity, Christianity, and benevolence; when they learn to do justice, God will accept their offering, (no man may think that I am against Missionaries for I am not, my object is to see justice done at home, before we go to convert the Heathens.)

miseries, deep down into which they have plunged them tell them, that they are an *inferior* and *distinct race* of beings, which they will be glad enough to re-call and swallow by and by. Fortune and misfortune, two inseparable compan-ions, lay rolled up in the wheel of events, which have from the creation of the world, and will continue to take place among men until God shall dash worlds together.

When we take a retrospective view of the arts and sciences—the wise legis-lators—the Pyramids, and other magnificent buildings—the turning of the channel of the river Nile, by the sons of Africa or of Ham, among whom learn-ing originated, and was carried thence into Greece, where it was improved upon and refined. Thence among the Romans, and all over the then enlight-ened parts of the world, and it has been enlightening the dark and benighted minds of men from then, down to this day. I say, when I view retrospectively, the renown of that once mighty people, the children of our great progenitor I am indeed cheered. Yea further, when I view that mighty son of Africa, HANNIBAL, one of the greatest generals of antiquity, who defeated and cut off so many thousands of the white Romans or murderers, and who carried his vic-torious arms, to the very gate of Rome, and I give it as my candid opinion, that had Carthage been well united and had given him good support, he would have carried that cruel and barbarous city by storm. But they were dis-united, as the coloured people are now, in the United States of America, the reason our nat-ural enemies are enabled to keep their feet on our throats.

Beloved brethren—here let me tell you, and believe it, that the Lord our God, as true as he sits on his throne in heaven, and as true as our Saviour died to redeem the world, will give you a Hannibal, and when the Lord shall have raised him up, and given him to you for your possession, O my suffering brethren! remember the divisions and consequent sufferings of *Carthage* and of *Hayti*. Read the history particularly of Hayti, and see how they were butchered by the whites, and do you take warning. The person whom God shall give you, give him your support and let him go his length, and behold in him the salva-tion of your God. God will indeed, deliver you through him from your de-plorable and wretched condition under the Christians of America. I charge you this day before my God to lay no obstacle in his way, but let him go.

The whites want slaves, and want us for their slaves, but some of them will curse the day they ever saw us. As true as the sun ever shone in its meridian splendor, my colour will root some of them out of the very face of the earth. They shall have enough of making slaves of, and butchering, and murdering us in the manner which they have. No doubt some may say that I write with a bad spirit, and that I being a black, wish these things to occur. Whether I write with a bad or a good spirit, I say if these things do not occur in their proper time, it is because the world in which we live does not exist, and we are de-ceived with regard to its existence.—It is immaterial however to me, who believe, or who refuse—though I should like to see the whites repent peradven-ture God may have mercy on them, some however, have gone so far that their cup must be filled.

But what need have I to refer to antiquity, when Hayti, the glory of the blacks and terror of tyrants, is enough to convince the most avaricious and stupid of wretches—which is at this time, and I am sorry to say it, plagued with that scourge of nations, the Catholic religion; but I hope and pray God that she may yet rid herself of it, and adopt in its stead the Protestant faith; also, I hope that she may keep peace within her borders and be united, keeping a strict look out for tyrants, for if they get the least chance to injure her, they will avail themselves of it, as true as the Lord lives in heaven. But one thing which gives me joy is, that they are men who would be cut off to a man, before they would yield to the combined forces of the whole world—in fact, if the whole world was combined against them, it could not do any thing with them, unless the Lord delivers them up.

Ignorance and treachery one against the other—a grovelling servile and abject submission to the lash of tyrants, we see plainly, my brethren, are not the natural elements of the blacks, as the Americans try to make us believe; but these are misfortunes which God has suffered our fathers to be enveloped in for many ages, no doubt in consequence of their disobedience to their Maker, and which do, indeed, reign at this time among us, almost to the destruction of all other principles: for I must truly say, that ignorance, the mother of treachery and deceit, gnaws into our very vitals. Ignorance, as it now exists among us, produces a state of things, Oh my Lord! too horrible to present to the world. Any man who is curious to see the full force of ignorance developed among the coloured people of the United States of America, has only to go into the southern and western states of this confederacy, where, if he is not a tyrant, but has the feelings of a human being, who can feel for a fellow creature, he may see enough to make his very heart bleed! He may see there, a son take his mother, who bore almost the pains of death to give him birth, and by the command of a tyrant, strip her as naked as she came into the world, and apply the cow-hide to her, until she falls a victim to death in the road! He may see a husband take his dear wife, not unfrequently in a pregnant state, and perhaps far advanced, and beat her for an unmerciful wretch, until his infant falls a lifeless lump at her feet! Can the Americans escape God Almighty? If they do, can he be to us a God of Justice? God is just, and I know it—for he has convinced me to my satisfaction—I cannot doubt him. My observer may see fathers beating their sons, mothers their daughters, and children their parents, all to pacify the passions of unrelenting tyrants. He may also, see them telling news and lies, making mischief one upon another. These are some of the productions of ignorance, which he will see practised among my dear brethren, who are held in unjust slavery and wretchedness, by avaricious and unmerciful tyrants, to whom, and their hellish deeds, I would suffer my life to be taken before I would submit. And when my curious observer comes to take notice of those who are said to be free, (which assertion I deny) and who are making some frivolous pretentions to common sense, he will see that branch of ignorance among the slaves assuming a more cunning and deceitful course of procedure.—He may see some of my brethren in league with tyrants, selling their own brethren into *hell upon earth,* not dissimilar to the exhibitions in Africa, but in a more secret, servile and abject manner. Oh Heaven! I am full! ! ! I can hardly move my pen! ! ! ! and as I expect some will try to put me to death, to strike terror into others, and to obliterate from their minds the notion of freedom, so as to keep my brethren the more secure in wretchedness, where they will be permitted to stay but a short time (whether tyrants believe it or not)—I shall give the world a development of facts, which are already witnessed in the courts of heaven. My observer may see some of those ignorant and treacherous creatures (coloured people) sneaking about in the large cities, endeavouring to find out all strange coloured people, where they work and where they reside, asking them questions, and trying to ascertain whether they are runaways or not, telling them, at the same time, that they always have been, are, and always will be, friends to their brethren; and, perhaps, that they themselves are absconders, and a thousand such treacherous lies to get the better information of the more ignorant! ! ! There have been and are at this day in Boston, New-York, Philadelphia, and Baltimore, coloured men, who are in league with tyrants, and who receive a great portion of their daily bread, of the moneys which they acquire from the blood and tears of their more miserable brethren, whom they scandalously delivered into the hands of our *natural enemies! ! ! ! !*

To show the force of degraded ignorance and deceit among us some farther, I will give here an extract from a paragraph, which may be found in the Columbian Centinel of this city, for September 9, 1829, on the first page of which, the curious may find an article, headed

"AFFRAY AND MURDER."
"Portsmouth, (Ohio) Aug. 22, 1829.

"A most shocking outrage was committed in Kentucky, about eight miles from this place, on 14th inst. A negro driver, by the name of Gordon, who had purchased in Maryland about sixty negroes, was taking them, assisted by an associate named Allen, and the wagoner who conveyed the baggage, to the Mississippi. The men were hand-cuffed and chained together, in the usual manner for driving those poor wretches, while the women and children were suffered to proceed without incumbrance. It appears that, by means of a file the negroes, unobserved, had succeeded in separating the iron which bound their hands, in such a way as to be able to throw them off at any moment. About 8 o'clock in the morning, while proceeding on the state road leading from Greenup to Vanceburg, two of them dropped their shackles and commenced a fight, when the wagoner (Petit) rushed in with his whip to compel them to desist. At this moment, every negro was found to be perfectly at liberty; and one of them seizing a club, gave Petit a violent blow on the head, and laid him dead at his feet; and Allen, who came to his assistance, met a similar fate, from the contents of a pistol fired by another of the gang. Gordon was then attacked, seized and held by one of the negroes, whilst another fired twice at him with a pistol, the ball of which each time grazed his head, but not proving effectual, he was beaten with clubs, and left for dead. They then commenced pillaging the wagon, and with an axe split open the trunk of Gordon, and rifled it of the money, about $2,400. Sixteen of the negroes then took to the woods; Gordon, in the mean time, not being materially injured, was enabled, by the assistance of one of the women, to mount his horse and flee; pursued, however, by one of the gang on another horse, with a drawn pistol; fortunately he escaped with his life barely, arriving at a plantation, as the negro came in sight; who then turned about and retreated.

"The neighbourhood was immediately rallied, and a hot pursuit given—which, we understand, has resulted in the capture of the whole gang and the recovery of the greatest part of the money. Seven of the negro men and one woman, it is said were engaged in the murders, and will be brought to trial at the next court in Greenupsburg."

Here my brethren, I want you to notice particularly in the above article, the *ignorant* and *deceitful actions* of this coloured woman. I beg you to view it candidly, as for ETERNITY! ! ! ! Here a *notorious wretch*, with two other confederates had SIXTY of them in a gang, driving them like *brutes*—the men all in chains and hand-cuffs, and by the help of God they got their chains and hand-cuffs thrown off, and caught two of the wretches and put them to death, and beat the other until they thought he was dead, and left him for dead; however, he deceived them, and rising from the ground, this *servile woman* helped him upon his horse, and he made his escape. Brethren, what do you think of this? Was it the natural *fine feelings* of this woman, to save such a wretch alive? I know that the blacks, take them half enlightened and ignorant, are more humane and merciful than the most enlightened and refined European that can be found in all the earth. Let no one say that I assert this because I am prejudiced on the side of my colour, and against the whites or Europeans. For what I write, I do it candidly, for my God and the good of both parties: Natural observations have taught me these things; there is a solemn awe in the hearts of the blacks, as it respects *murdering* men:* whereas the whites, (though they are great cowards) where they have the advantage, or think that there are any prospects of getting it, they murder all before them, in order to subject men to wretchedness and degradation under them. This is the natural result of pride and avarice. But I declare, the actions of this black woman are really insupportable. For my own part, I cannot think it was any thing but servile deceit, combined with the most gross ignorance: for we must remember that *humanity, kindness* and the *fear of the Lord*, does not consist in protecting *devils*. Here is a set of wretches, who had SIXTY of them in a gang, driving them around the country like *brutes*, to dig up gold and silver for them, (which they will get enough of yet.) Should the lives of such creatures be spared? Are God and Mammon in league? What has the Lord to do with a gang of desperate wretches, who go *sneaking about the country like robbers*—light upon his people

---

*Which is the reason the whites take the advantage of us.

wherever they can get a chance, binding them with chains and hand-cuffs, beat and murder them as they would *rattle-snakes?* Are they not the Lord's enemies? Ought they not to be destroyed? Any person who will save such wretches from destruction, is fighting against the Lord, and will receive his just recompense. The black men acted like *blockheads.* Why did they not make sure of the wretch? He would have made sure of them, if he could. It is just the way with black men—eight white men can frighten fifty of them; whereas, if you can only get courage into the blacks, I do declare it, that one good black man can put to death six white men; and I give it as a fact, let twelve black men get well armed for battle, and they will kill and put to flight fifty whites.—The reason is, the blacks, once you get them started, they glory in death. The whites have had us under them for more than three centuries, murdering, and treating us like brutes; and, as Mr. Jefferson wisely said, they have never *found us out*—they do not know, indeed, that there is an unconquerable disposition in the breasts of the blacks, which, when it is fully awakened and put in motion, will be subdued, only with the destruction of the animal existence. Get the blacks started, and if you do not have a gang of tigers and lions to deal with, I am a deceiver of the blacks and of the whites. How sixty of them could let that wretch escape unkilled, I cannot conceive—they will have to suffer as much for the two whom, they secured, as if they had put one hundred to death: if you commence, make sure work—do not trifle, for they will not trifle with you—they want us for their slaves, and think nothing of murdering us in order to subject us to that wretched condition—therefore, if there is an *attempt* made by us, kill or be killed. Now, I ask you, had you not rather be killed than to be a slave to a tyrant, who takes the life of your mother, wife, and dear little children? Look upon your mother, wife and children, and answer God Almighty; and believe this, that it is no more harm for you to kill a man, who is trying to kill you, than it is for you to take a drink of water when thirsty; in fact, the man who will stand still and let another murder him, is worse than an infidel, and, if he has common sense, ought not to be pitied. The actions of this deceitful and ignorant coloured woman, in saving the life of a desperate wretch, whose avaricious and cruel object was to drive her, and her companions in miseries, through the country like cattle, to make his fortune on their carcasses, are but too much like that of thousands of our brethren in these states: if any thing is whispered by one, which has any allusion to the melioration of their dreadful condition, they run and tell tyrants, that they may be enabled to keep them the longer in wretchedness and miseries. Oh! coloured people of these United States, I ask you, in the name of that God who made us, have we, in consequence of oppression, nearly lost the spirit of man, and, in no very trifling degree, adopted that of brutes? Do you answer, no?—I ask you, then, what set of men can you point me to, in all the world, who are so abjectly employed by their oppressors, as we are by our *natural enemies?* How can, Oh! how can those enemies but say that we and our children are not of the HUMAN FAMILY, but were made by our Creator to be an inheritance to them and theirs for ever? How can the slaveholders but say that they can bribe the best coloured person in the country, to sell his brethren for a trifling sum of money, and take that atrocity to confirm them in their avaricious opinion, that we were made to be slaves to them and their children? How could Mr. Jefferson but say,* "I advance it therefore as a suspicion only, that the blacks, whether originally a distinct race, or made distinct by time and circumstances, are *inferior* to the whites in the endowments both of body and mind?"—"It," says he, "is not against experience to suppose, that different species of the same genius, or varieties of the same species, may possess different qualifications." [Here, my brethren, listen to him.] ☞"Will not a lover of natural history, then, one who views the gradations in all the races of *animals* with the eye of philosophy, excuse an effort to keep those in the department of MAN as *distinct* as nature has formed them?"—I hope you will try to find out the meaning of this verse—its widest sense and all its bearings: whether you do or not, remember the whites do. This very verse, brethren, having emanated from Mr. Jefferson, a much greater philosopher the world never afforded, has in truth injured us more, and has been as great a barrier to our emancipation as any thing that has ever been advanced against us. I hope you will not let it pass unnoticed. He goes on further, and says: "This *unfortunate* difference of colour, and *perhaps* of *faculty*, is a powerful obstacle to the emancipation of these people. Many of their advocates, while they wish to vindicate the liberty of human nature are anxious also to preserve its *dignity* and *beauty*. Some of these, embarrassed by the question, 'What further is to be done with them?' join themselves in opposition with those who are actuated by sordid avarice only." Now I ask you candidly, my suffering brethren in time, who are candidates for the eternal worlds, how could Mr. Jefferson but have given the world these remarks respecting us, when we are so submissive to them, and so much servile deceit prevail among ourselves—when we so *meanly* submit to their murderous lashes, to which neither the Indians nor any other people under Heaven would submit? No, they would die to a man, before they would suffer such things from men who are no better than themselves, and *perhaps not so good*. Yes, how can our friends but be embarrassed, as Mr. Jefferson says, by the question, "What further is to be done with these people?" For while they are working for our emancipation, we are, by our treachery, wickedness and deceit, working against ourselves and our children—helping ours, and the enemies of God, to keep us and our dear little children in their infernal chains of slavery! ! ! Indeed, our friends cannot but relapse and join themselves "with those who are actuated by *sordid avarice* only! ! ! !" For my own part, I am glad Mr. Jefferson has advanced his positions for your sake; for you will either have to contradict or confirm him by your own actions, and not by what our friends have said or done for us; for those things are other men's labours, and do not satisfy the Americans, who are waiting for us to prove to them ourselves, that we are MEN, before they will be willing to admit the fact; for I pledge you my sacred word of honour, that Mr. Jefferson's remarks respecting us, have sunk deep into the hearts of millions of the whites, and never will be removed this side of

*See his Notes on Virginia, page 213.

eternity.—For how can they, when we are confirming him every day, by our *groveling submissions* and *treachery?* I aver, that when I look over these United States of America, and the world, and see the ignorant deceptions and consequent wretchedness of my brethren, I am brought oftimes solemnly to a stand, and in the midst of my reflections I exclaim to my God, "Lord didst thou make us to be slaves to our brethren, the whites?" But when I reflect that God is just, and that millions of my wretched brethren would meet death with glory—yea, more, would plunge into the very mouths of cannons and be torn into particles as minute as the atoms which compose the elements of the earth, in preference to a mean submission to the lash of tyrants, I am with streaming eyes, compelled to shrink back into nothingness before my Maker, and exclaim again, thy will be done, O Lord God Almighty.

Men of colour, who are also of sense, for you particularly is my APPEAL designed. Our more ignorant brethren are not able to penetrate its value. I call upon you therefore to cast your eyes upon the wretchedness of your brethren, and to do your utmost to enlighten them—*go to work and enlighten your brethren!*—Let the Lord see you doing what you can to rescue them and yourselves from degradation. Do any of you say that you and your family are free and happy, and what have you to do with the wretched slaves and other people? So can I say, for I enjoy as much freedom as any of you, if I am not quite as well off as the best of you. Look into our freedom and happiness, and see of what kind they are composed! ! They are of the very lowest kind—they are the very *dregs!*—they are the most servile and abject kind, that ever a people was in possession of! If any of you wish to know how FREE you are, let one of you start and go through the southern and western States of this country, and unless you travel as a slave to a white man (a servant is a *slave* to the man whom he serves) or have your free papers, (which if you are not careful they will get from you) if they do not take you up and put you in jail, and if you cannot give good evidence of your freedom, sell you into eternal slavery, I am not a living man: or any man of colour, immaterial who he is, or where he came from, if he is not *the fourth from the negro race! !* (as we are called) the white Christians of America will serve him the same they will sink him into wretchedness and degradation for ever while he lives. And yet some of you have the hardihood to say that you are free and happy! May God have mercy on your freedom and happiness! ! I met a coloured man in the street a short time since, with a string of boots on his shoulders: we fell into conversation, and in course of which, I said to him, what a miserable set of people we are! He asked, why?—Said I, we are so subjected under the whites, that we cannot obtain the comforts of life, but by cleaning their boots and shoes, old clothes, waiting on them, shaving them &c. Said he, (with the boots on his shoulders) "I am completely happy ! ! ! I never want to live any better or happier than when I can get a plenty of boots and shoes to clean! ! !" Oh! how can those who are actuated by avarice only, but think, that our Creator made us to be an inheritance to them for ever, when they see that our greatest glory is centered in such mean and low objects? Understand me, brethren, I do not mean to speak against the occupations by which we acquire enough and sometimes scarcely that, to render ourselves and families comfortable through life. I am subjected to the same inconvenience, as you all.—My objections are, to our *glorying* and being *happy* in such low employments; for if we are men, we ought to be thankful to the Lord for the past, and for the future. Be looking forward with thankful hearts to higher attainments than *wielding the razor* and *cleaning boots and shoes*. The man whose aspirations are not *above*, and even *below* these, is indeed, ignorant and wretched enough. I advanced it therefore to you, not as a *problematical*, but as an unshaken and for ever immovable *fact*, that your full glory and happiness, as well as all other coloured people under Heaven, shall never be fully consummated, but with the *entire emancipation of your enslaved brethren all over the world*. You may therefore, go to work and do what you can to rescue, or join in with tyrants to oppress them and yourselves, until the Lord shall come upon you all like a thief in the night. For I believe it is the will of the Lord that our greatest happiness shall consist in working for the salvation of our whole body. When this is accomplished a burst of glory will shine upon you, which will indeed astonish you and the world. Do any of you say this never will be done? I assure you that God will accomplish it—if nothing else will answer, he will hurl tyrants and devils into *atoms* and make way for his people. But O my brethren! I say unto you again, you must go to work and prepare the way of the Lord.

There is a great work for you to do, as trifling as some of you may think of it. You have to prove to the Americans and the world, that we are MEN, and not *brutes*, as we have been represented, and by millions treated. Remember, to let the aim of your labours among your brethren, and particularly the youths, be the dissemination of education and religion.* It is lamentable, that many of our children go to school, from four until they are eight or ten, and sometimes fifteen years of age, and leave school knowing but a little more about the grammar of their language than a horse does about handling a musket—and not a few of them are really so ignorant, that they are unable to answer a person correctly, general questions in geography, and to hear them read, would only be to disgust a man who has a taste for reading; which, to do well, as trifling as it may appear to some, (to the ignorant in particular) is a great part of learning. Some few of them, may make out to scribble tolerably well, over a half sheet of paper, which I believe has hitherto been a powerful obstacle in our way, to keep us from acquiring knowledge. An ignorant father, who knows no more than what nature has taught him, together with what little he acquires by the senses of hearing and seeing, finding his son able to write a neat hand, sets it down for

---

*Never mind what the ignorant ones among us may say, many of whom when you speak to them for their good, and try to enlighten their minds, laugh at you, and perhaps tell you plump to your face, that they want no instruction from you or any other Niger, and all such aggravating language. Now if you are a man of understanding and sound sense, I conjure you in the name of the Lord, and of all that is good, to impute their actions to ignorance, and wink at their follies, and do your very best to get around them some way or other, for remember they are your brethren; and I declare to you that it is for your interests to teach and enlighten them.

granted that he has as good learning as any body; the young, ignorant gump, hearing his father or mother, who perhaps may be ten times more ignorant, in point of literature, than himself, extolling his learning, struts about, in the full assurance, that his attainments in literature are sufficient to take him through the world, when, in fact, he has scarcely any learning at all! ! ! !

I promiscuously fell in conversation once, with an elderly coloured man on the topics of education, and of the great prevalency of ignorance among us: Said he, "I know that our people are very ignorant but my son has a good education: I spent a great deal of money on his education: he can write as well as any white man, and I assure you that no one can fool him," &c. Said I, what else can your son do, besides writing a good hand? Can he post a set of books in a mercantile manner? Can he write a neat piece of composition in prose or in verse? To these interrogations he answered in the negative. Said I, did your son learn, while he was at school, the width and depth of English Grammar? To which he also replied in the negative, telling me his son did not learn those things. Your son, said I, then, has hardly any learning at all— he is almost as ignorant, and more so, than many of those who never went to school one day in all their lives. My friend got a little put out, and so walking off, said that his son could write as well as any white man. Most of the coloured people, when they speak of the education of one among us who can write a neat hand, and who perhaps knows nothing but to scribble and puff pretty fair on a small scrap of paper, immaterial whether his words are gram- matical, or spelt correctly, or not; if it only looks beautiful, they say he has as good an education as any white man—he can write as well as any white man, &c. The poor, ignorant creature, hearing, this, he is ashamed, forever after, to let any person see him humbling himself to another for knowledge but going about trying to deceive those who are more ignorant than himself, he at last falls an ignorant victim to death in wretchedness. I pray that the Lord may undeceive my ignorant brethren, and permit them to throw away preten- sions, and seek after the substance of learning. I would crawl on my hands and knees through mud and mire, to the feet of a learned man, where I would sit and humbly supplicate him to instil into me, that which neither devils nor tyrants could remove, only with my life—for coloured people to acquire learning in this country, makes tyrants quake and tremble on their sandy foundation. Why, what is the matter? Why, they know that their infernal deeds of cruelty will be made known to the world. Do you suppose one man of good sense and learning would submit himself, his father, mother, wife and children, to be slaves to a wretched man like himself, who, instead of com- pensating him for his labours, chains, hand-cuffs and beats him and family al- most to death, leaving life enough in them, however, to work for, and call him master? No! no! he would cut his devilish throat from ear to ear, and well do slave-holders know it. The bare name of educating the coloured peo- ple, scares our cruel oppressors almost to death. But if they do not have enough to be frightened for yet, it will be, because they can always keep us ig- norant, and because God approbates their cruelties, with which they have been for centuries murdering us. The whites shall have enough of the blacks, yet, as true as God sits on his throne in Heaven.

Some of our brethren are so very full of learning, that you cannot mention any thing to them which they do not know better than yourself! !—nothing is strange to them! !—they knew every thing years ago!—if any thing should be mentioned in company where they are, immaterial how important it is respecting us or the world, if they had not divulged it; they make light of it, and affect to have known it long before it was mentioned and try to make all in the room, or wherever you may be, believe that your conversation is nothing! !—not worth hearing! All this is the result of ignorance and ill-breeding; for a man of good-breeding, sense and penetration, if he had heard a subject told twenty times over, and should happen to be in company where one should commence telling it again, he would wait with patience on its narrator, and see if he would tell it as it was told in his presence before—paying the most strict attention to what is said, to see if any more light will be thrown on the subject: for all men are not gifted alike in telling, or even hearing the most simple narration. These ignorant, vicious, and wretched men, contribute almost as much injury to our body as tyrants themselves, by doing so much for the promotion of ignorance amongst us; for they, making such pretensions to knowledge, such of our youth as are seeking after knowledge, and can get access to them, take them as criterions to go by, who will lead them into a channel, where, unless the Lord blesses them with the privilege of seeing their folly, they will be irretrievably lost forever, while in time! ! !

I must close this article by relating the very heart-rending fact, that I have examined school-boys and young men of colour in different parts of the country, in the most simple parts of Murray's English Grammar, and not more than one in thirty was able to give a correct answer to my interrogations. If any one contradicts me, let him step out of his door into the streets of Boston, New-York, Philadelphia, or Baltimore, (no use to mention any other, for the Christians are too charitable further south or west!)—I say, let him who disputes me, step out of his door into the streets of either of those four cities, and promiscuously collect one hundred school-boys, or young men of colour, *who have been to school,* and who are considered by the coloured people to have received an excellent education, because, perhaps, some of them can write a good hand, but who, notwithstanding their neat writing, may be almost as ignorant, in comparison, as a horse.—And, I say it, he will hardly find (in this enlightened day, and in the midst of this *charitable* people) five in one hundred, who, are able to correct the false grammar of their language.—The cause of this almost universal ignorance among us, I appeal to our schoolmasters to declare. Here is a fact, which I this very minute take from the mouth of a young coloured man, who has been to school in this state (Massachusetts) nearly nine years, and who knows grammar this day, *nearly* as well as he did the day he first entered the school-house, under a white master. This young man says: "My master would never allow me to study grammar." I asked him, why? "The school committee," said he "forbid the coloured children learning grammar—they would not allow any but the white children to study grammar." It is a notorious fact, that the major part of the white Americans, have, ever since we have been among them, tried to keep us ignorant, and make us believe that God made us and our children to be slaves to them and theirs. *Oh! my God, have mercy on Christian Americans! ! !*

Henry Highland Garnet
An Address to the Slaves of the United States of America

Brethren and Fellow Citizens: Your brethren of the North, East, and West have been accustomed to meet together in National Conventions, to sympathize with each other, and to weep over your unhappy condition. In these meetings we have addressed all classes of the free, but we have never, until this time, sent a word of consolation and advice to you. We have been contented in sitting still and mourning over your sorrows, earnestly hoping that before this day your sacred liberties would have been restored. But, we have hoped in vain. Years have rolled on, and tens of thousands have been borne on streams of blood and tears to the shores of eternity. While you have been oppressed, we have also been partakers with you; nor can we be free while you are enslaved. We, therefore, write to you as being bound with you.

Many of you are bound to us, not only by the ties of a common humanity, but we are connected by the more tender relations of parents, wives, husbands, and sisters, and friends. As such we most affectionately address you.

Slavery has fixed a deep gulf between you and us, and while it shuts out from you the relief and consolation which your friends would willingly render, it afflicts and persecutes you with a fierceness which we might not expect to see in the fiends of hell. But still the Almighty Father of mercies has left to us a glimmering ray of hope, which shines out like a lone star in a cloudy sky. Mankind are becoming wiser, and better—the oppressor's power is fading, and you, every day, are becoming better informed, and more numerous. Your grievances, brethren, are many. We shall not attempt, in this short address, to present to the world all the dark catalogue of the nation's sins, which have been committed upon an innocent people. Nor is it indeed necessary, for you feel them from day to day, and all the civilized world looks upon them with amazement.

Two hundred and twenty-seven years ago the first of our injured race were brought to the shores of America. They came not with glad spirits to select their homes in the New World. They came not with their own consent, to find an unmolested enjoyment of the blessings of this fruitful soil. The first dealings they had with men calling themselves Christians exhibited to them the worst features of corrupt and sordid hearts: and convinced them that no cruelty is too great, no villainy and no robbery too abhorrent for even enlightened men to perform, when influenced by avarice and lust. Neither did they come flying upon the wings of liberty to a land of freedom. But they came with broken hearts, from their beloved native land, and were doomed to unrequited toil and deep degradation. Nor did the evil of their bondage end at their emancipation by death. Succeeding generations inherited their chains, and millions have come from eternity into time, and have returned again to the world of spirits, cursed and ruined by American slavery.

The propagators of the system, or their immediate successors, very soon discovered its growing evil, and its tremendous wickedness, and secret promises were made to destroy it. The gross inconsistency of a people holding slaves, who had themselves "ferried o'er the wave" for freedom's sake, was too apparent to be entirely overlooked. The voice of Freedom cried, "Emancipate your slaves." Humanity supplicated with tears for the deliverance of the children of Africa. Wisdom urged her solemn plea. The bleeding captive plead his innocence, and pointed to Christianity who stood weeping at the cross. Jehovah frowned upon the nefarious institution, and thunderbolts, red with vengeance, struggled to leap forth to blast the guilty wretches who maintained it. But all was vain. Slavery had stretched its dark wings of death over the land, the Church stood silently by—the priests prophesied falsely, and the people loved to have it so. Its throne is established, and now it reigns triumphant.

Nearly three millions of your fellow-citizens are prohibited by law and public opinion (which in this country is stronger than law) from reading the Book of Life. Your intellect has been destroyed as much as possible, and every ray of light they have attempted to shut out from your minds. The oppressors themselves have become involved in the ruin. They have become weak, sensual, and rapacious—they have cursed you—they have cursed themselves—they have cursed the earth which they have trod.

The colonies threw the blame upon England. They said that the mother country entailed the evil upon them, and they would rid themselves of it if they could. The world thought they were sincere, and the philanthropic pitied them. But time soon tested their sincerity. In a few years the colonists grew strong, and severed themselves from the British Government. Their independence was declared, and they took their station among the sovereign powers of the earth. The declaration was a glorious document. Sages admired it, and the patriotic of every nation reverenced the God-like sentiments which it contained. When the power of Government returned to their hands, did they emancipate the slaves? No; they rather added new links to our chains. Were they ignorant of the principles of Liberty? Certainly they were not. The sentiments of their revolutionary orators fell in burning eloquence upon their hearts, and with one voice they cried, LIBERTY OR DEATH. Oh, what a sentence was that! It ran from soul to soul like electric fire, and nerved the arms of thousands to fight in the holy cause of Freedom. Among the diversity of opinions that are entertained in regard to physical resistance, there are but a few found to gainsay the stern declaration. We are among those who do not.

SLAVERY! How much misery is comprehended in that single word. What mind is there that does not shrink from its direful effects? Unless the image of

God be obliterated from the soul, all men cherish the love of liberty. The nice discerning political economist does not regard the sacred right more than the untutored African who roams in the wilds of Congo. Nor has the one more right to the full enjoyment of his freedom than the other. In every man's mind the good seeds of liberty are planted, and he who brings his fellow down so low, as to make him contented with a condition of slavery, commits the highest crime against God and man. Brethren, your oppressors aim to do this. They endeavor to make you as much like brutes as possible. When they have blinded the eyes of your mind—when they have embittered the sweet waters of life— when they have shut out the light which shines from the word of God—then, and not till then, has American slavery done its perfect work.

TO SUCH DEGRADATION IT IS SINFUL IN THE EXTREME FOR YOU TO MAKE VOLUNTARY SUBMISSION. The divine commandments you are in duty bound to reverence and obey. If you do not obey them, you will surely meet with the displeasure of the Almighty. He requires you to love Him supremely, and your neighbor as yourself—to keep the Sabbath day holy—to search the Scriptures—and bring up your children with respect for His laws, and to worship no other God but Him. But slavery sets all these at nought, and hurls defiance in the face of Jehovah. The forlorn condition in which you are placed does not destroy your obligation to God. You are not certain of heaven, because you allow yourselves to remain in a state of slavery, where you cannot obey the commandments of the Sovereign of the universe. If the ignorance of slavery is a passport to heaven, then it is a blessing, and no curse, and you should rather desire its perpetuity than its abolition. God will not receive slavery, nor ignorance, nor any other state of mind, for love and obedience to Him. Your condition does not absolve you from your moral obligation. The diabolical injustice by which your liberties are cloven down, NEITHER GOD NOR ANGELS, OR JUST MEN, COMMAND YOU TO SUFFER FOR A SINGLE MOMENT. THEREFORE IT IS YOUR SOLEMN AND IMPERATIVE DUTY TO USE EVERY MEANS, BOTH MORAL, INTELLECTUAL, AND PHYSICAL, THAT PROMISES SUCCESS. If a band of heathen men should attempt to enslave a race of Christians, and to place their children under the influence of some false religion, surely Heaven would frown upon the men who would not resist such aggression, even to death. If, on the other hand, a band of Christians should attempt to enslave a race of heathen men, and to entail slavery upon them, and to keep them in heathenism in the midst of Christianity, the God of heaven would smile upon every effort which the injured might make to disenthral themselves.

Brethren, it is as wrong for your lordly oppressors to keep you in slavery as it was for the man thief to steal our ancestors from the coast of Africa. You should therefore now use the same manner of resistance as would have been just in our ancestors when the bloody foot-prints of the first remorseless soul-thief was placed upon the shores of our fatherland. The humblest peasant is as free in the sight of God as the proudest monarch that ever swayed a sceptre. Liberty is a spirit sent out from God, and like its great Author, is no respecter of persons.

Brethren, the time has come when you must act for yourselves. It is an old and true saying that, "if hereditary bondmen would be free, they must themselves strike the blow." You can plead your own cause, and do the work of emancipation better than any others. The nations of the Old World are moving in the great cause of universal freedom, and some of them at least will, ere long, do you justice. The combined powers of Europe have placed their broad seal of disapprobation upon the African slave-trade. But in the slaveholding parts of the United States the trade is as brisk as ever. They buy and sell you as though you were brute beasts. The North has done much—her opinion of slavery in the abstract is known. But in regard to the South, we adopt the opinion of the *New York Evangelist*—"We have advanced so far, that the cause apparently waits for a more effectual door to be thrown open than has been yet." We are about to point you to that more effectual door. Look around you, and behold the bosoms of your loving wives heaving with untold agonies! Here the cries of your poor children! Remember the stripes your fathers bore. Think of the torture and disgrace of your noble mothers. Think of your wretched sisters, loving virtue and purity, as they are driven into concubinage and are exposed to the unbridled lusts of incarnate devils. Think of the undying glory that hangs around the ancient name of Africa— and forget not that you are native-born American citizens, and as such you are justly entitled to all the rights that are granted to the freest. Think how many tears you have poured out upon the soil which you have cultivated with unrequited toil and enriched with your blood; and then go to your lordly en-slavers and tell them plainly, that you *are determined to be free.* Appeal to their sense of justice, and tell them that they have no more right to oppress you than you have to enslave them. Entreat them to remove the grievous burdens which they have imposed upon you, and to remunerate you for your labor. Promise them renewed diligence in the cultivation of the soil, if they will render to you an equivalent for your services. Point them to the increase of happiness and prosperity in the British West Indies since the Act of Eman-cipation. Tell them in language which they cannot misunderstand of the ex-ceeding sinfulness of slavery, and of a future judgment, and of the righteous retributions of an indignant God. Inform them that all you desire is FREEDOM, and that nothing else will suffice. Do this, and forever after cease to toil for the heartless tyrants, who give you no other reward but stripes and abuse. If they then commence work of death, they, and not you, will be responsible for the consequences. You had far better all die—*die immediately*, than live slaves, and entail your wretchedness upon your posterity. If you would be free in this generation, here is your only hope. However much you and all of us may desire it, there is not much hope of redemption without the shedding of blood. If you must bleed, let it all come at once—rather *die freemen than live to be the slaves.* It is impossible, like the children of Israel, to make a grand ex-odus from the land of bondage. The Pharaohs are on both sides of the blood-red waters! You cannot move *en masse* to the dominions of the British Queen—nor can you pass through Florida and overrun Texas, and at last find peace in Mexico. The propagators of American slavery are spending their blood and treasure that they may plant the black flag in the heart of Mexico and riot in the halls of the Montezumas. In language of the Reverend Robert Hall, when addressing the volunteers of Bristol, who were rushing forth to repel the invasion of Napoleon, who threatened to lay waste the fair homes of England, "Religion is too much interested in your behalf not to shed over you her most gracious influences."

You will not be compelled to spend much time in order to become inured to hardships. From the first movement that you breathed the air of heaven, you have been accustomed to nothing else but hardships. The heroes of the American Revolution were never put upon harder fare than a peck of corn and few herrings per week. You have not become enervated by the luxuries of life. Your sternest energies have been beaten out upon the anvil of severe trial. Slavery has done this to make you subservient to its own purposes; but it has done more than this, it has prepared you for any emergency. If you receive good treatment, it is what you can hardly expect; if you meet with pain, sorrow, and even death, these are the common lot of the slaves.

Fellowmen! patient sufferers! behold your dearest rights crushed to the earth! See your sons murdered, and your wives, mothers and sisters doomed to prostitution. In the name of the merciful God, and by all that life is worth, let it no longer be a debatable question, whether it is better to choose *liberty* or *death*.

In 1822, Denmark Veazie, of South Carolina, formed a plan for the liberation of his fellowmen. In the whole history of human efforts to overthrow slavery, a more complicated and tremendous plan was never formed. He was betrayed by the treachery of his own people, and died a martyr to freedom. Many a brave hero fell, but history, faithful to her high trust, will transcribe his name on the same monument with Moses, Hampden, Tell, Bruce and Wallace, Toussaint L'Ouverture, Lafayette, and Washington. That tremendous movement shook the whole empire of slavery. The guilty soul-thieves were overwhelmed with fear. It is a matter of fact that at this time, and in consequence of the threatened revolution, the slave States talked strongly of emancipation. But they blew but one blast of the trumpet of freedom, and then laid it aside. As these men became quiet, the slave-holders ceased to talk about emancipation: and now behold your condition to-day! Angels sigh over it, and humanity has long since exhausted her tears in weeping on your account!

The patriotic Nathaniel Turner followed Denmark Veazie. He was goaded to desperation by wrong and injustice. By despotism, his name has been recorded on the list of infamy, and future generations will remember him among the noble and brave.

Next arose the immortal Joseph Cinque, the hero of the Amistad. He was a native African, and by the help of God he emancipated a whole shipload of his fellowmen on the high seas. And he now sings of liberty on the sunny hills of Africa and beneath his native palm-trees, where he hears the lion roar and feels himself as free as the king of the forest.

Next arose Madison Washington, that bright star of freedom, and took his station in the constellation of true heroism. He was a slave on board the brig *Creole*, of Richmond, bound to New Orleans, that great slave mart, with a hundred and four others. Nineteen struck for liberty or death. But one life was taken, and the whole were emancipated, and the vessel was carried into Nassau, New Providence.

Noble men! Those who have fallen in freedom's conflict, their memories will be cherished by the true-hearted and the God-fearing in all future generations; those who are living, their names are surrounded by a halo of glory.

Brethren, arise, arise! Strike for your lives and liberties. Now is the day and the hour. Let every slave throughout the land do this, and the days of slavery are numbered. You cannot be more oppressed than you have been—you cannot suffer greater cruelties than you have already. *Rather die freemen than live to be slaves*. Remember that you are FOUR MILLIONS!

It is in your power so to torment the God-cursed slaveholders that they will be glad to let you go free. If the scale was turned, and black men were the masters and white men the slaves, every destructive agent and element would be employed to lay the oppressor low. Danger and death would hang over their heads day and night. Yes, the tyrants would meet with plagues more terrible than those of Pharaoh. But you are a patient people. You act as though you were made for the special use of these devils. You act as though your daughters were born to pamper the lusts of your masters and overseers. And worse than all, you tamely submit while your lords tear your wives from your embraces and defile them before your eyes. In the name of God, we ask, are you men? Where is the blood of your fathers? Has it all run out of your veins? Awake, awake; millions of voices are calling you! Your dead fathers speak to you from their graves. Heaven, as with a voice of thunder, calls on you to arise from the dust.

Let your motto be resistance! *resistance!* RESISTANCE! No oppressed people have ever secured their liberty without resistance. What kind of resistance you had better make you must decide by the circumstances that surround you, and according to the suggestion of expediency. Brethren, adieu! Trust in the living God. Labor for the peace of the human race, and remember that you are FOUR MILLIONS!

Frederick Douglass

from *Narrative of the Life of Frederick Douglass, an American Slave, Written by Himself*

CHAPTER II

My master's family consisted of two sons, Andrew and Richard; one daughter, Lucretia, and her husband, Captain Thomas Auld. They lived in one house, upon the home plantation of Colonel Edward Lloyd. My master was Colonel Lloyd's clerk and superintendent. He was what might be called the overseers of the overseers. I spent two years of childhood on this plantation in my old master's family. It was here that I witnessed the bloody transaction recorded in the first chapter; and as I received my first impressions of slavery on this plantation, I will give some description of it, and of slavery as it there existed. The plantation is about twelve miles north of Easton, in Talbot county, and is situated on the border of Miles River. The principal products raised upon it were tobacco, corn, and wheat. These were raised in great abundance; so that, with the products of this and the other farms belonging to him, he was able to keep in almost constant employment a large sloop, in carrying them to market at Baltimore. This sloop was named Sally Lloyd, in honor of one of the colonel's daughters. My master's son-in-law, Captain Auld, was master of the vessel; she was otherwise manned by the colonel's own slaves. Their names were Peter, Isaac, Rich, and Jake. These were esteemed very highly by the other slaves, and looked upon as the privileged ones of the plantation; for it was no small affair, in the eyes of the slaves, to be allowed to see Baltimore.

Colonel Lloyd kept from three to four hundred slaves on his home plantation, and owned a large number more on the neighboring farms belonging to him. The names of the farms nearest to the home plantation were Wye Town and New Design. "Wye Town" was under the overseership of a man named Noah Willis. New Design was under the overseership of a Mr. Townsend. The overseers of these, and all the rest of the farms, numbering over twenty, received advice and direction from the managers of the home plantation. This was the great business place. It was the seat of government for the whole twenty farms. All disputes among the overseers were settled here. If a slave was convicted of any high misdemeanor, became unmanageable, or evinced a determination to run away, he was brought immediately here, severely whipped, put on board the sloop, carried to Baltimore, and sold to Austin Woolfolk or some other slave-trader, as a warning to the slaves remaining.

Here, too, the slaves of all the other farms received their monthly allowance of food, and their yearly clothing. The men and women slaves received, as their monthly allowance of food, eight pounds of pork, or its equivalent in fish, and one bushel of corn meal. Their yearly clothing consisted of two coarse linen shirts, one pair of linen trousers, like the shirts, one jacket, one pair of trousers for winter, made of coarse negro cloth, one pair of stockings, and one pair of shoes; the whole of which could not have cost more than seven dollars. The allowance of the slave children was given to their mothers, or the old women having the care of them. The children unable to work in the field had neither shoes, stockings, jackets, nor trousers, given to them; their clothing consisted of two coarse linen shirts per year. When these failed them, they went naked until the next allowance-day. Children from seven to ten years old, of both sexes, almost naked, might be seen at all seasons of the year.

There were no beds given the slaves, unless one coarse blanket be considered such, and none but the men and women had these. This, however, is not considered a very great privation. They find less difficulty from the want of beds, than from the want of time to sleep; for when their day's work in the field is done, the most of them having their washing, mending, and cooking to do, and having few or none of the ordinary facilities for doing either of these, very many of their sleeping hours are consumed in preparing for the field the coming day; and when this is done, old and young, male and female, married and single, drop down side by side, on one common bed,—the cold, damp floor,— each covering himself or herself with their miserable blankets; and here they sleep till they are summoned to the field by the driver's horn. At the sound of this, all must rise, and be off to the field. There must be no halting; every one must be at his or her post; and woe betides them who hear not this morning summons to the field; for if they are not awakened by the sense of hearing, they are by the sense of feeling; no age nor sex finds any favor. Mr. Severe, the overseer, used to stand by the door of the quarter, armed with a large hickory stick and heavy cowskin, ready to whip any one who was so unfortunate as not to hear, or, from any other cause, was prevented from being ready to start for the field at the sound of the horn.

Mr. Severe was rightly named: he was a cruel man. I have seen him whip a woman, causing the blood to run half an hour at the time; and this, too, in the midst of her crying children, pleading for their mother's release. He seemed to take pleasure in manifesting his fiendish barbarity. Added to his cruelty, he was a profane swearer. It was enough to chill the blood and stiffen the hair of an ordinary man to hear him talk. Scarce a sentence escaped him but that was commenced or concluded by some horrid oath. The field was the place to witness his cruelty and profanity. His presence made it both the field of blood and of blasphemy. From the rising till the going down of the sun, he was cursing, raving, cutting, and slashing among the slaves of the field, in the most frightful manner. His career was short. He died very soon after I went to Colonel Lloyd's; and he died as he lived, uttering, with his dying groans, bitter curses and horrid oaths. His death was regarded by the slaves as the result of a merciful providence.

Mr. Severe's place was filled by a Mr. Hopkins. He was a very different man. He was less cruel, less profane, and made less noise, than Mr. Severe. His course was characterized by no extraordinary demonstrations of cruelty. He whipped, but seemed to take no pleasure in it. He was called by the slaves a good overseer.

The home plantation of Colonel Lloyd wore the appearance of a country village. All the mechanical operations for all the farms were performed here. The shoemaking and mending, the blacksmithing, cartwrighting, coopering, weaving, and grain-grinding, were all performed by the slaves on the home plantation. The whole place wore a business-like aspect very unlike the neighboring farms. The number of houses, too, conspired to give it advantage over the neighboring farms. It was called by the slaves the *Great House Farm.* Few privileges were esteemed higher, by the slaves of the out-farms, than that of being selected to do errands at the Great House Farm. It was associated in their minds with greatness. A representative could not be prouder of his election to a seat in the American Congress, than a slave on one of the out-farms would be of his election to do errands at the Great House Farm. They regarded it as evidence of great confidence reposed in them by their overseers; and it was on this account, as well as a constant desire to be out of the field from under the driver's lash, that they esteemed it a high privilege, one worth careful living for. He was called the smartest and most trusty fellow, who had this honor conferred upon him the most frequently. The competitors for this office sought as diligently to please their overseers, as the office-seekers in the political parties seek to please and deceive the people. The same traits of character might be seen in Colonel Lloyd's slaves, as are seen in the slaves of the political parties.

The slaves selected to go to the Great House Farm, for the monthly allowance for themselves and their fellow-slaves, were peculiarly enthusiastic. While on their way, they would make the dense old woods, for miles around, reverberate with their wild songs, revealing at once the highest joy and the deepest sadness. They would compose and sing as they went along, consulting neither time nor tune. The thought that came up, came out—if not in the word, in the sound;—and as frequently in the one as in the other. They would sometimes sing the most pathetic sentiment in the most rapturous tone, and the most rapturous sentiment in the most pathetic tone. Into all of their songs they would manage to weave something of the Great House Farm. Especially would they do this, when leaving home. They would then sing most exultingly the following words:—

> "I am going away to the Great House Farm!
> O, yea! O, yea! O!"

This they would sing, as a chorus, to words which to many would seem unmeaning jargon, but which, nevertheless, were full of meaning to themselves. I have sometimes thought that the mere hearing of those songs would do more to impress some minds with the horrible character of slavery, than the reading of whole volumes of philosophy on the subject could do.

I did not, when a slave, understand the deep meaning of those rude and apparently incoherent songs. I was myself within the circle; so that I neither saw nor heard as those without might see and hear. They told a tale of woe which was then altogether beyond my feeble comprehension; they were tones loud, long, and deep; they breathed the prayer and complaint of souls boiling over with the bitterest anguish. Every tone was a testimony against slavery, and a prayer to God for deliverance from chains. The hearing of those wild notes always depressed my spirit, and filled me with ineffable sadness. I have frequently found myself in tears while hearing them. The mere recurrence to those songs, even now, afflicts me; and while I am writing these lines, an expression of feeling has already found its way down my cheek. To those songs I trace my first glimmering conception of the dehumanizing character of slavery. I can never get rid of that conception. Those songs still follow me, to deepen my hatred of slavery, and quicken my sympathies for my brethren in bonds. If any one wishes to be impressed with the soul-killing effects of slavery, let him go to Colonel Lloyd's plantation, and, on allowance-day, place himself in the deep pine woods, and there let him, in silence, analyze the sounds that shall pass through the chambers of his soul,—and if he is not thus impressed, it will only be because "there is no flesh in his obdurate heart."

I have often been utterly astonished, since I came to the north, to find persons who could speak of the singing, among slaves, as evidence of their contentment and happiness. It is impossible to conceive of a greater mistake. Slaves sing most when they are most unhappy. The songs of the slave represent the sorrows of his heart; and he is relieved by them, only as an aching heart is relieved by its tears. At least, such is my experience. I have often sung to drown my sorrow, but seldom to express my happiness. Crying for joy, and singing for joy, were alike uncommon to me while in the jaws of slavery. The singing of a man cast away upon a desolate island might be as appropriately considered as evidence of contentment and happiness, as the singing of a slave; the songs of the one and of the other are prompted by the same emotion.

CHAPTER VI

My new mistress proved to be all she appeared when I first met her at the door,—a woman of the kindest heart and finest feelings. She had never had a slave under her control previously to myself, and prior to her marriage she had been dependent upon her own industry for a living. She was by trade a weaver; and by constant application to her business, she had been in a good degree preserved from the blighting and dehumanizing effects of slavery. I was utterly astonished at her goodness. I scarcely knew how to behave towards her. She was entirely unlike any other white woman I had ever seen. I could not approach her as I was accustomed to approach other white ladies. My early instruction was all out of place. The crouching servility, usually so acceptable a quality in a slave, did not answer when manifested toward her. Her favor was not gained by it; she seemed to be disturbed by it. She did not deem it impudent or unmannerly for a slave to look her in the face. The meanest slave was put fully at ease in her presence, and none left without feeling better for having seen her. Her face was made of heavenly smiles, and her voice of tranquil music.

But, alas! this kind heart had but a short time to remain such. The fatal poison of irresponsible power was already in her hands, and soon commenced its infernal work. That cheerful eye, under the influence of slavery, soon became red with rage; that voice, made all of sweet accord, changed to one of harsh and horrid discord; and that angelic face gave place to that of a demon.

Very soon after I went to live with Mr. and Mrs. Auld, she very kindly commenced to teach me the A, B, C. After I had learned this, she assisted me in learning to spell words of three or four letters. Just at this point of my progress, Mr. Auld found out what was going on, and at once forbade Mrs. Auld to instruct me further, telling her, among other things, that it was unlawful, as well as unsafe, to teach a slave to read. To use his own words, further, he said, "If you give a nigger an inch, he will take an ell. A nigger should know nothing but to obey his master—to do as he is told to do. Learning would *spoil* the best nigger in the world. Now," said he, "if you teach that nigger (speaking of myself) how to read, there would be no keeping him. It would forever unfit him to be a slave. He would at once become unmanageable, and of no value to his master. As to himself, it could do him no good, but a great deal of harm. It would make him discontented and unhappy." These words sank deep into my heart, stirred up sentiments within that lay slumbering, and called into existence an entirely new train of thought. It was a new and special revelation, explaining dark and mysterious things, with which my youthful understanding had struggled, but struggled in vain. I now understood what had been to me a most perplexing difficulty—to wit, the white man's power to enslave the black man. It was a grand achievement, and I prized it highly. From that moment, I understood the pathway from slavery to freedom. It was just what I wanted, and I got it at a time when I the least expected it. Whilst I was saddened by the thought of losing the aid of my kind mistress, I was gladdened by the invaluable instruction which, by the merest accident, I had gained from my master. Though conscious of the difficulty of learning without a teacher, I set out with high hope, and a fixed purpose, at whatever cost of trouble, to learn how to read. The very decided manner with which he spoke, and strove to impress his wife with the evil consequences of giving me instruction, served to convince me that he was deeply sensible of the truths he was uttering. It gave me the best assurance that I might rely with the utmost confidence on the results which, he said, would flow from teaching me to read. What he most dreaded, that I most desired. What he most loved, that I most hated. That which to him was a great evil, to be carefully shunned, was to me a great good, to be diligently sought; and the argument which he so warmly urged, against my learning to read, only served to inspire me with a desire and determination to learn. In learning to read, I owe almost as much to the bitter opposition of my master, as to the kindly aid of my mistress. I acknowledge the benefit of both.

I had resided but a short time in Baltimore before I observed a marked difference, in the treatment of slaves, from that which I had witnessed in the country. A city slave is almost a freeman, compared with a slave on the plantation. He is much better fed and clothed, and enjoys privileges altogether unknown to the slave on the plantation. There is a vestige of decency, a sense of shame, that does much to curb and check those outbreaks of atrocious cruelty so commonly enacted upon the plantation. He is a desperate slaveholder, who will shock the humanity of his non-slaveholding neighbors with the cries of his lacerated slave. Few are willing to incur the odium attaching to the reputation of being a cruel master; and above all things, they would not be known as not giving a slave enough to eat. Every city slaveholder is anxious to have it known of him, that he feeds his slaves well; and it is due to them to say, that most of them do give their slaves enough to eat. There are, however, some painful exceptions to this rule. Directly opposite to us, on Philpot Street, lived Mr. Thomas Hamilton. He owned two slaves. Their names were Henrietta and Mary. Henrietta was about twenty-two years of age, Mary was about fourteen; and of all the mangled and emaciated creatures I ever looked upon, these two were the most so. His heart must be harder than stone, that could look upon these unmoved. The head, neck, and shoulders of Mary were literally cut to pieces. I have frequently felt her head, and found it nearly covered with festering sores, caused by the lash of her cruel mistress. I do not know that her master ever whipped her, but I have been an eye-witness to the cruelty of Mrs. Hamilton. I used to be in Mr. Hamilton's house nearly every day. Mrs. Hamilton used to sit in a large chair in the middle of the room, with a heavy cowskin always by her side, and scarce an hour passed during the day but was marked by the blood of one of these slaves. The girls seldom passed her without her saying, "Move faster, you *black gip!*" at the same time giving them a blow with the cowskin over the head or shoulders, often drawing the blood. She would then say, "Take that, you *black gip!*"—continuing, "If you don't move faster, I'll move you!" Added to the cruel lashings to which these slaves were subjected, they were kept nearly half-starved. They seldom knew what it was to eat a full meal. I have seen Mary contending with the pigs for the offal thrown into the street. So much was Mary kicked and cut to pieces, that she was oftener called "*pecked*" than by her name.

CHAPTER VII

I lived in Master Hugh's family about seven years. During this time, I succeeded in learning to read and write. In accomplishing this, I was compelled to resort to various stratagems. I had no regular teacher. My mistress, who had kindly commenced to instruct me, had, in compliance with the advice and direction of her husband, not only ceased to instruct, but had set her face against my being instructed by any one else. It is due, however, to my mistress to say of her, that she did not adopt this course of treatment immediately. She at first lacked the depravity indispensable to shutting me up in mental darkness. It was at least necessary for her to have some training in the exercise of irresponsible power, to make her equal to the task of treating me as though I were a brute.

My mistress was, as I have said, a kind and tender-hearted woman; and in the simplicity of her soul she commenced, when I first went to live with her, to treat me as she supposed one human being ought to treat another. In entering upon the duties of a slaveholder, she did not seem to perceive that I sustained to her the relation of a mere chattel, and that for her to treat me as a human being was not only wrong, but dangerously so. Slavery proved as injurious to her as it did to me. When I went there, she was a pious, warm, and tender-hearted woman. There was no sorrow or suffering for which she had not a tear. She had bread for the hungry, clothes for the naked, and comfort for every mourner that came within her reach. Slavery soon proved its ability to divest her of these heavenly qualities. Under its influence, the tender heart became stone, and the lamblike disposition gave way to one of tiger-like fierceness. The first step in her downward course was in her ceasing to instruct me. She now commenced to practise her husband's precepts. She finally became even more violent in her opposition than her husband himself. She was not satisfied with simply doing as well as he had commanded; she seemed anxious to do better. Nothing seemed to make her more angry than to see me with a newspaper. She seemed to think that here lay the danger. I have had her rush at me with a face made all up of fury, and snatch from me a newspaper, in a manner that fully revealed her apprehension. She was an apt woman; and a little experience soon demonstrated, to her satisfaction, that education and slavery were incompatible with each other.

From this time I was most narrowly watched. If I was in a separate room any considerable length of time, I was sure to be suspected of having a book, and was at once called to give an account of myself. All this, however, was too late. The first step had been taken. Mistress, in teaching me the alphabet, had given me the *inch*, and no precaution could prevent me from taking the *ell*.

The plan which I adopted, and the one by which I was most successful, was that of making friends of all the little white boys whom I met in the street. As many of these as I could, I converted into teachers. With their kindly aid, obtained at different times and in different places, I finally succeeded in learning to read. When I was sent of errands, I always took my book with me, and by going one part of my errand quickly, I found time to get a lesson before my return. I used also to carry bread with me, enough of which was always in the house, and to which I was always welcome; for I was much better off in this regard than many of the poor white children in our neighborhood. This bread I used to bestow upon the hungry little urchins, who, in return, would give me that more valuable bread of knowledge. I am strongly tempted to give the names of two or three of those little boys, as a testimonial of the gratitude and affection I bear them; but prudence forbids;—not that it would injure me, but it might embarrass them; for it is almost an unpardonable offence to teach slaves to read in this Christian country. It is enough to say of the dear little fellows, that they lived on Philpot Street, very near Durgin and Bailey's shipyard. I used to talk this matter of slavery over with them. I would sometimes say to them, I wished I could be as free as they would be when they got to be men. "You will be free as soon as you are twenty-one, *but I am a slave for life!* Have not I as good a right to be free as you have?" These words used to trouble them; they would express for me the liveliest sympathy, and console me with the hope that something would occur by which I might be free.

I was now about twelve years old, and the thought of being *a slave for life* began to bear heavily upon my heart. Just about this time, I got hold of a book entitled "The Columbian orator." Every opportunity I got, I used to read this book. Among much of other interesting matter, I found in it a dialogue between a master and his slave. The slave was represented as having run away from his master three times. The dialogue represented the conversation which took place between them, when the slave was retaken the third time. In this dialogue, the whole argument in behalf of slavery was brought forward by the master, all of which was disposed of by the slave. The slave was made to say some very smart as well as impressive things in reply to his master—things which had the desired though unexpected effect; for the conversation resulted in the voluntary emancipation of the slave on the part of the master.

In the same book, I met with one of Sheridan's mighty speeches on and in behalf of Catholic emancipation. These were choice documents to me. I read them over and over again with unabated interest. They gave tongue to interesting thoughts of my own soul, which had frequently flashed through my mind, and died away for want of utterance. The moral which I gained from the dialogue was the power of truth over the conscience of even a slaveholder. What I got from Sheridan was a bold denunciation of slavery, and a powerful vindication of human rights. The reading of these documents enabled me to utter my thoughts, and to meet the arguments brought forward to sustain slavery; but while they relieved me of one difficulty, they brought on another even more painful than the one of which I was relieved. The more I read, the more I was led to abhor and detest my enslavers. I could regard them in no other light than a band of successful robbers, who had left their homes, and gone to Africa, and stolen us from our homes, and in a strange land reduced us to slavery. I loathed them as being the meanest as well as the most wicked of men. As I read and contemplated the subject, behold! that very discontentment which Master Hugh had predicted would follow my learning to read had already come, to torment and sting my soul to unutterable anguish. As I writhed under it, I would at times feel that learning to read had been a curse rather than a blessing. It had given me a view of my wretched condition, without the remedy. I opened my eyes to the horrible pit, but to no ladder upon which to get out. In moments of agony, I envied my fellow-slaves for their stupidity. I have often wished myself a beast. I preferred the condition of the meanest reptile to my own. Any thing, no matter what, to get rid of thinking! It was this everlasting thinking of my condition that tormented me. There was no getting rid of it. It was pressed upon me by every object within sight or hearing, animate or inanimate. The silver trump of freedom had roused my soul to eternal wakefulness. Freedom now appeared, to disappear no more forever. It was heard in every sound, and seen in every thing. It was ever present to torment me with a sense of my wretched condition. I saw nothing without seeing it, I heard nothing without hearing it, and felt nothing without feeling it. It looked from every star, it smiled in every calm, breathed in every wind, and moved in every storm.

I often found myself regretting my own existence, and wishing myself dead; and but for the hope of being free, I have no doubt but that I should have killed myself, or done something for which I should have been killed. While in this state of mind, I was eager to hear any one speak of slavery. I was a ready listener. Every little while, I could hear something about the abolitionists. It was some time before I found what the word meant. It was always used in such connections as to make it an interesting word to me. If a slave ran away and succeeded in getting clear, or if a slave killed his master, set fire to a barn, or did any thing very wrong in the mind of a slaveholder, it was spoken of as the fruit of *abolition*. Hearing the word in this connection very often, I set about learning what it meant. The dictionary afforded me little or no help. I found it was "the act of abolishing;" but then I did not know what was to be abolished. Here I was perplexed. I did not dare to ask any one about its meaning, for I was satisfied that it was something they wanted me to know very little about. After a patient waiting, I got one of our city papers, containing an account of the number of petitions from the north, praying for the abolition of slavery in the District of Columbia, and of the slave trade between the States. From this time I understood the words *abolition* and *abolitionist*, and always drew near when that word was spoken, expecting to hear something of importance to myself and fellow-slaves. The light broke in upon me by degrees. I went one day down on the wharf of Mr. Waters; and seeing two Irishmen unloading a scow of stone, I went, unasked, and helped them. When we had finished, one of them came to me and asked me if I were a slave. I told him I was. He asked, "Are ye a slave for life?" I told him that I was. The good Irishman seemed to be deeply affected by the statement. He said to the other that it was a pity so fine a little fellow as myself should be a slave for life. He said it was a shame to hold me. They both advised me to run away to the north; that I should find friends there, and that I should be free. I pretended not to be interested in what they said, and treated them as if I did not understand them; for I feared they might be treacherous. White men have been known to encourage slaves to escape, and then, to get the reward, catch them and return them to their masters. I was afraid that these seemingly good men might use me so; but I nevertheless remembered their advice, and from that time I resolved to run away. I looked forward to a time at which it would be safe for me to escape. I was too young to think of doing so immediately; besides, I wished to learn how to write, as I might have occasion to write my own pass. I consoled myself with the hope that I should one day find a good chance. Meanwhile, I would learn to write.

The idea as to how I might learn to write was suggested to me by being in Durgin and Bailey's ship-yard, and frequently seeing the ship carpenters, after hewing, and getting a piece of timber ready for use, write on the timber the name of that part of the ship for which it was intended. When a piece of timber was intended for the larboard side, it would be marked thus—"L." When a piece was for the starboard side, it would be marked thus—"S." A piece for the larboard side forward, would be marked thus—"L. F." When a piece was for starboard side forward, it would be marked thus—"S. F." For larboard aft, it would be marked thus—"L. A." For starboard aft, it would be marked thus—"S. A." I soon learned the names of these letters, and for what they were intended when placed upon a piece of timber in the shipyard. I immediately commenced copying them, and in a short time was able to make the four letters named. After that, when I met with any boy who I knew could write, I would tell him I could write as well as he. The next word would be, "I don't believe you. Let me see you try it." I would then make the letters which I had been so fortunate as to learn, and ask him to beat that. In this way I got a good many lessons in writing, which it is quite possible I should never have gotten in any other way. During this time, my copy-book was the board fence, brick wall, and pavement; my pen and ink was a lump of chalk. With these, I learned mainly how to write. I then commenced and continued copying the Italics in Webster's Spelling Book, until I could make them all without looking at the book. By this time, my little Master Thomas had gone to school, and learned how to write, and had written over a number of copy-books. These had been brought home, and shown to some of our near neighbors, and then laid aside. My mistress used to go to class meeting at the Wilk Street meeting-house every Monday afternoon, and leave me to take care of the house. When left thus, I used to spend the time in writing in the spaces left in Master Thomas's copy-book, copying what he had written. I continued to do this until I could write a hand very similar to that of Master Thomas. Thus, after a long, tedious effort for years, I finally succeeded in learning how to write.

CHAPTER X

I left Master Thomas's house, and went to live with Mr. Covey, on the 1st of January, 1833. I was now, for the first time in my life, a field hand. In my new employment, I found myself even more awkward than a country boy appeared to be in a large city. I had been at my new home but one week before Mr. Covey gave me a very severe whipping, cutting my back, causing the blood to run, and raising ridges on my flesh as large as my little finger. The details of this affair are as follows: Mr. Covey sent me, very early in the morning of one of our coldest days in the month of January, to the woods, to get a load of wood. He gave me a team of unbroken oxen. He told me which was the in-hand ox, and which the off-hand one. He then tied the end of a large rope around the horns of the in-hand ox, and gave me the other end of it, and told me, if the oxen started to run, that I must hold on upon the rope. I had never driven oxen before, and of course I was very awkward. I, however, succeeded in getting to the edge of the woods with little difficulty; but I had got a very few rods into the woods, when the oxen took fright, and started full tilt, carrying the cart against trees, and over stumps, in the most frightful manner. I expected every moment that my brains would be dashed out against the trees. After running thus for a considerable distance, they finally upset the cart, dashing it with great force against a tree, and threw themselves into a dense thicket. How I escaped death, I do not know. There I was, entirely alone, in a thick wood, in a place new to me. My cart was upset and shattered, my oxen were entangled among the young trees, and there was none to help me. After a long spell of effort, I succeeded in getting my cart righted, my oxen disentangled, and again yoked to the cart. I now proceeded with my team to the place where I had, the day before, been chopping wood, and loaded my cart pretty heavily, thinking in this way to tame my oxen. I then proceeded on my way home. I had now consumed one half of the day. I got out of the woods safely, and now felt out of danger. I stopped my oxen to open the woods gate; and just as I did so, before I could get hold of my ox-rope, the oxen again started, rushed through the gate, catching it between the wheel and the body of the cart, tearing it to pieces, and coming within a few inches of crushing me against the gate-post. Thus twice, in one short day, I escaped death by the merest chance. On my return, I told Mr. Covey what had happened, and how it happened. He ordered me to return to the woods again immediately. I did so, and he followed on after me. Just as I got into the woods, he came up and told me to stop my cart, and that he would teach me how to trifle away my time, and break gates. He then went to a large gum-tree, and with his axe cut three large switches, and, after trimming them up neatly with his pocket-knife, he ordered me to take off my clothes. I made him no answer, but stood with my clothes on. He repeated his order. I still made him no answer, nor did I move to strip myself. Upon this he rushed at me with the fierceness of a tiger, tore off my clothes, and lashed me till he had worn out his switches, cutting me so savagely as to leave the marks visible for a long time after. This whipping was the first of a number just like it, and for similar offences.

I lived with Mr. Covey one year. During the first six months, of that year, scarce a week passed without his whipping me. I was seldom free from a sore back. My awkwardness was almost always his excuse for whipping me. We were worked fully up to the point of endurance. Long before day we were up, our horses fed, and by the first approach of day we were off to the field with our hoes and ploughing teams. Mr. Covey gave us enough to eat, but scarce time to eat it. We were often less than five minutes taking our meals. We were often in the field from the first approach of day till its last lingering ray had left us; and at saving-fodder time, midnight often caught us in the field binding blades.

Covey would be out with us. The way he used to stand it, was this. He would spend the most of his afternoons in bed. He would then come out fresh in the evening, ready to urge us on with his words, example, and frequently with the whip. Mr. Covey was one of the few slaveholders who could and did work with his hands. He was a hard-working man. He knew by himself just what a man or a boy could do. There was no deceiving him. His work went on in his absence almost as well as in his presence; and he had the faculty of making us feel that he was ever present with us. This he did by surprising us. He seldom approached the spot where we were at work openly, if he could do it secretly. He always aimed at taking us by surprise. Such was his cunning, that we used to call him, among ourselves, "the snake." When we were at work in the cornfield, he would sometimes crawl on his hands and knees to avoid detection, and all at once he would rise nearly in our midst, and scream out, "Ha, ha! Come, come! Dash on, dash on!" This being his mode of attack, it was never safe to stop a single minute. His comings were like a thief in the night. He appeared to us as being ever at hand. He was under every tree, behind every stump, in every bush, and at every window, on the plantation. He would sometimes mount his horse, as if bound to St. Michael's, a distance of seven miles, and in half an hour afterwards you would see him coiled up in the corner of the wood-fence, watching every motion of the slaves. He would, for this purpose, leave his horse tied up in the woods. Again, he would sometimes walk up to us, and give us orders as though he was upon the point of starting on a long journey, turn his back upon us, and make as though he was going to the house to get ready; and, before he would get half way thither, he would turn short and crawl into a fence-corner, or behind some tree, and there watch us till the going down of the sun.

Mr. Covey's *forte* consisted in his power to deceive. His life was devoted to planning and perpetrating the grossest deceptions. Every thing he possessed in the shape of learning or religion, he made conform to his disposition to deceive. He seemed to think himself equal to deceiving the Almighty. He would make a short prayer in the morning, and a long prayer at night; and, strange as it may seem, few men would at times appear more devotional than he. The exercises of his family devotions were always commenced with singing; and, as he was a very poor singer himself, the duty of raising the hymn generally came upon me. He would read his hymn, and nod at me to commence. I would at times do so; at others, I would not. My non-compliance would almost always produce much confusion. To show himself independent of me, he would start and stagger through with his hymn in the most discordant manner. In this state of mind, he prayed with more than ordinary spirit. Poor man! such was his disposition, and success at deceiving, I do verily believe that he sometimes deceived himself into the solemn belief, that he was a sincere worshipper of the most high God; and this, too, at a time when he may be said to have been guilty of compelling his woman slave to commit the sin of adultery. The facts in the case are these: Mr. Covey was a poor man; he was just commencing in life; he was only able to buy one slave; and, shocking as is the fact, he bought her, as he said, for *a breeder*. This woman was named Caroline. Mr. Covey bought her from Mr. Thomas Lowe, about six miles from St. Michael's. She was a large, able-bodied woman, about twenty years old. She had already given birth to one child, which proved her to be just what he wanted. After buying her, he hired a married man of Mr. Samuel Harrison, to live with him one year; and him he used to fasten up with her every night! The result was, that, at the end of the year, the miserable woman gave birth to twins. At this result Mr. Covey seemed to be highly pleased, both with the man and the wretched woman. Such was his joy, and that of his wife, that nothing they could do for Caroline during her confinement was too good, or too hard, to be done. The children were regarded as being quite an addition to his wealth.

If at any one time of my life more than another, I was made to drink the bitterest dregs of slavery, that time was during the first six months of my stay with Mr. Covey. We were worked in all weathers. It was never too hot or too cold; it could never rain, blow, hail, or snow, too hard for us to work in the field. Work, work, work, was scarcely more the order of the day than of the night. The longest days were too short for him, and the shortest nights too long for him. I was somewhat unmanageable when I first went there, but a few months of this discipline tamed me. Mr. Covey succeeded in breaking me. I was broken in body, soul, and spirit. My natural elasticity was crushed, my intellect languished, the disposition to read departed, the cheerful spark that lingered about my eye died; the dark night of slavery closed in upon me; and behold a man transformed into a brute!

Sunday was my only leisure time. I spent this in a sort of beast-like stupor, between sleep and wake, under some large tree. At times I would rise up, a flash of energetic freedom would dart through my soul, accompanied with a faint beam of hope, that flickered for a moment, and then vanished. I sank down again, mourning over my wretched condition. I was sometimes prompted to take my life, and that of Covey, but was prevented by a combination of hope and fear. My sufferings on this plantation seem now like a dream rather than a stern reality.

Our house stood within a few rods of the Chesapeake Bay, whose broad bosom was ever white with sails from every quarter of the habitable globe. Those beautiful vessels, robed in purest white, so delightful to the eye of freemen, were to me so many shrouded ghosts, to terrify and torment me with thoughts of my wretched condition. I have often, in the deep stillness of a summer's Sabbath, stood all alone upon the lofty banks of that noble bay, and traced, with saddened heart and tearful eye, the countless number of sails moving off to the mighty ocean. The sight of these always affected me powerfully. My thoughts would compel utterance; and there, with no audience but the Almighty, I would pour out my soul's complaint, in my rude way, with an apostrophe to the moving multitude of ships:—

"You are loosed from your moorings, and are free; I am fast in my chains, and am a slave! You move merrily before the gentle gale, and I sadly before the bloody whip! You are freedom's swift-winged angels, that fly round the world; I am confined in bands of iron! O that I were free! O, that I were on one of your gallant decks, and under your protecting wing! Alas! betwixt me and you, the turbid waters roll. Go on, go on. O, that I could also go! Could I but swim! If I could fly! O, why was I born a man, of whom to make a brute! The glad ship is gone; she hides in the dim distance. I am left in the hottest hell of unending slavery. O God, save me! God, deliver me! Let me be free! Is there any God! Why am I a slave? I will run away. I will not stand it. Get caught, or get clear, I'll try it. I had as well die with ague as the fever. I have only one life to lose. I had as well be killed running as die standing. Only think of it; one hundred miles straight north, and I am free! Try it? Yes! God helping me, I will. It can-not be that I shall live and die a slave. I will take to the water. This very bay shall yet bear me into freedom. The steamboats steered in a north-east course from North Point. I will do the same; and when I get to the head of the bay, I will turn my canoe adrift, and walk straight through Delaware into Pennsylva-nia. When I get there, I shall not be required to have a pass; I can travel with-out being disturbed. Let but the first opportunity offer, and, come what will, I am off. Meanwhile, I will try to bear up under the yoke. I am not the only slave in the world. Why should I fret? I can bear as much as any of them. Besides, I am but a boy, and all boys are bound to some one. It may be that my misery in slavery will only increase my happiness when I get free. There is a better day coming."

Thus I used to think, and thus I used to speak to myself; goaded almost to madness at one moment, and at the next reconciling myself to my wretched lot.

I have already intimated that my condition was much worse, during the first six months of my stay at Mr. Covey's, than in the last six. The circum-stances leading to the change in Mr. Covey's course toward me form an epoch in my humble history. You have seen how a man was made a slave; you shall see how a slave was made a man. On one of the hottest days of the month of August, 1833, Bill Smith, William Hughes, a slave named Eli, and myself, were engaged in fanning wheat. Hughes was clearing the fanned wheat from before the fan, Eli was turning, Smith was feeding, and I was carrying wheat to the fan. The work was simple, requiring strength rather than intellect; yet, to one entirely unused to such work, it came very hard. About three o'clock of that day, I broke down; my strength failed me; I was seized with a violent aching of the head, attended with extreme dizziness; I trembled in every limb. Finding what was coming, I nerved myself up, feeling it would never do to stop work. I stood as long as I could stagger to the hopper with grain. When I could stand no longer, I fell, and felt as if held down by an immense weight. The fan of course stopped; every one had his own work to do; and no one could do the work of the other, and have his own go at the same time.

Mr. Covey was at the house, about one hundred yards from the treading-yard where we were fanning. On hearing the fan stop, he left immediately, and came to the spot where we were. He hastily inquired what the matter was. Bill answered that I was sick, and there was no one to bring wheat to the fan. I had by this time crawled away under the side of the post and rail-fence by which the yard was enclosed, hoping to find relief by getting out of the sun. He then asked where I was. He was told by one of the hands. He came to the spot, and, after looking at me awhile, asked me what was the matter. I told him as well as

I could, for I scarce had strength to speak. He then gave me a savage kick in the side, and told me to get up. I tried to do so, but fell back in the attempt. He gave me another kick, and again told me to rise. I again tried, and succeeded in gaining my feet; but, stooping to get the tub with which I was feeding the fan, I again staggered and fell. While down in this situation, Mr. Covey took up the hickory slat with which Hughes had been striking off the half-bushel measure, and with it gave me a heavy blow upon the head, making a large wound, and the blood ran freely; and with this again told me to get up. I made no effort to comply, having now made up my mind to let him do his worst. In a short time after receiving this blow, my head grew better. Mr. Covey had now left me to my fate. At this moment I resolved, for the first time, to go to my master, enter a complaint, and ask his protection. In order to [do] this, I must that afternoon walk seven miles; and this, under the circumstances, was truly a severe undertaking. I was exceedingly feeble; made so as much by the kicks and blows which I received, as by the severe fit of sickness to which I had been subjected. I, however, watched my chance, while Covey was looking in an opposite direction, and started for St. Michael's. I succeeded in getting a considerable distance on my way to the woods, when Covey discovered me, and called after me to come back, threatening what he would do if I did not come. I disregarded both his calls and his threats, and made my way to the woods as fast as my feeble state would allow; and thinking I might be overhauled by him if I kept the road, I walked through the woods, keeping far enough from the road to avoid detection, and near enough to prevent losing my way. I had not gone far before my little strength again failed me. I could go no farther. I fell down, and lay for a considerable time. The blood was yet oozing from the wound on my head. For a time I thought I should bleed to death; and think now that I should have done so, but that the blood so matted my hair as to stop the wound. After lying there about three quarters of an hour, I nerved myself up again, and started on my way, through bogs and briers, barefooted and bareheaded, tearing my feet sometimes at nearly every step; and after a journey of about seven miles, occupying some five hours to perform it, I arrived at master's store. I then presented an appearance enough to affect any but a heart of iron. From the crown of my head to my feet, I was covered with blood. My hair was all clotted with dust and blood; my shirt was stiff with blood. My legs and feet were torn in sundry places with briers and thorns, and were also covered with blood. I suppose I looked like a man who had escaped a den of wild beasts, and barely escaped them. In this state I appeared before my master, humbly entreating him to interpose his authority for my protection. I told him all the circumstances as well as I could, and it seemed, as I spoke, at times to affect him. He would then walk the floor, and seek to justify Covey by saying he expected I deserved it. He asked me what I wanted. I told him, to let me get a new home; that as sure as I lived with Mr. Covey again, I should live with but to die with him; that Covey would surely kill me; he was in a fair way for it. Master Thomas ridiculed the idea that there was any danger of Mr. Covey's killing me, and said that he knew Mr. Covey; that he was a good man, and that he could not think of taking me from him; that, should he do so, he would lose the whole year's wages; that I belonged to Mr. Covey for one year, and that I must go back to him, come what might; and that I must not trouble him with any more stories, or that he would himself *get hold of me*. After threatening me thus, he gave me a very large dose of salts, telling me that I might remain in St. Michael's that night, (it being quite late,) but that I must be off back to Mr. Covey's early in the morning; and that if I did not, he would *get hold of me*, which meant that he would whip me. I remained all night, and, according to his orders, I started off to Covey's in the morning, (Saturday morning,) wearied in body and broken in spirit. I got no supper that night, or breakfast that morning. I reached Covey's about nine o'clock; and just as I was getting over the fence that divided Mrs. Kemp's fields from ours, out ran Covey with his cowskin, to give me another whipping. Before he could reach me, I succeeded in getting to the cornfield; and as the corn was very high, it afforded me the means of hiding. He seemed very angry, and searched for me a long time. My behavior was altogether unaccountable. He finally gave up the chase, thinking, I suppose, that I must come home for something to eat; he would give himself no further trouble in looking for me. I spent that day mostly in the woods, having the alternative before me,—to go home and be whipped to death, or stay in the woods and be starved to death. That night, I fell in with Sandy Jenkins, a slave with whom I was somewhat acquainted. Sandy had a free wife, who lived about four miles from Mr. Covey's; and it being Saturday, he was on his way to see her. I told him my circumstances, and he very kindly invited me to go home with him. I went home with him, and talked this whole matter over, and got his advice as to what course it was best for me to pursue. I found Sandy an old adviser. He told me, with great solemnity, I must go back to Covey; but that before I went, I must go with him into another part of the woods, where there was a certain *root*, which, if I would take some of it with me, carrying it *always on my right side*, would render it impossible for Mr. Covey, or any other white man, to whip me. He said he had carried it for years; and since he had done so, he had never received a blow, and never expected to while he carried it. I at first rejected the idea, that the simple carrying of a root in my pocket would have any such effect as he had said, and was not disposed to take it; but Sandy impressed the necessity with much earnestness, telling me it could do no harm, if it did no good. To please him, I at length took the root, and, according to his direction, carried it upon my right side. This was Sunday morning. I immediately started for home; and upon entering the yard gate, out came Mr. Covey on his way to meeting. He spoke to me very kindly, bade me drive the pigs from a lot near by, and passed on towards the church. Now, this singular conduct of Mr. Covey really made me begin to think that there was something in the *root* which Sandy had given me; and had it been on any other day than Sunday, I could have attributed the conduct to no other cause than the influence of that root; and as it was, I was half inclined to think the *root* to be something more than I at first had taken it to be. All went well till Monday morning. On this morning, the virtue of the *root* was fully tested. Long before daylight, I was called to go and rub, curry, and feed, the horses. I obeyed, and was glad to obey. But whilst thus engaged, whilst in the act of throwing down some blades from the loft, Mr. Covey entered the stable with a long rope; and just as I was half out of the loft, he caught hold of my legs, and was about tying me. As soon as I found what he was up to, I gave a sudden spring, and as I did so, he holding to my legs, I was brought sprawling on the stable floor. Mr. Covey seemed now to think he had me, and could do what he pleased; but at this moment—from whence came the spirit I don't know—I resolved to fight; and, suiting my action to the resolution, I seized Covey hard by the throat; and as I did so, I rose. He held on to me, and I to him. My resistance was so entirely unexpected, that Covey seemed taken all aback. He trembled like a leaf. This gave me assurance, and I held him uneasy, causing the blood to run where I touched him with the ends of my fingers. Mr. Covey soon called out to Hughes for help. Hughes came, and, while Covey held me, attempted to tie my right hand. While he was in the act of doing so, I watched my chance, and gave him a heavy kick close under the ribs. This kick fairly sickened Hughes, so that he left me in the hands of Mr. Covey. This kick had the effect of not only weakening Hughes, but Covey also. When he saw Hughes bending over with pain, his courage quailed. He asked me if I meant to persist in my resistance. I told him I did, come what might; that he had used me like a brute for six months, and that I was determined to be used so no longer. With that, he strove to drag me to a stick that was lying just out of the stable door. He meant to knock me down. But just as he was leaning over to get the stick, I seized him with both hands by his collar, and brought him by a sudden snatch to the ground. By this time, Bill came. Covey called upon him for assistance. Bill wanted to know what he could do. Covey said, "Take hold of him, take hold of him!" Bill said his master hired him out to work, and not to help to whip me; so he left Covey and myself to fight out own battle out. We were at it for nearly two hours. Covey at length let me go, puffing and blowing at a great rate, saying that if I had not resisted, he would not have whipped me half so much. The truth was, that he had not whipped me at all. I considered him as getting entirely the worst end of the bargain; for he had drawn no blood from me, but I had from him. The whole six months afterwards, that I spent with Mr. Covey, he never laid the weight of his finger upon me in anger. He would occasionally say, he didn't want to get hold of me again. "No," thought I, "you need not; for you will come off worse than you did before."

This battle with Mr. Covey was the turning-point in my career as a slave. It rekindled the few expiring embers of freedom, and revived within me a sense of my own manhood. It recalled the departed self-confidence, and inspired me again with a determination to be free. The gratification afforded by the triumph was a full compensation for whatever else might follow, even death itself. He only can understand the deep satisfaction which I experience, who has himself repelled by force the bloody arm of slavery. I felt as I never felt before. It was a glorious resurrection, for the tomb of slavery, to the heaven of freedom. My long-crushed spirit rose, cowardice departed, bold defiance took its place; and I now resolved that, however long I might remain a slave in form, the day has passed forever when I could be a slave in fact. I did not hesitate to let it be known of me, that the white man who expected to succeed in whipping, must also succeed in killing me.

From this time I was never again what might be called fairly whipped, though I remained a slave four years afterwards. I had several fights, but was never whipped.

It was for a long time a matter of surprise to me why Mr. Covey did not immediately have me taken by the constable to the whipping-post, and there regularly whipped for the crime of raising my hand against a white man in defence of myself. And the only explanation I can now think of does not entirely satisfy me; but such as it is, I will give it. Mr. Covey enjoyed the most unbounded reputation for being a first-rate overseer and negro-breaker. It was of considerable importance to him. That reputation was at stake; and had he sent me—a boy about sixteen years old—to the public whipping-post, his reputation would have been lost; so, to save his reputation, he suffered me to go unpunished.

My term of actual service to Mr. Edward Covey ended on Christmas day, 1833. The days between Christmas and New Year's day are allowed as holidays; and, accordingly, we were not required to perform any labor, more than to feed and take care of the stock. This time we regarded as our own, by the grace of our masters; and we therefore used or abused it nearly as we pleased. Those of us who had families at a distance, were generally allowed to spend the whole six days in their society. This time, however, was spent in various ways. The staid, sober, thinking and industrious ones of our number would employ themselves in making corn-brooms, mats, horse-collars, and baskets; and another class of us would spend the time in hunting opossums, hares, and coons. But by far the larger part engaged in such sports and merriments as playing ball, wrestling, running foot-races, fiddling, dancing, and drinking whiskey; and this latter mode of spending the time was by far the most agreeable to the feelings of our masters. A slave who would work during the holidays was considered by our masters as scarcely deserving them. He was regarded as one who rejected the favor of his master. It was deemed a disgrace not to get drunk at Christmas; and he was regarded as lazy indeed, who had not provided himself with the necessary means, during the year, to get whisky enough to last him through Christmas.

From what I know of the effect of these holidays upon the slave, I believe them to be among the most effective means in the hands of the slaveholder in keeping down the spirit of insurrection. Were the slaveholders at once to abandon this practice, I have not the slightest doubt it would lead to an immediate insurrection among the slaves. These holidays serve as conductors, or safety-valves, to carry off the rebellious spirit of enslaved humanity. But for these, the slave would be forced up to the wildest desperation; and woe betide the slaveholder, the day he ventures to remove or hinder the operation of those conductors! I warn him that, in such an event, a spirit will go forth in their midst, more to be dreaded than the most appalling earthquake.

The holidays are part and parcel of the gross fraud, wrong, and inhumanity of slavery. They are professedly a custom established by the benevolence of the slaveholders; but I undertake to say, it is the result of selfishness, and one of the grossest frauds committed upon the down-trodden slave. They do not give the slaves this time because they would not like to have their work during its continuance, but because they know it would be unsafe to deprive them of it. This will be seen by the fact, that the slaveholders like to have their slaves spend those days just in such a manner as to make them as glad of their ending as of their beginning. Their object seems to be, to disgust their slaves with freedom, by plunging them into the lowest depths of dissipation. For instance, the slaveholders not only like to see the slave drink of his own accord, but will adopt various plans to make him drunk. One plan is, to make bets on their slaves, as to who can drink the most whiskey without getting drunk; and in this way they succeed in getting whole multitudes to drink to excess. Thus, when the slave asks for virtuous freedom, the cunning slaveholder, knowing his ignorance, cheats him with a dose of vicious dissipation, artfully labelled with the name of liberty. The most of us used to drink it down, and the result was just what might be supposed: many of us were led to think that there was little to choose between liberty and slavery. We felt, and very properly too, that we had almost as well as slaves to man as to rum. So, when the holidays ended, we staggered up from the filth of our wallowing, took a long breath, and marched to the field,—feeling, upon the whole, rather glad to go, from what our master had deceived us into a belief was freedom, back to the arms of slavery.

I have said that this mode of treatment is a part of the whole system of fraud and inhumanity of slavery. It is so. The mode here adopted to disgust the slave with freedom, by allowing him to see only the abuse of it, is carried out in other things. For instance, a slave loves molasses; he steals some. His master, in many cases, goes off to town, and buys a large quantity; he returns, takes his whip, and commands the slave to eat the molasses, until the poor fellow is made sick at the very mention of it. The same mode is sometimes adopted to make the slaves refrain from asking for more food than their regular allowance. A slave runs through his allowance, and applies for more. His master is enraged at him; but, not willing to send him off without food, gives him more than is necessary, and compels him to eat it within a given time. Then, if he complains that he cannot eat it, he is said to be satisfied neither full nor fasting, and is whipped for being hard to please! I have an abundance of such illustrations of the same principle, drawn from my own observation, but think the cases I have cited sufficient. The practice is a very common one.

On the first of January, 1834, I left Mr. Covey, and went to live with Mr. William Freeland, who lived about three miles from St. Michael's. I soon found Mr. Freeland a very different man from Mr. Covey. Though not rich, he was what would be called an educated southern gentleman. Mr. Covey, as I have shown, was a well-trained negro-breaker and slave-driver. The former (slaveholder though he was) seemed to possess some regard for honor, some rever-

ence for justice, and some respect for humanity. The latter seemed totally insensible to all such sentiments. Mr. Freeland had many of the faults peculiar to
slaveholders, such as being very passionate and fretful; but I must do him the
justice to say, that he was exceedingly free from those degrading vices to which
Mr. Covey was constantly addicted. The one was open and frank, and we always knew where to find him. The other was a most artful deceiver, and could
be understood only by such as were skilful enough to detect his cunningly-
devised frauds. Another advantage I gained in my new master was, he made no
pretensions to, or profession of, religion; and this, in my opinion, was truly a
great advantage. I assert most unhesitatingly, that the religion of the south is a
mere covering for the most horrid crimes,—a justifier of the most appalling barbarity,—a sanctifier of the most hateful frauds,—and a dark shelter under,
which the darkest, foulest, grossest, and most infernal deeds of slaveholders find
the strongest protection. Were I to be again reduced to the chains of slavery,
next to that enslavement, I should regard being the slave of a religious master
the greatest calamity that could befall me. For of all slaveholders with whom I
have ever met, religious slaveholders are the worst. I have ever found them the
meanest and basest, and most cruel and cowardly, of all others. It was my unhappy lot not only to belong to a religious slaveholder, but to live in a community of such religionists. Very near Mr. Freeland lived the Rev. Daniel Weeden,
and in the same neighborhood lived the Rev. Rigby Hopkins. These were
members and ministers in the Reformed Methodist Church. Mr. Weeden
owned, among others, a woman slave, whose name I have forgotten. This
woman's back, for weeks, was kept literally raw, made so by the lash of this
merciless, *religious* wretch. He used to hire hands. His maxim was, Behave well
or behave ill, it is the duty of a master occasionally to whip a slave, to remind
him of his master's authority. Such was his theory, and such his practice.

Mr. Hopkins was even worse than Mr. Weeden. His chief boast was his
ability to manage slaves. The peculiar feature of his government was that of
whipping slaves in advance of deserving it. He always managed to have one or
more of his slaves to whip every Monday morning. He did this to alarm their
fears, and strike terror into those who escaped. His plan was to whip for the
smallest offences, to prevent the commission of large ones. Mr. Hopkins could
always find some excuse for whipping a slave. It would astonish one, unaccustomed to a slaveholding life, to see with what wonderful ease a slave-holder can
find things, of which to make occasion to whip a slave. A mere look, word, or
motion,—a mistake, accident, or want of power,—are all matters for which a
slave may be whipped at any time. Does a slave look dissatisfied? It is said, he
has the devil in him, and it must be whipped out. Does he speak loudly when
spoken to by his master? Then he is getting high-minded, and should be taken
down a button-hole lower. Does he forget to pull off his hat at the approach of
a white person? Then he is wanting in reverence, and should be whipped for it.
Does he ever venture to vindicate his conduct, when censured for it? Then he
is guilty of impudence,—one of the greatest crimes of which a slave can be
guilty. Does he ever venture to suggest a different mode of doing things from

that pointed out by his master? He is indeed presumptuous, and getting above himself; and nothing less than a flogging will do for him. Does he, while ploughing, break a plough,—or, while hoeing, break a hoe? It is owning to his carelessness, and for it a slave must always be whipped. Mr. Hopkins could always find something of this sort to justify the use of the lash, and he seldom failed to embrace such opportunities. There was not a man in the whole county, with whom the slaves who had the getting their own home, would not prefer to live, rather than with this Rev. Mr. Hopkins. And yet there was not a man any where round, who made higher professions of religion, or was more active in revivals,—more attentive to the class, love-feast, prayer and preaching meetings, or more devotional in his family,—that prayed earlier, later, louder, and longer,—than this same reverend slave-driver, Rigby Hopkins.

But to return to Mr. Freeland, and to my experience while in his employment. He, like Mr. Covey, gave us enough to eat; but, unlike Mr. Covey, he also gave us sufficient time to take our meals. He worked us hard, but always between sunrise and sunset. He required a good deal of work to be done, but gave us good tools with which to work. His farm was large, but he employed hands enough to work it, and with ease, compared with many of his neighbors. My treatment, while in his employment, was heavenly, compared with what I experienced at the hands of Mr. Edward Covey.

Mr. Freeland was himself the owner of but two slaves. Their names were Henry Harris and John Harris. The rest of his hands he hired. These consisted of myself, Sandy Jenkins,* and Handy Caldwell. Henry and John were quite intelligent, and in a very little while after I went there, I succeeded in creating in them a strong desire to learn how to read. This desire soon sprang up in the others also. They very soon mustered up some old spelling-books, and nothing would do but that I must keep a Sabbath school. I agreed to do so, and accordingly devoted my Sundays to teaching these my loved fellow-slaves how to read. Neither of them knew his letters when I went there. Some of the slaves of the neighboring farms found what was going on, and also availed themselves of this little opportunity to learn to read. It was understood, among all who came, that there must be as little display about it as possible. It was necessary to keep our religious masters at St. Michael's unacquainted with the fact, that, instead of spending the Sabbath in wrestling, boxing, and drinking whisky, we were trying to learn how to read the will of God; for they had much rather see us engaged in those degrading sports, than to see us behaving like intellectual, moral, and accountable beings. My blood boils as I think of the bloody manner in which Messrs. Wright Fairbanks and Garrison West, both class-leaders, in connection with many others, rushed in upon us with sticks and stones, and

---

*This is the same man who gave me the roots to prevent my being whipped by Mr. Covey. He was "a clever soul." We used frequently to talk about the fight with Covey, and as often as we did so, he would claim my success as the result of the roots which he gave me. This superstition is very common among the more ignorant slaves. A slave seldom dies but this his death is attributed to trickery.

broke up our virtuous little Sabbath school, at St. Michael's—all calling themselves Christians! humble followers of the Lord Jesus Christ! But I am again digressing.

I held my Sabbath school at the house of a free colored man, whose name I deem it imprudent to mention; for should it be known, it might embarrass him greatly, though the crime of holding the school was committed ten years ago. I had at one time over forty scholars, and those of the right sort, ardently desiring to learn. They were of all ages, though mostly men and women. I look back to those Sundays with an amount of pleasure not to be expressed. They were great days to my soul. The work of instructing my dear fellow-slaves was the sweetest engagement with which I was ever blessed. We loved each other, and to leave them at the close of the Sabbath was a severe cross indeed. When I think that these precious souls are to-day shut up in the prison-house of slavery, my feelings overcome me, and I am almost ready to ask, "Does a righteous God govern the universe? and for what does he hold the thunders in his right hand, if not to smite the oppressor, and deliver the spoiled out of the hand of the spoiler?" These dear souls came not to Sabbath school because it was popular to do so, nor did I teach them because it was reputable to be thus engaged. Every moment they spent in that school, they were liable to be taken up, and given thirty-nine lashes. They came because they wished to learn. Their minds had been starved by their cruel masters. They had been shut up in mental darkness. I taught them, because it was the delight of my soul to be doing something that looked like bettering the condition of my race. I kept up my school nearly the whole year I lived with Mr. Freeland; and, beside my Sabbath school, I devoted three evenings in the week, during the winter, to teaching the slaves at home. And I have the happiness to know, that several of those who came to Sabbath school learned how to read; and that one, at least, is now free through my agency.

The year passed off smoothly. It seemed only about half as long as the year which preceded it. I went through it without receiving a single blow. I will give Mr. Freeland the credit of being the best master I ever had, *till I became my own master*. For the ease with which I passed the year, I was, however, somewhat indebted to the society of my fellow-slaves. They were noble souls; they not only possessed loving hearts, but brave ones. We were linked and interlinked with each other. I loved them with a love stronger than any thing I have experienced since. It is sometimes said that we slaves do not love and confide in each other. In answer to this assertion, I can say, I never loved any or confided in any people more than my fellow-slaves, and especially those with whom I lived at Mr. Freeland's. I believe we would have died for each other. We never undertook to do any thing, of any importance, without a mutual consultation. We never moved separately. We were one; and as much so by our tempers and dispositions, as by the mutual hardships to which we were necessarily subjected by our condition as slaves.

At the close of the year 1834, Mr. Freeland again hired me of my master, for the year 1835. But, by this time, I began to want to live *upon free land* as well as *with Freeland*; and I was no longer content, therefore, to live with him or any other slaveholder. I began, with the commencement of the year, to prepare myself for a final struggle, which should decide my fate one way or the other. My tendency was upward. I was fast approaching manhood, and year after year had passed, and I was still a slave. These thoughts roused me—I must do something. I therefore resolved that 1835 should not pass without witnessing an attempt, on my part, to secure my liberty. But I was not willing to cherish this determination alone. My fellow-slaves were dear to me. I was anxious to have them participate with me in this, my life-giving determination. I therefore, though with great prudence, commenced early to ascertain their views and feelings in regard to their condition, and to imbue their minds with thoughts of freedom. I bent myself to devising ways and means for our escape, and meanwhile strove, on all fitting occasions, to impress them with the gross fraud and inhumanity of slavery. I went first to Henry, next to John, then to the others. I found, in them all, warm hearts and noble spirits. They were ready to hear, and ready to act when a feasible plan should be proposed. This was what I wanted. I talked to them of our want of manhood, if we submitted to our enslavement without at least one noble effort to be free. We met often, and consulted frequently, and told our hopes and fears, recounted the difficulties, real and imagined, which we should be called on to meet. At times we were almost disposed to give up, and try to content ourselves with our wretched lot; at others, we were firm and unbending in our determination to go. Whenever we suggested any plan, there was shrinking—the odds were fearful. Our path was beset with the greatest obstacles; and if we succeeded in gaining the end of it, our right to be free was yet questionable—we were yet liable to be returned to bondage. We could see no spot, this side of the ocean, where we could be free. We knew nothing about Canada. Our knowledge of the north did not extend farther than New York; and to go there, and be forever harassed with the frightful liability of being returned to slavery—with the certainty of being treated tenfold worse than before—the thought was truly a horrible one, and one which it was not easy to overcome. The case sometimes stood thus: At every gate through which we were to pass, we saw a watchman—at every ferry a guard—on every bridge a sentinel—and in every wood a patrol. We were hemmed in upon every side. Here were the difficulties, real or imagined—the good to be sought, and the evil to be shunned. On the one hand, there stood slavery, a stern reality, glaring frightfully upon us,—its robes already crimsoned with the blood of millions, and even now feasting itself greedily upon our own flesh. On the other hand, away back in the dim distance, under the flickering light of the north star, behind some craggy hill or snow-covered mountain, stood a doubtful freedom—half frozen—beckoning us to come and share its hospitality. This in itself was sometimes enough to stagger us; but when we permitted ourselves to survey the road, we were frequently appalled. Upon either side we saw grim death, assuming the most horrid shapes. Now it was starvation, causing us to eat our own flesh;—now we were contending with the waves, and were drowned;—now we were overtaken, and torn to pieces by the fangs of the terrible bloodhound. We were stung by scorpions, chased by wild beasts, bitten by snakes, and finally, after having nearly reached the desired spot,—after swimming rivers, encountering wild beasts, sleeping in the woods, suffering hunger and nakedness,—we were overtaken by our pursuers, and, in our resistance, we were shot dead upon the spot! I say, this picture sometimes appalled us, and made us

> "rather bear those ills we had,
> Than fly to others, that we knew not of."

In coming to a fixed determination to run away, we did more than Patrick Henry, when he resolved upon liberty or death. With us it was a doubtful liberty at most, and almost certain death if we failed. For my part, I should prefer death to hopeless bondage.

Sandy, one of our number, gave up the notion, but still encouraged us. Our company then consisted of Henry Harris, John Harris, Henry Bailey, Charles Roberts, and myself. Henry Bailey was my uncle, and belonged to my master. Charles married my aunt; he belonged to my master's father-in-law, Mr. William Hamilton.

The plan we finally concluded upon was, to get a large canoe belonging to Mr. Hamilton, and upon the Saturday night previous to Easter holidays, paddle directly up the Chesapeake Bay. On our arrival at the head of the bay, a distance of seventy or eighty miles from where we lived, it was our purpose to turn our canoe adrift, and follow the guidance of the north star till we got beyond the limits of Maryland. Our reason for taking the water route was, that we were less liable to be suspected as runaways; we hoped to be regarded as fishermen; whereas, if we should take the land route, we should be subjected to interruptions of almost every kind. Any one having a white face, and being so disposed, could stop us, and subject us to examination.

The week before our intended start, I wrote several protections, one for each of us. As well as I can remember, they were in the following words, to wit:—

"THIS is to certify that I, the undersigned, have given the bearer, my servant, full liberty to go to Baltimore, and spend the Easter holidays. Written with mine own hand, &c., 1835.

"WILLIAM HAMILTON,
"Near St. Michael's, in Talbot county, Maryland."

We were not going to Baltimore; but, in going up the bay, we went toward Baltimore, and these protections were only intended to protect us while on the bay.

As the time drew near for our departure, our anxiety became more and more intense. It was truly a matter of life and death with us. The strength of our determination was about to be fully tested. At this time, I was very active in explaining every difficulty, removing every doubt, dispelling every fear, and inspiring all with the firmness indispensable to success in our undertaking; assuring them that half was gained the instant we made the move; we had talked long enough; we were now ready to move; if not now, we never should be; and if we did not intend to move now, we had as well fold our arms, sit down, and acknowledge ourselves fit only to be slaves. This, none of us were prepared to acknowledge. Every man stood firm; and at our last meeting, we pledged ourselves afresh, in the most solemn manner, that, at the time appointed, we would certainly start in pursuit of freedom. This was in the middle of the week, at the end of which we were to be off. We went, as usual, to our several fields of labor, but with bosoms highly agitated with thoughts of our truly hazardous undertaking. We tried to conceal our feelings as much as possible; and I think we succeeded very well.

After a painful waiting, the Saturday morning, whose night was to witness our departure, came. I hailed it with joy, bring what of sadness it might. Friday night was a sleepless one for me. I probably felt more anxious than the rest, because I was, by common consent, at the head of the whole affair. The responsibility of success or failure lay heavily upon me. The glory of the one, and the confusion of the other, were alike mine. The first two hours of that morning were such as I never experienced before, and hope never to again. Early in the morning; we went, as usual, to the field. We were spreading manure; and all at once, while thus engaged, I was overwhelmed with an indescribable feeling, in the fulness of which I turned to Sandy, who was near by, and said, "We are betrayed!" "Well," said he, "that thought has this moment struck me." We said no more. I was never more certain of any thing.

The horn was blown as usual, and we went up from the field to the house for breakfast. I went for the form, more than for want of any thing to eat that morning. Just as I got to the house, in looking out at the lane gate, I saw four white men, with two colored men. The white men were on horseback, and the colored ones were walking behind, as if tied. I watched them a few moments till they got up to our lane gate. Here they halted, and tied the colored men to the gatepost. I was not yet certain as to what the matter was. In a few moments, in rode Mr. Hamilton, with a speed betokening great excitement. He came to the door, and inquired if Master William was in. He was told he was at the barn. Mr. Hamilton, without dismounting, rode up to the barn with extraordinary speed. In a few moments, he and Mr. Freeland returned to the house. By this time, the three constables rode up, and in great haste dismounted, tied their horses, and met Master William and Mr. Hamilton returning from the barn; and after talking awhile, they all walked up to the kitchen door. There was no one in the kitchen but myself and John. Henry and Sandy were up at the barn. Mr. Freeland put his head in at the door, and called me by name, saying, there were some gentlemen at the door who wished to see me. I stepped to the door, and inquired what they wanted. They at once seized me, and, without giving me any satisfaction, tied me—lashing my hands closely together. I insisted upon knowing what the matter was. They at length said, that they had learned

I had been in a "scrape," and that I was to be examined before my master; and if their information proved false, I should not be hurt.

In a few moments, they succeeded in tying John. They then turned to Henry, who had by this time returned, and commanded him to cross his hands. "I won't!" said Henry, in a firm tone, indicating his readiness to meet the consequences of his refusal. "Won't you?" said Tom Graham, the constable. "No, I won't!" said Henry, in a still stronger tone. With this, two of the constables pulled out their shining pistols, and swore, by their Creator, that they would make him cross his hands or kill him. Each cocked his pistol, and, with fingers on the trigger, walked up to Henry, saying, at the same time, if he did not cross his hands, they would blow his damned heart out. "Shoot me, shoot me!" said Henry; "you can't kill me but once. Shoot, shoot,—and be damned! *I won't be tied!*" This he said in a tone of loud defiance; and at the same time, with a motion as quick as lightning, he with one single stroke dashed the pistols from the hand of each constable. As he did this, all hands fell upon him, and, after beating him some time, they finally overpowered him, and got him tied.

During the scuffle, I managed, I know not how, to get my pass out, and, without being discovered, put it into the fire. We were all now tied; and just as we were to leave for Easton jail, Betsy Freeland, mother of William Freeland, came to the door with her hands full of biscuits, and divided them between Henry and John. She then delivered herself of a speech, to the following effect:—addressing herself to me, she said, "*You devil! You yellow devil!* it was you that put it into the heads of Henry and John to run away. But for you, you long-legged mulatto devil! Henry nor John would never have thought of such a thing." I made no reply, and was immediately hurried off towards St. Michael's. Just a moment previous to the scuffle with Henry, Mr. Hamilton suggested the propriety of making a search for the protections which he had understood Frederick had written for himself and the rest. But, just at the moment he was about carrying his proposal into effect, his aid was needed in helping to tie Henry; and the excitement attending the scuffle caused them either to forget, or to deem it unsafe, under the circumstances, to search. So we were not yet convicted of the intention to run away.

When we got about half way to St. Michael's, while the constables having us in charge were looking ahead, Henry inquired of me what he should do with his pass. I told him to eat it with his biscuit, and own nothing; and we passed the word around, "*Own nothing;*" and "*Own nothing!*" said we all. Our confidence in each other was unshaken. We were resolved to succeed or fail together, after the calamity had befallen us as much as before. We were now prepared for any thing. We were to be dragged that morning fifteen miles behind horses, and then to be placed in the Easton jail. When we reached St. Michael's, we underwent a sort of examination. We all denied that we ever intended to run away. We did this more to bring out the evidence against us, than from any hope of getting clear of being sold; for, as I have said, we were ready for that. The fact was, we cared but little where we went, so we went together. Our greatest concern was about separation. We dreaded that more than any thing this side of death. We found the evidence against us to be the testimony of one person; our master would not tell who it was; but we came to a unanimous decision among ourselves as to who their informant was. We were sent off to the jail at Easton. When we got there, we were delivered up to the sheriff, Mr. Joseph Graham, and by him placed in jail. Henry, John, and myself, were placed in one room together—Charles, and Henry Bailey, in another. Their object in separating us was to hinder concert.

We had been in jail scarcely twenty minutes, when a swarm of slave traders, and agents for slave traders, flocked into jail to look at us, and to ascertain if we were for sale. Such a set of beings I never saw before! I felt myself surrounded by so many fiends from perdition. A band of pirates never looked more like their father, the devil. They laughed and grinned over us, saying, "Ah, my boys! we have got you, haven't we?" And after taunting us in various ways, they one by one went into an examination of us, with intent to ascertain our value. They would impudently ask us if we would not like to have them for our masters. We would make them no answer, and leave them to find out as best they could. Then they would curse and swear at us, telling us that they could take the devil out of us in a very little while, if we were only in their hands.

While in jail, we found ourselves in much more comfortable quarters than we expected when we went there. We did not get much to eat, nor that which was very good; but we had a good clean room, from the windows of which we could see what was going on in the street, which was very much better than though we had been placed in one of the dark, damp cells. Upon the whole, we got along very well, so far as the jail and its keeper were concerned. Immediately after the holidays were over, contrary to all our expectations, Mr. Hamilton and Mr. Freeland came up to Easton, and took Charles, the two Henrys, and John, out of jail, and carried them home, leaving me alone. I regarded this separation as a final one. It caused me more pain than any thing else in the whole transaction. I was ready for any thing rather than separation. I supposed that they had consulted together, and had decided that, as I was the whole cause of the intention of the others to run away, it was hard to make the innocent suffer with the guilty; and that they had, therefore, concluded to take the others home, and sell me, as a warning to the others that remained. It is due to the noble Henry to say, he seemed almost as reluctant at leaving the prison as at leaving home to come to the prison. But we knew we should, in all probability, be separated, if we were sold; and since he was in their hands, he concluded to go peaceably home.

I was now left to my fate. I was all alone, and within the walls of a stone prison. But a few days before, and I was full of hope. I expected to have been safe in a land of freedom; but now I was covered with gloom, sunk down to the utmost despair. I thought the possibility of freedom was gone. I was kept in this way about one week, at the end of which, Captain Auld, my master, to my surprise and utter astonishment, came up, and took me out, with the intention of sending me, with a gentleman of his acquaintance, into Alabama. But, from some cause or other, he did not send me to Alabama, but concluded to send me back to Baltimore, to live again with his brother Hugh, and to learn a trade.

Thus, after an absence of three years and one month, I was once more permitted to return to my old home at Baltimore. My master sent me away, because there existed against me a very great prejudice in the community, and he feared I might be killed.

In a few weeks after I went to Baltimore, Master Hugh hired me to Mr. William Gardner, an extensive ship-builder, on Fell's Point. I was put there to learn how to calk. It, however, proved a very unfavorable place for the accomplishment of this object. Mr. Gardner was engaged that spring in building two large man-of-war brigs, professedly for the Mexican government. The vessels were to be launched in the July of that year, and in failure thereof, Mr. Gardner was to lose a considerable sum; so that when I entered, all was hurry. There was no time to learn any thing. Every man had to do that which he knew how to do. In entering the ship-yard, my orders from Mr. Gardner were, to do whatever the carpenters commanded me to do. This was placing me at the beck and call of about seventy-five men. I was to regard all these as masters. Their word was to be my law. My situation was a most trying one. At times I needed a dozen pair of hands. I was called a dozen ways in the space of a single minute. Three or four voices would strike my ear at the same moment. It was—"Fred., come help me to cant this timber here."—"Fred., come carry this timber yonder."—"Fred., bring that roller here."—"Fred., go get a fresh can of water."—"Fred., come help saw off the end of this timber."—"Fred., go quick, and get the crowbar."—"Fred., hold on the end of this fall."—"Fred., go to the blacksmith's shop, and get a new punch."—"Hurra, Fred.! run and bring me a cold chisel."—"I say, Fred., bear a hand, and get up a fire as quick as lightning under that steam-box."—"Halloo, nigger! come, turn this grindstone."—"Come, come! move, move! and *bowse* this timber forward."—"I say, darky, blast your eyes, why don't you heat up some pitch?"—"Halloo! halloo! halloo!" (Three voices at the same time.) "Come here!—Go there!—Hold on where you are! Damn you, if you move, I'll knock your brains out!"

This was my school for eight months; and I might have remained there longer, but for a most horrid fight I had with four of the white apprentices, in which my left eye was nearly knocked out, and I was horribly mangled in other respects. The facts in the case were these: Until a very little while after I went there, white and black ship-carpenters worked side by side, and no one seemed to see any impropriety in it. All hands seemed to be very well satisfied. Many of the black carpenters were freemen. Things seemed to be going on very well. All at once, the white carpenters knocked off, and said they would not work with free colored workmen. Their reason for this, as alleged, was, that if free colored carpenters were encouraged, they would soon take the trade into their own hands, and poor white men would be thrown out of employment. They therefore felt called upon at once to put a stop to it. And, taking advantage of Mr.

Gardner's necessities, they broke off, swearing they would work no longer, unless he would discharge his black carpenters. Now, though this did not extend to me in form, it did reach me in fact. My fellow-apprentices very soon began to feel it degrading to them to work with me. They began to put on airs, and talk about the "niggers" taking the country, saying we all ought to be killed; and, being encouraged by the journeymen, they commenced making my condition as hard as they could, by hectoring me around, and sometimes striking me. I, of course, kept the vow I made after the fight with Mr. Covey, and struck back again, regardless of consequences; and while I kept them from combining, I succeeded very well; for I could whip the whole of them, taking them separately. They, however, at length combined, and came upon me, armed with sticks, stones, and heavy handspikes. One came in front with a half brick. There was one at each side of me, and one behind me. While I was attending to those in front, and on either side, the one behind ran up with the handspike, and struck me a heavy blow upon the head. It stunned me. I fell, and with this they all ran upon me, and fell to beating me with their fists. I let them lay on for a while, gathering strength. In an instant, I gave a sudden surge, and rose to my hands and knees. Just as I did that, one of their number gave me, with his heavy boot, a powerful kick in the left eye. My eyeball seemed to have burst. When they saw my eye closed, and badly swollen, they left me. With this I seized the handspike, and for a time pursued them. But here the carpenters interfered, and I thought I might as well give it up. It was impossible to stand my hand against so many. All this took place in sight of not less than fifty white ship-carpenters, and not one interposed a friendly word; but some cried, "Kill the damned nigger! Kill him! kill him! He struck a white person." I found my only chance for life was in flight. I succeeded in getting away without an additional blow, and barely so; for to strike a white man is death by Lynch law,—and that was the law in Mr. Gardner's ship-yard; nor is there much of any other out of Mr. Gardner's ship yard.

I went directly home, and told the story of my wrongs to Master Hugh; and I am happy to say of him, irreligious as he was, his conduct was heavenly, compared with that of his brother Thomas under similar circumstances. He listened attentively to my narration of the circumstances leading to the savage outrage, and gave many proofs of his strong indignation at it. The heart of my once overkind mistress was again melted into pity. My puffed-out eye and blood-covered face moved her to tears. She took a chair by me, washed the blood from my face, and, with a mother's tenderness, bound up my head, covering the wounded eye with a lean piece of fresh beef. It was almost compensation for my suffering to witness, once more, a manifestation of kindness from this, my once affectionate old mistress. Master Hugh was very much enraged. He gave expression to his feelings by pouring out curses upon the heads of those who did the deed. As soon as I got a little the better of my bruises, he took me with him to Esquire Watson's, on Bond Street, to see what could be done about the matter. Mr. Watson inquired who saw the assault committed. Master Hugh told him it was done in Mr. Gardner's ship-yard, at mid-day, where there were a large company of men at work. "As to that," he said, "the deed was done, and there was no question as to who did it." His answer was, he could do nothing in the case, unless some white man would come forward and testify. He could issue no warrant on my word. If I had been killed in the presence of a thousand colored people, their testimony combined would have been insufficient to have arrested one of the murderers. Master Hugh, for once, was compelled to say this state of things was too bad. Of course, it was impossible to get any white man to volunteer his testimony in my behalf, and against the white young men. Even those who may have sympathized with me were not prepared to do this. It required a degree of courage unknown to them to do so; for just at that time, the slightest manifestation of humanity toward a colored person was denounced as abolitionism, and that name subjected its bearer to frightful liabilities. The watch-words of the bloody-minded in that region, and in those days, were, "Damn the abolitionists!" and "Damn the niggers!" There was nothing done, and probably nothing would have been done if I had been killed. Such was, and such remains, the state of things in the Christian city of Baltimore.

Master Hugh, finding he could get no redress, refused to let me go back again to Mr. Gardner. He kept me himself, and his wife dressed my wound till I was again restored to health. He then took me into the ship-yard of which he was foreman, in the employment of Mr. Walter Price. There I was immediately set to calking, and very soon learned the art of using my mallet and irons. In the course of one year from the time I left Mr. Gardner's, I was able to command the highest wages given to the most experienced calkers. I was now of some importance to my master. I was bringing him from six to seven dollars per week. I sometimes brought him nine dollars per week: my wages were a dollar and a half a day. After learning how to calk, I sought my own employment, made my own contracts, and collected the money which I earned. My pathway became much more smooth than before; my condition was now much more comfortable. When I could get no calking to do, I did nothing. During these leisure times, those old notions about freedom would steal over me again. When in Mr. Gardner's employment, I was kept in such a perpetual whirl of excitement, I could think of nothing, scarcely, but my life; and in thinking of my life, I almost forgot my liberty. I have observed this in my experience of slavery,—that whenever my condition was improved, instead of its increasing my contentment, it only increased my desire to be free, and set me to thinking of plans to gain my freedom. I have found that, to make a contented slave, it is necessary to make a thoughtless one. It is necessary to darken his moral and mental vision, and, as far as possible, to annihilate the power of reason. He must be able to detect no inconsistencies in slavery; he must be made to feel that slavery is right; and he can be brought to that only when he ceases to be a man.

I was now getting, as I have said, one dollar and fifty cents per day. I contracted for it; I earned it; it was paid to me; it was rightfully my own; yet, upon each returning Saturday night, I was compelled to deliver every cent of that money to Master Hugh. And why? Not because he earned it,—not because he had any hand in earning it,—not because I owed it to him,—nor because he possessed the slightest shadow of a right to it; but solely because he had the power to compel me to give it up. The right of the grim-visaged pirate upon the high seas is exactly the same.

from *My Bondage and My Freedom*

CHAPTER III

The Author's Parentage

If the reader will now be kind enough to allow me time to grow bigger, and afford me an opportunity for my experience to become greater, I will tell him something, by-and-by, of slave life, as I saw, felt, and heard it, on Col. Edward Lloyd's plantation, and at the house of old master, where I had now, despite of myself, most suddenly, but not unexpectedly, been dropped. Meanwhile, I will redeem my promise to say something more of my dear mother.

I say nothing of *father*, for he is shrouded in a mystery I have never been able to penetrate. Slavery does away with fathers, as it does away with families. Slavery has no use for either fathers or families, and its laws do not recognize their existence in the social arrangements of the plantation. When they *do* exist, they are not the outgrowths of slavery, but are antagonistic to that system. The order of civilization is reversed here. The name of the child is not expected to be that of its father, and his condition does not necessarily affect that of the child. He may be the slave of Mr. Tilgman; and his child, when born, may be the slave of Mr. Gross. He may be a *freeman*; and yet his child may be a *chattel*. He may be white, glorying in the purity of his Anglo-Saxon blood; and his child may be ranked with the blackest slaves. Indeed, he *may* be, and often *is*, master and father to the same child. He can be father without being a husband, and may sell his child without incurring reproach, if the child be by a woman in whose veins courses one thirty-second part of African blood. My father was a white man, or nearly white. It was sometimes whispered that my master was my father.

But to return, or rather, to begin. My knowledge of my mother is very scanty, but very distinct. Her personal appearance and bearing are ineffaceably stamped upon my memory. She was tall, and finely proportioned; of deep black, glossy complexion; had regular features, and among the other slaves, was remarkably sedate in her manners. There is in *"Prichard's Natural History of Man,"* the head of a figure—on page 157—the features of which so resemble those of my mother, that I often recur to it with something of the feeling which I suppose others experience when looking upon the pictures of dear departed ones.

Yet I cannot say that I was very deeply attached to my mother; certainly not so deeply as I should have been had our relations in childhood been different. We were separated, according to the common custom, when I was but an infant, and, of course, before I knew my mother from any one else.

The germs of affection with which the Almighty, in his wisdom and mercy, arms the helpless infant against the ills and vicissitudes of his lot, had been directed in their growth toward that loving old grandmother, whose gentle hand and kind deportment it was the first effort of my infantile understanding to comprehend and appreciate. Accordingly, the tenderest affection which a beneficent Father allows, as a partial compensation to the mother for the pains and lacerations of her heart, incident to the maternal relation, was, in my case, diverted from its true and natural object, by the envious, greedy, and treacherous hand of slavery. The slave-mother can be spared long enough from the field to endure all the bitterness of a mother's anguish, when it adds another name to a master's ledger, but *not* long enough to receive the joyous reward afforded by the intelligent smiles of her child. I never think of this terrible interference of slavery with my infantile affections, and its diverting them from their natural course, without feelings to which I can give no adequate expression.

I do not remember to have seen my mother at my grandmother's at any time. I remember her only in her visits to me at Col. Lloyd's plantation, and in the kitchen of my old master. Her visits to me there were few in number, brief in duration, and mostly made in the night. The pains she took, and the toil she endured, to see me, tells me that a true mother's heart was hers, and that slavery had difficulty in paralyzing it with unmotherly indifference.

My mother was hired out to a Mr. Stewart, who lived about twelve miles from old master's, and, being a field hand, she seldom had leisure, by day, for the performance of the journey. The nights and the distance were both obstacles to her visits. She was obliged to walk, unless chance flung into her way an opportunity to ride; and the latter was sometimes her good luck. But she always had to walk one way or the other. It was a greater luxury than slavery could afford, to allow a black slave-mother a horse or a mule, upon which to travel twenty-four miles, when she could walk the distance. Besides, it is deemed a foolish whim for a slave-mother to manifest concern to see her children, and, in one point of view, the case is made out—she can do nothing for them. She has no control over them; the master is even more than the mother, in all matters touching the fate of her child. Why, then, should she give herself any concern? She has no responsibility. Such is the reasoning, and such the practice. The iron rule of the plantation, always passionately and violently enforced in that neighborhood, makes flogging the penalty of failing to be in the field before sunrise in the morning, unless special permission be given to the absenting slave. "I went to see my child," is no excuse to the ear or heart of the overseer.

One of the visits of my mother to me, while at Col. Lloyd's, I remember very vividly, as affording a bright gleam of a mother's love, and the earnestness of a mother's care.

I had on that day offended "Aunt Katy," (called "Aunt" by way of re-spect,) the cook of old master's establishment. I do not now remember the nature of my offense in this instance, for my offenses were numerous in that quarter, greatly depending, however, upon the mood of Aunt Katy, as to their heinousness; but she had adopted, that day, her favorite mode of pun-ishing me, namely, making me go without food all day—that is, from after breakfast. The first hour or two after dinner, I succeeded pretty well in keep-ing up my spirits; but though I made an excellent stand against the foe, and fought bravely during the afternoon, I knew I must be conquered at last, un-less I got the accustomed reenforcement of a slice of corn bread, at sundown. Sundown came, but *no bread*, and, in its stead, there came the threat, with a scowl well suited to its terrible import, that she "meant to *starve the life out of me!*" Brandishing her knife, she chopped off the heavy slices for the other children, and put the loaf away, muttering, all the while, her savage designs upon myself. Against this disappointment, for I was expecting that her heart would relent at last, I made an extra effort to maintain my dignity; but when I saw all the other children around me with merry and satisfied faces, I could stand it no longer. I went out behind the house, and cried like a fine fellow! When tired of this, I returned to the kitchen, sat by the fire, and brooded over my hard lot. I was too hungry to sleep. While I sat in the corner, I caught sight of an ear of Indian corn on an upper shelf of the kitchen. I watched my chance, and got it, and, shelling off a few grains, I put it back again. The grains in my hand, I quickly put in some ashes, and covered them with embers, to roast them. All this I did at the risk of getting a brutal thumping, for Aunt Katy could beat, as well as starve me. My corn was not long in roasting, and, with my keen appetite, it did not matter even if the grains were not exactly done. I eagerly pulled them out, and placed them on my stool, in a clever little pile. Just as I began to help myself to my very dry meal, in came my dear mother. And now, dear reader, a scene occurred which was altogether worth beholding, and to me it was instructive as well as interesting. The friendless and hungry boy, in his extremest need—and when he did not dare to look for succor—found himself in the strong, pro-tecting arms of a mother; a mother who was, at the moment (being endowed with high powers of manner as well as matter) more than a match for all his enemies. I shall never forget the indescribable expression of her counte-nance, when I told her that I had had no food since morning; and that Aunt Katy said she "meant to starve the life out of me." There was pity in her glance at me, and a fiery indignation at Aunt Katy at the same time; and, while she took the corn from me, and gave me a large ginger cake, in its stead, she read Aunt Katy a lecture which she never forgot. My mother threatened her with complaining to old master in my behalf; for the latter, though harsh and cruel himself, at times, did not sanction the meanness, in-justice, partiality and oppressions enacted by Aunt Katy in the kitchen. That night I learned the fact, that I was not only a child, but *somebody's* child. The "sweet cake" my mother gave me was in the shape of a heart, with a rich, dark ring glazed upon the edge of it. I was victorious, and well off for the moment; prouder, on my mother's knee, than a king upon his throne. But my triumph was short. I dropped off to sleep, and waked in the morning only to find my mother gone, and myself left at the mercy of the sable virago, dominant in my old master's kitchen, whose fiery wrath was my constant dread.

I do not remember to have seen my mother after this occurrence. Death soon ended the little communication that had existed between us; and with it, I believe, a life—judging from her weary, sad, down-cast countenance and mute demeanor—full of heart-felt sorrow. I was not allowed to visit her during any part of her long illness; nor did I see her for a long time before she was taken ill and died. The heartless and ghastly form of *slavery* rises between mother and child, even at the bed of death. The mother, at the verge of the grave, may not gather her children, to impart to them her holy admonitions, and invoke for them her dying benediction. The bondwoman lives as a slave, and is left to die as a beast; often with fewer attentions than are paid to a favorite horse. Scenes of sacred tenderness, around the death-bed, never forgotten, and which often arrest the vicious and confirm the virtuous during life, must be looked for among the free, though they sometimes occur among the slaves. It has been a life-long, standing grief to me, that I knew so little of my mother; and that I was so early separated from her. The counsels of her love must have been beneficial to me. The side view of her face is imaged on my memory, and I take few steps in life, without feeling her presence; but the image is mute, and I have no striking words of her's treasured up.

I learned, after my mother's death, that she could read, and that she was the *only* one of all the slaves and colored people in Tuckahoe who enjoyed that advantage. How she acquired this knowledge, I know not, for Tuckahoe is the last place in the world where she would be apt to find facilities for learning. I can, therefore, fondly and proudly ascribe to her an earnest love of knowledge. That a "field hand" should learn to read, in any slave state, is remarkable; but the achievement of my mother, considering the place, was very extraordinary; and, in view of that fact, I am quite willing, and even happy, to attribute any love of letters I possess, and for which I have got—despite of prejudices—only too much credit, *not* to my admitted Anglo-Saxon paternity, but to the native genius of my sable, unprotected, and uncultivated *mother*—a woman, who belonged to a race whose mental endowments it is, at present, fashionable to hold in disparagement and contempt.

Summoned away to her account, with the impassible gulf of slavery between us during her entire illness, my mother died without leaving me a single intimation of *who* my father was. There was a whisper, that my master was my father; yet it was only a whisper, and I cannot say that I ever gave it credence. Indeed, I now have reason to think he was not; nevertheless, the fact remains, in all its glaring odiousness, that, by the laws of slavery, children, in all cases, are reduced to the condition of their mothers. This arrangement admits of the greatest license to brutal slaveholders, and their profligate sons, brothers, relations and friends, and gives to the pleasure of sin, the additional attraction of profit. A whole volume might be written on this single feature of slavery, as I have observed it.

One might imagine, that the children of such connections, would fare better, in the hands of their masters, than other slaves. The rule is quite the other way; and a very little reflection will satisfy the reader that such is the case. A man who will enslave his own blood, may not be safely relied on for magnanimity. Men do not love those who remind them of their sins—unless they have a mind to repent—and the mulatto child's face is a standing accusation against him who is master and father to the child. What is still worse, perhaps, such a child is a constant offense to the wife. She hates its very presence, and when a slaveholding woman hates, she wants not means to give that hate telling effect. Women—white women, I mean—are IDOLS at the south, not WIVES, for the slave woman are preferred in many instances; and if these *idols* but nod, or lift a finger, woe to the poor victim: kicks, cuffs and stripes are sure to follow. Masters are frequently compelled to sell this class of their slaves, out of deference to the feelings of their white wives; and shocking and scandalous as it may seem for a man to sell his own blood to the traffickers in human flesh, it is often an act of humanity toward the slave-child to be thus removed from his merciless tormentors.

It is not within the scope of the design of my simple story, to comment upon every phase of slavery not within my experience as a slave.

But, I may remark, that, if the lineal descendants of Ham are only to be enslaved, according to the scriptures, slavery in this country will soon become an unscriptual institution; for thousands are ushered into the world, annually, who—like myself—owe their existence to white fathers, and, most frequently, to their masters, and master's sons. The slave-woman is at the mercy of the fathers, sons or brothers of her master. The thoughtful know the rest.

After what I have now said of the circumstances of my mother, and my relations to her, the reader will not be surprised, nor be disposed to censure me, when I tell but the simple truth, viz: that I received the tidings of her death with no strong emotions of sorrow for her, and with very little regret for myself on account of her loss. I had to learn the value of my mother long after her death, and by witnessing the devotion of other mothers to their children.

There is not, beneath the sky, an enemy to filial affection so destructive as slavery. It had made my brothers and sisters strangers to me; it converted the mother that bore me, into a myth; it shrouded my father in mystery, and left me without an intelligible beginning in the world.

My mother died when I could not have been more than eight or nine years old, on one of old master's farms in Tuckahoe, in the neighborhood of Hillsborough. Her grave is, as the grave of the dead at sea, unmarked, and without stone or stake.

CHAPTER XVII

The Last Flogging

Sleep itself does not always come to the relief of the weary in body, and the broken in spirit; especially when past troubles only fore-shadow coming disasters. The last hope had been extinguished. My master, who I did not venture to hope would protect me as a *man*, had even now refused to protect me as *his property*; and had cast me back, covered with reproaches and bruises, into the hands of a stranger to that mercy which was the soul of the religion he professed. May the reader never spend such a night as that allotted to me, previous to the morning which was to herald my return to the den of horrors from which I had made a temporary escape.

I remained all night—sleep I did not—at St. Michael's; and in the morning (Saturday) I started off, according to the order of Master Thomas, feeling that I had no friend on earth, and doubting if I had one in heaven. I reached Covey's about nine o'clock; and just as I stepped into the field, before I had reached the house, Covey, true to his snakish habits, darted out at me from a fence corner, in which he had secreted himself, for the purpose of securing me. He was amply provided with a cowskin and a rope; and he evidently intended to *tie me up*, and to wreak his vengeance on me to the fullest extent. I should have been an easy prey, had he succeeded in getting his hands upon me, for I had taken no refreshment since noon on Friday; and this, together with the pelting, excitement, and the loss of blood, had reduced my strength. I, however, darted back into the woods, before the ferocious hound could get hold of me, and buried myself in a thicket, where he lost sight of me. The corn-field afforded me cover, in getting to the woods. But for the tall corn, Covey would have overtaken me, and made me his captive. He seemed very much chagrined that he did not catch me, and gave up the chase, very reluctantly; for I could see his angry movements, toward the house from which he had sallied, on his foray.

Well, now I am clear of Covey, and of his wrathful lash, for the present. I am in the wood, buried in its somber gloom, and hushed in its solemn silence; hid from all human eyes; shut in with nature and nature's God, and absent from all human contrivances. Here was a good place to pray; to pray for help for deliverance—a prayer I had often made before. But how could I pray? Covey could pray—Capt. Auld could pray—I would fain pray; but doubts (arising partly from my own neglect of the means of grace, and partly from the sham religion which everywhere prevailed, cast in my mind a doubt upon all religion, and led me to the conviction that prayers were unavailing and delusive) prevented my embracing the opportunity, as a religious one. Life, in itself, had almost become burdensome to me. All my outward relations were against me; I must stay here and starve, (I was already hungry,) or go home to Covey's, and have my flesh torn to pieces, and my spirit humbled under the cruel lash of Covey. This was the painful alternative presented to me. The day was long and irksome. My physical condition was deplorable. I was weak, from the toils of the previous day, and from the want of food and rest; and had been so little concerned about my appearance, that I had not yet washed the blood from my garments. I was an object of horror, even to myself. Life, in Baltimore, when most oppressive, was a paradise to this. What had I done, what had my parents done, that such a life as this should be mine? That day, in the woods, I would have exchanged my manhood for the brutehood of an ox.

Night came. I was still in the woods, unresolved what to do. Hunger had not yet pinched me to the point of going home, and I laid down in the leaves to rest; for I had been watching for hunters all day, but not being molested during the day. I expected no disturbance during the night. I had come to the conclusion that Covey relied upon hunger to drive me home; and in this I was quite correct—the facts showed that he had made no effort to catch me, since morning.

During the night, I heard the step of a man in the woods. He was coming toward the place where I lay. A person lying still has the advantage over one walking in the woods, in the day time, and this advantage is much greater at night. I was not able to engage in a physical struggle, and I had recourse to the common resort of the weak. I hid myself in the leaves to prevent discovery. But, as the night rambler in the woods drew nearer, I found him to be a *friend*, not an enemy; it was a slave of Mr. William Groomes, of Easton, a kind hearted fellow, named "Sandy." Sandy lived with Mr. Kemp that year, about four miles from St. Michael's. He, like myself, had been hired out by the year; but, unlike myself, had not been hired out to be broken. Sandy was the husband of a free woman, who lived in the lower part of "*Potpie Neck,*" and he was now on his way through the woods, to see her, and to spend the Sabbath with her.

As soon as I had ascertained that the disturber of my solitude was not an enemy, but the good-hearted Sandy—a man as famous among the slaves of the neighborhood for his good nature, as for his good sense—I came out from my hiding place, and made myself known to him. I explained the circumstances of the past two days, which had driven me to the woods, and he deeply compassionated my distress. It was a bold thing for him to shelter me, and I could not ask him to do so; for, had I been found in his hut, he would have suffered the penalty of thirty-nine lashes on his bare back, if not something worse. But, Sandy was too generous to permit the fear of punishment to prevent his relieving a brother bondman from hunger and exposure; and, therefore, on his own motion, I accompanied him to his home, or rather to the home of his wife—for the house and lot were hers. His wife was called up—for it was now about midnight—a fire was made, some Indian meal was soon mixed with salt and water, and an ash cake was baked in a hurry to relieve my hunger. Sandy's wife was not behind him in kindness—both seemed to esteem it a privilege to succor me; for, although I was hated by Covey and by my master, I was loved by the colored people, because *they* thought I was hated for my knowledge, and persecuted because I was feared. I was the *only* slave *now* in that region who could read and write. There had been one other man, belonging to Mr. Hugh Hamilton, who could read, (his name was "Jim,") but he, poor fellow, had, shortly after my coming into the neighborhood, been sold off to the far south. I saw Jim ironed, in the cart, to be carried to Easton for sale,—pinioned like a yearling for the slaughter. My knowledge was now the pride of my brother slaves; and, no doubt, Sandy felt something of the general interest in me on that account. The supper was soon ready, and though I have feasted since, with honorables, lord mayors and aldermen, over the sea, my supper on ash cake and cold water, with Sandy, was the meal, of all my life, most sweet to my taste, and now most vivid in my memory.

Supper over, Sandy and I went into a discussion of what was *possible* for me, under the perils and hardships which now overshadowed my path. The question was, must I go back to Covey, or must I now attempt to run away? Upon a careful survey, the latter was found to be impossible; for I was on a narrow neck of land, every avenue from which would bring me in sight of pursuers. There was the Chesapeake bay to the right, and "Pot-pie" river to the left, and St. Michael's and its neighborhood occupying the only space through which there was any retreat.

I found Sandy an old adviser. He was not only a religious man, but he professed to believe in a system for which I have no name. He was a genuine African, and had inherited some of the so called magical powers, said to be possessed by African and eastern nations. He told me that he could help me; that, in those very woods, there was an herb, which in the morning might be found, possessing all the powers required for my protection, (I put his thoughts in my own language;) and that, if I would take his advice, he would procure me the root of the herb of which he spoke. He told me further, that if I would take that root and wear it on my right side, it would be impossible for Covey to strike me a blow; that with this root about my person, no white man could whip me. He said he had carried it for years, and that he had fully tested its virtues. He had never received a blow from a slaveholder since he carried it; and he never expected to receive one, for he always meant to carry that root as a protection. He knew Covey well, for Mrs. Covey was the daughter of Mr. Kemp; and he (Sandy) had heard of the barbarous treatment to which I was subjected, and he wanted to do something for me.

Now all this talk about the root, was, to me, very absurd and ridiculous, if not positively sinful. I at first rejected the idea that the simple carrying a root on my right side, (a root, by the way, over which I walked every time I went into the woods,) could possess any such magic power as he ascribed to it, and I was, therefore, not disposed to cumber my pocket with it. I had a positive aversion to all pretenders to "*divination*." It was beneath one of my intelligence to countenance such dealings with the devil, as this power implied. But, with all my learning—it was really precious little—Sandy was more than a match for me. "My book learning," he said, "had not kept Covey off me," (a powerful argument just then,) and he entreated me, with flashing eyes, to try this. If it did me no good, it could do me no harm, and it would cost me nothing, any way. Sandy was so earnest, and so confident of the good qualities of this weed, that, to please him, rather than from any conviction of its excellence, I was induced to take it. He had been to me the good Samaritan, and had, almost providentially, found me, and helped me when I could not help myself; how did I know but that the hand of the Lord was in it? With thoughts of this sort, I took the roots from Sandy, and put them in my right hand pocket.

This was, of course, Sunday morning. Sandy now urged me to go home, with all speed, and to walk up bravely to the house, as though nothing had happened. I saw in Sandy too deep an insight into human nature, with all his superstition, not to have some respect for his advice; and perhaps, too, a slight gleam or shadow of his superstition had fallen upon me. At any rate, I started off toward Covey's, as directed by Sandy. having, the previous night, poured my griefs into Sandy's ears, and got him enlisted in my behalf, having made his wife a sharer in my sorrows, and having, also, become well refreshed by sleep and food, I moved off, quite courageously, toward the much dreaded Covey's. Singularly enough, just as I entered his yard gate, I met him and his wife, dressed in their Sunday best—looking as smiling as angels—on their way to church. The manner of Covey astonished me. There was something really benignant in his countenance. He spoke to me as never before; told me that the pigs had got into the lot, and he wished me to drive them out; inquired how I was, and seemed an altered man. This extraordinary conduct of Covey, really made me begin to think that Sandy's herb had more virtue in it than I, in my pride, had been willing to allow; and, had the day been other than Sunday, I should have attributed Covey's altered manner solely to the magic power of the root. I suspected, however, that the *Sabbath*, and not the *root*, was the real explanation of Covey's manner. His religion hindered him from breaking the Sabbath, but not from breaking my skin. He had more respect for the *day* than for the *man*, for whom the day was mercifully given; for while he would cut and slash my body during the week, he would not hesitate, on Sunday, to teach me the value of my soul, or the way of life and salvation by Jesus Christ.

All went well with me till Monday morning; and then, whether the root had lost its virtue, or whether my tormentor had gone deeper into the black art than myself, (as was sometimes said of him,) or whether he had obtained a special indulgence, for his faithful Sabbath day's worship, it is not necessary for me to know, or to inform the reader; but, this much I *may* say,—the pious and benignant smile which graced Covey's face on *Sunday*, wholly disappeared on *Monday*. Long before daylight, I was called up to go and feed, rub, and curry the horses. I obeyed the call, and I would have so obeyed it, had it been made at an earlier hour, for I had brought my mind to a firm resolve, during that Sunday's reflection, viz: to obey every order, however unreasonable, if it were possible, and, if Mr. Covey should then undertake to beat me, to defend and protect myself to the best of my ability. My religious views on the subject of resisting my master, had suffered a serious shock, by the savage persecution to which I had been subjected, and my hands were no longer tied by my religion. Master Thomas's indifference had severed the last link. I had now to this extent "backslidden" from this point in the slave's religious creed; and I soon had occasion to make my fallen state known to my Sunday-pious brother, Covey.

Whilst I was obeying his order to feed and get the horses ready for the field, and when in the act of going up the stable loft for the purpose of throwing down some blades, Covey sneaked into the stable, in his peculiar snake-like way, and seizing me suddenly by the leg, he brought me to the stable floor, giving my newly mended body a fearful jar. I now forgot my *roots*, and remembered my pledge to *stand up in my own defense*. The brute was endeavoring skillfully to get a slipknot on my legs, before I could draw up my feet. As soon as I found what he was up to, I gave a sudden spring, (my two day's rest had been of much service to me,) and by that means, no doubt, he was able to bring me to the floor so heavily. He was defeated in his plan of tying me. While down, he seemed to think he had me very securely in his power. He little thought he was—as the rowdies say—"in" for a "rough and tumble" fight; but such was the fact. Whence came the daring spirit necessary to grapple with a man who, eight-and-forty hours before, could, with his slightest word have made me tremble like a leaf in a storm, I do not know; at any rate, *I was resolved to fight*, and, what was better still, I was actually hard at it. The fighting madness had come upon me, and I found my strong fingers firmly attached to the throat of my cowardly tormentor; as heedless of consequences, at the moment, as though we stood as equals before the law. The very color of the man was forgotten. I felt as supple as a cat, and was ready for the snakish creature at every turn. Every blow of his was parried, though I dealt no blows in turn. I was strictly on the *defensive*, preventing him from injuring me, rather than trying to injure him. I flung him on the ground several times, when he meant to have hurled me there. I held him so firmly by the throat, that his blood followed my nails. He held me, and I held him.

All was fair, thus far, and the contest was about equal. My resistance was entirely unexpected, and Covey was taken all aback by it, for he trembled in every limb. "Are *you going to resist*, you scoundrel?" said he. To which, I returned a polite "*yes sir;*" steadily gazing my interrogator in the eye, to meet the first approach or dawning of the blow, which I expected my answer would call forth. But, the conflict did not long remain thus equal. Covey soon cried out lustily for help; not that I was obtaining any marked advantage over him, or was injuring him, but because he was gaining none over me, and was not able, single handed, to conquer me. He called for his cousin Hughes, to come to his assistance, and now the scene was changed. I was compelled to give blows, as well as to parry them; and, since I was, in any case, to suffer for resistance, I felt (as the musty proverb goes) that "I might as well be hanged for an old sheep as a lamb." I was still *defensive* toward Covey, but *aggressive* toward Hughes; and, at the first approach of the latter, I dealt a blow, in my desperation, which fairly sickened my youthful assailant. He went off, bending over with pain, and manifesting no disposition to come within my reach again. The poor fellow was in the act of trying to catch and tie my right hand, and while flattering himself with success, I gave him the kick which sent him staggering away in pain, at the same time that I held Covey with a firm hand.

Taken completely by surprise, Covey seemed to have lost his usual strength and coolness. He was frightened, and stood puffing and blowing, seemingly unable to command words or blows. When he saw that poor Hughes was standing half bent with pain—his courage quite gone—the cowardly tyrant asked if I "meant to persist in my resistance." I told him "I *did mean to resist, come what might;*" that I had been by him treated like a *brute*, during the last six months; and that I should stand it *no longer*. With that, he gave me a shake, and attempted to drag me toward a stick of wood, that was lying just outside the stable door. He meant to knock me down with it; but, just as he leaned over to get the stick, I seized him with both hands by the collar, and, with a vigorous and sudden snatch, I brought my assailant harmlessly, his full length, on the *not over* clean ground—for we were now in the cow yard. He had selected the place for the fight, and it was but right that he should have all the advantages of his own selection.

By this time, Bill, the hired man, came home. He had been to Mr. Hemsley's, to spend the Sunday with his nominal wife, and was coming home on Monday morning, to go to work. Covey and I had been skirmishing from before daybreak, till now, that the sun was almost shooting his beams over the eastern woods, and we were still at it. I could not see where the matter was to terminate. He evidently was afraid to let me go, lest I should again make off to the woods; otherwise, he would probably have obtained arms from the house, to frighten me. Holding me, Covey called upon Bill for assistance. The scene here, had something comic about it. "Bill," who knew *precisely* what Covey wished him to do, affected ignorance, and pretended he did not know what to do. "What shall I do, Mr. Covey," said Bill. "Take hold of him—take hold of him!" said Covey. With a toss of his head, peculiar to Bill, he said, "indeed, Mr. Covey, I want to go to work." "*This is* your work," said Covey; "take hold of him." Bill replied, with spirit, "My master hired me here, to work, and *not* to help you whip Frederick." It was now my turn to speak. "Bill," said I, "don't put your hands on me." To which he replied, "MY GOD! Frederick, I ain't goin' to tech ye," and Bill walked off, leaving Covey and myself to settle our matters as best we might.

But, my present advantage was threatened when I saw Caroline (the slave-woman of Covey) coming to the cow yard to milk, for she was a powerful woman, and could have mastered me very easily, exhausted as I now was. As soon as she came into the yard, Covey attempted to rally her to his aid. Strangely—and, I may add, fortunately—Caroline was in no humor to take a hand in any such sport. We were all in open rebellion, that morning. Caroline answered the command of her master to "*take hold of me,*" precisely as Bill had answered, but in *her*, it was at greater peril so to answer; she was the slave of Covey, and he could do what he pleased with her. It was *not* so with Bill, and Bill knew it. Samuel Harris, to whom Bill belonged, did not allow his slaves to be beaten, unless they were guilty of some crime which the law would punish. But, poor Caroline, like myself, was at the mercy of the merciless Covey; nor did she escape the dire effects of her refusal. He gave her several sharp blows.

Covey at length (two hours had elapsed) gave up the contest. Letting me go, he said,—puffing and blowing at a great rate—"now, you scoundrel, go to your work; I would not have whipped you half so much as I have had you not resisted." The fact was, *he had not whipped me at all.* He had not, in all the scuffle, drawn a single drop of blood from me. I had drawn blood from him; and, even without this satisfaction, I should have been victorious, because my aim had not been to injure him, but to prevent his injuring me.

During the whole six months that I lived with Covey, after this transaction, he never laid on me the weight of his finger in anger. He would, occasionally, say he did not want to have to get hold of me again—a declaration which I had no difficulty in believing; and I had a secret feeling, which answered, "you need not wish to get hold of me again, for you will be likely to come off worse in a second fight than you did in the first."

Well, my dear reader, this battle with Mr. Covey,—undignified as it was, and as I fear my narration of it is—was the turning point in my *"life as a slave."* It rekindled in my breast the smouldering embers of liberty; it brought up my Baltimore dreams, and revived a sense of my own manhood. I was a changed being after that fight. I was *nothing* before: I WAS A MAN NOW. It recalled to life my crushed self-respect and my self-confidence, and inspired me with a renewed determination to be A FREEMAN. A man, without force, is without the essential dignity of humanity. Human nature is so constituted, that it cannot *honor* a helpless man, although it can *pity* him; and even this it cannot do long, if the signs of power do not arise.

He only can understand the effect of this combat on my spirit, who has himself incurred something, hazarded something, in repelling the unjust and cruel aggressions of a tyrant. Covey was a tyrant, and a cowardly one, withal. After resisting him, I felt as I had never felt before. It was a resurrection from the dark and pestiferous tomb of slavery, to the heaven of comparative freedom. I was no longer a servile coward, trembling under the frown of a brother worm of the dust, but, my long-cowed spirit was roused to an attitude of manly independence. I had reached the point, at which I was *not afraid to die.* This spirit made me a freeman in *fact*, while I remained a slave in *form*. When a slave cannot be flogged he is more than half free. He has a domain as broad as his own manly heart to defend, and he is really *"a power on earth."* While slaves prefer their lives, with flogging, to instant death, they will always find christians enough, like unto Covey, to accommodate that preference. From this time, until that of my escape from slavery, I was never fairly whipped. Several attempts were made to whip me, but they were always unsuccessful. Bruises I did get, as I shall hereafter inform the reader; but the case I have been describing, was the end of the brutification to which slavery had subjected me.

The reader will be glad to know why, after I had so grievously offended Mr. Covey, he did not have me taken in hand by the authorities; indeed, why the law of Maryland, which assigns hanging to the slave who resists his master, was not put in force against me; at any rate, why I was not taken up, as is usual in such cases, and publicly whipped, for an example to other slaves, and as a means of deterring me from committing the same offense again. I confess, that the easy manner in which I got off, was, for a long time, a surprise to me, and I cannot, even now, fully explain the cause.

The only explanation I can venture to suggest, is the fact, that Covey was, probably, ashamed to have it known and confessed that he had been mastered by a boy of sixteen. Mr. Covey enjoyed the unbounded and very valuable reputation, of being a first rate overseer and *negro breaker*. By means of this reputation, he was able to procure his hands for *very trifling* compensation, and with very great ease. His interest and his pride mutually suggested the wisdom of passing the matter by, in silence. The story that he had undertaken to whip a lad, and had been resisted, was, of itself, sufficient to damage him; for his bearing should, in the estimation of slaveholders, be of that imperial order that should make such an occurrence *impossible*. I judge from these circumstances, that Covey deemed it best to give me the go-by. It is, perhaps, not altogether creditable to my natural temper, that, after this conflict with Mr. Covey, I did, at times, purposely aim to provoke him to an attack, by refusing to keep with the other hands in the field, but I could never bully him to another battle. I had made up my mind to do him serious damage, if he ever again attempted to lay violent hands on me.

"Hereditary bondmen, know ye not
Who would be free, themselves must strike the blow?"

Sojourner Truth
Address to the Ohio Women's Rights Convention

AR'N'T I A WOMAN?
SPEECH TO THE WOMEN'S RIGHTS CONVENTION
IN AKRON, OHIO, 1851

From The Anti-Slavery Bugle, June 21, 1851

One of the most unique and interesting speeches of the Convention was made by Sojourner Truth, an emancipated slave. It is impossible to transfer it to paper, or convey any adequate idea of the effect it produced upon the audience. Those only can appreciate it who saw her powerful form, her whole-souled, earnest gesture, and listened to her strong and truthful tones. She came forward to the platform and addressing the President said with great simplicity: "May I say a few words?" Receiving an affirmative answer, she proceeded:

I want to say a few words about this matter. I am a woman's rights. I have as much muscle as any man, and can do as much work as any man. I have plowed and reaped and husked and chopped and mowed, and can any man do more than that? I have heard much about the sexes being equal. I can carry as much as any man, and can eat as much too, if I can get it. I am as strong as any man that is now. As for intellect, all I can say is, if woman have a pint, and man a quart—why can't she have her little pint full? You need not be afraid to give us our rights for fear we will take too much,—for we can't take more than our pint'll hold. The poor men seem to be all in confusion, and don't know what to do. Why children, if you have woman's rights, give it to her and you will feel better. You will have your own rights, and they won't be so much trouble. I can't read, but I can hear. I have heard the bible and have learned that Eve caused man to sin. Well, if woman upset the world, do give her a chance to set it right side up again. The Lady has spoken about Jesus, how he never spurned woman from him, and she was right. When Lazarus died, Mary and Martha came to him with faith and love and besought him to raise their brother. And Jesus wept and Lazarus came forth. And how came Jesus into the world? Through God who created him and a woman who bore him. Man, where is your part? But the women are coming up blessed be God and a few of the men are coming up with them. But man is in a tight place, the poor slave is on him, woman is coming on him, he is surely between a hawk and a buzzard.

Martin R. Delaney

from *The Condition, Elevation, and Destiny of the Colored People of the United States, Politically Considered*

CHAPTER II.

Comparative Condition of the Colored People of the United States.

THE United States, untrue to her trust and unfaithful to her professed principles of republican equality, has also pursued a policy of political degradation to a large portion of her native born countrymen, and that class is the Colored People. Denied an equality not only of political, but of natural rights, in common with the rest of our fellow citizens, there is no species of degradation to which we are not subject.

Reduced to abject slavery is not enough, the very thought of which should awaken every sensibility of our common nature; but those of their descendants who are freemen even in the non-slaveholding States, occupy the very same position politically, religiously, civilly and socially, (with but few exceptions,) as the bondman occupies in the slave States.

In those States, the bondman is disfranchised, and for the most part so are we. He is denied all civil, religious, and social privileges, except such as he gets by mere sufferance, and so are we. They have no part nor lot in the government of the country, neither have we. They are ruled and governed without representation, existing as mere nonentities among the citizens, and excrescences on the body politic—a mere dreg in community, and so are we. Where then is our political superiority to the enslaved? none, neither are we superior in any other relation to society, except that we are defacto masters of ourselves and joint rulers of our own domestic household, while the bondman's self is claimed by another, and his relation to his family denied him. What the unfortunate classes are in Europe, such are we in the United States, which is folly to deny, insanity not to understand, blindness not to see, and surely now full time that our eyes were opened to these startling truths, which for ages have stared us full in the face.

It is time that we had become politicians, we mean, to understand the political economy and domestic policy of nations; that we had become as well as moral theorists, also the practical demonstrators of equal rights and self-government. Except we do, it is idle to talk about rights, it is mere chattering for the sake of being seen and heard—like the slave, saying something because his so called "master" said it, and saying just what he told him to say. Have we not now sufficient intelligence among us to understand our true position, to realise our actual condition, and determine for ourselves what is best to be done? If we have not now, we never shall have, and should at once cease prating about our equality, capacity, and all that.

Twenty years ago, when the writer was a youth, his young and yet uncultivated mind was aroused, and his tender heart made to leap with anxiety in anticipation of the promises then held out by the prime movers in the cause of our elevation.

In 1830 the most intelligent and leading spirits among the colored men in the United States, such as James Forten, Robert Douglass, I. Bowers, A. D. Shadd, John Peck, Joseph Cassey, and John B. Vashon of Pennsylvania; John T. Hilton, Nathaniel and Thomas Paul, and James G. Barbodoes of Massachusetts; Henry Sipkins, Thomas Hamilton, Thomas L. Jennings, Thomas Downing, Samuel E. Cornish, and others of New York; R. Cooley and others of Maryland, and representatives from other States which cannot now be recollected, the data not being at hand, assembled in the city of Philadelphia, in the capacity of a National Convention, to "devise ways and means for the bettering of our condition." These Conventions determined to assemble annually, much talent, ability, and energy of character being displayed; when in 1831 at a sitting of the Convention in September, from their previous pamphlet reports, much interest having been created throughout the country, they were favored by the presence of a number of whites, some of whom were able and distinguished men, such as Rev. R. R. Gurley, Arthur Tappan, Elliot Cresson, John Rankin, Simeon Jocelyn and others, among them William Lloyd Garrison, then quite a young man, all of whom were staunch and ardent Colonizationists, young Garrison at that time, doing his mightiest in his favorite work.

Among other great projects of interest brought before the convention at a previous sitting, was that of the expediency of a general emigration, as far as it was practicable, of the colored people to the British Provinces of North America. Another was that of raising sufficient means for the establishment and erection of a College for the proper education of the colored youth. These gentlemen long accustomed to observation and reflection on the condition of their people, saw at once, that there must necessarily be means used adequate to the end to be attained—that end being an unqualified equality with the ruling class of their fellow citizens. He saw that as a class, the colored people of the country were ignorant, degraded and oppressed, by far the greater portion of them being abject slaves in the South, the very condition of whom was almost enough, under the circumstances, to blast the remotest hope of success, and those who were freemen, whether in the South or North, occupied a subservient, servile, and menial position, considering it a favor to get into the service of the whites, and do their degrading offices. That the difference between the whites and themselves, consisted in the superior advantages of the one over the other, in point of attainments. That if a knowledge of the arts and sciences, the mechanical occupations, the industrial occupations, as farming, commerce, and all the various business enterprises, and learned professions were necessary for the superior position occupied by their rulers, it was also necessary for them. And very reasonably too, the first suggestion which occurred to them was, the advantages of a location, then the necessity of a qualification. They reasoned with themselves, that all distinctive differences made among men on account of their origin, is wicked, unrighteous, and cruel, and never shall receive countenance in any shape from us, therefore, the first acts of the measures entered into by them, was to protest, solemnly protest, against every unjust measure and policy in the country, having for its object the proscription of the colored people, whether state, national, municipal, social, civil, or religious.

But being far-sighted, reflecting, discerning men, they took a political view of the subject, and determined for the good of their people to be governed in their policy according to the facts as they presented themselves. In taking a glance at Europe, they discovered there, however unjustly, as we have shown in another part of this pamphlet, that there are and have been numerous classes proscribed and oppressed, and it was not for them to cut short their wise deliberations, and arrest their proceedings in contention, as to the cause, whether on account of language, the color of eyes, hair, skin, or their origin of country—because all this is contrary to reason, a contradiction to common sense, at war with nature herself, and at variance with facts as they stare us every day in the face, among all nations, in every country—this being made the pretext as a matter of *policy* alone—a fact worthy of observation, that wherever the objects of oppression are the most easily distinguished by any peculiar or general characteristics, these people are the more easily oppressed, because the war of oppression is the more easily waged against them. This is the case with the modern Jews and many other people who have strongly-marked, peculiar, or distinguishing characteristics. This arises in this wise. The policy of all those who proscribe any people, induces them to select as the objects of proscription, those who differed as much as possible, in some particulars, from themselves. This is to ensure the greater success, because it engenders the greater prejudice, or in other words, elicits less interest on the part of the oppressing class, in their favor. This fact is well understood in national conflicts, as the soldier or civilian, who is distinguished by his dress, mustache, or any other peculiar appendage, would certainly prove himself a madman, if he did not take the precaution to change his dress, remove his mustache, and conceal as much as possible his peculiar characteristics, to give him access among the repelling party. This is mere policy, nature having nothing to do with it. Still, it is a fact, a great truth well worthy of remark, and as such we adduce it for the benefit of those of our readers, unaccustomed to an enquiry into the policy of nations.

In view of these truths, our fathers and leaders in our elevation, discovered that as a policy, we the colored people were selected as the subordinate class in this country, not on account of any actual or supposed inferiority on their part, but simply because, in view of all the circumstances of the case, they were the very best class that could be selected. They would have as readily had any other class as subordinates in the country, as the colored people, but the condition of society *at the time*, would not admit of it. In the struggle for American Independence, there were among those who performed the most distinguished parts, the most common-place peasantry of the Provinces. English, Danish, Irish, Scotch, and others, were among those whose names blazoned forth as heroes in the American Revolution. But a single reflection will convince us, that no course of policy could have induced the proscription of the parentage and relatives of such men as Benjamin Franklin the printer, Roger Sherman the cobbler, the tinkers, and others of the signers of the Declaration of Independence. But as they were determined to have a subservient class, it will readily be conceived, that according to the state of society at the time, the better policy on their part was, to select some class, who from their political position—however much they may have contributed their aid as we certainly did, in the general struggle for liberty by force of arms—who had the least claims upon them, or who had the *least chance*, or was the *least potent* in urging their claims. This class of course was the colored people and Indians.

The Indians who in the early settlement of the continent, before an African captive had ever been introduced thereon, were reduced to the most abject slavery, toiling day and night in the mines, under the relentless hands of heartless Spanish taskmasters, but being a race of people raised to the sports of fishing, the chase, and of war, were wholly unaccustomed to labor, and therefore sunk under the insupportable weight, two millions and a half having fallen victims to the cruelty of oppression and toil suddenly placed upon their shoulders. And it was only this that prevented their farther enslavement as a class, after the provinces were absolved from the British Crown. It is true that their general enslavement took place on the islands and in the mining districts of South America, where indeed, the Europeans continued to enslave them, until a comparatively recent period; still, the design, the feeling, and inclination from policy, was the same to do so here, in this section of the continent.

Nor was it until their influence became too great, by the political position occupied by their brethren in the new republic, that the German and Irish peasantry ceased to be sold as slaves for a term of years fixed by law, for the repayment of their passage-money, the descendants of these classes of people for a long time being held as inferiors, in the estimation of the ruling class, and it was not until they assumed the rights and privileges guaranteed to them by the established policy of the country, among the leading spirits of whom were their relatives, that the policy towards them was discovered to be a bad one, and accordingly changed. Nor was it, as is frequently very erroneously asserted, by colored as well as white persons, that it was on account of hatred to the African, or in other words, on account of hatred to his color, that the African was selected as the subject of oppression in this country. This is sheer nonsense; being based on policy and nothing else, as shown in another place. The Indians, who being the most foreign to the sympathies of the Europeans on this continent, were selected in the first place, who, being unable to withstand the hardships, gave way before them.

But the African race had long been known to Europeans, in all ages of the world's history, as a long-lived, hardy race, subject to toil and labor of various kinds, subsisting mainly by traffic, trade, and industry, and consequently being as foreign to the sympathies of the invaders of the continent as the Indians, they were selected, captured, brought here as a laboring class, and as a matter of policy held as such. Nor was the absurd idea of natural inferiority of the African ever dreamed of, until recently adduced by the slave-holders and their abettors, in justification of their policy. This, with contemptuous indignation, we fling back into their face, as a scorpion to a vulture. And so did our patriots and leaders in the cause of regeneration know better, and never for a moment yielded to the base doctrine. But they had discovered the great fact, that a cruel policy was pursued towards our people, and that they possessed distinctive characteristics which made them the objects of proscription. These characteristics being strongly marked in the colored people, as in the Indians, by color, character of hair and so on, made them the more easily distinguished from other Americans, and the policies more effectually urged against us. For this reason they introduced the subject of emigration to Canada, and a proper institution for the education of the youth.

At this important juncture of their proceedings, the afore named white gentlemen were introduced to the notice of the Convention, and after gaining permission to speak, expressed their gratification and surprise at the qualification and talent manifested by different members of the Convention, all expressing their determination to give the cause of the colored people more serious reflection. Mr. Garrison, the youngest of them all, and none the less honest on account of his youthfulness, being but 26 years of age at the time, (1831) expressed his determination to change his course of policy at once, and espouse the cause of the elevation of the colored people here in their own country. We are not at present well advised upon this point, it now having escaped our memory, but we are under the impression that Mr. Jocelyn also, at once changed his policy.

During the winter of 1832, Mr. Garrison issued his "Thoughts on African Colonization," and near about the same time or shortly after, issued the first number of the "Liberator," in both of which, his full convictions of the enormity of American slavery, and the wickedness of their policy towards the colored people, were fully expressed. At the sitting of the Convention in this year, a number, perhaps all of these gentlemen were present, and those who had denounced the Colonization scheme, and espoused the cause of the elevation of the colored people in this country, or the Anti Slavery cause, as it was now termed, expressed themselves openly and without reserve.

Sensible of the high-handed injustice done to the colored people in the United States, and the mischief likely to emanate from the unchristian proceedings of the deceptious Colonization scheme, like all honest hearted penitents, with the ardor only known to new converts, they entreated the Convention, whatever they did, not to entertain for a moment, the idea of recommending emigration to their people, nor the establishment of separate institutions of learning. They earnestly contended, and doubtless honestly meaning what they said, that they (the whites) had been our oppressors and injurers, they had obstructed our progress to the high positions of civilization, and now, it was their bounden duty to make full amends for the injuries thus inflicted on an unoffending people. They exhorted the Convention to cease; as they had laid on the burden, they would also take it off; as they had obstructed our pathway, they would remove the hindrance. In a word, as they had oppressed and trampled down the colored people, they would now elevate them. These suggestions and promises, good enough to be sure, after they were made, were accepted by the Convention—though some gentlemen were still in favor of the first project as the best policy, Mr. A. D. Shadd of West Chester, Pa., as we learn from himself, being one among that number—ran through the country like wild-fire, no one thinking, and if he thought, daring to speak above his breath of going any where out of certain prescribed limits, or of sending a child to school, if it should but have the name of "colored" attached to it, without the risk of being termed a "traitor" to the cause of his people, or an enemy to the Anti Slavery cause.

At this important point in the history of our efforts, the colored men stopped suddenly, and with their hands thrust deep in their breeches-pockets, and their mouths gaping open, stood gazing with astonishment, wonder, and surprise, at the stupendous moral colossal statues of our Anti-Slavery friends and brethren, who in the heat and zeal of honest hearts, from a desire to make atonement for the many wrongs inflicted, promised a great deal more than they have ever been able half to fulfill, in thrice the period in which they expected it. And in this, we have no fault to find with our Anti-Slavery friends, and here wish it to be understood, that we are not laying any thing to their charge as blame, neither do we desire for a moment to reflect on them, because we heartily believe that all that they did at the time, they did with the purest and best of motives, and further believe that they now are, as they then were, the truest friends we have among the whites in this country. And hope, and desire, and request, that our people should always look upon *true* anti-slavery people, Abolitionists we mean, as their friends, until they have just cause for acting otherwise. It is true, that the Anti-Slavery, like all good causes, has produced some recreants, but the cause itself is no more to be blamed for that, than Christianity is for the malconduct of any professing hypocrite, nor the society of Friends, for the conduct of a broad-brimmed hat and shad-belly coated horse-thief, because he spoke *thee* and *thou* before stealing the horse. But what is our condition even amidst our Anti-Slavery friends? And here, as our sole intention is to contribute to the elevation of our people, we must be permitted to express our opinion freely, without being thought uncharitable.

In the first place, we should look at the objects for which the Anti-Slavery cause was commenced, and the promises or inducements it held out at the commencement. It should be borne in mind, that Anti-Slavery took its rise among *colored men*, just at the time they were introducing their greatest projects for their own elevation, and that our Anti-Slavery brethren were converts of the colored men, in behalf of their elevation. Of course, it would be expected that being baptized into the new doctrines, their faith would induce them to embrace the principles therein contained, with the strictest possible adherence.

The cause of dissatisfaction with our former condition, was, that we were proscribed, debarred, and shut out from every respectable position, occupying the places of inferiors and menials.

It was expected that Anti-Slavery, according to its professions, would extend to colored persons, as far as in the power of its adherents, those advantages nowhere else to be obtained among white men. That colored boys would get situations in their shops and stores, and every other advantage tending to elevate them as far as possible, would be extended to them. At least, it was expected, that in Anti-Slavery establishments, colored men would have the preference. Because, there was no other ostensible object in view, in the commencement of the Anti-Slavery enterprise, than the *elevation* of the *colored man*, by facilitating his efforts in attaining to equality with the white man. It was urged, and it was true, that the colored people were susceptible of all that the whites were, and all that was required was to give them a fair opportunity, and they would prove their capacity. That it was unjust, wicked, and cruel, the result of an unnatural prejudice, that debarred them from places of respectability, and that public opinion could and should be corrected upon this subject. That it was only necessary to make a sacrifice of feeling, and an innovation on the customs of society, to establish a different order of things,—that as Anti-Slavery men, they were willing to make these sacrifices, and determined to take the colored man by the hand, making common cause with him in affliction, and bear a part of the odium heaped upon him. That his cause was the cause of God—that "In as much as ye did it not unto the least of these my little ones, ye did it not unto me," and that as Anti-Slavery men, they would "do right if the heavens fell." Thus, was the cause espoused, and thus did we expect much. But in all this, we were doomed to disappointment, sad, sad disappointment. Instead of realising what we had hoped for, we find ourselves occupying the very same position in relation to our Anti-Slavery friends, as we do in relation to the pro-slavery part of the community—a mere secondary, underling position, in all our relations to them, and any thing more than this, is not a matter of course affair—it comes not by established anti-slavery custom or right, but like that which emanates from the proslavery portion of the community, by mere sufferance.

It is true, that the "Liberator" office, in Boston, has got Elijah Smith, a colored youth, at the cases—the "Standard," in New York, a young colored man, and the "Freeman," in Philadelphia, William Still, another, in the publication office, as "packing clerk;" yet these are but three out of the hosts that fill these offices in their various departments, all occupying places that could have been, and as we once thought, would have been, easily enough, occupied by colored men. Indeed, we can have no other idea about anti-slavery in this country, than that the legitimate persons to fill any and every position about an anti-slavery establishment are colored persons. Nor will it do to argue in extenuation, that white men are as justly entitled to them as colored men; because white men do not from *necessity* become anti-slavery men in order to get situations; they being white men, may occupy any position they are capable of filling—in a word, their chances are endless, every avenue in the country being opened to them. They do not therefore become abolitionists, for the sake of employment—at least, it is not the song that anti-slavery sung, in the first love of the new faith, proclaimed by its disciples.

And if it be urged that colored men are incapable as yet to fill these positions, all that we have to say is, that the cause has fallen far short; almost equivalent to a failure, of a tithe, of what it promised to do in half the period of its existence, to this time, if it have not as yet, now a period of twenty years, raised up colored men enough, to fill the offices within its patronage. We think it is not unkind to say, if it had been half as faithful to itself, as it should have been—its professed principles we mean; it could have reared and tutored from childhood, colored men enough by this time, for its own especial purpose. These we know could have been easily obtained, because colored people in general, are favorable to the anti-slavery cause, and wherever there is an adverse manifestation, it arises from sheer ignorance; and we have now but comparatively few such among us. There is one thing certain, that no colored person, except such as would reject education altogether, would be adverse to putting their child with an anti-slavery person, for educational advantages. This then, could have been done. But it has not been done, and let the cause of it be whatever it may, and let whoever may be to blame, we are willing to let all that pass, and extend to our anti-slavery brethren the right-hand of fellowship, bidding them God-speed in the propagation of good and wholesome sentiments—for whether they are practically carried out or not, the professions are in themselves all right and good. Like Christianity, the principles are holy and of divine origin. And we believe, if ever a man started right, with pure and holy motives, Mr. Garrison did; and that, had he the power of making the cause what it should be, it would all be right, and there never would have been any cause for the remarks we have made, though in kindness, and with the purest of motives. We are nevertheless, still occupying a miserable position in the community, wherever we live; and what we most desire is, to draw the attention of our people to this fact, and point out what, in our opinion, we conceive to be a proper remedy.

CHAPTER VI.

The United States Our Country.

OUR common country is the United States. Here were we born, here raised and educated; here are the scenes of childhood; the pleasant associations of our school going days; the loved enjoyments of our domestic and fireside relations, and the sacred graves of our departed fathers and mothers, and from here will we not be driven by any policy that may be schemed against us.

We are Americans, having a birthright citizenship—natural claims upon the country—claims common to all others of our fellow citizens—natural rights, which may, by virtue of unjust laws, be obstructed, but never can be annulled. Upon these do we place ourselves, as immovably fixed as the decrees of the living God. But according to the economy that regulates the policy of nations, upon which rests the basis of justifiable claims to all freemen's rights, it may be necessary to take another view of, and enquire into the political claims of colored men.

CHAPTER VII.

Claims of Colored Men as Citizens of the United States.

THE political basis upon which rests the establishment of all free nations, as the first act in their organization, is the security by constitutional provisions, of the fundamental claims of citizenship.

The legitimate requirement, politically considered, necessary to the justifiable claims for protection and full enjoyment of all the rights and privileges of an unqualified freeman, in all democratic countries is, that each person so endowed shall have made contributions and investments in the country. Where there is no investment there can be but little interest; hence an adopted citizen is required to reside a sufficient length of time, to form an attachment and establish some interest in the country of his adoption, before he can rightfully lay any claims to citizenship. The pioneer who leads in the discovery or settlement of a country, as the first act to establish a right therein, erects a building of whatever dimensions, and seizes upon a portion of the soil. The soldier, who braves the dangers of the battle-field, in defence of his country's rights, and the toiling laborer and husband-man, who cuts down and removes the forest, levels and constructs post-roads and other public highways—the mechanic, who constructs and builds up houses, villages, towns, and cities, for the conveniency of inhabitants—the farmer, who cultivates the soil for the production of bread-stuffs and forage, as food and feed for man and beast—all of these are among the first people of a democratic state, whose claims are legitimate as freemen of the commonwealth. A freeman in a political sense, is a citizen of unrestricted rights in the state, being eligible to the highest position known to their civil code. They are the preferred persons in whom may be invested the highest privileges, and to whom may be entrusted fundamentally the most sacred rights of the country; because, having made the greatest investments, they necessarily have the greatest interests; and consequently, are the safest hands into which to place so high and sacred a trust. Their interest being the country's, and the interest of the country being the interest of the people; therefore, the protection of their own interests necessarily protects the interests of the whole country and people. It is this simple but great principle of primitive rights, that forms the fundamental basis of citizenship in all free countries, and it is upon this principle, that the rights of the colored man in this country to citizenship are fixed.

The object of this volume is, to enlighten the minds of a large class of readers upon a subject with which they are unacquainted, expressed in comprehensible language, therefore we have studiously avoided using political and legal phrases, that would serve more to perplex than inform them. To talk about the barons, king John, and the Magna Charta, would be foreign to a work like this, and only destroy the interest that otherwise might be elicited in the subject. Our desire is, to arrest the attention of the American people in general, and the colored people in particular, to great truths as heretofore but little thought of. What claims then have colored men, based upon the principles set forth, as fundamentally entitled to citizenship? Let the living records of history answer the enquiry.

When Christopher Columbus, in 1492, discovered America, natives were found to pay little or no attention to cultivation, being accustomed by hereditary pursuit, to war, fishing, and the sports of the chase. The Spaniards and Portuguese, as well as other Europeans who ventured here, came as mineral speculators, and not for the purpose of improving the country.

As the first objects of speculation are the developments of the mineral wealth of every newly discovered country, so was it with this. Those who came to the new world, were not of the common people, seeking in a distant land the means of livelihood, but moneyed capitalists, the grandees and nobles, who reduced the natives to servitude by confining them to the mines. To have brought large numbers of the peasantry at that early period, from the monarchies of Europe, to the wilds of America, far distant from the civil and military powers of the home governments, would have been to place the means of self-control into their own hands, and invite them to rebellion against the crowns. The capitalist miners were few, compared to the number of laborers required; and the difficulty at that time of the transportation of suitable provisions for their sustenance, conduced much to the objection of bringing them here. The natives were numerous, then easily approached by the wily seductions of the Europeans, easily yoked and supported, having the means of sustenance at hand, the wild fruits and game of the forest, the fish of the waters and birds of the country. All these as naturally enough, European adventurers would be cautious against introducing into common use among hundreds of thousands of laborers, under all the influences incident to a foreign climate in a foreign country, in its primitive natural state. The Indians were then preferred for many reasons, as the common laborers on the continent, where nothing but the minning interests were thought of or carried on. This noble race of Aborigines, continued as the common slaves of the new world, to bear the yoke of foreign oppression, until necessity induced a substitute for them. They sunk by scores under the heavy weight of oppression, and were fast passing from the shores of time. At this, the foreigners grew alarmed, and of necessity, devised ways and means to obtain an adequate substitute. A few European laborers were brought into the country, but the influence of climate and mode of living, operated entirely against them. They were as inadequate to stand the climate, as the nobles were themselves.

From the earliest period of the history of nations, the African race had been known as an industrious people, cultivators of the soil. The grain fields of Ethiopia and Egypt were the themes of the poet, and their garners, the subject of the historian. Like the present America, all the world went to Africa, to get a supply of commodities. Their massive piles of masonry, their skilful architecture, their subterranean vaults, their deep and mysterious wells, their extensive artificial channels, their mighty sculptured solid rocks, and provinces of stone quarries; gave indisputable evidence, of the hardihood of that race of people.

Nor was Africa then, without the evidence of industry, as history will testify. All travelers who had penetrated towards the interior of the continent, have been surprised at the seeming state of civilization and evidences of industry among the inhabitants of that vast country. These facts were familiar to Europeans, who were continually trading on coast of Africa, as it was then the most important parts of adventure and research, known to the world. In later periods still, the history of African travelers, confirm all the former accounts concerning the industry of the people.

John and Richard Lander, two young English noblemen, in 1828, under the patronage of the English government, sailed to the western coast of Africa, on an expedition of research. In their voyage up the river Niger, their description of the scenes is extravagant. They represent the country on each side of the river, for several hundred miles up the valley, as being not only beautiful and picturesque, but the fields as in a high state of cultivation, clothed in the verdure of husbandry, waving before the gentle breezes, with the rich products of industry—maize, oats, rye, millet, and wheat, being among the fruits of cultivation. The fences were of various descriptions: hedge, wicker, some few pannel, and the old fashioned zig-zag, known as the "Virginia worm fence"—the hedge and worm fence being the most common. Their cattle were fine and in good order, looking in every particular, except perhaps in size, as well as European cattle on the best managed farms. The fruit groves were delightful to the eye of the beholder. Every variety common to the country, were there to be seen in a high state of cultivation. Their roads and public highways were in good condition, and well laid out, as by the direction of skillful supervising surveyors. The villages, towns, and cities, many of them, being a credit to the people. Their cities were well laid out, and presented evidence of educated minds and mechanical ingenuity. In many of the workshops in which they went, they found skillful workmen, in iron, copper, brass, steel, and gold; and their implements of husbandry and war, were as well manufactured by African sons of toil, as any in the English manufactories, save that they had not quite so fine a finish, garnish and embellishment. This is a description, given of the industry and adaptedness of the people of Africa, to labor and toil of every kind. As it was very evident, that where there were manufactories of various metals, the people must of necessity be inured to mining operations, so it was also very evident, that this people must be a very hardy and enduring people.

In 1442, fifty years previous to the sailing of Columbus in search of a new world, Anthony Gonzales, Portuguese, took from the gold coast of Guinea, ten Africans and a quantity of gold dust, which he carried back to Lisbon with him. These Africans were set immediately to work in the gardens of the emperor, which so pleased his queen, that the number were much augmented, all of whom were found to be skillful and industrious in agriculture.

In 1481, eleven years prior to the discovery by Columbus, the Portuguese built a fort on the Gold Coast, and there commenced mining in search of gold. During this time until the year 1502, a period of ten years, had there been no other evidence, there was sufficient time and opportunity, to give full practical demonstrations of the capacity of this people to endure toil, especially in the mining operations, and for this cause and this alone, were they selected in preference to any other race of men, to do the labor of the New World. They had proven themselves physically superior either to the European or American races—in fact, superior physically to any living race of men—enduring fatigue, hunger and thirst—enduring change of climate, habits, manners and customs, with infinitely far less injury to their physical and mental system, than any other people on the face of God's earth.

The following extract shows, that even up to the year 1676, the Indians were enslaved—but that little value were attached to them as laborers, as the price at which they were disposed and sold to purchasers, fully shows:

SLAVERY IN PROVIDENCE, R. I.—Immediately after the struggle between the natives and some of the New England settlers, known as "King Philip's war," it became necessary to dispose of certain Indian captives then in Providence. The method adopted was common in that day, but to us remarkable, as also the names of those who figured prominently therein. Only think of ROGER WILLIAMS sharing in the proceeds of a slave sale. The following is from the "Annals of Providence."

"A town meeting was held before Thomas Field's house, under a tree, by the water side, on the 14th of August, 1676. A committee was appointed to determine in what manner the Indians should be disposed of. They reported as follows:

"Inhabitants wanting, can have Indians at the price they sell at the Island of Rhode Island or elsewhere. All under five, to serve till thirty; above five and under ten, till twenty-eight; above ten to fifteen, till twenty-seven; above fifteen to twenty, till twenty-six; from twenty to thirty, shall serve eight years; all above thirty, seven years.

"We whose names are underwritten, being chosen by the town to see to the disposal of the Indians now in town, we agree that Roger Williams, N. Waterman, T. Fenner, H. Ashton, J. Morey, D. Abbot, J. Olney, V. Whitman, J. Whipple, sen., E. Pray, J. Pray, J. Angell, Jas. Angell, T. Arnold, A. Man, T. Field, E. Bennett, T. Clemence, W. Lancaster, W. Hopkins, W. Hawkins, W. Harris, Z. Field, S. Winsor, and Capt. Fenner, shall each have a whole share in the product. I Woodward and R. Pray, three-fourths of a share each. J. Smith, E. Smith, S. Whipple, N. Whipple and T. Walling each half a share."

Signed, "Roger Williams, Thomas Harris, sen., Thomas [X] Angell, Thomas Field, John Whipple, Jr."

To gratify curiosity as to the price of Indians on those terms, the following extracts are made from an account of sales about this time;

"To Anthony Low, five Indians, great and small, £8.

"To James Rogers, two, for twenty bushels of Indian corn.

"To Philip Smith, two, in silver, $4 10.

"To Daniel Allen, one, in silver, $2 10.

"To C. Carr, one, twelve bushels of Indian corn.

"To Elisha Smith, one, in wool, 100 lbs.

"To   "   "   one, for three fat sheep."

From 1492, the discovery of Hispaniola, to 1502, the short space of but four years, such was the mortality among the natives, that the Spaniards then holding rule there, "began to employ a few" Africans in the mines of the Island. The experiment was effective—a successful one. The Indian and African were enslaved together, when the Indian sunk, and the African stood. It was not until June the 24th of the year 1498, that the Continent was discovered by John Cabot, a Venitian, who sailed in August of the previous year 1497, from Bristol, under the patronage of Henry VII., King of England, with two vessels "freighted by the merchants of London and Bristol, with articles of traffic," his son Sebastian, and 300 men. In 1517, but the short period of thirteen years from the date of their first introduction, Carolus V., King of Spain, by the right of a patent, granted permission to a number of persons, annually, to supply to the Islands of Hispaniola, (St. Domingo,) Cuba, Jamaica, and Porto Rico, natives of Africa, to the number of four thousand annually. John Hawkins, an unprincipled Englishman—whose name should be branded with infamy—was the first person known to have engaged in so inhuman a traffic, and that living monster his mistress, Queen Elizabeth, engaged with him and shared in the profits.

The natives of Africa, on their introduction into a foreign country, soon discovered the loss of their accustomed food, and mode and manner of living. The Aborigines subsisted mainly by game and fish, with a few patches of maize or Indian corn near their wigwams, which were generally attended by the women, while the men were absent. The grains and fruits, such as they had been accustomed to, were not to be had among the Aborigines of the country, and this first induced the African to cultivate patches of ground in the neighborhood of the mines, for the raising of food for his own sustenance. This trait in their character was observed, and regarded by the Spaniards with considerable interest; and when on contracting with the English slave-dealer, Captain Hawkins, and others for new supplies of slaves, they were careful to request them to secure a quantity of the seeds and different products of the country, to bring with them to the New World. Many of these were cultivated to some extent, while those indigenous to America, were cultivated by them with considerable success. And up to this day, it is a custom on many of the slave plantations of the South, to allow the slave his "patch," and Saturday afternoon or Sabbath day, to cultivate it.

Shortly after the commencement of the shameful traffic in the blood and bones of men—the destiny and chastity of women by Captain Hawkins, and what was termed England's "Virgin Queen;" Elizabeth gave a license to Sir Walter Raleigh, to search for uninhabited lands, and seize upon all uninhabited by Christians. Sir Walter discovered the coast of North Carolina and Virginia, assigning the name of "Virginia" to the whole coast now composing the old state. A feeble colony was settled here, which did not avail, and it was not until the month of April, 1607, that the first permanent settlement was made in Virginia, under the patronage of letters patent from James I., King of England, to Thomas Gates and his associates.

This was the first settling of North America, and thirteen years anterior to the landing of the Pilgrims.

"No permanent settlement was effected in what is now called the United States, till the reign of James the First."—Ramsay's Hist. U. S., vol. I., p. 38.

"The month of April, 1607, is the epoch of the first permanent settlement on the coast of Virginia; the name then given to all that extent of country which forms thirteen States."—*Ib.* p. 39. The whole coast of the country was now explored, not for the purpose of trade and agriculture—because there were no products in the country—the natives not producing sufficient provisions to supply present wants, and, consequently, nothing to trade for; but like the speculations of their Spanish and Portuguese predecessors, on the islands and in South America, but for that of mining gold. Trade and the cultivation of the soil was foreign to their designs and intention on coming to the continent of the new world, and they were consequently, disappointed when failing of success. "At a time when the precious metals were conceived to be the peculiar and only valuable productions of the new world, when every mountain was supposed to contain a treasure, and every rivulet was searched for its golden sands, this appearance was fondly considered as an infallible indication of the mine. Every hand was eager to dig."   *   *   *

"There was now," says Smith, "no talk, no hope, no work; but dig gold, wash gold, refine gold. With this imaginary wealth, the first vessel returning to England was loaded, while the *culture of the land*, and every useful occupation was *totally neglected.*"   *   *   *

The colonists, thus left, were in miserable circumstances for want of provisions. The remainder of what they had brought with them, was so small in quantity, as to be soon expended—and so damaged in the course of a long voyage, as to be a source of disease.   *   *   *   In their expectation of getting gold, the people were disappointed, the glittering substance they had sent to England, proving to be a valueless mineral. "Smith, on his return to

Jamestown, found the colony reduced to thirty-eight persons, who, in despair, were preparing to abandon the country. He employed caresses, threats, and even violence, in order to prevent them from executing this fatal resolution." *Ibid.*, pp. 45–6. In November, 1620, the Pilgrims or Puritans made the harbor of Cape Cod, and after solemn vows and organization previous to setting foot on shore, they landed safely on "Plymouth Rock," December the 20th, about one month after. They were one hundred and one in number, and from the toils and hardships consequent to a severe season, in a strange country, in less than six months after their arrival, "forty-four persons, nearly one-half of their original number," had died.

    *   *   *   "In 1618, in the reign of James I., the British government established a regular trade on the coast of Africa. In the year 1620, negro slaves began to be imported into Virginia: a Dutch ship bringing twenty of them for sale."—Sampson's Hist. Dict., p. 348. The Dutch ship landed her cargo at New Bedford, (now Massachusetts,) as it will be remembered, that the whole coast, now comprising the "Old Thirteen," and original United States, was then called Virginia, so named by Sir Walter Raleigh, in honor of his royal Mistress and patron, Elizabeth, the Virgin Queen, under whom he received his royal patent commission of adventure and expedition.

Beginning their preparation in the slave-trade in 1618, just two years previous, giving time for successfully carrying out the project against the landing of the first emigrant settlers, it will be observed that the African captain, and the "Puritan" emigrants, landed upon the same section of the continent at the same time, 1620—the Pilgrims at Plymouth, and the captives at New Bedford, but a few miles comparatively south.

The country at this period, was one vast wilderness. "The continent of North America was then one continued forest."   *   *   *   There were no horses, cattle, sheep, hogs, or tame beasts of any kind. There were no domestic poultry.   *   *   *   There were no gardens, orchards, public roads, meadows, or cultivated fields.   *   *   *   They "often burned the woods that they could advantageously plant their corn." They had neither spice, salt, bread, butter, cheese, nor milk.   *   *   *   They had no set meals, but eat when they were hungry, and could find any thing to satisfy the cravings of nature.   *   *   *   Very little of their food was derived from the earth, except what it spontaneously produced.   *   *   *   The ground was both their seat and table. Their best bed was a skin.   *   *   *   They had neither steel, iron, nor any metallic instruments.   *   *   *   —Ramsay's Hist., pp. 39–40.

We adduce not these historical extracts to disparage our brother the Indian—far be it: whatever he may think of our race, according to the manner in which he has been instructed to look upon it, by our mutual oppressor the American nation; we admire his, for the many deeds of noble daring, for which the short history of his liberty-loving people are replete: we sympathise with them, because our brethren are the successors of their fathers in the degradation of American bondage—but we adduce them in evidence against the many aspersions charged against the African race, that their inferiority to the other races caused them to be reduced to servitude. For the purpose of proving that their superiority, and not inferiority, alone was the cause which first suggested to Europeans the substitution of Africans for that of aboriginal or Indian laborers in the mines; and that their superior skill and industry, first suggested to the colonists, the propriety of turning their attention to agricultural and other industrial pursuits, than that of mining.

It is very evident, from what has been adduced, the settlement of Captain John Smith, being in the course of a few months, reduced to thirty-eight, and that of Plymouth, from one hundred and one, to that of fifty-seven in six months—it is evident, that the whites nor the Indians were equal to the hard and almost insurmountable difficulties, that now stood wide-spread before them.

An endless forest, the impenetrable earth; the one to be removed, and the other to be excavated. Towns and cities to be built, and farms to be cultivated—all these presented difficulties too arduous for the European then here, and unknown to the Indian.

It is very evident, that at a period such as this, when the natives themselves had fallen victims to tasks imposed upon them by their usurpers, and the Europeans were sinking beneath the weight of climate and hardships; when food could not be had nor the common conveniences of life procured—when arduous duties of life were to be performed and none capable of doing them, but those who had previously by their labors, not only in their native country, but in the new, so proven themselves—as the most natural consequence, the Africans were resorted to, for the performance of every duty common to domestic life.

There were no laborers known to the colonists from Cape Cod to Cape Look Out, than those of the African race. They entered at once into the mines, extracting therefrom, the rich treasures that for a thousand ages lay hidden in the earth. And from their knowledge of cultivation, the farming interests in the North, and planting in the South, were commenced with a prospect never dreamed of before the introduction of this most extraordinary, hardy race of men: though pagans, yet skilled in all the useful duties of life. Farmers, herdsmen, and laborers in their own country, they required not to be taught to work, and how to do it—but it was only necessary to tell them to go to work, and they at once knew what to do, and how it should be done.

It is notorious, that in the planting States, the blacks themselves are the only skillful cultivators—the proprietor knowing little or nothing about the art, save that which he learns from the African husbandman, while his ignorant white overseer, who is merely there to see that the work is attended to, knows a great deal less. Tobacco, cotton, rice, hemp, indigo, the improvement in Indian corn, and many other important products, are all the result of African skill and labor in this country. And the introduction of the zigzag, or "Virginia Worm Fence," is purely of African origin. Nor was their skill as herdsmen inferior to their other attainments, being among the most accomplished trainers and horsemen in the world. Indeed, to this class of men may be indebted the entire country for the improvement South in the breed of horses. And any one who has travelled South, could not fail to have observed, that all of the leading trainers, jockies, and judges of horses, as well as riders, are men of African descent.

In speaking of the Bornouese, a people from among whom a great many natives have been enslaved by Arabian traders, and sold into foreign bondage, and of course many into this country, "It is said that Bornou can muster 15,000 Shonaas in the field mounted. They are the greatest breeders of cattle in the country, and annually supply Soudan with from two to three thousand horses." *   *   *   "Our road lying along one of them, gave me an excellent view of beautiful villages all round, and herds of cattle grazing in the open country." *   *   "Plantations of cotton or indigo now occupy the place where the houses formerly stood."   *   *   *   "The Souga market is well supplied with every necessary and luxury in request among the people of the interior." "The country still open and well cultivated, and the villages numerous. We met crowds of people coming from Karro with goods. Some carried them on their heads, others had asses or bullocks, according to their wealth."   *   * *   "The country still highly cultivated."   *   *   *   "We also passed several walled towns, quite deserted, the inhabitants having been sold by their conquerors, the Felatohs." "Women sat spinning cotton by the road side, offering for sale to the passing caravans, gussub water, roast-meat, sweet potatoes, coshen nuts," &c. (Dunham and Clapperton's Travels and Discoveries in North and Central Africa. Vol. 2, pp. 140. 230. 332, 333. 353.)

The forests gave way before them, and extensive verdant fields, richly clothed with produce, rose up as by magic before these hardy sons of toil. In the place of the unskillful and ill-constructed wigwam, houses, villages, towns and cities quickly were reared up in their stead. Being farmers, mechanics, laborers and traders in their own country, they required little or no instruction in these various pursuits. They were in fact, then, to the whole continent, what they are in truth now to the whole Southern section of the Union—the bone and sinews of the country. And even now, the existence of the white man, South, depends entirely on the labor of the black man—the idleness of the one, is sustained by the industry of the other. Public roads and highways are the result of their labor, as are also the first public works, as wharves, docks, forts, and all such improvements. Are not these legitimate investments in the common stock of the nation, which should command a proportionate interest?

We shall next proceed to review the contributions of colored men to other departments of the nation, and as among the most notorious and historical, we refer to colored American warriors.

Harriet E. Wilson
from *Our Nig*

CHAPTER I.

Mag Smith, My Mother.

Oh, Grief beyond all other griefs, when fate
First leaves the young heart lone and desolate
In the wide world, without that only tie
For which it loved to live or feared to die;
Lorn as the hung-up lute, that ne'er hath spoken
Since the sad day its master-chord was broken!

MOORE.

LONELY MAG SMITH! See her as she walks with downcast eyes and heavy heart. It was not always thus. She *had* a loving, trusting heart. Early deprived of parental guardianship, far removed from relatives, she was left to guide her tiny boat over life's surges alone and inexperienced. As she merged into womanhood, unprotected, uncherished, uncared for, there fell on her ear the music of love, awakening an intensity of emotion long dormant. It whispered of an elevation before unaspired to; of ease and plenty her simple heart had never dreamed of as hers. She knew the voice of her charmer, so ravishing, sounded far above her. It seemed like an angel's, alluring her upward and onward. She thought she could ascend to him and become an equal. She surrendered to him a priceless gem, which he proudly garnered as a trophy, with those of other victims, and left her to her fate. The world seemed full of hateful deceivers and crushing arrogance. Conscious that the great bond of union to her former companions was severed, that the disdain of others would be insupportable, she determined to leave the few friends she possessed, and seek an asylum among strangers. Her offspring came unwelcomed, and before its nativity numbered weeks, it passed from earth, ascending to a purer and better life.

"God be thanked," ejaculated Mag, as she saw its breathing cease; "no one can taunt *her* with my ruin."

Blessed release! may we all respond. How many pure, innocent children not only inherit a wicked heart of their own, claiming life-long scrutiny and restraint, but are heirs also of parental disgrace and calumny, from which only long years of patient endurance in paths of rectitude can disencumber them.

Mag's new home was soon contaminated by the publicity of her fall; she had a feeling of degradation oppressing her; but she resolved to be circumspect, and try to regain in a measure what she had lost. Then some foul tongue would jest of her shame, and averted looks and cold greetings disheartened her. She saw she could not bury in forgetfulness her misdeed, so she resolved to leave her home and seek another in the place she at first fled from.

Alas, how fearful are we to be first in extending a helping hand to those who stagger in the mires of infamy; to speak the first words of hope and warning to those emerging into the sunlight of morality! Who can tell what numbers, advancing just far enough to hear a cold welcome and join in the reserved converse of professed reformers, disappointed, disheartened, have chosen to dwell in unclean places, rather than encounter these "holier-than-thou" of the great brotherhood of man!

Such was Mag's experience; and disdaining to ask favor or friendship from a sneering world, she resolved to shut herself up in a hovel she had often passed in better days, and which she knew to be untenanted. She vowed to ask no favors of familiar faces; to die neglected and forgotten before she would be dependent on any. Removed from the village, she was seldom seen except as upon your introduction, gentle reader, with downcast visage, returning her work to her employer, and thus providing herself with the means of subsistence. In two years many hands craved the same avocation; foreigners who cheapened toil and clamored for a livelihood, competed with her, and she could not thus sustain herself. She was now above no drudgery. Occasionally old acquaintances called to be favored with help of some kind, which she was glad to bestow for the sake of the money it would bring her; but the association with them was such a painful reminder of by-gones, she returned to her hut morose and revengeful, refusing all offers of a better home than she possessed. Thus she lived for years, hugging her wrongs, but making no effort to escape. She had never known plenty, scarcely competency; but the present was beyond comparison with those innocent years when the coronet of virtue was hers.

Every year her melancholy increased, her means diminished. At last no one seemed to notice her, save a kind-hearted African, who often called to inquire after her health and to see if she needed any fuel, he having the responsibility of furnishing that article, and she in return mending or making garments.

"How much you earn dis week, Mag?" asked he one Saturday evening.

"Little enough, Jim. Two or three days without any dinner. I washed for the Reeds, and did a small job for Mrs. Bellmont; that's all. I shall starve soon, unless I can get more to do. Folks seem as afraid to come here as if they expected to get some awful disease. I do n't believe there is a person in the world but would be glad to have me dead and out of the way."

"No, no, Mag! do n't talk so. You shan't starve so long as I have barrels to hoop. Peter Greene boards me cheap. I'll help you, if nobody else will."

A tear stood in Mag's faded eye. "I'm glad," she said, with a softer tone than before, "if there is *one* who is n't glad to see me suffer. I b'lieve all Singleton wants to see me punished, and feel as if they could tell when I've been punished long enough. It's a long day ahead they'll set it, I reckon."

After the usual supply of fuel was prepared, Jim returned home. Full of pity for Mag, he set about devising measures for her relief. "By golly!" said he to himself one day—for he had become so absorbed in Mag's interest that he had fallen into a habit of musing aloud—"By golly! I wish she 'd *marry* me."

"Who?" shouted Pete Greene, suddenly starting from an unobserved corner of the rude shop.

"Where you come from, you sly nigger!" exclaimed Jim.

"Come, tell me, who is 't?" said Pete; "Mag Smith, you want to marry?"

"Git out, Pete! and when you come in dis shop again, let a nigger know it. Do n't steal in like a thief."

Pity and love know little severance. One attends the other. Jim acknowledged the presence of the former, and his efforts in Mag's behalf told also of a finer principle.

This sudden expedient which he had unintentionally disclosed, roused his thinking and inventive powers to study upon the best method of introducing the subject to Mag.

He belted his barrels, with many a scheme revolving in his mind, none of which quite satisfied him, or seemed, on the whole, expedient. He thought of the pleasing contrast between her fair face and his own dark skin; the smooth, straight hair, which he had once, in expression of pity, kindly stroked on her now wrinkled but once fair brow. There was a tempest gathering in his heart, and at last, to ease his pent-up passion, he exclaimed aloud, "By golly!" Recollecting his former exposure, he glanced around to see if Pete was in hearing again. Satisfied on this point, he continued: "She'd be as much of a prize to me as she'd fall short of coming up to the mark with white folks. I do n't care for past things. I've done things 'fore now I's 'shamed of. She 's good enough for me, any how."

One more glance about the premises to be sure Pete was away.

The next Saturday night brought Jim to the hovel again. The cold was fast coming to tarry its apportioned time. Mag was nearly despairing of meeting its rigor.

"How's the wood, Mag?" asked Jim.

"All gone; and no more to cut, any how," was the reply.

"Too bad!" Jim said. His truthful reply would have been, I'm glad.

"Anything to eat in the house?" continued he.

"No," replied Mag.

"Too bad!" again, orally, with the same *inward* gratulation as before.

"Well, Mag," said Jim, after a short pause, "you's down low enough. I do n't see but I've got to take care of ye. 'Sposin' we marry!"

Mag raised her eyes, full of amazement, and uttered a sonorous "What?"

Jim felt abashed for a moment. He knew well what were her objections.

"You's had trial of white folks, any how. They run off and left ye, and now none of 'em come near ye to see if you's dead or alive. I's black outside, I know, but I's got a white heart inside. Which you rather have, a black heart in a white skin, or a white heart in a black one?"

"Oh, dear!" sighed Mag; "Nobody on earth cares for *me*—"

"I do," interrupted Jim.

"I can do but two things," said she, "beg my living, or get it from you."

"Take me, Mag. I can give you a better home than this, and not let you suffer so."

He prevailed; they married. You can philosophize, gentle reader, upon the impropriety of such unions, and preach dozens of sermons on the evils of amalgamation. Want is a more powerful philosopher and preacher. Poor Mag. She has sundered another bond which held her to her fellows. She has descended another step down the ladder of infamy.

Harriet Jacobs
from *Incidents in the Life of a Slave Girl*

V

The Trials of Girlhood

DURING the first years of my service in Dr. Flint's family, I was accustomed to share some indulgences with the children of my mistress. Though this seemed to me no more than right, I was grateful for it, and tried to merit the kindness by the faithful discharge of my duties. But I now entered on my fifteenth year— a sad epoch in the life of a slave girl. My master began to whisper foul words in my ear. Young as I was, I could not remain ignorant of their import. I tried to treat them with indifference or contempt. The master's age, my extreme youth, and the fear that his conduct would be reported to my grandmother, made him bear this treatment for many months. He was a crafty man, and resorted to many means to accomplish his purposes. Sometimes he had stormy, terrific ways, that made his victims tremble; sometimes he assumed a gentleness that he thought must surely subdue. Of the two, I preferred his stormy moods, although they left me trembling. He tried his utmost to corrupt the pure principles my grandmother had instilled. He peopled my young mind with unclean images, such as only a vile monster could think of. I turned from him with disgust and hatred. But he was my master. I was compelled to live under the same roof with him—where I saw a man forty years my senior daily violating the most sacred commandments of nature. He told me I was his property; that I must be subject to his will in all things. My soul revolted against the mean tyranny. But where could I turn for protection? No matter whether the slave girl be as black as ebony or as fair as her mistress. In either case, there is no shadow of law to protect her from insult, from violence, or even from death; all these are inflicted by fiends who bear the shape of men. The mistress, who ought to protect the helpless victim, has no other feelings towards her but those of jealousy and rage. The degradation, the wrongs, the vices, that grow out of slavery, are more than I can describe. They are greater than you would willingly believe. Surely, if you credited one half the truths that are told you concerning the helpless millions suffering in this cruel bondage, you at the north would not help to tighten the yoke. You surely would refuse to do for the master, on your own soil, the mean and cruel work which trained bloodhounds and the lowest class of whites do for him at the south.

Every where the years bring to all enough of sin and sorrow; but in slavery the very dawn of life is darkened by these shadows. Even the little child, who is accustomed to wait on her mistress and her children, will learn, before she is twelve years old, why it is that her mistress hates such and such a one among the slaves. Perhaps the child's own mother is among those hated ones. She listens to violent outbreaks of jealous passion, and cannot help understanding what is the cause. She will become prematurely knowing in evil things. Soon she will learn to tremble when she hears her master's footfall. She will be compelled to realize that she is no longer a child. If God has bestowed beauty upon her, it will prove her greatest curse. That which commands admiration in the white woman only hastens the degradation of the female slave. I know that some are too much brutalized by slavery to feel the humiliation of their position; but many slaves feel it most acutely, and shrink from the memory of it. I cannot tell how much I suffered in the presence of these wrongs, nor how I am still pained by the retrospect. My master met me at every turn, reminding me that I belonged to him, and swearing by heaven and earth that he would compel me to submit to him. If I went out for a breath of fresh air, after a day of unwearied toil, his footsteps dogged me. If I knelt by my mother's grave, his dark shadow fell on me even there. The light heart which nature had given me became heavy with sad forebodings. The other slaves in my master's house noticed the change. May of them pitied me; but none dared to ask the cause. They had no need to inquire. They knew too well the guilty practices under that roof; and they were aware that to speak of them was an offence that never went unpunished.

I longed for some one to confide in. I would have given the world to have laid my head on my grandmother's faithful bosom, and told her all my troubles. But Dr. Flint swore he would kill me, if I was not as silent as the grave. Then, although my grandmother was all in all to me, I feared her as well as loved her. I had been accustomed to look up to her with a respect bordering upon awe. I was very young, and felt shamefaced about telling her such impure things, especially as I knew her to be very strict on such subjects. Moreover, she was a woman of a high spirit. She was usually very quiet in her demeanor; but if her indignation was once roused, it was not very easily quelled. I had been told that she once chased a white gentleman with a loaded pistol, because he insulted one of her daughters. I dreaded the consequences of a violent outbreak; and both pride and fear kept me silent. But though I did not confide in my grandmother, and even evaded her vigilant watchfulness and inquiry, her presence in the neighborhood was some protection to me. Though she had been a slave, Dr. Flint was afraid of her. He dreaded her scorching rebukes. Moreover, she was known and patronized by many people; and he did not wish to have his villainy made public. It was lucky for me that I did not live on a distant plantation, but in a town not so large that the inhabitants were ignorant of each other's affairs. Bad as are the laws and customs in a slaveholding community, the doctor, as a professional man, deemed it prudent to keep up some outward show of decency.

O, what days and nights of fear and sorrow that man caused me! Reader, it is not to awaken sympathy for myself that I am telling you truthfully what I suffered in slavery. I do it to kindle a flame of compassion in your hearts for my sisters who are still in bondage, suffering as I once suffered.

I once saw two beautiful children playing together. One was a fair white child; the other was her slave, and also her sister. When I saw them embracing each other, and heard their joyous laughter, I turned sadly away from the lovely sight. I foresaw the inevitable blight that would fall on the little slave's heart. I knew how soon her laughter would be changed to sighs. The fair child grew up to be a still fairer woman. From childhood to womanhood her pathway was blooming with flowers, and overarched by a sunny sky. Scarcely one day of her life had been clouded when the sun rose on her happy bridal morning.

How had those years dealt with her slave sister, the little playmate of her childhood? She, also, was very beautiful; but the flowers and sunshine of love were not for her. She drank the cup of sin, and shame, and misery, whereof her persecuted race are compelled to drink.

In view of these things, why are ye silent, ye free men and women of the north? Why do your tongues falter in maintenance of the right? Would that I had more ability! But my heart is so full, and my pen is so weak! There are noble men and women who plead for us, striving to help those who cannot help themselves. God bless them! God give them strength and courage to go on! God bless those, every where, who are laboring to advance the cause of humanity!

VI

The Jealous Mistress

I WOULD ten thousand times rather that my children should be the half-starved paupers of Ireland than to be the most pampered among the slaves of America. I would rather drudge out my life on a cotton plantation, till the grave opened to give me rest, than to live with an unprincipled master and a jealous mistress. The felon's home in a penitentiary is preferable. He may repent, and turn from the error of his ways, and so find peace; but it is not so with a favorite slave. She is not allowed to have any pride of character. It is deemed a crime in her to wish to be virtuous.

Mrs. Flint possessed the key to her husband's character before I was born. She might have used this knowledge to counsel and to screen the young and the innocent among her slaves; but for them she had no sympathy. They were the objects of her constant suspicion and malevolence. She watched her husband with unceasing vigilance; but he was well practised in means to evade it. What he could not find opportunity to say in words he manifested in signs. He invented more than were ever thought of in a deaf and dumb asylum. I let them pass, as if I did not understand what he meant; and many were the curses and threats bestowed on me for my stupidity. One day he caught me teaching myself to write. He frowned, as if he was not well pleased; but I suppose he came to the conclusion that such an accomplishment might help to advance his favorite scheme. Before long, notes were often slipped into my hand. I would return them, saying, "I can't read them, sir." "Can't you?" he replied; "then I must read them to you." He always finished the reading by asking, "Do you understand?" Sometimes he would complain of the heat of the tea room, and order his supper to be placed on a small table in the piazza. He would seat himself there with a well-satisfied smile, and tell me to stand by and brush away the flies. He would eat very slowly, pausing between the mouthfuls. These intervals were employed in describing the happiness I was so foolishly throwing away, and in threatening me with the penalty that finally awaited my stubborn disobedience. He boasted much of the forbearance he had exercised towards me, and reminded me that there was a limit to his patience. When I succeeded in avoiding opportunities for him to talk to me at home, I was ordered to come to his office, to do some errand. When there, I was obliged to stand and listen to such language as he saw fit to address to me. Sometimes I so openly expressed my contempt for him that he would become violently enraged, and I wondered why he did not strike me. Circumstanced as he was, he probably thought it was better policy to be forbearing. But the state of things grew worse and worse daily. In desperation I told him that I must and would apply to my grandmother for protection. He threatened me with death, and worse than death, if I made any complaint to her. Strange to say, I did not despair. I was naturally of a buoyant disposition, and always I had a hope of somehow getting out of his clutches. Like many a poor, simple slave before me, I trusted that some threads of joy would yet be woven into my dark destiny.

I had entered my sixteenth year, and every day it became more apparent that my presence was intolerable to Mrs. Flint. Angry words frequently passed between her and her husband. He had never punished me himself, and he would not allow any body else to punish me. In that respect, she was never satisfied; but, in her angry moods, no terms were too vile for her to bestow upon me. Yet I, whom she detested so bitterly, had far more pity for her than he had, whose duty it was to make her life happy. I never wronged her, or wished to wrong her; and one word of kindness from her would have brought me to her feet.

After repeated quarrels between the doctor and his wife, he announced his intention to take his youngest daughter, then four years old, to sleep in his apartment. It was necessary that a servant should sleep in the same room, to be on hand if the child stirred. I was selected for that office, and informed for what purpose that arrangement had been made. By managing to keep within sight of people, as much as possible, during the day time, I had hitherto succeeded in eluding my master, though a razor was often held to my throat to force me to change this line of policy. At night I slept by the side of my great aunt, where I felt safe. He was too prudent to come into her room. She was an old woman, and had been in the family many years. Moreover, as a married man, and a professional man, he deemed it necessary to save appearances in some degree. But he resolved to remove the obstacle in the way of his scheme; and he thought he had planned it so that he should evade suspicion. He was well aware how much I prized my refuge by the side of my old aunt, and he determined to dispossess me of it. The first night the doctor had the little child in his room alone. The next morning, I was ordered to take my station as nurse the following night. A kind Providence interposed in my favor. During the day Mrs. Flint heard of this new arrangement, and a storm followed. I rejoiced to hear it rage.

After a while my mistress sent for me to come to her room. Her first question was, "Did you know you were to sleep in the doctor's room?"

"Yes, ma'am."

"Who told you?"

"My master."

"Will you answer truly all the questions I ask?"

"Yes, ma'am."

"Tell me, then, as you hope to be forgiven, are you innocent of what I have accused you?"

"I am."

She handed me a Bible, and said, "Lay your hand on your heart, kiss this holy book, and swear before God that you tell me the truth."

I took the oath she required, and I did it with a clear conscience.

"You have taken God's holy word to testify your innocence," said she. "If you have deceived me, beware! Now take this stool, sit down, look me directly in the face, and tell me all that has passed between your master and you."

I did as she ordered. As I went on with my account her color changed frequently, she wept, and sometimes groaned. She spoke in tones so sad, that I was touched by her grief. The tears came to my eyes; but I was soon convinced that her emotions arose from anger and wounded pride. She felt that her marriage vows were desecrated, her dignity insulted; but she had no compassion for the poor victim of her husband's perfidy. She pitied herself as a martyr; but she was incapable of feeling for the condition of shame and misery in which her unfortunate, helpless slave was placed.

Yet perhaps she had some touch of feeling for me; for when the conference was ended, she spoke kindly, and promised to protect me. I should have been much comforted by this assurance if I could have had confidence in it; but my experiences in slavery had filled me with distrust. She was not a very refined woman, and had not much control over her passions. I was an object of her jealousy, and, consequently, of her hatred; and I knew I could not expect kindness or confidence from her under the circumstances in which I was placed. I could not blame her. Slaveholders' wives feel as other women would under similar circumstances. The fire of her temper kindled from small sparks, and now the flame became so intense that the doctor was obliged to give up his intended arrangement.

I knew I had ignited the torch, and I expected to suffer for it afterwards; but I felt too thankful to my mistress for the timely aid she rendered me to care much about that. She now took me to sleep in a room adjoining her own. There I was an object of her especial care, though not of her especial comfort, for she spent many a sleepless night to watch over me. Sometimes I woke up, and found her bending over me. At other times she whispered in my ear, as though it was her husband who was speaking to me, and listened to hear what I would answer. If she startled me, on such occasions, she would glide stealthily away; and the next morning she would tell me I had been talking in my sleep, and ask who I was talking to. At last, I began to be fearful for my life. It had been often threatened; and you can imagine, better than I can describe, what an unpleasant sensation it must produce to wake up in the dead of night and find a jealous woman bending over you. Terrible as this experience was, I had fears that it would give place to one more terrible.

My mistress grew weary of her vigils; they did not prove satisfactory. She changed her tactics. She now tried the trick of accusing my master of crime, in my presence, and gave my name as the author of the accusation. To my utter astonishment, he replied, "I don't believe it: but if she did acknowledge it, you tortured her into exposing me." Tortured into exposing him! Truly, Satan had no difficulty in distinguishing the color of his soul! I understood his object in making this false representation. It was to show me that I gained nothing by seeking the protection of my mistress; that the power was still all in his own hands. I pitied Mrs. Flint. She was a second wife, many years the junior of her husband; and the hoary-headed miscreant was enough to try the patience of a wiser and better woman. She was completely foiled, and knew not how to proceed. She would gladly have had me flogged for my supposed false oath; but, as I have already stated, the doctor never allowed any one to whip me. The old sinner was politic. The application of the lash might have led to remarks that would have exposed him in the eyes of his children and grandchildren. How often did I rejoice that I lived in a town where all the inhabitants knew each other! If I had been on a remote plantation, or lost among the multitude of a crowded city, I should not be a living woman at this day.

The secrets of slavery are concealed like those of the Inquisition. My master was, to my knowledge, the father of eleven slaves. But did the mothers dare to tell who was the father of their children? Did the other slaves dare to allude to it, except in whispers among themselves? No, indeed! They knew too well the terrible consequences.

My grandmother could not avoid seeing things which excited her suspicions. She was uneasy about me, and tried various ways to buy me; but the neverchanging answer was always repeated: "Linda does not belong to *me*. She is my daughter's property, and I have no legal right to sell her." The conscientious man! He was too scrupulous to *sell* me; but he had no scruples whatever about committing a much greater wrong against the helpless young girl placed under his guardianship, as his daughter's property. Sometimes my persecutor would ask me whether I would like to be sold. I told him I would rather be sold to any body than to lead such a life as I did. On such occasions he would assume the air of a very injured individual, and reproach me for my ingratitude. "Did I not take you into the house, and make you the companion of my own children?" he would say. "Have I ever treated you like a negro? I have never allowed you to be punished, not even to please your mistress. And this is the recompense I get, you ungrateful girl!" I answered that he had reasons of his own for screening me from punishment, and that the course he pursued made my mistress hate me and persecute me. If I wept, he would say, "Poor child! Don't cry! don't cry! I will make peace for you with your mistress. Only let me arrange matters in my own way. Poor, foolish girl! you don't know what is for your own good. I would cherish you. I would make a lady of you. Now go, and think of all I have promised you."

I did think of it.

Reader, I draw no imaginary pictures of southern homes. I am telling you the plain truth. Yet when victims make their escape from this wild beast of Slavery, northerners consent to act the part of bloodhounds, and hunt the poor fugitive back into his den, "full of dead men's bones, and all uncleanness." Nay, more, they are not only willing, but proud, to give their daughters in marriage to slaveholders. The poor girls have romantic notions of a sunny clime, and of the flowering vines that all the year round shade a happy home. To what disappointments are they destined! The young wife soon learns that the husband in whose hands she has placed her happiness pays no regard to his marriage vows. Children of every shade of complexion play with her own fair babies, and too well she knows that they are born unto him of his own household. Jealousy and hatred enter the flowery home, and it is ravaged of its loveliness.

Southern women often marry a man knowing that he is the father of many little slaves. They do not trouble themselves about it. They regard such children as property, as marketable as the pigs on the plantation; and it is seldom that they do not make them aware of this by passing them into the slavetrader's hands as soon as possible, and thus getting them out of their sight. I am glad to say there are some honorable exceptions.

I have myself known two southern wives who exhorted their husbands to free those slaves towards whom they stood in a "parental relation;" and their request was granted. These husbands blushed before the superior nobleness of their wives' natures. Though they had only counselled them to do that which it was their duty to do, it commanded their respect, and rendered their conduct more exemplary. Concealment was at an end, and confidence took the place of distrust.

Though this bad institution deadens the moral sense, even in white women, to a fearful extent, it is not altogether extinct. I have heard southern ladies say of Mr. Such a one, "He not only thinks it no disgrace to be the father of those little niggers, but he is not ashamed to call himself their master. I declare, such things ought not to be tolerated in any decent society!"

XII

Fear of Insurrection

NOT far from this time Nat Turner's insurrection broke out; and the news threw our town into great commotion. Strange that they should be alarmed, when their slaves were so "contented and happy"! But so it was.

It was always the custom to have a muster every year. On that occasion every white man shouldered his musket. The citizens and the so-called country gentlemen wore military uniforms. The poor whites took their places in the ranks in every-day dress, some without shoes, some without hats. This grand occasion had already passed; and when the slaves were told there was to be another muster, they were surprised and rejoiced. Poor creatures! They thought it was going to be a holiday. I was informed of the true state of affairs, and imparted it to the few I could trust. Most gladly would I have proclaimed it to every slave; but I dared not. All could not be relied on. Mighty is the power of the torturing lash.

By sunrise, people were pouring in from every quarter within twenty miles of the town. I knew the houses were to be searched; and I expected it would be done by country bullies and the poor whites. I knew nothing annoyed them so much as to see colored people living in comfort and respectability; so I made arrangements for them with especial care. I arranged every thing in my grandmother's house as neatly as possible. I put white quilts on the beds, and decorated some of the rooms with flowers. When all was arranged, I sat down at the window to watch. Far as my eye could reach, it rested on a motley crowd of soldiers. Drums and fifes were discoursing martial music. The men were divided into companies of sixteen, each headed by a captain. Orders were given, and the wild scouts rushed in every direction, wherever a colored face was to be found.

It was a grand opportunity for the low whites, who had no negroes of their own to scourge. They exulted in such a chance to exercise a little brief authority, and show their subserviency to the slaveholders; not reflecting that the power which trampled on the colored people also kept themselves in poverty, ignorance, and moral degradation. Those who never witnessed such scenes can hardly believe what I know was inflicted at this time on innocent men, women, and children, against whom there was not the slightest ground for suspicion. Colored people and slaves who lived in remote parts of the town suffered in an especial manner. In some cases the searchers scattered powder and shot among their clothes, and then sent other parties to find them, and bring them forward as proof that they were plotting insurrection. Every where men, women, and children were whipped till the blood stood in puddles at their feet. Some received five hundred lashes; others were tied hands and feet, and tortured with a bucking paddle, which blisters the skin terribly. The dwellings of the colored people, unless they happened to be protected by some influential white person, who was nigh at hand, were robbed of clothing and every thing else the marauders thought worth carrying away. All day long these unfeeling wretches went round, like a troop of demons, terrifying and tormenting the helpless. At night, they formed themselves into patrol bands, and went wherever they chose among the colored people, acting out their brutal will. Many women hid themselves in woods and swamps, to keep out of their way. If any of the husbands or fathers told of these outrages, they were tied up to the public whipping post, and cruelly scourged for telling lies about white men. The consternation was universal. No two people that had the slightest tinge of color in their faces dared to be seen talking together.

I entertained no positive fears about our household, because we were in the midst of white families who would protect us. We were ready to receive the soldiers whenever they came. It was not long before we heard the tramp of feet and the sound of voices. The door was rudely pushed open; and in they tumbled, like a pack of hungry wolves. They snatched at every thing within their reach. Every box, trunk, closet, and corner underwent a thorough examination. A box in one of the drawers containing some silver change was eagerly pounced upon. When I stepped forward to take it from them, one of the soldiers turned and said angrily, "What d'ye foller us fur? D'ye s'pose white folks is come to steal?"

I replied, "You have come to search; but you have searched that box, and I will take it, if you please."

At that moment I saw a white gentleman who was friendly to us; and I called to him, and asked him to have the goodness to come in and stay till the search was over. He readily complied. His entrance into the house brought in the captain of the company, whose business it was to guard the outside of the house, and see that none of the inmates left it. This officer was Mr. Litch, the wealthy slaveholder whom I mentioned, in the account of neighboring planters, as being notorious for his cruelty. He felt above soiling his hands with the search. He merely gave orders; and, if a bit of writing was discovered, it was carried to him by his ignorant followers, who were unable to read.

My grandmother had a large trunk of bedding and table cloths. When that was opened, there was a great shout of surprise; and one exclaimed, "Where'd the damned niggers git all dis sheet an' table clarf?"

My grandmother, emboldened by the presence of our white protector, said, "You may be sure we didn't pilfer 'em from *your* houses."

"Look here, mammy," said a grim-looking fellow without any coat, "you seem to feel mighty gran' 'cause you got all them 'ere fixens. White folks oughter have 'em all."

His remarks were interrupted by a chorus of voices shouting, "We's got 'em! We's got 'em! Dis 'ere yaller gal's got letters!"

There was a general rush for the supposed letter, which, upon examination, proved to be some verses written to me by a friend. In packing away my things, I had overlooked them. When their captain informed them of their contents, they seemed much disappointed. He inquired of me who wrote them. I told him it was one of my friends. "Can you read them?" he asked. When I told him I could, he swore, and raved, and tore the paper into bits. "Bring me all your letters!" said he, in a commanding tone. I told him I had none. "Don't be afraid," he continued, in an insinuating way. "Bring them all to me. Nobody shall do you any harm." Seeing I did not move to obey him, his pleasant tone changed to oaths and threats. "Who writes to you? half free niggers?" inquired he. I replied, "O, no; most of my letters are from white people. Some request me to burn them after they are read, and some I destroy without reading."

An exclamation of surprise from some of the company put a stop to our conversation. Some silver spoons which ornamented an old-fashioned buffet had just been discovered. My grandmother was in the habit of preserving fruit for many ladies in the town, and of preparing suppers for parties; consequently she had many jars of preserves. The closet that contained these was next invaded, and the contents tasted. One of them, who was helping himself freely, tapped his neighbor on the shoulder, and said, "Wal done! Don't wonder de niggers want to kill all de white folks, when dey live on 'sarves" [meaning preserves]. I stretched out my hand to take the jar, saying, "You were not sent here to search for sweetmeats."

"And what *were* we sent for?" said the captain, bristling up to me. I evaded the question.

The search of the house was completed, and nothing found to condemn us. They next proceeded to the garden, and knocked about every bush and vine, with no better success. The captain called his men together, and, after a short consultation, the order to march was given. As they passed out of the gate, the captain turned back, and pronounced a malediction on the house. He said it ought to be burned to the ground, and each of its inmates receive thirty-nine lashes. We came out of this affair very fortunately; not losing any thing except some wearing apparel.

Towards evening the turbulence increased. The soldiers, stimulated by drink, committed still greater cruelties. Shrieks and shouts continually rent the air. Not daring to go to the door, I peeped under the window curtain. I saw a mob dragging along a number of colored people, each white man, with his musket upraised, threatening instant death if they did not stop their shrieks. Among the prisoners was a respectable old colored minister. They had found a few parcels of shot in his house, which his wife had for years used to balance her scales. For this they were going to shoot him on Court House Green. What a spectacle was that for a civilized country! A rabble, staggering under intoxication, assuming to be the administrators of justice!

The better class of the community exerted their influence to save the innocent, persecuted people; and in several instances they succeeded, by keeping them shut up in jail till the excitement abated. At last the white citizens found that their own property was not safe from the lawless rabble they had summoned to protect them. They rallied the drunken swarm, drove them back into the country, and set a guard over the town.

The next day, the town patrols were commissioned to search colored people that lived out of the city; and the most shocking outrages were committed with perfect impunity. Every day for a fortnight, if I looked out, I saw horsemen with some poor panting negro tied to their saddles, and compelled by the lash to keep up with their speed, till they arrived at the jail yard. Those who had been whipped too unmercifully to walk were washed with brine, tossed into a cart, and carried to jail. One black man, who had not fortitude to endure scourging, promised to give information about the conspiracy. But it turned out that he knew nothing at all. He had not even heard the name of Nat Turner. The poor fellow had, however, made up a story, which augmented his own sufferings and those of the colored people.

The day patrol continued for some weeks, and at sundown a night guard was substituted. Nothing at all was proved against the colored people, bond or free. The wrath of the slaveholders was somewhat appeased by the capture of Nat Turner. The imprisoned were released. The slaves were sent to their masters, and the free were permitted to return to their ravaged homes. Visiting was strictly forbidden on the plantations. The slaves begged the privilege of again meeting at their little church in the woods, with their burying ground around it. It was built by the colored people, and they had no higher happiness than to meet there and sing hymns together, and pour out their hearts in spontaneous prayer. Their request was denied, and the church was demolished. They were permitted to attend the white churches, a certain portion of the galleries being appropriated to their use. There, when every body else had partaken of the communion, and the benediction had been pronounced, the minister said, "Come down, now, my colored friends." They obeyed the summons, and partook of the bread and wine, in commemoration of the meek and lowly Jesus, who said, "God is your Father, and all ye are brethren."

William Wells Brown

from *The Negro in the American Rebellion*

CHAPTER VI.

The John Brown Raid.

John Brown.—His Religious Zeal.—His Hatred to Slavery.—Organization of his Army.—Attack on Harper's Ferry.—His Execution.—John Brown's Companions, Green and Copeland.—The Executions.

THE year 1859 will long be memorable for the bold attempt of John Brown and his companions to burst the bolted door of the Southern house of bondage, and lead out the captives by a more effectual way than they had yet known: an attempt in which, it is true, the little band of heroes dashed themselves to bloody death, but, at the same time, shook the prison-walls from summit to foundation, and shot wild alarm into every tyrant-heart in all the slave-land. What were the plans and purposes of the noble old man is not precisely known, and perhaps will never be; but, whatever they were, there is reason to believe they had been long maturing,—brooded over silently and secretly, with much earnest thought, and under a solemn sense of religious duty. As early as the fall of 1857, he began to organize his band, chiefly from among the companions of his warfare against the "Border Ruffians" in Kansas. Nine or ten of these spent the winter of 1857–8 in Iowa, where a Col. Forbes was to have given them military instruction; but he, having fallen out with Brown, did not join them, and Aaron D. Stevens, one of the company, took his place.

About the middle of April, 1858, they left Iowa, and went to Chatham, Canada, where, on the 8th of May, was held a convention, called by a written circular, which was sent to such persons only as could be trusted. The convention was composed mostly of colored men, a few of whom were from the States, but the greater part residents in Canada, with no white men but the organized band already mentioned. A "Provisional Constitution," which Brown had previously prepared, was adopted; and the members of the convention took an oath to support it. Its manifest purpose was to insure a perfect organization of all who should join the expedition, whether free men or insurgent slaves, and to hold them under such strict control as to restrain them from every act of wanton or vindictive violence, all waste or needless destruction of life or property, all indignity or unnecessary severity to prisoners, and all immoral practices; in short, to keep the meditated movement free from every possibly avoidable evil ordinarily incident to the armed uprising of a long-oppressed and degraded people.

And let no one who glories in the revolutionary struggles of our fathers for their freedom deny the right of the American bondsman to imitate their high example. And those who rejoice in the deeds of a Wallace or a Tell, a Washington or a Warren; who cherish with unbounded gratitude the name of Lafayette for volunteering his aid in behalf of an oppressed people in a desperate crisis, and at the darkest hour of their fate,—cannot refuse equal merit to this strong, free, heroic man, who freely consecrated all his powers, and the labors of his whole life, to the help of the most needy, friendless, and unfortunate of mankind.

The picture of the Good Samaritan will live to all future ages, as the model of human excellence, for helping one whom he chanced to find in need.

John Brown did more: he went to *seek* those who were lost that he might save them.

On Sunday night, Oct. 16, John Brown, with twenty followers (five of them colored), entered the town of Harper's Ferry, in the State of Virginia; captured the place, making the United-States Armory his headquarters; sent his men in various directions in search of slaves with which to increase his force.

The whole thing, though premature in its commencement, struck a blow that rang on the fetters of the enslaved in every Southern State, and caused the oppressor to tremble for his own safety, as well as for that of the accursed institution.

John Brown's trial, heroism, and execution, an excellent history of which has been given to the public by Mr. James Redpath, saves me from making any lengthened statement here. His life and acts are matters of history, which will live with the language in which it is written. But little can be said of his companions in the raid on slavery. They were nearly all young men, unknown to fame, enthusiastic admirers of the old Puritan, entering heartily into all of his plans, obeying his orders, and dying bravely, with no reproach against their leader.

Of the five colored men, two only were captured alive,—Shields Green and John A. Copeland. The former was a native of South Carolina, having been born in the city of Charleston in the year 1832. Escaping to the North in 1857, he resided in Rochester, N.Y., until attracted by the unadorned eloquence and native magnetism of the hero of Harper's Ferry. The latter was from North Carolina, and was a mulatto of superior abilities, and a genuine lover of liberty and justice. The following letter, written a short time before his execution, needs no explanation:—

"CHARLESTOWN, VA., Dec. 10, 1859.

"MY DEAR BROTHER,—I now take my pen to write you a few lines to let you know how I am, and in answer to your kind letter of the 5th inst. Dear brother, I am, it is true, so situated at present as scarcely to know how to commence writing: not that my mind is filled with fear, or that it has become shattered in view of my near approach to death; not that I am terrified by the gallows which I see staring me in the face, and upon which I am so soon to stand and suffer death for doing what George Washington, the so-called father of this great but slavery-cursed country, was made a hero for doing while he lived, and when dead his name was immortalized, and his great and noble deeds in behalf of freedom taught by parents to their children. And now, brother, for having lent my aid to a general no less brave, and engaged in a cause no less honorable and glorious, I am to suffer death. Washington entered the field to fight for the freedom of the American people,—not for the white man alone, but for both black and white. Nor were they white men alone who fought for the freedom of this country. The blood of black men flowed as freely as that of white men. Yes, the *very first* blood that was spilt was that of a negro. It was the blood of that heroic man (though black he was), Crispus Attucks. And some of the *very last* blood shed was that of black men. To the truth of this, history, though prejudiced, is compelled to attest. *It is true* that black men did an equal share of the fighting for American independence; and they were assured by the whites that they should share equal benefits for so doing. But, after having performed their part honorably, they were by the whites most treacherously deceived,—they refusing to fulfil their part of the contract. But this you know as well as I do; and I will therefore say no more in reference to the claims which we, as colored men, have on the American people....

"It was a sense of the wrongs which we have suffered that prompted the noble but unfortunate Capt. Brown and his associates to attempt to give freedom to a small number, at least, of those who are now held by cruel and unjust laws, and by no less cruel and unjust men. To this freedom they were entitled by every known principle of justice and humanity; and, for the enjoyment of it, God created them. And now, dear brother, could I die in a more noble cause? Could I, brother, die in a manner and for a cause which would induce true and honest men more to honor me, and the angels more readily to receive me to their happy home of everlasting joy above? I imagine that I hear you, and all of you, mother, father, sisters and brothers, say, "No, there is not a cause for which we, with less sorrow, could see you die!"

"Your affectionate brother,
"JOHN A. COPELAND."

"The Baltimore Sun" says, "A few moments before leaving the jail, Copeland said, 'If I am dying for freedom, I could not die for a better cause. *I had rather die than be a slave!*' A military officer in charge on the day of the execution says, 'I had a position near the gallows, and carefully observed all. I can truly say I never witnessed more firm and unwavering fortitude, more perfect composure, or more beautiful propriety, than were manifested by young Copeland to the very last.'"

Shields Green behaved with equal heroism, ascending the scaffold with a firm and unwavering step, and died, as he had lived, a brave man, and expressing to the last his eternal hatred to human bondage, prophesying that slavery would soon come to a bloody end.

Angela Y. Davis
The Anti-Slavery Movement and the Birth of Women's Rights

When the true history of the anti-slavery cause shall be written, women will occupy a large space in its pages; for the cause of the slave has been peculiarly women's cause.

These are the words of an ex-slave, a man who became so closely associated with the nineteenth-century women's movement that he was accused of being a "women's rights man." Frederick Douglass, the country's leading Black abolitionist, was also the most prominent male advocate of women's emancipation in his times. Because of his principled support of the controversial women's movement, he was often held up to public ridicule. Most men of his era, finding their manhood impugned, would have automatically risen to defend their masculinity. But Frederick Douglass assumed an admirably anti-sexist posture and proclaimed that he hardly felt demeaned by the label "women's rights man. . . . I am glad to say that I have never been ashamed to be thus designated." Douglass' attitude toward his baiters may well have been inspired by his knowledge that white women had been called "nigger-lovers" in an attempt to lure them out of the anti-slavery campaign. And he knew that women were indispensable within the abolitionist movement—because of their numbers as well as "their efficiency in pleading the cause of the slave."

Why did so many women join the anti-slavery movement? Was there something special about abolitionism that attracted nineteenth-century white women as no other reform movement had been able to do? Had these questions been posed to a leading female abolitionist such as Harriet Beecher Stowe, she might have argued that women's maternal instincts provided a *natural* basis for their anti-slavery sympathies. This seems, at least, to be an implication of her novel *Uncle Tom's Cabin*, whose abolitionist appeal was answered by vast numbers of women.

When Stowe published *Uncle Tom's Cabin*, the nineteenth-century cult of motherhood was in full swing. As portrayed in the press, in the new popular literature and even in the courts of law, the perfect woman was the perfect mother. Her place was at home—never, of course, in the sphere of politics. In Stowe's novel, slaves, for the most part, are represented as sweet, loving, defenseless, if sometimes naughty children. Uncle Tom's "gentle domestic heart" was, so Stowe wrote, "the peculiar characteristic of his race." *Uncle Tom's*

Cabin is pervaded with assumptions of both Black and female inferiority. Most Black people are docile and domestic, and most women are mothers and little else. As ironic as it may seem, the most popular piece of anti-slavery literature of that time perpetuated the racist ideas which justified slavery and the sexist notions which justified the exclusion of women from the political arena where the battle against slavery would be fought.

The glaring contradiction between the reactionary content and the progressive appeal of *Uncle Tom's Cabin* was not so much a flaw in the author's individual perspective as a reflection of the contradictory nature of women's status in the nineteenth century. During the first decades of the century the industrial revolution caused U.S. society to undergo a profound metamorphosis. In the process, the circumstances of white women's lives were radically changed. By the 1830s many of women's traditional economic tasks were being taken over by the factory system. True, they were freed from some of their old oppressive jobs. Yet the incipient industrialization of the economy was simultaneously eroding women's prestige in the home—a prestige based on their previously *productive* and absolutely essential domestic labor. Their social status began to deteriorate accordingly. An ideological consequence of industrial capitalism was the shaping of a more rigorous notion of female inferiority. It seemed, in fact, that the more women's domestic duties shrank under the impact of industrialization, the more rigid became the assertion that "woman's place is in the home."

Actually, woman's place had always been in the home, but during the pre-industrial era, the economy itself had been centered in the home and its surrounding farmland. While men had tilled the land (often aided by their wives), the women had been manufacturers, producing fabric, clothing, candles, soap and practically all the other family necessities. Women's place had indeed been in the home—but not simply because they bore and reared children or ministered to their husbands' needs. They had been productive workers within the home economy and their labor had been no less respected than their men's. When manufacturing moved out of the home and into the factory, the ideology of womanhood began to raise the wife and mother as ideals. As workers, women had at least enjoyed economic equality, but as wives, they were destined to become appendages to their men, servants to their husbands. As mothers, they would be defined as passive vehicles for the replenishment of human life. The situation of the white housewife was full of contradictions. There was bound to be resistance.

The turbulent 1830s were years of intense resistance. Nat Turner's revolt, toward the beginning of the decade, unequivocally announced that Black men and women were profoundly dissatisfied with their lot as slaves and were determined, more than ever, to resist. In 1831, the year of Nat Turner's revolt, the organized abolitionist movement was born. The early thirties also brought "turn-outs" and strikes to the Northeastern textile factories, operated largely by young women and children. Around the same time, more prosperous white women began to fight for the right to education and for access to careers out-side their homes.

White women in the North—the middle-class housewife as well as the young "mill girl"—frequently invoked the metaphor of slavery as they sought to articulate their respective oppressions. Well-situated women began to de-nounce their unfulfilling domestic lives by defining marriage as a form of slav-ery. For working women, the economic oppression they suffered on the job bore a strong ressemblance to slavery. When the mill women in Lowell, Massa-chusetts, went out on strike in 1836, they marched through the town, singing:

> Oh, I cannot be a slave,
> I will not be a slave.
> Oh, I'm so fond of liberty,
> I will not be a slave.

As between women who were workers and those who came from prosper-ous middle-class families, the former certainly had more legitimate grounds for comparing themselves to slaves. Although they were nominally free, their working conditions and low wages were so exploitative as to automatically in-vite the comparison with slavery. Yet it was the women of means who invoked the analogy of slavery most literally in their effort to express the oppressive na-ture of marriage. During the first half of the nineteenth century the idea that the age-old, established institution of marriage could be oppressive was some-what novel. The early feminists may well have described marriage as "slavery" of the same sort Black people suffered primarily for the shock value of the com-parison—fearing that the seriousness of their protest might otherwise be missed. They seem to have ignored, however, the fact that their identification of the two institutions also implied that slavery was really no worse than mar-riage. But even so, the most important implication of this comparison was that white middle-class women felt a certain affinity with Black women and men, for whom slavery meant whips and chains.

During the 1830s white women—both housewives and workers—were ac-tively drawn into the abolitionist movement. While mill women contributed money from their meager wages and organized bazaars to raise further funds, the middle-class women became agitators and organizers in the anti-slavery cam-paign. By 1833, when the Philadelphia Female Anti-Slavery Society was born in the wake of the founding convention of the American Anti-Slavery Society, enough white women were manifesting their sympathetic attitudes toward the Black people's cause to have established the basis for a bond between the two oppressed groups.* In a widely publicized event that year, a young white woman emerged as a dramatic model of female courage and anti-racist mili-tancy. Prudence Crandall was a teacher who defied her white townspeople in Canterbury, Connecticut, by accepting a Black girl into her school. Her princi-

---

*The first female anti-slavery society was formed by Black women in 1832 in Salem, Massachusetts.

pled and unyielding stand throughout the entire controversy symbolized the possibility of forging a powerful alliance between the established struggle for Black Liberation and the embryonic battle for women's rights.

The parents of the white girls attending Prudence Crandall's school expressed their unanimous opposition to the Black pupil's presence by organizing a widely publicized boycott. But the Connecticut teacher refused to capitulate to their racist demands. Following the advice of Mrs. Charles Harris—a Black woman she employed—Crandall decided to recruit more Black girls, and if necessary, to operate an all-Black school. A seasoned abolitionist, Mrs. Harris introduced Crandall to William Lloyd Garrison, who published announcements about the school in the *Liberator*, his anti-slavery journal. The Canterbury townspeople countered by passing a resolution in opposition to her plans which proclaimed that "the government of the United States, the nation with all its institutions of right belong to the white men who now possess them." No doubt they did mean white *men* quite literally, for Prudence Crandall had not only violated their code of racial segregation, she had also defied the traditional attitudes concerning the conduct of a *white lady*.

> Despite all threats, Prudence Crandall opened the school . . . The Negro students stood bravely by her side.
> And then followed one of the most heroic—and most shameful—episodes in American history. The storekeepers refused to sell supplies to Miss Crandall. . . . The village doctor would not attend ailing students. The druggist refused to give medicine. On top of such fierce inhumanity, rowdies smashed the school windows, threw manure in the well and started several fires in the building.

Where did this young Quaker woman find her extraordinary strength and her astonishing ability to persevere in a dangerous situation of daily siege? Probably through her bonds with the Black people whose cause she so ardently defended. Her school continued to function until Connecticut authorities ordered her arrest. By the time she was arrested, Prudence Crandall had made such a mark on the epoch that even in apparent defeat, she emerged as a symbol of victory.

The Canterbury, Connecticut, events of 1833 erupted at the beginning of a new era. Like Nat Turner's revolt, like the birth of Garrison's *Liberator* and like the founding of the first national anti-slavery organization, these events announced the advent of an epoch of fierce social struggles. Prudence Crandall's unswerving defense of Black people's right to learn was a dramatic example—a more powerful example than ever could have been imagined—for white women who were suffering the birth pangs of political consciousness. Lucidly and eloquently, her actions spoke of vast possibilities for liberation if white women en masse would join hands with their Black sisters.

> Let Southern oppressors tremble—let their Northern apologists tremble—let all the enemies of the persecuted Blacks tremble . . . Urge me not to use moderation in

a cause like the present. I am in earnest—I will not equivocate—I will not excuse—I will not retreat a single inch—and *I will be heard.*

This uncompromising declaration was William Lloyd Garrison's personal statement to readers of the first issue of the *Liberator*. By 1833, two years later, this pioneering abolitionist journal had developed a significant readership, which consisted of a large group of Black subscribers and increasing numbers of whites. Prudence Crandall and others like her were loyal supporters of the paper. But white working women were also among those who readily agreed with Garrison's militant anti-slavery position. Indeed, once the anti-slavery movement was organized, factory women lent decisive support to the abolitionist cause. Yet the most visible white female figures in the anti-slavery campaign were women who were not compelled to work for wages. They were the wives of doctors, lawyers, judges, merchants, factory owners—in other words, women of the middle classes and the rising bourgeoisie.

In 1833 many of these middle-class women had probably begun to realize that something had gone terribly awry in their lives. As "housewives" in the new era of industrial capitalism, they had lost their economic importance in the home, and their social status as women had suffered a corresponding deterioration. In the process, however, they had acquired leisure time, which enabled them to become social reformers—active organizers of the abolitionist campaign. Abolitionism, in turn, conferred upon these women the opportunity to launch an implicit protest against their oppressive roles at home.

Only four women were invited to attend the 1833 founding convention of the American Anti-Slavery Society. The male organizers of this Philadelphia meeting stipulated, moreover, that they were to be "listeners and spectators" rather than full-fledged participants. This did not deter Lucretia Mott—one of the four women—from audaciously addressing the men at the convention on at least two occasions. At the opening session, she confidently arose from her "listener and spectator" seat in the balcony and argued against a motion to postpone the gathering because of the absence of a prominent Philadelphia man:

> Right principles are stronger than names. If our principles are right, why should we be cowards? Why should we wait for those who never have had the courage to maintain the inalienable rights of the slave?

A practicing Quaker minister, Lucretia Mott undoubtedly astounded the all-male audience, for in those days women never spoke out at public gatherings. Although the convention applauded her and moved on to its business as she suggested, at the conclusion of the meeting neither she nor the other women were invited to sign the Declaration of Sentiments and Purposes. Whether the women's signatures were expressly disallowed or whether it simply did not occur to the male leaders that women should be asked to sign, the men were extremely short-sighted. Their sexist attitudes prevented them from grasping the vast potential of women's involvement in the anti-slavery movement.

Lucretia Mott, who was not so short-sighted, organized the founding meeting of the Philadelphia Female Anti-Slavery Society in the immediate aftermath of the men's convention. She was destined to become a leading public figure in the anti-slavery movement, a woman who would be extensively admired for her overall courage and for her steadfastness in the face of raging racist mobs.

> In 1838, this frail-looking woman, dressed in the sober, starched garb of the Quakers, calmly faced the pro-slavery mob that burned down Pennsylvania Hall with the connivance of the mayor of Philadelphia.

Mott's commitment to abolitionism involved other dangers, for her Philadelphia home was a well-traveled Underground Railroad station, where such renowned fugitives as Henry "Box" Brown stopped off during the northward journey. On one occasion, Lucretia Mott herself assisted a slave woman to escape in a carriage under armed guard.

Like Lucretia Mott, many other white women with no previous political experience joined the abolitionist movement and literally received their baptism in fire. A pro-slavery mob burst into a meeting chaired by Maria Chapman Weston and dragged its speaker—William Lloyd Garrison—through the streets of Boston. A leader of the Boston Female Anti-Slavery Society, Weston realized that the white mob sought to isolate and perhaps violently attack the Black women in attendance, and thus insisted that each white woman leave the building with a Black woman at her side. The Boston Female Anti-Slavery Society was one of the numerous women's groups that sprang up in New England immediately after Lucretia Mott founded the Philadelphia society. If the number of women who were subsequently assaulted by racist mobs or who otherwise risked their lives could actually be determined, the figures would no doubt be astoundingly large.

As they worked within the abolitionist movement, white women learned about the nature of human oppression—and in the process, also learned important lessons about their own subjugation. In asserting their right to oppose slavery, they protested—sometimes overtly, sometimes implicitly—their own exclusion from the political arena. If they did not yet know how to present their own grievances collectively, at least they could plead the cause of a people who were also oppressed.

The anti-slavery movement offered women of the middle class the opportunity to prove their worth according to standards that were not tied to their role as wives and mothers. In this sense, the abolitionist campaign was a home where they could be valued for their concrete *works*. Indeed, their political involvement in the battle against slavery may have been as intense, as passionate and as total as it was because they were experiencing an exciting alternative to their domestic lives. And they were resisting an oppression which bore a certain resemblance to their own. Furthermore, they learned how to challenge male supremacy within the anti-slavery movement. They discovered that sexism, which seemed unalterable inside their marriages, could be questioned and fought in the arena of political struggle. Yes, white women would be called upon to defend fiercely their rights *as women* in order to fight for the emancipation of Black people.

As Eleanor Flexner's outstanding study of the women's movement reveals, women abolitionists accumulated invaluable political experiences, without which they could not have effectively organized the campaign for women's rights more than a decade later. Women developed fund-raising skills, they learned how to distribute literature, how to call meetings—and some of them even became strong public speakers. Most important of all, they became efficient in the use of the petition, which would become the central tactical weapon of the women's rights campaign. As they petitioned against slavery, women were compelled simultaneously to champion their own right to engage in political work. How else could they convince the government to accept the signatures of voteless women if not by aggressively disputing the validity of their traditional exile from political activity? And, as Flexner insists, it was necessary

> ...for the average housewife, mother, or daughter to overstep the limits of decorum, disregard the frowns, or jeers, or outright commands of her menfolk and... take her first petition and walk down an unfamiliar street, knocking on doors and asking for signatures to an unpopular plea. Not only would she be going out unattended by husband or brother; but she usually encountered hostility, if not outright abuse for her unwomanly behavior.

Of all the pioneering women abolitionists, it was the Grimke sisters from South Carolina—Sarah and Angelina—who most consistently linked the issue of slavery to the oppression of women. From the beginning of their tumultuous lecturing career, they were compelled to defend their rights as women to be public advocates of abolition—and by implication to defend the rights of all women to register publicly their opposition to slavery.

Born into a South Carolina slaveholding family, the Grimke sisters developed a passionate abhorrence of the "peculiar institution" and decided, as adults, to move North. Joining the abolitionist effort in 1836, they began to lecture in New England about their own lives and their daily encounters with the untold evils of slavery. Although the gatherings were sponsored by the female anti-slavery societies, increasing numbers of men began to attend. "Gentlemen, hearing of their eloquence and power, soon began timidly to slip into the back seats." These assemblies were unprecedented, for no other women had ever addressed mixed audiences on such a regular basis without facing derogatory cries and disruptive jeers hurled by men who felt that public speaking should be an exclusively male activity.

While the men attending the Grimkes' meetings were undoubtedly eager to learn from the women's experiences, the sisters were vengefully attacked by other male forces. The most devastating attack came from religious quarters: on July 28, 1837, the Council of Congregationalist Ministers of Massachusetts issued a pastoral letter severely chastising them for engaging in activities which subverted women's divinely ordained role:

> The power of woman is her dependence, flowing from the consciousness of that weakness which God has given her for her protection...

According to the ministers, the Grimkes' actions had created "dangers which at present threaten the female character with wide-spread and permanent injury." Moreover,

> We appreciate the unostentatious prayers of woman in advancing the cause of religion.... But when she assumes the place and tone of man as a public reformer..., she yields the power which God has given her for her protection, and her character becomes unnatural. If the vine, whose strength and beauty is to lean on the trellis-work, and half conceal its cluster, thinks to assume the independence and overshadowing nature of the elm, it will not only cease to bear fruit, but fall in shame and dishonor into the dust.

Framed by the largest Protestant denomination in Massachusetts, this pastoral letter had immense repercussions. If the ministers were correct, then Sarah and Angelina Grimke were committing the worst of all possible sins: they were challenging God's will. The echoes of this assault did not begin to fade until the Grimkes finally decided to terminate their lecturing career.

Neither Sarah nor Angelina had originally been concerned—at least not expressly—about questioning the social inequality of women. Their main priority had been to expose the inhuman and immoral essence of the slave system and the special responsibility women bore for its perpetuation. But once the male supremacist attacks against them were unleashed, they realized that unless they defended themselves as women—and the rights of women in general—they would be forever barred from the campaign to free the slaves. The more powerful orator of the two, Angelina Grimke challenged this assault on women in her lectures. Sarah, who was the theoretical genius, began a series of letters on *The Equality of the Sexes and the Condition of Women.*

Completed in 1838, Sarah Grimke's "Letters on the Equality of the Sexes..." contain one of the first extensive analyses of the status of women authored by a woman in the United States. Setting down her ideas six years before the publication of Margaret Fuller's well-known treatise on women, Sarah disputed the assumption that inequality between the sexes was commanded by God. "Men and women were created equal: they are both moral and accountable human beings." She directly contested the ministers' charge that women who seek to give leadership to social reform movements are unnatural, insisting instead that "whatever is right for man is right for woman."

The writings and lectures of these two outstanding sisters were enthusiastically received by many of the women who were active in the female anti-slavery movement. But some of the leading men in the abolitionist campaign claimed that the issue of women's rights would confuse and alienate those who were solely concerned about the defeat of slavery. Angelina's early response spelled out her (and her sister's) understanding of the strong threads tying women's rights to abolitionism:

> We cannot push Abolitionism forward with all our might untill we take up the stumbling block out of the road.... (T)o meet this question may appear to be turning out of the road.... It is not: we must meet it and meet it now.... Why, my dear brothers, can you not see the deep laid scheme of the clergy against us as lecturers?... If we surrender the right to speak in public this year, we must surrender the right to petition next year and the right to write the year after, and so on. What then can woman do for the slave, when she herself is under the feet of man and shamed into silence?

An entire decade before white women's mass opposition to the ideology of male supremacy received its organizational expression, the Grimke sisters urged women to resist the destiny of passivity and dependence which society had imposed upon them—in order to take their rightful place in the struggle for justice and human rights. Angelina's 1837 *Appeal to the Women of the Nominally Free States* forcefully argues this point:

> It is related of Buonaparte, that he one day rebuked a French lady for busying herself with politics. "Sire," replied she, "in a country where *women* are put to death, it is very natural that *women* should wish to know the reason why." And, dear sisters, in a country where women are degraded and brutalized, and where their exposed persons bleed under the lash—where they are sold in the shambles of "negro brokers"—robbed of their heard earnings—torn from their husbands, and forcibly plundered of their virtue and their offspring; surely in *such* a country, it is very natural that *women* should wish to know "the reason *why*"—especially when these outrages of blood and nameless horror are practiced in violation of the principles of our Constitution. We do not, then, and cannot concede the position, that because this is a *political subject* women ought to fold their hands in idleness, and close their eyes and ears to the "horrible things" that are practiced in our land. The denial of our duty to act is a bold denial of our right to act; and if we have no right to act, then may *we* well be termed "the white slaves of the North"—for like our brethren in bonds, we must seal our lips in silence and despair.

The above passage is also an illustration of the Grimke sisters' insistence that white women in the North and South acknowledge the special bond linking them with Black women who suffered the pain of slavery. Again:

> They are our country women—*they are our sisters;* and to us, as women, they have a right to look for sympathy with their sorrows, and effort and prayer for their rescue.

"The question of equality for women," as Eleanor Flexner put it, was not "a matter of abstract justice" for the Grimkes, "but of enabling women to join in an urgent task." Since the abolition of slavery was the most pressing political necessity of the times, they urged women to join in that struggle with the understanding that their own oppression was nurtured and perpetuated by the continued existence of the slave system. Because the Grimke sisters had such a profound consciousness of the inseparability of the fight for Black Liberation and the fight for Women's Liberation, they were never caught in the ideological snare of insisting that one struggle was absolutely more important than the other. They recognized the dialectical character of the relationship between the two causes.

More than any other women in the campaign against slavery, the Grimkes urged the constant inclusion of the issue of women's rights. At the same time they argued that women could never achieve their freedom independently of Black people. "I want to be identified with the Negro," said Angelina to a convention of patriotic women supporting the Civil War effort in 1863. "Until he gets his rights, we shall never have ours." Prudence Crandall had risked her life in defense of Black children's right to education. If her stand contained a promise of a fruitful and powerful alliance, bringing Black people and women together in order to realize their common dream of liberation, then the analysis presented by Sarah and Angelina Grimke was the most profound and most moving theoretical expression of that promise of unity.

Howard Zinn
Slavery Without Submission, Emancipation Without Freedom

The United States government's support of slavery was based on an overpowering practicality. In 1790, a thousand tons of cotton were being produced every year in the South. By 1860, it was a million tons. In the same period, 500,000 slaves grew to 4 million. A system harried by slave rebellions and conspiracies (Gabriel Prosser, 1800; Denmark Vesey, 1822; Nat Turner, 1831) developed a network of controls in the southern states, backed by the laws, courts, armed forces, and race prejudice of the nation's political leaders.

It would take either a full-scale slave rebellion or a full-scale war to end such a deeply entrenched system. If a rebellion, it might get out of hand, and turn its ferocity beyond slavery to the most successful system of capitalist enrichment in the world. If a war, those who made the war would organize its consequences. Hence, it was Abraham Lincoln who freed the slaves, not John Brown. In 1859, John Brown was hanged, with federal complicity, for attempting to do by small-scale violence what Lincoln would do by large-scale violence several years later—end slavery.

With slavery abolished by order of the government—true, a government pushed hard to do so, by blacks, free and slave, and by white abolitionists—its end could be orchestrated so as to set limits to emancipation. Liberation from the top would go only so far as the interests of the dominant groups permitted. If carried further by the momentum of war, the rhetoric of a crusade, it could be pulled back to a safer position. Thus, while the ending of slavery led to a reconstruction of national politics and economics, it was not a radical reconstruction, but a safe one—in fact, a profitable one.

The plantation system, based on tobacco growing in Virginia, North Carolina, and Kentucky, and rice in South Carolina, expanded into lush new cotton lands in Georgia, Alabama, Mississippi—and needed more slaves. But slave importation became illegal in 1808. Therefore, "from the beginning, the law went unenforced," says John Hope Franklin (*From Slavery to Freedom*). "The long, unprotected coast, the certain markets, and the prospects of huge profits were too much for the American merchants and they yielded to the temptation...." He estimates that perhaps 250,000 slaves were imported illegally before the Civil War.

How can slavery be described? Perhaps not at all by those who have not experienced it. The 1932 edition of a best-selling textbook by two northern liberal historians saw slavery as perhaps the Negro's "necessary transition to civilization." Economists or cliometricians (statistical historians) have tried to assess slavery by estimating how much money was spent on slaves for food and medical care. But can this describe the reality of slavery as it was to a human being who lived inside it? Are the *conditions* of slavery as important as the *existence* of slavery?

John Little, a former slave, wrote:

> They say slaves are happy, because they laugh, and are merry. I myself and three or four others, have received two hundred lashes in the day, and had our feet in fetters; yet, at night, we would sing and dance, and make others laugh at the rattling of our chains. Happy men we must have been! We did it to keep down trouble, and to keep our hearts from being completely broken: that is as true as the gospel! Just look at it,—must not we have been very happy? Yet I have done it myself—I have cut capers in chains.

A record of deaths kept in a plantation journal (now in the University of North Carolina Archives) lists the ages and cause of death of all those who died on the plantation between 1850 and 1855. Of the thirty-two who died in that period, only four reached the age of sixty, four reached the age of fifty, seven died in their forties, seven died in their twenties or thirties, and nine died before they were five years old.

But can statistics record what it meant for families to be torn apart, when a master, for profit, sold a husband or a wife, a son or a daughter? In 1858, a slave named Abream Scriven was sold by his master, and wrote to his wife: "Give my love to my father and mother and tell them good Bye for me, and if we Shall not meet in this world I hope to meet in heaven."

One recent book on slavery (Robert Fogel and Stanley Engerman, *Time on the Cross*) looks at whippings in 1840–1842 on the Barrow plantation in Louisiana with two hundred slaves: "The records show that over the course of two years a total of 160 whippings were administered, an average of 0.7 whippings per hand per year. About half the hands were not whipped at all during the period." One could also say: "Half of all slaves were whipped." That has a different ring. That figure (0.7 per hand per year) shows whipping was infrequent for any individual. But looked at another way, once every four or five days, *some* slave was whipped.

Barrow as a plantation owner, according to his biographer, was no worse than the average. He spent money on clothing for his slaves, gave them holiday celebrations, built a dance hall for them. He also built a jail and "was constantly devising ingenious punishments, for he realized that uncertainty was an important aid in keeping his gangs well in hand."

The whippings, the punishments, were work disciplines. Still, Herbert Gutman (*Slavery and the Numbers Game*) finds, dissecting Fogel and Engerman's statistics, "Over all, four in five cotton pickers engaged in one or more disorderly acts in 1840–41…. As a group, a slightly higher percentage of women than men committed seven or more disorderly acts." Thus, Gutman disputes the argument of Fogel and Engerman that the Barrow plantation slaves became "devoted, hard-working responsible slaves who identified their fortunes with the fortunes of their masters."

Slave revolts in the United States were not as frequent or as large-scale as those in the Caribbean islands or in South America. Probably the largest slave revolt in the United States took place near New Orleans in 1811. Four to five hundred slaves gathered after a rising at the plantation of a Major Andry. Armed with cane knives, axes, and clubs, they wounded Andry, killed his son, and began marching from plantation to plantation, their numbers growing. They were attacked by U.S. army and militia forces; sixty-six were killed on the spot, and sixteen were tried and shot by a firing squad.

The conspiracy of Denmark Vesey, himself a free Negro, was thwarted before it could be carried out in 1822. The plan was to burn Charleston, South Carolina, then the sixth-largest city in the nation, and to initiate a general revolt of slaves in the area. Several witnesses said thousands of blacks were implicated in one way or another. Blacks had made about 250 pike heads and bayonets and over three hundred daggers, according to Herbert Aptheker's account. But the plan was betrayed, and thirty-five blacks, including Vesey, were hanged. The trial record itself, published in Charleston, was ordered destroyed soon after publication, as too dangerous for slaves to see.

Nat Turner's rebellion in Southampton County, Virginia, in the summer of 1831, threw the slaveholding South into a panic, and then into a determined effort to bolster the security of the slave system. Turner, claiming religious visions, gathered about seventy slaves, who went on a rampage from plantation to plantation, murdering at least fifty-five men, women, and children. They gathered supporters, but were captured as their ammunition ran out. Turner and perhaps eighteen others were hanged.

Did such rebellions set back the cause of emancipation, as some moderate abolitionists claimed at the time? An answer was given in 1845 by James Hammond, a supporter of slavery:

> But if your course was wholly different—If you distilled nectar from your lips and discoursed sweetest music. . . . do you imagine you could prevail on us to give up a thousand millions of dollars in the value of our slaves, and a thousand millions of dollars more in the depreciation of our lands . . . ?

The slaveowner understood this, and prepared. Henry Tragle (*The Southampton Slave Revolt of 1831*), says:

> In 1831, Virginia was an armed and garrisoned state. . . . With a total population of 1,211,405, the State of Virginia was able to field a militia force of 101,488 men, including cavalry, artillery, grenadiers, riflemen, and light infantry! It is true that this was a "paper army" in some ways, in that the county regiments were not fully armed and equipped, but it is still an astonishing commentary on the state of the public mind of the time. During a period when neither the State nor the nation

faced any sort of exterior threat, we find that Virginia felt the need to maintain a security force roughly ten percent of the total number of its inhabitants: black and white, male and female, slave and free!

Rebellion, though rare, was a constant fear among slaveowners. Ulrich Phillips, a southerner whose *American Negro Slavery* is a classic study, wrote:

> A great number of southerners at all times held the firm belief that the negro population was so docile, so little cohesive, and in the main so friendly toward the whites and so contented that a disastrous insurrection by them would be impossible. But on the whole, there was much greater anxiety abroad in the land than historians have told of. . . .

Eugene Genovese, in his comprehensive study of slavery, *Roll, Jordan, Roll,* sees a record of "simultaneous accommodation and resistance to slavery." The resistance included stealing property, sabotage and slowness, killing overseers and masters, burning down plantation buildings, running away. Even the accommodation "breathed a critical spirit and disguised subversive actions." Most of this resistance, Genovese stresses, fell short of organized insurrection, but its significance for masters and slaves was enormous.

Running away was much more realistic than armed insurrection. During the 1850s about a thousand slaves a year escaped into the North, Canada, and Mexico. Thousands ran away for short periods. And this despite the terror facing the runaway. The dogs used in tracking fugitives "bit, tore, mutilated, and if not pulled off in time, killed their prey," Genovese says.

Harriet Tubman, born into slavery, her head injured by an overseer when she was fifteen, made her way to freedom alone as a young woman, then became the most famous conductor on the Underground Railroad. She made nineteen dangerous trips back and forth, often disguised, escorting more than three hundred slaves to freedom, always carrying a pistol, telling the fugitives, "You'll be free or die." She expressed her philosophy: "There was one of two things I had a right to, liberty or death; if I could not have one, I would have the other; for no man should take me alive. . . ."

One overseer told a visitor to his plantation that "some negroes are determined never to let a white man whip them and will resist you, when you attempt it; of course you must kill them in that case."

One form of resistance was not to work so hard. W. E. B. Du Bois wrote, in *The Gift of Black Folk:*

> As a tropical product with a sensuous receptivity to the beauty of the world, he was not as easily reduced to be the mechanical draft-horse which the northern European laborer became. He . . . tended to work as the results pleased him and refused to work or sought to refuse when he did not find the spiritual returns adequate; thus he was easily accused of laziness and driven as a slave when in truth he brought to modern manual labor a renewed valuation of life.

Ulrich Phillips described "truancy," "absconding," "vacations without leave," and "resolute efforts to escape from bondage altogether." He also described collective actions:

> Occasionally, however, a squad would strike in a body as a protest against severities. An episode of this sort was recounted in a letter of a Georgia overseer to his absent employer: "Sir, I write you a few lines in order to let you know that six of your hands has left the plantation—every man but Jack. They displeased me with their work and I give some of them a few lashes, Tom with the rest. On Wednesday morning, they were missing."

The instances where poor whites helped slaves were not frequent, but sufficient to show the need for setting one group against the other. Genovese says:

> The slaveholders...suspected that non-slaveholders would encourage slave disobedience and even rebellion, not so much out of sympathy for the blacks as out of hatred for the rich planters and resentment of their own poverty. White men sometimes were linked to slave insurrectionary plots, and each such incident rekindled fears.

This helps explain the stern police measures against whites who fraternized with blacks.

Herbert Aptheker quotes a report to the governor of Virginia on a slave conspiracy in 1802: "I have just received information that three white persons are concerned in the plot; and they have arms and ammunition concealed under their houses, and were to give aid when the negroes should begin." One of the conspiring slaves said that it was "the common run of poor white people" who were involved.

In return, blacks helped whites in need. One black runaway told of a slave woman who had received fifty lashes of the whip for giving food to a white neighbor who was poor and sick.

When the Brunswick canal was built in Georgia, the black slaves and white Irish workers were segregated, the excuse being that they would do violence against one another. That may well have been true, but Fanny Kemble, the famous actress and wife of a planter, wrote in her journal:

> But the Irish are not only quarrelers, and rioters, and fighters, and drinkers, and despisers of niggers—they are a passionate, impulsive, warm-hearted, generous people, much given to powerful indignations, which break out suddenly when not compelled to smoulder sullenly—pestilent sympathizers too, and with a sufficient dose of American atmospheric air in their lungs, properly mixed with a right proportion of ardent spirits, there is no saying but what they might actually take to sympathy with the slaves, and I leave you to judge of the possible consequences. You perceive, I am sure, that they can by no means be allowed to work together on the Brunswick Canal.

The need for slave control led to an ingenious device, paying poor whites—themselves so troublesome for two hundred years of southern history—to be overseers of black labor and therefore buffers for black hatred.

Religion was used for control. A book consulted by many planters was the *Cotton Plantation Record and Account Book*, which gave these instructions to overseers: "You will find that an hour devoted every Sabbath morning to their moral and religious instruction would prove a great aid to you in bringing about a better state of things amongst the Negroes."

As for black preachers, as Genovese puts its, "they had to speak a language defiant enough to hold the high-spirited among their flock but neither so inflammatory as to rouse them to battles they could not win nor so ominous as to arouse the ire of ruling powers." Practicality decided: "The slave communities, embedded as they were among numerically preponderant and militarily powerful whites, counseled a strategy of patience, of acceptance of what could not be helped, of a dogged effort to keep the black community alive and healthy—a strategy of survival that, like its African prototype, above all said yes to life in this world."

It was once thought that slavery had destroyed the black family. And so the black condition was blamed on family frailty, rather than on poverty and prejudice. Blacks without families, helpless, lacking kinship and identity, would have no will to resist. But interviews with ex-slaves, done in the 1930s by the Federal Writers Project of the New Deal for the Library of Congress, showed a different story, which George Rawick summarizes (*From Sundown to Sunup*):

> The slave community acted like a generalized extended kinship system in which all adults looked after all children and there was little division between "my children for whom I'm responsible" and "your children for whom you're responsible." ... A kind of family relationship in which older children have great responsibility for caring for younger siblings is obviously more functionally integrative and useful for slaves than the pattern of sibling rivalry and often dislike that frequently comes out of contemporary middle-class nuclear families composed of highly individuated persons. ... Indeed, the activity of the slaves in creating patterns of family life that were functionally integrative did more than merely prevent the destruction of personality. ... It was part and parcel, as we shall see, of the social process out of which came black pride, black identity, black culture, the black community, and black rebellion in America.

Old letters and records dug out by historian Herbert Gutman (*The Black Family in Slavery and Freedom*) show the stubborn resistance of the slave family to pressures of disintegration. A woman wrote to her son from whom she had been separated for twenty years: "I long to see you in my old age. ... Now my dear son I pray you to come and see your dear old Mother. ... I love you Cato you love your Mother—You are my only son. ..."

And a man wrote to his wife, sold away from him with their children: "Send me some of the children's hair in a separate paper with their names on the paper. ... I had rather anything to had happened to me most than ever to have been parted from you and the children. . . . Laura I do love you the same. . . ."

Going through records of slave marriages, Gutman found how high was the incidence of marriage among slave men and women, and how stable these marriages were. He studied the remarkably complete records kept on one South Carolina plantation. He found a birth register of two hundred slaves extending from the eighteenth century to just before the Civil War; it showed stable kin networks, steadfast marriages, unusual fidelity, and resistance to forced marriages.

Slaves hung on determinedly to their selves, to their love of family, their wholeness. A shoemaker on the South Carolina Sea Islands expressed this in his own way: "I'se lost an arm but it hasn't gone out of my brains."

This family solidarity carried into the twentieth century. The remarkable southern black farmer Nate Shaw recalled that when his sister died, leaving three children, his father proposed sharing their care, and he responded:

> That suits me, Papa. . . . Let's handle em like this: don't get the two little boys, the youngest ones, off at your house and the oldest one be at my house and we hold these little boys apart and won't bring em to see one another. I'll bring the little boy that I keep, the oldest one, around to your home amongst the other two. And you forward the others to my house and let em grow up knowin that they are brothers. Don't keep em separated in a way that they'll forget about one another. Don't do that, Papa.

Also insisting on the strength of blacks even under slavery, Lawrence Levine (*Black Culture and Black Consciousness*) gives a picture of a rich culture among slaves, a complex mixture of adaptation and rebellion, through the creativity of stories and songs:

> We raise de wheat,
> Dey gib us de corn;
> We bake de bread,
> Dey gib us de crust,
> We sif de meal,
> Dey gib us de huss;
> We peel de meat,
> Dey gib us de skin;
> And dat's de way
> Dey take us in;
> We skim de pot,
> Dey gib us de liquor,
> An say dat's good enough for nigger.

There was mockery. The poet William Cullen Bryant, after attending a corn shucking in 1843 in South Carolina, told of slave dances turned into a pretended military parade, "a sort of burlesque of our militia trainings. . . ."

Spirituals often had double meanings. The song "O Canaan, sweet Canaan, I am bound for the land of Canaan" often meant that slaves meant to get to the North, their Canaan. During the Civil War, slaves began to make up new spirituals with bolder messages: "Before I'd be a slave, I'd be buried in my grave, and go home to my Lord and be saved." And the spiritual "Many Thousand Go":

> No more peck o' corn for me, no more, no more,
> No more driver's lash for me, no more, no more. . . .

Levine refers to slave resistance as "pre-political," expressed in countless ways in daily life and culture. Music, magic, art, religion, were all ways, he says, for slaves to hold on to their humanity.

While southern slaves held on, free blacks in the North (there were about 130,000 in 1830, about 200,000 in 1850) agitated for the abolition of slavery. In 1829, David Walker, son of a slave, but born free in North Carolina, moved to Boston, where he sold old clothes. The pamphlet he wrote and printed, *Walker's Appeal*, became widely known. It infuriated southern slaveholders; Georgia offered a reward of $10,000 to anyone who would deliver Walker alive, and $1,000 to anyone who would kill him. It is not hard to understand why when you read his *Appeal*.

There was no slavery in history, even that of the Israelites in Egypt, worse than the slavery of the black man in America, Walker said. ". . . show me a page of history, either sacred or profane, on which a verse can be found, which maintains, that the Egyptians heaped the insupportable insult upon the children of Israel, by telling them that they were not of the human family."

Walker was scathing to his fellow blacks who would assimilate: "I would wish, candidly . . . to be understood, that I would not give a pinch of snuff to be married to any white person I ever saw in all the days of my life."

Blacks must fight for their freedom, he said:

> Let our enemies go on with their butcheries, and at once fill up their cup. Never make an attempt to gain our freedom or natural right from under our cruel oppressors and murderers, until you see your way clear—when that hour arrives and you move, be not afraid or dismayed. . . . God has been pleased to give us two eyes, two hands, two feet, and some sense in our heads as well as they. They have no more right to hold us in slavery than we have to hold them. . . . Our sufferings will come to an end, in spite of all the Americans this side of eternity. Then we will want all the learning and talents among ourselves, and perhaps more, to govern ourselves.—"Every dog must have its day," the American's is coming to an end.

One summer day in 1830, David Walker was found dead near the doorway of his shop in Boston.

Some born in slavery acted out the unfulfilled desire of millions. Frederick Douglass, a slave, sent to Baltimore to work as a servant and as a laborer in the shipyard, somehow learned to read and write, and at twenty-one, in the year 1838, escaped to the North, where he became the most famous black man of his time, as lecturer, newspaper editor, writer. In his autobiography, *Narrative of the Life of Frederick Douglass*, he recalled his first childhood thoughts about his condition:

> Why am I a slave? Why are some people slaves, and others masters? Was there ever a time when this was not so? How did the relation commence?
>
> Once, however, engaged in the inquiry, I was not very long in finding out the true solution of the matter. It was not color, but crime, not God, but man, that afforded the true explanation of the existence of slavery; nor was I long in finding out another important truth, viz: what man can make, man can unmake. . . .
>
> I distinctly remember being, even then, most strongly impressed with the idea of being a free man some day. This cheering assurance was an inborn dream of my human nature—a constant menace to slavery—and one which all the powers of slavery were unable to silence or extinguish.

The Fugitive Slave Act passed in 1850 was a concession to the southern states in return for the admission of the Mexican war territories (California, especially) into the Union as nonslave states. The Act made it easy for slaveowners to recapture ex-slaves or simply to pick up blacks they claimed had run away. Northern blacks organized resistance to the Fugitive Slave Act, denouncing President Fillmore, who signed it, and Senator Daniel Webster, who supported it. One of these was J. W. Loguen, son of a slave mother and her white owner. He had escaped to freedom on his master's horse, gone to college, and was now a minister in Syracuse, New York. He spoke to a meeting in that city in 1850:

> The time has come to change the tones of submission into tones of defiance—and to tell Mr. Fillmore and Mr. Webster, if they propose to execute this measure upon us, to send on their blood-hounds. . . . I received my freedom from Heaven, and with it came the command to defend my title to it. . . . I don't respect this law—I don't fear it—I won't obey it! It outlaws me, and I outlaw it. . . . I will not live a slave, and if force is employed to re-enslave me, I shall make preparations to meet the crisis as becomes a man. . . . Your decision tonight in favor of resistance will give vent to the spirit of liberty, and it will break the bands of party, and shout for joy all over the North. . . . Heaven knows that this act of noble daring will break out somewhere—and may God grant that Syracuse be the honored spot, whence it shall send an earthquake voice through the land!

The following year, Syracuse had its chance. A runaway slave named Jerry was captured and put on trial. A crowd used crowbars and a battering ram to break into the courthouse, defying marshals with drawn guns, and set Jerry free.

Part Three—Reconstruction

13th, 14th, and 15th Amendments to the Constitution of the United States

AMENDMENT XIII [1865]

Section 1

Neither slavery nor involuntary servitude, except as a punishment for crime whereof the party shall have been duly convicted, shall exist within the United States, or any place subject to their jurisdiction.

Section 2

Congress shall have power to enforce this article by appropriate legislation.

AMENDMENT XIV [1868]

Section 1

All persons born or naturalized in the United States, and subject to the jurisdiction thereof, are citizens of the United States and of the State wherein they reside. No State shall make or enforce any law which shall abridge the privileges or immunities of citizens of the United States; nor shall any State deprive any person of life, liberty, or property, without due process of law; nor deny to any person within its jurisdiction the equal protection of the laws.

Section 2

Representatives shall be apportioned among the several States according to their respective numbers, counting the whole number of persons in each State, excluding Indians not taxed. But when the right to vote at any election for the choice of electors for President and Vice President of the United States, Representatives in Congress, the Executive and Judicial officers of a State, or the members of the Legislature thereof, is denied to any of the male inhabitants of such State, being twenty-one years of age, and citizens of the United States or in any way abridged, except for participation in rebellion, or other crime, the basis of representaton therein shall be reduced in the proportion which the number of such male citizens shall bear to the whole number of male citizens twenty-one years of age in such State.

Section 3

No person shall be a Senator or Representative in Congress, or elector of President and Vice President, or hold any office, civil or military, under the United States, or under any State, who, having previously taken an oath, as a member of Congress, or as an officer of the United States, or as a member of any State legislature, or as an executive or judicial officer of any State, to support the Constitution of the United States, shall have engaged in insurrection or rebellion against the same, or given aid or comfort to the enemies thereof. But Congress may by a vote of two-thirds of each House, remove such disability.

Section 4

The validity of the public debt of the United States, authorized by law, including debts incurred for payment of pensions and bounties for services in suppressing insurrection or rebellion, shall not be questioned. But neither the United States nor any State shall assume or pay any debt or obligation incurred in aid of insurrection or rebellion against the United States, or any claim for the loss or emancipation of any slave; but all such debts, obligations, and claims shall be held illegal and void.

Section 5

The Congress shall have the power to enforce, by appropriate legislation, the provisions of this article.

AMENDMENT XV [1870]

Section 1

The right of citizens of the United States to vote shall not be denied or abridged by the United States or by any State on account of race, color, or previous condition of servitude.

Section 2

The Congress shall have power to enforce this article by appropriate legislation.

Elizabeth Keckley
from *Behind the Scenes: Thirty Years a Slave and Four Years in the White House*

CHAPTER IX.

Behind the Scenes.

Some of the freedmen and freedwomen had exaggerated ideas of liberty. To them it was a beautiful vision, a land of sunshine, rest, and glorious promise. They flocked to Washington, and since their extravagant hopes were not realized, it was but natural that many of them should bitterly feel their disappointment. The colored people are wedded to associations, and when you destroy these you destroy half of the happiness of their lives. They make a home, and are so fond of it that they prefer it, squalid though it be, to the comparative ease and luxury of a shifting, roaming life. Well, the emancipated slaves, in coming North, left old associations behind them, and the love for the past was so strong that they could not find much beauty in the new life so suddenly opened to them. Thousands of the disappointed, huddled together in camps, fretted and pined like children for the "good old times." In visiting them in the interests of the Relief Society of which I was president, they would crowd around me with pitiful stories of distress. Often I heard them declare that they would rather go back to slavery in the South, and be with their old masters, than to enjoy the freedom of the North. I believe they were sincere in these declarations, because dependence had become a part of their second nature, and independence brought with it the cares and vexations of poverty.

I was very much amused one day at the grave complaints of a good old, simple-minded woman, fresh from a life of servitude. She had never ventured beyond a plantation until coming North. The change was too radical for her, and she could not exactly understand it. She thought, as many others thought, that Mr. and Mrs. Lincoln were the government, and that the President and his wife had nothing to do but to supply the extravagant wants of every one that applied to them. The wants of this old woman, however, were not very extravagant.

"Why, Missus Keckley," said she to me one day, "I is been here eight months, and Missus Lingom an't even give me one shife. Bliss God, childen, if I had ar know dat de Government, and Mister and Missus Government, was going to do dat ar way, I neber would 'ave comed here in God's wurld. My old missus us't gib me two shifes eber year."

I could not restrain a laugh at the grave manner in which this good old woman entered her protest. Her idea of freedom was two or more old shifts every year. Northern readers may not fully recognize the pith of the joke. On the Southern plantation, the mistress, according to established custom, every year made a present of certain under-garments to her slaves, which articles were always anxiously looked forward to, and thankfully received. The old woman had been in the habit of receiving annually two shifts from her mistress, and she thought the wife of the President of the United States very mean for overlooking this established custom of the plantation.

While some of the emancipated blacks pined for the old associations of slavery, and refused to help themselves, others went to work with commendable energy, and planned with remarkable forethought. They built themselves cabins, and each family cultivated for itself a small patch of ground. The colored people are fond of domestic life, and with them domestication means happy children, a fat pig, a dozen or more chickens, and a garden. Whoever visits the Freedmen's Village now in the vicinity of Washington will discover all of these evidences of prosperity and happiness. The schools are objects of much interest. Good teachers, white and colored, are employed, and whole brigades of bright-eyed dusky children are there taught the common branches of education. These children are studious, and the teachers inform me that their advancement is rapid. I number among my personal friends twelve colored girls employed as teachers in the schools at Washington. The Colored Mission Sabbath School, established through the influence of Gen. Brown at the Fifteenth Street Presbyterian Church, is always an object of great interest to the residents of the Capital, as well as to the hundreds of strangers visiting the city.

In 1864 the receptions again commenced at the White House. For the first two years of Mr. Lincoln's administration, the President selected a lady to join in the promenade with him, which left Mrs. Lincoln free to choose an escort from among the distinguished gentlemen that always surrounded her on such occasions. This custom at last was discontinued by Mrs. Lincoln.

"Lizabeth!"—I was sewing in her room, and she was seated in a comfortable arm-chair—"Lizabeth, I have been thinking over a little matter. As you are well aware, the President, at every reception, selects a lady to lead the promenade with him. Now it occurs to me that this custom is an absurd one. On such occasions our guests recognize the position of the President as first of all; consequently, he takes the lead in everything; well, now, if they recognize his position they should also recognize mine. I am his wife, and should lead with him. And yet he offers his arm to any other lady in the room, making her first with him and placing me second. The custom is an absurd one, and I mean to abolish it. The dignity that I owe to my position, as Mrs. President, demands that I should not hesitate any longer to act."

Mrs. Lincoln kept her word. Ever after this, she either led the promenade with the President, or the President walked alone or with a gentleman. The change was much remarked, but the reason why it was made, I believe, was never generally known.

In 1864 much doubt existed in regard to the re-election of Mr. Lincoln, and the White House was besieged by all grades of politicians. Mrs. Lincoln was often blamed for having a certain class of men around her.

"I have an object in view, Lizabeth," she said to me in reference to this matter. "In a political canvass it is policy to cultivate every element of strength. These men have influence, and we require influence to re-elect Mr. Lincoln. I will be clever to them until after the election, and then, if we remain at the White House, I will drop every one of them, and let them know very plainly that I only made tools of them. They are an unprincipled set, and I don't mind a little double-dealing with them."

"Does Mr. Lincoln know what your purpose is?" I asked.

"God! no; he would never sanction such a proceeding, so I keep him in the dark, and will tell him of it when all is over. He is too honest to take the proper care of his own interests, so I feel it to be my duty to electioneer for him."

Mr. Lincoln, as every one knows, was far from handsome. He was not admired for his graceful figure and finely moulded face, but for the nobility of his soul and the greatness of his heart. His wife was different. He was wholly unselfish in every respect, and I believe that he loved the mother of his children very tenderly. He asked nothing but affection from her, but did not always receive it. When in one of her wayward impulsive moods, she was apt to say and do things that wounded him deeply. If he had not loved her, she would have been powerless to cloud his thoughtful face, or gild it with a ray of sunshine as she pleased. We are indifferent to those we do not love, and certainly the President was not indifferent to his wife. She often wounded him in unguarded moments, but calm reflection never failed to bring regret.

Mrs. Lincoln was extremely anxious that her husband should be re-elected President of the United States. In endeavoring to make a display becoming her exalted position, she had to incur many expenses. Mr. Lincoln's salary was inadequate to meet them, and she was forced to run in debt, hoping that good fortune would favor her, and enable her to extricate herself from an embarrassing situation. She bought the most expensive goods on credit, and in the summer of 1864 enormous unpaid bills stared her in the face.

"What do you think about the election, Lizabeth?" she said to me one morning.

"I think that Mr. Lincoln will remain in the White House four years longer," I replied, looking up from my work.

"What makes you think so? Somehow I have learned to fear that he will be defeated."

"Because he has been tried, and has proved faithful to the best interests of the country. The people of the North recognize in him an honest man, and they are willing to confide in him, at least until the war has been brought to a close. The Southern people made his election a pretext for rebellion, and now to replace him by some one else, after years of sanguinary war, would look too much like a surrender of the North. So, Mr. Lincoln is certain to be re-elected.

He represents a principle, and to maintain this principle the loyal people of the loyal States will vote for him, even if he had no merits to commend him."

"Your view is a plausible one, Lizabeth, and your confidence gives me new hope. If he should be defeated, I do not know what would become of us all. To me, to him, there is more at stake in this election than he dreams of."

"What can you mean, Mrs. Lincoln? I do not comprehend."

"Simply this. I have contracted large debts, of which he knows nothing, and which he will be unable to pay if he is defeated."

"What are your debts, Mrs. Lincoln?"

"They consist chiefly of store bills. I owe altogether about twenty-seven thousand dollars; the principal portion at Stewart's, in New York. You understand, Lizabeth, that Mr. Lincoln has but little idea of the expense of a woman's wardrobe. He glances at my rich dresses, and is happy in the belief that the few hundred dollars that I obtain from him supply all my wants. I must dress in costly materials. The people scrutinize every article that I wear with critical curiosity. The very fact of having grown up in the West, subjects me to more searching observation. To keep up appearances, I must have money—more than Mr. Lincoln can spare for me. He is too honest to make a penny outside of his salary; consequently I had, and still have, no alternative but to run in debt."

"And Mr. Lincoln does not even suspect how much you owe?"

"God, no!"—this was a favorite expression of hers—"and I would not have him suspect. If he knew that his wife was involved to the extent that she is, the knowledge would drive him mad. He is so sincere and straightforward himself, that he is shocked by the duplicity of others. He does not know a thing about any debts, and I value his happiness, not to speak of my own, too much to allow him to know anything. This is what troubles me so much. If he is re-elected, I can keep him in ignorance of my affairs; but if he is defeated, then the bills will be sent in, and he will know all;" and something like a hysterical sob escaped her.

Mrs. Lincoln sometimes feared that the politicians would get hold of the particulars of her debts, and use them in the Presidential campaign against her husband; and when this thought occurred to her, she was almost crazy with anxiety and fear.

When in one of these excited moods, she would fiercely exclaim—

"The Republican politicians must pay my debts. Hundreds of them are getting immensely rich off the patronage of my husband, and it is but fair that they should help me out of my embarrassment. I will make a demand of them, and when I tell them the facts they cannot refuse to advance whatever money I require."

W. E. B. Du Bois

from *Black Reconstruction in America, 1860–1880*

VIII. TRANSUBSTANTIATION OF A POOR WHITE

How Andrew Johnson, unexpectedly raised to the Presidency, was suddenly set between a democracy which included poor whites and black men, and an autocracy that included Big Business and slave barons; and how torn between impossible allegiances, he ended in forcing a hesitant nation to choose between the increased political power of a restored Southern oligarchy and votes for Negroes

Like Nemesis of Greek tragedy, the central problem of America after the Civil War, as before, was the black man: those four million souls whom the nation had used and degraded, and on whom the South had built an oligarchy similar to the colonial imperialism of today, erected on cheap colored labor and raising raw material for manufacture. If Northern industry before the war had secured a monopoly of the raw material raised in the South for its new manufactures; and if Northern and Western labor could have maintained their wage scale against slave competition, the North would not have touched the slave system. But this the South had frustrated. It had threatened labor with nation-wide slave competition and had sent its cotton abroad to buy cheap manufactures, and had resisted the protective tariff demanded by the North.

It was this specific situation that had given the voice of freedom a chance to be heard: freedom for new-come peasants who feared the competition of slave labor; peasants from Europe, New England and the poor white South; freedom for all men black and white through that dream of democracy in which the best of the nation still believed.

The result was war because of the moral wrong, the economic disaster and the democratic contradiction of making human labor real estate; war, because the South was determined to make free white labor compete with black slaves, monopolize land and raw material in the hands of a political aristocracy, and extend the scope of that power; war, because the industrial North refused to surrender its raw material and one of its chief markets to Europe; war, because white American labor, while it refused to recognize black labor as equal and human, had to fight to maintain its own humanity and ideal of equality.

The result of the war left four million human beings just as valuable for the production of cotton and sugar as they had been before the war—but during the war, as laborers and soldiers, these Negroes had made it possible for the

North to win, and without their actual and possible aid, the South would never have surrendered; and not least, these four million free men formed in the end the only possible moral justification for an otherwise sordid and selfish orgy of murder, arson and theft.

Now, early in 1865, the war is over. The North does not especially want free Negroes; it wants trade and wealth. The South does not want a particular interpretation of the Constitution. It wants cheap Negro labor and the political and social power based on it. Had there been no Negroes, there would have been no war. Had no Negroes survived the war, peace would have been difficult because of hatred, loss and bitter grief. But its logical path would have been straight.

The South would have returned to its place in Congress with less than its former representation because of the growing North and West. These areas of growing manufacture and agriculture, railroad building and corporations, would have held the political power over the South until the South united with the new insurgency of the West or the old Eastern democratic ideals. Industrialization might even have brought a third party representing labor and raised the proletariat to dominance.

Of this, in 1865 there were only vague signs, and in any case, the former Southern aristocracy would not easily have allied itself with immigrant labor, while the Southern poor whites would have needed long experience and teaching. Thus, the North in the absence of the Negro would have had a vast debt, a problem of charity, distress and relief, such reasonable amnesty as would prevent the old Southern leaders from returning immediately to power, the recognition of the reorganized states, and then work and forgetting.

"Let us have peace." But there was the black man looming like a dark ghost on the horizon. He was the child of force and greed, and the father of wealth and war. His labor was indispensable, and the loss of it would have cost many times the cost of the war. If the Negro had been silent, his very presence would have announced his plight. He was not silent. He was in unusual evidence. He was writing petitions, making speeches, parading with returned soldiers, reciting his adventures as slave and freeman. Even dumb and still, he must be noticed. His poverty had to be relieved, and emancipation in his case had to mean poverty. If he had to work, he had to have land and tools. If his labor was in reality to be free labor, he had to have legal freedom and civil rights. His ignorance could only be removed by that very education which the law of the South had long denied him and the custom of the North had made exceedingly difficult. Thus civil status and legal freedom, food, clothes and tools, access to land and help to education, were the minimum demands of four million laborers, and these demands no man could ignore, Northerner or Southerner, Abolitionist or Copperhead, laborer or captain of industry. How did the nation face this paradox and dilemma?

Led by Abraham Lincoln, the nation had looked back to the status before the war in order to find a path to which the new nation and the new condition of the freedmen could be guided. Only one forward step President Lincoln insisted upon and that was the real continued freedom of the emancipated slave; but the abolition-democracy went beyond this because it was convinced that here was no logical stopping place; and it looked forward to civil and political rights, education and land, as the only complete guarantee of freedom, in the face of a dominant South which hoped from the first, to abolish slavery only in name.

In the North, a new and tremendous dictatorship of capital was arising. There was only one way to curb and direct what promised to become the greatest plutocratic government which the world had ever known. This way was first to implement public opinion by the weapon of universal suffrage—a weapon which the nation already had in part, but which had been virtually impotent in the South because of slavery, and which was at least weakened in the North by the disfranchisement of an unending mass of foreign-born laborers. Once universal suffrage was achieved, the next step was to use it with such intelligence and power that it would function in the interest of the mass of working men.

To accomplish this end there should have been in the country and represented in Congress a union between the champions of universal suffrage and the rights of the freedmen, together with the leaders of labor, the small landholders of the West, and logically, the poor whites of the South. Against these would have been arrayed the Northern industrial oligarchy, and eventually, when they were re-admitted to Congress, the representatives of the former Southern oligarchy.

This union of democratic forces never took place. On the contrary, they were torn apart by artificial lines of division. The old anti-Negro labor rivalry between white and black workers kept the labor elements after the war from ever really uniting in a demand to increase labor power by Negro suffrage and Negro economic stability. The West was seduced from a vision of peasant-proprietors, recruited from a laboring class, into a vision of labor-exploiting farmers and land speculation which tended to transform the Western farmers into a petty bourgeoisie fighting not to overcome but to share spoils with the large land speculators, the monopolists of transportation, and the financiers. Wherever a liberal and democratic party started to differentiate itself from this group, the only alliance offered was the broken oligarchy of the South, with its determination to reenslave Negro labor.

The effective combination which ensued was both curious and contradictory. The masters of industry, the financiers and monopolists, had in self-defense to join with abolition-democracy in forcing universal suffrage on the South, or submit to the reassertion of the old land-slave feudalism with increased political power.

Such a situation demanded an economic guardianship of freedmen, and the first step to this meant at least the beginning of a dictatorship by labor. This, however, had to be but temporary union and was bound to break up before long. The break was begun by the extraordinary corruption, graft and theft that became more and more evident in the country from 1868 on, as a result of the wild idea that industry and progress for the people of the United States were compatible with the selfish sequestration of profit for private individuals and powerful corporations.

But those who revolted from the party of exploitation and high finance did not see allies in the dictatorship of labor in the South. Rather they were entirely misled by the complaint of property from the Southern oligarchy. They failed to become a real party of economic reform and became a reaction of small property-holders against corporations; of a petty bourgeoisie against a new economic monarchy. They immediately joined Big Business in coming to an understanding with the South in 1876, so that by force and fraud the South overthrew the dictatorship of the workers.

But this was only the immediate cause. If there had been no widespread political corruption, North and South, there would still have arisen an absolute difference between those who were trying to conduct the new Southern state governments in the interest of the mass of laborers, black and white, and those North and South who were determined to exploit labor, both in agriculture and industry, for the benefit of an oligarchy. Such an oligarchy was in effect back of the military dictatorship which supported these very Southern labor governments, and which had to support them either as laborers or by developing among them a capitalist class. But as soon as there was understanding between the Southern exploiter of labor and the Northern exploiter, this military support would be withdrawn; and the labor governments, in spite of what they had accomplished for the education of the masses, and in spite of the movements against waste and graft which they had inaugurated, would fail. Under such circumstances, they had to fail, and in a large sense the immediate hope of American democracy failed with them.

Let us now follow this development more in detail. In 1863 and 1864, Abraham Lincoln had made his tentative proposals for reconstructing the South. He had left many things unsaid. The loyal-minded, consisting of as few as one-tenth of the voters whom Lincoln proposed to regard as a state, must naturally, to survive, be supported by the United States Army, until a majority of the inhabitants acquiesced in the new arrangements. It was Lincoln's fond hope that this acquiescence might be swift and clear, but no one knew better than he that it might not.

He was careful to say that Congress would certainly have voice as to the terms on which they would recognize the newly elected Senators and Representatives. This proposal met the general approval of the country, but Congress saw danger and enacted the Wade-Davis Bill. This did not recognize Negro suffrage, and was not radically different from the Lincoln plan, except that the final power and assent of Congress were more prominently set forth.

Lincoln did not oppose it. He simply did not want his hands permanently tied. The bill failed, leaving Lincoln making a careful study of the situation, and promising another statement. He was going forward carefully, hoping for some liberal movement to show itself in the South, and delicately urging it. In the election of 1864, the country stood squarely back of him. The Northern democracy carried only New Jersey, Delaware and Kentucky. But he died, and Andrew Johnson took his place.

Thus, suddenly, April 15, 1865, Andrew Johnson found himself President of the United States, six days after Lee's surrender, and a month and a half after the 38th Congress had adjourned, March 3.

It was the drear destiny of the Poor White South that, deserting its economic class and itself, it became the instrument by which democracy in the nation was done to death, race provincialism deified, and the world delivered to plutocracy. The man who led the way with unconscious paradox and contradiction was Andrew Johnson.

Lately the early life and character of Andrew Johnson have been abundantly studied. He was a fanatical hater of aristocracy. "Through every public act of his runs one consistent, unifying thread of purpose—the advancement of the power, prosperity and liberty of the masses at the expense of intrenched privilege. The slaveholding aristocracy he hated with a bitter, enduring hatred born of envy and ambition. 'If Johnson were a snake,' said his rival, the well-born Isham G. Harris, 'he would lie in the grass to bite the heels of the rich men's children.' The very thought of an aristocrat caused him to emit venom and lash about him in fury."

His political methods were those of the barn-storming demagogue.

"Johnson's speeches were tissues of misstatement, misrepresentation, and insulting personalities, directed to the passions and unreasoning impulses of the ignorant voters; assaults upon aristocrats combined with vaunting of his own low origin and the dignity of manual labor." Yet a biographer says that Johnson was "the only President who practiced what he preached, drawing no distinction between rich and poor, or high and low...."

"Do not these facts furnish an explanation of Johnson's life? Do they not show why he had the courage to go up against caste and cheap aristocracy, why he dared to stand for the under-dog, whether Catholic, Hebrew, foreigner, mechanic, or child; and to cling like death to the old flag and the Union?...

" 'Gladly I would lay down my life,' he wrote, 'if I could so engraft democracy into our general government that it would be permanent.' "

To all this there is one great qualification. Andrew Johnson could not include Negroes in any conceivable democracy. He tried to, but as a poor white, steeped in the limitations, prejudices, and ambitions of his social class, he could not; and this is the key to his career.

Johnson sat in Congress from 1843 to 1853, and was Senator from 1857 to 1862. He favored the annexation of Texas as a gateway for Negro emigration. He was against a high tariff, championed free Western lands for white labor, and favored the annexation of Cuba for black slave labor.

McConnell introduced a homestead bill into Congress in January, 1846. Johnson's bill came in March. He returned to Tennessee as Governor, but induced the legislature to instruct members of Congress to vote for his bill. The bill finally passed the House but was defeated in the Senate, and this was repeated for several sessions. Meantime, Johnson found himself in curious company. He was linked on the one hand to the Free Soilers, and in 1851 went to New York to address a Land Reform Association. On the other hand, the South called him socialistic and Wigfall of Texas dubbed him: "The vilest of Republicans, the reddest of Reds, a sans-culotte, for four years past he has been trying to please the North with his Homestead and other bills." The Abolitionists meanwhile looked askance because Johnson favored the bill for annexing Cuba.

He voted against the Pacific railroad, owned eight slaves and said at one time: "You won't get rid of the Negro except by holding him in slavery." In the midst of such vacillation and contradiction, small wonder that Lane referred to Johnson's "triumphant ignorance and exulting stupidity." Yet Johnson hewed doggedly to certain lines. In 1860, he was advocating his homestead bill again. It finally passed both House and Senate, but Buchanan vetoed it as unconstitutional. Johnson called the message "monstrous and absurd." At last, in June, 1862, after the South had withdrawn from Congress, Johnson's bill was passed and Lincoln signed it.

Yet it was this same Johnson who said in the 36th Congress that if the Abolitionists freed the slaves and let them loose on the South, "the non-slaveholder would join with the slave-owner and extirpate them," and "if one should be more ready to join than another it would be myself."

Johnson early became a follower of Hinton Helper and used his figures. *The Impending Crisis* was "Andrew Johnson's vade mecum—his arsenal of facts."

Johnson made two violent speeches against secession in 1860–61, with bitter personalities against Jefferson Davis, Judah Benjamin and their fellows. He called them rebels and traitors; the galleries yelled and the presiding officers threatened to clear them. Johnson shouted: "I would have them arrested, and if convicted, within the meaning and scope of the Constitution, by the Eternal God, I would execute them; Sir, treason must be punished; its enormity and the extent and depth of the offense must be made known!"

Clingman of North Carolina said that Johnson's speech brought on the Civil War. Alexander Stephens said that it solidified the North. Letters came in to congratulate and to encourage "the only Union Senator from the South." Labor rallied to him. A Baltimore laborer wrote that "the poor working man will no doubt be called on to fight the battles of the rich." From Memphis another wrote: "It was labor that achieved our independence and the laborers are ready to maintain it." The New York Working Man's Association passed a resolution of thanks.

Lincoln set about winning Tennessee, and as a step toward it, asked Andrew Johnson to go and act as Military Governor, and restore the state. Johnson resigned from the Senate and went to Tennessee early in March, 1862. He arrived in Nashville March 12, and took possession of the State House. His courage and sacrifice eventually redeemed the state and restored it to the Union.

Several times Johnson spoke on slavery and the Negro. When he asked that plantations be divided in the South and lands opened in the West, he had in mind white men, who would thus become rich or at least richer. But for Negroes, he had nothing of the sort in mind, except the bare possibility that, if given freedom, they might continue to exist and not die out.

Johnson said in January, 1864, at Nashville in reply to a question as to whether he was in favor of emancipation:

"As for the Negro I am for setting him free but at the same time I assert that this is a white man's government.... If whites and blacks can't get along together arrangements must be made to colonize the blacks.... In 1843, when I was candidate for Governor, it was said, 'That fellow Johnson is a demagogue, is an Abolitionist.'... Because I advocated a white basis for representation—apportioning members of Congress according to the number of qualified voters, instead of embracing Negroes, they called me an Abolitionist.... What do we find today? Right goes forward; truth triumphs; justice is supreme; and slavery goes down.

"In fact, the Negroes are emancipated in Tennessee today, and the only remaining question for us to settle, as prudent and wise men, is in assigning the Negro his new relation. Now, what will that be? The Negro will be thrown upon society, governed by the same laws that govern communities, and be compelled to fall back upon his own resources, as all other human beings are.... Political freedom means liberty to work, and at the same time enjoy the products of one's labor.... If he can rise by his own energies, in the name of God, let him rise. In saying this, I do not argue that the Negro race is equal to the Anglo-Saxon.... If the Negro is better fitted for the inferior condition of society, the laws of nature will assign him there!"

As a reward for Johnson's services and to unite the sections Lincoln chose Johnson as his running mate in 1864. Before the campaign June 10, from the St. Cloud Hotel, Johnson gave his philosophy of Reconstruction:

"One of the chief elements of this rebellion is the opposition of the slave aristocracy to being ruled by men who have risen from the ranks of the people. This aristocracy hated Mr. Lincoln because he was of humble origin, a railsplitter in early life. One of them, the private secretary of Howell Cobb, said to me one day, after a long conversation, 'We people of the South will not submit to be governed by a man who has come up from the ranks of the common people, as Abe Lincoln has.' He uttered the essential feeling and spirit of this Southern rebellion. Now it has just occurred to me, if this aristocracy is so violently opposed to being governed by Mr. Lincoln, what in the name of conscience will it do with Lincoln and Johnson?...

"I am for emancipation for two reasons: First, because it is right in itself; and second, because in the emancipation of the slaves, we break down an odious and dangerous aristocracy; I think that we are freeing more whites than blacks in Tennessee.

"I want to see slavery broken up, and when its barriers are torn down, I want to see industrious, thrifty immigrants pouring in from all parts of the country. Come on! we need your labor, your skill, your capital....

"Ah, these Rebel leaders have a strong personal reason for holding out—to save their necks from the halter. And these leaders must feel the power of the government. Treason must be made odious, and the traitor must be punished and impoverished. Their great plantations must be seized and divided into small farms, and sold to honest, industrious men. The day for protecting the lands and Negroes of these authors of rebellion is past. It is high time it was."

During the campaign he addressed a torchlight procession of thousands of Negroes and whites. He said, October, 1864:

"Who has not heard of the great estates of Mack Cockrill, situated near this city, estates whose acres are numbered by the thousand, whose slaves were once counted by the score? And of Mack Cockrill, their possessor, the great slave-owner and, of course, the leading rebel, who lives in the very wantonness of wealth, wrung from the sweat and toil and stolen wages of others, and who gave fabulous sums to aid Jeff Davis in overturning this Government?...

"Who has not heard of the princely estates of General W. D. Harding, who, by means of his property alone, outweighed in influence any other man in Tennessee, no matter what were that other's worth, or wisdom, or ability. Harding, too, early espoused the cause of treason and made it his boast that he had contributed, and directly induced others to contribute, millions of dollars in aid of that unholy cause....It is wrong that Mack Cockrill and W. D. Harding, by means of forced and unpaid labor, should have monopolized so large a share of the lands and wealth of Tennessee; and I say if their immense plantations were divided up and parceled out amongst a number of free, industrious, and honest farmers, it would give more good citizens to the Commonwealth, increase the wages of our mechanics, enrich the markets of our city, enliven all the arteries of trade, improve society, and conduce to the greatness and glory of the State.

"The representatives of this corrupt, and if you will permit me almost to swear a little, this damnable aristocracy, taunt us with our desire to see justice done, and charge us with favoring Negro equality. Of all living men they should be the last to mouth that phrase; and, even when uttered in their hearing, it should cause their cheeks to tinge and burn with shame. Negro equality, indeed! Why, pass any day along the sidewalks of High Street where these aristocrats more particularly dwell—these aristocrats, whose sons are now in the bands of guerillas and cut-throats who prowl and rob and murder around our city—pass by their dwellings, I say, and you will see as many mulatto as Negro children, the former bearing an unmistakable resemblance to their aristocratic owners....Thank God, the war has ended all this...a war that has freed more whites than blacks....Suppose the Negro is set free and we have less cotton, we will raise more wool, hemp, flax and silk....It is all an idea that the world can't get along without cotton. And, as is suggested by my friend behind me, whether we attain perfection in the raising of cotton or not, I think we ought to stimulate the cultivation of hemp (great and renewed laughter); for we ought to have more of it and a far better material, a stronger fiber, with which to make a stronger rope. For, not to be malicious or malignant, I am free to say that I believe many who were driven into this Rebellion, are repentant; but I say of the leaders, the instigators, the conscious, intelligent traitors, they ought to be hung."

" 'Looking at this vast crowd of colored people,' continued the Governor, 'and reflecting through what a storm of persecution and obloquy they are compelled to pass, I am almost induced to wish that, as in the days of old, a Moses might arise who should lead them safely to their promised land of freedom and happiness.'

" 'You are our Moses,' shouted several voices, and the exclamation was caught up and cheered until the Capitol rung again....

" 'Well, then,' replied the speaker, 'humble and unworthy as I am, if no other better shall be found, I will indeed be your Moses, and lead you through the Red Sea of war and bondage to a fairer future of liberty and peace. I speak now as one who feels the world his country, and all who love equal rights his friends. I speak, too, as a citizen of Tennessee. I am here on my own soil; and here I mean to stay and fight this great battle of truth and justice to a triumphant end. Rebellion and slavery shall, by God's good help, no longer pollute our State. Loyal men, whether white or black, shall alone control her destinies; and when this strife in which we are all engaged is past, I trust, I know, we shall have a better state of things, and shall all rejoice that honest labor reaps the fruit of its own industry, and that every man has a fair chance in the race of life.' "

Winston interpreted the latter part of this speech as directed to the whites, when clearly he was speaking directly to the colored people; but he was afterward unwilling to live up to its promises. As a matter of fact, he favored emancipation "in order to save the Union and to free the white man and no further. 'Damn the Negroes,' he once said when charged with race equality. 'I am fighting those traitorous aristocrats, their masters.' "

Johnson appeared to take the oath of office as Vice-President so drunk he was taken into prolonged seclusion after a maudlin speech; his resignation was discussed. He was not a habitual drunkard, although he drank "three or four glasses of Robertson's Canada Whiskey" some days. In 1848 Johnson writes that he had been "on a kind of bust—not a big drunk." Both of Johnson's sons became drunkards and were cut off before they reached middle life. Yet Lincoln was right:

"Oh, well, don't you bother about Andy Johnson's drinking. He made a bad slip the other day, but I have known Andy a great many years, and he ain't no drunkard." Johnson was deeply humiliated by the inauguration episode and perhaps here began his alienation from those who might have influenced him best.

Charles A. Dana, Assistant Secretary of War, says that he met Vice-President Johnson in Richmond. "He took me aside and spoke with great earnestness about the necessity of not taking the Confederates back without some conditions or without some punishment. He insisted that their sins had been enormous, and that if they were let back into the Union without any punishment the effect would be very bad. He said they might be very dangerous in the future. The Vice-President talked to me in this strain for fully twenty minutes, I should think—an impassioned, earnest speech on the subject of punishing rebels."

His sudden induction as President was marked by modesty and genuine feeling. Carl Schurz says that the inaugural speech of Andrew Johnson, in 1865, was very pleasing to the liberals of the North, and made them believe that he was going to allow the Negro to have some part in the reconstruction of the states.

For a month after coming to the Presidency, Johnson indulged in speechmaking, and his words were still so severe that the anti-slavery people became uneasy, feeling that Johnson would give his attention primarily to punishing the whites rather than protecting the Negroes. April 21, 1865, he said in an interview with some citizens of Indiana:

"They [the Rebel leaders] must not only be punished, but their social power must be destroyed.... And I say that, after making treason odious, every Union man and the government should be remunerated out of the pockets of those who have inflicted this great suffering upon the country." This was exactly the thesis of Thaddeus Stevens enunciated in September of the same year.

A number of Virginians visited Johnson in July and complained that they were seeking credits in the North and West, but could get no consideration while they remained under the ban of the government. The President replied: "'It was the wealthy men who dragooned the people into secession; I know how this thing was done. You rich men used the press and bullied your little men to force the state into secession.' He spoke as a poor white for poor whites and the planters left in gloom."

He kept on insisting upon punishment for the South, and not only personal punishment but economic punishment, so that many conservatives were afraid that they had elected to the Presidency a radical who would seriously attack the South.

This would have been true but for one thing: the Southern poor white had his attitude toward property and income seriously modified by the presence of the Negro. Even Abraham Lincoln was unable for a long time to conceive of free, poor, black citizens as voters in the United States. The problem of the Negroes, as he faced it, worried him, and he made repeated efforts to see if in some way they could not be sent off to Africa or to foreign lands. Johnson had no such broad outlook. Negroes to him were just Negroes, and even as he expressed his radical ideas of helping the poor Southerners, he seldom envisaged Negroes as a part of the poor.

Lincoln came to know Negroes personally. He came to recognize their manhood. He praised them generously as soldiers, and suggested that they be admitted to the ballot. Johnson, on the contrary, could never regard Negroes as men. "He has all the narrowness and ignorance of a certain class of whites who have always looked upon the colored race as out of the pale of humanity."

The Northern press had been quite satisfied with Lincoln's attitude. He had served liberty and America well. "Lincoln," said Senator Doolittle, repre-

senting industry in the West, "would have dealt with the Rebels as an indulgent father deals with his erring children. Johnson would deal with them more
like a stern and incorruptible judge. Thus in a moment has the scepter of power
passed from the hand of flesh to the hand of iron."

At a cabinet meeting with Mr. Lincoln on the last day of his life, Friday,
April 14, Stanton submitted the draft of a plan for the restoration of governments in the South. The draft applied expressly to two states, but was intended
as a model for others. The President suggested a revision, and the subject was
postponed until Tuesday the 18th.

Andrew Johnson became President, and on Sunday, April 16, Stanton read
his draft to Sumner and other gentlemen. Sumner interrupted the reading with
the inquiry: " 'Whether any provision was made for enfranchising the colored
men,' saying, also, that 'unless the black man is given the right to vote his freedom is a mockery.' Stanton deprecated the agitation of the subject... but Sumner insisted that the black man's right to vote was 'the essence—the great
essential.' Stanton's draft, now confined to North Carolina, was considered in
the Cabinet May 9, when it appeared with a provision for suffrage in the election of members of a constitutional convention for the State. It included 'the
loyal citizens of the United States.' This paragraph, it appears, Stanton had accepted April 16, as an amendment from Sumner and Colfax....He admitted
that it was intended to include Negroes as well as white men."

Stanton invited an expression of opinion; several members of the Cabinet
were absent. Stanton, Dennison and Speed favored the inclusion; McCulloch,
Welles and Usher were against it. The President expressed no opinion, but
Sumner was certain of the President's decision in favor of Negro suffrage.

Sumner sought to keep close to Johnson. He and Chase had an interview
with him a week after he had taken the oath of office. Johnson was reserved but
sympathetic and they left light-hearted. A few days later, when the President
and Senator Sumner were alone together, the President said: " 'On this question [that of suffrage] there is no difference between us; you and I are alike.'
Sumner expressed his joy and gratitude that the President had taken this position, and that as a consequence there would thus be no division in the Union
party; and the President replied, 'I mean to keep you all together.' As he
walked away that evening, Sumner felt that the battle of his own life was
ended."

He wrote to Bright, May 1, 1865, encouragingly: "Last evening, I had a
long conversation with him [Johnson], mainly on the rebel states and how they
shall be tranquillized. Of course my theme is justice to the colored race. He accepted this idea completely, and indeed went so far as to say 'that there is no
difference between us.' You understand that the question whether rebel states
shall be treated as military provinces or territories is simply one of form, with a
view to the great result. It is the result that I aim at! and I shall never stickle on
any intermediate question if that is secured. He deprecates haste; is unwilling
that states should be precipitated back; thinks there must be a period of probation, but that meanwhile all loyal people, without distinction of color, must be

treated as citizens, and must take part in any proceedings for reorganization. He doubts at present the expediency of announcing this from Washington lest it should give a handle to party, but is willing it should be made known to the people in the rebel states. The Chief Justice started yesterday on a visit to North Carolina, South Carolina, Florida and New Orleans, and will on his way touch the necessary strings, so far as he can. I anticipate much from this journey. His opinions are fixed, and he is well informed with regard to those of the President. I would not be too sanguine, but I should not be surprised if we had this great question settled before the next meeting of Congress—I mean by this that we had such expression of opinion and acts as will forever conclude it. My confidence is founded in part upon the essential justice of our aims and the necessity of the case. With the President as well disposed as he shows himself, and the Chief Justice as positive, we must prevail. Will not all this sanctify our war beyond any in history?"

The next day writing to Lieber, Sumner quoted Johnson as saying that "colored persons are to have the right to suffrage; that no state can be precipitated into the Union; that rebel states must go through a term of probation. All this he had said to me before. Ten days ago, the Chief Justice and myself visited him in the evening to speak of these things. I was charmed by his sympathy, which was entirely different from his predecessor's. The Chief Justice is authorized to say wherever he is what the President desires, and to do everything he can to promote organization without distinction of color. The President desires that the movement should appear to proceed from the people. This is in conformity with his general ideas; but he thinks it will disarm the party at home. I told him that while I doubted if the work could be effectively done without federal authority, I regarded the *modus operandi* as an inferior question; and that I should be content, provided equality before the law was secured for all without distinction of color. I said during this winter that the rebel states could not come back, except on the footing of the Declaration of Independence, and the complete recognition of human rights. I feel more than ever confident that all this will be fulfilled. And then what a regenerated land! I had looked for a bitter contest on this question; but with the President on our side, it will be carried by simple avoirdupois."

Chase wrote Johnson from South Carolina the same month: "Suffrage to loyal blacks; I find that readiness and even desire for it is in proportion to the loyalty of those who express opinions. Nobody dissents, vehemently; while those who have suffered from rebellion and rejoice with their whole hearts in the restoration of the National Authority, are fast coming to the conclusion they will find their own surest safety in the proposed extension....

"All seem embarrassed about first steps. I do not entertain the slightest doubt that they would all welcome some simple recommendation from yourself, and would adopt readily any plan which you would suggest....

"I am anxious that *you* should have the lead in this work. It is my deliberate judgment that nothing will so strengthen you with the people or bring so much honor to your name throughout the world as some such short address as I suggested before leaving Washington. Just say to the people: 'Reorganize your state governments. I will aid you in the enrollment of the loyal citizens; you will not expect me to discriminate among men equally loyal; once enrolled, vote for delegates to the Convention to reform your State Constitution. I will aid you in collecting and declaring their suffrages. Your convention and your-selves must do the rest; but you may count on the support of the National Gov-ernment in all things constitutionally expedient.' "

In April and May of 1866, Tennessee had confined the right to vote to whites. The Tennessee Senate refused a suffrage bill which allowed all blacks and whites of legal age to vote, but excluded after 1875 all who could not read. Sumner wanted Johnson to insist on Negro suffrage in Tennessee, but Johnson explained that if he were in Tennessee he would take a stand, but that he could not in Washington.

Sumner remained in Washington half through May and saw the President almost daily, always seizing opportunity to present his views on Reconstruction, and insisting on suffrage for Negroes.

Just before leaving Washington, Sumner had a final interview with the President. He found him cordial and apparently unchanged. Sumner apologized for repeating his views expressed before. Johnson said, with a smile, "Have I not always listened to you?" Sumner, as he left, "assured his friends and correspon-dents that the cause he had at heart was safe" with Andrew Johnson.

Disturbing signs, however, began to occur. Carl Schurz wrote in May con-cerning the plans of Southern leaders in Mississippi, Georgia and North Car-olina. Thaddeus Stevens was alarmed at the President's recognition of the Pierpont government of Virginia. A caucus was, therefore, called at the Na-tional Hotel at Washington, May 12, to prevent the administration from going completely astray. Wade and Sumner said the President was in no danger, and that he was in favor of Negro suffrage.

Sumner may have been over-sanguine and read into Johnson's words more than Johnson intended, but it is certain that Sumner received a definite un-derstanding that President Johnson stood for real emancipation and Negro suffrage.

Here then was Andrew Johnson in 1865, born at the bottom of society, and during his early life a radical defender of the poor, the landless and the exploited. In the heyday of his early political career, he railed against land monopoly in the South, and after the Civil War, wanted the land of the monopolists divided among peasant proprietors.

Suddenly, by the weird magic of history, he becomes military dictator of a nation. He becomes the man by whom the greatest moral and economic revo-lution that ever took place in the United States, and perhaps in modern times, was to be put into effect. He becomes the real emancipator of four millions of black slaves, who have suffered more than anything that he had experienced in his earlier days. They not only have no lands; they have not owned even their bodies, nor their clothes, nor their tools. They have been exploited down to the ownership of their own families; they have been poor by law, and ignorant by force. What more splendid opportunity could the champion of labor and the exploited have had to start a nation towards freedom?

Johnson took over Lincoln's cabinet with an Anti-Abolitionist Whig, a Pro-Slavery Democrat, and a liberal student of industry, among others. This cabinet lasted a little over a year when early in July, 1866, three members, Dennison, Harlan and Speed, resigned, being unwilling to oppose Congress.

In all their logical sequence, the Reconstruction policies now associated with Johnson's name were laid down by Seward, and his logic overwhelmed Johnson. As Stevens explained: "Seward entered into him, and ever since they have been running down steep places into the sea."

The Cabinet met at Seward's house May 9, and on May 29, Johnson issued a Proclamation of Amnesty which showed the Seward influence. Indeed, nothing was left, apparently, of Johnson's liberalism, except the exclusion from amnesty, not simply of the leaders of the Confederacy, but of the rich—those worth $20,000 or more. Seward opposed this, but it was the only thing that he yielded to Johnson's liberalism. He early convinced Johnson that Reconstruction was a matter for the President to settle and especially he opened the door to his thorough conversion when the power of further pardons was put into Johnson's hand.

Part Four—The Jim Crow Era

Frances E. W. Harper

Bury Me in a Free Land

Make me a grave where'er you will,
In a lowly plain or a lofty hill;
Make it among earth's humblest graves,
But not in a land where men are slaves.

I could not rest, if around my grave
I heard the steps of a trembling slave;
His shadow above my silent tomb
Would make it a place of fearful gloom.

I could not sleep, if I heard the tread
Of a coffle-gang to the shambles led,
And the mother's shriek of wild despair
Rise, like a curse, on the trembling air.

I could not rest, if I saw the lash
Drinking her blood at each fearful gash;
And I saw her babes torn from her breast,
Like trembling doves from their parent nest.

I'd shudder and start, if I heard the bay
Of a bloodhound seizing his human prey;
And I heard the captive plead in vain,
As they bound, afresh, his galling chain.

If I saw young girls from their mother's arms
Bartered and sold for their youthful charms,
My eye would flash with a mournful flame,
My death-pale cheek grow red with shame.

I would sleep, dear friends, where bloated Might
Can rob no man of his dearest right;
My rest shall be calm in any grave
Where none can call his brother a slave.

I ask no monument, proud and high,
To arrest the gaze of the passers by;
All that my yearning spirit craves
Is—*Bury me not in a land of slaves!*

Aunt Chloe's Politics

Of course, I don't know very much
    About these politics,
But I think that some who run 'em
    Do mighty ugly tricks.

I've seen 'em honey-fugle round,
    And talk so awful sweet,
That you'd think them full of kindness,
    As an egg is full of meat.

Now I don't believe in looking
    Honest people in the face,
And saying when you're doing wrong,
    That "I haven't sold my race."

When we want to school our children,
    If the money isn't there,
Whether black or white have took it,
    The loss we all must share.

And this buying up each other
    Is something worse than mean,
Though I thinks a heap of voting,
    I go for voting clean.

Songs for the People

Let me make the songs for the people,
    Songs for the old and young;
Songs to stir like a battle-cry
    Wherever they are sung.

Not for the clashing of sabres,
    For carnage nor for strife;
But songs to thrill the hearts of men
    With more abundant life.

Let me make the songs for the weary,
    Amid life's fever and fret,
Till hearts shall relax their tension,
    And careworn brows forget.

Let me sing for little children,
    Before their footsteps stray,
Sweet anthems of love and duty,
    To float o'er life's highway.

I would sing for the poor and aged,
    When shadows dim their sight;
Of the bright and restful mansions,
    Where there shall be no night.

Our world, so worn and weary,
    Needs music, pure and strong,
To hush the jangle and discords
    Of sorrow, pain, and wrong.

Music to soothe all its sorrow,
    Till war and crime shall cease;
And the hearts of men grown tender
    Girdle the world with peace.

Woman's Political Future

If before sin had cast its deepest shadows or sorrow had distilled its bitterest tears, it was true that it was not good for man to be alone, it is no less true, since the shadows have deepened and life's sorrows have increased, that the world has need of all the spiritual aid that woman can give for the social advancement and moral development of the human race. The tendency of the present age, with its restlessness, religious upheavals, failures, blunders, and crimes, is toward broader freedom, an increase of knowledge, the emancipation of thought, and a recognition of the brotherhood of man; in this movement woman, as the companion of man, must be a sharer. So close is the bond between man and woman that you can not raise one without lifting the other. The world can not move without woman's sharing in the movement, and to help give a right impetus to that movement is woman's highest privilege.

If the fifteenth century discovered America to the Old World, the nineteenth is discovering woman to herself. Little did Columbus imagine, when the New World broke upon his vision like a lovely gem in the coronet of the universe, the glorious possibilities of a land where the sun should be our engraver, the winged lightning our messenger, and steam our beast of burden. But as mind is more than matter, and the highest ideal always the true real, so to woman comes the opportunity to strive for richer and grander discoveries than ever gladdened the eye of the Genoese mariner.

Not the opportunity of discovering new worlds, but that of filling this old world with fairer and higher aims than the greed of gold and the lust of power, is hers. Through weary, wasting years men have destroyed, dashed in pieces, and overthrown, but to-day we stand on the threshold of woman's era, and woman's work is grandly constructive. In her hand are possibilities whose use or abuse must tell upon the political life of the nation, and send their influence for good or evil across the track of unborn ages.

As the saffron tints and crimson flushes of morn herald the coming day, so the social and political advancement which woman has already gained bears the promise of the rising of the full-orbed sun of emancipation. The result will be not to make home less happy, but society more holy; yet I do not think the mere extension of the ballot a panacea for all the ills of our national life. What we need to-day is not simply more voters, but better voters. To-day there are red-handed men in our republic, who walk unwhipped of justice, who richly deserve to exchange the ballot of the freeman for the wristlets of the felon; brutal and cowardly men, who torture, burn, and lynch their fellow-men, men whose defenselessness should be their best defense and their weakness an ensign of protection. More than the changing of institutions we need the development of a national conscience, and the upbuilding of national character. Men may boast of the aristocracy of blood, may glory in the aristocracy of talent, and be proud of the aristocracy of wealth, but there is one aristocracy which must ever outrank them all, and that is the aristocracy of character; and it is the women of a country who help to mold its character, and to influence if not determine its destiny; and in the political future of our nation woman will not have done what she could if she does not endeavor to have our republic stand foremost among the nations of the earth, wearing sobriety as a crown and righteousness as a garment and a girdle. In coming into her political estate woman will find a mass of illiteracy to be dispelled. If knowledge is power, ignorance is also power. The power that educates wickedness may manipulate and dash against the pillars of any state when they are undermined and honeycombed by injustice.

I envy neither the heart nor the head of any legislator who has been born to an inheritance of privileges, who has behind him ages of education, dominion, civilization, and Christianity, if he stands opposed to the passage of a national education bill, whose purpose is to secure education to the children of those who were born under the shadow of institutions which made it a crime to read.

To-day women hold in their hands influence and opportunity, and with these they have already opened doors which have been closed to others. By opening doors of labor woman has become a rival claimant for at least some of the wealth monopolized by her stronger brother. In the home she is the priestess, in society the queen, in literature she is a power, in legislative halls lawmakers have responded to her appeals, and for her sake have humanized and liberalized their laws. The press has felt the impress of her hand. In the pews of the church she constitutes the majority; the pulpit has welcomed her, and in the school she has the blessed privilege of teaching children and youth. To her is apparently coming the added responsibility of political power; and what she now possesses should only be the means of preparing her to use the coming power for the glory of God and the good of mankind; for power without righteousness is one of the most dangerous forces in the world.

Political life in our country has plowed in muddy channels, and needs the infusion of clearer and cleaner waters. I am not sure that women are naturally so much better than men that they will clear the stream by the virtue of their womanhood; it is not through sex but through character that the best influence of women upon the life of the nation must be exerted.

I do not believe in unrestricted and universal suffrage for either men or women. I believe in moral and educational tests. I do not believe that the most ignorant and brutal man is better prepared to add value to the strength and durability of the government than the most cultured, upright, and intelligent woman. I do not think that willful ignorance should swamp earnest intelligence at the ballot-box, nor that educated wickedness, violence, and fraud should cancel the votes of honest men. The unsteady hands of a drunkard can not cast the ballot of a freeman. The hands of lynchers are too red with blood to determine the political character of the government for even four short years. The ballot in the hands of woman means power added to influence. How well she will use that power I can not foretell. Great evils stare us in the face that need to be throttled by the combined power of an upright manhood and an enlightened womanhood; and I know that no nation can gain its full measure of enlightenment and happiness if one-half of it is free and the other half is fettered. China compressed the feet of her women and thereby retarded the steps of her men. The elements of a nation's weakness must ever be found at the hearthstone.

More than the increase of wealth, the power of armies, and the strength of fleets is the need of good homes, of good fathers, and good mothers.

The life of a Roman citizen was in danger in ancient Palestine, and men had bound themselves with a vow that they would eat nothing until they had killed the Apostle Paul. Pagan Rome threw around that imperiled life a bulwark of living clay consisting of four hundred and seventy human hearts, and Paul was saved. Surely the life of the humblest American citizen should be as well protected in America as that of a Roman citizen was in heathen Rome. A wrong done to the weak should be an insult to the strong. Woman coming into her kingdom will find enthroned three great evils, for whose overthrow she should be as strong in a love of justice and humanity as the warrior is in his might. She will find intemperance sending its flood of shame, and death, and sorrow to the homes of men, a fretting leprosy in our politics, and a blighting curse in our social life; the social evil sending to our streets women whose laughter is sadder than their tears, who slide from the paths of sin and shame to the friendly shelter of the grave; and lawlessness enacting in our republic deeds over which angels might weep, if heaven knows sympathy.

How can any woman send petitions to Russia against the horrors of Siberian prisons if, ages after the Inquisition has ceased to devise its tortures, she has not done all she could by influence, tongue, and pen to keep men from making bonfires of the bodies of real or supposed criminals?

O women of America! into your hands God has pressed one of the sublimest opportunities that ever came into the hands of the women of any race or people. It is yours to create a healthy public sentiment; to demand justice, simple justice, as the right of every race; to brand with everlasting infamy the lawless and brutal cowardice that lynches, burns, and tortures your own countrymen.

To grapple with the evils which threaten to undermine the strength of the nation and to lay magazines of powder under the cribs of future generations is no child's play.

Let the hearts of the women of the world respond to the song of the herald angels of peace on earth and good will to men. Let them throb as one heart unified by the grand and holy purpose of uplifting the human race, and humanity will breathe freer, and the world grow brighter. With such a purpose Eden would spring up in our path, and Paradise be around our way.

Anna Julia Cooper
from *A Voice from the South by a Black Woman of the South*

HAS AMERICA A RACE PROBLEM; IF SO, HOW CAN IT BEST BE SOLVED?

There are two kinds of peace in this world. The one produced by suppression, which is the passivity of death; the other brought about by a proper adjustment of living, acting forces. A nation or an individual may be at peace because all opponents have been killed or crushed; or, nation as well as individual may have found the secret of true harmony in the determination to live and let live.

A harmless looking man was once asked how many there were in his family.

"Ten," he replied grimly; "my wife's a one and I a zero." In that family there was harmony, to be sure, but it was the harmony of a despotism—it was the quiet of a muzzled mouth, the smoldering peace of a volcano crusted over.

Now I need not say that peace produced by suppression is neither natural nor desirable. Despotism is not one of the ideas that man has copied from nature. All through God's universe we see eternal harmony and symmetry as the unvarying result of the equilibrium of opposing forces. Fair play in an equal fight is the law written in Nature's book. And the solitary bully with his foot on the breast of his last antagonist has no warrant in any fact of God.

The beautiful curves described by planets and suns in their courses are the resultant of conflicting forces. Could the centrifugal force for one instant triumph, or should the centripetal grow weary and give up the struggle, immeasurable disaster would ensue—earth, moon, sun would go spinning off at a tangent or must fall helplessly into its master sphere. The acid counterbalances and keeps in order the alkali; the negative, the positive electrode. A proper equilibrium between a most inflammable explosive and the supporter of combustion, gives us water, the bland fluid that we cannot dispense with. Nay, the very air we breathe, which seems so calm, so peaceful, is rendered innocuous only by the constant conflict of opposing gases. Were the fiery, never-resting, all-corroding oxygen to gain the mastery we should be burnt to cinders in a trice. With the sluggish, inert nitrogen triumphant, we should die of inanition.

These facts are only a suggestion of what must be patent to every student of history. Progressive peace in a nation is the result of conflict; and conflict, such as is healthy, stimulating, and progressive, is produced through the co-existence of radically opposing or racially different elements. Bellamy's ox-like men pictured in *Looking Backward*, taking their daily modicum of provender from the grandmotherly government, with nothing to struggle for, no wrong to put down, no reform to push through, no rights to vindicate and uphold, are nice folks to read about; but they are not natural; they are not progressive. God's world is not governed that way. The child can never gain strength save by resistance, and there can be no resistance if all movement is in one direction and all opposition made forever an impossibility.

I confess I can see no deeper reason than this for the specializing of racial types in the world. Whatever our theory with reference to the origin of species and the unity of mankind, we cannot help admitting the fact that no sooner does a family of the human race take up its abode in some little nook between mountains, or on some plain walled in by their own hands, no sooner do they begin in earnest to live their own life, think their own thoughts, and trace out their own arts, than they begin also to crystallize some idea different from and generally opposed to that of other tribes or families.

Each race has its badge, its exponent, its message, branded in its forehead by the great Master's hand which is its own peculiar keynote, and its contribution to the harmony of nations.

Left entirely alone,—out of contact, that is with other races and their opposing ideas and conflicting tendencies, this cult is abnormally developed and there is unity without variety, a predominance of one tone at the expense of moderation and harmony, and finally a sameness, a monotonous dullness which means stagnation,—death.

It is this of which M. Guizot complains in Asiatic types of civilization; and in each case he mentions I note that there was but one race, one free force predominating.

In Lect. II. Hist. of Civ. he says:

"In Egypt the theocratic principle took possession of society and showed itself in its manners, its monuments and in all that has come down to us of Egyptian civilization. In India the same phenomenon occurs—a repetition of the almost exclusively prevailing influence of theocracy. In other regions the domination of a conquering caste; where such is the case the principle of force takes entire possession of society. In another place we discover society under the entire influence of the democratic principle. Such was the case in the commercial republics which covered the coasts of Asia Minor and Syria, in Ionia and Phœnicia. In a word whenever we contemplate the civilization of the ancients, we find them all impressed with *one ever prevailing character of unity*, visible in their institutions, their ideas and manners; *one sole influence seems to govern and determine all things.* . . . In one nation, as in Greece, the unity of the social principle led to a development of wonderful rapidity; no other people ever ran so brilliant a career in so short a time. But Greece had hardly become glorious before she appeared worn out. Her decline was as sudden as her rise had been rapid. It seems as if the principle which called Greek civilization into life was exhausted. No other came to invigorate it or supply its place. In India and Egypt where again only one principle of civilization prevailed (*one race predominant you see*) society became stationary. Simplicity produced monotony. Society continued to exist, but there was no progression. It remained torpid and inactive."

Now I beg you to note that in none of these systems was a RACE PROBLEM possible. The dominant race had settled that matter forever. Asiatic society was fixed in cast iron molds. Virtually there was but one race inspiring and molding the thought, the art, the literature, the government. It was against this shrivelling caste prejudice and intolerance that the zealous Buddha set his face like a flint. And I do not think it was all blasphemy in Renan when he said Jesus Christ was first of democrats, i. e., a believer in the royalty of the individual, a preacher of the brotherhood of man through the fatherhood of God, a teacher who proved that the lines on which worlds are said to revolve are *imaginary*, that for all the distinctions of blue blood and black blood and red blood—*a man's a man for a' that*. Buddha and the Christ, each in his own way, wrought to rend asunder the clamps and bands of caste, and to thaw out the ice of race tyranny and exclusiveness. The Brahmin, who was Aryan, spurned a suggestion even, from the Sudra, who belonged to the hated and proscribed Turanian race. With a Pariah he could not eat or drink. They were to him outcasts and unclean. Association with them meant contamination; the hint of their social equality was blasphemous. Respectful consideration for their rights and feelings was almost a physical no less than a moral impossibility.

No more could the Helots among the Greeks have been said to contribute anything to the movement of their times. The dominant race had them effectually under its heel. It was the tyranny and exclusiveness of these nations, therefore, which brought about their immobility and resulted finally in the barrenness of their one idea. From this came the poverty and decay underlying their civilization, from this the transitory, ephemeral character of its brilliancy.

To quote Guizot again: "Society belonged to *one exclusive* power which could bear with no other. Every principle of a different tendency was proscribed. The governing principle would nowhere suffer by its side the manifestation and influence of a rival principle. This character of unity in their civilization is equally impressed upon their literature and intellectual productions. Those monuments of Hindoo literature lately introduced into Europe seem all struck from the same die. They all seem the result of one same fact, the expression of one idea. Religious and moral treatises, historical traditions, dramatic poetry, epics, all bear the same physiognomy. The same character of unity and monotony shines out in these works of mind and fancy, as we discover in their life and institutions." Not even Greece with all its classic treasures is made an exception from these limitations produced by exclusivness.

But the course of empire moves one degree westward. Europe becomes the theater of the leading exponents of civilization, and here we have a *Race Problem*,—if, indeed, the confused jumble of races, the clash and conflict, the din and devastation of those stormy years can be referred to by so quiet and so dignified a term as "problem." Complex and appalling it surely was. Goths and Huns, Vandals and Danes, Angles, Saxons, Jutes—could any prophet foresee that a vestige of law and order, of civilization and refinement would remain after this clumsy horde of wild barbarians had swept over Europe?

"Where is somebody'll give me some white for all this yellow?" cries one with his hands full of the gold from one of those magnificent monuments of antiquity which he and his tribe had just pillaged and demolished. Says the historian: "Their history is like a history of kites and crows." Tacitus writes: "To shout, to drink, to caper about, to feel their veins heated and swollen with wine, to hear and see around them the riot of the orgy, this was the first need of the barbarians. The heavy human brute gluts himself with sensations and with noise."

Taine describes them as follows:

"Huge white bodies, cool-blooded, with fierce blue eyes, reddish flaxen hair; ravenous stomachs, filled with meat and cheese, heated by strong drinks. Brutal drunken pirates and robbers, they dashed to sea in their two-sailed barks, landed anywhere, killed everything; and, having sacrificed in honor of their gods the tithe of all their prisoners, leaving behind the red light of their burning, went farther on to begin again."

A certain litany of the time reads: "From the fury of the Jutes, Good Lord deliver us." "Elgiva, the wife of one of their kings," says a chronicler of the time, "they hamstrung and subjected to the death she deserved;" and their heroes are frequently represented as tearing out the heart of their human victim and eating it while it still quivered with life.

A historian of the time, quoted by Taine, says it was the custom to buy men and women in all parts of England and to carry them to Ireland for sale. The buyers usually made the women pregnant and took them to market in that condition to ensure a better price. "You might have seen," continues the historian, "long files of young people of both sexes and of great beauty, bound with ropes and daily exposed for sale. They sold as slaves in this manner, their nearest relatives and even their own children."

What could civilization hope to do with such a swarm of sensuous, bloodthirsty vipers? Assimilation was horrible to contemplate. They will drag us to their level, quoth the culture of the times. Deportation was out of the question; and there was no need to talk of their emigrating. The fact is, the barbarians were in no hurry about moving. They didn't even care to colonize. They had come to stay. And Europe had to grapple with her race problem till time and God should solve it.

And how was it solved, and what kind of civilization resulted?

Once more let us go to Guizot. "Take ever so rapid a glance," says he, "at modern Europe and it strikes you at once as diversified, confused, and stormy. All the principles of social organization are found existing together within it; powers temporal, and powers spiritual, the theocratic, monarchic, aristocratic, and democratic elements, all classes of society *in a state of continual struggle* without any one having sufficient force to master the others and take sole possession of society." Then as to the result of this conflict of forces: "Incomparably more rich and diversified than the ancient, European civilization has within it the promise of *perpetual progress*. It has now endured more than fifteen centuries and in all that time has been in a state of progression, not so rapidly as the Greek nor yet so ephemeral. While in other civilizations the exclusive domination of a principle (*or race*) led to tyranny, in Europe the diversity of social elements (*growing out of the contact of different races*) the incapability of any one to exclude the rest, gave birth to the LIBERTY which now prevails. This inability of the various principles to exterminate one another compelled each to endure the others and made it necessary for them in order to live in common to enter into a sort of mutual understanding. Each consented to have only that part of civilization which equitably fell to its share. Thus, while everywhere else the predominance of one principle produced tyranny, the variety and warfare of the elements of European civilization gave birth to *reciprocity and liberty*."

There is no need to quote further. This is enough to show that the law holds good in sociology as in the world of matter, *that equilibrium, not repression among conflicting forces is the condition of natural harmony, of permanent progress, and of universal freedom*. That exclusiveness and selfishness in a family, in a community, or in a nation is suicidal to progress. Caste and prejudice mean immobility. One race predominance means death. The community that closes its gates against foreign talent can never hope to advance beyond a certain point. Resolve to keep out foreigners and you keep out progress. Home talent develops its one idea and then dies. Like the century plant it produces its one flower, brilliant and beautiful it may be, but it lasts only for a night. Its forces have exhausted themselves in that one effort. Nothing remains but to wither and to rot.

It was the Chinese wall that made China in 1800 A. D. the same as China in the days of Confucius. Its women have not even yet learned that they need not bandage their feet if they do not relish it. The world has rolled on, but within that wall the thoughts, the fashions, the art, the tradition, and the beliefs are those of a thousand years ago. Until very recently, the Chinese were wholly out of the current of human progress. They were like gray headed infants—a man of eighty years with the concepts and imaginings of a babe of eight months. A civilization measured by thousands of years with a development that might be comprised within as many days—arrested development due to exclusive living.

But European civilization, rich as it was compared to Asiatic types, was still not the consummation of the ideal of human possibilities. One more degree westward the hand on the dial points. In Europe there was conflict, but the elements crystallized out in isolated nodules, so to speak. Italy has her dominant principle, Spain hers, France hers, England hers, and so on. The proximity is close enough for interaction and mutual restraint, though the acting forces are at different points. To preserve the balance of power, which is nothing more than the equilibrium of warring elements, England can be trusted to keep an eye on her beloved step-relation-in-law, Russia,—and Germany no doubt can be relied on to look after France and some others. It is not, however, till the scene changes and America is made the theater of action, that the interplay of forces narrowed down to a single platform.

Hither came Cavalier and Roundhead, Baptist and Papist, Quaker, Ritualist, Freethinker and Mormon, the conservative Tory, the liberal Whig, and the radical Independent,—the Spaniard, the Frenchman, the Englishman, the Italian, the Chinaman, the African, Swedes, Russians, Huns, Bohemians, Gypsies, Irish, Jews. Here surely was a seething caldron of conflicting elements. Religious intolerance and political hatred, race prejudice and caste pride—

"Double, double, toil and trouble;
Fire burn and cauldron bubble."

Conflict, Conflict, Conflict.

America for Americans! This is the white man's country! The Chinese must go, shrieks the exclusionist. Exclude the Italians! Colonize the blacks in Mexico or deport them to Africa. Lynch, suppress, drive out, kill out! America for Americans!

"*Who are Americans?*" comes rolling back from ten million throats. Who are to do the packing and delivering of the goods? Who are the homefolks and who are the strangers? Who are the absolute and original tenants in fee-simple?

The red men used to be owners of the soil,—but they are about to be pushed over into the Pacific Ocean. They, perhaps, have the best right to call themselves "Americans" by law of primogeniture. They are at least the oldest inhabitants of whom we can at present identify any traces. If early settlers from abroad merely are meant and it is only a question of squatters' rights—why, the Mayflower, a pretty venerable institution, landed in the year of Grace 1620, and the first delegation from Africa just one year ahead of that,—in 1819. The first settlers seem to have been almost as much mixed as we are on this point; and it does not seem at all easy to decide just what individuals we mean when we yell "America for the Americans." At least the cleavage cannot be made by hues and noses, if we are to seek for the genuine F. F. V.'s as the inhabitants best entitled to the honor of that name.

The fact is this nation was foreordained to conflict from its incipiency. Its elements were predestined from their birth to an irrepressible clash followed by the stable equilibrium of opposition. Exclusive possession belongs to none. There never was a point in its history when it did. There was never a time since America became a nation when there were not more than race, more than one party, more than one belief contending for supremacy. Hence no one is or can be supreme. All interests must be consulted, all claims conciliated. Where a hundred free forces are lustily clamoring for recognition and each wrestling mightily for the mastery, individual tyrannies must inevitably be chiselled down, individual bigotries worn smooth and malleable, individual prejudices either obliterated or concealed. America is not from choice more than of necessity republic in form and democratic in administration. The will of the majority must rule simply because no class, no family, no individual has ever been able to prove sufficient political legitimacy to impose their yoke on the country. All attempts at establishing oligarchy must be made by wheedling and cajoling, pretending that not supremacy but service is sought. The nearest approach to outspoken self-assertion is in the conciliatory tones of candid compromise. "I will let you enjoy that if you will not hinder me in the pursuit of this" has been the American sovereign's home policy since his first Declaration of Independence was inscribed as his policy abroad. Compromise and concession, liberality and toleration were the conditions of the nation's birth and are the *sine qua non* of its continued existence. A general amnesty and universal reciprocity are the only *modus vivendi* in a nation whose every citizen is his own king, his own priest and his own pope.

De Tocqueville, years ago, predicted that republicanism must fail in America. But if republicanism fails, America fails, and somehow I can not think this colossal stage was erected for a tragedy. I must confess to being an optimist on the subject of my country. It is true we are too busy making history, and have been for some years past, to be able to write history yet, or to understand and interpret it. Our range of vision is too short for us to focus and image our conflicts. Indeed Von Holtz, the clearest headed of calm spectators, says he doubts if the history of American conflict can be written yet even by a disinterested foreigner. The clashing of arms and the din of battle, the smoke of cannon and the heat of combat, are not yet cleared away sufficiently for us to have the judicial vision of historians. Our jottings are like newspaper reports written in the saddle, mid prancing steeds and roaring artillery.

But of one thing we may be sure: the God of battles is in the conflicts of history. The evolution of civilization is His care, eternal progress His delight. As the European was higher and grander than the Asiatic, so will American civilization be broader and deeper and closer to the purposes of the Eternal than any the world has yet seen. This the last page is to mark the climax of history, the bright consummate flower unfolding *charity toward all and malice toward none,*—the final triumph of universal reciprocity born of universal conflict with forces that cannot be exterminated. Here at last is an arena in which every agony has a voice and free speech. Not a spot where no wrong can exist, but where each feeblest interest can cry with Themistocles, "*Strike, but hear me!*" Here you will not see as in Germany women hitched to a cart with donkeys; not perhaps because men are more chivalrous here than there, but because woman can speak. Here labor will not be starved and ground to powder, because the laboring man can make himself heard. Here races that are weakest can, *if they so elect*, make themselves felt.

The supremacy of one race,—the despotism of a class or the tyranny of an individual can not ultimately prevail on a continent held in equilibrium by such conflicting forces and by so many and such strong fibred races as there are struggling on this soil. Never in America shall one man dare to say as Germany's somewhat bumptious emperor is fond of proclaiming: "There is only one master in the country and I am he. I shall suffer no other beside me. Only to God and my conscience am I accountable." The strength of the opposition tones down and polishes off all such ugly excrescencies as that. "I am the State," will never be proclaimed above a whisper on a platform where there is within arm's length another just as strong, possibly stronger, who holds, or would like to hold that identical proposition with reference to himself. In this arena then is to be the last death struggle of political tyranny, of religious bigotry, and intellectual intolerance, of caste illiberality and class exclusiveness. And the last monster that shall be throttled forever methinks is race prejudice. Men will here learn that a race, as a family, may be true to itself without seeking to exterminate all others. That for the note of the feeblest there is room, nay a positive need, in the harmonies of God. That the principles of true democracy are founded in universal reciprocity, and that "A man's a man" was written when God first stamped His own image and superscription on His child and breathed into his nostrils the breath of life. And I confess I can pray for no nobler destiny for my country than that it may be the stage, however far distant in the future, whereon these ideas and principles shall ultimately mature; and culminating here at whatever cost of production shall go forth hence to dominate the world.

Methought I saw a mighty conflagration, plunging and heaving, surging and seething, smoking and rolling over this American continent. Strong men and wise men stand helpless in mute consternation. Empty headed babblers add the din of their bray to the crashing and crackling of the flames. But the hungry flood rolls on. The air is black with smoke and cinders. The sky is red with lurid light. Forked tongues of fiery flame dart up and lick the pale stars, and seem to laugh at men's feebleness and frenzy. As I look on I think of Schiller's sublime characterization of fire: "Frightful becomes this God-power, when it snatches itself free from fetters and stalks majestically forth on its own career—the free daughter of Nature." Ingenuity is busy with newly patented snuffers all warranted to extinguish the flame. The street gamin with a hooked wire pulls out a few nuggets that chanced to be lying on the outskirts where they were cooked by the heat; and gleefully cries "What a nice fire to roast my chestnuts," and like little Jack Horner, "what a nice boy am I!"

Meantime this expedient, that expedient, the other expedient is suggested by thinkers and theorizers hoping to stifle the angry, roaring, devouring demon and allay the mad destruction.

> "Wehe wenn sie losgelassen,
>   Wachsend ohne Widerstand,
> Durch die volkbelebten Gassen
>   Walzt den ungeheuren Brand!"

But the strength of the Omnipotent is in it. The hand of God is leading it on. It matters not whether you and I in mad desperation cast our quivering bodies into it as our funeral pyre; or whether, like the street urchins, we pull wires to secure the advantage of the passing moment. We can neither help it nor hinder; only

"Let thy gold be cast in the furnace,
    Thy red gold, precious and bright.
Do not fear the hungry fire
    With its caverns of burning light."

If it takes the dearest idol, the pet theory or the darling 'ism', the pride, the self-ishness, the prejudices, the exclusiveness, the bigotry and intolerance, the conceit of self, of race, or of family superiority,—nay, if it singe from thee thy personal gratifications in thy distinction by birth, by blood, by sex—everything,—and leave thee nothing but thy naked manhood, solitary and unadorned,—let them go—let them go!

"And thy gold shall return more precious,
Free from every spot and stain,
For gold must be tried by fire."

And the heart of nations must be tried by pain; and their polish, their true culture must be wrought in through conflict.

Has America a Race Problem?

Yes.

What are you going to do about it?

Let it alone and mind my own business. It is God's problem and He will solve it in time. It is deeper than Gehenna. What can you or I do!

Are there then no duties and special lines of thought growing out of the present conditions of this problem?

Certainly there are. *Imprimis;* let every element of the conflict see that it represent a positive force so as to preserve a proper equipoise in the conflict. No shirking, no skulking, no masquerading in another's uniform. Stand by your guns. And be ready for the charge. The day is coming, and now is, when America must ask each citizen not "who was your grandfather and what the color of his cuticle," but "*What can you do?*" Be ready each individual element,—each race, each class, each family, each man to reply "*I engage to undertake an honest man's share.*"

God and time will work the problem. You and I are only to stand for the quantities *at their best*, which he means us to represent.

Above all, for the love of humanity stop the mouth of those learned theorizers, the expedient mongers, who come out annually with their new and improved method of getting the answer and clearing the slate: amalgamation, deportation, colonization and all the other ations that were ever devised or dreampt of. If Alexander wants to be a god, let him; but don't have Alexander hawking his patent plan for universal deification. If all could or would follow Alexander's plan, just the niche in the divine cosmos meant for man would be vacant. And we think that men have a part to play in this great drama no less than gods, and so if a few are determined to be white—amen, so be it; but don't let them argue as if there were no part to be played in life by black men and black women, and as if to become white were the sole specific and panacea for all the ills that flesh is heir to—the universal solvent for all America's irritations. And again, if an American family of whatever condition or hue takes a notion to reside in Africa or in Mexico, or in the isles of the sea, it is most un-American for any power on this continent to seek to gainsay or obstruct their departure; but on the other hand, no power or element of power on this continent, least of all a self-constituted tribunal of "recent arrivals," possesses the right to begin figuring beforehand to calculate what it would require *to send* ten millions of citizens, whose ancestors have wrought here from the planting of the nation, to the same places at so much per head—at least till some one has consulted those heads.

We would not deprecate the fact, then, that America has a Race Problem. It is guaranty of the perpetuity and progress of her institutions, and insures the breadth of her culture and the symmetry of her development. More than all, let us not disparage the factor which the Negro is appointed to contribute to that problem. America needs the Negro for ballast if for nothing else. His tropical warmth and spontaneous emotionalism may form no unseemly counterpart to the cold and calculating Anglo-Saxon. And then his instinct for law and order, his inborn respect for authority, his inaptitude for rioting and anarchy, his gentleness and cheerfulness as a laborer, and his deep-rooted faith in God will prove indispensable and invaluable elements in a nation menaced as America is by anarchy, socialism, communism, and skepticism poured in with all the jail birds from the continents of Europe and Asia. I believe with our own Dr. Crummell that "the Almighty does not preserve, rescue, and build up a lowly people merely for ignoble ends." And the historian of American civilization will yet congratulate this country that she has had a Race Problem and that descendants of the black race furnished one of its largest factors.

Ida B. Wells-Barnett
from *A Red Record*

CHAPTER I.

The Case Stated.

The student of American sociology will find the year 1894 marked by a pronounced awakening of the public conscience to a system of anarchy and outlawry which had grown during a series of ten years to be so common, that scenes of unusual brutality failed to have any visible effect upon the humane sentiments of the people of our land.

Beginning with the emancipation of the Negro, the inevitable result of unbridled power exercised for two and a half centuries, by the white man over the Negro, began to show itself in acts of conscienceless outlawry. During the slave regime, the Southern white man owned the Negro body and soul. It was to his interest to dwarf the soul and preserve the body. Vested with unlimited power over his slave, to subject him to any and all kinds of physical punishment, the white man was still restrained from such punishment as tended to injure the slave by abating his physical powers and thereby reducing his financial worth. While slaves were scourged mercilessly, and in countless cases inhumanly treated in other respects, still the white owner rarely permitted his anger to go so far as to take a life, which would entail upon him a loss of several hundred dollars. The slave was rarely killed, he was too valuable; it was easier and quite as effective, for discipline or revenge, to sell him "Down South."

But Emancipation came and the vested interests of the white man in the Negro's body were lost. The white man had no right to scourge the emancipated Negro, still less has he a right to kill him. But the Southern white people had been educated so long in that school of practice, in which might makes right, that they disdained to draw strict lines of action in dealing with the Negro. In slave times the Negro was kept subservient and submissive by the frequency and severity of the scourging, but, with freedom, a new system of intimidation came into vogue; the Negro was not only whipped and scourged; he was killed.

Not all nor nearly all of the murders done by white men, during the past thirty years in the South, have come to light, but the statistics as gathered and preserved by white men, and which have not been questioned, show that during these years more than ten thousand Negroes have been killed in cold blood, without the formality of judicial trial and legal execution. And yet, as evidence of the absolute impunity with which the white man dares to kill a Negro, the same record shows that during all these years, and for all these murders only three white men have been tried, convicted, and executed. As no white man has been lynched for the murder of colored people, these three executions are the only instances of the death penalty being visited upon white men for murdering Negroes.

Naturally enough the commission of these crimes began to tell upon the public conscience, and the Southern white man, as a tribute to the nineteenth century civilization, was in a manner compelled to give excuses for his barbarism. His excuses have adapted themselves to the emergency, and are aptly outlined by that greatest of all Negroes, Frederick Douglass, in an article of recent date, in which he shows that there have been three distinct eras of Southern barbarism, to account for which three distinct excuses have been made.

The first excuse given to the civilized world for the murder of unoffending Negroes was the necessity of the white man to repress and stamp out alleged "race riots." For years immediately succeeding the war there was an appalling slaughter of colored people, and the wires usually conveyed to northern people and the world the intelligence, first, that an insurrection was being planned by Negroes, which, a few hours later, would prove to have been vigorously resisted by white men, and controlled with a resulting loss of several killed and wounded. It was always a remarkable feature in these insurrections and riots that only Negroes were killed during the rioting, and that all the white men escaped unharmed.

From 1865 to 1872, hundreds of colored men and women were mercilessly murdered and the almost invariable reason assigned was that they met their death by being alleged participants in an insurrection or riot. But this story at last wore itself out. No insurrection ever materialized; no Negro rioter was ever apprehended and proven guilty, and no dynamite ever recorded the black man's protest against oppression and wrong. It was too much to ask thoughtful people to believe this transparent story, and the southern white people at last made up their minds that some other excuse must be had.

Then came the second excuse, which had its birth during the turbulent times of reconstruction. By an amendment to the Constitution the Negro was given the right of franchise, and, theoretically at least, his ballot became his invaluable emblem of citizenship. In a government "of the people, for the people, and by the people," the Negro's vote became an important factor in all matters of state and national politics. But this did not last long. The southern white man would not consider that the Negro had any right which a white man was bound to respect, and the idea of a republican form of government in the southern states grew into general contempt. It was maintained that "This is a white man's government," and regardless of numbers the white man should rule. "No Negro domination" became the new legend on the sanguinary banner of the sunny South, and under it rode the Ku Klux Klan, the Regulators, and the lawless mobs, which for any cause chose to murder one man or a dozen as suited their purpose best. It was a long, gory campaign; the blood chills and the heart almost loses faith in Christianity when one thinks of Yazoo, Hamburg, Edgefield, Copiah, and the countless massacres of defenseless Negroes, whose only crime was the attempt to exercise their right to vote.

But it was a bootless strife for colored people. The government which had made the Negro a citizen found itself unable to protect him. It gave him the right to vote, but denied him the protection which should have maintained that right. Scourged from his home; hunted through the swamps; hung by midnight raiders, and openly murdered in the light of day, the Negro clung to his right of franchise with a heroism which would have wrung admiration from the hearts of savages. He believed that in that small white ballot there was a subtle something which stood for man-hood as well as citizenship, and thousands of brave black men went to their graves, exemplifying the one by dying for the other.

The white man's victory soon became complete by fraud, violence, intimidation and murder. The franchise vouchsafed to the Negro grew to be a "barren ideality," and regardless of numbers, the colored people found themselves voiceless in the councils of those whose duty it was to rule. With no longer the fear of "Negro Domination" before their eyes, the white man's second excuse became valueless. With the Southern governments all subverted and the Negro actually eliminated from all participation in state and national elections, there could be no longer an excuse for killing Negroes to prevent "Negro Domination."

Brutality still continued; Negroes were whipped, scourged, exiled, shot and hung whenever and wherever it pleased the white man so to treat them, and as the civilized world with increasing persistency held the white people of the South to account for its outlawry, the murderers invented the third excuse— that Negroes had to be killed to avenge their assaults upon women. There could be framed no possible excuse more harmful to the Negro and more unanswerable if true in its sufficiency for the white man.

Humanity abhors the assailant of womanhood, and this charge upon the Negro at once placed him beyond the pale of human sympathy. With such unanimity, earnestness and apparent candor was this charge made and reiterated that the world has accepted the story that the Negro is a monster which the Southern white man has painted him. And to-day, the Christian world feels, that while lynching is a crime, and lawlessness and anarchy the certain precursors of a nation's fall, it can not by word or deed, extend sympathy or help to a race of outlaws, who might mistake their plea for justice and deem it an excuse for their continued wrongs.

The Negro has suffered much and is willing to suffer more. He recognizes that the wrongs of two centuries can not be righted in a day, and he tries to bear his burden with patience for to-day and be hopeful for to-morrow. But there comes a time when the veriest worm will turn, and the Negro feels to-day that after all the work he has done, all the sacrifices he has made, and all the suffering he has endured, if he did not, now, defend his name and manhood from this vile accusation, he would be unworthy even of the contempt of mankind. It is to this charge he now feels he must make answer.

If the Southern people in defense of their lawlessness, would tell the truth and admit that colored men and women are lynched for almost any offense, from murder to a misdemeanor, there would not now be the necessity for this defense. But when they intentionally, maliciously and constantly belie the record and bolster up these faleshoods by the words of legislators, preachers, governors and bishops, then the Negro must give to the world his side of the awful story.

A word as to the charge itself. In considering the third reason assigned by the Southern white people for the butchery of blacks, the question must be asked, what the white man means when he charges the black man with rape. Does he mean the crime which the statutes of the civilized states describe as such? Not by any means. With the Southern white man, any mesalliance existing between a white woman and a colored man is a sufficient foundation for the charge of rape. The Southern white man says that it is impossible for a voluntary alliance to exist between a white woman and a colored man, and therefore, the fact of an alliance is a proof of force. In numerous instances where colored men have have been lynched on the charge of rape, it was positively known at the time of lynching, and indisputably proven after the victim's death, that the relationship sustained between the man and woman was voluntary and clandestine, and that in no court of law could even the charge of assault have been successfully maintained.

It was for the assertion of this fact, in the defense of her own race, that the writer hereof became an exile; her property destroyed and her return to her home forbidden under penalty of death, for writing the following editorial which was printed in her paper, the Free Speech, in Memphis, Tenn., May 21, 1892:

"Eight Negroes lynched since last issue of the 'Free Speech' one at Little Rock, Ark., last Saturday morning where the citizens broke (?) into the penitentiary and got their man; three near Anniston, Ala., one near New Orleans; and three at Clarksville, Ga., the last three for killing a white man, and five on the same old racket—the new alarm about raping white women. The same programme of hanging, then shooting bullets into the lifeless bodies was carried out to the letter. Nobody in this section of the country believes the old threadbare lie that Negro men rape white women. If Southern white men are not careful, they will over-reach themselves and public sentiment will have a reaction; a conclusion will then be reached which will be very damaging to the moral reputation of their women."

But threats cannot suppress the truth, and while the Negro suffers the soul deformity, resultant from two and a half centuries of slavery, he is no more guilty of this vilest of all vile charges than the white man who would blacken his name.

During all the years of slavery, no such charge was ever made, not even during the dark days of the rebellion, when the white man, following the fortunes of war went to do battle for the maintenance of slavery. While the master was away fighting to forge the fetters upon the slave, he left his wife and children with no protectors save the Negroes themselves. And yet during those years of trust and peril, no Negro proved recreant to his trust and no white man returned to a home that had been dispoiled.

Likewise during the period of alleged "insurrection," and alarming "race riots," it never occurred to the white man, that his wife and children were in danger of assault. Nor in the Reconstruction era, when the hue and cry was against "Negro Domination," was there ever a thought that the domination would ever contaminate a fireside or strike to death the virtue of womanhood. It must appear strange indeed, to every thoughtful and candid man, that more than a quarter of a century elapsed before the Negro began to show signs of such infamous degeneration.

In his remarkable apology for lynching, Bishop Haygood, of Georgia, says: "No race, not the most savage, tolerates the rape of woman, but it may be said without reflection upon any other people that the Southern people are now and always have been most sensitive concerning the honor of their women— their mothers, wives, sisters and daughters." It is not the purpose of this defense to say one word against the white women of the South. Such need not be said, but it is their misfortune that the chivalrous white men of that section, in order to escape the deserved execration of the civilized world, should shield themselves by their cowardly and infamously false excuse, and call into question that very honor about which their distinguished priestly apologist claims they are most sensitive. To justify their own barbarism they assume a chivalry which they do not possess. True chivalry respects all womanhood, and no one who reads the record, as it is written in the faces of the million mulattoes in the South, will for a minute conceive that the southern white man had a very chivalrous regard for the honor due the women of his own race or respect for the womanhood which circumstances placed in his power. That chivalry which is "most sensitive concerning the honor of women" can hope for but little respect from the civilized world, when it confines itself entirely to the women who happen to be white. Virtue knows no color line, and the chivalry which depends upon complexion of skin and texture of hair can command no honest respect.

When emancipation came to the Negroes, there arose in the northern part of the United States an almost divine sentiment among the noblest, purest and best white women of the North, who felt called to a mission to educate and Christianize the millions of southern ex-slaves. From every nook and corner of the North, brave young white women answered that call and left their cultured homes, their happy associations and their lives of ease, and with heroic determination went to the South to carry light and truth to the benighted blacks. It was a heroism no less than that which calls for volunteers for India, Africa and the Isles of the sea. To educate their unfortunate charges; to teach them the Christian virtues and to inspire in them the moral sentiments manifest in their own lives, these young women braved dangers whose record reads more like fiction than fact. They became social outlaws in the South. The peculiar sensitiveness of the southern white men for women, never shed its protecting influence about them. No friendly word from their own race cheered them in their work; no hospitable doors gave them the companionship like that from which they had come. No chivalrous white man doffed his hat in honor or respect. They were "Nigger teachers"—unpardonable offenders in the social ethics of the South, and were insulted, persecuted and ostracised, not by Negroes, but by the white manhood which boasts its chivalry toward women.

And yet these northern women worked on, year after year, unselfishly, with a heroism which amounted almost to martyrdom. Threading their way through dense forests, working in schoolhouse, in the cabin and in the church, thrown at all times and in all places among the unfortunate and lowly Negroes, whom they had come to find and to serve, these northern women, thousands and thousands of them, have spent more than a quarter of a century in giving to the colored people their splendid lessons for home and heart and soul. Without protection, save that which innocence gives to every good woman, they went about their work, fearing no assault and suffering none. Their chivalrous protectors were hundreds of miles away in their northern homes, and yet they never feared any "great dark faced mobs," they dared night or day to "go beyond their own roof trees." They never complained of assaults, and no mob was ever called into existence to avenge crimes against them. Before the world adjudges the Negro a moral monster, a vicious assailant of womanhood and a menace to the sacred precincts of home, the colored people ask the consideration of the silent record of gratitude, respect, protection and devotion of the millions of the race in the South, to the thousands of northern white women who have served as teachers and missionaries since the war.

The Negro may not have known what chivalry was, but he knew enough to preserve inviolate the womanhood of the South which was entrusted to his hands during the war. The finer sensibilities of his soul may have been crushed out by years of slavery, but his heart was full of gratitude to the white women of the North, who blessed his home and inspired his soul in all these years of freedom. Faithful to his trust in both of these instances, he should now have the impartial ear of the civilized world, when he dares to speak for himself as against the infamy wherewith he stands charged.

It is his regret, that, in his own defense, he must disclose to the world that degree of dehumanizing brutality which fixes upon America the blot of a national crime. Whatever faults and failings other nations may have in their dealings with their own subjects or with other people, no other civilized nation stands condemned before the world with a series of crimes so peculiarly national. It becomes a painful duty of the Negro to reproduce a record which shows that a large portion of the American people avow anarchy, condone murder and defy the contempt of civilization.

These pages are written in no spirit of vindictiveness, for all who give the subject consideration must concede that far too serious is the condition of that civilized government in which the spirit of unrestrained outlawry constantly increases in violence, and casts its blight over a continually growing area of territory. We plead not for the colored people alone, but for all victims of the terrible injustice which puts men and women to death without form of law. During the year 1894, there were 132 persons executed in the United States by due form of law, while in the same year, 197 persons were put to death by mobs who gave the victims no opportunity to make a lawful defense. No comment need be made upon a condition of public sentiment responsible for such alarming results.

The purpose of the pages which follow shall be to give the record which has been made, not by colored men, but that which is the result of compilations made by white men, of reports sent over the civilized world by white men in the South. Out of their own mouths shall the murderers be condemned. For a number of years the Chicago Tribune, admittedly one of the leading journals of America, has made a specialty of the compilation of statistics touching upon lynching. The data compiled by that journal and published to the world January 1st, 1894, up to the present time has not been disputed. In order to be safe from the charge of exaggeration, the incidents hereinafter reported have been confined to those vouched for by the Tribune.

CHAPTER VI.

History of Some Cases of Rape.

It has been claimed that the Southern white women have been slandered because, in defending the Negro race from the charge that all colored men, who are lynched, only pay penalty for assaulting women. It is certain that lynching mobs have not only refused to give the Negro a chance to defend himself, but have killed their victim with a full knowledge that the relationship of the alleged assailant with the woman who accused him, was voluntary and clandestine. As a matter of fact, one of the prime causes of the Lynch Law agitation has been a necessity for defending the Negro from this awful charge against him. This defense has been necessary because the apologists for outlawry insist that in no case has the accusing woman been a willing consort of her paramour, who is lynched because overtaken in wrong. It is well known, however, that such is the case. In July of this year, 1894, John Paul Bocock, a Southern white man living in New York, and assistant editor of the New York Tribune, took occasion to defy the publication of any instance where the lynched Negro was the victim of a white woman's falsehood. Such cases are not rare, but the press and people conversant with the facts, almost invariably suppress them.

The New York Sun of July 30th, 1894, contained a synopsis of interviews with leading congressmen and editors of the South. Speaker Crisp, of the House of Representatives, who was recently a Judge of the Supreme Court of Georgia, led in declaring that lynching seldom or never took place, save for vile crime against women and children. Dr. Hoss, editor of the leading organ of the Methodist Church South, published in its columns that it was his belief that more than three hundred women had been assaulted by Negro men within three months. When asked to prove his charges, or give a single case upon which his "belief" was founded, he said that he could do so, but the details were unfit for publication. No other evidence but his "belief" could be adduced to substantiate this grave charge, yet Bishop Haygood, in the Forum of October, 1893, quotes this "belief" in apology for lynching, and voluntarily adds: "It is my opinion that this is an underestimate." The "opinion" of this man, based upon a "belief," had greater weight coming from a man who has posed as a friend to "Our Brother in Black," and was accepted as authority. An interview of Miss Frances E. Willard, the great apostle of temperance, the daughter of abolitionists and a personal friend and helper of many individual colored people, has been quoted in support of the utterance of this calumny against a weak and defenseless race. In the New York Voice of October 23, 1890, after a tour in the South, where she was told all these things by the "best white people," she said: "The grogshop is the Negro's center of power. Better whisky and more of it is the rallying cry of great, dark-faced mobs. The colored race multiplies like the locusts of Egypt. The grogshop is its center of power. The safety of woman, of childhood, the home, is menaced in a thousand localities at this moment, so that men dare not go beyond the sight of their own roof-tree."

These charges so often reiterated, have had the effect of fastening the odium upon the race of a peculiar propensity for this foul crime. The Negro is thus forced to a defense of his good name, and this chapter will be devoted to the history of some of the cases where assault upon white women by Negroes is charged. He is not the aggressor in this fight, but the situation demands that the facts be given, and they will speak for themselves. Of the 1,115 Negro men, women and children hanged, shot and roasted alive from January 1st, 1882, to January 1st, 1894, inclusive, only 348 of that number were charged with rape. Nearly 700 of these persons were lynched for any other reason which could be manufactured by a mob wishing to indulge in a lynching bee.

A White Woman's Falsehood.

The Cleveland, Ohio, Gazette, January 16, 1892, gives an account of one of these cases of "rape."

Mrs. J. C. Underwood, the wife of a minister of Elyria, Ohio, accused an Afro-American of rape. She told her husband that during his absence in 1888, stumping the state for the Prohibition Party, the man came to the kitchen door, forced his way in the house and insulted her. She tried to drive him out with a heavy poker, but he overpowered and chloroformed her, and when she revived her clothing was torn and she was in a horrible condition. She did not know the man, but could identify him. She subsequently pointed out William Offett, a married man, who was arrested, and, being in Ohio, was granted a trial.

The prisoner vehemently denied the charge of rape, but confessed he went to Mrs. Underwood's residence at her invitation and was criminally intimate with her at her request. This availed him nothing against the sworn testimony of a minister's wife, a lady of the highest respectability. He was found guilty, and entered the penitentiary, December 14, 1888, for fifteen years. Sometime afterwards the woman's remorse led her to confess to her husband that the man was innocent. These are her words: "I met Offett at the postoffice. It was raining. He was polite to me, and as I had several bundles in my arms he offered to carry them home for me, which he did. He had a strange fascination for me, and I invited him to call on me. He called, bringing chestnuts and candy for the children. By this means we got them to leave us alone in the room. Then I sat on his lap. He made a proposal to me and I readily consented. Why I did so I do not know, but that I did is true. He visited me several times after that and each time I was indiscreet. I did not care after the first time. In fact I could not have resisted, and had no desire to resist."

When asked by her husband why she told him she had been outraged, she said: "I had several reasons for telling you. One was the neighbors saw the fellow here, another was, I was afraid I had contracted a loathsome disease, and still another was that I feared I might give birth to a Negro baby. I hoped to save my reputation by telling you a deliberate lie." Her husband, horrified by the confession, had Offett, who had already served four years, released and secured a divorce.

There have been many such cases throughout the South, with the difference that the Southern white men in insensate fury wreak their vengeance without intervention of law upon the Negro who consorts with their women.

Tried to Manufacture an Outrage.

The Memphis (Tenn.) Ledger, of June 8, 1892, has the following: "If Lillie Bailey, a rather pretty white girl, seventeen years of age, who is now at the city hospital, would be somewhat less reserved about her disgrace there would be some very nauseating details in the story of her life. She is the mother of a little coon. The truth might reveal fearful depravity or the evidence of a rank outrage. She will not divulge the name of the man who has left such black evidence of her disgrace, and in fact says it is a matter in which there can be no interest to the outside world. She came to Memphis nearly three months ago, and was taken in at the Woman's Refuge in the southern part of the city. She remained there until a few weeks ago when the child was born. The ladies in charge of the Refuge were horrified. The girl was at once sent to the city hospital, where she has been since May 30th. She is a country girl. She came to Memphis from her father's farm, a short distance from Hernando, Miss. Just when she left there she would not say. In fact she says she came to Memphis from Arkansas, and says her home is in that state. She is rather good looking, has blue eyes, a low forehead and dark red hair. The ladies at the Woman's Refuge do not know anything about the girl further than what they learned when she was an inmate of the institution; and she would not tell much. When the child was born an attempt was made to get the girl to reveal the name of the Negro who had disgraced her, she obstinately refused and it was impossible to elicit any information from her on the subject."

Note the wording: "The truth might reveal fearful depravity or rank outrage." If it had been a white child or if Lillie Bailey had told a pitiful story of Negro outrage, it would have been a case of woman's weakness or assault and she could have remained at the Woman's Refuge. But a Negro child and to withhold its father's name and thus prevent the killing of another Negro "rapist" was a case of "fearful depravity." Had she revealed the father's name, he would have been lynched and his taking off charged to an assault upon a white woman.

Burned Alive for Adultery.

In Texarkana, Arkansas, Edward Coy was accused of assaulting a white woman. The press dispatches of February 18, 1892, told in detail how he was tied to a tree, the flesh cut from his body by men and boys, and after coal oil was poured over him, the woman he had assaulted gladly set fire to him, and 15,000 persons saw him burn to death. October 1st, the Chicago Inter Ocean contained the following account of that horror from the pen of the "Bystander"—Judge Albion W. Tourgee—as the result of his investigations:

"1. The woman who was paraded as victim of violence was of bad character; her husband was a drunkard and a gambler.

"2. She was publicly reported and generally known to have been criminally intimate with Coy for more than a year previous.

"3. She was compelled by threats, if not by violence, to make the charge against the victim.

"4. When she came to apply the match Coy asked her if she would burn him after they had 'been sweethearting' so long.

"5. A large majority of the 'superior' white men prominent in the affair are the reputed fathers of mulatto children.

"These are not pleasant facts, but they are illustrative of the vital phase of the so-called 'race question,' which should properly be designated an earnest inquiry as to the best methods by which religion, science, law and political power may be employed to excuse injustice, barbarity and crime done to a people because of race and color. There can be no possible belief that these people were inspired by any consuming zeal to vindicate God's law against miscegenationists of the most practical sort. The woman was a willing partner in the victim's guilt, and being of the 'superior' race must naturally have been more guilty."

Not Identified but Lynched.

February 11th, 1893, there occurred in Shelby county, Tennessee, the fourth Negro lynching within fifteen months. The three first were lynched in the city of Memphis for firing on white men in self-defense. This Negro, Richard Neal, was lynched a few miles from the city limits, and the following is taken from the Memphis (Tenn.) Scimitar:

"As the Scimitar stated on Saturday the Negro, Richard Neal, who raped Mrs. Jack White near Forest Hill, in this county, was lynched by a mob of about 200 white citizens of the neighborhood. Sheriff McLendon, accompanied by Deputies Perkins, App and Harvey and a Scimitar reporter, arrived on the scene of the execution about 3:30 in the afternoon. The body was suspended from the first limb of a post oak tree by a new quarter inch grass rope. A hangman's knot, evidently tied by an expert, fitted snugly under the left ear of the corpse, and a new name string pinioned the victim's arms behind him. His legs were not tied. The body was perfectly limber when the Sheriff's posse cut it down and retained enough heat to warm the feet of Deputy Perkins, whose road cart was converted into a hearse. On arriving with the body at Forest Hill the Sheriff made a bargain with a stalwart young man with a blonde mustache and deep blue eyes, who told the Scimitar reporter that he was the leader of the mob, to haul the body to Germantown for $3.

"When within half-a-mile of Germantown the Sheriff and posse were overtaken by Squire McDonald of Collierville, who had come down to hold the inquest. The Squire had his jury with him, and it was agreed for the convenience of all parties that he should proceed with the corpse to Germantown and conduct the inquiry as to the cause of death. He did so, and a verdict of death from hanging by parties unknown was returned in due form.

"The execution of Neal was done deliberately and by the best people of the Collierville, Germantown and Forest Hill neighborhoods, without passion or exhibition of anger.

"He was arrested on Friday about ten o'clock, by Constable Bob Cash, who carried him before Mrs. White. She said: 'I think he is the man. I am almost certain of it. If he isn't the man he is exactly like him.'

"The Negro's coat was torn also, and there were other circumstances against him. The committee returned and made its report, and the chairman put the question of guilt or innocence to a vote.

"All who thought the proof strong enough to warrant execution were invited to cross over to the other side of the road. Everybody but four or five negroes crossed over.

"The committee then placed Neal on a mule with his arms tied behind him, and proceeded to the scene of the crime, followed by the mob. The rope, with a noose already prepared, was tied to the limb nearest the spot where the unpardonable sin was committed, and the doomed man's mule was brought to a standstill beneath it.

"Then Neal confessed. He said he was the right man, but denied that he used force or threats to accomplish his purpose. It was a matter of purchase, he claimed, and said the price paid was twenty-five cents. He warned the colored men present to beware of white women and resist temptation, for to yield to their blandishments or to the passions of men, meant death.

"While he was speaking, Mrs. White came from her home and calling Constable Cash to one side, asked if he could not save the Negro's life. The reply was, 'No,' and Mrs. White returned to the house.

"When all was in readiness, the husband of Neal's victim leaped upon the mule's back and adjusted the rope around the Negro's neck. No cap was used, and Neal showed no fear, nor did he beg for mercy. The mule was struck with a whip and bounded out from under Neal, leaving him suspended in the air with his feet about three feet from the ground."

Delivered to the Mob by the Governor of the State.

John Peterson, near Denmark, S. C., was suspected of rape, but escaped, went to Columbia, and placed himself under Gov. Tillman's protection, declaring he too could prove an alibi by white witnesses. A white reporter hearing his declaration volunteered to find these witnesses, and telegraphed the governor that he would be in Columbia with them on Monday. In the meantime the mob at Denmark, learning Peterson's whereabouts, went to the governor and demanded the prisoner. Gov. Tillman, who had during his canvass for re-election the year before, declared that he would lead a mob to lynch a Negro that assaulted a white woman, gave Peterson up to the mob. He was taken back to Denmark, and the white girl in the case as positively declared that he was not the man. But the verdict of the mob was that "the crime had been committed and somebody had to hang for it, and if he, Peterson, was not guilty of that he was of some other crime," and he was hung, and his body riddled with 1,000 bullets.

Lynched as a Warning.

Alabama furnishes a case in point. A colored man named Daniel Edwards, lived near Selma, Alabama, and worked for a family of a farmer near that place. This resulted in an intimacy between the young man and a daughter of the householder, which finally developed in the disgrace of the girl. After the birth of the child, the mother disclosed the fact that Edwards was its father. The relationship had been sustained for more than a year, and yet this colored man was apprehended, thrown into jail from whence he was taken by a mob of one hundred neighbors and hung to a tree and his body riddled with bullets. A dispatch which describes the lynching, ends as follows. "Upon his back was found pinned this morning the following: 'Warning to all Negroes that are too intimate with white girls. This the work of one hundred best citizens of the South Side.'"

There can be no doubt from the announcement made by this "one hundred best citizens" that they understood full well the character of the relationship which existed between Edwards and the girl, but when the dispatches were sent out, describing the affair, it was claimed that Edwards was lynched for rape.

Suppressing the Truth.

In a county in Mississippi during the month of July the Associated Press dispatches sent out a report that the sheriff's eight year old daughter had been assaulted by a big, black, burly brute who had been promptly lynched. The facts which have since been investigated show that the girl was more than eighteen years old and that she was discovered by her father in this young man's room who was a servant on the place. But these facts the Associated Press has not given to the world, nor did the same agency acquaint the world with the fact that a Negro youth who was lynched in Tuscumbia, Ala., the same year on the same charge told the white girl who accused him before the mob, that he had met her in the woods often by appointment. There is a young mulatto in one of the State prisons of the South to-day who is there by charge of a young white woman to screen herself. He is a college graduate and had been corresponding with, and clandestinely visiting her until he was surprised and run out of her room en deshabille by her father. He was put in prison in another town to save his life from the mob and his lawyer advised that it were better to save his life by pleading guilty to charges made and being sentenced for years, than to attempt a defense by exhibiting the letters written him by this girl. In the latter event, the mob would surely murder him, while there was a chance for his life by adopting the former course. Names, places and dates are not given for the same reason.

The excuse has come to be so safe, it is not surprising that a Philadelphia girl, beautiful and well educated, and of good family, should make a confession published in all the daily papers of that city October, 1894, that she had been stealing for some time, and that to cover one of her thefts, she had said she had been bound and gagged in her father's house by a colored man, and money stolen therefrom by him. Had this been done in many localities, it would only have been necessary for her to "identify" the first Negro in that vicinity, to have brought about another lynching bee.

A Vile Slander with Scant Retraction.

The following published in the Cleveland (Ohio) Leader of Oct. 23d, 1894, only emphasizes our demand that a fair trial shall be given those accused of crime, and the protection of the law be extended until time for a defense be granted.

"The sensational story sent out last night from Hicksville that a Negro had outraged a little four-year-old girl proves to be a base canard. The correspondents who went into the details should have taken the pains to investigate, and the officials should have known more of the matter before they gave out such grossly exaggerated information.

"The Negro, Charles O'Neil, had been working for a couple of women and, it seems, had worked all winter without being remunerated. There is a little girl, and the girl's mother and grandmother evidently started the story with idea of frightening the Negro out of the country and thus balancing accounts. The town was considerably wrought up and for a time things looked serious. The accused had a preliminary hearing to-day and not an iota of evidence was produced to indicate that such a crime had been committed, or that he had even attempted such an outrage. The village marshal was frightened nearly out of his wits and did little to quiet the excitement last night.

"The affair was an outrage on the Negro, at the expense of innocent childhood, a brainless fabrication from start to finish."

The original story was sent throughout this country and England, but the Cleveland Leader, so far as known, is the only journal which has published these facts in refutation of the slander so often published against the race.

Not only is it true that many of the alleged cases of rape against the Negro, are like the foregoing, but the same crime committed by white men against Negro women and girls, is never punished by mob or the law. A leading journal in South Carolina openly said some months ago that "it is not the same thing for a white man to assault a colored woman as for a colored man to assault a white woman, because the colored woman had no finer feelings nor virtue to be outraged!" Yet colored women have always had far more reason to complain of white men in this respect than ever white women have had of Negroes.

Illinois Has a Lynching.

In the month of June, 1893, the proud commonwealth of Illinois joined the ranks of Lynching States. Illinois, which gave to the world the immortal heroes, Lincoln, Grant and Logan, trailed its banner of justice in the dust—dyed its hands red in the blood of a man not proven guilty of crime.

June 3, 1893, the country about Decatur, one of the largest cities of the state was startled with the cry that a white woman had been assaulted by a colored tramp. Three days later a colored man named Samuel Bush was arrested and put in jail. A white man testified that Bush, on the day of the assault, asked him where he could get a drink and he pointed to the house where the farmer's wife was subsequently said to have been assaulted. Bush said he went to the well but did not go near the house, and did not assault the woman. After he was arrested the alleged victim did not see him to identify him—he was presumed to be guilty.

The citizens determined to kill him. The mob gathered, went to the jail, met with no resistance, took the suspected man, dragged him out tearing every stitch of clothing from his body, then hanged him to a telegraph pole. The grand jury refused to indict the lynchers though the names of over twenty persons who were leaders in the mob were well known. In fact twenty-two persons were indicted, but the grand jurors and the prosecuting attorney disagreed as to the form of the indictments, which caused the jurors to change their minds. All indictments were reconsidered and the matter was dropped. Not one of the dozens of men prominent in that murder have suffered a whit more inconvenience for the butchery of that man, than they would have suffered for shooting a dog.

Color Line Justice.

In Baltimore, Maryland, a gang of white ruffians assaulted a respectable colored girl who was out walking with a young man of her own race. They held her escort and outraged the girl. It was a deed dastardly enough to arouse Southern blood, which gives its horror of rape as excuse for lawlessness, but she was a colored woman. The case went to the courts and they were acquitted.

In Nashville, Tennessee, there was a white man, Pat Hanifan, who outraged a little colored girl, and from the physical injuries received she was ruined for life. He was jailed for six months, discharged, and is now a detective in that city. In the same city, last May, a white man outraged a colored girl in a drug store. He was arrested and released on bail at the trial. It was rumored that five hundred colored men had organized to lynch him. Two hundred and fifty white citizens armed themselves with Winchesters and guarded him. A cannon was placed in front of his home, and the Buchanan Rifles (State Militia) ordered to the scene for his protection. The colored mob did not show up. Only two weeks before, Eph. Grizzard, who had only been charged with rape upon a white woman, had been taken from the jail, with Governor Buchanan and the police and militia standing by, dragged through the streets in broad daylight, knives plunged into him at every step, and with every fiendish cruelty that a frenzied mob could devise, he was at last swung out on the bridge with hands cut to pieces as he tried to climb up the stanchions. A naked, bloody example of the bloodthirstiness of the nineteenth century civilization of the Athens of the South! No cannon nor military were called out in his defense. He dared to visit a white woman.

At the very moment when these civilized whites were announcing their determination "to protect their wives and daughters," by murdering Grizzard, a white man was in the same jail for raping eight-year-old Maggie Reese, a colored girl. He was not harmed. The "honor" of grown women who were glad enough to be supported by the Grizzard boys and Ed Coy, as long as the liaison was not known, needed protection; they were white. The outrage upon helpless childhood needed no avenging in this case; she was black.

A white man in Guthrie, Oklahoma Territory, two months after inflicted such injuries upon another colored girl that she died. He was not punished, but an attempt was made in the same town in the month of June to lynch a colored man who visited a white woman.

In Memphis, Tennessee, in the month of June, Ellerton L. Dorr, who is the husband of Russell Hancock's widow, was arrested for attempted rape on Mattie Cole, a neighbor's cook; he was only prevented from accomplishing his purpose by the appearance of Mattie's employer. Dorr's friends say he was drunk and not responsible for his actions. The grand jury refused to indict him and he was discharged.

In Tallahassee, Florida, a colored girl, Charlotte Gilliam, was assaulted by white men. Her father went to have a warrant for their arrest issued, but the judge refused to issue it.

In Bowling Green, Virginia, Moses Christopher, a colored lad, was charged with assault, September 10. He was indicted, tried, convicted and sentenced to death in one day. In the same state at Danville, two weeks before—August 29, Thomas J. Penn, a white man, committed a criminal assault upon Lina Hanna, a twelve-year-old colored girl, but he has not been tried, certainly not killed either by the law or the mob.

In Surrey county, Virginia, C. L. Brock, a white man, criminally assaulted a ten-year-old colored girl, and threatened to kill her if she told. Notwithstanding, she confessed to her aunt, Mrs. Alice Bates, and the white brute added further crime by killing Mrs. Bates when she upbraided him about his crime upon her niece. He emptied the contents of his revolver into her body as she lay. Brock has never been apprehended, and no effort has been made to do so by the legal authorities.

But even when punishment is meted out by law to white villians for this horrible crime, it is seldom or never that capital punishment is invoked. Two cases just clipped from the daily papers will suffice to show how this crime is punished when committed by white offenders and black.

LOUISVILLE, KY., October 19.—Smith Young, colored, was to-day sentenced to be hanged. Young criminally assaulted a six-year-old child about six months ago.

Jacques Blucher, the Pontiac Frenchman who was arrested at that place for a criminal assault on his daughter Fanny on July 29 last, pleaded nolo contendere when placed on trial at East Greenwich, near Providence, R. I., Tuesday, and was sentenced to five years in State Prison.

Charles Wilson was convicted of assault upon seven-year-old Mamie Keys in Philadelphia, in October, and sentenced to ten years in prison. He was white. Indianapolis courts sentenced a white man in September to eight years in prison for assault upon a twelve-year old white girl.

April 24, 1893, a lynching was set for Denmark, S. C., on the charge of rape. A white girl accused a Negro of assault, and the mob was about to lynch him. A few hours before the lynching three reputable white men rode into the town and solemnly testified that the accused Negro was at work with them 25 miles away on the day and at the hour the crime had been committed. He was accordingly set free. A white person's word is taken as absolutely for as against a Negro.

Henry McNeal Turner
The Barbarous Decision of the Supreme Court

Editor of the New York Voice:

Amidst multitudinous duties I find, calling my attention, your note of recent date, asking me to briefly refer to the "Civil Rights Decisions," which, since their delivery has drawn from me expressions which many are pleased to call severe adverse strictures upon the highest court in this country, and upon all of its judges save one, Mr. Justice Harlan. It is to me a matter of that kind of surprise called wonder suddenly excited to find a single, solitary individual who belongs in the United States, or who has been here for any considerable time, unacquainted with those famous FIVE DEATH DEALING DECISIONS. Indeed, sir, those decisions have had, since the 15th day of October, A. D. 1883, the day of their pronouncement, more of my study than any other civil subject. I incline to the opinion that I have an argument which, taken as a concomitant of the learned dissenting sentiments of that eminent jurist, Mr. Justice Harlan, would to a rational mind make the judgment of Justice Bradley and his associates a deliquescence—a bubble on the wave of equity—a legal nothing. You bid me in my reply to observe brevity. Shortness and conciseness seem to be the ever present rule when the Negro and his case is under treatment. However, I am satisfied that in saying this, I do not convey your reason for commanding me to condense, "boil down." The more I ponder the non-agreeing words of that member of our chief assize, who had the moral courage to bid defiance to race prejudice, the more certain am I that no words of mine, condemnatory of that decision, have been sufficiently harsh.

March 1st, 1875, Congress passed an act entitled "An act for the prevention of discrimination on the ground of race, color or previous condition of servitude," said act being generally known as the Civil Rights Bill, introduced during the lifetime of the Negro's champion, the immortal Charles Sumner. The act provided:

"SECTION 1. That all persons within the jurisdiction of the United States shall be entitled to the full and equal enjoyment of the accommodations, advantages, facilities, and privileges of inns, public conveyances on land or water, theatres, and other places of public amusements—subject only to the conditions and limitations established by law and applicable alike to citizens of every color and race, regardless of any previous condition of servitude.

"SEC. 2. That any person, who shall violate the foregoing section by denying to any citizen, except for reasons by law applicable to citizens of every race and color, and regardless of any previous condition of servitude, the full enjoyment of any of the accommodations, advantages, facilities or privileges in said section enumerated, or by aiding or inciting such denial, shall for every such offense forfeit and pay the sum of five hundred dollars to the person aggrieved thereby, to be recovered in an action of debt, with full costs; and shall also, for every such offence, be deemed guilty of a misdemeanor, and, upon conviction thereof, shall be fined not less than five hundred, nor more than one thousand dollars, or shall be imprisoned not less than thirty days nor more than one year. Provided, that all persons may elect to sue for the penalty aforesaid, or to proceed under their rights at common law and by State statutes; and having so elected to proceed in the one mode or the other, their right to proceed in the other jurisdiction shall be barred. But this provision shall not apply to criminal proceedings, either under this act or the criminal law of any State. And provided further, that a judgment for the penalty in favor of the party aggrieved, or a judgment upon an indictment, shall be a bar to either prosecution respectively."

Here we have the exact language of the law:

First, what is forbidden; second, the penalty; third, the mode for gaining redress; and fourth, the defendant's security against excessive punishment. The questions that come forward and will not down are: Was this law just? Did this law violate the principle which should be foremost in every hall of legislation—hurt no one, give unto every man his just due? Should the color of one's skin deny him privileges any more than the color of one's hair, seeing that the individual had nothing to do with the cause for the one or for the other? Before attempting to answer the above questions, which must and will suggest themselves to every *compos mentis*, we state the constitutional amendments upon which the act under consideration was founded and upheld. We cannot see how one so learned in the law as Mr. Justice Bradley is presumed to be, by reason of his exalted position, can see only the Fourteenth Amendment, as the part of the Constitution, relied on. It is undeniably patent to all that the Thirteenth Amendment more nearly expresses the foundation for the "act." The language of the Thirteenth Amendment says:

SECTION 1. "Neither slavery nor involuntary servitude, except as a punishment for a crime, whereof the party shall have duly been convicted, shall exist within the United States, or any place subject to their jurisdiction." This amendment in its second section, declares that "Congress shall have the power to enforce this article by appropriate legislation." Under this article, alone, I am satisfied that our National Legislature had full warrant and authority to enact the law now abrogated. The Fourteenth Amendment to the Constitution provides that "All persons born or naturalized in the United States, and subject to the jurisdiction thereof, are citizens of the United States, and of the State wherein they reside. No State shall make or enforce any law which shall abridge the privileges or immunities of the citizens of the United States; nor shall any State deprive any person of life, liberty or property without due process of law, nor deny to any person in its jurisdiction the equal protection of the laws." Upon these two amendments, say these wise judges, depends the constitutionality of the act or law under discussion.

In October, 1882, five cases were filed or submitted: United States *vs.* Stanley, from Kansas; United States *vs.* Ryan, from California; United States *vs.* Nichols, from Missouri; United States *vs.* Singleton, from New York; and Robinson and wife *vs.* Memphis and Charleston Railroad Company, from Tennessee. Our learned (?) judges occupied a year in considering what their dicta should be. October 15, 1883, found Justice Bradley in his place, on the bench prepared to voice the opinion of the court as to the rights of more than seven millions of human beings. Mr. Solicitor-General Phillips had delivered his argument for the life of the law to be maintained. The argument of the Solicitor-General had been supplemented by the eloquent efforts of Mr. William M. Randolph, on behalf of Robinson and wife. Numerous authorities were cited to show that where the Constitution guarantees a right, Congress is empowered to pass the legislation appropriate to give effect to that right. It was also maintained and established by judicial precedents, that the constitutionality of the act was not harmed by the nice distinction of "guaranteed rights," instead of "created rights." Justice Bradley consumes seventeen pages, to do what in his conscientious (?) opinion he believes to be right. Justice Harlan, in opposing the position taken by Mr. Bradley, occupies thirty-seven pages. After reciting the law countenancing the actions instituted by the sorely aggrieved persons, the first question which propounded itself to the member reading the opinion was: "Are these sections constitutional?" After taking space and time to tell what it is not the essence of the law to do, the Honorable Judge in *obiter dictum* language says: "But the responsibility of an independent judgment is now thrown upon this court; and we are bound to exercise it according to the best lights we have."

Why this apologetic language? Are we not acquainted with the functions and duties of our court of last resort? Do we not know that the judges thereof are appointed for life, subject only to their good behavior? This deciding judge says: "The power is sought, first in the Fourteenth Amendment; and the views and arguments of distinguished senators, advanced whilst the law was under consideration, claiming authority to pass it by virtue of that amendment, are the principal arguments adduced in favor of the power. We have carefully considered those arguments, as was due to the eminent ability of those who put them forward, and have felt, in all its force, the weight of authority which always invests a law that Congress deems itself competent to pass." It is not said that arguments opposed to the passage of the act were noticed. It is not said that this Honorable Judge, long before this question of law was brought before him, had predetermined its non-constitutionality.

It is not hinted that this Republican Supreme Court had caused it to be noised abroad what their "finding" would be if the "law" was inquired into. The court, it is said, could see, and only see, negroes in Kansas and Missouri intermingling with white persons in hotels and inns; negroes in California and New

York associating on equal terms with Caucasians in theaters; and negroes in the presence of those free from the taint of African blood in the parlor-cars of Tennessee. These sights completely blinded the eyes of the, at other times, learned judges, and one of their number, not too full of indignation for utterance, proclaimed aloud, these things may not be, these pictures shall not in future be produced; the law is unconstitutional; and all of the other members, save one said, amen. Negroes may come as servants into all of the hotels, inns, theaters and parlor-cars, but they shall never be received as equals—as are other persons. A negro woman with a white baby in her arms may go to the table in the finest and most aristocratic hotel, and there, as a servant, be permitted to associate with all present, of whatever nationality. The same woman, unaccompanied by said baby, or coming without the distinguished rank of servant, is given to understand that she can not enter. And what is more, by the Bradley infamous decision, may be by force of arms prevented from entering. A negro, whose father is a white man, and whose mother's father was white, if marked sufficiently to tell that he is somewhat negro is denied admission into certain places; the same resorts or places of entertainment being readily granted to the inky dark negro who is accompanying an invalid white man. The gambler, cutthroat, thief, despoiler of happy homes and the cowardly assassin need only to have white faces in order to be accommodated with more celerity and respect than are our lawyers, doctors, teachers and humble preachers. Talk about the "Dred Scott" decision; why it was only a mole-hill in comparison with this obstructing Rocky Mountain to the freedom of citizenship. I am charged by your Pennsylvania correspondent with saying that, "By the decision of the Republican Supreme Court colored people may be turned out of hotels, cheated, abused and insulted on steamboats and railroads without legal redress." I am of the opinion that the reporter on your paper who published the above quotation as coming from me, made no mistake unless it was that of making it more mild than I intended. When I use the term, "cheated," I mean that colored persons are required to pay first-class fare and in payment therefor are given no-class treatment, or at least the kind which no other human being, paying first-class fare, is served. Some conveyances, excepted, I must say to their credit. Bohemians, Scandinavians, Greasers, Italians and Mongolians all precede negroes. When Mr. Justice Harlan shall have retired from the bench by reason of age and infirmity, I pray him to accept, take and carry with him into his retirement the boiled-down essence of the love of more than eight million negroes, who delight to honor an individual whose vertebrae is strong enough to stem the tide of race prejudice. His decision dissenting in favor of equal and exact justice to all men will last always, will never be forgotten as long as there is a descendant of the American negro on the earth; I have no doubt that the feelings of Justice Harlan when seeking rest upon his soft couch on the night of that fateful day in October, were different to the emotions present with Judge Bradley. The latter had doomed seven million human beings and their posterity to "stalls" and "nooks," donating inferiority; the other had attempted to protect them from American barbarism and vandalism. Seven million persons, many of whom are not only related to Justice Bradley's race by affinity, but by consanguinity, cannot move the bowels of his compassion to the extent of framing or constructing even one sentence in all of that notorious decision which fairly can be interpreted as a friendly regard for the rights of those struggling souls who cried to God, while carrying the burden of bondage for more than two hundred and forty years. God will some day raise up another Lincoln, another Thad. Stevens and another Charles Sumner. In my opinion, if Jesus was on earth, he would say, when speaking of eight members of the Supreme Court and the decision which worked such acerb and cruel wrong upon my people, "Father, forgive them; they know not what they do."

Mr. Justice Harlan, in his protesting language, says many things which stand non-controvertible and may some day be remembered only to be thought about when it is too late. He says: "The opinion in these cases proceeds, it seems to me, upon grounds entirely too narrow and artificial. I cannot resist the conclusion that the substance and spirit of the recent amendments of the Constitution have been sacrificed by a subtle and ingenious verbal criticism." He then quotes an authority which is so old and well established that the memory of man goeth not to the contrary, which says: "It is not the words of the law, but the internal sense of it that makes the law; the letter of the law is the body; the sense and reason of the law is the soul." Continuing, he says:

> Constitutional provisions, adopted in the interest of liberty, and for the purpose of securing, through national legislation, if need be, rights inhering in a state of freedom, and belonging to American citizenship, have been so construed as to defeat the ends the people desired to accomplish, which they attempted to accomplish, and which they thought they had accomplished by changes in their fundamental law. By this, I do not mean that the determination of these cases should have been materially controlled by considerations of mere expediency or policy. I mean only, in this form, to express an earnest conviction that the court has departed from the familiar rule requiring, in the interpretation of constitutional provisions, that full effect be given to the intent with which they were adopted. The court adjudges, I think, erroneously, that Congress is without power, under either the Thirteenth or Fourteenth Amendment, to establish such regulations, and that the first and second sections of the statute are, in all their parts, unconstitutional and void.

Then follows a great number of authorities maintaining his position. No sane man can read the record, law and authorities relating to these cases, without forming a conclusion that cannot be brushed away, that the bench of judges were narrow even to wicked ingeniousness, superinduced by color-phobeism. Sane men know that the gentlemen in Congress who voted for this act of 1875 understood full well the condition of our country, as did the powers amending the Constitution abolishing slavery. The intention was to entirely free, not to partly liberate. The desire was to remove the once slave so far from his place of bondage, that he would not even remember it, if such a thing were possible. Congress stepped in and said, he shall vote, he shall serve on juries, he shall testify in court, he shall enter the professions, he shall hold offices, he shall be treated like other men, in all places the conduct of which is regulated by law, he shall in no way be reminded by partial treatment, by discrimination, that he was once a "chattel," a "thing." Certainly Congress had a right to do this. The power that made the slave a man instead of a "thing" had the right to fix his status. The height of absurdity, the chief point in idiocy, the brand of total imbecility, is to say that the Negro shall vote a privilege into existence which one citizen may enjoy for pay, to the exclusion of another, coming in the same way, but clothed in the vesture covering the earth when God first looked upon it. Are colored men to vote grants to railroads upon which they cannot receive equal accommodation? When we ask redress, we are told the State must first pass a law prohibiting us from enjoying certain priviliges and rights, and that after such laws have been passed by the State, we can apply to the United States courts to have such laws declared null and void by *quo warranto* proceedings. The Supreme Court, when applied to, will say to the State, you must not place such laws on your statute book. You can continue your discrimination on account of color. You can continue to place the badge of slavery on persons having more than one-eighth part of Negro blood in their veins, and so long as your State legislatures do not license you so to do, you are safe. For if they (the Negroes) come to us for redress, we will talk about the autonomy of the State must be held inviolate, referring them back to you for satisfaction.

Do you know of anything more degrading to our country, more damnable? The year after this decision the Republican party met with defeat, because it acquiesced by its silence in that abominable decision, nor did it lift a hand to strike down that diabolical sham of judicial monstrosity, neither in Congress nor the great national convention which nominated Blaine and Logan. God, however, has placed them in power again, using the voters and our manner of electing electors as instruments in His hands. God would have men do right, harm no one, and to render to every man his just due. Mr. Justice Harlan rightly says that the Thirteenth Amendment intended that the white race should have no privilege whatsoever pertaining to citizenship and freedom, that was not alike extended and to be enjoyed by those persons who, though the greater part of them were slaves, were invited by an act of Congress to aid in saving from overthrow a government which, theretofore by all of its departments, had treated them as an inferior race, with no legal rights or privileges except such as the white race might choose to grant. It is an indisputable fact that the amendment last mentioned may be exerted by legislation of a direct and primary character for the eradication, not simply of the institution of slavery, but of its badges and incidents indicating that the individual was once a slave. The Supreme Court must decide the interstate commerce law to be unconstitutional on account of interference with the State's autonomy, for it must be remembered that Mrs. Robinson, a citizen of Mississippi, bought a ticket from Grand Junction, Tennessee, to Lynchburg, Virginia, and when praying for satisfaction for rough and contumacious treatment, received at the hands of the company's agent, she was informed by the court, that the court was without power to act. Congress had constitutional power to pursue a runaway slave into all the States by legislation, to punish the man that would dare to conceal the slave. Congress could find the poor fellow seeking God's best blessing to man, liberty, and return him to his master, but Congress cannot, so says our honorable court, give aid sufficient to the poor black man, to prove beyond all doubt to him that he is as free as any other citizen. Mr. Justice Harlan says:

> The difficulty has been to compel a recognition of the legal right of the black race to take the rank of citizens, and to secure the enjoyment of privileges belonging under the law to them as a component part of the people for whose welfare government is ordained. At every step in this direction, the Nation has been confronted with class tyranny, which is of all tyrannies the most intolerable, for it is ubiquitous in its operation, and weighs perhaps most heavily on those whose obscurity or distance would draw them from the notice of a single despot. Today it is the colored race which is denied by corporations and individuals wielding public authority, rights fundamental in their freedom and citizenship. AT SOME FUTURE TIME IT MAY BE THAT SOME OTHER RACE WILL FALL UNDER THE BAN OF RACE DISCRIMINATION.

This last preceding sentence sounds like prophecy from on high. Will the day come when Justice Bradley will want to hide from his decree of the 15th day of October, 1883, and say *non est factum?* I conclude with great reluctance these brief lines, assuring you that the subject is just opened and if desired by you, I will be glad to give it elaborate attention. I ask no rights and privileges for my race in this country, which I would not contend for on behalf of the white people were the conditions changed, or were I to find proscribed white men in Africa where black rules.

A word more and I am done, as you wish brevity. God may forgive this corps of unjust judges, but I never can, their very memories will also be detested by my children's children, nor am I alone in this detestation. The eight millions of my race and their posterity will stand horror-frozen at the very mention of their names. The scenes that have passed under my eyes upon the public highways, the brutal treatment of helpless women which I have witnessed, since that decision was proclaimed, is enough to move heaven to tears and raise a loud acclaim in hell over the conquest of wrong. But we will wait and pray, and look for a better day, for God still lives and the LORD OF HOSTS REIGNS.

I am, sir, yours, for the Fatherhood of God, and the Brotherhood of man.

Atlanta, Georgia, January 4, 1889

Booker T. Washington

from *Up From Slavery*

CHAPTER XIV

The Atlanta Exposition Address

The Atlanta Exposition, at which I had been asked to make an address as a representative of the Negro race, as stated in the last chapter, was opened with a short address from Governor Bullock. After other interesting exercises, including an invocation from Bishop Nelson, of Georgia, a dedicatory ode by Albert Howell, Jr., and addresses by the President of the Exposition and Mrs. Joseph Thompson, the President of the Woman's Board, Governor Bullock introduced me with the words, "We have with us to-day a representative of Negro enterprise and Negro civilization."

When I arose to speak, there was considerable cheering, especially from the coloured people. As I remember it now, the thing that was uppermost in my mind was the desire to say something that would cement the friendship of the races and bring about hearty coöperation between them. So far as my outward surroundings were concerned, the only thing that I recall distinctly now is that when I got up, I saw thousands of eyes looking intently into my face. The following is the address which I delivered:—

MR. PRESIDENT AND GENTLEMEN OF THE BOARD OF DIRECTORS AND CITIZENS.

One-third of the population of the South is of the Negro race. No enterprise seeking the material, civil, or moral welfare of this section can disregard this element of our population and reach the highest success. I but convey to you, Mr. President and Directors, the sentiment of the masses of my race when I say that in no way have the value and manhood of the American Negro been more fittingly and generously recognized than by the managers of this magnificent Exposition at every stage of its progress. It is a recognition that will do more to cement the friendship of the two races than any occurrence since the dawn of our freedom.

Not only this, but the opportunity here afforded will awaken among us a new era of industrial progress. Ignorant and inexperienced, it is not strange that in the first years of our new life we began at the top instead of at the bottom; that a seat in Congress or the state legislature was more sought than real estate or industrial skill; that the political convention or stump speaking had more attractions than starting a dairy farm or truck garden.

A ship lost at sea for many days suddenly sighted a friendly vessel. From the mast of the unfortunate vessel was seen a signal, "Water, water; we die of thirst!" The answer from the friendly vessel at once came back, "Cast down your bucket where you are." A second time the signal, "Water, water; send us water!" ran up from the distressed vessel, and was answered, "Cast down your bucket where you are." And a third and fourth signal for water was answered, "Cast down your bucket where you are." The captain of the distressed vessel, at last heeding the injunction, cast down his bucket, and it came up full of fresh, sparkling water from the mouth of the Amazon River. To those of my race who depend on bettering their condition in a foreign land or who underestimate the importance of cultivating friendly relations with the Southern white man, who is their next-door neighbour, I would say: "Cast down your bucket where you are"—cast it down in making friends in every manly way of the people of all races by whom we are surrounded.

Cast it down in agriculture, mechanics, in commerce, in domestic service, and in the professions. And in this connection it is well to bear in mind that whatever other sins the South may be called to bear, when it comes to business, pure and simple, it is in the South that the Negro is given a man's chance in the commercial world, and in nothing is this Exposition more eloquent than in emphasizing this chance. Our greatest danger is that in the great leap from slavery to freedom we may overlook the fact that the masses of us are to live by the productions of our hands, and fail to keep in mind that we shall prosper in proportion as we learn to dignify and glorify common labour and put brains and skill into the common occupations of life; shall prosper in proportion as we learn to draw the line between the superficial and the substantial, the ornamental gewgaws of life and the useful. No race can prosper till it learns that there is as much dignity in tilling a field as in writing a poem. It is at the bottom of life we must begin, and not at the top. Nor should we permit our grievances to overshadow our opportunities.

To those of the white race who look to the incoming of those of foreign birth and strange tongue and habits for the prosperity of the South, were I permitted I would repeat what I say to my own race, "Cast down your bucket where you are." Cast it down among the eight millions of Negroes whose habits you know, whose fidelity and love you have tested in days when to have proved treacherous meant the ruin of your firesides. Cast down your bucket among these people who have, without strikes and labour wars, tilled your fields, cleared your forests, builded your railroads and cities, and brought forth treasures from the bowels of the earth, and helped make possible this magnificent representation of the progress of the South. Casting down your bucket among my people, helping and encouraging them as you are doing on these grounds, and to education of head, hand, and heart, you will find that they will buy your surplus land, make blossom the waste places in your fields, and run your factories. While doing this, you can be sure in the future, as in the past, that you and your families will be surrounded by the most patient, faithful, law-abiding, and unresentful people that the world has seen. As we have proved our loyalty to you in the past, in nursing your children, watching by the sick-bed of your mothers and fathers, and often following them with tear-dimmed eyes to their graves, so in the future, in our humble way, we shall stand by you with a devotion that no foreigner can approach, ready to lay down our lives, if need be, in defence of yours, interlacing our industrial, commercial, civil, and religious life with yours in a way that shall make the interests of both races one. In all things that are purely social we can be as separate as the fingers, yet one as the hand in all things essential to mutual progress.

There is no defence or security for any of us except in the highest intelligence and development of all. If anywhere there are efforts tending to curtail the fullest growth of the Negro, let these efforts be turned into stimulating, encouraging, and making him the most useful and intelligent citizen. Effort or means so invested will pay a thousand percent interest. These efforts will be twice blessed—"blessing him that gives and him that takes."

There is no escape through law of man or God from the inevitable:—

The laws of changeless justice bind
   Oppressor with oppressed;
And close as sin and suffering joined
   We march to fate abreast.

Nearly sixteen millions of hands will aid you in pulling the load upward, or they will pull against you the load downward. We shall constitute one-third and more of the ignorance and crime of the South, or one-third its intelligence and progress; we shall contribute one-third to the business and industrial prosperity of the South, or we shall prove a veritable body of death, stagnating, depressing, retarding every effort to advance the body politic.

Gentlemen of the Exposition, as we present to you our humble effort at an exhibition of our progress, you must not expect overmuch. Starting thirty years ago with ownership here and there in a few quilts and pumpkins and chickens (gathered from miscellaneous sources), remember the path that has led from these to the inventions and production of agricultural implements, buggies, steam-engines, newspapers, books, statuary, carving, paintings, the management of drug-stores and banks, has not been trodden without contact with thorns and thistles. While we take pride in what we exhibit as a result of our independent efforts, we do not for a moment forget that our part in this exhibition would fall far short of your expectations but for the constant help that has come to our educational life, not only from the Southern states, but especially from Northern philanthropists, who have made their gifts a constant stream of blessing and encouragement.

The wisest among my race understand that the agitation of questions of social equality is the extremest folly, and that progress in the enjoyment of all the privileges that will come to us must be the result of severe and constant struggle rather than of artificial forcing. No race that has anything to contribute to the markets of the world is long in any degree ostracized. It is important and right that all privileges of the law be ours, but it is vastly more important that we be prepared for the exercises of these privileges. The opportunity to earn a dollar in a factory just now is worth infinitely more than the opportunity to spend a dollar in an opera-house.

In conclusion, may I repeat that nothing in thirty years has given us more hope and encouragement, and drawn us so near to you of the white race, as this opportunity offered by the Exposition; and here bending, as it were, over the altar that represents the results of the struggles of your race and mine, both starting practically empty-handed three decades ago, I pledge that in your effort to work out the great and intricate problem which God has laid at the doors of the South, you shall have at all times the patient, sympathetic help of my race; only let this be constantly in mind, that, while from representations in these buildings of the product of field, of forest, of mine, of factory, letters, and art, much good will come, yet far above and beyond material benefits will be that higher good, that, let us pray God, will come, in a blotting out of sectional differences and racial animosities and suspicions, in a determination to administer absolute justice, in a willing obedience among all classes to the mandates of law. This, this, coupled with our material prosperity, will bring into our beloved South a new heaven and a new earth.

The first thing that I remember, after I had finished speaking, was that Governor Bullock rushed across the platform and took me by the hand, and that others did the same. I received so many and such hearty congratulations that I found it difficult to get out of the building. I did not appreciate to any degree, however, the impression which my address seemed to have made, until the next morning, when I went into the business part of the city. As soon as I was recognized, I was surprised to find myself pointed out and surrounded by a crowd of men who wished to shake hands with me. This was kept up on every street on to which I went, to an extent which embarrassed me so much that I went back to my boarding-place. The next morning I returned to Tuskegee. At the station in Atlanta, and at almost all of the stations at which the train stopped between that city and Tuskegee, I found a crowd of people anxious to shake hands with me.

The papers in all parts of the United States published the address in full, and for months afterward there were complimentary editorial references to it. Mr. Clark Howell, the editor of the Atlanta *Constitution*, telegraphed to a New York paper, among other words, the following, "I do not exaggerate when I say that Professor Booker T. Washington's address yesterday was one of the most notable speeches, both as to character and as to the warmth of its reception, ever delivered to a Southern audience. The address was a revelation. The whole speech is a platform upon which blacks and whites can stand with full justice to each other."

The Boston *Transcript* said editorially: "The speech of Booker T. Washington at the Atlanta Exposition, this week, seems to have dwarfed all the other proceedings and the Exposition itself. The sensation that it has caused in the press has never been equalled."

I very soon began receiving all kinds of propositions from lecture bureaus, and editors of magazines and papers, to take the lecture platform, and to write articles. One lecture bureau offered me fifty thousand dollars, or two hundred dollars a night and expenses, if I would place my services at its disposal for a given period. To all these communications I replied that my life-work was at Tuskegee; and that whenever I spoke it must be in the interests of the Tuskegee school and my race, and that I would enter into no arrangements that seemed to place a mere commercial value upon my services.

Some days after its delivery I sent a copy of my address to the President of the United States, the Hon. Grover Cleveland. I received from him the following autograph reply:—

> Gray Gables, Buzzard's Bay, Mass.,
> October 6, 1895.

BOOKER T. WASHINGTON, ESQ.:

MY DEAR SIR: I thank you for sending me a copy of your address delivered at the Atlanta Exposition.

I thank you with much enthusiasm for making the address. I have read it with intense interest, and I think the Exposition would be fully justified if it did not do more than furnish the opportunity for its delivery. Your words cannot fail to delight and encourage all who wish well for your race; and if our coloured fellow-citizens do not from your utterances gather new hope and form new determinations to gain every valuable advantage offered them by their citizenship, it will be strange indeed.

> Yours very truly,
> GROVER CLEVELAND.

Later I met Mr. Cleveland, for the first time, when, as President, he visited the Atlanta Exposition. At the request of myself and others he consented to spend an hour in the Negro Building, for the purpose of inspecting the Negro exhibit and of giving the coloured people in attendance an opportunity to shake hands with him. As soon as I met Mr. Cleveland I became impressed with his simplicity, greatness, and rugged honesty. I have met him many times since then, both at public functions and at his private residence in Princeton, and the more I see of him the more I admire him. When he visited the Negro Building in Atlanta he seemed to give himself up wholly, for that hour, to the coloured people. He seemed to be as careful to shake hands with some old coloured "auntie" clad partially in rags, and to take as much pleasure in doing so, as if he were greeting some millionnaire. Many of the coloured people took advantage of the occasion to get him to write his name in a book or on a slip of paper. He was as careful and patient in doing this as if he were putting his signature to some great state document.

Mr. Cleveland has not only shown his friendship for me in many personal ways, but has always consented to do anything I have asked of him for our school. This he has done, whether it was to make a personal donation or to use his influence in securing the donations of others. Judging from my personal acquaintance with Mr. Cleveland, I do not believe that he is conscious of possessing any colour prejudice. He is too great for that. In my contact with people I find that, as a rule, it is only the little, narrow people who live for themselves, who never read good books, who do not travel, who never open up their souls in a way to permit them to come into contact with other souls—with the great outside world. No man whose vision is bounded by colour can come into contact with what is highest and best in the world. In meeting men, in many places, I have found that the happiest people are those who do the most for others; the most miserable are those who do the least. I have also found that few things, if any, are capable of making one so blind and narrow as race prejudice. I often say to our students, in the course of my talks to them on Sunday evenings in the chapel, that the longer I live and the more experience I have of the world, the more I am convinced that, after all, the one thing that is most worth living for—and dying for, if need be—is the opportunity of making some one else more happy and more useful.

The coloured people and the coloured newspapers at first seemed to be greatly pleased with the character of my Atlanta address, as well as with its reception. But after the first burst of enthusiasm began to die away, and the coloured people began reading the speech in cold type, some of them seemed to feel that they had been hypnotized. They seemed to feel that I had been too liberal in my remarks toward the Southern whites, and that I had not spoken out strongly enough for what they termed the "rights" of the race. For a while there was a reaction, so far as a certain element of my own race was concerned, but later these reactionary ones seemed to have been won over to my way of believing and acting.

While speaking of changes in public sentiment, I recall that about ten years after the school at Tuskegee was established, I had an experience that I shall never forget. Dr. Lyman Abbott, then the pastor of Plymouth Church, and also editor of the *Outlook* (then the *Christian Union*), asked me to write a letter for his paper giving my opinion of the exact condition, mental and moral, of the coloured ministers in the South, as based upon my observations. I wrote the letter, giving the exact facts as I conceived them to be. The picture painted was a rather black one—or, since I am black, shall I say "white"? It could not be otherwise with a race but a few years out of slavery, a race which had not had time or opportunity to produce a competent ministry.

What I said soon reached every Negro minister in the country, I think, and the letters of condemnation which I received from them were not few. I think that for a year after the publication of this article every association and every conference or religious body of any kind, of my race, that met, did not fail before adjourning to pass a resolution condemning me, or calling upon me to retract or modify what I had said. Many of these organizations went so far in their resolutions as to advise parents to cease sending their children to Tuskegee. One association even appointed a "missionary" whose duty it was to warn the people against sending their children to Tuskegee. This missionary had a son in the school, and I noticed that, whatever the "missionary" might have said or done with regard to others, he was careful not to take his son away from the institution. Many of the coloured papers, especially those that were the organs of religious bodies, joined in the general chorus of condemnation or demands for retraction.

During the whole time of the excitement, and through all the criticism, I did not utter a word of explanation or retraction. I knew that I was right, and that time and the sober second thought of the people would vindicate me. It was not long before the bishops and other church leaders began to make a careful investigation of the conditions of the ministry, and they found out that I was right. In fact, the oldest and most influential bishop in one branch of the Methodist Church said that my words were far too mild. Very soon public sentiment began making itself felt, in demanding a purifying of the ministry. While this is not yet complete by any means, I think I may say, without egotism, and I have been told by many of our most influential ministers, that my words had much to do with starting a demand for the placing of a higher type of men in the pulpit. I have had the satisfaction of having many who once condemned me thank me heartily for my frank words.

The change of the attitude of the Negro ministry, so far as regards myself, is so complete that at the present time I have no warmer friends among any class than I have among the clergymen. The improvement in the character and life of the Negro ministers is one of the most gratifying evidences of the progress of the race. My experience with them, as well as other events in my life, convince me that the thing to do, when one feels sure that he has said or done the right thing, and is condemned, is to stand still and keep quiet. If he is right, time will show it.

In the midst of the discussion which was going on concerning my Atlanta speech, I received the letter which I give below, from Dr. Gilman, the President of Johns Hopkins University, who had been made chairman of the judges of award in connection with the Atlanta Exposition:—

Johns Hopkins University, Baltimore,
President's Office, September 30, 1895.
DEAR MR. WASHINGTON: Would it be agreeable to you to be one of the Judges of Award in the Department of Education at Atlanta? If so, I shall be glad to place your name upon the list. A line by telegraph will be welcomed.
Yours very truly,
D. C. GILMAN.

I think I was even more surprised to receive this invitation than I had been to receive the invitation to speak at the opening of the Exposition. It was to be a part of my duty, as one of the jurors, to pass not only upon the exhibits of the coloured schools, but also upon those of the white schools. I accepted the position, and spent a month in Atlanta in performance of the duties which it entailed. The board of jurors was a large one, consisting in all of sixty members. It was about equally divided between Southern white people and Northern white people. Among them were college presidents, leading scientists and men of letters, and specialists in many subjects. When the group of jurors to which I was assigned met for organization, Mr. Thomas Nelson Page, who was one of the number, moved that I be made secretary of that division, and the motion was unanimously adopted. Nearly half of our division were Southern people. In performing my duties in the inspection of the exhibits of white schools I was in every case treated with respect, and at the close of our labours I parted from my associates with regret.

I am often asked to express myself more freely than I do upon the political condition and the political future of my race. These recollections of my experience in Atlanta give me the opportunity to do so briefly. My own belief is, although I have never before said so in so many words, that the time will come when the Negro in the South will be accorded all the political rights which his ability, character, and material possessions entitle him to. I think, though, that the opportunity to freely exercise such political rights will not come in any large degree through outside or artificial forcing, but will be accorded to the Negro by the Southern white people themselves, and that they will protect him in the exercise of those rights. Just as soon as the South gets over the old feeling that it is being forced by "foreigners," or "aliens," to do something which it does not want to do, I believe that the change in the direction that I have indicated is going to begin. In fact, there are indications that it is already beginning in a slight degree.

Let me illustrate my meaning. Suppose that some months before the opening of the Atlanta Exposition there had been a general demand from the press and public platform outside the South that a Negro be given a place on the opening programme, and that a Negro be placed upon the board of jurors of award. Would any such recognition of the race have taken place? I do not think so. The Atlanta officials went as far as they did because they felt it to be a pleasure, as well as a duty, to reward what they considered merit in the Negro race. Say what we will, there is something in human nature which we cannot blot out, which makes one man, in the end, recognize and reward merit in another, regardless of colour or race.

I believe it is the duty of the Negro—as the greater part of the race is already doing—to deport himself modestly in regard to political claims, depending upon the slow but sure influences that proceed from the possession of property, intelligence, and high character for the full recognition of his political rights. I think that the according of the full exercise of political rights is going to be a matter of natural, slow growth, not an over-night, gourd-vine affair. I do not believe that the Negro should cease voting, for a man cannot learn the exercise of self-government by ceasing to vote, any more than a boy can learn to swim by keeping out of the water, but I do believe that in his voting he should more and more be influenced by those of intelligence and character who are his next-door neighbours.

I know coloured men who, through the encouragement, help, and advice of Southern white people, have accumulated thousands of dollars' worth of property, but who, at the same time, would never think of going to those same persons for advice concerning the casting of their ballots. This, it seems to me, is unwise and unreasonable, and should cease. In saying this I do not mean that the Negro should truckle, or not vote from principle, for the instant he ceases to vote from principle he loses the confidence and respect of the Southern white man even.

I do not believe that any state should make a law that permits an ignorant and poverty-stricken white man to vote, and prevents a black man in the same condition from voting. Such a law is not only unjust, but it will react, as all unjust laws do, in time; for the effect of such a law is to encourage the Negro to secure education and property, and at the same time it encourages the white man to remain in ignorance and poverty. I believe that in time, through the operation of intelligence and friendly race relations, all cheating at the ballot-box in the South will cease. It will become apparent that the white man who begins by cheating a Negro out of his ballot soon learns to cheat a white man out of his, and that the man who does this ends his career of dishonesty by the theft of property or by some equally serious crime. In my opinion, the time will come when the South will encourage all of its citizens to vote. It will see that it pays better, from every standpoint, to have healthy, vigorous life than to have that political stagnation which always results when one-half of the population has no share and no interest in the Government.

As a rule, I believe in universal, free suffrage, but I believe that in the South we are confronted with peculiar conditions that justify the protection of the ballot in many of the states, for a while at least, either by an educational test, a property test, or by both combined; but whatever tests are required, they should be made to apply with equal and exact justice to both races.

Paul Lawrence Dunbar

from *The Sport of the Gods*

VII

In New York

To the provincial coming to New York for the first time, ignorant and un-known, the city presents a notable mingling of the qualities of cheeriness and gloom. If he have any eye at all for the beautiful, he cannot help experiencing a thrill as he crosses the ferry over the river filled with plying craft and catches the first sight of the spires and buildings of New York. If he have the right stuff in him, a something will take possession of him that will grip him again every time he returns to the scene and will make him long and hunger for the place when he is away from it. Later, the lights in the busy streets will bewilder and entice him. He will feel shy and helpless amid the hurrying crowds. A new emotion will take his heart as the people hasten by him,—a feeling of loneli-ness, almost of grief, that with all of these souls about him he knows not one and not one of them cares for him. After a while he will find a place and give a sigh of relief as he settles away from the city's sights behind his cosey blinds. It is better here, and the city is cruel and cold and unfeeling. This he will feel, perhaps, for the first half-hour, and then he will be out in it all again. He will be glad to strike elbows with the bustling mob and be happy at their indiffer-ence to him, so that he may look at them and study them. After it is all over, after he has passed through the first pangs of strangeness and homesickness, yes, even after he has got beyond the stranger's enthusiasm for the metropolis, the real fever of love for the place will begin to take hold upon him. The subtle, in-sidious wine of New York will begin to intoxicate him. Then, if he be wise, he will go away, any place,—yes, he will even go over to Jersey. But if he be a fool, he will stay and stay on until the town becomes all in all to him; until the very streets are his chums and certain buildings and corners his best friends. Then he is hopeless, and to live elsewhere would be death. The Bowery will be his ro-mance, Broadway his lyric, and the Park his pastoral, the river and the glory of it all his epic, and he will look down pityingly on all the rest of humanity.

It was the afternoon of a clear October day that the Hamiltons reached New York. Fannie had some misgivings about crossing the ferry, but once on the boat these gave way to speculations as to what they should find on the other side. With the eagerness of youth to take in new impressions, Joe and Kitty were more concerned with what they saw about them than with what their future would hold, though they might well have stopped to ask some such questions. In all the great city they knew absolutely no one, and had no idea which way to go to find a stopping-place.

They looked about them for some coloured face, and finally saw one among the porters who were handling the baggage. To Joe's inquiry he gave them an address, and also proffered his advice as to the best way to reach the place. He was exceedingly polite, and he looked hard at Kitty. They found the house to which they had been directed, and were a good deal surprised at its apparent grandeur. It was a four-storied brick dwelling on Twenty-seventh Street. As they looked from the outside, they were afraid that the price of staying in such a place would be too much for their pockets. Inside, the sight of the hard, gaudily upholstered instalment-plan furniture did not disillusion them, and they continued to fear that they could never stop at this fine place. But they found Mrs. Jones, the proprietress, both gracious and willing to come to terms with them.

As Mrs. Hamilton—she began to be Mrs. Hamilton now, to the exclusion of Fannie—would have described Mrs. Jones, she was a "big yellow woman." She had a broad good-natured face and a tendency to run to bust.

"Yes," she said, "I think I could arrange to take you. I could let you have two rooms, and you could use my kitchen until you decided whether you wanted to take a flat or not. I has the whole house myself, and I keeps roomers. But latah on I could fix things so's you could have the whole third floor ef you wanted to. Most o' my gent'men 's railroad gent'men, they is. I guess it must 'a' been Mr. Thomas that sent you up here."

"He was a little bright man down at de deepo."

"Yes, that's him. That's Mr. Thomas. He's always lookin' out to send some one here, because he's been here three years hisself an' he kin recommend my house."

It was a relief to the Hamiltons to find Mrs. Jones so gracious and home-like. So the matter was settled, and they took up their abode with her and sent for their baggage.

With the first pause in the rush that they had experienced since starting away from home, Mrs. Hamilton began to have time for reflection, and their condition seemed to her much better as it was. Of course, it was hard to be away from home and among strangers, but the arrangement had this advantage,—that no one knew them or could taunt them with their past trouble. She was not sure that she was going to like New York. It had a great name and was really a great place, but the very bigness of it frightened her and made her feel alone, for she knew that there could not be so many people together without a deal of wickedness. She did not argue the complement of this, that the amount of good would also be increased, but this was because to her evil was the very present factor in her life.

Joe and Kit were differently affected by what they saw about them. The boy was wild with enthusiasm and with a desire to be a part of all that the metropolis meant. In the evening he saw the young fellows passing by dressed in their spruce clothes, and he wondered with a sort of envy where they could be going. Back home there had been no place much worth going to, except church and one or two people's houses. But these young fellows seemed to show by their manners that they were neither going to church nor a family visiting. In the moment that he recognised this, a revelation came to him,—the knowledge that his horizon had been very narrow, and he felt angry that it was so. Why should those fellows be different from him? Why should they walk the streets so knowingly, so independently, when he knew not whither to turn his steps? Well, he was in New York, and now he would learn. Some day some greenhorn from the South should stand at a window and look out envying him, as he passed, red-cravated, patent-leathered, intent on some goal. Was it not better, after all, that circumstances had forced them thither? Had it not been so, they might all have stayed home and stagnated. Well, thought he, it's an ill wind that blows nobody good, and somehow, with a guilty under-thought, he forgot to feel the natural pity for his father, toiling guiltless in the prison of his native State.

Whom the Gods wish to destroy they first make mad. The first sign of the demoralisation of the provincial who comes to New York is his pride at his insensibility to certain impressions which used to influence him at home. First, he begins to scoff, and there is no truth in his views nor depth in his laugh. But by and by, from mere pretending, it becomes real. He grows callous. After that he goes to the devil very cheerfully.

No such radical emotions, however, troubled Kit's mind. She too stood at the windows and looked down into the street. There was a sort of complacent calm in the manner in which she viewed the girls' hats and dresses. Many of them were really pretty, she told herself, but for the most part they were not better than what she had had down home. There was a sound quality in the girl's make-up that helped her to see through the glamour of mere place and recognise worth for itself. Or it may have been the critical faculty, which is prominent in most women, that kept her from thinking a five-cent cheesecloth any better in New York than it was at home. She had a certain self-respect which made her value herself and her own traditions higher than her brother did his.

When later in the evening the porter who had been kind to them came in and was introduced as Mr. William Thomas, young as she was, she took his open admiration for her with more coolness than Joe exhibited when Thomas offered to show him something of the town some day or night.

Mr. Thomas was a loquacious little man with a confident air born of an intense admiration of himself. He was the idol of a number of servant-girls' hearts, and altogether a decidedly dashing back-area-way Don Juan.

"I tell you, Miss Kitty," he burst forth, a few minutes after being introduced, "they ain't no use talkin', N' Yawk'll give you a shakin' up 'at you won't soon forget. It's the only town on the face of the earth. You kin bet your life they ain't no flies on N' Yawk. We git the best shows here, we git the best concerts—say, now, what's the use o' my callin' it all out?—we simply git the best of everything."

"Great place," said Joe wisely, in what he thought was going to be quite a man-of-the-world manner. But he burned with shame the next minute because his voice sounded so weak and youthful. Then too the oracle only said "Yes" to him, and went on expatiating to Kitty on the glories of the metropolis.

"D'jever see the statue o' Liberty? Great thing, the statue o' Liberty. I'll take you 'round some day. An' Cooney Island—oh, my, now that's the place; and talk about fun! That's the place for me."

"La, Thomas," Mrs. Jones put in, "how you do run on! Why, the strangers'll think they'll be talked to death before they have time to breathe."

"Oh, I guess the folks understan' me. I'm one o' them kin' o' men 'at believe in whooping things up right from the beginning. I'm never strange with anybody. I'm a N' Yawker, I tell you, from the word go. I say, Mis' Jones, let's have some beer, an' we'll have some music purty soon. There's a fellah in the house 'at plays 'Rag-time' out o' sight."

Mr. Thomas took the pail and went to the corner. As he left the room, Mrs. Jones slapped her knee and laughed until her bust shook like jelly.

"Mr. Thomas is a case, sho'," she said; "but he likes you all, an' I'm mighty glad of it, fu' he's mighty curious about the house when he don't like the roomers."

Joe felt distinctly flattered, for he found their new acquaintance charming. His mother was still a little doubtful, and Kitty was sure she found the young man "fresh."

He came in pretty soon with his beer, and a half-dozen crabs in a bag.

"Thought I'd bring home something to chew. I always like to eat something with my beer."

Mrs. Jones brought in the glasses, and the young man filled one and turned to Kitty.

"No, thanks," she said with a surprised look.

"What, don't you drink beer? Oh, come now, you'll get out o' that."

"Kitty don't drink no beer," broke in her mother with mild resentment. "I drinks it sometimes, but she don't. I reckon maybe de chillen better go to bed."

Joe felt as if the "chillen" had ruined all his hopes, but Kitty rose.

The ingratiating "N' Yawker" was aghast.

"Oh, let 'em stay," said Mrs. Jones heartily; "a little beer ain't goin' to hurt 'em. Why, sakes, I know my father gave me beer from the time I could drink it, and I knows I ain't none the worse fu' it."

"They'll git out o' that, all right, if they live in N' Yawk," said Mr. Thomas, as he poured out a glass and handed it to Joe. "You neither?"

"Oh, I drink it," said the boy with an air, but not looking at his mother.

"Joe," she cried to him, "you must ricollect you ain't at home. What 'ud yo' pa think?" Then she stopped suddenly, and Joe gulped his beer and Kitty went to the piano to relieve her embarrassment.

"Yes, that's it, Miss Kitty, sing us something," said the irrepressible Thomas, "an' after while we'll have that fellah down that plays 'Rag-time.' He's out o' sight, I tell you."

With the pretty shyness of girlhood, Kitty sang one or two little songs in the simple manner she knew. Her voice was full and rich. It delighted Mr. Thomas.

"I say, that's singin' now, I tell you," he cried. "You ought to have some o' the new songs. D' jever hear 'Baby, you got to leave'? I tell you, that's a hot one. I'll bring you some of 'em. Why, you could git a job on the stage easy with that voice o' yourn. I got a frien' in one o' the comp'nies an' I'll speak to him about you."

"You ought to git Mr. Thomas to take you to the th'atre some night. He goes lots."

"Why, yes, what's the matter with to-morrer night? There's a good coon show in town. Out o' sight. Let's all go."

"I ain't nevah been to nothin' lak dat, an' I don't know," said Mrs. Hamilton.

"Aw, come, I'll git the tickets an' we'll all go. Great singin', you know. What d' you say?"

The mother hesitated, and Joe filled the breach.

"We'd all like to go," he said. "Ma, we'll go if you ain't too tired."

"Tired? Pshaw, you'll furgit all about your tiredness when Smithkins gits on the stage. Y' ought to hear him sing, 'I bin huntin' fu' wo'k'! You'd die laughing."

Mrs. Hamilton made no further demur, and the matter was closed.

Awhile later the "Rag-time" man came down and gave them a sample of what they were to hear the next night. Mr. Thomas and Mrs. Jones two-stepped, and they sent a boy after some more beer. Joe found it a very jolly evening, but Kit's and the mother's hearts were heavy as they went up to bed.

"Say," said Mr. Thomas when they had gone, "that little girl's a peach, you bet; a little green, I guess, but she'll ripen in the sun."

W. E. B. Du Bois
from *The Souls of Black Folk*

I

Of Our Spiritual Strivings

O water, voice of my heart, crying in the sand,
All night long crying with a mournful cry,
As I lie and listen, and cannot understand
The voice of my heart in my side or the voice of the sea,
O water, crying for rest, is it I, is it I?
All night long the water is crying to me.

Unresting water, there shall never be rest
Till the last moon droop and the last tide fail,
And the fire of the end begin to burn in the west;
And the heart shall be weary and wonder and cry like the sea,
All life long crying without avail,
As the water all night long is crying to me.

ARTHUR SYMONS.

Between me and the other world there is ever an unasked question: unasked by some through feelings of delicacy; by others through the difficulty of rightly framing it. All, nevertheless, flutter round it. They approach me in a half-hesitant sort of way, eye me curiously or compassionately, and then, instead of saying directly, How does it feel to be a problem? they say, I know an excellent colored man in my town; or, I fought at Mechanicsville; or, Do not these Southern outrages make your blood boil? At these I smile, or am interested, or reduce the boiling to a simmer, as the occasion may require. To the real question, How does it feel to be a problem? I answer seldom a word.

And yet, being a problem is a strange experience,—peculiar even for one who has never been anything else, save perhaps in babyhood and in Europe. It is in the early days of rollicking boyhood that the revelation first bursts upon one, all in a day, as it were. I remember well when the shadow swept across me. I was a little thing, away up in the hills of New England, where the dark Housatonic winds between Hoosac and Taghkanic to the sea. In a wee wooden schoolhouse, something put it into the boys' and girls' heads to buy gorgeous visiting-cards—ten cents a package—and exchange. The exchange was merry, till one girl, a tall newcomer, refused my card,—refused it peremptorily, with a glance. Then it dawned upon me with a certain suddenness that I was different from the others; or like, mayhap, in heart and life and longing, but shut out from their world by a vast veil. I had thereafter no desire to tear down that veil, to creep through; I held all beyond it in common contempt, and lived above it in a region of blue sky and great wandering shadows. That sky was bluest when I could beat my mates at examination-time, or beat them at a foot-race, or even beat their stringy heads. Alas, with the years all this fine contempt began to fade; for the worlds I longed for, and all their dazzling opportunities, were theirs, not mine. But they should not keep these prizes, I said; some, all, I would wrest from them. Just how I would do it I could never decide: by reading law, by healing the sick, by telling the wonderful tales that swam in my head,—some way. With other black boys the strife was not so fiercely sunny: their youth shrunk into tasteless sycophancy, or into silent hatred of the pale world about them and mocking distrust of everything white; or wasted itself in a bitter cry, Why did God make me an outcast and a stranger in mine own house? The shades of the prison-house closed round about us all: walls strait and stubborn to the whitest, but relentlessly narrow, tall, and unscalable to sons of night who must plod darkly on in resignation, or beat unavailing palms against the stone, or steadily, half hopelessly, watch the streak of blue above.

After the Egyptian and Indian, the Greek and Roman, the Teuton and Mongolian, the Negro is a sort of seventh son, born with a veil, and gifted with second-sight in this American world,—a world which yields him no true self-consciousness, but only lets him see himself through the revelation of the other world. It is a peculiar sensation, this double-consciousness, this sense of always looking at one's self through the eyes of others, of measuring one's soul by the tape of a world that looks on in amused contempt and pity. One ever feels his two-ness,—an American, a Negro; two souls, two thoughts, two unreconciled strivings; two warring ideals in one dark body, whose dogged strength alone keeps it from being torn asunder.

The history of the American Negro is the history of this strife,—this longing to attain self-conscious manhood, to merge his double self into a better and truer self. In this merging he wishes neither of the older selves to be lost. He would not Africanize America, for America has too much to teach the world and Africa. He would not bleach his Negro soul in a flood of white American-ism, for he knows that Negro blood has a message for the world. He simply wishes to make it possible for a man to be both a Negro and an American, without being cursed and spit upon by his fellows, without having the doors of Opportunity closed roughly in his face.

This, then, is the end of his striving: to be a co-worker in the kingdom of culture, to escape both death and isolation, to husband and use his best powers and his latent genius. These powers of body and mind have in the past been strangely wasted, dispersed, or forgotten. The shadow of a mighty Negro past flits through the tale of Ethiopia the Shadowy and of Egypt the Sphinx. Throughout history, the powers of single black men flash here and there like falling stars, and die sometimes before the world has rightly gauged their brightness. Here in America, in the few days since Emancipation, the black man's turning hither and thither in hesitant and doubtful striving has often made his very strength to lose effectiveness, to seem like absence of power, like weakness. And yet it is not weakness,—it is the contradiction of double aims. The double-aimed struggle of the black artisan—on the one hand to escape white contempt for a nation of mere hewers of wood and drawers of water, and on the other hand to plough and nail and dig for a poverty-stricken horde—could only result in making him a poor craftsman, for he had but half a heart in either cause. By the poverty and ignorance of his people, the Negro minister or doctor was tempted toward quackery and demagogy; and by the criticism of the other world, toward ideals that made him ashamed of his lowly tasks. The would-be black *savant* was confronted by the paradox that the knowledge his people needed was a twice-told tale to his white neighbors, while the knowledge which would teach the white world was Greek to his own flesh and blood. The innate love of harmony and beauty that set the ruder souls of his people a-dancing and a-singing raised but confusion and doubt in the soul of the black artist; for the beauty revealed to him was the soul-beauty of a race which his larger audience despised, and he could not articulate the message of another people. This waste of double aims, this seeking to satisfy two unreconciled ideals, has wrought sad havoc with the courage and faith and deeds of ten thousand thousand people,— has sent them often wooing false gods and invoking false means of salvation, and at times has even seemed about to make them ashamed of themselves.

Away back in the days of bondage they thought to see in one divine event the end of all doubt and disappointment; few men ever worshipped Freedom with half such unquestioning faith as did the American Negro for two centuries. To him, so far as he thought and dreamed, slavery was indeed the sum of all villainies, the cause of all sorrow, the root of all prejudice; Emancipation was the key to a promised land of sweeter beauty than ever stretched before the eyes of wearied Israelites. In song and exhortation swelled one refrain—Liberty; in his tears and curses the God he implored had Freedom in his right hand. At last it came,—suddenly, fearfully, like a dream. With one wild carnival of blood and passion came the message in his own plaintive cadences:—

> "Shout, O children!
> Shout, you're free!
> For God has bought your liberty!"

Years have passed away since then,—ten, twenty, forty; forty years of national life, forty years of renewal and development, and yet the swarthy spectre sits in its accustomed seat at the Nation's feast. In vain do we cry to this our vastest social problem:—

> "Take any shape but that, and my firm nerves
> Shall never tremble!"

The Nation has not yet found peace from its sins; the freedman has not yet found in freedom his promised land. Whatever of good may have come in these years of change, the shadow of a deep disappointment rests upon the Negro people,—a disappointment all the more bitter because the unattained ideal was unbounded save by the simple ignorance of a lowly people.

The first decade was merely a prolongation of the vain search for freedom, the boon that seemed ever barely to elude their grasp,—like a tantalizing will-o'-the-wisp, maddening and misleading the headless host. The holocaust of war, the terrors of the Ku-Klux Klan, the lies of carpet-baggers, the disorganization of industry, and the contradictory advice of friends and foes, left the bewildered serf with no new watchword beyond the old cry for freedom. As the time flew, however, he began to grasp a new idea. The ideal of liberty demanded for its attainment powerful means, and these the Fifteenth Amendment gave him. The ballot, which before he had looked upon as a visible sign of freedom, he now regarded as the chief means of gaining and perfecting the liberty with which war had partially endowed him. And why not? Had not votes made war and emancipated millions? Had not votes enfranchised the freedmen? Was anything impossible to a power that had done all this? A million black men started with renewed zeal to vote themselves into the kingdom. So the decade flew away, the revolution of 1876 came, and left the half-free serf weary, wondering, but still inspired. Slowly but steadily, in the following years, a new vision began gradually to replace the dream of political power,—a powerful movement, the rise of another ideal to guide the unguided, another pillar of fire by night after a clouded day. It was the ideal of "book-learning"; the curiosity, born of compulsory ignorance, to know and test the power of the cabalistic letters of the white man, the longing to know. Here at last seemed to have been discovered the mountain path to Canaan; longer than the highway of Emancipation and law, steep and rugged, but straight, leading to heights high enough to overlook life.

Up the new path the advance guard toiled, slowly, heavily, doggedly; only those who have watched and guided the faltering feet, the misty minds, the dull understandings, of the dark pupils of these schools know how faithfully, how piteously, this people strove to learn. It was weary work. The cold statistician wrote down the inches of progress here and there, noted also where here and there a foot had slipped or some one had fallen. To the tired climbers, the horizon was ever dark, the mists were often cold, the Canaan was always dim and far away. If, however, the vistas disclosed as yet no goal, no resting-place, little but flattery and criticism, the journey at least gave leisure for reflection and self-examination; it changed the child of Emancipation to the youth with dawning self-consciousness, self-realization, self-respect. In those sombre forests of his striving his own soul rose before him, and he saw himself,—darkly as through a veil; and yet he saw in himself some faint revelation of his power, of his mission. He began to have a dim feeling that, to attain his place in the world, he must be himself, and not another. For the first time he sought to analyze the burden he bore upon his back, that dead-weight of social degradation partially masked behind a half-named Negro problem. He felt his poverty; without a cent, without a home, without land, tools, or savings, he had entered into competition with rich, landed, skilled neighbors. To be a poor man is hard, but to be a poor race in a land of dollars is the very bottom of hardships. He felt the weight of his ignorance,—not simply of letters, but of life, of business, of the humanities; the accumulated sloth and shirking and awkwardness of decades and centuries shackled his hands and feet. Nor was his burden all poverty and ignorance. The red stain of bastardy, which two centuries of systematic legal defilement of Negro women had stamped upon his race, meant not only the loss of ancient African chastity, but also the hereditary weight of a mass of corruption from white adulterers, threatening almost the obliteration of the Negro home.

A people thus handicapped ought not to be asked to race with the world, but rather allowed to give all its time and thought to its own social problems. But alas! while sociologists gleefully count his bastards and his prostitutes, the very soul of the toiling, sweating black man is darkened by the shadow of a vast despair. Men call the shadow prejudice, and learnedly explain it as the natural defence of culture against barbarism, learning against ignorance, purity against crime, the "higher" against the "lower" races. To which the Negro cries Amen! and swears that to so much of this strange prejudice as is founded on just homage to civilization, culture, righteousness, and progress, he humbly bows and meekly does obeisance. But before that nameless prejudice that leaps beyond all this he stands helpless, dismayed, and well-nigh speechless; before that personal disrespect and mockery, the ridicule and systematic humiliation, the distortion of fact and wanton license of fancy, the cynical ignoring of the better and the boisterous welcoming of the worse, the all-pervading desire to inculcate disdain for everything black, from Toussaint to the devil,—before this there rises a sickening despair that would disarm and discourage any nation save that black host to whom "discouragement" is an unwritten word.

But the facing of so vast a prejudice could not but bring the inevitable self-questioning, self-disparagement, and lowering of ideals which ever accompany repression and breed in an atmosphere of contempt and hate. Whisperings and portents came borne upon the four winds: Lo! we are diseased and dying, cried the dark hosts; we cannot write, our voting is vain; what need of education, since we must always cook and serve? And the Nation echoed and enforced this self-criticism, saying: Be content to be servants, and nothing more; what need of higher culture for half-men? Away with the black man's ballot, by force or fraud,—and behold the suicide of a race! Nevertheless, out of the evil came something of good,—the more careful adjustment of education to real life, the

clearer perception of the Negroes' social responsibilities, and the sobering realization of the meaning of progress.

So dawned the time of *Sturm und Drang*: storm and stress to-day rocks our
little boat on the mad waters of the world-sea; there is within and without the
sound of conflict, the burning of body and rending of soul; inspiration strives
with doubt, and faith with vain questionings. The bright ideals of the past,—
physical freedom, political power, the training of brains and the training of
hands,—all these in turn have waxed and waned, until even the last grows dim
and overcast. Are they all wrong,—all false? No, not that, but each alone was
over-simple and incomplete,—the dreams of a credulous race-childhood, or the
fond imaginings of the other world which does not know and does not want to
know our power. To be really true, all these ideals must be melted and welded
into one. The training of the schools we need to-day more than ever,—the
training of deft hands, quick eyes and ears, and above all the broader, deeper,
higher culture of gifted minds and pure hearts. The power of the ballot we need
in sheer self-defence,—else what shall save us from a second slavery? Freedom,
too, the long-sought, we still seek,—the freedom of life and limb, the freedom
to work and think, the freedom to love and aspire. Work, culture, liberty,—all
these we need, not singly but together, not successively but together, each
growing and aiding each, and all striving toward that vaster ideal that swims
before the Negro people, the ideal of human brotherhood, gained through the
unifying ideal of Race; the ideal of fostering and developing the traits and talents of the Negro, not in opposition to or contempt for other races, but rather
in large conformity to the greater ideals of the American Republic, in order
that some day on American soil two world-races may give each to each those
characteristics both so sadly lack. We the darker ones come even now not altogether empty-handed: there are to-day no truer exponents of the pure human
spirit of the Declaration of Independence than the American Negroes; there is
no true American music but the wild sweet melodies of the Negro slave; the
American fairy tales and folk-lore are Indian and African; and, all in all, we
black men seem the sole oasis of simple faith and reverence in a dusty desert of
dollars and smartness. Will America be poorer if she replace her brutal dyspep-
tic blundering with light-hearted but determined Negro humility? or her coarse
and cruel wit with loving jovial good-humor? or her vulgar music with the soul
of the Sorrow Songs?

Merely a concrete test of the underlying principles of the great republic is
the Negro Problem, and the spiritual striving of the freedmen's sons is the travail of souls whose burden is almost beyond the measure of their strength, but
who bear it in the name of an historic race, in the name of this the land of their
fathers' fathers, and in the name of human opportunity.

And now what I have briefly sketched in large outline let me on coming
pages tell again in many ways, with loving emphasis and deeper detail, that
men may listen to the striving in the souls of black folk.

III

Of Mr. Booker T. Washington and Others

From birth till death enslaved; in word, in deed, unmanned!
. . . .
Hereditary bondsmen! Know ye not
Who would be free themselves must strike the blow?

BYRON.

Easily the most striking thing in the history of the American Negro since 1876 is the ascendancy of Mr. Booker T. Washington. It began at the time when war memories and ideals were rapidly passing; a day of astonishing commercial development was dawning; a sense of doubt and hesitation overtook the freedmen's sons,—then it was that his leading began. Mr. Washington came, with a simple definite programme, at the psychological moment when the nation was a little ashamed of having bestowed so much sentiment on Negroes, and was concentrating its energies on Dollars. His programme of industrial education, conciliation of the South, and submission and silence as to civil and political rights, was not wholly original; the Free Negroes from 1830 up to wartime had striven to build industrial schools, and the American Missionary Association had from the first taught various trades; and Price and others had sought a way of honorable alliance with the best of the Southerners. But Mr. Washington first indissolubly linked these things; he put enthusiasm, unlimited energy, and perfect faith into this programme, and changed it from a by-path into a veritable Way of Life. And the tale of the methods by which he did this is a fascinating study of human life.

It startled the nation to hear a Negro advocating such a programme after many decades of bitter complaint; it startled and won the applause of the South, it interested and won the admiration of the North; and after a confused murmur of protest, it silenced if it did not convert the Negroes themselves.

To gain the sympathy and coöperation of the various elements comprising the white South was Mr. Washington's first task; and this, at the time Tuskegee was founded, seemed, for a black man, well-nigh impossible. And yet ten years later it was done in the word spoken at Atlanta: "In all things purely social we can be as separate as the five fingers, and yet one as the hand in all things essential to mutual progress." This "Atlanta Compromise" is by all odds the most notable thing in Mr. Washington's career. The South interpreted it in different ways: the radicals received it as a complete surrender of the demand for civil and political equality; the conservatives, as a generously conceived working basis for mutual understanding. So both approved it, and to-day its author is certainly the most distinguished Southerner since Jefferson Davis, and the one with the largest personal following.

Next to this achievement comes Mr. Washington's work in gaining place and consideration in the North. Others less shrewd and tactful had formerly essayed to sit on these two stools and had fallen between them; but as Mr. Washington knew the heart of the South from birth and training, so by singular insight he intuitively grasped the spirit of the age which was dominating the North. And so thoroughly did he learn the speech and thought of triumphant commercialism, and the ideals of material prosperity, that the picture of a lone black boy poring over a French grammar amid the weeds and dirt of a neglected home soon seemed to him the acme of absurdities. One wonders what Socrates and St. Francis of Assisi would say to this.

And yet this very singleness of vision and thorough oneness with his age is a mark of the successful man. It is as though Nature must needs make men narrow in order to give them force. So Mr. Washington's cult has gained unquestioning followers, his work has wonderfully prospered, his friends are legion, and his enemies are confounded. To-day he stands as the one recognized spokesman of his ten million fellows, and one of the most notable figures in a nation of seventy millions. One hesitates, therefore, to criticise a life which, beginning with so little, has done so much. And yet the time is come when one may speak in all sincerity and utter courtesy of the mistakes and shortcomings of Mr. Washington's career, as well as of his triumphs, without being thought captious or envious, and without forgetting that it is easier to do ill than well in the world.

The criticism that has hitherto met Mr. Washington has not always been of this broad character. In the South especially has he had to walk warily to avoid the harshest judgments,—and naturally so, for he is dealing with the one subject of deepest sensitiveness to that section. Twice—once when at the Chicago celebration of the Spanish-American War he alluded to the color-prejudice that is "eating away the vitals of the South," and once when he dined with President Roosevelt—has the resulting Southern criticism been violent enough to threaten seriously his popularity. In the North the feeling has several times forced itself into words, that Mr. Washington's counsels of submission overlooked certain elements of true manhood, and that his educational programme was unnecessarily narrow. Usually, however, such criticism has not found open expression, although, too, the spiritual sons of the Abolitionists have not been prepared to acknowledge that the schools founded before Tuskegee, by men of broad ideals and self-sacrificing spirit, were wholly failures or worthy of ridicule. While, then, criticism has not failed to follow Mr. Washington, yet the prevailing public opinion of the land has been but too willing to deliver the solution of a wearisome problem into his hands, and say, "If that is all you and your race ask, take it."

Among his own people, however, Mr. Washington has encountered the strongest and most lasting opposition, amounting at times to bitterness, and even to-day continuing strong and insistent even though largely silenced in outward expression by the public opinion of the nation. Some of this opposition is, of course, mere envy; the disappointment of displaced demagogues and the spite of narrow minds. But aside from this, there is among educated and thoughtful colored men in all parts of the land a feeling of deep regret, sorrow, and apprehension at the wide currency and ascendancy which some of Mr. Washington's theories have gained. These same men admire his sincerity of purpose, and are willing to forgive much to honest endeavor which is doing something worth the doing. They coöperate with Mr. Washington as far as they conscientiously can; and, indeed, it is no ordinary tribute to this man's tact and power that, steering as he must between so many diverse interests and opinions, he so largely retains the respect of all.

But the hushing of the criticism of honest opponents is a dangerous thing. It leads some of the best of the critics to unfortunate silence and paralysis of effort, and others to burst into speech so passionately and intemperately as to lose listeners. Honest and earnest criticism from those whose interests are most nearly touched,—criticism of writers by readers, of government by those governed, of leaders by those led,—this is the soul of democracy and the safeguard of modern society. If the best of the American Negroes receive by outer pressure a leader whom they had not recognized before, manifestly there is here a certain palpable gain. Yet there is also irreparable loss,—a loss of that peculiarly valuable education which a group receives when by search and criticism it finds and commissions its own leaders. The way in which this is done is at once the most elementary and the nicest problem of social growth. History is but the record of such group-leadership; and yet how infinitely changeful is its type and character! And of all types and kinds, what can be more instructive than the leadership of a group within a group?—that curious double movement where real progress may be negative and actual advance be relative retrogression. All this is the social student's inspiration and despair.

Now in the past the American Negro has had instructive experience in the choosing of group leaders, founding thus a peculiar dynasty which in the light of present conditions is worth while studying. When sticks and stones and beasts form the sole environment of a people, their attitude is largely one of determined opposition to and conquest of natural forces. But when to earth and brute is added an environment of men and ideas, then the attitude of the imprisoned group may take three main forms,—a feeling of revolt and revenge; an attempt to adjust all thought and action to the will of the greater group; or, finally, a determined effort at self-realization and self-development despite environing opinion. The influence of all of these attitudes at various times can be traced in the history of the American Negro, and in the evolution of his successive leaders.

Before 1750, while the fire of African freedom still burned in the veins of the slaves, there was in all leadership or attempted leadership but the one motive of revolt and revenge,—typified in the terrible Maroons, the Danish blacks, and Cato of Stono, and veiling all the Americas in fear of insurrection. The liberalizing tendencies of the latter half of the eighteenth century brought, along with kindlier relations between black and white, thoughts of ultimate adjustment and assimilation. Such aspiration was especially voiced in the earnest songs of Phyllis, in the martyrdom of Attucks, the fighting of Salem and Poor, the intellectual accomplishments of Banneker and Derham, and the political demands of the Cuffes.

Stern financial and social stress after the war cooled much of the previous humanitarian ardor. The disappointment and impatience of the Negroes at the persistence of slavery and serfdom voiced itself in two movements. The slaves in the South, aroused undoubtedly by vague rumors of the Haytian revolt, made three fierce attempts at insurrection,—in 1800 under Gabriel in Virginia, in 1822 under Vesey in Carolina, and in 1831 again in Virginia under the terrible Nat Turner. In the Free States, on the other hand, a new and curious attempt at self-development was made. In Philadelphia and New York color-prescription led to a withdrawal of Negro communicants from white churches and the formation of a peculiar socio-religious institution among the Negroes known as the African Church,—an organization still living and controlling in its various branches over a million of men.

Walker's wild appeal against the trend of the times showed how the world was changing after the coming of the cotton-gin. By 1830 slavery seemed hopelessly fastened on the South, and the slaves thoroughly cowed into submission. The free Negroes of the North, inspired by the mulatto immigrants from the West Indies, began to change the basis of their demands; they recognized the slavery of slaves, but insisted that they themselves were freemen, and sought assimilation and amalgamation with the nation on the same terms with other men. Thus, Forten and Purvis of Philadelphia, Shad of Wilmington, Du Bois of New Haven, Barbadoes of Boston, and others, strove singly and together as men, they said, not as slaves; as "people of color," not as "Negroes." The trend of the times, however, refused them recognition save in individual and exceptional cases, considered them as one with all the despised blacks, and they soon found themselves striving to keep even the rights they formerly had of voting and working and moving as freemen. Schemes of migration and colonization arose among them; but these they refused to entertain, and they eventually turned to the Abolition movement as a final refuge.

Here, led by Remond, Nell, Wells-Brown, and Douglass, a new period of self-assertion and self-development dawned. To be sure, ultimate freedom and assimilation was the ideal before the leaders, but the assertion of the manhood rights of the Negro by himself was the main reliance, and John Brown's raid was the extreme of its logic. After the war and emancipation, the great form of Frederick Douglass, the greatest of American Negro leaders, still led the host. Self-assertion, especially in political lines, was the main programme, and behind Douglass came Elliot, Bruce, and Langston, and the Reconstruction politicians, and, less conspicuous but of greater social significance Alexander Crummell and Bishop Daniel Payne.

Then came the Revolution of 1876, the suppression of the Negro votes, the changing and shifting of ideals, and the seeking of new lights in the great night. Douglass, in his old age, still bravely stood for the ideals of his early manhood,—ultimate assimilation *through* self-assertion, and on no other terms. For a time Price arose as a new leader, destined, it seemed, not to give up, but to restate the old ideals in a form less repugnant to the white South. But he passed away in his prime. Then came the new leader. Nearly all the former ones had become leaders by the silent suffrage of their fellows, had sought to lead their own people alone, and were usually, save Douglass, little known outside their race. But Booker T. Washington arose as essentially the leader not of one race but of two,—a compromiser between the South, the North, and the Negro. Naturally the Negroes resented, at first bitterly, signs of compromise which surrendered their civil and political rights, even though this was to be exchanged for larger chances of economic development. The rich and dominating North, however, was not only weary of the race problem, but was investing largely in Southern enterprises, and welcomed any method of peaceful coöperation. Thus, by national opinion, the Negroes began to recognize Mr. Washington's leadership; and the voice of criticism was hushed.

Mr. Washington represents in Negro thought the old attitude of adjustment and submission; but adjustment at such a peculiar time as to make his programme unique. This is an age of unusual economic development, and Mr. Washington's programme naturally takes an economic cast, becoming a gospel of Work and Money to such an extent as apparently almost completely to overshadow the higher aims of life. Moreover, this is an age when the more advanced races are coming in closer contact with the less developed races, and the race-feeling is therefore intensified; and Mr. Washington's programme practically accepts the alleged inferiority of the Negro races. Again, in our own land, the reaction from the sentiment of war time has given impetus to race-prejudice against Negroes, and Mr. Washington withdraws many of the high demands of Negroes as men and American citizens. In other periods of intensified prejudice all the Negro's tendency to self-assertion has been called forth; at this period a policy of submission is advocated. In the history of nearly all other races and peoples the doctrine preached at such crises has been that manly self-respect is worth more than lands and houses, and that a people who voluntarily surrender such respect, or cease striving for it, are not worth civilizing.

In answer to this, it has been claimed that the Negro can survive only through submission. Mr. Washington distinctly asks that black people give up, at least for the present, three things,—

First, political power,
Second, insistence on civil rights,
Third, higher education of Negro youth,

—and concentrate all their energies on industrial education, the accumulation of wealth, and the conciliation of the South. This policy has been courageously and insistently advocated for over fifteen years, and has been triumphant for perhaps ten years. As a result of this tender of the palm-branch, what has been the return? In these years there have occurred:

1. The disfranchisement of the Negro.
2. The legal creation of a distinct status of civil inferiority for the Negro.
3. The steady withdrawal of aid from institutions for the higher training of the Negro.

These movements are not, to be sure, direct results of Mr. Washington's teachings; but his propaganda has, without a shadow of doubt, helped their speedier accomplishment. The question then comes: Is it possible, and probable, that nine millions of men can make effective progress in economic lines if they are deprived of political rights, made a servile caste, and allowed only the most meagre chance for developing their exceptional men? If history and reason give any distinct answer to these questions, it is an emphatic No. And Mr. Washington thus faces the triple paradox of his career:

1. He is striving nobly to make Negro artisans business men and property-owners; but it is utterly impossible, under modern competitive methods, for workingmen and property-owners to defend their rights and exist without the right of suffrage.
2. He insists on thrift and self-respect, but at the same time counsels a silent submission to civic inferiority such as is bound to sap the manhood of any race in the long run.
3. He advocates common-school and industrial training, and depreciates institutions of higher learning; but neither the Negro common-schools, nor Tuskegee itself, could remain open a day were it not for teachers trained in Negro colleges, or trained by their graduates.

This triple paradox in Mr. Washington's position is the object of criticism by two classes of colored Americans. One class is spiritually descended from Toussaint the Savior, through Gabriel, Vesey, and Turner, and they represent the attitude of revolt and revenge; they hate the white South blindly and distrust the white race generally, and so far as they agree on definite action, think that the Negro's only hope lies in emigration beyond the borders of the United States. And yet, by the irony of fate, nothing has more effectually made this programme seem hopeless than the recent course of the United States toward weaker and darker peoples in the West Indies, Hawaii, and the Philippines,— for where in the world may we go and be safe from lying and brute force?

The other class of Negroes who cannot agree with Mr. Washington has hitherto said little aloud. They deprecate the sight of scattered counsels, of internal disagreement; and especially they dislike making their just criticism of a useful and earnest man an excuse for a general discharge of venom from small-minded opponents. Nevertheless, the questions involved are so fundamental and serious that it is difficult to see how men like the Grimkes, Kelly Miller,

J. W. E. Bowen, and other representatives of this group, can much longer be silent. Such men feel in conscience bound to ask of this nation three things:

1. The right to vote.
2. Civic equality.
3. The education of youth according to ability.

They acknowledge Mr. Washington's invaluable service in counselling patience and courtesy in such demands; they do not ask that ignorant black men vote when ignorant whites are debarred, or that any reasonable restrictions in the suffrage should not be applied; they know that the low social level of the mass of the race is responsible for much discrimination against it, but they also know, and the nation knows, that relentless color-prejudice is more often a cause than a result of the Negro's degradation; they seek the abatement of this relic of barbarism, and not its systematic encouragement and pampering by all agencies of social power from the Associated Press to the Church of Christ. They advocate, with Mr. Washington, a broad system of Negro common schools supplemented by thorough industrial training; but they are surprised that a man of Mr. Washington's insight cannot see that no such educational system ever has rested or can rest on any other basis than that of the well-equipped college and university, and they insist that there is a demand for a few such institutions throughout the South to train the best of the Negro youth as teachers, professional men, and leaders.

This group of men honor Mr. Washington for his attitude of conciliation toward the white South; they accept the "Atlanta Compromise" in its broadest interpretation; they recognize, with him, many signs of promise, many men of high purpose and fair judgment, in this section; they know that no easy task has been laid upon a region already tottering under heavy burdens. But, nevertheless, they insist that the way to truth and right lies in straightforward honesty, not in indiscriminate flattery; in praising those of the South who do well and criticising uncompromisingly those who do ill; in taking advantage of the opportunities at hand and urging their fellows to do the same, but at the same time in remembering that only a firm adherence to their higher ideals and aspirations will ever keep those ideals within the realm of possibility. They do not expect that the free right to vote, to enjoy civic rights, and to be educated, will come in a moment; they do not expect to see the bias and prejudices of years disappear at the blast of a trumpet; but they are absolutely certain that the way for a people to gain their reasonable rights is not by voluntarily throwing them away and insisting that they do not want them; that the way for a people to gain respect is not by continually belittling and ridiculing themselves; that, on the contrary, Negroes must insist continually, in season and out of season, that voting is necessary to modern manhood, that color discrimination is barbarism, and that black boys need education as well as white boys.

In failing thus to state plainly and unequivocally the legitimate demands of their people, even at the cost of opposing an honored leader, the thinking classes of American Negroes would shirk a heavy responsibility,—a responsibility to themselves, a responsibility to the struggling masses, a responsibility to the darker races of men whose future depends so largely on this American experiment, but especially a responsibility to this nation,—this common Fatherland. It is wrong to encourage a man or a people in evil-doing; it is wrong to aid and abet a national crime simply because it is unpopular not to do so. The growing spirit of kindliness and reconciliation between the North and South after the frightful differences of a generation ago ought to be a source of deep congratulation to all, and especially to those whose mistreatment caused the war; but if that reconciliation is to be marked by the industrial slavery and civic death of those same black men, with permanent legislation into a position of inferiority, then those black men, if they are really men, are called upon by every consideration of patriotism and loyalty to oppose such a course by all civilized methods, even though such opposition involves disagreement with Mr. Booker T. Washington. We have no right to sit silently by while the inevitable seeds are sown for a harvest of disaster to our children, black and white.

First, it is the duty of black men to judge the South discriminatingly. The present generation of Southerners are not responsible for the past, and they should not be blindly hated or blamed for it. Furthermore, to no class is the indiscriminate endorsement of the recent course of the South toward Negroes more nauseating than to the best thought of the South. The South is not "solid"; it is a land in the ferment of social change, wherein forces of all kinds are fighting for supremacy; and to praise the ill the South is to-day perpetrating is just as wrong as to condemn the good. Discriminating and broad-minded criticism is what the South needs,—needs it for the sake of her own white sons and daughters, and for the insurance of robust, healthy mental and moral development.

To-day even the attitude of the Southern whites toward the blacks is not, as so many assume, in all cases the same; the ignorant Southerner hates the Negro, the workingmen fear his competition, the money-makers wish to use him as a laborer, some of the educated see a menace in his upward development, while others—usually the sons of the masters—wish to help him to rise. National opinion has enabled this last class to maintain the Negro common schools, and to protect the Negro partially in property, life, and limb. Through the pressure of the money-makers, the Negro is in danger of being reduced to semi-slavery, especially in the country districts; the workingmen, and those of the educated who fear the Negro, have united to disfranchise him, and some have urged his deportation; while the passions of the ignorant are easily aroused to lynch and abuse any black man. To praise this intricate whirl of thought and prejudice is nonsense; to inveigh indiscriminately against "the South" is unjust; but to use the same breath in praising Governor Aycock, exposing Senator Morgan, arguing with Mr. Thomas Nelson Page, and denouncing Senator Ben Tillman, is not only sane, but the imperative duty of thinking black men.

It would be unjust to Mr. Washington not to acknowledge that in several instances he has opposed movements in the South which were unjust to the Negro; he sent memorials to the Louisiana and Alabama constitutional conventions, he has spoken against lynching, and in other ways has openly or silently set his influence against sinister schemes and unfortunate happenings. Notwithstanding this, it is equally true to assert that on the whole the distinct impression left by Mr. Washington's propaganda is, first, that the South is justified in its present attitude toward the Negro because of the Negro's degradation; secondly, that the prime cause of the Negro's failure to rise more quickly is his wrong education in the past; and, thirdly, that his future rise depends primarily on his own efforts. Each of these propositions is a dangerous half-truth. The supplementary truths must never be lost sight of: first, slavery and race-prejudice are potent if not sufficient causes of the Negro's position; second, industrial and common-school training were necessarily slow in planting because they had to await the black teachers trained by higher institutions,—it being extremely doubtful if any essentially different development was possible, and certainly a Tuskegee was unthinkable before 1880; and, third, while it is a great truth to say that the Negro must strive and strive mightily to help himself, it is equally true that unless his striving be not simply seconded, but rather aroused and encouraged, by the initiative of the richer and wiser environing group, he cannot hope for great success.

In his failure to realize and impress this last point, Mr. Washington is especially to be criticised. His doctrine has tended to make the whites, North and South, shift the burden of the Negro problem to the Negro's shoulders and stand aside as critical and rather pessimistic spectators; when in fact the burden belongs to the nation, and the hands of none of us are clean if we bend not our energies to righting these great wrongs.

The South ought to be led, by candid and honest criticism, to assert her better self and do her full duty to the race she has cruelly wronged and is still wronging. The North—her co-partner in guilt—cannot salve her conscience by plastering it with gold. We cannot settle this problem by diplomacy and suaveness, by "policy" alone. If worse come to worst, can the moral fibre of this country survive the slow throttling and murder of nine millions of men?

The black men of America have a duty to perform, a duty stern and delicate,—a forward movement to oppose a part of the work of their greatest leader. So far as Mr. Washington preaches Thrift, Patience, and Industrial Training for the masses, we must hold up his hands and strive with him, rejoicing in his honors and glorying in the strength of this Joshua called of God and of man to lead the headless host. But so far as Mr. Washington apologizes for injustice, North or South, does not rightly value the privilege and duty of voting, belittles the emasculating effects of caste distinctions, and opposes the higher training and ambition of our brighter minds,—so far as he, the South, or the Nation, does this,—we must unceasingly and firmly oppose them. By every civilized and peaceful method we must strive for the rights which the world accords to men, clinging unwaveringly to those great words which the sons of the Fathers would fain forget: "We hold these truths to be self-evident: That all men are created equal; that they are endowed by their Creator with certain unalienable rights; that among these are life, liberty, and the pursuit of happiness."

A. Philip Randolph
A New Crowd—A New Negro

Throughout the world among all peoples and classes, the clock of social progress is striking the high noon of the Old Crowd. And why?

The reason lies in the inability of the old crowd to adapt itself to the changed conditions, to recognize and accept the consequences of the sudden, rapid and violent social changes that are shaking the world. In wild desperation, consternation and despair, the proud scions of regal pomp and authority, the prophets and high-priests of the old order, view the steady and menacing rise of the great workingclass. Yes, the Old Crowd is passing, and with it, its false, corrupt and wicked institutions of oppression and cruelty; its ancient prejudices and beliefs and its pious, hypocritical and venerated idols.

Its all like a dream! In Russia, one-hundred and eighty million of peasants and workmen—disinherited, writhing under the ruthless heel of the Czar, for over three hundred years, awoke and revolted and drove their hateful oppressors from power. Here a New Crowd arose—the Bolsheviki, and expropriated their expropriators. They fashioned and established a new social machinery—the soviet—to express the growing class consciousness of teaming millions, disillusioned and disenchanted. They also chose new leaders—Lenin and Trotsky to invent and adopt scientific methods of social control; to marshal, organize and direct the revolutionary forces in constructive channels to build a New Russia.

The "iron battalions of the proletariat" are shaking age-long and historic thrones of Europe. The Hohenzollerns of Europe no longer hold mastery over the destinies of the German people. The Kaiser, once proud, irresponsible and powerful; wielding his sceptre in the name of the "divine right of kings," has fallen, his throne has crumbled and he now sulks in ignominy and shame—expelled from his native land, a man without a country. And Nietzsche, Treitschke, Bismarck, and Bernhardi, his philosophic mentors are scrapped, discredited and discarded, while the shadow of Marx looms in the distance. The revolution in Germany is still unfinished. The Eberts and Scheidermanns rule for the nonce; but a New Crowd is rising. The hand of the Sparticans must raise a New Germany out of the ashes of the old.

Already, Karolyi of the old regime of Hungary, abdicates to Bela Kun, who wirelessed greetings to the Russian Federated Socialist Soviet Republic. Meanwhile the triple alliance consisting of the National Union of Railwaymen, the National Transport Workers' Federation and the Miners' Federation, threaten to paralyze England with a general strike. The imminence of industrial disaster hangs like a pall over the Lloyd George government. The shop stewards' committee or the rank and file in the works, challenge the sincerity and methods of the old pure and simple unions leaders. British labor would build a New England. The Seine Feiners are the New Crowd in Ireland fighting for self-determination. France and Italy, too, bid soon to pass from the control of scheming and intriguing diplomats into the hands of a New Crowd. Even Egypt, raped for decades, prostrate under the juggernaut of financial imperialism, rises in revolution to expel a foreign foe.

And the natural question arises: What does it all mean to the Negro?

First it means that he, too, must scrap the Old Crowd. For not only is the Old Crowd useless, but like the vermiform appendix, it is decidedly injurious, it prevents all real progress.

Before it is possible for the Negro to prosecute successfully a formidable offensive for justice and fair play, he must tear down his false leaders, just as the people of Europe are tearing down their false leaders. Of course, some of the Old Crowd mean well. But what matter it though poison be administered to the sick intentionally or out of ignorance. The result is the same—death. And our indictment of the Old Crowd is that: it lacks the knowledge of methods for the attainment of ends which it desires to achieve. For instance the Old Crowd never counsels the Negro to organize and strike against low wages and long hours. It cannot see the advisability of the Negro, who is the most exploited of the American workers, supporting a workingman's political party.

The Old Crowd enjoins the Negro to be conservative, when he has nothing to conserve. Neither his life nor his property receives the protection of the government which conscripts his life to "make the world safe for democracy." The conservative in all lands are the wealthy and the ruling class. The Negro is in dire poverty and he is no part of the ruling class.

But the question naturally arises: who is the Old Crowd?

In the Negro schools and colleges the most typical reactionaries are Kelly, Miller, Moton and William Pickens. In the press Du Bois, James Weldon Johnson, Fred R. Moore, T. Thomas Fortune, Roscoe Conkling Simmons and George Harris are compromising the case of the Negro. In politics Chas. W. Anderson, W. H. Lewis, Ralph Tyler, Emmet Scott, George E. Haynes and the entire old line palliating, me-to-boss gang of Negro Republican politicians, are hopelessly ignorant and distressingly unwitting of their way.

In the church the old crowd still preaches that "the meek will inherit the earth," "if the enemy strikes you on one side of the face, turn the other," and "you may take all this world but give me Jesus." "Dry Bones," "The Three Hebrew Children in the Firy Furnace" and "Jonah in the Belly of the Whale," constitute the subjects of the Old Crowd, for black men and women who are over-worked and under-paid, lynched, jim-crowed and disfranchised—a people who are yet languishing in the dungeons of ignorance and superstition. Such then is the Old Crowd. And this is not strange to the student of history, economics, and sociology.

A man will not oppose his benefactor. The Old Crowd of Negro leaders has been and is subsidized by the Old Crowd of White Americans—a group which viciously opposes every demand made by organized labor for an opportunity to live a better life. Now, if the Old Crowd of white people opposes every demand of white labor for economic justice, how can the Negro expect to get that which is denied the white working class? And it is well nigh beyond the realm of controversy that economic justice is at the basis of social and political equality.

For instance, there is no organization of national prominence which ostensibly is working in the interest of the Negro which is not dominated by the Old Crowd of white people. And they are controlled by the white people because they receive their funds—their revenue from them. It is, of course, a matter of common knowledge that Du Bois does not determine the policy of the National Association for the Advancement of Colored People; nor does Kinckle Jones or George E. Haynes control the National Urban League. The organizations are not responsible to Negroes because Negroes do not maintain them.

This brings us to the question as to who shall assume the reins of leadership when the Old Crowd falls.

As among all other peoples, the New Crowd must be composed of young men who are educated, radical and fearless. Young Negro radicals must control the press, church, schools, politics and labor. The condition for joining the New Crowd are: ability, radicalism and sincerity. The New Crowd views with much expectancy the revolutions ushering in a New World. The New Crowd is uncompromising. Its tactics are not defensive but offensive. It would not send notes after a Negro is lynched. It would not appeal to white leaders. It would appeal to the plain working people everywhere. The New Crowd sees that the war came, that the Negro fought, bled and died; that the war has ended, and he is not yet free.

The New Crowd would have no armistice with lynch-law; no truce with jim crowism and disfranchisement; no peace until the Negro receives complete social, economic and political justice. To this end the New Crowd would form an alliance with white radicals such as the I.W.W., the Socialists and the Non-Partisan League, to mold a new society, a society of equals, without class, race, caste or religious distinctions.

Rudolf Fisher
The Caucasian Storms Harlem

It might not have been such a jolt had my five years' absence from Harlem been spent otherwise. But the study of medicine includes no courses in cabareting; and, anyway, the Negro cabarets in Washington, where I studied, are all uncompromisingly black. Accordingly I was entirely unprepared for what I found when I returned to Harlem recently.

I remembered one place especially where my own crowd used to hold forth; and, hoping to find some old-timers there still, I sought it out one midnight. The old, familiar plunkety-plunk welcomed me from below as I entered. I descended the same old narrow stairs, came into the same smoke-misty basement, and found myself a chair at one of the ancient white-porcelain, mirror-smooth tables. I drew a deep breath and looked about, seeking familiar faces. "What a lot of 'fays!" I thought, as I noticed the number of white guests. Presently I grew puzzled and began to stare, then I gaped—and gasped. I found myself wondering if this was the right place—if, indeed, this was Harlem at all. I suddenly became aware that, except for the waiters and members of the orchestra, I was the only Negro in the place.

After a while I left it and wandered about in a daze from night-club to night-club. I tried the Nest, Small's, Connie's Inn, the Capitol, Happy's, the Cotton Club. There was no mistake; my discovery was real and was repeatedly confirmed. No wonder my old crowd was not to be found in any of them. The best of Harlem's black cabarets have changed their names and turned white.

Such a discovery renders a moment's recollection irresistible. As irresistible as were the cabarets themselves to me seven or eight years ago. Just out of college in a town where cabarets where something only read about. A year of graduate work ahead. A Summer of rest at hand. Cabarets. Cabarets night after night, and one after another. There was no cover-charge then, and a fifteen-cent bottle of Whistle lasted an hour. It was just after the war—the heroes were home—cabarets were the thing.

How the Lybia prospered in those happy days! It was the gathering place of the swellest Harlem set: if you didn't go to the Lybia, why, my dear, you just didn't belong. The people you saw at church in the morning you met at the Lybia at night. What romance in those war-tinged days and nights! Officers from Camp Upton, with pretty maids from Brooklyn! Gay lieutenants, handsome captains—all whirling the lively onestep. Poor non-coms completely ignored; what sensible girl wanted a corporal or even a sergeant? That white, old-fashioned house, standing alone in 138th street, near the corner of Seventh avenue—doomed to be torn down a few months thence—how it shook with the dancing and laughter of the dark merry crowds!

But the first place really popular with my friends was a Chinese restaurant in 136th street, which had been known as Hayne's Café and then became the Oriental. It occupied an entire house of three stories, and had carpeted floors and a quiet, superior air. There was excellent food and incredibly good tea and two unusual entertainers: a Cuban girl, who could so vary popular airs that they sounded like real music, and a slender little "brown" with a voice of silver and a way of singing a song that made you forget your food. One could dance in the Oriental if one liked, but one danced to a piano only, and wound one's way between linen-clad tables over velvety, noiseless floors.

Here we gathered: Fritz Pollard, All-American halfback, selling Negro stock to prosperous Negro physicians; Henry Creamer and Turner Layton, who had written "After You've Gone" and a dozen more songs, and were going to write "Strut, Miss Lizzie;" Paul Robeson, All-American end, on the point of tackling law, quite unaware that the stage would intervene; Preacher Harry Bragg, Harvard Jimmie MacLendon and half a dozen others. Here at a little table, just inside the door, Bert Williams had supper every night, and afterward sometimes joined us upstairs and sang songs with us and lampooned the Actors' Equity Association, which had barred him because of his color. Never did white guests come to the Oriental except as guests of Negroes. But the manager soon was stricken with a psychosis of some sort, became a black Jew, grew himself a bushy, square-cut beard, donned a skull-cap and abandoned the Oriental. And so we were robbed of our favorite resort, and thereafter became mere rounders.

II

Such places, those real Negro cabarets that we met in the course of our rounds! There was Edmonds' in Fifth avenue at 130th street. It was a sure-enough honky-tonk, occupying the cellar of a saloon. It was the social center of what was then, and still is, Negro Harlem's kitchen. Here a tall brown-skin girl, unmistakably the one guaranteed in the song to make a preacher lay his Bible down, used to sing and dance her own peculiar numbers, vesting them with her own originality. She was known simply as Ethel, and was a genuine drawing-card. She knew her importance, too. Other girls wore themselves ragged trying to rise above the inattentive din of conversation, and soon, literally, yelled themselves hoarse; eventually they lost whatever music there was in their voices and acquired that familiar throaty roughness which is so frequent among blues singers, and which, though admired as characteristically African, is as a matter of fact nothing but a form of chronic laryngitis. Other girls did these things, but not Ethel. She took it easy. She would stride with great leisure and self-assurance to the center of the floor, stand there with a half-contemptuous nonchalance, and wait. All would become silent at once. Then she'd begin her song, genuine blues, which, for all their humorous lines, emanated tragedy and heart-break:

Woke up this mawnin'
The day was dawnin'
And I was sad and blue, so blue, Lord—
Didn' have nobody
To tell my troubles to—

It was Ethel who first made popular the song, "Tryin' to Teach My Good Man Right from Wrong," in the slow, meditative measures in which she complained:

I'm gettin' sick and tired of my railroad man
I'm gettin' sick and tired of my railroad man—
Can't get him when I want him—
I get him when I can.

It wasn't long before this song-bird escaped her dingy cage. Her name is a vaudeville attraction now, and she uses it all—Ethel Waters. Is there anyone who hasn't heard her sing "Shake That Thing!"?

A second place was Connor's in 135th street near Lenox avenue. It was livelier, less languidly sensuous, and easier to breathe in that Edmonds'. Like the latter, it was in a basement, reached by the typical narrow, headlong stairway. One of the girls there specialized in the Jelly-Roll song, and mad habitués used to fling petitions of greenbacks at her feet—pretty nimble feet they were, too—when she sang that she loved 'em but she had to turn 'em down. Over in a corner a group of 'fays would huddle and grin and think they were having a wild time. Slumming. But they were still very few in those days.

And there was the Oriental, which borrowed the name that the former Hayne's Café had abandoned. This was beyond Lenox avenue on the south side of 135th street. An upstairs place, it was nevertheless as dingy as any of the cellars, and the music fairly fought its way through the babble and smoke to one's ears, suffering in transit weird and incredible distortion. The prize pet here was a slim, little lad, unbelievably black beneath his high-brown powder, wearing a Mexican bandit costume with a bright-colored head-dress and sash. I see him now, poor kid, in all his glory, shimmying for enraptured women, who marveled at the perfect control of his voluntary abdominal tremors. He used to let the women reach out and put their hands on his sash to palpate those tremors—for a quarter.

Finally, there was the Garden of Joy, an open-air cabaret between 138th and 139th streets in Seventh avenue, occupying a plateau high above the sidewalk—a large, well-laid, smooth wooden floor with tables and chairs and a tinny orchestra, all covered by a propped-up roof, that resembled an enormous lampshade, directing bright light downward and outward. Not far away the Abyssinian Church used to hold its Summer camp-meetings in a great round circus-tent. Night after night there would arise the mingled strains of blues and spirituals, those peculiarly Negro forms of song, the one secular and the other religious, but both born of wretchedness in travail, both with their soarings of exultation and sinkings of despair. I used to wonder if God, hearing them both, found any real distinction.

There were the Lybia, then, and Hayne's, Connor's, the Oriental, Edmonds' and the Garden of Joy, each distinctive, standing for a type, some living up to their names, others living down to them, but all predominantly black. Regularly I made the rounds among these places and saw only incidental white people. I have seen them occasionally in numbers, but such parties were out on a lark. They weren't in their natural habitat and they often weren't any too comfortable.

But what of Barron's, you say? Certainly they were at home there. Yes, I know about Barron's. I have been turned away from Barron's because I was too dark to be welcome. I have been a member of a group that was told, "No more room," when we could see plenty of room. Negroes were never actually wanted in Barron's save to work. Dark skins were always discouraged or barred. In short, the fact about Barron's was this: it simply wasn't a Negro cabaret; it was a cabaret run by Negroes for whites. It wasn't even on the lists of those who lived in Harlem—they'd no more think of going there than of going to the Winter Garden Roof. But these other places were Negro through and through. Negroes supported them, not merely in now-and-then parties, but steadily, night after night.

III

Now, however, the situation is reversed. It is I who go occasionally and white people who go night after night. Time and again, since I've returned to live in Harlem, I've been one of a party of four Negroes who went to this or that Harlem cabaret, and on each occasion we've been the only Negro guests in the place. The managers don't hesitate to say that it is upon these predominant white patrons that they depend for success. These places therefore are no longer mine but theirs. Not that I'm barred, any more than they were seven or eight years ago. Once known, I'm even welcome, just as some of them used to be. But the complexion of the place is theirs, not mine. I? Why, I am actually stared at, I frequently feel uncomfortable and out of place, and when I go out on the floor to dance I am lost in a sea of white faces. As another observer has put it to me since, time was when white people went to Negro cabarets to see how Negroes acted; now Negroes go to these same cabarets to see how white people act. Negro clubs have recently taken to hiring a place outright for a presumably Negro party; and even then a goodly percentage of the invited guests are white.

One hurries to account for this change of complexion as a reaction to the Negro invasion of Broadway not long since. One remembers "Shuffle Along" of four years ago, the first Negro piece in the downtown district for many a moon. One says, "Oh yes, Negroes took their stuff to the whites and won attention and praise, and now the whites are seeking this stuff out on its native soil." Maybe. So I myself thought at first. But one looks for something of opposite- ness in a genuine reaction. One would rather expect the reaction to the Negro invasion of Broadway to be apathy. One would expect that the same thing re- peated under different names or in imitative fragments would meet with colder and colder reception, and finally with none at all.

A little recollection will show that just what one would expect was what happened. Remember "Shuffle Along's" successors: "Put and Take," "Liza," "Strut Miss Lizzie," "Runnin' Wild," and the others? True, none was so good as "Shuffle Along," but surely they didn't deserve all the roasting they got. "Liza" flared but briefly, during a holiday season. "Put and Take" was a loss, "Strut Miss Lizzie" strutted about two weeks, and the humor of "Runnin' Wild" was derided as Neo-Pleistocene. Here was reaction for—wholesale withdrawal of favor. One can hardly conclude that such withdrawal culminated in the present swamping of Negro cabarets. People so sick of a thing would hardly go out of their way to find it.

And they *are* sick of it—in quantity at least. Only one Negro entertain- ment has survived this reaction of apathy in any permanent fashion. This is the series of revues built around the personality of Florence Mills. Without that bright live personality the Broadway district would have been swept clean last season of all-Negro bills. Here is a girl who has triumphed over a hundred ob- stacles. Month after month she played obscure, unnoticed rôles with obscure, unknown dark companies. She was playing such a minor part in "Shuffle Along" when the departure of Gertrude Saunders, the craziest blues-singer on earth, unexpectedly gave her the spotlight. Florence Mills cleaned up. She cleaned up so thoroughly that the same public which grew weary of "Shuffle Along" and sick of its successors still had an eager ear for her. They have yet, and she neither wearies nor disappoints them. An impatient Broadway audi- ence awaits her return from Paris, where she and the inimitable Josephine Baker have been vying with each other as sensations. She is now in London on the way home, but London won't release her; the enthusiasm over her exceeds anything in the memory of the oldest reviewers.

Florence Mills, moreover, is admired by her own people too, because, far from going to her head, her success has not made her forgetful. Not long ago, the rumor goes, she made a fabulous amount of money in the Florida real-estate boom, and what do you suppose she plans to do with it? Build herself an Italian villa somewhere up the Hudson? Not at all. She plans to build a first-rate Negro theatre in Harlem.

But that's Florence Mills. Others have encountered indifference. In vain has Eddie Hunter, for instance, tried for a first-class Broadway showing, despite the fact that he himself has a new kind of Negro-comedian character to por- tray—the wise darkey, the "bizthniss man," the "fly" rascal who gets away with murder, a character who amuses by making a goat of others instead of by mak- ing a goat of himself. They say that some dozen Negro shows have met with similar denials. Yet the same people, presumably, whose spokesmen render these decisions flood Harlem night after night and literally crowd me off the dancing-floor. If this is a reaction, it is a reaction to a reaction, a swinging back of the pendulum from apathy toward interest. Maybe so. The cabarets may present only those special Negro features which have a particular and peculiar appeal, leaving out the high-yaller display that is merely feebly imitative. But a reaction to a reaction—that's differential calculus.

IV

Some think it's just a fad. White people have always more or less sought Negro entertainment as diversion. The old shows of the early nineteen hundreds, Williams and Walker and Cole and Johnson, are brought to mind as examples. The howling success—literally that—of J. Leubrie Hill around 1913 is another; on the road his "Darktown Follies" played in numerous white theatres. In Harlem it played at the black Lafayette and, behold, the Lafayette temporarily became white. And so now, it is held, we are observing merely one aspect of a meteoric phenomenon, which simply presents itself differently in different circumstances: Roland Hayes and Paul Robeson, Jean Toomer and Walter White, Charles Gilpin and Florence Mills—"Green Thursday," "Porgy," "In Abraham's Bosom"—Negro spirituals—the startling new African groups proposed for the Metropolitan Museum of Art. Negro stock is going up, and everybody's buying.

This doesn't sound unreasonable when it refers to certain things. Interest in the shows certainly presents many features of a fad. As in some epidemic fevers, there are sudden onset, swift contagion, brief duration, and a marked tendency to recur. Consider "Shuffle Along," for example, as a fad. Interest waned, as it will with fads. Disruption was hastened by internal dissension in the company: Sissle and Blake had written the songs and insisted on keeping the royalties therefrom, and Miller and Lyles had helped make the songs famous and contended that they too deserved a share of the proceeds. There was a deadlock and a split. "In Bamville" went one way and "Runnin' Wild" another, but neither went the prosperous way of the parent fad, "Shuffle Along."

Meanwhile, Creamer and Layton, among others, had found that the fad no longer infected. But if America was barren ground was not Europe virgin soil?

So, while Creamer remained to run the Cotton Club, Layton packed off to England, where already Hayes had done admirably in recital and Robeson was becoming well known on the stage. Layton and his new partner, Tandy Johnstone, were amazed at their success in England, and there they are at this writing. They earn more in a week there than they used to in many months over here. They have transplanted their fad into other susceptible communities—communities likely to become immune less swiftly. They are London vaudeville headliners, and their jazz has captivated the British. These entertainers will probably not soon lose that peculiar knack of striking a popular response. Turner Layton's father was for many years assistant director of music in the Washington public schools, and it is said that this imposing gentleman could get music out of a hall full of empty chairs. There may be something hereditary therefore in the way in which the most lifeless instrument responds to Turner's touch.

Followed Sissle and Blake to England, whence they have recently returned successful. Noble Sissle was the friend and companion of Jim Europe, who organized the New York Clef Club and was the most popular Negro musician of his day. After Europe's unfortunate death, Sissle and Eubie Blake became an extremely popular vaudeville team. Earlier, Blake used to play the piano for house-parties and dances around Baltimore, and later played in cabarets. Certain of his Baltimore friends point to him proudly now, and well they may: the accuracy and agility with which his fingers scamper over the keyboard is always a breath-taking wonder. Sissle and Blake, too, have learned the lessons taught by struggle and disaster. Time was when the "Shuffle Along" company, coming to Washington from New York for a Sunday afternoon engagement at the world's best Negro theatre, the Lincoln, entered the town with all the triumphal glamor of a circus. Almost every principal in the show had his or her own automobile, and they weren't designed or painted with an eye for modest retirement. The principals drove down from New York in their cars, if you please; which was entirely their own business, of course. The point is that they *could*. Sissle and Blake, it appears, still can. Such is the profitable contagion of a fad.

Pending a contemplated reunion of these unusual teams, Miller and Lyles have been playing with various Broadway revues. These comical fellows are both college graduates, and eminently respectable and conservative in private life. It is, by the way, a noteworthy thing about all of these men, Creamer, Johnstone, Layton, Sissle, Blake, Miller, and Lyles, that one never hears the slightest murmur of social criticism about any one of them. They have managed to conduct themselves off stage entirely above reproach. It is no accident that the private lives of these dark-skinned stars are so circumspect. It is part of the explanation of their success.

V

It is only a part, however; and the fad-like characteristics of their experience may be another part. It may be a season's whim, then, this sudden, contagious interest in everything Negro. If so, when I go into a familiar cabaret, or the place where a familiar cabaret used to be, and find it transformed and relatively colorless, I may be observing just one form that the season's whim has taken.

But suppose it is a fad—to say that explains nothing. How came the fad? What occasions the focusing of attention on this particular thing—rounds up and gathers these seasonal whims, and centers them about the Negro? Cabarets are peculiar, mind you. They're not like theatres and concert halls. You don't just go to a cabaret and sit back and wait to be entertained. You get out on the floor and join the pow-wow and help entertain yourself. Granted that white people have long enjoyed the Negro entertainment as a diversion, is it not something different, something more, when they bodily throw themselves into Negro entertainment in cabarets? "Now Negroes go to their own cabarets to see how white people act."

And what do we see? Why, we see them actually playing Negro games. I watch them in that epidemic Negroism, the Charleston. I look on and envy them. They camel and fish-tail and turkey, they geche and black-bottom and scronch, they skate and buzzard and mess-around—and they do them all better than I! This interest in the Negro is an active and participating interest. It is almost as if a traveler from the North stood watching an African tribe-dance, then suddenly found himself swept wildly into it, caught in its tidal rhythm.

Willingly would I be an outsider in this if I could know that I read it aright—that out of this change in the old familiar ways some finer thing may come. Is this interest akin to that of the Virginians on the veranda of a planta-tion's big-house—sitting genuinely spellbound as they hear the lugubrious strains floating up from the Negro quarters? Is it akin to that of the African ex-plorer, Stanley, leaving a village far behind, but halting in spite of himself to catch the boom of its distant drum? Is it significant of basic human responses, the effect of which, once admitted, will extend far beyond cabarets? Maybe these Nordics at last have tuned in on our wavelength. Maybe they are at last learning to speak our language.

Marcus Garvey
The Future As I See It

It comes to the individual, the race, the nation, once in a life-time to decide upon the course to be pursued as a career. The hour has now struck for the individual Negro as well as the entire race to decide the course that will be pursued in the interest of our own liberty.

We who make up the Universal Negro Improvement Association have decided that we shall go forward, upward and onward toward the great goal of human liberty. We have determined among ourselves that all barriers placed in the way of our progress must be removed, must be cleared away for we desire to see the light of a brighter day.

THE NEGRO IS READY

The Universal Negro Improvement Association for five years has been proclaiming to the world the readiness of the Negro to carve out a pathway for himself in the course of life. Men of other races and nations have become alarmed at this attitude of the Negro in his desire to do things for himself and by himself. This alarm has become so universal that organizations have been brought into being here, there and everywhere for the purpose of deterring and obstructing this forward move of our race. Propaganda has been waged here, there and everywhere for the purpose of misinterpreting the intention of this organization; some have said that this organization seeks to create discord and discontent among the races; some say we are organized for the purpose of hating other people. Every sensible, sane and honest-minded person knows that the Universal Negro Improvement Association has no such intention. We are organized for the absolute purpose of bettering our condition, industrially, commercially, socially, religiously and politically. We are organized not to hate other men, but to lift ourselves, and to demand respect of all humanity. We have a program that we believe to be righteous; we believe it to be just, and we have made up our minds to lay down ourselves on the altar of sacrifice for the realization of this great hope of ours, based upon the foundation of righteousness. We declare to the world that Africa must be free, that the entire Negro race must be emancipated from industrial bondage, peonage and serfdom; we make no compromise, we make no apology in this our declaration. We do not desire to create offense on the part of other races, but we are determined that we shall be heard, that we shall be given the rights to which we are entitled.

THE PROPAGANDA OF OUR ENEMIES

For the purpose of creating doubts about the work of the Universal Negro Improvement Association, many attempts have been made to cast shadow and gloom over our work. They have even written the most uncharitable things about our organization; they have spoken so unkindly of our effort, but what do we care? They spoke unkindly and uncharitably about all the reform movements that have helped in the betterment of humanity. They maligned the great movement of the Christian religion; they maligned the great liberation movements of America, of France, of England, of Russia; can we expect, then, to escape being maligned in this, our desire for the liberation of Africa and the freedom of four hundred million Negroes of the world?

We have unscrupulous men and organizations working in opposition to us. Some trying to capitalize the new spirit that has come to the Negro to make profit out of it to their own selfish benefit; some are trying to set back the Negro from seeing the hope of his own liberty, and thereby poisoning our people's mind against the motives of our organization; but every sensible far-seeing Negro in this enlightened age knows what propaganda means. It is the medium of discrediting that which you are opposed to, so that the propaganda of our enemies will be of little avail as soon as we are rendered able to carry to our peoples scattered throughout the world the true message of our great organization.

"CROCODILES" AS FRIENDS

Men of the Negro race, let me say to you that a greater future is in store for us; we have no cause to lose hope, to become faint-hearted. We must realize that upon ourselves depend our destiny, our future; we must carve out that future, that destiny, and we who make up the Universal Negro Improvement Association have pledged ourselves that nothing in the world shall stand in our way, nothing in the world shall discourage us, but opposition shall make us work harder, shall bring us closer together so that as one man the millions of us will march on toward that goal that we have set for ourselves. The new Negro shall not be deceived. The new Negro refuses to take advice from anyone who has not felt with him, and suffered with him. We have suffered for three hundred years, therefore we feel that the time has come when only those who have suffered with us can interpret our feelings and our spirit. It takes the slave to interpret the feelings of the slave; it takes the unfortunate man to interpret the spirit of his unfortunate brother; and so it takes the suffering Negro to interpret the spirit of his comrade. It is strange that so many people are interested in the Negro now, willing to advise him how to act, and what organizations he should join, yet nobody was interested in the Negro to the extent of not making him a slave for two hundred and fifty years, reducing him to industrial peonage and serfdom after he was freed; it is strange that the same people can be so interested in the Negro now, as to tell him what organization he should follow and what leader he should support.

Whilst we are bordering on a future of brighter things, we are also at our danger period, when we must either accept the right philosophy, or go down by following deceptive propaganda which has hemmed us in for many centuries.

DECEIVING THE PEOPLE

There is many a leader of our race who tells us that everything is well, and that all things will work out themselves and that a better day is coming. Yes, all of us know that a better day is coming; we all know that one day we will go home to Paradise, but whilst we are hoping by our Christian virtues to have an entry into Paradise we also realize that we are living on earth, and that the things that are practiced in Paradise are not practiced here. You have to treat this world as the world treats you; we are living in a temporal, material age, an age of activity, an age of racial, national selfishness. What else can you expect but to give back to the world what the world gives to you, and we are calling upon the four hundred million Negroes of the world to take a decided stand, a determined stand, that we shall occupy a firm position; that position shall be an emancipated race and a free nation of our own. We are determined that we shall have a free country; we are determined that we shall have a flag; we are determined that we shall have a government second to none in the world.

AN EYE FOR AN EYE

Men may spurn the idea, they may scoff at it; the metropolitan press of this country may deride us; yes, white men may laugh at the idea of Negroes talking about government; but let me tell you there is going to be a government, and let me say to you also that whatsoever you give, in like measure it shall be returned to you. The world is sinful, and therefore man believes in the doctrine of an eye for an eye, a tooth for a tooth. Everybody believes that revenge is God's, but at the same time we are men, and revenge sometimes springs up, even in the most Christian heart.

Why should man write down a history that will react against him? Why should man perpetrate deeds of wickedness upon his brother which will return to him in like measure? Yes, the Germans maltreated the French in the Franco-Prussian war of 1870, but the French got even with the Germans in 1918. It is history, and history will repeat itself. Beat the Negro, brutalize the Negro, kill the Negro, burn the Negro, imprison the Negro, scoff at the Negro, deride the Negro, it may come back to you one of these fine days, because the supreme destiny of man is in the hands of God. God is no respecter of persons, whether that person be white, yellow or black. Today the one race is up, tomorrow it has fallen; today the Negro seems to be the footstool of the other races and nations of the world; tomorrow the Negro may occupy the highest rung of the great human ladder.

But, when we come to consider the history of man, was not the Negro a power, was he not great once? Yes, honest students of history can recall the day when Egypt, Ethiopia and Timbuctoo towered in their civilizations, towered above Europe, towered above Asia. When Europe was inhabited by a race of cannibals, a race of savages, naked men, heathens and pagans, Africa was peopled with a race of cultured black men, who were masters in art, science and literature; men who were cultured and refined; men who, it was said, were like the gods. Even the great poets of old sang in beautiful sonnets of the delight it afforded the gods to be in companionship with the Ethiopians. Why, then, should we lose hope? Black men, you were once great; you shall be great again. Lose not courage, lose not faith, go forward. The thing to do is to get organized; keep separated and you will be exploited, you will be robbed, you will be killed. Get organized, and you will compel the world to respect you. If the world fails to give you consideration, because you are black men, because you are Negroes, four hundred millions of you shall, through organization, shake the pillars of the universe and bring down creation, even as Samson brought down the temple upon his head and upon the heads of the Philistines.

AN INSPIRING VISION

So Negroes, I say, through the Universal Negro Improvement Association, that there is much to live for. I have a vision of the future, and I see before me a picture of a redeemed Africa, with her dotted cities, with her beautiful civilization, with her millions of happy children, going to and fro. Why should I lose hope, why should I give up and take a back place in this age of progress? Remember that you are men, that God created you Lords of this creation. Lift up yourselves, men, take yourselves out of the mire and hitch your hopes to the stars; yes, rise as high as the very stars themselves. Let no man pull you down, let no man destroy your ambition, because man is but your companion, your equal; man is your brother; he is not your lord; he is not your sovereign master.

We of the Universal Negro Improvement Association feel happy; we are cheerful. Let them connive to destroy us; let them organize to destroy us; we shall fight the more. Ask me personally the cause of my success, and I say opposition; oppose me, and I fight the more, and if you want to find out the sterling worth of the Negro, oppose him, and under the leadership of the Universal Negro Improvement Association he shall fight his way to victory, and in the days to come, and I believe not far distant, Africa shall reflect a splendid demonstration of the worth of the Negro, of the determination of the Negro, to set himself free and to establish a government of his own.

Langston Hughes
Goodbye Christ

Listen, Christ,
You did alright in your day, I reckon—
But that day's gone now.
They ghosted you up a swell story, too,
Called it Bible—
But it's dead now,
The popes and the preachers've
Made too much money from it.
They've sold you to too many

Kings, generals, robbers, and killers—
Even to the Tzar and the Cossacks,
Even to Rockefeller's Church,
Even to THE SATURDAY EVENING POST.
You ain't no good no more.
They've pawned you
Till you've done wore out.

Goodbye,
Christ Jesus Lord God Jehova,
Beat it on away from here now.
Make way for a new guy with no religion at all—
A real guy named
Marx Communist Lenin Peasant Stalin Worker ME—

I said, ME!
Go ahead on now,
You're getting in the way of things, Lord.
And please take Saint Ghandi with you when you go,
And Saint Pope Pius,
And Saint Aimee McPherson,
And big black Saint Becton
Of the Consecrated Dime.
And step on the gas, Christ!
Move!

Don't be so slow about movin'!
The world is mine from now on—
And nobody's gonna sell ME
To a king, or a general,
Or a millionaire.

The Negro Speaks of Rivers

I've known rivers:
I've known rivers ancient as the world and older than the flow of human blood
    in human veins.

My soul has grown deep like the rivers.

I bathed in the Euphrates when dawns were young.
I built my hut near the Congo and it lulled me to sleep.
I looked upon the Nile and raised the pyramids above it.
I heard the singing of the Mississippi when Abe Lincoln went down to New
    Orleans, and I've seen its muddy bosom turn all golden in the sunset.

I've known rivers:
Ancient, dusky rivers.

My soul has grown deep like the rivers.

The Weary Blues

Droning a drowsy syncopated tune,
Rocking back and forth to a mellow croon,
    I heard a Negro play.
Down on Lenox Avenue the other night
By the pale dull pallor of an old gas light
    He did a lazy sway. . . .
    He did a lazy sway. . . .
To the tune o' those Weary Blues.
With his ebony hands on each ivory key
He made that poor piano moan with melody.
    O Blues!
Swaying to and fro on his rickety stool
He played that sad raggy tune like a musical fool.

Sweet Blues!
Coming from a black man's soul.
    O Blues!
In a deep song voice with a melancholy tone
I heard that Negro sing, that old piano moan—
    "Ain't got nobody in all this world,
        Ain't got nobody but ma self.
        I's gwine to quit ma frownin'
        And put ma troubles on the shelf."

Thump, thump, thump, went his foot on the floor.
He played a few chords then he sang some more—
    "I got the Weary Blues
        And I can't be satisfied.
        Got the Weary Blues
        And can't be satisfied—
        I ain't happy no mo'
        And I wish that I had died."
And far into the night he crooned that tune.
The stars went out and so did the moon.
The singer stopped playing and went to bed
While the Weary Blues echoed through his head.
He slept like a rock or a man that's dead.

Harlem [1]

Here on the edge of hell
Stands Harlem—
Remembering the old lies,
The old kicks in the back,
The old "Be patient"
They told us before.

Sure, we remember.
Now when the man at the corner store
Says sugar's gone up another two cents,
And bread one,
And there's a new tax on cigarettes—
We remember the job we never had,
Never could get,
And can't have now
Because we're colored.

So we stand here
On the edge of hell
In Harlem
And look out on the world
And wonder
What we're gonna do
In the face of what
We remember.

Ballad of the Landlord

Landlord, landlord,
My roof has sprung a leak.
Don't you 'member I told you about it
Way last week?

Landlord, landlord,
These steps is broken down.
When you come up yourself
It's a wonder you don't fall down.

Ten Bucks you say I owe you?
Ten Bucks you say is due?
Well, that's Ten Bucks more'n I'll pay you
Till you fix this house up new.

What? You gonna get eviction orders?
You gonna cut off my heat?
You gonna take my furniture and
Throw it in the street?

Um-huh! You talking high and mighty.
Talk on—till you get through.
You ain't gonna be able to say a word
If I land my fist on you.

Police! Police!
Come and get this man!
He's trying to ruin the government
And overturn the land!

Copper's whistle!
Patrol bell!
Arrest.

Precinct Station.
Iron cell.
Headlines in press:

MAN THREATENS LANDLORD
∴
TENANT HELD NO BAIL
∴
JUDGE GIVES NEGRO 90 DAYS IN COUNTY JAIL.

The Backlash Blues

Mister Backlash, Mister Backlash,
Just who do you think I am?
Tell me, Mister Backlash,
Who do you think I am?
You raise my taxes, freeze my wages,
Send my son to Vietnam.

You give me second-class houses,
Give me second-class schools,
Second-class houses
And second-class schools.
You must think us colored folks
Are second-class fools.

When I try to find a job
To earn a little cash,
Try to find myself a job
To earn a little cash,
All you got to offer
Is a white backlash.

But the world is big,
The world is big and round,
Great big world, Mister Backlash,
Big and bright and round—
And it's full of folks like me who are
Black, Yellow, Beige, and Brown.

Mister Backlash, Mister Backlash,
What do you think I got to lose?
Tell me, Mister Backlash,

What you think I got to lose?
I'm gonna leave you, Mister Backlash,
Singing your mean old backlash blues.

>   *You're the one,*
>   *Yes, you're the one*
>   *Will have the blues.*

Bombings in Dixie

It's not enough to mourn
And not enough to pray.
Sackcloth and ashes, anyhow,
Save for another day.

The Lord God Himself
Would hardly desire
That men be burned to death—
And bless the fire.

Claude McKay

If We Must Die

If we must die, let it not be like hogs
Hunted and penned in an inglorious spot,
While round us bark the mad and hungry dogs,
Making their mock at our accursed lot.
If we must die, O let us nobly die,
So that our precious blood may not be shed
In vain; then even the monsters we defy
Shall be constrained to honor us though dead!
O kinsmen! we must meet the common foe!
Though far outnumbered let us show us brave,
And for their thousand blows deal one deathblow!
What though before us lies the open grave?
Like men we'll face the murderous, cowardly pack,
Pressed to the wall, dying, but fighting back!

The White House

Your door is shut against my tightened face,
And I am sharp as steel with discontent;
But I possess the courage and the grace
To bear my anger proudly and unbent.
The pavement slabs burn loose beneath my feet,
A chafing savage, down the decent street;
And passion rends my vitals as I pass,
Where boldly shines your shuttered door of glass.
Oh, I must search for wisdom every hour,
Deep in my wrathful bosom sore and raw,
And find in it the superhuman power
To hold me to the letter of your law!
Oh, I must keep my heart inviolate
Against the potent poison of your hate.

To the White Fiends

Think you I am not fiend and savage too?
Think you I could not arm me with a gun
And shoot down ten of you for every one
Of my black brothers murdered, burnt by you?
Be not deceived, for every deed you do
I could match—out-match: am I not Afric's son,
Black of that black land where black deeds are done?
But the Almighty from the darkness drew
My soul and said: Even thou shalt be a light
Awhile to burn on the benighted earth,
Thy dusky face I set among the white
For thee to prove thyself of higher worth;
Before the world is swallowed up in night,
To show thy little lamp: go forth, go forth!

America

Although she feeds me bread of bitterness,
And sinks into my throat her tiger's tooth,
Stealing my breath of life, I will confess
I love this cultured hell that tests my youth!
Her vigor flows like tides into my blood,
Giving me strength erect against her hate.
Her bigness sweeps my being like a flood.
Yet as a rebel fronts a king in state,
I stand within her walls with not a shred
Of terror, malice, not a word of jeer.
Darkly I gaze into the days ahead,
And see her might and granite wonders there,
Beneath the touch of Tune's unerring hand,
Like pureless treasures sinking in the sand.

Anne Spencer
White Things

Most things are colorful things—the sky, earth, and sea.
  Black men are most men; but the white are free!
White things are rare things; so rare, so rare
They stole from out a silvered world—somewhere.
Finding earth-plains fair plains, save greenly grassed,
They strewed white feathers of cowardice, as they passed;
  The golden stars with lances fine,
  The hills all red and darkened pine,
They blanched with their wand of power;
And turned the blood in a ruby rose
To a poor white poppy-flower.

They pyred a race of black, black men,
And burned them to ashes white; then,
Laughing, a young one claimed a skull,
For the skull of a black is white, not dull,
  But a glistening awful thing
  Made, it seems, for this ghoul to swing
In the face of God with all his might,
And swear by the hell that sired him:
  "Man-maker, make white!"

Georgia Douglas Johnson
Common Dust

And who shall separate the dust
What later we shall be:
Whose keen discerning eye will scan
And solve the mystery?

The high, the low, the rich, the poor,
The black, the white, the red,
And all the chromatique between,
Of whom shall it be said:

Here lies the dust of Africa;
Here are the sons of Rome;
Here lies the one unlabelled,
The world at large his home!

Can one then separate the dust?
Will mankind lie apart,
When life has settled back again
The same as from the start?

Alice Dunbar-Nelson
The Proletariat Speaks

I love beautiful things:
Great trees, bending green winged branches to a velvet lawn,
Fountains sparkling in white marble basins,
Cool fragrance of lilacs and roses and honeysuckle

Or exotic blooms, filling the air with heart-contracting odors;
Spacious rooms, cool and gracious with statues and books,
Carven seats and tapestries, and old masters,
Whose patina shows the wealth of centuries.

And so I work
In a dusty office, whose grimed windows
Look out on an alley of unbelievable squalor,
Where mangy cats, in their degradation, spurn
Swarming bits of meat and bread;
Where odors, vile and breath-taking, rise in fetid waves
Filling my nostrils, scorching my humid, bitter cheeks.

I love beautiful things:
Carven tables laid with lily-hued linen
And fragile china and sparkling iridescent glass;
Pale silver, etched with heraldries,
Where tender bits of regal dainties tempt,
And soft-stepped service anticipates the unspoken wish.

And so I eat
In the food-laden air of a greasy kitchen,
At an oil-clothed table:
Plate piled high with food that turns my head away,
Lest a squeamish stomach reject too soon
The lumpy gobs it never needed.
Or in a smoky cafeteria, balancing a slippery tray
To a table crowded with elbows
Which lately the busboy wiped with a grimy rag.

I love beautiful things:
Soft linen sheets and silken coverlet,
Sweet cool of chamber opened wide to fragrant breeze;

Rose-shaded lamps and golden atomizers,
Spraying Parisian fragrance over my relaxed limbs,
Fresh from a white marble bath, and sweet cool spray.

And so I sleep
In a hot hall-room whose half-opened window,
Unscreened, refuses to budge another inch,
Admits no air, only insects, and hot choking gasps
That make me writhe, nun-like, in sackcloth sheets and lumps of straw
And then I rise
To fight my way to a dubious tub,
Whose tiny, tepid stream threatens to make me late;
And hurrying out, dab my unrefreshed face
With bits of toiletry from the ten cent store.

Virginia A. Houston
Class Room

Behind him a picture.
Blue-gray skies,
Phantom clouds
Chasing a topsy-turvy ship
Across an indigo sea . . .

And on those joyous sails
A mirrored image of a bald head,
Shattering my dream
Of faraway, mysterious lands,
Gold-red sunsets,
Silver-white nights,
Of seas shattering against
A sun-splashed deck.

The whisper of the sea in my ears
And the whistle of the wind in the sails
Are replaced by the wheezy murmur
Of an anti-Freudian.

Dorothea Mathews
The Lynching

He saw the rope, the moving mob,
And suddenly thought of quiet things;
The way the river-ripples sob,
The silver flight of pigeon's wings
Free in the blue September air;
And that the night was warm and brown—
Under the trees the shadows hung;
The little stars of God looked down.

Helene Johnson
Bottled

Upstairs on the third floor
Of the 135th Street library
In Harlem, I saw a little
Bottle of sand, brown sand,
Just like the kids make pies
Out of down at the beach.
But the label said: "This
Sand was taken from the Sahara desert."
Imagine that! The Sahara desert!
Some bozo's been all the way to Africa to get some sand.

And yesterday on Seventh Avenue
I saw a darky dressed to kill
In yellow gloves and swallowtail coat
And swirling a cane. And everyone
Was laughing at him. Me too,
At first, till I saw his face
When he stopped to hear a
Organ grinder grind out some jazz.
Boy! You should a seen that darky's face!
It just shone. Gee, he was happy!
And he began to dance. No
Charleston or Black Bottom for him.
No sir. He danced just as dignified
And slow. No, not slow either.
Dignified and *proud!* You couldn't
Call it slow, not with all the
Cuttin' up he did. You would a died to see him.

The crowd kept yellin' but he didn't hear,
Just kept on dancin' and twirlin' that cane
And yellin' out loud every once in a while.
I know the crowd thought he was coo-coo.
But say, I was where I could see his face,
And somehow, I could see him dancin' in a jungle,
A real honest-to-cripe jungle, and he wouldn't leave on them

Trick clothes—those yaller shoes and yaller gloves
And swallowtail coat. He wouldn't have on nothing.
And he wouldn't be carrying no cane.
He'd be carrying a spear with a sharp fine point
Like the bayonets we had "over there."
And the end of it would be dipped in some kind of
Hoo-doo poison. And he'd be dancin' black and naked and gleaming.
And he'd have rings in his ears and on his nose
And bracelets and necklaces of elephants' teeth.
Gee, I bet he'd be beautiful then all right.
No one would laugh at him then, I bet.
Say! That man that took that sand from the Sahara desert
And put it in a little bottle on a shelf in the library,
That's what they done to this shine, ain't it? Bottled him.
Trick shoes, trick coat, trick cane, trick everything—all glass—
But inside—
Gee, that poor shine!

Gwendolyn B. Bennett
Heritage

I want to see the slim palm-trees,
Pulling at the clouds
With little pointed fingers. . . .

I want to see lithe Negro girls
Etched dark against the sky
While sunset lingers.

I want to hear the silent sands,
Singing to the moon
Before the Sphinx-still face. . . .

I want to hear the chanting
Around a heathen fire
Of a strange black race.

I want to breathe the Lotus flow'r,
Sighing to the stars
With tendrils drinking at the Nile. . . .

I want to feel the surging
Of my sad people's soul,
Hidden by a minstrel-smile.

Angelina Weld Grimke

El Beso

Twilight—and you
Quiet—the stars;
Snare of the shine of your teeth,
Your provocative laughter,
The gloom of your hair;
Lure of you, eye and lip;
Yearning, yearning,
Languor, surrender;
   Your mouth,
And madness, madness,
Tremulous, breathless, flaming,
The space of a sigh;
Then awakening—remembrance,
Pain, regret—your sobbing;
And again, quiet—the stars,
Twilight—and you.

Sterling D. Spero and Abram L. Harris
from *The Black Worker*

CHAPTER XVIII

The "New" Negro and Post-War Unrest

THE competition into which Negroes and whites were suddenly thrown as a result of the southern Negro migrations was more direct and on a larger scale than had ever occurred. It was in the nature of a revolution that could not take place without some disaster. The whites resented the intrusion and the underbidding of black labor. But the Negro, too, had his grievances. Although he enjoyed greater economic and industrial opportunity, he found the North less of a haven than he had anticipated. Advancement in industry was not as rapid and as frequent as he had visualized. Residential segregation and high rents, racial discrimination, and social ostracism were found to be characteristic of the North no less than of the South. Yet he had escaped political disfranchisement, illiteracy, and poor schools, and the inhibitions to freedom of thought and expression that Negroes experience in the South. In this atmosphere the Negro imbibed the spirit of race consciousness. He was no less antagonistic to the white worker than the latter was to him. Thus the migration provoked mutual racial antagonism through the competition between Negroes and whites for jobs and threw into relief much of the dissatisfaction and unrest long pent up in the Negro masses. Unrest and racial hostility were intensified by the problem of housing the rapidly expanding Negro population.

The shortage of houses in sections reserved for Negroes forced newcomers to bid for homes in white residential sections. An increase in rents naturally followed, and the effect of high rent was not only felt by the Negro but also by the whites. Because of a belief in the undesirability of Negro neighbors the whites felt impelled to seek houses in other sections of the city where property values, likewise, responded to the pressure of new demand. Very often in these sections, where new real estate developments did not keep pace with the demand or the available houses were insufficient to relieve the pressure of demand, purchase prices and rentals were higher than in the sections abandoned to the Negro. When the whites' retreat from the Negro invasion was temporarily checked by the unavailability of houses elsewhere, and the protest of home owners and tenants' leagues failed to dissuade landlords and real estate agents from plying their lucrative trade among Negroes, violence and intimidation were used. The first victims of the whites' anger were members of the Negro upper classes who were economically able to acquire homes in white neighborhoods. But whenever the life or property of a Negro who had moved into a white section was threatened, the Negro masses rose up to protect him. In the Washington, East St. Louis, and Chicago race riots, which were to a large degree caused by competition between Negroes and whites for jobs and houses, the Negro masses demonstrated very clearly that they would meet violence with violence. This determination of the Negro masses to fight back when one of their race was injured or threatened with injury was the expression of a spirit of revolt that accompanied the migrations, the smouldering embers of which were fanned into a militant race consciousness by the writings of the younger Negro intellectuals such as Claude McKay[1] and the editors of radical publications like the *Crusader*, the *Messenger*, and the *Challenge*, which loomed into prominence just after the World War.[2]

Typical of the intellectual stimulation given to this surging consciousness of the Negro masses was the following verse:

> This must not be!
> The time is past when black men
> Laggard Sons of Ham,
> Shall tamely bow and weakly cringe
> In servile manner full of shame.
>
> Lift up your heads!
> Be proud! be brave!
> Though black, the same red blood
> Flows through your veins
> As through your paler brothers.
> . . . .
> Your toil enriched the Southern lands;
> Your anguish has made sweet the sugar cane;
> Your sweat has moistened the growing corn,
> And drops of blood from the cruel master's whip
> Has caused the white cotton to burst forth in mute protest.
>
> Demand, come not mock suppliant!
> Demand, and if not given—take!
> Take what is rightfully yours;

[1]McKay, the distinguished poet, is known for his adherence to economic radicalism as much as by his poetry and recent novels. He saw in the acceptance of Bolshevism by the white American workers the emancipation of the "black toilers." See his poem, "If We Must Die," which well expresses the belligerent and bitter state of Negro feeling during the post-war period. *The Book of American Negro Poetry*, edited by James Weldon Johnson, 1922.

[2]*The Investigation Activities of the Department of Justice*, Senate Documents, 66th Congress, 1st Session, 1919, Vol. 12, pp. 161–87. Exhibit No. 10.

An eye for an eye;
A soul for soul;
Strike, black man, strike!
This shall not be!

This bit of verse, like much of the literature of the period, is not only an expression of race consciousness but also of economic discontent. And it would seem to follow that some of the racial conflict which orginated in economic facts would have been forestalled had organized labor brought Negro and white workers into closer affiliation before the migrations. But organized labor's traditional view of the Negro as a strike breaker and its laissez-faire attitude toward Negro organization as well as toward other important questions rendered it helpless. The Negro was left to himself to make whatever adjustments he could in his new economic environment. The racial movements and philosophies that sprang up among the Negro population during the five years that followed the World War bore the earmarks of economic unrest and social dissatisfaction for which the inertia of the labor movement and American race psychology were responsible. They were generated by economic competition, racial antagonism, the Negro's awakened self-reliance and race consciousness and his new intellectual freedom. The movements took one of the following forms: economic radicalism, racial self-sufficiency, or Negro Zionism.

The last mentioned movement, Negro Zionism, popularly known as the "Back to Africa Movement," was sponsored by Marcus Garvey, a Jamaican Negro, through his Universal Negro Improvement Association and African Communities (Imperial) League. This was an all-Negro movement built upon pride of race and the exaltation of things black.[3] Negro economic self-sufficiency was a revival of the individualism enunciated by Booker T. Washington. A typical expression of this doctrine in the post-war period was contained in a leaflet circulated by the International Negro Civic Association of New York. The association protested that millionaires were being made in Harlem every five years; that Negroes ought to own Harlem or leave it; that a Negro boy has as much right behind a bank window as a white boy, but that the Negro race had to build banks before this would be possible; and that rents were "murderous" but, owning no houses, the Negro must pay what is asked or be "scrapped."[4] The self-sufficiency movement was closely related to the Garvey movement in that the two of them idealized a sort of self-contained racial economy. One looked to Africa as the place where its dreams were to be realized, while the other hoped to build in America.

The first mentioned movement, economic radicalism, was inaugurated about 1918 by Chandler Owen and Asa Philip Randolph, the editors of the *Messenger*, a magazine of "scientific radicalism." Owen and Randolph had for-

[3]For Garvey's philosophy see Chapter VII.

[4]*Revolutionary Radicalism*, a report of the Joint Legislative Committee of the State of New York Investigating Seditious Activities, 1920, Vol. II, Pt. 1, p. 1518.

merly been employed as editors of the *Hotel Messenger*, a journal published by
the Headwaiters and Sidewaiters' Society of Greater New York. A rift occurred
between the editors and the society when the editors persisted in commenting
upon the sidewaiters' inadequate wages and disagreeable working conditions.[5]
The ruptured relations led to the founding of the "militant and revolutionary"
Messenger in 1917. The new magazine avowed itself to be the organ of labor
unionism and socialism among Negroes.[6] Associated with Randolph and Owen
in the task of intellectually emancipating the workingmen, were W. A.
Domingo, editor of the *Emancipator*, whose motto was "to preach deliverance
to the slaves," William N. Colson, the Reverend George Frazier Miller,
Richard B. Moore, and Cyril Briggs.[7] Later Moore and Briggs withdrew and affiliated with the Communist party of America. These were the vanguard of the
"New" Negro whom the *Messenger* editor described as "the product of the same
world-wide forces that have brought into being the great liberal and radical
movements that are now seizing the reins of political, economic and social
power in all the civilized countries of the world." The "New" Negro "unlike the
old Negro" was not to be "lulled into a false sense of security with political
spoils and patronage." He demanded "the full product of his toil." His immediate aim was "more wages, shorter hours and better working conditions."
He stood for "absolute social equality, education, physical action in self-
defense, freedom of speech, press and assembly, and the right of Russia to self-
determination."[8]

The "New" Negroes or economic radicals were the first expression of socialism in the Negro world.[9] They maintained that the Socialist party represented the interests of workingmen and, since 99 per cent of the Negro people
were workers, the Negro's logical alignment was with the Socialist party. Fur-

---

[5]*Messenger*, Nov. 1917, p. 21. Chief among the latter was the rather general practice among headwaiters to compel the sidewaiters to purchase uniforms from them. At this time when employment agencies were just beginning to play an important part in supplying the hotels with labor,
the recruiting of waiters for the large hotels at winter and summer resorts was done very largely by
the Negro headwaiter. For performing this service the headwaiter levied a revenue upon the side-
waiter and obtained it by means of his monopoly in the sale of waiters' uniforms. A headwaiter
would have a shipment of uniforms consigned to him by a wholesaler. He would then compel the
waiters whom he had employed to purchase the uniforms at a price often doubling and even
trebling the consigned value. The difference between the consigned price, which was never paid
to the wholesaler until after sale of the uniforms, and the price at which they retailed was pock-
eted by the headwaiter as agent's fee or the price of a risk which he never bore. Very little risk entered such transactions, as a waiter usually signed a statement authorizing the hotel management
to deduct the price from his pay for delivery to the headwaiter.

[6]*Messenger*, July, 1918, p. 7.

[7]See *Revolutionary Radicalism*, p. 1483.

[8]*Messenger*, Aug., 1920, p. 73.

[9]The Negro radical movement in New York was foreshadowed by Hubert Harrison, a West Indian
Negro, whose activity in Revolutionary working-class circles and influence in various intellectual
clubs in Harlem laid the foundation for the later propaganda of the *Messenger* editors. See the
Negro Champion, June 23, 1928, p. 3.

thermore, the Socialist party's advocacy of collective ownership entitled it to the Negro's political support. Under municipal socialism, educated Negroes, it was contended, would have a better chance to obtain the higher positions that are denied them under private ownership.[10]

This type of appeal was, of course, non-Marxian. It was directed toward enlisting the support of the middle-class Negro. At the same time it revealed the racial motivation underlying the *Messenger* radicals' acceptance of socialism. For they attributed race prejudice to capitalism. They held that in an individualistic economic system, competition for jobs and the profitableness of race prejudice to the capitalist class were incentives to race conflict. Therefore the removal of the motive for creating racial strife was conditioned upon the socialization of industry and the nationalization of land, in short, upon the elimination of economic individualism and competition through social revolution.[11]

To have confined their propaganda to the Negro bourgeoisie would have caused the Negro radicals to compromise with the theories to which they were committed. Their acceptance of the theory of the class struggle and their application of it to the race question caused them to champion labor solidarity between white and black workers. The argument for labor solidarity was the Negro and white workers' identity of economic interest, i e., "the getting of more wages, shorter hours, and better working conditions," and the fact that unorganized workers, whether white or black, are potential scabs upon organized labor. But from the standpoint of socialism, the most potent argument used by the *Messenger* radicals in disseminating the doctrine of labor solidarity was capital's ignoring of color and race in its exploitation of labor.[12] It is therefore not at all singular that the *Messenger* radicals were aided in their espousal of industrial unionism and labor solidarity between white and black workers by such socialistic unions as the Amalgamated Clothing Workers, the International Ladies' Garment Workers, the Brewery Workers, and the Industrial Workers of the World.[13] Whether the anarcho-syndicalist industrialism of the I. W. W., or the socialist-industrial unionism of the Amalgamated was more in accord with the Negro radicals' trade-union philosophy is not clear from their writings. Practical strategy, however, in the organization of all Negro workers in some radical class-conscious union could but lead them to admonish the Negro worker to affiliate with the I. W. W., since the jurisdiction of the Amal-

[10]*Messenger*, July, 1918, p. 14.

[11]"The Cause of and Remedy for Race Riots," a *Messenger* editorial quoted in *Revolutionary Radicalism*, Vol. II, Pt. 1, p. 1479.

[12]*Messenger*, July, 1918, p. 14.

[13]Among the organizations enumerated as the financial supporters of the *Messenger* during 1922, were the New York Joint Board of the Amalgamated Clothing Workers, the International Ladies Garment Workers, New York Joint Board of Cloak Makers, the Workingmen's Circle, the Jewish *Daily Forward*, New York District Painters' Council, and the Marine Transport Workers (affiliated with the I. W. W.), *Messenger*, April, 1922, p. 390. See earlier editions for complimentary advertisements of liberal and radical unions.

gamated Clothing Workers covers only one industry, whereas the I. W. W. looked forward to organizing the workers in all branches of industry. In addition to the I. W. W.'s claim to wider industrial jurisdiction, its liberal attitude on the race question, combined with the *Messenger* radicals' naïve conviction that the world was at that time moving toward industrial unionism, caused them to place their faith in the I. W. W. not only as the embryo of a new social order, but as the possible formidable rival to the American Federation of Labor.[14] And the "proletarian" zeal that had stimulated the insurgency within the labor movement during the nineties, and which now seemed destined to force the rebuilding of unionism on some basis other than that of trade autonomy and the neglect of those workers traditionally viewed as unorganizable, now led the Negro radicals to vent much wrath upon the American Federation of Labor. "The dissolution of the American Federation of Labor," they contended, "would inure to the benefit of the labor movement in this country in particular and the international labor movement in general. It is organized upon unsound principles. It holds that there can be a partnership between labor and capital. . . . It stands for pure and simple unionism as against industrial unionism. . . . The present American Federation of Labor is the most wicked machine for the propagation of race prejudice in the country."[15]

In 1918 when the conference between the Executive Council of the A. F. of L. and the committee[16] of Negro leaders headed by Eugene Kinckle Jones of the National Urban League failed to bring about positive measures for organizing the Negro, the radicals became convinced of the inherent weakness of craft unionism and therefore confirmed in their opposition to the Federation. One cannot be certain, however, as to which of the two elements—the philosophy of class-conscious unionism or militant race psychology—was the determining cause of the opposition. Perhaps one was as basic a motive as the other, since they levelled their criticisms not only against the Federation but against the Negro representatives to the conference. In describing the activity of the Negro representatives they pointed out that:

> . . . the dominating influences . . . were Robert Russa Moton, Emmett J. Scott, Eugene Kinckle Jones . . . George E. Haynes and a few other Negroes of similar type. Robert Russa Moton and Emmett Scott came from Tuskegee. On the trustee board of Tuskegee are Rosenwald, Rockefeller, Carnegie, and a long line of similarly wealthy persons. Eugene Kinckle Jones and George Haynes come from the Urban League. On its executive board are William G. Wilcox, E. R. A. Seligman, A. S. Frissell, Paul D. Cravath with such honorary members as William H. Taft, Chas. D. Hillis, Robert Russa Moton, along with John D. Rockefeller as a heavy financial contributor. . . . Such financiers as these and their associates are largely employers of labor. Their object is to get the greatest amount of work out of laborers—white

---

[14]*Messenger*, May-June, 1919, pp. 6 and 7.

[15]*Ibid.*, p. 7.

[16]See above, pp. 107–11, 142–43.

and black—for the lowest possible wages. . . . The point is that Rockefeller, Carnegie, Frissell, and Seligman do not hire people to work against their interests. Nor have they made any mistake in employing the Negro leaders named above. The financial interests that gave us the Ludlow massacre, Bayonne, Bisbee deportations and the like of white men because they had formed labor organizations . . . need to be looked at with suspicion when they begin to accord a helping hand to do for Negro laborers what they import thugs and gunmen to prevent white laborers from doing.[17]

These sentiments contained the sum and substance of the Negro radicals' often expressed dissatisfaction with the older Negro political and intellectual leaders who were either held to be tools of the capitalist class or ignorant as to modern political and economic problems. The logic which dictated their antipathy to the Negro representatives to the conference with A. F. of L. officials in particular, and to Negro leaders in general was an adaptation of Marxian economic determinism—a vulgar version of it, perhaps—to the race question. The use of such logic was the inevitable reaction from the convergence of militant race psychology and the ideology of proletarian class consciousness. And the Negro radicals applied this logic to the race question and to Negro leadership as relentlessly as they applied it to the labor movement.

The *Messenger* radicals were not content to remain mere critics of the labor movement or of the intellectuals who pointed the way to Negro economic advancement. They desired to construct the vehicle for reaching the goal. This took the form of several measures for promoting Negro economic welfare and for organizing Negro workers in unions.

Their first actual participation in the labor movement came in the autumn of 1917 when Owen and Randolph organized the United Brotherhood of Elevator and Switchboard Operators. After three weeks, the organization was reported to have had a membership of about 600 out of an approximate total of 10,000 Negro operators in New York.[18] The demands of the organization were the eight-hour day, weekly pay, and a minimum wage of $18 per week. To obtain these demands, Owen and Randolph, as organizers, counseled a strike and a drive for 8,000 members. The effectiveness of the proposed strike was thought to be assured by the general scarcity of labor due to the war, the labor demands of the munition factories, the cessation of immigration, and the fact that the Negro elevator operators held a monopoly of the jobs in New York and Brooklyn.[19] But the strike did not materialize. The *Messenger* radicals soon lost interest. And the operators affiliated with the American Federation of Labor as the Elevator Operators' and Starters' Union, Local 16,030. After this nothing more was heard of the organization. Subsequently Owen and Randolph proclaimed

[17]*Messenger*, July, 1918, p. 20. For Roger Baldwin's criticism of the editor's analysis, see *Messenger*, Aug., 1921, p. 229.

[18]*Messenger*, Nov., 1917, pp. 14 and 20.

[19]*Ibid.*

the time "ripe for a great mass movement among Negroes" which should assume the form of "labor unions, farmers' protective unions, coöperative business, and socialism."[20] When the National Brotherhood Workers of America[21] was organized at Washington in the spring of 1919, it seemed that this prophecy was about to be fulfilled. According to one of the originators, R. T. Sims, the Brotherhood welcomed the association of the *Messenger* radicals because of a general belief in their intellectual qualifications for dealing with questions affecting labor and race relations. The desirability of their fellowship was further enhanced by the fact that coöperation with some established magazine as a means for quickly popularizing the new organization and, thereby, augmenting its membership was felt to be imperative. Owen and Randolph were elected to the general executive council, and their magazine became the official organ of the Brotherhood Workers. The resolutions adopted by the first convention calling for organization of every Negro into industrial, labor, or trade unions in all skilled and unskilled occupations,[22] are suggestive of the Negro radicals' influence. Other resolutions dealing with Mexican intervention, the Russian blockade, class war prisoners, and the coöperative movement were no doubt initiated by them. But this was the height of their influence. The magazine was never effective in increasing the desired membership. Randolph and Owen were accused of being more interested in the financial support of their magazine than[23] in building an economic organization. Apparently, when the infant organization revealed that its own need for financial succor was greater than its capacity to give it, the *Messenger* editors and the Brotherhood parted company long before the natural death of the organization some time in 1921.

In May, 1920, the radicals launched the Friends of Negro Freedom.[24] This was to be a national organization of local branches throughout the country. The purpose of the Friends was the unionization of the Negro migrant, the protection of Negro tenants, the advancement of coöperation, and the organization of forums for publicly educating the masses.[25] A novel feature of the organization was the plan to fight racial discrimination with the boycott. Only a few isolated locals were set up, and the Friends enjoyed a paper existence for about three years. About the same time that the Friends of Negro Freedom was initiated, the National Association for the Promotion of Labor Unionism among Negroes was conceived. Owen was president and Randolph, secretary. The advisory board comprised such prominent white labor radicals and intellectuals as Joseph D. Cannon, Joseph Baskin, Charles W. Erwin, Edward F.

[20]*Ibid.*, May-June, 1919, p. 8.

[21]See discussion of the National Brotherhood Workers of America in Chapter VI, pp. 117–19.

[22]*Messenger*, Dec., 1919, pp. 17–19.

[23]Correspondence with R. T. Sims.

[24]*Messenger*, April-May, 1920, p. 4.

[25]*Ibid.*, Feb., 1923, p. 529.

Cassidy, M. Feinstone, Julius Gerber, Morris Hillquit, James H. Maurer, Andrew Weiners, Max Pine, Joseph Schlossberg, Rose Schneidermann, and A. J. Shiplacoff.[26] From the available records,[27] it seems that the National Association soon ceased to function after Randolph and Owen's futile attempt to organize the Negro laundry workers and a branch of the Journeymen Bakers' and Confectioners' International Union.[28]

Finally, in 1923, the *Messenger* declared that "while out of the unions, Negroes complain against the bar erected by certain unions . . . after they join the unions, they still complain about race prejudice within the unions. Still there is no machinery which can be set in motion either to get the Negroes in the unions . . . or to see that those who are in get justice both from the point of view of getting jobs in their trade and being elected officials in their unions. Thus to the end of creating and stimulating in the Negro worker a larger, more active and substantial interest in the principles, policies, and tactics of the labor movement in general . . . an organization known as the United Negro Trades should be formed. . . ." The United Negro Trades was to function in the Negro's behalf just as the United Hebrew Trades and the Italian Chamber of Labor functioned in behalf of the Jewish and Italian workers, respectively.[29] Obviously, the United Negro Trades was patterned after the National Brotherhood Workers. The only difference between the two organizations was that the United Negro Trades was more ephemeral than the Brotherhood.

Those to whom *Messenger* radicalism had signified a sort of new Negro dispensation[30] were disillusioned when in 1924 the *Messenger*, because of accumulated financial reverses, ceased to function as the organ of "scientific radicalism" and became the "World's Greatest Negro Monthly." But the editors had shown earlier symptoms of retreat. Although Randolph ran for secretary of state of the state of New York on the American Labor party's[31] ticket in 1922, it was evident that economic radicalism was then on the verge of bankruptcy. In the summer of 1922 the *Messenger* had led a fight for the deportation of Marcus Garvey as an undesirable alien. The controversy degenerated into a fight between West Indian and American Negroes, causing William Domingo, himself a West Indian, to resign from the editorial board. Cyril Briggs[32] and Richard Moore, never on the editorial board but supporters of *Messenger* radicalism, had become hostile in view of their affiliation with the Communist party of America. Shortly afterward Owen shifted his scene of activity to

[26]*Ibid.*, Aug., 1920, p. 62.

[27]The *Messenger* was notoriously irregular in publication. Only incomplete files are available.

[28]*Messenger*, Sept., 1920, p. 95.

[29]*Messenger*, July, 1923, p. 757.

[30]See, for example, Mary White Ovington's letter to the editors, *Messenger*, July, 1918, p. 14.

[31]A short-lived coalition of socialists and progressive trade Unionists. See *Messenger*, Oct., 1922, p. 497. Also the *American Labor Year Book*, 1919–1920, p. 2021.

[32]Briggs originated the African Blood Brotherhood before his affiliation with the communists. See Abram L. Harris, "The Negro Problem as Viewed by Negro Leaders," *Current History*, June, 1923.

Chicago, although he did not relinquish his rights in the magazine. During 1925 and 1926 the Brotherhood of Sleeping Car Porters was formed and Randolph was chosen general organizer. And the *Messenger*, now purged of its radicalism, became, under the "Menckenian" editorship of George Schuyler, the official journal of the porters' union until the organization was no longer financially able to support it. Under the necessity of hewing close to trade-union strategy in organizing the porters, Randolph forgot his social radicalism. The despised American Federation of Labor which the *Messenger* editors had once condemned for its ineptitude, was now courted by Randolph with the hope of having the Federation charter the Brotherhood of Porters as one of its independent national unions. Randolph's indecisive strategy in the organization of the porters and his over-weaning ambition to play the role of scholar, economist, journalist, race leader, and union organizer all in one are suggestive of the shortcomings of economic radicalism five years after its complete abandonment. One is prompted to ask: Were the economic radicals a sport phenomenon, the momentary efflorescence of Negro unrest?[33] Or, were they sincere adherents to the philosophy of class struggle, who, despite their belief in the revolutionary dissolution of capitalism as a prerequisite to complete realization of their ideals, attempted to direct Negro unrest into channels of constructive economic reforms?

The obstacles which economic radicalism had to overcome in order to gain some acceptance in Negro life were: (1) the Negro's orthodox religious traditions; (2) the growing prevalence of Negro middle-class ideology;[34] and (3) racial antagonism between white and black workers.

To overcome the influence of religion was in itself a task of huge proportions. In attacking the question the radicals accused the Negro church of failing to educate the people. They said: "the church must become an open educational forum where problems of hygiene, labor, government, racial relationships, etc., are discussed. . . . The Negro ministry must get education of information instead of education of inspiration. It needs less Bible and more economics, history, sociology and physical science."[35]

Such criticism of the church did not necessarily run counter to the Negro's faith in orthodox religion. As a matter of fact large sections of the Negro popu-

---

[33]A strong evidence of this unrest and the Negro economic radical's part in it is contained in the Lusk Commission's Report on Seditious Activities, to wit: "The most interesting as well as one of the most important features of radical and revolutionary propaganda is the appeal made to those elements of our population that have a just cause of complaint with the treatment they have received in this country. . . . In recent years opportunity for employment in industry has induced large numbers of Negroes to come to this state [New York] from the South as well as from the West Indies. While in general the Negro in New York State has been treated well, the treatment accorded him in many parts of the country has engendered a spirit of resentment which has been capitalized by agents and agitators of the Socialist Party of America, the I. W. W. and other radical groups." *Revolutionary Radicalism*, Vol. II, Pt. 1, p. 1476.

[34]For discussion, see pp. 50–52, 424–25, 431, 465–67.

[35]*Messenger*, Oct., 1919, p. 6.

lation were becoming responsive to this type of attack because of resentment against economic and social disadvantages and because of the complacence of the church in the face of these disadvantages. One can, therefore, easily dismiss the viewpoint advanced by Dr. George E. Haynes[36] that the *Messenger* radicals' attack upon the Negro church and the Negro leaders weakened their influence, especially when similar attacks by Marcus Garvey only served to augment his following. Yet few Negroes were then or are today tolerant of atheism. In an editorial on Thanksgiving the *Messenger*, declared: "We do not thank God for anything nor do our thanks include gratitude for which most persons usually give thanks at this period. With us we are thankful for different things and to a different Deity. Our Deity is the toiling masses of the world and the things for which we thank are their achievement." They were thankful for the Russian, German, Austrian, and Bulgarian Revolutions; for world unrest, labor solidarity, the "relegation of trade unionism," and the rise of industrial unionism; for the "New Crowd Negro" who was taking his place in socialist politics; and "for the speedy on-coming of the new order of society in which Thanksgiving will be relieved of its cynicism and hypocrisy—when people may be thankful every day in the year."[37]

The attempt to combine religious radicalism with their radical economic philosophy, rather than their mild attack on the social shortcomings of the Negro church was most potent among the factors responsible for their failure, for any Negro movement which rests upon a social theory strongly tinged with atheism is not likely to receive large support from Negroes. While the economic radicals' atheism ran counter to the Negro's religious traditions, their advocacy of proletarian class consciousness and labor solidarity could hardly strike a responsive chord among new industrial workers whose experience seemed to contradict the doctrine of identical interest between themselves and the white workers. As put by W. E. B. Du Bois: "Theoretically we are a part of the world proletariat in the sense that we are mainly an exploited class of cheap laborers; but practically we are not a part of the white proletariat and are not recognized by that proletariat to any great extent. We are the victims of their physical oppression, social ostracism, economic exclusion, and personal hatred; and when in self defense we seek sheer subsistence we are howled down as scabs."[38]

Race prejudice has inhibited effective coöperation of Negroes and whites in the industrial world. To escape economic circumscription imposed by race feeling, the Negro has cultivated the good graces of those in whom the power of the disposal of opportunity lies. The more fortunate among the Negro have entered the professions and self-employment. Today it is generally assumed that: (1) Negro material welfare rests upon the establishment of business enterprise as the basis of a sort of self-contained economy furnishing jobs to Negroes

[36]George E. Haynes, *The Trend of the Races* (1922), p. 14, footnote 1.

[37]*Messenger*, Dec., 1919, p. 4.

[38]*Crisis*, Aug., 1921, p. 151.

and erecting a Negro middle-class; (2) the benefactions of wealthy philanthropists will continue; and (3) the Negro masses' traditional allegiance to the
employing and financially dominant classes will be maintained. To expect a
people who have such a background and who have been chiefly employed in
agriculture and domestic service to embrace social radicalism when white
workers with older industrial traditions have not, is to expect the miraculous.
Because of economic and political unrest a people inured to conservatism and
habituated to servility might willingly adopt a militant and race-conscious
leadership dedicated to the acquisition of their political rights and the protection of their civil liberties. They are not likely to give lasting support to a form
of leadership which predicates betterment upon the reorganization of industrial
society.

Another outstanding weakness of *Messenger* radicalism was the attempt of
the leaders to combine socialist propaganda with racial journalism and practical economic reform. It is evident that many of their reforms would have
ameliorated some of the Negro's industrial problems. But as reformers they
subordinated constructive planning and management to socialist propaganda
and racial protest which, though often degenerating into mere vituperation,[39]
contained much valid criticism of social politics. Upon the death of one reform
they conjured up another. They could initiate movements but lacked the
power of sustaining them. This dismayed their friends and convinced their opponents of their instability. This was their undoing.

The fact that the soil necessary to the growth of economic radicalism was
lacking among Negro workers, and indeed among white workers as well,
seemed never to have occurred to Owen and Randolph. Only one[40] of the economic radicals expressed an appreciation of the resistance that the Negro's cultural background set up against socialism. Owen and Randolph's failure to see
it explains their failure to see the futility of Marxian propaganda in Negro life.
But this disability was not peculiar to the Negro exponents of socialism. It has
been one of the outstanding shortcomings of American socialism in general.
American socialists have just begun to realize that their doctrines were foreign
importations which did not interpret American conditions.

[39]For example, see attacks on Negro leaders, *Messenger*, Jan., 1918, p. 23; July, 1918, pp. 8 and 28;
March, 1919, p. 23; and Sept., 1919, p. 9.

[40]W. A. Domingo. See his "Socialism Imperilled, or the Negro—a Potential Menace to American
Radicalism." Quoted in *Revolutionary Radicalism*, Vol. II, Pt. 1, p. 1494.

Zora Neale Hurston
The Gilded Six-Bits

It was a Negro yard around a Negro house in a Negro settlement that looked to the payroll of the G and G Fertilizer works for its support.

But there was something happy about the place. The front yard was parted in the middle by a sidewalk from gate to door-step, a sidewalk edged on either side by quart bottles driven neck down into the ground on a slant. A mess of homey flowers planted without a plan but blooming cheerily from their helter-skelter places. The fence and house were whitewashed. The porch and steps scrubbed white.

The front door stood open to the sunshine so that the floor of the front room could finish drying after its weekly scouring. It was Saturday. Everything clean from the front gate to the privy house. Yard raked so that the strokes of the rake would make a pattern. Fresh newspaper cut in fancy edge on the kitchen shelves.

Missie May was bathing herself in the galvanized washtub in the bedroom. Her dark-brown skin glistened under the soapsuds that skittered down from her wash rag. Her stiff young breasts thrust forward aggressively like broad-based cones with the tips lacquered in black.

She heard men's voices in the distance and glanced at the dollar clock on the dresser.

"Humph! Ah'm way behind time t'day! Joe gointer be heah 'fore Ah git mah clothes on if Ah don't make haste."

She grabbed the clean meal sack at hand and dried herself hurriedly and began to dress. But before she could tie her slippers, there came the ring of singing metal on wood. Nine times.

Missie May grinned with delight. She had not seen the big tall man come stealing in the gate and creep up the walk grinning happily at the joyful mischief he was about to commit. But she knew that it was her husband throwing silver dollars in the door for her to pick up and pile beside her plate at dinner. It was this way every Saturday afternoon. The nine dollars hurled into the open door, he scurried to a hiding place behind the cape jasmine bush and waited.

Missie May promptly appeared at the door in mock alarm.

"Who dat chunkin' money in mah do'way?" She demanded. No answer from the yard. She leaped off the porch and began to search the shrubbery.

She peeped under the porch and hung over the gate to look up and down the road. While she did this, the man behind the jasmine darted to the chinaberry tree. She spied him and gave chase.

"Nobody ain't gointer be chuckin' money at me and Ah not do 'em nothin'," she shouted in mock anger. He ran around the house with Missie May at his heels. She overtook him at the kitchen door. He ran inside but could not close it after him before she crowded in and locked with him in a rough and tumble. For several minutes the two were a furious mass of male and female energy. Shouting, laughing, twisting, turning, tussling, tickling each other in the ribs; Missie May clutching onto Joe and Joe trying, but not too hard, to get away.

"Missie May, take yo' hand out mah pocket!" Joe shouted out between laughs.

"Ah ain't, Joe, not lessen you gwine gimme whateve' it is good you got in yo' pocket. Turn it go, Joe, do Ah'll tear yo' clothes."

"Go on tear 'em. You de one dat pushes de needles round heah. Move yo' hand Missie May."

"Lemme git dat paper sack out yo' pocket. Ah bet its candy kisses."

"Tain't. Move yo' hand. Woman ain't go no business in a man's clothes nohow. Go way."

Missie May gouged way down and gave an upward jerk and triumphed.

"Unhhunh! Ah got it. It 'tis so candy kisses. Ah knowed you had somethin' for me in yo' clothes. Now Ah got to see whut's in every pocket you got."

Joe smiled indulgently and let his wife go through all of his pockets and take out the things that he had hidden there for her to find. She bore off the chewing gum, the cake of sweet soap, the pocket handkerchief as if she had wrested them from him, as if they had not been bought for the sake of this friendly battle.

"Whew! dat play-fight done got me all warmed up." Joe exclaimed. "Got me some water in de kittle?"

"Yo' water is on de fire and yo' clean things is cross de bed. Hurry up and wash yo'self and git changed so we kin eat. Ah'm hongry." As Missie said this, she bore the steaming kettle into the bedroom.

"You ain't hongry, sugar," Joe contradicted her. "Youse jes' a little empty. Ah'm de one whut's hongry. Ah could eat up camp meetin', back off 'ssociation, and drink Jurdan dry. Have it on de table when Ah git out de tub."

"Don't you mess wid mah business, man. You git in yo' clothes. Ah'm a real wife, not no dress and breath. Ah might not look lak one, but if you burn me, you won't git a thing but wife ashes."

Joe splashed in the bedroom and Missie May fanned around in the kitchen. A fresh red and white checked cloth on the table. Big pitcher of buttermilk beaded with pale drops of butter from the churn. Hot fried mullet, crackling bread, ham hock atop a mound of string beans and new potatoes, and perched on the window-sill a pone of spicy potato pudding.

Very little talk during the meal but that little consisted of banter that pretended to deny affection but in reality flaunted it. Like when Missie May reached for a second helping of the tater pone. Joe snatched it out of her reach.

After Missie May had made two or three unsuccessful grabs at the pan, she begged, "Aw, Joe gimme some mo' dat tater pone."

"Nope, sweetenin' is for us men-folks. Y'all pritty lil frail eels don't need nothin 'lak dis. You too sweet already."

"Please, Joe."

"Naw, naw. Ah don't want you to git no sweeter than whut you is already. We goin' down de road a lil piece t'night so you go put on yo' Sunday-go-to-meetin' things."

Missie May looked at her husband to see if he was playing some prank. "Sho nuff, Joe?"

"Yeah. We goin' to de ice cream parlor."

"Where de ice cream parlor at, Joe?"

"A new man done come heah from Chicago and he done got a place and took and opened it up for a ice cream parlor, and bein' as it's real swell, Ah wants you to be one de first ladies to walk in dere and have some set down."

"Do Jesus, Ah ain't knowed nothin' 'bout it. Who de man done it?"

"Mister Otis D. Slemmons, of spots and places—Memphis, Chicago, Jacksonville, Philadelphia and so on."

"Dat heavy-set man wid his mouth full of gold teethes?"

"Yeah. Where did you see 'im at?"

"Ah went down to de sto' tuh git a box of lye and Ah seen 'im standin' on de corner talkin' to some of de mens, and Ah come on back and went to scrubbin' de floor, and he passed and tipped his hat whilst Ah was scourin' de steps. Ah thought Ah never seen *him* befo'."

Joe smiled pleasantly. "Yeah, he's up to date. He got de finest clothes Ah ever seen on a colored man's back."

"Aw, he don't look no better in his clothes than you do in yourn. He got a puzzlegut on 'im and he so chuckle-headed, he got a pone behind his neck."

Joe looked down at his own abdomen and said wistfully, "Wisht Ah had a build on me lak he got. He ain't puzzle-gutted, honey. He jes' got a corperation. Dat make 'm look lak a rich white man. All rich mens is got some belly on 'em."

"Ah seen de pitchers of Henry Ford and he's a spare-built man and Rockefeller look lak he ain't got but one gut. But Ford and Rockefeller and dis Slemmons and all de rest kin be as many-gutted as dey please, Ah'm satisfied wid you jes' lak you is, baby. God took pattern after a pine tree and built you noble. Youse a pritty man, and if Ah knowed any way to make you mo' pritty still Ah'd take and do it."

Joe reached over gently and toyed with Missie May's ear. "You jes' say dat cause you love me, but Ah know Ah can't hold no light to Otis D. Slemmons. Ah ain't never been nowhere and Ah ain't got nothin' but you."

Missie May got on his lap and kissed him and he kissed back in kind. Then he went on. "All de womens is crazy 'bout 'im everywhere he go."

"How you know dat, Joe?"

"He tole us so hisself."

"Dat don't make it so. His mouf is cut cross-ways, ain't it? Well, he kin lie jes' lak anybody else."

"Good Lawd, Missie! You womens sho is hard to sense into things. He's got a five-dollar gold piece for a stick-pin and he got a ten-dollar gold piece on his watch chain and his mouf is jes' crammed full of gold teethes. Sho wisht it wuz mine. And whut make it so cool, he got money 'cumulated. And womens give it all to 'im."

"Ah don't see whut de womens see on 'im. Ah wouldn't give 'im a wink if de sheriff wuz after 'im."

"Well, he tole us how de white womens in Chicago give 'im all dat gold money. So he don't 'low nobody to touch it at all. Not even put dey finger on it. Dey tole 'im not to. You kin make 'miration at it, but don't tetch it."

"Whyn't he stay up dere where dey so crazy 'bout 'im?"

"Ah reckon dey done made 'im vast-rich and he wants to travel some. He say dey wouldn't leave 'im hit a lick of work. He got mo' lady people crazy 'bout him than he kin shake a stick at."

"Joe, Ah hates to see you so dumb. Dat stray nigger jes' tell y'all anything and y'all b'lieve it."

"Go 'head on now, honey and put on yo' clothes. He talkin' 'bout his pritty womens—Ah want 'im to see *mine.*"

Missie May went off to dress and Joe spent the time trying to make his stomach punch out like Slemmons' middle. He tried the rolling swagger of the stranger, but found that his tall bone-and-muscle stride fitted ill with it. He just had time to drop back into his seat before Missie May came in dressed to go.

On the way home that night Joe was exultant. "Didn't Ah say ole Otis was swell? Can't he talk Chicago talk? Wuzn't dat funny whut he said when great big fat ole Ida Armstrong come in? He asted me, 'Who is dat broad wid de forte shake?' Dat's a new word. Us always thought forty was a set of figgers but he showed us where it means a whole heap of things. Sometimes he don't say forty, he jes' say thirty-eight and two and dat mean de same thing. Know whut he tole me when Ah wuz payin' for our ice cream? He say, 'Ah have to hand it to you, Joe. Dat wife of yours is jes' thirty-eight and two. Yessuh, she's forte!' Ain't he killin'?"

"He'll do in case of a rush. But he sho is got uh heap uh gold on 'im. Dat's de first time Ah ever seed gold money. It lookted good on him sho nuff, but it'd look a whole heap better on you."

"Who, me? Missie May youse crazy! Where would a po' man lak me git gold money from?"

Missie May was silent for a minute, then she said, "Us might find some goin' long de road some time. Us could."

"Who would be losin' gold money round heah? We ain't even seen none dese white folks wearin' no gold money on dey watch chain. You must be figgerin' Mister Packard or Mister Cadillac goin' pass through heah."

"You don't know whut been lost 'round heah. Maybe somebody way back in memorial times lost they gold money and went on off and it ain't never been found. And then if we wuz to find it, you could wear some 'thout havin' no gang of womens lak dat Slemmons say he got."

Joe laughed and hugged her. "Don't be so wishful 'bout me. Ah'm satisfied de way Ah is. So long as Ah be yo' husband, Ah don't keer 'bout nothin' else. Ah'd ruther all de other womens in de world to be dead than for you to have de toothache. Less we go to bed and git our night rest."

It was Saturday night once more before Joe could parade his wife in Slemmons' ice cream parlor again. He worked the night shift and Saturday was his only night off. Every other evening around six o'clock he left home, and dying dawn saw him hustling home around the lake where the challenging sun flung a flaming sword from east to west across the trembling water.

That was the best part of life—going home to Missie May. Their whitewashed house, the mock battle on Saturday, the dinner and ice cream parlor afterwards, church on Sunday nights when Missie outdressed any woman in town—all, everything was right.

One night around eleven the acid ran out at the G. and G. The foreman knocked off the crew and let the steam die down. As Joe rounded the lake on his way home, a lean moon rode the lake in a silver boat. If anybody had asked Joe about the moon on the lake, he would have said he hadn't paid it any attention. But he saw it with his feelings. It made him yearn painfully for Missie. Creation obsessed him. He thought about children. They had been married for more than a year now. They had money put away. They ought to be making little feet for shoes. A little boy child would be about right.

He saw a dim light in the bedroom and decided to come in through the kitchen door. He could wash the fertilizer dust off himself before presenting himself to Missie May. It would be nice for her not to know that he was there until he slipped into his place in bed and hugged her back. She always liked that.

He eased the kitchen door open slowly and silently, but when he went to set his dinner bucket on the table he bumped it into a pile of dishes, and something crashed to the floor. He heard his wife gasp in fright and hurried to reassure her.

"Iss me, honey. Don't get skeered."

There was a quick, large movement in the bedroom. A rustle, a thud, and a stealthy silence. The light went out.

What? Robbers? Murderers? Some varmint attacking his helpless wife, perhaps. He struck a match, threw himself on guard and stepped over the door-sill into the bedroom.

The great belt on the wheel of Time slipped and eternity stood still. By the match light he could see the man's legs fighting with his breeches in his frantic desire to get them on. He had both chance and time to kill the intruder in his helpless condition—half in and half out of his pants—but he was too weak to take action. The shapeless enemies of humanity that live in the hours of Time had waylaid Joe. He was assaulted in his weakness. Like Samson awakening after his haircut. So he just opened his mouth and laughed.

The match went out and he struck another and lit the lamp. A howling wind raced across his heart, but underneath its fury he heard his wife sobbing and Slemmons pleading for his life. Offering to buy it with all that he had. "Please, suh, don't kill me. Sixty-two dollars at de sto'. Gold money."

Joe just stood. Slemmons looked at the window, but it was screened. Joe stood out like a rough-backed mountain between him and the door. Barring him from escape, from sunrise, from life.

He considered a surprise attack upon the big clown that stood there laughing like a chessy cat. But before his fist could travel an inch, Joe's own rushed out to crush him like a battering ram. Then Joe stood over him.

"Git into yo' damn rags, Slemmons, and dat quick."

Slemmons scrambled to his feet and into his vest and coat. As he grabbed his hat, Joe's fury overrode his intentions and he grabbed at Slemmons with his left hand and struck at him with his right. The right landed. The left grazed the front of his vest. Slemmons was knocked a somersault into the kitchen and fled through the open door. Joe found himself alone with Missie May, with the golden watch charm clutched in his left fist. A short bit of broken chain dangled between his fingers.

Missie May was sobbing. Wails of weeping without words. Joe stood, and after awhile he found out that he had something in his hand. And then he stood and felt without thinking and without seeing with his natural eyes. Missie May kept on crying and Joe kept on feeling so much and not knowing what to do with all his feelings, he put Slemmons' watch charm in his pants pocket and took a good laugh and went to bed.

"Missie May, whut you cryin' for?"

"Cause Ah love you so hard and Ah know you don't love *me* no mo'."

Joe sank his face into the pillow for a spell then he said huskily, "You don't know de feelings of dat yet, Missie May."

"Oh Joe, honey, he said he wuz gointer give me dat gold money and he jes' kept on after me—"

Joe was very still and silent for a long time. Then he said, "Well, don't cry no mo', Missie May. Ah got yo' gold piece for you."

The hours went past on their rusty ankles. Joe still and quiet on one bedrail and Missie May wrung dry of sobs on the other. Finally the sun's tide crept upon the shore of night and drowned all its hours. Missie May with her face stiff and streaked towards the window saw the dawn come into her yard. It was day. Nothing more. Joe wouldn't be coming home as usual. No need to fling open the front door and sweep off the porch, making it nice for Joe. Never no more breakfast to cook; no more washing and starching of Joe's jumper-jackets and pants. No more nothing. So why get up?

With this strange man in her bed, she felt embarrassed to get up and dress. She decided to wait till he had dressed and gone. Then she would get up, dress quickly and be gone forever beyond reach of Joe's looks and laughs. But he never moved. Red light turned to yellow, then white.

From beyond the no-man's land between them came a voice. A strange voice that yesterday had been Joe's.

"Missie May, ain't you gonna fix me no breakfus'?"

She sprang out of bed. "Yeah, Joe. Ah didn't reckon you wuz hongry."

No need to die today. Joe needed her for a few more minutes anyhow.

Soon there was a roaring fire in the cook stove. Water bucket full and two chickens killed. Joe loved fried chicken and rice. She didn't deserve a thing and good Joe was letting her cook him some breakfast. She rushed hot biscuits to the table as Joe took his seat.

He ate with his eyes on his plate. No laughter, no banter.

"Missie May, you ain't eatin' yo' breakfus'."

"Ah don't choose none, Ah thank yuh."

His coffee cup was empty. She sprang to refill it. When she turned from the stove and bent to set the cup beside Joe's plate, she saw the yellow coin on the table between them.

She slumped into her seat and wept into her arms.

Presently Joe said calmly, "Missie May, you cry too much. Don't look back lak Lot's wife and turn to salt."

The sun, the hero of every day, the impersonal old man that beams as brightly on death as on birth, came up every morning and raced across the blue dome and dipped into the sea of fire every evening. Water ran down hill and birds nested.

Missie knew why she didn't leave Joe. She couldn't. She loved him too much, but she could not understand why Joe didn't leave her. He was polite, even kind at times, but aloof.

There were no more Saturday romps. No ringing silver dollars to stack beside her plate. No pockets to rifle. In fact the yellow coin in his trousers was like a monster hiding in the cave of his pockets to destroy her.

She often wondered if he still had it, but nothing could have induced her to ask nor yet to explore his pockets to see for herself. Its shadow was in the house whether or no.

One night Joe came home around midnight and complained of pains in the back. He asked Missie to rub him down with liniment. It had been three months since Missie had touched his body and it all seemed strange. But she rubbed him. Grateful for the chance. Before morning, youth triumphed and Missie exulted. But the next day, as she joyfully made up their bed, beneath her pillow she found the piece of money with the bit of chain attached.

Alone to herself, she looked at the thing with loathing, but look she must. She took it into her hands with trembling and saw first thing that it was no gold piece. It was a gilded half dollar. Then she knew why Slemmons had forbidden anyone to touch his gold. He trusted village eyes at a distance not to recognize his stick-pin as a gilded quarter, and his watch charm as a four-bit piece.

She was glad at first that Joe had left it there. Perhaps he was through with her punishment. They were man and wife again. Then another thought came clawing at her. He had come home to buy from her as if she were any woman in the long house. Fifty cents for her love. As if to say that he could pay as well as Slemmons. She slid the coin into his Sunday pants pocket and dressed herself and left his house.

Halfway between her house and the quarters she met her husband's mother, and after a short talk she turned and went back home. Never would she admit defeat to that woman who prayed for it nightly. If she had not the substance of marriage she had the outside show. Joe must leave *her*. She let him see she didn't want his old gold four-bits too.

She saw no more of the coin for some time though she knew that Joe could not help finding it in his pocket. But his health kept poor, and he came home at least every ten days to be rubbed.

The sun swept around the horizon, trailing its robes of weeks and days. One morning as Joe came in from work, he found Missie May chopping wood. Without a word he took the ax and chopped a huge pile before he stopped.

"You ain't got no business choppin' wood, and you know it."

"How come? Ah been choppin' it for de last longest."

"Ah ain't blind. You makin' feet for shoes."

"Won't you be glad to have a lil baby chile, Joe?"

"You know dat 'thout astin' me."

"Iss gointer be a boy chile and de very spit of you." "You reckon, Missie May?"

"Who else could it look lak?"

Joe said nothing, but he thrust his hand deep into his pocket and fingered something there.

It was almost six months later Missie May took to bed and Joe went and got his mother to come wait on the house.

Missie May delivered a fine boy. Her travail was over when Joe came in from work one morning. His mother and the old women were drinking great bowls of coffee around the fire in the kitchen.

The minute Joe came into the room his mother called him aside.

"How did Missie May make out?" he asked quickly.

"Who, dat gal? She strong as a ox. She gointer have plenty mo'. We done fixed her wid de sugar and lard to sweeten her for de nex' one."

Joe stood silent awhile.

"You ain't ast 'bout de baby, Joe. You oughter be mighty proud cause he sho is de spittin' image of yuh, son. Dat's yourn all right, if you never git another one, dat un is yourn. And you know Ah'm mighty proud too, son, cause Ah never thought well of you marryin' Missie May cause her ma used tuh fan her foot round right smart and Ah been mighty skeered dat Missie May was gointer git misput on her road."

Joe said nothing. He fooled around the house till late in the day then just before he went to work, he went and stood at the foot of the bed and asked his wife how she felt. He did this every day during the week.

On Saturday he went to Orlando to make his market. It had been a long time since he had done that.

Meat and lard, meal and flour, soap and starch. Cans of corn and tomatoes. All the staples. He fooled around town for awhile and bought bananas and apples. Way after while he went around to the candy store.

"Hellow, Joe," the clerk greeted him. "Ain't seen you in a long time."

"Nope, Ah ain't been heah. Been round in spots and places."

"Want some of them molasses kisses you always buy?"

"Yessuh." He threw the gilded half dollar on the counter. "Will dat spend?"

"Whut is it, Joe? Well, I'll be doggone! A gold-plated four-bit piece. Where'd you git it, Joe?"

"Offen a stray nigger dat come through Eatonville. He had it on his watch chain for a charm—goin' round making out iss gold money. Ha ha! He had a quarter on his tie pin and it wuz all golded up too. Tryin' to fool people. Makin' out he so rich and everything. Ha! Ha! Tryin' to tole off folkses wives from home."

"How did you git it, Joe? Did he fool you, too?"

"Who, me? Naw suh! He ain't fooled me none. Know whut Ah done? He come round me wid his smart talk. Ah hauled off and knocked 'im down and took his old four-bits way from 'im. Gointer buy my wife some good ole lasses kisses wid it. Gimme fifty cents worth of dem candy kisses."

"Fifty cents buys a mighty lot of candy kisses, Joe. Why don't you split it up and take some chocolate bars, too. They eat good, too."

"Yessuh, dey do, but Ah wants all dat in kisses. Ah got a lil boy chile home now. Tain't a week old yet, but he kin suck a sugar tit and maybe eat one them kisses hisself."

Joe got his candy and left the store. The clerk turned to the next customer. "Wisht I could be like these darkies. Laughin' all the time. Nothin' worries 'em."

Back in Eatonville, Joe reached his own front door. There was the ring of singing metal on wood. Fifteen times. Missie May couldn't run to the door, but she crept there as quickly as she could.

"Joe Banks, Ah hear you chunkin' money in mah do'way. You wait till Ah got mah strength back and Ah'm gointer fix you for dat."

Mae V. Cowdery
Insatiate

If my love were meat and bread
And sweet cool wine to drink,
They would not be enough,
For I must have a finer table spread
To sate my entity.

If her lips were rubies red,
Her eyes two sapphires blue,
Her fingers ten sticks of white jade,
Coral tipped . . . and her hair of purple hue
Hung down in a silken shawl . . .
They would not be enough
To fill the coffers of my need.

If her thoughts were arrows
Ever speeding true
Into the core of my mind,
And her voice round notes of melody
No nightingale or lark
Could ever hope to sing . . .
Not even these would be enough
To keep my constancy.

But if my love did whisper
Her song into another's ear
Or place the tip of one pink nail
Upon another's hand,
Then would I forever be
A willing prisoner . . .
Chained to her side by uncertainty!

Lines to a Sophisticate

Never would I seek
To capture you with tempestuous ardor
Nor hold you at arm's length
In carnal anticipation. . . .
But like a wine of rare vintage
I would savor and sip slowly
That I might know each separate scent
Of your elusive fragrance.

Never would I seek to capture all your beauty
And imprison it in the mouldy bottle of my lust;
Rather would I pour it into the chalice of my love
And let its bouquet escape to mingle with the air
That I might breathe again your perfume
Long after you are gone. . . .

Part Five—Civil Rights and Black Power

Chester Himes
from *If He Hollers Let Him Go*

CHAPTER II

I WENT out to the garage, threw up the door, backed halfway out to the street on the starter, telling myself at the time I oughtn' to do it. I had a '42 Buick Roadmaster I'd bought four months ago, right after I'd gotten to be a leader-man, and every time I got behind the wheel and looked down over the broad, flat, mile-long hood I thought about how the rich white folks out in Beverly couldn't even buy a new car now and got a certain satisfaction. I straightened out and dug off with a jerk, turned the corner at forty, pushed it on up in the stretch on Fifty-fourth between San Pedro and Avalon, with my nerves tightening, telling me to take it slow before I got into a battle royal with some cracker motor-cycle cop, and my mind telling me to hell with them, I was a key man in a shipyard, as important as anybody now.

Homer and Conway were waiting in front of the drug-store at the corner of Fifty-fourth and Central.

'You're kinda tardy, playboy,' Homer said, climbing in beside Conway.

I turned the corner into Central and started digging. 'She wouldn't let me go,' I said.

'You mean you had that last dollar left,' Conway said.

I squeezed between a truck and an oncoming streetcar, almost brushing, and Homer said, 'See that. Now he's tryna kill us. He don't mind dying hisself, but why he got to kill you and me too?'

'Just like that safety man said, gambling thirty seconds against thirty years,' Conway said.

I pulled up in front of the hotel at Fifty-seventh and my other three riders, Smitty, Johnson and Pigmeat climbed in the back.

Before I started I turned to Pigmeat and said, 'I own some parts of you, don't I, buddy?'

'Get over, goddamnit!' Johnson snarled at Smitty in the back seat and pushed him. 'You want all the seat?'

'Don't call me no "buddy," man,' Pigmeat said to me. 'When I escaped from Mississippi I swore I'd lynch the first sonabitch that called me a "buddy".'

'There these niggers is fighting already,' Homer said, shaking his head. 'Whenever niggers gets together that's the first thing they gonna do.'

Smitty squirmed over to give Johnson more room. 'By God, here's a man wakes up evil every morning. Ain't just *some* mornings; this man wakes up evil *every* morning.' He looked around at Johnson. 'What's the matter with you, man, do your old lady beat you?'

Homer thought they were going to fight. He decided to be peacemaker. 'Now you know how Johnson is,' he said to Smitty. 'That's just his way. You know he don't mean no harm.'

As soon as Smitty found out somebody was ready to argue he began getting bad sure enough. 'How do I know how he is?' he shouted. 'Does he know how I is? Hell, everybody evil on Monday morning. I'm evil too. He ain't no eviler'n me.'

'Shut up!' Conway yelled. 'Bob's tryna say something.' Then he turned to me. 'Don't you know what a "buddy" is, Bob? A "buddy" drinks bilge water, eats crap, and runs rabbits. That's what a peckerwood means when he calls you "buddy".'

'I ain't kidding, fellow,' I told Pigmeat.

He started scratching for his wallet. 'Now that's a Senegalese for you,' he complained. 'Gonna put me out his car 'bout three lousy bucks. Whatcha gonna do with a fellow like that?' He passed me three ones.

'This is for last week,' I said, taking them. 'What about this week?'

'Aw, man, I'll give it to you Friday,' he grumbled. 'You raise more hell 'bout three lousy bucks——'

I mashed the starter and dug off without hearing the rest of it. Johnson had started beefing about the job, and now they all had it.

'How come it is we always got to get the hardest jobs?' Smitty asked. 'If somebody'd take a crap on deck Kelly'd come and get our gang to clean it up.'

'I been working in this yard two years—Bob'll tell you—and all I done yet is the jobs don't nobody else wanta do,' Conway said. 'I'm gonna quit this yard just as sure as I live and nothing don't happen and get me a job at Cal Ship.'

'They don't want you over there neither,' Pigmeat said.

'They don't even want a coloured man to go to the school here any more,' Homer put in. 'Bessie ask Kelly the other day 'bout going to school—she been here three months now—and he told her they still filled up. And a peck come right after—I was standing right there—and he signed him up right away.'

'You know they don't want no more nig—no more of us getting no mechanic's pay,' Pigmeat said. 'You know that in front. What she gotta do is keep on after him.'

'If I ever make up my mind to quit,' Johnson said, 'he the first sonabitch I'm gonna whup. I'm gonna whup his ass till it ropes like okra.'

Conway said, 'I ain't gonna let you. He mine. I been saving that red-faced peckerwood too long to give 'im up now. I'm gonna whip 'im till he puke; then I'm gonna let 'im get through puking; then I'm gonna light in on him and whip 'im till he poot....' He kept on as if it was getting good to him. 'Then I'm gonna let 'im get through pooting; then I'm gonna light in on 'im and whip 'im till he——' They were all laughing now.

'You can't whip him until you get him,' I called over my shoulder.

'You tell 'em, Bob,' Smitty said. 'We gonna see Kelly in a half-hour, then we gonna see what Conway do.'

'I ain't said I was gonna whip the man this morning,' Conway backtracked. 'I said when I *quit*—that's what I said.'

The red light caught me at Manchester; and that made me warm. It never failed; every time I got in a hurry I got caught by every light. I pulled up in the outside lane, abreast a V-8 and an Olds, shifted back to first, and got set to take the lead. When the light turned green it caught a white couple in the middle of the street. The V-8 full of white guys dug off and they started to run for it; and the two white guys in the Olds blasted at them with the horn, making them jump like grasshoppers. But when they looked up and saw we were coloured they just took their time, giving us a look of cold hatred.

I let out the clutch and stepped on the gas. Goddamn 'em, I'll grind 'em into the street, I thought. But just before I hit them something held me. I tamped the brake.

'What the hell!' Johnson snarled, picking himself up off the floor.

I sat there looking at the white couple until they had crossed the sidewalk, giving them stare for stare, hate for hate. Horns blasted me from behind, guys in the middle lanes looked at me as they passed; but all I could see was two pecks who didn't hate me no more than I hated them. Finally I went ahead, just missed sideswiping a new Packard Clipper. My arms were rubbery and my fingers numb; I was weak as if I'd been heaving sacks of cement all day in the sun.

After that everything got under my skin. I was coming up fast in the middle lane and some white guy in a Nash coupé cut out in front of me without signalling. I had to burn rubber to keep from taking off his fender; and the car behind me tapped my bumper. I didn't know whether he had looked in the rearview mirror before he pulled out or not, but I knew if he had, he could have seen we were a carful of coloured—and that's the way I took it. I kept on his tail until I could pull up beside him, then I leaned out the window and shouted, 'This ain't Alabama, you peckerwood son of a bitch. When you want to pull out of line, stick out your hand.'

He gave me a quick glance, then looked straight ahead. After that he ignored me. That made me madder than if he'd talked back. I stuck with him clear out to Compton. A dozen times I had a chance to bump him into an oncoming truck. Then I began feeling virtuous and let him go.

But at the entrance to the Shell Refinery the white cop directing traffic caught sight of us and stopped me on a dime. The white workers crossing the street looked at the big new car full of black faces and gave off cold hostility. I gave them look for look.

'What's the matter with these pecks this morning?' Homer said. 'Is everybody evil?'

By now it was a quarter of eight. It was twelve miles to the yard. I gritted my teeth and started digging again; I swore the next person who tried to stop me I'd run him down. But traffic on all harbour roads was heavy the whole day through, and during the change of shifts at the numerous refineries and ship-yards it was mad, fast, and furious.

It was a bright June morning. The sun was already high. If I'd been a white boy I might have enjoyed the scramble in the early morning sun, the tight competition for a twenty-foot lead on a thirty-mile highway. But to me it was racial. The huge industrial plants flanking the ribbon of road—shipyards, re-fineries, oil wells, steel mills, construction companies—the thousands of rush-ing workers, the low-hanging barrage balloons, the close hard roar of Diesel trucks and the distant drone of patrolling planes, the sharp, pungent smell of exhaust that used to send me driving clear across Ohio on a sunny summer morning, and the snow-capped mountains in the background, like picture post-cards, didn't mean a thing to me. I didn't even see them; all I wanted in the world was to push my Buick Roadmaster over some peckerwood's face.

Time and again I cut in front of some fast-moving car, making rubber burn and brakes scream and drivers curse, hoping a paddy would bump my fender so I'd have an excuse to get out and clip him with my tyre iron. My eyes felt red and sticky and my mouth tasted brown. I turned into the tightly patrolled har-bour road, doing a defiant fifty.

Conway said at large, 'Oh, Bob's got plenny money, got just too much money. He don't mind paying a fine.'

Nobody answered him. By now we were all too evil to do much talking. We came into the stretch of shipyards—Consolidated, Bethlehem, Western Pipe and Steel—caught an open mile, and I went up to sixty. White guys looked at us queerly as we went by. We didn't get stopped but we didn't make it. It was five after eight when we pulled into the parking lot at Atlas Ship. I found a spot and parked and we scrambled out, nervous because we were late, and belligerent because we didn't want anybody to say anything about it.

The parking-lot attendant waited until I had finished locking the car, then came over and told me I had to move, I'd parked in the place reserved for com-pany officials. I looked at him with a cold, dead fury, too spent even to hit him. I let my breath out slowly, got back into the car, and moved it. The other fel-lows had gone into the yard. I had to stop at Gate No. 2 to get a late card.

The gatekeeper said, 'Jesus Christ, all you coloured boys are late this morning.'

A guard standing near by leered at me. 'What'd y'all do las' night, boy? I bet y'all had a ball down on Central Avenue.'

I started to tell him I was up all night with his mother, but I didn't feel up to the trouble. I punched my card without giving a sign that I had heard. Then I cut across the yard to the outfitting dock. We were working on a repair ship—it was called a floating dry dock—for the Navy. My gang was installing the ventilation in the shower compartment and the heads, as the toilets were called.

At the entrance to the dock the guard said, 'Put out that cigarette, boy. What's the matter you coloured boys can't never obey no rules?'

I tossed it over on the wooden craneway, still burning. He muttered some-thing as he went over to step on it.

The white folks had sure brought their white to work with them that morning.

CHAPTER III

I CLIMBED the outside wooden gangway from the dock and went aboard through the gangway port, an accommodation opening in the shell that put me on the third of the five decks. The compartment I entered was the machine shop; forward was the carpenter shop; aft were the various lockers, toolrooms, storerooms, and such, and finally the third-deck showers and latrine—all a part of the ship itself—where my gang was working.

The decks were low, and with the tools and equipment of the workers, the thousand and one lines of the welders, the chippers, the blowers, the burners, the light lines, the wooden staging, combined with the equipment of the ship, the shapes and plates, the ventilation trunks and ducts, reducers, dividers, transformers, the machines, lathes, mills, and such, half yet to be installed, the place looked like a littered madhouse. I had to pick every step to find a foot-size clearance of deck space, and at the same time to keep looking up so I wouldn't tear off an ear or knock out an eye against some overhanging shape. Every two or three steps I'd bump into another worker. The only time anybody ever apologized was when they knocked you down.

Bessie, one of the helpers in my gang, met me at the midship bulkhead with the time cards.

'Are you evil too?' she greeted.

'Not at you, beautiful,' I grimaced.

All I knew about her was that she was brown-skinned, straightened-haired, and medium-sized; she wore a hard hat, clean cotton waists, blue denim slacks, and a brown sweater. I'd never looked at her any closer.

'You folks got me almost scared to come to work,' she was saying.

I ducked through the access opening without answering, came to a manhole, went down a jack ladder to the second deck, threaded through a maze of shapes to the sheet-metal toolroom. The Kelly that Conway had been whipping in the car was our supervisor. He was a thin, wiry, nervous Irishman with a blood-red, beaked face and close-set bright blue eyes. He had fought like hell to keep me from being made a leaderman, and we never had too much to say to each other.

I tossed the cards on the desk before the clerk with the late cards on top. She picked them up without saying anything. Kelly looked up from a blueprint he was studying with Chuck, a white leaderman, and his face got redder. He turned back to the print without saying anything, and I turned to go out. He had given me enough jobs to last my gang another week and I didn't see any need to say anything to him either. But before I got out he stopped me.

'How's that coloured gang of yours coming along, Bob?'

It was a moment before I turned around. I had to decide first whether to tell him to go to hell or not. Finally I said, 'Fine, Kelly, fine! My coloured gang is coming along fine.' I started to ask him how were the white gangs coming along, but I caught myself in time.

'You coloured boys make good workers when you learn how,' he said. 'I ain't got no fault to find with you at all.'

Chuck gave me a sympathetic grin.

'Now that's fine,' I said. I opened my mouth to say, 'What do you think about the way we're blasting at Ireland?' but I didn't say it.

I turned to the crib girl and said, 'Let me have S-14.'

She was a fat, ducky, blue-eyed farm girl with round red cheeks and brownish hair. She widened her eyes with an inquiring look. 'What's that?'

'A print.'

'What's a print?' she asked.

She hadn't been on the job very long so I said patiently, 'A print is a blueprint. They're in that cabinet there. You have the key. Will you unlock the cabinet and give me the print—the blueprint—marked S-14?'

She unlocked the cabinet reluctantly, giving quick side glances at Kelly to see if he'd say anything, and when she saw that S-14 was marked 'Not to be taken from office,' she turned to Kelly and asked, 'Can he see this?'

My head began heating up again. Kelly looked up and nodded. She took down the print and handed it to me. 'You'll have to look at it here,' she said.

All the leadermen took out prints. I wanted to explain it to her, knowing that she was new on the job. But she had tried my patience, so I said, 'Listen, little girl, don't annoy me this morning.'

She looked inquiringly at Kelly again, but he didn't look up. I walked out with the print. She called, 'Hey!' indecisively, but I didn't look around.

A white helper was soldering a seam in a trunk while a white mechanic looked on. The mechanic and I had been in the department together for the past two years, but we had never spoken. He looked at me as I passed, I looked at him; we kept the record straight. I went up the jack ladder and came out on the third deck again.

There were a lot of women workers on board, mostly white. Whenever I passed the white women looked at me, some curiously, some coyly, some with open hostility. Some just stared with blank hard eyes. Few ever moved aside to let me pass; I just walked around them. On the whole the older women were friendlier than the younger. Now and then some of the young white women gave me an opening to make a pass, but I'd never made one: at first because the coloured workers seemed as intent on protecting the white women from the coloured men as the white men were, probably because they wanted to prove to the white folks they could work with white women without trying to make them; and then, after I'd become a leaderman, because I, like a damn fool, felt a certain responsibility about setting an example. Now I had Alice and the white chicks didn't interest me; I thought Alice was better than any white woman who ever lived.

When I ducked to pass through the access opening in the transverse bulkhead I noticed some words scrawled above and straightened up to read them:

'Don't duck, Okie, you're tough.' I was grinning when I ducked through the hole and straightened up, face to face with a tall white girl in a leather welder's suit.

She was a peroxide blonde with a large-featured, overly made-up face, and she had a large, bright-painted, fleshy mouth, kidney-shaped, thinner in the middle than at the ends. Her big blue babyish eyes were mascaraed like a burlesque queen's and there were tiny wrinkles in their corners and about the flare of her nostrils, calipering down about the edges of her mouth. She looked thirty and well sexed, rife but not quite rotten. She looked as if she might have worked half those years in a cat house, and if she hadn't she must have given a lot of it away.

We stood there for an instant, our eyes locked, before either of us moved; then she deliberately put on a frightened, wide-eyed look and backed away from me as if she was scared stiff, as if she was a naked virgin and I was King Kong. It wasn't the first time she had done that. I'd run into her on board a half-dozen times during the past couple of weeks and each time she'd put on that scared-to-death act. I was used to white women doing all sorts of things to tease or annoy the coloured men so I hadn't given it a second thought before.

But now it sent a blinding fury through my brain. Blood rushed to my head like gales of rain and I felt my face burn white-hot. It came up in my eyes and burned at her; she caught it and kept staring at me with that wide-eyed phoney look. Something about her mouth touched it off, a quirk made the curves change as if she got a sexual thrill, and her mascaraed eyelashes fluttered.

Lust shook me like an electric shock; it came up in my mouth, filling it with tongue, and drained my whole stomach down into my groin. And it poured out of my eyes in a sticky rush and spurted over her from head to foot.

The frightened look went out of her eyes and she blushed right down her face and out of sight beneath the collar of her leather jacket, and I could imagine it going down over her over-ripe breasts and spreading out over her milk-white stomach. When she turned out of my stare I went sick to the stomach and felt like vomiting. I had started toward the ladder going to the upper deck, but instead I turned past her, slowing down and brushing her. She didn't move. I kept on going, circling.

Someone said, 'Hiya, Bob,' but I didn't hear him until after I'd half climbed, half crawled a third of the way up the jack ladder. Then I said, 'Yeah.' I came out on the fourth deck, passed two white women who looked away disdainfully, climbed to the weather deck. A little fat brown-skinned girl with hips that shook like jelly leaned against the bulwark in the sun. 'Hello,' she cooed, dishing up everything she had to offer in that first look.

'Hello, baby,' I said. The sickness went. I leaned close to her and whispered, 'Still keeping it for me?'

She giggled and said half seriously, 'You don't want none.'

I'd already broken two dates with her and I didn't want to make another one. 'I'll see you at lunch,' I said, moving quickly off.

I found a clean spot in the sun and spread out the print. I wanted an overall picture of the whole ventilation system; I was tired of having my gant kicked down in first one stinking hole and then another. But before I'd gotten a chance to look George came up and said Johnson and Conway were about to get into a fight.

'Hell, let 'em fight,' I growled. 'What the hell do I care, I ain't their papa.'

But I got up and went down to the third deck again to see what it was all about. It was cramped quarters aft, a labyrinth of narrow, hard-angled companionways, jammed with staging, lines, shapes, and workers who had to be contortionists first of all. I ducked through the access opening, squeezed by the electricians' staging, pushed a helper out of my way, and started through the opening into the shower room. Just as I stuck my head inside a pipe fitter's tacker struck an arc and I jerked out of the flash. Behind me someone moved the nozzle of the blower that was used to ventilate the hole, and the hard stream of air punched my hard hat off like a fist. In grabbing for it I bumped my head against the angle of the bulkhead. My hat sailed into the middle of the shower room where my gang was working, and I began cursing in a steady streak.

Bessie gave me a dirty look, and Pigmeat said, 'We got Bob throwing his hat in before him. We're some tough cats.'

The air was so thick with welding fumes, acid smell, body odour, and cigarette smoke; even the stream from the blower couldn't get it out. I had fifteen in my gang, twelve men and three women, and they were all working in the tiny, cramped quarters. Two fire pots were going, heating soldering irons. Somebody was drilling. Two or three guys were hand-riveting. A chipper was working on the deck above. It was stifling hot, and the din was terrific.

I picked up my hat and stuck it back on my head. Peaches was sitting on the staging at the far end, legs dangling, eating an apple and at peace with the world. She was a short-haired, dark brown, thick-lipped girl with a placid air— that's as much as I'd seen.

'Where's Smitty?' I asked her. She was his helper.

'I don't know,' she said without moving.

Willie said, 'While you're here, Bob, you can show me where to hang these stays and save me having to go get the print.' He was crouched on the staging beneath the upper deck, trying to hang his duct.

I knew he couldn't read blueprints, but he was drawing a mechanic's pay. I flashed my light on the job and said, 'Hang the first two by the split and the other two just back of the joint. What's your X?'

'That's what I don't know,' he said. 'I ain't seen the print yet.'

'It's three-nine off the bulkhead,' I said.

Behind me Arkansas said, 'Conway, you're an evil man. You don't get along with nobody. How you get along with him, Zula Mae?'

'He's all right,' she said. She was Conway's helper. 'You just got to understand him.'

'See,' Conway said. 'She's my baby.'

Arkansas gave her a disdainful look. 'That's 'cause she still think you her boss. Don't you let this guy go boss you 'round, you hear.'

'He don't boss me 'round,' she defended.

'You just tryna make trouble between me and my helper,' Conway said. 'I'm the easiest man here to get along with. Everybody gets along with me.'

'You from Arkansas?' Arkansas asked.

'How you know I ain't from California?' Conway said.

'Ain't nobody in here from California,' Arkansas said. 'What city in Arkansas you from?'

'He's from Pine Bluff,' Johnson said. 'Can't you tell a Pine Bluff nig—Pine Bluffian when you see him?'

'Hear the Moroccan,' Conway sneered. 'Johnson a Moroccan, he ain't no coloured man.'

'You got any folks in Fort Worth, Conway?' Arkansas asked.

'I ain't got many folks,' Conway said. 'We a small family.'

'You got a grandpa, ain't you?' Arkansas persisted.

'Had one,' Conway said.

'Then how you know?' Arkansas pointed out.

Peaches was grinning.

'You going back?' Homer asked.

Arkansas looked at him. 'Who you talking to? Me?'

'You'll do. You going back?'

'Back where?'

'Back to Arkansas?'

'Yeah, I'm going back—when the horses, they pick the cotton, and the mules, they cut the corn; when the white chickens lay black eggs and the white folks is Jim Crowed while the black folks is——'

He broke off as Smitty came in with a white leaderman named Donald. They didn't see me. He showed Donald where he had cut an opening in his duct for an intake vent, and Donald said he'd cut four inches off the X.

'That's where Bob told me to cut,' he said.

Donald shook his head noncommittally; he was a nice guy and he didn't want to say I was wrong. I'd often wondered if he was a Communist. He had a round moonface, pleasant but unsmiling, and that sharp speculative look behind rimless spectacles that some Communists have.

I stepped into the picture then. 'When did I tell you to cut out there?' I asked Smitty.

Donald turned red. 'Hello, Bob,' he said. 'Smitty said you was off today.'

'Jesus Christ, can't you coloured boys do anything right?' Kelly said from behind me. He had slipped in unnoticed.

Air began lumping in my chest and my eyes started burning. I looked at Kelly. I ought to bust him right on the side of his scrawny red neck, I thought. I'd kill him as sure as hell. Instead I ground out, 'Any mechanic might have made the same mistake. Any mechanic but a white mechanic,' I added.

He didn't get it. 'Yeah, but you boys make too many mistakes. You got to cut it out.'

Donald started moving off. 'I ain't made a single mistake this month, Mr. Kelly.' Conway grinned up at him from where he knelt on the floor, soldering a seam.

Pigmeat nudged me. 'See what I mean? Got 'em skunt back to his ears. He thinks the man a dentist.'

Kelly heard him but acted as if he didn't. He said to Conway, 'I wasn't talking about you. You're a good boy, a good worker. I was talking 'bout some of these other boys.'

In the silence that followed Peaches said, 'Oh, Conway gonna get a raise,' before she could catch herself, having thought we'd keep on talking and she wouldn't be heard. Somebody laughed.

I kept looking at Kelly without saying anything. He turned suddenly and started out. When he had gone Smitty said, 'How come he always got to pick on you? He don't never jump on none of these white leadermen. You know as much as they do.'

I unfolded my rule and tapped the duct he was working on. 'Cut your bottom line ten inches from the butt joint,' I directed, trying to keep my voice steady. He was just a simple-minded, Uncle Tom-ish nigger, I told myself; he couldn't help it. 'You'll have a four-inch gap. Take this duct over to the shop and get a production welder to weld in an insert plate and grind the burrs down as smooth as possible.' I turned and started out, then stopped. 'And remember I'm your leaderman,' I added.

Ben was standing in the opening, grinning at me. He was a light-brown-skinned guy in his early thirties, good-looking with slightly Caucasian features and straight brown hair. He was a graduate of U.C.L.A. and didn't take anything from the white folks and didn't give them anything. If he had been on the job for more than nine months he'd probably have been the leaderman instead of me; he probably knew more than I did, anyway.

I grinned back at him.

He said, 'Tough, Bob, but you got to take it.'

Richard Wright
from *White Man Listen!*

2. TRADITION AND INDUSTRIALIZATION

The Historic Meaning of the Plight of the Tragic Elite in Asia and Africa

So great a legion of ideological interests is choking the media of communication of the world today that I deem it advisable to define the terms in which I speak and for whom. In the heated, charged, and violently partisan atmosphere in which we live at this moment, all public utterances are dragged willy-nilly into the service of something or somebody. Even the most rigorously determined attitudes of objectivity and the most passionate avowals of good faith have come to be suspect. And especially is this true of the expressions of those of us who have been doomed to live and act in a tight web of racial and economic facts, facts viewed by many through eyes of political or religious interest, facts examined by millions with anxiety and even hysteria.

Knowing the suspicious, uneasy climate in which our twentieth-century lives are couched, I, as a Western man of color, strive to be as objective as I can when I seek to communicate. But, at once, you have the right to demand of me: What does being objective mean? Is it possible to speak at all today and not have the meaning of one's words construed in six different ways?

For example, he who advocates the use of mass educational techniques today can be, and usually is, accused of harboring secret Soviet sympathies, despite the fact that his advocacy of the means of mass education aims at a quick spreading of literacy so that Communism cannot take root, so that vast populations trapped in tribal or religious loyalties cannot be easily duped by self-seeking demagogues. He who urgently counsels the establishment of strong, central governments in the so-called underdeveloped countries, in the hope that those countries can quickly pull themselves out of the mire and become swiftly modernized and industrialized and thereby set upon the road to democracy, free speech, a secular state, universal suffrage, etc., can be and commonly is stigmatized as: "Well, he's no Communist, *but...*" He who would invoke, as sanction for experimental political action, a desire to seek the realization of the basic ideals of the Western world in terms of unorthodox and as yet untried institutional structures—instrumentalities for short-cutting long, drawn-out historical processes—as a means of constructing conditions for the creation of individual freedom, can be branded as being "emotionally unstable and having tendencies that *could* lead, therefore, to Communism." He who would question, with all the good faith in the world, whether the philosophical ideas and assumptions of John Stuart Mill and John Locke are valid for all times, for all peoples, and for all countries with their vastly differing traditions and backgrounds, with the motive of psychologically freeing men's minds so that they can seek new conditions and instrumentalities for freedom, can be indicted as an enemy of democracy.

Confronted with a range of negative hostility of this sort, knowing that the society of the Western world is so frantically defensive that it would seek to impose conformity at any price, what is an honest man to do? Should he keep silent and thereby try to win a degree of dubious safety for himself? Should he endorse static defensiveness as the price of achieving his own personal security? The game isn't worth the candle, for, in doing so, he buttresses that which would eventually crush not only him, but that which would negate the very conditions of life out of which freedom can spring. In such a situation one's silence implies that one has surrendered one's intellectual faculties to fear, that one has voluntarily abdicated life itself, that one has gratuitously paralyzed one's possibilities of action. Since any and all events can be lifted by men of bad faith out of their normal contexts and projected into others and thus consequently condemned, since one's thoughts can be interpreted in terms of such extreme implications as to reduce them to absurdity or subversion, obviously a mere declaration of one's good intentions is not enough. In an all-pervading climate of intellectual evasion or dishonesty, everything becomes dishonest; suspicion subverts events and distorts their meaning; mental reservations alter the character of facts and rob them of validity and utility. In short, if good will is lacking, everything is lost and a dialogue between men becomes not only useless, but dangerous, and sometimes even incriminating.

To imagine that straight communication is no longer possible is to declare that the world we seek to defend is no longer worth defending, that the battle for human freedom is already lost. I'm assuming, however naively, that such is not quite yet the case. I cannot, of course, assume that universal good will reigns, but I have the elementary right, the bounden duty even, to assume that man, when he has the chance to speak and act without fear, still wishes to be man, that is, he harbors the dream of being a free and creative agent.

Then, first of all, let us honestly admit that there is no such thing as objectivity, no such objective fact as objectivity. Objectivity is a fabricated concept, a synthetic intellectual construction devised to enable others to know the general conditions under which one has done something, observed the world or an event in that world.

So, before proceeding to give my opinions concerning Tradition and Industrialization, I shall try to state as clearly as possible where I stand, the mental climate about me, the historic period in which I speak, and some of the elements in my environment and my own personality which propel me to communicate. The basic assumption behind all so-called objective attitudes is this: If others care to assume my mental stance and, through empathy, duplicate the atmosphere in which I speak, if they can imaginatively grasp the factors in my environment and a sense of the impulses motivating me, they will, if they are of a mind to, be able to see, more or less, what I've seen, will be capable of apprehending the same general aspects and tones of reality that comprise my world, that world that I share daily with all other men. By revealing the assumptions behind my statements, I'm striving to convert you to my outlook, to its essential humaneness, to the generality and reasonableness of my arguments.

Obviously no striving for an objectivity of attitude is ever complete. Tomorrow, or the day after, someone will discover some fact, some element, or a nuance that I've forgotten to take into account, and, accordingly, my attitude will have to be revised, discarded, or extended, as the case may be. Hence, there is no such thing as an absolute objectivity of attitude. The most rigorously determined attitude of objectivity is, at best, relative. We are human; we are the slaves of our assumptions, of time and circumstance; we are the victims of our passions and illusions; and the most that our critics can ask of us is this: Have you taken your passions, your illusions, your time, and your circumstances into account? That is what I am attempting to do. More than that no reasonable man of good will can demand.

First of all, my position is a split one. I'm black. I'm a man of the West. These hard facts are bound to condition, to some degree, my outlook. I see and understand the West; but I also see and understand the non- or anti-Western point of view. How is this possible? This double vision of mine stems from my being a product of Western civilization and from my racial identity, long and deeply conditioned, which is organically born of my being a product of that civilization. Being a Negro living in a white Western Christian society, I've never been allowed to blend, in a natural and healthy manner, with the culture and civilization of the West. This contradiction of being both Western and a man of color creates a psychological distance, so to speak, between me and my environment. I'm self-conscious. I admit it. Yet I feel no need to apologize for it. Hence, though Western, I'm inevitably critical of the West. Indeed, a vital element of my Westernness resides in this chronically skeptical, this irredeemably critical, outlook. I'm restless. I question not only myself, but my environment. I'm eager, urgent. And to be so seems natural, human, and good to me. Life without these qualities is inconceivable, less than human. In spite of myself, my imagination is constantly leaping ahead and trying to reshape the world I see (basing itself strictly on the materials of the world in which I live each day) toward a form in which all men could share my creative restlessness. Such an outlook breeds criticism. And my critical attitude and detachment are born of my position. I and my environment are one, but that oneness has in it, at its very core, an abiding schism. Yet I regard my position as natural, as normal, though others, that is, Western whites, anchored in tradition and habit, would have to make a most strenuous effort of imagination to grasp it.

Yet, I'm not non-Western. I'm no enemy of the West. Neither am I an Easterner. When I look out upon those vast stretches of this earth inhabited by brown, black, and yellow men—sections of the earth in which religion dominates, to the exclusion of almost everything else, the emotional and mental landscape—my reactions and attitudes are those of the West. I see both worlds from another and third point of view. (This outlook has nothing to do with any so-called Third Force; I'm speaking largely in historical and psychological terms.)

I'm numbed and appalled when I know that millions of men in Asia and Africa assign more reality to their dead fathers than to the crying claims of their daily lives: poverty, political degradation, illness, ignorance, etc. I shiver when I learn that the infant mortality rate, say, in James Town (a slum section of Accra, the capital of the Gold Coast in British West Africa) is fifty per cent in the first year of life; and, further, I'm speechless when I learn that this inhuman condition is explained by the statement, "The children did not wish to stay. Their ghost-mothers called them home." And when I hear that explanation I know that there can be no altering of social conditions in those areas until such religious rationalizations have been swept from men's minds, no matter how devoutly they are believed in or defended. Indeed, the teeming religions gripping the minds and consciousness of Asians and Africans offend me. I can conceive of no identification with such mystical visions of life that freeze millions in static degradation, no matter how emotionally satisfying such degradation seems to those who wallow in it. But, because the swarming populations in those continents are two-time victims—victims of their own religious projections and victims of Western imperialism—my sympathies are unavoidably with, and unashamedly for, them. For this sympathy I offer no apology.

Yet, when I turn to face the environment that cradled and nurtured me, I experience a sense of dismaying shock, for that Western environment is soaked in and stained with the most blatant racism that the contemporary world knows. It is a racism that has almost become another kind of religion, a religion of the materially dispossessed, of the culturally disinherited. Rooted in my own disinheritedness, I know instinctively that this clinging to, and defense of, racism by Western whites are born of their psychological nakedness, of their having, through historical accident, partially thrown off the mystic cauls of Asia and Africa that once too blinded and dazed them. A deeply conscious victim of white racism could even be strangely moved to compassion for that white man who, having lost his mystic vision of a stern Father God, a dazzling Virgin, and a Dying Son Who promises to succor him after death, settles upon racism! What a poor substitute! What a shabby, vile, and cheap home the white heart finds when it seeks shelter in racism! One would think that sheer pride would deter Western whites from such emotional debasement!

I stand, therefore, mentally and emotionally looking in both directions, being claimed by a negative identification on one side, and being excluded by a feeling of repulsion on the other.

Since I'm detached from, because of racial conditions, the West, why do I bother to call myself Western at all? What is it that prompts me to make an identification with the West despite the contradiction involved? The fact is that I really have no choice in the matter. Historical forces more powerful than I am have shaped me as a Westerner. I have not consciously elected to be a

Westerner; I have been made into a Westerner. Long before I had the freedom to choose, I was molded a Westerner. It began in childhood. And the process continues.

Hence, standing shoulder to shoulder with the Western white man, speaking his tongue, sharing his culture, participating in the common efforts of the Western community, I say frankly to that white man: "I'm Western, just as Western as you are, maybe more; but I don't completely agree with you."

What do I mean, then, when I say that I'm Western? I shall try to define what the term means to me. I shan't here, now, try to define what being Western means to all Westerners. I shall confine my definition only to that aspect of the West with which I identify, that aspect that makes me feel, act, and live Western.

The content of my Westernness resides fundamentally, I feel, in my secular outlook upon life. I believe in a separation of Church and State. I believe that the State possesses a value in and for itself. I feel that man—just sheer brute man, just as he is—has a meaning and value over and above all sanctions or mandates from mystical powers, either on high or from below. I am convinced that the humble, fragile dignity of man, buttressed by a tough-souled pragmatism, implemented by methods of trial and error, can sufficiently sustain and nourish human life, can endow it with ample and durable meaning. I believe that all ideas have a right to circulate in the market place without restriction. I believe that all men should have the right to have their say without fear of the political "powers that be," without having to dread the punitive measures or the threat of invisible forces which some castes of men claim as their special domain—men such as priests and churchmen. (My own position compels me to grant those priests and churchmen the right to have their say, but not at the expense of having my right to be heard annulled.) I believe that art has its own autonomy, a self-sufficiency that extends beyond, and independent of, the spheres of political or priestly power or sanction. I feel that science exists without any a priori or metaphysical assumptions. I feel that human personality is an end in and for itself. In short, I believe that man, for good or ill, is his own ruler, his own sovereign, his own keeper. I hold human freedom as a supreme right and good for all men, my conception of freedom being the right of all men to exercise their natural and acquired powers as long as the exercise of those powers does not hinder others from doing the same.

These are my assumptions, my values, my morality, if you insist upon that word. Yet I hold these values at a time in history when they are threatened. I stand in the middle of that most fateful of all the world's centuries: the twentieth century. Nuclear energy, the center of the sun, is in the hands of men. In most of the land mass of Asia and Africa the traditional and customary class relations of feudal, capitalistic societies have been altered, frequently brutally shattered, by murder and terror. Most of the governments of the earth today rule, by one pretext or another, by open or concealed pressure upon the individual, by black lists, intimidation, fiat, secret police, and machine guns. Among intellectual circles the globe over the desperate question has been raised: "What is man?" In the East as in the West, wealth and the means of production have been taken out of private hands, families, clans, and placed at the disposal of committees and state bureaucrats. The consciousness of most men on earth is filled with a sense of shame, of humiliation, of memories of past servitude and degradation—and a sense of fear that that condition of servitude and degradation will return. The future for most men is an apprehensive void which has created the feeling that it has to be impetuously, impulsively filled, given a new content at all costs. With the freeing of Asia and most of Africa from Western rule, more active and unbridled religion now foments and agitates the minds and emotions of men than at any time since 1455! Man's world today lies in the pythonlike coils of vast irrational forces which he cannot control. This is the mental climate out of which I speak, a climate that tones my being and pitches consciousness on a certain plane of tension. These are the conditions under which I speak, conditions that condition me.

Now, the above assumptions and facts would and do color my view of history, that record of the rise and fall of traditions and religions. All of those past historical forces which have, accidentally or intentionally, helped to create the basis of freedom in human life, I extol, revere and count as my fervent allies. Those conditions of life and of history which thwart, threaten and degrade the values and assumptions I've listed, I reject and consider harmful, something to be doggedly resisted.

Now, I'm aware that to some tender, sensitive minds such a decalogue of beliefs is chilling, arid, almost inhuman. And especially is this true of those multitudes inhabiting the dense, artistically cluttered Catholic countries of present-day Europe. To a richly endowed temperament such a declaration is akin to an invitation to empty out all the precious values of the past; indeed, to many millions such a declaration smacks of an attack upon what they have been taught to consider and venerate as civilization itself. The emotionally thin-skinned cannot imagine, even in the middle of our twentieth century, a world without external emotional props to keep them buttressed to a stance of constant meaning and justification, a world filled with overpowering mother and father and child images to anchor them in emotional security, to keep a sense of the warm, intimate, sustaining influence of the family alive. And I can readily conceive of such temperaments willing to condemn my attitude as being barbarian, willful, or perverse. What such temperaments do not realize is that my decalogue of beliefs does not imply that I've turned my back in scorn upon the past of mankind in so crude or abrupt a manner as they feel or think. Men who can slough off the beautiful mythologies, the enthralling configurations of external ceremonies, manners, and codes of the past are not necessarily unacquainted with, or unappreciative of, them; they have *interiorized* them, have reduced them to mental traits, psychological problems. I know, however, that such a fact is small comfort to those who love the past, who long to be caught up in rituals that induce blissful self-forgetfulness, and who would find the meaning of their lives in them. I confess frankly that I cannot solve this problem for everybody; I state further that it is my profound conviction that emotional independence is a clear and distinct human advance, a gain for all mankind and, if that gain and advance seem inhuman, there is nothing that can rationally be done about it. Freedom needs no apology.

Naturally, a man holding such values will view history in a rather novel light. How do these values compel me to regard the claims of Western imperialism? What virtue or evil do I assign to the overrunning of Asia and Africa by Western Christian white men? What about color prejudice? What about the undeniable technical and industrial power and superiority of the white West? How do I feel about the white man's vaunted claim—and I'm a product, reluctant, to be sure, of that white man's culture and civilization—that he has been called by his God to rule the world and to have all overriding considerations over the rest of mankind, that is, colored men?

And, since the Christian religion, by and large, has tacitly endorsed racism by the nature of its past historical spread and its present sway, how do I view that religion whose irrational core can propel it toward such ends, whether that religion be in Europe, Asia, or Africa? And, since tradition is generally but forms of frozen or congealed religion, how do I regard tradition?

I've tried to lead you to my angle of vision slowly, step by step, keeping nothing back. If I insist over and over again upon the personal perspective, it is because my weighing of external facts is bound organically with that personal perspective. My point of view is a Western one, but a Western one that conflicts at several vital points with the present, dominant outlook of the West. Am I ahead of or behind the West? My personal judgment is that I'm ahead. And I do not say that boastfully; such a judgment is implied by the very nature of those Western values that I hold dear.

Let me dig deeper into my personal position. I was born a black Protestant in that most racist of all the American states: Mississippi. I lived my childhood under a racial code, brutal and bloody, that white men proclaimed was ordained of God, said was made mandatory by the nature of their religion. Naturally, I rejected that religion and would reject any religion which prescribes for me an inferior position in life; I reject that tradition and any tradition which proscribes my humanity. And, since the very beginnings of my life on this earth were couched in this contradiction, I became passionately curious as to why Christians felt it imperative to practice such wholesale denials of humanity. My seeking carried me back to a crucial point in Western history where a clearly enunciated policy on the part of the Church spelt my and others' doom. In 1455 the Pope divided the world between Spain and Portugal and decreed that those two nations had not only the right, but the consecrated duty of converting or enslaving all infidels. Now, it just so happened that at that time all the infidels, from the white Western Christian point of view, were in Asia, Africa, the many islands of the Atlantic, the Pacific, and the then unknown Americas—and it just so happened that they were all people of color.

Further reading of history brought me abreast of a strong countercurrent of opposition to that Church that had imperialistically condemned all colored mankind. When I discovered that John Calvin and Martin Luther were stalwart rebels against the domination of a Church that had condemned and damned the majority of the human race, I felt that the impulses, however confused, animating them were moving in the direction of a fuller concept of human dignity and freedom. But the Protestantism of Calvin and Luther did not go far enough; they underestimated the nature of the revolution they were trying to make. Their fight against the dead weight of tradition was partial, limited. Racism was historically and circumstantially embedded in their rejection of the claims of the Church that they sought to defeat. Calvin and Luther strove for freedom, but it was inevitably and inescapably only for their kind, that is, European whites. So, while recognizing the positive but limited nature of Calvin's and Luther's contribution, I had to look elsewhere for a concept of man that would not do violence to my own concept of, and feeling for, life.

What did magnetize me toward the emotional polarizations of Calvin and Luther was the curious psychological strength that they unknowingly possessed, a strength that propelled them, however clumsily, toward the goal of emotional independence. These two bold European insurgents had begun, though they called it by another name, a stupendous *introjection* of the religious symbols by which the men of their time lived. They were proponents of that tide that was moving from simple, naive credence toward self-skepticism, from a state of sensual slavery to the sights, sounds, and colors of the external world toward a stance of detachment. By some quirk of mental strength, they felt stronger than their contemporaries and could doubt and even doff the panoply of religious rituals and ceremonies and could either live without much of them or could, gropingly to be sure, stand psychologically alone to an amazing degree. In the lives of Calvin and Luther there had begun a dual process: on one hand, the emptying of human consciousness of its ancient, infantile, subjective accretions, and, on the other, a denuding of an anthropocentric world of the poetry that man had projected upon it. A two-way doubt of the world and of man's own self had set in, and this putting man and his world in question would not pause until it had enthroned itself in a new consciousness. Western man was taking that first step toward a new outlook that would not terminate until it had flowered in the bleak stretches of an undiscovered America which, ironically, was peopled by red-skinned "savages" who could not dream of doubting their own emotions or questioning the world that impinged upon their sensibilities. (The partially liberated Pilgrims slew those religiously captured "savages"!) Not understanding the implications of the needs prompting them, Calvin and Luther did not realize that what they were trying to do had already been neatly, clearly, and heroically done before by the brave and brooding Greeks who, overwhelmed by contradictory experiences and the antinomic currents of their own passions, had lifted their dazed eyes toward an empty Heaven and uttered those bitterly tragic words that were to become the motto of abandoned Western man:

"What do we do now?"

The Protestant is a queer animal who has never fully understood himself, has never guessed that he is an abortive freeman, an issue of historical birth that never quite came to full life. It has been conveniently forgotten that the Protestant is a product and a result of *oppression*, which might well account for his inability to latch directly onto the Greek heritage and thereby save himself a lot of useless and stupid thrashing about in history. Stripped by the heavy, intolerant conditions of Catholic rule of much of his superfluous emotional baggage, the emerging Protestant rebel, harassed by his enemies and haunted by his own guilt, was doomed to *react* rather than *act*, to *protest* rather than *affirm*, never fully grasping what was motivating him until he had been swept by history so far beyond his original problem that he had forgotten its initial content of meaning. The Protestant was being called to a goal the terrifying nature of which he had neither the courage nor the strength to see or understand. The Protestant is the brave blind man cursed by destiny with a burden which he has not the inner grace to accept wholeheartedly.

The ultimate consequences of Calvin's and Luther's rebellious doctrines and seditious actions, hatched and bred in emotional confusion, unwittingly created the soil out of which grew something that Calvin and Luther did not dream of. (And this is not the last time that I shall call your attention to an odd characteristic of the Western world; the men of the West seem prone in their actions to achieve results that contradict their motives. They have a genius for calling things by wrong names; they seek to save souls and become involved in murder; they attempt to enthrone God as an absolute and they achieve the establishment of the prerequisites of science and atheistic thought; they seem wedded to a terribly naive and childlike outlook upon the world and themselves, and they are filled with consternation when their actions produce results that they did not foresee.) Determined to plant the religious impulse in each individual's heart declaring that each man could stand face to face with God, Calvin and Luther blindly let loose mental and emotional forces which, in turn, caused a vast revolution in the social, cultural, governmental, and economic conditions under which Western man lived—a revolution that finally negated their own racial attitudes! The first and foremost of these conditions were the guaranteeing of individual conscience and judgment, an act which loosened, to a degree, the men of Europe from custom and tradition, from the dead hand of the past, evoking a sense of future expectation, infinitely widening man's entire horizon. And yet this was achieved by accident! That's the irony of it. Calvin and Luther, preoccupied with metaphysical notions, banished dread from men's minds and allowed them to develop that courageous emotional strength which sanctioned and spurred the amassing of a vast heap of positive fact relating to daily reality. As a result of Calvin's and Luther's heresy, man began to get a grip upon his external environment. Science and industry were born and, through their rapid growth, each enriched the other and nullified the past notions of social structures, negated norms of nobility, of tradition, of priestly values, and fostered new social classes, new occupations, new experiences, new structures of government, new pleasures, hungers, dreams, in short, a whole new and unheard of universe. A Church world was transformed into a worldly world, any man's world, a world in which even black, brown, and yellow men could have the possibility to live and breathe.

Yet, while living with these facts, Europeans still believed in and practiced a racism that the very logic of the world they were creating told them was irrational and insane!

Buttressed by their belief that their God had entrusted the earth into their keeping, drunk with power and possibility, waxing rich through trade in commodities, human and non-human, with awesome naval and merchant marines at their disposal, their countries filled with human debris anxious for any adventures, psychologically armed with new facts, white Western Christian civilization, with a long, slow, and bloody explosion, hurled itself upon the sprawling masses of humanity in Asia and Africa.*

Perhaps now you'll expect me to pause and begin a vehement and moral denunciation of Europe. No. The facts are complex. In that process of Europe's overrunning of the rest of mankind a most bewildering mixture of motives, means, and ends took place. White men, spurred by religious and areligious motives—that is, to save the souls of a billion or so heathens and to receive the material blessings of God while doing so—entered areas of the earth where religion ruled with an indigenous absoluteness that did not even obtain in Europe.

Are we here confronted with a simple picture of virtue triumphing over villainy, of right over wrong, of the superior over the inferior, of the biologically fit blond beast over biologically botched brown, yellow, and black men? That is what Europe felt about it. But I do not think that that is a true picture of what really happened. Again I call your attention to the proneness of white Europe, under the influence of a strident, romantic individualism, to do one thing and call that thing by a name that no one but itself could accept or recognize.

What, then, happened? Irrationalism met irrationalism. The irrationalism of Europe met the irrationalism of Asia and Africa, and the resulting confusion has yet to be unraveled and understood. Europe called her adventure imperialism, the spread of civilization, missions of glory, of service, of destiny even. Asians and Africans called it colonization, blood-sucking, murder, butchery, slavery. There is no doubt that both sides had some measure of truth in their claims. But I state that neither side quite knew what was happening and neither side was conscious of the real process that was taking place. The truth lay beyond the blurred ken of both the European and his Asian and African victim.

I have stated publicly, on more than one occasion, that the economic spoils of European imperialism do not bulk so large or important to me. I know that today it is the fashion to list the long and many economic advantages that Europe gained from its brutal and bloody impact upon hundreds of millions of Asians and Africans. The past fifty years have created a sprawling literature of

*See The Psychological Reactions of Oppressed People.

the fact that the ownership of colonies paid princely dividends. I have no doubt of it. Yet that fact does not impress me as much as still another and more obscure and more important fact. What rivets my attention in this clash of East and West is that an irrational Western world helped, unconsciously and unintentionally to be sure, to smash the irrational ties of religion and custom and tradition in Asia and Africa. THIS, IN MY OPINION, IS THE CENTRAL HISTORIC FACT! The European said that he was saving souls, yet he kept himself at a distance from the brown, black, and yellow skins that housed the souls that he claimed that he so loved and so badly wanted to save. Thank the white man's God for that bit of racial and color stupidity! His liberating effect upon Asia and Africa would not have been so thorough had he been more human.

Yes, there were a few shrewd Europeans who wanted the natives to remain untouched, who wished to see what they called the "nobility" of the black, brown, and yellow lives remain intact. The more backward and outlandish the native was, the more the European loved him. This attitude can be boiled down to one simple wish: The imperialist wanted the natives to sleep on in their beautifully poetic dreams so that the ruling of them could be more easily done. They devised systems of administration called "indirect rule," "assimilation," "gradual constitutional government," etc., but they all meant one simple thing; a white man's military peace, a white man's political order, and a white man's free trade, whether that trade involved human bodies or tin or oil.

Again, I say that I do not denounce this. Had even the white West known what it was really doing, it could not have done a better job of beginning to launch the liberation of the masses of Asia and Africa from their age-old traditions.

Being ignorant of what they were really doing, the men of Europe failed to fill the void that they were creating in the very heart of mankind, thereby compounding their strange historical felony.

There are Europeans today who look longingly and soulfully at the situation developing in the world and say: "But, really, we love 'em. We are friends of theirs!" To attitudes like that I can only say: "My friends, look again. Examine the heritage you left behind. Read the literature that your fathers and your fathers' fathers wrote about those natives. Your fathers were naive but honest men."

How many souls did Europe save? To ask that question is to make one laugh! Europe was tendering to the great body of mankind a precious gift which she, in her blindness and ignorance, in her historical shortsightedness, was not generous enough to give her own people! Today, a *knowing* black, brown, or yellow man can say:

"Thank you, Mr. White Man, for freeing me from the rot of my irrational traditions and customs, though you are still the victim of your own irrational customs and traditions!"

There was a boon wrapped in that gift of brutality that the white West showered upon Asia and Africa. Over the centuries, meticulously, the white men took the sons and daughters of the chiefs and of the noble houses of Asia and Africa and instilled in them the ideas of the West so the eventual West-ernized Asian and African products could become their collaborators. Yet they had no thought of how those Westernized Asians and Africans would fare when cast, like fishes out of water, back into their poetic cultures. (These un-employed Asians and Africans eventually became national revolutionaries, of course!) Shorn of all deep-seated faiths, these Westernized Asians and Africans had to sink or swim with no guides, no counsel. Over and above this, the Euro-peans launched vast industrial enterprises in almost all of the lands that they controlled, vast enterprises that wrought profound alterations in the Asian-African ways of life and thought. *In sum, white Europeans set off a more deep-going and sudden revolution in Asia and Africa than had ever obtained in all of the history of Europe.* And they did this with supreme confidence. On one occasion Christian English gentlemen chartered a royal company for one thousand years to buy and sell black slaves! Oh, what hope they had!

I declare that merely rational motives could not have sustained the white men who damaged and destroyed the ancient Asian-African cultures and social structures; they had perforce to believe that they were the tools of cosmic pow-ers, that they were executing the will of God, or else they would not have had the cruel daring to try to harness the body of colored mankind into their per-sonal service. The sheer magnitude of their depredations and subjugations ought to have given them pause, but it never did to any effective degree. Only a blind and ignorant militancy could have sustained such insane ventures, such outlandish dreams. Indeed, one could say that it was precisely because the white Westerner had partially lost his rooting in his own culture that he could remain so insensitive to the dangerous unleashing of human forces of so vast and catastrophic a sweep. Had he been more at home in his own world of values, sheer prudence would have made him quail before the earth-shaking human energies which he so rashly and diligently cut loose from their moorings.

Today the intelligent sons and daughters of the old-time European free-booters, despoilers, and imperial pirates tremble with moral consternation at what their forefathers did. Says Gunnar Myrdal, in his *An International Econ-omy*, page 168 (Harper and Brothers: New York, 1956):

"The horrible vision often enters my mind of the ultimate results of our continuing and rapidly speeding up the practice, well established in some coun-tries during the era of colonialism, of tossing together even bigger crowds of il-literate proletarians—these new proletariats being even more uprooted than they were in the stagnant villages where they lived in the remnants of some culture and some established mores."

Who *took* here? Who *gave*? It is too complicated a process to admit of such simple questions. But the Europeans naively called it soul-saving, money-making, modern administration, missions of civilization, *Pax Britannica*, and a host of other equally quaint appellations. History is a strange story. Men enact history with one set of motives and the consequences that flow from such moti-vated actions often have nothing whatsoever to do with such motives. What irony will history reveal when those pages of Europe's domination of Asia and Africa are finally and honestly written! That history will depict a ghastly racial tragedy; it will expose a blind spot on the part of white Westerners that will make those who read that history laugh with a sob in their throats. The white Western world, until relatively recently the most secular and free part of the earth—with a secularity and freedom that was the secret of its power (science and industry)—labored unconsciously and tenaciously for five hundred years to make Asia and Africa (that is, the elite in those areas) more secular-minded than the West!

In the minds of hundreds of millions of Asians and Africans the traditions of their lives have been psychologically condemned beyond recall. Hundreds of millions live uneasily with beliefs of which they have been made ashamed. I say, "*Bravo!*" for that clumsy and cruel deed. Not to the motives, mind you, behind those deeds, motives which were all too often ignoble and base. But I do say "Bravo!" to the consequences of Western plundering, a plundering that created the conditions for the possible rise of rational societies for the greater majority of mankind.

But enough of ironic comparisons. Where do we stand today? That part of the heritage of the West that I value—man stripped of the past and free for the future—has now been established as lonely bridgeheads in Asia and Africa in the form of a Western-educated elite, an elite that is more Western, in most cases, than the West. Tragic and lonely and all too often misunderstood are these men of the Asian-African elite. The West hates and fears that elite, and I must, to be honest, say that the instincts of the West that prompt that hate and fear are, on the whole, correct. For this elite in Asia and Africa constitutes islands of free men, the FREEST MEN IN ALL THE WORLD TODAY. They stand poised, nervous, straining at the leash, ready to go, with no weight of the dead past clouding their minds, no fears of foolish customs benumbing their consciousness, eager to build industrial civilizations. What does this mean? It means that the spirit of the Enlightenment, of the Reformation, which made Europe great, now has a chance to be extended to all mankind! A part of the non-West is now akin to a part of the West. East and West have become compounded. The partial overcoming of the forces of tradition and oppressive religions in Europe resulted, in a round-about manner, in a partial overcoming of tradition and religion in decisive parts of Asia and Africa. The unspoken assumption in this history has been: WHAT IS GOOD FOR EUROPE IS GOOD FOR ALL MANKIND! I say: So be it.

I approve of what has happened. My only regret is that Europe could not have done what she did in a deliberate and intentional manner, could not have planned it as a global project. My wholehearted admiration would have gone out to the spirit of a Europe that had had the imagination to have launched this mighty revolution out of the generosity of its heart, out of a sense of lofty responsibility. Europe could then stand proudly before all the world and say: "Look at what we accomplished! We remade man in our image! Look at the new form of life that we brought into being!" And I'm sure that had that happened, the majority of mankind would have been Western in a sense that no atom or hydrogen bombs can make a man Western. But, alas, that chance, that rare and noble opportunity, is gone forever. Europe missed the boat.

How can the spirit of the Enlightenment and the Reformation be extended now to all men? How can this accidental boon be made global in effect? That is the task that history now imposes upon us. Can a way be found, purged of racism and profits, to melt the rational areas and rational personnel of Europe with those of Asia and Africa? How can the curtains of race, color, religion, and tradition—all of which hamper man's mastery of his environment—be collectively rolled back by free men of the West and non-West? Is this a Utopian dream? Is this mere wishing? No. It is more drastic than that. The nations of Asia and Africa and Europe contain too much of the forces of the irrational for anyone to think that the future will take care of itself. The islands of the rational in the East are too tenuously held to permit of optimism. And the same is true of Europe. (We have but to recall reading of ideas to "burn up entire continents" to doff our illusions.) The truth is that our world—a world for all men, black, brown, yellow, and white—will either be all rational or totally irrational. For better or worse, it will eventually be one world.

How can these rational regions of the world be maintained? How can the pragmatically useful be made triumphant? Does this entail a surrender of the hard-bought national freedoms on the part of non-Western nations? I'm convinced that that will not happen, for these Asian and African nations, led by Western-educated leaders, love their freedom as much as the West loves its own. They have had to struggle and die for their freedom and they value it passionately. It is unthinkable that they, so recently freed from color and class domination of the West, would voluntarily surrender their sovereignty. Let me state the problem upside down. What Western nation would dream of abdicating its sovereignty and collaborating with powers that once so recently ruled them in the name of interests that were not their own—powers that created a vast literature of hate against them? Such an act would be irrational in the extreme. And the Western-educated leaders of non-Western nations are filled with too much distrust of an imperial-minded West to permit of any voluntary relinquishing of their control over their destinies.

Is there no alternative? *Must* there be a victorious East or a victorious West? If one or the other must win completely, then the fragile values won so blindly and accidentally and at so great a cost and sacrifice will be lost for us all. Where is the crux of this matter? Who is to act first? Who *should* act first? The burden of action rests, I say, with the West. For it was the West, however naively, that launched this vast historical process of the transformation of mankind. And of what must the action of the West consist? The West must aid and, yes, abet the delicate and tragic elite in Asia and Africa to establish rational areas of living. THE WEST, IN ORDER TO KEEP BEING WESTERN, FREE, AND SOMEWHAT RATIONAL, MUST BE PREPARED TO ACCORD TO THE ELITE OF ASIA AND AFRICA A FREEDOM WHICH IT ITSELF NEVER PERMITTED IN ITS OWN DOMAIN. THE ASIAN AND AFRICAN ELITE MUST BE GIVEN ITS HEAD! The West must perform an act of faith and do this. Such a mode of action has long been implied in the very nature of the ideas which the West has instilled into that Asian-African elite. The West must trust that part of itself that it has thrust, however blunderingly, into Asia and Africa. Nkrumah, Nasser, Sukarno, and Nehru, and the Western-educated heads of these newly created national states, must be given *carte blanche* to modernize their lands without overlordship of the West, and we must understand the methods that they will feel compelled to use.

Never, you will say. That is impossible, you will declare. Oh, I'm asking a hard thing and I know it. I'm Western, remember, and I know how horribly implausible my words sound to Westerners so used to issuing orders and having those orders obeyed at gun point. But what rational recourse does the West possess other than this? None.

If the West cannot do this, it means that the West does not believe in itself, does not trust the ideas which it has cast into the world. Yes, Sukarno, Nehru, Nasser and others will necessarily use quasi-dictatorial methods to hasten the process of social evolution and to establish order in their lands—lands which were left spiritual voids by a too-long Western occupation and domination. Why pretend to be shocked at this? You would do the same if you were in their place. You have done it in the West over and over again. You do it in every war you fight, in every crisis, political or economic, you have. And don't you feel and know that, as soon as order has been established by your Western-educated leaders, they will, in order to be powerful, surrender the personal power that they have had to wield?*

Let us recognize what our common problem really is. Let us rethink what the issue is. This problem is vast and complicated. Merely to grasp it takes an act of the imagination. This problem, though it has racial overtones, is not racial. Though it has religious aspects, it is not religious. Though it has strong economic motives, it is not wholly economic. And though political action will, no doubt, constitute the main means, the *modus operandi*, of its solution, the problem is not basically political.

The problem is freedom. How can Asians and Africans be free of their stultifying traditions and customs and become industrialized, and powerful, if you like, like the West?

I say that the West cannot ask the elite of Asia and Africa, even though educated in the West, to copy or ape what has happened in the West. Why? Because the West has never really been honest with itself about how it overcame its own traditions and blinding customs.

Let us look at some examples of Western interpretation of its own history. A Civil War was fought in America and American school children are taught

---

*Here is a paradox: Nehru is as powerful as an emperor; Nkrumah is a *de facto* dictator; yet both men are staunch democrats and are using their vast personal power to sponsor measures that will undermine their "cult of the personality"! The key to their motives is that they seek power not for themselves, but for their people!

that it was to free the black slaves. It was not. It was to establish a republic, to create conditions of economic freedom, to clear the ground for the launching of an industrial society. (Naturally, slavery had to go in such a situation. I'm emphasizing the positive historic aspects, not the negative and inevitable ones!) The French fought a long and bloody Revolution and French school children are taught that it was for Liberty, Equality, and Fraternity. Yet we know that it was for the right of a middle class to think, to buy and sell, to enable men with talent to rise in their careers, and to push back (which was inevitable and implied) the power of the Church and the nobility. The English, being more unintentionally forthright than others, never made much bones about the fact that the freedom that they fought for was a freedom of trade.

Do these misinterpretations of Western history by the West negate the power and net historical gains of the Western world? No. It is not what the West said it did, but what the results really were that count in the long run.

Why have I raised these points of Western contradictions? Because, when non-Westerners, having the advantage of seeing more clearly—being psychologically *outside* of the West—what the West did, and when non-Westerners seek to travel that same road, the West raises strong objections, moral ones. I've had a white Westerner tell me: "You know, we must stay in Africa to protect the naked black natives. If we leave, the blacks we have educated will practice fascism against their own people." So this man was in a position to endorse the shooting down of a black elite because that black elite wanted to impose conditions relating to the control of imports and exports, something which his country practiced every day with hordes of armed policemen to enforce the laws regulating imports and exports!

The same objections are leveled against Nkrumah in the Gold Coast, against Sukarno in Indonesia, against Nasser in Egypt, against Nehru in India. Wise Westerners would insist that stern measures be taken by the elite of Asia and Africa to overcome the irrational forces of racism, superstition, etc. But if a selfish West hamstrings the elite of Asia and Africa, distrusts their motives, a spirit of absolutism will rise in Asia and Africa and will provoke a spirit of counterabsolutism in the West. In case that happens, all will be lost. We shall all, Asia and Africa as well as Europe, be thrown back into an age of racial and religious wars, and the precious heritage—the freedom of speech, the secular state, the independent personality, the autonomy of science—which is not Western or Eastern, but human, will be snuffed out of the minds of men.

The problem is freedom from a dead past. And freedom to build a rational future. How much are we willing to risk for freedom? I say let us risk everything. Freedom begets freedom. Europe, I say to you before it is too late: Let the Africans and Asians whom you have educated in Europe have their freedom, or you will lose your own in trying to keep freedom from them.

But how can this be done? Have we any recent precedent for such procedure? Is my suggestion outlandish? Unheard of? No. A ready answer and a vivid example are close at hand. A scant ten years ago we concluded a tragically desperate and costly war in Europe to beat back the engulfing tides of an irrational fascism. During those tense and eventful days I recall hearing Winston Churchill make this appeal to the Americans, when Britain was hard-pressed by hordes of German and Italian fascists:

"Give us the tools and we'll finish the job."

Today I say to the white men of Europe:

"You have, however misguidedly, trained and educated an elite in Africa and Asia. You have implanted in their hearts the hunger for freedom and rationality. Now this elite of yours—your children, one might say—is hard-pressed by hunger, disease, poverty, by stagnant economic conditions, by unbalanced class structures of their societies, by surging tides of racial shame, by oppressive and irrational tribal religions. You men of Europe made an abortive beginning to solve that problem. You failed. Now, I say to you: Men of Europe, give that elite the tools and let it finish that job!"

FREEDOM IS INDIVISIBLE.

W. E. B. Du Bois
American Negroes and Africa's Rise to Freedom

In the United States in 1860 there were some 17,000,000 persons of African descent. In the eighteenth century they had regarded Africa as their home to which they would eventually return when free. They named their institutions "African" and started migration to Africa as early as 1815. But the American Negroes were soon sadly disillusioned: first their immigrants to Liberia found that Africans did not regard them as Africans; and then it became clear by 1830 that colonization schemes were a device to rid America of free Africans so as to fasten slavery more firmly to support the Cotton Kingdom.

Negroes therefore slowly turned to a new ideal: to strive for equality as American citizens, determined that when Africa needed them they would be equipped to lead them into civilization. Meantime, however, American Negroes learned from their environment to think less and less of their fatherland and its folk. They learned little of its history or its present conditions. They began to despise the colored races along with the white Americans and to acquiesce in color prejudice.

From 1825 to 1860 the American Negro went through hell. He yelled in desperation as the slave power tried to make the whole union a slave nation and then to extend its power over the West Indies; he became the backbone of the abolition movement; he led thousands of fugitives to freedom; he died with John Brown and made the North victorious in the Civil War. For a few years he led democracy in the South until a new and powerful capitalism disfranchised him by 1876.

Meantime a great change was sweeping the earth. Socialism was spreading; first in theory and experiment for a half century and then at last in 1917 in Russia where a communist state was founded. The world was startled and frightened. The United States joined 16 other nations to prevent this experiment which all wise men said would fail miserably in a short time. But it did not fail. It defended its right to try a new life, and staggered on slowly but surely began to prove to all who would look that communism could exist and prosper.

What effect did this have on American Negroes? By this time their leaders had become patriotic Americans, imitating white Americans without criticism. If Americans said that communism had failed, then it had failed. And this of course Americans did say and repeat. Big business declared communism a crime and communists and socialists criminals. Some Americans and some Negroes did not believe this; but they lost employment or went to jail.

Meantime, many thoughtful white Americans, fearing the advance of socialism and communism not only in Europe but in America under the "New Deal," conceived a new tack. They said the American color line cannot be held in the face of communism. It is quite possible that we can help beat communism if in America we begin to loosen if not break the color line.

The movement started and culminated in a Supreme Court decision which was a body blow to color discrimination, and certainly if enforced would take the wind out of the sails of critics of American democracy.

To Negroes the government said, it will be a fine thing now if you tell foreigners that our Negro problem is settled; and in such case we can help with your expenses of travel. A remarkable number of Negroes of education and standing found themselves able to travel and testify that American Negroes now had no complaints.

Then came three disturbing facts: (1) The Soviet Union was forging ahead in education and science and it drew no color line. (2) Outside the Soviet Union, in England, France and all West Europe, especially Scandinavia, socialism was spreading: state housing, state ownership of railroads, telegraphs and telephones, subways, buses and other public facilities; social medicine, higher education, old age care, insurance and many other sorts of relief; even in the United States, the New Deal was socialism no matter what it was called. (3) The former slave South had no intention of obeying the Supreme Court. To the Bourbon South it was said: don't worry, the law will not be enforced for a decade if not a century. Most Negroes still cannot vote, their schools are poor and the black workers are exploited, diseased and at the bottom of the economic pile. Trade unions north as well as south still discriminate against black labor. But finally a new and astonishing event was the sudden rise of Africa.

My own study had for a long time turned toward Africa. I planned a series of charts in 1900 for the Paris Exposition, which gained a Grand Prize. I attended a Pan-African conference in London and was made secretary of the meeting and drafted its resolutions.

In 1911 the Ethical Culture Societies of the world called a races congress in London and made Felix Adler and me secretaries for America. In 1915 I published my first book on African history and there was much interest and discussion. In 1919 I planned a Pan-African Congress, but got little support. Blaise Diagne of Senegal, whose volunteers had saved France from the first onslaught of the Germans in World War I, induced Clemenceau to allow the Congress despite the opposition of the United States and Britain. It was a small meeting, but it aroused a West African Congress the next year which was the beginning of independence of Ghana and Nigeria.

In 1921 I called a second Pan-African Congress to meet in London, Paris and Brussels. This proved a large and influential meeting, with delegates from the whole Negro world. The wide publicity it gained led to the organization of congresses in many parts of Africa by the natives. Our attempt to form a permanent organization located in Paris was betrayed but I succeeded in assembling a small meeting in London and Lisbon in 1923. I tried a fourth congress in Tunis but France forbade it. At last in 1927 I called the Fourth Pan-African Congress in New York. It was fairly well attended by American Negroes but few Africans. Then the Second World War approached and the work was interrupted.

Meanwhile methods changed and ideas expanded. Africans themselves began to demand more voice in colonial government and the Second World War had made their cooperation so necessary to Europe that at the end actual and unexpected freedom for African colonies was in sight.

Moreover there miraculously appeared Africans able to take charge of these governments. American Negroes of former generations had always calculated that when Africa was ready for freedom, American Negroes would be ready to lead them. But the event was quite opposite. The African leaders proved to be Africans, some indeed educated in the United States, but most of them trained in Europe and in Africa itself. American Negroes for the most part showed neither the education nor the aptitude for the magnificent opportunity which was suddenly offered. Indeed, it now seems that Africans may have to show American Negroes the way to freedom.

The rise of Africa in the last 15 years has astonished the world. Even the most doubting of American Negroes have suddenly become aware of Africa and its possibilities and particularly of the relation of Africa to the American Negro. The first reaction was typically American. Since 1910 American Negroes had been fighting for equal opportunity in the United States. Indeed, Negroes soon faced a curious paradox.

Now equality began to be offered; but in return for equality, Negroes must join American business in its domination of African cheap labor and free raw materials. The educated and well-to-do Negroes would have a better chance to make money if they would testify that Negroes were not discriminated against and join in American red-baiting.

American Negroes began to appear in Africa, seeking chances to make money and testifying to Negro progress. In many cases their expenses were paid by the State Department. Meantime Negro American colleges ceased to teach socialism and the Negro masses believed with the white masses that communism is a crime and all socialists conspirators.

Africans know better. They have not yet all made up their minds what side to take in the power contest between East and West but they recognize the accomplishments of the Soviet Union and the rise of China.

Meantime American Negroes in their segregated schools and with lack of leadership have no idea of this world trend. The effort to give them equality has been over-emphasized and some of our best scholars and civil servants have been bribed by the State Department to testify abroad and especially in Africa to the success of capitalism in making the American Negro free. Yet it was British capitalism which made the African slave trade the greatest commercial venture in the world; and it was American slavery that raised capitalism to its domination in the nineteenth century and gave birth to the Sugar Empire and the Cotton Kingdom. It was new capitalism which nullified Abolition and keeps us in serfdom.

The Africans know this. They have in many cases lived in America. They have in other cases been educated in the Soviet Union and even in China. They will make up their minds on communism and not listen solely to American lies. The latest voice to reach them is from Cuba.

Would it not be wise for American Negroes themselves to read a few books and do a little thinking for themselves? It is not that I would persuade Negroes to become communists, capitalists or holy rollers; but whatever belief they reach, let it for God's sake be a matter of reason and not of ignorance, fear, and selling their souls to the devil.

Martin Luther King, Jr.
Letter From Birmingham Jail

My Dear Fellow Clergymen:

While confined here in the Birmingham city jail, I came across your recent statement calling my present activities "unwise and untimely." Seldom do I pause to answer criticism of my work and ideas. If I sought to answer all the criticisms that cross my desk, my secretaries would have little time for anything other than such correspondence in the course of the day, and I would have no time for constructive work. But since I feel that you are men of genuine good will and that your criticisms are sincerely set forth, I want to try to answer your statement in what I hope will be patient and reasonable terms.

I think I should indicate why I am here in Birmingham, since you have been influenced by the view which argues against "outsiders coming in." I have the honor of serving as president of the Southern Christian Leadership Conference, an organization operating in every southern state, with headquarters in Atlanta, Georgia. We have some eighty-five affiliated organizations across the South, and one of them is the Alabama Christian Movement for Human Rights. Frequently we share staff, educational, and financial resources with our affiliates. Several months ago the affiliate here in Birmingham asked us to be on call to engage in a nonviolent direct-action program if such were deemed necessary. We readily consented, and when the hour came we lived up to our promise. So I, along with several members of my staff, am here because I was invited here. I am here because I have organizational ties here.

But more basically, I am in Birmingham because injustice is here. Just as the prophets of the eighth century B.C. left their villages and carried their "thus saith the Lord" far beyond the boundaries of their home towns, and just as the Apostle Paul left his village of Tarsus and carried the gospel of Jesus Christ to the far corners of the Greco-Roman world, so am I compelled to carry the gospel of freedom beyond my own home town. Like Paul, I must constantly respond to the Macedonian call for aid.

Moreover, I am cognizant of the interrelatedness of all communities and states. I cannot sit idly by in Atlanta and not be concerned about what happens in Birmingham. Injustice anywhere is a threat to justice everywhere. We are caught in an inescapable network of mutuality, tied in a single garment of destiny. Whatever affects one directly, affects all indirectly. Never again can we afford to live with the narrow, provincial "outside agitator" idea. Anyone who lives inside the United States can never be considered an outsider anywhere within its bounds.

You deplore the demonstrations taking place in Birmingham. But your statement, I am sorry to say, fails to express a similar concern for the conditions that brought about the demonstrations. I am sure that none of you would want to rest content with the superficial kind of social analysis that deals merely with effects and does not grapple with underlying causes. It is unfortunate that demonstrations are taking place in Birmingham, but it is even more unfortunate that the city's white power structure left the Negro community with no alternative.

In any nonviolent campaign there are four basic steps: collection of the facts to determine whether injustices exist; negotiation; self-purification; and direct action. We have gone through all these steps in Birmingham. There can be no gainsaying the fact that racial injustice engulfs this community. Birmingham is probably the most thoroughly segregated city in the United States. Its ugly record of brutality is widely known. Negroes have experienced grossly unjust treatment in the courts. There have been more unsolved bombings of Negro homes and churches in Birmingham than in any other city in the nation. These are the hard, brutal facts of the case. On the basis of these conditions, Negro leaders sought to negotiate with the city fathers. But the latter consistently refused to engage in good-faith negotiation.

Then, last September, came the opportunity to talk with leaders of Birmingham's economic community. In the course of the negotiations, certain promises were made by the merchants—for example, to remove the stores' humiliating racial signs. On the basis of these promises, the Reverend Fred Shuttlesworth and the leaders of the Alabama Christian Movement for Human Rights agreed to a moratorium on all demonstrations. As the weeks and months went by, we realized that we were the victims of a broken promise. A few signs, briefly removed, returned; the others remained.

As in so many past experiences, our hopes had been blasted, and the shadow of deep disappointment settled upon us. We had no alternative except to prepare for direct action, whereby we would present our very bodies as a means of laying our case before the conscience of the local and the national community. Mindful of the difficulties involved, we decided to undertake a process of self-purification. We began a series of workshops on nonviolence, and we repeatedly asked ourselves: "Are you able to accept blows without retaliating?" "Are you able to endure the ordeal of jail?" We decided to schedule our direct-action program for the Easter season, realizing that except for Christmas, this is the main shopping period of the year. Knowing that a strong economic-withdrawal program would be the by-product of direct action, we felt that this would be the best time to bring pressure to bear on the merchants for the needed change.

Then it occurred to us that Birmingham's mayoral election was coming up in March, and we speedily decided to postpone action until after election day. When we discovered that the Commissioner of Public Safety, Eugene "Bull"

Connor, had piled up enough votes to be in the run-off, we decided again to postpone action until the day after the run-off so that the demonstrations could not be used to cloud the issues. Like many others, we wanted to see Mr. Connor defeated, and to this end we endured postponement after postponement. Having aided in this community need, we felt that our direct-action program could be delayed no longer.

You may well ask, "Why direct action? Why sit-ins, marches, and so forth? Isn't negotiation a better path?" You are quite right in calling for negotiation. Indeed, this is the very purpose of direct action. Nonviolent direct action seeks to create such a crisis and foster such a tension that a community which has constantly refused to negotiate is forced to confront the issue. It seeks so to dramatize the issue that it can no longer be ignored. My citing the creation of tension as part of the work of the nonviolent-resister may sound rather shocking. But I must confess that I am not afraid of the word "tension." I have earnestly opposed violent tension, but there is a type of constructive, nonviolent tension which is necessary for growth. Just as Socrates felt that it was necessary to create a tension in the mind so that individuals could rise from the bondage of myths and half-truths to the unfettered realm of creative analysis and objective appraisal, so must we see the need for nonviolent gadflies to create the kind of tension in society that will help men rise from the dark depths of prejudice and racism to the majestic heights of understanding and brotherhood.

The purpose of our direct-action program is to create a situation so crisis-packed that it will inevitably open the door to negotiation. I therefore concur with you in your call for negotiation. Too long has our beloved Southland been bogged down in a tragic effort to live in monologue rather than dialogue.

One of the basic points in your statement is that the action that I and my associates have taken in Birmingham is untimely. Some have asked: "Why didn't you give the new city administration time to act?" The only answer that I can give to this query is that the new Birmingham administration must be prodded about as much as the outgoing one, before it will act. We are sadly mistaken if we feel that the election of Albert Boutwell as mayor will bring the millennium to Birmingham. While Mr. Boutwell is a much more gentle person than Mr. Connor, they are both segregationists, dedicated to maintenance of the status quo. I have hoped that Mr. Boutwell will be reasonable enough to see the futility of massive resistance to desegregation. But he will not see this without pressure from devotees of civil rights. My friends, I must say to you that we have not made a single gain in civil rights without determined legal and nonviolent pressure. Lamentably, it is an historical fact that privileged groups seldom give up their privileges voluntarily. Individuals may see the moral light and voluntarily give up their unjust posture; but, as Reinhold Niebuhr has reminded us, groups tend to be more immoral than individuals.

We know through painful experience that freedom is never voluntarily given by the oppressor; it must be demanded by the oppressed. Frankly, I have yet to engage in a direct-action campaign that was "well timed" in the view of those who have not suffered unduly from the disease of segregation. For years now I have heard the word "Wait!" It rings in the ear of every Negro with piercing familiarity. This "Wait" has almost always meant "Never." We must come to see, with one of our distinguished jurists, that "justice too long delayed is justice denied."

We have waited for more than 340 years for our constitutional and God-given rights. The nations of Asia and Africa are moving with jetlike speed toward gaining political independence, but we still creep at horse-and-buggy pace toward gaining a cup of coffee at a lunch counter. Perhaps it is easy for those who have never felt the stinging darts of segregation to say, "Wait." But when you have seen vicious mobs lynch your mothers and fathers at will and drown your sisters and brothers at whim; when you have seen hate-filled policemen curse, kick, and even kill your black brothers and sisters; when you see the vast majority of your twenty million Negro brothers smothering in an airtight cage of poverty in the midst of an affluent society; when you suddenly find your tongue twisted and your speech stammering as you seek to explain to your six-year-old daughter why she can't go to the public amusement park that has just been advertised on television, and see tears welling up in her eyes when she is told that Funtown is closed to colored children, and see ominous clouds of inferiority beginning to form in her little mental sky, and see her beginning to distort her personality by developing an unconscious bitterness toward white people; when you have to concoct an answer for a five-year-old son who is asking, "Daddy, why do white people treat colored people so mean?"; when you take a cross-country drive and find it necessary to sleep night after night in the uncomfortable corners of your automobile because no motel will accept you; when you are humiliated day in and day out by nagging signs reading "white" and "colored"; when your first name becomes "nigger," your middle name becomes "boy" (however old you are) and your last name becomes "John," and your wife and mother are never given the respected title "Mrs."; when you are harried by day and haunted by night by the fact that you are a Negro, living constantly at tiptoe stance, never quite knowing what to expect next, and are plagued with inner fears and outer resentments; when you are forever fighting a degenerating sense of "nobodiness"—then you will understand why we find it difficult to wait. There comes a time when the cup of endurance runs over, and men are no longer willing to be plunged into the abyss of despair. I hope, sirs, you can understand our legitimate and unavoidable impatience.

You express a great deal of anxiety over our willingness to break laws. This is certainly a legitimate concern. Since we so diligently urge people to obey the Supreme Court's decision of 1954 outlawing segregation in the public schools, at first glance it may seem rather paradoxical for us consciously to break laws. One may well ask: "How can you advocate breaking some laws and obeying others?" The answer lies in the fact that there are two types of laws: just and unjust. I would be the first to advocate obeying just laws. One has not only a legal but a moral responsibility to obey just laws. Conversely, one has a moral responsibility to disobey unjust laws. I would agree with St. Augustine that "an unjust law is no law at all."

Now, what is the difference between the two? How does one determine whether a law is just or unjust? A just law is a man-made code that squares with the moral law or the law of God. An unjust law is a code that is out of harmony with the moral law. To put it in the terms of St. Thomas Aquinas: An unjust law is a human law that is not rooted in eternal law and natural law. Any law that uplifts human personality is just. Any law that degrades human personality is unjust. All segregation statutes are unjust because segregation distorts the soul and damages the personality. It gives the segregator a false sense of superiority and the segregated a false sense of inferiority. Segregation, to use the terminology of the Jewish philosopher Martin Buber, substitutes an "I-it" relationship for an "I-thou" relationship and ends up relegating persons to the status of things. Hence segregation is not only politically, economically, and sociologically unsound, it is morally wrong and sinful. Paul Tillich has said that sin is separation. Is not segregation an existential expression of man's tragic separation, his awful estrangement, his terrible sinfulness? Thus it is that I can urge men to obey the 1954 decision of the Supreme Court, for it is morally right; and I can urge them to disobey segregation ordinances, for they are morally wrong.

Let us consider a more concrete example of just and unjust laws. An unjust law is a code that a numerical or power majority group compels a minority group to obey but does not make binding on itself. This is *difference* made legal. By the same token, a just law is a code that a majority compels a minority to follow and that it is willing to follow itself. This is *sameness* made legal.

Let me give another explanation. A law is unjust if it is inflicted on a minority that, as a result of being denied the right to vote, had no part in enacting or devising the law. Who can say that the legislature of Alabama which set up that state's segregation laws was democratically elected? Throughout Alabama all sorts of devious methods are used to prevent Negroes from becoming registered voters, and there are some counties in which, even though Negroes constitute a majority of the population, not a single Negro is registered. Can any law enacted under such circumstances be considered democratically structured?

Sometimes a law is just on its face and unjust in its application. For instance, I have been arrested on a charge of parading without a permit. Now, there is nothing wrong in having an ordinance which requires a permit for a parade. But such an ordinance becomes unjust when it is used to maintain segregation and to deny citizens the First-Amendment privilege of peaceful assembly and protest.

I hope you are able to see the distinction I am trying to point out. In no sense do I advocate evading or defying the law, as would the rabid segregationist. That would lead to anarchy. One who breaks an unjust law must do so openly, lovingly, and with a willingness to accept the penalty. I submit that an individual who breaks a law that conscience tells him is unjust, and who willingly accepts the penalty of imprisonment in order to arouse the conscience of the community over its injustice, is in reality expressing the highest respect for law.

Of course, there is nothing new about this kind of civil disobedience. It was evidenced sublimely in the refusal of Shadrach, Meshach, and Abednego to obey the laws of Nebuchadnezzar, on the ground that a higher moral law was at stake. It was practiced superbly by the early Christians, who were willing to face hungry lions and the excruciating pain of chopping blocks rather than submit to certain unjust laws of the Roman Empire. To a degree, academic freedom is a reality today because Socrates practiced civil disobedience. In our own nation, the Boston Tea Party represented a massive act of civil disobedience.

We should never forget that everything Adolf Hitler did in Germany was "legal" and everything the Hungarian freedom fighters did in Hungary was "illegal." It was "illegal" to aid and comfort a Jew in Hitler's Germany. Even so, I am sure that, had I lived in Germany at the time, I would have aided and comforted my Jewish brothers. If today I lived in a Communist country where certain principles dear to the Christian faith are suppressed, I would openly advocate disobeying that country's anti-religious laws.

I must make two honest confessions to you, my Christian and Jewish brothers. First, I must confess that over the past few years I have been gravely disappointed with the white moderate. I have almost reached the regrettable conclusion that the Negro's great stumbling block in his stride toward freedom is not the White Citizen's Counciler or the Ku Klux Klanner, but the white moderate, who is more devoted to "order" than to justice; who prefers a negative peace which is the absence of tension to a positive peace which is the presence of justice; who constantly says, "I agree with you in the goal you seek, but I cannot agree with your methods of direct action"; who paternalistically believes he can set the timetable for another man's freedom; who lives by a mythical concept of time and who constantly advises the Negro to wait for a "more convenient season." Shallow understanding from people of good will is more frustrating than absolute misunderstanding from people of ill will. Lukewarm acceptance is much more bewildering than outright rejection.

I had hoped that the white moderate would understand that law and order exist for the purpose of establishing justice and that when they fail in this purpose they become the dangerously structured dams that block the flow of social progress. I had hoped that the white moderate would understand that the present tension in the South is a necessary phase of the transition from an obnoxious negative peace, in which the Negro passively accepted his unjust plight, to a substantive and positive peace, in which all men will respect the dignity and worth of human personality. Actually, we who engage in nonviolent direct action are not the creators of tension. We merely bring to the surface the hidden tension that is already alive. We bring it out in the open, where it can be seen and dealt with. Like a boil that can never be cured so long as it is covered up but must be opened with all its ugliness to the natural medicines of air and light, injustice must be exposed, with all the tension its exposure creates, to the light of human conscience and the air of national opinion, before it can be cured.

In your statement you assert that our actions, even though peaceful, must be condemned because they precipitate violence. But is this a logical assertion? Isn't this like condemning a robbed man because his possession of money precipitated the evil act of robbery? Isn't this like condemning Socrates because his unswerving commitment to truth and his philosophical inquiries precipitated the act by the misguided populace in which they made him drink hemlock? Isn't this like condemning Jesus because his unique God-consciousness and never-ceasing devotion to God's will precipitated the evil act of crucifixion? We must come to see that, as the federal courts have consistently affirmed, it is wrong to urge an individual to cease his efforts to gain his basic constitutional rights because the quest may precipitate violence. Society must protect the robbed and punish the robber.

I had also hoped that the white moderate would reject the myth concerning time in relation to the struggle for freedom. I have just received a letter from a white brother in Texas. He writes: "All Christians know that the colored people will receive equal rights eventually, but it is possible that you are in too great a religious hurry. It has taken Christianity almost two thousand years to accomplish what it has. The teachings of Christ take time to come to earth." Such an attitude stems from a tragic misconception of time, from the strangely irrational notion that there is something in the very flow of time that will inevitably cure all ills. Actually, time itself is neutral; it can be used either destructively or constructively. More and more I feel that the people of ill will have used time much more effectively than have the people of good will. We will have to repent in this generation not merely for the hateful words and actions of the bad people, but for the appalling silence of the good people. Human progress never rolls in on wheels of inevitability; it comes through the tireless efforts of men willing to be co-workers with God, and without this hard work, time itself becomes an ally of the forces of social stagnation. We must use time creatively, in the knowledge that the time is always ripe to do right. Now is the time to make real the promise of democracy and transform our pending national elegy into a creative psalm of brotherhood. Now is the time to lift our national policy from the quicksand of racial injustice to the solid rock of human dignity.

You speak of our activity in Birmingham as extreme. At first I was rather disappointed that fellow clergymen would see my nonviolent efforts as those of an extremist. I began thinking about the fact that I stand in the middle of two opposing forces in the Negro community. One is a force of complacency, made up in part of Negroes who, as a result of long years of oppression, are so drained of self-respect and a sense of "somebodiness" that they have adjusted to segregation; and in part of a few middle-class Negroes who, because of a degree of academic and economic security and because in some ways they profit by segregation, have become insensitive to the problems of the masses. The other force is one of bitterness and hatred, and it comes perilously close to advocating violence. It is expressed in the various black nationalist groups that are springing up across the nation, the largest and best-known being Elijah Muhammad's Muslim movement. Nourished by the Negro's frustration over the continued existence of racial discrimination, this movement is made up of people who have lost faith in America, who have absolutely repudiated Christianity, and who have concluded that the white man is an incorrigible "devil."

I have tried to stand between these two forces, saying that we need emulate neither the "do-nothingism" of the complacent nor the hatred and despair of the black nationalist. For there is the more excellent way of love and nonviolent protest. I am grateful to God that, through the influence of the Negro church, the way of nonviolence became an integral part of our struggle.

If this philosophy had not emerged, by now many streets of the South would, I am convinced, be flowing with blood. And I am further convinced that if our white brothers dismiss as "rabblerousers" and "outside agitators" those of us who employ nonviolent direct action, and if they refuse to support our nonviolent efforts, millions of Negroes will, out of frustration and despair, seek solace and security in black-nationalist ideologies—a development that would inevitably lead to a frightening racial nightmare.

Oppressed people cannot remain oppressed forever. The yearning for freedom eventually manifests itself, and that is what has happened to the American Negro. Something within has reminded him of his birthright of freedom, and something without has reminded him that it can be gained. Consciously or unconsciously, he has been caught up by the *Zeitgeist*, and with his black brothers of Africa and his brown and yellow brothers of Asia, South America, and the Caribbean, the United States Negro is moving with a sense of great urgency toward the promised land of racial justice. If one recognizes this vital urge that has engulfed the Negro community, one should readily understand why public demonstrations are taking place. The Negro has many pent-up resentments and latent frustrations, and he must release them. So let him march; let him make prayer pilgrimages to the city hall; let him go on freedom rides— and try to understand why he must do so. If his repressed emotions are not released in nonviolent ways, they will seek expression through violence; this is not a threat but a fact of history. So I have not said to my people, "Get rid of your discontent." Rather, I have tried to say that this normal and healthy discontent can be channeled into the creative outlet of nonviolent direct action. And now this approach is being termed extremist.

But though I was initially disappointed at being categorized as an extremist, as I continued to think about the matter I gradually gained a measure of satisfaction from the label. Was not Jesus an extremist for love: "Love your enemies, bless them that curse you, do good to them that hate you, and pray for them which despitefully use you, and persecute you." Was not Amos an extremist for justice: "Let justice roll down like waters and righteousness like an ever-flowing stream." Was not Paul an extremist for the Christian gospel: "I bear in my body the marks of the Lord Jesus." Was not Martin Luther an extremist: "Here I stand; I cannot do otherwise, so help me God." And John Bunyan: "I will stay in jail to the end of my days before I make a butchery of my conscience." And Abraham Lincoln: "This nation cannot survive half slave and half free." And Thomas Jefferson: "We hold these truths to be self-evident, that all men are created equal...." So the question is not whether we will be extremists, but what kind of extremists we will be. Will we be extremists for hate or for love? Will we be extremists for the preservation of injustice or for the extension of justice? In that dramatic scene on Calvary's hill three men were crucified. We must never forget that all three were crucified for the same crime—the crime of extremism. Two were extremists for immorality, and thus fell below their environment. The other, Jesus Christ, was an extremist for love, truth, and goodness, and thereby rose above his environment. Perhaps the South, the nation, and the world are in dire need of creative extremists.

I had hoped that the white moderate would see this need. Perhaps I was too optimistic; perhaps I expected too much. I suppose I should have realized that few members of the oppressor race can understand the deep groans and passionate yearnings of the oppressed race, and still fewer have the vision to see that injustice must be rooted out by strong, persistent, and determined action. I am thankful, however, that some of our white brothers in the South have grasped the meaning of this social revolution and committed themselves to it. They are still all too few in quantity, but they are big in quality. Some—such as Ralph McGill, Lillian Smith, Harry Golden, James McBridge Dabbs, Ann Braden, and Sarah Patton Boyle—have written about our struggle in eloquent and prophetic terms. Others have marched with us down nameless streets of the South. They have languished in filthy, roach-infested jails, suffering the abuse and brutality of policemen who view them as "dirty nigger-lovers." Unlike so many of their moderate brothers and sisters, they have recognized the urgency of the moment and sensed the need for powerful "action" antidotes to combat the disease of segregation.

Let me take note of my other major disappointment. I have been so greatly disappointed with the white church and its leadership. Of course, there are some notable exceptions. I am not unmindful of the fact that each of you has taken some significant stands on this issue. I commend you, Reverend Stallings, for your Christian stand on this past Sunday, in welcoming Negroes to your worship service on a nonsegregated basis. I commend the Catholic leaders of this state for integrating Spring Hill College several years ago.

But despite these notable exceptions, I must honestly reiterate that I have been disappointed with the church. I do not say this as one of those negative critics who can always find something wrong with the church. I say this as a minister of the gospel, who loves the church; who was nurtured in its bosom; who has been sustained by its spiritual blessings and who will remain true to it as long as the cord of life shall lengthen.

When I was suddenly catapulted into the leadership of the bus protest in Montgomery, Alabama, a few years ago, I felt we would be supported by the white church. I felt that the white ministers, priests, and rabbis of the South would be among our strongest allies. Instead, some have been outright opponents, refusing to understand the freedom movement and misrepresenting its leaders; all too many others have been more cautious than courageous and have remained silent behind the anesthetizing security of stainedglass windows.

In spite of my shattered dreams, I came to Birmingham with the hope that the white religious leadership of this community would see the justice of our cause and, with deep moral concern, would serve as the channel through which our just grievances could reach the power structure. I had hoped that each of you would understand. But again I have been disappointed.

I have heard numerous southern religious leaders admonish their worshipers to comply with a desegregation decision because it is the law, but I have longed to hear white ministers declare: "Follow this decree because integration is morally right and because the Negro is your brother." In the midst of blatant injustices inflicted upon the Negro, I have watched white churchmen stand on the sideline and mouth pious irrelevancies and sanctimonious trivialities. In the midst of a mighty struggle to rid our nation of racial and economic injustice, I have heard many ministers say: "Those are social issues, with which the gospel has no real concern." And I have watched many churches commit themselves to a completely otherworldly religion which makes a strange, un-Biblical distinction between body and soul, between the sacred and the secular.

I have traveled the length and breadth of Alabama, Mississippi, and all the other southern states. On sweltering summer days and crisp autumn mornings I have looked at the South's beautiful churches with their lofty spires pointing heavenward. I have beheld the impressive outlines of her massive religious-education buildings. Over and over I have found myself asking: "What kind of people worship here? Who is their God? Where were their voices when the lips of Governor Barnett dripped with words of interposition and nullification? Where were they when Governor Wallace gave a clarion call for defiance and hatred? Where were their voices of support when bruised and weary Negro men and women decided to rise from the dark dungeons of complacency to the bright hills of creative protest?"

Yes, these questions are still in my mind. In deep disappointment I have wept over the laxity of the church. But be assured that my tears have been tears of love. There can be no deep disappointment where there is not deep love. Yes, I love the church. How could I do otherwise? I am in the rather unique position of being the son, the grandson, and the great-grandson of preachers. Yes, I see the church as the body of Christ. But, oh! How we have blemished and scarred that body through social neglect and through fear of being non-conformists.

There was a time when the church was very powerful—in the time when the early Christians rejoiced at being deemed worthy to suffer for what they believed. In those days the church was not merely a thermometer that recorded the ideas and principles of popular opinion; it was a thermostat that transformed the mores of society. Whenever the early Christians entered a town, the people in power became disturbed and immediately sought to convict the Christians for being "disturbers of the peace" and "outside agitators." But the Christians pressed on, in the conviction that they were "a colony of heaven," called to obey God rather than man. Small in number, they were big in commitment. They were too God-intoxicated to be "astronomically intimidated." By their effort and example they brought an end to such ancient evils as infanticide and gladiatorial contests.

Things are different now. So often the contemporary church is a weak, ineffectual voice with an uncertain sound. So often it is an arch-defender of the status quo. Far from being disturbed by the presence of the church, the power structure of the average community is consoled by the church's silent—and often even vocal—sanction of things as they are.

But the judgment of God is upon the church as never before. If today's church does not recapture the sacrificial spirit of the early church, it will lose its authenticity, forfeit the loyalty of millions, and be dismissed as an irrelevant social club with no meaning for the twentieth century. Every day I meet young people whose disappointment with the church has turned into outright disgust.

Perhaps I have once again been too optimistic. Is organized religion too inextricably bound to the status quo to save our nation and the world? Perhaps I must turn my faith to the inner spiritual church, the church within the church, as the true *ekklesia* and the hope of the world. But again I am thankful to God that some noble souls from the ranks of organized religion have broken loose from the paralyzing chains of conformity and joined us as active partners in the struggle for freedom. They have left their secure congregations and walked the streets of Albany, Georgia, with us. They have gone down the highways of the South on tortuous rides for freedom. Yes, they have gone to jail with us. Some have been dismissed from their churches, have lost the support of their bishops and fellow ministers. But they have acted in the faith that right defeated is stronger than evil triumphant. Their witness has been the spiritual salt that has preserved the true meaning of the gospel in these troubled times. They have carved a tunnel of hope through the dark mountain of disappointment.

I hope the church as a whole will meet the challenge of this decisive hour. But even if the church does not come to the aid of justice, I have no despair about the future. I have no fear about the outcome of our struggle in Birmingham, even if our motives are at present misunderstood. We will reach the goal of freedom in Birmingham and all over the nation, because the goal of America is freedom. Abused and scorned though we may be, our destiny is tied up with America's destiny. Before the pilgrims landed at Plymouth, we were here. Before the pen of Jefferson etched the majestic words of the Declaration of Independence across the pages of history, we were here. For more than two centuries our forebears labored in this country without wages; they made cotton king; they built the homes of their masters while suffering gross injustice and shameful humiliation—and yet out of a bottomless vitality they continued to thrive and develop. If the inexpressible cruelties of slavery could not stop us, the opposition we now face will surely fail. We will win our freedom because the sacred heritage of our nation and the eternal will of God are embodied in our echoing demands.

Before closing I feel impelled to mention one other point in your statement that has troubled me profoundly. You warmly commended the Birmingham police force for keeping "order" and "preventing violence." I doubt that you would have so warmly commended the police force if you had seen its dogs sinking their teeth into unarmed, nonviolent Negroes. I doubt that you would so quickly commend the policemen if you were to observe their ugly and inhumane treatment of Negroes here in the city jail; if you were to watch them push and curse old Negro women and young Negro girls; if you were to see them slap and kick old Negro men and young boys; if you were to observe them, as they did on two occasions, refuse to give us food because we wanted to sing our grace together. I cannot join you in your praise of the Birmingham police department.

It is true that the police have exercised a degree of discipline in handling the demonstrators. In this sense they have conducted themselves rather "nonviolently" in public. But for what purpose? To preserve the evil system of segregation. Over the past few years I have consistently preached that nonviolence demands that the means we use must be as pure as the ends we seek. I have tried to make clear that it is wrong to use immoral means to attain moral ends. But now I must affirm that it is just as wrong, or perhaps even more so, to use moral means to preserve immoral ends. Perhaps Mr. Connor and his policemen have been rather nonviolent in public, as was Chief Pritchett in Albany, Georgia, but they have used the moral means of nonviolence to maintain the immoral end of racial injustice. As T. S. Eliot has said, "The last temptation is the greatest treason: To do the right deed for the wrong reason."

I wish you had commended the Negro sit-inners and demonstrators of Birmingham for their sublime courage, their willingness to suffer, and their amazing discipline in the midst of great provocation. One day the South will recognize its real heroes. They will be the James Merediths, with the noble sense of purpose that enables them to face jeering and hostile mobs, and with the agonizing loneliness that characterizes the life of the pioneer. They will be old, oppressed, battered Negro women, symbolized in a seventy-two-year-old woman in Montgomery, Alabama, who rose up with a sense of dignity and with her people decided not to ride segregated buses, and who responded with ungrammatical profundity to one who inquired about her weariness: "My feets is tired, but my soul is at rest." They will be the young high school and college students, the young ministers of the gospel and a host of their elders, courageously and nonviolently sitting in at lunch counters and willingly going to jail for conscience' sake. One day the South will know that when these disinherited children of God sat down at lunch counters, they were in reality standing up for what is best in the American dream and for the most sacred values in our Judaeo-Christian heritage, thereby bringing our nation back to those great wells of democracy which were dug deep by the founding fathers in their formulation of the Constitution and the Declaration of Independence.

Never before have I written so long a letter. I'm afraid it is much too long to take your precious time. I can assure you that it would have been much shorter if I had been writing from a comfortable desk, but what else can one do when he is alone in a narrow jail cell, other than write long letters, think long thoughts, and pray long prayers?

If I have said anything in this letter that overstates the truth and indicates an unreasonable impatience, I beg you to forgive me. If I have said anything that understates the truth and indicates my having a patience that allows me to settle for anything less than brotherhood, I beg God to forgive me.

I hope this letter finds you strong in the faith. I also hope that circumstances will soon make it possible for me to meet each of you, not as an integrationist or a civil-rights leader but as a fellow clergyman and a Christian brother. Let us all hope that the dark clouds of racial prejudice will soon pass away and the deep fog of misunderstanding will be lifted from our fear-drenched communities, and in some not too distant tomorrow the radiant stars of love and brotherhood will shine over our great nation with all their scintillating beauty.

Yours for the cause of Peace and Brotherhood,
MARTIN LUTHER KING, JR.

Malcolm X
Not just an American problem, but a world problem

FIRST, brothers and sisters, I want to start by thanking you for taking the time to come out this evening and especially for the invitation for me to come up to Rochester and participate in this little informal discussion this evening on matters that are of common interest to all elements in the community, in the entire Rochester community. My reason for being here is to discuss the Black revolution that is going on, that's taking place on this earth, the manner in which it's taking place on the African continent, and the impact that it's having in Black communities, not only here in America but in England and in France and in other of the former colonial powers today.

Many of you probably read last week I made an effort to go to Paris and was turned away. And Paris doesn't turn anybody away. You know anybody is supposed to be able to go to France, it's supposed to be a very liberal place. But France is having problems today that haven't been highly publicized. And England is also having problems that haven't been highly publicized, because America's problems have been so highly publicized. But all of these three partners, or allies, have troubles in common today that the Black American, or Afro-American, isn't well enough up on.

And in order for you and me to know the nature of the struggle that you and I are involved in, we have to know not only the various ingredients involved at the local level and national level, but also the ingredients that are involved at the international level. And the problems of the Black man here in this country today have ceased to be a problem of just the American Negro or an American problem. It has become a problem that is so complex, and has so many implications in it, that you have to study it in its entire world, in the world context or in its international context, to really see it as it actually is. Otherwise you can't even follow the local issue, unless you know what part it plays in the entire international context. And when you look at it in that context, you see it in a different light, but you see it with more clarity.

And you should ask yourself why should a country like France be so concerned with a little insignificant American Negro that they would prohibit him from going there, when almost anybody else can go to that country whenever they desire. And it's primarily because the three countries have the same problems. And the problem is this: That in the Western Hemisphere, you and I haven't realized it, but we aren't exactly a minority on this earth. In the Western Hemisphere there are—there's the people in Brazil, two-thirds of the people in Brazil are dark-skinned people, the same as you and I. They are people of African origin, African ancestry—African background. And not only in Brazil, but throughout Latin America, the Caribbean, the United States, and Canada, you have people here who are of African origin.

Many of us fool ourselves into thinking of Afro-Americans as those only who are here in the United States. America is North America, Central America, and South America. Anybody of African ancestry in South America is an Afro-American. Anybody in Central America of African blood is an Afro-American. Anybody here in North America, including Canada, is an Afro-American if he has African ancestry—even down in the Caribbean, he's an Afro-American. So when I speak of the Afro-American, I'm not speaking of just the 22 million of us who are here in the United States. But the Afro-American is that large number of people in the Western Hemisphere, from the southernmost tip of South America to the northern-most tip of North America, all of whom have a common heritage and have a common origin when you go back to the roots of these people.

Now, there are four spheres of influence in the Western Hemisphere, where Black people are concerned. There's the Spanish influence, which means that Spain formerly colonized a certain area of the Western Hemisphere. There's the French sphere of influence, which means that area that she formerly colonized. The area that the British formerly colonized. And then those of us who are in the United States.

The area that was formerly colonized by the Spanish is commonly referred to as Latin America. They have many dark-skinned people there, of African ancestry. The area which the French colonized here in the Western Hemisphere is largely referred to as the French West Indies. And the area that the British colonized are those that are commonly referred to as the British West Indies, and also Canada. And then again, there's the United States. So we have these four different classifications of Black people, or nonwhite people, here in the Western Hemisphere.

Because of the poor economy of Spain, and because it has ceased to be an influence on the world scene as it formerly was, not very many of the people from—not very many of the black-skinned people from the Spanish sphere of influence migrate to Spain. But because of the high standard of living in France and England, you find many of the Black people from the British West Indies have been migrating to Great Britain, many of the Black people from the French West Indies migrate to France, and then you and I are already here.

So it means that the three major allies, the United States, Britain, and France, have a problem today that is a common problem. But you and I are never given enough information to realize that they have a common problem. And that common problem is the new mood that is reflected in the overall division of the Black people within continental France, within the same sphere of England, and also here in the United States. So that—and this mood has been changing to the same degree that the mood on the African continent has been changing. So when you find the African revolution taking place, and by African revolution I mean the emergence of African nations into independence that has been going on for the past ten or twelve years, has absolutely affected the mood of the Black people in the Western Hemisphere. So much so that when they migrate to England, they pose a problem for the English. And when they migrate to France, they pose a problem for the French. And when they—already here in the States—but when they awaken, and this same mood is reflected in the Black man in the States, then it poses a problem to the white man here in America.

And don't you think that the problem that the white man in America has is unique. France is having the same problem. And Great Britain is having the same problem. But the only difference between the problem in France and Britain and here is there have been many Black leaders that have risen up here in the Western Hemisphere, in the United States, that have created so much sort of militancy that has frightened the American whites. But that has been absent in France and England. And it has only been recently that the American Negro community and the British West Indian community, along with the African community in France, have begun to organize among themselves, and it's frightening France to death. And the same thing is happening in England. It is—up until recently it was disorganized completely. But recently, the West Indians in England, along with the African community in England, along with the Asians in England began to organize and work in coordination with each other, in conjunction with each other. And this has posed England a very serious problem.

So I had to give you that background, in order for you to understand some of the current problems that are developing here on this earth. And in no time can you understand the problems between Black and white people here in Rochester or Black and white people in Mississippi or Black and white people in California, unless you understand the basic problem that exists between Black and white people—not confined to the local level, but confined to the international, global level on this earth today. When you look at it in that context, you'll understand. But if you only try to look at it in the local context, you'll never understand. You have to see the trend that is taking place on this earth. And my purpose for coming here tonight is to try and give you as up-to-date an understanding of it all as is possible.

As many of you know, I left the Black Muslim movement and during the summer months, I spent five of those months on the—in the Middle East and on the African continent. During this time I visited many countries, first of which was Egypt, and then Arabia, then Kuwait, Lebanon, Sudan, Kenya, Ethiopia, Zanzibar, Tanganyika—which is now Tanzania—Nigeria, Ghana, Guinea, Liberia, Algeria. And then the five months that I was away I had an opportunity to hold lengthy discussions with President Nasser in Egypt, President Julius Nyerere in Tanzania, Jomo Kenyatta in Kenya, Milton Obote in Uganda, Azikiwe in Nigeria, Nkrumah in Ghana, and Sékou Touré in Guinea.

And during conversations with these men, and other Africans on that continent, there was much information exchanged that definitely broadened my understanding, and I feel, broadened my scope. For since coming back from over there, I have had no desire whatsoever to get bogged down in any picayune arguments with any bird-brained or small-minded people who happen to belong to organizations, based upon facts that are very misleading and don't get you anywhere when you have problems as complex as ours that are trying to get solved.

So I'm not here tonight to talk about some of these movements that are clashing with each other. I'm here to talk about the problem that's in front of all of us. And to have—and to do it in a very informal way. I never like to be tied down to a formal method or procedure when talking to an audience, because I find that usually the conversation that I'm involved in revolves around race, or things racial, which is not my fault. I didn't create the race problem. And you know, I didn't come to America on the *Mayflower* or at my own volition. Our people were brought here involuntarily, against our will. So if we pose the problem now, they shouldn't blame us for being here. They brought us here.

[*Applause*]

One of the reasons I feel that it is best to remain very informal when discussing this type of topic, when people are discussing things based on race, they have a tendency to be very narrow-minded and to get emotional and all involved in—especially white people. I have found white people that usually are very intelligent, until you get them to talking about the race problem. Then they get blind as a bat and want you to see what they know is the exact opposite of the truth. [*Applause*]

So what I would rather we try and do is be very informal, where we can relax and keep an open mind, and try and form the pattern or the habit of seeing for ourselves, hearing for ourselves, thinking for ourselves, and then we can come to an intelligent judgment for ourselves.

To straighten out my own position, as I did earlier in the day at Colgate, I'm a Muslim, which only means that my religion is Islam. I believe in God, the Supreme Being, the creator of the universe. This is a very simple form of religion, easy to understand. I believe in one God. It's just a whole lot better. But I believe in one God, and I believe that that God had one religion, has one religion, always will have one religion. And that that God taught all of the prophets the same religion, so there is no argument about who was greater or who was better: Moses, Jesus, Muhammad, or some of the others. All of them were prophets who came from one God. They had one doctrine, and that doctrine was designed to give clarification of humanity, so that all of humanity would see that it was one and have some kind of brotherhood that would be practiced here on this earth. I believe in that.

I believe in the brotherhood of man. But despite the fact that I believe in the brotherhood of man, I have to be a realist and realize that here in America we're in a society that doesn't practice brotherhood. It doesn't practice what it preaches. It preaches brotherhood, but it doesn't practice brotherhood. And because this society doesn't practice brotherhood, those of us who are Muslim—those of us who left the Black Muslim movement and regrouped as Muslims, in a movement based upon orthodox Islam—we believe in the brotherhood of Islam.

But we also realize that the problem facing Black people in this country is so complex and so involved and has been here so long, unsolved, that it is absolutely necessary for us to form another organization. Which we did, which is a nonreligious organization in which—is known as the Organization of Afro-American Unity, and it is so structured organizationally to allow for active participation of any Afro-American, any Black American, in a program that is designed to eliminate the negative political, economic, and social evils that our people are confronted by in this society. And we have that set up because we realize that we have to fight against the evils of a society that has failed to produce brotherhood for every member of that society. This in no way means that we're antiwhite, antiblue, antigreen, or antiyellow. We're antiwrong. We're antidiscrimination. We're antisegregation. We're against anybody who wants to practice some form of segregation or discrimination against us because we don't happen to be a color that's acceptable to you. . . . [*Applause*]

We don't judge a man because of the color of his skin. We don't judge you because you're white; we don't judge you because you're black; we don't judge you because you're brown. We judge you because of what you do and what you practice. And as long as you practice evil, we're against you. And for us, the most—the worst form of evil is the evil that's based upon judging a man because of the color of his skin. And I don't think anybody here can deny that we're living in a society that just doesn't judge a man according to his talents, according to his know-how, according to his possibility—background, or lack of academic background. This society judges a man solely upon the color of his skin. If you're white, you can go forward, and if you're Black, you have to fight your way every step of the way, and you still don't get forward. [*Applause*]

We are living in a society that is by and large controlled by people who believe in segregation. We are living in a society that is by and large controlled by a people who believe in racism, and practice segregation and discrimination and racism. We believe in a—and I say that it is controlled, not by the well-meaning whites, but controlled by the segregationists, the racists. And you can see by the pattern that this society follows all over the world. Right now in Asia you have the American army dropping bombs on dark-skinned people. You can't say that—it's as though you can justify being that far from home, dropping bombs on somebody else. If you were next door, I could see it, but you can't go that far away from this country and drop bombs on somebody else and justify your presence over there, not with me. [*Applause*]

It's racism. Racism practiced by America. Racism which involves a war against the dark-skinned people in Asia, another form of racism involving a war against the dark-skinned people in the Congo...as it involves a war against the dark-skinned people in Mississippi, Alabama, Georgia, and Rochester, New York. [*Applause*]

So we're not against people because they're white. But we're against those who practice racism. We're against those who drop bombs on people because their color happens to be of a different shade than yours. And because we're against it, the press says we're violent. We're not for violence. We're for peace. But the people that we're up against are for violence. You can't be peaceful when you're dealing with them. [*Applause*]

They accuse us of what they themselves are guilty of. This is what the criminal always does. They'll bomb you, then accuse you of bombing yourself. They'll crush your skull, then accuse you of attacking him. This is what the racists have always done—the criminal, the one who has criminal processes developed to a science. Their practice is criminal action. And then use the press to make you victim—look like the victim is the criminal, and the criminal is the victim. This is how they do it. [*Applause*]

And you here in Rochester probably know more about this than anybody anywhere else. Here's an example of how they do. They take the press, and through the press, they beat the system....Or through the white public. Because the white public is divided. Some mean good, and some don't mean good. Some are well meaning, and some are not well meaning. This is true. You got some that are not well meaning, and some are well meaning. And usually those that are not well meaning outnumber those that are well meaning. You need a microscope to find those that are well meaning. [*Applause*]

So they don't like to do anything without the support of the white public. The racists, that are usually very influential in the society, don't make their move without first going to get public opinion on their side. So they use the press to get public opinion on their side. When they want to suppress and oppress the Black community, what do they do? They take the statistics, and through the press, they feed them to the public. They make it appear that the role of crime in the Black community is higher than it is anywhere else.

What does this do? [*Applause*] This message—this is a very skillful message used by racists to make the whites who aren't racists think that the rate of crime in the Black community is so high. This keeps the Black community in the image of a criminal. It makes it appear that anyone in the Black community is a criminal. And as soon as this impression is given, then it makes it possible, or paves the way to set up a police-type state in the Black community, getting the full approval of the white public when the police come in, use all kind of brutal measures to suppress Black people, crush their skulls, sic dogs on them, and things of that type. And the whites go along with it. Because they think that everybody over there's a criminal anyway. This is what—the press does this. [*Applause*]

This is skill. This skill is called—this is a science that's called "image making." They hold you in check through this science of imagery. They even make you look down upon yourself, by giving you a bad image of yourself. Some of our own Black people who have eaten this image themselves and digested it—until they themselves don't want to live in the Black community. They don't want to be around Black people themselves. [*Applause*]

It's a science that they use, very skillfully, to make the criminal look like the victim, and to make the victim look like the criminal. Example: In the United States during the Harlem riots, I was in Africa, fortunately. [*Laughter*] During these riots, or because of these riots, or after the riots, again the press, very skillfully, depicted the rioters as hoodlums, criminals, thieves, because they were abducting some property.

Now mind you, it is true that property was destroyed. But look at it from another angle. In these Black communities, the economy of the community is not in the hands of the Black man. The Black man is not his own landlord. The buildings that he lives in are owned by someone else. The stores in the community are run by someone else. Everything in the community is out of his hands. He has no say-so in it whatsoever, other than to live there, and pay the highest rent for the lowest-type boarding place, [*Applause*] pays the highest prices for food, for the lowest grade of food. He is a victim of this, a victim of economic exploitation, political exploitation, and every other kind.

Now, he's so frustrated, so pent-up, so much explosive energy within him, that he would like to get at the one who's exploiting him. But the one who's exploiting him doesn't live in his neighborhood. He only owns the house. He only owns the store. He only owns the neighborhood. So that when the Black man explodes, the one that he wants to get at isn't there. So he destroys the property. He's not a thief. He's not trying to steal your cheap furniture or your cheap food. He wants to get at you, but you're not there. [*Applause*]

And instead of the sociologists analyzing it as it actually is, trying to understand it as it actually is, again they cover up the real issue, and they use the press to make it appear that these people are thieves, hoodlums. No! They are the victims of organized thievery, organized landlords who are nothing but thieves, merchants who are nothing but thieves, politicians who sit in the city hall and who are nothing but thieves in cahoots with the landlords and the merchants. [*Applause*]

But again, the press is used to make the victim look like the criminal and make the criminal look like the victim.... This is imagery. And just as this imagery is practiced at the local level, you can understand it better by an international example. The best recent example at the international level to bear witness to what I'm saying is what happened in the Congo. Look at what happened. We had a situation where a plane was dropping bombs on African villages. An African village has no defense against the bombs. And an African village is not sufficient threat that it has to be bombed! But planes were dropping bombs on African villages. When these bombs strike, they don't distinguish between enemy and friend. They don't distinguish between male and female. When these bombs are dropped on African villages in the Congo, they are dropped on Black women, Black children, Black babies. These human beings were blown to bits. I heard no outcry, no voice of compassion for these thousands of Black people who were slaughtered by planes. [*Applause*]

Why was there no outcry? Why was there no concern? Because, again, the press very skillfully made the victims look like they were the criminals, and the criminals look like they were the victims. [*Applause*]

They refer to the villages as "rebel held," you know. As if to say, because they are rebel-held villages, you can destroy the population, and it's okay. They also refer to the merchants of death as "American-trained, anti-Castro Cuban pilots." This made it okay. Because these pilots, these mercenaries—you know what a mercenary is, he's not a patriot. A mercenary is not someone who goes to war out of patriotism for his country. A mercenary is a hired killer. A person who kills, who draws blood for money, anybody's blood. You kill a human being as easily as you kill a cat or a dog or a chicken.

So these mercenaries, dropping bombs on African villages, caring nothing as to whether or not there are innocent, defenseless women and children and babies being destroyed by their bombs. But because they're called "mercenaries," given a glorified name, it doesn't excite you. Because they are referred to as "American-trained" pilots, because they are American-trained, that makes them okay. "Anti-Castro Cubans," that makes them okay. Castro's a monster, so anybody who's against Castro is all right with us, and anything they can do from there, that's all right with us....They put your mind right in a bag and take it wherever they want, as well. [*Applause*]

But it's something that you have to look at and answer for. Because they are American planes, American bombs, escorted by American paratroopers, armed with machine guns. But, you know, they say they're not soldiers, they're just there as escorts, like they started out with some advisers in South Vietnam. Twenty thousand of them—just advisers. These are just "escorts." They're able to do all of this mass murder and get away with it by labeling it "humanitarian," an act of humanitarianism. Or "in the name of freedom," "in the name of liberty." All kinds of high-sounding slogans, but it's cold-blooded murder, mass murder. And it's done so skillfully, so you and I, who call ourselves sophisticated in this twentieth century, are able to watch it, and put the stamp of approval upon it. Simply because it's being done to people with black skin, by people with white skin.

They take a man who is a cold-blooded murderer, named [Moise] Tshombe. You've heard of him, Uncle Tom Tshombe. [*Laughter and applause*] He murdered the prime minister, the rightful prime minister, [Patrice] Lumumba. He murdered him. [*Applause*] Now here's a man who's an international murderer, selected by the State Department and placed over the Congo and propped into position by your tax dollars. He's a killer. He's hired by our government. He's a hired killer. And to show the type of hired killer he is, as soon as he's in office, he hires more killers in South Africa to shoot down his own people. And you wonder why your American image abroad is so bankrupt.

Notice I said, "Your American image abroad is so bankrupt."

They make this man acceptable by saying in the press that he's the only one that can unite the Congo. Ha. A murderer. They won't let China in the United Nations because they say she declared war on UN troops in Korea. Tshombe declared war on UN troops in Katanga. You give him money and prop him up. You don't use the same yardstick. You use the yardstick over here, change it over here.

This is true—everybody can see you today. You make yourself look sick in the sight of the world trying to fool people that you were at least once wise with your trickery. But today your bag of tricks have absolutely run out. The whole world can see what you're doing.

The press whips up hysteria in the white public. Then it shifts gears and starts working trying to get the sympathy of the white public. And then it shifts gears and gets the white public to support whatever criminal action they're getting ready to involve the United States in.

Remember how they referred to the hostages as "white hostages." Not "hostages." They said these "cannibals" in the Congo had "white hostages." Oh, and this got you all shook up. White nuns, white priests, white missionaries. What's the difference between a white hostage and a Black hostage? What's the difference between a white life and a Black life? You must think there's a difference, because your press specifies whiteness. "Nineteen white hostages" cause you to grieve in your heart. [Laughter and applause]

During the months when bombs were being dropped on Black people by the hundreds and the thousands, you said nothing. And you did nothing. But as soon as a few—a handful of white people who didn't have any business getting caught up in that thing in the first place—[Laughter and applause]—as soon as their lives became involved, you got concerned.

I was in Africa during the summer when they—when the mercenaries and the pilots were shooting down Black people in the Congo like flies. It wouldn't even get mentioned in the Western press. It wasn't mentioned. If it was mentioned, it was mentioned in the classified section of the newspaper. Someplace where you'd need a microscope to find it.

And at that time the African brothers, at first they weren't taking hostages. They only began to take hostages when they found that these pilots were bombing their villages. And then they took hostages, moved them into the village, and warned the pilots that if you drop bombs on the village, you'll hit your own people. It was a war maneuver. They were at war. They only held a hostage in a village to keep the mercenaries from murdering on a mass scale the people of those villages. They weren't keeping them as hostages because they were cannibals. Or because they thought their flesh was tasty. Some of those missionaries had been over there for forty years and didn't get eaten up. [Laughter and applause] If they were going to eat them they would have eaten them when they were young and tender. [Laughter and applause] Why you can't even digest that old white meat on an old chicken. [Laughter]

It's imagery. They use their ability to create images, and then they use these images that they've created to mislead the people. To confuse the people and make the people accept wrong as right and reject right as wrong. Make the people actually think that the criminal is the victim and the victim is the criminal.

Even as I point this out, you may say, "What does this all have to do with the Black man in America? And what does it have to do with the Black and white relations here in Rochester?"

You have to understand it. Until 1959 the image of the African continent was created by the enemies of Africa. Africa was a land dominated by outside powers. A land dominated by Europeans. And as these Europeans dominated the continent of Africa, it was they who created the image of Africa that was projected abroad. And they projected Africa and the people of Africa in a negative image, a hateful image. They made us think that Africa was a land of jungles, a land of animals, a land of cannibals and savages. It was a hateful image.

And because they were so successful in projecting this negative image of Africa, those of us here in the West of African ancestry, the Afro-American, we looked upon Africa as a hateful place. We looked upon the African as a hateful person. And if you referred to us as an African it was like putting us as a servant, or playing house, or talking about us in the way we didn't want to be talked.

Why? Because those who oppress know that you can't make a person hate the root without making them hate the tree. You can't hate your own and not end up hating yourself. And since we all originated in Africa, you can't make us hate Africa without making us hate ourselves. And they did this very skillfully.

And what was the result? They ended up with 22 million Black people here in America who hated everything about us that was African. We hated the African characteristics, the African characteristics. We hated our hair. We hated our nose, the shape of our nose, and the shape of our lips, the color of our skin. Yes we did. And it was you who taught us to hate ourselves simply by shrewdly maneuvering us into hating the land of our forefathers and the people on that continent.

As long as we hated those people, we hated ourselves. As long as we hated what we thought they looked like, we hated what we actually looked like. And you call me a hate teacher. Why, you taught us to hate ourselves. You taught the world to hate a whole race of people and have the audacity now to blame us for hating you simply because we don't like the rope that you put around our necks. [*Applause*]

When you teach a man to hate his lips, the lips that God gave him, the shape of the nose that God gave him, the texture of the hair that God gave him, the color of the skin that God gave him, you've committed the worst crime that a race of people can commit. And this is the crime that you've committed.

Our color became a chain, a psychological chain. Our blood—African blood—became a psychological chain, a prison, because we were ashamed of it.

We believe—they would tell it to your face, and say they weren't; they were! We felt trapped because our skin was black. We felt trapped because we had African blood in our veins.

This is how you imprisoned us. Not just bringing us over here and making us slaves. But the image that you created of our motherland and the image that you created of our people on that continent was a trap, was a prison, was a chain, was the worst form of slavery that has ever been invented by a so-called civilized race and a civilized nation since the beginning of the world.

You still see the result of it among our people in this country today. Because we hated our African blood, we felt inadequate, we felt inferior, we felt helpless. And in our state of helplessness, we wouldn't work for ourselves. We turned to you for help, and then you wouldn't help us. We didn't feel adequate. We turned to you for advice and you gave us the wrong advice. Turned to you for direction and you kept us going in circles.

But a change has come about. In us. And what from? Back in '55 in Indonesia, at Bandung, they had a conference of dark-skinned people. The people of Africa and Asia came together for the first time in centuries. They had no nuclear weapons, they had no air fleets, no navy. But they discussed their plight and they found that there was one thing that all of us had in common— oppression, exploitation, suffering. And we had a common oppressor, a common exploiter.

If a brother came from Kenya and called his oppressor an Englishman; and another came from the Congo, he called his oppressor a Belgian; another came from Guinea, he called his oppressor French. But when you brought the oppressors together there's one thing they all had in common, they were all from Europe. And this European was oppressing the people of Africa and Asia.

And since we could see that we had oppression in common and exploitation in common, sorrow and sadness and grief in common, our people began to get together and determined at the Bandung Conference that it was time for us to forget our differences. We had differences. Some were Buddhists, some were Hindus, some were Christians, some were Muslim, some didn't have any religion at all. Some were socialists, some were capitalists, some were communists, and some didn't have any economy at all. But with all of the differences that existed, they agreed on one thing, the spirit of Bandung was, from there on in, to deemphasize the areas of difference and emphasize the areas that we had in common.

And it was the spirit of Bandung that fed the flames of nationalism and freedom not only in Asia, but especially on the African continent. From '55 to '60 the flames of nationalism, independence on the African continent, became so bright and so furious, they were able to burn and sting anything that got in its path. And that same spirit didn't stay on the African continent. It somehow or other—it slipped into the Western Hemisphere and got into the heart and the mind and the soul of the Black man in the Western Hemisphere who supposedly had been separate from the African continent for almost 400 years.

But the same desire for freedom that moved the Black man on the African continent began to burn in the heart and the mind and the soul of the Black man here, in South America, Central America, and North America, showing us we were not separated. Though there was an ocean between us, we were still moved by the same heartbeat.

The spirit of nationalism on the African continent—It began to collapse; the powers, the colonial powers, they couldn't stay there. The British got in trouble in Kenya, Nigeria, Tanganyika, Zanzibar, and other areas of the continent. The French got in trouble in the entire French Equatorial North Africa, including Algeria. Became a trouble spot for France. The Congo wouldn't any longer permit the Belgians to stay there. The entire African continent became explosive from '54–'55 on up to 1959. By 1959 they couldn't stay there any longer.

It wasn't that they wanted to go. It wasn't that all of a sudden they had become benevolent. It wasn't that all of a sudden they had ceased wanting to exploit the Black man of his natural resources. But it was the spirit of independence that was burning in the heart and mind of the Black man. He no longer would allow himself to be colonized, oppressed, and exploited. He was willing to lay down his life and take the lives of those who tried to take his, which was a new spirit.

The colonial powers didn't leave. But what did they do? Whenever a person is playing basketball, if—you watch him—the players on the opposing team trap him and he doesn't want to get rid of, to throw the ball away, he has to pass it to someone who's in the clear, who's on the same team as he. And since Belgium and France and Britain and these other colonial powers were trapped—they were exposed as colonial powers—they had to find someone who was still in the clear, and the only one in the clear so far as the Africans were concerned was the United States. So they passed the ball to the United States. And this administration picked it up and ran like mad ever since. [*Laughter and applause*]

As soon as they grabbed the ball, they realized that they were confronted with a new problem. The problem was that the Africans had awakened. And in their awakening they were no longer afraid. And because the Africans were not afraid, it was impossible for the European powers to stay on that continent by force. So our State Department, grabbing the ball and in their new analysis, they realized that they had to use a new strategy if they were going to replace the colonial powers of Europe.

What was their strategy? The friendly approach. Instead of coming over there with their teeth gritted, they started smiling at the Africans. "We're your friends." But in order to convince the African that he was their friend he had to start off pretending like they were our friend.

You didn't get the man to smile at you because you were bad, no. He was trying to impress your brother on the other side of the water. He smiled at you to make his smile consistent. He started using a friendly approach over there. A benevolent approach. A philanthropic approach. Call it benevolent colonialism. Philanthropic imperialism. Humanitarianism backed up by dollarism. Tokenism. This is the approach that they used. They didn't go over there well meaning. How could you leave here and go on the African continent with the Peace Corps and Cross Roads and these other outfits when you're hanging Black people in Mississippi? How could you do it? [*Applause*]

How could you train missionaries, supposedly over there to teach them about Christ, when you won't let a Black man in your Christ's church right here in Rochester, much less in the South. [*Applause*] You know that's something to think about. It gets me hot when I think about it. [*Laughter*]

From 1954 to 1964 can easily be looked upon as the era of the emerging African state. And as the African state emerged from '54 to '64, what impact, what effect did it have on the Afro-American, the Black American? As the Black man in Africa got independent, it put him in a position to be master of making his own image. Up until 1959 when you and I thought of an African, we thought of someone naked, coming with the tom-toms, with bones in his nose. Oh yeah!

This was the only image you had in your mind of an African. And from '59 on when they begin to come into the UN and you'd see them on the television you'd get shocked. Here was an African who could speak better English than you. He made more sense than you. He had more freedom than you. Why places where you couldn't go—[*Applause*]—places where you couldn't go, all he had to do was throw on his robes and walk right past you. [*Laughter and applause*]

It had to shake you up. And it was only when you'd become shook up that you began to really wake up. [*Laughter*]

So as the African nations gained their independence and the image of the African continent began to change, the things agreed as the image of Africa switched from negative to positive. Subconsciously. The Black man throughout the Western Hemisphere, in his subconscious mind, began to identify with that emerging positive African image.

And when he saw the Black man on the African continent taking a stand, it made him become filled with the desire also to take a stand. The same image, the same—just as the African image was negative—and you hear about old hat in the hand, compromising, fearful looks—we were the same way. But when we began to read about Jomo Kenyatta and the Mau Mau and others, then you find Black people in this country began to think along the same line. And more closely along the same line than some of them really want to admit.

When they saw—just as they had to change their approach with the people on the African continent, they also then began to change their approach with our people on this continent. As they used tokenism and a whole lot of other friendly, benevolent, philanthropic approaches on the African continent, which were only token efforts, they began to do the same thing with us here in the States.

Tokenism. They came up with all kinds of programs that weren't really designed to solve anybody's problems. Every move they made was a token move. They never made a real down-to-earth move at one time to really solve the problem. They came up with a Supreme Court desegregation decision that they haven't put into practice yet. Not even in Rochester, much less in Mississippi. [*Applause*]

They fooled the people in Mississippi by trying to make it appear that they were going to integrate the University of Mississippi. They took one Negro to the university backed up with about 6,000—15,000 troops, I think it was. And I think it cost them $6 million. [*Laughter*]

And three or four people got killed in the act. And it was only an act. Now, mind you, after one of them got in, they said there's integration in Mississippi. [*Laughter*]

They stuck two of them in the school in Georgia and said there's integra-tion in Georgia. Why you should be ashamed. Really, if I was white, I'd be so ashamed I'd crawl under a rug. [*Laughter and applause*] And I'd feel so low while I was under that rug I wouldn't even leave a hump. [*Laughter*]

This tokenism, this tokenism was a program that was designed to protect the benefits of only a handful of handpicked Negroes. And these handpicked Negroes were given big positions, and then they were used to open up their mouths to tell the world, "Look at how much progress we're making." He should say, look at how much progress he is making. For while these handpicked Ne-groes were eating high on the hog, rubbing elbows with white folk, sitting in Washington, D.C., the masses of Black people in this country continued to live in the slum and in the ghetto. The masses, [*Applause*] the masses of Black people in this country remain unemployed, and the masses of Black people in this country continue to go to the worst schools and get the worst education.

Along during the same time appeared a movement known as the Black Muslim movement. The Black Muslim movement did this: Up until the time the Black Muslim movement came on the scene, the NAACP was regarded as radical. [*Laughter*] They wanted to investigate it. They wanted to investigate it. CORE and all the rest of them were under suspect, under suspicion. King wasn't heard of. When the Black Muslim movement came along talking that kind of talk that they talked, the white man said, "Thank God for the NAACP." [*Laughter and applause*]

The Black Muslim movement has made the NAACP acceptable to white folks. It made its leaders acceptable. They then began to refer to them as re-sponsible Negro leaders. [*Laughter*] Which meant they were responsible to white folk. [*Applause*] Now I am not attacking the NAACP. I'm just telling you about it. [*Laughter*] And what makes it so bad, you can't deny it. [*Laughter*]

So this is the contribution that that movement made. It frightened a lot of people. A lot of people who wouldn't act right out of love begin to act right out of fear. Because Roy [Wilkins] and [James] Farmer and some of the others used to tell white folk, look if you don't act right by us you're going to have to listen to them. They used us to better their own position, their own bargaining posi-tion. No matter what you think of the philosophy of the Black Muslim move-ment, when you analyze the part that it played in the struggle of Black people during the past twelve years you have to put it in its proper context and see it in its proper perspective.

The movement itself attracted the most militant, the most dissatisfied, the most uncompromising elements of the Black community. And also the youngest elements of the Black community. And as this movement grew, it attracted such a militant, uncompromising, dissatisfied element.

The movement itself was supposedly based upon the religion of Islam and therefore supposedly a religious movement. But because the world of Islam or the orthodox Muslim world would never accept the Black Muslim movement as a bona fide part of it, it put those of us who were in it in a sort of religious vacuum. It put us in a position of identifying ourselves by a religion, while the world in which that religion was practiced rejected us as not being bona fide practicers, practitioners of that religion.

Also the government tried to maneuver us and label us as political rather than religious so that they could charge us with sedition and subversion. This is the only reason. But although we were labeled political, because we were never permitted to take part in politics we were in a vacuum politically. We were in a religious vacuum. We were in a political vacuum. We were actually alienated, cut off from all type of activity with even the world that we were fighting against.

We became a sort of a religious-political hybrid, all to ourselves. Not involved in anything but just standing on the sidelines condemning everything. But in no position to correct anything because we couldn't take action.

Yet at the same time, the nature of the movement was such that it attracted the activists. Those who wanted action. Those who wanted to do something about the evils that confronted all Black people. We weren't particularly concerned with the religion of the Black man. Because whether he was a Methodist or a Baptist or an atheist or an agnostic, he caught the same hell.

So we could see that we had to have some action, and those of us who were activists became dissatisfied, disillusioned. And finally dissension set in and eventually a split. Those who split away were the real activists of the movement who were intelligent enough to want some kind of program that would enable us to fight for the rights of all Black people here in the Western Hemisphere.

But at the same time we wanted our religion. So when we left, the first thing we did we regrouped into a new organization known as the Muslim Mosque, headquartered in New York. And in that organization we adopted the real, orthodox religion of Islam, which is a religion of brotherhood. So that while accepting this religion and setting up an organization which could practice that religion—and immediately this particular Muslim Mosque was recognized and endorsed by the religious officials of the Muslim world.

We realized at the same time we had a problem in this society that went beyond religion. And it was for that reason we set up the Organization of Afro-American Unity in which anybody in the community could participate in an action program designed to bring about complete recognition and respect of Black people as human beings.

And the motto of the Organization of Afro-American Unity is By Any Means Necessary. We don't believe in fighting a battle that's going to—in which the ground rules are to be laid down by those who suppress us. We don't believe that we can win in a battle where the ground rules are laid down by those who exploit us. We don't believe that we can carry on a struggle trying to win the affection of those who for so long have oppressed and exploited us.

We believe that our fight is just. We believe that our grievances are just. We believe that the evil practices against Black people in this society are criminal and that those who engage in such criminal practices are to be looked upon themselves as nothing but criminals. And we believe that we are within our rights to fight those criminals by any means necessary.

This doesn't mean that we're for violence. But we do—we have seen that the federal government has shown its inability, its absolute unwillingness, to protect the lives and the property of Black people. We have seen where organized white racists, Klansmen, Citizens' Councilmen, and others can come into the Black community and take a Black man and make him disappear and nothing be done about it. We have seen that they can come in—[*Applause*]

We reanalyzed our condition. When we go back to 1939, Black people in America were shining shoes. Some of the most educated were shining in Michigan, where I came from, in Lansing, the capital. The best jobs you could get in the city were carrying trays out at the country club to feed white people. And usually the waiter at the country club was looked upon as the town big shot 'cause he had a good job around "good" white folks, you know. [*Laughter*]

He had the best education, but he'd be shining shoes right at the State House, the capitol. Shining the governor's shoes, and the attorney general's shoes, and this made him in the know, you know, 'cause he could shine white folks' shoes who were in big places. Whenever the people downtown wanted to know what was going on in the Black community, he was their boy. He was what's known as the "town Negro," the Negro leader. And those who weren't shining shoes, the preachers, also had a big voice in the community. That's all they'd let us do is shine shoes, wait on tables, and preach. [*Laughter*]

In 1939, before Hitler went on the rampage, or rather at the time—yeah, before Hitler went on the rampage, a Black man couldn't even work in the factory. We were digging ditches on WPA. Some of you all have forgotten too quick. We were ditchdigging on the WPA. Our food came from the welfare, they were stamped "not to be sold." I got so many things from the store called "not to be sold," I thought that was a store some place. [*Laughter*]

This is the condition the Black man was in, and that's till 1939....Until the war started, we were confined to these menial tasks. When the war started, they wouldn't even take us in the army. A Black man wasn't drafted. Was he or was he not? No! You couldn't join the navy. Remember that? Wouldn't draft one. This was as late as 1939 in the United States of America!

They taught you to sing "sweet land of liberty" and the rest of that stuff. No! You couldn't join the army. You couldn't join the navy. They wouldn't even draft you. They only took white folks. They didn't start drafting us until the Negro leader opened up his big mouth, [*Laughter*] talking about, "If white folks must die, we must die too." [*Laughter and applause*]

The Negro leader got a whole lot of Negroes killed in World War II who never had to die. So when America got into the war, immediately she was faced with a manpower shortage. Up until the time of the war, you couldn't get inside of a plant. I lived in Lansing, where Oldsmobile's factory was and Reo's. There was about three in the whole plant and each one of them had a broom. They had education. They had gone to school. I think one had gone to college. But he was a "broomologist." [*Laughter*]

When times got tough and there was a manpower shortage, then they let us in the factory. Not through any effort of our own. Not through any sudden moral awakening on their part. They needed us. They needed manpower. Any kind of manpower. And when they got desperate and in need, they opened up the factory door and let us in.

So we began to learn to run machines. Then we began to learn how to run machines, when they needed us. Put our women in as well as our men. As we learned to operate the machines, we began to make more money. As we began to make more money, we were able to live in a little better neighborhood. When we moved to a little better neighborhood, we went to a little better school. And when we went to that better school, we got a little better education and got in a little better position to get a little better job.

It was no change of heart on their part. It was no sudden awakening of their moral consciousness. It was Hitler. It was Tojo. It was Stalin. Yes, it was pressure from the outside, at the world level, that enabled you and me to make a few steps forward.

Why wouldn't they draft us and put us in the army in the first place? They had treated us so bad, they were afraid that if they put us in the army and give us a gun and showed us how to shoot it—[*Laughter*] they feared that they wouldn't have to tell us what to shoot at. [*Laughter and applause*]

And probably they wouldn't have had. It was their conscience. So I point this out to show that it was not change of heart on Uncle Sam's part that permitted some of us to go a few steps forward. It was world pressure. It was threat from outside. Danger from outside that made it—that occupied his mind and forced him to permit you and me to stand up a little taller. Not because he wanted us to stand up. Not because he wanted us to go forward. He was forced to.

And once you properly analyze the ingredients that opened the doors even to the degree that they were forced open, when you see what it was, you'll better understand your position today. And you'll better understand the strategy that you need today. Any kind of movement for freedom of Black people based solely within the confines of America is absolutely doomed to fail. [*Applause*]

As long as your problem is fought within the American context, all you can get as allies is fellow Americans. As long as you call it civil rights, it's a domestic problem within the jurisdiction of the United States government. And the United States government consists of segregationists, racists. Why the most powerful men in the government are racists. This government is controlled by thirty-six committees. Twenty congressional committees and sixteen senatorial committees. Thirteen of the twenty congressmen that make up the congressional committees are from the South. Ten of the sixteen senators that control the senatorial committees are from the South. Which means, that of the thirty-six committees that govern the foreign and domestic directions and temperament of the country in which we live, of the thirty-six, twenty-three of them are in the hands of racists. Outright, stone-cold, dead segregationists. This is what you and I are up against. We are in a society where the power is in the hands of those who are the worst breed of humanity.

Now how are we going to get around them? How are we going to get justice in a Congress that they control? Or a Senate that they control? Or a White House that they control? Or from a Supreme Court that they control?

Look at the pitiful decision that the Supreme Court handed down. Brother, look at it! Don't you know these men on the Supreme Court are masters of legal—not only of law, but legal phraseology. They are such masters of the legal language that they could very easily have handed down a desegregation decision on education so worded that no one could have gotten around. But they come up with that thing worded in such a way that here ten years have passed, and there's all kind of loopholes in it. They knew what they were doing. They pretend to give you something while knowing all the time you can't utilize it.

They come up last year with a civil rights bill that they publicized all around the world as if it would lead us into the promised land of integration. Oh yeah! Just last week, the Right Reverend Dr. Martin Luther King come out of the jail house and went to Washington, D.C., saying he's going to ask every day for new legislation to protect voting rights for Black people in Alabama. Why? You just had legislation. You just had a civil rights bill. You mean to tell me that that highly publicized civil rights bill doesn't even give the federal government enough power to protect Black people in Alabama who don't want to do anything but register? Why it's another foul trick, 'cause they...tricked us year in and year out. Another foul trick. [*Applause*]

So, since we see—I don't want you to think I'm teaching hate. I love everybody who loves me. [*Laughter*] But I sure don't love those who don't love me. [*Laughter*]

Since we see all of this subterfuge, this trickery, this maneuvering—it's not only at the federal level, the national level, the local level, all levels. The young generation of Blacks that's coming up now can see that as long as we wait for the Congress and the Senate and the Supreme Court and the president to solve our problems, you'll have us waiting on tables for another thousand years. And there aren't no days like those.

Since the civil rights bill—I used to see African diplomats at the UN crying out against the injustice that was being done to Black people in Mozambique, in Angola, the Congo, in South Africa, and I wondered why and how they could go back to their hotels and turn on the TV and see dogs biting

Black people right down the block and policemen wrecking the stores of Black people with their clubs right down the block, and putting water hoses on Black people with pressure so high it tear our clothes off, right down the block. And I wondered how they could talk all that talk about what was happening in Angola and Mozambique and all the rest of it and see it happen right down the block and get up on the podium in the UN and not say anything about it.

But I went and discussed it with some of them. And they said that as long as the Black man in America calls his struggle a struggle of civil rights—that in the civil rights context, it's domestic and it remains within the jurisdiction of the United States. And if any of them open up their mouths to say anything about it, it's considered a violation of the laws and rules of protocol. And the difference with the other people was that they didn't call their grievances "civil rights" grievances, they called them "human rights" grievances. "Civil rights" are within the jurisdiction of the government where they are involved. But "human rights" is part of the charter of the United Nations.

All the nations that signed the charter of the UN came up with the Declaration of Human Rights and anyone who classifies his grievances under the label of "human rights" violations, those grievances can then be brought into the United Nations and be discussed by people all over the world. For as long as you call it "civil rights" your only allies can be the people in the next community, many of whom are responsible for your grievance. But when you call it "human rights" it becomes international. And then you can take your troubles to the World Court. You can take them before the world. And anybody anywhere on this earth can become your ally.

So one of the first steps that we became involved in, those of us who got into the Organization of Afro-American Unity, was to come up with a program that would make our grievances international and make the world see that our problem was no longer a Negro problem or an American problem but a human problem. A problem for humanity. And a problem which should be attacked by all elements of humanity. A problem that was so complex that it was impossible for Uncle Sam to solve it himself and therefore we want to get into a body or conference with people who are in such positions that they can help us get some kind of adjustment for this situation before it gets so explosive that no one can handle it.

Thank you. [*Applause*]

LeRoi Jones
The Slave

CHARACTERS

WALKER VESSELS, tall, thin Negro about forty.

GRACE, blonde woman about same age. Small, thin, beautiful.

BRADFORD EASLEY, tall, broad white man, with thinning hair, about forty-five.

> The action takes place in a large living room, tastefully furnished the way an intelligent university professor and his wife would furnish it.

> Room is dark at the beginning of the play, except for light from explosions, which continue, sometimes close, sometimes very far away, throughout both acts, and well after curtain of each act.

PROLOGUE

WALKER.
> [Coming out dressed as an old field slave, balding, with white hair, and an old ragged vest. (Perhaps he is sitting, sleeping, initially-nodding and is awakened by faint cries, like a child's.) He comes to the center of the stage slowly, and very deliberately, puffing on a pipe, and seemingly uncertain of the reaction any audience will give his speech]

Whatever the core of our lives. Whatever the deceit. We live where we are, and seek nothing but ourselves. We are liars, and we are murderers. We invent death for others. Stop their pulses publicly. Stone possible lovers with heavy worlds we think are ideas...and we know, even before these shapes are realized, that these worlds, these depths or heights we fly to smoothly, as in a dream, or slighter, when we stare dumbly into space, leaning our eyes just behind a last quick moving bird, then sometimes the place and twist of what we are will push and sting, and what the crust of our stance has become will ring in our ears and shatter that piece of our eyes that is never closed. An ignorance. A stupidity. A stupid longing not to know...which is automatically fulfilled. Automatically triumphs. Automatically makes us killers or foot-dragging celebrities at the core of any filth. And it is a deadly filth that passes as whatever thing we feel is too righteous to question, too deeply felt to deny.
> [Pause to relight pipe]
I am much older than I look...or maybe much younger. Whatever I am or seem...
> [Significant pause]

to you, then let that rest. But figure, still, that you might not be right. Figure, still, that you might be lying...to save yourself. Or myself's image, which might set you crawling like a thirsty dog, for the meanest of drying streams. The meanest of ideas.

[*Gentle, mocking laugh*]

Yeah. Ideas. Let that settle! Ideas. Where they form. Or whose they finally seem to be. Yours? The other's? Mine?

[*Shifts uneasily, pondering the last*]

No, no more. Not mine. I served my slow apprenticeship...and maybe came up lacking. Maybe. Ha. Who's to say, really? Huh? But figure, still, ideas are still in the world. They need judging. I mean, they don't come in that singular or wild, that whatever they are, just because they're beautiful and brilliant, just because they strike us full in the center of the heart....My God!

[*Softer*]

My God, just because, and even this, believe me, even if, that is, just because they're *right*...doesn't mean anything. The very rightness stinks a lotta times. The very rightness.

[*Looks down and speaks softer and quicker*]

I am an old man. An old man.

[*Blankly*]

The waters and wars. Time's a dead thing really...and keeps nobody whole. An old man, full of filed rhythms. Terrific, eh? That I hoarded so much dignity? An old man full of great ideas. Let's say theories. As: Love is an instrument of knowledge. Oh, not my own. Not my own...is right. But listen now....Brown is not brown except when used as an intimate description of personal phenomenological fields. As your brown is not my brown, et cetera, that is, we need, ahem, a meta-language. We need some thing not included here.

[*Spreads arms*]

Your ideas? An old man can't be expected to be right. If I'm old. If I really claim that embarrassment.

[*Saddens...brightens*]

A poem? Lastly, that, to distort my position? To divert you...in your hour of need. Before the thing goes on. Before you get your lousy chance. Discovering racially the funds of the universe. Discovering the last image of the thing. As the sky when the moon is broken. Or old, old blues people moaning in their sleep, singing, man, oh, nigger, nigger, you still here, as hard as nails, and takin' no shit from nobody. He say, yeah, yeah, he say yeah, yeah. He say, yeah, yeah...goin' down slow, man. Goin' down slow. He say...yeah, heh...

[*Running down, growing anxiously less articulate, more "field hand" sounding, blankly lyrical, shuffles slowly around, across the stage, as the lights dim and he enters the set proper and assumes the position he will have when the play starts...still moaning...*]

ACT I

The Scene: A light from an explosion lights the room dimly for a second and the outline of a figure is seen half sprawled on a couch. Every once in a while another blast shows the figure in silhouette. He stands from time to time, sits, walks nervously around the room

examining books and paintings. Finally, he climbs a flight of stairs, stays for a few min-
utes, then returns. He sits smoking in the dark, until some sound is heard outside the
door. He rises quickly and takes a position behind the door, a gun held out stiffly. GRACE
and EASLEY *open the door, turn on the light, agitated and breathing heavily.* GRACE *quiet*
and weary. EASLEY *talking in harsh angry spurts.*

EASLEY. Son of a bitch. Those black son of a bitches. Why don't they at least
stop and have their goddamned dinners? Goddamn son of a bitches. They're
probably gonna keep that horseshit up all goddamn night. Goddamnit. Goddamn it!
[He takes off a white metal hat and slings it across the room. It bangs loudly against the
brick of the fireplace]

GRACE. Brad! You're going to wake up the children!

EASLEY. Oh, Christ!...But if they don't wake up under all that blasting, I don't
think that tin hat will do it.
[He unbuttons his shirt, moves wearily across the room, still mumbling under his breath
about the source of the explosions]
Hey, Grace...you want a drink? That'll fix us up.
[He moves to get the drink and spots WALKER *leaning back against the wall, half smiling,*
also very weary, but still holding the gun, stomach high, and very stiffly. EASLEY *freezes,*
staring at WALKER'*s face and then the gun, and then back to* WALKER'*s face. He makes no*
sound. The two men stand confronting each other until GRACE *turns and sees them]*

GRACE. Sure, I'll take a drink...one of the few real pleasures left in the West-
ern world.
[She turns and drops her helmet to the floor, staring unbelievingly]
Ohh!

WALKER.
[Looks over slowly at GRACE *and waves as from a passing train. Then he looks back at*
EASLEY; *the two men's eyes are locked in the same ugly intensity.* WALKER *beckons to* GRACE]
The blinds.

GRACE. Walker!
[She gets the name out quietly, as if she is trying to hold so many other words in]
Walker...the gun!

WALKER.
[Half turning to look at her. He looks back at EASLEY, *then lets the gun swing down easily*
toward the floor. He looks back at GRACE, *and tries to smile]*
Hey, momma. How're you?

EASLEY.
[At WALKER, *and whatever else is raging in his own head]*
Son of a bitch!

GRACE. What're you doing here, Walker? What do you want?

WALKER.
[Looking at EASLEY *from time to time]*

Nothing. Not really. Just visiting.

[Grins]

I was in the neighborhood; thought I'd stop by and see how the other half lives.

GRACE. Isn't this dangerous?

[She seems relieved by WALKER's *relative good spirits and she begins to look for a cigarette.* EASLEY *has not yet moved. He is still staring at* WALKER]

WALKER. Oh, it's dangerous as a bitch. But don't you remember how heroic I am?

EASLEY.

[Handing GRACE *a cigarette, then waiting to light it]*

Well, what the hell do you want, hero?

[Drawn out and challenging]

WALKER.

[With same challenge]

Nothing you have, fellah, not one thing.

EASLEY. Oh?

[Cynically]

Is *that* why you and your noble black brothers are killing what's left of this city?

[Suddenly broken]

I should say... what's left of this country... or world.

WALKER. Oh, fuck you

[Hotly]

fuck you... just fuck you, that's all. Just fuck you!

[Keeps voice stiffly contained, but then it rises sharply]

I mean really, just fuck you. Don't, goddamnit, don't tell me about any god-damn killing of anything. If that's what's happening. I mean if this shitty town is being flattened... let it. It needs it.

GRACE. Walker, shut up, will you?

[Furious from memory]

I had enough of your twisted logic in my day... you remember? I mean like your heroism. The same kind of memory. Or Lie. Do you remember which? Huh?

[Starting to weep]

WALKER.

[Starts to comfort her]

Grace... look... there's probably nothing I can say to make you understand me ... now.

EASLEY.

[Steps in front of WALKER *as he moves toward* GRACE . . . *feigning a cold sophistication]*

Uh... no, now come, Jefe, you're not going to make one of those embrace the weeping ex-wife dramas, are you? Well, once a bad poet always a bad poet... even in the disguise of a racist murderer!

WALKER.
[Not quite humbled]
Yeah.
[Bends head, then he brings it up quickly, forcing the joke]
Even disguised as a racist murderer...I remain a bad poet. Didn't St. Thomas say that? Once a bad poet always a bad poet...or was it Carl Sandburg, as some kind of confession?

EASLEY. You're not still writing...now, are you? I should think the political, now military estates would be sufficient. And you always used to speak of the Renaissance as an evil time.
[Begins making two drinks]
And now you're certainly the gaudiest example of Renaissance man I've heard of.
[Finishes making drinks and brings one to GRACE. WALKER watches him and then as he starts to speak he walks to the cabinet, picks up the bottle, and empties a good deal of it]

GRACE.
[Looking toward WALKER even while EASLEY extends the drink toward her]
Walker...you are still writing, aren't you?

WALKER. Oh, God, yes. Want to hear the first lines of my newest work?
[Drinks, does a theatrical shiver]
Uh, how's it go...? Oh, "Straddling each dolphin's back/And steadied by a fin,/Those innocents relive their death,/Their wounds open again."

GRACE.
[Staring at him closely]
It's changed quite a bit.

WALKER. Yeah...it's changed to Yeats.
[Laughs very loudly]
Yeah, Yeats.... Hey, professor, anthologist, lecturer, loyal opposition, et cetera, et cetera, didn't you recognize those words as being Yeats's? Goddamn, I mean if you didn't recognize them...who the hell would? I thought you knew all kinds of shit.

EASLEY.
[Calmly]
I knew they were Yeats'.

WALKER.
[Tilting the bottle again quickly]
Oh, yeah? What poem?

EASLEY. The second part of "News for the Delphic Oracle."

WALKER.
[Hurt]
"News for the Delphic Oracle." Yeah. That's right.
[To GRACE]

You know that, Grace? Your husband knows all about everything. The second part of "News for the Delphic Oracle."

[Rhetorically]

Intolerable music falls. Nymphs and satyrs copulate in the foam.

[Tilts bottle again, some liquor splashes on the floor]

EASLEY.

[Suddenly straightening and stopping close to WALKER]

Look...LOOK! You arrogant maniac, if you get drunk or fall out here, so help me, I'll call the soldiers or somebody...and turn you over to them. I swear I'll do that.

GRACE. Brad!

WALKER. Yeah, yeah, I know. That's your job. A liberal education, and a long history of concern for minorities and charitable organizations can do that for you.

EASLEY.

[Almost taking hold of WALKER's clothes]

No! I mean this, friend! Really! If I get the slightest advantage, some cracker soldier will be bayoneting you before the night is finished.

WALKER.

[Slaps EASLEY across the face with the back of his left hand, pulling the gun out with his right and shoving it as hard as he can against EASLEY's stomach. EASLEY slumps, and the cruelty in WALKER's face at this moment also frightens GRACE]

"My country, 'tis of thee. Sweet land of liber-ty."

[Screams off key like drunken opera singer]

Well, let's say liberty and ignorant vomiting faggot professors.

[To GRACE]

Right, lady? Isn't that right? I mean you ought to know, 'cause you went out of your way to marry one.

[Turns to GRACE and she takes an involuntary step backward. And in a cracked ghostlike voice that he wants to be loud...]

Huh? Huh? And then fed the thing my children.

[He reaches stiffly out and pushes her shoulder, intending it to be strictly a burlesque, but there is quite a bit of force in the gesture. GRACE falls back, just short of panic, but WALKER bunches his shoulders and begins to jerk his finger at the ceiling; one eye closed and one leg raised, jerking his finger absurdly at the ceiling, as if to indicate something upstairs that was to be kept secret]

Ah, yes, the children...

[Affecting an imprecise "Irish" accent]

sure and they looked well enough...

[Grins]

and white enough, roosting in that kennel. Hah, I hope you didn't tell Faggy, there, about those two lovely ladies.

[EASLEY is kneeling on the floor holding his stomach and shaking his head]

Ahh, no, lady, let's keep that strictly in the family. I mean among those of us who screw.

[*He takes another long drink from the bottle, and "threatens" EASLEY's head in a kind of burlesque*]

For Lawrence, and all the cocksmen of my underprivileged youth. When we used to chase that kind of frail little sissy-punk down Raymond Boulevard and compromise his sister-in-laws in the cloak room... It's so simple to work from the bottom up. To always strike, and know, from the blood's noise that you're right, and what you're doing is right, and even *pretty*.

[*Suddenly more tender toward GRACE*]

I swear to you, Grace, I did come into the world pointed in the right direction. Oh, shit, I learned so many words for what I've wanted to say. They all come down on me at once. But almost none of them are mine.

[*He straightens up, turning quickly toward the still kneeling EASLEY, and slaps him as hard as he can across the face, sending his head twisting around*]

Bastard! A poem for your mother!

GRACE.

[*Lets out a short pleading cry*]

Ohh! Get away from him, Walker! Get away from him,

[*Hysterically*]

you nigger murderer!

WALKER.

[*Has started to tilt the bottle again, after he slaps EASLEY, and when GRACE shouts at him, he chokes on the liquor, spitting it out, and begins laughing with a kind of hysterical amusement*]

Oh! Ha, ha, ha... you mean... Wow!

[*Trying to control laughter, but it is an extreme kind of release*]

No kidding? Grace, Gracie! Wow! I wonder how long you had that stored up.

GRACE.

[*Crying now, going over to EASLEY, trying to help him up*]

Brad. Brad. Walker, why'd you come here? Why'd you come here? Brad?

WALKER.

[*Still laughing and wobbling clumsily around*]

Nigger murderer? Wowee. Gracie, are you just repeating your faggot husband, or did you have that in you a long time? I mean... for all the years we were together? Hooo! Yeah.

[*Mock seriously*]

Christ, it could get to be a weight after a time, huh? When you taught the little girls to pray... you'd have to whisper, "And God bless Mommy, and God bless Daddy, the nigger murderer." Wow, that's some weight.

GRACE. Shut up, Walker. Just shut up, and get out of here, away from us, please. I don't want to hear you... I don't need to hear you, again. Remember, I heard it all before, baby... you don't get me again.

[*She is weeping and twisting her head, trying at the same time to fully revive EASLEY, who is still sitting on the floor with legs sprawled apart, both hands held to the pit of his stomach, his head nodding back and forth in pain*]

Why'd you come here...just to do this? Why don't you leave before you kill somebody?

[*Trying to hold back a scream*]

Before you kill another white person?

WALKER.

[*Sobering, but still forcing a cynical hilarity*]

Ah...the party line. Stop him before he kills another white person! Heh. Yeah. Yeah. And that's not such a bad idea, really....I mean, after all, only you and your husband there are white in this house. Those two lovely little girls upstairs are niggers. You know, circa 1800, one drop makes you whole?

GRACE. Shut up, Walker!

[*She leaps to her feet and rushes toward him*]

Shut your ugly head!

[*He pushes her away*]

EASLEY.

[*Raising his head and shouting as loud as he can manage*]

You're filth, boy. Just filth. Can you understand that anything and everything you do is stupid, filthy, or meaningless! Your inept formless poetry. Hah. Poetry? A flashy doggerel for inducing all those unfortunate troops of yours to spill their blood in your behalf. But I guess that's something! Ritual drama, we used to call it at the university. The poetry of ritual drama.

[*Pulls himself up*]

And even that's giving that crap the benefit of the doubt. Ritual filth would have been the right name for it.

WALKER. Ritual drama...

[*Half musing*]

yeah, I remember seeing that phrase in an old review by one of your queer academic friends....

[*Noticing EASLEY getting up*]

Oh well, look at him coming up by his bootstraps. I didn't mean to hit you that hard, Professor Easley, sir...I just don't know my own strent'.

[*Laughs and finishes the bottle...starts as if he is going to throw it over his shoulder, then he places it very carefully on the table. He starts dancing around and whooping like an "Indian"*]

More! Bwana, me want more fire water!

EASLEY. As I said, Vessels, you're just filth. Pretentious filth.

WALKER.

[*Dances around a bit more, then stops abruptly in front of EASLEY; so close they are almost touching. He speaks in a quiet menacing tone*]

The liquor, turkey. The liquor. No opinions right now. Run off and get more liquor, *sabe?*

GRACE.

[*Has stopped crying and managed to regain a cynical composure*]

I'll get it, Brad. Mr. Vessels is playing the mad scene from Native Son.
  [Turns to go]
A second-rate Bigger Thomas.

WALKER.
  [Laughs]
Yeah. But remember when I used to play a second-rate Othello? Oh, wow...
you remember that, don't you, Professor No-Dick? You remember when I used
to walk around wondering what that fair sister was thinking?
  [Hunches EASLEY]
Oh, come on now, you remember that....I was Othello...Grace there was
Desdemona...and you were Iago...
  [Laughs]
or at least between classes, you were Iago. Hey, who were you during classes? I
forgot to find that out. Ha, the key to my downfall. I knew you were Iago be-
tween classes, when I saw you, but I never knew who you were during classes.
Ah ah, that's the basis of an incredibly profound social axiom. I quote:...and
you better write this down, Bradford, so you can pass it on to your hipper col-
leagues at the university...
  [Laughs]
I mean if they ever rebuild the university. What was I saying to you, enemy?
Oh yeah...the axiom. Oh...

GRACE.
  [Returning with a bottle]
You still at it, huh, Bigger?

WALKER. Yeah, yeah...
  [Reaches for bottle]
lemme see. I get it....If a white man is Iago when you see him...uhh...
chances are he's eviler when you don't.
  [Laughs]

EASLEY. Yes, that was worthy of you.

WALKER. It *was* lousy, wasn't it?

GRACE. Look
  [Trying to be earnest]
Walker, pour yourself a drink...as many drinks as you need...and then leave,
will you? I don't see what you think you're accomplishing by hanging around us.

EASLEY. Yes...I was wondering who's taking care of your mighty army while
you're here in the enemy camp? How can the black liberation movement spare
its illustrious leader for such a long stretch?

WALKER.
  *[Sits abruptly on couch and stretches both legs out, drinking big glass of bourbon. Begins
  speaking in pidgin "Japanese"]*

Oh, don't worry about that, doomed American dog. Ha. You see and hear those shells beating this town flat, don't you? In fact, we'll probably be here en masse in about a week. Why don't I just camp here and wait for my brothers to get here and liberate the whole place? Huh?
[Laughs]

GRACE. Walker, you're crazy!

EASLEY. I think he's got more sense than that.

WALKER.
[Starting to make up a song]
Ohhh! I'll stay here and rape your wife...as I so often used to do...as I so often used...

GRACE. Your mind is gone, Walker...completely gone.
[She turns to go upstairs. A bright blast rocks the house and she falls against the wall]

WALKER.
[Thrown forward to the floor, rises quickly to see how GRACE is]
Hey, you all right, lady?

EASLEY. Grace!
[He has also been rocked, but he gets to GRACE first]
Don't worry about my wife, Vessels. That's my business.

GRACE. I'm O.K., Brad. I was on my way upstairs to look in on the girls. It's a wonder they're not screaming now.

WALKER. They were fine when I looked in earlier. Sleeping very soundly.

EASLEY. You were upstairs?

WALKER.
[Returning to his seat, with another full glass]
Of course I went upstairs, to see my children. In fact, I started to take them away with me, while you patriots were out.
[Another close blast]
But I thought I'd wait to say hello to the mommy and stepdaddy.

EASLEY. You low bastard.
[Turning toward WALKER and looking at GRACE at the same time]

GRACE. No...you're not telling the truth now, Walker.
[Voice quavering and rising]
You came here just to say that. Just to see what your saying that would do to me.
[Turns away from him]
You're a bad liar, Walker. As always...a very bad liar.

WALKER. You know I'm not lying. I want those children. You know that, Grace.

EASLEY. I know you're drunk!

GRACE. You're lying. You don't want those children. You just want to think you want them for the moment...to excite one of those obscure pathological instruments you've got growing in your head. Today, you want to feel like you want the girls. Just like you wanted to feel hurt and martyred by your misdirected cause, when you first drove us away.

WALKER. Drove you away? You knew what I was in to. You could have stayed. You said you wanted to pay whatever thing it cost to stay.

EASLEY. How can you lie like this, Vessels? Even I know you pushed Grace until she couldn't retain her sanity and stay with you in that madness. All the bigoted racist imbeciles you started to cultivate. Every white friend you had knows that story.

WALKER. You shut up....I don't want to hear anything you've got to say.

GRACE. There are so many bulbs and screams shooting off inside you, Walker. So many lies you have to pump full of yourself. You're split so many ways... your feelings are cut up into skinny horrible strips...like umbrella struts... holding up whatever bizarre black cloth you're using this performance as your self's image. I don't even think you know who you are any more. No, I don't think you *ever* knew.

WALKER. I know what I can use.

GRACE. No, you never even found out who you were until you sold the last of your loves and emotions down the river...until you killed your last old friend... and found out *what* you were. My God, it must be hard being you, Walker Vessels. It must be a sick task keeping so many lying separate uglinesses together... and pretending they're something you've made and understand.

WALKER. What I can use, madam...what I can use. I move now trying to be certain of that.

EASLEY. You're talking strangely. What is this, the pragmatics of war? What are you saying...use? I thought you meant yourself to be a fantastic idealist? All those speeches and essays and poems...the rebirth of idealism. That the Western white man had forfeited the most impressive characteristic of his culture... the idealism of rational liberalism...and that only the black man in the West could restore that quality to Western culture, because he still understood the necessity for it. Et cetera, et cetera. Oh, look, I remember your horseshit theories, friend. I remember. And now the great black Western idealist is talking about use.

WALKER. Yeah, yeah. Now you can call me the hypocritical idealist nigger murderer. You see, what I want is more titles.

GRACE. And saying you want the children is another title...right? Every time you say it, one of those bulbs goes off in your head and you think you can focus on still another attribute, another beautiful quality in the total beautiful structure of the beautiful soul of Walker Vessels, sensitive Negro poet, savior of his people, deliverer of Western idealism...commander-in-chief of the forces of righteousness...Oh, God, et cetera, et cetera.

WALKER. Grace Locke Vessels Easley...whore of the middle classes.

EASLEY.
   [*Turning suddenly as if to offer combat*]
Go and fuck yourself.

GRACE. Yes, Walker, by all means...go and fuck yourself.
   [*And softer*]
Yes, do anything...but don't drag my children into your scheme for martyrdom and immortality, or whatever else it is makes you like you are...just don't... don't even mention it.

EASLEY.
   [*Moving to comfort her*]
Oh, don't get so worried, Grace...you know he just likes to hear himself talk... more than anything...he just wants to hear himself talk, so he can find out what he's supposed to have on his mind.
   [*To WALKER*]
He knows there's no way in the world he could have those children. No way in the world.

WALKER.
   [*Feigning casual matter-of-fact tone*]
Mr. Easley, Mrs. Easley, those girls' last name is Vessels. Whatever you think is all right. I mean I don't care what you think about me or what I'm doing...the whole mess. But those beautiful girls you have upstairs there are my daughters. They even look like me. I've loved them all their lives. Before this there was too much to do, so I left them with you.
   [*Gets up, pours another drink*]
But now...things are changed...I want them with me.
   [*Sprawls on couch again*]
I want them with me very much.

GRACE. You're lying. Liar, you don't give a shit about those children. You're a liar if you say otherwise. You never never never cared at all for those children. My friend, you have never cared for anything in the world that I know of but what's in there behind your eyes. And God knows what ugliness that is... though there are thousands of people dead or homeless all over this country who begin to understand a little. And not just white people...you've killed so many of your own people too. It's a wonder they haven't killed you.

EASLEY.
   [*Walks over to WALKER*]
Get up and get out of here! So help me...if you don't leave here now...I'll call the soldiers. They'd just love to find you.

[WALKER doesn't move]

Really, Vessels, I'll personally put a big hole in that foul liberation movement right now...I swear it.

[He turns to go to the phone]

WALKER.

[At first as if he is good-natured]

Hey, hey...Professor Easley, I've got this gun here, remember? Now don't do that...in fact if you take another step, I'll blow your goddamn head off. And I mean that, Brad, turn around and get back here in the center of the room.

GRACE.

[Moves for the stairs]

Ohhh!

WALKER. Hey, Grace, stop...you want me to shoot this fairy, or what? Come back here!

GRACE. I was only going to see about the kids.

WALKER. I'm their father...I'm thinking about their welfare, too. Just come back here. Both of you sit on this couch where I'm sitting, and I'll sit in that chair over there near the ice tray.

EASLEY. So now we get a taste of Vessels, the hoodlum.

WALKER. Uh, yeah. Another title, boss man. But just sit the fuck down for now.

[Goes to the window. Looks at his watch]

I got about an hour.

GRACE. Walker, what are you going to do?

WALKER. Do? Well, right now I'm going to have another drink.

EASLEY. You know what she means.

GRACE. You're not going to take the children, are you? You wouldn't just take them, would you? You wouldn't do that. You can't hate me so much that you'd do that.

WALKER. I don't hate you at all, Grace. I hated you when I wanted you. I haven't wanted you for a long time. But I do want those children.

GRACE. You're lying!

WALKER. No, I'm not lying...and I guess that's what's cutting you up...because you probably know I'm not lying, and you can't understand that. But I tell you now that I'm not lying, and that in spite of all the things I've done that have helped kill love in me, I still love those girls.

EASLEY. You mean, in spite of all the people you've killed.

WALKER. O.K., O.K., however you want it...however you want it, let it go at that. In spite of all the people I've killed. No, better, in spite of the fact that I,

Walker Vessels, single-handedly, and with no other adviser except my own ego, promoted a bloody situation where white and black people are killing each other; despite the fact that I know that this is at best a war that will only change, ha, the complexion of tyranny...

   [Laughs sullenly]

In spite of the fact that I have killed for all times any creative impulse I will ever have by the depravity of my murderous philosophies...despite the fact that I am being killed in my head each day and by now have no soul or heart or warmth, even in my long killer fingers, despite the fact that I have no other thing in the universe that I love or trust, but myself...despite or in spite, the respite, my dears, my dears, hear me, O Olympus, O Mercury, God of thieves, O Damballah, chief of all the dead religions of pseudo-nigger patriots hoping to open big restaurants after de wah...har har...in spite, despite, the resistance in the large cities and the small towns, where we have taken, yes, dragged piles of darkies out of their beds and shot them for being in Rheingold ads, despite the fact that all of my officers are ignorant motherfuckers who have never read any book in their lives, despite the fact that I would rather argue politics, or litera-ture, or boxing, or anything, with you, dear Easley, with you...

   [Head slumps, weeping]

despite all these things and in spite of all the drunken noises I'm making, despite...in spite of...I want those girls, very, very much. And I will take them out of here with me.

EASLEY. No, you won't...not if I can help it.

WALKER. Well, you can't help it.

GRACE.
   [Jumps up]
What? Is no one to reason with you? Isn't there any way something can exist without you having the final judgment on it? Is the whole world yours...to deal with or destroy? You're right! You feel! You have the only real vision of the world. You love! No one else exists in the world except you, and those who can help you. Everyone else is nothing or else they're something to be de-stroyed. I'm your enemy now...right? I'm wrong. You are the children's father... but I'm no longer their mother. Every one of your yesses or nos is intended by you to reshape the world after the image you have of it. They *are* my children! I am their mother! But because somehow I've become your enemy, I suddenly no longer qualify. Forget you're their mother, Grace. Walker has decided that you're no longer to perform that function. So the whole business is erased as if it never existed. I'm *not* in your head, Walker. Neither are those kids. We are all flesh and blood and deserve to live...even unabstracted by what you think we ought to be in the general scheme of things. Even alien to it. I left you... and took the girls because you'd gone crazy. You're crazy now. This stupid ugly killing you've started will never do anything, for anybody. And you and all your people will be wiped out, you know that. And you'll have accomplished noth-

ing. Do you want those two babies to be with you when you're killed so they can witness the death of a great man? So they can grow up and write articles for a magazine sponsored by the Walker Vessels Society?

WALKER. Which is still better than being freakish mulattoes in a world where your father is some evil black thing you can't remember. Look, I was going to wait until the fighting was over...
   [Reflective]
until we had won, before I took them. But something occurred to me for the first time, last night. It was the idea that we might not win. Somehow it only got through to me last night. I'd sort've taken it for granted...as a solved problem, that the fighting was the most academic of our problems, and that the real work would come necessarily after the fighting was done. But...

EASLEY. Things are not going as well for you as you figured.

WALKER. No. It will take a little longer, that's all. But this city will fall soon. We should be here within a week. You see, I could have waited until then. Then just marched in, at the head of the triumphant army, and seized the children as a matter of course. In fact I don't know why I didn't, except I did want to see you all in what you might call your natural habitats. I thought maybe I might be able to sneak in just as you and my ex-wife were making love, or just as you were lining the girls up against the wall to beat them or make them repeat after you, "Your daddy is a racist murderer." And then I thought I could murder both of you on the spot, and be completely justified.

GRACE. You've convinced yourself that you're rescuing the children, haven't you?

WALKER. Just as you convinced yourself you were rescuing them when you took them away from me.

EASLEY. She was!

WALKER. Now so am I.

GRACE. Yes
   [Wearily]
I begin to get some of your thinking now. When you mentioned killing us. I'm sure you thought the whole thing up in quite heroic terms. How you'd come through the white lines, murder us, and rescue the girls. You probably went over that...or had it go through your head on that gray film, a thousand times until it was some kind of obligatory reality.
   [WALKER laughs]

EASLEY. The kind of insane reality that brought about all the killing.

WALKER. Christ, the worst thing that ever happened to the West was the psychological novel...believe me.

EASLEY. When the Nazis were confronted with Freud, they claimed his work was of dubious value.

WALKER. Bravo!

GRACE. It's a wonder you *didn't* murder us!

WALKER.
[Looking suddenly less amused]
Oh…have I forfeited my opportunity?

EASLEY.
[Startled reaction]
You're not serious? What reason…what possible reason would there be for killing us? I mean I could readily conceive of your killing me, but the two of us, as some kind of psychological unit. I don't understand that. You said you didn't hate Grace.

GRACE.
[To press WALKER]
He's lying again, Brad. Really, most times he's not to be taken seriously. He was making a metaphor before…one of those ritual-drama metaphors…
[Laughs, as does BRAD]
You said it before…just to hear what's going on in his head. Really, he's not to be taken seriously.
[She hesitates, and there is a silence]
Unless there's some way you can kill him.

WALKER.
[Laughs, then sobers, but begins to show the effects of the alcohol]
Oh, Grace, Grace. Now you're trying to incite your husbean…which I swear is hardly Christian. I'm really surprised at you. But more so because you completely misunderstand me now…or maybe I'm not so surprised. I guess you never did know what was going on. That's why you left. You thought I betrayed you or something. Which really knocked me on my ass, you know? I was preaching hate the white man…get the white man off our backs…if necessary, kill the white man for our rights…whatever the hell that finally came to mean. And don't, now, for God's sake start thinking he's disillusioned, he's cynical, or any of the rest of these horseshit liberal definitions of the impossibility or romanticism of idealism. But those things I said…and would say now, pushed you away from me. I couldn't understand that.

GRACE. You couldn't understand it? What are you saying?

WALKER. No, I couldn't understand it. We'd been together a long time, before all that happened. What I said…what I thought I had to do…I knew you, if any white person in the world could, I knew you would understand. And then you didn't.

GRACE. You began to align yourself with the worst kind of racists and second-rate hack political thinkers.

WALKER. I've never aligned myself with anything or anyone I hadn't thought up first.

GRACE. You stopped telling me everything!

WALKER. I never stopped telling you I loved you...or that you were my wife!

GRACE.
[Almost broken]
It wasn't enough, Walker. It wasn't enough.

WALKER. God, it should have been.

GRACE. Walker, you were preaching the murder of all white people. Walker, I was, am, white. What do you think was going through my mind every time you were at some rally or meeting whose sole purpose was to bring about the destruction of white people?

WALKER. Oh, goddamn it, Grace, are you so stupid? You were my wife...I loved you. You mean because I loved you and was married to you...had had children by you, I wasn't supposed to say the things I felt. I was crying out against three hundred years of oppression; not against individuals.

EASLEY. But it's individuals who are dying.

WALKER. It was individuals who were doing the oppressing. It was individuals who were being oppressed. The horror is that oppression is not a concept that can be specifically transferable. From the oppressed, down on the oppressor. To keep the horror where it belongs...on those people who we can speak of, even in this last part of the twentieth century, as evil.

EASLEY. You're so wrong about everything. So terribly, sickeningly wrong. What can you change? What do you hope to change? Do you think Negroes are better people than whites...that they can govern a society *better* than whites? That they'll be more judicious or more tolerant? Do you think they'll make fewer mistakes? I mean really, if the Western white man has proved one thing... it's the futility of modern society. So the have-not peoples become the haves. Even so, will that change the essential functions of the world? Will there be more love or beauty in the world...more knowledge...because of it?

WALKER. Probably. Probably there will be more...if more people have a chance to understand what it is. But that's not even the point. It comes down to baser human endeavor than any social-political thinking. What does it matter if there's more love or beauty? Who the fuck cares? Is that what the Western ofay thought while he was ruling...that his rule somehow brought more love and beauty into the world? Oh, he might have thought that concomitantly, while sipping a gin rickey and scratching his ass...but that was not ever the point. Not even on the Crusades. The point is that you had your chance, darling, now these other folks have theirs.
[Quietly]
Now they have theirs.

EASLEY. God, what an ugly idea.

WALKER.
> [*Head in hands*]

I know. I know.
> [*His head is sagging, but he brings it up quickly. While it is down,* EASLEY *crosses* GRACE *with a significant look*]

But what else you got, champ? What else you got? I remember too much horse-shit from the other side for you to make much sense. Too much horseshit. The cruelty of it, don't you understand, now? The complete ugly horseshit cruelty of it is that there doesn't have to be a change. It'll be up to individuals on that side, just as it was supposed to be up to individuals on this side. Ha!...Who failed! Just like you failed, Easley. Just like you failed.

EASLEY. Failed? What are you talking about?

WALKER.
> [*Nodding*]

Well, what do you think? You never did anything concrete to avoid what's going on now. Your sick liberal lip service to whatever was the least filth. Your high aesthetic disapproval of the political. Letting the sick ghosts of the thirties strangle whatever chance we had.

EASLEY. What are you talking about?

WALKER. What we argued about so many times...befo' de wah.

EASLEY. And you see...what I predicted has happened. Now, in whatever cruel, and you said it, cruel political synapse you're taken with, or anyone else is taken with, with sufficient power I, any individual, any person who thinks of life as a purely anarchic relationship between man and God...or man and his work...any consciousness like that is destroyed...along with your *enemies*. And you, for whatever right or freedom or sickening cause you represent, kill me. Kill what does not follow.

WALKER. Perhaps you're right. But I have always found it hard to be neutral when faced with ugliness. Especially an ugliness that has worked all my life to twist me.

GRACE. And so you let it succeed!

WALKER. The aesthete came long after all the things that really formed me. It was the easiest weight to shed. And I couldn't be merely a journalist...a social critic. No social protest...right is in the act! And the act itself has some place in the world...it makes some place for itself. Right? But you all accuse me, not understanding that what you represent, you, my wife, all our old intellectual cut-throats, was something that was going to die anyway. One way or another. You'd been used too often, backed off from reality too many times. Remember the time, remember that time long time ago, in the old bar when you and Louie Rino were arguing with me, and Louie said then that he hated people who wanted to change the world. You remember that?

EASLEY. I remember the fight.

WALKER. Yeah, well, I know I thought then that none of you would write any poetry either. I knew that you had moved too far away from the actual mean-ings of life...into some lifeless cocoon of pretended intellectual and emotional achievement, to really be able to see the world again. What was Rino writing before he got killed? Tired elliptical little descriptions of what he could see out the window.

EASLEY. And how did he die?

WALKER. An explosion in the school where he was teaching.
    [Nodding]

EASLEY. One of your terrorists did it.

WALKER. Yeah, yeah.

EASLEY. He was supposed to be one of your closest friends.

WALKER. Yeah, yeah.

GRACE. Yeah, yeah, yeah, yeah.
    [With face still covered]

WALKER. We called for a strike to show the government we had all the white intellectuals backing us.
    [Nodding]
Hah, and the only people who went out were those tired political hacks. No one wanted to be intellectually compromised.

EASLEY. I didn't go either.
    [Hunches GRACE, starts to ease out of his chair]
And it was an intellectual compromise. No one in their right mind could have backed your program completely.

WALKER. No one but Negroes.

EASLEY. Well, then, they weren't in their right minds. You'd twisted them.

WALKER. The country twisted 'em.
    [Still nodding]
The country had twisted them for so long.
    [Head almost touching his chest]

EASLEY.
    [Taking very cautious step toward WALKER, still talking]
The politics of self-pity.
    [Indicates to GRACE that she is to talk]

WALKER.
    [Head down]
Yeah. Yeah.

EASLEY. The politics of self-pity.

GRACE.
[Raising her head slowly to watch, almost petrified]
A murderous self-pity. An extraordinarily murderous self-pity.
[There is another explosion close to the house. The lights go out for a few seconds. They come on, and EASLEY is trying to return to his seat, but WALKER's head is still on his chest]

WALKER.
[Mumbles]
What'd they do, hit the lights? Goddamn lousy marksmen.
[EASLEY starts again]
Lousy marksmen . . . and none of 'em worth shit.
[Now, another close explosion. The lights go out again. They come on; EASLEY is standing almost halfway between the couch and WALKER. WALKER's head is still down on his chest. EASLEY crouches to move closer. The lights go out again]

Black

[More explosions]

ACT II

Explosions are heard before the curtain goes up. When curtain rises, room is still in darkness, but the explosion does throw some light. Figures are still as they were at the end of first act; light from explosions outlines them briefly.

WALKER. Shit.
[Lights come up. WALKER's head is still down, but he is nodding from side to side, cursing something very drunkenly. EASLEY stands very stiffly in the center of the room, waiting to take another step. GRACE sits very stiffly, breathing heavily, on the couch, trying to make some kind of conversation, but not succeeding. WALKER has his hand in his jacket pocket, on the gun]

GRACE. It is self-pity, and some weird ambition, Walker.
[Strained silence]
But there's no reason . . . the girls should suffer. There's . . . no reason.
[EASLEY takes a long stride, and is about to throw himself at WALKER, when there is another explosion, and the lights go out again, very briefly. When they come up, EASLEY is set to leap, but WALKER's head comes abruptly up. He stares drunkenly at EASLEY, not moving his hand. For some awkward duration of time the two men stare at each other, in almost the same way as they had at the beginning of the play. Then GRACE screams]

GRACE. Walker!
[WALKER looks at her slightly, and EASLEY throws himself on him. The chair falls backward and the two men roll on the floor. EASLEY trying to choke WALKER. WALKER trying to get the gun out of his pocket]

GRACE. Walker! Walker!
[Suddenly, WALKER shoves one hand in EASLEY's face, shooting him without taking the gun from his pocket. EASLEY slumps backward, his face twisted, his mouth open and

working. WALKER *rolls back off* EASLEY, *pulling the gun from his pocket. He props himself against the chair, staring at the man's face]*

GRACE. Walker.
[Her shouts have become whimpers, and she is moving stiffly toward EASLEY*]*
Walker. Walker.

EASLEY.
[Mouth is still working . . . and he is managing to get a few sounds, words, out]

WALKER.
[Still staring at him, pulling himself up on the chair]
Shut up, you!
[To EASLEY*]*
You shut up. I don't want to hear anything else from you. You just die, quietly. No more talk.

GRACE. Walker!
[She is screaming again]
Walker!
[She rushes toward EASLEY, *but* WALKER *catches her arm and pushes her away]*
You're an insane man. You hear me, Walker?
[He is not looking at her, he is still staring down at EASLEY*]*
Walker, you're an insane man.
[She screams]
You're an insane man.
[She slumps to the couch, crying]
An insane man...

WALKER. No profound statements, Easley. No horseshit like that. No elegance. You just die quietly and stupidly. Like niggers do. Like they are now.
[Quieter]
Like I will. The only thing I'll let you say is, "I only regret that I have but one life to lose for my country." You can say that.
[Looks over at GRACE*]*
Grace! Tell Bradford that he can say, "I only regret that I have but one life to lose for my country." You can say that, Easley, but that's all.

EASLEY.
[Straining to talk]
Ritual drama. Like I said, ritual drama...
[He dies.

WALKER *stands staring at him. The only sounds are an occasional explosion, and* GRACE's *heavy brittle weeping]*

WALKER. He could have said, "I only regret that I have but one life to lose for my country." I would have let him say that... but no more. No more. There is no reason he should go out with any kind of dignity. I couldn't allow that.

GRACE. You're out of your mind.
[Slow, matter-of-fact]

WALKER. Meaning?

GRACE. You're out of your mind.

WALKER.
[Wearily]
Turn to another station.

GRACE. You're out of your mind.

WALKER. I said, turn to another station...will you? Another station! Out of my mind is not the point. You ought to know that.
[Brooding]
The way things are, being out of your mind is the only thing that qualifies you to stay alive. The only thing. Easley was in his right mind. Pitiful as he was. That's the reason he's dead.

GRACE. He's dead because you killed him.

WALKER. Yeah. He's dead because I killed him. Also, because he thought he ought to kill me.
[Looking over at the dead man]
You want me to cover him up?

GRACE. I don't want you to do anything, Walker...but leave here.
[Raising her voice]
Will you do that for me...or do you want to kill me too?

WALKER. Are you being ironic? Huh?
[He grabs her arm, jerking her head up so she has to look at him]
Do you think you're being ironic? Or do you want to kill me, too?...
[Shouting]
You're mighty right I want to kill you. You're mighty goddamn right. Believe me, self-righteous little bitch, I want to kill you.

GRACE.
[Startled, but trying not to show it]
The cause demands it, huh? The cause demands it.

WALKER. Yeah, the cause demands it.

GRACE.
[She gets up and goes to EASLEY, kneeling beside the body]
The cause demands it, Brad. That's why Walker shot you...because the cause demands it.
[Her head droops but she doesn't cry. She sits on her knees, holding the dead man's hand]
I guess the point is that now when you take the children I'll be alone.
[She looks up at WALKER]
I guess that's the point, now. Is that the point, Walker? Me being alone...as you have been now for so long? I'll bet that's the point, huh? I'll bet you came

here to do exactly what you did…kill Brad, then take the kids, and leave me alone…to suffocate in the stink of my memories.

[She is trying not to cry]

Just like I did to you. I'm sure that's the point. Right?

[She leaps up suddenly at WALKER]

You scum! You murdering scum.

[They grapple for a second, then WALKER slaps her to the floor. She kneels a little way off from EASLEY's body]

WALKER. Yeh, Grace. That's the point. For sure, that's the point.

GRACE. You were going to kill Brad, from the first. You knew that before you even got here.

WALKER. I'd thought about it.

GRACE.

[Weeping, but then she stops and is quiet for a minute]

So what's supposed to happen then…I mean after you take the kids and leave me here alone? Huh? I know you've thought about that, too.

WALKER. I have. But you know what'll happen much better than I do. But maybe you don't. What do you think happened to me when you left? Did you ever think about that? You must have.

GRACE. You had your cause, friend. Your cause, remember. And thousands of people following you, hoping that shit you preached was right. I pitied you.

WALKER. I know that. It took me awhile, but then I finally understood that you did pity me. And that you were somewhere, going through whatever mediocre routine you and Easley called your lives…pitying me. I figured that, finally, you weren't really even shocked by what was happening…what had happened. You were so secure in the knowledge that you were good, and compassionate… and right, that most of all…you were certain, my God, so certain…emotionally and intellectually, that you were right, until the only idea you had about me was to pity me.

[He wheels around to face her squarely]

God, that pissed me off. You don't really know how furious that made me. You and that closet queen, respected, weak-as-water intellectual, pitying me. God. God!

[Forcing the humor]

Miss Easley, honey, I could have killed both of you every night of my life.

GRACE. Will you kill me now if I say right here that I still pity you?

WALKER.

[A breathless half-broken little laugh]

No. No, I won't kill you.

GRACE. Well, I pity you, Walker. I really do.

WALKER. Only until you start pitying yourself.

GRACE. I wish I could call you something that would hurt you.

WALKER. So do I.

GRACE.
[Wearily]
Nigger.

WALKER. So do I.
[Looks at his watch]
I've got to go soon.

GRACE. You're still taking the girls.
[She is starting to push herself up from the floor.

WALKER. stares at her, then quickly over his shoulder at the stairway. He puts his hand in the pocket where the gun is, then he shakes his head slowly]

GRACE.
[Not seeing this gesture]
You're still taking the children?
[WALKER shakes his head slowly. An explosion shakes the house a little]

GRACE. Walker. Walker.
[She staggers to her feet, shaking with the next explosion]
Walker? You shook your head?
[WALKER stands very stiffly looking at the floor.

GRACE starts to come to him, and the next explosion hits very close or actually hits the house. Beams come down; some of the furniture is thrown around. GRACE falls to the floor. WALKER is toppled backward. A beam hits GRACE across the chest. Debris falls on WALKER. There are more explosions, and then silence]

GRACE. Walker! Walker!
[She is hurt very badly and is barely able to move the debris that is covering her]
Walker! The girls! Walker! Catherine! Elizabeth! Walker, the girls!
[WALKER finally starts to move. He is also hurt badly, but he is able to move much more freely than GRACE. He starts to clear away the debris and make his way to his knees]

GRACE. Walker?

WALKER. Yeah? Grace?

GRACE. Walker, the children... the girls... see about the girls.
[She is barely able to raise one of her arms]
The girls, Walker, see about them.

WALKER.
[He is finally able to crawl over to GRACE, and pushes himself unsteadily up on his hands]
You're hurt pretty badly? Can you move?

GRACE. The girls, Walker, see about the girls.

WALKER. Can you move?

GRACE. The girls, Walker...
[She is losing strength]
Our children!

WALKER.
[He is silent for a while]
They're dead, Grace. Catherine and Elizabeth are dead.
[He starts up stairs as if to verify his statement. Stops, midway, shakes his head; retreats]

GRACE.
[Looking up at him frantically, but she is dying]
Dead? Dead?
[She starts to weep and shake her head]
Dead?
[Then she stops suddenly, tightening her face]
How... how do you know, Walker? How do you know they're dead?
[WALKER's head is drooping slightly]
How do you know they're dead, Walker? How do you...
[Her eyes try to continue what she is saying, but she slumps, and dies in a short choking spasm.

WALKER looks to see that she is dead, then resumes his efforts to get up. He looks at his watch. Listens to see if it is running. Wipes his face. Pushes the floor to get up. Another explosion sounds very close and he crouches quickly, covering his head. Another explosion. He pushes himself up, brushing sloppily at his clothes. He looks at his watch again, then starts to drag himself toward the door]
They're dead, Grace!
[He is almost shouting]
They're dead.
[He leaves, stumbling unsteadily through the door. He is now the old man at the beginning of the play. There are more explosions. Another one very close to the house. A sudden aggravated silence, and then there is a child heard crying and screaming as loud as it can. More explosions]

Black

[More explosions, after curtain for some time]

James Baldwin

from *The Fire Next Time*

DOWN AT THE CROSS

Letter from a Region in My Mind

Take up the White Man's burden—
Ye dare not stoop to less—
Nor call too loud on Freedom
To cloak your weariness;
By all ye cry or whisper,
By all ye leave or do,
The silent, sullen peoples
Shall weigh your Gods and you.

—KIPLING

Down at the cross where my Saviour died,
Down where for cleansing from sin I cried,
There to my heart was the blood applied,
Singing glory to His name!

—HYMN

I underwent, during the summer that I became fourteen, a prolonged religious crisis. I use the word "religious" in the common, and arbitrary, sense, meaning that I then discovered God, His saints and angels, and His blazing Hell. And since I had been born in a Christian nation, I accepted this Deity as the only one. I supposed Him to exist only within the walls of a church—in fact, of *our* church—and I also supposed that God and safety were synonymous. The word "safety" brings us to the real meaning of the word "religious" as we use it. Therefore, to state it in another, more accurate way, I became, during my fourteenth year, for the first time in my life, afraid—afraid of the evil within me and afraid of the evil without. What I saw around me that summer in Harlem was what I had always seen; nothing had changed. But now, without any warning, the whores and pimps and racketeers on the Avenue had become a personal menace. It had not before occurred to me that I could become one of them, but now I realized that we had been produced by the same circumstances. Many of my comrades were clearly headed for the Avenue, and my father said that I was headed that way, too. My friends began to drink and smoke, and embarked—at first avid, then groaning—on their sexual careers. Girls, only slightly older than I was, who sang in the choir or taught Sunday school, the children of holy parents, underwent, before my eyes, their incredible metamorphosis, of which the most bewildering aspect was not their budding breasts or their rounding behinds but something deeper and more subtle, in their eyes, their heat, their odor, and the inflection of their voices. Like the strangers on the Avenue, they became, in the twinkling of an eye, unutterably different and fantastically *present*. Owing to the way I had been raised, the abrupt discomfort that all this aroused in me and the fact that I had no idea what my voice or my mind or my body was likely to do next caused me to consider myself one of the most depraved people on earth. Matters were not helped by the fact that these holy girls seemed rather to enjoy my terrified lapses, our grim, guilty, tormented experiments, which were at once as chill and joyless as the Russian steppes and hotter, by far, than all the fires of Hell.

Yet there was something deeper than these changes, and less definable, that frightened me. It was real in both the boys and the girls, but it was, somehow, more vivid in the boys. In the case of the girls, one watched them turning into matrons before they had become women. They began to manifest a curious and really rather terrifying single-mindedness. It is hard to say exactly how this was conveyed: something implacable in the set of the lips, something farseeing (seeing what?) in the eyes, some new and crushing determination in the walk, something peremptory in the voice. They did not tease us, the boys, any more; they reprimanded us sharply, saying, "You better be thinking about your soul!" For the girls also saw the evidence on the Avenue, knew what the price would be, for them, of one misstep, knew that they had to be protected and that we were the only protection there was. They understood that they must act as God's decoys, saving the souls of the boys for Jesus and binding the bodies of the boys in marriage. For this was the beginning of our burning time, and "It is better," said St. Paul—who elsewhere, with a most unusual and stunning exactness, described himself as a "wretched man"—"to marry than to burn." And I began to feel in the boys a curious, wary, bewildered despair, as though they were now settling in for the long, hard winter of life. I did not know then what it was that I was reacting to; I put it to myself that they were letting themselves go. In the same way that the girls were destined to gain as much weight as their mothers, the boys, it was clear, would rise no higher than their fathers. School began to reveal itself, therefore, as a child's game that one could not win, and boys dropped out of school and went to work. My father wanted me to do the same. I refused, even though I no longer had any illusions about what an education could do for me; I had already encountered too many college-graduate handymen. My friends were now "downtown," busy, as they put it, "fighting the man." They began to care less about the way they looked, the way they dressed, the things they did; presently, one found them in twos and threes and fours, in a hallway, sharing a jug of wine or a bottle of whisky, talking, cursing, fighting, sometimes weeping: lost, and unable to say what it was that oppressed them, except that they knew it was "the man"—the white man. And there seemed to be no way whatever to remove this cloud that stood between them and the sun, between them and love and life and power, between them and whatever it was that they wanted. One did not have to be very bright to realize how little one could do to change one's situation; one did not have to be abnormally sensitive to be worn down to a cutting edge by the incessant and gratuitous humiliation and danger one encountered every working day, all day long. The humiliation did not apply merely to working days, or workers; I was thirteen and was crossing Fifth Avenue on my way to the Forty-second Street library, and the cop in the middle of the street muttered as I passed him, "Why don't you niggers stay uptown where you belong?" When I was ten, and didn't look, certainly, any older, two policemen amused themselves with me by frisking me, making comic (and terrifying) speculations concerning my ancestry and probable sexual prowess, and for good measure, leaving me flat on my back in one of Harlem's empty lots. Just before and then during the Second World War, many of my friends fled into the service, all to be changed there, and rarely for the better, many to be ruined, and many to die. Others fled to other states and cities—that is, to other ghettos. Some went on wine or whisky or the needle, and are still on it. And others, like me, fled into the church.

For the wages of sin were visible everywhere, in every wine-stained and urine-splashed hallway, in every clanging ambulance bell, in every scar on the faces of the pimps and their whores, in every helpless, newborn baby being brought into this danger, in every knife and pistol fight on the Avenue, and in every disastrous bulletin: a cousin, mother of six, suddenly gone mad, the children parcelled out here and there; an indestructible aunt rewarded for years of hard labor by a slow, agonizing death in a terrible small room; someone's bright son blown into eternity by his own hand; another turned robber and carried off to jail. It was a summer of dreadful speculations and discoveries, of which these were not the worst. Crime became real, for example—for the first time—not as a possibility but as *the* possibility. One would never defeat one's circumstances by working and saving one's pennies; one would never, by working, acquire that many pennies, and, besides, the social treatment accorded even the most successful Negroes proved that one needed, in order to be free, something more than a bank account. One needed a handle, a lever, a means of inspiring fear. It was absolutely clear that the police would whip you and take you in as long as they could get away with it, and that everyone else—housewives, taxi-drivers, elevator boys, dishwashers, bartenders, lawyers, judges, doctors, and grocers—would never, by the operation of any generous human feeling, cease to use you as an outlet for his frustrations and hostilities. Neither civilized reason nor Christian love would cause any of those people to treat you as they presumably wanted to be treated; only the fear of your power to retaliate would cause them to do that, or to seem to do it, which was (and is) good enough. There appears to be a vast amount of confusion on this point, but I do not know many Negroes who are eager to be "accepted" by white people, still less to be loved by them; they, the blacks, simply don't wish to be beaten over the head by the whites every instant of our brief passage on this planet. White people in this country will have quite enough to do in learning how to accept and love themselves and each other, and when they have achieved this—which will not be tomorrow and may very well be never—the Negro problem will no longer exist, for it will no longer be needed.

People more advantageously placed than we in Harlem were, and are, will no doubt find the psychology and the view of human nature sketched above dismal and shocking in the extreme. But the Negro's experience of the white world cannot possibly create in him any respect for the standards by which the white world claims to live. His own condition is overwhelming proof that white people do not live by these standards. Negro servants have been smuggling odds and ends out of white homes for generations, and white people have been delighted to have them do it, because it has assuaged a dim guilt and testified to the intrinsic superiority of white people. Even the most doltish and servile Negro could scarcely fail to be impressed by the disparity between his situation and that of the people for whom he worked; Negroes who were neither doltish nor servile did not feel that they were doing anything wrong when they robbed white people. In spite of the Puritan-Yankee equation of virtue with well-being, Negroes had excellent reasons for doubting that money was made or kept by any very striking adherence to the Christian virtues; it certainly did not work that way for black Christians. In any case, white people, who had robbed black people of their liberty and who profited by this theft every hour that they lived, had no moral ground on which to stand. They had the judges, the juries, the shotguns, the law—in a word, power. But it was a criminal power, to be feared but not respected, and to be outwitted in any way whatever. And those virtues preached but not practiced by the white world were merely another means of holding Negroes in subjection.

It turned out, then, that summer, that the moral barriers that I had supposed to exist between me and the dangers of a criminal career were so tenuous as to be nearly nonexistent. I certainly could not discover any principled reason for not becoming a criminal, and it is not my poor, God-fearing parents who are to be indicted for the lack but this society. I was icily determined—more determined, really, than I then knew—never to make my peace with the ghetto but to die and go to Hell before I would let any white man spit on me, before I would accept my "place" in this republic. I did not intend to allow the white people of this country to tell me who I was, and limit me that way, and polish me off that way. And yet, of course, at the same time, I *was* being spat on and defined and described and limited, and could have been polished off with no effort whatever. Every Negro boy—in my situation during those years, at least—who reaches this point realizes, at once, profoundly, because he wants to live, that he stands in great peril and must find, with speed, a "thing," a gimmick, to lift him out, to start him on his way. *And it does not matter what the gimmick is.* It was this last realization that terrified me and—since it revealed that the door opened on so many dangers—helped to hurl me into the church. And, by an unforeseeable paradox, it was my career in the church that turned out, precisely, to be my gimmick.

For when I tried to assess my capabilities, I realized that I had almost none. In order to achieve the life I wanted, I had been dealt, it seemed to me, the worst possible hand. I could not become a prizefighter—many of us tried but very few succeeded. I could not sing. I could not dance. I had been well conditioned by the world in which I grew up, so I did not yet dare take the idea of becoming a writer seriously. The only other possibility seemed to involve my becoming one of the sordid people on the Avenue, who were not really as sordid as I then imagined but who frightened me terribly, both because I did not want to live that life and because of what they made me feel. Everything inflamed me, and that was bad enough, but I myself had also become a source of fire and temptation. I had been far too well raised, alas, to suppose that any of the extremely explicit overtures made to me that summer, sometimes by boys and girls but also, more alarmingly, by older men and women, had anything to do with my attractiveness. On the contrary, since the Harlem idea of seduction is, to put it mildly, blunt, whatever these people saw in me merely confirmed my sense of my depravity.

It is certainly sad that the awakening of one's senses should lead to such a merciless judgment of oneself—to say nothing of the time and anguish one spends in the effort to arrive at any other—but it is also inevitable that a literal attempt to mortify the flesh should be made among black people like those with whom I grew up. Negroes in this country—and Negroes do not, strictly or legally speaking, exist in any other—are taught really to despise themselves from the moment their eyes open on the world. This world is white and they are black. White people hold the power, which means that they are superior to blacks (intrinsically, that is: God decreed it so), and the world has innumerable ways of making this difference known and felt and feared. Long before the Negro child perceives this difference, and even longer before he understands it, he has begun to react to it, he has begun to be controlled by it. Every effort made by the child's elders to prepare him for a fate from which they cannot protect him causes him secretly, in terror, to begin to await, without knowing that he is doing so, his mysterious and inexorable punishment. He must be "good" not only in order to please his parents and not only to avoid being punished by them; behind their authority stands another, nameless and impersonal, infinitely harder to please, and bottomlessly cruel. And this filters into the child's consciousness through his parents' tone of voice as he is being exhorted, punished, or loved; in the sudden, uncontrollable note of fear heard in his mother's or his father's voice when he has strayed beyond some particular boundary. He does not know what the boundary is, and he can get no explanation of it, which is frightening enough, but the fear he hears in the voices of his elders is more frightening still. The fear that I heard in my father's voice, for example, when he realized that I really *believed* I could do anything a white boy could do, and had every intention of proving it, was not at all like the fear I heard when one of us was ill or had fallen down the stairs or strayed too far from the house. It was another fear, a fear that the child, in challenging the white world's assumptions, was putting himself in the path of destruction. A child cannot, thank Heaven, know how vast and how merciless is the nature of power, with what unbelievable cruelty people treat each other. He reacts to the fear in his parents' voices because his parents hold up the world for him and he has no protection without them. I defended myself, as I imagined, against the fear my father made me feel by remembering that he was very old-fashioned. Also, I prided myself on the fact that I already knew how to outwit him. To defend oneself against a fear is simply to insure that one will, one day, be conquered by it; fears must be faced. As for one's wits, it is just not true that one can live by them—not, that is, if one wishes really to live. That summer, in any case, all the fears with which I had grown up, and which were now a part of me and controlled my vision of the world, rose up like a wall between the world and me, and drove me into the church.

As I look back, everything I did seems curiously deliberate, though it certainly did not seem deliberate then. For example, I did not join the church of which my father was a member and in which he preached. My best friend in school, who attended a different church, had already "surrendered his life to the Lord," and he was very anxious about my soul's salvation. (I wasn't, but any human attention was better than none.) One Saturday afternoon, he took me to his church. There were no services that day, and the church was empty, except for some women cleaning and some other women praying. My friend took me into the back room to meet his pastor—a woman. There she sat, in her robes, smiling, an extremely proud and handsome woman, with Africa, Europe, and the America of the American Indian blended in her face. She was perhaps forty-five or fifty at this time, and in our world she was a very celebrated woman. My friend was about to introduce me when she looked at me and smiled and said, "Whose little boy are you?" Now this, unbelievably, was precisely the phrase used by pimps and racketeers on the Avenue when they suggested, both humorously and intensely, that I "hang out" with them. Perhaps part of the terror they had caused me to feel came from the fact that I unquestionably wanted to be *somebody's* little boy. I was so frightened, and at the mercy of so many conundrums, that inevitably, that summer, *someone* would have taken me over; one doesn't, in Harlem, long remain standing on any auction block. It was my good luck—perhaps—that I found myself in the church racket instead of some other, and surrendered to a spiritual seduction long before I came to any carnal knowledge. For when the pastor asked me, with that marvellous smile, "Whose little boy are you?" my heart replied at once, "Why, yours."

The summer wore on, and things got worse. I became more guilty and more frightened, and kept all this bottled up inside me, and naturally, inescapably, one night, when this woman had finished preaching, everything came roaring, screaming, crying out, and I fell to the ground before the altar. It was the strangest sensation I have ever had in my life—up to that time, or since. I had not known that it was going to happen, or that it could happen. One moment I was on my feet, singing and clapping and, at the same time, working out in my head the plot of a play I was working on then; the next moment, with no transition, no sensation of falling, I was on my back, with the lights beating down into my face and all the vertical saints above me. I did not know what I was doing down so low, or how I had got there. And the anguish that filled me cannot be described. It moved in me like one of those floods that devastate counties, tearing everything down, tearing children from their parents and lovers from each other, and making everything an unrecognizable waste. All I really remember is the pain, the unspeakable pain; it was as though I were yelling up to Heaven and Heaven would not hear me. And if Heaven would not hear me, if love could not descend from Heaven—to wash me, to make me clean—then utter disaster was my portion. Yes, it does indeed mean something—something unspeakable—to be born, in a white country, an Anglo-Teutonic, antisexual country, black. You very soon, without knowing it, give up all hope of communion. Black people, mainly, look down or look up but do not look at each other, not at you, and white people, mainly, look away. And the universe is simply a sounding drum; there is no way, no way whatever, so it seemed then and has sometimes seemed since, to get through a life, to love your wife and children, or your friends, or your mother and father, or to be loved. The universe, which is not merely the stars and the moon and the planets, flowers, grass, and trees, but *other people*, has evolved no terms for your existence, has made no room for you, and if love will not swing wide the gates, no other power will or can. And if one despairs—as who has not?—of human love, God's love alone is left. But God—and I felt this even then, so long ago, on that tremendous floor, unwillingly—is white. And if His love was so great, and if He loved all His children, why were we, the blacks, cast down so far? Why? In spite of all I said thereafter, I found no answer on the floor—not *that* answer, anyway—and I was on the floor all night. Over me, to bring me "through," the saints sang and rejoiced and prayed. And in the morning, when they raised me, they told me that I was "saved."

Well, indeed I was, in a way, for I was utterly drained and exhausted, and released, for the first time, from all my guilty torment. I was aware then only of my relief. For many years, I could not ask myself why human relief had to be achieved in a fashion at once so pagan and so desperate—in a fashion at once so unspeakably old and so unutterably new. And by the time I was able to ask myself this question, I was also able to see that the principles governing the rites and customs of the churches in which I grew up did not differ from the principles governing the rites and customs of other churches, white. The principles were Blindness, Loneliness, and Terror, the first principle necessarily and actively cultivated in order to deny the two others. I would love to believe that the principles were Faith, Hope, and Charity, but this is clearly not so for most Christians, or for what we call the Christian world.

I was saved. But at the same time, out of a deep, adolescent cunning I do not pretend to understand, I realized immediately that I could not remain in the church merely as another worshipper. I would have to give myself something to do, in order not to be too bored and find myself among all the wretched unsaved of the Avenue. And I don't doubt that I also intended to best my father on his own ground. Anyway, very shortly after I joined the church, I became a preacher—a Young Minister—and I remained in the pulpit for more than three years. My youth quickly made me a much bigger drawing card than my father. I pushed this advantage ruthlessly, for it was the most effective means I had found of breaking his hold over me. That was the most frightening time of my life, and quite the most dishonest, and the resulting hysteria lent great passion to my sermons—for a while. I relished the attention and the relative immunity from punishment that my new status gave me, and I relished, above all, the sudden right to privacy. It had to be recognized, after all, that I was still a schoolboy, with my schoolwork to do, and I was also expected to prepare at least one sermon a week. During what we may call my heyday, I preached much more often than that. This meant that there were hours and even whole days when I could not be interrupted—not even by my father. I had immobilized him. It took rather more time for me to realize that I had also immobilized myself, and had escaped from nothing whatever.

The church was very exciting. It took a long time for me to disengage myself from this excitement, and on the blindest, most visceral level, I never really have, and never will. There is no music like that music, no drama like the drama of the saints rejoicing, the sinners moaning, the tambourines racing, and all those voices coming together and crying holy unto the Lord. There is still, for me, no pathos quite like the pathos of those multicolored, worn, somehow triumphant and transfigured faces, speaking from the depths of a visible, tangible, continuing despair of the goodness of the Lord. I have never seen anything to equal the fire and excitement that sometimes, without warning, fill a church, causing the church, as Leadbelly and so many others have testified, to "rock." Nothing that has happened to me since equals the power and the glory that I sometimes felt when, in the middle of a sermon, I knew that I was somehow, by some miracle, really carrying, as they said, "the Word"—when the church and I were one. Their pain and their joy were mine, and mine were theirs—they surrendered their pain and joy to me, I surrendered mine to them—and their cries of "Amen!" and "Hallelujah!" and "Yes, Lord!" and "Praise His name!" and "Preach it, brother!" sustained and whipped on my solos until we all became equal, wringing wet, singing and dancing, in anguish and rejoicing, at the foot of the altar. It was, for a long time, in spite of—or, not inconceivably, because of—the shabbiness of my motives, my only sustenance, my meat and drink. I rushed home from school, to the church, to the altar, to be alone there, to commune with Jesus, my dearest Friend, who would never fail me, who knew all the secrets of my heart. Perhaps He did, but I didn't, and the bargain we struck, actually, down there at the foot of the cross, was that He would never let me find out.

He failed His bargain. He was a much better Man than I took Him for. It happened, as things do, imperceptibly, in many ways at once. I date it—the slow crumbling of my faith, the pulverization of my fortress—from the time, about a year after I had begun to preach, when I began to read again. I justified this desire by the fact that I was still in school, and I began, fatally, with Dostoevsky. By this time, I was in a high school that was predominantly Jewish. This meant that I was surrounded by people who were, by definition, beyond any hope of salvation, who laughed at the tracts and leaflets I brought to school, and who pointed out that the Gospels had been written long after the death of Christ. This might not have been so distressing if it had not forced me to read the tracts and leaflets myself, for they were indeed, unless one believed their message already, impossible to believe. I remember feeling dimly that there was a kind of blackmail in it. People, I felt, ought to love the Lord *because* they loved Him, and not because they were afraid of going to Hell. I was forced, reluctantly, to realize that the Bible itself had been written by men, and translated by men out of languages I could not read, and I was already, without quite admitting it to myself, terribly involved with the effort of putting words on paper. Of course, I had the rebuttal ready: These men had all been operating under divine inspiration. *Had* they? *All* of them? And I also knew by now, alas, far more about divine inspiration than I dared admit, for I knew how I worked myself up into my own visions, and how frequently—indeed, incessantly—the visions God granted to me differed from the visions He granted to my father. I did not understand the dreams I had at night, but I knew that they were not holy. For that matter, I knew that my waking hours were far from holy. I spent most of my time in a state of repentance for things I had vividly desired to do but had not done. The fact that I was dealing with Jews brought the whole question of color, which I had been desperately avoiding, into the terrified center of my mind. I realized that the Bible had been written by white men. I knew that, according to many Christians, I was a descendant of Ham, who had been cursed, and that I was therefore predestined to be a slave. This had nothing to do with anything I was, or contained, or could become; my fate had been sealed forever, from the beginning of time. And it seemed, indeed, when one looked out over Christendom, that this was what Christendom effectively believed. It was certainly the way it behaved. I remembered the Italian priests and bishops blessing Italian boys who were on their way to Ethiopia.

Again, the Jewish boys in high school were troubling because I could find no point of connection between them and the Jewish pawnbrokers and landlords and grocerystore owners in Harlem. I knew that these people were Jews— God knows I was told it often enough—but I thought of them only as white. Jews, as such, until I got to high school, were all incarcerated in the Old Testament, and their names were Abraham, Moses, Daniel, Ezekiel, and Job, and Shadrach, Meshach, and Abednego. It was bewildering to find them so many miles and centuries out of Egypt, and so far from the fiery furnace. My best friend in high school was a Jew. He came to our house once, and afterward my father asked, as he asked about everyone, "Is he a Christian?"—by which he meant "Is he saved?" I really do not know whether my answer came out of innocence or venom, but I said coldly, "No. He's Jewish." My father slammed me across the face with his great palm, and in that moment everything flooded back—all the hatred and all the fear, and the depth of a merciless resolve to kill my father rather than allow my father to kill me—and I knew that all those sermons and tears and all that repentance and rejoicing had changed nothing. I wondered if I was expected to be glad that a friend of mine, or anyone, was to be tormented forever in Hell, and I also thought, suddenly, of the Jews in another Christian nation, Germany. They were not so far from the fiery furnace after all, and my best friend might have been one of them. I told my father, "He's a better Christian than you are," and walked out of the house. The battle between us was in the open, but that was all right; it was almost a relief. A more deadly struggle had begun.

Being in the pulpit was like being in the theater; I was behind the scenes and knew how the illusion was worked. I knew the other ministers and knew the quality of their lives. And I don't mean to suggest by this the "Elmer Gantry" sort of hypocrisy concerning sensuality; it was a deeper, deadlier, and more subtle hypocrisy than that, and a little honest sensuality, or a lot, would have been like water in an extremely bitter desert. I knew how to work on a congregation until the last dime was surrendered—it was not very hard to do—and I knew where the money for "the Lord's work" went. I knew, though I did not wish to know it, that I had no respect for the people with whom I worked. I could not have said it then, but I also knew that if I continued I would soon have no respect for myself. And the fact that I was "the young Brother Baldwin" increased my value with those same pimps and racketeers who had helped to stampede me into the church in the first place. They still saw the little boy they intended to take over. They were waiting for me to come to my senses and realize that I was in a very lucrative business. They knew that I did not yet realize this, and also that I had not yet begun to suspect where my own needs, *coming up* (they were very patient), could drive me. They themselves did know the score, and they knew that the odds were in their favor. And, really, I knew it, too. I was even lonelier and more vulnerable than I had been before. And the blood of the Lamb had not cleansed me in any way whatever. I was just as black as I had been the day that I was born. Therefore, when I faced a congregation, it began to take all the strength I had not to stammer, not to curse, not to tell them to throw away their Bibles and get off their knees and go home and organize, for example, a rent strike. When I watched all the children, their copper, brown, and beige faces staring up at me as I taught Sunday school, I felt that I was committing a crime in talking about the gentle Jesus, in telling them to reconcile themselves to their misery on earth in order to gain the crown of eternal life. Were only Negroes to gain this crown? Was Heaven, then, to be merely another ghetto? Perhaps I might have been able to reconcile myself even to this if I had been able to believe that there was any loving-kindness to be found in the haven I represented. But I had been in the pulpit too long and I had seen too many monstrous things. I don't refer merely to the glaring fact that the minister eventually acquires houses and Cadillacs while the faithful continue to scrub floors and drop their dimes and quarters and dollars into the plate. I really mean that there was no love in the church. It was a mask for hatred and self-hatred and despair. The transfiguring power of the Holy Ghost ended when the service ended, and salvation stopped at the church door.

When we were told to love everybody, I had thought that that meant *everybody*. But no. It applied only to those who believed as we did, and it did not apply to white people at all. I was told by a minister, for example, that I should never, on any public conveyance, under any circumstances, rise and give my seat to a white woman. White men never rose for Negro women. Well, that was true enough, in the main—I saw his point. But what was the point, the purpose, of *my* salvation if it did not permit me to behave with love toward others, no matter how they behaved toward me? What others did was their responsibility, for which they would answer when the judgment trumpet sounded. But what *I* did was *my* responsibility, and I would have to answer, too—unless, of course, there was also in Heaven a special dispensation for the benighted black, who was not to be judged in the same way as other human beings, or angels. It probably occurred to me around this time that the vision people hold of the world to come is but a reflection, with predictable wishful distortions, of the world in which they live. And this did not apply only to Negroes, who were no more "simple" or "spontaneous" or "Christian" than anybody else—who were merely more oppressed. In the same way that we, for white people, were the descendants of Ham, and were cursed forever, white people were, for us, the descendants of Cain. And the passion with which we loved the Lord was a measure of how deeply we feared and distrusted and, in the end, hated almost all strangers, always, and avoided and despised ourselves.

But I cannot leave it at that; there is more to it than that. In spite of everything, there was in the life I fled a zest and a joy and a capacity for facing and surviving disaster that are very moving and very rare. Perhaps we were, all of us—pimps, whores, racketeers, church members, and children—bound together by the nature of our oppression, the specific and peculiar complex of risks we had to run; if so, within these limits we sometimes achieved with each other a freedom that was close to love. I remember, anyway, church suppers and outings, and, later, after I left the church, rent and waistline parties where rage and sorrow sat in the darkness and did not stir, and we ate and drank and talked and laughed and danced and forgot all about "the man." We had the liquor, the chicken, the music, and each other, and had no need to pretend to be what we were not. This is the freedom that one hears in some gospel songs, for example, and in jazz. In all jazz, and especially in the blues, there is something tart and ironic, authoritative and double-edged. White Americans seem to feel that happy songs are *happy* and sad songs are *sad*, and that, God help us, is exactly the way most white Americans sing them—sounding, in both cases, so helplessly, defenselessly fatuous that one dare not speculate on the temperature of the deep freeze from which issue their brave and sexless little voices. Only people who have been "down the line," as the song puts it, know what this music is about. I think it was Big Bill Broonzy who used to sing "I Feel So Good," a really joyful song about a man who is on his way to the railroad station to meet his girl. She's coming home. It is the singer's incredibly moving exuberance that makes one realize how leaden the time must have been while she was gone. There is no guarantee that she will stay this time, either, as the singer clearly knows, and, in fact, she has not yet actually arrived. Tonight, or tomorrow, or within the next five minutes, he may very well be singing "Lonesome in My Bedroom," or insisting, "Ain't we, ain't we, going to make it all right? Well, if we don't today, we will tomorrow night." White Americans do not understand the depths out of which such an ironic tenacity comes, but they suspect that the force is sensual, and they are terrified of sensuality and do not any longer understand it. The word "sensual" is not intended to bring to mind quivering dusky maidens or priapic black studs. I am referring to something much simpler and much less fanciful. To be sensual, I think, is to respect and rejoice in the force of life, of life itself, and to be *present* in all that one does, from the effort of loving to the breaking of bread. It will be a great day for America, incidentally, when we begin to eat bread again, instead of the blasphemous and tasteless foam rubber that we have substituted for it. And I am not being frivolous now, either. Something very sinister happens to the people of a country when they begin to distrust their own reactions as deeply as they do here, and become as joyless as they have become. It is this individual uncertainty on the part of white American men and women, this inability to renew themselves at the fountain of their own lives, that makes the discussion, let alone elucidation, of any conundrum—that is, any reality—so supremely difficult. The person who distrusts himself has no touchstone for reality—for this touchstone can be only oneself. Such a person interposes between himself and reality nothing less than a labyrinth of attitudes. And these attitudes, furthermore, though the person is usually unaware of it (is unaware of so much!), are historical and public attitudes. They do not relate to the present any more than they relate to the person. Therefore, whatever white people do not know about Negroes reveals, precisely and inexorably, what they do not know about themselves.

from *No Name in the Street*

[MALCOLM X]

Alex Haley wrote *The Autobiography of Malcolm X*. Months before the foregoing, in New York, he and Elia Kazan and I had agreed to do it as a play—and I still wish we had. We were vaguely aware that Hollywood was nibbling for a book, but, as Hollywood is always nibbling, it occurred to no one, certainly not to me, to take these nibbles seriously. It simply was not a subject which Hollywood could manage, and I didn't see any point in talking to them about it. But the book was sold to an independent producer, named Marvin Worth, who would produce it for Columbia Pictures. By this time, I was already in London; and I was also on the spot. For, while I didn't believe Hollywood could do it, I didn't quite see, since they declared themselves sincerely and seriously willing to attempt it, how I could duck the challenge. What it came to, in fact, was an enormous question: to what extent was I prepared again to gamble on the good faith of my countrymen?

In that time, now so incredibly far behind us, when the Black Muslims meant to the American people exactly what the Black Panthers mean today, and when they were described in exactly the same terms by that High Priest, J. Edgar Hoover, and when many of us believed or made ourselves believe that the American state still contained within itself the power of self-confrontation, the power to change itself in the direction of honor and knowledge and freedom, or, as Malcolm put it, "to atone," I first met Malcolm X. Perhaps it says a great deal about the black American experience, both negatively and positively, that so many should have believed so hard, so long, and paid such a price for believing: but what this betrayed belief says about white Americans is very accurately and abjectly summed up by the present, so-called Nixon Administration.

I had heard a great deal about Malcolm, as had everyone else, and I was a little afraid of him, as was everyone else, and I was further handicapped by having been out of the country for so long. When I returned to America, I again went south, and thus, imperceptibly, found myself mainly on the road. I saw Malcolm before I met him. I had just returned from someplace like Savannah, I was giving a lecture somewhere in New York, and Malcolm was sitting in the first or second row of the hall, bending forward at such an angle that his long arms nearly caressed the ankles of his long legs, staring up at me. I very nearly panicked. I knew Malcolm only by legend, and this legend, since I was a Harlem street boy, I was sufficiently astute to distrust. I distrusted the legend because we, in Harlem, have been betrayed so often. Malcolm might be the torch white people claimed he was—though, in general, white America's evaluations of these matters would be laughable and even pathetic did not these evaluations have such wicked results—or he might be the hustler I remembered from my pavements. On the other hand, Malcolm had no reason to trust me, either—and so I stumbled through my lecture, with Malcolm never taking his eyes from my face.

It must be remembered that in those great days I was considered to be an "integrationist"—this was never, quite, my own idea of myself—and Malcolm was considered to be a "racist in reverse." This formulation, in terms of power—and power is the arena in which racism is acted out—means absolutely nothing: it may even be described as a cowardly formulation. The powerless, by definition, can never be "racists," for they can never make the world pay for what they feel or fear except by the suicidal endeavor which makes them fanatics or revolutionaries, or both; whereas, those in power can be urbane and charming and invite you to those which they know you will never own. The powerless must do their own dirty work. The powerful have it done for them.

Anyway: somewhat later, I was the host, or moderator, for a radio program starring Malcolm X and a sit-in student from the Deep South. I was the moderator because both the radio station and I were afraid that Malcolm would simply eat the boy alive. I didn't want to be there, but there was no way out of it. I had come prepared to throw various camp stools under the child, should he seem wobbly; to throw out the life-line whenever Malcolm should seem to be carrying the child beyond his depth. Never has a moderator been less needed. Malcolm understood that child and talked to him as though he were talking to a younger brother, and with that same watchful attention. What most struck me was that he was not at all trying to proselytize the child: he was trying to make him think. He was trying to do for the child what he supposed, for too long a time, that the Honorable Elijah had done for him. But I did not think of that until much later. I will never forget Malcolm and that child facing each other, and Malcolm's extraordinary gentleness. And that's the truth about Malcolm: he was one of the gentlest people I have ever met. And I am sure that the child remembers him that way. That boy, by the way, battling so valiantly for civil rights, might have been, for all I can swear to, Stokely Carmichael or Huey Newton or Bobby Seale or Rap Brown or one of my nephews. That's how long or how short—*oh, pioneers!*—the apprehension of betrayal takes: "If you are an American citizen," Malcolm asked the boy, "why have you got to fight for your rights as a citizen? To be a citizen means that you have the rights of a citizen. If you haven't got the rights of a citizen, then you're not a citizen." "It's not as simple as that," the boy said. "Why not?" asked Malcolm.

I was, in some way, in those years, without entirely realizing it, the Great Black Hope of the Great White Father. I was *not* a racist—so I thought; Malcolm *was* a racist, so *he* thought. In fact, we were simply trapped in the same situation, as poor Martin was later to discover (who, in those days, did not talk to Malcolm and was a little nervous with me). As the GBH of the GWF, anyway, I appeared on a television program, along with Malcolm and several other hopes, including Mr. George S. Schuyler. It was pretty awful. If I had ever hoped to become a racist, Mr. Schuyler dashed my hopes forever, then and there. I can scarcely discuss this program except to say that Malcolm and I very quickly dismissed Mr. Schuyler and virtually everyone else, and, as the old street rats and the heirs of Baptist ministers, played the program off each other.

Nothing could have been more familiar to me than Malcolm's style in debate. I had heard it all my life. It was vehemently non-stop and Malcolm was young and looked younger; this caused his opponents to suppose that Malcolm was reckless. Nothing could have been less reckless, more calculated, even to those loopholes he so often left dangling. These were not loopholes at all, but hangman's knots, as whoever rushed for the loophole immediately discovered. Whenever this happened, the strangling interlocutor invariably looked to me, as being the more "reasonable," to say something which would loosen the knot. Mr. Schuyler often *did* say something, but it was always the wrong thing, giving Malcolm yet another opportunity. All I could do was elaborate on some of Malcolm's points, or modify, or emphasize, or seem to try to clarify, but there was no way I could disagree with him. The others were discussing the past or the future, or a country which may once have existed, or one which may yet be brought into existence—Malcolm was speaking of the bitter and unanswerable present. And it was too important that this be heard for anyone to attempt to soften it. It was important, of course, for white people to hear it, if they were still able to hear; but it was of the utmost importance for black people to hear it, for the sake of their morale. It was important for them to know that there was someone like them, in public life, telling the truth about their condition. Malcolm considered himself to be the spiritual property of the people who produced him. He did not consider himself to be their saviour, he was far too modest for that, and gave that role to another; but he considered himself to be their servant and in order not to betray that trust, he was willing to die, and died. Malcolm was not a racist, not even when he thought he was. His intelligence was more complex than that; furthermore, if he had been a racist, not many in this racist country would have considered him dangerous. He would have sounded familiar and even comforting, his familiar rage confirming the reality of white power and sensuously inflaming a bizarre species of guilty eroticism without which, I am beginning to believe, most white Americans of the more or less liberal persuasion cannot draw a single breath. What made him unfamiliar and dangerous was not his hatred for white people but his love for blacks, his apprehension of the horror of the black condition, and the reasons for it, and his determination so to work on their hearts and minds that they would be enabled to see their condition and change it themselves.

For this, after all, not only were no white people needed; they posed, *en bloc*, the very greatest obstacle to black self-knowledge and had to be considered a menace. But white people have played so dominant a role in the world's history for so long that such an attitude toward them constitutes the most disagreeable of novelties; and it may be added that, though they have never learned how to live with the darker brother, they do not look forward to having to learn how to live without him. Malcolm, finally, was a genuine revolutionary, a virile impulse long since fled from the American way of life—in himself, indeed, he was a kind of revolution, both in the sense of a return to a former principle, and in the sense of an upheaval. It is pointless to speculate on his probable fate had he been legally white. Given the white man's options, it is probably just as well for all of us that he was legally black. In some church someday, so far unimagined and unimaginable, he will be hailed as a saint. Of course, this day waits on the workings of the temporal power which Malcolm understood, at last, so well. Rome, for example, has just desanctified some saints and invented, if one dares to use so utilitarian a word in relation to so divine an activity, others, and the Pope has been to Africa, driven there, no doubt, however belatedly, by his concern for the souls of black folk: who dares imagine the future of such a litany as *black like me*! Malcolm, anyway, had this much in common with all real saints and prophets, he had the power, if not to drive the money-changers from the temple, to tell the world what they were doing there.

For reasons I will never understand, on the day that I realized that a play based on *The Autobiography* was not going to be done, that sooner or later I would have to say yes or no to the idea of doing a movie, I flew to Geneva. I will never know why I flew to Geneva, which is far from being my favorite town. I will never know how it is that I arrived there with no toilet articles whatever, no toothbrush, no toothpaste, no razor, no hairbrush, no comb, and virtually no clothes. Furthermore, I have a brother-in-law and a sister-in-law living in Geneva of whom I'm very fond and it didn't even occur to me that they were there. All that I seem to have brought with me is *The Autobiography*. And I sat in the hotel bedroom all the weekend long, with the blinds drawn, reading and rereading—or, rather, endlessly traversing—the great jungle of Malcolm's book.

The problems involved in a cinematic translation were clearly going to be formidable, and wisdom very strongly urged that I have nothing to do with it. It could not possibly bring me anything but grief. I still would have much preferred to have done it as a play, but that possibility was gone. I had grave doubts and fears about Hollywood. I had been there before, and I had not liked it. The idea of Hollywood doing a truthful job on Malcolm could not but seem preposterous. And yet—I didn't want to spend the rest of my life thinking: *It could have been done if you hadn't been chicken.* I felt that Malcolm would never have forgiven me for that. He had trusted me in life and I believed he trusted me in death, and that trust, as far as I was concerned, was my obligation.

From Geneva, I eventually went to London, to join my brother and sister. It was from London that I wired Kazan to say that the play was off, and I was doing the movie. This was only to take K. off the hook, for I wired no one else, had made no agreement to do the movie, and was very troubled and uncertain in my own mind....

[THE BLACK PANTHERS]

In February, the Panthers in Oakland gave a birthday party for the incarcerated Huey Newton. They asked me to "host" this party, and so I flew to Oakland. The birthday party was, of course, a rally to raise money for Huey's defense, and it was a way of letting the world know that the sorely beleaguered Panthers had no intention of throwing in the towel. It was also a way of letting the world—and Huey—know how much they loved and honored the very young man who, along with Bobby Seale, had organized The Black Panther Party for Self Defense, in the spring of 1966. That was the original name of the Party, and the name states very succinctly the need which brought the Party into existence.

It is a need which no black citizen of the ghetto has to have spelled out. When, as white cops are fond of pointing out to me, ghetto citizens "ask for more cops, not less," what they are asking for is more police protection: for crimes committed by blacks against blacks have never been taken very seriously. Furthermore, the prevention of crimes such as these is not the reason for the policeman's presence. That black people need protection *against* the police is indicated by the black community's reaction to the advent of the Panthers. Without community support, the Panthers would have been merely another insignificant street gang. It was the reaction of the black community which triggered the response of the police: these young men, claiming the right to bear arms, dressed deliberately in guerrilla fashion, standing nearby whenever a black man was accosted by a policeman to inform the black man of his rights and insisting on the right of black people to self defense, were immediately marked as "troublemakers."

But white people seem affronted by the black distrust of white policemen, and appear to be astonished that a black man, woman, or child can have any reason to fear a white cop. One of the jurors challenged by Charles Garry during the *voir dire* proceedings before Huey's trial had this to say:

"As I said before, that I feel, and it is my opinion that racism, bigotry, and segregation is something that we have to wipe out of our hearts and minds, and not on the street. I have had an opinion that—and been taught never to resist a police officer, that we have courts of law in which to settle—no matter how much I thought I was in the right, the police officer would order me to do something, I would do it expecting if I thought I was right in what I was doing, that I could get justice in the courts"—And, in response to Garry's question, "Assuming the police officer pulled a gun and shot you, what would you do about it?" the prospective juror, at length, replied, "Let me say this. I do not believe a police officer will do that."

This is a fairly vivid and accurate example of the American piety at work. The beginning of the statement is revealing indeed: "———racism, bigotry, and segregation is something we have to wipe out of our hearts and minds and not on the street." One can wonder to whom the "we" here refers, but there isn't any question as to the object of the tense, veiled accusation contained in "not on the street." Whoever the "we" is, it is probably not the speaker—to leave it at that: but the anarchy and danger "*on the street*" are the fault of the blacks. Unnecessarily: for the police are honorable, and the courts are just.

It is no accident that Americans cling to this dream. It involves American self-love on some deep, disastrously adolescent level. And Americans are very carefully and deliberately conditioned to believe this fantasy: by their politicians, by the news they get and the way they read it, by the movies, and the television screen, and by every aspect of the popular culture. If I learned nothing else in Hollywood, I learned how abjectly the purveyors of the popular culture are manipulated. The brainwashing is so thorough that blunt, brutal reality stands not a chance against it; the revelation of corruption in high places, as in the recent "scandals" in New Jersey, for example, has no effect whatever on the American complacency; nor have any of our recent assassinations had any more effect than to cause Americans to arm—thus proving their faith in the law!—and double-lock their doors. No doubt, behind these locked doors, with their weapons handy, they switch on the tube and watch "The F.B.I.," or some similarly reassuring fable. It means nothing, therefore, to say to so thoroughly insulated a people that the forces of crime and the forces of law and order work hand in hand in the ghetto, bleeding it day and night. It means nothing to say that, in the eyes of the black and the poor certainly, the principal distinction between a policeman and a criminal is to be found in their attire. A criminal can break into one's house without warning, at will, and harass or molest everyone in the house, and even commit murder, and so can a cop, and they do; whoever operates whatever hustle in the ghetto without paying off the cops does not stay in business long; and it will be remembered—Malcolm certainly remembered it—that the dope trade flourished in the ghetto for years without ever being seriously molested. Not until white boys and girls began to be hooked—not until the plague in the ghetto spread outward, as plagues do—was there any public uproar. As long as it was only the niggers who were killing themselves and paying white folks handsomely for the privilege, the forces of law and order were silent. The very structure of the ghetto is a nearly irresistible temptation to criminal activity of one kind or another: it is a very rare man who does not victimize the helpless. There is no pressure on the landlord to be responsible for the upkeep of his property: the only pressure on him is to collect his rent; that is, to bleed the ghetto. There is no pressure on the butcher to be honest: if he can sell bad meat at a profit, why should he not do so? buying cheap and selling dear is what made this country great. If the storekeeper can sell, on the installment plan, a worthless "bedroom suite" for six or seven times its value, what is there to prevent him from doing so, and who will ever hear, or credit, his customer's complaint? in the unlikely event that the customer has any notion of where to go to complain. And the ghetto is a goldmine for the insurance companies. A dime a week, for five or ten or twenty years, is a lot of money, but rare indeed is the funeral paid for by the insurance. I myself do not know of any. Some member of my family had been carrying insurance at a dime a week for years and we finally persuaded her to drop it and cash in the policy—which was now worth a little over two hundred dollars. And let me state candidly, and I know, in this instance, that I do not speak only for myself, that every time I hear the black people of this country referred to as "shiftless" and "lazy," every time it is implied that the blacks deserve their condition here. (Look at the Irish! look at the Poles! Yes. Look at them.) I think of all the pain and sweat with which these greasy dimes were earned, with what trust they were given, in order to make the difficult passage somewhat easier for the living, in order to show honor to the dead, and I then have no compassion whatever for this country, or my countrymen.

Into this maelstrom, this present elaboration of the slave quarters, this rehearsal for a concentration camp, we place, armed, not for the protection of the ghetto but for the protection of American investments there, some blank American boy who is responsible only to some equally blank elder patriot—Andy Hardy and his pious father. Richard Harris, in his *New Yorker* article, "The Turning Point," observes that "Back in 1969, a survey of three hundred police departments around the country had revealed that less than 1 percent required any college training. Three years later, a pilot study ordered by the president showed that most criminals were mentally below average, which suggested that that policemen who failed to stop or find them might not be much above it."

The white cop in the ghetto is as ignorant as he is frightened, and his entire concept of police work is to cow the natives. He is not compelled to answer to these natives for anything he does; whatever he does, he knows that he will be protected by his brothers, who will allow nothing to stain the honor of the force. When his working day is over, he goes home and sleeps soundly in a bed miles away—miles away from the niggers, for that is the way he really thinks of black people. And he is assured of the rightness of his course and the justice of his bigotry every time Nixon, or Agnew, or Mitchell—or the governor of the state of California—open their mouths.

Watching the northern reaction to the Black Panthers, observing the abject cowardice with which the northern populations allow them to be menaced, jailed, and murdered, and all this with but the faintest pretense to legality, can fill one with great contempt for that emancipated North which, but only yesterday, was so full of admiration and sympathy for the heroic blacks in the South. Luckily, many of us were skeptical of the righteous northern sympathy then, and so we are not overwhelmed or disappointed now. Luckily, many of us have always known, as one of my brothers put it to me something like twenty-four years ago, that "the spirit of the South is the spirit of America." Now, exactly like the Germans at the time of the Third Reich, though innocent men are being harassed, jailed, and murdered, in all the northern cities, the citizens know nothing, and wish to know nothing, of what is happening around them. Yet the advent of the Panthers was as inevitable as the arrival of that day in Montgomery, Alabama, when Mrs. Rosa Parks refused to stand up on that bus and give her seat to a white man. That day had been coming for a very long time; danger upon danger, and humiliation upon humiliation, had piled intolerably high and gave Mrs. Parks her platform. If Mrs. Parks had merely had a headache that day, and if the community had had no grievances, there would have been no bus boycott and we would never have heard of Martin Luther King.

Just so with the Panthers: it was inevitable that the fury would erupt, that a black man, openly, in the sight of all his fellows, should challenge the policeman's gun, and not only that, but the policeman's right to be in the ghetto at all, and that man happened to be Huey. It is not conceivable that the challenge thus thrown down by this rather stubby, scrubbed-looking, gingerbread-colored youth could have had such repercussions if he had not been articulating the rage and repudiating the humiliation of thousands, more, millions of men.

Huey, on that day, the day which prompted Bobby Seale to describe Huey as "the baddest motherfucker in history," restored to the men and women of the ghetto their honor. And, for this reason, the Panthers, far from being an illegal or a lawless organization, are a great force for peace and stability in the ghetto. But, as this suggests an unprecedented measure of autonomy for the ghetto citizens, no one in authority is prepared to face this overwhelmingly obvious fact. White America remains unable to believe that black America's grievances are real; they are unable to believe this because they cannot face what this fact says about themselves and their country; and the effect of this massive and hostile incomprehension is to increase the danger in which all black people live here, especially the young. No one is more aware of this than the Black Panther leadership. This is why they are so anxious to create work and study programs in the ghetto—everything from hot lunches for school children to academic courses in high schools and colleges to the content, format, and distribution of the Black Panther newspapers. All of these are antidotes to the demoralization which is the scourge of the ghetto, are techniques of self-realization. This is also why they are taught to bear arms—not, like most white Americans, because they fear their neighbors, though indeed they have the most to fear, but in order, this time, to protect *their* lives, *their* women and children, *their* homes, rather than the life and property of an Uncle Sam who has rarely been able to treat his black nephews with more than a vaguely benign contempt. For the necessity, now, which I think nearly all black people see in different ways, is the creation and protection of a nucleus which will bring into existence a new people.

The Black Panthers made themselves visible—made themselves targets, if you like—in order to hip the black community to the presence of a new force in its midst, a force working toward the health and liberation of the community. It was a force which set itself in opposition to that force which uses people as things and which grinds down men and women and children, not only in the ghetto, into an unrecognizable powder. They announced themselves especially as a force for the rehabilitation of the young—the young who were simply perishing, in and out of schools, on the needle, in the Army, or in prison. The black community recognized this energy almost at once and flowed toward it and supported it; a people's most valuable asset is the well-being of their young.

Nothing more thoroughly reveals the actual intentions of this country, domestically and globally, than the ferocity of the repression, the storm of fire and blood which the Panthers have been forced to undergo merely for declaring themselves as men—men who want "land, bread, housing, education, clothing, justice, and peace." The Panthers thus became the native Vietcong, the ghetto became the village in which the Vietcong were hidden, and in the ensuing search-and-destroy operations, everyone in the village became suspect.

Under such circumstances, the creation of a new people may seem as unlikely as fashioning the proverbial bricks without straw. On the other hand, though no one appears to learn very much from history, the rulers of empires assuredly learn the least. This unhappy failing will prove to be especially aggravated in the case of the American rulers, who have never heard of history and who have never read it, who do not know what the passion of a people can withstand or what it can accomplish, or how fatal is the moment, for the kingdom, when the passion is driven underground. They do not, for that matter, yet realize that they have already been forced to do two deadly things. They have been forced to reveal their motives, themselves, in all their unattractive nakedness; hence the reaction of the blacks, on every level, to the "Nixon Administration," which is of a stunning, unprecedented unanimity. The administration, increasingly, can rule only by fear: the fears of the people who elected them, and the fear that the administration can inspire. In spite of the tear gas, mace, clubs, helicopters, bugged installations, spies, *provocateurs*, tanks, machine guns, prisons, and detention centers, this is a shaky foundation. And they have helped to create a new pantheon of black heroes. Black babies will be born with new names hereafter and will have a standard to which to aspire new in this country, new in the world. The great question is what this will cost. The great effort is to minimize the damage. While I was on the Coast, Eldridge Cleaver and Bobby Seale and David Hilliard were still free, Fred Hampton and Mark Clark were still alive. Now, every day brings a new setback, frequently a bloody one. The government is absolutely determined to wipe the Black Panthers from the face of the earth: which is but another way of saying that it is absolutely determined to keep the nigger in his place. But this merciless and bloody repression, which is carried out, furthermore, with a remarkable contempt for the sensibilities and intelligence of the black people of this nation—for who can believe the police reports?—causes almost all blacks to realize that neither the government, the police, nor the populace are able to distinguish between a Black Panther, a black school child, or a black lawyer. And this reign of terror is creating a great problem in prisons all over this country. "Now, look," said a harassed prison official to Bobby Seale, "you got a lot of notoriety. We don't want no organizing here, or nothing else. We ain't got no Panthers, we ain't got no Rangers, we ain't got no Muslims. All we got is in-mates." All he's got is trouble. All he's got is black people who know why they're in prison, and not all of them can be kept in solitary. These blacks have unforgiving relatives, to say nothing of unforgiving children, at every level of American life. The government cannot afford to trust a single black man in this country, nor can they penetrate any black's disguise, or apprehend how devious and tenacious black patience can be, and any black man that they appear to trust is useless to them, for he will never be trusted by the blacks. It is true that our weapons do not appear to be very formidable, but, then, they never have. Then, as now, our greatest weapon is silence. As black poet Robert E. Hayden puts it in his poem to Harriet Tubman, "Runagate, Runagate": *Mean mean mean to be free.*

Harold Cruse
from *The Crisis of the Negro Intellectual*

THE INTELLECTUALS AND FORCE AND VIOLENCE

The American social system is unlike any other in world history. America is a nation that has been pragmatically created, a nation that has emerged from the old into something new and original, never seen before. The inner-dynamics of American social change were, from the very outset, self-contained. Thus in relation to foreign ideologies the world over, America is almost a closed system. It grows, develops, and even reacts to outside social currents, according to the persuasions of its own self-contained, inner dynamic. Not only has America absorbed wave after wave of immigrants, she also absorbs all the radical ideologies of immigrants and Americanizes them by negation. Considering what has happened to revolutionary Marxism, introduced into America by German immigrants back in the 1840's, Roosevelt's New Deal of the 1930's inveigled the Communist revolutionaries into a united front, emasculated them, stole their programs, and patronized them with semi-official recognition. But after brain-picking and tolerating these radicals in order to neutralize them, the Federal power then turned on them with a vengeance, cast them out into the cold, and then prosecuted them for the sin of political prostitution.

All of this would seem to suggest that the American social system is immune to the trials of social revolution. But this is far from true, as any modern economist knows; for social revolution as such does not necessarily correspond to any preconceived formulas extracted from some foreign revolution of decades past. Each new social revolution is unique. There have been a variety of social revolutions but there will be still *others*.

The modern world emerged painfully out of a series of such revolutions, all of them rather protracted and all of them characterized by much force and violence. The United States emerged as an independent nation through the force and violence of the American Revolution. And even before 1775 this revolution was being prepared by the force and violence the British, French and Indians inflicted on each other. Afterwards, the American nation grew and expanded through many decades of forceful and violent conquest. The entire nineteenth-century history of the United States is a violent one: Indian wars, slave uprisings, Civil War, more Indian wars, race violence and labor violence. After the forcible pacification of the Indians, both labor and racial violence continued into the twentieth century.

The traditionally violent nature of American society has its roots in several factors: its expansive frontier ideology, its racial composition, and its labor-capital relationships. Writing about American labor of the late nineteenth and early twentieth centuries, Theodore Draper says: "The relations between labor and capital were largely undefined and uncontrollable except by sheer force on both sides. Employers fought labor organization by every possible means. Strikes were ruthlessly crushed by armed guards, police, sheriffs, militia, and federal troops."[1] The violence that attended early American labor relations was due much more to the indigenous qualities of America than to the importation of the foreign revolutionary doctrine of anarchism. In fact, the use of force and violence did not become a controversial issue even for the professional revolutionaries themselves until the period around 1906, when three labor leaders, one of whom was William D. (Big Bill) Haywood of the IWW, were arrested for complicity in the bombing-murder of the governor of Idaho. Of this arrest and the labor unrest leading up to it, Draper says: "They were finally released, but the entire labor movement had to come to their defense, since the overshadowing issue of the case was the responsibility of the labor movement for the violence which had characterized the great American strikes for two decades."[2]

From this point on until 1912, the question of force and violence so agitated all revolutionary and reform socialists, that the Socialist party of America was forced to resolve the matter. "Long a matter of dispute as a theoretical issue," writes Draper, force and violence "now had to be settled as a matter of practical politics."[3] During the Socialist party's convention in the spring of 1912, "Article II, Section 6, of the party's constitution was changed to expel anyone 'who opposes political action or advocates crime, sabotage, or other methods of violence as a weapon of the working class.' "[4] This amendment was upheld by a referendum vote of thirteen thousand to four thousand. Haywood was expelled from the Socialist party's National Executive Committee for holding to the view that the capitalist system should be overthrown "by forcible means if necessary." From 1912 to 1913 about fifteen percent of the membership left the Socialist party along with Haywood—whose real home was in the IWW, the most extreme revolutionary faction of the labor movement. Many of those who sympathized with Haywood's position on force and violence belonged to the developing radical leftwing which formed the nucleus of what later became the American Communist Party in 1919. But it was not long before the newly-formed Communists themselves began to play down all overt references to the use of force and violence in their political activities.

[1] *The Roots of American Communism, op. cit.*, p. 13.

[2] *Ibid.*, p. 21.

[3] *Ibid.*, p. 45.

[4] *Ibid.*, p. 46.

So, for about forty years, the question of revolutionary force and violence became mostly an academic issue in American radical politics. The indictment of the Communist Party of America in 1948 was not for overt acts of force and violence, but, among other things, for conspiring and organizing to "teach and advocate the overthrow and destruction of the Government of the United States by force and violence."[5] In 1952, William Z. Foster stated the official position of his Party: "The Communist Party, although it does not advocate violence in the worker's struggles, cannot, however, declare that there will be no violence in the establishment of socialism in this country."[6] In the struggle for socialism, the Communists believe that "a peaceful path of development is quite possible for certain capitalist countries." According to Foster, this was Joseph Stalin's view as far back as 1928.

Today, the Trotskyist Socialist Workers Party considers itself the only true revolutionary Marxist party (at least in theory) which hews strictly to the line of class-struggle politics. However, a closer examination will reveal that Trotskyists differ from Communists only in the matter of form. Their theoretical positions differ only in an academic degree, inasmuch as both Marxist factions suffer the same limitations imposed on them by the peculiarities of American capitalism which has, for all intents and purposes, negated class struggle on the part of the workers against the capitalists. The same can be said for all radical factions in American society today who claim allegiance to the Marxist tradition.

Force and violence has become a principal question within the Negro movement proper (as distinct from Negro groups allied with other white-oriented trends). Like the early pre-Communist white labor movements, the American Negro movement has experienced a long series of violent eras on the racial front, going all the way back to the slave rebellions of Nat Turner and Denmark Vesey. These historical episodes of force and violence in Negro history have become hallowed as prototypal examples of the revolutionary potential in the Negro presence in America. Everyone from Communist whites to nationalist blacks sees in these slave uprisings anything they want to see. Although Turner and Vesey never heard of Marx and Engels (and would not have known either one from a slavemaster), there are certain Communist historians who try to see a direct line from the slave revolts in Virginia to the projected socialist revolution wherein Negroes in the twentieth century will storm the capitalist stronghold. On the other hand, certain Black Nationalists of today see in these same revolts the beginnings of the Black Nationalist movement. But mere rebellions are not revolutions in themselves—especially in America. So far in America, rebellions both black and white have been piecemeal and sporadic social reactions in response to, or in reaction against, the American capitalistic revolution as it progresses. The African, by being enslaved, was drawn into the exchange machinery of the capitalistic (industrial) revolution

---

[5]*History of the Communist Party, USA, op. cit.*, p. 509.
[6]*Ibid.*, p. 552.

as a human commodity. His revolt under slavery was simply a revolt against being brutally enslaved, inasmuch as all slaves in all historical eras have been known to revolt.

When seen in historical perspective, all American rebellions and uprisings have come in waves under changing capitalistic conditions and have different objectives from previous waves. Although the Negro in the South of today is still seeking the freedom that the ex-slave expected, this modern rebellion is taking place under different capitalistic conditions and is in great degree a profound response to those very conditions. Add to these regional conditions in the South proper, the penetrating influences of the larger world-embracing political conditions, and you have what some have called the revolution of rising expectations. Yet, the Negro movement is not yet a revolutionary movement, no matter what the radical idealists say about it. This movement cannot become revolutionary until it articulates objectives which transcend its present aims—racial integration. The very fact that many radicals and revolutionaries attempt to connect the present-day Negro rebellion with the slave rebellions only serves to reveal its limitations. At least the slaves knew exactly what they wanted—the abolition of the slave system. Today every Negro in or out of the freedom movement knows he wants "freedom," but actually not one knows what he *really* wants out of present-day America. Therefore, to hark romantically back to the slave rebellions for the purpose of bolstering present-day revolutionary morale is rather pointless. Moreover, it only shows just how far the modern Negro in America has retrogressed in revolutionary virtue when his leadership can talk him into accepting non-violence as a means of achieving his aims. Today, the Negro movement's most radical wing (which calls itself a non-violent committee) has recently worked hand in hand with another segment that upholds the virtues of passive resistance.

For fifty-odd years the NAACP has nurtured a race of people on policies of constitutionalism and legal redress. But, during the late 1950's, in a civil rights episode in Monroe, North Carolina, these legalistic traditions served to reintroduce the old, historical problem of force and violence in a curious and interesting way.*

Robert F. Williams had taken over a defunct NAACP branch in Monroe, reorganized it, and put the branch on a functioning basis with a program of desegregating certain public facilities. Williams' actions brought on the bitter resistance of the Ku Klux Klan, who resorted to traditional terror tactics in an attempt to frighten Williams into submission. But Williams, an ex-Marine, retaliated by organizing his followers into a rifle club and drilling them into an effective armed corps against the attacks of the Klan. Without going into all the details of the Monroe affair, it is enough to say that the town became an armed camp of high tensions between black and white. There was a long reign of ter-

---

*For a more detailed account of the Monroe, North Carolina, case, see: Truman Nelson, *People With Strength—The Story of Monroe, North Carolina*, published by the author. Also: Robert F. Williams, *Negroes With Guns* (New York: Marzani and Munsell, 1962).

ror, jailings and beatings. In the course of these happenings, Williams was moved to make a public statement to the effect that Negroes might have to stop lynching with lynching. This marked the first time that a local NAACP branch leader in the South had openly espoused meeting violence with violence, and it brought Williams into a policy conflict with the NAACP. The organization censured Williams for expressing views contrary to Association policy which could "be used by segregationists to spread the false impression that the NAACP supported lynching and violence."[7] One month after his statement Williams was suspended from the NAACP for six months by the board of directors. Later, Williams publicly altered his original statement to mean that *"Negroes should have the right of armed self-defense against attack."*[8] Whichever way Robert Williams meant to use violence, that is, offensively or defensively, his armed self-defense tactic became the ideological spark that ignited a hidden potential within the newly emerging phase of the Negro movement. But this potential did not really begin to show itself until about five years later. Other ingredients had to be added.

In analyzing the Williams-Monroe affair it is interesting to note that Williams' conflict with the NAACP's official policy in 1959 resembles somewhat the old Socialist party's conflict with the left-wing labor radicals over force and violence back in 1912. There is a resemblance but there is also an important difference. The old IWW leader, William Haywood, actually espoused *offensive* direct action with the aim of overthrowing the capitalist system "by forcible means if necessary." Williams did not, and could not, espouse offensive direct action by any means possible for any tangible objective. He merely espoused self-defense—a retaliatory action. This approach grew out of the objective nature of race relations because Williams was not contemplating overthrowing anything, much less the capitalist system. The Negro movement is fundamentally a *protest* movement, not a revolutionary movement. Furthermore, the adoption of armed self-defense does not, in itself, transform what was a protest movement into a revolutionary movement. This is true despite the fact that many of Williams's most ardent supporters in the North consider his adoption of self-defense a revolutionary accomplishment. If Williams had, at the same time, changed his *social* objective, he might have fulfilled this definition. His objective remained exactly what it was before—desegregation. And desegregation of public facilities was also the aim of the official NAACP leadership. Thus Williams differed not in aims but in tactics when he opted for armed self-defense. But this raised an important question for the entire Negro movement—one that has not yet been answered: Could armed self-defense really lead to desegregation?

The Northern-based revolutionaries who supported Williams were so eager to see Monroe, North Carolina, as the take-off location for a new revolutionary wave, that they forgot that Monroe was merely one isolated spot on the civil

---

[7]*The New York Times*, May 7, 1959, p. 22.

[8]*Ibid.*, May 8, 1959, p. 16; June 9, 1959, p. 31; July 18, 1959, p. 5.

rights map. Because Williams defied the conservative, legalistic, and non-violent traditions of the NAACP, his supporters began to act as if armed self-defense was the latest thing in revolutionary effectiveness and also the final answer to all tactical questions for the future. Few asked themselves why it was necessary for the issue to be raised so as to suggest that the right to self-defense was a privilege that Negroes could not assume without asking the sanction of the NAACP, the public authorities and the President, or without publicizing beforehand that self-defense is a God-given right of every living man. Once more it was demonstrated how deeply ingrained is the protest tradition in Negro thinking. Even Williams' plea for the right of self-defense was, in itself, another form of protest.

It is difficult to believe that Williams had any illusions that he was going to change the policies of the NAACP, but he acted as if he did. Otherwise he would have seen clearly that the NAACP was an inhospitable place for himself and his views. He might have realized that what he had in mind had much broader implications than the immediate situation in Monroe, a small community that could not stand alone. He might have seen that his aims required a larger scope of organization, broader planning and a longer-range strategical vision. The Monroe episode actually raised important questions: How does armed self-defense relate to the civil rights movement as a whole? How would armed self-defense apply in the North, South, East or West? How would armed self-defense relate to the non-violent or the passive resistance forces? How does armed self-defense apply in certain Northern locations where desegregation of swimming pools or public libraries (as in Monroe) is not a force-and-violence issue? Or how would armed self-defense relate to Northern cities where police brutality *is* a force-and-violence issue—because it is a form of violence inflicted by an arm of the state against Negroes in particular? Lastly, but not least, how does armed self-defense relate to the various blends of Black Nationalism flourishing today?

However, as long as the Negro movement, in all its various tendencies and segments, remains essentially a protest movement seeking civil rights, its objectives will remain more moral and ethical than tangible. One can objectively shoot a Klansman "defensively" or "offensively," but to succeed in shooting one's way into voting rights, jobs, and "desegregated" public facilities calls for much deeper thought than certain revolutionaries seem to imagine.

The issue of armed self-defense, as projected by Williams in 1959, presaged the emergence of other factors deeply hidden within the Negro movement. It was not until after 1959 that these factors began to reveal themselves. Part of this fateful evolution was the rise of what John Henrik Clarke of *Freedomways* called "The New Afro-American Nationalism." As distinct from the more publicized Nation of Islam movement, this new nationalism was represented in the ideas of a new, young generation born in the late 1930's and early 1940's. This generation grew up in time to be deeply impressed by the emergence of the African states, the Cuban Revolution, Malcolm X and Robert Williams himself. They were witnessing a revolutionary age of the liberation of oppressed peoples. Thus, they were led to connect their American situation with those foreign revolutionary situations. They did not know, of course, that to attempt to apply foreign ideologies to the United States was more easily imagined than accomplished. They did not know that the revolutionary Marxists had attempted this and had come to grief. In fact, they did not even know what a Marxist was, even though they were destined to have to contend with them in their own little movements. They did not realize how little they actually understood about what they saw happening, nor did they have the slightest idea of how much they had to learn about the past forty-odd years before they could even begin to understand the revolutionary age in which they lived. They also were unaware that many of the older generation did not understand *them* or what they implied as a new, young generation. Before long, they would even be misinterpreted on *Freedomways* magazine by John Henrik Clarke, who would describe the "new Afro-America nationalism" as proletarian, when, in fact, it was crowded with young intellectuals, artists, writers, poets, and musicians. These young people were actually coming of age into a great intellectual, political, creative and theoretical vacuum. They would enter the arena of activity in search of leadership and find little but confusion, since leaders were few and destined to be evanescent. But despite all this, they would learn. One of the most outstanding of them, LeRoi Jones, learned in such a personal way as to epitomize within himself all the other things his generation learned either empirically or vicariously.

Several years before anyone had heard of Robert Williams or Monroe, LeRoi Jones had moved into Greenwich Village from his hometown of Newark in New Jersey. This was during the middle 1950's. At the time, Jones appeared very quiet, unassuming, reticent, even meek—although curious about everything. But thinking back, one wonders if perhaps his inner personality had not been grossly misinterpreted. I, for example, met Jones from time to time, here and there, without expending too much attention on him. A person of my background would have been incomprehensible to Jones anyway; and, as for Jones—he was then just another addition to the black intellectual scene of Greenwich Village—and rather late at that. From that point on, Jones made the "beat generation" scene. His name became linked with that of Jack Kerouac, and he soon began to make his name as a Beat Poet of talent. But at the same time there were others of Jones's generation emerging in Harlem—the "natives" of the black ghetto. Later, Jones would meet up with these, but not before he went through more conditioning. But his conditioning was to be for certain social objectives that others of his generation could not clearly see. They were acting intuitively and the outlines of the future were vague and undefinable, as this generation had the impossible inheritance of three decades of conflicting ideologies not their own. But the late 1950's and the present 1960's became what can be called the new era of black ideological transformation, especially among the newest wave of intellectuals.

The great transformation in LeRoi Jones was brought on by the Cuban Revolution. In July, 1960, I accompanied Jones to Cuba to "see for ourselves" what it was all about. It was the first time since Jones came to the Village scene that I had had the opportunity to observe him intimately and he had by then become rather contemptuous of individuals not of his generation. In his article about his trip, "Cuba Libre," he wrote mockingly of certain individuals in the writers' contingent as being "nineteen-fortyish" and "nineteen-thirtyish" (as if to say that the really "in" thing was to be "nineteen-fiftyish"). Jones was also disappointed by the fact that many of the "name" writers he was eager to meet did not accept the invitation to Cuba with him. At that time, though Jones considered himself a Beat and a nonconformist he was still very impressed with "name" writers. The only people on this contingent to Cuba who had any kind of reputation for being *engagé*—either literarily and/or politically—were Robert Williams, Julian Mayfield, John Henrik Clarke and myself. At any rate, his actual experiences in Cuba amply compensated Jones for the lack of representative Negro writers in his delegation.*

In Havana it was noted that Jones made a very favorable impression on the revolutionary intelligentsia of the Castro regime. Although they were all white Cubans, it was remarkable to see how much they and Jones had in common—they actually talked the same "language." As I was "nineteen-fortyish," I noticeably held back all outward exuberance for the Cuban situation. I was admittedly pro-Castro, but there were too many Communists around acting imperious and important. Moreover, there was the obvious and unclarified position of the Cuban Negro to consider. Yet we were all treated with such overwhelming deference, consideration and privilege, it was difficult to be critical. The crowning event of this trip was the long journey from Havana to Sierra Maestre. Riding with us in a string of modern air-conditioned coaches was a large corps from the international press of Europe, Latin America, United States (*Look* magazine), and the Far East.

In this instance, the ideology of a new revolutionary wave in the world at large, had lifted us out of the anonymity of lonely struggle in the United States to the glorified rank of visiting dignitaries. For Jones's impressionable generation this revolutionary indoctrination, this ideological enchantment, was almost irresistible. And here, vicariously, a crucial question was engendered: *What did it all mean and how did it relate to the Negro in America?* It did demonstrate incontrovertibly the relevance of force and violence to successful revolutions, especially abroad. Beyond that, neither Robert Williams who tried mightily, nor Jones's generation, have adequately explained it in Afro-American terms.

But we hardly thought about that on the morning of July 26, 1960, at the foot of the Sierra Maestre mountains. We were caught up in a revolutionary outpouring of thousands upon thousands of people making their way up the mountain roads to the shrine of the Revolution, under the hottest sun-drenching any of us Americans had probably ever experienced. Jones and I stood shoulder-to-shoulder in a Cuban rebel army truck, packed to its side-

*See "Cuba Libre," *Evergreen Review*, November-December, 1960, pp. 139–159.

ribbings with liberated Castroites whose euphoria we could feel profoundly, but not experience. Nothing in our American experience had ever been as arduous and exhausting as this journey. Our reward was the prize of revolutionary protocol that favored those victims of capitalism away from home. We were escorted by a guard of armed rebels to the official platform and presented to Fidel Castro. There we were seated in the company of the rebel elite as Castro tuned up and spoke for four hours to the Sierra Maestre hills covered with people as far as the eye could see. Robert Williams was the nominal leader of our contingent, but Jones was the most interesting personality. During the whole time I watched him closely and wondered what he was thinking. I wondered how this Greenwich Village Beat poet would relate politically, artistically, ideologically to this foreign revolution.

These questions were soon to be answered back in the United States, beginning with certain events of 1961 when Jones ventured from the Village to the Harlem scene. In the meantime, however, Jones had formed personal associations with the John O. Killens literary faction through Julian Mayfield and John Henrik Clarke, via Havana. It probably did not occur to Jones either there, or back in New York, that he could never thrive literarily or ideologically with this leftwing faction. Artistically, they and Jones were poles apart. What held them together in a temporary and functional alliance was their attachment to Robert Williams and his Monroe affair, and the Cuban Revolution. But not a single one of them succeeded in analyzing the implications of their new alliance, just as none of them seriously analyzed the meaning of Williams's armed self-defense tactic. What did Negro creative intellectuals have to do with Williams and armed self-defense? Was the Negro writers' role simply to support Robert Williams verbally or organizationally? If so, this was no more than was expected from everybody else. Since for the most part, all Negro writers functioned out of New York, what did the situation there (Harlem, that is) have to do with Monroe, North Carolina—where desegregation, despite armed self-defense, was simply trying to catch up with Northern desegregation won by law? Whose movement was more important overall— Monroe's or Harlem's—or did they complement each other? Since no one seriously attempted to explore these matters, it was not at all surprising that Robert Williams and a couple of his intellectual supporters got badly botched-up in their communications between Harlem and Monroe; as a result, they were forced into exile, leaving behind them one Harlem woman who became the hostage for the authorities.

There were several factors involved in the Monroe, North Carolina, fiasco. In the first place, all kinds of factions descended on Williams and his self-defense cohorts. There were leftwing Trotskyists, Freedom Riders and representatives of other civil rights groups—all pro-integrationist forces. On the other hand, there were also nationalist-oriented individuals from Harlem, not to speak of certain writers with muddled views on integrationism and nationalism. They all saw something in Monroe that did not actually exist—an immediate revolutionary situation.

But the Monroe defeat highlighted certain Northern dilemmas—among them, the question of the new Afro-American nationalism. In the North, the bulk of Williams's supporters in the young generation were nationalists. Neither Clarke nor Mayfield, however, belonged to this group, and even Jones had not yet fully arrived. Robert Williams himself was never a nationalist, but an avowed integrationist, a fact that later created much propaganda confusion. For the young nationalists celebrated Williams as their leader, since his self-defense stand coincided with their rising interests in the adoption of force and violence tactics in the North. But in the North, armed self-defense would not be against an unofficial force such as the Klan, but would arise in opposition to the police, the Army and the National Guard—official arms of the State power.

It should be noted in passing that Williams would have welcomed the intervention of the Federal National Guard in Monroe, but that same intervention was not welcomed in Watts, Los Angeles, for obvious reasons. Watts was not Monroe and the force and violence occurring there was on a far different level. Although force and violence could be a revolutionary ingredient, self-defense as Williams projected it, is *not* revolutionary, even with arms. It is exactly what it says it is—defensive—at best, a holding action. Misconceptions about this have led to other fiascos and failures. For example, in Harlem, uprisings are ignited spontaneously over one issue (such as police brutality), but are actually deeply rooted in the general social conditions. Yet the slogan of armed self-defense was militantly raised so as to provoke the police into more severe repressive actions by giving them a ready-made excuse to shoot to kill. Needless to say, not a single one of the basic economic, political, or cultural aspects of the Harlem social conditions that feed the riotous proclivities of the population are ever touched on by the revolutionaries, who misapply the slogan of armed self-defense. The failure of the intellectuals is that they do not attempt to clarify these issues.

Another reason why the tactic of armed self-defense, in the North, is so inappropriate is that historically Black Nationalism has never upheld the use of force and violence. This is another compelling reason why Garveyism, to which many of the young nationalists hark back, is today passé. Garvey was not a revolutionary but a reformist. Garvey's scheme for a "peaceful return to Africa" creates both practical and theoretical problems for today's new Afro-American nationalists who study Garveyism historically, but are less and less inclined to peaceful methods. But the emergence of free African states with political autonomy has done Garvey's work for him; even so, most of the West Indians from Garvey's homeland in Jamaica leave home not to return to Africa, but to emigrate to the British Isles. This is a fact that the Garveyites do not like to discuss, but that must force the new, young nationalists to realize that ultimately, *their* situation must have an American, not an African, solution. This means that Afro-American nationalism must be geared organically to the native American revolutionary dynamic toward social change. Today, Afro-American nationalism is *the* main force behind that social dynamic, and as such, the last social link to the unsolved American nationality dilemma.

488 Part 5/Civil Rights and Black Power

However, this social dynamic comprises many factors—practical, organizational, institutional, and theoretical—and each one is essential to the whole. Force and violence enters the picture only to the degree that American (white) institutions resist the pressures towards social change exerted by the Afro-American social dynamic. Strong resistance there has been and will be; yet, ironically, much of this resistance, though less overt and demonstrative than methods of force and violence, *is just as effective*. But in terms of the peculiarities of the American social system, there must evolve a more profound understanding of the real meaning of this resistance. It is much more than mere reluctance to grant racial democracy and equal rights, as the civil righters would have it. Overall, it is the natural resistance a malfunctioning social organism throws up against being rehabilitated, reconstructed, and made functional—*i.e.*, to perfect its "democratic" potential. Sick social systems, like sick bodies, tend to resist curative treatment. Historically, however, it has been amply demonstrated that America, as well as the Afro-American to whom she is wedded, are both condemned to be free: The American social system is fated to evolve according to its own innate and internal social dynamic, despite all the internal resistance exerted to the contrary. In this process, then, force and violence is part but not the whole of the strategy. The quality of resistance exerted against social change determines the quality of self-defense tactics. But the *main* front tactics must always be organizational and institutional. As the economist P.J.D. Wiles points out, revolutions occur only in those societies that resist new institutionalisms.

One of the keys to understanding the effectiveness of any tactic, idea, strategy or trend in the Negro movement, is to determine how well the American system can absorb it and, thus, negate its force. To repeat, the American social system quite easily absorbs all foreign, and even native, radical doctrines and neutralizes them. The same applies to the doctrines of the Negro movement. In fact, it applies all the more, simply because this movement is more native than others and therefore more intimately connected to the inner American social dynamic. We have seen that most of the tactics of the civil rights trends are so easily absorbed by the system as to lose their original motivational impetus; their objectives become more and more diffuse and intangible. When the issue of armed self-defense was first raised, the young Afro-American nationalists enthusiastically embraced this revolutionary innovation. But not long after Robert Williams departed into exile, a new armed self-defense organization—The Deacons of Defense—emerged in Louisiana. However it was not long before the Deacons were absorbed by the civil rights movement, both North and South. The Deacons did not, and could not, espouse any revolutionary aims beyond defending themselves and the rights of civil rights workers to pursue their aims of orderly integration. This new self-defense development did not venture beyond the original position of Williams in Monroe, but there was a difference: In Monroe the integrationist civil righters came to the rescue of Williams; in Bogalusa, Louisiana, the Deacons came to the rescue of harried civil rights workers. In effect, the Deacons became the broad organizational development that Williams should have pursued in the first place, instead of getting trapped into premature actions in isolated Monroe. Even so, the Deacons' objective remained the same—desegregation. Except for the use of armed self-defense, the NAACP could not disagree. The Northern Afro-American nationalists hailed the Deacons for their stand, but the Deacons are no more nationalistic than Robert Williams. Nationalism is, essentially, a Northern urban phenomenon which today attempts to form links with the South through the adoption of new Southern tactics. But since these naturally are most applicable in the South, tactics like self-defense become the property of the interracial integrationist trend, and are thus absorbed. As a result, when the civil rights movement gets bogged down in the South so does the concept of armed self-defense. In this way, the entire Negro movement as a whole becomes the tactical prisoner of its inherent pragmatism. This strategical defect will not be overcome until the new Afro-American nationalism of the North develops a theoretical grasp of its own leadership function within the Afro-American social dynamic. But sadly, LeRoi Jones and those of his generation did not fully understand this.

The fact that Jones and his active contemporaries were, to a great degree, creative, artistic intellectuals did not alleviate their problem. They were not the proletarians who went into the Nation of Islam to be rehabilitated. They represented a new breed of Afro-American nationalist. With its commitment to force and violence, and its support by the young creative intellectuals, the new Afro-American nationalism has historically unique facets. This does not mean, of course, that the participants fully understand all the ramifications of their movement—far from it. These young intellectuals are the victims of historical discontinuity. Marxist Communism (aided by the Great Depression), the Jewish Left and liberal seduction of the 1930's, the Jewish-Christian liberal paternalism of the 1940's and 1950's, have all combined to eradicate the living threads between the young Negro generations of the late 1950's and the 1960's, and their predecessors in the 1920's.

As a result, this new generation is called upon to make up for lost time— about forty-five years of it. They must achieve an historical perspective on what happened since about 1920, in order to transcend politically, economically and culturally every social objective projected by the Negro movement since that time. In other words, their social objectives in terms of program must be adequate to the potential of their own social dynamic *at this moment* in American history.

The first indication that LeRoi Jones and his generation were willing but not ready, came in Harlem in 1961. It became obvious that Jones and his young Harlem group did not understand their own social dynamic. They were interested, after a fashion, in politics, economics and culture, but not at all interested in political, economic, and cultural organizations *per se*. The Jones who could set up the Black Arts Theater and School in 1965 was not the Jones of 1961. Although Jones and his trend considered themselves the new wave, once they had set up their organizations they proceeded to do the exact same thing every other civil rights trend was doing—they went out on protest demonstrations. They felt they were different not only because they were young, but for other largely intuitive, ill-defined reasons. Jones once threatened to picket the NAACP, for no other apparent reason than that it represented the old guard, of which Jones was contemptuous.

From the very outset, in 1961, Jones's generation had to go through a process that revealed their ambivalence toward two concerns—their relation to whites, and to Black Nationalism of the traditional kind. As forerunners of the new Afro-American nationalism, they were in trouble over these two questions. Jones, for example, was dubious at first about what he called the Harlem Black Nats (nationalists). His first Harlem organization, the "On Guard for Freedom Committee," was an interracial group. This committee was the creation of Jones and one of his close Negro colleagues, Calvin Hicks; part of its membership came out of Jones's original group, the "Organization of Young Men" (OYM), a "downtown" movement. However, when some of the young nationalists of his Harlem committee objected to the presence of whites at their membership meetings, Jones disagreed. He said at one meeting that he could not see why it was necessary to restrict whites from participation. More than that, he said he could not understand why Harlem Negroes should hate whites. Jones was still a long way from his militant anti-white stand of 1965. He was wrestling with the unsolved problems of his intellectual antecedents which, for him, has to be posed in terms that equated pro-blackness with a hatred of whiteness. Long before Jones came on the scene this had been one of the Negro intellectual's most severe "hang-ups."

Negro intellectuals have been sold a bill of goods on interracialism by white Communists and white liberals. As a result of this, a peculiar form of what might be called the psychology of political interracialism (for want of a better term) has been inculcated in the Negro's mind. Even before the average Negro attempts to undertake any action himself, he assumes, almost involuntarily, that he must not, cannot, dare not exclude whites, because he cannot succeed without them. He has been so conditioned that he cannot separate personal and individual associations with individual whites in the everyday business of striving and existing, from that interior business that is the specific concern of his group's existence. Every other ethnic group in America, a "nation of nations," has accepted the fact of its separateness and used it to its own social advantage. But the Negro's conditioning has steered him into that perpetual state of suspended tension wherein ninety-five per cent of his time and energy is expended on fighting prejudice in whites. As a result, he has neither the time nor the inclination to realize that all of the effort spent fighting prejudice will not obviate those fundamental things an ethnic group must do for itself. This situation results from a psychology that is rooted in the Negro's symbiotic "blood-ties" to the white Anglo-Saxon. It is the culmination of that racial drama of love and hate between slave and master, bound together in the purgatory of plantations. Today the African foster-child in the American racial equation must grow to manhood, break the psychological umbilical ties to intellectual paternalism. The American Negro has never yet been able to break entirely free of the ministrations of his white masters to the extent that he is willing to exile himself, in search of wisdom, into the wastelands of the American desert. That is what must be done, if he is to deal with the Anglo-Saxon as the independent political power that he, the Negro, potentially is.

What has further complicated this emergence of Afro-American ethnic consciousness is the Jewish involvement in this interracial process over the last fifty-odd years. The role of American Jews as political mediator between Negro and Anglo-Saxon must be terminated by Negroes themselves. This inter-group arrangement is fraught with serious dangers to all concerned. The status of Jews in America is a white Christian-Jewish affair, and the ultimate status of the Negro in America is a white Christian-Negro affair since Negroes and Christians are the more populous groups.

But with LeRoi Jones and his young Afro-American nationalists, anti-interracialism was equated not only with anti-whiteness, but with *hatred* of whiteness. In other words, Negroes had become so deeply mired in an institutionalized form of political interracialism that they could not break with it unless sufficient hatred were mustered to avoid the necessity of apologizing to whites for excluding them. That this was a paranoia-producing rationalization was not understood. If Negroes were actually thinking and functioning on a mature political level, then the exclusion of whites—organizationally and politically—should be based not on hatred but on strategy. It would be much like the tradition that no one outside one's immediate family is ever admitted into a discussion of intimate family problems. It is, therefore, an unfortunate development in Negro life that political interracialism has become so doctrinaire that certain nationalistic Negroes have been forced to resort to race hate in order to block out the negative effect of interracialism on ethnic consciousness. All race hate is self-defeating in the long run because it distorts the critical faculties. Thus it happened that when LeRoi Jones finally came to the point of rejecting interracialism in Harlem in 1965, his erstwhile white friends and associates called him anti-white and a fosterer of race hate and black extremism. But a few of Jones's young collaborators had swung much further toward such extremes than Jones, and in fact rejected Jones as too moderate and pro-white.

This extremist faction represented a concept of force and violence that went far beyond the mere armed self-defense of Robert Williams in 1959. It represented a tendency toward violence that is bred out of the desperation and alienation of the Harlem ghetto; a poisonous brew of hate, hopelessness, racial envy and class inferiority complexes. It has passed even the stage of blind hate to become a form of ghetto paranoia, directed not only toward whites, but at a more immediate target—the middle-class Negro, the "bourgies." More than that, some of the young nationalists have evinced a new black form of anti-intellectualism. The Negro intellectual, too, is suspect, because he is either middle class in origins, accepted by the middle class, or has middle-class leanings. Much of this anti-intellectualism crops up in those whose desire to resort to force and violence takes on such "terroristic" designs as destruction of symbolic objects for mere propaganda effect. Hence, the new Afro-American nationalism has emerged with both a positive rational wing and an anarchistic wing with nihilistic overtones. Revolutionary nationalism in black America has developed a form of black Bakuninism.

Unavoidably, Jones' On Guard for Freedom group collapsed, for neither Jones nor his collaborators were prepared to deal with the political, economic, and cultural imperatives of their movement. Because they were unable to start off on an all-black basis, their organizational interracialism got them ensnared, as always happens in such instances, by the white Marxist Left—both Communists and Trotskyists. This was fatal for the simple reason that neither Communists nor Trotskyists could offer either program or direction to Afro-American nationalism. This had to come from the young intellectuals themselves or it would never come. But without knowledge of the Marxist factional background in America, and without seeing the necessity of breaking with institutionalized interracialism, Jones and company were wide open for infiltration. Like all new generations in all endeavors, they had to learn by themselves; they could not be told anything by those who knew better, for having learned many bitter lessons during the past two decades. It also demonstrated that because Negro intellectuals establish no institutions which can be sustained from one generation to the next, they cannot even hand down to succeeding generations the lessons of their failures. Thus the Harlem political organization that Jones tried to establish had a certain precedence but no continuity. Since the new wave believed they owed little or nothing to the past—or more precisely, to the older generation—they made light of the fact that any new group starting in Harlem is bequeathed a raft of acute social problems, which must be reevaluated.

At the very outset, three years before the Harlem uprising of 1964, Jones' group was warned that Harlem was due for another outbreak of violence. Therefore, unless a fundamental survey of the economic problems of Harlem rehabilitation was pursued, no amount of protest demonstrations, petitions, and militant speeches would mean a thing. Needless to say, this proposal was ignored and not even discussed—because its meaning was not understood. Here was the spectacle of a group of young men, some of them college graduates, who dared to aspire to black revolution without even a glimmer of knowledge about the economics of social change. More important, they lacked the curiosity, interest or willingness to learn and study all the factors of the community situation at hand from a political, economic and cultural point of view. How could anyone talk seriously about social change without a thorough investigation of these social factors? But the blind aplomb with which Jones and his group ignored any suggestions and proceeded to outline a series of protest actions, revealed the disturbing depth and scope of technical unpreparedness of Negroes in highly organized society.

In the Negro community there is no tradition of intellectual skill in the social sciences beyond social work. As a prime victim of laissez-faire capitalism and its social imperatives, the Negro intellectual is pro-capitalistic in his every reflex. He does not see that the concepts of social equality for the entire Negro group, and unqualified capitalism, are contradictory and incompatible. The ideology of the Negro movement, in all its trends, protests against the *ill-effects* of capitalist society but *not* against the society itself. This undermines the rational and organizational viability of the Negro movement and encourages the irrationality of nationalist anarchism and nihilism. It brings the Negro movement and all of its factions face to face with the hard social dynamics of American capitalism. This inner capitalistic dynamic, if left to its own momentum, subordinates and absorbs everything, including the Negro movement and its pro-capitalistic ideology. It can be no other way. As such, without an anti-capitalistic ideology, the Negro movement is doomed to be rolled back into submission. Nothing but welfare state politics and economics will be administered from above, in response to the lingering and sporadic Negro protests from below.

It took Jones and his young Afro-American nationalists four more years to arrive at the realization that it had to establish institutions inside the Harlem ghetto in order to implement a positive program. The institution established was not economic or political, but cultural—the Black Arts Repertory Theater and School. However, no sooner was this institution established than it had to appeal to a federally sponsored economic program for survival—the HARYOU Anti-Poverty Program. Thus, the Jones group was forced to enter an uneven struggle with a federal agency over the dispensation of funds, without having prepared for such an eventuality with a grassroots economic institution of its own in the community. If such a Harlem-based economics planning group had been established, Jones would have been able to wage a more effective *political* struggle with the HARYOU administration and the Federal government over the funding of anti-poverty programs.

The most important conclusion about the Jones movement is that these young intellectuals have been unable to clarify for themselves what the specific role is of the Negro intellectuals as a class in this era. From 1960 to 1965, Jones himself went through a very unique creative development as poet, novelist, and dramatist. But this represented an individual rather than a class development; the latter is more important. For unless the Negro intellectual's role as a class is defined (or redefined), the entire Negro movement—all the way from integrationists to nationalists—is doomed to be bogged down and wasted, through confusion and lack of direction. Even when Jones and his group finally established the Black Arts Theater and School, it was merely a faltering step in the right direction. No real Harlem cultural objectives for this school were defined; nor was the peculiar role of the young intellectuals in this school analyzed, clarified and planned. True to form, it was a pragmatic step without substantial theoretical inspiration. For sadly, Negro intellectuals as a class have no cultural philosophy on which to base such a theory.

One of the main reasons Jones's On Guard group was prevented from analyzing their own role as new wave intellectuals, was their preoccupation with the Robert Williams self-defense mystique in the South. Amidst all the other domestic and international influences, such as Africa and Cuba, Williams stood out as the great American symbol of black resistance. More than that, Williams was also personally identified with the Cuban experience—making him all the more magnetic a figure. However, Monroe represented a Southern trend, while Jones's movement was definitely Northern—with no specific "Northern" program beyond civil rights integration. Thus, the attempted liaison between North and South was in fact highly impractical and adventuristic. What was presented was the spectacle of a collection of Northern romantics playing at revolution, to the extent of shipping arms to Monroe and *publishing the fact in a Northern leftwing newspaper*; for even before the Jones group could establish itself, the Northern liaison with Monroe was already under the control of white leftwingers in New York, as Williams himself had come North and bypassed Harlem in favor of leftwing support in downtown Manhattan.

The upshot of the entire Monroe affair was a series of uncontrollable events, which led to the kidnapping charge levied against Williams and his supporters. From this point on, the white leftwing in New York took over the Williams defense case for propaganda purposes, and was immediately split into two factions—dominated by Trotskyists on the one hand, and pro-Communists on the other. Considering their irreconcilable tenets, one can imagine the divisive and disorienting effects these two political factions would exert on a Negro movement. The young chairman of one of these defense groups—the Monroe Defense Committee—was Jones's friend Calvin Hicks, of the On Guard group.* After the formation of the Monroe Defense Committee, headed by Hicks, another white radical splinter faction ran a story about the Monroe affair under the heading "Afro-American Leadership is the Issue! Why Two Defense Committees?"[9] In this article, Calvin Hicks was quoted as follows:

> We are more than willing to accept the support of our white progressive friends, as our own list of supporters should prove. But right now these particular friends want to dominate us rather than just support us.
>
> They even offered us considerable financial assistance—and later withdrew it when we insisted upon our own leadership.
>
> We were shocked at this, and pretty angry at the time. But I still do not entirely blame them for their actions because it is extremely hard for them to understand why we feel the way we do.

The article said further that "some of these [white] progressives actually stated that they would not support a committee with only a [Negro] leadership." But Hicks concluded, that "considering that various white progressives helped Williams with funds and in other ways, it also seems logical that they

---

*The rival group, the Committee to Aid the Monroe Defenders (CAMD), was the Trotskyist group.

[9]The *Workers World*, September 29, 1961, p. 3. N.B. Organ of a splinter group from the Socialist Workers Party (Trotskyist); the *Workers World* group stood between the Trotskyist and Stalinist (Communist) parties.

should continue to support the defense committee without demanding leadership of it."

Note that Calvin Hicks has never departed any further from political interracialism than to demand that it be black-led. The On Guard group itself never went beyond this demand. It did not occur to Hicks that what he wanted was impossible—white participation and financial support without white leadership. The lesson that the young Afro-American nationalists had to learn was that they had to pay their own way, still another aspect of the economics question they managed to evade.

The story of the On Guard group and the two Monroe Defense Committees is a graphic lesson in the frustrating politics of interracialism. It was compounded and confounded by the mélange of incipient nationalism in the North, armed self-defense in the South, and integrationism plus leftwing political and propagandistic intervention. As a practical and expedient way out of the confusion, Calvin Hicks was able to substitute Williams's movement for the Harlem program his On Guard group was able to create for itself. But all it amounted to in the end was just another Northern protest that swiftly petered out. Not only did the original On Guard group pass out of existence, so did the two rival committees on Monroe defense. The new Afro-American nationalists had a long way to go before they could master the tactical and strategical problems of working out of Harlem. Rather than analyze the Monroe situation, they oversimplified it. However, once the white leftwing gets its hands on a Negro propaganda issue, oversimplification is unavoidable.

Without an ideology relevant to America, white leftwingers are forced to attempt to take over the control of any incipient Negro trend that appears revolutionary. Thus the Marxist factions took over the Monroe armed self-defense movement. The fact that these arms were to be used by Negroes to protect themselves against whites who were also workers (the alleged allies of the Negro) did not at all disturb the zeal of the Marxists. They were going to bake their own revolutionary cake and entice Negroes to eat it with them, without stopping to debate certain fine points of revolutionary theory out of Marx, Engels, Lenin, Stalin or Trotsky.

The American propaganda apparatus has created the great social myth that the Negro protest movement is, in fact, the Black Revolution in progress. This is stretching the word revolution to include anything from "pray ins" to the March on Washington. It is true that, to many whites, the very fact that so many Negroes are protesting all at one time in so many different places, is unsettling enough to induce certain opinion-molders to believe their own alarmist propaganda. Ghetto uprisings like Harlem and Watts lend credence to the spectre of revolution even more. But as long as these uprisings are sporadic, the American capitalistsic welfare state will absorb them and, more than that, pay for the damage in the same way the government pays for the destruction caused by hurricanes and floods. Uprisings are merely another form of extreme protest action soon to be included under the heading of Natural Calamities.

People who call the Negro protest movement a black revolution do not really understand their own system, for a real social revolution in their country would involve a social dynamic of many correlated parts. Such a revolution would have very little in common with the foreign revolutions they have read about. It would amount to a massive social transformation of a kind unheard of before, and the elements for it already exist within the society either actively or latently.

The Negro movement acts out its many-sided role under the influence of, and as a part of, the structural imperatives of the American system. This movement cannot function in any other way as it progresses from one stage to another. Its future failures or successes will depend on to what degree the movement succeeds (or fails) in mastering the imperatives of its own social dynamic. The more the Negro movement falls prey to the myths created by the system—that it is revolutionary when it is not—the longer will it take for this movement to create an advanced leadership. The more the movement absorbs the American myths, the more the American system will absorb the impetus and elements of the movement, and the more internal leadership disorientation will result.

Negro leadership generally functions, even during protest, with one foot out and the other foot inside the Establishment. Being neither "in," nor without hope of getting "in," Negro leadership encounters the difficulty of fighting and protesting against the very social system it wants to join. This means, in effect, that Negro leadership is not really fighting *against* the system, but against being *left out of it*. Therefore, what really worries the Establishment is not so much the cacophony of protest, but the problem of how to absorb the movement without too much stress and strain. The general staff of the capitalistic welfare state understands this situation much better than the muddled minds that run the civil rights movement. The administrative "brains" at the top of the American system may be pragmatically shallow, but not too shallow to understand that the Negro protest movement is not really a revolutionary movement, but rather a response to another kind of American revolution, the capitalistic revolution that threatens to alter social relations in the Southern states. Industrialization has driven Negroes off the farms and plantations into the urban centers; it has mechanized farms, built industries and increased trade. The Negro response to this process has been inspired both by rising expectations and the instability of being uprooted. If Negro leadership fails to understand both the complexities of this capitalistic dynamic and the potential power of the Afro-American social dynamic as an entity, then the entire movement is wide open to being absorbed and controlled by welfare state antipoverty programs and their ilk.

If Negro leadership, especially the new young generation, also understood the history of the white Marxist Left, then they would better understand American capitalism and the Marxist Left's real position within it. They would see how the myth of the Negro revolution is used by both capitalism and the white Left. However, the inner dynamic of American capitalism has nullified any possibility of the Marxist Left leading a revolution according to its theories. Consequently, out of sheer political insolvency and desperation, the white Left swallows the myth of the Black Revolution and reads revolution into every actual or potential Negro uprising. The joke is that the leftwing buys its way into a procapitalistic movement on the hope that what the establishment calls a revolution, will in fact become one later on. But the white Left does not possess a single idea, tactic or strategy in its theoretical arsenal that can make the Negro protest movement a revolutionary one. All it can achieve is to intervene and foster such tactics as will get some persevering Negro activist leader jailed, framed, or exiled for utterly romantic reasons. As of now, the same capitalistic dynamic that absorbed and negated the white Left of the 1930's, has blunted the forward thrust of broad segments of the civil rights movement (including self-defense uprisings).

Association with white Marxists warps the social perception of leftwing Negro intellectuals to the extent that they also fail to see the factors of their own dynamic. Over the past forty-five years many of the best Negro minds have passed in, through, and out of the Marxist Left. Their creative and social perceptions have been considerably dulled in the process, and their collective, cumulative failures over the decades have contributed to the contemporary poverty and insolvency of Negro intellectuals as a class. When the intellectual output, the level of social insight, and the lackluster quality and scarcity of the Negro intellectuals' creative enterprises are stacked against the potentialities of the Negro ethnic group in America, the Negro intellectual class is seen as a colossal fraud. The Negro intellectual may have been sold out in America, but he has participated all too readily in the grand design of his own deception.

Julian Mayfield, who was to become deeply and disastrously involved in the Monroe movement, once wrote in defense of James Baldwin: "Would that the artist could be a scholar and vice versa, but he rarely is."[10] He did not advise that artists in this complex world who are not scholars should not become spokesmen in matters where scholarship is required. As a ranking member of the Harlem leftwing literary and cultural elite (although a late arrival), Mayfield never had to deal with the question of force and violence from a Left point of view until the Monroe affair. As a literary artist who would prefer that scholarship be left to others, Mayfield perhaps was not aware of how his Communist peers had reacted to the first Harlem uprising of 1935. Like the Watts outbursts of thirty years later, this Harlem demonstration of force and violence was directed mainly against the presence of white-owned business establishments. The difference was that no arms were used. Because of the fact that the bulk of businesses in Harlem were Jewish-owned, at least one leading white Communist of 1935 called the uprising an anti-Semitic pogrom. All of the Communists (black and white) were against this outbreak and it is said that a few were actively involved in efforts to put it down. Here, in a decade of economic desperation, was a bitter irony: Communist revolutionaries—who

---

[10]Mayfield, "And Then Came Baldwin," *Harlem, U.S.A.*, ed. John Henrik Clarke (East Berlin: Seven Seas Publishers, 1960), p. 160.

claimed to be against exploitation in all forms—were in fact opposing an uprising against exploitation. In view of the fact that in 1936 the Communist-laden
National Negro Congress was formed with an economic program it did not pursue, the Harlem uprising of 1935 clearly demonstrated why Marxist politics
cannot deal with the economic "roots" of black revolution.*

The emergence of Robert Williams in 1959 brought Mayfield into contact
with the new Afro-American nationalist trend. The Cuban experience, of
course, was an overwhelming factor in the metamorphosis of this trend, and
Williams personified the sympathetic link between the Castroites and the
Negro struggle. Williams and his followers—Jones, Mayfield, Clarke, et al.—
were all deeply moved by these sentiments of solidarity, despite the fact that
not a single Cuban leader, from Castro on down, had the slightest grasp of the
complexity of the Negro struggle in the United States. Conversely, neither did
Williams, Jones, and company seriously examine the real position of the Cuban
Negro in the Cuban Revolution.

Back in New York, the white Marxists made propaganda for their respective factions from the Cuban Revolution (not, incidentally, a revolution made
by Cuban Marxists). The Trotskyists published a pamphlet entitled "How
Cuba Uprooted Race Discrimination," which Williams' followers upheld without question. Mayfield wrote an article on the same topic in a Negro newspaper.[†] However in 1964, a young Cuban Negro patriot, Carlos More, published a
lengthy, detailed document entitled "Have Black People [Cubans] a Place in
the Cuban Revolution?"[††] In this critique More took the Cuban Marxists to
task on their attitudes towards Cuban Negroes who fought in a revolution that
Cuban Communists did not make. None of Robert Williams' Negro Left supporters has pursued this question any further, because none would dare to criticize the American Communists the way Carlos More criticized the Cuban
Communists.

---

*In 1935 the Communists explained the Harlem riots as "resentment against hunger, relief cuts
sweep Harlem" but refused to admit that the real focus of the outbreak was against white businesses and outside economic control of the ghetto. The *Daily Worker* ran a front page appeal—
"Negro and White Workers! United Against Race Riot Provocation," on March 19, 1935. It took
the Communist Party thirty years, plus the Watts uprising, to admit that ghetto uprisings are not
provoked by outside agitation but by internal black-white relations. See Herbert Aptheker on
"The Watts Ghetto Uprising," *Political Affairs*, October and November, 1965. See also, "Communications—The Meaning of Watts," Ben Dobbs and Herbert Aptheker discussion, *Political Affairs*,
January, 1966, pp. 53–57.

[†]In 1961, Julian Mayfield wrote: "I can say without hesitation that the new government, in the
brief time it has been in power, has substantially eliminated racial discrimination on the island."
See his "The Cuban Challenge," *Freedomways*, Summer, 1961, p. 187.

[††]In this article, More charges: "Thus far Cuba, contrary to all claims, *there has not been a revolution*—which explains the total absence of proletarians and Afro-Cubans in the affairs of the 'dictatorship of the proletariat' and of the 'government of the people'—What has, in fact, happened has
been the displacement of a fictional national bourgeoisie in favor of a *real one*." See Carlos More,
"Le Peuple Noir a-t-il sa Place dans la Révolution Cubaine?" *Presence Africaine*, Fourth Quarter,
1964, p. 228.

In 1961 Mayfield had published an article called "Challenge to Negro Leadership—The Case of Robert Williams." The importance of this article lies in the fact that it was the first attempt on the part of any member of John O. Killens' Harlem literary and cultural group to extend their creativity into the field of social analysis. Significantly, it took the new issue of force and violence, with a self-defense theme, to prod a member of this group off the protest platform. In this effort Mayfield extended his inquiry to include the Negro movement as a whole: "For some time now it has been apparent that the traditional leadership of the American Negro community—a leadership which has been largely middleclass in origin and orientation—is in danger of losing its claim to speak for the masses of Negroes."[11]

Thus at the very outset Mayfield establishes the theoretical premise of his analysis by repeating what had for years been used and overused as a class truism. Negro civil rights leadership is middle class, the Negro masses are working class; hence the leadership has forfeited its right to speak for the masses because it is middle class. What makes this class reference important for Mayfield is that it is Marxist in tone even though *Commentary* is not a Left publication. This would mean also that all of the Killens group's leftwing friends would read the article with interest, if not with full approbation. However, the author's political upbringing left his thinking full of holes.

By "middle class," Mayfield actually meant the NAACP leadership—the section of the black bourgeoisie with whom Williams came into conflict over "meeting lynching with lynching," "self-defense," etc. But he neglected to mention that the Communist Party had officially switched its position in 1959 to that of full support of this same NAACP line of unqualified racial integration. He also failed to mention that neither Williams nor he was the least bit opposed to the NAACP's middle-class-oriented integration. Hence, the Williams case, for Mayfield, represented not an issue of aims, but of methods (as it had also for Williams, in 1961). Thus the main conclusion Mayfield drew in his article was that the methods of middle-class Negro leadership (the NAACP) were losing their relevance to the needs of the masses because they were not revolutionary. After reviewing and forecasting events in the Southern situation he ended on a note of prophecy: "Then to the fore may come Robert Williams and other young men and women like him, who have concluded that the only way to win a revolution is to be a revolutionary."[12]

Despite Mayfield's insouciance it is not a simple matter for an avowed integrationist leader, even of Williams's fiber, to become a revolutionary and tear himself completely out of the context of the protest movement. Integration, in itself, is not a revolutionary idea. If it were, one would have to say that the Supreme Court of the United States is a revolutionary tribunal. But Mayfield was able to bypass all of these conceptual difficulties because he saw in the

[11]Julian Mayfield, "Challenge to Negro Leadership—The Case of Robert Williams," New York, *Commentary*, April, 1961, p. 297. Used by permission.

[12]*Ibid.*, p. 305.

Southern movement a new revolutionary trend already in motion. In light of his own recent inspiration by the Cuban Revolution, it is easy to imagine what cataclysmic visions were conjured up in his mind about the situation in the United States. Where-abouts in our troubled Southland would our "Sierra Maestre" be found? Perhaps in Monroe, North Carolina. In his article, Mayfield simply transferred the old Left prophecies about the proletarian awakening to the Southern movement (with suitable variations). For example, he wrote: "But sooner than anyone now supposes, three factors may create a social climate in the South in which a Robert Williams will play a leading role. They are the growing militancy of Negro students; the intransigence of the Southern White oligarchy; and the depressed Negro workingclass and peasantry."[13]

This analysis must have greatly warmed the hearts of all of Mayfield's Marxist mentors in the tired old Communist ranks—from Herbert Aptheker to Shirley Graham DuBois. Word for word, the above would not have been out of place in *Political Affairs*, the Party's official organ (that is, with the exception of the classification "peasantry," which Mayfield borrowed from the Cuban experience). The American Communists were not in the habit of calling Negro farmers and sharecroppers "peasants," but Mayfield was bent on imagining class affinities between Cuban and American Negroes in the light of the new revolutionary wave. But not to appear to be overly carried away, Mayfield admonished:

> Predictions are risky at best, but it seems safe to say that as these forces come into sharper conflict in what is essentially an attempt to overthrow an entrenched political and economic power, the Negro leadership class will be faced with a crisis, for its purely legalistic (or passive-resistance) approach will clearly not be able to control the dynamics of the Negro struggle. Then to the fore may come [a] Robert Williams.[14]

Mayfield's article had the Trotskyists in the "Fair Play for Cuba Committee" all in a revolutionary dither, which made up for the fact that Mayfield's Communist friends were not officially pro-Williams, but were supporting the NAACP. Since Mayfield was supporting the Cuba Committee but not the Trotskyists in it, they in turn tried to woo Mayfield into their camp by giving him great play in their press. In all this factional intrigue over who would represent Cuba in the United States, the Communists came out second best; so Julian Mayfield was left in the interesting position of trying to ride different horses going in opposite directions—Robert Williams and the Communist Left. As one venerable, diehard Communist argued when questioned about his Party's latest switch on the Negro—"Well, we have to go where the *people* are. And the people are following the NAACP's integration line." These people

[13]*Ibid.*
[14]*Ibid.*

were obviously not the same ones Mayfield was talking about in his article, or else the conflict had not sharpened to the point of overthrowing "an entrenched political and economic power." But the people whom a Robert Williams might eventually lead, Mayfield felt would "have nothing to barter in the labor market but their willingness to work.... It is not [for their] children that all the school desegregation furore is about."[15]

True...and then not quite true...because Negro children of all classes in the South are affected by school desegregation more or less depending on their locality. But in Monroe, Robert Williams was an integrationist just like any other NAACP-er he disagreed with over self-defense; and whatever effects school desegregation had on his followers, they were certainly behind Williams in his efforts to desegregate a Monroe swimming pool. Everything that happened in Monroe stemmed from the integration question, and many flaws in Mayfield's analysis are rooted in his inability to explore contradictory factors.

Reading old Left ideas into a new racial situation, Mayfield utterly failed to perceive the larger implications of what indeed was new. He saw the new Negro movement as a challenge to traditional middle-class leadership without understanding that it too was, with few exceptions, also strongly middle-class-oriented. In Montgomery, Alabama, the bus strike movement that started out as a grassroots affair was taken over by Martin L. King and his middle-class orientation. The first phases of the Birmingham up-rising were very orderly processions led by King for essentially middle-class objectives. King's followers did not welcome the working-class uprising that followed, in riotous disorder. Williams' Monroe events were merely a notable exception to the general rule which started out within the framework of the NAACP's program.

The Negro movement has been historically propelled by a succession of new waves of middle-class origins or motivations, each wave professing to be more militant than the last—or, as Mayfield put it—the last "traditional" leadership. (What is radical today is traditional tomorrow.) Hence, what is really crucial about Negro leadership is not its class origins but its program. So far the only programs (good, bad, or indifferent) have come from bourgeois Negroes or those with bourgeois aspirations. The real problem, then, is that even when more militant and effective leadership does arrive from other than bourgeois class origins, it must have bourgeois support or else it can get nowhere. This is because effective social movements require educated people with knowledge and technical skills which the proletariat, or the masses, do not possess. It is only the educated, trained, and technically-qualified who can deal directly with the state apparatus. In America, when members of the masses acquire education and skills, they cease, forthwith, to be proletarians. Even if the Marxists would rather evade these facts about class differences, they are crucial truths in the Negro struggle.

[15]*Ibid.*

When Marxist leftwingers speak of the coming proletarian revolution (even in fancy), they know that according to the script, this projects something apocalyptic in scope, a fundamental mass assault on capitalistic property relations, the abolition of the capitalist class in toto. But do they really believe this, now? If so, it is pointless to debate such irrational beliefs. Yet, one must insist on asking—How can a social movement that is demanding more and better jobs, homes, education and other privileges—all of which are benefits that lie within the social grasp of the lower- and the upper-middle-class frame of reference—be characterized as a movement that is consciously seeking the abolition of capitalistic property relations at the same time? Such a movement is not aimed at overthrowing anything; although Negroes want jobs, they want them *within the existing economic framework*, for the simple reason that Negroes actually know no other kind of economic system, real or imaginary.

Essentially, the Negro's outlook is determined by the material conditions of the American capitalistic dynamic. The Marxists would have to agree with this assertion inasmuch as it corresponds to one of their prime postulates. However, it is also true that no foreign revolutionary ideology can really penetrate the Negro psychology, especially if it is anti-capitalistic to the point of interfering with the desire to "make good" in the world. Moreover, American capitalism is also able to offer the masses (and even members of the intelligentsia) large doses of spoon-fed socialism. These fringe benefits of American capitalism—welfare relief, health insurance, old-age benefits, anti-poverty programs, etc.—are much higher in dollar value than the wages of many productive workers in the underdeveloped world whose countries are building anti-capitalistic socialism. Thus it is the height of romantic folly to believe that the American masses, of any color, could be motivated to revolutionary actions to achieve something they already have in one degree or another. Whatever the American Negro has achieved economically, whether capitalistic or socialistic, he has won under capitalistic conditions. He will struggle for more only within that framework—unless he is induced otherwise through experience. So far, despite all the talk about the Black Revolution, he has not been educated for anything else. He is a child of the era of New Deal capitalism and all that that economic philosophy implies. It will take much more than the tactics of a Robert Williams or the social analysis of a Julian Mayfield to goad any future Negro protest wave to attempt to "overthrow an entrenched political and economic power" of American capitalism, either North or South.

The black revolutionaries of the 1960's forget that it was the Supreme Court Decision of the 1950's that gave initial sanction and set the stage for the new-wave civil rights movement that later became the Black Revolution. This surely exposes the Negro's heritage insofar as it is rooted in the patronage of New Deal capitalism. Although that decision hardly made the Court a revolutionary body (for it would never hand down a juridical decision that might turn wheels of social change the legislative and executive branches could not control), it did demonstrate the power of the Federal government. And it is in the Federal government that the integrationists—from the NAACP to King to

Williams—place their ultimate faith. Even after his condemnation of the Federal government and the courts for failure to bring a "halt to lynching in the South," Williams, according to Mayfield, was "convinced that the Federal government offers the only real hope the Negro has of winning any large measure of his civil rights."[16] This means, of course, that a Robert Williams who feels this way will hardly ever come to the point of the revolutionary overthrow of that very institution in which he places ultimate hope for salvation. Moreover, that "entrenched political and economic power" which Mayfield foresees being overthrown in the future is, in reality, the power of the base of a structure at whose pinnacle towers the very same Federal power. The integrationists seek the intervention of this Federal power on behalf of all civil rights issues, and it is precisely on this possibility of Federal intervention that the whole revolutionary prognosis of a Mayfield falters. The Federal government is able to move in on an armed self-defense clash between Negroes and Whites just as effectively as it moved in on Little Rock, Arkansas, to uphold school integration. No vision of the proletarian revolution, whether in Mayfield's black tones or in white Leftist white tones, can seriously project overthrowing the Federal structure. It is so powerfully "big" that even the conservative rightwing is worried to the point of extremist apoplexy—and they are certainly more highly organized in every department than either the Negro movement or the white Left. The Marxists cannot admit this reality about the American Federal structure and, at the same time, hold fast to the Marxian schema about proletarian overthrow, so they do not admit it. But no more can they admit the possibility of another native American inner dynamic for social change *unrelated* to the Marxian schema. Hence, they fall victims to the American dynamic and are absorbed just as is the Negro movement. This is the price the white Marxists pay for their doctrinaire intolerance, exclusiveness and the provincialism of their nineteenth-century creed. It is the price the Negro movement pays for not being intolerant and exclusive *enough*, and for not having a social creed to be doctrinaire *about*—unless, of course, it is racial integration. This makes the American Negro intellectual the first great prototype of the American universalist: He has no social philosophy of his own, but accepts everybody else's philosophies without question. Beneath the Marxist veneer of a Julian Mayfield lies a tradition of intellectual retrogression from an age of renaissance to an age of mid-century crisis. It is only because the slogans, the appeals, the protests and declarations are dressed up with contemporary allusions to civil rights headlines and international events, that the poverty in ideas is not exposed beneath the hollow phrases.

[16]*Ibid.*, p. 300.

Eldridge Cleaver
from *Soul on Ice*

ON BECOMING

Folsom Prison
June 25, 1965

Nineteen fifty-four, when I was eighteen years old, is held to be a crucial turning point in the history of the Afro-American—for the U.S.A. as a whole—the year segregation was outlawed by the U.S. Supreme Court. It was also a crucial year for me because on June 18, 1954, I began serving a sentence in state prison for possession of marijuana.

The Supreme Court decision was only one month old when I entered prison, and I do not believe that I had even the vaguest idea of its importance or historical significance. But later, the acrimonious controversy ignited by the end of the separate-but-equal doctrine was to have a profound effect on me. This controversy awakened me to my position in America and I began to form a concept of what it meant to be black in white America.

Of course I'd always known that I was black, but I'd never really stopped to take stock of what I was involved in. I met life as an individual and took my chances. Prior to 1954, we lived in an atmosphere of novocain. Negroes found it necessary, in order to maintain whatever sanity they could, to remain somewhat aloof and detached from "the problem." We accepted indignities and the mechanics of the apparatus of oppression without reacting by sitting-in or holding mass demonstrations. Nurtured by the fires of the controversy over segregation, I was soon aflame with indignation over my newly discovered social status, and inwardly I turned away from America with horror, disgust and outrage.

In Soledad state prison, I fell in with a group of young blacks who, like myself, were in vociferous rebellion against what we perceived as a continuation of slavery on a higher plane. We cursed everything American—including baseball and hot dogs. All respect we may have had for politicians, preachers, lawyers, governors, Presidents, senators, congressmen was utterly destroyed as we watched them temporizing and compromising over right and wrong, over legality and illegality, over constitutionality and unconstitutionality. We knew that in the end what they were clashing over was us, what to do with the blacks, and whether or not to start treating us as human beings. I despised all of them.

The segregationists were condemned out of hand, without even listening to their lofty, finely woven arguments. The others I despised for wasting time in debates with the segregationists: why not just crush them, put them in prison—they were defying the law, weren't they? I defied the law and they put me in prison. So why not put all those dirty mothers in prison too? I had gotten caught with a shopping bag full of marijuana, a shopping bag full of love—I was in love with the weed and I did not for one minute think that anything was wrong with getting high. I had been getting high for four or five years and was convinced, with the zeal of a crusader, that marijuana was superior to lush—yet the rulers of the land seemed all to be lushes. I could not see how they were more justified in drinking than I was in blowing the gage. I was a grasshopper, and it was natural that I felt myself to be unjustly imprisoned.

While all this was going on, our group was espousing atheism. Unsophisticated and not based on any philosophical rationale, our atheism was pragmatic. I had come to believe that there is no God; if there is, men do not know anything about him. Therefore, all religions were phony—which made all preachers and priests, in our eyes, fakers, including the ones scurrying around the prison who, curiously, could put in a good word for you with the Almighty Creator of the universe but could not get anything down with the warden or parole board—they could usher you through the Pearly Gates *after you were dead*, but not through the prison gate *while you were still alive and kicking*. Besides, men of the cloth who work in prison have an ineradicable stigma attached to them in the eyes of convicts because they escort condemned men into the gas chamber. Such men of God are powerful arguments in favor of atheism. Our atheism was a source of enormous pride to me. Later on, I bolstered our arguments by reading Thomas Paine and his devastating critique of Christianity in particular and organized religion in general.

Through reading I was amazed to discover how confused people were. I had thought that, out there beyond the horizon of my own ignorance, unanimity existed, that even though I myself didn't know what was happening in the universe, other people certainly did. Yet here I was discovering that the whole U.S.A. was in a chaos of disagreement over segregation/integration. In these circumstances I decided that the only safe thing for me to do was go for myself. It became clear that it was possible for me to take the initiative: instead of simply *reacting* I could *act*. I could unilaterally—whether anyone agreed with me or not—repudiate all allegiances, morals, values—even while continuing to exist within this society. My mind would be free and no power in the universe could force me to accept something if I didn't want to. But I would take my own sweet time. That, too, was a part of my new freedom. I would accept nothing until it was proved that it was good—for me. I became an extreme iconoclast. Any affirmative assertion made by anyone around me became a target for tirades of criticism and denunciation.

This little game got good to me and I got good at it. I attacked all forms of piety, loyalty, and sentiment: marriage, love, God, patriotism, the Constitution, the founding fathers, law, concepts of right-wrong-good-evil, all forms of ritualized and conventional behavior. As I pranced about, club in hand, seeking new idols to smash, I encountered really for the first time in my life, with any seriousness, The Ogre, rising up before me in a mist. I discovered, with alarm, that The Ogre possessed a tremendous and dreadful power over me, and I didn't understand this power or why I was at its mercy. I tried to repudiate The Ogre, root it out of my heart as I had done God, Constitution, principles, morals, and values—but The Ogre had its claws buried in the core of my being and refused to let go. I fought frantically to be free, but The Ogre only mocked me and sank its claws deeper into my soul. I knew then that I had found an important key, that if I conquered The Ogre and broke its power over me I would be free. But I also knew that it was a race against time and that if I did not win I would certainly be broken and destroyed. I, a black man, confronted The Ogre—the white woman.

In prison, these things withheld from and denied to the prisoner become precisely what he wants most of all, of course. Because we were locked up in our cells before darkness fell, I used to lie awake at night racked by painful craving to take a leisurely stroll under the stars, or to go to the beach, to drive a car on a freeway, to grow a beard, or to make love to a woman.

Since I was not married conjugal visits would not have solved my problem. I therefore denounced the idea of conjugal visits as inherently unfair; single prisoners needed and deserved *action* just as married prisoners did. I advocated establishing a system under Civil Service whereby salaried women would minister to the needs of those prisoners who maintained a record of good behavior. If a married prisoner preferred his own wife, that would be his right. Since California was not about to inaugurate either conjugal visits or the Civil Service, one could advocate either with equal enthusiasm and with the same result: nothing.

This may appear ridiculous to some people. But it was very real to me and as urgent as the need to breathe, because I was in my bull stage and lack of access to females was absolutely a form of torture. I suffered. My mistress at the time of my arrest, the beautiful and lonely wife of a serviceman stationed overseas, died unexpectedly three weeks after I entered prison; and the rigid, dehumanized rules governing correspondence between prisoners and free people prevented me from corresponding with other young ladies I knew. It left me without any contact with females except those in my family.

In the process of enduring my confinement, I decided to get myself a pinup girl to paste on the wall of my cell. I would fall in love with her and lavish my affections upon her. She, a symbolic representative of the forbidden tribe of women, would sustain me until I was free. Out of the center of *Esquire*, I married a voluptuous bride. Our marriage went along swell for a time: no quarrels, no complaints. And then, one evening when I came in from school, I was shocked and enraged to find that the guard had entered my cell, ripped my sugar from the wall, torn her into little pieces, and left the pieces floating in the commode: it was like seeing a dead body floating in a lake. Giving her a proper burial, I flushed the commode. As the saying goes, I sent her to Long Beach. But I was genuinely beside myself with anger: almost every cell, excepting those of the homosexuals, had a pin-up girl on the wall and the guards didn't bother them. Why, I asked the guard the next day, had he singled me out for special treatment?

"Don't you know we have a rule against pasting up pictures on the walls?" he asked me.

"Later for the rules," I said. "You know as well as I do that that rule is not enforced."

"Tell you what," he said, smiling at me (the smile put me on my guard), "I'll compromise with you: get yourself a colored girl for a pinup—no white women—and I'll let it stay up. Is that a deal?"

I was more embarrassed than shocked. He was laughing in my face. I called him two or three dirty names and walked away. I can still recall his big moon-face, grinning at me over yellow teeth. The disturbing part about the whole incident was that a terrible feeling of guilt came over me as I realized that I had chosen the picture of the white girl over the available pictures of black girls. I tried to rationalize it away, but I was fascinated by the truth involved. Why hadn't I thought about it in this light before? So I took hold of the question and began to inquire into my feelings. Was it true, did I really prefer white girls over black? The conclusion was clear and inescapable: I did. I decided to check out my friends on this point and it was easy to determine, from listening to their general conversation, that the white woman occupied a peculiarly prominent place in all of our frames of reference. With what I have learned since then, this all seems terribly elementary now. But at the time, it was a tremendously intriguing adventure of discovery.

One afternoon, when a large group of Negroes was on the prison yard shooting the breeze, I grabbed the floor and posed the question: which did they prefer, white women or black? Some said Japanese women were their favorite, others said Chinese, some said European women, others said Mexican women—they all stated a preference, and they generally freely admitted their dislike for black women.

"I don't want nothing black but a Cadillac," said one.

"If money was black I wouldn't want none of it," put in another.

A short little stud, who was a very good lightweight boxer with a little man's complex that made him love to box heavyweights, jumped to his feet. He had a yellowish complexion and we called him Butterfly.

"All you niggers are sick!" Butterfly spat out. "I don't like no stinking white woman. My grandma is a white woman and I don't even like her!"

But it just so happened that Butterfly's crime partner was in the crowd, and after Butterfly had his say, his crime partner said, "Aw, sit on down and quit that lying, lil o' chump. What about that gray girl in San Jose who had your nose wide open? Did you like her, or were you just running after her with your tongue hanging out of your head because you hated her?"

Partly because he was embarrassed and partly because his crime partner was a heavyweight, Butterfly flew into him. And before we could separate them and disperse, so the guard would not know who had been fighting, Butterfly bloodied his crime partner's nose. Butterfly got away but, because of the blood, his crime partner got caught. I ate dinner with Butterfly that evening and questioned him sharply about his attitude toward white women. And after an initial evasiveness he admitted that the white woman bugged him too. "It's a sickness," he said. "All our lives we've had the white woman dangled before our eyes like a carrot on a stick before a donkey: look but don't touch." (In 1958, after I had gone out on parole and was returned to San Quentin as a parole violator with a new charge, Butterfly was still there. He had become a Black Muslim and was chiefly responsible for teaching me the Black Muslim philosophy. Upon his release from San Quentin, Butterfly joined the Los Angeles Mosque, advanced rapidly through the ranks, and is now a full-fledged minister of one of Elijah Muhammad's mosques in another city. He successfully completed his parole, got married—to a very black girl—and is doing fine.)

From our discussion, which began that evening and has never yet ended, we went on to notice how thoroughly, as a matter of course, a black growing up in America is indoctrinated with the white race's standard of beauty. Not that the whites made a conscious, calculated effort to do this, we thought, but since they constituted the majority the whites brainwashed the blacks by the very processes the whites employed to indoctrinate themselves with their own group standards. It intensified my frustrations to know that I was indoctrinated to see the white woman as more beautiful and desirable than my own black woman. It drove me into books seeking light on the subject. In Richard Wright's *Native Son*, I found Bigger Thomas and a keen insight into the problem.

My interest in this area persisted undiminished and then, in 1955, an event took place in Mississippi which turned me inside out: Emmett Till, a young Negro down from Chicago on a visit, was murdered, allegedly for flirting with a white woman. He had been shot, his head crushed from repeated blows with a blunt instrument, and his badly decomposed body was recovered from the river with a heavy weight on it. I was, of course, angry over the whole bit, but one day I saw in a magazine a picture of the white woman with whom Emmett Till was said to have flirted. While looking at the picture, I felt that little tension in the center of my chest I experience when a woman appeals to me. I was disgusted and angry with myself. Here was a woman who had caused the death of a black, possibly because, when he looked at her, he also felt the same tensions of lust and desire in his chest—and probably for the same general reasons that I felt them. It was all unacceptable to me. I looked at the picture again and again, and in spite of everything and against my will and the hate I felt for the woman and all that she represented, she appealed to me. I flew into a rage at myself, at America, at white women, at the history that had placed those tensions of lust and desire in my chest.

Two days later, I had a "nervous breakdown." For several days I ranted and raved against the white race, against white women in particular, against white America in general. When I came to myself, I was locked in a padded cell with not even the vaguest memory of how I got there. All I could recall was an eternity of pacing back and forth in the cell, preaching to the unhearing walls.

I had several sessions with a psychiatrist. His conclusion was that I hated my mother. How he arrived at this conclusion I'll never know, because he knew nothing about my mother; and when he'd ask me questions I would answer him with absurd lies. What revolted me about him was that he had heard me denouncing the whites, yet each time he interviewed me he deliberately guided the conversation back to my family life, to my childhood. That in itself was all right, but he deliberately blocked all my attempts to bring out the racial question, and he made it clear that he was not interested in my attitude toward whites. This was a Pandora's box he did not care to open. After I ceased my diatribes against the whites, I was let out of the hospital, back into the general inmate population just as if nothing had happened. I continued to brood over these events and over the dynamics of race relations in America.

During this period I was concentrating my reading in the field of economics. Having previously dabbled in the theories and writings of Rousseau, Thomas Paine, and Voltaire, I had added a little polish to my iconoclastic stance, without, however, bothering too much to understand their affirmative positions. In economics, because everybody seemed to find it necessary to attack and condemn Karl Marx in their writings, I sought out his books, and although he kept me with a headache, I took him for my authority. I was not prepared to understand him, but I was able to see in him a thoroughgoing critique and condemnation of capitalism. It was like taking medicine for me to find that, indeed, American capitalism deserved all the hatred and contempt that I felt for it in my heart. This had a positive, stabilizing effect upon me—to an extent because I was not about to become stable—and it diverted me from my previous preoccupation: morbid broodings on the black man and the white woman. Pursuing my readings into the history of socialism, I read, with very little understanding, some of the passionate, exhortatory writings of Lenin; and I fell in love with Bakunin and Nechayev's *Catechism of the Revolutionist*—the principles of which, along with some of Machiavelli's advice, I sought to incorporate into my own behavior. I took the *Catechism* for my bible and, standing on a oneman platform that had nothing to do with the reconstruction of society, I began consciously incorporating these principles into my daily life, to employ tactics of ruthlessness in my dealings with everyone with whom I came into contact. And I began to look at white America through these new eyes.

Somehow I arrived at the conclusion that, as a matter of principle, it was of paramount importance for me to have an antagonistic, ruthless attitude toward white women. The term *outlaw* appealed to me and at the time my parole date was drawing near, I considered myself to be mentally free—I was an "outlaw." I had stepped outside of the white man's law, which I repudiated with scorn and self-satisfaction. I became a law unto myself—my own legislature, my own supreme court, my own executive. At the moment I walked out of the prison gate, my feelings toward white women in general could be summed up in the following lines:

To a White Girl

I love you
Because you're white,
Not because you're charming
Or bright.
Your whiteness
Is a silky thread
Snaking through my thoughts
In redhot patterns
Of lust and desire.

I hate you
Because you're white.
Your white meat
Is nightmare food.
White is
The skin of Evil.
You're my Moby Dick,
White Witch,
Symbol of the rope and hanging tree,
Of the burning cross.
Loving you thus
And hating you so,
My heart is torn in two.
Crucified.

I became a rapist. To refine my technique and *modus operandi*, I started out by practicing on black girls in the ghetto—in the black ghetto where dark and vicious deeds appear not as aberrations or deviations from the norm, but as part of the sufficiency of the Evil of a day—and when I considered myself smooth enough, I crossed the tracks and sought out white prey. I did this consciously, deliberately, willfully, methodically—though looking back I see that I was in a frantic, wild, and completely abandoned frame of mind.

Rape was an insurrectionary act. It delighted me that I was defying and trampling upon the white man's law, upon his system of values, and that I was defiling his women—and this point, I believe, was the most satisfying to me because I was very resentful over the historical fact of how the white man has used the black woman. I felt I was getting revenge. From the site of the act of rape, consternation spreads outwardly in concentric circles. I wanted to send waves of consternation throughout the white race. Recently, I came upon a quotation from one of LeRoi Jones' poems, taken from his book *The Dead Lecturer*:

A cult of death need of the simple striking arm under
the street lamp. The cutters from under their rented
earth. Come up, black dada nihilismus. Rape the white
girls. Rape their fathers. Cut the mothers' throats.

I have lived those lines and I know that if I had not been apprehended I
would have slit some white throats. There are, of course, many young blacks
out there right now who are slitting white throats and raping the white girl.
They are not doing this because they read LeRoi Jones' poetry, as some of his
critics seem to believe. Rather, LeRoi is expressing the funky facts of life.

After I returned to prison, I took a long look at myself and, for the first
time in my life, admitted that I was wrong, that I had gone astray—astray not
so much from the white man's law as from being human, civilized—for I could
not approve the act of rape. Even though I had some insight into my own motivations, I did not feel justified. I lost my self-respect. My pride as a man dis-
solved and my whole fragile moral structure seemed to collapse, completely
shattered.

That is why I started to write. To save myself.

I realized that no one could save me but myself. The prison authorities
were both uninterested and unable to help me. I had to seek out the truth and
unravel the snarled web of my motivations. I had to find out who I am and
what I want to be, what type of man I should be, and what I could do to become the best of which I was capable. I understood that what had happened to
me had also happened to countless other blacks and it would happen to many,
many more.

I learned that I had been taking the easy way out, running away from problems. I also learned that it is easier to do evil than it is to do good. And I have
been terribly impressed by the youth of America, black and white. I am proud
of them because they have reaffirmed my faith in humanity. I have come to feel
what must be love for the young people of America and I want to be part of the
good and greatness that they want for all people. From my prison cell, I have
watched America slowly coming awake. It is not fully awake yet, but there is
soul in the air and everywhere I see beauty. I have watched the sit-ins, the freedom raids, the Mississippi Blood Summers, demonstrations all over the country, the FSM movement, the teach-ins, and the mounting protest over Lyndon
Strangelove's foreign policy—all of this, the thousands of little details, show
me it is time to straighten up and fly right. That is why I decided to concentrate on my writings and efforts in this area. We are a very sick country—I, perhaps, am sicker than most. But I accept that. I told you in the beginning that I
am extremist by nature—so it is only right that I should be extremely sick.

I was very familiar with the Eldridge who came to prison, but that Eldridge
no longer exists. And the one I am now is in some ways a stranger to me. You
may find this difficult to understand but it is very easy for one in prison to lose
his sense of self. And if he has been undergoing all kinds of extreme, involved,
and unregulated changes, then he ends up not knowing who he is. Take the

point of being attractive to women. You can easily see how a man can lose his arrogance or certainty on that point while in prison! When he's in the free world, he gets constant feedback on how he looks from the number of female heads he turns when he walks down the street. In prison he gets only hate-stares and sour frowns. Years and years of bitter looks. Individuality is not nourished in prison, neither by the officials nor by the convicts. It is a deep hole out of which to climb.

What must be done, I believe, is that all these problems—particularly the sickness between the white woman and the black man—must be brought out into the open, dealt with and resolved. I know that the black man's sick attitude toward the white woman is a revolutionary sickness: it keeps him perpetually out of harmony with the system that is oppressing him. Many whites flatter themselves with the idea that the Negro male's lust and desire for the white dream girl is purely an esthetic attraction, but nothing could be farther from the truth. His motivation is often of such a bloody, hateful, bitter, and malignant nature that whites would really be hard pressed to find it flattering. I have discussed these points with prisoners who were convicted of rape, and their motivations are very plain. But they are very reluctant to discuss these things with white men who, by and large, make up the prison staffs. I believe that in the experience of these men lies the knowledge and wisdom that must be utilized to help other youngsters who are heading in the same direction. I think all of us, the entire nation, will be better off if we bring it all out front. A lot of people's feelings will be hurt, but that is the price that must be paid.

It may be that I can harm myself by speaking frankly and directly, but I do not care about that at all. Of course I want to get out of prison, badly, but I shall get out some day. I am more concerned with what I am going to be after I get out. I know that by following the course which I have charted I will find my salvation. If I had followed the path laid down for me by the officials, I'd undoubtedly have long since been out of prison—but I'd be less of a man. I'd be weaker and less certain of where I want to go, what I want to do, and how to go about it.

The price of hating other human beings is loving oneself less.

THE BLACK MAN'S STAKE IN VIETNAM

The most critical tests facing Johnson are the war in Vietnam and the Negro revolution at home. The fact that the brains in the Pentagon see fit to send 16 per cent black troops to Vietnam is one indication that there is a structural relationship between these two arenas of conflict. And the initial outrageous refusal of the Georgia Legislature to seat representative-elect Julian Bond, because he denounced the aggressive U.S. role in Vietnam, shows, too, the very intimate relationship between the way human beings are being treated in Vietnam and the treatment they are receiving here in the United States.

We live today in a system that is in the last stages of the protracted process of breaking up on a worldwide basis. The rulers of this system have their hands full. Injustice is being challenged at every turn and on every level. The rulers perceive the greatest threat to be the national liberation movements around the world, particularly in Asia, Africa, and Latin America. In order for them to wage wars of suppression against these national liberation movements abroad, they must have peace and stability and unanimity of purpose at home. But at home there is a Trojan Horse, a Black Trojan Horse that has become aware of itself and is now struggling to get on its feet. It, too, demands liberation.

What is the purpose of the attention that the rulers are now focusing on the Trojan Horse? Is it out of a newfound love for the horse, or is it because the rulers need the horse to be quiet, to be still, and not cause the rulers, already with their backs pressed to the wall, any trouble or embarrassment while they force the war in Vietnam? Indeed, the rulers have need of the horse's power on the fields of battle. What the black man in America must keep constantly in mind is that the doctrine of white supremacy, which is a part of the ideology of the world system the power structure is trying to preserve, lets the black men in for the greatest portion of the suffering and hate which white supremacy has dished out to the non-white people of the world for hundreds of years. The white-supremacy-oriented white man feels less compunction about massacring "niggers" than he does about massacring any other race of people on earth. This historically indisputable fact, taken with the present persistent efforts of the United States to woo the Soviet Union into an alliance against China, spells *DANGER* to all the peoples of the world who have been victims of white supremacy. If this sweethearting proves successful, if the United States is finally able to make a match with Russia, or if the U.S. can continue to frighten the Soviet Union into reneging on its commitments to international socialist solidarity (about which the Soviets are always trumpeting, while still allowing the imperialist aggressors to daily bomb the Democratic Republic of North Vietnam), and if the U.S. is able to unleash its anxious fury and armed might against the rising non-white giant of China, which is the real target of U.S. policy in Vietnam and the Object-Evil of U.S. strategy the world over—if the U.S. is successful in these areas, then it will be the black man's turn again to face the lyncher and burner of the world: and face him alone.

Black Americans are too easily deceived by a few smiles and friendly gestures, by the passing of a few liberal-sounding laws which are left on the books to rot unenforced, and by the mushy speechmaking of a President who is a past master of talking out of the thousand sides of his mouth. Such poetry does not *guarantee* the safe future of the black people in America. The black people must have a guarantee, they must be *certain*, they must be sure beyond all doubt that the reign of terror is ended and not just suspended, and that the future of their people is secure. And the only way they can ensure this is to gain organizational unity and communication with their brothers and allies around the world, on an international basis. They must have this power. There is no other way. Anything else is a sellout of the future of their people. The world of today was fashioned yesterday. What is involved here, what is being decided right now, is the shape of power in the world tomorrow.

The American racial problem can no longer be spoken of or solved in isolation. The relationship between the genocide in Vietnam and the smiles of the white man toward black Americans is a direct relationship. Once the white man solves his problem in the East he will then turn his fury again on the black people of America, his longtime punching bag. The black people have been tricked again and again, sold out at every turn by misleaders. After the Civil War, America went through a period similar to the one we are now in. The Negro problem received a full hearing. Everybody knew that the black man had been denied justice. No one doubted that it was time for changes and that the black man should be made a first-class citizen. But Reconstruction ended. Blacks who had been elevated to high positions were brusquely kicked out into the streets and herded along with the mass of blacks into the ghettos and black belts. The lyncher and the burner received virtual license to murder blacks at will. White Americans found a new level on which to cool the blacks out. And with the help of such tools as Booker T. Washington, the doctrine of segregation was clamped firmly onto the backs of the blacks. It has taken a hundred years to struggle up from that level of cool-out to the miserable position that black Americans now find themselves in. Time is passing. The historical opportunity which world events now present to black Americans is running out with every tick of the clock.

This is the last act of the show. We are living in a time when the people of the world are making their final bid for full and complete freedom. Never before in history has this condition prevailed. Always before there have been more or less articulate and aware pockets of people, portions of classes, etc., but today's is an era of mass awareness, when the smallest man on the street is in rebellion against the system which has denied him life and which he has come to understand robs him of his dignity and self-respect. Yet he is being told that it will take time to get programs started, to pass legislation, to educate white people into accepting the idea that black people want and deserve freedom. But it is physically impossible to move as fast as the black man would like to move. Black men are deadly serious when they say FREEDOM NOW. Even if the white man wanted to eradicate all traces of evil overnight, he would not be able to do it because the economic and political system will not permit it. All talk about going too fast is treasonous to the black man's future.

What the white man must be brought to understand is that the black man in America today is fully aware of his position, and he does not intend to be tricked again into another hundred-year forfeit of freedom. Not for a single moment or for any price will the black men now rising up in America settle for anything less than their full proportionate share and participation in the sovereignty of America. The black man has already come to a realization that to be free it is necessary for him to throw his life—everything—on the line, because the oppressors refuse to understand that it is now impossible for them to come up with another trick to squelch the black revolution. The black man can't afford to take a chance. He can't afford to put things off. He must stop the whole show *NOW* and get his business straight, because if he does not do it now, if he fails to grasp securely the reins of this historic opportunity, there may be no tomorrow for him.

The black man's interest lies in seeing a free and independent Vietnam, a strong Vietnam which is not the puppet of international white supremacy. If the nations of Asia, Latin America, and Africa are strong and free, the black man in America will be safe and secure and free to live in dignity and self-respect. It is a cold fact that while the nations of Africa, Asia, and Latin America were shackled in colonial bondage, the black American was held tightly in the vise of oppression and not permitted to utter a sound of protest of any effect. But when these nations started bidding for their freedom, it was then that black Americans were able to seize the chance; it was then that the white man yielded what little he did—out of sheer necessity. The only lasting salvation for the black American is to do all he can to see to it that the African, Asian, and Latin American nations are free and independent.

In this regard, black Americans have a big role to play. They are a Black Trojan Horse within white America and they number in excess of 23,000,000 strong. That is a lot of strength. But it is a lot of weakness if it is disorganized and at odds with itself. Right now it is deplorably disorganized, and the overriding need is for unity and organization. Unity is on all black lips. Today we stand on the verge of sweeping change in this wretched landscape of a thousand little fragmented and ineffectual groups and organizations unable to work together for the common cause. *The need for one organization that will give one voice to the black man's common interest* is felt in every bone and fiber of black America.

Yesterday, after firmly repudiating racism and breaking his ties with the Black Muslim organization, the late Malcolm X launched a campaign to transform the American black man's struggle from the narrow plea for "civil rights" to the universal demand for human rights, with the ultimate aim of bringing the United States government to task before the United Nations. This, and the idea of the Organization of Afro-American Unity, was Malcolm's dying legacy to his people. It did not fall on barren ground. Already, black American leaders have met with the ambassadors of black Africa at a luncheon at UN headquarters. The meaning of this momentous event is lost on no one. The fact that it was the issue of Julian Bond, his denunciation of U.S. aggression in Vietnam, and the action of racist elements in the Georgia legislature which brought the leaders of black Africa and black America together is prophetic of an even clearer recognition by black men that their interests are also threatened by the U.S. war of suppression in Vietnam. This dovetailing of causes and issues is destined to bring to fruition the other dream which Malcolm's assassination prevented him from realizing—the Organization of Afro-American Unity, or perhaps a similar organization under a different name. Black Americans now realize that they must organize for the power to change the foreign and domestic policies of the U.S. government. They must let their voice be heard on these issues. They must let the world know where they stand.

It is no accident that the U.S. government is sending all those black troops to Vietnam. Some people think that America's point in sending 16 per cent black troops to Vietnam is to kill off the cream of black youth. But it has another important result. By turning her black troops into butchers of the Vietnamese people, America is spreading hate against the black race throughout Asia. Even black Africans find it hard not to hate black Americans for being so stupid as to allow themselves to be used to slaughter another people who are fighting to be free. Black Americans are considered to be the world's biggest fools to go to another country to fight for something they don't have for themselves.

It bothers white racists that people around the world love black Americans but find it impossible to give a similar warm affection to white Americans. The white racist knows that he is the Ugly American and he wants the black American to be Ugly, too, in the eyes of the world: misery loves company! When the people around the world cry "Yankee, Go Home!" they mean the white man, not the black man who is a recently freed slave. The white man is deliberately trying to make the people of the world turn against black Americans, because he knows that the day is coming when black Americans will need the help and support of their brothers, friends, and natural allies around the world. If through stupidity or by following hand-picked leaders who are the servile agents of the power structure, black Americans allow this strategy to succeed against them, then when the time comes and they need this help and support from around the world, it will not be there. All of the international love, respect, and goodwill that black Americans now have around the world will have dried up. They themselves will have buried it in the mud of the rice paddies of Vietnam.

Gwendolyn Brooks
Riot

A riot is the language of the unheard.
　　　　—Martin Luther King

John Cabot, out of Wilma, once a Wycliffe,
all whitebluerose below his golden hair,
wrapped richly in right linen and right wool,
almost forgot his Jaguar and Lake Bluff;
almost forgot Grandtully (which is The
Best Thing That Ever Happened To Scotch); almost
forgot the sculpture at the Richard Gray
and Distelheim; the kidney pie at Maxim's,
the Grenadine de Boeuf at Maison Henri.

Because the Negroes were coming down the street.

Because the Poor were sweaty and unpretty
(not like Two Dainty Negroes in Winnetka)
and they were coming toward him in rough ranks.
In seas. In windsweep. They were black and loud.
And not detainable. And not discreet.

Gross. Gross. *"Que tu es grossier!"* John Cabot
itched instantly beneath the nourished white
that told his story of glory to the World.
"Don't let It touch me! the blackness! Lord!" he whispered
to any handy angel in the sky.
But, in a thrilling announcement, on It drove
and breathed on him: and touched him. In that breath
the fume of pig foot, chitterling and cheap chili,
malign, mocked John. And, in terrific touch, old
averted doubt jerked forward decently,
cried "Cabot! John! You are a desperate man,
and the desperate die expensively today."

John Cabot went down in the smoke and fire
and broken glass and blood, and he cried "Lord!
Forgive these nigguhs that know not what they do."

Mari Evans

I Am a Black Woman

I am a black woman
the music of my song
some sweet arpeggio of tears
is written in a minor key
and I
can be heard humming in the night
Can be heard
           humming
in the night.

I saw my mate leap screaming to the sea
and I/with these hands/cupped the lifebreath
from my issue in the canebrake
I lost Nat's swinging body in a rain of tears
and heard my son scream all the way from Anzio
for Peace he never knew. . . . I
learned Da Nang and Pork Chop Hill
in anguish
Now my nostrils know the gas
and these trigger tire/d fingers
seek the softness in my warrior's beard

I
am a black woman
tall as a cypress
strong
beyond all definition still
defying place
and time
and circumstance
   assailed
      impervious
         indestructible
Look
  on me and be
renewed

Sam Greenlee
from *The Spook Who Sat by the Door*

12

It had been a harsh winter, with subzero temperatures a regular thing. There would be an occasional respite while the big, soft snow covered the city and for a short time covered the grime and dirt and ugliness of Chicago with its virginal whiteness, but within hours after the last flake fell, the virginal snow would be a greasy, dirt-grimed whorelike snow and then the temperature would drop and film the streets with mirrorlike glaze, turning the city snow into something that crunched underfoot like an old cereal in a new box labeled super and all-new. There was nothing super and all-new about Chicago and it is not a place for people who concern themselves with the weather, winter or summer. The wind would whip in from the lake, bearing airborne razors of ice that sliced the flesh. There were regular gray skies and little sun. The sky seemed to sit just above the Tribune Tower and it would sometimes descend to the city streets when the warm-air masses moved up across the plains from the Gulf of Mexico to turn the city into a fog-bound, slushy swamp full of mud-splattered people who groped their way in the dense muck, mire and moody low-sitting cloud, like amoebas in search of a guide to nowhere.

When there was sun, it would come from afar in a hazy, cloudless sky, giving a harsh, cold and biting light, the lack of clouds permitting what little warmth remained to flee toward the planets above, the people below creating little clouds of their own as they breathed and gasped, moving through the brutal city. Because the weather was so menacing, the Cobras were not missed from their usual haunts and there was no need to interrupt training by having some of the gang members on the block. It was too cold to be there and the police and social workers did not worry where they might be since the word was that the Cobras were no longer a bopping gang. And since lower-class Negroes are visible only when convenient or menacing, the Cobras disappeared and no one concerned themselves with what they might be doing that cold and forbidding winter.

They were learning the lessons of the oppressed throughout history in striking back at their oppressors; the linguistics of deception; subterfuge, to strike when least expected and then fade into the background; to hound, harass, worry and weaken the strong and whittle away at the strength and power that kept them where they were. Just before the rumble near the railroad tracks, the winter ended as abruptly as it had begun and spring was in Chicago with no warning, the flowers blooming, the trees suddenly budding, the grass turning green, the dirty snow melting and disappearing into the sewers. Spring meant baseball and track, walks in the parks for young lovers and examinations for the students reluctant to remain in the libraries and overheated apartments with textbooks that had become symbolic of the prison of a nasty Chicago winter.

It was time for examinations for Freeman's small band of revolutionaries-in-training. They were becoming restless with the constant drills, the routines; they wanted to "get it on." The rumble had convinced Freeman that they had not softened and that they could be counted on to follow orders. There were two more tests that were necessary and the change in weather permitted them.

Freeman continued to contribute to his playboy image; pretending to enjoy parties that bored him, dating women he did not like, flattering men he detested, doing and saying and acting things that sickened him. But there was never a hint that he was anything other than he appeared to be and those of his committed friends who were now active in the "movement" and who remembered Freeman as a tireless firebrand in the struggle for civil rights now regarded him with contempt as a hopeless sellout. They stopped asking him to attend meetings, contribute to their campaigns, man their picket lines or join their marches. They were his barometer and he judged his performance by their personal reaction to him. The women thought him an eligible bachelor, if a bit of a chaser. The men thought him harmless and appreciated that he did not try to steal their women; Freeman thought that there was little to choose from among the black middle-class chicks available and that risking the wrath of an insecure middle-class Negro, whose only available test of manhood was confined to the boundaries of his bed, was a waste of time and energy. Like Willy Loman, but for different reasons, it was important that Freeman be well liked, and he was.

He made speeches in the white suburbs concerning juvenile delinquency in the ghetto, as the executive director of his foundation. He knew that his speeches were intended for entertainment rather than enlightenment and he spiced them with the white man's statistics concerning Negro crime. He did not point out that Negro crime was largely confined to the ghetto, because he knew those nice white people wanted to feel threatened by the nasty Negroes in the ghettoes they never need see, except in the picture magazines, on television or when behind a mop, broom or tray. He was urbane, witty and fake-informative.

His Lotus was known over most of the South Side and although he had to put on its hardtop so as not to muss the hair or wigs of his dates, he enjoyed it very much, as much as any part of his cover. He cultivated the police and politicians and the members of his board of directors. Freeman was constantly pointed out as an example of what a Negro could accomplish if he tried hard enough. He was considered an example of Negro progress and no one concerned themselves with the increasing unemployment in the ghetto, the fact that Negroes continued to fall behind in national economic statistics. Freeman was a good salve for the nonexistent conscience of the white man; that vacuum the editorials spoke of as having been aroused by the "Negro Revolt." Freeman told them what they wanted to hear and was just argumentative enough in cocktail parties to have whites refer to him as "militant, but responsible." Freeman was the best Tom in town. His cover was as good as it ever figured to be and would probably not be blown before he could get his program under way. It was time to begin. He gathered his lieutenants at his apartment, plus a few other members of the Cobras, including Pretty Willie Du Bois.

"This summer is the scene, but we need a few things first; most of all bread. We been building up the war chest with what we been stealing, plus whatever we make peddling shit in New York, but we don't have near enough. Sugar Hips, how we stand?"

"We got a balance of $8432.86."

"Right. That ain't enough for what we have to do, so we have to get more. We take it from whitey and we get it from where he keeps it." Freeman spread plans on his cocktail table. "These are the floor plans for the bank in the shopping center on 115th and Halstead. We ought to be able to get a bit more than a hundred thousand dollars. They have a closed-circuit TV and automatic cameras, plus a very sophisticated alarm system. When they touch it off, it alerts the nearest precinct station, but makes no noise.

"There are only two guards, one on the floor, the other on a balcony above, behind one-way, bulletproof glass, with ports for firing to the floor below, but we hit the bank when it's crowded and he won't be able to fire for fear of hitting some innocent bystander. The only tight moment is when you move out and he might get a clear shot as you go through the door, but you'll move to the door with a couple of people as a shield, then shove them back in and make it. He'll be able to hear you up there and make it clear that if he starts firing at any time, you start wasting the crowd.

"It's a short hop to the Negro section in Princeton Park and since it's all middle-class nice, the cops are not likely to search it. That's where we hide out, in the house of Pretty Willie's mother, who's in New Orleans for the Mardi Gras. Besides, they're not going to be looking for niggers, anyway, but for white men."

They looked at him with curiosity. He drained his bottle of Carlsberg before he spoke.

"Pretty Willie leads it. He takes Red Beans, Benny Rooster, Po' Monty and Pussy Head."

They looked at one another and smiled, except Pretty Willie. Freeman had named the lightest-colored members of the Cobras.

"No, goddamnit; I ain't white, I'm a nigger," said Willie.

"Sure, baby, we know that, but that day whitey is going to think you're white. They'll be looking for everybody except us. Niggers don't rob banks, man, you know that. With a gun in your hand, telling Mr. Charlie what to do, to give you his money, why, man, you got to be white," said Dean.

"Look, baby, you know we need the bread and you know none of the rest of us can do it. They must not have more than twenty niggers with accounts there and if five walk in at the same time, they're going to be suspicious. You the only one in the gang can do it because, although your soul is black, your skin is white," added Scott.

"No!" said Willie.

"Man," said Stud. "Don't you see how beautiful it is? I mean, you're turning him around. We all know you a nigger and so does whitey when you on the block with your skinny-brim hat, hangin' out with the cats. He never treat you any different from the rest of us, 'cause you ain't black? Hell no, he gives you a harder time. Now, you got a chance to turn it around."

"No."

Dean spoke up. "Turk, give us a chance to talk about it. Willie, you don't have to do it if you don't want to." He looked at Freeman for confirmation. Freeman nodded. "And, nobody going to put you down if you don't." He swept the room with hard eyes. "We all know you hung-up 'bout not being black, just like some hung-up 'cause they is black. So come on down to the poolroom and we talk about it a little. You don't want to do it, you don't do it and we do it some other way. OK, Turk?" Freeman nodded again. "Crazy, let's split. Stud, you go see your ol' lady, 'cause you might get bugged and want to get physical and there ain't going to be no shit like that, dig. 'Sides, I ain't sure you could whip Pretty Willie, anyway."

They all laughed and relaxed, including Willie and Stud. They were both good enough not to have to worry about the difference. They finished the beer, took the bottles into the kitchen and filed out.

Three days later Freeman received a call from Dean.

"Turk, it all right. Pretty Willie do it. Funny thing, he kind of happy 'bout it now. Never seen the cat smile so much."

"OK, come on by tonight. We'll need about two weeks to get it down pat and it will have to be before the weather turns good. The worse, the better."

It only took them ten days of coaching to get the details right, but a warm-air mass moved up from the Gulf and turned Chicago into a muddy, messy swamp of slush and snow that would freeze at night in the grotesque shapes that had been molded by tires during the day. They waited a week before the snow came again and then the temperature dropped swiftly one moonless night, hovering around zero and turning the icy streets into a glassy surface that sent cars spinning if braked too suddenly. The sky was a slate gray the next morning, seeming to hover just above the rooftops, heavy and leaden, threatening to fall on the ugly city below.

They left for the shopping center at noon, by separate routes, and by that time the temperature had risen and a fine wind-blown snow slanted to cover the icy streets. Freeman drove a Mini-Minor with Scandinavian ice tires on the front wheels, the front-wheel drive gripping the ice firmly. It was modified to serve as a delivery truck for a small dry cleaner's, whose owner ate lunch at home and napped afterward. They had timed him and he never returned to work before three in the afternoon. They had stolen the car and changed the front tires. Freeman drove alone into the big parking lot not more than a hundred yards from the bank. The others arrived in a Willys station wagon, its four-wheel drive giving it stability on the icy streets. Freeman watched as they approached the bank separately. He could see into the bank through the big glass doors. There were about three dozen people inside, other than the employees. Not many, but enough.

He watched Pretty Willie walk in last and without hesitation pull his gun. Mouths opened to scream and shout, but no sound reached Freeman outside. They had been lucky and one of the guards was at lunch. The other reached for his gun and Willie dropped him with a bullet in the thigh. Monty was the closest to the guard; he kicked his gun away and then kicked him in the head until he lay quiet. Two of the others vaulted the cashier's counter and began stuffing money into canvas laundry bags. Willie watched the ports above for the sign of a gun barrel, unaware that the guard was absent. No one else moved. First Pussy Head, then Rooster moved from around the counter, bags full of money in each hand. Freeman started the car and wheeled swiftly in front of the bank, the back of the small truck toward the doors. They moved out of the bank and into the truck and Freeman drove off quickly. Dean, across the street and using the hood of the Willys wagon as a gun rest, fired a deer rifle with scope sights high into the glass doors, pinning the occupants to the floor. He emptied the chamber and got into the truck, following the Mini north on Halsted. Freeman drove to Ninety-fifth and turned east, coming to rest in front of Willie's house after zigzagging to it from five blocks away. They moved swiftly into the house with the money and he drove away and left the car in a residential neighborhood and was picked up by Stud Davis in another car. They had left the stolen Mini in a white neighborhood.

In fifteen minutes Freeman was home sipping twelve-year-old scotch, waiting for the bathtub to fill with very hot water.

Later that evening he watched the news on television and heard the announcer describe the daring daylight robbery of the bank. They were all listed as Caucasian in the police description of the bandits. Freeman smiled. A nigger with a gun in a bank with a lot of money had to be white because niggers snatched purses and rolled drunks—any cop could tell you that—they just didn't rob banks.

Freeman now had an army and a treasury. He needed an arsenal and he knew where he could get that. Then he could start messing with white folks.

Spring came early as if in apology for the fierce winter, the sun bright in pale blue skies, fat white clouds floating overhead, the ore boats moving lazily to the steel mills at the lake's southern tip. The buds burst, the city turned green, and the grime did not seem so noticeable, the noise of the El not so annoying, the stench of the fumes from the buses not so poisonous. For a few days in spring and fall Chicago seems almost fit for human habitation.

Baseballs, footballs, basketballs filled the air in the ghetto, the spherical symbols of a possible escape from the ghetto cage. The junkies stood and sat in the warm sun, their dope-filled blood moving sluggishly in their veins, the ugly world taking on a warm glow, everything soft and pretty prior to their moving through the streets at night looking for loot to support their habit. The winos drank their sweet wine beneath the El tracks, their hoarse voices rising with laughter as the sweet alcohol filled them; the unemployed who still stubbornly hoped were in the Loop and at the factories on the periphery of the city looking for jobs that did not exist; their more realistic black brothers stood and joked in front of the poolrooms, sat in front of countless TV sets in countless bars or drank beer from quart bottles in paper bags. The squad cars moved slowly through the ghetto, stopping here and there to collect their graft. Whores arose, dressed and moved into the unfamiliar sunlight toward a restaurant and late afternoon breakfast. Whites moved through the ghetto like maggots on a carcass: cops, social workers, schoolteachers, bill collectors, the supervisors and collectors of the syndicate, the owners of taverns, furniture stores, currency exchanges, television stores. The ghetto moved into the streets—from the hovels where they had huddled during the winter—where they would stay until the Chicago cold forced them to return to their small smelly rooms for another winter.

They moved through Washington Park on a cool moonless night toward the big National Guard Armory that stood on Cottage Grove Avenue on the Park side. Freeman led two strike teams of five each, Stud Davis in charge of one, Pretty Willie heading the second, Dean as Freeman's second-in-command. There was a wire fence separating the armory from the park. They scaled the fence easily. Freeman motioned to Stud, and Davis and three others moved silently toward the bored guard. There would be two guards walking the armory perimeter and four more inside for relief. They were regular army, their commander a master sergeant who drove home to Winnetka along the outer drive each night. The first heard nothing, right up until the time he was grabbed from behind and borne to the ground by Stud. The second turned his head before he was hit, but had no time to yell. The rest were simply locked in the guardroom, bound and gagged after being confronted by the silent men with their faces covered by nylon stockings.

Freeman forced the lock on the room holding the arms. He had chosen this armory because it was a white unit in the segregated Illinois guard and they figured to have more modern equipment than in either of the Negro armories. He found that they were in luck and in addition to M-1's there were grease guns, pistols, M-14 and M-16 rifles and several thousand rounds of ammunition for the weapons. He moved quickly through the storeroom, selecting the weapons they would use: grease guns, Colt .45 automatics and ammunition for both fragmentation, smoke and tear-gas grenades, grenade launchers, gas masks, four Spring-field .03 sniper rifles with scopes and ammo for them, eight bazookas and rockets. He was disappointed to find no plastic explosives, only TNT and detonators, but it was better than nothing.

He moved through the room, indicating what should be moved into the yard outside the armory. He chose a grease gun, slipped a full magazine into it, jacked a round into the chamber and slipped the safety on. He waited outside, the gun at the ready while his men moved the arms and ammunition. The empty green and white CTA bus blinked its lights two blocks away and he motioned to Pretty Willie to open the gates on the Cottage Grove side of the building.

The bus was driven by a Cobra. It took less than twenty minutes to load the bus and since a CTA garage was less than three blocks south of the armory on Cottage Grove, no one thought it strange to see an empty bus on the street. Within an hour, the arms and ammunition were cached and Freeman was ready. He need only wait for the hot, humid summer and an arrogant, head-whipping cop to spark the riots. It was like waiting for the sun to shine in the Sahara Desert. Freeman did not think that there would be much searching of the ghetto for the arms because niggers didn't steal government property and defy the FBI any more than they robbed banks.

Maya Angelou

from *I Know Why the Caged Bird Sings*

19

The last inch of space was filled, yet people continued to wedge themselves along the walls of the Store. Uncle Willie had turned the radio up to its last notch so that youngsters on the porch wouldn't miss a word. Women sat on kitchen chairs, dining-room chairs, stools and upturned wooden boxes. Small children and babies perched on every lap available and men leaned on the shelves or on each other.

The apprehensive mood was shot through with shafts of gaiety, as a black sky is streaked with lightning.

"I ain't worried 'bout this fight. Joe's gonna whip that cracker like it's open season."

"He gone whip him till that white boy call him Momma."

At last the talking was finished and the string-along songs about razor blades were over and the fight began.

"A quick jab to the head." In the Store the crowd grunted. "A left to the head and a right and another left." One of the listeners cackled like a hen and was quieted.

"They're in a clench, Louis is trying to fight his way out."

Some bitter comedian on the porch said, "That white man don't mind hugging that niggah now, I betcha."

"The referee is moving in to break them up, but Louis finally pushed the contender away and it's an uppercut to the chin. The contender is hanging on, now he's backing away. Louis catches him with a short left to the jaw."

A tide of murmuring assent poured out the doors and into the yard.

"Another left and another left. Louis is saving that mighty right..." The mutter in the Store had grown into a baby roar and it was pierced by the clang of a bell and the announcer's "That's the bell for round three, ladies and gentlemen."

As I pushed my way into the Store I wondered if the announcer gave any thought to the fact that he was addressing as "ladies and gentlemen" all the Negroes around the world who sat sweating and praying, glued to their "master's voice."

There were only a few calls for R. C. Colas, Dr. Peppers, and Hire's root beer. The real festivities would begin after the fight. Then even the old Christian ladies who taught their children and tried themselves to practice turning the other cheek would buy soft drinks, and if the Brown Bomber's victory was a particularly bloody one they would order peanut patties and Baby Ruths also.

Bailey and I lay the coins on top of the cash register. Uncle Willie didn't allow us to ring up sales during a fight. It was too noisy and might shake up the atmosphere. When the gong rang for the next round we pushed through the near-sacred quiet to the herd of children outside.

"He's got Louis against the ropes and now it's a left to the body and a right to the ribs. Another right to the body, it looks like it was low ... Yes, ladies and gentlemen, the referee is signaling but the contender keeps raining the blows on Louis. It's another to the body, and it looks like Louis is going down."

My race groaned. It was our people falling. It was another lynching, yet another Black man hanging on a tree. One more woman ambushed and raped. A Black boy whipped and maimed. It was hounds on the trail of a man running through slimy swamps. It was a white woman slapping her maid for being forgetful.

The men in the Store stood away from the walls and at attention. Women greedily clutched the babes on their laps while on the porch the shufflings and smiles, flirtings and pinching of a few minutes before were gone. This might be the end of the world. If Joe lost we were back in slavery and beyond help. It would all be true, the accusations that we were lower types of human beings. Only a little higher than the apes. True that we were stupid and ugly and lazy and dirty and, unlucky and worst of all, that God Himself hated us and ordained us to be hewers of wood and drawers of water, forever and ever, world without end.

We didn't breathe. We didn't hope. We waited.

"He's off the ropes, ladies and gentlemen. He's moving towards the center of the ring." There was no time to be relieved. The worst might still happen.

"And now it looks like Joe is mad. He's caught Carnera with a left hook to the head and a right to the head. It's a left jab to the body and another left to the head. There's a left cross and a right to the head. The contender's right eye is bleeding and he can't seem to keep his block up. Louis is penetrating every block. The referee is moving in, but Louis sends a left to the body and it's the uppercut to the chin and the contender is dropping. He's on the canvas, ladies and gentlemen."

Babies slid to the floor as women stood up and men leaned toward the radio.

"Here's the referee. He's counting. One, two, three, four, five, six, seven ... Is the contender trying to get up again?"

All the men in the store shouted, "NO."

"—eight, nine, ten." There were a few sounds from the audience, but they seemed to be holding themselves in against tremendous pressure.

"The fight is all over, ladies and gentlemen. Let's get the microphone over to the referee ... Here he is. He's got the Brown Bomber's hand, he's holding it up ... Here he is ..."

Then the voice, husky and familiar, came to wash over us—"The winnah, and still heavyweight champeen of the world ... Joe Louis."

Champion of the world. A Black boy. Some Black mother's son. He was the strongest man in the world. People drank Coca-Colas like ambrosia and ate candy bars like Christmas. Some of the men went behind the Store and poured white lightning in their soft-drink bottles, and a few of the bigger boys followed them. Those who were not chased away came back blowing their breath in front of themselves like proud smokers.

It would take an hour or more before the people would leave the Store and head for home. Those who lived too far had made arrangements to stay in town. It wouldn't do for a Black man and his family to be caught on a lonely country road on a night when Joe Louis had proved that we were the strongest people in the world.

Bobby Seale
from *Seize the Time*

THE PANTHER PROGRAM

One day Huey said, "It's about time we get the organization off the ground, and do it now."

This was in the latter part of September 1966. From around the first of October to the fifteenth of October, in the poverty center in North Oakland, Huey and I began to write out a ten-point platform and program of the Black Panther Party. Huey himself articulated it word for word. All I made were suggestions.

Huey said, "We need a program. We have to have a program for the people. A program that relates to the people. A program that the people can understand. A program that the people can read and see, and which expresses their desires and needs at the same time. It's got to relate to the philosophical meaning of where in the world we are going, but the philosophical meaning will also have to relate to something specific."

That was very important with Huey. So, Huey divided it up into "What We Want" and "What We Believe." "What We Want" are the practical, specific things that we need and that should exist. At the same time, we expressed philosophically, but concretely, what we believe. So we read the program one to one. Point One of "What We Want" and Point One of "What We Believe." Point Two of "What We Want" and Point Two of "What We Believe." This is the way the people should look at it. It puts together concisely all the physical needs and all the philosophical principles in some basic instructive thing that they can understand, instead of a bunch of esoteric bullshit.

I don't care what kind of cat is on the block—if he doesn't relate to anything else, he can relate to the ten-point platform and program of the Black Panther Party.

Huey said, "Black people and especially brothers on the block have to have some political consciousness."

We wrote it out and Melvin Newton, Huey's brother, came over and proofed it for corrections in grammar. We put it together, and we took all the paper we needed out of the poverty program supplies late at night at the poverty office. We were writing out the ten-point platform and program inside the back office.

Huey said, "Now, what's the first thing we want?" And Huey answered his own question. "WE WANT FREEDOM."

And I wrote down, "We want freedom."

Then he said, "We want the power to determine the destiny of our black community."

I said, "Right, brother, that's good. What's the next thing?"

"We want full employment for our people."

"What else?"

"Nothing else."

"OK, brother, right."

I thought about it and he was right. That's what we want. We want full employment for our people. This is a basic program for our people, because the people are going to relate to the fact that this is exactly what they want and they ain't going to settle for nothing else—they ain't going to settle for a bunch of esoteric bullshit and a long essay.

Then Huey said, "We want the white racist businessman to end the robbery and exploitation of the black community." So, we wrote that down.

Then we wrote, "We want decent housing, fit for shelter of human beings."

"What else, brother Huey?"

Huey sat there and he thought for a few shakes. He said, "Now we got to get off into the area of education. I think that's important. We got employment, the power of our own community, and decent housing. Now we want decent education that teaches us about the true nature of this decadent American system, and education that teaches us about our true history and our role in present-day society."

After that he went right into, "We want all black men to be exempt from military service."

That's the way we put it. We didn't have to go into anything else because we knew that the black people on the block would understand and that's what we want. Basically nothing else.

Then Huey said, "Look at the racist power structure. We have to deal with that. We have to understand that we want an immediate end to police brutality and murder of black people."

I wrote that exactly like it was.

Huey went on to the next one. "We want all black men and women to be released from the federal, county, state, and city jails and prisons."

I said, "Right," and wrote that down.

Then brother Huey said, "We want every black man brought to trial to be tried in a court by a jury of his peer group as it is defined by the Constitution of this United States."

For a black man this means people from the black community.

Then Huey said, "Let's summarize these points. We want land, we want bread, we want housing, we want education, we want clothing, we want justice, and we want some peace."

That's the way Huey put it and I wrote it down. We went over the ten points and put in our commas and periods, and then we got into "What We Believe." We went through everything we believed that was correlative to everything that we wanted.

Huey said, "This ten-point platform and program is what we want and what we believe. These things did not just come out of the clear blue sky. This is what black people have been voicing all along for over 100 years since the Emancipation Proclamation and even before that. These things are directly related to the things we had before we left Africa."

When we got all through writing the program, Huey said, "We've got to have some kind of structure. What do you want to be," he asked me, "Chairman or Minister of Defense?"

"Doesn't make any difference to me," I said. "What do you want to be, Chairman or Minister of Defense?"

"I'll be the Minister of Defense," Huey said, "and you'll be the Chairman."

"That's fine with me," I told him, and that's just the way that shit came about, how Huey became the Minister of Defense and I became the Chairman of the Black Panther Party. Just like that.

With the ten-point platform and program and the two of us, the Party was officially launched on October 15, 1966, in a poverty program office in the black community in Oakland, California.

We got my wife and Huey's girl friend La Verne together, and they typed it out for us on stencils inside that poverty program office. The next night we took them and we ran off over a thousand copies of that ten-point platform and program.

Huey said, "The brothers and sisters have to relate to this because this is what they want. This is what they've told me. This is what they've told every other leader in this country."

You always have to understand that Huey understood the difference between reform and revolution. Huey understood that you answer the momentary desires and needs of the people, that you try to instruct them and politically educate them, that these are their basic political desires and needs, and from the people themselves will rage a revolution to make sure that they have these basic desires and needs fulfilled.

That's what Huey P. Newton put forth, and that's what Huey P. Newton understood to be political, and that's what Huey P. Newton understood to be the reason why people who are oppressed will wage a revolution. That's what I remember, that's what I know, that's what I feel, and that's what I'll never forget about Huey. He never forgot about the people. He'd bring it right down to the food, and the bread and employment, decent housing, decent education—the way the motherfuckers, the President, and all, fucked over us in the military service; the pigs, the murder, and brutality; the courts; the brothers who are in jail, how they had to be released.

While he was in jail, a year-and-a-half later, Huey said to add something to Point Ten. He was reading brother Eldridge Cleaver's thing about a black plebiscite in the United States conducted by the United Nations (which is di-rectly related to what Malcolm X said). Huey related not to the personality alone of Malcolm, or Mao Tse Tung, or Fanon. He related to what all these revolutionary leaders of the world said we must do, what we must establish, what we must institutionalize. That's very important. This is the way the pro-gram was written. Huey always had the people's desires and political needs in mind. He always had the revolutionary tactics and the revolutionary means in mind as to how the people must go about getting these things, getting these basic desires and needs.

This is where the shit boils down to—to what the people want and not what some intellectual personally wants or some cultural nationalists, like LeRoi Jones, want, or some jive-ass underground RAM motherfucker wants, or what some jive motherfucker in some college studying bullshit says, talking es-oteric shit about the basic social-economic structure, and the adverse condi-tions that we're subjected to so that no black man even understands. Huey was talking about some full employment, some decent housing, some education, about stopping those pigs from brutalizing us and murdering us.

Then Huey came on the street with some guns. About a month and a half after this program was written, Huey P. Newton tried to tell the intellectuals that it's time, it's time to go forth in the revolutionary struggle. That it's no time to be bullshitting. "Pick up some guns and don't be bullshitting." Huey wanted brothers off the block—brothers who had been out there robbing banks, brothers who had been pimping, brothers who had been peddling dope, brothers who ain't gonna take no shit, brothers who had been fighting pigs—because he knew that once they get themselves together in the area of political education (and it doesn't take much because the political education is the ten-point platform and program), Huey P. Newton knew that once you organize the brothers he ran with, he fought with, he fought against, who he fought harder than they fought him, once you organize those brothers, you get niggers, you get black men, you get revolutionaries who are too much.

We went off into this ten-point platform and Huey went forth to take a pulse beat of the black community, using Oakland, California where there's nearly 40 percent blacks and as a black community typical of any other in this nation. I don't give a damn if a black brother's in the South because we have brothers from the South all the way up here in Oakland, and we have brothers from New York, brothers from Chicago, what have you. Huey understood that Oakland was a typical black community, so we took the ten-point platform and program—a thousand copies of it—and went to the black community with them. He didn't just pass out the platform in people's hands. He stopped, talked, and discussed the points on the ten-point platform with all the black brothers and sisters off the block, and with mothers who had been scrubbing Miss Ann's kitchen. We talked to brothers and sisters in colleges, in high schools, who were on parole, on probation, who'd been in jails, who'd just got-ten out of jail, and brothers and sisters who looked like they were on their way to jail. They would cite cases. Huey was always interested in any kind of case anyone who looked like he was going to jail had inside of the courts. Huey was always interested in that. Huey would talk about this brother possibly being railroaded off into jail or prison. Huey knew this because he experienced it and because he understood the brother's predicament in terms of the power structure railroading him there.

So, we had a thousand copies of the ten-point platform and program being circulated through the black community by myself and Huey P. Newton. Little Bobby Hutton came along, and for one-and-a-half months, Bobby stuck with me and Huey, helping us articulate this ten-point platform and program, and the fact that we have to arm ourselves against these pigs who've been murdering us and brutalizing us, how we have to arm ourselves against these racists, Birchites, and Ku Klux Klaners infested in the police departments, the pig departments who "occupy our communities," as Huey P. Newton says, "like a foreign troop." We have to defend ourselves against them because they are breaking down our doors, shooting black brothers on the streets, and brutalizing sisters on the head. They are wearing guns mostly to intimidate the people from forming organizations to really get our basic political desires and needs answered. The power structure uses the facist police against people moving for freedom and liberation. It keeps our people divided, but the program will be what we unite the people around and to teach our people self-defense.

When we started passing the platform around the poverty center there, they'd ask, "Why do you want to be a vicious animal like a panther?"

Huey would break in. "The nature of a panther is that he never attacks. But if anyone attacks him or backs him into a corner, the panther comes up to wipe that aggressor or that attacker out, absolutely, resolutely, wholly, thoroughly, and completely." They didn't *want* to understand that.

Here is the ten-point platform and program as it appears each week in our paper:

OCTOBER 1966

BLACK PANTHER PARTY
PLATFORM AND PROGRAM

WHAT WE WANT
WHAT WE BELIEVE

1. We want freedom. We want power to determine the destiny of our Black Community.

We believe that black people will not be free until we are able to determine our destiny.

2. We want full employment for our people.

We believe that the federal government is responsible and obligated to give every man employment or a guaranteed income. We believe that if the white American businessmen will not give full employment, then the means of production should be taken from the businessmen and placed in the community so that the people of the community can organize and employ all of its people and give a high standard of living.

3. We want an end to the robbery by the white man of our Black Community.

We believe that this racist government has robbed us and now we are demanding the overdue debt of forty acres and two mules. Forty acres and two mules was promised 100 years ago as restitution for slave labor and mass murder of black people. We will accept the payment in currency which will be distributed to our many communities. The Germans are now aiding the Jews in Israel for the genocide of the Jewish people. The Germans murdered six million Jews. The American racist has taken part in the slaughter of over fifty million black people; therefore, we feel that this is a modest demand that we make.

4. We want decent housing, fit for shelter of human beings.

We believe that if the white landlords will not give decent housing to our black community, then the housing and the land should be made into cooperatives so that our community, with government aid, can build and make decent housing for its people.

5. We want education for our people that exposes the true nature of this decadent American society. We want education that teaches us our true history and our role in the present-day society.

We believe in an educational system that will give to our people a knowledge of self. If a man does not have knowledge of himself and his position in society and the world, then he has little chance to relate to anything else.

6. We want all black men to be exempt from military service.

We believe that black people should not be forced to fight in the military service to defend a racist government that does not protect us. We will not fight and kill other people of color in the world who, like black people, are being victimized by the white racist government of America. We will protect ourselves from the force and violence of the racist police and the racist military, by whatever means necessary.

7. We want an immediate end to POLICE BRUTALITY and MURDER of black people.

We believe we can end police brutality in our black community by organizing black self-defense groups that are dedicated to defending our black community from racist police oppression and brutality. The Second Amendment to the Constitution of the United States gives a right to bear arms. We therefore believe that all black people should arm themselves for self-defense.

8. We want freedom for all black men held in federal, state, county and city prisons and jails.

We believe that all black people should be released from the many jails and prisons because they have not received a fair and impartial trial.

9. *We want all black people when brought to trial to be tried in court by a jury of their peer group or people from their black communities, as defined by the Constitution of the United States.*

We believe that the courts should follow the United States Constitution so that black people will receive fair trials. The Fourteenth Amendment of the U.S. Constitution gives a man a right to be tried by his peer group. A peer is a person from a similar economic, social, religious, geographical, environmental, historical, and racial background. To do this the court will be forced to select a jury from the black community from which the black defendant came. We have been and are being tried by all-white juries that have no understanding of the "average reasoning man" of the black community.

10. *We want land, bread, housing, education, clothing, justice, and peace. And as our major political objective, a United Nations-supervised plebiscite to be held throughout the black colony in which only black colonial subjects will be allowed to participate, for the purpose of determining the will of black people as to their national destiny.*

When, in the course of human events, it becomes necessary for one people to dissolve the political bands which have connected them with another, and to assume, among the powers of the earth, the separate and equal station to which the laws of nature and nature's God entitle them, a decent respect to the opinions of mankind requires that they should declare the causes which impel them to the separation.

We hold these truths to be self-evident, that all men are created equal; that they are endowed by their Creator with certain unalienable rights; that among these are life, liberty, and the pursuit of happiness. That, to secure these rights, governments are instituted among men, deriving their just powers from the consent of the governed; that, whenever any form of government becomes destructive of these ends, it is the right of the people to alter or to abolish it, and to institute a new government, laying its foundation on such principles, and organizing its powers in such form, as to them shall seem most likely to effect their safety and happiness. Prudence, indeed, will dictate that governments long established should not be changed for light and transient causes; and, accordingly, all experience hath shown, that mankind are more disposed to suffer, while evils are sufferable, than to right themselves by abolishing the forms to which they are accustomed. But, when a long train of abuses and usurpations, pursuing invariably the same object, evinces a design to reduce them under absolute despotism, it is their right, it is their duty, to throw off such government, and to provide new guards for their future security.

WHY WE ARE NOT RACISTS

The Black Panther Party is not a black racist organization, not a racist organization at all. We understand where racism comes from. Our Minister of Defense, Huey P. Newton, has taught us to understand that we have to oppose all kinds of racism. The Party understands the imbedded racism in a large part of white America and it understands that the very small cults that sprout up every now and then in the black community have a basically black racist philosophy.

The Black Panther Party would not stoop to the low, scurvy level of a Ku Klux Klansman, a white supremacist, or the so-called "patriotic" white citizens organizations, which hate black people because of the color of their skin. Even though some white citizens organizations will stand up and say, "Oh, we don't hate black people. It's just that we're not gonna let black people do this, and we're not gonna let black people do that." This is scurvy demagoguery, and the basis of it is the old racism of tabooing everything, and especially of tabooing the body. The black man's mind was stripped by the social environment, by the decadent social environment he was subjected to in slavery and in the years after the so-called Emancipation Proclamation. Black people, brown people, Chinese people, and Vietnamese people are called gooks, spicks, niggers, and other derogatory names.

What the Black Panther Party has done in essence is to call for an alliance and coalition with all of the people and organizations who want to move against the power structure. It is the power structure who are the pigs and hogs, who have been robbing the people; the avaricious, demagogic ruling-class elite who move the pigs upon our heads and who order them to do so as a means of maintaining their same old exploitation.

In the days of worldwide capitalistic imperialism, with that imperialism also manifested right here in America against many different peoples, we find it necessary, as human beings, to oppose misconceptions of the day, like integration.

If people want to integrate—and I'm assuming they will fifty or 100 years from now—that's their business. But right now we have the problem of a ruling-class system that perpetuates racism and uses racism as a key to maintain its capitalistic exploitation. They use blacks, especially the blacks who come out of the colleges and the elite class system, because these blacks have a tendency to flock toward a black racism which is parallel to the racism the Ku Klux Klan or white citizens groups practice.

It's obvious that trying to fight fire with fire means there's going to be a lot of burning. The best way to fight fire is with water because water douses the fire. The water is the solidarity of the people's right to defend themselves together in opposition to a vicious monster. Whatever is good for the man, can't be good for us. Whatever is good for the capitalistic ruling-class system, can't be good for the masses of the people.

We, the Black Panther Party, see ourselves as a nation within a nation, but not for any racist reasons. We see it as a necessity for us to progress as human beings and live on the face of this earth along with other people. We do not fight racism with racism. We fight racism with solidarity. We do not fight exploitative capitalism with black capitalism. We fight capitalism with basic socialism. And we do not fight imperialism with more imperialism. We fight imperialism with proletarian internationalism. These principles are very functional for the Party. They're very practical, humanistic, and necessary. They should be understood by the masses of the people.

We don't use our guns, we have never used our guns to go into the white community to shoot up white people. We only defend ourselves against anybody, be they black, blue, green, or red, who attacks us unjustly and tries to murder us and kill us for implementing our programs. All in all, I think people can see from our past practice, that ours is not a racist organization but a very progressive revolutionary party.

Those who want to obscure the struggle with ethnic differences are the ones who are aiding and maintaining the exploitation of the masses of the people: poor whites, poor blacks, browns, red Indians, poor Chinese and Japanese, and the workers at large.

Racism and ethnic differences allow the power structure to exploit the masses of workers in this country, because that's the key by which they maintain their control. To divide the people and conquer them is the objective of the power structure. It's the ruling class, the very small minority, the few avaricious, demagogic hogs and rats who control and infest the government. The ruling class and their running dogs, their lackeys, their bootlickers, their Toms and their black racists, their cultural nationalists—they're all the running dogs of the ruling class. These are the ones who help to maintain and aid the power structure by perpetuating their racist attitudes and using racism as a means to divide the people. But it's really the small, minority ruling class that is dominating, exploiting, and oppressing the working and laboring people.

All of us are laboring-class people, employed or unemployed, and our unity has got to be based on the practical necessities of life, liberty, and the pursuit of happiness, if that means anything to anybody. It's got to be based on the practical things like the survival of people and people's right to self-determination, to iron out the problems that exist. So in essence it is not at all a race struggle. We're rapidly educating people to this. In our view it is a class struggle between the massive proletarian working class and the small, minority ruling class. Working-class people of all colors must unite against the exploitative, oppressive ruling class. So let me emphasize again—we believe our fight is a class struggle and not a race struggle.

Addison Gayle, Jr.
from *The Black Aesthetic*

CULTURAL STRANGULATION:
BLACK LITERATURE AND THE WHITE AESTHETIC

"This assumption that of all the hues of God, whiteness is inherently and obviously better than brownness or tan leads to curious acts. . . ."

W. E. B. DuBois

The expected opposition to the concept of a "Black Aesthetic" was not long in coming. In separate reviews of *Black Fire*, an anthology edited by LeRoi Jones and Larry Neal, critics from the Saturday Review and the New York Review of Books presented the expected rebuttal. Agreeing with Ralph Ellison that sociology and art are incompatible mates, these critics, nevertheless, invoked the cliches of the social ideology of the "we shall overcome" years in their attempt to steer Blacks from "the path of literary fantasy and folly."

Their major thesis is simple: There is no Black aesthetic because there is no white aesthetic. The Kerner Commission Report to the contrary, America is not two societies but one. Therefore, Americans of all races, colors and creeds share a common cultural heredity. This is to say that there is one predominant culture—the American culture—with tributary national and ethnic streams flowing into the larger river. Literature, the most important by-product of this cultural monolith, knows no parochial boundaries. To speak of a Black literature, a Black aesthetic, or a Black state, is to engage in racial chauvinism, separatist bias, and Black fantasy.

The question of a white aesthetic, however, is academic. One has neither to talk about it nor define it. Most Americans, black and white, accept the existence of a "White Aesthetic" as naturally as they accept April 15th as the deadline for paying their income tax—with far less animosity towards the former than the latter. The white aesthetic, despite the academic critics, has always been with us: for long before Diotima pointed out the way to heavenly beauty to Socrates, the poets of biblical times were discussing beauty in terms of light and dark—the essential characteristics of a white and black aesthetic—and establishing the dichotomy of superior *vs.* inferior which would assume body and form in the 18th century. Therefore, more serious than a definition, is the problem of tracing the white aesthetic from its early origins and afterwards, outlining the various changes in the basic formula from culture to culture and from nation to nation. Such an undertaking would be more germane to a book than an essay; nevertheless, one may take a certain starting point and, using selective nations and cultures, make the critical point, while calling attention to the necessity of a more comprehensive study encompassing all of the nations and cultures of the world.

Let us propose Greece as the logical starting point, bearing in mind Will Durant's observation that "all of Western Civilization is but a footnote to Plato," and take Plato as the first writer to attempt a systematic aesthetic. Two documents by Plato, *The Symposium* and *The Republic*, reveal the twin components of Plato's aesthetic system.

In *The Symposium*, Plato divides the universe into spheres. In one sphere, the lower, one finds the forms of beauty; in the other, the higher, beauty, as Diotima tells Socrates, is absolute and supreme. In *The Republic*, Plato defines the poet as an imitator (a third-rate imitator—a point which modern critics have long since forgotten) who reflects the heavenly beauty in the earthly mirror. In other words, the poet recreates beauty as it exists in heaven; thus the poet, as Neo-Platonists from Aquinas to Coleridge have told us, is the custodian of beauty on earth.

However, Plato defines beauty only in ambiguous, mystical terms; leaving the problem of a more circumscribed, secular definition to philosophers, poets, and critics. During most of the history of the Western world, these aestheticians have been white; therefore, it is not surprising that, symbolically and literally, they have defined beauty in terms of whiteness. (An early contradiction to this tendency is the Marquis DeSade who inverted the symbols, making black beautiful, but demonic, and white pure, but sterile—the Marquis is considered by modern criticism to have been mentally deranged.)

The distinction between whiteness as beautiful (good) and blackness as ugly (evil) appears early in the literature of the middle ages—in the Morality Plays of England. Heavily influenced by both Platonism and Christianity, these plays set forth the distinctions which exist today. To be white was to be pure, good, universal, and beautiful; to be black was to be impure, evil, parochial, and ugly.

The characters and the plots of these plays followed this basic format. The villain is always evil, in most cases the devil; the protagonist, or hero, is always good, in most cases, angels or disciples. The plot then is simple; good (light) triumphs over the forces of evil (dark). As English literature became more sophisticated, the symbols were made to cover wider areas of the human and literary experience. To love was divine; to hate, evil. The fancied mistress of Petrarch was the purest of the pure; Grendel's mother, a creature from the "lower regions and marshes," is, like her son, a monster; the "bad" characters in Chaucer's *Canterbury Tales* tell dark stories; and the Satan of *Paradise Lost* must be vanquished by Gabriel, the angel of purity.

These ancients, as Swift might have called them, established their dichotomies as a result of the influences of Neo-Platonism and Christianity.

Later, the symbols became internationalized. Robert Burton, in *The Anatomy of Melancholy*, writes of "dark despair" in the seventeenth century, and James Boswell describes melancholia, that state of mind common to intellectuals of the 17th and 18th centuries, as a dark, dreaded affliction which robbed men of their creative energies. This condition—dark despair or melancholia—was later popularized in what is referred to in English literature as its "dark period"—the period of the Grave Yard School of poets and the Gothic novels.

The symbols thus far were largely applied to conditions, although characters who symbolized evil influences were also dark. In the early stages of English literature, these characters were mythological and fictitious and not representative of people of specific racial or ethnic groups. In the 18th century English novel, however, the symbolism becomes ethnic and racial.

There were forerunners. As early as 1621, Shakespeare has Iago refer to Othello as that "old Black ewe," attaching the mystical sexual characteristic to blackness which would become the motive for centuries of oppressive acts by white Americans. In *The Tempest*, Shakespeare's last play, Caliban, though not ostensibly black, is nevertheless a distant cousin of the colonial Friday in Daniel Defoe's *Robinson Crusoe*.

Robinson Crusoe was published at a historically significant time. In the year 1719, the English had all but completed their colonization of Africa. The slave trade in America was on its way to becoming a booming industry; in Africa, Black people were enslaved mentally as well as physically by such strange bedfellows as criminals, businessmen, and Christians. In the social and political spheres, a rationale was needed, and help came from the artist—in this case, the novelist—in the form of *Robinson Crusoe*. In the novel, Defoe brings together both Christian and Platonic symbolism, sharpening the dichotomy between light and dark on the one hand, while on the other establishing a criterion for the inferiority of Black people as opposed to the superiority of white.

One need only compare Crusoe with Friday to validate both of these statements. Crusoe is majestic, wise, white and a colonialist; Friday is savage, ignorant, black and a colonial. Therefore, Crusoe, the colonialist, has a double task. On the one hand he must transform the island (Africa—unproductive, barren, dead) into a little England (prosperous, life-giving, fertile), and he must recreate Friday in his own image, thus bringing him as close to being an Englishman as possible. At the end of the novel, Crusoe has accomplished both undertakings; the island is a replica of "mother England"; and Friday has been transformed into a white man, now capable of immigrating to the land of the gods.

From such mystical artifacts has the literature and criticism of the Western world sprung; and based upon such narrow prejudices as those of Defoe, the art of Black people throughout the world has been described as parochial and inferior. Friday was parochial and inferior until, having denounced his own culture, he assimilated another. Once this was done, symbolically, Friday underwent a change. To deal with him after the conversion was to deal with him in terms of a character who had been civilized and therefore had moved beyond racial parochialism.

However, Defoe was merely a hack novelist, not a thinker. It was left to shrewder minds than his to apply the rules of the white aesthetic to the practical areas of the Black literary and social worlds, and no shrewder minds were at work on this problem than those of writers and critics in America. In America, the rationale for both slavery and the inferiority of Black art and culture was supplied boldly, without the trappings of 18th century symbolism.

In 1867, in a book entitled *Nojoque: A Question for a Continent*, Hinton Helper provided the vehicle for the cultural and social symbols of inferiority under which Blacks have labored in this country. Helper intended, as he states frankly in his preface, "to write the negro out of America." In the headings of the two major chapters of the book, the whole symbolic apparatus of the white aesthetic handed down from Plato to America is graphically revealed: the heading of one chapter reads: "Black: A Thing of Ugliness, Disease"; another heading reads: "White: A Thing of Life, Health, and Beauty."

Under the first heading, Helper argues that the color black "has always been associated with sinister things such as mourning, the devil, the darkness of night." Under the second, "White has always been associated with the light of day, divine transfiguration, the beneficent moon and stars...the fair complexion of romantic ladies, the costumes of Romans and angels, and the white of the American flag so beautifully combined with blue and red without ever a touch of the black that has been for the flag of pirates."

Such is the American critical ethic based upon centuries of distortion of the Platonic ideal. By not adequately defining beauty, and implying at least that this was the job of the poet, Plato laid the foundation for the white aesthetic as defined by Daniel Defoe and Hinton Helper. However, the uses of that aesthetic to stifle and strangle the cultures of other nations is not to be attributed to Plato, but, instead, to his hereditary brothers far from the Aegean. For Plato knew his poets. They were not, he surmised, a very trusting lot and, therefore, by adopting an ambiguous position on symbols, he limited their power in the realm of aesthetics. For Plato, there were two kinds of symbols: natural and proscriptive. Natural symbols corresponded to absolute beauty as created by God; proscriptive symbols, on the other hand, were symbols of beauty as proscribed by man, which is to say that certain symbols are said to mean such and such by man himself.

The irony of the trap in which the Black artist has found himself throughout history is apparent. Those symbols which govern his life and art are proscriptive ones, set down by minds as diseased as Hinton Helper's. In other words, beauty has been in the eyes of an earthly beholder who has stipulated that beauty conforms to such and such a definition. To return to Friday, Defoe stipulated that civilized man was what Friday had to become, proscribed certain characteristics to the term "civilized," and presto, Friday, in order not to be regarded as a "savage under Western eyes," was forced to conform to this ideal. How well have the same stipulative definitions worked in the artistic sphere! Masterpieces are made at will by each new critic who argues that the subject of his doctoral dissertation is immortal. At one period of history, John Donne, according to the critic Samuel Johnson, is a second rate poet; at another period, according to the critic T. S. Eliot, he is one of the finest poets in the language. Dickens, argues Professor Ada Nisbet, is one of England's most representative novelists, while for F. R. Leavis, Dickens' work does not warrant him a place in *The Great Tradition.*

When Black literature is the subject, the verbiage reaches the height of the ridiculous. The good "Negro Novel," we are told by Robert Bone and Herbert Hill, is that novel in which the subject matter moves beyond the limitations of narrow parochialism. Form is the most important criterion of the work of art when Black literature is evaluated, whereas form, almost non-existent in Dostoyevsky's *Crime and Punishment,* and totally chaotic in Kafka's *The Trial,* must take second place to the supremacy of thought and message.

Richard Wright, says Theodore Gross, is not a major American novelist; while Ralph Ellison, on the strength of one novel, is. LeRoi Jones is not a major poet, Ed Bullins not a major playwright, Baldwin incapable of handling the novel form—all because white critics have said so.

Behind the symbol is the object or vehicle, and behind the vehicle is the definition. It is the definition with which we are concerned, for the extent of the cultural strangulation of Black literature by white critics has been the extent to which they have been allowed to define the terms in which the Black artist will deal with his own experience. The career of Paul Laurence Dunbar is the most striking example. Having internalized the definitions handed him by the American society, Dunbar would rather not have written about the Black experience at all, and three of his novels and most of his poetry support this argument. However, when forced to do so by his white liberal mentors, among them was the powerful critic, William Dean Howells, Dunbar deals with Blacks in terms of buffoonery, idiocy and comedy.

Like so many Black writers, past and present, Dunbar was trapped by the definitions of other men, never capable of realizing until near the end of his life, that those definitions were not god-given, but man-given; and so circumscribed by tradition and culture that they were irrelevant to an evaluation of either his life or his art.

In a literary conflict involving Christianity, Zarathustra, Friedrich Nietzsche's iconoclast, calls for "a new table of the laws." In similar iconoclastic fashion, the proponents of a Black Aesthetic, the idol smashers of America, call for a set of rules by which Black literature and art is to be judged and evaluated. For the historic practice of bowing to other men's gods and definitions has produced a crisis of the highest magnitude, and brought us, culturally, to the limits of racial armageddon. The trend must be reversed.

The acceptance of the phrase "Black is Beautiful" is the first step in the destruction of the old table of the laws and the construction of new ones, for the phrase flies in the face of the whole ethos of the white aesthetic. This step must be followed by serious scholarship and hard work; and Black critics must dig beneath the phrase and unearth the treasure of beauty lying deep in the untoured regions of the Black experience—regions where others, due to historical conditioning and cultural deprivation, cannot go.

Lucille Clifton
the lost baby poem

the time i dropped your almost body down
down to meet the waters under the city
and run one with the sewage to the sea
what did i know about waters rushing back
what did i know about drowning
or being drowned

you would have been born into winter
in the year of the disconnected gas
and no car   we would have made the thin
walk over genesee hill into the canada wind
to watch you slip like ice into strangers' hands
you would have fallen naked as snow into winter
if you were here i could tell you these
and some other things

if i am ever less than a mountain
for your definite brothers and sisters
let the rivers pour over my head
let the sea take me for a spiller
of seas   let black men call me stranger
always   for your never named sake

later i'll say
i spent my life
loving a great man

later
my life will accuse me
of various treasons

not black enough
too black
eyes closed when they should have been open
eyes open when they should have been closed

will accuse me for unborn babies
and dead trees

later
when i defend again and again
with this love
my life will keep silent
listening to
my body breaking

Derrick Morrison
Black Liberation and the Coming American Socialist Revolution

THE COMBINED CHARACTER OF THE COMING AMERICAN REVOLUTION

Two events of supreme significance occurred in May 1954. Even though they occurred 10,000 miles apart, they were very much connected with one another. The two events represented the surfacing of three-fourths of humanity, a surfacing from the depths to which they had been relegated by European and North American imperialism. The first event occurred on May 7, 1954. On that day the Vietnam Doc Lap Dong Minh, better known as the Vietminh, defeated the French army at Dien Bien Phu. The victory at Dien Bien Phu represented the first time an imperialist army was single-handedly defeated by a colonized people. To be sure, there was the Korean War, which lasted from 1950 to 1953. But the decisive factor in Korea was the People's Republic of China. Had it not been for the intervention of the Chinese workers' state, the forces of imperialism, organized through the United Nations, would have overrun all of Korea.

At the same time, the Vietnamese victory at Dien Bien Phu registered the power of the national question on an international scale. The Vietnamese demonstrated, as had the Russians, Chinese, and North Koreans, that the demand of oppressed peoples for self-determination can only be fulfilled by a socialist revolution and the construction of a workers' state.

The other event of importance in May 1954 took place ten days after the Vietnamese victory at Dien Bien Phu. On May 17 the Supreme Court of the United States ruled that racial segregation in the public schools was illegal. This decision was a complete reversal of a decision handed down by the Supreme Court more than fifty years earlier. In 1896 the Supreme Court had declared that racial segregation in the public schools was lawful. At that time European and North American imperialism were in the process of subduing and subjugating the peoples of Africa, Asia, and Latin America. And since imperialism was militarily victorious everywhere, there was no respect, not even a semblance of respect, for the rights of Black, Brown, Red, or Yellow people.

This general attitude of disrespect, this general North American and European assumption that Third World people are not human beings but beasts of burden, plagued not only Africa, Asia, and Latin America, but also the descendants of Africans, Asians, and Latin Americans here in the United States. If the Black man and woman in Africa had no rights that white people were bound to respect, then it was no different with the Black man and woman in the United States. So in 1896 the Supreme Court denied the right of Black people to a decent education by allowing segregation in the public schools. This decision was part of a systematic campaign to reduce the Black man and woman to the position of noncitizenship.

But the whole system of racial suppression and oppression, better known as colonialism, began to crumble after a series of events in the twentieth century. The two world wars and the Russian, Chinese, and Eastern European revolutions had a crippling and damaging effect on the imperialist system. As the imperialist system declined, the fortunes of the colonized began to rise. They began to take their destinies into their own hands, challenging the right of imperialism to rule over them. This uprising of the colonized forced the imperialists to adopt new tactics, to recognize the right of formal independence in order to stop the drive toward real independence.

The impact of these new tactics inside the United States led to the removal of laws sanctioning the most overt forms of racial segregation. The intent of the United States government was to give the impression of freedom to the Black man and woman, but not the substance of freedom. And it is in this light, in the light of global public relations, that we can understand why the Supreme Court reversed itself and came out for an end to segregation in the public schools on May 17, 1954.

Even though this decision was intended to give only the impression of equal rights for the Black man and woman, Black people took it to mean that the government was finally going to do something about their segregated condition. Black people took it to mean that the government was finally going to grant them some social, economic, and political mobility. This was the state of mind that the Supreme Court decision generated among Black people. This was the state of mind which gave birth to the civil-rights movement.

The civil-rights movement, beginning with the Montgomery, Alabama, bus boycott in 1955 and the sit-ins in 1960, was the first stage in the national awakening of Afro-America after the Second World War. It was the first thrust forward in what has become known today as Afro-America's struggle for self-determination.

The civil-rights movement was unique in that it broke from the NAACP strategy of total reliance upon the court system to rectify the condition of the Black man and woman. Rather than throw all of their apples into a court-litigation bag, the new civil-rights organizations combined court fights with mass actions in the streets.

This tendency toward mass action, toward the independent mobilization of Black people in the streets, was the most important aspect of the civil-rights movement. The movement was not really about what is popularly termed "integration." That is to say, Black people didn't mount these mass actions in order to sit next to a white person in a restaurant, or to sit on a white toilet stool, or to drink from a white drinking fountain, or to live next to white people in a white neighborhood. Getting next to white folks was not the major thrust of the movement, even though many civil-rights spokesmen may have interpreted the struggle in that way.

What the masses wanted was desegregation, not integration. The masses wanted the right to sit anywhere in a restaurant they chose. They wanted the right to go to any school, to sit anywhere on the bus they chose. They wanted the right to sit on any toilet stool or drink from any water fountain they chose. And they wanted the right to live anywhere they chose. This was the essence of the movement. Black people wanted the same rights that are guaranteed to every citizen of this nation-state. And they knew what these rights were since they were very clearly codified in the Constitution and in the Bill of Rights. These are the documents that the government claims as the basis for all its laws and regulations. All that Black people were demanding was that these documents be enforced equally.

But the important thing was that the movement was not just putting forth demands and then waiting for action upon them by the political, economic, and social institutions of the bourgeoisie. What the activists in SCLC and SNCC did was to combine this reliance upon bourgeois institutions with direct action by the masses.

This independent mobilization of the Black masses, through sit-ins, boycotts, and demonstrations, had a logic of its own, a logic which was not comprehended by most of the participants or their leaders. The effect of the mobilizations was to give the Black masses a sense of organization and a glimpse of their potential strength. Just the sight of several thousand people demonstrating in a small southern town began to break down the isolation and atomization in the Black community. People who had been trying to solve social problems in an individual way began to sense the power of the mass. Instead of laying the blame for social problems upon themselves, or their brother or their sister, they began to lay the blame where it belongs—on the society itself. Black people everywhere, as they saw their situation getting national and international attention, began to become cautiously optimistic. This optimism was magnified even more as the overt forms of segregation began to fall.

The mobilizations gave Black people a sense of confidence and reliance upon themselves. Slowly but surely, illusions began to crumble about the promises and civil-rights rhetoric of the government and its politicians. The continued mobilizations taught Black people that the government's practice did not measure up to its righteous rhetoric.

While the FBI stood around "taking notes," white-racist violence continued unabated.

As Black people saw through the superficial changes, they saw that the lines of difference between the federal government and state governments became murky and blurred. As the struggle deepened and spread northward, militants found out that there was very little difference between a northern Democrat and a southern Dixiecrat.

Thus the consciousness generated by these independent mobilizations over civil-rights issues began to affect the whole outlook of Black people toward society. For many Black people, these mobilizations demonstrated that racial oppression is not a question of morality, or brotherhood, or a question of good men fighting evil men. These mobilizations demonstrated that racial oppression is rooted in the very fabric of this society, that it is institutionalized, systematized, and calculated into the American way of life.

As a result of these independent mobilizations conducted over civil rights, Black people began to move to a higher level of independence in thought and in action. This new level of independence from white bourgeois institutions was reflected in the acquisition of nationalist, or Black, consciousness. From the vantage point of Black consciousness, Black people began to realize the need for independence in all areas of life from this decadent white-capitalist society. This new nationalist consciousness grew as a result of two developments: the ghetto rebellions and the transformation of the major civil-rights organizations, such as SNCC and CORE, into nationalist organizations.

The combativity of the civil-rights movement had begun to bring to the surface all of the resentments and grievances that Black people had against capitalist society. As illusion after illusion about liberals and liberalism was stripped from the minds of the masses through struggle, Black people became more assertive, more aggressive. When the last shred of faith in gradualism was blown to the wind, all of the anger and pent-up resentment burst through the surface with a volcanic fury.

Nobody, with the exception of Malcolm X, expected and predicted the ghetto explosions. Everything was peace and progress until the Black uprisings in Watts, Newark, and Detroit.

Here is how Malcolm X predicted these explosions at a Militant Labor Forum in January 1965:

> But by the end of 1964, we had to agree that instead of the Year of Promise, instead of those promises materializing, they substituted devices to create the illusion of progress; 1964 was the Year of Illusion and Delusion. We received nothing but a promise....In 1963, one of their devices to let off the steam of frustration was the march on Washington. They used that to make us think we were making progress. Imagine, marching to Washington and getting nothing for it whatsoever....
>
> In 1963, it was the march on Washington. In 1964, what was it? The civil-rights bill. They murdered a Negro in Georgia and did nothing about it; murdered two whites and a Negro in Mississippi and did nothing about it. So that the civil-rights bill has produced nothing where we're concerned. It was only a valve, a vent, that was designed to enable us to let off our frustrations. But the bill itself was not designed to solve our problems.
>
> Since we see what they did in 1963, and we saw what they did in 1964, what will they do now, in 1965? If the march on Washington was supposed to lessen the

explosion, and the civil-rights bill was designed to lessen the explosion—That's all it was designed to do; it wasn't designed to solve the problems; it was designed to lessen the explosion. Everyone in his right mind knows there should have been an explosion. You can't have all those ingredients, those explosive ingredients that exist in Harlem and elsewhere where our people suffer, and not have an explosion. So these are devices to lessen the danger of the explosion, but not designed to remove the material that's going to explode. [*Malcolm X Speaks* (Merit Publishers: New York), pp. 158–59).]

The ghetto rebellions caught the civil-rights organizations and leaders totally unaware. They did not understand the chain reaction that they had set in motion. But as they began to see that no perceptible change had occurred in the lives of the masses, the new stage of independence reached by the ghetto rebellions became very attractive. SNCC and CORE made the transition from civil-rights consciousness to nationalist consciousness. This transition was expressed in the cry for "Black Power." These two organizations not only made the transition to nationalist consciousness but also became the leaders and articulators of this nascent nationalist movement.

This independent mobilization of Black people around nationalist consciousness escalated with U.S. aggression against Vietnam. The resistance of the Vietnamese to U.S. imperialism has played and will continue to play a big role in the development of nationalist consciousness among Black people. For thousands of Black GIs, Vietnam has transformed their whole outlook toward this society.

As Black nationalism spreads and deepens its grip on the psyches of Black people, the vanguard role of Black people in changing this society becomes very clear. The best example is provided by the Black student movement. The students are the most organized and politicized sector of the Black community. The independent organization of Black college and high school students has proceeded further than that of any other sector of the Black community. By examining the Black student movement, we can get an example in microcosm of the impact that the independent organization of the entire Black community will have on the whole of capitalist society.

On the campus, the struggle for Black studies or for the Black university has radically transformed the relationship of the entire student body to the university administration. The struggle for the Black university prepared the ground and set the precedent for the May 1970 upsurge over the antiwar university.

The independent organization of Black students not only provided leadership for Black students but also led masses of white students into combat against university administrations. Upheavals such as these occurred at San Francisco State, the University of California at Berkeley, Brandeis, the University of Houston, the University of Washington in Seattle, City College of New York and many more.

As a result of this independent organization of Black students, initial demands for merely establishing the right of all-Black student organizations to exist grew into demands that whole departments and schools be devoted to the study of the Black man and woman and that these departments and schools be under the control of the Black student community.

This is the logic and dynamic of nationalist consciousness in the campus setting. The nationalist consciousness of Black students has also made them very much aware of the difference in interests of the students and the authoritarian university administration. That is to say, the independent organization of Black students created not only an awareness of themselves as *Blacks* but also an awareness of themselves as *students*. The action of Black students brought many other students to this same awareness. Their struggles educated many about how the white capitalist class controls and uses the university as just another cog in the imperialist machine.

This independent mobilization of Black students is only a shadow of what the independent mobilization of the total Black community would be like. If one can sense that, then one can sense the power of a mass independent Black political party basing itself on a set of transitional demands.

We now see independent organization spreading to various sectors of the Black community. And as each sector achieves some degree of independent organization, there follows a struggle around demands that are transitional in nature. But in the course of each struggle, Blacks reflect an awareness of being oppressed not only because they are Black but also because they are welfare-mothers, or tenants, or women, or workers, or GIs.

In the army, for example, the independent organization of Black GIs leads not only to struggle against white-racist oppression but also to struggle against oppression as GIs. In the case of GIs United at Fort Jackson, South Carolina, Black and Brown GIs got together first to fight racist persecution. After this independent mobilization of their strength, they became the most militant fighters in the struggle against the war and for GI rights. This is the logic and dynamic of the struggle. The Black GI organization that recently came together in Heidelberg, Germany, called the Unsatisfied Black Soldiers, fights not only against racism and brutality but also against bad conditions, and calls for the immediate withdrawal of U.S. troops from Vietnam. As the independent organization of Black GIs proceeds, it will provide leadership for both white and Black GIs. Such organizations will make it harder for white GIs to be both racist and antiwar.

Nationalist consciousness has begun to stimulate Black workers, both as Blacks and as workers. The plantation conditions faced by Black workers at the point of production are no longer being tolerated. Symptomatic of this situation is the fact that in some cases Black auto and steel workers are resorting to armed self-defense inside the factories. Just recently at a Chrysler auto plant in Detroit, a Black auto worker with two years' seniority came to work and found that his job had been given to a man with less seniority and less experience.

When he protested this slap at his dignity and worth as a human being, he was suspended by his foreman. At being suspended by his Black foreman, the worker experienced a virtual emotional explosion. His job was his life. When he could get no relief from his white union shop steward, the Black worker went home, got his M-1 rifle, smuggled it into the plant and went looking for his foreman. After the smoke cleared that day, two plant foremen, one Black and one white, and a white skilled tradesman had been blown away. This example gives only a glimpse of the pent-up anger and fury generated in these modern-day plantations called automobile plants.

Along with these isolated acts, there is also occurring the growth of Black caucuses within the trade-union movement. In Detroit, the League of Revolutionary Black Workers continues to operate a number of plant caucuses and, in some cases, intervenes in local union elections with candidates of its own.

The impact of nationalist consciousness on Black workers and the unions has come through in recent strike struggles. In the postal-workers' strike, the militancy and drive of the strike was provided by the Black workers. And there is no doubt that the militancy of the nationalist-minded Black workers pushed the white workers to new levels of enthusiasm about the strike.

In another instance, a Teamsters local of United Parcel Service workers in New York went on strike because Black workers were not allowed to wear the red, black, and green button symbolizing the flag of Black liberation. Management had allowed the workers to wear buttons symbolizing the American flag. But as soon as Black workers, who constitute 35 percent of the union, started showing up for work with nationalist buttons, management outlawed all buttons.

This denial of the right to wear the button of their choice is what precipitated the strike. Curiously enough, the demand of the Teamsters local was that the workers be allowed to wear any button they chose. This strike—which was a political strike, not an economic strike—even caused a one-day solidarity strike by United Parcel Service workers in Secaucus, New Jersey. And while these UPS workers in New York were on strike, they weren't laying low. Several hundred demonstrated in front of city hall and in front of the courthouse to protest fines levied on the union for the strike. In the demonstration, both the American flag and the Black liberation flag were carried.

Here we see nationalist consciousness shaking up the unions, making them instruments of struggle. These actions underscore Trotsky's statement that in the epoch of imperialism, the national struggle becomes one of the most important forms of the class struggle.

The import of this statement is strikingly confirmed by the recent events in Jackson, Mississippi. This was the first strike of municipal workers in the history of Jackson. This particular local of the American Federation of State, County and Municipal Employees was all Black. The white workers didn't feel the need of a union since they were given wages much higher than those of the Black workers. One day all of the Black workers went on strike, demanding union recognition, a wage increase, an antidiscrimination clause, grievance procedures, a health plan, and other benefits. Here Blacks combined nationalist demands with class demands. In fact, the nationalist demands were class demands, and the class demands were nationalist demands.

By striking, the workers had hoped to gain national attention and support for their cause. Instead they were treacherously sold out by the national leadership of AFSCME whose field representative told them to go back to work. Because the workers were combining nationalist demands with the demand for union recognition, the field representative said that this wasn't a strike. And with this denial of national support, the strike was effectively broken.

Thus the strike showed just how far these liberal union bureaucrats will go. It also illustrated that the national question will play a most important role in the regeneration of the unions into organs of struggle.

These examples of struggle by Black workers illustrate the dual or combined character of the struggle for Black liberation. In combination with the struggle for self-determination, the working-class character of the Black community will make the national question a most explosive force on the political scene in the United States. In the United States the national question revolves around a proletarian mass, unlike Eastern Europe, Africa, Asia, and Latin America where the national question revolves around a peasant mass.

There is another difference between the national question here and elsewhere. Unlike the nations of Eastern Europe and Asia, the Black nation was forged in the heat of North American capitalist expansion. The slaves came from many different African ethnic groups, each with its own heritage, tradition and language. But the process of enslavement destroyed these ethnic groups and welded the African slaves into one people with a common heritage of white-racist exploitation and oppression.

In Latin America, we could even say that it was Spanish and Portuguese colonization that produced many of the nation-states. The United States itself is a nation that was produced by the expansion of English capitalism. In fact, all of the nations in the Western Hemisphere were produced by the historical unevenness between Europe and the Americas. Within the nation-states carved out of the Americas, there was unevenness between the European settlers, the Native Americans, and the African slaves. The product of this unevenness was the superexploitation and oppression of the Native Americans and the African slaves.

That superexploitation and oppression of the African slaves produced a nation within a nation. Within the United States, the bourgeois-democratic revolution, which was completed for white people, was never completed for Black people. Capitalist society in the United States had never been able to digest Black people as citizens.

The first phase of the bourgeois-democratic revolution began when the Declaration of Independence was issued in 1776. Although Blacks fought and died in the first American Revolution, they did not enjoy the fruits of victory.

In the Constitution, a Black person was calculated to be three-fifths of a human being. This was the basis of southern representation in the Congress. Yet the Blacks were slaves and not citizens. Despite the fact that the slaves figured in on the congressional representation, a slave could not cast three-fifths of a vote. It was upon the backs of the slaves that the southern slave-holders consolidated their control of the nation.

The conflict between the need to expand bourgeois property relations and the plantation system led to the second American revolution in 1861, which ended with the destruction of slavery. However, the former slaves—even though 200,000 fought in the Civil War and provided the margin of victory for the North—did not get possession of the land. The campaign for "forty acres and a mule," which was an expression of this urge for land, never got off the ground.

Because it was the Republican administration that signed the Emancipation Proclamation, the newly freed slaves considered this instrument of capitalist rule to be their party. This was a natural reaction. However, the Blacks did not develop any independent political organization when the Republicans pulled back from the land question. If the Republicans had broken up the landed estates and redistributed the land, this would have caused not only a race revolution but a class revolution as well. Land could not have been given to the Blacks without a similar distribution to the poor whites. And the Republicans were not prepared to accept the consequences of such a step. Therefore, since the relationship of forces was not in their favor, the four-and-a-half million Blacks became sharecroppers and landed serfs rather than landholders.

The opposite of this situation had occurred sixty years before in Haiti, when a half-million former slaves, under the leadership of the Black general Dessalines, declared their independence from France. This declaration of Haitian independence on December 31, 1803, culminated fourteen years of war and revolution. It was during this fourteen-year period that the Blacks were able to mold and build an army independent of the French under the dynamic leadership of Toussaint L'Ouverture.

The four-year Civil War in the United States, however, was too short a period for a similar development in the South. It was not long enough to allow the development of Black guerrilla groups or a Black army of emancipation in the South. Had there been serious warfare between the slaveholders and the poor whites during the Civil War, the North American Blacks might have been able to seize the land and develop a significant amount of independent organization. Such an event would have changed the whole course of North American and world history. This more-than-partial completion of the bourgeois-democratic revolution in relation to Black people would have weakened the whole schema of racial oppression in this country. Blacks would have been a more integral part of the United States. The class struggle would have developed along much sharper and much clearer lines, which would have slowed the growth of North American imperialism.

But this was not the case. The North American bourgeoisie was too strong. Blacks were forced to depend upon the Republican Party. And when this instrument of the new industrial elite had consolidated northern hegemony, Black people were left in the lurch, left to fend for themselves against the southern oligarchy. Thus Reconstruction was ended, and the task of completing the bourgeois-democratic revolution in relation to the Black man and woman carried over into the twentieth century.

Because the democratic revolution was left to the twentieth century, to the epoch of imperialism—as the theory of permanent revolution tells us—it becomes a task that only the socialist revolution can complete. The noncompletion of democracy for the Black man and woman allows no other course. And because there is no other course, the struggle for self-determination is part and parcel of the struggle for socialist revolution in the United States.

So we see that the unevenness bred by North American capitalism, the unevenness between the descendants of Africa and the descendants of Europe, will give the coming revolution a combined character. This revolution will combine national tasks with socialist tasks, and socialist tasks with national tasks. Unlike some pseudo-Marxists and shallow-minded leftists, we see no contradiction between Black nationalist consciousness and class consciousness. In fact, the deeper the penetration of nationalism into the consciousness of Black people, the better will be the development of the class struggle. Because we stand upon the theory of permanent revolution, and see this as the age of permanent revolution, we know that bourgeois society can neither accommodate the national question nor grant self-determination.

We therefore welcome and look forward to the independent mobilization and organization of Black people. The greater the independent organization of Black people, the easier it will be for Black people to acquire socialist consciousness.

Wasn't this the case in Cuba? Because the July 26 Movement, which was a nationalist movement, was organized totally independent of U.S. imperialism, it was able to accept socialist revolution as the only way to solve its national tasks. Even though the July 26 Movement started out with a petty-bourgeois and confused ideology, an ideology predicated on reforming Cuban society, the *independent organization* of the movement in the intransigent pursuit of its nationalist goals was the decisive factor.

Today in the Middle East, the power of the Palestinian commando movement flows from the fact that it is organized independent of imperialism and the Arab states.

So, as with the Cubans and the Palestinians, the power of Black people will flow from the depth of independent organization. The primary reason that SNCC collapsed was its dependence upon white liberals for organizational and financial resources. The weakness of the Black Panther Party can be attributed to its organizational and financial dependence upon white petty-bourgeois radicals of the Peace and Freedom and Yippie variety. The Panthers fell into a fatal trap. They found it was easier to appeal to the sympathies of white liberals and radicals than to organize the Black community. Their heavy Maoist-Stalinist rap and pick-up-the-gun rhetoric was aimed more at meeting the expectations of their ultraleft white supporters than the needs of the Black community for political leadership.

The best example of independence so far remains Brother Malcolm X. Malcolm was trying to build an independent organization of, by, and for Black people. And in doing so, Malcolm moved very much in the direction of a transitional program for Black liberation. This is what Malcolm was trying to codify in the "Statement of Basic Aims and Objectives of the Organization of Afro-American Unity." I suggest the book *By Any Means Necessary* for further reading on this subject.

What we advocate in terms of advancing the struggle for self-determination is the independent organization of the oppressed nation. From the vantage point of independent Black organizations, Black people will be better able to judge who is for them and who is against them. As Black people, through struggle, gain an understanding that self-determination can only be won through the construction of a workers' state, they will come to join the ranks of the multinational revolutionary socialist party.

The task of winning Black people to the revolutionary party involves the decisive question of whether there will be a socialist revolution in the United States. If we understand that the nature of that revolution will be a combined one, involving both the class and national questions, then it becomes impossible to conceive of any revolution in the United States without a great deal of participation and leadership coming from Black people and the other oppressed Third World national minorities. We can state simply that either the coming socialist revolution will be a combined one, or there won't be revolution at all.

To state it another way, revolution is not just an objective event, but a subjective one as well. Part of making a revolution is discovering objective historical laws, such as the theory of the permanent revolution, *which point to the revolution.* But unless those laws are given subjective expression in the program of a vanguard party, the revolution remains on paper.

A very good case in point is the first socialist revolution in history, the Russian Revolution. This revolution had a combined character because of the oppression of national minorities by the czarist state. Support for the right to self-determination was rooted in the theory and practice of the Bolshevik Party. This clearly distinguished them from the Mensheviks and the Provisional Government between February and October of 1917. And, more important, their position on the national question enabled the Bolsheviks to triumph in the civil war that took place after the revolution.

Just as revolutionary socialists comprehend that the dialectical unity between the national and class questions is a precondition for making revolution, so the North American capitalist class understands the necessity of separating these two questions if it is to continue to rule. The ruling class, the reformists and the labor bureaucrats all try to separate and compartmentalize racial oppression and class exploitation. Their contention is that the national question can be solved within the confines of capitalist society. They hold the same view of class conflict. In order to keep people busy trying to find solutions to class conflict and race conflict short of revolution, the two questions must never be linked together. This is what the AFSCME bureaucrat was opposed to. He was unalterably opposed to any attempt by the Jackson workers to use the union as a vehicle in the struggle against racial oppression. The consequences would have been too explosive. And the same goes for the ruling class, the class that is responsible for the training of the labor bureaucrats. The ruling class always maintains that there is some middle ground, that there is room "to reason" on the national question.

But just how far they are willing to go to reason was illustrated in Detroit. Right after the uprising there in 1967, the automobile bourgeoisie made all types of promises of change. To bring about these changes, they created the New Detroit Committee. Among those on the New Detroit Committee sat Henry Ford II and James Roche, the chairman of General Motors. This committee was supposed to rebuild the burnt-out areas in Detroit. Ford and Roche held out the promise of jobs for the hard-core Black unemployed. The New Detroit Committee brought together the bigwigs of business, labor and the government to solve the problems of the Black community. Detroit was in a good position to tackle these problems because it is the center of the automobile industry.

But after three years—with the air cleared of the hot and heavy rhetoric of the NDC—the problems remain the same. The burnt-out areas are just empty lots. No new housing has been constructed. The promise of jobs by the automobile industry was just a cruel joke. You need ninety days of work to get into the union. The brothers who were hired were then fired on the eighty-ninth day. And then thousands of brothers who had made it were laid off early this year because of the recession that hit the industry.

Thus, despite the absorption of many Black workers by the automobile industry, Blacks still occupy the bulk of the reserve army of labor. The reserve army of labor is the last hired and the first fired. These workers are the last ones in on an economic upswing, but the first ones out in the beginning of an economic slump.

The example of Detroit only highlights the fact that the U.S. ruling class is in permanent crisis over the national question. And because of this permanent crisis, there will be permanent struggle.

In this permanent crisis, the bourgeoisie will make use of its apparatus of deception and its apparatus of repression. The apparatus of deception tells people that the vast riches and wealth of North America can be theirs if only they work hard and get the right breaks. The existence of such riches and wealth eggs the struggle on. People continue to try to shape the reality of their existence to the illusions about how to achieve the good things in life. This contradiction—trying to make what the Man says real—acts as a generator of struggle amongst the masses of Black people.

The fact that motion is breaking out among other sectors of the society—women, Chicanos, Puerto Ricans, Native Americans and Asian-Americans—will deepen and extend the struggle for Black self-determination. And what must be added to this is the fact that struggle and motion continue all over the world—in Vietnam, Ireland, Africa and Latin America. All these factors mean that there will be no letup in the struggle for Black self-determination. Contrary to what the ultralefts believe, doom, disaster, repression and fascism do not loom around the corner. The ruling class's apparatus of deception has yet to be exhausted.

This is not to say that the bourgeoisie will not resort to repression. The countless police murders of Black militants are testimony to this fact. But in this period, the bourgeoisie uses its repression to divide the militants from the masses. The ruling class wants to isolate, contain, and snuff out the lives of those revolutionary militants who have the potential of leading masses of people in struggle. It is this potential linkup that they dread. But use of ultraleft rhetoric by militant Black groups only aids the ruling class in smashing that potential linkup with the masses. This "pick-up-the-gun" rhetoric provides handles for the ruling class in attacking these groups.

As long as the masses of Black people see themselves as the audience and the revolutionary nationalists as the actors and actresses, there will be no linkup. Only through a united front based on transitional demands does everybody come onto the stage. And when everybody comes onto the stage, repression and anything else can be defeated.

An example of this is the recent defense of militants in the Republic of New Africa. These militants were charged with the murder of a cop. The blowing away of this cop occurred in a police attack on a convention of the Republic of New Africa last year. Because of a united-front defense built by the League of Revolutionary Black Workers, in combination with impressive legal tactics, all three defendants were acquitted. This shows that with the activation of the Black community repression can be rolled back and successful struggles mounted.

The theme running through all of the actions in the Black community is the question of control. It is around this demand for Black control that various sectors of the Black community are organizing themselves independently of the white capitalist power structure. And it is in the process of struggle that these various sectors come to grips with and hammer out a set of transitional demands.

The transitional program itself arises from and is based upon struggle. The Black university concept came out of the struggle for Black control of Black education; various demands are arising from the struggle of Black caucuses in the trade-union movement. But what is important is that, out of the struggle for Black control of the Black community, there will arise popular organs of struggle through which the masses can express themselves. And in the course of building those popular organs around the different aspects of Black oppression, the groundwork will be laid for the building of a Black political party.

Now the struggle for Black control of the Black community is in the process of being nationalized. That is to say, the demand for Black control is applicable to wherever Black people are at. What brings about this centralization of the demand is the increasing urbanization of Black people in the North, South, East, and West. This urban setting provides the backdrop for the demand.

In the South, the struggle is becoming increasingly explosive over the demand for Black control of Black education. What is happening is that desegregation of schools is being used by the white power structure to displace Black teachers and Black administrators. Before desegregation, schools in the Black community had teaching staffs and administrative staffs that were all-Black in composition. And, of course, in the white community the schools had teaching staffs and administrative staffs that were totally white. But because the power over this whole school system rested in an all-white board of education, this was segregation, not separation. The Blacks were powerless. And because of this state of powerlessness, desegregation is now wiping out jobs for Black teachers and administrators.

This is most clearly the case in North Carolina and Georgia. In these two states, struggle has erupted over the racist application of the desegregation process. This struggle has not only hit the racist hiring procedures but also protested the blatantly racist abuse of Black students in predominantly white or newly desegregated schools. In these desegregated schools, all types of discriminations are dropped on Black students. They are denied entrance into extracurricular activity, such as clubs and sports. The teachers tolerate no questioning of the racist subject matter that is fed in the classroom. This discrimination collides very sharply with the nationalist consciousness of Black students. Out of this collision comes struggle, as in North Carolina and Albany, Georgia, recently.

As this struggle for control is organized over the issue of education, it will become the starting point for other struggles around Black control. In West Point, Mississippi, through a combination of uprisings and organization, Black residents now control all of the economic activity in their community. From this vantage point of economic control, the Blacks, who make up 42 percent of West Point's population, are now seeking to take political control by electing a Black man to the office of mayor. This candidate is a thirty-year-old former SNCC worker who came to West Point in 1964.

The struggle for control is also broadening very rapidly in the North and in the West. Just recently, militant Puerto Ricans occupied the administrative offices of Lincoln Hospital. Lincoln Hospital is one of the butcher shops in a heavily Puerto Rican community in the Bronx in New York City. The militants were demanding that Puerto Rican patients be treated as human beings and that the hospital deal with the ills of the community, such as lead poisoning and drug addiction. This was followed by some Harlem militants seizing part of Harlem Hospital, demanding that the hospital deal with drug addiction.

At the last NAACP convention, that organization went on record for mass demonstrations at construction sites in order to get Black people hired into the building trades. The power of such mobilizations was revealed last year in Pittsburgh and Chicago.

The cutting edge of the struggle for Black control still remains in the schools. The continued breakdown and disintegration of the school system poses the question of Black community control. Last spring in New York City, the mere attempt by Black parents to set up a grievance table in a high school led to a struggle that lasted several months.

It is becoming all too clear to the Black community that an end must come to white control of Black education. And for this reason, the mass mobilizations over control of the schools will continue. The power of such mobilizations in respect to the total mobilization of the community is made quite clear by the Chicano struggle.

The victory of La Raza Unida Party in Crystal City, Texas, grew out of a mobilization of the Chicano community over Chicano control of the schools. It was through this mobilization over the schools that economic boycotts were conducted, voter registration drives conducted, and the road paved to enable the Chicano community to gain control of the board of education in Crystal City. La Raza Unida Party is an example of the logic of the struggle for self-determination.

The party arose out of popular organs of struggle built in the struggle for community control. In Texas, the popular youth organ that led the way in the formation of La Raza Unida Party was MAYO, the Mexican American Youth Organization. In Colorado, the popular organ of struggle around which La Raza Unida Party was formed was the Crusade for Justice.

MAYO and the Crusade for Justice are organizations of mass action. The logic of their struggle for independence in one sphere led to struggle for independence in all spheres. And if a La Raza Unida Party is formed in California, it is obvious that the organs of mass action will play a most decisive role in its constitution. The example of La Raza Unida demonstrates the best way to coordinate and unify the multifarious struggle for self-determination.

To conclude, I want to quote from a statement Trotsky made in 1933 and to broaden that statement in the light of recent events. Where Trotsky said "Negro," we can insert "Puerto Rican, Chicano, and Black":

> I believe that by the unheard-of political and theoretical backwardness and the unheard-of economic advance the awakening of the working class will proceed quite rapidly. The old ideological covering will burst, all questions will emerge at once, and since the country is so economically mature the adaptation of the political and theoretical to the economic level will be achieved very rapidly. It is then

possible that the [Puerto Ricans, Chicanos, and Blacks] will become the most advanced section. We have already a similar example in Russia. The Russians were the European [Puerto Ricans, Chicanos, and Blacks]. It is very possible that the [Puerto Ricans, Chicanos, and Blacks] also through the self-determination will proceed to the proletarian dictatorship in a couple of gigantic strides, ahead of the great bloc of white workers. They will then furnish the vanguard. I am absolutely sure that they will in any case fight better than the white workers. That, however, can happen only provided the Communist party carries on an uncompromising merciless struggle not against the supposed national prepossessions of the [Puerto Ricans, Chicanos, and Blacks] but against the colossal prejudices of the white workers and gives it no concession whatever. [*Leon Trotsky on Black Nationalism and Self-Determination* (Pathfinder Press: New York, 1972), p. 18.]

Carolyn M. Rogers
and when the revolution came

(for Rayfield and Lillie and the whole rest)

and when the revolution came
the militants said
niggers wake up
you got to comb yo hair
the natural way
            and the church folks say oh yeah? sho 'nuff . . .
and they just kept on going to church
gittin on they knees and praying
and tithing and building and buying

and when the revolution came
the militants said
niggers you got to change
the way you dress
and the church folk say oh yeah?
            and they just kept on going to church
with they knit suits and flowery bonnets
and gittin on they knees and praying
and tithing and building and buying

and when the revolution came
the militants said
you got to give up
white folks and the
            church folk say oh yeah? well?
never missed what we never had
and they jest kept on going to church
with they nice dresses and suits and
praying and building and buying

and when the revolution came
the militants say you got to give up
pork and eat only brown rice and
health food and the
            church folks said uh hummmm

and they just kept on eating they chitterlings and
going to church and praying and tithing and
building and buying

and when the revolution came
the militants said
all you church going niggers
got to give up easter and christmas
and the bible
cause that's the white man's religion
and the church folks said well well well well well

and then the militants said we got to
build black institutions where our children
call each other sister and brother
and can grow beautiful, black and strong and grow in black grace
and the church folks said yes, lord Jesus we been calling each other
sister and brother a long time

and the militants looked around
after a while and said hey, look at all
these fine buildings we got scattered throughout
the black communities some of em built wid schools and nurseries
who do they belong to?

and the church folks said, yeah.
we been waiting fo you militants
to realize that the church is an eternal rock
now why don't you militants jest come on in
we been waiting for you
we can show you how to build
    anything that needs building
and while we're on our knees, at that.

Part Six—The Post-Industrial, Post-Civil Rights Era

Audre Lorde
Power

The difference between poetry and rhetoric
is being
ready to kill
yourself
instead of your children.

I am trapped on a desert of raw gunshot wounds
and a dead child dragging his shattered black
face off the edge of my sleep
blood from his punctured cheeks and shoulders
is the only liquid for miles and my stomach
churns at the imagined taste while
my mouth splits into dry lips
without loyalty or reason
thirsting for the wetness of his blood
as it sinks into the whiteness
of the desert where I am lost
without imagery or magic
trying to make power out of hatred and destruction
trying to heal my dying son with kisses
only the sun will bleach his bones quicker.

The policeman who shot down a 10-year-old in Queens
stood over the boy with his cop shoes in childish blood
and a voice said "Die you little motherfucker" and
there are tapes to prove that. At his trial
this policeman said in his own defense
"I didn't notice the size or nothing else
only the color," and
there are tapes to prove that, too.

Today that 37-year-old white man with 13 years of police forcing
has been set free
by 11 white men who said they were satisfied
justice had been done
and one black woman who said
"They convinced me" meaning

they had dragged her 4'10" black woman's frame
over the hot coals of four centuries of white male approval
until she let go the first real power she ever had
and lined her own womb with cement
to make a graveyard for our children.

I have not been able to touch the destruction within me.
But unless I learn to use
the difference between poetry and rhetoric
my power too will run corrupt as poisonous mold
or lie limp and useless as an unconnected wire
and one day I will take my teenaged plug
and connect it to the nearest socket
raping an 8year-old white woman
who is somebody's mother
and as I beat her senseless and set a torch to her bed
a greek chorus will be singing in 3/4 time
"Poor thing. She never hurt a soul. What beasts they are."

William Julius Wilson
from *The Declining Significance of Race*

6 PROTESTS, POLITICS, AND THE CHANGING
BLACK CLASS STRUCTURE

In the preindustrial period of American race relations, very nearly all blacks had not only to confront the day-to-day problems associated with subordination by racial status but also those stemming from subordination by social class. Whether one focuses on the vast majority of enslaved blacks or on the small number of free blacks, their uniformly low economic class position reinforced the racists' views that blacks were not only culturally inferior to whites but biogenetically inferior as well. The question of whether the black experience in this period is better explicated in terms of class or in terms of race has little meaning, for throughout most of the preindustrial period to be black was to be severely deprived of both social and economic resources. Accordingly, if there was meaningful collective variation in the black experience, it pertained to the difference in being a slave as opposed to being a free black, particularly to being a free black in the nineteenth-century antebellum North.

The slave experience was conditioned by the structured relationships with the slave masters—relationships that not only epitomized the extreme differences in racial status and power but also became increasingly paternalistic after the ban on the African slave trade. The very structure of the relationship between master and slave, not to mention the isolation of the latter on rural plantations, effectively prevented the development of a racially militant collective awareness. There were, of course, a few sporadic slave revolts organized by free blacks and slaves who happened to reside in the cities and who were neither under nor influenced by the close, day-to-day plantation supervision. However, the conditions conducive to a successful revolt, or even a large number of attempted revolts, did not exist in the antebellum South. Unlike slaves in Brazil and the Caribbean, bondsmen in the Old South failed to forge a revolutionary tradition or to generate revolts of significant frequency, duration, size, and historical-political magnitude. The structural factors that account for these differences are general conditions that could be meaningfully applied in comparative explanations of slave revolts in other societies. Basically, as Genovese points out, slave insurrections flourished in areas where plantations were very large, where there was a high ratio of slaves to free persons, where the ruling class was divided, where slaves had a chance to acquire military experience, and where the master-slave relations were more business-oriented than paternalistic. None of these factors prevailed in the Old South. Throughout the period of slavery, therefore, blacks were hardly in a position to mount a serious attack against the institution of slavery. They even had to depend on their paternalistic bond with the masters for protection against the abuses of the white lower class which had helplessly, but resentfully, watched slavery erode its economic position in the South.

For free blacks in the antebellum North the situation was somewhat different. They, unlike most southern blacks, were not at the mercy of an overseer or master; they could not be bought and sold; and their families could not be arbitrarily broken up by whites. Although the overwhelming majority of northern free blacks were trapped in menial positions, and although they were frequently victimized by white working-class racial antagonism, a few were able to improve their socioeconomic position. Indeed some northern blacks established successful businesses and accumulated property. By 1860 an increasing number of northern blacks were making use of educational opportunities both in all-black schools and in a small number of integrated schools. Moreover, educated blacks did not passively accept attempts to deprive them of equal rights. The rigid racial order never permitted the types of overt protest characteristic of the late twentieth century, but educated northern blacks did organize and petition, publish newspapers voicing their opposition to racial exploitation, join with white abolitionists to advance civil rights, press political candidates to take a stand against slavery, speak out against political oppression, launch suffrage campaigns, and organize Negro convention movements to devise plans to eliminate racial oppression. Although these protest activities had little real effect, they symbolized the beginning of an organized free black opposition to racial oppression, opposition which varied in intensity, complexity, and style under the changing social conditions of the late nineteenth and twentieth centuries. The protests also underlined the fact that on the eve of the Civil War a small black elite had emerged in the North whose improved class status coincided with increased expressions of dissatisfaction with racial injustice. But it was not until the industrial period of American race relations that one could meaningfully speak of the development of a black middle class and could witness a much clearer manifestation of class-based racial protests.

Industrial Race Relations and the Emergence of a Black Middle Class

The change from a preindustrial to an industrial system of production facilitated and directly contributed to the growth of the urban black community. As Negroes began migrating in significant numbers from the rural South to the nation's burgeoning industrial centers, black enclaves sprang up in various parts of those cities. These Negro neighborhoods reflected both class subordination and racial segregation. Blacks were trapped in the most deteriorated or run-down residential sections not only because of poverty but also because of a stringent pattern of housing discrimination. That the typical black migrant did not escape poverty when he arrived in the city in the first quarter of the twentieth century, although the standard of living in the city was still higher than in the rural South, is seen in the overwhelming concentration of Negroes in the low-status occupations such as domestic and service jobs. Even after black workers entered the goods-producing industries in fairly significant numbers during the World War I period, they rarely advanced beyond the most menial jobs.

Although the vast majority of urban blacks represented the very bottom of the occupational ladder and had few, if any, prospects for occupational advancement, during the first quarter of the twentieth century a class structure within the segregated black community had slowly but definitely taken shape. Essentially, a Negro business and professional class developed hand in hand with the growth of black organizations and institutions to meet the needs of and serve the rapidly expanding black urban population. Before the turn of the century only a handful of blacks (in cities such as Chicago, New York, Washington, D.C., Philadelphia, and Baltimore) could be identified as having an economic and status position uniquely and significantly different from the masses. This group constituted, in the words of Allan Spear, "a proud and exclusive elite—men and women who traced their ancestry to ante-bellum free blacks and who frequently had close economic and social ties with the white community." They were firmly committed to the view that America's racial problems could be relieved through integration. In the late nineteenth century their leader was the great abolitionist and integrationist Frederick Douglass, and in the early twentieth century the militant black intellectual W. E. B. Dubois inspired some of them.

However, during the first two decades of the twentieth century, the old black elite was gradually displaced by a new leadership of black businessmen and professionals whose base was in the growing, but segregated, black community and who had little contact or association with the white community. Unlike the old integration-oriented elite (whose contacts in the white community went back not only to the fluid period of race relations from 1870 to 1890 but also to the abolitionist era of the late antebellum period) this new leadership abandoned the dream of integration. As the South was rapidly developing a rigid pattern of Jim Crow segregation, and as race relations in the North deteriorated at the turn of the century, the emerging Negro business and professional class turned inward and espoused the philosophy of self-help and racial solidarity, eloquently articulated on a national level by Booker T. Washington. This small but growing group of black businessmen, ministers, politicians, journalists, and other professionals, excluded from the white community, "worked to create a cohesive and self-sufficient black metropolis. They were the architects of the institutional ghetto." Their hopes for a viable and autonomous black community were quickly dashed, however. Most black businesses were unable to survive because they were undercapitalized and could not obtain credit from white banks. Black social agencies were hardly in a position to confront the problems of the impoverished ghetto because they lacked the financial resources to develop satisfactory facilities and to hire adequate professional staffs. And black politicians, excluded from meaningful participation in the powerful urban political machines, could only offer token patronage. Thus, concludes Spear, "The dream of a black controlled community, growing out of the frustrations of the turn-of-the-century race relations and nurtured by the population growth of the World War I era and the 1920's, collapsed with the Depression—to be revived, in different form of course, in the 1960's."

The Changing Shape of the Black Class Structure

The Depression of the 1930s not only wiped out many of the small black businesses established during the two previous decades, it also created even greater miseries for the huge black lower-class population. Indeed, in some of the southern cities as many as three-fourths of the black population were on relief. However, the New Deal policies of Franklin D. Roosevelt's administration brought sudden relief to many of the impoverished black masses and significantly contributed to the growth of occupational differentiation within the black community. Blacks were employed for the first time as statisticians, lawyers, engineers, architects, economists, office managers, case aids, librarians, and interviewers. Lower-level white-collar positions for secretaries, clerks, and stenographers also became available. Despite the fact that many of these jobs involved administering governmental programs for blacks, they represented the first real breakthrough in a racially segregated labor market.

The role of the state in providing such employment opportunities for blacks is not surprising in view of the increased black political resources generated by their growing concentration in northern cities. But more about that in a later section of this chapter; I have yet to discuss what was one of the most significant contributions to black occupational differentiation during and following the New Deal era, the improved relationship between black workers and labor unions.

The passage of protective union legislation during the New Deal era created a favorable climate for collective bargaining and, as I pointed out in Chapter 4, precipitated a change in organized labor's relationships with black workers. The importance of the changing union attitudes and practices toward blacks is perhaps best conveyed in Bayard Rustin's observation:

> Although the new industrial unions were certainly not free of the prejudicial attitudes and policies which permeated the entire society, they made a practice of organizing black and white workers as equals wherever possible. Today this may not seem important, but at the time it was a gesture of revolutionary significance. No other mass institution in American society was so fully open to the participation of blacks; for the first time, Negroes could play an active role in an institution which vigorously sought to change the direction of society.

The increased black participation in labor unions was probably one of the major reasons why the proportion of blacks in semi-skilled and skilled positions increased from 17.2 percent in 1940 to 29.1 percent in 1950 (see table 13). However, to talk about the greater representation of blacks in higher-paying

TABLE 13   Percentage of Employed Black Males (Fourteen Years Old and Over) in Major Occupations in 1940, 1950, 1960, and 1970

Occupation	1940	1950	1960	1970
Professional and technical workers	1.8	2.1	4.6	7.0
Proprietors, managers, and officials	1.3	2.2	1.9	3.0
Clerical, sales, etc.	2.0	4.3	6.8	10.2
Craftsmen, foremen, etc.	4.5	7.8	10.7	15.2
Operatives	12.7	21.3	26.6	29.4
Service workers and laborers	37.1	38.1	38.4	32.0
Farm workers	41.0	24.0	12.3	4.4

Source: U.S. Bureau of the Census, *Census of the Population: 1940*, Characteristics of the Nonwhite Population by Race, Table 8; *Census of the Population: 1950*, vol. 4, Special Reports, Nonwhite Population by Race, Table 9; *Census of the Population: 1960*, Subject Reports, Nonwhite Population by Race, Final Report PC(2)-1C, Table 32; *Census of the Population: 1970*, Subject Reports, Final Report PC(2)-1B, Negro Population, Table 7.

blue-collar jobs is to describe just one of the ways in which blacks experienced occupational change during the decade of the 1940s. If we follow E. Franklin Frazier's lead and identify a black middle class in terms of those who are employed in the white-collar jobs and in the craftsmen and foremen positions, then the proportion of black males in those occupations increased from 9.6 percent in 1940 to 16.4 percent in 1950. Moreover, the proportion of black males in working-class jobs (semiskilled operative positions) increased from 12.7 percent in 1940 to 21.3 percent in 1950. Finally, the percentage of black males in essentially lower-class jobs (service workers, farm workers, and unskilled laborers) decreased from 78.1 percent in 1940 to 62.1 percent in 1950.

Thus, on the basis of the occupational distribution of employed males, it appears that roughly only one-third of the black population could be classified as either working class or middle class at mid-twentieth century. Still, when one considers that the percentage of black males in working- and middle-class jobs increased from 22.3 in 1940 to 37.6 in 1950, it is quite clear that a sizable number of blacks experienced occupational mobility during the decade of the 1940s. Aside from the previously mentioned factors of more liberal union policies and employment in government industries, black job opportunities also increased during World War II because of the labor shortages and the passage of the Fair Employment Practices Act that outlawed discrimination in the industrial plants holding federal contracts. Although many black workers lost their jobs following the war because defense industries declined and white veterans returned to the civilian labor force, "the conditions remained more favorable for Negro advancement than they had been before the war. Negro servicemen and workers in war industries gained valuable training and experience that enabled them to compete more effectively and their employment in large numbers in the unionized industries during the war left them in a stronger position in the labor market."

The most dramatic changes in black mobility, however, occurred during the decades of the 1950s and 1960s. Whereas 16.4 percent of black males were employed in middle-class occupations in 1950, 24 percent held such jobs in 1960 and 35.3 percent in 1970. Whereas 21.3 percent of black males were in essentially working-class jobs in 1950, 26.6 percent were so employed in 1960 and 29.4 percent in 1970. Finally, whereas 62.1 percent of all black employed males were in basically lower-class jobs in 1950, 50.7 percent held such jobs in 1960 and only 36.4 percent in 1970.

There are several factors involved in this remarkable shift in the black occupational structure. It is clear that the expansion of the economy, that is, the growth of the corporate and government sectors during the 1950s and 1960s, increased white-collar job opportunities for more talented or educated blacks. Moreover, the increased involvement of blacks in unions facilitated their entry into the higher-paying semiskilled and skilled blue-collar jobs. Furthermore, the equal employment legislation, first on the municipal and state levels after World War II and then on the federal level in the 1960s, removed many of the artificial barriers to black employment. Finally, the movement of blacks from the rural South to the industrial centers of the nation sharply decreased the number of blacks working on farms (from 41 percent in 1940 to 4.4 percent in 1970), where so much of black poverty had been concentrated throughout the twentieth century.

Although the changes in the black occupational structure since 1940 quite clearly show a consistent pattern of job upgrading, there are firm indications, as I have emphasized, that in the period of modern industrialization, the chances of continued economic improvement for the black poor are rapidly decreasing. I specifically have in mind the sharp rise in the black unemployment rate for the young and poorly trained ghetto blacks who are entering or have recently entered the labor market and face structural barriers to the higher-paying positions in the central corporate and government industries. Their unemployment rates sharply exceed the rates of other groups in the labor force regardless of swings in the business cycle. Moreover, they have evidenced a steady decline in their labor force participation rates in recent years which means that many of them have given up looking for work altogether. Furthermore, the effects of the advanced industrial, segmented labor market can be gauged by examining the rapid increase in the educational level of workers in the lower-paying occupations (unskilled laborers, service workers, semiskilled operatives) in which blacks are heavily concentrated. This means that persons with only a high school education or less may be increasingly consigned to the most inferior jobs. There is already an indication that the movement of blacks out of lower-paying to higher-paying jobs has slowed considerably in the 1970s. However, given the fact that the nation has been in the throes of a recession during this period, one would hardly expect the rate of black occupational mobility in the first half of the 1970s to keep pace with the rate recorded during the 1960s. As shown in table 14, the rate of black occupational upgrading from 1970 to 1974 is considerably below that of 1964 to 1970. However, although blacks continue

TABLE 14   Percentage of Employed Persons Sixteen Years and Over, by Occupation Group and Color for 1964, 1970, and 1974

	1964		1970		1974	
Occupation	White	Black and other races	White	Black and other races	White	Black and other races
Professional and technical	13.0	6.8	14.8	9.1	14.8	10.4
Managers and administrators	11.7	2.6	11.4	3.5	11.2	4.1
Sales workers	6.6	1.7	6.7	2.1	6.8	2.3
Clerical workers	16.3	7.7	18.0	13.2	17.8	15.2
Craft and similar workers	13.7	7.1	13.5	8.2	13.8	9.4
Operatives	18.4	20.5	17.0	23.7	15.5	21.9
Service workers and laborers	14.6	45.2	14.8	36.3	16.4	34.0
Farm workers	5.8	8.4	4.0	3.4	3.6	2.7

Source: U.S. Department of Labor, *Manpower Report of the President* (Washington, D.C.: Government Printing Office, 1975).

to experience a faster rate of job improvement than whites, the movement of blacks into the higher-paying white-collar and skilled crafts positions is occurring at a faster rate (5.9 percent) than the movement of blacks out of low-paying service worker and laborer jobs (2.3 percent); the percentage difference between the growth of middle-class jobs and the decline of lower-class jobs was only 1.6 between 1964 and 1970, with black white-collar and skilled craft workers increasing by 10.3 percent and service workers and unskilled laborers decreasing by 8.9 percent.

There are other indications that the poor blacks' economic situation is deteriorating. After a steady decrease in the percentage of black families below the low-income level (from 48.1 percent in 1959 to 29.4 percent in 1968) the proportion of poor black families has remained around 28 percent from 1969 (27.9 percent) to 1974 (27.8 percent). Moreover, female heads of poor black households increased from 56 percent in 1970 to 67 percent in 1974, and 75 percent of poor black female-headed families received some or all of their income from public assistance in 1973.

Reflecting the increase in black female-headed families, the percentage of black children living with both parents decreased markedly from 64 in 1970 to 56 in 1974. However, as shown in Table 15, for both black and white families, the percentage of children living with both parents is strongly associated with income level. This relationship is even stronger among black families than among white families. For example, in 1974, only 18 percent of the children in black families with incomes of less than $4,000 lived with both parents, while 90 percent of the children in families with incomes of $15,000 or more lived with both parents. The comparable figures for white families are 39 percent and

TABLE 15   *Own Children under Eighteen Years by Presence of Parents and Family Income, 1974 (Income, in current dollars, refers to income received during 1973)*

Family Income	Own Black Children Total (thousands)	% living with Both	One	Own White Children Total (thousands)	% living with Both	One
Under $4,000	2,031	18	82	3,382	39	61
$4,000–$5,999	1,472	35	65	3,413	66	34
$6,000–$7,999	1,273	53	47	4,260	77	23
$8,000–$9,999	914	78	22	5,321	88	12
$10,000 and over	2,910	88	12	38,949	96	4
$10,000–$14,999	1,600	86	14	16,179	94	6
$15,000 and over	1,310	90	10	22,770	97	3

Source: U.S. Bureau of the Census, "The Social and Economic Status of the Black Population in The United States, 1974," *Current Population Reports*, Series P-23 no. 54, (Washington, D.C.: Government Printing Office, 1975).

Note: Universe is own unmarried children under eighteen years old living in families where at least one parent is present.

97 percent. Accordingly, to suggest categorically that the problem of female-headed households is characteristic of black families is to overlook the powerful influence of economic class background. The increase in female-headed households among poor blacks is a consequence of the fact that the poorly trained and educated black males have increasingly restricted opportunities for higher-paying jobs and thus find it increasingly difficult to satisfy the expectations of being a male breadwinner. Moreover, as Carol Stack, in her sensitive analysis of poor black families, has pointed out, "caretaker agencies such as public welfare are insensitive to individual attempts for social mobility. A woman may be immediately cut off the welfare roles when a husband returns from prison, the army, or if she gets married. Thus, the society's welfare system collaborates in weakening the position of the black male."

Not only is there a stronger relationship between female-headed households and social class among black families than among white families, but there is also a more unequal income distribution among black families than among white families. In 1970, the economist Andrew Brimmer pointed out that the lowest two-fifths of nonwhite families in 1969 contributed only 15.3 percent to the total nonwhite income, whereas the lowest two-fifths of white families provided 18.7 percent of the total white income; conversely, the upper two-fifths among white families contributed 63.7 percent of the total white income, whereas the upper two-fifths among nonwhite families provided 68.2 percent of the total nonwhite income. After reviewing income data in the

1960s, Brimmer concludes that, unlike among whites, the income gap among blacks seems to be widening.

There has been an uneven development of economic resources in the black community that is not reflected in the changes in the black occupational distribution over the last several decades. For unlike more affluent blacks, the black poor have been plagued by higher unemployment rates, lower labor-force participation rates, higher welfare rates, and, more recently, a slower movement out of poverty. For all these reasons, one has to give considerable credence to Brimmer's warning that there is a deepening economic schism in the black community, a schism that has become especially evident during the economic recession period of the 1970s. And since the structural barriers to occupational advancement were evident even during the high business-activity years in the late 1960s, even an economic recovery is not likely to reverse the pattern of unemployment, underemployment, poverty, welfare, and female-headed households. In short, there are clear indications that the economic gap between the black underclass (close to a third of the black population) and the higher-income blacks will very likely widen and solidify.

Ideology, Racial Protest, and the Changing Black Class Structure

If history tells us anything about the black experience it is that the different expressions of black protest tend often to be a by-product of economic class position. Although it is difficult at this point to determine the effect of the present economic gap between the black poor and the more affluent blacks on racial ideology and protest, there are some concrete observations that can be made about social class and the recent black protest movements.

One major effect of the changes in the black occupational structure after 1940 was the revival of the integrationist ideology and concern for civil rights that had preoccupied black leaders prior to the pessimistic period of self-help and racial solidarity at the turn of the century. "This generation of clerks, teachers, and postmen," states historian John Bracey, "had achieved a sufficient degree of economic security to be able to direct their attention to issues such as integrated education, open housing and free access to public accommodations, and they had the financial resources to support organizations like the N.A.A.C.P., the Urban League, and the numerous local human relations committees that acted in their behalf."

The civil rights organizations effectively pressed for the passage of enforceable bills against discrimination in northern states. In 1945 the New York state legislature enacted the Ives-Quinn Bill, which established the State Commission Against Discrimination, and New Jersey created a division against racial discrimination in the Department of Education. In 1946 Massachusetts established a Fair Employment Practices Commission, and by 1965 twenty-five states and numerous municipalities had established similar commissions. It was no coincidence that in many of the states in which civil rights laws were passed blacks had achieved significant political strength as a result of their increasing concentration in key industrial centers. Indeed, organizations such as the NAACP stressed the importance of the black vote when they pressed politicians to support civil rights legislation.

The mobilization of black political resources was not confined to the state and local levels, however. For example, the NAACP stepped up its litigation efforts and in 1954 won a favorable ruling in *Brown* v. *Board of Education* that overturned the "separate but equal" doctrine established in the *Plessy* v. *Ferguson* decision of 1896, and the proliferation of civil rights protests helped to generate the 1964 civil rights bill and the 1965 voting rights bill.

These federal, state, and municipal civil rights acts were mainly due to the efforts of the black professional groups (ministers, lawyers, teachers), students, and, particularly in the 1960s, sympathetic white liberals. Lower-income blacks had little involvement in civil rights politics up to the mid-1960s. As indicated in Chapter 4, blacks throughout the industrial period of race relations were denied access to the structural avenues for political participation (the urban political machines) and could only exert their influence through the extra-institutional civil rights movement. The movement had, as Martin Kilson has noted, a class and status bias and it tended to operate with little direct relationship to the black ghetto. It was not until the latter half of the 1960s that the ghetto blacks significantly determined the nature and direction of black politics.

The prelude to the active involvement of ghetto blacks in politics was the nonviolent resistance campaigns of the early 1960s. The distinctive feature of these protests, which took the form of sit-ins, freedom rides, and the like, was that they were led and organized by educated blacks, many of whom were college students. These black activists recognized and clearly articulated the view that because of the increasing black political resources, the pressures of nonviolent protests, and the United States' concern for world-wide opinion of her racial crisis, the government was likely to react to a disciplined nonviolent movement for civil rights with the enactment of antidiscrimination laws. They were correct. The passage of the 1964 civil rights bill (which outlawed, among other things, discrimination in public facilities, public accommodations, and employment) clearly demonstrated the success of the nonviolent protests against racial injustice. This legislation and the voting rights bill of 1965 (which was intended to enforce the Fifteenth Amendment to the Constitution) and the civil rights bill of 1968 (which banned discrimination in the rental or sale of homes, except for single-family houses sold by the owner himself) were particularly relevant to the growing black middle class that was not concerned about the day-to-day problems of economic survival. However, this legislation did not sufficiently address the unique problems of de facto segregation and social class subordination confronting ghetto blacks.

Nonetheless, although the racial issues that were defined and articulated by black activists in the early 1960s reflected the orientations and specific needs of the growing black middle class, the civil rights protests did in fact heighten lower-class black awareness of racial inequality. With electronic media penetrating the ghetto and covering all aspects of the civil rights protest movement, including the often violent resistance to racial change by white southerners, ghetto blacks, like blacks in all walks of life throughout the country, developed an impatience with the pace of racial change. Indeed it was the violent southern white resistance to racial protest that probably had the greatest effect in increasing militancy among various segments of the black population in the middle 1960s. It is not surprising that white southerners, particularly the white lower class, provided such firm resistance to the civil rights movement. Blacks made up nearly 40 percent of the southern population in the years following the Civil War; they were central to the economy as cheap laborers; and they were highly visible in virtually every region of the South. They proved to be particularly worrisome for the white lower-class masses, who were also victimized by poverty and illiteracy. It was this concern that motivated the most threatened of white southerners to attempt to eliminate black competition after the collapse of Reconstruction. And they did it well. The Jim Crow system of segregation was virtually unchallenged until the 1950s. As long as blacks "kept their place," white southerners exhibited little outward hostility. But the 1954 Supreme Court decision and the nonviolent demonstrations in the South threatened the "southern way of life," and the most violent resistance to racial change came from lower-class whites who felt that they had the most to lose by black encroachment. As white resistance to civil rights protests increased in the South, black bitterness, disgust, and disappointment over the pace of racial change also increased. In the urban ghetto these feelings were dramatically expressed in a series of violent revolts that erupted across the nation in the late 1960s.

It would be difficult to explain the ghetto revolts of the 1960s without relating them to the black disillusionment and anger following the violent white resistance to racial change. However, as I have argued elsewhere, this sense of anger and frustration was combined with specific grievances over unemployment, underemployment, inferior education, inadequate housing, and police brutality. Although these conditions have characterized ghetto living throughout the twentieth century, they seemed all the more intolerable to poor urban blacks in the face of their greater sensitivity to and awareness of racial oppression. As black leaders began to articulate these problems and focus on ways to solve them, the issue of civil rights, which had preoccupied middle-class blacks, was overshadowed by concerns that related more specifically to class subordination in the urban ghetto. Thus, in the late 1960s, some black leaders dramatically proclaimed that, for the black underclass, the question of human rights is far more fundamental than the question of civil rights. The late Martin Luther King was one of the first civil rights leaders to recognize the unique problems of poor Negroes, when he raised the pointed question, "What good is it to be allowed to eat in a restaurant if you can't afford a hamburger?"

If nothing else, the ghetto revolts of the late 1960s helped to shift the philosophy of the black protest movement. People who had been active in the civil rights movement began to focus on ways to erase the cycle of poverty, unemployment, and poor education. At the same time the federal government's

"War on Poverty," initiated partly in response to the riots, provided one major mechanism for the institutionalization of ghetto-based politics. Over two thousand community action programs were formed around the country. Although the result was not intended by federal authorities, these programs were often transformed from community service agencies into local political structures staffed and directed by lower-class militants. Across the country the lower-class leaders used these agencies in efforts to politicize the heretofore politically inactive ghetto blacks (welfare mothers, gangs, unskilled and semiskilled workers, school dropouts).

Black professional politicians were also caught up in this new mobilization of political power. With the increased politicization of the black lower class, black middle-class politicians found it necessary to articulate in a more forceful manner the particular needs and problems of their constituencies. This resulted in a shift from a middle-class-based politics to a lower-class-based politics, a shift from a politics whose issues emerged from the concerns of professional civil rights organizations and which focused primarily on problems of race discrimination, to a politics whose issues were defined in response to the urban unrest of the 1960s and which focused on problems of de facto segregation, class subordination, welfare state measures, and human survival in the ghetto.

The changing emphasis in black politics was also accompanied by the revival of the philosophy of racial solidarity growing out of the Black Power movement. Although the Black Power movement, like similar racial solidarity movements of the past, was a response to the frustrations encountered in the scope, pace, and quality of racial change (particularly the resistance to race protest in the South which led leaders such as Stokely Carmichael and H. Rap Brown to question the nonviolent resistance philosophy of moral persuasion and interracialism), its basic ideology guided many of the efforts to politically mobilize the black community. Thus for some black militants the development of black political power not only pertains to control of the basic institutions in the black community but also to political control of the central city. The significance and meaning of such political power in the age of modern industrialization is a subject to which I now turn.

Black Political Control of the Declining Central City

The dilemma for urban blacks is that they are gaining political influence in large urban areas (in 1975 blacks were mayors of eleven large metropolitan cities with populations of one hundred thousand or more) at the very time when the political power and influence of the cities are on the wane. The growth of corporate manufacturing, of retail and wholesale trade on the metropolitan periphery; the steady migration of impoverished minorities to the central city; the continuous exodus of the more affluent families to the suburbs; and, consequently, the relative decline of the central-city tax base have made urban politicians increasingly dependent on state and federal sources of funding in order to maintain properly the services that are vital for community health and stability. Whereas state and federal funds contributed about 25 percent to major-city revenues a decade ago, their contribution today amounts to about 50 percent. Thus America's metropolises are increasingly controlled by politicians whose constituencies do not necessarily live in those cities.

It is this *politics of dependency* that changes the meaning and reduces the significance of the greater black participation in urban political processes. And the militant cry of "black control of the central city" has a hollow ring when one confronts the hard reality of the deepening urban fiscal crisis that has developed in the wake of industry dispersion and urban population shifts. When we consider facts such as those which show that the aggregate income of families and unrelated individuals entering the central city between 1970 and 1973 was only 26 billion dollars, whereas the income of those *leaving* was roughly 55 billion dollars, it becomes clear that the internal resources needed by urban politicians to deal with the problems of the city continue to decrease. To suggest therefore that the solution to the problems of the black poor is dependent on blacks gaining political control of the central city is to ignore the fact that the fundamental bases of the urban crisis are not amenable to urban political solutions. Perhaps Katznelson best sums the matter up when he argues that:

> Neither demographic patterns nor poverty rates are caused in the cities, nor are they susceptible to much manipulation at that level. Urban authorities and citizens can hardly control the characteristics of the national economy, including its rate of growth and the nature of the demand for labor; nor can they control characteristics of the industry in which an individual is employed such as profit rates, technology, unionization and the industry's relationship to government, or individual characteristics like age, ethnicity and class, which affect employability. Migration patterns, too, depend heavily on "push" factors over which the receiving cities have virtually no control.

Despite the fact that racial friction is more a symptom than a cause of the declining central city, the urban crisis is often depicted or described as a racial crisis, and the proposed solutions advanced in different quarters (for example, black political control of the city, school desegregation, and residential integration) are often directed at altering the patterns of racial interaction or dominance. Nonetheless, the way that urban families are affected by or are responding to the problems of urban living are more a function of their economic class position than of their racial status. Thus, the declining growth of the manufacturing, wholesale, and retail industries in the central city creates problems for many lower-income whites and blacks but has had little impact on the white and black middle class, whose members have access to the higher-paying white-collar jobs in the expanding service-producing industries in the central city. Moreover, the deterioration of the urban public schools is not as much a problem for middle-income whites and blacks because they have the live option of private-school education; and although middle-class blacks have greater difficulty than middle-class whites in finding housing, their economic resources provide them with more opportunities to find desirable housing and neighborhoods within either the central city or the suburbs than both lower-income blacks and lower-income whites. Since the greater options open to black and white middle-income groups make them less susceptible to racial confrontation in the central city, it is the lower-income groups which are the direct recipients of racial antagonism emanating from the continuing struggle for moderately priced housing in the remaining stable neighborhoods, for access to the more adequate public schools, for the use of inexpensive recreational areas, and for political control of the central city.

Conclusion

In the first part of this chapter I tried to show how the growth of a black middle-class population accompanied the shift from a preindustrial to an industrial system of production. In the early twentieth century a Negro professional and business class developed to meet the needs of and serve the rapidly expanding black population. Disillusioned by the racial setbacks in both the North and the South at the turn of the century, this group of professionals and businessmen trumpeted the ideology of racial solidarity and pressed for the creation of a viable, self-sufficient black metropolis, only to see their hopes shattered by the ravages of the Depression. However, the New Deal marked the beginning of a progressive pattern of occupational upgrading of the black population. Specifically, the more liberal racial policies of labor unions, the increasing black employment in government, the expansion of black job opportunities in the private sector during and following World War II (as a result of the Fair Employment Practices Act and the labor shortage during the war and the expansion of the economy following the war) sharply increased the ranks of working-class and middle-class blacks by mid-twentieth century. Continued expansion of the economy during the 1950s and 1960s, the increased black union membership, the municipal, state, and federal equal employment legislation, and the continued migration of blacks from the rural South to the industrial cities of the nation resulted in an even greater increase of blacks from lower-paying to higher-paying jobs. By 1970 the black occupational structure, which only three decades earlier reflected an overwhelming concentration of Negroes in the low-paying service worker, unskilled laborer, and farm worker jobs, revealed a substantial majority of black workers in white-collar positions and higher-paying blue-collar positions.

I have been careful to point out, however, that the impressive occupational gains made by blacks during these three decades have been partly offset by the effects of basic structural changes in our modern industrial economy, changes that are having differential impact on the different income groups in the black community. Unlike more affluent blacks, many of whom continued to experience improved economic opportunity even during the recession period of the 1970s, the black underclass has evidenced higher unemployment rates, lower labor-force participation rates, higher welfare rates, and, more recently, a sharply declining movement out of poverty. The net effect has been a deepening economic schism in the black community that could very easily widen and solidify.

Considering the changes in the black occupational structure from the industrial to the modern industrial period of American race relations, I have tried to show the connection between social class and the recent black protest movement. I pointed out that, as the ranks of the black middle class swelled, as more and more blacks achieved economic security, attention was directed to issues such as integration and civil rights politics, issues that had preoccupied black leaders prior to the pessimistic period of racial solidarity at the turn of the century. Thus, it was the more educated blacks who led the civil rights campaigns in the late 1950s and early 1960s, and effectively used civil rights politics in achieving the passage of various municipal, state, and federal civil rights laws. However, I argued that although the civil rights movement reflected the needs and interests of the black middle class, it did not sufficiently address the unique problems of class subordination and de facto segregation in the black ghetto. Indeed ghetto blacks had little direct involvement in the civil rights protests. However, the very activity of the civil rights activists had the effect of increasing lower-class black awareness of and impatience with racial oppression. And these feelings exploded in a proliferation of ghetto riots in the late 1960s. If nothing else, the revolts led black leaders to redefine the problems of poor blacks and paved the way for a shift from a middle-class-based black politics to a lower-class-based black politics. This shift in black politics was also accompanied by the new strategies of black political power that grew out of the Black Power movement, including the avowed goal, in some quarters, of gaining black political control of the central city.

However, as I emphasized, blacks are gaining urban political influence at the very time when the city, as a base of political power, is on the decline. And, the problems created by population shifts, industry dispersion, and other basic economic changes cannot be sufficiently addressed by urban political solutions.

Audre Lorde
from *Sister Outsider*

POETRY IS NOT A LUXURY

THE QUALITY OF LIGHT by which we scrutinize our lives has direct bearing upon the product which we live, and upon the changes which we hope to bring about through those lives. It is within this light that we form those ideas by which we pursue our magic and make it realized. This is poetry as illumination, for it is through poetry that we give name to those ideas which are—until the poem—nameless and formless, about to be birthed, but already felt. That distillation of experience from which true poetry springs births thought as dream births concept, as feeling births idea, as knowledge births (precedes) understanding.

As we learn to bear the intimacy of scrutiny and to flourish within it, as we learn to use the products of that scrutiny for power within our living, those fears which rule our lives and form our silences begin to lose their control over us.

For each of us as women, there is a dark place within, where hidden and growing our true spirit rises, "beautiful/and tough as chestnut/stanchions against (y)our nightmare of weakness/"* and of impotence.

These places of possibility within ourselves are dark because they are ancient and hidden; they have survived and grown strong through that darkness. Within these deep places, each one of us holds an incredible reserve of creativity and power, of unexamined and unrecorded emotion and feeling. The woman's place of power within each of us is neither white nor surface; it is dark, it is ancient, and it is deep.

When we view living in the european mode only as a problem to be solved, we rely solely upon our ideas to make us free, for these were what the white fathers told us were precious.

But as we come more into touch with our own ancient, non-european consciousness of living as a situation to be experienced and interacted with, we learn more and more to cherish our feelings, and to respect those hidden sources of our power from where true knowledge and, therefore, lasting action comes.

*From "Black Mother Woman," first published in *From A Land Where Other People Live* (Broadside Press, Detroit, 1973), and collected in *Chosen Poems: Old and New* (W. W. Norton and Company, New York, 1982) p. 53.

At this point in time, I believe that women carry within ourselves the possibility for fusion of these two approaches so necessary for survival, and we come closest to this combination in our poetry. I speak here of poetry as a revelatory distillation of experience, not the sterile word play that, too often, the white fathers distorted the word *poetry* to mean—in order to cover a desperate wish for imagination without insight.

For women, then, poetry is not a luxury. It is a vital necessity of our existence. It forms the quality of the light within which we predicate our hopes and dreams toward survival and change, first made into language, then into idea, then into more tangible action. Poetry is the way we help give name to the nameless so it can be thought. The farthest horizons of our hopes and fears are cobbled by our poems, carved from the rock experiences of our daily lives.

As they become known to and accepted by us, our feelings and the honest exploration of them become sanctuaries and spawning grounds for the most radical and daring of ideas. They become a safe-house for that difference so necessary to change and the conceptualization of any meaningful action. Right now, I could name at least ten ideas I would have found intolerable or incomprehensible and frightening, except as they came after dreams and poems. This is not idle fantasy, but a disciplined attention to the true meaning of "it feels right to me." We can train ourselves to respect our feelings and to transpose them into a language so they can be shared. And where that language does not yet exist, it is our poetry which helps to fashion it. Poetry is not only dream and vision; it is the skeleton architecture of our lives. It lays the foundations for a future of change, a bridge across our fears of what has never been before.

Possibility is neither forever nor instant. It is not easy to sustain belief in its efficacy. We can sometimes work long and hard to establish one beachhead of real resistance to the deaths we are expected to live, only to have that beachhead assaulted or threatened by those canards we have been socialized to fear, or by the withdrawal of those approvals that we have been warned to seek for safety. Women see ourselves diminished or softened by the falsely benign accusations of childishness, of nonuniversality, of changeability, of sensuality. And who asks the question: Am I altering your aura, your ideas, your dreams, or am I merely moving you to temporary and reactive action? And even though the latter is no mean task, it is one that must be seen within the context of a need for true alteration of the very foundations of our lives.

The white fathers told us: I think, therefore I am. The Black mother within each of us—the poet—whispers in our dreams: I feel, therefore I can be free. Poetry coins the language to express and charter this revolutionary demand, the implementation of that freedom.

However, experience has taught us that action in the now is also necessary, always. Our children cannot dream unless they live, they cannot live unless they are nourished, and who else will feed them the real food without which their dreams will be no different from ours? "If you want us to change the world someday, we at least have to live long enough to grow up!" shouts the child.

Sometimes we drug ourselves with dreams of new ideas. The head will save us. The brain alone will set us free. But there are no new ideas still waiting in the wings to save us as women, as human. There are only old and forgotten ones, new combinations, extrapolations and recognitions from within ourselves—along with the renewed courage to try them out. And we must constantly encourage ourselves and each other to attempt the heretical actions that our dreams imply, and so many of our old ideas disparage. In the forefront of our move toward change, there is only poetry to hint at possibility made real. Our poems formulate the implications of ourselves, what we feel within and dare make real (or bring action into accordance with), our fears, our hopes, our most cherished terrors.

For within living structures defined by profit, by linear power, by institutional dehumanization, our feelings were not meant to survive. Kept around as unavoidable adjuncts or pleasant pastimes, feelings were expected to kneel to thought as women were expected to kneel to men. But women have survived. As poets. And there are no new pains. We have felt them all already. We have hidden that fact in the same place where we have hidden our power. They surface in our dreams, and it is our dreams that point the way to freedom. Those dreams are made realizable through our poems that give us the strength and courage to see, to feel, to speak, and to dare.

If what we need to dream, to move our spirits most deeply and directly toward and through promise, is discounted as a luxury, then we give up the core—the fountain—of our power, our womanness; we give up the future of our worlds.

For there are no new ideas. There are only new ways of making them felt—of examining what those ideas feel like being lived on Sunday morning at 7 A.M., after brunch, during wild love, making war, giving birth, mourning our dead—while we suffer the old longings, battle the old warnings and fears of being silent and impotent and alone, while we taste new possibilities and strengths.

THE MASTER'S TOOLS WILL NEVER DISMANTLE THE MASTER'S HOUSE

I AGREED TO TAKE PART in a New York University Institute for the Humanities conference a year ago, with the understanding that I would be commenting upon papers dealing with the role of difference within the lives of american women: difference of race, sexuality, class, and age. The absence of these considerations weakens any feminist discussion of the personal and the political.

It is a particular academic arrogance to assume any discussion of feminist theory without examining our many differences, and without a significant input from poor women, Black and Third World women, and lesbians. And yet, I stand here as a Black lesbian feminist, having been invited to comment within the only panel at this conference where the input of Black feminists and lesbians is represented. What this says about the vision of this conference is sad, in a country where racism, sexism, and homophobia are inseparable. To read this program is to assume that lesbian and Black women have nothing to say about existentialism, the erotic, women's culture and silence, developing feminist theory, or heterosexuality and power. And what does it mean in personal and political terms when even the two Black women who did present here were literally found at the last hour? What does it mean when the tools of a racist patriarchy are used to examine the fruits of that same patriarchy? It means that only the most narrow perimeters of change are possible and allowable.

The absence of any consideration of lesbian consciousness or the consciousness of Third World women leaves a serious gap within this conference and within the papers presented here. For example, in a paper on material relationships between women, I was conscious of an either/or model of nurturing which totally dismissed my knowledge as a Black lesbian. In this paper there was no examination of mutuality between women, no systems of shared support, no interdependence as exists between lesbians and women-identified women. Yet it is only in the patriarchal model of nurturance that women "who attempt to emancipate themselves pay perhaps too high a price for the results," as this paper states.

For women, the need and desire to nurture each other is not pathological but redemptive, and it is within that knowledge that our real power is rediscovered. It is this real connection which is so feared by a patriarchal world. Only within a patriarchal structure is maternity the only social power open to women.

Interdependency between women is the way to a freedom which allows the *I* to *be*, not in order to be used, but in order to be creative. This is a difference between the passive *be* and the active *being*.

Advocating the mere tolerance of difference between women is the grossest reformism. It is a total denial of the creative function of difference in our lives. Difference must be not merely tolerated, but seen as a fund of necessary polarities between which our creativity can spark like a dialectic. Only then does the necessity for interdependency become unthreatening. Only within that interdependency of different strengths, acknowledged and equal, can the power to seek new ways of being in the world generate, as well as the courage and sustenance to act where there are no charters.

Within the interdependence of mutual (nondominant) differences lies that security which enables us to descend into the chaos of knowledge and return with true visions of our future, along with the concomitant power to effect those changes which can bring that future into being. Difference is that raw and powerful connection from which our personal power is forged.

As women, we have been taught either to ignore our differences, or to view them as causes for separation and suspicion rather than as forces for change. Without community there is no liberation, only the most vulnerable and temporary armistice between an individual and her oppression. But community must not mean a shedding of our differences, nor the pathetic pretense that these differences do not exist.

Those of us who stand outside the circle of this society's definition of acceptable women; those of us who have been forged in the crucibles of difference—those of us who are poor, who are lesbians, who are Black, who are older—know that *survival is not an academic skill*. It is learning how to stand alone, unpopular and sometimes reviled, and how to make common cause with those others identified as outside the structures in order to define and seek a world in which we can all flourish. It is learning how to take our differences and make them strengths. *For the master's tools will never dismantle the master's house*. They may allow us temporarily to beat him at his own game, but they will never enable us to bring about genuine change. And this fact is only threatening to those women who still define the master's house as their only source of support.

Poor women and women of Color know there is a difference between the daily manifestations of marital slavery and prostitution because it is our daughters who line 42nd Street. If white american feminist theory need not deal with the differences between us, and the resulting difference in our oppressions, then how do you deal with the fact that the women who clean your houses and tend your children while you attend conferences on feminist theory are, for the most part, poor women and women of Color? What is the theory behind racist feminism?

In a world of possibility for us all, our personal visions help lay the groundwork for political action. The failure of academic feminists to recognize difference as a crucial strength is a failure to reach beyond the first patriarchal lesson. In our world, divide and conquer must become define and empower.

Why weren't other women of Color found to participate in this conference? Why were two phone calls to me considered a consultation? Am I the only possible source of names of Black feminists? And although the Black panelist's paper ends on an important and powerful connection of love between women, what about interracial cooperation between feminists who don't love each other?

In academic feminist circles, the answer to these questions is often, "We did not know who to ask." But that is the same evasion of responsibility, the same cop-out, that keeps Black women's art out of women's exhibitions, Black women's work out of most feminist publications except for the occasional "Special Third World Women's Issue," and Black women's texts off your reading lists. But as Adrienne Rich pointed out in a recent talk, white feminists have educated themselves about such an enormous amount over the past ten years, how come you haven't also educated yourselves about Black women and the differences between us—white and Black—when it is key to our survival as a movement?

Women of today are still being called upon to stretch across the gap of male ignorance and to educate men as to our existence and our needs. This is an old and primary tool of all oppressors to keep the oppressed occupied with the master's concerns. Now we hear that it is the task of women of Color to educate white women—in the face of tremendous resistance—as to our existence, our differences, our relative roles in our joint survival. This is a diversion of energies and a tragic repetition of racist patriarchal thought.

Simone de Beauvoir once said: "It is in the knowledge of the genuine conditions of our lives that we must draw our strength to live and our reasons for acting."

Racism and homophobia are real conditions of all our lives in this place and time. *I urge each one of us here to reach down into that deep place of knowledge inside herself and touch that terror and loathing of any difference that lives there. See whose face it wears.* Then the personal as the political can begin to illuminate all our choices.

Sonia Sanchez
from *homegirls and handgrenades*

REFLECTIONS AFTER THE JUNE 12TH MARCH FOR DISARMAMENT

I have come to you tonite out of the depths
   of slavery
   from white hands peeling black skins over
   america;
I have come out to you from reconstruction eyes
   that closed on black humanity
   that reduced black hope to the dark
   huts of america;
I have come to you from the lynching years,
   the exploitation of black men and women by
   a country that allowed the swinging of
   strange fruits from southern trees;
I have come to you tonite thru the
   delaney years, the du bois years, the
   b.t. washington years, the robeson
   years, the garvey years, the
   depression years, the you can't eat
   or sit or live just die here years,
   the civil rights years, the black power
   years, the black nationalist years, the
   affirmative action years, the liberal
   years, the neo-conservative years;
I have come to say that those years
   were not in vain, the ghosts of our
   ancestors searching this american dust for
   rest were not in vain, black women
   walking their lives in clots were not
   in vain, the years walked
   sideways in a foresaken land were not
   in vain;
I have come to you tonite as an equal,
   as a comrade, as a black woman
   walking down a corridor of tears,

looking neither to the left or the right,
pulling my history with bruised
heels,
beckoning to the illusion of america
daring you to look me in the eyes to
see these faces, the exploitation of a
people because of skin pigmentation;
I have come to you tonite because no people
have been asked to be modern day people
with the history of slavery, and still
we walk, and still we talk, and
still we plan, and still we hope and
still we sing;
I have come to you tonite because there are
inhumanitarians in the world. they are not
new. they are old. they go back into history.
they were called explorers, soldiers, mercenaries,
imperialists, missionaries, adventurers,
but they looked at the world for what
it would give up to them and they violated
the land and the people, they looked
at the land and sectioned it up for
private ownership, they looked at the
people and decided how to manipulate
them thru fear and ignorance, they looked
at the gold and began to hoard and
worship it;
I have come to you because it is time
for us all to purge capitalism from
our dreams, to purge materialism
from our eyes, from the planet earth
to deliver the earth again into the hands
of the humanitarians;
I have come to you tonite not just for the stoppage
of nuclear proliferation, nuclear
plants, nuclear bombs, nuclear
waste, but to stop the proliferation
of nuclear minds, of nuclear generals
of nuclear presidents, of nuclear scientists,
who spread human and nuclear waste
over the world;
I come to you because the world needs to be
saved for the future generations who must
return the earth to peace, who will not
be startled by a man's/woman's skin color;

I come to you because the world needs sanity
    now, needs men and women who will
    not work to produce nuclear weapons,
    who will give up their need for excess
    wealth and learn how to share the
    world's resources, who will never
    again as scientists invent again just
    for the sake of inventing;
I come to you because we need to turn our
    eyes to the beauty of this planet, to the
    bright green laughter of trees, to the beautiful
    human animals waiting to smile their unprostituted smiles;
I have come to you to talk about our inexperience
    at living as human beings, thru death marches and camps,
    thru middle passages and slavery
    and thundering countries raining hungry faces;
I am here to move against
    leaving our shadows implanted on the
    earth while our bodies disintegrate in
    nuclear lightning;
I am here between the voices of our ancestors
    and the noise of the planet,
    between the surprise of death and life;
I am here because I shall not give the
    earth up to non-dreamers and earth molesters;
I am here to say to you:
    my body is full of veins
    like the bombs waiting to burst
    with blood.
    we must learn to suckle life not
    bombs and rhetoric
    rising up in redwhiteandblue patriotism;
I am here. and my breath/our breaths
    must thunder across this land
    arousing new breaths. new life.
    new people, who will live in peace
    and honor.

MIA'S

(*missing in action and other atlantas*)

this morning i heard the cuckoo bird calling
and i saw children wandering like quicksand
over the exquisite city

scooping up summer leaves in enema bags
self-sustaining warriors spitting
long metal seeds on porcelain bricks.

atlanta:
              city of cathedrals and colleges
              rustling spirituals in the morning air
              while black skulls splinter the nite
              and emmett till bones drop in choruses.

littleman. where you running to?
yes. you. youngblood.
touching and touched at random
running towards places where legions ride.

              yo man. you want some
              action. i'm yo/main man.
              buy me. i can give it to you
              wholesale.

heyladycarryyobagsfoyou?
50¢costyouonly50¢.yo.man.
washyocar.idoagoodjob.
heymanwhyyousocold?
yoman.youneedyobasement
cleaned?meandmypartner
doyouupdecent. yoman.

johannesburg:
              squatting like a manicured mannequin
              while gathering ghosts clockwise
              and policing men, using up their tongues
              pronounce death syllables
              in the nite.

              august 18:
30 yr. old african arrested
on the highway. taken to
port elizabeth. examined.
found to be in good health.
placed in a private cell
for questioning.

              sept. 7:
varicose cells. full of
assassins. beating their
red arms against the walls.
and biko. trying to ration

his blood spills permanent
blood in a port elizabeth cell.
and biko's body sings heavy
with cracks.

   sept. 13:
hear ye. hear ye. hear ye.
i regret to announce that stephen
biko is dead. he was refused
food since sept. 5th. we did
all we could for the man.
he has hanged himself while sleeping
we did all we could for him.
he fell while answering our questions
we did all we could for the man.
he washed his face and hung him
self out to dry
we did all we could for him.
he drowned while drinking his supper
we did all we could for the man.
he fell
       hangedhimself   starved
drowned himself
we did all we could for him.
it's hard to keep someone alive
who won't even cooperate.
hear ye.

can i borrow yo/eyes south africa?
can i redistribute yo/legs america?
multiplying multinationally over the world.

    yebo madola*
    yebo bafazi
        i say
    yebo madola
    yebo bafazi

el salvador:
    country of vowelled ghosts.
    country of red bones
    a pulse beat gone mad
    with death.
    redwhiteandblue guns splintering the

*come on men and women

nite with glass
redwhiteandblue death squads running on borrowed
knees cascading dreams.

quiero ser libre
pues libre naci
       i say
quiero ser libre
pues libre naci

they came to the village that nite. all day the
birds had pedalled clockwise drowning their
feet in clouds. the old men and women
talked of foreboding. that it was a bad sign.
and they crossed themselves in two as
their eyes concluded design.
they came that nite to the village.
calling peace. liberty. freedom.
their tongues lassoing us with
circus patriotism
their elbows wrapped in blood paper
they came penises drawn
their white togas covering their
stained glass legs
their thick hands tatooing decay
on los campaneros till their
young legs rolled out from under them
to greet death
they came leaving a tatoo of hunger
over the land.

quiero ser libre
pues libre naci

so i plant myself in the middle
of my biography
of dying drinking working dancing people
their tongues swollen with slavery
waiting and i say
yebo madola
yebo bafazi
cmon men and women
peel your guerilla veins toward
this chorus line of beasts who will sell
the morning air passing thru your bones
cmon. men. and. women.

plant yourself in the middle of your
blood with no transfusions for
reagan or botha or bush or
d'aubuisson.

plant yourself in the eyes of the
children who have died carving out their
own childhood.
plant yourself in the dreams of the people
scattered by morning bullets.
let there be everywhere our talk.
let there be everywhere our eyes.
let there be everywhere our thoughts.
let there be everywhere our love.
let there be everywhere our actions.
breathing hope and victory
into their unspoken questions
summoning the dead to life again
to the hereafter of freedom.

cmon. men. women.
i want to be free.

Molefi Asante
from *Afrocentricity*

CHAPTER 2

The Constituents of Power

Language Liberation

An ideology for liberation must find its existence in ourselves, it cannot be external to us, and it cannot be imposed by those other than ourselves; it must be derived from our particular historical and cultural experience. Our liberation from the captivity of racist language is the first order of the intellectual. *There can be no freedom until there is a freedom of the mind.* As Lorenzo Turner understood, language is essentially the control of thought. It becomes impossible for us to direct our future until we control our language. The sense of language is in precision of vocabulary and structure for a particular social context. If we allow others to box us into their concepts, then we will always talk and act like them. Black language must possess instrumentality, that is, it must be able to do something for our liberation; such a position is not foreign to our particular or collective international struggle. Liberation is fundamentally a seizure of the instruments of control. If the language is not functional, then it should have no place in our vocabulary. In every revolution, the people have first seized the instruments of idea formation and then property production.

History is instructive for us. In the thirteen American colonies, the rebels took *liberty* and *parliamentary representation* and gave them definitions foreign to the ruling classes. In 1789, in the French Revolution, the so-called first modern revolution, the people took *liberté*, *égalité*, and *fraternité* and made them instruments for a collective will to power. The Soviet Union's revolution of 1917 could not have succeeded without the creative eloquence of Trotsky and Lenin. They understood that to free the masses from abject slavery it was necessary to teach them to think in different terms. In Algeria, in Cuba, in Mozambique, in Zimbabwe, and in Angola the same pattern appears. We cannot seek only to be opposites of the oppressor, that simply makes us "reactionaries," and "reactionaries" are conservative not progressive. The aim of systematic nationalism is to make the language ours, to claim a new language, not merely an opposite language.

Africans have shown a remarkable ability to humanize any language we have spoken whether it was Portuguese, English, Spanish, French, or Russian. What Nicolas Guillen did to Spanish, what Alexander Pushkin did to Russian, what Langston Hughes did to English, and what Aime Cesaire, the greatest of all poets, did to French, suggest that it is in the soul of our people to seize and redirect language toward liberating ideas and thought.

African-Americans are an historic people. We have met the challenges of an alien culture, a racist mentality, and an exploitative enterprise with our African ability to transform reality with words and actions. We must nourish this capability. Maulana Karenga argues that "no people can turn its history and humanity over to alien hands and expect social justice and respect" (Karenga, 1979). Language is the essential instrument of social cohesion. Social cohesion is the fundamental element of liberation.

All language is epistemic. Our language provides our understanding of our reality. *A revolutionary language must not befuddle; it cannot be allowed to confuse.* Critics must actively pursue the clarification of public language when they believe it is designed to whiten the issues. We know through science and rhetoric; they are parallel systems of epistemology. Rhetoric is art and art is as much a way of knowing as science.

When the oppressor seeks to use language for the manipulation of our reality; Nommo, for ourselves, and of ourselves, must continue the correct path of critical analysis. Such a path is not dictated necessarily by the oppressor's rhetoric but *Njia* for the Afro-American intellectual. Objectivism, born of the history, culture, and materials of our existence must be at the base of our talk and our essaying.

It is necessary to understand the power of this concept. Some of our poets and preachers have understood it. We must gather the materials and sources from ourselves first. We must then move to enlarge upon our precepts and concepts by constant clarification and progressivism. The language of the exploiter is vile, corrupt, and vulgar. For him racism is nonexistent because it is now merely discrimination or pragmatically the inequality of opportunity. We cannot permit this easy slide into exploitative rhetoric. *There is no such thing as a black racism against whites; racism is based on fantasy; black views of whites are based on fact.* Racist language makes the victim the criminal. We must repudiate that thinking.

The use of the terms *ethnicity*, *disadvantaged*, *minority*, and *ghetto* are antithetical to our political consciousness which is indivisible from the international political struggle against racism. Our American situation has never been defined as "ethnic" until now when it is beneficial for the oppressor. This is new and must be understood. Our situation has been one where racism victimizes Africans as a race. Racism is the fundamental contradiction in African-American existence. It is also the case in Brazil, South Africa, and Namibia. It is too early for us to allow that to be forgotten. But this twist in talk is due to the fact that race functions as a fundamental category of class in the United States. The ruling classes in America have moved to interpret European ethnics as similar to blacks in their predicament. Such rhetoric generates class conflict which hides racism, the primary reality of American society. Class conflict does exist, yet such conflict is also manipulated by language in a society where rulers are isolated from the ruled. Language serves as an instrument of social restraint. There are certain things you do not say to some people and surely some things you do not do to them. Our breaking away from the structures of the oppressor's language will be instructive at a class as well as at the race level.

Those among us who have been trapped into using Marxist language have understood neither our history nor that of Marxism. While it is possible for socialism to find expression in places outside of its original intellectual context, no context is ever the same. Each context invites a variation in the doctrine; and some contexts may find the expression of the doctrine unnatural. Needless to say, it cannot and has not been imposed on those contexts which would have responded more naturally to other political expressions. Mozambique is not Cuba is not China and so forth. An adaptive process takes precedence over the presence of the doctrine. This is true of capitalism as well. But those among us who become dogmatic in any doctrine except on founded upon principles and assumption derived from our historical context will always make the wrong analysis. You cannot use the language of socialism only and expect to escape ambiguity.

Systematic nationalism does not negate socialism (Asante, 1978). Socialism provides us with some possibilities of freedom from class exploitation but our political liberation must come primarily from notions forged from our social experiences. Our language must reflect liberation as well. We have been exploited, discriminated, oppressed, humiliated, and assassinated. Our political doctrines must speak to that reality. Since language is the instrument for conveying that truth, our language must be aggressive, and innovative. As inventive people, we must make sure that our linguistic inventions are functional in a socially and politically cohesive way. This means we must rid our language of degrading terms which have been inherited from our oppressor.

Our history is replete with political cycles as evidenced by the historical discontinuity of our struggle. The basic political quality, exemplified in our perpetual will to freedom frequently has been diverted by subversion, discontinuous explications, and personality phenomena into rarefied and stratified discussions which have little basis in experience, the most radical of empiricisms. Systematic nationalism has occupied and will continue to reign supreme in our ideological confrontation with racist language and behavior because of its groundedness in the folk beliefs of our people, its historical locus in creative struggle, and the power of the rhetoric which it commands. Social and political conquest are the results of intellectual and spiritual conquest, and time does not change the fact.

The complexity of our intellectual heritage defies brief recapitulation. Yet when we contemplate the politics of communication and continual restructuring of black language to accommodate the intensification of struggle we must remember the contributions of Damas, Blyden, Padmore, Locke, W.E.B. Du Bois, Malcolm X, C.L.R. James. We are the inheritors of a noble tradition. Add to this tradition the wealth of values passed from generation to generation, and we have a formidable cultural inheritance as well.

However, we cannot peddle good feelings. We must judge relevance, evaluate the historical realism, and apply appropriate models for liberation. I seek a language whose axiological basis resides in history but those pragmatic manifestations are in our present reality. History is self compliments; the present puts us face to face with ourselves as we are. Our history cannot be left for others to write but neither should our present be turned over to others. All oppressor nations attempt to create taboos or legal prohibitions to block languages which might change the way people think. Such oppressor societies try to perpetuate their own politics by blocking competing language forms.

Lessons from History

The Third Reich created the *Regenspropagandaministerium*. Information ministries frequently have been turned to suppressive uses. In the United States we must combat a huge bureaucracy which has a life of its own. Pronouncements, memoranda, and policies are generated by the internal energy of the system so that an individual working in the bureau becomes merely an informational link in the process already begun. There seems to be no beginning or ending. *The force of our truth must be so deafening that even the bureaucrats will have to change their language to accommodate the reality.* This was being accomplished during the 1960's and 1970's. What happened of course was that the media stole the irony and facilitated acceptance of "right on" with a bic ballpen advertisement "write on." Lyndon Johnson was to "overcome" and "Black is beautiful, so is green" became Reverend Ike parody. The white Left wanted all power to the people, and so did the white Right. Black power alone seemed to have escaped this whitening process, but even here we had Nixonians rushing to explain that it meant black capitalism.

The vicious South African supremacist state has stolen liberating language through the manipulation of the communication process. They have employed two methods of control: (1) the modification of the meaning of words and (2) the suppression of opposition language. Consequently, the people battle against distortions, fallacies, and lies, as well as physical oppression. However, the people will win because the spirit of resistance to evil is ultimately more creative than the evil will to destroy.

The language of personal racism expressed in *de facto*, and *de jure* situations was called institutional racism by Stokely Carmichael and Charles Hamilton. Their creative exposition, based upon the people's historical objections, and mass action campaigns, produced institutional changes. The government mandated affirmative action programs and it seemed as if institutional racism was being legislated out of existence. The talk went right along with the legislation. Those of us who had marched, been jailed and clubbed thought that progress was being made. But only the rhetoric of oppression has changed. Personal racism remains unabated. What happened was that *institutional racism* gave way to *process racism*.

Process racism as a metamorphosis of institutional racism dominates the society. Jimmy Carter's Georgia church dispensed with an institutional stand against blacks and adopted a process stand by setting up a screening committee. The idea is to give the impression of running while standing still. Our aggressive language must attack, not institutional or process racism but personal racism. Scholars must study the psyches of racists, their lifestyles and the value-beliefs systems in order to devise language strategies to deal with reactionary postures.

Our task is *elephant*. The massiveness of it can be met by skillful rhetoricians understanding the immensity of the problem. A mobilizing language would elevate nationalism above religious sects, sex roles, and social class distinctions. As nationalism counteracted ethnic divisions and social class in Mozambique and Zimbabwe it can also do in African America. Everyone from merchant to laborer, from Christian to Muslim, from intellectual to illiterate, and from aspiring socialist to aspiring capitalist must be mobilized by a new language of consciousness. Malcolm X acknowledged this when he said we were attacked because of our blackness and not because we were Baptist, Methodist, or Muslim. Religious and class struggles must be subordinated to national struggle in an aggressive stance toward racism. Such substantive rhetoric, even acted out in the formation of group cohesion, cannot eliminate all internal contradictions. What is necessary, however, is that the national cause becomes the principal interest of the people and all other interests become subordinate considerations.

In the resurgence of nationalism, which is an arm of pan-Africanism, we cannot permit the hijacking of the movement by those who understand neither our history nor our struggle. Our last cycle was a lesson in history. Strident rhetoric between different political organizations professing the liberation of the people gave aid and comfort to the enemy forces. Despite the rhetoric it is clear now that the Black Panthers foreshadowed the decline of nationalism in the late sixties. Streetwise brothers and sisters learned the proper tenets of Marx and Mao but failed to study David Walker, Henry Garnet, Marcus Garvey, Kwame Nkrumah and Malcolm X. Bobby Seale, co-founder of the Panthers, often found himself trying to moderate the rhetoric of Mao's four works and other teachings. Thus, a brilliant community program which inspired thousands was stagnated because it lacked an historical perspective. Seale recognized this more than Huey Newton and sought to elevate the consciousness of radical black history. Nonetheless, their rhetoric remained without the historical content so necessary for a correct interpretation of our American experience.

Afrocentric writers restructure the language to tell the truth. Our logicians and rhetoricians must not let us fall into any linguistic chasms. The major human rights problem in the world today in terms of extent of exploitation, class suffering and racial oppression is in southern Africa. We cannot allow ourselves to be beguiled by any rhetoric which elevates the suffering of Russian Jews any higher than the plight of Africans in Azania. It is our task to *endarken* the people that national struggle Azania is a part of our struggle. We must demonstrate that those who minimize the suffering in Azania are blinded by racism, and to the fact that Mandela is a victim of white racism. Thousands suffer with him in South African jails. Let us build a language of truth. Upon the base of this language can be erected the pyramids of progressive national liberation.

The communication of our national will to liberty through adequate actions and symbols is the single most important fact in cultural liberation. Whether in the use of language or other symbols the propagation of culture views and senses distinguishes one society from another. The cardinality of productive forces, technologically derived modes of dissemination, pre-empts all other concerns with the nature of our political rhetoric. The control of mass media technology, electronic and print, by reactionary forces around the world must be neutralized by the persistence of our historically and culturally derived mechanism of political propagation. We must create, innovate, and bombard the communication channels with positive images, which will constitute a revolutionary response to racist repression. In voice, percussion, writing, and images we should express the totality of our American experience, knowing both its separateness from and its connectedness to a Pan-African world. Certain distinctions, to be sure, exist within societies because of the *emphasis* placed on the productive forces and the political objectives. The imperialism of rhetoric, couched in either capitalist or socialist terms, must be curbed by an aggressive language which finds it *fons et origo* in our natural will to freedom. A language, dedicated to such an end, regularly expanded with relevant ideas and symbols, is crucial to our liberation from racist concepts. So when you greet one another say, "Peace, freedom belongs to you."

Types of Intelligence

Three types of intelligence exist in the world: *creative intelligence, recreative intelligence,* and *consumer intelligence.* The most valuable type of intelligence is that which communicates with the whole earth by remaining open to associations, ideas, spaces, and possibilities. Disciplined attitudes rooted in Afrocentric images and symbols can create endless combinations; there are numerous examples from our history of the constructive potential of creative combinations.

Re-creative intellectuals are able to take the vision of the creative intellectuals to new heights. They do this by constantly seizing upon ideas and propagating them with great clarity. Thus Malcolm X was the reproductive mind for the work of Elijah Muhammad; Halisi and Baraka propagated the works of Karenga; Lenin and Mao expounded the principles of Marx; Jesus had twelve initial teachers; Muhammad sent Abu Bakr and others to the various parts of the world; King had his Abernathy and Jackson. These reproductive minds may be creative in other areas but in the situations mentioned they were recreative. Some of the greatest people known in the history of the world are reproductive minds. In Afrocentricity there will be numerous poets, scholars, teachers, artists, and philosophers who will surpass those who laid the foundation in terms of propagation.

The third type of intelligence is that of the practical intellectual who neither creates nor recreates but rather consumes and utilizes ideas. In an Afrocentric society, all intelligence is accepted as containing the God-force. Yet it is understood that not everyone can appropriate its power for every purpose. Some people are actualizing and recreative, and still others are actively practicing and consuming. There is nothing inherently wrong with consumption; one must know what is being consumed.

With this analysis of intelligence it becomes possible for us to see the connectedness of intelligence to nature and culture. The Afrocentric perspective envisions one wholistic, organic process. Thus, all political, artistic, economic, ethical, and aesthetic issues are connected to the context of Afrocentric knowledge. Everything that you do; all that you are and will become is intricately wrapped with the Kente of culture. Mind and matter, spirit and fact, truth and opinion, are all aspects or dimensions of one vital process.

There can be no good intelligence except as it is reflected in the nature of things. All propositions, statements about good, truth, falsehood and evil, rest with the Afrocentric concept of nature. What is the nature of things? For us, naturalism in of itself is inert and does not explain our spirituality, or vitality, our creative and dynamic energy. Idealism begins with too much abstractness to account for process; static concepts box in our vital nature as a people.

All things are possible as actions; all objects are integral to nature as objects; and all phenomena are potentially good or evil according to their cultural use. Afrocentricity views all things as integrated with culture and nature. We are one. Facts, then, are not intelligence or knowledge about things. The knowledge of a thing can only come through an act of judgment involving concept and ideology. What concept do you possess and in what ideological framework is it contained? These questions speak to the direction, intensity, purpose, and identity of the seeker. Reality exists not merely as a reality of facts but a reality of creation and perception.

Intellectual Vigilance

Afrocentricity maintains intellectual vigilance as the proper posture toward all scholarship which ignores the origin of civilization in the highlands of East Africa. Our need is to advance the theory of Afrocentricity through critical attention to what is written and spoken by those who profess knowledge regardless to their ancestry. Arnold Toynbee, for example, wrote that whites founded four ancient civilizations while blacks found none. This is not merely Eurocentricity; it is malicious racism of the type we have confronted and exposed for the last two hundred years. We know because of our Afrocentric consciousness that only one ancient civilization could be considered European in origin, Greece. And Greece itself is a product of its interaction with African civilizations. Among ancient civilizations Africans gave the world, Ethiopia, Nubia, Egypt, Cush, Axum, Ghana, Mali, and Songhay. These ancient civilizations are responsible for medicine, science, the concept of monarchies and divine-kingships, and an Almighty God. Afrocentricity establishes a profound movement in critical reading as well as critical thinking. To the degree that we begin to examine the literary perspectives of black and white writers we will understand the power of symbols.

Our collective consciousness must question writers who use symbols and objects which do not contribute meaningfully to our victory. How could a black writer be allowed to use symbols which contradict our existence and we not raise our voices? Afrocentric criticism must hold especially accountable the works of African, continental or diasporan. We have failed to be critical of the Alvin Aileys and Arthur Mitchells in dance for example because we felt that we should not criticize blacks who are creative. The times are surely different and we must now open the floodgates of protest against any non-Afrocentric stances taken by writers, authors, and other intellectuals or artists. Afrocentricity sustains our lives through self affirmation.

The Provable Bases

Afrocentricity reorganizes our frame of reference so that we become the center of analysis and synthesis. As such, it becomes the source of regeneration of our values and beliefs. Indeed, this movement recaptures the collective will responsible for ancient Egypt and Nubia. The past, however, only tells us what is possible; it cannot fight for us except in a psychological sense. We accept the psychological support and laud ourselves for having ancestors who gave us such a powerful legacy. How can Hansel and Gretel or Jack and Jill continue to be the names, with all that those names imply, of our children's clubs? What insidious animal eats away at our brains and causes us to sleep when our own children are being stolen away from us? What is a child to believe when he or she grows up? Is it to be that we were so preoccupied with a whiteness that we could not reinforce our own heritage for them, even if only in names of our clubs? Understand gently, what we choose to call ourselves and our organizations reflects on our own consciousness. Every act must be deliberately chosen for its historic purpose and mission. Nothing that is done can ever be glossed over again; it must be considered in terms of its implications for the future. Our time is now.

The breakdown of our central political organizations from the disintegration of Egypt during the coming of the foreigners all the way to the enslavement of Africans represents one massive slide away from our center. Since the colonial era, many countries have adopted all of the symbols and behaviors of decadent Western societies. Thus, in the Diaspora and on the continent we become victims of Eurocentric behaviors. Instead of modeling governments on the traditional values and patterns of our people, we follow systems which have proved themselves neither in their native lands nor among us. And those structures which have existed for thousands of years are often abandoned in favor of an imported ideology. Because of this lack of consciousness the people will demand a return to the basic principles which have always placed us at the center. Afrocentricity does not champion reactionary postures and it is not regresssive. Nevertheless Afrocentricity seeks to modify even African traditions where necessary to meet the demands of modern society. A halt is called to the disintegration of our collective consciousness by introducing Afrocentricity at every step. This is necessary to shock the unconsciousness into awakening postures.

Some of us have been asleep so long and so deeply that we were not able to heed the words of Cheikh Anta Diop and Chancellor Williams (Diop, 1974, 1978; Williams, 1974). But when the New York Times came out with the story that Nubia had an older civilization than Egypt it validated the Afrocentric histories of Diop, Ben-Jochannan, and Williams in the minds of even the most stubborn Eurocentric Africans (Ben-Jochannan, 1972). Numerous writers have challenged the basic premises of Afrocentricity by expounding a Eurocentric viewpoint of everything from culture to the origin of civilization. The African writers who have mimicked such Eurocentric formulas are unable to think in an Afrocentric frame of mind. As a result, they relinquish their thoughts and research to Eurocentric purposes, and consequently deny their own humanity. Enslavement of the mind is the most pernicious kind of enslavement because the person so enslaved will never be able to see clearly for himself. Breaking the mental chains only occurs when a person learns to take two sets of notes on almost everything encountered in the Western world. If they say that Shakespeare is the greatest writer, know Cesaire, Du Bois, Hughes, Soyinka, Guillen, Ngugu, Pushkin. If they say that ballet is classical dance, know that it is no more classical than Adowa or a Mfundalai Shairi Dansi. If they say Bach is universal, know that Bach cannot be anymore universal than John Coltrane or Duke Ellington. After one has established a sound basis for knowledge, other truths will find their way. In this manner the frames of reference change and become liberatory for us, expanding our horizons to ourselves.

The brother who thought he was getting over, meaning, showing how white he had become replied to the student that he was really a writer who just happened to be black. There is no such animal as that. One is always born with a certain heritage and identity; to deny it is to deny yourself. Garth Fagan of The Bucket Dance Company made such an antihuman statement when asked about being a black choreographer. Although his inspiration is most definitely African he copped out and told the New York Voice (June, 1987) that "he happened to be black." The reaction of most people was "I guess you did!" A symbol revolution based upon Afrocentricity is necessary for the salvation of our sanity as a people.

When a writer seeks to write about life, death, birth, love, happiness, or sadness, the first thing that should come to mind is himself, his people, and their motifs. If he writes about his own people, he is writing about a universal experience of people. Do not be captured by a sense of universality given to you by the Eurocentric viewpoint; such a viewpoint is contradictory to your own ultimate reality. Isolate, define, and promote those values, symbols, and experiences which affirm you. Only through this type of affirmation can we really and truly find our renewal; this is why I speak of it as a reconstruction instead of a redefinition. Actually what we have to do is not difficult because the guidelines are clearly established in our past. We must continue to be excellent, provocative, organized, educated, and dependable. Understand something, these qualities represent our natural state. We are already practicing the attributes; now we must perfect them in ourselves and others.

Afrocenticity does not condone inefficiency in its name. Our history gives us enough examples to demonstrate this point. Those who have truly acted from their own Afrocentric centers have always had admirable records of excellence and efficiency. Consider the work of David Walker who was so inspired by the convention held in Boston that the next year, 1828, he began to write and have broadcast his dynamic pamphlet, *An Appeal to the Colored Citizens of the World*. Walker did it because he loved himself, and consequently he loved the people whose son he was. What he did was profound in its power and excellence. It took courage, commitment, and time. David Walker's victory was achieved in the face of nearly overwhelming odds for a freedom fighter in his time. He planned, strategized, and succeeded in having copies of his powerful pamphlet distributed as far south as Georgia. Every victory over fascism, apartheid, and racism has been won by rational fanatics who have shown their commitment to excellence. You must develop the will to see a project through to conclusion. Don't start a class and then stop it because you did not think it through; and don't request information and then refuse to pick it up and use it. These are all typical anti-Afrocentric behaviors. They do not reflect yourself at the center. You are always the center of what you do.

The chain of reasoning that leads to the denunciation of racism starts with your ultimate reality which is blackness. Indeed the racist must be allowed to act; he cannot act unchecked unless we allow him to act. Thus, when you have any hint of racism occurring in your presence, confront it immediately and directly. Be sure of your ground, then attack the racist with convincing arguments. You can always be sure of your ground if you have a clear conception of who you are and what you will and will not allow to be said or done to others like yourself. I used Afrocentricity as a reference point and spoke up firmly and directly. The matter was resolved.

We need not act belligerently in cases where we put our center to work for us. Our facts act for us. Langston Hughes was more universal than Robert Frost; and he had a more pleasant and humanistic personality, too. With this fact I do not have to beat someone over the head; I simply state my truth. That is the way to practice Afrocentricity. There is little need to make grand stands on issues. Our facts are in our history, use them. Their facts are in their history, and they have certainly used theirs. Denounce racism by the strength of moral and political will. Our collective will secures the victory that we reach with our historical and cultural facts. Allow Shango, Obatala, Simple, Legba, Chaka, Nzingha, Candace, Oduduwa, and Menes to announce your superior knowledge. When you sit in classes and listen to lecturers speak of Keats, Yeats, Twain, Wordsworth, Frost, Eliot, and Goethe, you had better be able to call upon Baraka, Shange, Welsh, Guillen, Cesaire, Abiola, Ngugi, and Okai. Not to call upon these spirit voices when you are bombarded with alien shadows makes you a victim of the most detestable isolation and alienation from your own past and present.

In a revolutionary context, the force which secures the strongest commitment to Afrocentricity will always occupy the central position of power. This is true for political parties among us that are engaged in warfare against white minority regimes. When the core is clear, other things become clear. Peripheral concepts will hover around the fringes of power but the real core must be Afrocentric for effectiveness. The more we shave off the fringes, the more pronounced and sufficient our Afrocentricity. Pure Afrocentricity is a compelling force (Welsh, 1978). Yet we are naturally propelled toward it by our unyielding humanism. Express symbols to the survival of human spirit in the midst of materialism, we are positive motion. In art, science, medicine, engineering, and literature we are the vanguards for humanism and sensitivity.

Afrocentricity can stand its ground among any ideology or religion: Marxism, Islam, Christianity, Buddhism, or Judaism. Your Afrocentricity will emerge in the presence of these other ideologies because it is from you. It is a truth, even though it may not be their truth. This singularity of purpose is close to Afrocentricity because it does not ignore logic and emotion. They are inseparable in this context and most Africans no matter how distorted their realities will accept the cultural basis of Afrocentricity. It is like a fish swimming in water, it cannot escape the water. Its choice is whether to swim or not, that is, to activate. There is nothing the fish can do about the existence of the water. This is why the contemporary philosopher Karenga says "Our Africanity is our ultimate reality." As a people, our most cherished and valuable achievements are the achievements of spirit. With an Afrocentric spirit, all things can be made to happen, it is the source of genuine revolutionary commitment.

Lucille Clifton
move

On May 13, 1985 Wilson Goode, Philadelphia's first Black mayor, authorized the bombing of 6221 Osage Avenue after the complaints of neighbors, also Black, about the Afrocentric back-to-nature group headquartered there and calling itself Move. All the members of the group wore dreadlocks and had taken the surname Africa. In the bombing eleven people, including children, were killed and sixty-one homes in the neighborhood were destroyed.

they had begun to whisper
among themselves   hesitant
to be branded neighbor to the wild
haired women the naked children
reclaiming a continent
away

move

he hesitated
then turned his smoky finger
toward africa toward the house
he might have lived in might have
owned or saved had he not turned
away

move

the helicopter rose at the command
higher at first then hesitating
then turning toward the center
of its own town only a neighborhood
away

move

she cried as the child stood
hesitant in the last clear sky
he would ever see the last
before the whirling blades the whirling smoke
and sharp debris carried all clarity
away

move

if you live in a mind
that would destroy itself
to comfort itself
if you would stand fire
rather than difference
do not hesitate
move
away

Manning Marable
from *Beyond Black and White*

How do we transcend the theoretical limitations and social contradictions of the politics of racial identity? The challenge begins by constructing new cultural and political "identities," based on the realities of America's changing multicultural, democratic milieu. The task of constructing a tradition of unity between various groups of color in America is a far more complex and contradictory process than progressive activists or scholars have admitted, precisely because of divergent cultural traditions, languages and conflicting politics of racial identity—on the part of Latinos, African-Americans, Asian Americans, Pacific Island Americans, Arab Americans, American Indians and others. Highlighting the current dilemma in the 1990s, is the collapsing myth of "brown-black solidarity."

Back in the 1960s and early 1970s, with the explosion of the civil-rights and black power movements in the African-American community, activist formations with similar objectives also emerged among Latinos. The Black Panther Party and the League of Revolutionary Black Workers, for example, found their counterparts among Chicano militants in La Raza Unida Party in Texas, and the Crusade for Justice in Colorado. The Council of La Raza and the Mexican American Legal Defense Fund began to push for civil-rights reforms within government, and for expanding influence for Latinos within the Democratic Party, paralleling the same strategies of Jesse Jackson's Operation PUSH and the NAACP Legal Defense Fund.

With the growth of a more class-conscious black and Latino petty bourgeoisie—ironically, a social product of affirmative action and civil-rights gains—tensions between these two large communities of people of color began to deteriorate. The representatives of the African-American middle class consolidated their electoral control of the city councils and mayoral posts of major cities throughout the country. Black entrepreneurship increased, as the black American consumer market reached a gross sales figure of $270 billion by 1991, an amount equal to the gross domestic product of the fourteenth wealthiest nation on earth. The really important "symbolic triumphs" of this privileged strata of the African-American community were not the dynamic 1984 and 1988 presidential campaigns of Jesse Jackson; they were instead the electoral victory of Democratic "moderate" Doug Wilder as Virginia governor in 1990, and the appointment of former-Jackson-lieutenant-turned-moderate Ron Brown as head of the Democratic National Committee. Despite the defeats represented by Reaganism and the absence of affirmative-action enforcement, there was a sense that the strategy of "symbolic representation" had cemented this stratum's hegemony over the bulk of the black population. Black politicians like Doug Wilder and television celebrity journalists such as black-nationalist-turned-Republican Tony Brown weren't interested in pursuing coalitions between blacks and other people of color. Multiracial, multiclass alliances raised too many questions about the absence of political accountability between middle-class "leaders" and their working-class and low-income "followers." Even Jesse Jackson shied away from addressing a black-Latino alliance except in the most superficial terms.

By the late 1980s and early 1990s, however, the long-delayed brown-black dialogue at the national level began crystallizing into tensions around at least four critical issues. First, after the census of 1990, scores of congressional districts were reapportioned with African-American or Latino pluralities or majorities, guaranteeing greater minority-group representation in Congress. However, in cities and districts where Latinos and blacks were roughly divided, and especially in those districts which blacks had controlled in previous years but in which Latinos were now in the majority, disagreements often led to fractious ethnic conflicts. Latinos claimed that they were grossly underrepresented within the political process. African-American middle-class leaders argued that "Latinos" actually represented four distinct groups with little to no shared history or common culture: Mexican Americans, concentrated overwhelmingly in the southwestern states; Hispanics from the Caribbean, chiefly Puerto Ricans and Dominicans, most of whom had migrated to New York City and the northeast since 1945; Cuban Americans, mostly middle- to upper-class exiles of Castro's Cuba, and who voted heavily Republican; and the most recent Spanish-speaking emigrants from Central and South America. Blacks insisted that Cuban Americans were definitely not an "underprivileged minority," and as such did not merit minority set-aside economic programs, affirmative-action and equal-opportunity programs. The cultural politics of Afrocentrism made it difficult for many African-Americans to recognize that they might share any common interest with Latinos.

Second, immigration issues are also at the center of recent Latino–black conflicts. Over one-third of the Latino population of more that 24 million in the USA consists of undocumented workers. Some middle-class African-American leaders have taken the politically conservative viewpoint that undocumented Latino workers deprive poor blacks of jobs within the low-wage sectors of the economy. Third, bilingual education and efforts to impose linguistic and cultural conformity upon all sectors of society (such as "English-only" referenda) have also been issues of contention. Finally, the key element that drives these topics of debate is the rapid transformation of America's non-white demography. Because of relatively higher birth rates than the general population and substantial immigration, within less than two decades Latinos as a group will outnumber African-Americans as the largest minority group in the USA. Even by 1990, about one out of nine US households spoke a non-English language at home, predominately Spanish.

Black middle-class leaders who were accustomed to advocating the interests of their constituents in simplistic racial terms were increasingly confronted by Latinos who felt alienated from the system and largely ignored and underrepresented by the political process. Thus in May 1991, Latinos took to the streets in Washington DC, hurling bottles and rocks and looting over a dozen stores, in response to the shooting by the local police of a Salvadorian man whom they claimed had wielded a knife. African-American mayor Sharon Pratt Dixon ordered over one thousand police officers to patrol the city's Latino neighborhoods, and used tear gas to quell the public disturbances. In effect, a black administration in Washington DC used the power of the police and courts to suppress the grievances of Latinos—just as the white administration had done against black protesters during the urban uprisings of 1968.

The tragedy here is that too little is done by either African-American or Latino "mainstream" leaders, who practice racial-identity politics to transcend their parochialism and to redefine their agendas on common ground. Latinos and blacks alike can agree on an overwhelming list of issues—such as the inclusion of multicultural curricula in public schools, improvements in public health care, job training initiative, the expansion of public transportation and housing for low- to moderate-income people; and greater fairness and legal rights within the criminal justice system. Despite the image that Latinos as a group are more "economically privileged" than African-Americans, Mexican American families earn only slightly more than black households, and Puerto Rican families earn less than black Americans on average. Economically, Latinos and African-Americans have both experienced the greatest declines in real incomes and some of the greatest increases in poverty rates within the USA. From 1973 to 1990, for example, the incomes for families headed by a parent under thirty years of age declined by 28 per cent for Latino families and by 48 per cent for African-American families. The poverty rates for young families in these same years rose 44 per cent for Latinos and 58 per cent for blacks.

There is also substantial evidence that Latinos continue to experience discrimination in elementary, secondary and higher education which is in many respects more severe than that experienced by African-Americans. Although high-school graduation rates for the entire population have steadily improved, the rates for Latinos have declined consistently since the mid 1980s. In 1989, for instance, 76 per cent of all African-Americans and 82 per cent of all whites aged between eighteen and twenty-four had graduated from high school. By contrast, the graduation rate for Latinos in 1989 was 56 per cent. By 1992, the high-school completion rate for Latino males dropped to its lowest level, 47.8 per cent, since 1972—the year such figures began to be compiled by the American Council on Education. In colleges and universities, the pattern of Latino inequality was the same. In 1991, 34 per cent of all whites and 24 per cent of all African-Americans aged between eighteen and twenty-four were enrolled in college. Latino college enrollment for the same age group was barely 18 per cent. As of 1992, approximately 22 per cent of the non-Latino adult population in the USA possessed at least a four-year college degree. College graduation rates for Latino adults were just 10 per cent. Thus, on a series of public policy issues—access to quality education, economic opportunity, the availability of human services, and civil rights—Latinos and African-Americans share a core set of common concerns and long-term interests. What is missing is the dynamic vision and political leadership necessary to build something more permanent than temporary electoral coalitions between these groups.

A parallel situation exists between Asian Americans, Pacific Americans and the black American community. Two generations ago, the Asian American population was comparatively small, except in states such as California, Washington, and New York. With the end of discriminatory immigration restrictions on Asians in 1965, however, the Asian American population began to soar dramatically, changing the ethnic and racial character of urban America. For example, in the years 1970 to 1990 the Korean population increased from 70,000 to 820,000. Since 1980, about 33,000 Koreans have entered the USA each year, a rate of immigration exceeded only by Latinos and Filipinos. According to the 1990 census, the Asian American and Pacific Islander population in the USA exceeds 7.3 million.

Some of the newer Asian immigrants in the 1970s and 1980s were of middle-class origin with backgrounds in entrepreneurship, small manufacturing and the white-collar professions. Thousands of Asian American small-scale, family-owned businesses began to develop in black and Latino neighborhoods, in many instances taking the place of the Jewish merchants in the ghettoes a generation before. It did not take long before Latino and black petty hostilities and grievances against this new ethnic entrepreneurial group crystallized into deep racial hatred. When African-American rapper Ice Cube expressed his anger against Los Angeles's Korean American business community in the 1991 song "Black Korea," he was also voicing the popular sentiments of many younger blacks:

> So don't follow me up and down your market, or your little chop-suey ass will be a target of the nationwide boycott. Choose with the people, that's what the boy got. So pay respect to the black fist, or we'll burn down your store, right down to a crisp, and then we'll see you, 'cause you can't turn the ghetto into Black Korea.

Simmering ethnic tensions boiled into open outrage in Los Angeles when a black teenage girl was killed by Korean American merchant Soon Ja Du. Although convicted of voluntary manslaughter, Du was sentenced to probation and community service only. Similarly, in the early 1990s African-Americans launched economic boycotts of, and political confrontations with, Korean American small merchants in New York. Thus, in the aftermath of the blatant miscarriage of justice in Los Angeles last year—the acquittal of four white police officers for the violent beating of Rodney King—the anger and outrage within the African-American community was channeled not against the state and the corporations, but against small Korean American merchants. Throughout Los Angeles, over 1,500 Korean-American-owned stores were destroyed, burned or looted. Following the urban uprising, a fiercely anti-Asian sentiment continued to permeate sections of Los Angeles. In 1992–93 there have been a series of incidents of Asian Americans being harassed or beaten in southern California. After the rail-system contract was awarded to a Japanese company, a chauvinistic movement was launched to "buy American." Asian Americans are still popularly projected to other nonwhites as America's successful "model minorities," fostering resentment, misunderstandings and hostilities among people of color. Yet black leaders have consistently failed to explain to African-Americans that Asian-Americans as a group do not own the major corporations or banks which control access to capital. They do not own massive amounts of real estate, control the courts or city governments, have ownership of the mainstream media, dominate police forces, or set urban policies.

While African-Americans, Latinos and Asian-Americans scramble over which group should control the mom-and-pop grocery store in their neighborhood, almost no one questions the racist "redlining" policies of large banks which restrict access to capital to nearly all people of color. Black and Latino working people usually are not told by their race-conscious leaders and middle-class "symbolic representatives" that institutional racism has also frequently targeted Asian Americans throughout US history—from the recruitment and exploitation of Asian laborers, to a series of lynchings and violent assaults culminating in the mass incarceration of Japanese Americans during World War II, to the slaying of Vincent Chin in Detroit and the violence and harassment of other Asian Americans. A central ideological pillar of "whiteness" is the consistent scapegoating of the "oriental menace." As legal scholar Mari Matsuda observes:

> There is an unbroken line of poor and working Americans turning their anger and frustration into hatred of Asian Americans. Every time this happens, the real villains—the corporations and politicians who put profits before human needs—are allowed to go about their business free from public scrutiny, and the anger that could go to organizing for positive social change goes instead to Asian-bashing.

What is required is a radical break from the narrow, race-based politics of the past, which characterized the core assumptions about black empowerment since the mid nineteenth century. We need to recognize that the two perspectives of racial-identity politics that are frequently juxtaposed, integration/assimilation and nationalist/separatism, are actually two sides of the same ideological and strategic axis. To move into the future will require that we bury the racial barriers of the past, for good. The essential point of departure is the deconstruction of the idea of "whiteness," the ideology of white power, privilege and elitism which remains heavily embedded within the dominant culture, social institutions and economic arrangements of the society. But we must do more than critique the white pillars of race, gender and class domination. We must rethink and restructure the central social categories of collective struggle by which we conceive and understand our own political reality. We must redefine "blackness" and other traditional racial categories to be more inclusive of contemporary ethnic realities.

To be truly liberating, a social theory must reflect the actual problems of a historical conjuncture with a commitment to rigor and scholastic truth. "Afrocentrism" fails on all counts to provide that clarity of insight into the contemporary African-American urban experience. It looks to a romantic, mythical reconstruction of yesterday to find some understanding of the cultural basis of today's racial and class challenges. Yet that critical understanding of reality cannot begin with an examination of the lives of Egyptian Pharaohs. It must begin by critiquing the vast structure of power and privilege which characterizes the political economy of post-industrial capitalist America. According to the Center on Budget and Policy Priorities, during the Reagan–Bush era of the 1980s the poorest one-fifth of all Americans earned about $7,725 annually, and experienced a decline in before-tax household incomes of 3.8 per cent over the decade. The middle fifth of all US households earned about $31,000 annually, with an income gain of 3.1 per cent during the 1980s. Yet the top fifth of household incomes reached over $105,200 annually by 1990, with before-tax incomes growing by 29.8 per cent over the 1980s. The richest 5 per cent of all American households exceeded $206,000 annually, improving their incomes by 44.9 per cent under Reagan and Bush. The wealthiest 1 per cent of all US households reached nearly $550,000 per year, with average before-tax incomes increasing by 75.3 per cent. In effect, since 1980 the income gap between America's wealthiest 1 per cent and the middle class *nearly doubled*. As the Center on Budget and Policy Priorities relates, the wealthiest 1 per cent of all Americans—roughly 2.5 million people—receive "nearly as much income after taxes as the bottom 40 per cent, about 100 million people. While wealthy households are taking a larger share of the national income, the tax burden has been shifted down the income pyramid." A social theory of a reconstructed, multicultural democracy must advance the reorganization and ownership of capital resources, the expansion of production in minority areas, and provision of guarantees for social welfare—such as a single-payer, national health-care system.

The factor of "race" by itself does not and cannot explain the massive transformation of the structure of capitalism in its post-industrial phase, or the destructive redefinition of "work" itself, as we enter the twenty-first century. Increasingly in Western Europe and America, the new division between "haves" and "have nots" is characterized by a new segmentation of the labor force. The division is between those workers who have maintained basic economic security and benefits—such as full health insurance, term life insurance, pensions, educational stipends or subsidies for the employee's children, paid vacations, and so forth—and those marginal workers who are either unemployed, or part-time employees, or who labor but have few if any benefits. Since 1982, "temporary employment" or part-time hirings without benefits have increased 250 per cent across the USA, while all employment has grown by less than 20 per cent. Today, the largest private employer in the USA is Manpower, Inc., the world's largest temporary employment agency, with 560,000 workers. By the year 2000, half of all American workers will be classified as part-time employees, or, as they are termed within IBM, "the peripherals." The reason for this massive restructuring of labor relations is capital's search for surplus value or profits.

Increasingly, disproportionately high percentages of Latino and African-American workers will be trapped within this second-tier of the labor market. Black, Latino, Asian-American, and low-income white workers all share a stake in fighting for a new social contract relating to work and social benefits: the right to a good job should be guaranteed in the same way as the human right to vote; the right to free high-quality health care should be as secure as the freedom of speech. The radical changes within the domestic economy require that black leadership reaches out to other oppressed sectors of the society, creating a common program for economic and social justice. Vulgar Afrocentrism looks inward; the new black liberation of the twenty-first century must look outward, embracing those people of color and oppressed people of divergent ethnic backgrounds who share our democratic vision.

The multicultural democratic critique must consider the changing demographic, cultural and class realities of modern post-industrial America. By the year 2000, one-third of the total US population will consist of people of color. Within seventy years, roughly half of America's entire population will be Latino, American Indian, Pacific American, Arab American and African-American. The ability to create a framework for multicultural democracy, inter-group dialogue, and interaction within and between the most progressive leaders, grassroots activists, intellectuals and working people of these communities will determine the future of American society itself. Our ability to transcend racial chauvinism and inter-ethnic hatred and the old definitions of "race," to recognize the class commonalities and joint social-justice interests of all groups in the restructuring of this nation's economy and social order, will be the key to constructing a nonracist democracy, transcending ancient walls of white violence, corporate power and class privilege. By dismantling the narrow politics of racial identity and selective self-interest, by going beyond "black" and "white," we may construct new values, new institutions and new visions of an America beyond traditional racial categories and racial oppression.

Sanyika Shakur
from *Monster*

When Tamu and my sister, Kendis, came to visit my brother and me on Sunday, I told them about Muhammad and the way he talked. I asked Bro to accompany me Monday night to services, and he agreed to.

On Monday Muhammad did as he had the week before, only this time he spoke more about the Black Panther party and its threat to the U.S. government. Seeing me and Li'l Monster there, he intentionally expounded on the lives of George and Jonathan Jackson, both members of the party. Jonathan was murdered in a heroic attempt to liberate three prisoners, including the Soledad Brothers—of which his Brother-Comrade, George, was one. Comrade George was assassinated the following year in a bungled attempt to escape from San Quentin.

"How old are you?" Muhammad asked, pointing at Li'l Monster.

"Seventeen," replied Li'l Bro.

"Jonathan Jackson was seventeen when he walked into the Marin County Courthouse and took the judge and D.A. hostage."

He paused a minute for effect.

"What set you from?" Muhammad asked me.

"Eight Tray Gangster," I replied.

"George Jackson was the field marshal for the Black Panther party. He was eighteen when he was captured. He was given one year to life for a seventy-dollar gas station robbery. He served eleven years before he was killed by pigs. He was twenty-nine years old."

He turned to Li'l Monster. "What you in here for?"

"For murder."

"Who you kill?"

"Some Sixties—"

"Black people!" Muhammad shouted.

"Yeah, but—"

"George Jackson corrected, not killed, *corrected* three pigs and two Nazis before he himself was murdered!"

Muhammad seemed possessed.

"This is what I'm trying to tell you. As you kill each other, the real enemy is steadily killing you. Your generation has totally turned inward and is now self-destructive. You are less of a threat when you fight one another, you dig?"

We sat upright, clinging to his words.

"Jonathan knew chemistry, demolition, and martial arts. He was a manchild, a revolutionary. He felt responsible for the future of his people."

We sat there, stunned by the parallel between us and George and Jonathan Jackson. What made us sit up and take note of what Muhammad was saying about our self-destructive behavior was that he never talked down to us, always *to* us. He didn't like what we were doing, but he respected us as young warriors. He never once told us to disarm. His style of consciousness-raising was in total harmony with the ways in which we had grown up in our communities, in this country, on this planet. Muhammad's lessons were local, national, and international.

I put the word out that all Crips should come to Muslim services and hear Muhammad talk. Within three weeks attendance increased from nine to twenty-seven to forty and finally to eighty! The staff became alarmed, asking questions and even sitting in on some of the services, trying to grasp our sudden attraction to Islamic services. They never caught it.

Islam is a way of life, just like banging. We could relate to what Muhammad was saying, especially when he spoke about jihad—struggle. Of course we heard what we wanted to hear. We knew that Islam or revolution was not a threat to us as warriors. Muhammad didn't seek to make us passive or weak. On the contrary, he encouraged us to "stand firm," "stay armed," and "stay black." He encouraged us not to shoot one another, if possible, but to never hesitate to "correct a pig who transgressed against the people." After every service let out, it was a common sight to see fifty to eighty New Afrikan youths mobbing back to their units shouting "Jihad till death!" and "Death to the oppressor!"

The Protestant following totally evaporated. Reverend Jackson could not figure out where his constituents had gone. In these times, gang conflicts involving New Afrikans were at an all-time low. Mr. Hernandez began to pull on the strings of his informants, which, without fail, led him to me.

One day he called me into his office for a fact-finding chat. He offered me a seat, but I declined. He then began his little probe.

"So, Mr. Scott—or is it Abdul or Ali Baba?"

I said nothing.

"Yes, well anyway I have called you in here because it is my understanding that you have been trying to subvert the institutional security."

The term "institutional security" is so far-reaching that whenever there is nothing to lock a prisoner down or harass him for, staff, correction officers, and most any figure of authority in any institution will pull out this ambiguous term. It is precisely this wording that has me locked deep within the bowels of Pelican Bay today. I am a threat, and proud of it. If I wasn't a threat, I'd be doing something wrong.

"Institutional what?" I asked, not yet familiar with the terminology.

"Security, Scott, security."

"Man, you trippin'—"

"No, Scott, *you* are tripping!" he yelled, slapping both hands hard on the table.

"I don't know what you talkin' 'bout," I answered with a blank stare.

"Oh, you don't, huh? Well how do you explain twenty-three Eight Trays, fourteen Hoovers, eleven East Coasts and a lesser assortment of other bangers cropped up in Moslem church for the past month, huh? Explain that!"

"Man, I ain't explainin' shit."

"Oh, no? Well how 'bout if I keep your bad ass on the Rock forever, huh? How 'bout that?"

"I already been there two months for some shit that didn't involve me—"

"You are a *damn* liar, you ordered that boy Layton to jump on Cox. And you been involved in a host of other shit. So don't tell me what you *ain't* done."

"You know what, Hernandez, do what you gotta do," I said low and slow, to let him know that I wasn't hardly giving a fuck about what he was stressing on.

"Yeah, I'll do that, I'll just do that. But you remember this when you go up for parole."

"Can I leave now?" I asked, bored with his threats.

Actually the Rock wasn't all that bad. I ate all my meals in the cage, showered every other day, and came out once a day for an hour, usually in the morning. I was able to have my radio and a few tapes. At that time I was exploring the blues. Jimmy Reed was my favorite. I still got my weekly visits, though I couldn't decide who I wanted to have come. At Y.T.S. they allowed prisoners to have only one female on their visiting list, other than mothers and sisters. Tamu really was not my first choice, China was. But she didn't have the mobility to be there every week, and riding the bus was suicidal. So I took her off my visiting list and replaced her with Ayanna, who was also from the 'hood. Her mother had moved her out to Pomona to get her out of the gang environment, and she now lived in close proximity to Y.T.S. Our visits went like clockwork, but eventually we grew tired of each other, so I took her off my list. For a short time I replaced Ayanna with Felencia, Tray Ball's sister. This didn't work out too well either, because she wanted me to stop gangbanging and I just wasn't having it. I was not giving up my career for no female, so I ended up putting Tamu back on the list. As long as I got my visits and could keep my music, the Rock wasn't shit.

In my cell on the Rock, I reread for the hundredth time *Message to the Oppressed*. Malcolm came on strong:

> We declare our right on this earth to be a man, to be a human being, to be given the rights of a human being in this society, on this earth, in this day, which we intend to bring into existence BY ANY MEANS NECESSARY.

As I read on I felt the words seeping deeper into me, their power coursing through my body, giving me strength to push on. I was changing, I felt it. For once I didn't challenge it or see it as being a threat to the established mores of the 'hood, though, of course, it was. Muhammad's teachings corresponded with my condition of being repressed on the Rock. Never could I have been touched by such teachings in the street.

The prison setting, although repressive, was a bit too free. But on the Rock, the illusion of freedom vanished, and in its place was the harsh actuality of oppression and the very real sense of powerlessness over destiny. Because there was no shooting war to concentrate on, your worst enemy was easily replaced by the figure presently doing you the most harm. In prisons this figure is more often than not an American. An American who locks you in a cage, counts you to make sure you haven't escaped, holds a weapon on you, and, in many instances, shoots you. Add to this the fact that most of us grew up in an eighty percent New Afrikan community policed—or occupied—by an eighty-five percent American pig force that is clearly antagonistic to any male in the community, displaying this antagonism at every opportunity by any means necessary with all the brute force and sadistic imagination they can muster.

It was quite easy then for Muhammad's teachings to hit me in the heart. However, my attraction to the facts involving our national oppression was grounded in emotionalism, and eight years of evolutionary development in Crip culture could hardly be rolled back by one pamphlet and a few trips to Islamic services. But I did feel the strength. I called off the move on the Sixties after Tray Ball killed himself. Everyone asked why, but I really had no answer. I told them that we'd handle it in a little while.

Stagalee was my neighbor on the Rock; he and I would talk through a small hole in the wall. I sent him over the *Message to the Oppressed* pamphlet and solicited a response from him about its contents.

"Cuz," I said bending down so as to talk through the hole, "what you think 'bout that paper I sent over there?"

"I don't know, some of these words too hard fo' me, cuz. But I can see that this is some powerful shit."

"Well, what you could catch, what did you think?"

"Cuz, really, I think Muhammad is some kind of terrorist or somethin'."

"Stag, you trippin'. Muhammad ain't no terrorist. Shit, Muhammad is down for us."

"Who?" he asked, "the set?"

"Hell naw, nigga, black people!"

"Ah, cuz, fuck all that, 'cause soon he gonna be tellin' us to stop bangin' and shit—"

"Stag, Stag." I tried to slow him down.

"Naw, cuz, I can't see me being no Muslim. I just can't see it. They be standing on corners selling pies and shit. Do you know how long one of us would live standin' on a corner, not even in our 'hood? Monster, let me catch a Sissy, Muslim or not, and I'ma blow that nigga up!"

"I don't know, homie, I just feel that there is something there."

"Yeah, muthafucka, a bean pie!" Stag answered and broke out laughing.

"Stall it out, cuz," I said, feeling myself getting angry.

"Monster, you ain't thinkin' 'bout being no Muslim, is you? Cuz, don't do it. Muhammad cool and everythang, but cuz, you Monster Kody. Ain't nobody gonna let you live in peace. Plus the set needs you, cuz. Here, cuz."

Stag had rolled up the pamphlet and was pushing it through the hole.

"Naw, cuz, I ain't thinkin' 'bout turnin' no Muslim. I'm just sayin' that what Muhammad be stressin' is real."

"Right, right."

"Well, I'ma step back and get some z's. I'll rap to you later. Three minutes."

"Three minutes."

I lay on my bed with the rolled-up pamphlet on my chest and thought about what Stag had said.

"You Monster Kody. Ain't nobody gonna let you live in peace.... The set needs you..."

My young consciousness screamed back in an attempt to exert itself.

"Who *is* Monster Kody?...*I* am Monster Kody...a person, a young man, a black man...Anything else?...No, not that I know of...*What* is Monster Kody?...A Crip, an Eight Tray, a Rollin' Sixty killer...a black man...Black man, black man, BLACK MAN..."

The words reverberated again and again.

"Nobody gonna let you live in peace..."

"*Who* ain't gonna let you live in peace?"

"Black men, black men, black men..."

"*Why?!*" my consciousness shouted back. "WHY?!"

I had no answer. The confusion gave me a headache. I knew that I was reaching a crossroad, but I didn't know how to handle it. Should I accept it or reject it? In a perverted sort of way I enjoyed being Monster Kody. I lived for the power surge of playing God, having the power of life and death in my hands. Nothing I knew of could compare with riding in a car with three other homeboys with guns, knowing that they were as deadly and courageous as I was. To me, at that time in my life, this was power. It made me feel responsible for either killing someone or letting them live. The thought of controlling something substantial—like land—never occurred to me. The thought of responsibility for the welfare of my daughter or a nation, New Afrika, never crossed my mind. I was only responsible to my 'hood and my homeboys. Now I was being subjected to a wider reality than I had ever known.

Then I heard it. As I was struggling with this dilemma I grasped the point that Muhammad was trying to make.

"When you were born you were born black. That's all. Then, later on, you turned Crip, dig?"

In this light I found clarity. But, I asked myself, what was Muhammad really asking of us? Did I have to be a Muslim to be black? I surmised that it was like being a Crip or a Blood, as opposed to being a hook or a civilian. Where I came from, in order to be down you had to be "in." Did I have to be "in"—that is, a Muslim—to be down with blackness? Surely much thought and internal debate had to go into this issue.

My thing was this: I didn't believe there was a God. I just had no faith in what I couldn't see, feel, taste, hear, or smell. All my life I have seen the power of life and death in the hands of men and boys. If I shot at someone and I hit him and he died, who took his life? Me or God? Was it predestined that on this day at this time I would specifically push this guy out of existence? I never believed that. I believed that I hunted him, caught him, and killed him. I had lived in too much disorder to believe that there was an actual design to this world. So I had a problem with believing in anything other than myself.

My interest here was drawn by the militancy of Malcolm X and Muhammad, not by the spirituality of Islam. The first book I got was *Soul on Ice* by Eldridge Cleaver. Most of it was too hard to grasp, but what I did get was militant and strong. I found that this was my preference.

I was subsequently taken off the Rock and put back in Unit Three, in company U-V. While attending school for my G.E.D., I met a brother named Walter Brown. Bro—who worked at Y.T.S. as a teacher but functioned better as a guiding light—had been a prisoner himself in the 1960s. He was stern but flexible and held great influence over most of us who were considered O.G.s. Brown was militant but responsible. Not to imply that militants are irresponsible, but Brown was specifically responsible for the upbringing of us—young, New Afrikan males. His degree of effectiveness can be measured by the fact that he was designated to "teach" parole classes. That gave him access to prisoners for one week, one hour a day, before they were paroled. This skimpy time frame could not possibly have helped prisoners deal with the multi-complex phenomena of society. Most of what was taught was useless, old institutional garbage that was not applicable to the streets. Brown, however, was beyond that and taught hard-core reality-politics that drew those of us who listened closer to the brink of consciousness. Some of us, those who Brown felt had potential, would stop by his class long before pre-parole and sit and listen to him talk about the raw reality of America.

"Kody," Brown would say, "these white folks ain't playin', man. They will lock you up, lock you down, lock you in just like they have locked you out of this society. If you haven't got any marketable skills to sustain an income on your own, man, your chances of survival are slim. You are high-risk living—actually just existing. You young, black, unskilled, strong...you smoke cigarettes?"

"Naw, just bo'."

"Well, that's good enough. You use drugs, you drink, and to top it off you gangbang! Man, how you gonna make it?"

"Man, I don't know..."

Brown, like Muhammad, had a great impact on my development, though it took a few years to appreciate their contribution. The strongest New Afrikan men I had known up until that time were bangers. Verbalizing was not an issue. Shoot first and let the victims' relatives ask questions later. Guns were our tools of communication. If we liked you, you weren't shot and we'd go to any length to shoot whomever disliked you. If you were not liked, you were hunted, if necessary, and shot—period. Instantaneous communication. That's all I had known for years. Words, I thought, could never take the place of guns to communicate like or dislike. But here I was, totally absorbed in the spoken words of Muhammad and Brown, and the written word of Malcolm X. Each emotional lash was tantamount to the resounding echo of gunfire. But unlike gunfire, no one was killed. This was my first encounter with brothers who could kill with words. Their words were not mere talk, either. Action followed in the wake of their theories, and their presence demanded respect long before their words were spoken.

Cornel West
from *Keeping Faith*

5

The Dilemma of the Black Intellectual

The peculiarities of the American social structure, and the position of the in-
tellectual class within it, make the functional role of the negro intellectual a
special one. The negro intellectual must deal intimately with the white power
structure and cultural apparatus, and the inner realities of the black world at
one and the same time. But in order to function successfully in this role, he
has to be acutely aware of the nature of the American social dynamic and
how it monitors the ingredients of class stratifications in American society. . . .
Therefore the functional role of the negro intellectual demands that he
cannot be absolutely separated from either the black or white world.

Harold Cruse
The Crisis of the Negro Intellectual (1967)

The contemporary black intellectual faces a grim predicament. Caught between an insolent American society and an insouciant black community, the
African American who takes seriously the life of the mind inhabits an isolated
and insulated world. This condition has little to do with the motives and intentions of black intellectuals; rather it is an objective situation created by circumstances not of their own choosing. In this meditative essay, I will explore this
dilemma of the black intellectual and suggest various ways of understanding
and transforming it.

On Becoming a Black Intellectual

The choice of becoming a black intellectual is an act of self-imposed marginality; it assures a peripheral status in and to the black community. The quest for
literacy indeed is a fundamental theme in African American history and a
basic impulse in the black community. But for blacks, as with most Americans,
the uses for literacy are usually perceived to be for more substantive pecuniary
benefits than those of the writer, artist, teacher or professor. The reasons some
black people choose to become serious intellectuals are diverse. But in most
cases these reasons can be traced back to a common root: a conversionlike experience with a highly influential teacher or peer that convinced one to dedi-
cate one's life to the activities of reading, writing and conversing for the

purposes of individual pleasure, personal worth and political enhancement of black (and often other oppressed) people.

The way in which one becomes a black intellectual is highly problematic. This is so because the traditional roads others travel to become intellectuals in American society have only recently been opened to black people—and remain quite difficult. The main avenues are the academy or the literate subcultures of art, culture and politics. Prior to the acceptance of black undergraduate students to elite white universities and colleges in the late sixties, select black educational institutions served as the initial stimulus for potential black intellectuals. And in all honesty, there were relatively more and better black intellectuals then than now. After a decent grounding in a black college, where self-worth and self-confidence were affirmed, bright black students then matriculated to leading white institutions to be trained by liberal, sympathetic scholars, often of renowned stature. Stellar figures such as W. E. B. Du Bois, E. Franklin Frazier and John Hope Franklin were products of this system. For those black intellectuals-to-be who missed college opportunities for financial or personal reasons, there were literate subcultures—especially in the large urban centers—of writers, painters, musicians and politicos for unconventional educational enhancement. Major personages such as Richard Wright, Ralph Ellison and James Baldwin were products of this process.

Ironically, the present-day academy and contemporary literate subcultures present more obstacles for young blacks than those in decades past. This is so for three basic reasons. First, the attitudes of white scholars in the academy are quite different from those in the past. It is much more difficult for black students, especially graduate students, to be taken seriously as *potential scholars and intellectuals* owing to the managerial ethos of our universities and colleges (in which less time is spent with students) and to the vulgar (racist) perceptions fueled by affirmative action programs which pollute many black student–white professor relations.

Second, literate subcultures are less open to blacks now than they were three or four decades ago, not because white avant-garde journals or leftist groups are more racist today, but rather because heated political and cultural issues, such as the legacy of the Black Power movement, the Israeli-Palestinian conflict, the invisibility of Africa in American political discourse, have created rigid lines of demarcation and distance between black and white intellectuals. Needless to say, black presence in leading liberal journals like the *New York Review of Books* and the *New York Times Book Review* is negligible—nearly nonexistent. And more leftist periodicals such as *Dissent, Socialist Review, the Nation* and *Telos,* or avant-garde scholarly ones like *Diacritics, Salmagundi, Partisan Review* and *Raritan* do not do much better. Only *Monthly Review,* the *Massachusetts Review, Boundary 2* and *Social Text* make persistent efforts to cover black subject matter and have regular black contributors. The point here is not mere finger-pointing at negligent journals (though it would not hurt matters), but rather an attempt to highlight the racially separatist publishing patterns and practices of American intellectual life which are characteristic of the chasm between black and white intellectuals.

Third, the general politicization of American intellectual life (in the academy and outside), along with the rightward ideological drift, constitutes a hostile climate for the making of black intellectuals. To some extent, this has always been so, but the ideological capitulation of a significant segment of former left-liberals to the new-style conservatism and old-style imperialism has left black students and black professors with few allies in the academy and in influential periodicals. This hostile climate requires that black intellectuals fall back upon their own resources—institutions, journals and periodicals—which, in turn, reinforce the de facto racially separatist practices of American intellectual life.

The tragedy of black intellectual activity is that the black institutional support for such activity is in shambles. The quantity and quality of black intellectual exchange is at its worst since the Civil War. There is no major black academic journal; no major black intellectual magazine; no major black periodical of highbrow journalism; not even a major black newspaper of national scope. In short, the black infrastructure for intellectual discourse and dialogue is nearly nonexistent. This tragedy is, in part, the price for integration—which has yielded mere marginal black groups within the professional disciplines of a fragmented academic community. But this tragedy also has to do with the refusal of black intellectuals to establish and sustain their own institutional mechanisms of criticism and self-criticism, organized in such a way that people of whatever color would be able to contribute to them. This refusal over the past decade is significant in that it has lessened the appetite for, and the capacity to withstand, razor-sharp criticism among many black intellectuals whose formative years were passed in a kind of intellectual vacuum. So besides the external hostile climate, the tradition of serious black intellectual activity is also threatened from within.

The creation of an intelligentsia is a monumental task. Yet black churches and colleges, along with white support, served as resources for the first black intellectuals with formal training. The formation of high-quality habits of criticism and international networks of serious intellectual exchange among a relatively isolated and insulated intelligentsia is a gargantuan endeavor. Yet black intellectuals have little choice: either continued intellectual lethargy on the edges of the academy and literate subcultures unnoticed by the black community, or insurgent creative activity on the margins of the mainstream ensconced within bludgeoning new infrastructures.

Black Intellectuals and the Black Community

The paucity of black infrastructures for intellectual activity results, in part, from the inability of black intellectuals to gain respect and support from the black community—and especially the black middle class. In addition to the general anti-intellectual tenor of American society, there is a deep distrust and suspicion of black intellectuals within the black community. This distrust and suspicion stem not simply from the usual arrogant and haughty disposition of intellectuals toward ordinary folk, but, more importantly, from the widespread refusal of black intellectuals to remain, in some visible way, organically linked with African American cultural life. The relatively high rates of exogamous marriage, the abandonment of black institutions and the preoccupation with Euro-American intellectual products are often perceived by the black community as intentional efforts to escape the negative stigma of blackness or are viewed as symptoms of self-hatred. And the minimal immediate impact of black intellectual activity on the black community and American society reinforces common perceptions of the impotence, even uselessness, of black intellectuals. In good American fashion, the black community lauds those black intellectuals who excel as *political activists* and *cultural artists*; the life of the mind is viewed as neither possessing intrinsic virtues nor harboring emancipatory possibilities—solely short-term political gain and social status.

This truncated perception of intellectual activity is widely held by black intellectuals themselves. Given the constraints upon black upward social mobility and the pressures for status and affluence among middle-class peers, many black intellectuals principally seek material gain and cultural prestige. Since these intellectuals are members of an anxiety-ridden and status-hungry black middle class, their proclivities are understandable and, to some extent, justifiable. For most intellectuals are in search of recognition, status, power and often wealth. Yet for black intellectuals this search requires immersing oneself in and addressing oneself to the very culture and society which degrade and devalue the black community from whence one comes. And, to put it crudely, most black intellectuals tend to fall within the two camps created by this predicament: "successful" ones, distant from (and usually condescending toward) the black community, and "unsuccessful" ones, disdainful of the white intellectual world. But both camps remain marginal to the black community—dangling between two worlds with little or no black infrastructural bases. Therefore, the "successful" black intellectual capitulates, often uncritically, to the prevailing paradigms and research programs of the white bourgeois academy, and the "unsuccessful" black intellectual remains encapsulated within the parochial discourses of African American intellectual life. The alternatives of meretricious pseudo-cosmopolitanism and tendentious, cathartic provincialism loom large in the lives of black intellectuals. And the black community views both alternatives with distrust and disdain—and with good reason. Neither alternative has had a positive impact on the black community. The major black intellectuals from W. E. B. Du Bois and St. Clair Drake to Ralph Ellison and Toni Morrison have shunned both alternatives.

This situation has resulted in the major obstacle confronting black intellectuals: the inability to transmit and sustain the requisite institutional mechanisms for the persistence of a discernible intellectual tradition. The racism of American society, the relative lack of black community support, and hence the dangling status of black intellectuals have prevented the creation of a rich heritage of intellectual exchange, intercourse and dialogue. There indeed have been grand black intellectual achievements, but such achievements do not substitute for tradition.

I would suggest that there are two *organic* intellectual traditions in African American life: *the black Christian tradition of preaching* and *the black musical tradition of performance*. Both traditions, though undoubtedly linked to the life of the mind, are oral, improvisational and histrionic. Both traditions are rooted in black life and possess precisely what the literate forms of black intellectual activity lack: institutional matrices over time and space within which there are accepted rules of procedure, criteria for judgment, canons for assessing performance, models of past achievement and present emulation and an acknowledged succession and accumulation of superb accomplishments. The richness, diversity and vitality of the traditions of black preaching and black music stand in strong contrast to the paucity, even poverty, of black literate intellectual production. There simply have been no black literate intellectuals who have mastered their craft commensurate with the achievements of Louis Armstrong, Charlie Parker or Rev. Manuel Scott—just as there are no black literate intellectuals today comparable to Miles Davis, Sarah Vaughn or Rev. Gardner Taylor. This is so not because there have been or are no first-rate black literate intellectuals, but rather because without strong institutional channels to sustain traditions, great achievement is impossible. And, to be honest, black America has yet to produce a great literate intellectual with the exception of Toni Morrison. There indeed have been superb ones—Du Bois, Frazier, Ellison, Baldwin, Hurston—and many good ones. But none can compare to the heights achieved by black preachers and musicians.

What is most troubling about black literate intellectual activity is that as it slowly evolved out of the black Christian tradition and interacted more intimately with secular Euro-American styles and forms, it seemed as if by the latter part of the twentieth century maturation would set in. Yet, as we approach the last few years of this century, black literate intellectual activity has declined in both quantity and quality. As I noted earlier, this is so primarily because of relatively greater black integration into postindustrial capitalist America with its bureaucratized elite universities, dull middlebrow colleges and decaying high schools, which have little concern for or confidence in black students as potential intellectuals. Needless to say, the predicament of the black intellectual is inseparable from that of the black community—especially the black middle-class community—in American society. And only a fundamental transformation of American society can possibly change the situation of the black community and the black intellectual. And though my own Christian skepticism regarding human totalistic schemes for change chastens my deep socialist sentiments regarding radically democratic and libertarian socioeconomic and cultural arrangements, I shall forego these larger issues and focus on more specific ways to enhance the quantity and quality of black literate intellectual activity in the USA. This focus shall take the form of sketching four models for black intellectual activity, with the intent to promote the crystallization of infrastructures for such activity.

The Bourgeois Model: Black Intellectual as Humanist

For black intellectuals, the bourgeois model of intellectual activity is problematic. On the one hand, the racist heritage—aspects of the exclusionary and repressive effects of white academic institutions and humanistic scholarship—puts black intellectuals on the defensive: there is always the need to assert and defend the humanity of black people, including their ability and capacity to reason logically, think coherently and write lucidly. The weight of this inescapable burden for black students in the white academy has often determined the content and character of black intellectual activity. In fact, black intellectual life remains largely preoccupied with such defensiveness, with "successful" black intellectuals often proud of their white approval and "unsuccessful" ones usually scornful of their white rejection. This concern is especially acute among the first generation of black intellectuals accepted as teachers and scholars within elite white universities and colleges, largely a post-1968 phenomenon. Only with the publication of the intimate memoirs of these black intellectuals and their students will we have the gripping stories of how this defensiveness cut at much of the heart of their intellectual activity and creativity within white academic contexts. Yet, however personally painful such battles have been, they had to be fought, given the racist milieu of American intellectual and academic life. These battles will continue, but with far fewer negative consequences for the younger generation because of the struggles by the older black trailblazers.

On the other hand, the state of siege raging in the black community requires that black intellectuals accent the practical dimension of their work. And the prestige and status, as well as the skills and techniques provided by the white bourgeois academy, render it attractive for the task at hand. The accentuation of the practical dimension holds for most black intellectuals regardless of ideological persuasion—even more than for the stereotypical, pragmatic, American intellectual. This is so not simply because of the power-seeking lifestyles and status-oriented dispositions of many black intellectuals, but also because of their relatively small number, which forces them to play multiple roles vis-à-vis the black community and, in addition, intensifies their need for self-vindication—the attempt to justify to themselves that, given such unique opportunities and privileges, they are spending their time as they ought—which often results in activistic and pragmatic interests.

The linchpin of the bourgeois model is academic legitimation and placement. Without the proper certificate, degree and position, the bourgeois model loses its raison d'être. The influence and attractiveness of the bourgeois model permeate the American academic system; yet the effectiveness of the bourgeois model is credible for black intellectuals only if they possess sufficient legitimacy and placement. Such legitimacy and placement will give one access to select networks and contacts which may facilitate black impact on public policies. This seems to have been the aim of the first generation of blacks trained in elite white institutions (though not permitted to teach there), given their predominant interests in the social sciences.

The basic problem with the bourgeois model is that it is existentially and intellectually stultifying for black intellectuals. It is existentially debilitating because it not only generates anxieties of defensiveness on the part of black intellectuals; it also thrives on them. The need for hierarchical ranking and the deep-seated racism shot through bourgeois humanistic scholarship cannot provide black intellectuals with either the proper ethos or conceptual framework to overcome a defensive posture. And charges of intellectual inferiority can never be met upon the opponent's terrain—to try to do so only intensifies one's anxieties. Rather the terrain itself must be viewed as part and parcel of an antiquated form of life unworthy of setting the terms of contemporary discourse.

The bourgeois model sets intellectual limits, in that one is prone to adopt uncritically prevailing paradigms predominant in the bourgeois academy because of the pressures of practical tasks and deferential emulation. Every intellectual passes through some kind of apprenticeship stage in which s/he learns the language and style of the authorities, but when s/he is already viewed as marginally talented s/he may be either excessively encouraged or misleadingly discouraged to examine critically paradigms deemed marginal by the authorities. This hostile environment results in the suppression of one's critical analyses and in the limited use of one's skills in a manner considered legitimate and practical.

Despite its limitations, the bourgeois model is inescapable for most black intellectuals. This is so because most of the important and illuminating discourses in the country take place in white bourgeois academic institutions and because the more significant intellectuals teach in such places. Many of the elite white universities and colleges remain high-powered schools of education, learning and training principally due to large resources and civil traditions that provide the leisure time and atmosphere necessary for sustained and serious intellectual endeavor. So aside from the few serious autodidactic black intellectuals (who often have impressive scope but lack grounding and depth), black intellectuals must pass through the white bourgeois academy (or its black imitators).

Black academic legitimation and placement can provide a foothold in American intellectual life so that black infrastructures for intellectual anxiety can be created. At present, there is a small yet significant black presence within the white bourgeois academic organizations, and it is able to produce newsletters and small periodicals. The next step is to institutionalize more broadly black intellectual presence, as the Society of Black Philosophers of New York has done, by publishing journals anchored in a discipline (crucial for the careers of prospective professors) yet relevant to other disciplines. It should be noted that such a black infrastructure for intellectual activity should attract persons of whatever hue or color. Black literary critics and especially black psychologists are far ahead of other black intellectuals in this regard, with journals

630   Part 6/The Post-Industrial, Post-Civil Rights Era

such as the *Black American Literature Forum*, the *College Language Association* and the *Journal of Black Psychology*.

Black academic legitimation and placement also can result in black control over a portion of, or significant participation within, the larger white infrastructures for intellectual activity. This has not yet occurred on a broad scale. More black representation is needed on the editorial boards of significant journals so that a larger black intellectual presence is permitted. This process is much slower and has less visibility, yet, given the hegemony of the bourgeois model, it must be pursued by those so inclined.

The bourgeois model is, in some fundamental and ultimate sense, more part of the problem than the solution in regard to black intellectuals. Yet, since we live our lives daily and penultimately within this system, those of us highly critical of the bourgeois model must try to subvert it, in part, from within the white bourgeois academy. For black intellectuals—in alliance with nonblack progressive intellectuals—this means creating and augmenting infrastructures for black intellectual activity.

The Marxist Model: Black Intellectual as Revolutionary

Among many black intellectuals, there is a knee-jerk reaction to the severe limitations of the bourgeois model (and capitalist society)—namely, to adopt the Marxist model. This adoption satisfies certain basic needs of the black intelligentsia: the need for social relevance, political engagement and organizational involvement. The Marxist model also provides entry into the least xenophobic white intellectual subculture available to black intellectuals.

The Marxist model privileges the activity of black intellectuals and promotes their prophetic role. As Harold Cruse has noted, such privileging is highly circumscribed and rarely accents the theoretical dimension of black intellectual activity. In short, the Marxist privileging of black intellectuals often reeks of condescension that confines black prophetic roles to spokespersons and organizers; only rarely are they allowed to function as creative thinkers who warrant serious critical attention. It is no accident that the relatively large numbers of black intellectuals attracted to Marxism over the past sixty years have yet to produce a major black Marxist theoretician with the exception of C. L. R. James. Only W. E. B. Du Bois's *Black Reconstruction* (1935), Oliver Cox's *Caste, Class and Race* (1948) and, to some degree, Harold Cruse's *The Crisis of the Negro Intellectual* (1967) are even candidates for such a designation. This is so not because of the absence of black intellectual talent in the Marxist camp but rather because of the absence of the kind of tradition and community (including intense critical exchange) that would allow such talent to flower.

In stark contrast to the bourgeois model, the Marxist model neither generates black intellectual defensiveness nor provides an adequate analytical apparatus for short-term public policies. Rather the Marxist model yields black intellectual self-satisfaction which often inhibits growth; it also highlights social structural constraints with little practical direction regarding conjunctural opportunities. This self-satisfaction results in either dogmatic submission to and upward mobility within sectarian party or preparty formations or marginal placement in the bourgeois academy equipped with cantankerous Marxist rhetoric and sometimes insightful analysis utterly divorced from the integral dynamics, concrete realities and progressive possibilities of the black community. The preoccupation with social structural constraints tends to produce either preposterous chiliastic projections or paralyzing pessimistic pronouncements. Such projections and pronouncements have as much to do with the self-image of black Marxist intellectuals as with the prognosis for black liberation.

It is often claimed "that Marxism is the false consciousness of the radical-ized, bourgeois intelligentsia." For black intellectuals, the Marxist model func-tions in a more complex manner than this glib formulation permits. On the one hand, the Marxist model is liberating for black intellectuals in that it pro-motes critical consciousness and attitudes toward the dominant bourgeois para-digms and research programs. Marxism provides attractive roles for black intellectuals—usually highly visible leadership roles—and infuses new meaning and urgency into their work. On the other hand, the Marxist model is debili-tating for black intellectuals because the cathartic needs it satisfies tend to sti-fle the further development of black critical consciousness and attitudes.

The Marxist model, despite its shortcomings, is more part of the solution than part of the problem for black intellectuals. This is so because Marxism is the brook of fire—the purgatory—of our postmodern times. Black intellectuals must pass through it, come to terms with it, and creatively respond to it if black intellectual activity is to reach any recognizable level of sophistication and refinement.

The Foucaultian Model: Black Intellectual as Postmodern Skeptic

As Western intellectual life moves more deeply into crisis and as black intellec-tuals become more fully integrated into intellectual life—or into "the culture of careful and critical discourse" (as the late Alvin Gouldner called it)—a new model appears on the horizon. This model, based primarily upon the influential work of the late Michel Foucault, unequivocably rejects the bourgeois model and eschews the Marxist model. It constitutes one of the most exciting intel-lectual challenges of our day: the Foucaultian project of historical nominalism. This detailed investigation into the complex relations of knowledge and power, discourses and politics, cognition and social control compels intellectuals to re-think and redefine their self-image and function in our contemporary situation.

The Foucaultian model and project are attractive to black intellectuals pri-marily because they speak to the black postmodern predicament, defined by the rampant xenophobia of bourgeois humanism predominant in the whole acad-emy, the waning attraction to orthodox reductionist and scientific versions of Marxism, and the need for reconceptualization regarding the specificity and complexity of African American oppression. Foucault's deep antibourgeois sentiments, explicit post-Marxist convictions and profound preoccupations with those viewed as radically "Other" by dominant discourses and traditions are quite seductive for politicized black intellectuals wary of antiquated panaceas for black liberation.

Foucault's specific analyses of the "political economy of truth"—the study of the discursive ways in which and institutional means by which "regimes of truth" are constituted by societies over space and time—result in a new conception of the intellectual. This conception no longer rests upon the smooth transmittance of "the best that has been thought and said," as in the bourgeois humanist model, nor on the engaged utopian energies of the Marxist model. Rather the postmodern situation requires "the specific intellectual" who shuns the labels of scientificity, civility and prophecy and instead delves into the specificity of the political, economic and cultural matrices within which regimes of truth are produced, distributed, circulated and consumed. No longer should intellectuals deceive themselves by believing—as do humanist and Marxist intellectuals—that they are struggling "on behalf" of the truth; rather the problem is the struggle over the very status of truth and the vast institutional mechanisms which account for this status. The favored code words of "science," "taste," "tact," "ideology," "progress" and "liberation" of bourgeois humanism and Marxism are no longer applicable to the self-image of postmodern intellectuals. Instead, the new key terms become those of "regime of truth," "power/knowledge" and "discursive practices."

Foucault's notion of the specific intellectual rests upon his demystification of conservative, liberal and Marxist rhetorics which restore, resituate and reconstruct intellectuals' self-identities so that they remain captive to and supportive of institutional forms of domination and control. These rhetorics authorize and legitimate, in different ways, the privileged status of intellectuals, which not only reproduces ideological divisions between intellectual and manual labor but also reinforces disciplinary mechanisms of subjection and subjugation. This self-authorizing is best exemplified in the claims made by intellectuals that they "safeguard" the achievement of highbrow culture or "represent" the "universal interests" of particular classes and groups. In African American intellectual history, similar self-authorizing claims such as "the talented tenth," "prophets in the wilderness," "articulators of a black aesthetic," "creators of a black renaissance" and "vanguard of a revolutionary movement" are widespread.

The Foucaultian model promotes a leftist form of postmodern skepticism; that is, it encourages an intense and incessant interrogation of power-laden discourses in the service of neither restoration, reformation nor revolution, but rather of revolt. And the kind of revolt enacted by intellectuals consists of the disrupting and dismantling of prevailing "regimes of truth"—including their repressive effects—of present-day societies. This model suits the critical, skeptical, and historical concerns of progressive black intellectuals and provides a sophisticated excuse for ideological and social distance from insurgent black movements for liberation. By conceiving intellectual work as oppositional political praxis, it satisfies the leftist self-image of black intellectuals, and, by making a fetish of critical consciousness, it encapsulates black intellectual activity within the comfortable bourgeois academy of postmodern America.

The Insurgency Model: Black Intellectual as Critical Organic Catalyst

Black intellectuals can learn much from each of the three previous models, yet should not uncritically adopt any one of them. This is so because the bourgeois, Marxist and Foucaultian models indeed relate to, but do not adequately speak to, the uniqueness of the black intellectual predicament. This uniqueness remains relatively unexplored, and will remain so until black intellectuals articulate a new "regime of truth" linked to, yet not confined by, indigenous institutional practices permeated by the kinetic orality and emotional physicality, the rhythmic syncopation, the protean improvisation and the religious, rhetorical and antiphonal repetition of African American life. Such articulation depends, in part, upon elaborate black infrastructures which put a premium on creative and cultivated black thought; it also entails intimate knowledge of prevailing Euro-American "regimes of truth" which must be demystified, deconstructed and decomposed in ways which enhance and enrich future black intellectual life. The new "regime of truth" to be pioneered by black thinkers is neither a hermetic discourse (or set of discourses), which safeguards mediocre black intellectual production, nor the latest fashion of black writing, which is often motivated by the desire to parade for the white bourgeois intellectual establishment. Rather it is inseparable from the emergence of new cultural forms which prefigure (and point toward) a post-Western civilization. At present, such talk may seem mere dream and fantasy. So we shall confine ourselves to the first step: black insurgency and the role of the black intellectual.

The major priority of black intellectuals should be the creation or reactivation of institutional networks that promote high-quality critical habits primarily for the purpose of black insurgency. An intelligentsia without institutionalized critical consciousness is blind, and critical consciousness severed from collective insurgency is empty. The central task of postmodern black intellectuals is to stimulate, hasten and enable alternative perceptions and practices by dislodging prevailing discourses and powers. This can be done only by intense intellectual work and engaged insurgent praxis.

The insurgency model for black intellectual activity builds upon, yet goes beyond, the previous three models. From the bourgeois model, it recuperates the emphasis on human will and heroic effort. Yet the insurgency model refuses to conceive of this will and effort in individualistic and elitist terms. Instead of the solitary hero, embattled exile and isolated genius—the intellectual as star, celebrity, commodity—this model privileges collective intellectual work that contributes to communal resistance and struggle. In other words, it creatively accents the voluntarism and heroism of the bourgeois model, but it rejects the latter's naiveté about the role of society and history. From the Marxist model it recovers the stress on structural constraints, class formations and radical democratic values. Yet the insurgency model does not view these constraints, formations and values in economistic and deterministic terms. Instead of the a priori privileging of the industrial working class and the metaphysical positing of a relatively harmonious socialist society, there is the wholesale assault on varieties of social hierarchy and the radical democratic (and libertarian) mediation, not elimination, of social heterogeneity. In short, the insurgency model ingeniously incorporates the structural, class and democratic concerns of the Marxist model, yet it acknowledges the latter's naiveté about culture.

Lastly, from the Foucaultian model, the insurgency model recaptures the preoccupation with worldly skepticism, the historical constitution of "regimes of truth," and the multifarious operations of "power/knowledge." Yet the insurgency model does not confine this skepticism, this truth-constituting and detailed genealogical inquiry to micronetworks of power. Instead of the ubiquity of power (which simplifies and flattens multidimensional social conflict) and the paralyzing overreaction to past utopianisms, there is the possibility of effective resistance and meaningful societal transformation. The insurgency model carefully highlights the profound Nietzschean suspicion and the illuminating oppositional descriptions of the Foucaultian model, though it recognizes the latter's naiveté about social conflict, struggle and insurgency—a naiveté primarily caused by the rejection of any form of utopianism and any positing of a telos.

Black intellectual work and black collective insurgency must be rooted in the specificity of African American life and history; but they also are inextricably linked to the American, European and African elements which shape and mold them. Such work and insurgency are explicitly particularist though not exclusivist—hence they are international in outlook and practice. Like their historical forerunners, black preachers and black musical artists (with all their strengths and weaknesses), black intellectuals must realize that the creation of "new" and alternative practices results from the heroic efforts of collective intellectual work and communal resistance which shape and are shaped by present structural constraints, workings of power and modes of cultural fusion. The distinctive African American cultural forms such as the black sermonic and prayer styles, gospel, blues and jazz should inspire, but not constrain, future black intellectual production; that is, the process by which they came to be should provide valuable insights, but they should serve as models neither to imitate nor emulate. Needless to say, these forms thrive on incessant critical innovation and concomitant insurgency.

The Future of the Black Intellectual

The predicament of the black intellectual need not be grim and dismal. Despite the pervasive racism of American society and anti-intellectualism of the black community, critical space and insurgent activity can be expanded. This expansion will occur more readily when black intellectuals take a more candid look at themselves, the historical and social forces that shape them, and the limited though significant resources of the community from whence they come. A critical "self-inventory" that scrutinizes the social positions, class locations and cultural socializations of black intellectuals is imperative. Such scrutiny should be motivated by neither self-pity nor self-satisfaction. Rather this "self-inventory" should embody the sense of critique and resistance applicable to the black community, American society and Western civilization as a whole. James Baldwin has noted that the black intellectual is "a kind of bastard of the West." The future of the black intellectual lies neither in a deferential disposition toward the Western parent nor a nostalgic search for the African one. Rather it resides in a critical negation, wise preservation and insurgent transformation of this black lineage which protects the earth and projects a better world.

Georgia Persons
from *Dilemmas of Black Politics*

BLACK MAYORALTIES AND THE NEW BLACK POLITICS: FROM INSURGENCY TO RACIAL RECONCILIATION

Introduction

The November 1989 elections appeared to have marked the beginning of a new era in black electoral politics. Several African-Americans were elected as mayors of major American cities—New York, New Haven, Seattle, Cleveland, and Durham, North Carolina—and in a most historic development, L. Douglas Wilder was elected as the nation's first black governor in the state of Virginia. The fact that in each case these men won in majority white jurisdictions made these developments only somewhat unique as blacks (Congressmen Dellums of California, and Wheat of Missouri, for example) had previously been elected in majority white election districts. However, what gave the 1989 elections such prominence were their manifestations as a clustering of events which collectively posed a challenge to dominant theories of American electoral politics generally and black politics specifically. Prior to these elections, the predominant pattern and constraint in the election of black candidates had been their emergence from concentrated, predominantly black (population) locales, with the corollary of a strong and persistent reluctance of white voters to support black candidates.

Coupled with this seemingly anomalous development, the factor which sparked concern and debate, first among analysts of black politics and later incorporating journalist/observers and laypersons alike,[1] was the apparent deliberate absence of familiar appeals to black voters, as well as the absence or diminution by the winning candidates of campaign issues which could be interpreted as addressing "the black agenda." Thus, in effect, the 1989 elections conveyed a new set of signals, a new political message. Interpretations of the strategic contents and significance of the 1989 elections as manifestations of an emergent political strategy of deracialization is the specific focus of Chapter 4 in this volume. For the purposes of this chapter, the 1989 elections serve as a reflective backdrop for attempting to understand the evolution of the new black politics. The analysis and discussion presented in this chapter assume that the 1989 elections constituted a significant political development with implications for the future practice of black politics, and constituted as well a new and important reference point for the analysis and understanding of politics in America.

From the vantage point of early 1990, the 1989 elections appeared to portend, or at least to crystallize in our understanding of things past, the end of an era in black political struggle. The possible end of an era and the implications inherent in such a magnitude of change provoke concern and the quest for explanatory factors, because profound questions of the status of blacks in America remain unanswered. Yet, one also senses other profound changes under way which promise to affect, in non-negligible ways, the future status of blacks in America. Some of these changes are occurring external to the black community, such as the growing number of newly immigrant groups and their increasing influence socially and politically. The social and political emergence of newly immigrant groups is not only altering the ethnic mosaic of major urban areas, but in many instances strains the social order and threatens to redistribute political power, just as blacks had achieved some limited successes in exacting rewards from the political system. Moreover, the socio-political dynamics of a culturally significant and politically distinct, multiethnic society are likely to be far different than those attendant to a society which, in relationship to the quest for black political empowerment, was in the main, culturally and politically defined by a bifurcation along racial lines of black and white.

Other dynamics, which are indeed ominous, are present within the black community. There is a widening gap between the black underclass and the rest of black America (Wilson 1978; 1987). This widening gap seems impervious to the social and political thrusts around which the black community has been mobilized and directed for the past several decades. In short, the successes of black political empowerment seem unable to deliver on the expectations and promises so fervently anticipated a few decades ago. Yet, what we have conceptualized as the new black politics simultaneously appears to be facing imminent transition and possible eclipse, leaving significantly unaltered the status of large segments of the black community.

The *primary* objective of this chapter is to illuminate a single question: in examining the evolution of black mayoralties, what developments, or patterns of developments, signalled the nature of strategic changes embodied in the 1989 elections? The focus is on black mayoralties as the embodiment of the major achievements and constraints of the new black politics. The focus on black mayoralties particularly affords illumination of the evolution of the new black politics from its early manifestation as an insurgent movement to its seeming "maturation" as a variant of "politics as usual," in which the significance of traditional racial appeals and social reform efforts apparently have been diminished.

In examining the collective evolution of big-city black mayoralties, three simultaneous and overlapping developmental paths are apparent:

1. A *pattern of insurgency* characterized by challenges to the prevailing political order, embrace of a social reform agenda, and utilization of a pattern of racial appeals to mobilize a primary support group of black voters;

2. A *pattern of racial reconciliation* in which, in some cases, black candidates woo white voters by simply diminishing, avoiding, or perverting racial appeals, while in other situations black candidates exploit the images of insurgent-style candidates to enhance by contrast their own appeal as racial moderates; in both instances black candidates expect to reap the benefits of racial symbolism and concomitant black voter support in a white-on-black contest;

3. A *pattern of institutionalization* which underlies all black mayoral successes in that the number of black mayoral successes has increased over time, and their longevity and succession in office have increased, reflecting their grounding, though in varied manifestations, in the systemic fabric of American politics.

The argument is advanced here that, within the context of the institutionalization of black mayoralties, and simultaneously the parent phenomenon of the new black politics, the apparently anomalous nature of the 1989 elections, in fact, reflects an ongoing evolution from a pattern of spirited insurgency to a pattern of attempts at racial reconciliation evident in black mayoral politics specifically, and black politics generally. Data for this chapter were drawn from extant studies of black mayoralties and the author's own research on black mayoralties in Atlanta, Washington, D.C., Gary, Newark, and other cities.

The Rise of the New Black Politics

If we seek to understand change of significant magnitude, we need to understand the past as the standard against which to assess and interpret the new. What analysts and laypersons alike have, for more than two decades, characterized as the new black politics—its promises and expectations—has defined for many a *preferred conception* of black politics; though as the point will be made later, this conception has not in reality embraced all of what has in effect passed—to use a racially laden pun—as black politics. In its conceptions and early manifestation the new black politics represented a major strategic shift in tactics used by blacks. Analysts generally identify three shifts in black strategic activities which have occurred in the recent past: the first of which occurred between 1955 and 1957 in the movement for civil rights; the second in 1966–1967 with the black liberation movement, and the third in the period 1970–1972 with the movement to black electoral politics (Walters 1980). The latter and current period has been characterized as the era of "the new black politics" (Preston et al. 1982). The new black politics sought to shift black strategic efforts away from various modes of protest and civil disobedience to electoral politics as the means of achieving black political and social empowerment. Varying forms of representation are presumed to bestow varying benefits upon the group seeking representation (Pitkin 1967). It was assumed that with the achievement of descriptive *and* substantive representation, that is, the election to office of individuals who mirrored the racial background *and* political

philosophies of blacks, that significant social and political benefits would accrue to the black community.

The new black politics represented primarily a strategic concensus, the
pursuit of electoral politics, that has proven to be a consensus open to rather
broad interpretations in terms of specific strategies. However, in its initial conception, the new black politics was a strategy presumed to be anchored in a
consensus on objectives as well; indeed assumed to be so strongly shared within
the black leadership corps that it constituted a cause of the intensity of the
civil rights movement. The early promises and expectations of the new black
politics were eloquently captured in an ambitious definition proffered by
William Nelson:

> At bottom the new black politics is a politics of social and economic transforma-
> tion based on the mobilization of community power....
>
> The new black politics represents an effort by black political leaders to capitalize
> on the increasing size of the black electorate; the strategic position of black voters
> in many cities, counties, and congressional districts, and the growing political con-
> sciousness of the black community. It constitutes an immensely serious effort to
> build bases of electoral strength in the black community *and organize black political
> interests around the power of the vote* (emphasis added) (Nelson 1982).

Perhaps the singular achievement of the new black politics has been the
election of black mayors in many of the major cities in America as well as in
hundreds of small towns, totalling some 293 black mayors in early 1990. Prior
to the election of Douglas Wilder as governor of Virginia, big-city black mayors
were the most visible black elected officials; their responsibilities to the citizenry are much greater and more comprehensive than that of most other local
officials, and their influence less subject to dilution than representatives in
Congress. Thus the election of a black mayor, particularly a big-city black
mayor, constitutes a major socio-political achievement, a highly symbolic
achievement, as well as highly visible evidence of black strategic efforts. Yet
prior to the 1989 elections, questions were being raised about the efficacy of
black mayors (Preston 1990), reflecting recognition that the expectations and
promises of their regimes were not being realized.

The Institutionalization of Black Mayoralties
and a Changing Political Order

Institutionalization as a Political and Social Process

Social scientists use the concept of institutionalization to capture a dynamic in
the processes of socio-political development when political leadership, governmental bodies, the rules and procedures of governance, and general methods of
politics become accepted and widely supported by the polity (Polsby 1968). Institutionalization is assumed to have occurred when methods of politics, political leadership, governmental institutions, rules and procedures of governance

reach a significant level of stability, as characterized by orderly, predictable, and infrequent changes, and in some cases, obtain a presumed permanent status. Institutionalization is characterized by predictability in patterns of recruitment of political leadership, professionalization of personnel and standards within governmental bureaucracies, infrequent and orderly change, and adaptability of political processes and institutions to change. The key factors to successful institutionalization are broad-based public support and acceptance, stability of functions, procedures, and political leadership resulting in a stable leadership corps.

The concept of institutionalization has been used explicitly as an analytical framework for studies of the U.S. Congress, which is said to have institutionalized over time as turnover in its membership has declined, as members have served longer terms, and as representation has become more stable (Polsby 1968). The concept has also been used extensively in the study of developing societies, particularly in reference to the processes of political development in post-colonial regimes, as the procedures and institutions of representative democracy have taken hold (Nordlinger 1971). It is therefore a useful concept for understanding the interplay of social and political dynamics pertinent to the realization of politically defined objectives.

The concept of institutionalization is particularly useful in observing and understanding the process of representation of diverse interests. It is useful as well in understanding changes in institutional arrangements in response to broad-based social change. Institutionalization thus implies a developmental process incorporating changes and adjustments in the dynamics and structures of political processes over time, bolstered by the critical element of broad-based, mass-level acceptance and support. As such, it is something of a "settling in" process for a new political order, a movement towards stability and permanency, and not an immediate occurrence. Thus, in regard to black mayoralties, the mere election of a large number of black mayors is not automatically tantamount to institutionalization, although such electoral successes may well be manifestations of broad-based public acceptance and thus reflect some of the preconditions of institutionalization.

Today, when one speaks of the election of a black mayor, reference is not necessarily made to the comparatively simple development of 1967 when the nation's first black mayors were elected. In the late 1960s and early 1970s, the election of a black mayor was generally the outcome of a black candidate challenging the "white power structure" in a bruising, racially charged contest. Twenty years later, the election of a black mayor may occur as the result of a number of different political configurations: (1) the election of a first black mayor for a given locale based on the mobilization of a majority or critical near-majority black population (the dominant pattern of the early cases); (2) the election of a first black mayor in a predominantly white setting (this variant emerged early in Los Angeles in 1973 and has now been repeated in several locales); (3) the election of a black successor to an incumbent black mayor whose statutory term in office has ended; or (4) the election of a black successor in the unseating of an incumbent black mayor. Thus, there is now considerable diversity in the circumstances surrounding the election of black mayors, yet all reflecting the results of a pursuit of electoral politics.

In regard to big-city (population 150,000 and above) black mayors, there have been roughly five electoral waves. The first wave occurred with the election of black mayors in Cleveland and Gary in 1967, and Newark in 1970. Cleveland lost its first black mayoralty in an unsuccessful effort to elect a second black mayor in 1972. The second wave occurred with the election of black mayors in Detroit, Atlanta, and Los Angeles in 1973, and the District of Columbia in 1974.[2] The third wave brought black mayors to New Orleans and Oakland in 1977, and Birmingham in 1979. The fourth wave occurred in 1983 with the election of Harold Washington in Chicago, Wilson Goode in Philadelphia, and Harvey Gantt in Charlotte, North Carolina. The black mayoralty in Chicago was lost in 1989, subsequent to the death of Harold Washington during his second term in office. In Charlotte, Harvey Gantt was defeated for reelection by a white female Republican. Baltimore was added in 1987, initially by default with the election of then Mayor Shaeffer to the state governorship, and the automatic ascendancy of the black deputy mayor to the position of mayor. Harvard-trained attorney and Rhodes scholar, Kurt Schmoke became the first elected black mayor of Baltimore in 1987. The fifth and most recent wave occurred in November 1989 with the election of black mayors in New York City, New Haven, Seattle, Durham, North Carolina, and again in Cleveland, Ohio (see Table 3.1).

During the 20 years or so since the election of the first black mayor in a major city, several electoral junctures have been reached, including: successful reelections in many cities; long-term incumbencies of first black mayors in Detroit, Los Angeles, (Gary and Newark); voluntary succession in Atlanta; and involuntary succession in Gary, Newark, and New Orleans.[3] These electoral waves and junctures embody the developmental paths of insurgency, racial reconciliation, and institutionalization.

Insurgency as Strategy and Style

Among black mayoral aspirants, particularly in the early stages of the new black politics strategy, insurgency served as the predominant campaign strategy; and later insurgency served as a style of leadership for many elected mayors. Generally, insurgency as strategy has been associated with the initial election of a black mayor in a given locale, and as a leadership style, has been adopted and retained by first black mayors throughout their tenure in office. (The retention of insurgency as a leadership style in long-term black mayoral incumbencies is discussed below.) Insurgency was characterized by direct challenges to the prevailing political order, encompassing explicit criticisms and attacks on elected officials, institutional processes, civic leadership structures, and the resulting mobilization of interests and bias in local political contexts.

As a tactical strategy, insurgency was driven by imperatives of time and place, and the prevailing demographics. The nature of the times was such that

TABLE 3.1   *Black Mayors of Cities with Populations Over 50,000, (1990)*

Name	City	Population	% Black
David Dinkins	New York City	7,071,000	25.0
Thomas Bradley	Los Angeles, CA	3,259,000	17.0
W. Wilson Goode	Philadelphia, PA	1,642,000	40.2
Coleman Young	Detroit, MI	1,086,000	63.1
Kurt Schmoke	Baltimore, MD	763,000	54.8
Marion Barry	Washington, D.C.	626,000	70.0
Michael White	Cleveland, OH	573,800	45.0
Sidney Barthelemy	New Orleans, LA	554,000	55.3
Norman Rice	Seattle, WA	493,800	9.5
Maynard Jackson	Atlanta, GA	421,000	66.6
Lionel Wilson	Oakland, CA	356,000	46.9
Sharpe James	Newark, NJ	316,000	46.9
Richard Arrington	Birmingham, AL	277,000	55.6
Richard Dixon	Dayton, OH	181,000	37.0
Jessie Ratley	Newport News, VA	154,000	31.5
Carrie Perry	Hartford, CT	137,000	33.9
Thomas Barnes	Gary, IN	136,000	70.8
John Daniels	New Haven, CT	129,000	31.0
Chester Jenkins	Durham, NC	110,000	47.0
Edward Vincent	Inglewood, CA	102,000	57.3
Noel Taylor	Roanoke, VA	100,000	22.0
Walter Tucker	Compton, CA	93,000	74.8
Melvin Primas	Camden, NJ	82,000	53.0
John Hatcher, Jr.	East Orange, NJ	77,000	83.6
George Livingston	Richmond, CA	77,000	47.9
Edna W. Summers	Evanston Township	72,000	21.4
Walter L. Moore	Pontiac, MI	70,000	34.2
Ronald Blackwood	Mt. Vernon, NY	68,000	48.7
E. Pat Larkins	Pompano Beach, FL	66,000	17.2
Carl E. Officer	East St. Louis, IL	51,000	95.6

Source: Joint Center for Political Studies. Washington, D.C., U.S. Bureau of the Census. 1986 population estimates.

blacks were not only systematically excluded from elected positions and other posts within local political establishments, but their exclusion was also supported by a prevailing ethos which rendered their desires and efforts to obtain access to the political process to be illegitimate demands on the local political order. Prevailing patterns of voting behavior were such that a black candidate could not expect to receive more than a very small percentage of white votes, dictating an almost exclusive reliance on black voters, many of whom were not registered or generally unaccustomed to participating in politics, especially politics that deliberately threatened the prevailing political order. Given this convergence of conditions and circumstances, even in the absence of specifically social reform issues, insurgent black candidates were perceived as social reform-ers, a residual benefit which continues to accrue to most black aspirants for po-litical office.

The early pattern of insurgency pitted a black candidate against a white candidate in a racially heated contest (Nelson and Meranto 1977). The basic pattern has been one of mobilization based on racial appeals with the successful black candidate garnering a solid black bloc vote supplemented with the crossover of a small percentage (rarely exceeding 20 percent) of white voters (Bullock 1984). Thus, the overwhelming majority of early black mayors were elected in cities with a majority of near-majority black population. In most cases of the initial election of a black mayor, either substantive issues were sub-ordinated to overt racial appeals (frequently by both black and white candi-dates), or positions espoused by black candidates were of a social reform nature, racially exhortatory, and clearly directed towards black voters. White candi-dates in these races resorted to "save our city" racial appeals or adopted a newly "race-neutral" position of desiring to "represent all of the people" (Hahn et al. 1976; Pettigrew 1976).

As a strategy *insurgency promoted black political mobilization and provoked white resistance.* The result in most locales was that, subsequent to the election of a black mayor, the initial period of transition and displacement was charac-terized by severe racial polarization (Levine 1974; Eisinger 1980). Racial polar-ization subsided over time, but in many locales remained sufficiently ingrained to make for a tendency among whites and blacks to define most issues within a racial context (Persons 1985). However, severe racial conflict has not been a constant attendant to the election of first black mayors, although reasons for this significant deviation are not clear. The case of Atlanta, which became se-verely racially polarized, disputes the theory of the mediating effects of a previ-ously prevailing biracial coalition (Persons 1985). The racially polarized 1983 election in Chicago, almost 20 years after the nation's first election of a big-city black mayor, disputes the temporal factor as an explanation, as does the con-trast of the Philadelphia election of 1983 in which racial polarization did not occur. A highly plausible explanation may rest on whether the black mayoral contender espoused an explicitly social reform agenda or otherwise made strong and explicit appeals to the black community, thereby clearly challenging the prevailing political order.

In the case of Chicago, much more was at stake than a comparatively sim-ple racial and political displacement. Harold Washington ran against the white ethnic-dominated political machine, which had variously dominated Chicago politics for almost half a century, and the prospect of his election carried a par-ticularly severe threat (Akalimat and Gills 1984). Moreover, Chicago has long been held by many observers to harbor a most invidious form of racial tensions, in no small part attributable to the organizing tactics of the old line political machine that was founded and sustained by drawing on heightened ethnic ap-peals, making exclusion and oppression of blacks both politically expedient and socially acceptable. Thus the socio-political dynamics in Chicago in 1983 were very similar in nature and effect to those which prevailed in many cities two decades or more earlier.

The early black mayoral elections signalled a potentially significant level of social reform. These elections meant major change in the most important and visible local leadership corps. They also meant the representation and entry of new claimants to local political arenas. Most early black mayors explicitly articulated a social reform agenda in their campaigns, emphasizing issues of police brutality, the hiring of blacks in municipal jobs, increased contracting to minority vendors, improved low-income housing choices, improved and equitable delivery of public services, and a more open government relative to groups formerly shut out of the local governing process. While strong social reform agendas clearly caused concern among white voters, such an explicitly articulated agenda was not always necessary for mobilizing the black vote. In most initial black mayoral elections, for most black voters, the symbolic significance of the potential of elect a black mayor tended to override concerns for the specifics of issue positions. Moreover, in most black versus white mayoral contests, most black voters have understandably automatically associated descriptive representation (electing a representative who mirrored their racial and general social characteristics) with substantive representation (the support for and advocacy of issues and interests of greatest concern to them). Well beyond the early stage of insurgency politics, some black mayoral candidates and candidates for other offices as well have factored the significance of this symbolism into their strategies and, discounting the importance of explicitly stated substantive issues for black voters, have directed issue-specific appeals almost exclusively to white voters (Ransom 1987; Keiser 1990).

After the initial election, the crucial next step in the process of institutionalization is reelection. This is a particularly critical step for insurgent black mayors if social reform efforts are to be established. Some new dynamics emerge at this electoral juncture, presenting something of a strategic dilemma for the incumbent. However, perhaps the most interesting development is that at the stage of reelection we begin to see the many faces of the coin of race and its varied uses in black politics. Reelection efforts of insurgents have been characterized by the continued resistance of a significant number of white voters to black mayoral rule, manifested in efforts to develop more effective strategies against a second black electoral victory (Watson 1984). This occurred in Atlanta in 1978, and Chicago in 1987. In both instances, overtly racist campaigns were launched by white challengers to "save our city" from continued black governance. Moreover, there is the added problem of maintaining the monolithic clout of a well-mobilized black community in the face of major white and black challengers. First black mayors know well the dynamics of a black versus white contest, having experienced this in their initial elections, and having benefitted from having a "white ogre" as an opponent. One might thus conclude that the dynamics of a reelection contest involving a strong black challenger might require an adjustment in strategy; this is not necessarily the case.

The pairing of two black contenders in a multicandidate race suggests a need to create a distinction between the two while preserving the monolithic black vote in support of a single black candidate. This leads to a highly tenuous situation for both black candidates, as a split in the black vote may result in a loss of the mayoralty to a white candidate. The black challenger may, of course, seek to build a pivotal base of support among white voters with a smaller supplement of black votes. Such a strategy by a black challenger would simply reverse the conventional first black mayor strategy.

Coleman Young of Detroit faced this situation in his first reelection bid in 1977. Young's black opponent sought to make Coleman Young the issue: his frequently abrasive political style, his lifestyle, and his frequent use of rough language were labeled as inappropriate for the leadership of Detroit. Young's strategy was to label his black opponent as a "black, white hope." Young's black challenger had received only five percent of the black vote in the primary, but had forced Young into a runoff on the strength of his white support (Rich 1989). The appellation of "black, white hope" embodied the message which many incumbent black mayors, at one time or another, have sought to convey: competition is a threat to the tenuous political hold of black mayoralties and may result in a major setback for the black community—the loss of the newly won mayoralty to a white contender. The strategy of Young's challenger also has become a familiar one as the appeal of the mayoralty has become a means of fulfilling the personal and political ambitions of many black aspirants. In the Detroit case of 1977, racial appeals of essentially the same type as were used in the initial election continued to serve the incumbent despite the change to a black versus black contest. For strategic purposes the black challenger was depicted as the surrogate "white ogre," an interesting turn of the coin of race, and an interesting means of sustaining insurgency.

Also interesting is the fact that in some locales, structural factors, that is, the absence of statutory limits on the number of consecutive terms a mayor may serve, have played a major role in institutionalizing insurgency through facilitating long-term incumbencies of first black mayors. The result has been that some first black mayors have succeeded in "institutionalizing" their individual presences in office. This has been the case in Detroit and Los Angeles where incumbent black mayors have been reelected for five consecutive four-year terms. (Los Angeles is not here characterized as an insurgency mayoralty.) Similar situations prevailed in Gary and Newark until both incumbents were defeated in 1986 and 1987, respectively. (The latter two cases are discussed later in regard to the dynamics of black mayoral succession.)

We might assume that long-term black mayoral incumbency might provide insights into the experiences of black mayoralties beyond the immediacy of the racially charged, initial transition and displacement to a period of normalcy, when the routine issues of governance come to dominate the local political agenda in a less racial context. Based on a study of the Young mayoralty in Detroit (Rich 1989), one can identify two major, somewhat distinct dynamics of long-term incumbency. First, there is the continuation of racial appeals in mobilizing the black community with the use of a kind of racial ostracism in efforts to differentiate the incumbent from his black challengers. Concomitantly, there is the continuation of clear, racial divisions in voting patterns regardless of the race of the challenger. In other words, the insurgent incurs the wrath of many white voters and that condition prevails indefinitely. Second, there is a distinct change over time in the type of issues that dominate the local political agenda, with a shift away from general social reform issues to basic issues concerning the overall economy of the city and its fiscal stability. However, despite successful mayoral efforts in garnering the active support of white economic elites in responding to these issues, and despite the fact that the white business community belatedly provided very strong support for the Young mayoralty, the majority of the mass-level white electorate remained generally unsupportive. For example, a crucial vote on a tax increase to save the city of Detroit from insolvency in 1981 was supported by white business elites, but won exclusively in the black wards of the city.

For the primary support group of black voters who sustain long-term insurgencies, the full range of advantages are not clear. Long-term insurgencies may assist the larger process of institutionalization by transcending the difficult period of initial transition and displacement to firmly establish a new, more inclusive political order. On the other hand, longterm incumbencies may well discourage or otherwise eliminate viable black successors. The long-term dominance of a single black mayor may serve to stymie the development of a black leadership corps independent of the incumbent, resulting in a decline in the number and efficacy of black activists who seek to monitor local government, and help keep it accountable and inclusive. Thus, by adversely impacting the local black leadership structure, the longevity of a single black mayor may serve to obstruct democratization and accountability, and may thereby hinder the move towards institutionalization of substantive black interests and participation.

There are also indications that the "institutionalization" of a single black mayor may otherwise have transforming effects on the local political arena. The District of Columbia is a case in point. Both scholarly and lay observers point to the existence of a machine-style politics attendant to the three-term mayoralty of Marion Barry, crediting Barry with influencing political and electoral processes across the board, including city council and school board elections. The Barry machine repeatedly undermined viable black mayoral successors by arousing mass-level black concerns about the danger of creating prime conditions for a "white takeover." Barry successfully used insurgency to build and sustain a political machine that was held together in the traditional mode of political machines: by patronage in the dispensation of city jobs and contracts, and firm control of the political mobilization, recruitment, and candidate slating processes. The retention of insurgency as a leadership style for long-term incumbents is no doubt attributable to the reluctance of a political leader to risk an obvious change in tactics and style, or perhaps a perceived inability to relinquish this posture, given the political exigencies prevalent in a particular political context. For whatever strategic or other considerations, insurgency is a continuing use of the coin of race even when population dynamics and other factors do not afford the likelihood of a white takeover (Persons and Henderson 1990).

We see that insurgency has served as a useful strategic resource in the mobilization of the black population requisite to the election of most first black mayors. In a game of low-resource electoral politics, insurgency tactics are a powerful means of creating vitally needed political resources. Having adopted the political style of an insurgent, many black mayors, in tending to their maintenance needs, use the spirit of insurgency as necessary, as long as it is a winning currency. We also see that as a matter of style and image, insurgency can be utilized as a way of undermining and delegitimizing all challengers, black and white, to an incumbent first black mayor. However, as a strategic political tempo and leadership style, insurgency can be difficult to maintain over time. It can effectively give way, in some cases, to the exigencies of governance, lose its social reform content, and subsequently serve as a rhetorical tactic for rallying necessary black electoral support. In some cases its demise is facilitated by the dynamics of black mayoral succession.

Black Mayoral Succession and the Passing of the Old Order

Black mayoral succession is of great significance in the process of institutionalization as it suggests the move towards permanency in securing the black political presence in American urban politics: One of the more interesting aspects of black mayoral succession is that this sequence has to date been a limited one. Perhaps indicative of a still nascent institutional process is the fact that the still dominant pattern in the election of black mayors remains the first-time election of black mayors in an increasing number of cities. However, the succession stage has not been stymied due so much to a large loss of black mayoralties as it has been equally stymied by long-term incumbencies of several first black mayoralties.

It appears that the black mayoral succession stage constitutes the defining stage of the new black politics. At this stage we see a fully charged political dynamic in which the new black politics as a sociopolitical phenomenon has been launched and is effectively "on its own." Thus, we see the emergence of critical contradictions internal to the black community that constrain the fostering of serious system challenging action. We also see critical decisions being made by key players in the political game, which in effect set the tone and thrust for the future practice of black politics. Specifically, assessment of the succession stage yields added insights into the following:

1. The pairing of two blacks in the absence of a "white ogre" or a surrogate "white ogre"
2. The move towards racial reconciliation as a strategic means of differentiating politically between black competitors

3. Situations in which white voters hold the decisive swing vote even with black population majorities
4. The emergence of nascent, class-based cleavages within the black community, resulting in the subordination of political thrusts by low-income blacks to the imperative of black solidarity as manifested in black bloc voting
5. Yet another face of the coin of race with the use of race as its stereotypical stigma by black candidates seeking racial reconciliation as a strategic move

There are two variants of black mayoral succession, both of which have occurred to date. Voluntary succession occurs when an incumbent leaves office at the end of a term as set by statute, or otherwise declines to seek reelection and is succeeded by a black. Involuntary succession occurs when an incumbent is defeated or otherwise removed from office and is succeeded by a black. Although the succession sequence has been a limited one to date, the city of Atlanta has experienced its second succession election. The discussion below focuses first on the dynamics of voluntary succession in Atlanta and New Orleans, and second on involuntary succession in Gary and Newark.

Voluntary Succession: Atlanta and New Orleans

In Atlanta, the October, 1981, election to succeed first black mayor Maynard Jackson was at once a serious test of the black community's ability to hold on to the mayoralty and a bitter reminder to whites of their displaced political status. For many whites the election became a "last ditch" effort to recapture city hall. The reported sentiment of many white elites was that the Jackson succession election was the last hope of electing a white mayor of Atlanta in the then foreseeable future. Nonetheless, in a style peculiar to Atlanta's historical political culture, the succession campaign was expected to be carried out in a manner devoid of any racial overtones. As one observer put it, "everything was racial, but nothing was racist!"

There were three major challengers in the Atlanta succession race: former Congressman Andrew Young and former Public Safety Commissioner A. Reginald Eaves, both black; and one white candidate, popular state legislator Sidney Marcus. Despite the fact that the black population had reached the level of 56.6 percent, making a black victory a theoretical certainty, this situation did not preclude a white victory in the event of a severely split black vote. This possibility was enhanced by the fact that Young and Eaves appealed to different segments of the black electorate; Young to solidly middle- and upper-middle-class blacks, and Eaves to low-income and marginal middle-class blacks. This nascent class cleavage has long been intermittently evident in Atlanta's politics as many low-income blacks, excluded from the historically discriminating black social and economic elite circles, at times have sought to displace those blacks who were, relatively speaking, "to the manor born."

Eaves was clearly identified with the insurgent regime of Maynard Jackson's first mayoralty, and had been the lightning rod of white ire and much discomfort among the old-line black leadership. Eaves had been appointed the "superchief" by Jackson, with authority over the police, fire, and emergency management departments. This move led to prolonged racial polarization, a legal challenge to the constitutionality of the city charter, and Eaves' eventual resignation under a cloud of scandal surrounding promotional examinations for police officers. Thus an Eaves candidacy continued the thrust and political tempo of insurgency.

Interestingly, *The Atlanta Constitution* ran a major news analysis series on poverty in Atlanta during the campaign, in conjunction with an assessment of the changes that had occurred during the previous eight years of black mayoral rule. It is not clear what the motivations were for the series, but it could have served to further incite a counter-mobilization among low-income blacks, thereby enhancing the possibility of electing a white candidate. The legal requirement that a mayoral winner receive a real majority (as opposed to a plurality) of the total vote all but dictated that one of the black candidates would face the white challenger in a runoff, given the racial demographics of the city and the generally racial voting patterns that had characterized the city's politics in the past. Eaves would have been, by far, the easier black candidate to defeat in a runoff with a white challenger, as many middle-class blacks would likely have supported the moderate white candidate out of a sense of "voting responsibly without regard to race." However, Young was the leader in the general election[4] with 41 percent of the vote. Marcus and Eaves received 39 and 20 percent, respectively.

In the succession runoff race, Atlanta was back to mayoral "politics as usual" with a black versus white contest in which the stakes were starkly clear. Most observers agreed that there were no major issue differences between Young and Marcus, and not surprisingly, substantive issues gave way to explicitly racial overtures. In the end, Andrew Young was endorsed by the *Atlanta Constitution* and won with 55.1 percent of the vote. There was roughly a 10–15 percent crossover vote for both Young and Marcus. Otherwise, voting occurred along racial lines, giving Young a decisive advantage because of the black population majority in the city (*Atlanta Constitution* 10/29/81). The business community had supported the white candidate, displaying a continued resistance to black control of city hall, which historically was controlled by the white business community via politically moderate white mayors. In that regard, the dynamics of the succession election demonstrated that the transition and adjustment to black mayoral governance in Atlanta had not been complete.

However, despite the refusal of the white business community to support Andrew Young's bid for mayor, in a grand gesture of racial reconciliation in the early days of his mayoralty, Young informed the white business community that he could not govern without their support (Stone 1989, 110). Insurgency was dead.

In contrast to the heated succession race, Andrew Young's reelection race in 1985 was a political nonevent. All three challengers to Young were political neophytes and virtually unknown. There was no "great white hope" candidate, nor was there a serious black challenger. Young easily won with 83 percent of the total vote in a race with a very low turnout of 32.3 percent compared to a 64.0 percent turnout in the 1981 runoff election (*Atlanta Constitution* 10/28/85).

In the New Orleans succession election of 1986, there were also three major challengers: two blacks, State Senator William Jefferson, and Sidney Barthelemy, a former city councilman and former state senator; and white candidate Sam LeBlanc, a senior-level local government employee. Despite a black population of 51 percent, a split in the black vote in New Orleans could have easily resulted in a white victory. As in the Atlanta case, nascent class-based cleavages were evident in the New Orleans succession race. New Orleans has the distinction of having three socially and politically significant "racial groups": whites, blacks, and Creoles, who are very fair-skinned blacks (Schexnider 1982). Jefferson appealed mainly to low-income and dark-skinned blacks, while Barthelemy appealed to the largely middle-class Creole group. Barthelemy also assiduously courted the white vote.

As had happened in the Atlanta succession race, the specter of the New Orleans succession race as the last opportunity to elect a white mayor appeared strongly to influence the dynamics of the campaign. While whites could not independently elect a white mayor, they could nevertheless determine which black candidate would win the mayoralty. Thus Barthelemy assiduously courted the white vote and won the primary with 41 percent of the white vote, despite the presence of a white candidate, and faced Jefferson in the runoff. This black versus black contest had thus become a significantly class-based contest between low-income blacks and middle-class blacks (who are disproportionately Creole). Substantive issues in the runoff contest were upstaged by issues of personality, and the racial factor, around which the outcome of the election pivoted.

Initially, New Orleans' first black mayor, Morial, had unsuccessfully sought to get the voters to change the city charter to allow him to seek a third term in office. This effort and Morial's generally combative style had generated significant antagonism among whites. Thus, when Morial endorsed Jefferson, Jefferson was viewed by many whites as the black candidate to defeat. Barthelemy won the runoff with 58 percent of the total vote, 85 percent of the white vote, and 25 percent of the black vote. Analysts and observers suggest that with the near certainty of another black mayor, New Orleans white voters aligned themselves with the black candidate who was not "cut from the same political cloth" as the city's first black mayor (Watson 1984). The heavy white crossover vote was not only pivotal, but decisive.

In both the Atlanta and New Orleans succession races, the nascent black class cleavages were fleeting, and dissipated with the transformation of the election contest into the traditional black versus white contest. This does not, however, suggest the insignificance of this cleavage. Rather, the nascent and apparent fleeting nature of black class cleavage likely reflects the cross-cutting conflicts created by the perceived, overpowering significance of black racial

solidarity and bloc voting. This exemplifies how the need for black racial solidarity, as a precondition for repeating even symbolic black political gains, tends
to submerge the diversity of interests within the black community.

As has been noted earlier, the coin of race has many faces. While black
mayoral candidates will use racial appeals to mobilize the black community to
the point of labelling a black challenger a surrogate "white ogre," some black
candidates will also use race as a specter of fear in mobilizing white voters
against a black candidate with a "radicalized" or insurgent image. One variation of this occurred in the New Orleans succession election, another variation
occurred in the second succession election in Atlanta.

The second succession election in Atlanta occurred in October, 1989, and
pitted first black mayor Maynard Jackson against Fulton County Commission
Chairman Michael Lomax, also black. Lomax had originally come to Atlanta
as a special assistant to Jackson during Jackson's first term as mayor. Using his
experience in city hall under Jackson, Lomax remained in the city to plow his
own political fortunes. While Lomax had done well on the county commission,
and was generally well received in both the black and white communities in
the county, he had always been plagued with the image of an ultra-elitist who
was basically uncomfortable being around most blacks of all socio-economic
statuses. Lomax's image problem was, in turn, reflected in his standing in the
polls taken during the mayoral campaign.

The earliest polls taken during the campaign showed Lomax trailing Jackson by 22 percentage points. Five months prior to the October election, Jackson had increased his lead by 34 percentage points, with a 58 to 24 percent lead
over Lomax (*Atlanta Constitution* 5/7/89). Lomax had been able to increase his
standing among whites, but was unable to claim support from a majority of any
racial or income group. Lomax's standing among whites was not insignificant:
he led Jackson among white voters 44 to 32 percent. Jackson led among black
voters, 69 to 16 percent. Blacks comprised 61 percent of Atlanta's registered
voters, while whites comprised 39 percent, a demographic mix which actually
permitted blacks to vote in bloc and independently elect the city's mayor.
There were no white challengers in this second succession race.

Former Mayor Jackson was by far the more popular of the two candidates
although both Jackson and Lomax were seen as being well qualified to be
mayor. Jackson enjoyed broad support among all demographic groups. Interestingly, Jackson also enjoyed solid support from the white business community.
In his first term, Jackson had clashed with this group and reconciliation had
not occurred prior to his leaving office. However, Jackson had moved early in
his new campaign to cement good relations with this group, and he had succeeded. The white business community had responded positively with political
support, and substantial financial support as well. During his years in private
law practice Jackson had moved to the prestigious and overwhelmingly white,
north side of Atlanta. Place of residency and race are by design such important
co-factors in political and social sensibilities among Atlantans that this was not
an insignificant move on Jackson's part (Bayor 1989). To his benefit, Jackson

projected an air of consummate confidence, maturity, and leadership ability, all enhanced by an imposing physical presence. Lomax appeared too young in comparison. The challenge for Lomax was to create a major chink in Jackson's political armor and he chose a most interesting tactic. Lomax chose to exploit the social and political tensions, which were also largely racial in nature, that had attended Jackson's term as the city's first black mayor, a tactic that simultaneously permitted Lomax to enhance his own strength among white voters.

Lomax chose to exploit the crime issue and to attack Jackson on the high crime rate which had prevailed during part of his first mayoralty. Like most big cities, the high crime rate during Jackson's first term was nothing new, but rather reflected a pattern of highs and lows over the years. In fact, the city was experiencing a crime wave which placed it first in the nation, even during the second succession campaign. The issue of crime during Jackson's first term was also connected to his firing of a white police chief and the appointment of the city's first black police chief. This action singularly led to severe and prolonged racial conflict in the city (Persons 1985; Eisinger 1980). Thus, to raise the issue of crime during Jackson's first mayoralty was to reopen old political and social wounds.

More importantly, Lomax chose a television advertisement campaign to exploit the issue. One ad featured a white woman declaring her fears about the safety of the streets of Atlanta under a new Jackson mayoralty. Another ad featured former State Governor Carl Sanders recalling the death of his secretary, who was murdered on the city's streets one evening after working late. Another ad featured prominent black Atlanta businessman Jesse Hill declaring his concern for the safety of Atlanta's streets during a new Jackson mayoralty. Lomax, in effect, sought to consolidate white voter support by manipulating the racially charged issue of crime in a predominantly black city. The net result was that in a contest between two black challengers, absent a "white ogre" or surrogate, there was still a return to racial and racist appeals. Jackson won with little difficulty, after Lomax withdrew just prior to the date on which he would have had to declare officially his candidacy for mayor and simultaneously relinquish his county council chairmanship.

In the first Atlanta succession race we see the demise of insurgency as it becomes clearly identified with the specific plight of low-income blacks in the Eaves candidacy, and we witness its subordination to the overriding consideration of racial solidarity and the subsequent triumph of the representational interests of the black middle class. We also witness the death of insurgency by abdication in the Andrew Young victory. In the second Atlanta succession race, we see yet another face of the coin of race with race used as a stigma by the weaker of two black contestants and as a grand gesture of empathy with the stereotypical fears of many white voters. We also see a former black insurgent win with both the overwhelming support of blacks and the overwhelming financial support and political endorsements of the white business community. The common thread in each of these variations is the move towards racial reconciliation, first as a means of political differentiation, and later as a more distinctly philosophical perspective not born of any clear "strategic necessity." In the New Orleans succession race, black class cleavages emerged as well in an association with insurgent politics. However, black middle-class representational interests triumphed due to political differentiation tactics by a black contestant, and a corresponding vote by whites against black insurgency politics. The era of black insurgent politics had passed, just two decades since its emergence.

Involuntary Succession: Newark and Gary

Within the span of a twelve-month period, two of the country's longest-serving first black mayors were defeated in reelection bids; Gibson in Newark in May, 1986, and Hatcher in Gary in May, 1987. Both incumbents faced strong black challengers in the absence of a white challenger, and thereby were faced with a relatively new and different set of dynamics in their reelection bids. In Newark, which is roughly 47 percent black, all three challengers to Gibson were black in a non-partisan, mayoral contest. In Gary, Hatcher's challengers for the Democratic nomination in a heavily Democratic, 78 percent black city were also all black. In both Newark and Gary, the most important factor in these succession contests seems to have been the absence of a "white ogre." In both cases, this missing element appears to have catalyzed a different dynamic, which significantly contributed to defeat and involuntary succession.

Gibson was initially elected mayor of Newark in 1970, winning with 60 percent of the vote in the heady and hopeful period (three years) following the Newark riots. He was reelected in 1974 with 55 percent of the vote in a bitter, racially charged contest against Anthony Imperiale, whom Gibson had defeated in his initial win. Gibson won again in 1978 with 68 percent of the vote. Gibson faced a black challenger in his fourth race in 1982, winning with 52 percent of the vote despite the fact that he and his major challenger were under federal indictments on charges of corruption. In 1986, the deficiencies in Gibson's record became a liability. Unfortunately, the generally continuing decline of the Newark economy was paralleled by Gibson's tenure in office.

Gibson's 16 years in office provided a convenient time frame for asessing the economic well-being of the city. Between 1970 and 1985, the city had a population loss of 68,050 residents, a decline of 17.8 percent. The steel fabrication plants, breweries, and other factories, which once boosted the local economy, had closed or declined. Unemployment in Newark in 1986 was 11.2 percent overall, and triple that for some segments of the black community. During the period 1970–1986, the number of movie theaters in Newark had declined from 14 to 6; hotels from 32 to 6; bowling alleys from 15 to 0; restaurants from 937 to 246; and food stores from 377 to 184 (*The New York Times* 5/24/87). Interestingly, *The New York Times* asserted that Newark's economy had begun to rebound with a burgeoning downtown and plans for major corporate relocations from Manhattan to Newark. However, many of Newark's neighborhoods remained blighted and the office real estate boom was not expected to aid the poor.

Gibson had made clear his political ambitions over the years. He had twice, but unsuccessfully, sought the Democratic nomination for governor, in 1981 and 1985. He had achieved the stature of a nationally prominent politician in Democratic party circles, which had been both necessary and beneficial to the city during Democratic administrations. Those ties had facilitated the rewarding of the low-income black voter base so crucial in the calculus of national Democratic party politics. However, under the Reagan regime, the city of Newark, like most major cities, had lost substantial federal funds previously provided under the Community Development Block Grant program and the Comprehensive Employment and Training Act program among others. Thus Gibson was rendered vulnerable against a strong black challenger and defeated by Sharpe James, who emphasized economic revitalization, improving the image of the city, increasing the housing stock, and more effectively combatting crime. Ironically, in many respects, the issues resonated Gibson's campaign in 1970. In another interesting irony, Gibson was endorsed by his old white opponent, Anthony Imperiale. Sharpe James carried all five of the city's wards, garnering 55 percent of the total vote to Gibson's 40 percent (*The New York Times* 5/15/86).

In 1986 there was no racist "ogre" to assure automatic black support for Gibson based on an obscuring of issues by the shield of racial solidarity. There are no indications that Gibson's opponent made special efforts to woo the support of the white community, despite the fact that the black population comprised slightly less than 50 percent of the total population. The combined black and Hispanic population totaled 70 percent of the electorate. The white vote was not pivotal to victory in this election. The mayoral contest thus pivoted around substantive issues regarding the future of the city, as espoused by two black contestants, with the record of the long-term black incumbent used pejoratively as a central theme. Interestingly, the black challenger's theme did not reflect a politically conservative turn, for the black incumbent was no longer perceived as radical. The challenger's theme was explicitly directed toward issues deemed critical to the needs of the black community in particular, and towards improving the image and economic vitality of the city in general, much as Gibson had promised over the years. The critical exception in 1986 was that the record of the long-term black incumbent was the standard against which blame was assessed, and the challenger was welcomed as a "refreshing breath" of new leadership.

In relationship to the Newark succession election of 1986, the outcome of the Gary succession election in 1987 was very much one of *déjà vu*. Richard Hatcher, initially elected in 1967, was the longest serving black mayor in America. Like Gibson, Hatcher had the misfortune of presiding over a city that declined along with the steel industry, upon which its economy depended. Gary had also lost substantial population, 60,000 or 29 percent, since 1967, as well as its taxi service, movie houses, many restaurants, and many other businesses (*Indiana Crusader* 3/14/87). Hatcher, too, was indisputably a black politician of national prominence and stature, and was widely respected beyond Gary for his efforts on behalf of the national struggle for black political empowerment. Many national-level black politicians campaigned on his behalf, but to no avail. Hatcher lost to a black challenger who promised to improve the functioning of the city government and the general welfare of its citizenry.

In part, Hatcher's embattled position significantly reflected the consequences of the long-standing refusal of major components of the white elite structure to accept the transition to black mayoral governance. Hatcher had never won the support of the white business community or the white ethnic-dominated Democratic party. In the case of the business community, their split with city hall had actually preceeded Hatcher in that they had earlier objected to mayoral efforts in support of striking steel workers (Lane 1979). They were, of course, not satisfied with Hatcher's initial election and when Hatcher faced reelection in 1971, in a last-ditch effort to forestall their political displacement, the white business community and the party machine endorsed a black moderate candidate in opposition to Hatcher. Apparently in response to the prospects of an extended period of insurgent black mayoral leadership in Gary, the business community moved to abandon the city by building a mall in the adjacent suburb of Merrillville. Within fewer than 10 years after Hatcher's initial election, all 4 department stores, more than 100 smaller businesses and 2 major banks had closed operation in Gary and moved to the suburban mall (Lane 1979).

Moreover, Gary was a classic example of a company town, originally established as the locus for a major U.S. Steel operation and company housing areas for its employees. U.S. Steel and ancillary industries dominated the economy of Gary and the Lake County region. Subsequently, the fortunes of the Gary economy waxed and waned with the fortunes of U.S. Steel. Unfortunately, the waning of the local steel-based economy in Gary paralleled many of Hatcher's later years in office. For example, during the period of 1979–1982, employment at U.S. Steel in Gary dropped from 25,000 to 8000, and by 1987 had declined still further to 6000 (*Post Tribune* 1/17/86). Although Hatcher had not inherited a hollow prize, as some analysts predicted that black mayors would (Feemstra 1969), in the end, he was left to preside over one.

While black political rule had not come exclusively at the price of a loss of economic vitality (as there was no causal relationship between black political dominance and the decline of the steel industry), ironically, blacks in Gary were forced to entertain the option of trading political dominance for the prospect of improving the economic lot of the city. Thus, when the state legislature proposed a consolidation of the many separate governments in Lake County into the single political entity of Metrolake, which would have subordinated Gary residents politically and racially, many blacks in Gary speculated that such consolidation was perhaps what the city needed for economic revitalization. Metrolake would have consolidated some 70 governmental entities into a single metropolitan government of 405,000 in population, with 60 percent white and 40 percent black, excluding Merrillville. Although the consolidation effort failed, Mayor Hatcher was able to garner only minimal support at public rallies in opposition to the consolidation (*Post Tribune* 10/28/86, 11/3/86).

In the end there were many ironies in Hatcher's defeat. First, according to some observers, conditions in the city were in objective ways considerably better than four years earlier when, in 1983, Hatcher had narrowly won reelection. Crime was down, there was a generally better economic climate, large layoffs of city patronage workers had stopped, and some new jobs had been created in the local economy (Isadore 5/31/88). While many in the black community considered Hatcher their personal savior, many black elected officials and other local black leaders asserted that they had been "iced" by Hatcher over the years as he had moved to consolidate his power base. Thomas Barnes, Hatcher's successor, had been a member of Hatcher's initial team of key campaign workers in 1967, had been elected to three terms as the town tax assessor, but had broken with Hatcher in 1983 to support Thomas Crump, who lost by 2,700 votes. Hatcher had run an entire slate of black candidates for office in 1984 and they were all defeated, including U.S. Representative Katie Hall (Caitlin 1985). Hatcher's image as a political leader suffered a major defeat.

Hatcher had not been able (or necessarily willing, according to some) to establish ties with the Republican-dominated state legislature, and in early 1986, the state taxation board granted U.S. Steel of Gary a reduction of $16 million in its property tax assessments, leading to a 10 percent shortfall for the city of Gary and its school system. The state taxation board had previously refused to allow the city to raise taxes (*Post Tribune* 1/16/86). Hatcher was faulted by many for not seeking support from the state legislature until 1983, far into his mayoralty, when it was effectively too late. Others understood that Hatcher was very distrustful of whites in the state legislature and in the Gary suburban areas. Barnes, on the other hand, had worked to build support among whites in suburban areas and enjoyed considerable popularity among them. Hatcher was, in part, hampered by his record of insurgency-style politics and apparently by his own conception of the dictates of independent, insurgent black politics. Hatcher's primary support group of black voters had become ambivalent about his leadership. In 1987, he had great difficulty mobilizing his supporters and Barnes won the Gary mayoralty with 56 percent of the vote, carrying all but one of the city's voting districts.

In significant ways, the involuntary succession of long-term insurgents in Gary and Newark reflect the limitations and inflexibility of insurgent styles of political leadership at the level of city government, given the rather dependent nature of the city. We also get insights into the plight of black mayoral leadership in older northern cities with economies historically based on heavy industries, which have in recent years declined in concert with the declining status of the United States in world trade. However, Coleman Young's tenure in Detroit offers an interesting contrast in regard to the sustentation of insurgent-style leadership. Over the years, Young has engaged in an interesting mix of roles, as both social reformer concerned with social welfare issues, and as a fiscal conservative. He has also courted the local business community, including Republican businesspeople and politicians, while maintaining the loyalty of his primary support base among black voters. He used city funds to finance the acquisition of land for a new General Motors plant inside the city, rather than lose it to a suburban jurisdiction. These and many other actions taken by Young have been highly controversial for one reason or another (Hill 1983). However, Coleman Young's tenure has been distinguished by one major objective. He has held on to that which defined Detroit as an economic entity: its image and position as the center of the U.S. automobile industry. Depending on one's perspective, one might conclude that the black residents of Detroit have paid a very high price in shouldering the responsibilities of governance. Summing up the evolution of Detroit's politics under Coleman Young, Wilbur Rich offers a poignant statement of the apparent ineluctable nature of change in the new black politics: "Detroit's politics have changed. No longer black politics, they are the current politics of Detroit. People who were black leaders are now city leaders." (Rich 1989, 267).

Summary: Racial Reconciliation and the Passing of the Old Order

The election and collective experience of black mayors have taken place within the context of currents of broader socio-political change. Black mayors were first elected in the wake of the civil rights movement and the period of major unrest of the late 1960s. The brief, but no less strident, period of the black power movement which followed also contributed to the context out of which emerged the new black politics. Thus, it was expected that those black mayors would be activists and strong social reform advocates. They could be no less.

However, time makes for change, and the era of the insurgent black mayor as social reformer seems to have passed. The passing of the old order seems to occur at the point of succession. Although there is significant overlapping of the old dynamics, the emergence of a new dynamic becomes evident at this stage. There are several reasons for this apparent change. Succession occurs at a point distant in time from the "fever pitch" of racial tensions attendant to the election of first black mayors. Thus, the racial appeals formula is sometimes not as potent in its effect. Also, many succession races frequently enjoy a solid black population majority, diminishing somewhat the importance and necessity of racial appeals. While racial voting persists, it persists with somewhat less passion. For blacks, there is probably the realization that the likely major changes, certainly the major particularistic benefits, have generally been reaped. Black mayors at that point also appear to have learned a very sobering lesson on the limits of local governmental power to transform the social order. Having learned the realities of political power, they are less strident in social reform advocacy. For some whites, the point of succession may become the strategic last stand in terms of retaining the mayoralty for the foreseeable future. However, whites, too, appear to have learned a sobering, but reassuring, lesson at the point of succession: that black mayoral leadership may well be the new political reality, and that new reality is not one of political, social, or economic doom for whites.

While the point of succession in many cases appears to be the benchmark of major change, to a substantial degree the impetus for change is simply a temporal factor; the passage of time and attendant broader currents of change. It is evident that change in perceptions, and self-definition of roles occur over time for long-term incumbent black mayors, though they attempt to sustain the rhetorical tempo of insurgency. Long-term incumbents have been overtaken by broader currents of change: declining economies in their respective cities, the declining fortunes of the national Democratic party, and the vulnerability these two factors created during a Republican regime which deemphasized cities and urban problems. Long-term incumbents who have thrived somewhat during this time period, Coleman Young of Detroit for example, have done so by embracing a more expansive definition of the role of mayor. For many black politicians, holding office has come to mean more or less than seeking social reforms, and has come to mean assuming responsibility for the full mantle of governance. That means assuming responsibility for the total social, political, and economic well-being of the city. The new or nascent ethos appears to be one of saving the city, as a civic duty and responsibility, and as a means of benefitting the entire electorate, and perhaps as a means of proving that black leaders can indeed take on the full mantle of governance. There are some indications as well that the black electorate is increasingly expecting or demanding a broader approach to governance. Although there were many overlapping and interrelated factors, these new demands appear to have been the central message of the involuntary successions in Gary and Newark.

Another aspect of the new normalcy is the forging of strong alliances between black mayors and the white business community. This has occurred in both succession mayoralties in Atlanta and in the New Orleans succession mayoralty as well, and the long-term incumbencies in Detroit and Washington, D.C. This is something of an ironic development because early black mayors actually ran against the white business community, who in many cases, had dominated city hall in a fashion which deliberately barred inclusion of blacks and accommodation of their interests. Perhaps this change is as much indicative of the ineluctable triumph of conservatism as anything else.

Although the element of race remains disproportionately a factor in black mayoral elections, the element of race has taken on varied dimensions over time. First, in many mayoral contests, race is the prime currency, a currency to be manipulated by black and white candidates. Race is more a currency in some locales where there is a sizable black population. In some contexts, the black population is not only accustomed and responsive to racial appeals in political mobilization efforts, but due to historical patterns of white-dominated exclusionary governance, many blacks expect sincere articulation and representation of their interests to be made within a racial context. Second, it is the case that race is manipulated by incumbent blacks to serve their own maintenance needs in office, sometimes in the absence of any clear racist threat. White candidates have manipulated the element of race in efforts to retain or establish a dominant political position. The element of race also gets manipulated by some black candidates seeking to mobilize the white voter against a black whose image can be "radicalized." Finally, race gets used in its traditional stigma, in which one black candidate depicts another as synonymous with stereotypical fears whites hold against blacks.

As major currents of socio-political change have spawned and defined black mayoralties, one might reasonably expect that they would be affected by the nascent national trends towards black crossover politics. Black crossover politics must be defined in relationship to the style of black politics that preceded it. The new black politics was a politics based on racial appeals, tied to a concentrated black population base, with candidates promising descriptive and substantive representation for their black constituents, supported by a relatively small contingent of white supporters. In contrast, black crossover politics is primarily race-neutral in its appeal, at most making an appeal for racial harmony, and crossover candidates may or may not seek election in predominantly black locales. Also, crossover candidates do not advocate an identifiably black agenda.

How then might the evolution or institutionalization of black mayoralties have permitted anticipation of the strategic changes embodied in the 1989 elections? The elections of 1989 have been variously referred to as black crossover politics, the politics of deracialization, and rather ominously as "the death of black politics." In their essence, the elections of 1989 were the crystallization of the black politics of racial reconciliation. Given what had been the emergent and defining characteristics of the new black politics, and the continuing racial order in American politics, black politicians seeking major crossover appeal had to adopt some variant of racial reconciliation. Thus, black crossover politics is primarily race-neutral. It is a politics in which the black candidate diminishes the significance of his race and proffers appeals based on partisanship, a modified populism, or other traditional, non-racial themes.

The major consequences of black crossover politics will likely be the total delegitimizing of insurgent-style politics. Insurgency has effectively long been dead, but its spirit has been kept alive by tactics of long-term black incumbents, the effective internalization of insurgency, and its embodiment as a social reform strategy (the collective and preferred conception of the new black politics). This preferred conception has been buttressed by a kind of obsession with scoring; with increasing the number of black elected officials nationwide, again assuming that descriptive representation is synonmous with substantive representation, or that somehow sufficient numbers of black representatives would pose an effective challenge against the system and make for a realization of the black agenda. However, scoring has been the proverbial, political double-edged sword.

While the black presence in American politics has traditionally been associated with the threat of system-challenging action, the new crossover politics significantly disassociates the black presence from system challenge and instead emphasizes the "positive symbolism" of race. In short, racial reconciliation in all its variations, was born of insurgency. It is the alternative to insurgent politics. In its latest manifestation, the politics of racial reconciliation is a strategically pristine, political counteroffer, with a lagniappe. For whites it provides an opportunity to embrace demonstrably the principles of full participatory equality for all Americans regardless of race; for blacks it provides major symbolic gratification and necessary opportunities to take pride in the achievements of blacks to more and higher political offices. That this variant of racial reconciliation is apparently devoid even of a generalized black agenda is indeed a profound dilemma of black politics in the present era.

References

Alkalimat, Abdul and Doug Gills. 1984. "*Black Power* v. *Racism:* Harold Washington Becomes Mayor." In *The New Black Vote.* Ed. Rod Bush. 53–179. San Francisco: Synthesis Publications.

Bayor, Ronald H. 1989. "Urban Renewal, Public Housing and the Racial Shaping of Atlanta." *Journal of Policy History* 1(4).

Bullock, Charles. 1984. "Racial Crossover Voting and the Election of Black Officials." *Journal of Politics* 46 (February): 238–51.

Caitlin, Robert. 1985. "Organizational Effectiveness and Black Political Participation: The Case of Katie Hall." *Phylon* 41(3): 179–92.

Eisinger, Peter K. 1980. *The Politics of Displacement: Racial and Ethnic Transition in Three American Cities.* New York: Academic Press.

Feemstra, L. Paul. 1969. "Black Control of Central Cities." *Journal of American Institute of Planners.* 4: 75–79.

Hahn, Harlan, David Klingman, and Harry Pachon. 1976. "Cleavages, Coalitions, and the Black Candidate: The Los Angeles Mayoralty Elections of 1969 and 1973." *Western Political Quarterly* 29 (December): 507–520.

Hill, Richard Child. 1983. "Crisis in the Motor City: The Politics of Economic Development in Detroit." In *Restructuring the City.* Susan Fainstein, et al. New York: Longman, 80–125.

Isadore, Chris. 1988. *The Post Tribune.* Personal Interview, May 31.

Keiser, Richard A. 1990. "The Rise of a Biracial Coalition in Philadelphia." In *Racial Politics in American Cities.* Eds. Rufus P. Browning et al. New York: Longman.

Lane, James. 1979. *City of the Century: Gary from 1900–1975.* Bloomington, IN: Indiana University Press.

Levine, Charles H. 1974. *Racial Politics and the American Mayor: Power, Polarization, and Performance.* Lexington, MA: Lexington Books.

Nelson, William E. 1982. "Cleveland: The Rise and Fall of the New Black Politics." In *The New Black Politics: The Search for Political Power.* 1st ed., eds. Michael Preston et al. 187–208. New York: Longman.

Nelson, William E. and Philip Meranto. 1977. *Electing Black Mayors: Political Action in the Black Community.* Columbus, OH: Ohio State University Press.

Nordlinger, Eric A. 1971. "Political Development: Time Sequences and Rates of Change." In *Political Development and Social Change.* 2nd ed., eds. Finkle and Richard W. Gable. New York: John Wiley & Sons.

Persons, Georgia A. 1985. "Reflections on Mayoral Leadership: The Impact of Changing Issues and Changing Times." *Phylon* 46(3) (September): 205–218.

Persons, Georgia A. and Lenneal Henderson, Jr. 1990. "Mayor of the Colony: Effective Mayoral Leadership as a Matter of Public Perception." *National Political Science Review* 2.

Pettigrew, Thomas F. 1976. "Black Mayoralty Campaigns." In *Urban Governance and Minorities.* Ed. Herrington Bryce. New York: Praeger.

Pitkin, Hanna F. 1967. *The Concept of Representation.* Berkeley: University of California Press.

Polsby, Nelson W. 1968. "Institutionalization of the U.S. House of Representatives" *American Political Science Review* 62(1): 144–68.

Preston, Michael B. 1990. "1990 Big City Black Mayors: Have They Made a Difference? A Symposium." *National Political Science Review*, 2: 129–195.

Preston, Michael, B., Lenneal J. Henderson, Jr., and Paul Puryear, eds. 1982. *The New Black Politics: The Search for Political Power*, 1st ed. New York: Longman.

Ransom, Bruce. 1987. "Black Independent Electoral Politics in Philadelphia: The Election of Mayor W. Wilson Goode." In *The New Black Politics: The Search for Political Power.* 2nd ed., eds. Michael B. Preston, Lenneal J. Henderson, Jr. New York: Longman.

Rich, Wilbur. 1989. *Coleman Young and Detroit Politics: From Social Activist to Power Broker.* Detroit, MI: Wayne State University Press.

Schexnider, Alvin J. 1982. "Political Mobilization in the South: The Election of a Black Mayor in New Orleans." In *The New Black Politics: The Search for Political Power.* 1st ed., eds. Michael B. Preston, Lenneal J. Henderson, Jr., and Paul Puryear. New York: Longman.

Stone, Clarence. 1989. *Regime Politics: Governing Atlanta 1946–1988.* Lawrence, KS: University Press of Kansas.

Walters, Ronald W. 1980. "The Challenge of Black Leadership: An Analysis of the Problem of Strategy Shift." *The Urban League Review* 5(1) (Summer): 77–88.

Watson, Sharon. 1984. "The Second Time Around: A Profile of Black Mayoral Reelection Campaigns." *Phylon* 45 (Fall): 166–178.

Wilson, William J. 1978. *The Declining Significance of Race: Blacks and Changing American Institutions.* Chicago: University of Chicago Press.

———. 1987. *The Truly Disadvantaged: The Inner City, the Underclass, and Public Policy.* Chicago: University of Chicago Press.

Notes

1. The November 1989 elections were the focus of heated debate at the 1990 Annual Meeting of the National Conference of Black Political Scientists held in March, 1990, in Atlanta. The debate from the conference became the focus of a media-sponsored debate, with particular focus on Virginia Governor L. Douglas Wilder.

2. The District of Columbia's first black mayor, Walter Washington, was initially appointed by President Lyndon Baines Johnson (who also appointed the entire city council), when the city was being governed completely by the federal government. Washington subsequently sought and won election under the 1973 Home Rule Charter. In his bid for reelection, Washington lost in a three-way race to Marion Barry, who had formerly served as president of the D.C. School Board. Prior to the (limited) Home Rule Charter of 1973, the only local elective offices open to D.C. residents were seats on the school board.

3. New Orleans is characterized as an involuntary succession since the first black mayor, the late Earnest Morial, sought a change in the city charter to permit him to serve more

than two, consecutive four-year terms. This proposal was defeated in a referendum vote, effectively forcing Morial from office.

4. Atlanta's mayoral elections are non-partisan. Therefore, the initial election is the general election with a runoff required by state law if no candidate receives more than 50 percent (plus 1) of the total vote.

Tricia Rose

from *Black Noise*

CHAPTER ONE
VOICES FROM THE MARGINS

Rap Music and Contemporary Black Cultural Production

Public Enemy's "Can't Truss It" opens with rapper Flavor Flav shouting "Confusion!" over a heavy and energetic bass line. The subsequent lyrics suggest that Flavor Flav is referring to lead rapper Chuck D's story about the legacy of slavery, that it has produced extreme cultural confusion. He could just as easily be describing the history of rap. Rap music is a confusing and noisy element of contemporary American popular culture that continues to draw a great deal of attention to itself. On the one hand, music and cultural critics praise rap's role as an educational tool, point out that black women rappers are rare examples of aggressive pro-women lyricists in popular music, and defend rap's ghetto stories as real-life reflections that should draw attention to the burning problems of racism and economic oppression, rather than to questions of obscenity. On the other hand, news media attention on rap seems fixated on instances of violence at rap concerts, rap producers' illegal use of musical samples, gangsta raps' lurid fantasies of cop killing and female dismemberment, and black nationalist rappers' suggestions that white people are the devil's disciples. These celebratory and inflammatory aspects in rap and the media coverage of them bring to the fore several long-standing debates about popular music and culture. Some of the more contentious disputes revolve around the following questions: Can violent images incite violent action, can music set the stage for political mobilization, do sexually explicit lyrics contribute to the moral "breakdown" of society, and finally, is this really *music* anyway?

And, if these debates about rap music are not confusing enough, rappers engage them in contradictory ways. Some rappers defend the work of gangster rappers and at the same time consider it a negative influence on black youths. Female rappers openly criticize male rappers' sexist work and simultaneously defend the 2 Live Crew's right to sell misogynist music. Rappers who criticize America for its perpetuation of racial and economic discrimination also share conservative ideas about personal responsibility, call for self-improvement strategies in the black community that focus heavily on personal behavior as the cause and solution for crime, drugs, and community instability.

Rap music brings together a tangle of some of the most complex social, cultural, and political issues in contemporary American society. Rap's contradictory articulations are not signs of absent intellectual clarity; they are a common feature of community and popular cultural dialogues that always offer more than one cultural, social, or political viewpoint. These unusually abundant polyvocal conversations seem irrational when they are severed from the social contexts where everyday struggles over resources, pleasure, and meanings take place.

Rap music is a black cultural expression that prioritizes black voices from the margins of urban America. Rap music is a form of rhymed storytelling accompanied by highly rhythmic, electronically based music. It began in the mid-1970s in the South Bronx in New York City as a part of hip hop, an African-American and Afro-Caribbean youth culture composed of graffiti, breakdancing, and rap music. From the outset, rap music has articulated the pleasures and problems of black urban life in contemporary America. Rappers speak with the voice of personal experience, taking on the identity of the observer or narrator. Male rappers often speak from the perspective of a young man who wants social status in a locally meaningful way. They rap about how to avoid gang pressures and still earn local respect, how to deal with the loss of several friends to gun fights and drug overdoses, and they tell grandiose and sometimes violent tales that are powered by male sexual power over women. Female rappers sometimes tell stories from the perspective of a young woman who is skeptical of male protestations of love or a girl who has been involved with a drug dealer and cannot sever herself from his dangerous life-style. Some raps speak to the failures of black men to provide security and attack men where their manhood seems most vulnerable: the pocket. Some tales are one sister telling another to rid herself from the abuse of a lover.

Like all contemporary voices, the rapper's voice is imbedded in powerful and dominant technological, industrial, and ideological institutions. Rappers tell long, involved, and sometimes abstract stories with catchy and memorable phrases and beats that lend themselves to black sound bite packaging, storing critical fragments in fast-paced electrified rhythms. Rap tales are told in elaborate and ever-changing black slang and refer to black cultural figures and rituals, mainstream film, video and television characters, and little-known black heroes. For rap's language wizards, all images, sounds, ideas, and icons are ripe for recontextualization, pun, mockery, and celebration. Kool Moe Dee boasts that each of his rhymes is like a dissertation, Kid-N-Play have quoted Jerry Lee Lewis's famous phrase "great balls of fire," Big Daddy Kane brags that he's raw like sushi (and that his object of love has his nose open like a jar of Vicks), Ice Cube refers to his ghetto stories as "tales from the darkside," clearly referencing the television horror show with the same name. Das Efx's raps include Elmer Fud's characteristic "OOOH I'm steamin'!" in full character voice along with a string of almost surreal collagelike references to Bugs Bunny and other television characters. At the same time, the stories, ideas, and thoughts articulated in rap lyrics invoke and revise stylistic and thematic elements that are deeply wedded to a number of black cultural storytelling forms, most prominently toasting and the blues. Ice-T and Big Daddy Kane pay explicit homage to Rudy Ray Moore as

"Dolomite," Roxanne Shante toasts Millie Jackson, and black folk wisdom and folktales are given new lives and meanings in contemporary culture.

Rap's stories continue to articulate the shifting terms of black marginality in contemporary American culture. Even as rappers achieve what appears to be central status in commercial culture, they are far more vulnerable to censorship efforts than highly visible white rock artists, and they continue to experience the brunt of the plantationlike system faced by most artists in the music and sports industries. Even as they struggle with the tension between fame and rap's gravitational pull toward local urban narratives, for the most part, rappers continue to craft stories that represent the creative fantasies, perspectives, and experiences of racial marginality in America.

Rap went relatively unnoticed by mainstream music and popular culture industries until independent music entrepreneur Sylvia Robinson released "Rappers Delight" in 1979. Over the next five years rap music was "discovered" by the music industry, the print media, the fashion industry, and the film industry, each of which hurried to cash in on what was assumed to be a passing fad. During the same years, Run DMC (who recorded the first gold rap record *Run DMC* in 1984), Whodini, and the Fat Boys became the most commercially successful symbols of rap music's sounds and style.

By 1987, rap music had survived several death knells, Hollywood mockery, and radio bans and continued to spawn new artists, such as Public Enemy, Eric B. & Rakim, and L.L. Cool J. At the same time, women rappers, such as MC Lyte and Salt 'N' Pepa, encouraged by Roxanne Shante's early successes, made inroads into rap's emerging commercial audience. Between 1987 and 1990 a number of critical musical and industry changes took place. Public Enemy became rap's first superstar group, and media attention to its black nationalist political articulations intensified. The success of De La Soul's playful Afrocentricity, tongue in cheek spoof of rap's aggressive masculinity and manipulation of America's television culture encouraged the Native Tongues wing of rap that opened the door to such future groups as A Tribe Called Quest, Queen Latifah, Brand Nubian, and Black Sheep. Ice-T put the Los Angeles gangsta rap style on the national map, which encouraged the emergence of NWA, Ice Cube, Too Short, and others.

At the industry level, the effects of rap's infiltration were widespread. Black filmmaker Spike Lee's commercially successful use of b-boys, b-girls, hip hop music, and style in the contemporary urban terrain as primary themes in *She's Gotta Have It* and *Do the Right Thing* fired up Hollywood's new wave of black male ghetto films, most notably, *Colors, New Jack City, Boyz in the Hood, Juice* and *Menace II Society*. By 1989, MTV began playing rap music on a relatively regular basis, and multimillion unit rap sales by the Beastie Boys, Tone Loc, M.C. Hammer and Vanilla Ice convinced music industry executives that rap music, for all of its "blackness" in attitude, style, speech, music, and thematics, was a substantial success with white teenagers.

Rap's black cultural address and its focus on marginal identities may appear to be in opposition to its crossover appeal for people from different racial or ethnic groups and social positions. How can this black public dialogue speak to the thousands of young white suburban boys and girls who are critical to the record sales successes of many of rap's more prominent stars? How can I suggest that rap is committed culturally and emotionally to the pulse, pleasures, and problems of black urban life in the face of such diverse constituencies?

To suggest that rap is a black idiom that prioritizes black culture and that articulates the problems of black urban life does not deny the pleasure and participation of others. In fact, many black musics before rap (e.g., the blues, jazz, early rock 'n' roll) have also become American popular musics precisely because of extensive white participation; white America has always had an intense interest in black culture. Consequently, the fact that a significant number of white teenagers have become rap fans is quite consistent with the history of black music in America and should not be equated with a shift in rap's discursive or stylistic focus away from black pleasure and black fans. However, extensive white participation in black culture has also always involved white appropriation and attempts at ideological recuperation of black cultural resistance. Black culture in the United States has always had elements that have been at least bifocal—speaking to both a black audience and a larger predominantly white context. Rap music shares this history of interaction with many previous black oral and music traditions.

Like generations of white teenagers before them, white teenage rap fans are listening in on black culture, fascinated by its differences, drawn in by mainstream social constructions of black culture as a forbidden narrative, as a symbol of rebellion. Kathy Ogren's study of jazz in the 1920s shows the extensive efforts made by white entertainers and fans to imitate jazz music, dance styles, and language as well as the alarm such fascination caused on the part of state and local authority figures. Lewis Erenberg's study of the development of the cabaret illustrates the centrality of jazz music to the fears over blackness associated with the burgeoning urban nightlife culture. There are similar and abundant cases for rock 'n' roll as well.

Fascination with African-American culture is not new, nor can the dynamics and politics of pleasure across cultural "boundaries" in segregated societies be overlooked. Jazz, rock 'n' roll, soul, and R&B each have large devoted white audience members, many of whom share traits with Norman Mailer's "white negroes," young white listeners trying to perfect a model of correct white hipness, coolness, and style by adopting the latest black style and image. Young white listeners' genuine pleasure and commitment to black music are necessarily affected by dominant racial discourses regarding African Americans, the politics of racial segregation, and cultural difference in the United States. Given the racially discriminatory context within which cultural syncretism takes place, some rappers have equated white participation with a process of dilution and subsequent theft of black culture. Although the terms dilution and theft do not capture the complexity of cultural incorporation and syncretism, this interpretation has more than a grain of truth in it. There is abundant evidence that white artists imitating black styles have greater economic opportunity and access to larger audiences than black innovators. His-torical accounts of the genres often position these subsequently better known artists as the central figures, erasing or marginalizing the artists and contexts within which the genre developed. The process of incorporation and margin-alization of black practitioners has also fostered the development of black forms and practices that are less and less accessible, forms that require greater knowledge of black language and styles in order to participate. Be Bop, with its insider language and its "willfully harsh, anti-assimilationist sound" is a clear example of this response to the continuation of plantation system logic in American culture. In addition to the sheer pleasure black musicians derive from developing a new and exciting style, these black cultural reactions to American culture suggest a reclaiming of the definition of blackness and an attempt to retain aesthetic control over black cultural forms. In the 1980s, this re-claiming of blackness in the popular realm is complicated by access to new reproduction technologies and revised corporate relations in the music industry.

In a number of ways, rap has followed the patterns of other black popular musics, in that at the outset it was heavily rejected by black and white middle-class listeners; the assumption was that it would be a short-lived fad; the mainstream record industry and radio stations rejected it; its marketing was pioneered by independent entrepreneurs and independent labels; and once a smidgen of commercial viability was established the major labels at-tempted to dominate production and distribution. These rap-related patterns were augmented by more general music industry consolidation in the late 1970s that provided the major music corporations with greater control over the market. By 1990 virtually all major record chain store distribution is con-trolled by six major record companies: CBS, Polygram, Warner, BMG, Capitol-EMI, and MCA.

However, music industry consolidation and control over distribution is complicated by three factors: the expansion of local cable access, sophisticated and accessible mixing, production, and copying equipment, and a new relation-ship between major and independent record labels. In previous eras when independent labels sustained the emergence of new genres against industry re-jection, the eventual absorption of these genres by larger companies signalled the dissolution of the independent labels. In the early 1980s, after rap spurred the growth of new independent labels, the major labels moved in and at-tempted to dominate the market but could not consolidate their efforts. Artists signed to independent labels, particularly Tommy Boy, Profile, and Def Jam continued to flourish, whereas acts signed directly to the six majors could not produce comparable sales. It became apparent that the independent labels had a much greater understanding of the cultural logic of hip hop and rap music, a logic that permeated decisions ranging from signing acts to promotional meth-ods. Instead of competing with smaller, more street-savvy labels for new rap acts, the major labels developed a new strategy: buy the independent labels, allow them to function relatively autonomously, and provide them with production resources and access to major retail distribution. Since the emergence of Public Enemy and their substantial cross-genre success in the late 1980s, rappers have generally been signed to independent labels (occasionally black owned and sometimes their own labels) and marketed and distributed by one of the six major companies. In this arrangement, the six majors reap the benefits of a genre that can be marketed with little up-front capital investment, and the artists are usually pleased to have access to the large record and CD chain stores that would otherwise never consider carrying their work.

In the 1980s, the trickle-down effect of technological advances in electronics brought significantly expanded access to mixing, dubbing, and copying equipment for consumers and black market retailers. Clearly, these advances provided aspiring musicians with greater access to recording and copying equipment at less expense. They also substantially improved the market for illegal dubbing of popular music for street corner sale at reduced cost. (Illegally recorded cassette tapes cost approximately $5.00, one-half the cost of label issues.) These lower quality tapes are usually sold in poorer, densely populated communities where reduced cost is a critical sales factor. Rap music is a particularly popular genre for bootleg tapes in urban centers.

Even though actual sales demographics for rap music are not available, increasing sales figures for rap musicians (several prominent rap artists have sales over 500,000 units per album), suggest that white teenage rap consumers have grown steadily since the emergence of Public Enemy in 1988. Middle-class white teenage rap consumers appear to be an increasingly significant audience. This can be inferred from location sales via market surveys and Soundscan, a new electronic scan system installed primarily in large, mostly suburban music chain stores. It is quite possible, however, that the percentage of white rap consumers in relation to overall sales is being disproportionately represented, because bootleg street sales coupled with limited chain music store outlets in poor communities makes it very difficult to assess the demographics for actual sales of rap music to urban black and Hispanic consumers. In addition to inconsistent sales figures, black teen rap consumers may also have a higher "pass-along rate," that is, the rate at which one purchased product is shared among consumers. In my conversations with James Bernard, an editor at The Source (a major hip hop culture magazine with a predominantly black teen readership), The Source's pass-along rate is approximately 1 purchase for every 11–15 readers. According to Bernard, this rate is at least three to four times higher than the average magazine industry pass-along rate. It is conceivable, then, that a similar pass-along rate exists among rap music CD and cassette consumption, especially among consumers with less disposable income.

Cable television exploded during the 1980s and had a significant effect on the music industry and on rap music. Launched in August 1981 by Warner Communications and the American Express Company, MTV became the fastest growing cable channel and as Garofalo points out, "soon became the most effective way for a record to get national exposure." Using its rock format and white teen audience as an explanation for its almost complete refusal to play videos by black artists (once pressure was brought to bear they added Michael Jackson and Prince), MTV finally jumped on the rap music band-wagon. It was not until 1989, with the piloting of "Yo! MTV Raps" that any black artists began to appear on MTV regularly. Since then, as Jamie Malanowski reports, " 'Yo MTV Raps' [has become] one of MTV's most popu-lar shows, is dirt cheap to produce and has almost single-handedly dispelled the giant tastemaking network's reputation for not playing black artists."

Since 1989, MTV has discovered that black artists in several genres are marketable to white suburban teenagers and has dramatically revised its for-matting to include daily rap shows, Street Block (dance music), and the rota-tion of several black artists outside of specialized-genre rotation periods. However, MTV's previous exclusion of black artists throughout the mid-1980s, inspired other cable stations to program black music videos. Black Entertain-ment Television (BET), the most notable alternative to MTV, continues to air a wide variety of music videos by black artists as one of its programming main-stays. And local and syndicated shows (e.g., "Pump It Up!" based in Los Ange-les and "Video Music Box" based in New York), continue to play rap music videos, particularly lower budget, and aggressively black nationalist rap videos deemed too angry or too antiwhite for MTV.

MTV's success has created an environment in which the reception and marketing of music is almost synonymous with the production of music videos. Fan discussions of popular songs and the stories they tell are often accompanied by a reading of the song's interpretation in music video. Music video is a col-laboration in the production of popular music; it revises meanings, provides preferred interpretations of lyrics, creates a stylistic and physical context for re-ception; and valorizes the iconic presence of the artist. Can we really imagine, nonetheless understand, the significance of Michael Jackson's presence as a popular cultural icon without interpreting his music video narratives? The same holds true for Madonna, Janet Jackson, U2, Whitney Houston, Nirvana, and Guns N Roses among others. The visualization of music has far-reaching effects on musical cultures and popular culture generally, not the least of which is the increase in visual interpretations of sexist power relationships, the mode of visual storytelling, the increased focus on how a singer looks rather than how he or she sounds, the need to craft an image to accompany one's music, and ever-greater pressure to abide by corporate genre-formatting rules.

The significance of music video as a partner in the creation or reception of popular music is even greater in the case of rap music. Because the vast major-ity of rap music (except by the occasional superstar) has been virtually frozen out of black radio programming—black radio representatives claim that it scares off high-quality advertising—and because of its limited access to large performance venues, music video has been a crucial outlet for rap artist audi-ences and performer visibility. Rap music videos have animated hip hop cultural style and aesthetics and have facilitated a cross-neighborhood, cross-country (transnational?) dialogue in a social environment that is highly segre-gated by class and race.

The emergence of rap music video has also opened up a previously nonexistent creative arena for black visual artists. Rap music video has provided a creative and commercially viable arena where black film, video, set design, costume, and technical staff and trainees can get the crucial experience and connections to get a foot in the world of video and film production. Before music video production for black musicians, these training grounds, however exploitative, were virtually inaccessible to black technicians. The explosion of music video production, especially black music video, has generated a pool of skilled young black workers in the behind-the-scenes nonunion crews (union membership is overwhelmingly white and male), who are beginning to have an impact on current black film production.

Shooting in the Ghetto: locating rap music video production

Rap video has also developed its own style and its own genre conventions. These conventions visualize hip hop style and usually affirm rap's primary thematic concerns: identity and location. Over most of its brief history (rap video production began in earnest in the mid-to-late 1980s), rap video themes have repeatedly converged around the depiction of the local neighborhood and the local posse, crew, or support system. Nothing is more central to rap's music video narratives than situating the rapper in his or her milieu and among one's crew or posse. Unlike heavy metal videos, for example, which often use dramatic live concert footage and the concert stage as the core location, rap music videos are set on buses, subways, in abandoned buildings, and almost always in black urban inner-city locations. This usually involves ample shots of favorite street corners, intersections, playgrounds, parking lots, school yards, roofs, and childhood friends. When I asked seasoned music video director Kevin Bray what comprised the three most important themes in rap video, his immediate response was, "Posse, posse, and posse.... They'll say, 'I want my shit to be in my hood. Yeah, we got this dope old parking lot where I used to hang out when I was a kid.'" The hood is not a generic designation; videos featuring South Central Los Angeles rappers such as Ice Cube, Ice-T, and NWA very often capture the regional specificity of spatial, ethnic, temperate, and psychological facets of black marginality in Los Angeles, whereas Naughty by Nature's videos feature the ghetto specificity of East Orange, New Jersey.

Rappers' emphasis on posses and neighborhoods has brought the ghetto back into the public consciousness. It satisfies poor young black people's profound need to have their territories acknowledged, recognized, and celebrated. These are the street corners and neighborhoods that usually serve as lurid backdrops for street crimes on the nightly news. Few local people are given an opportunity to speak, and their points of view are always contained by expert testimony. In rap videos, young mostly male residents speak for themselves and for the community, they speak when and how they wish about subjects of their choosing. These local turf scenes are not isolated voices; they are voices from a variety of social margins that are in dialogue with one another. As Bray points out, "If you have an artist from Detroit, the reason they want to shoot at least one video on their home turf is to make a connection with, say, an East Coast New York rapper. It's the dialogue. It's the dialogue between them about where they're from."

However, the return of the ghetto as a central black popular narrative has also fulfilled national fantasies about the violence and danger that purportedly consume the poorest and most economically fragile communities of color. Some conservative critics such as George Will have affirmed the "reality" of some popular cultural ghetto narratives and used this praise as a springboard to call for more police presence and military invasionlike policies. In other cases, such as that of white rapper Vanilla Ice, the ghetto is a source of fabricated white authenticity. Controversy surrounding Ice, one of rap music's most commercially successful artists, highlights the significance of "ghetto blackness" as a model of "authenticity" and hipness in rap music. During the winter of 1989, Vanilla Ice summoned the wrath of the hip hop community not only by successfully marketing himself as a white rapper but also by "validating" his success with stories about his close ties to black poor neighborhoods, publicly sporting his battle scars from the black inner city. According to *Village Voice* columnist Rob Tannenbaum, Robert Van Winkle (aka Vanilla Ice) told Stephen Holden of the *New York Times* that "he 'grew up in the ghetto,' comes from a broken home, hung out mainly with blacks while attending the same Miami high school as Luther Campbell of 2 Live Crew, and was nearly killed in a gang fight." Yet, in a copyrighted, front page story in the Dallas *Morning News*, Ken P. Perkins charges, among other things, that Mr. Van Winkle is instead a middle-class kid from Dallas, Texas. Vanilla Ice's desire to be a "white negro" (or, as some black and white hip hop fans say, a Wigger—a white nigger), to "be black" in order to validate his status as a rapper hints strongly at the degree to which ghetto-blackness is a critical code in rap music. Vanilla Ice not only pretended to be from the ghetto, but he also pretended to have produced the music for his mega-hit "Ice, Ice Baby." In keeping with his pretenses, he only partially credited—and paid no royalties to—black friend and producer Mario Johnson, aka Chocolate(!), who actually wrote the music for "Ice, Ice Baby" and a few other cuts from Vanilla's fifteen times platinum record *To the Extreme*. After a lengthy court battle, Chocolate is finally getting paid in full.

Convergent forces are behind this resurgence of black ghetto symbolism and representation. Most important, the ghetto *exists* for millions of young black and other people of color—it is a profoundly significant social location. Using the ghetto as a source of identity—as rapper Trech would say, if you're not from the ghetto, don't ever come to the ghetto—undermines the stigma of poverty and social marginality. At the same time, the ghetto badman posture-performance is a protective shell against real unyielding and harsh social policies and physical environments. Experience also dictates that public attention is more easily drawn to acts, images, and threats of black male violence than to any other form of racial address. The ghetto produces a variety of meanings for diverse audiences, but this should not be interpreted to mean that intragroup black meanings and uses are less important than larger social receptions. Too often, white voyeuristic pleasure of black cultural imagery or such imagery's role in the performance of ghetto crisis for the news media, are interpreted as their primary value. Even though rappers are aware of the diversity of their audiences and the context for reception, their use of the ghetto and its symbolic significances is primarily directed at other black hip hop fans. If white teen and adult viewers were the preferred audience, then it wouldn't matter which ghetto corner framed images of Trech from rap group Naughty by Nature, especially as most white popular cultural depictions of ghetto life are drained of relevant detail, texture, and complexity. Quite to the contrary, rap's ghetto imagery is too often intensely specific and locally significant, making its preferred viewer someone who can read ghettocentricity with ghetto sensitivity.

The fact that rappers' creative desires or location requests are frequently represented in music videos should not lead one to believe that rappers control the music video process. Music video production is a complex and highly mediated process dictated by the record company in what is sometimes a contentious dialogue with the artists' management, the chosen video director, and video producer. Even though the vast majority of the music video production budget is advanced from the artists' royalties (rap video budgets can range from a low $5,000 to an unusual $100,000 with an average video costing about $40,000), the artist has very little final decision-making control over the video process. Generally speaking, once the single is chosen, a group of music video directors are solicited by the record company, management, and artist to submit video ideas or treatments, and an estimated budget range is projected. After listening to the rapper's work, the video directors draft narrative treatments that usually draw on the rap artists' desires, strengths, lyrical focus, and the feel of the music while attempting to incorporate his or her own visual and technical strengths and preferred visual styles. Once a director is selected, the treatment and budget are refined, negotiated, and the video is cast and produced.

In the first few years of rap video production, the record companies were less concerned about music video's creative process, leaving artists and directors more creative decision-making power. As rappers developed more financial viability, record companies became increasingly invasive at the editing stage, going even so far as to make demands about shot selection and sequencing. This intervention has been facilitated by record companies' increasing sophistication about the video production process. Recently, record companies have begun hiring ex-freelance video producers as video commissioners whose familiarity with the production process aids the record company in channeling and constraining directors, producers, and artist decisions. For veteran music video director Charles Stone, these commercial constraints define music video, in the final analysis, as a commercial product: "Commercial expectations are always an undercurrent. Questions like, does the artist look good, is the artist's image being represented—are always a part of your decision-making process. You have to learn how to protect yourself from excessive meddling, but some negotiation with record companies and artist management always takes place."

With rap's genre and stylistic conventions and artists' desires flanking one side of the creative process and the record company's fiscal and artist management's marketing concerns shoring up the other, music video directors are left with a tight space within which to exercise their creativity. Still, video directors find imaginative ways to engage the musical and lyrical texts and enter into dialogue with the rappers' work. For Bray and other directors, the best videos have the capacity to offer new interpretations after multiple viewings, they have the spontaneity and intertextuality of the music, and most importantly, as Bray describes, the best videos are "sublime visual interpretations of the lyrics which work as another instrument in the musical arrangement; the music video is a visual instrument." Sometimes this visual instrumentation is a thematic improvisation on the historical point of reference suggested by the musical samples. So, a cool jazz horn sample might evoke a contemporary refashioning of a jazz club or cool jazz coloring or art direction. Stone often relies on text and animation to produce creative interpretations of musical works. "Using word overlay," Stone says, "is particularly compatible with rap's use of language. Both are candid and aggressive uses of words, and both play with words' multiple meanings." His selective and unconventional use of animation often makes rappers seem larger than life and can visually emphasize the superheroic powers suggested by rappers' lyrical delivery and performance.

Satisfying the record companies, artists, and managers is only half the battle; MTV, the most powerful video outlet, has its own standards and guidelines for airing videos. These guidelines, according to several frustrated directors, producers, and video commissioners, are inconsistent and unwritten. The most consistent rule is the "absolutely not" list (that some people claim has been subverted by powerful artists and record companies). The "absolutely not" list includes certain acts of violence, some kinds of nudity and sex, profanity and epithets (e.g., "nigger" or "bitch" no matter how these words are being used). The list of censored words and actions expands regularly.

Independent video producer Gina Harrell notes that the process of establishing airing boundaries takes place on a case-by-case basis. MTV is frequently sent a rough cut for approval as part of the editing process to determine if they will *consider* airing the video, and often several changes, such as word reversals, scene cuts, and lyrical rewrites, must be made to accommodate their standards: "Afterwards, you wind up with very little to work with. There is so much censorship now, and from the other end, the record company's video commissioners are much more exacting about what they want the end result to be. It has extended the editing process and raised production costs. Basically, there are too many cooks in the kitchen." There is, not surprisingly, special concern over violence: "The cop issue has really affected rap music video. You can't shoot anybody in a video, you can hold up a gun, but you can't show who you're pointing at. So you can hold up a gun in one frame and then cut to the person being shot in the next frame, but you can't have a person shooting at another person in the same frame." Even so, many artists refuse to operate in a self-censoring fashion and continue to push on these fluid boundaries by shooting footage that they expect will be censored.

MTV's sex policies are equally vague. Although MTV has aired such a video as Wrecks-N-Effect's "Rumpshaker," whose concept is a series of closeup and sometimes magnified distortions of black women's bikini-clad gyrating behinds and breasts, it refused to allow A Tribe Called Quest to say the word *prophylactic* in the lyrical soundtrack for the video "Bonita Applebum," a romantic and uncharacteristically emotionally honest portrayal of teen desire and courtship. MTV denied Stone's request to show condoms in the video, even though the song's mild references to sex and his video treatment were cast in safe sex language. Given the power of cultural conservatives to "strike the fear of god" in music industry corporations, most video producers and directors are bracing themselves for further restrictions.

Rap music and video have been wrongfully characterized as thoroughly sexist but rightfully lambasted for their sexism. I am thoroughly frustrated but not surprised by the apparent need for some rappers to craft elaborate and creative stories about the abuse and domination of young black women. Perhaps these stories serve to protect young men from the reality of female rejection; maybe and more likely, tales of sexual domination falsely relieve their lack of self-worth and limited access to economic and social markers for heterosexual masculine power. Certainly, they reflect the deep-seated sexism that pervades the structure of American culture. Still, I have grown weary of rappers' stock retorts to charges of sexism in rap: "There are 'bitches' or 'golddiggers' out there, and that's who this rap is about," or "This is just a story, I don't *mean anything* by it." I have also grown impatient with the cowardly silence of rappers who I know find this aspect of rap troubling.

On the other hand, given the selective way in which the subject of sexism occupies public dialogue, I am highly skeptical of the timing and strategic deployment of outrage regarding rap's sexism. Some responses to sexism in rap music adopt a tone that suggests that rappers have infected an otherwise sexism-free society. These reactions to rap's sexism deny the existence of a vast array of accepted sexist social practices that make up adolescent male gender role modeling that results in social norms for adult male behaviors that are equally sexist, even though they are usually expressed with less profanity. Few popular analyses of rap's sexism seem willing to confront the fact that sexual and institutional control over and abuse of women is a crucial component of developing a heterosexual masculine identity. In some instances, the music has become a scapegoat that diverts attention away from the more entrenched problem of redefining the terms of heterosexual masculinity.

Rap's sexist lyrics are also part of a rampant and viciously normalized sexism that dominates the corporate culture of the music business. Not only do women face gross pay inequities, but also they face extraordinary day-to-day sexual harassment. Male executives expect to have sexual and social access to women as one of many job perks, and many women, especially black women, cannot establish authority with male coworkers or artists in the business unless they are backed up by male superiors. Independent video producers do not have this institutional backup and, therefore, face exceptionally oppressive work conditions. Harrell has left more than one position because of recurrent, explicit pressure to sleep with her superiors and finds the video shoots an even more unpredictably offensive and frustrating terrain:

> For instance, during a meeting with Def Jam executives on a video shoot, a very famous rapper started lifting up my pants leg trying to rub my leg. I slapped his hand away several times. Later on he stood onstage sticking his tongue out at me in a sexually provocative way—everyone was aware of what he was doing, no one said a word. This happens quite a bit in the music business. Several years ago I had begun producing videos for a video director who made it clear that I could not continue to work with him unless I slept with him. I think that women are afraid to respond legally or aggressively, not only because many of us fear professional recriminations, but also because so many of us were molested when we were children. Those experiences complicate our ability to defend ourselves.

These instances are not exceptions to the rule—they are the rule, even for women near the very top of the corporate ladder. As Carmen Ashhurst-Watson, president of Rush Communications (a multimedia offshoot of Def Jam Records) relates: "The things that Anita Hill said she heard from Clarence Thomas over a four-year period, I might hear in a morning."

Mass media outlets need to be challenged into opening dialogue about pervasive and oppressive sexual conditions in society and into facilitating more frank discussion about sexist gender practices and courtship rituals. The terms of sexual identities, sexual oppression, and their relationship to a variety of forms of social violence need unpacking and closer examination. Basically, we need more discussions about sex, sexism, and violence, not less.

MTV and the media access it affords is a complex and ever-changing facet of mass-mediated and corporation-controlled communication and culture. To refuse to participate in the manipulative process of gaining access to video, recording materials, and performing venues is to almost guarantee a negligible audience and marginal cultural impact. To participate in and try to manipulate the terms of mass-mediated culture is a double-edged sword that cuts both ways—it provides communication channels within and among largely disparate groups and requires compromise that often affirms the very structures much of rap's philosophy seems determined to undermine. MTV's acceptance and gatekeeping of rap music has dramatically increased rap artists' visibility to black, white, Asian, and Latino teenagers, but it has also inspired antirap censorship groups and fuels the media's fixation on rap and violence.

Commercial marketing of rap music represents a complex and contradictory aspect of the nature of popular expression in a corporation-dominated information society. Rap music and hip hop style have become common and campaign hooks for McDonald's, Burger King, Coke, Pepsi, several athletic shoe companies, clothing chain stores, MTV, antidrug campaigns, and other global corporate efforts ad nauseam. Rap music has grown into a multimillion dollar record, magazine, and video industry with multiplatinum world renowned rappers, disc jockeys, and entertainers. Dominating the black music charts, rap music and rap music cousins, such as Hip House, New Jack Swing (a dance style of R&B with rap music rhythms and drum beats), have been trendsetters for popular music in the U.S. and around the world. Rap's musical and visual style have had a profound impact on all contemporary popular music. Rock artists have begun using sampling styles and techniques developed by rappers; highly visible artists, such as Madonna, Janet Jackson, and New Kids on the Block wear hip hop fashions, use hip hop dances in their stage shows and rap lyrics and slang words in their recordings.

Yet, rap music is also Black American TV, a public and highly accessible place, where black meanings and perspectives—even as they are manipulated by corporate concerns—can be shared and validated among black people. Rap is dependent on technology and mass reproduction and distribution. As Andrew Ross has observed, popular music is capable of transmitting, disseminating, and rendering "visible 'black' meanings, *precisely because of*, and not in spite of, its industrial forms of production, distribution, and consumption." Such tensions between rap's highly personal, conversational intimacy and the massive institutional and technological apparatuses on which rap's global voice depends are critical to hip hop, black culture, and popular cultures around the world in the late twentieth century. Inside of these commercial constraints, rap offers alternative interpretations of key social events such as the Gulf War, The Los Angeles uprising, police brutality, censorship efforts, and community-based education. It is the central cultural vehicle for open social reflection on poverty, fear of adulthood, the desire for absent fathers, frustrations about black male sexism, female sexual desires, daily rituals of life as an unemployed teen hustler, safe sex, raw anger, violence, and childhood memories. It is also the home of innovative uses of style and language, hilariously funny carnivalesque and chitlin-circuit-inspired dramatic skits, and ribald storytelling. In short, it is black America's most dynamic contemporary popular cultural, intellectual, and spiritual vessel.

Rap's ability to draw the attention of the nation, to attract crowds around the world in places where English is rarely spoken are fascinating elements of rap's social power. Unfortunately, some of this power is linked to U.S.-based cultural imperialism, in that rappers benefit from the disproportionate exposure of U.S. artists around the world facilitated by music industry marketing muscle. However, rap also draws international audiences because it is a powerful conglomeration of voices from the margins of American society speaking about the terms of that position. Rap music, like many powerful black cultural forms before it, resonates for people from vast and diverse backgrounds. The cries of pain, anger, sexual desire, and pleasure that rappers articulate speak to hip hop's vast fan base for different reasons. For some, rappers offer symbolic prowess, a sense of black energy and creativity in the face of omnipresent oppressive forces; others listen to rap with an ear toward the hidden voices of the oppressed, hoping to understand America's large, angry, and "unintelligible" population. Some listen to the music's powerful and life-affirming rhythms, its phat beats and growling bass lines, revelling in its energy, seeking strength from its cathartic and electric presence. Rap's global industry-orchestrated (but not industry-created) presence illustrates the power of the language of rap and the salience of the stories of oppression and creative resistance its music and lyrics tell. The drawing power of rap is precisely its musical and narrative commitment to black youth and cultural resistance, and nothing in rap's commercial position and cross-cultural appeal contradicts this fact. Rap's margin(ality) is represented in the contradictory reaction rap receives in mainstream American media and popular culture. It is at once part of the dominant text and, yet, always on the margins of this text; relying on and commenting on the text's center and always aware of its proximity to the border.

Rap music and hip hop culture are cultural, political, and commercial forms, and for many young people they are the primary cultural, sonic, and linguistic windows on the world. After the Los Angeles riots, author Mike Davis attended an Inglewood Crip and Blood gang truce meeting in which gang members voiced empassioned testimonials and called for unity and political action. Describing their speeches, Davis said: "These guys were very eloquent, and they spoke in a rap rhythm and with rap eloquence, which I think kind of shook up the white television crews." Later, he noted that the gang truce and the political struggles articulated in that meeting were "translated into the [hip hop] musical culture." Hip hop, Davis concluded, "is the fundamental matrix of self-expression for this whole generation."

Manning Marable
History and Black Consciousness

The central theme of black American history has been the constant struggle to overcome the barriers of race and the reality of unequal racial identities between black and white. This racial bifurcation has created parallel realities or racial universes, in which blacks and whites may interact closely with one another but perceive social reality in dramatically different ways. These collective experiences of discrimination, and this memory of resistance and oppression, have given rise to several overlapping group strategies or critical perspectives within the African-American community, which have as their objective the ultimate empowerment of black people. In this sense, the contours of struggle for black people have given rise to a very specific consciousness: a sense of our community, its needs and aspirations for itself. The major ideological debates which map the dimensions of the political mind of black America have always been about the orientation and objectives of black political culture and consciousness. The great historical battles between Booker T. Washington, the architect of the "Atlanta Compromise" of 1895, and W.E.B. Du Bois, the founder of the NAACP, and the conflicts between Du Bois and black nationalist leader Marcus Garvey, were fought largely over the manner in which the black community would define for itself the political and economic tools necessary for its empowerment and future development. Sometimes the battle lines in these struggles for black leadership and for shaping the consciousness of the African-American community were defined by class divisions. More generally, the lines of separation had less to do with class than with the internalized definitions of what "race" meant to African-Americans themselves in the context of black political culture.

Ironically, the historical meaning and reality of race was always fundamentally a product of class domination. Race, in the last analysis, is neither biologically nor genetically derived. It is a structure rooted in white supremacy, economic exploitation and social privilege. It evolved in the process of slavery and the transatlantic slave trade. Racism has power only as a set of institutional arrangements and social outcomes which perpetuate the exploitation of black labor and the subordination of the black community's social and cultural life. But all of this is masked by institutional racism to those who experience the weight of its oppression. The oppressed perceive domination through the language and appearance of racial forms, although such policies and practices always served a larger class objective. As a result, the political culture of black America is organized around racial themes, either an effort to overcome or escape the manifestations of institutional racism, or to build alternative institutions which empower black people within environments of whiteness. The approach of political empowerment is distinctly racial, rather than class-oriented.

Most historians characterized the central divisions within black political culture as the 150-year struggle between "integration" and "separation." In 1925, this division was perceived as separating Du Bois and the NAACP from the Garveyites. In 1995, the division is used to distinguish such pragmatic multicultural liberals as Henry Louis Gates, director of Harvard University's Afro-American Studies department, from the architect of Afrocentrism, Temple University Professor Molefi Asante. However, this theoretical model has serious limitations. The simple fact is that the vast majority of African-American people usually would not define themselves as either Roy Wilkins-style integrationists or black separatists like City University of New York Black Studies director Leonard Jeffries. Most blacks have perceived integration or black nationalism as alternative strategies which might serve the larger purpose of empowering their community and assisting in the deconstruction of institutions perpetuating racial inequality. As anthropologist Leith Mullings and I have argued (Chapter 17 above), a more accurate description of black political culture would identify three strategic visions; these can be termed "inclusion" or integration, "black nationalism," and "transformation."

Since the rise of the free Negro community in the North during the antebellum era, inclusion has been the central impulse for reform among black Americans. The inclusionists have sought to minimize or even eradicate the worst effects and manifestations of racism within the African-American community. They have mobilized resources to alter or abolish legal restrictions on the activities of blacks, and have agitated to achieve acceptance of racial diversity by the white majority. Essentially, the inclusionists have operated philosophically and ideologically as "liberals": they usually believe that the state is inherently a "neutral apparatus," open to the pressure and persuasion of competing interest groups. They have attempted to influence public opinion and mass behavior on issues of race by changing public policies, and educational and cultural activity. But the theoretical guiding star of the inclusionists has been what I term "symbolic representation." They firmly believe that the elevation and advancement of select numbers of well-educated, affluent and/or powerful blacks into positions of authority helps to dismantle the patterns and structures of racial discrimination. The theory is that if blacks are well represented inside government, businesses and social institutions, then this will go a long way toward combatting the traditional practices of inequality and patterns of discrimination. Black representatives within the system of power would use their leverage to carry out policies that benefited the entire African-American population.

Embedded deeply within the logic of inclusionism were two additional ideas. First, the intellectual foundations of inclusionism drew a strong parallel between the pursuit of freedom and the acquisition of private property. To unshackle oneself from the bonds of inequality was, in part, to achieve the material resources necessary to improve one's life and the lives of those in one's family. This meant that freedom was defined by one's ability to gain access to resources and to the pre-requisites of power. Implicitly, the orientation of inclusionism reinforced the logic and legitimacy of America's economic system and class structure, seeking to assimilate blacks within them. Second, inclusionists usually had a cultural philosophy of integration within the aesthetic norms and civil society created by the white majority. Inclusionists sought to transcend racism by acting in ways which whites would not find objectionable or repulsive. The more one behaved in a manner which emulated whites, the less likely one might encounter the negative impact and effects of Jim Crow. By assimilating the culture of whites and by minimizing the cultural originality and creativity of African-Americans, one might find the basis for a "universalist" dialogue that transcends the ancient barriers of color. Historically, the inclusionists can be traced to those groups of former slaves in colonial America who assimilated themselves into majority white societies, who forgot African languages and traditions and tried to participate fully in the social institutions that whites had built for themselves. In the nineteenth century, the inclusionists' outstanding leader was Frederick Douglass. Today, the inclusionists include most of the traditional leadership of the civil-rights organizations such as the National Association for the Advancement of Colored People and the National Urban League, the bulk of the Congressional Black Caucus and most African-American elected officials, and the majority of the older and more influential black middle class, professionals and managerial elites.

On balance, the inclusionists' strategy sought to transcend race by creating a context wherein individuals could be judged on the basis of what they accomplished rather than on the color of their skin. This approach minimized the extensive interconnectedness between color and inequality; it tended to conceive racism as a kind of social disease rather than the logical and coherent consequence of institutional arrangements, private property and power relations, reinforced by systemic violence. The inclusionists seriously underestimated the capacity and willingness of white authorities to utilize coercion to preserve and defend white privilege and property. Integration, in short, was a strategy to avoid the worst manifestations of racism, without upsetting the deep structures of inequality which set into motion the core dynamics of white oppression and domination.

Although the inclusionist perspective dominates the literature that interprets black history, it never consolidated itself as a consensus framework for the politics of the entire black community. A sizable component of the African-American population always rejected integration as a means of transcending institutional racism. This alternative vision was black nationalism. Black nationalism sought to overturn racial discrimination by building institutions controlled and owned by blacks, providing resources and services to the community. The nationalists distrusted the capacity of whites as a group to overcome the debilitating effects of white privilege, and questioned the inclusionists' simple-minded faith in the power of legal reforms. Nationalists rejected the culture and aesthetics of white Euro-America in favor of what today would be termed an Afrocentric identity. Historically, the initial nationalist impulse for black group autonomous development really began with those slaves who ran away from the plantations and farms of whites, and who established "maroons," frontier enclaves or villages of defiant African-Americans, or who mounted slave rebellions. Malcolm X and Marcus Garvey, among others, are within this cultural, intellectual and political tradition. However, like the inclusionists, the nationalists often tended to reify race, perceiving racial categories as static and ahistorical, rather than fluid and constantly subject to renegotiation and reconfiguration. They struggled to uproot race, but were frequently imprisoned themselves by the language and logic of inverted racial thinking. They utilized racial categories to mobilize their core constituencies without fully appreciating their own internal contradictions.

The black nationalist tradition within black political culture was, and remains, tremendously complex, rich and varied. At root, its existential foundations were the national consciousness and collective identity of people of African descent, as they struggled against racism and class exploitation. But, as in any form of nationalism, this tradition of resistance and group consciousness expressed itself politically around many different coordinates and tendencies. Within black nationalism is the separatist current, which tends to perceive the entire white community as racially monolithic and articulates racial politics with starkly confrontational and antagonistic overtones. Today, one could point to educator Len Jeffries' controversial descriptions of European Americans as "ice people"—cold, calculating, materialistic—and African-Americans as "sun people"—warm, generous, humanistic—as a separatist-oriented, conservative social theory within the nationalist tradition. The Nation of Islam's theory of Yacub, first advanced under the leadership of Elijah Muhammad, projected an image of whites as "devils," incapable of positive change. At the other end of the nationalist spectrum were radicals like Hubert H. Harrison, Cyril V. Briggs and Huey P. Newton, and militant groups such as the League of Revolutionary Black Workers from the late 1960s, who incorporated a class analysis and the demand for socialism within their politics. To this radical tendency, black nationalism had to rely on the collaboration of other oppressed people regardless of the color of their skin, languages or nationalities. Between these two tendencies is the black nationalism of the rising black petty bourgeoisie, which utilizes racial segregation as a barrier to facilitate capital accumulation from the mostly working-class, black consumer market. Nationalist rhetoric such as "buy black" becomes part of the appeal employed by black entrepreneurs to generate profits. All of these contradictory currents are part of the complex historical terrain of black nationalism.

The basic problem confronting both inclusionism and black nationalism is that the distinct social structure, political economy and ethnic demography which created both strategic visions for black advancement has been radically transformed, especially in the past quarter of a century. Segregation imposed a kind of social uniformity on the vast majority of black people, regardless of their class affiliation, education or social condition. The stark brutality of legal Jim Crow, combined with the unforgiving and vicious character of the repression that was essential to such a system, could only generate two major reactions: a struggle to be acknowledged and accepted despite one's racial designation, or a struggle to create an alternative set of cultural, political and social axioms which could sustain a distinctly different group identity against "whiteness." But as the social definition of what it means to be "different" in the USA has changed, the whole basis for both of these traditional racial outlooks within African-American society becomes far more contentious and problematic.

Many people from divergent ethnic backgrounds, speaking various languages and possessing different cultures, now share a common experience of inequality in the USA—poor housing, homelessness, inadequate health care, underrepresentation within government, lagging incomes and high rates of unemployment, discrimination in capital markets, and police brutality on the streets. Yet there is an absence of unity between these constituencies, in part because their leaders are imprisoned ideologically and theoretically by the assumptions and realities of the past. The rhetoric of racial solidarity, for instance, can be used to mask class contradictions and divisions within the black, Latino and Asian American communities. Symbolic representation can be manipulated to promote the narrow interest of minority elected officials who may have little commitment to advancing the material concerns of the most oppressed sectors of multicultural America.

What is also missing is a common language of resistance. Race as a social construction generates its own internal logic and social expressions of pain, anger and alienation within various communities. These are often barriers to an understanding of the larger social and economic forces at work which undermine our common humanity. From the cultural threads of our own experiences, we must find parallel patterns and symbols of struggle which permit us to draw connections between various groups within society. This requires the construction of a new lexicon of activism, a language which transcends the narrow boundaries of singular ethnic identity and embraces a vision of democratic pluralism.

The immediate factors involved in a general strategic rethinking of the paradigms for black American struggle are also international. A generation ago, black Americans with an internationalist perspective might see themselves as part of the diverse nonaligned movement of Third World nations, strategically distanced between capitalist America and Communist Russia. Like legal racial segregation, the system of Soviet Communism and the Soviet Union itself no longer exist. Apartheid as a system of white privilege and political totalitarianism no longer exists, as the liberation forces of Nelson Mandela and the African National Congress struggle to construct a multiracial democracy. The Sandinistas of Nicaragua lost power, as their model of a pluralistic, socialist-oriented society was overturned, at least for the time being. Throughout the rest of the Third World, from Ghana to Vietnam, socialists moved rapidly to learn the language of markets and foreign investment, and were forced to curtail egalitarian programs and accommodate themselves to the ideological requirements of the "New World Order" and the demands of transnational capital. Millions of people of color were on the move, one of the largest migrations in human history. Rural and agricultural populations migrated to cities in search of work and food; millions traveled from the Third World periphery to the metropolitan cores of Western Europe and North America to occupy the lowest levels of labor. In many instances, these new groups were socially stigmatized and economically dominated, in part by the older categories of "race" and the social divisions of "difference" which separated the newest immigrants from the white "mainstream."

Nevertheless, within this changing demographic/ethnic mix which increasingly characterizes the urban environments of Western Europe and North America, the older racial identities and categories have begun in many instances to break down, with new identities and group symbols being formulated by various "minorities." In the United Kingdom by the 1970s, immigrants—of radically divergent ethnic backgrounds and languages—from the Caribbean, Asia and Africa began to term themselves "black" as a political entity. In the US, the search for both disaggregation and rearticulation of group identity and consciousness among people of color is also occurring, although along different lines due to distinct historical experiences and backgrounds. In the Hawaiian islands, for example, many of the quarter of a million native Hawaiians support the movement for political sovereignty and self-determination. But do native Hawaiians have more in common culturally and politically with American Indians or Pacific islanders? What are the parallels and distinctions between the discrimination experienced by Mexican Americans in the US Southwest, and African-Americans under slavery and Jim Crow segregation? Do the more than five million Americans of Arab, Kurdish, Turkish and Iranian nationality and descent have a socioeconomic experience in the USA which puts them in conflict with native-born African-Americans, or is there sufficient commonality of interest and social affinity to provide the potential framework for principled activism and unity?

Similar questions about social distinctions rooted in mixed ethnic heritages and backgrounds could be raised within the black community itself. At least three out of four native-born Americans of African descent in the USA have to some extent a racial heritage which is also American Indian, European, Asian and/or Hispanic. Throughout much of the Americas, racial categories were varied and complex, reflecting a range of social perceptions based on physical appearance, color, hair texture, class, social status and other considerations. In the USA prior to the civil-rights movement, with a few exceptions, the overwhelmingly dominant categorization was "black" and "white." In the late 1970s, the federal government adopted a model for collecting census data based on four "races"—black, Asian, American Indian and white—and two ethnic groups, Hispanic and non-Hispanic, which could be of whatever "racial" identity. Today, all of these categories are being contested and questioned.

Some of the hundreds of thousands of African-Americans and whites who intermarry have begun to call for a special category for their children—"multiracial." By 1994, three states required a "multiracial" designation on public-school forms, and Georgia has established the "multiracial" category on its mandatory state paperwork. The "multiracial" designation, if popularized and structured into the state bureaucracy, could have the dangerous effect of siphoning off a segment of what had been the "black community" into a distinct and potentially privileged elite, protected from the normal vicissitudes and ordeals experienced by black folk under institutional racism. It could become a kind of "passing" for the twenty-first century, standing apart from the definition of blackness. Conversely, as more immigrants from the African continent and the Caribbean intermarry with native-born black Americans, notions of what it means to be "black" become culturally and ethnically far more pluralistic and international. The category of "blackness" becomes less parochial and more expansive, incorporating the diverse languages, histories, rituals and aesthetic textures of new populations and societies.

Inside the United States, other political and social factors have contributed to the reframing of debates on race and our understanding of the social character of the black community. In just the past five years, we have experienced the decline and near-disappearance of Jesse Jackson's Rainbow Coalition and efforts to liberalize and reform the Democratic Party from within; the explosive growth of a current of conservative black nationalism and extreme racial separatism within significant sections of the African-American community; the vast social uprising of the Los Angeles rebellion in April and May 1992, triggered by a Not Guilty verdict on police officers who had viciously beaten a black man; and the political triumph of mass conservatism in the 1994 congressional elections, due primarily to an overwhelmingly Republican vote by millions of angry white males. Behind these trends and events, from the perspective of racial history, was an even larger dilemma: the failure of the modern black American freedom movement to address or even to listen to the perspectives and political insights of the "hip-hop" generation, those African-Americans born and/or socialized after the March on Washington of 1963 and the passage of the Civil Rights Act a year later. The hip-hop generation was largely pessimistic about the quality and character of black leadership, and questioned the legitimacy and relevancy of organizations like the NAACP. Although the hip-hop movement incorporated elements of black nationalism into its wide array of music and art, notably through its iconization of Malcolm X in 1990–93, it nevertheless failed to articulate a coherent program or approach to social change which addressed the complex diversities of black civil society. Both inclusionism and black nationalism had come to represent fragmented social visions and archaic agendas, which drew eclectically from racial memory. Both ideologies failed to appreciate how radically different the future might be for black people, especially in the context of a post-Cold War, postmodern, post-industrial future. The sad and sorry debacle surrounding the public vilification and firing of NAACP former national secretary Benjamin

Chavis, for example, illustrated both the lack of internal democracy and accountability of black political institutions, as well as the absence of any coherent program which could speak meaningfully to the new social, political and cultural realities.

The urgent need to redefine the discourse and strategic orientation of the black movement is more abundantly clear in the mid 1990s than ever before. Proposition 187 in California, which denied medical, educational, and social services to undocumented immigrants, as well as the current national debates about affirmative action and welfare, all have one thing in common: the cynical and deliberate manipulation of racial and ethnic stereotypes by the far right. White conservatives understand the power of "race." They have made a strategic decision to employ code-words and symbols which evoke the deepest fears and anxieties of white middle-class and working-class Americans with regard to African-American issues and interests.

The reasons for this strategy are not difficult to discern. Since the emergence of Reaganism in the United States, corporate capitalism has attempted to restrict the redistributive authority and social-program agenda of the state. Many of the reform programs, from the legal desegregation of society in the 1960s to the Johnson administration's "War on Poverty," were created through pressure from below. The initiation of affirmative-action programs for women and minorities and the expansion of the welfare state contributed to some extent to a more humane and democratic society. The prerogatives of capital were not abolished by any means, but the democratic rights of minorities, women and working people were expanded. As capitalist investment and production became more global, the demand for cheap labor increased dramatically. Capital aggressively pressured Third World countries to suppress or outlaw unions, reduce wage levels, and eliminate the voices of left opposition. Simultaneously, millions of workers were forced to move from rural environments into cities in the desperate search for work. The "Latinization" of cities, from Los Angeles to New York, is a product of this destructive, massive economic process.

In the United States since the early 1980s, corporate capital has pushed aggressively for lower taxes, deregulation, a relaxation of affirmative action and environmental protection laws, and generally more favorable social and political conditions for corporate profits. Over the past twenty years, this has meant that real incomes of working people in the United States, adjusted for inflation, have fallen significantly. Between 1947 and 1973, the average hourly and weekly earnings of US production and nonsupervisory workers increased dramatically—from $6.75 per hour to $12.06 per hour (in 1993 inflation-adjusted dollars). But after 1973, production workers lost ground—from $12.06 per hour in 1979 to $11.26 per hour in 1989 to only $10.83 per hour in 1993. According to the research of the Children's Defense Fund, the greatest losses occurred among families with children under the age of eighteen where the household head was also younger than the age of thirty. The inflation-adjusted income of white households in this category fell 22 per cent between 1973 and 1990. For young Latino families with children, the decline during these years was 27.9 per cent. For young black families, the drop was a devastating 48.3 per cent.

During the Reagan administration, the United States witnessed a massive redistribution of wealth upward, unequaled in our history. In 1989, the top 1 per cent of all US households received 16.4 per cent of all US incomes in salaries and wages; it possessed 48.1 per cent of the total financial wealth of the country. In other words, the top 1 per cent of all households controlled a significantly greater amount of wealth than the bottom 95 per cent of all US households (which controlled only 27.7 per cent). These trends produced a degree of economic uncertainty and fear for millions of households unparalleled since the Great Depression. White working-class families found themselves working harder, yet falling further behind. "Race" in this uncertain political environment easily became a vehicle for orienting politics toward the right. If a white worker cannot afford a modest home in the suburbs such as his or her parents could have purchased thirty years ago, the fault is attributed not to falling wages but to affirmative action. If the cost of public education spirals skyward, white teenagers and their parents often conclude that the fault is not due to budget cuts but to the fact that "undeserving" blacks and Hispanics have taken the places of "qualified" white students.

As significant policy debates focus on the continuing burden of race within society, the black movement is challenged to rethink its past and to restructure radically the character of its political culture. Race is all too often a barrier to understanding the central role of class in shaping personal and collective outcomes within a capitalist society. Black social theory must transcend the theoretical limitations and programmatic contradictions of the old assimilationist/integrationist paradigm on the one hand, and of separatist black nationalism on the other. We have to replace the bipolar categories, rigid racial discourses and assumptions of the segregationist past with an approach toward politics and social dialogue which is pluralistic, multicultural, and nonexclusionary. In short, we must go beyond black and white, seeking power in a world which is increasingly characterized by broad diversity in ethnic and social groupings, but structured hierarchically in terms of privilege and social inequality. We must go beyond black and white, but never at the price of forgetting the bitter lessons of our collective struggles and history, never failing to appreciate our unique cultural and aesthetic gifts or lacking an awareness of our common destiny with others of African descent. We must find a language that clearly identifies the role of class as central to the theoretical and programmatic critique of contemporary society. And we must do this in a manner which reaches out to the newer voices and colors of US society—Latinos, Asian Americans, Pacific Island Americans, Middle East Americans, American Indians, and others.

We have entered a period in which our traditional definitions of what it has meant to be "black" must be transformed. The old racial bifurcation of white versus black no longer accurately or adequately describes the social composition and ethnic character of the United States. Harlem, the cultural capital of black America, is now more than 40 per cent Spanish-speaking. Blackness as an identity now embraces a spectrum of nationalities, languages, and ethnicities, from the Jamaican and Trinidadian cultures of the West Indies to the Hispanicized blackness of Panama and the Dominican Republic. More than ever before, we must recognize the limitations and inherent weaknesses of a model of politics which is grounded solely or fundamentally in racial categories. The diversity of ethnicities which constitute the urban United States today should help us to recognize the basic common dynamics of class undergirding the economic and social environment of struggle for everyone.

Historically, there is an alternative approach to the politics and social analysis of black empowerment which is neither inclusionist nor nationalist. This third strategy can be called "transformationist." Essentially, transformationists within the racial history of America have sought to deconstruct or destroy the ideological foundations, social categories and institutional power of race. Transformationists have sought neither incorporation nor assimilation into a white mainstream, nor the static isolation of racial separation; instead they have advocated a restructuring of power relations and authority between groups and classes, in such a manner as to make race potentially irrelevant as a social force. This critical approach to social change begins with a radical understanding of culture. The transformationist sees culture not as a set of artefacts or formal rituals, but as the human content and product of history itself. Culture is both the result of and the consequences of struggle; it is dynamic and ever-changing, yet structured around collective memories and traditions. The cultural history of black Americans is, in part, the struggle to maintain their own group's sense of identity, social cohesion and integrity, in the face of policies which have been designed to deny both their common humanity and particularity. To transform race in American life, therefore, demands a dialectical approach toward culture which must simultaneously preserve and destroy. We must create the conditions for a vital and creative black cultural identity—in the arts and literature, in music and film—which also has the internal confidence and grace of being to draw parallels and assume lines of convergence with other ethnic traditions. But we must destroy and uproot the language and logic of inferiority and racial inequality, which sees blackness as a permanent caste and whiteness as the eternal symbol of purity, power and privilege.

The transformationist tradition is also grounded in a radical approach to politics and the state. Unlike the integrationists, who seek "representation" within the system as it is, or the nationalists, who generally favor the construction of parallel racial institutions controlled by blacks, the transformationists basically seek the redistribution of resources and the democratization of state power along more egalitarian lines. A transformationist approach to politics begins with the formulation of a new social contract between people and the state which asks: "What do people have a right to expect from their government in terms of basic human needs which all share in common?" Should all citizens have a right to vote, but have no right to employment? Should Americans have a right to freedom of speech and unfettered expression, but no right to universal public health care? These are some of the questions that should be at the heart of the social policy agenda of a new movement for radical multicultural democracy.

The transformationist tradition in black political history embraces the radical abolitionists of the nineteenth century, the rich intellectual legacy of W.E.B. Du Bois, and the activism of militants from Paul Robeson to Fannie Lou Hamer. But it is also crucial to emphasize that these three perspectives—inclusion, black nationalism, and transformation—are not mutually exclusive or isolated from one another. Many integrationists have struggled to achieve racial equality through the policies of liberal desegregation, and have moved toward more radical means as they became disenchanted with the pace of social change. The best example of integrationist transformationism is provided by the final two years of Martin Luther King, Jr.'s public life: anti-Vietnam War activism; advocacy of a "Poor People's March" on Washington DC; the mobilization of black sanitation workers in Memphis, Tennessee; and support for economic democracy. Similarly, many other black activists began their careers as black nationalists, and gradually came to the realization that racial inequality cannot be abolished until and unless the basic power structure and ownership patterns of society are transformed. This requires at some level the establishment of principled coalitions between black people and others who experience oppression or social inequality. The best example of a black nationalist who acquired a transformationist perspective is, of course, Malcolm X, who left the Nation of Islam in March 1964 and created the Organization of Afro-American Unity several months later. In the African diaspora, a transformationist perspective in politics and social theory is best expressed in the writings of Amilcar Cabral, C.L.R. James and Walter Rodney.

In the wake of the "failure" of world socialism, the triumph of mass conservatism in politics, and the ideological hegemony of the values of markets, private enterprise and individual self-interest, black politics has to a great extent retreated from the transformationist perspective in recent years. It is difficult, if not impossible, to talk seriously about group economic development, collective interests and the radical restructuring of resources along democratic lines. Yet I am convinced that the road toward black empowerment in the multinational corporate and political environment of the post-Cold War would require a radical leap in social imagination, rather than a retreat to the discourse and logic of the racial past.

Our greatest challenge in rethinking race as ideology is to recognize how we unconsciously participate in its recreation and legitimization. Despite the legal desegregation of American civil society a generation ago, the destructive power and perverse logic of race still continues. Most Americans continue to perceive social reality in a manner which grossly underestimates the role of social class, and legitimates the categories of race as central to the ways in which privilege and authority are organized. We must provide the basis for a progressive alternative to the interpretation of race relations, moving the political culture of black America from a racialized discourse and analysis to a critique of inequality which has the capacity and potential to speak to the majority of American people. This leap in theory and social analysis must be made, if black America has any hope of transcending its current impasse of powerlessness and systemic inequality. As C.L.R. James astutely observed: "The race question is subsidiary to the class question in politics, and to think of imperialism in terms of race is disastrous. But to neglect the racial factor as merely incidental is an error only less grave than to make it fundamental."

Robin D. G. Kelley
from *Yo Mama's Disfunktional!*

LOOKING FOR THE "REAL" NIGGA: SOCIAL SCIENTISTS CONSTRUCT THE GHETTO

Perhaps the supreme irony of black American existence is how broadly black people debate the question of cultural identity among themselves while getting branded as a cultural monolith by those who would deny us the complexity and complexion of a community, let alone a nation. If Afro-Americans have never settled for the racist reductions imposed upon them—from chattel slaves to cinematic stereotype to sociological myth—it's because the black collective conscious not only knew better but also knew more than enough ethnic diversity to subsume these fictions.

—GREG TATE,
Flyboy in the Buttermilk

The biggest difference between us and white folks is that we know when we are playing.

—ALBERTA ROBERTS,
QUOTED IN JOHN LANGSTON GWALTNEY, *Drylongso*

"I think this anthropology is just another way to call me a nigger." So observed Othman Sullivan, one of many informants in John Langston Gwaltney's classic study of black culture, *Drylongso*. Perhaps a kinder, gentler way to put it is that anthropology, not unlike most urban social science, has played a key role in marking "blackness" and defining black culture to the "outside" world. Beginning with Robert Park and his protégés to the War on Poverty-inspired ethnographers, a battery of social scientists have significantly shaped the current dialogue on black urban culture. Today sociologists, anthropologists, political scientists, and economists compete for huge grants from Ford, Rockefeller, Sage, and other foundations to measure everything measurable in order to get a handle on the newest internal threat to civilization. With the discovery of the so-called underclass, terms like *nihilistic*, *dysfunctional*, and *pathological* have become the most common adjectives to describe contemporary black urban culture. The question they often pose, to use Mr. Othman Sullivan's words, is what *kind* of "niggers" populate the inner cities?

Unfortunately, too much of this rapidly expanding literature on the underclass provides less an understanding of the complexity of people's lives and cultures than a bad blaxploitation film or an Ernie Barnes painting. Many social scientists are not only quick to generalize about the black urban poor on the basis of a few "representative" examples, but more often than not, they do not let the natives speak. A major part of the problem is the way in which many mainstream social scientists studying the underclass define *culture*. Relying on a narrowly conceived definition of culture, most of the underclass literature uses *behavior* and *culture* interchangeably.

My purpose, then, is to offer some reflections on how the culture concept employed by social scientists has severely impoverished contemporary debates over the plight of urban African Americans and contributed to the construction of the ghetto as a reservoir of pathologies and bad cultural values. Much of this literature not only conflates behavior with culture, but when social scientists explore "expressive" cultural forms or what has been called "popular culture" (such as language, music, and style), most reduce it to expressions of pathology, compensatory behavior, or creative "coping mechanisms" to deal with racism and poverty. While some aspects of black expressive cultures certainly help inner city residents deal with and even resist ghetto conditions, most of the literature ignores what these cultural forms mean for the practitioners. Few scholars acknowledge that what might also be at stake here are aesthetics, style, and pleasure. Nor do they recognize black urban culture's hybridity and internal differences. Given the common belief that inner city communities are more isolated than ever before and have completely alien values, the notion that there is one discrete, identifiable black urban culture carries a great deal of weight. By conceiving black urban culture in the singular, interpreters unwittingly reduce their subjects to cardboard typologies who fit neatly into their own definition of the "underclass" and render invisible a wide array of complex cultural forms and practices.

"It's Just a Ghetto Thang": The Problem of Authenticity and the Ethnographic Imagination

A few years ago Mercer Sullivan decried the disappearance of "culture" from the study of urban poverty, attributing its demise to the fact that "overly vague notions of the culture of poverty brought disrepute to the culture concept as a tool for understanding the effects of the concentration of poverty among cultural minorities." In some respects, Sullivan is right: the conservatives who maintain that persistent poverty in the inner city is the result of the behavior of the poor, the product of some cultural deficiency, have garnered so much opposition from many liberals and radicals that few scholars are willing even to discuss culture. Instead, opponents of the "culture of poverty" idea tend to focus on structural transformations in the U.S. economy, labor force composition, and resultant changes in marriage patterns to explain the underclass.

However, when viewed from another perspective, culture never really disappeared from the underclass debate. On the contrary, it has been as central to the work of liberal structuralists and radical Marxists as it has been to that of the conservative culturalists. While culturalists insist that the behavior of the urban poor explains their poverty, the structuralists argue that the economy explains their behavior as well as their poverty. For all their differences, there is general agreement that a common, debased culture is what defines the "underclass," what makes it a threat to the future of America. Most interpreters of the "underclass" treat behavior as not only a synonym for culture but also as the determinant for class. In simple terms, what makes the "underclass" a class is members' common behavior—not their income, their poverty level, or the kind of work they do. It is a definition of class driven more by moral panic than by systematic analysis. A cursory look at the literature reveals that there is no consensus as to precisely what behaviors define the underclass. Some scholars, like William Julius Wilson, have offered a more spatial definition of the underclass by focusing on areas of "concentrated poverty," but obvious problems result when observers discover the wide range of behavior and attitudes in, say, a single city block. What happens to the concept when we find people with jobs engaging in illicit activities and some jobless people depending on church charity? Or married employed fathers who spend virtually no time with their kids and jobless unwed fathers participating and sharing in child care responsibilities? How does the concept of underclass behavior hold up to Kathryn Edin's findings that many so-called welfare-dependent women must also work for wages in order to make ends meet? More importantly, how do we fit criminals (many first-time offenders), welfare recipients, single mothers, absent fathers, alcohol and drug abusers, and gun-toting youth all into one "class"?

When we try to apply the same principles to people with higher incomes, who are presumed to be "functional" and "normative," we ultimately expose the absurdity of it all. Political scientist Charles Henry offers the following description of pathological behavior for the very folks the underclass is supposed to emulate. This tangle of deviant behavior, which he calls the "culture of wealth," is characterized by a "rejection or denial of physical attributes" leading to "hazardous sessions in tanning parlors" and frequent trips to weight-loss salons; rootlessness; antisocial behavior; and "an inability to make practical decisions" evidenced by their tendency to own several homes, frequent private social and dining clubs, and by their vast amount of unnecessary and socially useless possessions. "Finally," Henry adds, "the culture of the rich is engulfed in a web of crime, sexism, and poor health. Drug use and white collar crime are rampant, according to every available index....In sum, this group is engaged in a permanent cycle of divorce, forced child separations through boarding schools, and rampant materialism that leads to the dreaded Monte Carlo syndrome. Before they can be helped they must close tax loopholes, end subsidies, and stop buying influence."

As absurd as Henry's satirical reformulation of the culture of poverty might appear, this very instrumentalist way of understanding culture is deeply rooted even in the more liberal social science approaches to urban poverty. In the mid- to late 1960s, a group of progressive social scientists, mostly ethnographers, challenged the more conservative culture-of-poverty arguments and insisted that black culture was itself a necessary adaptation to racism and poverty, a set of coping mechanisms that grew out of the struggle for material and psychic survival. Ironically, while this work consciously sought to recast ghetto dwellers as active agents rather than passive victims, it has nonetheless reinforced monolithic interpretations of black urban culture and significantly shaped current articulations of the culture concept in social science approaches to poverty.

With the zeal of colonial missionaries, these liberal and often radical ethnographers (mostly white men) set out to explore the newly discovered concrete jungles. Inspired by the politics of the 1960s and mandated by Lyndon Johnson's War on Poverty, a veritable army of anthropologists, sociologists, linguists, and social psychologists set up camp in America's ghettos. In the Harlem and Washington Heights communities where I grew up in the mid- to late 1960s, even our liberal white teachers who were committed to making us into functional members of society turned out to be foot soldiers in the new ethnographic army. With the overnight success of published collections of inner city children's writings like *The Me Nobody Knows* and Caroline Mirthes's *Can't You Hear Me Talking to You?*, writing about the intimate details of our home life seemed like our most important assignment. (And we made the most of it by enriching our mundane narratives with stories from *Mod Squad, Hawaii Five-O*, and *Speed Racer*.)

Of course, I do not believe for a minute that most of our teachers gave us these kinds of exercises hoping to one day appear on the *Merv Griffin Show*. But, in retrospect at least, the explosion of interest in the inner city cannot be easily divorced from the marketplace. Although these social scientists came to mine what they believed was *the* "authentic Negro culture," there was real gold in them thar ghettos since white America's fascination with the pathological urban poor translated into massive book sales.

Unfortunately, most social scientists believed they knew what "authentic Negro culture" was before they entered the field. The "real Negroes" were the young jobless men hanging out on the corner passing the bottle, the brothers with the nastiest verbal repertoire, the pimps and hustlers, and the single mothers who raised streetwise kids who began cursing before they could walk. Of course, there were other characters, like the men and women who went to work every day in foundries, hospitals, nursing homes, private homes, police stations, sanitation departments, banks, garment factories, assembly plants, pawn shops, construction sites, loading docks, storefront churches, telephone companies, grocery and department stores, public transit, restaurants, welfare offices, recreation centers; or the street vendors, the cab drivers, the bus drivers, the ice cream truck drivers, the seamstresses, the numerologists and fortune tellers, the folks who protected or cleaned downtown buildings all night long. These are the kinds of people who lived in my neighborhood in West

Harlem during the early 1970s, but they rarely found their way into the ethnographic text. And when they did show up, social scientists tended to reduce them to typologies—"lames," "strivers," "mainstreamers," "achievers," or "revolutionaries."

Perhaps these urban dwellers were not as interesting, as the hard-core ghetto poor, or more likely, they stood at the margins of a perceived or invented "authentic" Negro society. A noteworthy exception is John Langston Gwaltney's remarkable book, *Drylongso: A Self-Portrait of Black America* (1981). Based on interviews conducted during the 1970s with black working-class residents in several Northeastern cities, *Drylongso* is one of the few works on urban African Americans by an African American anthropologist that appeared during the height of ghetto ethnography. Because Gwaltney is blind, he could not rely on the traditional methods of observation and intereepretation. Instead— and this is the book's strength—he allowed his informants to speak for themselves about what *they* see and do. They interpret their own communities, African American culture, white society, racism, politics and the state, and the very discipline in which Gwaltney was trained—anthropology. What the book reveals is that the natives are aware that anthropologists are constructing them, and they saw in Gwaltney—who relied primarily on family and friends as informants—an opportunity to speak back. One, a woman he calls Elva Noble, said to him: "I'm not trying to tell you your job, but if you ever do write a book about us, then I hope you really do write about things the way they really are. I guess that depends on you to some extent but you know that there are more of us who are going to work every day than there are like the people who are git'n over." While his definition of a "core black culture" may strike some as essentialist, it emphasizes diversity and tolerance for diversity. Gwaltney acknowledges the stylistic uniqueness of African American culture, yet he shows that the central facet of this core culture is the deep-rooted sense of community, common history, and collective recognition that there is indeed an African American culture and a "black" way of doing things. Regardless of the origins of a particular recipe, or the roots of a particular religion or Christian denomination, the cook and the congregation have no problem identifying these distinct practices and institutions as "black."

Few ghetto ethnographers have understood or developed Gwaltney's insights into African American urban culture. Whereas Gwaltney's notion of a core culture incorporates a diverse and contradictory range of practices, attitudes, and relationships that are dynamic, historically situated, and ethnically hybrid, social scientists of his generation and after—especially those at the forefront of poverty studies—treat culture as if it were a set of behaviors. They assume that there is one identifiable ghetto culture, and what they observed was *it*. These assumptions, which continue to shape much current social science and most mass media representations of the "inner city," can be partly attributed to the way ethnographers are trained in the West. As James Clifford observed, anthropologists studying non-Western societies are not only compelled to describe the communities under interrogation as completely foreign to their own society, but if a community is to be worthy of study as a group it must posses an identifiable, homogeneous culture. I think, in principle at least, the same holds true for interpretations of black urban America. Ethnographers can argue that inner city residents, as a "foreign" culture, do not share "mainstream" values. Social scientists do not treat behavior as situational, an individual response to a specific set of circumstances; rather, inner city residents act according to their own unique cultural "norms."

For many of these ethnographers, the defining characteristic of African American urban culture was relations between men and women. Even Charles Keil, whose *Urban Blues* is one of the few ethnographic texts from that period to not only examine aesthetics and form in black culture but take "strong exception to the view that lower-class Negro life style and its characteristic rituals and expressive roles are the products of overcompensation for masculine self-doubt," nonetheless concludes that "the battle of the sexes" is precisely what characterizes African American urban culture. Expressive cultures, then, were not only constructed as adaptive, functioning primarily to cope with the horrible conditions of ghetto life, but were conceived largely as expressions of masculinity. In fact, the linking of men with expressive cultures was so pervasive that the pioneering ethnographies focusing on African American women and girls—notably the work of Joyce Ladner and Carol Stack—do not explore this realm, whether in mixed-gender groupings or all-female groups. They concentrated more on sex roles, relationships, and family survival rather than expressive cultures.

Two illuminating examples are the debate over the concept of "soul" and the verbal art form known to most academics as "the dozens." In the ethnographic imagination, "soul" and "the dozens" were both examples par excellence of authentic black urban culture as well as vehicles for expressing black masculinity. The bias toward expressive male culture must be understood within a particular historical and political context. In the midst of urban rebellions, the masculinist rhetoric of black nationalism, the controversy over the Moynihan report, and the uncritical linking of "agency" and resistance with men, black men took center stage in poverty research.

Soul was so critical to the social science discourse on the adaptive culture of the black urban poor that Lee Rainwater edited an entire book about it, and Ulf Hannerz structured his study of Washington, D.C. on it. According to these authors, *soul* is the expressive lifestyle of black men adapting to economic and political marginality. This one word supposedly embraces the entire range of "Negro lower class culture"; it constitutes "essential Negroness." Only authentic Negroes had soul. In defining *soul*, Hannerz reduces aesthetics, style, and the dynamic struggle over identity to a set of coping mechanisms. Among his many attempts to define *soul*, he insists that it is tied to the instability of black male-female relationships. He deduced evidence for this from his findings that "success with the opposite sex is a focal concern in lower-class Negro life," and the fact that a good deal of popular black music—soul music—was preoccupied with courting or losing a lover.

Being "cool" is an indispensable component of soul; it is also regarded by these ethnographers as a peculiarly black expression of masculinity. Indeed, the entire discussion of cool centers entirely on black men. Cool as an aesthetic, as a style, as an art form expressed through language and the body, is simply not dealt with. Cool, not surprisingly, is merely another mechanism to cope with racism and poverty. According to Lee Rainwater and David Schulz, it is nothing more than a survival technique intended to "make yourself interesting and attractive to others so that you are better able to manipulate their behavior along lines that will provide some immediate gratification." To achieve cool simply entails learning to lie and putting up a front of competence and success. But like a lot of adaptive strategies, cool is self-limiting. While it helps young black males maintain an image of being "in control," according to David Schulz, it can also make "intimate relationships" more difficult to achieve.

Hannerz reluctantly admits that no matter how hard he tried, none of the "authentic ghetto inhabitants" he had come across could define *soul*. He was certain that soul was "essentially Negro," but concluded that it really could not be defined, for to do that would be to undermine its meaning: it is something one possesses, a ticket into the "in crowd." If you need a definition you do not know what it means. It's a black (male) thang; you'll never understand. But Hannerz obviously felt confident enough to venture his own definition, based on his understanding of African American culture, that *soul* was little more than a survival strategy to cope with the harsh realities of the ghetto. Moreover, he felt empowered to determine which black people had the right to claim the mantle of authenticity: when LeRoi Jones and Lerone Bennett offered their interpretation of soul, Hannerz rejected their definitions, in part because they were not, in his words, "authentic Negroes."

By constructing the black urban world as a single culture whose function is merely to survive the ghetto, Rainwater, Hannerz, and most of their colleagues at the time ultimately collapsed a wide range of historically specific cultural practices and forms and searched for a (*the*) concept that could bring them all together. Such an interpretation of culture makes it impossible for Hannerz and others to see soul not as a thing but as a discourse through which African Americans, at a particular historical moment, claimed ownership of the symbols and practices of their own imagined community. This is why, even at the height of the Black Power movement, African American urban culture could be so fluid, hybrid, and multinational. In Harlem in the 1970s, Nehru suits were as popular and as "black" as dashikis, and martial arts films placed Bruce Lee among a pantheon of black heroes that included Walt Frazier and John Shaft. As debates over the black aesthetic raged, the concept of soul was an assertion that there are "black ways" of doing things, even if those ways are contested and the boundaries around what is "black" are fluid. How it manifests itself and how it shifts is less important than the fact that the boundaries exist in the first place. At the very least, *soul* was a euphemism or a creative way of identifying what many believed was a black aesthetic or black style, and it was a synonym for black itself or a way to talk about being black without reference to color, which is why people of other ethnic groups could have soul.

Soul in the 1960s and early 1970s was also about transformation. It was almost never conceived by African Americans as an innate, genetically derived feature of black life, for it represented a shedding of the old "Negro" ways and an embrace of "Black" power and pride. The most visible signifier of soul was undoubtedly the Afro. More than any other element of style, the Afro put the issue of hair squarely on the black political agenda, where it has been ever since. The current debates over hair and its relationship to political consciousness really have their roots in the Afro. Not surprisingly, social scientists at the time viewed the Afro through the limited lens of Black Power politics, urban uprisings, and an overarching discourse of authenticity. And given their almost exclusive interest in young men, their perspective on the Afro was strongly influenced by the rhetoric and iconography of a movement that flouted black masculinity. Yet, once we look beyond the presumably male-occupied ghetto streets that dominated the ethnographic imagination at the time, the story of the Afro's origins and meaning complicates the link to soul culture.

First, the Afro powerfully demonstrates the degree to which soul was deeply implicated in the marketplace. What passed as "authentic" ghetto culture was as much a product of market forces and the commercial appropriation of urban styles as experience and individual creativity. And very few black urban residents/consumers viewed their own participation in the marketplace as undermining their own authenticity as bearers of black culture. Even before the Afro reached its height of popularity, the hair care industry stepped in and began producing a vast array of chemicals to make one's "natural" more natural. One could pick up Raveen Hair Sheen, Afro Sheen, Ultra Sheen, Head Start vitamin and mineral capsules, to name a few. The Clairol Corporation (whose CEO supported the Philadelphia Black Power Conference in 1967) did not hesitate to enter the "natural" business. Listen to this Clairol ad published in *Essence Magazine* (November 1970):

> No matter what they say...Nature Can't Do It Alone! Nothing pretties up a face like a beautiful head of hair, but even hair that's born this beautiful needs a little help along the way....A little brightening, a little heightening of color, a little extra sheen to liven up the look. And because that wonderful natural look is still the most wanted look...the most fashionable, the most satisfying look you can have at any age...anything you do must look natural, natural, natural. And this indeed is the art of Miss Clairol.

Depending on the particular style, the Afro could require almost as much maintenance as chemically straightened hair. And for those women (and some men) whose hair simply would not cooperate or who wanted the flexibility to shift from straight to nappy, there was always the Afro wig. For nine or ten dollars, one could purchase a variety of different wig styles, ranging from the "Soul-Light Freedom" wigs to the "Honey Bee Afro Shag," made from cleverly labeled synthetic materials such as "Afrylic" or "Afrilon."

Secondly, the Afro's roots really go back to the bourgeois high fashion circles in the late 1950s. The Afro was seen by the black and white elite as a kind of new female exotica. Even though its intention, among some circles at least, was to achieve healthier hair and express solidarity with newly independent African nations, the Afro entered public consciousness as a mod fashion statement that was not only palatable to bourgeois whites but, in some circles, celebrated. There were people like Lois Liberty Jones, a consultant, beauty culturist, and lecturer, who claimed to have pioneered the natural as early as 1952! She originated "Coiffures Aframericana" concepts of hair styling which she practiced in Harlem for several years from the early 1960s. More importantly, it was the early, not the late, 1960s, when performers like Odetta, Miriam Makeba, Abby Lincoln, Nina Simone, and the artist Margaret Burroughs began wearing the "au naturelle" style—medium to short Afros. Writer Andrea Benton Rushing has vivid memories of seeing Odetta at the Village Gate long before Black Power entered the national lexicon. "I was mesmerized by her stunning frame," she recalled, "in its short kinky halo. She had a regal poise and power that I had never seen in a 'Negro' (as we called ourselves back then) woman before—no matter how naturally 'good' or diligently straightened her hair was." Many other black women in New York, particularly those who ran in the interracial world of Manhattan sophisticates, were first introduced to the natural through high fashion models in au naturelle shows, which were the rage at the time.

Helen Hayes King, associate editor of *Jet*, came in contact with the au naturelle style at an art show in New York, in the late 1950s. A couple of years later, she heard Abby Lincoln speak about her own decision to go natural at one of these shows and, with prompting from her husband, decided to go forth to adopt the 'fro. Ironically, one of the few salons in Chicago specializing in the au naturelle look was run by a white male hairdresser in the exclusive Northside community. He actually lectured King on the virtues of natural hair: "I don't know why Negro women with delicate hair like yours burn and process all the life out of it. . . . If you'd just wash it, oil it and take care of it, it would be so much healthier. . . . I don't know how all this straightening foolishness started anyhow." When she returned home to the Southside, however, instead of compliments she received strange looks from her neighbors. Despite criticism and ridicule by her co-workers and friends, she stuck with her au naturelle, not because she was trying to make a political statement or demonstrate her solidarity with African independence movements. "I'm not so involved in the neo-African aspects of the 'au naturelle' look," she wrote, "nor in the get-back-to-your-heritage bit." Her explanation was simple: the style was chic and elegant and in the end she was pleased with the feel of her hair. It is fitting to note that most of the compliments came from whites.

What is also interesting about King's narrative is that it appeared in the context of a debate with Nigerian writer Theresa Ogunbiyi over whether black women should straighten their hair or not, which appeared in a 1963 issue of

Negro Digest. In particular, Ogunbiyi defended the right of a Lagos firm to forbid employees to plait their hair; women were required to wear straight hair. She rejected the idea that straightening hair destroys national custom and heritage: "I think we carry this national pride a bit too far at times, even to the detriment of our country's progress." Her point was that breaking with tradition *is* progress, especially since Western dress and hairstyles are more comfortable and easier to work in. "When I wear the Yoruba costume, I find that I spend more time than I can afford, re-tying the headtie and the bulky wrapper round my waist. And have you tried typing in an 'Agbada'? I am all for nationalisation but give it to me with some comfort and improvement."

Andrea Benton Rushing's story is a slight variation on King's experience. She, too, was a premature natural hair advocate. When she stepped out of the house sporting her first Afro, perhaps inspired by Odetta or prompted by plain curiosity, her "relatives thought I'd lost my mind and, of course, my teachers at Juilliard stole sideways looks at me and talked about the importance of appearance in auditions and concerts." Yet, while the white Juilliard faculty and her closest family members found the new style strange and inappropriate, brothers on the block in her New York City neighborhood greeted her with praise: " 'Looking good, sister,' 'Watch out, African queen!' " She, too, found it ironic that middle-class African woman on the continent chose to straighten their hair. During a trip to Ghana years later, she recalled the irony of having her Afro braided in an Accra beauty parlor while "three Ghanaians (two Akan-speaking government workers and one Ewe microbiologist)...were having their chemically-straightened hair washed, set, combed out, and sprayed in place."

No matter what spurred on the style or who adopted it, however, the political implications of the au naturelle could not be avoided. After all, the biggest early proponents of the style tended to be women artists whose work identified with the black freedom movement and African liberation. In some respects, women such as Abby Lincoln, Odetta, and Nina Simone were part of what might be called black bohemia. They participated in a larger community—based mostly in New York—of poets, writers, musicians of the 1950s, for whom the emancipation of their own artistic form coincided with the African freedom movement. *Ebony, Jet*, and *Sepia* magazines were covering Africa, and African publications such as *Drum* were being read by those ex-Negroes in the States who could get their hands on it. The Civil Rights movement, the struggle against apartheid in South Africa, and the emergence of newly independent African nations found a voice in recordings by various jazz artists, including Randy Weston's *Uhuru Afrika*, Max Roach's *We Insist: Freedom Now Suite* (featuring Abby Lincoln, Roach's wife), Art Blakey's "Message from Kenya" and "Ritual," and John Coltrane's "Liberia," "Dahomey Dance," and "Africa." Revolutionary political movements, combined with revolutionary experiments in artistic creation—the simultaneous embrace and rejection of tradition—forged the strongest physical and imaginary links between Africa and the diaspora.

Thus, it is not surprising that Harold Cruse, in one of his seminal essays on the coming of the new black nationalism, anticipated the importance of the style revolution and the place of the au naturelle in it. As early as 1962, Cruse predicted that in the coming years "Afro-Americans...will undoubtedly make a lot of noise in militant demonstrations, cultivate beards and sport their hair in various degrees of la mode au naturel, and tend to be cultish with African- and Arab-style dress."

Of course, he was right. By the mid-1960s, however, the Afro was no longer associated with downtown chic but with uptown rebellion. It was sported by rock-throwing black males and black-leathered militants armed to the teeth. Thus, once associated with feminine chic, the Afro suddenly became the symbol of black manhood, the death of the "Negro" and birth of the militant, virulent Black man. The new politics, combined with media representations of Afro-coifed black militants, profoundly shaped the ethnographic imagination. As new narratives were created to explain the symbolic significance of the natural style, women were rendered invisible. The erasure of women, I would argue, was not limited to histories of style politics but to ghetto ethnography in general.

The masculinism of soul in contemporary ghetto ethnography has survived to this day, despite the last quarter-century of incisive black feminist scholarship. The ethnographic and sociological search for soul has made a comeback recently under a new name: the "cool pose." In a recent book, Richard Majors and Janet Mancini Bilson have recycled the arguments of Lee Rainwater, Ulf Hannerz, Elliot Liebow, and David Schulz, and have suggested that the "cool pose" captures the essence of young black male expressive culture. Like earlier constructors of soul, they too believe that the "cool pose" is an adaptive strategy to cope with the particular forms of racism and oppression black males face in America. "Cool pose is a ritualized form of masculinity that entails behaviors, scripts, physical posturing, impression management, and carefully crafted performances that deliver a single, critical message: pride, strength, and control." Echoing earlier works, the cool pose is also a double-edged sword since it allegedly undermines potential intimacy with females. By playing down the aesthetics of cool and reducing the cool pose to a response by heterosexual black males to racism, intraracial violence, and poverty, the authors not only reinforce the idea that there is an essential black urban culture created by the oppressive conditions of the ghetto but ignore manifestations of the cool pose in the public "performances" of black women, gay black men, and the African American middle class.

A more tangible example of black urban expressive culture that seemed to captivate social scientists in the 1960s is "the dozens." Yet, in spite of the amount of ink devoted to the subject, it has also been perhaps the most misinterpreted cultural form coming out of African American communities. Called at various times in various places "capping," "sounding," "ranking," "bagging," or "dissing," virtually all leading anthropologists, sociologists, and linguists agree that it is a black male form of "ritual insult," a verbal contest involving any number of young black men who compete by talking about each other's mama. There is less agreement, however, about how to interpret the sociological and psychological significance of the dozens. In keeping with the dominant social science interpretations of the culture concept, so-called ritual insults among urban black youth were either another adaptive strategy or an example of social pathology.

The amazing thing about the sociological and ethnographic scholarship on the dozens, from John Dollard's ruminations in 1939 to the more recent misreadings by Roger Lane and Carl Nightingale, is the consistency with which it repeats the same errors. For one, the almost universal assertion that the dozens is a "ritual" empowers the ethnographer to select what appears to be more formalized verbal exchanges (e.g., rhyming couplets) and ascribe to them greater "authenticity" than other forms of playful conversation. In fact, by framing the dozens as ritual, most scholars have come to believe that it is first and foremost a "contest" with rules, players, and mental scorecards rather than the daily banter of many (not all) young African Americans. Anyone who has lived and survived the dozens (or whatever name you want to call it) cannot imagine turning to one's friends and announcing, "Hey, let's go outside and play the dozens." Furthermore, the very use of the term *ritual* to describe everyday speech reinforces the exoticization of black urban populations, constructing them as Others whose investment in this cultural tradition is much deeper than trying to get a laugh.

These problems, however, are tied to larger ones. For example, white ethnographers seemed oblivious to the fact that their very presence shaped what they observed. Asking their subjects to "play the dozens" while an interloper records the "session" with a tape recorder and notepad has the effect of creating a ritual performance for the sake of an audience, of turning spontaneous, improvised verbal exchanges into a formal practice. More significantly, ethnographers have tailor-made their own interpretation of the dozens by selecting what they believe were the most authentic sites for such verbal duels— street corners, pool halls, bars, and parks. In other words, they sought out male spaces rather than predominantly female and mixed-gender spaces to record the dozens. It is no wonder that practically all commentators on the dozens have concluded that it is a boy thing. The fact is, evidence suggests that young women engaged in these kinds of verbal exchanges as much as their male counterparts, both with men and between women. And they were no less profane. By not searching out other mixed-gender and female spaces such as school buses, cafeterias, kitchen tables, beauty salons, and house parties, ethnographers have overstated the extent to which the dozens were the sole property of men.

Folklorist Roger Abrahams, who pioneered the study of the dozens in his book on black vernacular folklore "from the streets of Philadelphia," is one of the few scholars to appreciate the pleasure and aesthetics of such verbal play. Nevertheless, he argues that one of the primary functions of the dozens is to compensate for a lack of masculinity caused by too many absent fathers and domineering mothers, which is why the main target of insults is an "opponent's" mother. "By exhibiting his wit, by creating new and vital folkloric expression, [the dozens player] is able to effect a temporary release from anxiety for both himself and his audience. By creating playgrounds for playing out aggressions, he achieves a kind of masculine identity for himself and his group in a basically hostile environment." David Schulz offers an even more specific interpretation of the dozens as a form of masculine expression in an environment dominated by dysfunctional families. He writes: "Playing the dozens occurs at the point when the boy is about to enter puberty and suffer his greatest rejection from his mother as a result of his becoming a man. The dozens enables him to develop a defense against this rejection and provides a vehicle for his transition into the manipulative world of the street dominated by masculine values expressed in gang life." It then serves as a "ritualized exorcism" that allows men to break from maternal dominance and "establish their own image of male superiority celebrated in street life."

Allow me to propose an alternative reading of the dozens. The goal of the dozens and related verbal games is deceptively simple: to get a laugh. The pleasure of the dozens is not the viciousness of the insult but the humor, the creative pun, the outrageous metaphor. Contrary to popular belief, mothers are not the sole target; the subjects include fathers, grandparents, brothers, sisters, cousins, friends, food, skin color, smell, and hairstyles. I am not suggesting that "your mama" is unimportant in the whole structure of these verbal exchanges. Nor am I suggesting that the emphasis on "your mama" has absolutely nothing to do with the ways in which patriarchy is discursively reproduced. However, we need to understand that "your mama" in this context is almost never living, literal, or even metaphoric. "Your mama" is a generic reference, a code signaling that the dozens have begun—it signifies a shift in speech. "Your mama" is also a mutable, nameless body of a shared imagination that can be constructed and reconstructed in a thousand different shapes, sizes, colors, and circumstances. The emphasis on "your mama" in most interpretations of the dozens has more to do with the peculiar preoccupation of social science with Negro family structure than anything else. Besides, in many cases the target is immaterial; your mama, your daddy, your greasy-headed granny are merely vehicles through which the speaker tries to elicit a laugh and display her skills. In retrospect, this seems obvious, but amid the complicated readings of masculine overcompensation and ritual performance, only a handful of writers of the period—most of whom were African Americans with no affiliation with the academy—recognized the centrality of humor. One was Howard Seals, who self-published a pamphlet on the dozens in 1969 titled *You Ain't Thuh Man Yuh Mamma Wuz*. In an effort to put to rest all the sociological overinterpretation, Seals explains: "The emotional tone to be maintained is that of hilariously, outrageously funny bantering." Compare Seals's comment with linguist William Labov, who, while recognizing the humor, ultimately turns laughter into part of the ritual and thus reinforces the process of Othering:

The primary mark of positive evaluation is laughter. We can rate the effectiveness of a sound in a group session by the number of members of the audience who laugh.

A really successful sound will be evaluated by overt comments...the most common forms are: "Oh!," "Oh shit!" "God damn!," or "Oh lord!" By far the most common is "Oh shit!" The intonation is important: when approval is to be signalled the vowel of each word is quite long, with a high sustained initial pitch, and a slow-falling pitch contour.

Without a concept of, or even an interest in, aesthetics, style, and the visceral pleasures of cultural forms, it should not be surprising that most social scientists explained black urban culture in terms of coping mechanisms, rituals, or oppositional responses to racism. And trapped by an essentialist interpretation of culture, they continue to look for that elusive "authentic" ghetto sensibility, the true, honest, unbridled, pure cultural practices that capture the raw, ruffneck "reality" of urban life. Today, that reality is rap. While studies of rap and Hip Hop culture have been useful in terms of nudging contemporary poverty studies to pay attention to expressive cultures, they have not done much to advance the culture concept in social science. Like its progenitor, the dozens, rap or Hip Hop has been subject to incredible misconception and overinterpretation. Despite the brilliant writing of cultural critics like Tricia Rose, Greg Tate, George Lipsitz, Brian Cross, James Spady, dream hampton, Seth Fernando, Jonathan Scott, Juan Flores, Toure, and others, a number of scholars have returned to or revised the interpretive frameworks developed by the previous generation of ethnographers.

For example, in a very recent book on poor black youth in post-war Philadelphia, Carl Nightingale suggests that the presumed loss of oral traditions like toasting (long, often profane vernacular narrative poetry performed orally) and the dozens, and the rise of rap music and similar commercialized expressive cultures partly explains the increase in violence among young black males. The former, he argues, has played a positive role in curbing violence while the latter is responsible for heightening aggression. He thus calls on young black men to return to these earlier, presumably precommercial cultural forms to vent emotions. Nightingale advocates resurrecting the ring shout, drumming, singing the blues, even toasting, to express black male pain and vulnerability.

The suggestion that rap music has undermined black cultural integrity is made even more forcefully in a recent article by Andre Craddock-Willis. He criticizes nearly all rap artists—especially hard-core gangsta rappers—for not knowing the "majesty" of the blues. The Left, he insists, "must work to gently push these artists to understand the tradition whose shoulders they stand on, and encourage them to comprehend struggle, sacrifice, vision and dedication— the cornerstones for the Black musical tradition." (A tradition, by the way, that includes the great Jelly Roll Morton, whose 1938 recording of "Make Me a Pallet on the Floor" included lines like: "Come here you sweet bitch, give me that pussy, let me get in your drawers/I'm gonna make you think you fuckin' with Santa Claus.")

On the flip side are authors who insist that rap music is fundamentally the authentic, unmediated voice of ghetto youth. Tommy Lott's recent essay, "Marooned in America: Black Urban Youth Culture and Social Pathology," offers a powerful critique of neoconservative culture-of-poverty theories and challenges assumptions that the culture of the so-called underclass is pathological, but he nevertheless reduces expressive culture to a coping strategy to deal with the terror of street life. For Lott, the Hip Hop nation is the true voice of the black lumpenproletariat whose descriptions of street life are the real thing. "As inhabitants of extreme-poverty neighborhoods," he writes, "many rap artists and their audiences are entrenched in a street life filled with crime, drugs, and violence. Being criminal-minded and having street values are much more suitable for living in their environment." Of course, most rap music is not about a nihilistic street life but about rocking the mike, and the vast majority of rap artists (like most inner city youth) were not entrenched in the tangled web of crime and violence. Yet, he is convinced that Hip Hop narratives of ghetto life "can only come from one's experiences on the streets. Although, at its worst, this knowledge is manifested through egotistical sexual boasting, the core meaning of the rapper's use of the term 'knowledge' is to be *politically* astute, that is, to have a full understanding of the conditions under which black urban youth must survive."

By not acknowledging the deep visceral pleasures black youth derive from making and consuming culture, the stylistic and aesthetic conventions that render the form and performance more attractive than the message, these authors reduce expressive culture to a political text to be read like a less sophisticated version of *The Nation* or *Radical America*. But what counts more than the story is the "storytelling"—an emcee's verbal facility on the mic, the creative and often hilarious use of puns, metaphors, similes, not to mention the ability to kick some serious slang (or what we might call linguistic inventiveness). As microphone fiend Rakim might put it, the function of Hip Hop is to "move the crowd." For all the implicit and explicit politics of rap lyrics, Hip Hop must be understood as a sonic force more than anything else.

Despite their good intentions, ignoring aesthetics enables these authors not only to dismiss "egotistical sexual boasting" as simply a weakness in political ideology but also to mistakenly interpret narratives of everyday life as descriptions of personal experience rather than a revision of older traditions of black vernacular poetry and/or appropriations from mainstream popular culture. To begin with rap music as a mirror image of daily life ignores the influences of urban toasts and published "pimp narratives," which became popular during the late 1960s and early 1970s. In many instances the characters are almost identical, and on occasion rap artists pay tribute to toasting by lyrically "sampling" these early pimp narratives.

Moreover, the assumption that rappers are merely street journalists does not allow for the playfulness and storytelling that is so central to Hip Hop specifically, and black vernacular culture generally. For example, violent lyrics in rap music are rarely meant to be literal. Rather, they are more often than not metaphors to challenge competitors on the microphone. The mic becomes a Tech-9 or AK-47, imagined drive-bys occur from the stage, flowing lyrics become hollow-point shells. Classic examples are Ice Cube's "Jackin' for Beats," a humorous song that describes sampling other artists and producers as outright armed robbery, and Ice T's "Pulse of the Rhyme" or "Grand Larceny" (which brags about stealing a show). Moreover, exaggerated and invented boasts of criminal acts should sometimes be regarded as part of a larger set of signifying practices. Growing out of a much older set of cultural practices, these masculinist narratives are essentially verbal duels over who is the "baddest." They are not meant as literal descriptions of violence and aggression, but connote the playful use of language itself.

Of course, the line between rap music's gritty realism, storytelling, and straight-up signifyin(g) is not always clear to listeners, nor is it supposed to be. Hip Hop, particularly gangsta rap, also attracts listeners for whom the "ghetto" is a place of adventure, unbridled violence, erotic fantasy, and/or an imaginary alternative to suburban boredom. White music critic John Leland, who claimed that Ice Cube's turn toward social criticism "killed rap music," praised the group NWA because they "dealt in evil as fantasy: killing cops, smoking hos, filling quiet nights with a flurry of senseless buckshot." This kind of voyeurism partly explains NWA's huge white following and why their album *Efil4zaggin* shot to the top of the charts as soon as it was released. As one critic put it, "In reality, NWA have more in common with a Charles Bronson movie than a PBS documentary on the plight of the inner-cities." NWA members have even admitted that some of their recent songs were not representations of reality "in the hood" but inspired by popular films like *Innocent Man* starring Tom Selleck, and *Tango and Cash.*

Claims to have located the authentic voice of black ghetto youth are certainly not unique. Several scholars insist that Hip Hop is the pure, unadulterated voice of a ghetto that has grown increasingly isolated from "mainstream" society. Missing from this formulation is rap music's incredible hybridity. From the outset, rap music embraced a variety of styles and cultural forms, from reggae and salsa to heavy metal and jazz. Hip Hop's hybridity reflected, in part, the increasingly international character of America's inner cities resulting from immigration, demographic change, and new forms of information, as well as the inventive employment of technology in creating rap music. By using two turntables, and later digital samplers, deejays played different records, isolated the "break beats" or what they identified as the funkiest part of a song, and boldly mixed a wide range of different music and musical genres to create new music. And despite the fact that many of the pioneering deejays, rappers, and break dancers were African American, West Indian, and Puerto Rican and strongly identified with the African diaspora, rap artists wrecked all the boundaries between "black" and "white" music. Deejay Afrika Islam remembers vividly the time when Hip Hop and punk united for a moment and got busy at the New Wave clubs in New York during the early 1980s. Even before the punk rockers sought a relationship with uptown Hip Hop deejays, Afrika Islam recalls, in the Bronx they were already playing "everything from Aerosmith's 'Walk This Way' to Dunk and the Blazers." Grand Master Caz, whose lyrics were stolen by the Sugarhill Gang and ended up in *Rapper's Delight* (the first successful rap record in history), grew up in the Bronx listening to soft rock and mainstream pop music. As he explained in an interview, "Yo, I'd bug you out if I told you who I used to listen to. I used to listen to Barry Manilow, Neil Diamond, and Simon and Garfunkel. I grew up listening to that. WABC. That's why a lot of the stuff that my group did, a lot of routines that we're famous for all come from all white boy songs."

If you saw a picture of Caz, this statement would seem incongruous. He looks the part of an authentic black male, a real ruffneck, hoodie, "G," nigga, criminal, menace. And yet, he is a product of a hybrid existence, willing to openly talk about Simon and Garfunkel in a book that I could only purchase from a Nation of Islam booth on 125th Street in Harlem. He is also the first to call what he does "black music," structured noise for which the beat, no matter where it is taken from, is everything. Moreover, like the breakers who danced to his rhymes, the kids who built his speakers, the deejay who spun the records, Caz takes credit for his creativity, his artistry, his "work." This is the "black urban culture" which has remained so elusive to social science; it is the thing, or rather the process, that defies concepts like "coping strategy," "adaptative," "authentic," "nihilistic," and "pathological."

Revising the Culture Concept: Hybridity, Style, and Aesthetics in Black Urban Culture

Aside from the tendency to ignore expressive/popular cultural forms, and limit the category of culture to (so-called dysfunctional) behavior, the biggest problem with the way social scientists employ the culture concept in their studies of the black urban poor is their inability to see what it all means *to the participants and practitioners*. In other words, they do not consider what Clinton (George, that is) calls the "pleasure principle." If I may use a metaphor here, rather than hear the singer they analyze the lyrics; rather than hear the drum they study the song title. Black music, creativity and experimentation in language, that walk, that talk, that style, must also be understood as sources of visceral and psychic pleasure. Though they may also reflect and speak to the political and social world of inner city communities, expressive cultures are not simply mirrors of social life or expressions of conflicts, pathos, and anxieties.

Paul Willis's concept of "symbolic creativity" provides one way out of the impasse created by such a limited concept of culture. As Willis argues, constructing an identity, communicating with others, and achieving pleasure are all part of symbolic creativity—it is literally the labor of creating art in everyday life. Despite his distrust of and vehement opposition to "aesthetics," he realizes that, in most cases, the explicit meaning or intention of a particular cultural form is not the thing that makes it attractive. The appeal of popular music, for example, is more than lyrical: "Songs bear meaning and allow symbolic work not just as speech acts, but also as structures of sound with unique rhythms, textures and forms. Thus, it is not always what is sung, but the *way* it is sung, within particular conventions or musical genres which gives a piece of music its communicative power and meaning." Indeed, words like *soul* and *funk* were efforts to come up with a language to talk about that visceral element in music, even if they did ultimately evolve into market categories. Over two decades ago, black novelist Cecil Brown brilliantly captured this "thing," this symbolic creativity, the pleasure principle, soul, or whatever you want to call it. Writing about the godfather of soul, James Brown, he argued that his lyrics are less important than how they are uttered, where they are placed rhythmically, and "how he makes it sound." "What, for instance, does 'Mother Popcorn' mean? But what difference does it make when you're dancing to it, when you are feeling it, when you are it and it you (possession). It's nothing and everything at once; it is what black (hoodoo) people who never studied art in school mean by art."

Yet to say it is a "black" thing doesn't mean it is made up entirely of black things. As Greg Tate makes clear in his recent collection of essays, *Flyboy in the Buttermilk*, and in the epigraph to this chapter, interpreters of the African American experience—in our case social scientists—must bear a large share of the responsibility for turning ghetto residents into an undifferentiated mass. We can no longer ignore the fact that information technology, new forms of mass communication, and immigration have made the rest of the world more accessible to inner city residents than ever before. Contemporary black urban culture is a hybrid that draws on Afrodiasporic traditions, popular culture, the vernacular of previous generations of Southern and Northern black folk, new and old technologies, and a whole lot of imagination. Once again, James Clifford's ruminations on the "predicament of culture" are useful for exposing the predicament of social science. He writes: "To tell...local histories of cultural survival and emergence, we need to resist deep-seated habits of mind and systems of authenticity. We need to be suspicious of an almost-automatic tendency to relegate non-Western (read: black) peoples and objects to the pasts of an increasingly homogeneous humanity."

Angela Y. Davis
Race and Criminalization

BLACK AMERICANS AND THE PUNISHMENT INDUSTRY

In this post–civil rights era, as racial barriers in high economic and political realms are apparently shattered with predictable regularity, race itself becomes an increasingly proscribed subject. In the dominant political discourse it is no longer acknowledged as a pervasive structural phenomenon, requiring the continuation of such strategies as affirmative action, but rather is represented primarily as a complex of prejudicial attitudes, which carry equal weight across all racial boundaries. Black leadership is thus often discredited and the identification of race as a public, political issue itself called into question through the invocation of, and application of the epithet "black racist" to, such figures as Louis Farrakhan and Khalid Abdul Muhammad. Public debates about the role of the state that once focused very sharply and openly on issues of "race" and racism are now expected to unfold in the absence of any direct acknowledgment of the persistence—and indeed further entrenchment—of racially structured power relationships. Because race is ostracized from some of the most impassioned political debates of this period, their racialized character becomes increasingly difficult to identify, especially by those who are unable—or do not want—to decipher the encoded language. This means that hidden racist arguments can be mobilized readily across racial boundaries and political alignments. Political positions once easily defined as conservative, liberal, and sometimes even radical therefore have a tendency to lose their distinctiveness in the face of the seductions of this camouflaged racism.

President Clinton chose the date of the Million Man March, convened by Minister Louis Farrakhan of the Nation of Islam, to issue a call for a "national conversation on race," borrowing ironically the exact words of Lani Guinier (whose nomination for assistant attorney general in charge of civil rights he had previously withdrawn because her writings focused too sharply on issues of race).[1] Guinier's ideas had been so easily dismissed because of the prevailing ideological equation of the "end of racism" with the removal of all allusions to race. If conservative positions argue that race consciousness itself impedes the process of solving the problem of race—i.e., achieving race blindness—then Clinton's speech indicated an attempt to reconcile the two, positing race consciousness as a means of moving toward race blindness. "There are too many today, white and black, on the left and the right, on the street corners and radio waves, who seek to sow division for their own purposes. To them I say: 'No more. We must be one.' "

While Clinton did acknowledge "the awful history and stubborn persistence of racism," his remarks foregrounded those reasons for the "racial divide" that "are rooted in the fact that we still haven't learned to talk frankly, to listen carefully and to work together across racial lines." Race, he insisted, is not about government, but about the hearts of people. Of course, it would be absurd to deny the degree to which racism infects in deep and multiple ways the national psyche. However, the relegation of race to matters of the heart tends to render it increasingly difficult to identify the deep structural entrenchment of contemporary racism.

When the structural character of racism is ignored in discussions about crime and the rising population of incarcerated people, the racial imbalance in jails and prisons is treated as a contingency, at best as a product of the "culture of poverty," and at worst as proof of an assumed black monopoly on criminality. The high proportion of black people in the criminal justice system is thus normalized and neither the state nor the general public is required to talk about and act on the meaning of that racial imbalance. Thus Republican and Democratic elected officials alike have successfully called for laws mandating life sentences for three-time "criminals," without having to answer for the racial implications of these laws. By relying on the alleged "race-blindness" of such laws, black people are surreptitiously constructed as racial subjects, thus manipulated, exploited, and abused, while the structural persistence of racism—albeit in changed forms—in social and economic institutions, and in the national culture as a whole, is adamantly denied.

Crime is thus one of the masquerades behind which "race," with all its menacing ideological complexity, mobilizes old public fears *and* creates new ones. The current anticrime debate takes place within a reified mathematical realm—a strategy reminiscent of Malthus's notion of the geometrical increase in population and the arithmetical increase in food sources, thus the inevitability of poverty and the means of suppressing it: war, disease, famine, and natural disasters. As a matter of fact, the persisting neo-Malthusian approach to population control, which, instead of seeking to solve those pressing social problems that result in real pain and suffering in people's lives, calls for the elimination of those suffering lives—finds strong resonances in the public discussion about expurgating the "nation" of crime. These discussions include arguments deployed by those who are leading the call for more prisons and employ statistics in the same fetishistic and misleading way as Malthus did more than two centuries ago. Take for example James Wooten's comments in the *Heritage Foundation State Backgrounder*:

> If the 55% of the estimated 800,000 current state and federal prisoners who are violent offenders were subject to serving 85% of their sentence, and assuming that those violent offenders would have committed 10 violent crimes a year while on the street, then the number of crimes prevented each year by truth in sentencing

would be 4,000,000. That would be over 2/3 of the 6,000,000 violent crimes reported.[2]

In *Reader's Digest*, Senior Editor Eugene H. Methvin writes:

> If we again double the present federal and state prison population—to somewhere between 1 million and 1.5 million and leave our city and county jail population at the present 400,000, we will break the back of America's 30 year crime wave.[3]

The real human beings—a vastly disproportionate number of whom are black and Latino/a men and women—designated by these numbers in a seemingly race-neutral way are deemed fetishistically exchangeable with the crimes they have or will allegedly commit. The real impact of imprisonment on their lives never need be examined. The inevitable part played by the punishment industry in the reproduction of crime never need be discussed. The dangerous and indeed fascistic trend toward progressively greater numbers of hidden, incarcerated human populations is itself rendered invisible. All that matters is the elimination of crime—and you get rid of crime by getting rid of people who, according to the prevailing racial common sense, are the most likely people to whom criminal acts will be attributed. Never mind that if this strategy is seriously and consistently pursued, the majority of young black men and a fast-growing proportion of young black women will spend a good portion of their lives behind walls and bars in order to serve as a reminder that the state is aggressively confronting its enemy.[4]

While I do not want to locate a response to these arguments on the same level of mathematical abstraction and fetishism I have been problematizing, it is helpful, I think, to consider how many people are presently incarcerated or whose lives are subject to the direct surveillance of the criminal justice system. There are already approximately 1 million people in state and federal prisons in the United States, not counting the 500,000 in city and county jails or the 600,000 on parole or the 3 million people on probation or the 60,000 young people in juvenile facilities. Which is to say that there are presently over 5.1 million people either incarcerated, on parole, or on probation. Many of those presently on probation or parole would be behind bars under the conditions of the recently passed crime bill. According to the Sentencing Project, even before the passage of the crime bill, black people were 7.8 times more likely to be imprisoned than whites.[5] The Sentencing Project's most recent report[6] indicates that 32.2 percent of young black men and 12.3 percent of young Latino men between the ages of twenty and twenty-nine are either in prison, in jail, or on probation or parole. This is in comparison with 6.7 percent of young white men. A total of 827,440 young African-American males are under the supervision of the criminal justice system, at a cost of $6 billion per year. A major strength of the 1995 report, as compared to its predecessor, is its acknowledgment that the racialized impact of the criminal justice system is also gendered and that the relatively smaller number of African-American women drawn into the system should not relieve us of the responsibility of understanding the encounter of gender and race in arrest and incarceration practices. Moreover, the increases in women's contact with the criminal justice system have been even more dramatic that those of men.

> The 78% increase in criminal justice control rates for black women was more than double the increase for black men and for white women, and more than nine times the increase for white men.... Although research on women of color in the criminal justice system is limited, existing data and research suggest that it is the combination of race and sex effects that is at the root of the trends which appear in our data. For example, while the number of blacks and Hispanics in prison is growing at an alarming rate, the rate of increase for women is even greater. Between 1980 and 1992 the female prison population increased 276%, compared to 163% for men. Unlike men of color, women of color thus belong to two groups that are experiencing particular dramatic growth in their contact with the criminal justice system.[7]

It has been estimated that by the year 2000 the number of people imprisoned will surpass 4 million, a grossly disproportionate number of whom will be black people, and that the cost will be over $40 billion a year,[8] a figure that is reminiscent of the way the military budget devoured—and continues to devour—the country's resources. This out-of-control punishment industry is an extremely effective criminalization industry, for the racial imbalance in incarcerated populations is not recognized as evidence of structural racism, but rather is invoked as a consequence of the assumed criminality of black people. In other words, the criminalization process works so well precisely because of the hidden logic of racism. Racist logic is deeply entrenched in the nation's material and psychic structures. It is something with which we all are very familiar. The logic, in fact, can persist, even when direct allusions to "race" are removed.

Even those communities that are most deeply injured by this racist logic have learned how to rely upon it, particularly when open allusions to race are not necessary. Thus, in the absence of broad, radical grassroots movements in poor black communities so devastated by new forms of youth-perpetrated violence, the ideological options are extremely sparse. Often there are no other ways to express collective rage and despair but to demand that police sweep the community clean of crack and Uzis, and of the people who use and sell drugs and wield weapons. Ironically, Carol Moseley-Braun, the first black woman senator in our nation's history, was an enthusiastic sponsor of the Senate Anti-crime Bill, whose passage in November 1993 paved the way for the August 25, 1994, passage of the bill by the House. Or perhaps there is little irony here. It may be precisely because there is a Carol Moseley-Braun in the Senate and a Clarence Thomas in the Supreme Court—and concomitant class differentiations and other factors responsible for far more heterogeneity in black communities than at any other time in this country's history—that implicit consent to antiblack racist logic (not to speak of racism toward other groups) becomes far more widespread among black people. Wahneema Lubiano's explorations of the complexities of state domination as it operates within and through the subjectivities of those who are the targets of this domination facilitates an understanding of this dilemma.[9]

Borrowing the title of Cornel West's recent work, race *matters*. Moreover, it matters in ways that are far more threatening and simultaneously less discernible than those to which we have grown accustomed. Race matters inform, more than ever, the ideological and material structures of U.S. society. And, as the current discourses on crime, welfare, and immigration reveal, race, gender, and class matter enormously in the continuing elaboration of public policy and its impact on the real lives of human beings.

And how does race matter? Fear has always been an integral component of racism. The ideological reproduction of a fear of black people, whether economically or sexually grounded, is rapidly gravitating toward and being grounded in a fear of crime. A question to be raised in this context is whether and how the increasing fear of crime—this ideologically produced fear of crime—serves to render racism simultaneously more invisible and more virulent. Perhaps one way to approach an answer to this question is to consider how this fear of crime effectively summons black people to imagine black people as the enemy. How many black people present at this conference have successfully extricated ourselves from the ideological power of the figure of the young black male as criminal—or at least seriously confronted it? The lack of a significant black presence in the rather feeble opposition to the "three strikes, you're out" bills, which have been proposed and/or passed in forty states already, evidences the disarming effect of this ideology.

California is one of the states that has passed the "three strikes, you're out" bill. Immediately after the passage of that bill, Governor Pete Wilson began to argue for a "two strikes, you're out" bill. Three, he said, is too many. Soon we will hear calls for "one strike, you're out." Following this mathematical regression, we can imagine that at some point the hard-core anticrime advocates will be arguing that to stop the crime wave, we can't wait until even one crime is committed. Their slogan will be: "Get them before the first strike!" And because certain populations have already been criminalized, there will be those who say, "We know who the real criminals are—let's get them before they have a chance to act out their criminality."

The fear of crime has attained a status that bears a sinister similarity to the fear of communism as it came to restructure social perceptions during the fifties and sixties. The figure of the "criminal"—the racialized figure of the criminal—has come to represent the most menacing enemy of "American society." Virtually anything is acceptable—torture, brutality, vast expenditures of public funds—as long as it is done in the name of public safety. Racism has always found an easy route from its embeddedness in social structures to the psyches of collectives and individuals precisely because it mobilizes deep fears. While explicit, old-style racism may be increasingly socially unacceptable—precisely as a result of antiracist movements over the last forty years—this does not mean that U.S. society has been purged of racism. In fact, racism is more deeply embedded in socioeconomic structures, and the vast populations of incarcerated people of color is dramatic evidence of the way racism systematically structures economic relations. At the same time, this structural racism is rarely recognized as "racism." What we have come to recognize as open, explicit racism has in many ways begun to be replaced by a secluded, camouflaged kind of racism, whose influence on people's daily lives is as pervasive and systematic as the explicit forms of racism associated with the era of the struggle for civil rights.

The ideological space for the proliferations of this racialized fear of crime has been opened by the transformations in international politics created by the fall of the European socialist countries. Communism is no longer the quintessential enemy against which the nation imagines its identity. This space is now inhabited by ideological constructions of crime, drugs, immigration, and welfare. Of course, the enemy within is far more dangerous than the enemy without, and a black enemy within is the most dangerous of all.

Because of the tendency to view it as an abstract site into which all manner of undesirables are deposited, the prison is the perfect site for the simultaneous production and concealment of racism. The abstract character of the public perception of prisons militates against an engagement with the real issues afflicting the communities from which prisoners are drawn in such disproportionate numbers. This is the ideological work that the prison performs—it relieves us of the responsibility of seriously engaging with the problems of late capitalism, of transnational capitalism. The naturalization of black people as criminals thus also erects ideological barriers to an understanding of the connections between late-twentieth-century structural racism and the globalization of capital.

The vast expansion of the power of capitalist corporations over the lives of people of color and poor people in general has been accompanied by a waning anticapitalist consciousness. As capital moves with ease across national borders, legitimized by recent trade agreements such as NAFTA and GATT, corporations are allowed to close shop in the United States and transfer manufacturing operations to nations providing cheap labor pools. In fleeing organized labor in the U.S. to avoid paying higher wages and benefits, they leave entire communities in shambles, consigning huge numbers of people to joblessness, leaving them prey to the drug trade, destroying the economic base of these communities, thus affecting the education system, social welfare—and turning the people who live in those communities into perfect candidates for prison. At the same time, they create an economic demand for prisons, which stimulates the economy, providing jobs in the correctional industry for people who often come from the very populations that are criminalized by this process. It is a horrifying and self-reproducing cycle.

Ironically, prisons themselves are becoming a source of cheap labor that attracts corporate capitalism—as yet on a relatively small scale—in a way that parallels the attraction unorganized labor in Third World countries exerts. A statement by Michael Lamar Powell, a prisoner in Capshaw, Alabama, dramatically reveals this new development:

> I cannot go on strike, nor can I unionize. I am not covered by workers' compensation of the Fair Labor Standards Act. I agree to work late-night and weekend shifts. I do just what I am told, no matter what it is. I am hired and fired at will, and I am not even paid minimum wage: I earn one dollar a month. I cannot even voice grievances or complaints, except at the risk of incurring arbitrary discipline or some covert retaliation.
>
> You need not worry about NAFTA and your jobs going to Mexico and other Third World countries. I will have at least five percent of your jobs by the end of this decade.
>
> I am called prison labor. I am The New American Worker.[10]

This "new American worker" will be drawn from the ranks of a racialized population whose historical superexploitation—from the era of slavery to the present—has been legitimized by racism. At the same time, the expansion of convict labor is accompanied in some states by the old paraphernalia of ankle chains that symbolically links convict labor with slave labor. At least three states—Alabama, Florida, and Arizona—have reinstituted the chain gang. Moreover, as Michael Powell so incisively reveals, there is a new dimension to the racism inherent in this process, which structurally links the superexploitation of prison labor to the globalization of capital.

In California, whose prison system is the largest in the country and one of the largest in the world, the passage of an inmate labor initiative in 1990 has presented businesses seeking cheap labor with opportunities uncannily similar to those in Third World countries. As of June 1994, a range of companies were employing prison labor in nine California prisons. Under the auspices of the Joint Venture Program, work now being performed on prison grounds includes computerized telephone messaging, dental apparatus assembly, computer data entry, plastic parts fabrication, electronic component manufacturing at the Central California Women's facility at Chowchilla, security glass manufacturing, swine production, oak furniture manufacturing, and the production of stainless steel tanks and equipment. In a California Corrections Department brochure designed to promote the program, it is described as "an innovative public-private partnership that makes good business sense."[11] According to the owner of Tower Communications, whom the brochure quotes,

> The operation is cost effective, dependable and trouble free.... Tower Communications has successfully operated a message center utilizing inmates on the grounds of a California state prison. If you're a business leader planning expansion, considering relocation because of a deficient labor pool, starting a new enterprise, look into the benefits of using inmate labor.

The employer benefits listed by the brochure include

> federal and state tax incentives; no benefit package (retirement pay, vacation pay, sick leave, medical benefits); long term lease agreements at far below market value costs; discount rates on Workers Compensation; build a consistent, qualified work force; on call labor pool (no car breakdowns, no babysitting problems); option of hiring job-ready ex-offenders and minimizing costs; becoming a partner in public safety.

There is a major, yet invisible, racial supposition in such claims about the profitability of a convict labor force. The acceptability of the superexploitation of convict labor is largely based on the historical conjuncture of racism and incarceration practices. The already disproportionately black convict labor force will become increasingly black if the racially imbalanced incarceration practices continue.

The complicated yet unacknowledged structural presence of racism in the U.S. punishment industry also includes the fact that the punishment industry which sequesters ever-larger sectors of the black population attracts vast amounts of capital. Ideologically, as I have argued, the racialized fear of crime has begun to succeed the fear of communism. This corresponds to a structural tendency for capital that previously flowed toward the military industry to now move toward the punishment industry. The ease with which suggestions are made for prison construction costing in the multibillions of dollars is reminiscent of the military buildup: economic mobilization to defeat communism has turned into economic mobilization to defeat crime. The ideological construction of crime is thus complemented and bolstered by the material construction of jails and prisons. The more jails and prisons are constructed, the greater the fear of crime, and the greater the fear of crime, the stronger the cry for more jails and prisons, ad infinitum.

The law enforcement industry bears remarkable parallels to the military industry (just as there are anti-Communist resonances in the anti-crime campaign). This connection between the military industry and the punishment industry is revealed in a *Wall Street Journal* article entitled "Making Crime Pay: The Cold War of the '90s":

> Parts of the defense establishment are cashing in, too, scenting a logical new line of business to help them offset military cutbacks. Westinghouse Electric Corp., Minnesota Mining and Manufacturing Co., GDE Systems (a division of the old General Dynamics) and Alliant Techsystems Inc., for instance, are pushing crime-fighting equipment and have created special divisions to retool their defense technology for America's streets.

According to the article, a conference sponsored by the National Institute of Justice, the research arm of the Justice Department, was organized around the theme "Law Enforcement Technology in the 21st Century." The secretary of defense was a major presenter at this conference, which explored topics like "the role of the defense industry, particularly for dual use and conversion":

> Hot topics: defense-industry technology that could lower the level of violence involved in crime fighting. Sandia National Laboratories, for instance, is experimenting with a dense foam that can be sprayed at suspects, temporarily blinding and deafening them under breathable bubbles. Stinger Corporation is working on "smart guns," which will fire only for the owner, and retractable spiked barrier strips to unfurl in front of fleeing vehicles. Westinghouse is promoting the "smart car," in which mini-computers could be linked up with big mainframes at the police department, allowing for speedy booking of prisoners, as well as quick exchanges of information.[12]

Again, race provides a silent justification for the technological expansion of law enforcement, which, in turn, intensifies racist arrest and incarceration practices. This skyrocketing punishment industry, whose growth is silently but powerfully sustained by the persistence of racism, creates an economic demand for more jails and prisons and thus for similarly spiraling criminalization practices, which, in turn fuels the fear of crime.

Most debates addressing the crisis resulting from overcrowding in prisons and jails focus on male institutions. Meanwhile, women's institutions and jail space for women are proportionately proliferating at an even more astounding rate than men's. If race is largely an absent factor in the discussions about crime and punishment, gender seems not even to merit a place carved out by its absence. Historically, the imprisonment of women has served to criminalize women in a way that is more complicated than is the case with men. This female criminalization process has had more to do with the marking of certain groups of women as undomesticated and hypersexual, as women who refuse to embrace the nuclear family as paradigm. The current liberal-conservative discourse around welfare criminalizes black single mothers, who are represented as deficient, manless, drug-using breeders of children, and as reproducers of an attendant culture of poverty. The woman who does drugs is criminalized both because she is a drug user and because, as a consequence, she cannot be a good mother. In some states, pregnant women are being imprisoned for using crack because of possible damage to the fetus.

According to the U.S. Department of Justice, women are far more likely than men to be imprisoned for a drug conviction.[13] However, if women wish to receive treatment for their drug problems, often their only option, if they cannot pay for a drug program, is to be arrested and sentenced to a drug program via the criminal justice system. Yet when U.S. Surgeon General Joycelyn Elders alluded to the importance of opening discussion on the decriminalization of drugs, the Clinton administration immediately disassociated itself from her remarks. Decriminalization of drugs would greatly reduce the numbers of incarcerated women, for the 278 percent increase in the numbers of black women in state and federal prisons (as compared to the 186 percent increase in the numbers of black men) can be largely attributed to the phenomenal rise in drug-related and specifically crack-related imprisonment. According to the Sentencing Project's 1995 report, the increase amounted to 828 percent.[14]

Official refusals to even consider decriminalization of drugs as a possible strategy that might begin to reverse present incarceration practices further bolsters the ideological staying power of the prison. In his well-known study of the history of the prison and its related technologies of discipline, Michel Foucault pointed out that an evolving contradiction is at the very heart of the historical project of imprisonment.

> For a century and a half, the prison has always been offered as its own remedy:... the realization of the corrective project as the only method of overcoming the impossibility of implementing it.[15]

As I have attempted to argue, within the U.S. historical context, racism plays a pivotal role in sustaining this contradiction. In fact, Foucault's theory regarding the prison's tendency to serve as its own enduring justification becomes even more compelling if the role of race is also acknowledged. Moreover, moving beyond the parameters of what I consider the double impasse implied by his theory—the discursive impasse his theory discovers and that of the theory itself—I want to conclude by suggesting the possibility of radical race-conscious strategies designed to disrupt the stranglehold of criminalization and incarceration practices.

In the course of a recent collaborative research project with U.C. Santa Barbara sociologist Kum-Kum Bhavnani, in which we interviewed thirty-five women at the San Francisco County Jail, the complex ways in which race and gender help to produce a punishment industry that reproduces the very problems it purports to solve became dramatically apparent. Our interviews focused on the women's ideas about imprisonment and how they themselves imagine alternatives to incarceration. Their various critiques of the prison system and of the existing "alternatives," all of which are tied to reimprisonment as a last resort, led us to reflect more deeply about the importance of retrieving, retheorizing, and reactivating the radical abolitionist strategy first proposed in connection with the prison-reform movements of the sixties and seventies.

We are presently attempting to theorize women's imprisonment in ways that allow us to formulate a radical abolitionist strategy departing from, but not restricted in its conclusions to, women's jails and prisons. Our goal is to formulate alternatives to incarceration that substantively reflect the voices and agency of a variety of imprisoned women. We wish to open up channels for their involvement in the current debates around alternatives to incarceration, while not denying our own role as mediators and interpreters and our own political positioning in these debates. We also want to distinguish our explorations of alternatives from the spate of "alternative punishments" or what are now called "intermediate sanctions" presently being proposed and/or implemented by and through state and local correctional systems.

This is a long-range project that has three dimensions: academic research, public policy, and community organizing. In other words, for this project to be successful, it must build bridges between academic work, legislative and other policy interventions, and grassroots campaigns calling, for example, for the decriminalization of drugs and prostitution—and for the reversal of the present proliferation of jails and prisons.

Raising the possibility of abolishing jails and prisons as the institutionalized and normalized means of addressing social problems in an era of migrating corporations, unemployment and homelessness, and collapsing public services, from health care to education, can hopefully help to interrupt the current law-and-order discourse that has such a grip on the collective imagination, facilitated as it is by deep and hidden influences of racism. This late-twentieth-century "abolitionism," with its nineteenth-century resonances, may also lead to a historical recontextualization of the practice of imprisonment. With the passage of the Thirteenth Amendment, slavery was abolished for all except convicts—and in a sense the exclusion from citizenship accomplished by the slave system has persisted within the U.S. prison system. Only three states allow prisoners to vote, and approximately 4 million people are denied the right to vote because of their present or past incarceration. A radical strategy to abolish jails and prisons as the normal way of dealing with the social problems of late capitalism is not a strategy for abstract abolition. It is designed to force a rethinking of the increasingly repressive role of the state during this era of late capitalism and to carve out a space for resistance.

Notes

1. See, for instance, the *Austin-American Statesman*, October 17, 1995.
2. Charles S. Clark, "Prison Overcrowding," *Congressional Quarterly Researcher* 4, no. 5 (Feb. 4, 1994): 97–119.
3. Ibid.
4. Marc Mauer, "Young Black Men and the Criminal Justice System: A Growing National Problem," Washington, D.C.: The Sentencing Project, February 1990.
5. Alexander Cockburn, *Philadelphia Inquirer*, August 29, 1994.
6. Marc Mauer and Tracy Huling, "Young Black Americans and the Criminal Justice System: Five Years Later," Washington, D.C.: The Sentencing Project, October 1995.
7. Ibid., 18.
8. *See* Cockburn.
9. *See* Lubiano's essay in this volume, as well as "Black Ladies, Welfare Queens, and State Minstrels: Ideological War by Narrative Means," in *Race-ing Justice, En-gendering Power: Essays on Anita Hill, Clarence Thomas, and the Construction of Social Reality*, ed. Toni Morrison (New York: Pantheon, 1992), 323–63.
10. Unpublished essay, "Modern Slavery American Style," 1995.
11. I wish to acknowledge Julie Brown, who acquired this brochure from the California Department of Correction in the course of researching the role of convict labor.
12. *Wall Street Journal*, May 12, 1994.

13. Lawrence Rence, A. Greenfield, Stephanie Minor-Harper, *Women in Prison* (Washington, D.C.: U.S. Dept. of Justice, Office of Justice Programs, Bureau of Statistics, 1991).
14. Mauer and Huling, "Young Black Americans," 19.
15. Michel Foucault, *Discipline and Punish: The Birth of the Prison*, trans. Alan Sheridan (New York: Vintage, 1979), 395.

Adolph Reed, Jr.
Demobilization in the New Black Political Regime

IDEOLOGICAL CAPITULATION AND RADICAL FAILURE IN THE POSTSEGREGATION ERA

It is ironic that the exponential increases in black public-office holding since the 1970s have been accompanied by a deterioration of the material circumstances of large segments of the black citizenry. Comment on that irony comes both from those on the Left who underscore the insufficiency of capturing public office and from those on the Right who disparage the pursuit of public action on behalf of blacks or push oblique claims about black incompetence. In the middle are liberal social scientists and journalists who construe this inverse association as a puzzling deviation from the orthodox narrative of American interest-group pluralism. The liberal and conservative tendencies especially are often elaborated through a rhetoric that juxtaposes black political power and white economic power, treating them almost as naturalized racial properties, rather than as contingent products of social and political institutions.

At the same time, a different anomaly bedevils those on the Left who presume that oppression breeds political resistance to power relations enforced through the state apparatus. The intensification of oppression over the 1980s—seen, for example, in worsening of material conditions and an expanding regime of social repression—has not produced serious oppositional political mobilization. This is the key problem for articulation of a progressive black urban politics in the 1990s.

Making sense of these anomalies requires examining critical characteristics of post-segregation-era black politics. Although the disparate fortunes of black officialdom and its constituents are not causally linked, their relation sheds light on popular demobilization. This relation connects with each of the three features of the contemporary political landscape that hinder progressive black mobilization: (1) political incorporation and its limits, (2) the hegemony of underclass discourse as a frame for discussing racial inequality and poverty, and (3) the Left's failure to think carefully and critically about black politics and the ways that it connects with the role of race in the American stratification system.

The Limits of Incorporation

Systemic incorporation along four dimensions has been the most significant development in black urban politics since the 1960s. First, enforcement of the Voting Rights Act has increased the efficacy of black electoral participation;

invalidation of cruder forms of racial gerrymandering and biased electoral systems, as well as redress against intimidation, have made it easier for black voters to elect candidates.[1]

Second, a corollary of that electoral efficacy, has been the dramatic increase of black elected officials. Their existence has become a fact of life in U.S. politics and has shaped the modalities of race relations management. Black elected officials tend to operate within already existing governing coalitions at the local level and within the imperatives of the Democratic party's internal politics, as well as with an eye to their constituents. The logic of incumbency, moreover, is race-blind and favors reelection above all else. Not surprisingly, black officeholders tend to be disposed to articulate their black constituents' interests in ways that are compatible with those other commitments.

Third, black people have increasingly assumed administrative control of the institutions of urban governance. Housing authorities, welfare departments, school systems, even public safety departments are ever more likely to be run by black officials, and black functionaries are likely to be prominent at all levels within those organizations.[2] Those agencies have their own attentive constituencies within the black electorate, radiating out into the family and friendship networks of personnel. And a substratum of professional, often geographically mobile public functionaries with commitments to public management ideologies may now constitute a relatively autonomous interest configuration within black politics. This dimension of incorporation short-circuits critiques of those agencies' operations crafted within the racially inflected language most familiar to black insurgency. A critique that pivots on racial legitimacy as a standard for evaluating institutional behavior cannot be effective—as a basis for either organizing opposition or stimulating critical public debate—in a situation in which blacks conspicuously run the institutions. Because they have their own black constituencies and greater access to resources for shaping public opinion, public officials have the advantage in any debate that rests simplistically on determining racial authenticity.

A fourth and related dimension of incorporation is the integration of private civil rights and uplift organizations into a regime of race relations management driven by incrementalist, insider negotiation.[3] The tracings of this process could be seen dramatically at the national level during the Jimmy Carter administration with the inclusion of Jesse Jackson's Operation Push and the National Urban League as line item accounts in Department of Labor budgets. The boundaries between state agendas and elites and those of black non-government organizations may even be more porous at the local level, where personnel commonly move back and forth from one payroll system to another and where close coordination with local interest groupings is woven more seamlessly into the texture of everyday life.

An effect has arguably been further to skew the black politically attentive public toward the new regime of race relations management. On the one hand, generation of a professional world of public/private race relations engineers drawn from politically attentive elements of the black population channels issue-articulation and agenda-formation processes in black politics in ways reflecting the regime's common sense. On the other hand, insofar as the nongovernmental organizations and their elites carry the historical sediment of adversarial, protest politics, their integration into the new regime further ratifies its protocols as the only thinkable politics.

These trajectories of incorporation have yielded real benefits for the black citizenry. They have enhanced income and employment opportunity and have injected a greater measure of fairness into the distribution of public benefits in large and small ways. Black citizens have greater access now to the informal networks through which ordinary people use government to get things done—find summer jobs for their children, obtain zoning variances and building permits, get people out of jail, remove neighborhood nuisances, or site parks and libraries. Objectives that not long ago required storming city council meetings now can be met through routine processes. These accomplishments often are dismissed in some quarters on the Left as trivial and evidence of co-optation. Certainly, such characterizations are true "in the last analysis," but we don't live and can't do effective politics "in the last analysis." For them to function effectively as co-optation, for example, the fruits of incorporation cannot be trivial for those who partake or expect to be able to partake of them. The inclination to dismiss them reflects instead problematic tendencies within the Left to trivialize and simultaneously to demonize the exercise of public authority.

The new regime of race relations management as realized through the four-pronged dynamic of incorporation has exerted a *demobilizing* effect on black politics precisely by virtue of its capacities for delivering benefits and for defining what benefits political action can legitimately be used to pursue. Ease in voting and in producing desired electoral outcomes legitimizes that form as the primary means of political participation, which naturally seems attractive compared with others that require more extensive and intensive commitment of attention and effort. A result is to narrow the operative conception of political engagement to one form, and the most passive one at that.

Incumbent public officials generically have an interest in dampening the possibilities for new or widespread mobilization because of its intrinsic volatility. Uncontrolled participation can produce unpleasant electoral surprises and equally can interfere with the reigning protocols through which public agencies discharge their functions. As popular participation narrows, the inertial logic of incumbency operates to constrict the field of political discourse. Incumbents respond to durable interests, and they seek predictability, continuity, and a shared common sense. This translates into a preference for a brokered "politics as usual" that limits the number and range of claims on the policy agenda. Such a politics preserves the thrust of inherited policy regimes and reinforces existing patterns of systemic advantage by limiting the boundaries of the politically reasonable.[4] The same is true for the insider-negotiation processes through which the nongovernmental organizations now define their roles, and those organizations often earn their insider status by providing a convincing alternative to popular political mobilization.

Underclass Rhetoric and the Disappearance of Politics

Fueled largely by sensationalist journalism and supposedly tough-minded, policy-oriented social scientists, underclass rhetoric became over the 1980s the main frame within which to discuss inner-city poverty and inequality. The pundits and scholars who created this "underclass" define the stratum's membership in a variety of slightly differing ways; however, they all circle around a basic characterization that roots it among inner-city blacks and Hispanics, and they share a consensual assessment that the underclass makes up about 20 percent of the impoverished population in inner cities.[5]

The underclass notion is a contemporary extrapolation from a Victorian petit bourgeois fantasy world, and it is almost invariably harnessed to arguments for reactionary and punitive social policy. Even at its best—that is, when it is connected with some agenda other than pure stigmatization and denial of public responsibility—this rhetoric is depoliticizing and thus demobilizing in at least three ways.

First, the underclass frame does not direct attention to the political-economic dynamics that produce and reproduce dispossession and its entailments but focuses instead on behavioral characteristics alleged to exist among the victims of those dynamics. The result is to immerse discussion of inequality, poverty, and racial stratification in often overlapping rhetorics of individual or collective pathogenesis and knee-jerk moral evaluation. Conservatives bask in the simplicity of a discourse that revolves around racialized stigmatization of people as good, bad, or defective.[6] Even those versions propounded by liberals, like that offered by William Julius Wilson, which purport to provide structurally grounded accounts of inner-city inequality, describe the "underclass" in primarily behavioral terms.[7]

In both conservative and putatively liberal versions, the underclass rhetoric reinforces tendencies to demobilization by situating debate about poverty and inequality not in the public realm of politics—which would warrant examination of the role of public action in the reproduction of an unequal distribution of material costs and benefits (for example, federal and local housing and redevelopment policies that feed ghettoization and favor suburbs over inner cities, that favor homeowners over renters in the face of widespread and blatant racial discrimination in access to mortgages, and subsidies for urban deindustrialization and disinvestment)—but on the ostensibly private realm of individual values and behavior, pivoting specifically on images of male criminality and female slovenliness and irresponsible sexuality. The specter of drugs and gangs is omnipresent as well, underscoring the composite image of a wanton, depraved Other and automatically justifying any extreme of official repression and brutality. Even when acknowledged as unfounded, invocation of suspicion of the presence of drugs and gangs exculpates arbitrary violation of civil liberties in inner cities and police brutality to the extent of homicide.

Insofar as this focus opens to public policy at all, it tilts toward social and police repression, as in ubiquitous proposals for draconian "welfare reform" that seek only to codify the punitive moralism propelling the underclass narrative. That essentially racialized agenda is not likely to fuel broad political mobilization among black Americans, not in service to progressive agendas, at any rate.

Second, the underclass rhetoric reinforces demobilization because of its very nature as a third-person discourse. As a rhetoric of stigmatization, it is deployed about rather than by any real population. No one self-identifies as a member of the underclass. To that extent, as well as because the rhetoric presumes their incompetence, exhortations of the stigmatized population to undertake any concerted political action on their own behalf are unthinkable.

Its association with "self-help" ideology is in fact the third way that the underclass narrative undercuts popular mobilization. Because behavioral pathology appears in that narrative as at least the proximate source of poverty, inequality, and even contemporary racial discrimination, the programmatic responses that arise most naturally within its purview are those geared to correcting the supposed defects of the target population. This biases programmatic discussion toward bootstrap initiatives that claim moral rehabilitation of impoverished individuals and communities as part of their mission.

In this context two apparently different streams of neo-Jeffersonian romanticism—those associated respectively with the 1960s' New Left and Reaganism—converge on an orientation that eschews government action on principle in favor of voluntarist, "community-based" initiatives. Particularly when steeped in a language of "empowerment," this antistatist convergence overlaps current manifestations of a conservative, bootstrap tendency among black elites that stretches back at least through Booker T. Washington at the turn of the century. Indeed, it was the Reagan administration's evil genius to appeal to that tendency by shifting from a first-term tactic that projected combative black voices, like Thomas Sowell and Clarence Pendleton, to a more conciliatory style exemplified by Glenn Loury. In Reagan's second term the administration apparently opted for a different posture as a new group of its black supporters, led by Loury and Robert Woodson of the National Center for Neighborhood Enterprise, stepped into the spotlight. Although this wave of black Reaganauts could be pugnacious with adversaries, they were far more inclined than their predecessors to make overtures to the entrenched race relations elite. Those overtures disarmed partisan skepticism by emphasizing the black middle class's supposedly special responsibility for correcting the underclass and the problems associated with it.[8]

Underwriting this version of self-help are three interlocked claims: (1) that black inner cities are beset by grave and self-regenerative problems of social breakdown and pathology that have undermined the possibility of normal civic life, (2) that these problems are beyond the reach of positive state action, and (3) that they can be addressed only by private, voluntarist black action led by the middle class. Over the late 1980s and early 1990s these three claims—each dubious enough on its own, all justified at most by appeal to lurid anecdotes, self-righteous prejudices, and crackerbarrel social theory—congealed into hegemonic wisdom. Black public figures supposedly identified with the Left, like Jesse Jackson, Roger Wilkins, and Cornel West, have become as devout prose-lytizers of this catechistic orthodoxy as are rightists like Woodson, Loury, and Clarence Thomas.[9]

The rise and consolidation of the Democratic Leadership Council and the "New Liberalism" as dominant within the Democratic party no doubt rein-forced and were reinforced by black self-help bromides' elevation to the status of conventional wisdom. On the one hand, black self-help rhetoric historically has been associated with presumptions that blacks have no hope for allies in pursuit of justice through public policy, and the successful offensive of Demo-cratic "centrists" and neoliberals—predicated in large part on flight from iden-tification with both perceived black interests and downwardly redistributive social policy—certainly lends credence to the impression that the federal gov-ernment is not a dependable ally of black objectives. Even the celebrated declamations by New Liberal consciences Bill Bradley and John Kerry for racial justice and tolerance were mainly, after brief statements against bigotry, ex-tended characterizations of impoverished inner cities as savage hearts of dark-ness, saturated in self-destructive violence and pathology; the speeches carried no particular warrant for action addressing inequality and its effects except calls for moral uplift.

Despite its foundation on notions of grassroots activism, the self-help regime is best seen as community mobilization for political demobilization. Each attempt by a neighborhood or church group to scrounge around the phil-anthropic world and the interstices of the federal system for funds to build low-income housing or day-care or neighborhood centers or to organize programs that compensate for inadequate school funding, public safety, or trash pickup, simultaneously concedes the point that black citizens cannot legitimately pur-sue those benefits through government. This is a very dangerous concession in an ideological context defined largely by a logic that, like that in the post-Reconstruction era of the last century, could extend to an almost genocidal ex-pulsion of black citizens toward a bantustanized periphery of society.

We cannot concede the important ground of black people's equal propri-etorship of public institutions with all other citizens; affirming the legitimacy of black Americans' demands on the state—on an equal basis with those who re-ceive defense contracts, homeownership subsidies, investment tax credits, flood protection, and a host of other benefits from government—is also affirming black Americans' equal membership in the polity. The more ground we give on this front, the more the latter-day versions of the Southern Redeemers will take. Frederick Douglass put it succinctly, "The limits of tyrants are prescribed by the endurance of those whom they oppress."

The problem with self-help ideology is that it reifies community initiative, freighting it with an ideological burden that reduces to political quietism and a programmatic mission it is ill equipped to fulfill. It is absurd to present neigh-borhood and church initiatives as appropriate responses to the effects of government-supported disinvestment, labor market segmentation, widespread and well-documented patterns of discrimination in employment and housing as well as in the trajectory of direct and indirect public spending, and an all-out corporate assault on the social wage.

Its endorsement by public officials is a particularly ironic aspect of the self-help rhetoric. That endorsement amounts to an admission of failure, an acknowledgment that the problems afflicting their constituents are indeed beyond the scope of the institutional apparatus under their control, that black officials are in fact powerless to provide services to inner-city citizens effectively through those institutions.

A key to overcoming the demobilizing effects of self-help ideology, as well as those of underclass rhetoric more generally, lies in stimulation of strategic debate—grounded in the relation between social conditions affecting the black population and public policy and the larger political-economic tendencies to which it responds—within and about black political activity. This in turn requires attending to the complex dynamics of interest and ideological differentiation that operate within black politics, taking into account the who-gets-what-when-where-how dimension of politics as it appears among black political agents and interest configurations. In principle, the Left should be intimately engaged in this project, which is the stock-in-trade of Left political analysis.

The Left and Black Politics

By outlawing official segregation and discriminatory restrictions on political participation, the Voting Rights Act and the 1964 Civil Rights Act rendered obsolete the least common denominator—opposition to Jim Crow—that for more than a half-century had given black political activity coherence and a pragmatic agenda plausibly understood to be shared uniformly among the black citizenry.[10] (This effect no doubt is a factor—along with the spread of self-help ideology and the aging of the population that can recall the ancien régime—driving contemporary nostalgia for the sense of community that supposedly flourished under segregation. That perception was always more apparent than real; the coherence and cohesiveness were most of all artifacts of the imperatives of the Jim Crow system and the struggle against it. In black politics as elsewhere, what appears as political cohesiveness has been the assertion of one tendency over others coexisting and competing with it—in this case, first, white elites' successful projection of Booker T. Washington's capitulationist program and then, for the half-century after Washington's death, the primacy of the focus on attacking codified segregation.) The Voting Rights Act, additionally, ensued in opening new possibilities, concrete objectives and incentives for political action, and new, more complex relations with mainstream political institutions, particularly government and the Democratic party at all levels.

In the decade after 1965 black political activity came increasingly to revolve around gaining, enhancing, or maintaining official representation in public institutions and the distribution of associated material and symbolic benefits. The greatest increases in black elective-office holding occurred during those years. That period also saw the rise of black urban governance, both in black-led municipal regimes and in growing black authority in the urban administrative apparatus.

At the same time this shift exposed a long-standing tension in black political discourse between narrower and broader constructions of the practical agenda for realizing racially democratic interests. The narrower view has focused political objectives on singular pursuit of racial inclusion, either accepting the structure and performance of political and economic institutions as given or presuming that black representation is an adequate basis for correcting what might be unsatisfactory about them. The essence of this view was distilled, appropriately, in two pithy formulations in the late 1960s: the slogan demanding "black faces in previously all-white places" and the proposition that, as an ideal, black Americans should make up 12 percent of corporate executives, 12 percent of the unemployed, and 12 percent of everything in between.[11] The broader tendency is perhaps best seen as an ensemble of views joined by inclination toward structural critique. This tendency sees simple racial inclusion as inadequate and argues for tying political action to insurgent programs that seek either to transform existing institutions or to reject them altogether in favor of race nationalist or social revolutionary alternatives.

The tension between these two views has been a recurring issue in black politics, overlapping and crosscutting—and, arguably, being mistaken for—other fault lines that appear more commonly in the historiography of black political debate (for example, the militant/moderate, protest/accommodationist, and integrationist/nationalist dichotomies).[12] In the 1960s, however, the combination of broad popular mobilization and heightened prospects for victory against legally enforced exclusion made this tension more prominent than at any prior time except during the 1930s and early 1940s, when Ralph Bunche and other Young Turks pushed sharp, Marxist-inspired critiques into the main lines of black debate.

Black accession to responsible positions in the apparatus of public management enabled for the first time—save for fleeting moments in Reconstruction—a discourse focused on the concrete, nuts-and-bolts, incrementalist exercise of public authority. Three factors compel the new pragmatic orientation toward incrementalism. First, the inclusionist program had developed largely as an insider politics, seeking legitimacy in part through emphasis of loyalty, particularly in the cold war context, to prevailing political and economic arrangements except insofar as those were racially exclusionary. To that extent it has been predisposed to take existing systemic and institutional imperatives as given. Second, experience in War on Poverty and Great Society programs socialized the pool of potential black officials into the public management system's entrenched protocols and operating logic, initiating them into existing policy processes. This socialization spurred articulation of a rhetoric exalting realpolitik and keying strategic consideration only to advancement of black representation among beneficiaries within existing institutional regimes.[13] This notion of political pragmatism not only reinforces incremental-ism; it also requires a shifting construction of "black" interests to conform to options set in a received policy and issue framework. For instance, Mayor May-nard Jackson strained to define one of the alternatives in a developers' fight over siting a new Atlanta airport as the black choice, although building a sec-ond airport on either location would have had no discernibly positive impact on black Atlantans; public support for the project on any site, moreover, would amount to a redistribution of fiscal resources away from the city's black popula-tion to developers and remote, generally hostile metropolitan economic inter-ests.[14] Finally, inclusionist politics affords no larger vision around which to orient a critical perspective on either the operations and general functions of political institutions or the general thrust of public policy. This characteristic, which might appear as political myopia, is rationalizable as pragmatic; in any event, it further reinforces incrementalism by screening out broader issues and concerns.

The hegemony of incrementalism has facilitated elaboration of a political discourse that sidesteps a critical problem at the core of post-segregation-era black politics: the tension between black officials' institutional legitimation and their popular electoral legitimation. The institutions that black officials administer are driven by the imperatives of managing systemic racial subordi-nation, but the expectations they cultivate among their constituents define the role of black administrative representation in those institutions as a de facto challenge to racial subordination.

So by the 1990s it was commonplace to see black housing authority direc-tors' policy innovations run to advocating lockdowns and random police sweeps, black school superintendents discussing their duties principally through a rhetoric of discipline and calling for punishment of parents of transgressors in their charge, black mayors and legislators locked into a victim-blaming inter-pretive frame accenting drug abuse and criminality as the only actionable social problems—and all falling back on the bromides about family breakdown and moral crisis among their constituents to explain the inadequacy of public ser-vices. This rhetoric obscures their capitulation to business-led programs of re-gressive redistribution—tax breaks and other subsidies, as well as general subservience to development interests in planning and policy formulation—that contribute further to fiscal strain, thus justifying still further service cuts, which increase pressure for giving more to development interests to stimulate "growth" that supposedly will build the tax base, and so on. From this perspec-tive, Sharon Pratt Kelly's Washington, D.C., mayoralty is emblematic; her tenure was distinguished only by repeated service and personnel cuts and her 1993 call for the National Guard to buttress municipal police efforts—even as the District of Columbia already has one of the highest police-to-citizen ratios in the United States. There could hardly be a more striking illustration of the extent to which minority public officials are the equivalent of Bantustan administrators. Incrementalism serves as blinders, sword, and shield. It blocks alternative courses from view, delegitimizes criticism with incantations of realpolitik, and provides a Pontius Pilate defense of any action by characterizing officials as incapable of acting on their circumstances.[15]

Continued debate with the oppositional tendency in black politics could have mitigated the corrosive effects of incrementalist hegemony. Such debate might have broadened somewhat the perspective from which black officials themselves define pragmatic agendas. It might have stimulated among black citizens a practical, policy-oriented public discourse that would either have supported black officials in the articulation of bold initiatives and/or held them accountable to autonomously generated programmatic agendas and concerns.

Yet few would dispute the argument that radicalism has been routed in postsegregation black politics. Some fit that fact into a naturalistic reading of incorporation: radicalism automatically wanes as avenues open for regular political participation. Others concede incrementalist, petit bourgeois hegemony in electoral politics but claim that radicalism's social base has not been destroyed but only displaced to other domains—dormant mass anger, Louis Farrakhan's apparent popularity, rap music and other extrusions of youth culture, literary production, and the like—suggesting a need to reconceptualize politics to reflect the significance of such phenomena. Both sorts of response, however, evade giving an account of how the radical tendency was expunged from the black political mainstream, which is critically important for making sense of the limitations of inherited forms of black radicalism and for the task of constructing a progressive black politics in the present.

The oppositional tendency in postsegregation black politics was hampered by an aspect of its origin in black power ideology. Radicals—all along the spectrum, ranging from cultural nationalist to Stalinoid Marxist—began from a stance that took the "black community" as the central configuration of political interest and the source of critical agency. This stance grew from black power rhetoric's emphasis on "community control" and its projection of the "community" as touchstone of legitimacy and insurgent authenticity. This formulation is a presumptive claim for the existence of a racial population that is organically integrated and that operates as a collective subject in pursuit of unitary interests. That claim, which persists as a grounding principle in black strategic discourse, is problematic in two linked ways that bear on elaboration of a critical politics.

First, positing a black collectivity as an organic political agent preempts questions of interest differentiation. If the "community" operates with a single will and a single agenda, then there is neither need nor basis for evaluating political programs or policies with respect to their impact on differing elements of the black population. Any initiative enjoying conspicuous support from any group of black people can be said plausibly to reflect the community's preference or interest; the metaphorical organicism that drives the "black community" formulation presumes that what is good for one is good for all.

Similarly, because the organic black community is construed as naturalistic, the notion precludes discussion of both criteria of political representation and the definition of constituencies. Those issues become matters for concern when the relevant polity is perceived to be made up of diverse and not necessarily compatible interests and/or when the relation between representatives and represented is seen as contingent and mediated rather than cellular or isomorphic. By contrast, in the black community construct those who appear as leaders or spokespersons are not so much representatives as pure embodiments of collective aspirations.

As the stratum of black public officials emerged, black power radicalism's limitations became visible. Blacks' accession to prominence within the institutional apparatus of urban administration did not appreciably alter the mission or official practices of the institutions in their charge. Putting black faces in previously all-white places was not sufficient for those who identified with institutional transformation along populist lines or who otherwise rejected the status quo of race relations management. Yet, because black power's communitarian premises reified group identity and could not accommodate structural differentiation among Afro-Americans, the only critical frame on which radicals could draw consensually was the language of racial authenticity.

By the end of the 1960s, black power's inadequacy as a basis for concrete political judgment had begun to fuel radicals' self-conscious turn to creation and adoption of "ideologies"—global political narratives encompassing alternative vision, norms, and strategic programs—that promised to provide definite standpoints for critical judgment and platforms for political mobilization. This development underwrote a logic of sectarianism that embedded a cleavage between Marxists and cultural nationalists as the pivotal tension in black oppositional politics.

Ironically, the impetus propelling the ideological turn—the need to compensate for the inadequacies of black power's simplistic communitarianism—was thwarted by failure to break with the essential flaw, the stance positing the "black community" as the source of political legitimation and its attendant rhetoric of authenticity. Indeed, the turn to ideology may have reinforced propensities to rely on communitarian mystification because the flight into theoreticism made the need to claim connections with popular action all the more urgent.

The quandary faced by the oppositional politics that evolved from black power produced two main organizational responses: the National Black Political Assembly (NBPA) and the African Liberation Support Committee (ALSC).[16] The NBPA, which grew from the 1972 National Black Political Convention at Gary, was spearheaded by the cultural nationalist camp and was an attempt to unite activists and elected officials in support of a common, generically black agenda. Reflecting the view that there is a racial political interest that transcends other affiliations or commitments, the NBPA was organized on Imamu Amiri Baraka's principle of "unity without uniformity." ALSC was the outgrowth of an ad hoc African Liberation Day Coordinating Committee that had organized the first African Liberation Day national mobilization, also in 1972. Creation of ALSC reflected a concern to formalize a presence to act in support of African liberation movements, particularly in the Portugese colonies, Rhodesia, South Africa, and southwest Africa. Like the NBPA, ALSC was in principle ecumenically black. ALSC differed, however, in its focus on popular mobilization; its agenda centered on mass political education and agitation, largely in concert with organizing an annual African Liberation Day demonstration, as well as fund-raising for annual allocations to designated liberation movements. To that extent ALSC was more an activist organization and was somewhat less oriented to building formal relationships with mainstream politicians. Both organizations represented radicals' desire to define a space for oppositional politics in the postsegregation context; both were attempts to create organizational bases that could institutionalize racially autonomous radicalism in the new Afro-American political culture and facilitate pursuit of practical agendas consonant with black power ideological positions. There was also substantial overlap in radicals' participation in the two organizations.

Even with their best intentions, however, the radicals in ALSC failed to connect with an effective social base. Efforts to create a popular constituency by perfecting and propagating one or another abstract ideology required that people disengage from their worlds of lived experience and undergo a process of ontological change not unlike conversion. Neither Marxists nor nationalists offered programs with demonstrable payoffs comparable to those promised by mainstream politicians; more important, neither radical camp provided concretely persuasive or inspiring critiques of mainstream agendas. To that extent, they held out no reason to compel the leap of faith for which they called. In those circumstances radicals were incapable of braking or modifying mainstream politicians' assertion of hegemony, and ALSC collapsed entirely into sectarian infighting. By 1977 all that remained was a squabble over the organization's carcass, as three factions simultaneously held competing "national" African Liberation Day demonstrations in Washington.

In both Marxist and nationalist camps the ideological turn was an imposition on rather than a product of analysis of the forces animating black American politics. As a consequence, radicals were never moved to confront the ideal of effective political agency that they had brought forward from black power rhetoric—the reified notion of the "black community" and the language of racial authenticity attendant to it. Because the black community idea is a mystification, it gives no solid standpoint from which to situate policies or political programs.

So expired the last gasp of the autonomous black radicalism spawned in the 1960s. Paroxysms continued here and there. The Communist Workers party's 1979 shootout with the Ku Klux Klan in Greensboro, North Carolina, for instance, was the culmination of a sectarian spiral that reached back through ALSC to a pan-Africanist and black power activism rooted in dynamic labor and poor people's organizations. Individuals and networks adjusted to the new regime and attempted to advance progressive interests within it; some simply were incorporated. Nevertheless, by the time Jimmy Carter was elected president no signs of institutionalized opposition were visible in black political life except on a sectarian fringe; all traces of alternatives to the incrementalist program of black officialdom had been expunged from Afro-American civic discourse. In 1977, for example, Mayor Maynard Jackson was able to fire two thousand striking black Atlanta sanitation workers without significant dissent; he won reelection in the same year with over three-fourths of the vote.[17] The victory of the new regime was so complete that in the early 1980s liberal social scientists ratified it in whiggish accounts that represented the contemporary status quo as the precise goal toward which the previous generation of black activism had unfolded smoothly, willfully, and ineluctably. This fundamentally Orwellian victor's narrative canonized as the only thinkable reality—the teleological fulfillment of black political aspiration—what was in fact the outcome of contingency and contestation, thus denying space for radical critique in both present and past.

The purblindness that has omitted post-black-power radicalism from accounts of the transition "from protest to politics" partly reflects a perspective that derives from either prior commitment to incrementalist politics or premises that apprehend black political activity in relation to a simple inclusion/exclusion axis. From either vantage point it seems natural and automatic that the mainstream, incrementalist agenda would become hegemonic upon removal of fetters blocking regular, systemically conventional forms of political participation. Omission occurs also, however, because the radical tendencies that emerged from black power sensibilities were purely endogenous to black politics. Consonant with their black power origins, radicals actively sought to maintain a racially exclusive universe of critical political discourse; they generally neither pursued interaction with whites nor were centrally concerned with interracialism as an issue. Therefore, those strains of autonomous black radicalism were largely invisible to white observers, who as a rule do not attend closely to machinations internal to black politics.

Whites' failure to discern endogenous tendencies among Afro-Americans extends across the political spectrum and has clearly undermined the Left's ability to generate an appropriate strategic approach to black political activity. At least since the Students for a Democratic Society's 1969 proclamation of the Black Panther party as the "vanguard of the black revolution" two problematic features have organized white Left discourse about Afro-American politics: (1) a reluctance to see black political interests and activity as internally differentiated in ways that are grounded in social structure and (2) a converging focus on willingness to align with whites as the primary criterion for making judgments about individuals or currents in black politics. The first problem stems from and reinforces the familiar assumption of the existence of an organic "black community." In white strategic discourse this notion not only has the same evasive and counterproductive qualities as it does in black political rhetoric; it also implies that black life is opaque to those outside it. Knowledge appears to require identifying individuals or groups who reflect the authentic mood, sentiments, will, or preferences of the reified community. This impulse places a premium on articulate black spokespersons to act as emissaries to the white Left. By definition, such emissaries—even if they adopt a different posture—satisfy the interracialism criterion, and the operative premises and biases leave no space for interrogating the claims to authenticity or popular legitimacy that underlie the role of racial emissary.

This circumstance led to the irony that in the 1980s—thanks in part to the consolidation of Democratic Socialists of America, which provided a national forum—the institutional apparatus of the white Left began designating and projecting one black figure after another as the voice of black radical activism, long after the last embers of organized oppositional activism had been expunged. In the absence of independent knowledge or nuanced insight regarding black politics, assessment of claims to authenticity ultimately relies on the appeal that a given claimant's persona or stance offers to white auditors. Critical evaluation tends toward designation of good and bad, true and false black leaders. This failing has underwritten in one venue after another—as, for example, in the case of former New York City mayor. David Dinkins—a cycle of exaggerated estimation of the progressive commitments of black mainstream politicians followed by crashing disillusionment when they fail to live up to expectations. This cycle not only impedes practical strategic analysis; it has also greased the skids of this generation's "god-that-failed" rightward political slide. Treatment of blacks as bearers of a deeper humanity and higher morality opens to a rhetoric of betrayal, and the imagery shifts to venality and immorality—thus synecdochically justifying resistance to black political aspirations.

The costly and dangerous entailments of the white Left's approach to black politics reached a national apotheosis in the knee-jerk embrace of Jesse Jackson's campaign of self-promotion. In 1984 Jackson, who had been a consummate insider for at least a decade, proclaimed himself an outsider, parlaying a well-publicized southern speaking tour into a Potemkin movement. He traded precisely on gullibility about the organic black community to project himself as the literal embodiment of a popular black insurgency.

The Left generally—black and white—accepted Jackson's propaganda on face value, in part through simple wish fulfillment but in part also out of opportunistic attempts to ride on his coattails. Black activists' hopes to co-opt Jackson's initiative demonstrated naiveté regarding their ability to manipulate politicians to advance their ends. Having established himself as the supposed champion of a Rainbow Coalition of the "locked out," between 1984 and 1988 Jackson abandoned his outsider posture and tightened his links with black regular Democrats. He had pried open a space for himself, momentarily at least, as primus inter pares in the national black political elite and had attained a quasi official status in the Democratic hierarchy—both mainly on the strength of his claim to represent a popular black constituency. This claim was legitimized by the enthusiastic assent of his activist supporters, who sought through his cachet to create just such a constituency.

As it had for the NBPA and ALSC in the mid-1970s, this gambit backfired for the Rainbow Coalition activists. Radicals hardly succeeded in using Jackson to gain access to a popular base; instead, he used and discarded them. Significantly, skepticism in the white Left about the Jackson phenomenon revolved primarily around the extent to which he would attempt to fashion a multiracial constituency. There was no significant effort to undertake critique of Jackson's essentially personalistic appeal to black voters or to make sense of his role in black politics. From this perspective, for instance, Jackson's move between 1984 and 1988 boosted his progressive credentials because of his elaborate, if pro forma and symbolic, multiracialist gestures in the latter campaign—even though those gestures were crafted to project his image as a responsible insider.[18]

The combination of opportunism and evasive romanticism that blocked critical evaluation of Jackson's enterprise also left both black and white insurgents without effective response to its denouement. After all the symbolic rhetoric, photo ops with striking workers, and canned leftist position papers, Jackson bargained at the Democratic convention for an airplane to use in campaigning for nominee Michael Dukakis and payoffs for cronies—benefits even skimpier and more narrowly personal than the ornamental fruits of his brokerage in 1984. Between 1988 and 1994 he provided ample evidence of his self-aggrandizing and conservative agenda—launch of a talk show career, quixotic definition of statehood for the District of Columbia as the most important civil rights issue of our time, the "Shadow Senator" farce, pouting refusal to commit to or dissent from any candidate in the 1992 Democratic nominating process, and worst of all his proclamation that black criminality is the central problem in contemporary Afro-American life.

In both of his campaigns radicals endorsed Jackson's rhetoric of hope and inspiration as a way to sidestep grappling with empirically dubious claims about his impact on black voter registration and turnout and his candidacy's electoral coattail effects. In the process these evasions obscured the possibility that, despite his constant allegations that the Democratic party takes black voters for granted, Jackson's campaign facilitated just such an outcome. Especially in 1988, when it was clear from the beginning that Jackson would have nearly unanimous black support, the other contenders for the nomination made only perfunctory appeals to black voters during the primaries. Without Jackson's presence in the field at least some of the other candidates may have courted black Democrats, if only to gain a comparative electoral advantage in the South. With the black primary vote—and that of the party's left wing as well—conceded to Jackson, however, the others simply could avoid addressing black interests until the convention, at which point the eventual winner could broker some concessions to Jackson in the name of Afro-American and progressive concerns.

In this regard also, Jackson's campaign may well have strengthened the party's rightist faction, formalized as the Democratic Leadership Council (DLC) in the aftermath of Mondale's defeat.[19] The two Jackson campaigns were arguably purely beneficial for the Democratic Right. Jackson's insurgency maximized black visibility yet posed no genuine threat programmatically, because at the same time it demobilized blacks' participation in the debate over the party's future substantively and strategically. It demobilized black Democrats substantively by defining their interests solely in relation to Jackson's personal fortunes and strategically by funneling black action through his insider's style of brokerage politics. By 1992 the rightist narrative had become nearly hegemonic in the Democratic party and in the society at large, thanks principally to its continual, virtually unchallenged repetition as fact by sympathetic journalists and academics.

Of course, the Jackson insurgency did not generate the DLC camp, which would have sought to stigmatize blacks and the Left anyway. The critical problem is that Jackson's radical supporters reproduced the pattern of opportunism and abstract purism that has consistently evaded toughminded analysis of the practical forces driving American politics and black politics in particular. As a result, they were unable to respond frankly and forthrightly to Jackson's increasingly crude, personalistic maneuverings after 1988. In acquiescing to a frame that designates Jackson ascriptively as the embodiment of progressive interests, leftists and black activists sacrificed the political distance that would give a critical foundation from which to assess his behavior.

Certainly, by the time the 1992 Democratic field was set, there was no real Left option; Kerry, Clinton, and Tsongas all operated entirely within the new rightist conventions, and even the short-lived Harkin candidacy—perhaps the last gasp of the party's labor-Left wing—was ambivalent in practice if not rhetoric about catering to the white middle class. In this environment no challenge appeared when the well-organized Clinton forces swept through, remonstrating with black elites to support their candidate without questions because his nomination was a fait accompli. The Clinton campaign exploited a long-standing problem in black political life, the tendency to conflate descriptive representation and representation of substantive interests. By defining representation among campaign leadership and prospective appointments as the key shorthand expression of openness to black concerns, Clinton and his black supporters manipulated this tendency—which Jackson's insistent personalism had ensconced as the coin of militant black critique—to avoid confronting the material implications of his rightist "New Democrat" agenda for black Americans.

Considering a counterfactual may highlight the limits of the Jackson phenomenon more clearly. What forms could an effective Left insurgent Democratic candidacy have taken? In the first place it would have had to proceed from an institutional base within the party's left wing and from a coherent, well-articulated programmatic agenda—not the whim of a random individual. Any such insurgency most likely would have little chance of actually winning the nomination; its objectives would have to be gaining specific programmatic concessions, exerting a leftward pull on political debate, and perhaps strengthening and building progressive networks within the party and outside. And those objectives require relative clarity of political vision and concreteness of strategy. The focus would have to be on advancing a specific program or critique rather than an individual. The candidate-centered bias in U.S. electoral politics creates openings to co-optation for which an insurgent movement would have to compensate by fastening the candidacy as much as possible to a concrete agenda. The Jackson candidacies met none of these criteria.

In the current situation black (and white) radicalism has retreated ever more hermetically into the university, and the unaddressed tendency to wish fulfillment has reached new extremes, so that oppositional politics becomes little more than a pose livening up the march through the tenure ranks. The context of desperation and utter defeat enveloping activist politics outside the academy has not only reinforced the retreat to the campus; it has also removed practical fetters on the compensatory imagination guiding the creation of intentionally oppositional academic discourses. In this context the notion of radicalism is increasingly removed from critique and substantive action directed toward altering entrenched patterns of subordination and inequality mediated through public policy.

The characteristics of this dynamic are mainly crystallized in the turn to a rhetoric pivoting on an idea of "cultural politics." The discourse of cultural politics does not differentiate between public, collective activity explicitly challenging patterns of political and socioeconomic hierarchy and the typically surreptitious, often privatistic practices of "everyday resistance"—the mechanisms through which subordinates construct moments of dignity and autonomy and enhance their options within relations of oppression without attacking them head on. The failure to make any such distinction—or making and then eliding it—dramatizes the fate that befalls black radicalism's separation of abstract theorizing from concrete political action when academic hermeticism eliminates the imperative to think about identifying and mobilizing a popular constituency. Participating in youth fads, maintaining fraternal organizations, vesting hopes in prayer or root doctors, and even quilt making thus become indistinguishable from slave revolts, activism in Reconstruction governments, the Montgomery bus boycott, grassroots campaigns for voter registration, and labor union or welfare rights agitation as politically meaningful forms of "resistance."[20]

Conclusion

The collapse of popularly based radicalism in the 1970s underlies the failure of a critical politics to develop as a significant force, even in response to the Reagan-Bush years' heavy-handed assault on the interests of racial equality. The demise of that autonomous radical strain has had important and extensive consequences. For instance, the absence of a populist activism has eliminated a constraint on the incrementalist, demobilizing tendencies of systemic incorporation. To that extent, it has distorted the development of what might have been, as some thought, a functional division of labor or, what was more likely, a creative tension between the new black public officialdom and attentive black constituencies. That tension could well have broadened processes of interest articulation and differentiation in black politics and brought them into the realm of public debate.

Contrary to the communitarian reflex on which Afro-American political discourse has pivoted for a generation, stimulation of overt interest-group dynamics—organized on the basis of neighborhood, class, gender, occupation, or other aspects of social status, as well as a variety of interest groups whose memberships overlapped and other coalitional activity—could enrich democratic participation by encouraging controversy among black Americans over the concrete, tangible implications of policy issues. A sharply focused civic discourse grounded on the interplay of clearly articulated interests could feed political mobilization, both electoral and otherwise, by highlighting the human impact of government action and the stakes of political activity in general. Elaboration of a political discourse based explicitly on a consideration of the differential allocation of costs and benefits of public policy within an attentive, relatively mobilizable polity could also increase public officials' accountability to the black constituencies they purportedly represent.

It certainly seems possible that systemic incorporation might have occurred on terms that embedded more seriously progressive vision and momentum in black politics than has been the case. Either because electoral processes may have produced individuals independently more attuned to progressive black agendas or because of the need to respond to popular pressure, an outcome could have been a stratum of mainstream politicians and officials at least marginally more inclined to press aggressively against the Left boundaries of dominant policy streams and to use the visibility of office as a bully pulpit from which to help shape the contours of black action and discourse in a leftward direction.

A sophisticated, sharp, and popularly grounded progressive black presence in the national Democratic coalition also could have exerted a more effectively countervailing force against the "retreat from McGovernism" narrative and program as they developed from Carter forward. A coherent black response along social democratic lines could have helped both to discredit the conservative Democrats' initiative on substantive grounds and to galvanize a broader, class-based counterattack.

The keys to generation of such a politics, now as then, include breaking with the mystification of an organic black community. Recognition that all black people are not affected in the same ways by public policy and government practice is central to construction of a civic discourse that revolves tough-mindedly around determining who benefits and who loses from public action.

Breaking with the communitarian mythology also means rejecting a first-person/third-person rhetoric concerning black Americans' relation to the institutions of public authority. The perception of black people as passive recipients of the actions of a government fundamentally alien to them reflected a material reasonableness during most of the Jim Crow era; it has been superseded by full enfranchisement and systemic incorporation since passage of the

initial Voting Rights Act. In fact, as the history of black mobilization for governance during Reconstruction shows, the segregation era marked a shift—expressing the realities of systematic expulsion from civic life—from a
presumption that the Thirteenth, Fourteenth, and Fifteenth Amendments authenticated Afro-Americans' claims to equal proprietorship of American political institutions. In positing a reified "we," however, the black community
formulation sets up "America"—and, therefore, official institutions—as a
"they" to which black people relate most authentically as a collectivity, not as
individual citizens.

With regard to specific foci for political action that could support progressive mobilization, a critical task is transcendence of a simplistic inclusion/exclusion axis for strategic thinking, with respect to both positive programs and
critical responses to dominant initiatives. This implies recognition that vigorous pursuit of an affirmative action/set-aside agenda is necessary but not sufficient for advancing the interests of racial democracy. Progressives' strategic
thinking in black politics should be based more than it is on public policy and
government institutions, with specific attention given to actual and potential
effects of each on black Americans. Examples of pertinent issues and policy
areas are the relation of government action to deindustrialization and its roots
in global capitalist reorganization; the racially and intraracially differential impact of federal and local housing, transportation, redevelopment, and revenue
policy; and the racist, anti-civil-libertarian programmatic rhetoric and presumptions undergirding the criminal justice system. Similarly important initiatives could include the fight against privatization of public services, the fight
for equalization of school funding, stimulation of open discussion, where appropriate, of metropolitan tax base sharing, and metropolitanization of functions
on an equitable basis, in ways that ensure minority constituents' capacities to
participate effectively by electing representatives of their choice.

The interests of constituents and incumbents are not always identical on
issues like reapportionment and packing of legislative districts. Progressives'
mandate should be to expand the electorate, an objective in which incumbents
often have little interest. In addition, efforts to register new voters have begun
to yield diminishing returns in recent years, suggesting that conventional
methods may have nearly exhausted the population of the unregistered who
might be added to the rolls with relative ease.

In relation to a political strategy focused on issues of policy and governance, black academic radicals' romance of inner-city youth seems mistaken.
Although politicizing young people certainly is important, making them the
central point of strategic discourse amounts to leading from a position of weakness. They are among the most alienated and the least connected segments of
the black population, with the least practical understanding of how the world
works, the thinnest commitments, the greatest volatility, and the most transient social status. Their energy and openness to experimentation only partially
offset these limitations.

A more efficacious strategy would center on segments of the population that are already politically attentive, people who presume efficacy in political action. To that extent, a more rational and effective course would be to undertake a struggle for the hearts and minds of the black working and lower middle classes who attend to political affairs. These are in a way the most centrally placed strata of the Afro-American population. They overlap—through family, friendship, and neighborhood networks, as well as in their own life courses—the ranks of the unemployed and recipients of those forms of public assistance designated for the poor. These are also the people who actively reproduce the character of black political discourse by trying to make sense of the world and constructing their own interests within the inadequate and self-defeating frames of underclass and self-help rhetoric, with which they are bombarded and on which they confer legitimacy by use in the absence of better alternatives. A crucial objective must be to provide such alternatives.

Similarly, a practical Left agenda might profitably include cultivation of such progressive or even guild consciousness as can be identified among the stratum of minority public functionaries and service providers. This is perhaps the most politically sophisticated element of the Afro-American population, the most knowledgeable regarding the real workings of political institutions. Yet they also, by and large, operate without an adequate alternative to the reactionary and victim-blaming frames that presently prevail. Many of them, of course, do so quite happily and will not be susceptible to Left critique; the stratum is, after all, petit bourgeois. Some fraction of them, perhaps mainly among staff-level professionals, however, are committed to ideals of public service and use of government for progressively redistributive purposes. Their pragmatic understanding of government and policy processes could also significantly benefit elaboration of a credible, systematic, and practicable Left program. One approach to undercutting the effects of the current rightist hegemony among them, moreover, might be to attempt to organize coalitions of service providers and constituents of their institutions' services. It should prove less difficult to reach alienated young people in an adult environment characterized by political debate and mobilization.

An approach of this sort provides the best possibility for transcending a simplistic politics that offers as critical touchstones only an abstract, disembodied racism or the victim-blaming self-help line. "Racism" has become too often an empty reification, an alternative to unraveling the complex, frequently indirect processes through which racial inequality is reproduced. Racial stratification is not enacted simply in the indignity of a black professor's inability to get a cab in Manhattan or being mistaken for a parking lot attendant, in discrimination in access to employment, business loans, mortgages, rental housing, or consumer discounts, or even in the demonization of black and brown poor people and the police terror routinely visited upon minority citizens. These problems—from the more petty to the more grave—must be attacked, of course. But racial inequality is also built into the "natural" logic of labor and real estate markets; it inheres, for example, in culturally constructed and politically enforced notions of the appropriate prices for different units of labor power and in the ways that parcels of land are valorized. Racial inequality has been a central organizing premise of federal, state, and local public policy for at least a century, as housing, development, tax, defense, and social welfare policymaking have almost unfailingly reproduced and reinforced it.

The deeper structures of racial stratification are not accessible to the hortatory and demobilizing style of insider negotiation and communitarian mythology around which black political activity has been organized. What is required is the aggressive mobilization of black citizens to pursue specific interests in concert with articulation of a larger programmatic agenda centered in the use of public power—the state apparatus—to realize and enforce concrete visions of social justice. This in turn requires resuscitation of a climate of popular debate in black politics, proceeding from an assumption of civic entitlement and ownership of the society's public institutions.

This is the combined opportunity and challenge presented by the successes of the civil rights movement; it has so far not been met in black politics. Especially now, as the forces of horrible reaction—both black and white—gather steam once again precisely around such premises, it is vitally important to reject emphatically all explicit or tacit claims that black Americans are somehow citizens with an asterisk. Rejection must proceed not only by argument but most of all through the matter-of-fact acting out of black citizenship—through struggling, that is, to use and shape public institutions to advance black interests.

Notes

1. See Frank Parker, *Black Votes Count* (Chapel Hill: University of North Carolina Press, 1990); James W. Button, *Blacks and Social Change* (Princeton, N.J.: Princeton University Press, 1989); and Chandler Davidson and Bernard Grofman, eds., *Quiet Revolution in the South* (Princeton, N.J.: Princeton University Press, 1994).
2. Peter Eisinger, "Black Mayors and the Politics of Racial Economic Advancement," in *Readings in Urban Politics: Past, Present and Future*, ed. Harlan Hahn and Charles Levine (New York: Longman, 1984); Eisinger, "Black Empowerment in Municipal Jobs: The Impact of Black Political Power," *American Political Science Review* 76 (June 1982): 380–92.
3. Earl Picard, "New Black Economic Development Strategy," *Telos*, Summer 1984, 53–64.
4. See Clarence N. Stone, "Social Stratification, Nondecision-Making, and the Study of Community Power," *American Politics Quarterly* 10 (July 1982): 275–302.
5. For a critique, see Adolph Reed Jr., "The 'Underclass' as Myth and Symbol: The Poverty of Discourse about Poverty," *Radical America* 24 (Winter 1991/92): 21–40; Brett Williams, "Poverty among African Americans in the Urban United States," *Human Organization* 51 (Summer 1992): 164–74; Leslie Innis and Joe R. Feagin, "The Black 'Underclass' Ideology in Race Relations Analysis," *Social Justice* 16 (Winter 1989): 13–33.

6. See Lawrence Mead, *Beyond Entitlement: The Social Obligations of Citizenship* (New York: Free Press, 1986).

7. William Julius Wilson, *The Truly Disadvantaged: The Inner City, The Underclass, and Public Policy* (Chicago: University of Chicago Press, 1987).

8. See, for example, Murray Friedman, "The New Black Intellectuals," *Commentary* 69 (June 1980): 46–52; Glenn Loury, "Who Speaks for Black Americans?" *Commentary* 83 (January 1987): 34–38.

9. See Joint Center for Political Studies, *Black Initiative and Governmental Responsibility* (Washington, D.C.: JCPS, 1987); Eugene Rivers, "On the Responsibility of Intellectuals in the Age of Crack," *Boston Review*, September/October 1992; Anthony Appiah, Eugene Rivers, Cornel West, bell hooks, Henry Louis Gates Jr., Margaret Burnham, and special expert Glenn Loury, "On the Responsibility of Intellectuals (in the Age of Crack)," *Boston Review*, January/February 1993.

10. Bayard Rustin's famous essay, "From Protest to Politics," *Commentary* 39 (February 1965): 25–31, noted at the time the challenge that the civil rights movement's successes posed for progressive black interests.

11. See Nathan Wright, *Black Power and Urban Unrest* (New York: Hawthorn, 1967)

12. See Howard Brotz, *Negro Social and Political Thought, 1850–1920* (New York: Basic Books, 1966), 1–33.

13. Robert J. Kerstein and Dennis R. Judd, "Achieving Less Influence with More Democracy: The Permanent Legacy of the War on Poverty," *Social Science Quarterly* 61 (September 1980): 208–20.

14. Adolph Reed Jr., "A Critique of Neo-Progressivism in Theorizing about Development Policy: A Case from Atlanta," in *The Politics of Urban Development*, ed. Clarence N. Stone and Heywood Sanders (Lawrence: University of Kansas Press, 1987).

15. See "Murder Capital: A Mayor's Call for Help," *Newsweek*, November 1, 1993; Don Terry. "A Graver Jackson's Cry: Overcome the Violence," *New York Times*, November 13, 1993; William Raspberry, "Jesse Jackson Calls on Nation's Blacks to 'Tell It' Like It Is," *Chicago Tribune*, October 11, 1993.

16. The Black Panther party's absence from this account may seem curious. It is nonetheless justified. The BPP was in effect the creature of a transitional moment between simple black power rhetoric and the clearly articulated formation of incrementalist mainstream and radical wings. The BPP crested as an autonomous black political organization in the late 1960s, before the institutional entailments of systemic incorporation had begun to take their ultimate forms. By the time the practical outlines of the new regime were clearly discernible, the party was in disarray practically everywhere except Oakland, California.

17. Clarence N. Stone, *Regime Politics: Governing Atlanta, 1946–1988* (Lawrence: University of Kansas Press, 1989), 93, 166; Mack H. Jones, "Black Political Empowerment in Atlanta: Myth and Reality," *Annals of the American Academy of Political and Social Science* 439 (September 1978): 90–117.

18. See Leslie Cagan, "Rainbow Realignment," *Zeta*, May 1989; Thulani Davis and James Ridgeway, "Jesse Jackson's New Math: Does It Add Up to a Winner?" *Village Voice*, December 22, 1987.

19. Thomas Byrne Edsall and Mary D. Edsall, *Chain Reaction: The Impact of Race, Rights and Taxes on American Politics* (New York: Norton, 1991); William Crotty, "Who Needs Two Republican Parties?" in *The Democrats Must Lead: The Case for a Progres-*

sive Democratic Party, ed. James MacGregor Burns, William Crotty, Lois Lovelace Duke, and Lawrence D. Lovejoy (Boulder, Colo.: Westview Press, 1992).

20. See, for example, George Lipsitz, "The Mardi Gras Indians: Carnival and Counter-Narrative in Black New Orleans," *Cultural Critique*, Fall 1988, 99–121; Elsa Barkley-Brown. "African-American Women's Quilting: A Framework for Conceptualizing and Teaching African-American Women's History," *Signs* 14 (Summer 1989); 921–29; and Michelle Wallace and Gina Dent, eds., *Black Popular Culture* (Seattle, Wash.: Bay Press, 1992).

Earl Smith
African American Intercollegiate Athletes

College athletics programs provide opportunities for growth and development, fuel school spirit and community involvement, and open doors for students who otherwise would not have had a chance to attend college—benefits that we, of course, proudly trumpet. But far too often, and with increasing frequency, college athletics has been a source of embarrassment. . . . When the National Collegiate Athletic Association releases its annual data on graduation rates of varsity athletes in the so-called revenue sports—football and men's basketball—presidents join, if not lead, the predictable chorus of educators and editorials expressing outrage at the abysmal results. We publicly deplore, for instance, statistics revealing that only 4 out of 10 basketball players graduate in 6 years or less. But what, if anything, are we doing about the problem?

—Joe B. Wyatt, President, Vanderbilt University[1]

INTRODUCTION

The subject of this essay, a problem in the sociology of sport, has long been of special interest to me. The essay is about African American student-athletes.[2] While there have been debates surrounding the relationship between education and athletics and many have been both longstanding and some are now legendary,[3] for me the intellectual interest came when I least expected it.

EDUCATIONAL MALPRACTICE

When I started teaching a "sociology of sport" course in 1983 at Washington State University, I was unaware of the controversies surrounding intercollegiate sports. Soon thereafter, I learned that Dexter Manley, an Oklahoma State

---

[1]Joe B. Wyatt, 1999, "Our Moral Duty to Clean Up College Athletics." *Chronicle of Higher Education*, August 13th, op-ed, back page.

[2]Student-athlete refers to college students who attend post-secondary institutions on athletic scholarships. See, especially, Timothy Davis, 1992, "Examining Educational Malpractice Jurisprudence: Should a Cause of Action Be Created for Student-Athletes?" *Denver University Law Review* 69, note 7, p. 58.

[3]John Thelin, 1994, *Games Colleges Play: Scandal and Reform in Intercollegiate Athletics*. Baltimore: Johns Hopkins University Press, p. 26.

"graduate", drafted 5th in the first round of the National Football League draft in 1981, told a Senate panel that upon leaving Oklahoma State he could not read. I became very aware of many concerns that faculty have about college athletics and began to systematically study some of these issues. A major concern of mine is the lack of attention athletic programs pay to the student side of their athletes' responsibilities. This deficit is long-standing, and especially troubling as it pertains to African American student athletes.

For example, the Carnegie Commission Report of 1929 entitled *American College Athletics* could state:

> The heart of the problem facing college sports was commercialization: an interlocking network that included expanded press coverage, public interest, alumni involvement, and recruiting abuses. The victim was the student-athlete in particular, the diminishing of educational and intellectual values in general.

Some of the same concerns that are evident in the 1929 Carnegie Commission report are still with us today.[4] Former President of Occidental College Dr. John B. Slaughter, writing about the responsibilities of college and university presidents for change within intercollegiate athletic programs at their institutions, felt that university chief executive officers had allowed the list of problems and scandals to grow into a very long list of problems and scandals. He put it thus:[5]

> While far more of these programs are conducted with integrity than are not, the ones that get press and media attention are those in which avarice, dishonesty, and the exploitation of athletes have replaced the high moral values and benefits of competition upon which intercollegiate athletics were founded. Unfortunately, the list of those perpetrators of wrongdoing has grown inexorably long.

So, while the debate about college athletics and its place within higher education has had an airing, this essay will focus on similar issues with the understanding that the concern herein is the role that ethics and honor (E & H) plays in all intercollegiate sports.

We would be remiss if we were not concerned with the substantial problems inherent in intercollegiate sport programs. These include, but are not limited to, classroom cheating, cheating in the recruitment of student-athletes, academic fraud, sexual abuse and drug use and abuse. The late Ernest Boyer, scholar extraordinary, could write in his influential book *College: The Under-*

---

[4]In a followup study conducted on behalf of the *New York Times* in 1931 it was found that not one of the 112 colleges studied in 1929 by the Carnegie Commission had changed its practices. See, also, Knight Foundation Commission report of 1991 entitled: *Keeping the Faith with the Student Athlete: A New Model for Intercollegiate Athletics.*

[5]John B. Slaughter, 1989, "Where was the President? A President's Responsibility for Change in Intercollegiate Athletics." Pp. 179–191 in Richard Lapchick and John B. Slaughter (Ed.), *The Rules of the Game: Ethics in College Sport.* New York: Macmillan Publishers.

graduate Experience in America that in regards to ambivalence over standards that

> Integrity cannot be divided. If high standards of conduct are expected of students, colleges must have impeccable integrity themselves. Otherwise, the lessons of the "hidden curriculum" will shape the undergraduate experience (p. 184).

This deterioration of high standards cannot be allowed to happen. If deterioration takes place in the realm of the type and stature of athletes brought to the college campus, it will soon take place in the classroom as well.

Intercollegiate sports, unlike any other activity that students participate in, continue to offer students a chance to change, for the better, the quality of their lives. Yet, because institutions of higher learning net millions of dollars in receipts—from the sale of athletic contests, for example, the marketing of high profile team sports like basketball and football, to the sale of athletic clothing—there ever remains the need to be diligent against unscrupulous activities. Among these I would include gambling by students, even student-athletes, to improper sports agent contact with student-athletes who are still participating under National Collegiate Athletic Association (hereafter NCAA) rules governing student-athletes.[6] These temptations have proven to be real over the course of the last decade or longer, and raise serious ethical issues and questions.

Never again can colleges and universities error on the side of illegalities, bad decisions, immorality and unethical behavior as they did in the Kevin Ross case. Ross, an African American student-athlete, enrolled at Creighton University as a 6'9" basketball player. He had scored 9 of a possible 36 on his ACT test. At the time the average score at Creighton was 23. When the initial application was rejected, a Vice President and officials in the athletic department got the decision overturned and Ross began his collegiate career taking courses such as "Theory of Basketball", "Introduction to Ceramics" and "Theory of Track & Field." Ross was advanced to his sophomore year. The problem is that when the sports program at Creighton was finished with Ross, he was dropped from school and later diagnosed as being functionally illiterate. The case gained national attention when Ross began taking classes (actually attending) with elementary school children in Chicago.[7]

Students are in school to be educated. No one would argue against this fact. Yet, it is the issue of priorities that needs to be addressed as intercollegiate athletics makes an attempt to walk a path that is not only narrow and straight but, at the same time, is both ethical and honest.[8]

[6]Kenneth Shropshire, 1990, *Agents of Opportunity: Sports Agents and Corruption in Collegiate Sports.* Philadelphia: University of Pennsylvania Press.

[7]Timothy Davis, 1992, "Examining Educational Malpractice Jurisprudence: Should a Cause of Action be Created for Student-Athletes?" *Denver University Law Review* 69:57–96.

[8]Proceedings: National Alliance for College Athletic Reform, conference at Drake University, March 24–25, 2000.

For a long time now student-athletes' academic abilities have been questioned. The nature of this concern is longstanding. The contemporary era is more insistent in seeing to it that students who come to college to play sports also graduate from college when their playing time is over. Moreso these days, student-athletes take five to six years to complete their education. And many never complete their education. This is especially true of the African American male student-athlete and becoming increasingly true of African American female student-athletes.

The most recent data from the NCAA shows that student athletes graduate at similar rates as nonathletes. Nationally, the figure is somewhere around fifty-eight (58) percent. The data also show that student-athletes in the so-called revenue producing sports of football and basketball have graduation rates that are lower than the average.

Particularly troublesome are the rates for African American males who play basketball. Welch Suggs in the September 10th 1999 edition of the *Chronicle of Higher Education* examined these data and found the following:

> 33 per cent of Division 1 black male basketball players who enrolled as freshmen in 1992 received their degrees within six years.[9]

While the history of the African American athlete within collegiate institutions has followed a curious path, these data show that open admissions, affirmative action, the decline in systematic segregation all may not have helped the educational quest of African Americans pursuing this goal via athletics. Aside from those scholars who are carefully researching the education/athletic relationship, the general public, including students, are not aware of the deep problems in this arena. It is only when the high profile cases hit the media spotlight, such as Dexter Manley or Kevin Ross (mentioned above) that you begin to see a cry to do something.[10]

Do what? When athletic programs as big as Syracuse University, University of South Carolina, Baylor University, Brigham Young, La Salle University, Gonzaga University, and the University of Louisville to the little known programs at the University of Idaho and Southern University play athletes for five and six years and then fail to graduate even one, what can be done?[11] Several institutions remain suspect for their continued cheating violations and other indiscretions yet we always see teams from these schools participating, year

[9]Welch Suggs, 1999, "Graduation Rates Hit Lowest Level in 7 Years for Athletes in Football and Basketball: Percentage of black team members earning degrees is lower than at any time in the decade." *Chronicle of Higher Education*, September 10th.

[10]A careful overview of the education/athletics relationship is in my forthcoming book entitled *The Sporting World of African American Athletes: From Jackie Roosevelt Robinson to Michael "Air" Jordan*.

[11]Betsy Peoples, 2000, "Basketball Fouls: Bottom 50, A New Low for College Hoops." *Emerge Magazine*, April, pp. 45–46.

in and year out. There is something very unethical about this institutional behavior.

Almost everyone accepts the proposition that intercollegiate athletic programs are a consequential part of the mission of a college and/or university today. But are these programs *more important* than the education mission itself? I don't think so.

VIOLENCE

College athletic coaches and administrators must also stem the on-the-field and off-the-field violence that has begun to impact the intercollegiate sports scene.

Approximately four years back Virginia Tech lost the 1996 Orange Bowl to perennial football powerhouse Nebraska. Between May 1996 and May 1997 eighteen (18) members of Tech's football program were arrested. Two players were arrested for rape.[12,13]

In April 2000 eight (8) members of the proud Providence College basketball program stalked three students for a few days and then pummeled these classmates to the point of unconsciousness, leaving one student in need of reconstructive surgery. Two of the students needed the surgery for broken jaws and a broken nose.[14]

If, as some assert, the violence that shadows intercollegiate athletic programs is a pre-college issue, it would stand to reason that the personnel responsible for recruiting the athletes to campus must do a better job of the tasks they are assigned. Otherwise, the need to win games will always receive priority over recruiting good students who are also good athletes.

A disproportionate number of the student-athletes who get into trouble are football and basketball players. African American student-athletes dominate at these two sports.

The case of Lawrence Phillips, Nebraska, is not an exception to the rule. Phillips was a star runningback for the top ranked Nebraska Cornhuskers. He was also a batterer. Phillips was convicted of the felony of beating Kate McEwen while both were enrolled at the university. Phillips received no jail time, was briefly suspended from the team by then coach Tom Osborne (now a U.S. Senator) and went on to be drafted 6th by the St. Louis Rams.

At the height of his prowess on the football field Phillips was living off-campus and with McEwen. During a two year period (1994–1996) Phillips re-

[12]Jeffrey Benedict, 1997, "Colleges Must Act Firmly When Scholarship Athletes Break the Law." *Chronicle of Higher Education*, May 9, p. B6.

[13]Todd Crossett, 1995, "Male Student Athletes Reported for Sexual Assault." *Journal of Sport and Social Issues*, 19: 126–140. (The authors conducted an empirical study of the records of college judicial programs and found that scholarship athletes were more often involved in campus rape cases than nonathletes).

[14]Jack Curry, 2000, "A Vicious Fight Casts Its Shadow." *New York Times*, May 11th. One student needed his eye socket repaired and another had to have a metal plate inserted into his face.

peatedly brutalized McEwen. In a court affidavit filed on August 16th, 1996 in the Jackson County Federal Court in Kansas, McEwen revealed the assaults upon her person handed out by Phillips.

When they broke up, Phillips cut her tires, choked her, threatened to shoot her, sexually assaulted her and on September 10, 1995 she reports the following:

> Phillips beat me and kicked me while I was at a friend's house. He grabbed me and pulled me down three flights of stairs and slammed my head into a wall.[15]

According to police reports he had been abusing McEwen for a long time before the September 10th report was filed.

It is this type of behavior that requires football programs (and not tennis or golf or baseball programs) to house football teams in local hotels the Friday night before home games. The cost, per annum, for such lodging is astronomical.

This problem has profound implications for African American student-athletes: violence and criminal conduct indelibly marks the African American athlete.

$ GREED $

Nike hasn't called and told us when to start our games. Athletes don't miss classes because of Nike. If intercollegiate athletics has sold its soul, it wasn't to shoe and apparel companies. They sold it a long time ago, to television.

—Joe Robinson, Athletic director at the University
of Michigan until August 1997[16]

College athletics has become a big business. Beginning in 1950, and increasing in direct involvement in commercial interlocking business relations since then, the NCAA has signed million dollar contracts with commercial television (in 1951 the deal was with Westinghouse Electric) outlets to broadcast its college games. The data in Table 1 are an illustration of the modern era relationship of intercollegiate sports and television.

The former football powerhouse Notre Dame remains as of this writing the only institution to have its own TV deal. Notre Dame signed a seven year, $45 million dollar deal with NBC and since then the on-the-field performance has declined and the off-the-field student-athlete antics have increased.

Ara Parasegian the legendary Notre Dame coach—with the "halo" qualities of the great Green Bay packers coach Vince Lombardi—was said to be impeccable. He won football games with style. He taught discipline and respect.

---

[15]The grim details of the Phillips case are found in the book by Jeff Benedict and Don Yaeger. 1998. *Pros and Cons: The Criminals who Play in the NFL*. New York: Warner Books.

[16]Cited on p. 125 in Zimbalist, *Unpaid Professionals*.

TABLE I   *Major Division 1A Football Conference Television Deals, 1996–2000*

Conference/School	TV Network	Contract Amount (in millions $)
ACC	ABC/ESPN	70
Big East	CBS	65
Big Ten/Pac-10	ABC	115
SEC	CBS	85
Notre Dame	NBC	38 (7yrs, worth $45 mil)

Source: Zimbalist, 1999, p. 103

Yet, the tradition he built at Notre Dame was tainted when boosters' greed turned to tampering with the rules that govern intercollegiate athletics.[17] The student athletes on the football team received jewelry, sex, clothing, and air trips to Las Vegas vacation spots all paid for by a booster by the name of Ms. Kimberly Dunbar who embezzled $1.4 million dollars from her employer to pay for the gifts.[18]

The greed goes both ways. Colleges get wrapped up in the money game and go after athletes who have proven track records as winners. (If they do not have the winning track record, the culture of the sport stereotype is invoked and the players are *supposed* to be winners.)[19] They come to campus as semi-professionals and are slotted under the rubric of "student-athlete," carrying all the baggage that comes with that title. No other student who gives time, service and energy to the university carries such a label. Students participate in the affairs of the university in a variety of ways: some students are full-time band members, some with scholarships, debate club members and in some institutions the tradition of the intellectual game known as the "college bowl" still exists. None of these students carry a label akin to student-athlete. None receive the perks of student-athletes and, depending on the institution they attend, their activities are often just as significant as those of some sponsored sport programs.

The student-athletes who are men (and increasingly women) spend an enormous amount of time on their sports both in and out of season. In the money-producing sports of basketball and football the players can spend up to 25 to 30 hours per week training with the team. They must be compensated via the "scholarship" route but increasingly as the money tree grows the athletes and their families request more and more for themselves.

[17]David Maraniss, 1999, *When Pride Still Mattered: A Life of Vince Lombardi.* New York: Simon & Schuster.

[18]This is a story that will make its way to the Big Screen someday. See, especially, Joe Drape, 1998, "ND Halo Loses Some Glow After Recent Revelations." *New York Times,* August 14th.

[19]The best research on the sport stereotype is found in the work of Arizona State psychologist Professor Jeff Stone. See Jeff Stone et al., 1999, "Stereotype Threat Effects on Black and White Athletic Performance." *Journal of Personality and Social Psychology* 77:1213–1227.

From initial recruitment through graduation, the greed runs a path that no respecting citizen would want to know about. Student athletes gamble on games. They steal from department stores. And, finally many of them end up in court or jail or both for abusing their college girlfriends.[20]

John Wooden, the legendary basketball coach at the University of California at Los Angeles (UCLA) left the game before his championship teams could become tainted, chasing the money. Wooden amassed ten (10) NCAA basketball championships in twelve (12) years, and won seven (7) of those championships in a row. The days of coaches like John Wooden are over in intercollegiate sports. The players and their parents, athletic directors, boosters, posse, and fans all have a say in determining what the coach can or cannot do. That is to say, the ethics of good coaching that helps shape adulthood for young men and women, their morality, perspective on fairness and civility and fair play among young student-athletes, is being lost to greed.[21]

There is no better illustration to make the point than this: All college sporting events take a back seat to the Final Four NCAA Basketball Elimination Tournament. But, does this tournament have anything to do with higher education other than the names of the universities across the players' chests?

Men's basketball has played 2nd fiddle to college football for years and still remains in that position. Yet, basketball is gaining ground on football as the national sporting event to watch on TV. The biggest jump from contributing financially approximately nine (9) percent to the overall athletic revenues in 1960 to approximately 25 percent in 1998 is directly related to the Final Four basketball tournament.

In a "war" with the National Invitational Tournament (NIT), the NCAA made an all-out bid to destabilize the NIT and take over first place as the preeminent post-season basketball tournament. It worked!

Beginning with the 1990 season the NCAA signed an unheard of contract worth at minimum $1 billion dollars with CBS for the rights to the Final Four tournament. Another $5 billion is in the package for TV rights to local, regional and national games. The most recent contract calls for an eight-year deal (1995–2002) worth at least $1.75 billion. A good portion of that money is generated via the fee paid for TV advertising at $600,000 for 30-second spots!

The math on all of this is very complicated so let's say that the conference payouts, TV money, advertising, sale of school apparel and logos all contribute to the big money and high profile commercial sports. We can then assume that most of this greed has little to do with education and very little of the money goes directly to the players. This causes a slate of problems in and of itself.

For example, another dimension to all of this has not been discussed, and I will do that now. UCLA's JaRon Rush and his brother Kareem, who plays for

[20]Dan Wetzel and Don Yaeger, 2000, *Sole Influence: Basketball, Corporate Greed, and the Corruption of America's Youth.* New York: Warner Books.

[21]John Wooden, 1997, *WOODEN: A Lifetime of Observations and Reflections On and Off the Court.* Lincolnwood, Illinois: Contemporary Books.

the University of Missouri, were suspended during the 1999–2000 season for accepting gifts from Kansas City summer league coach Myron Piggie.

Piggie, a former crack dealer,[22] was charged April 13, 2000 in an indictment, with paying the Rush brothers, Oklahoma State's Andre Williams, former Duke player Corey Maggette and ex-Wichita high school superstar Korleone Young more than $35,000 while they were playing for him between high school seasons, jeopardizing their college eligibility and thus defrauding the programs that ultimately signed them.

This case fueled calls to clean up the summer game, in which sponsors, nonscholastic coaches and shoe companies have come to wield considerable influence over players, and yet without the rules, regulations and leadership that govern intercollegiate sports.[23]

The players are tainted long before they reach campus and once they do, all of the pre-college relationships and dealings follow them. Many stay in school a year or two, then depart, leaving a trail of debris behind them. Even institutions that have considerably good academic/athletic histories and no NCAA violation charges are having to alter the way they relate to players, and agents, because of the amount of money now involved in collegiate sports.[24]

WAKE FOREST UNIVERSITY

One of the distinguishing characteristics of Wake Forest University (hereafter WFU), making it different from many of the NCAA 900-plus member institutions,[25] is that the athletic department does not run the university; athletics are not supreme over academics.[26]

In the modern era of the University and its athletic programs this is not accidental. Furthermore, it is no more visible than the relationship that the Uni-

---

[22]Dan Wetzel and Don Yaeger, 2000, *Sole Influence: Basketball, Corporate Greed, and the Corruption of America's Youth*. New York: Warner Books, p. xii.

[23]Steve Weiberg. "A new ballgame: NCAA takes another shot at trying to clean up its tarnished reputation." *USA Today*, April 27, 2000, p. 3C.

[24]I am thinking here mainly of Duke that had for the first time in the storied history of their basketball program, two or three underclass players leave the school early (1998) for the professional NBA.

[25]Most of the research, writing, and commission reports, etc., about the NCAA are usually in reference to the "big-time sports" of football and basketball (also known as the money sports) within Division 1. In many institutions the athletic department is organized to function almost autonomously from the larger university structure.

[26]Murray Sperber (Indiana University) in his best selling book *College Sports, Inc*. notes that many Division 1 universities pay lip service to academics. See, also, the critical op-ed by *Sports Illustrated* writer Rick Reilly (*SI*, "Class Struggle at Ohio State", August 31, 1998, p. 156) on Ohio State University and their star football player, Andy Katzenmoyer, the 1997 Butkus Award winner (for best linebacker in college football). When Katzenmoyer's GPA slipped below 2.0 the athletic department arranged for him to take three summer courses. The courses: Golf, Music and AIDS Awareness. See also, Frederick Klein, 1997, "Student Athlete Raises Questions About Education." *Wall Street Journal*, p. B11.

TABLE 2   *Wake Forest U Graduation Rates for All Students & Student-Athletes (Entering Class of 1992)*

All students		All		White men		Black men		White women		Black women	
92–93	91–92	92–93	91–92	92–93	91–92	92–93	91–92	92–93	91–92	92–93	91–92
82%	85%	69%	76%	70%	85%	57%	46%	78%	86%	100%	100%

Source: *Chronicle of Higher Education*, September 10, 1999

versity has with the football program under the leadership of Coach Jim Caldwell. Under Caldwell, the football program has begun to turn around and in the 1999–2000 season they won six games and lost five. The season was capped off with an Aloha Bowl victory on Christmas day over Arizona State.

In Division 1 football circles the credo is "win—at any cost." What is impressive, if not rare, is that WFU still adheres to a level of integrity that weds academics and athletics. WFU has a graduation rate of approximately 85% and among student-athletes in all sports that provide athletic scholarships, WFU has one of the highest graduation rates in the country at approximately seventy-six percent (76%).

One measure of the quality of the academic/athletic relationship at WFU is that some student-athletes combine their athletic talent with being good students. Several student-athletes have distinguished themselves as academic All Americans and one has been awarded the Arthur Ashe Jr. Sports Scholar Award (see Table 3). These awards of academic excellence do not come easily nor are they given to anyone for simply trying (see Table 4).

It is safe to say that athletes as students come first at WFU. At no time in the history of the sports program would you find the following:

> In spring training my sophomore year, I broke my neck, four vertebrae. "Hey, coach," I said, "my neck don't feel good." "There's nothing wrong with your neck, you jackass," he said. So the numb went away a little, and I made a tackle. When I went to get up, my body got up but my head just stayed there, right on the ground. The coach says, "Hey, get this jackass off the field." So the trainer puts some ice on my neck and after practice they took me up to the infirmary for an X-ray. The doctor said, "Son, your neck is broken. You got here ten minutes later, you'd be dead."

TABLE 3   *Arthur Ashe Jr., Student-Athlete Award*

Year	Name	Major	Sport
1996	Ndoma-Ogar, Elton SR.	Hlth/Sport Sci	Football

Source: Paul Robeson Center for Academic and Athletic Prowess, University of Michigan, April 7, 2000

TABLE 4   *GTE Academic All-Americans*

Year	Name	Sport
1959	Aubrey Currie	Football
1959	Larry Fleisher	Football
1985	Amy Privette	W Basketball
1986	Amy Privette	W Basketball
1987	Amy Privette	W Basketball
1988	William Masse	Baseball
1988	Donald Heck	Soccer
1994	Stephanie Neill	Golf
1995	Andy Bloom	Track & Field
1996	Rusty LaRue	M Basketball
1996	Andy Bloom	Track & Field
1997	David Lardieri	Baseball

Source: WFU Athletics, March 2000

Dead! Man, that scared me. I mean those colleges let you lie right out there on the field and die. That's something to think about.[27]

Controversy continues to wrack intercollegiate athletics. Some of the persistent criticisms begin with the meeting that President Theodore "Teddy" Roosevelt held at the White House on October 9, 1905 with representatives from Harvard, Princeton and Yale to discuss the growing violence in football. According to the historian John R. Thelin in *Games Colleges Play: Scandal and Reform in Intercollegiate Athletics*, it is this meeting that led to some of the first major reform movements in college sports.[28] When the Carnegie Commission released its 1929 report it gave considerable attention to the growing "commercialization" in intercollegiate sports programs. Following the report's release, cheating and financial scandals increased.

These are some of the persistent problems that continue to plague college sports. Athletic directors, coaches, faculty, and administrators at WFU must insure that safeguards are in place for the future to safeguard heeding to the temptations of "win—at any cost."

CONCLUSION

Historically, presidents and other college administrators have not maintained a continuing, focused involvement in the activities of their athletics departments.

—Joe B. Wyatt, President, Vanderbilt University[29]

---

[27]Charlie Taylor, a former football player at Arizona State, cited in Zimbalist, p. 217.

[28]John R. Thelin, 1994, *Games Colleges Play*. Baltimore, Maryland: The Johns Hopkins University Press.

[29]Joe B. Wyatt, 1999, "Our Moral Duty to Clean Up College Athletics." *Chronicle of Higher Education*. August 13th, op-ed, back page.

The study of sport provides an excellent opportunity to empirically examine many of the issues that confront American society. This is especially true when examining issues of ethics and honor within the university system of intercollegiate athletics.

In this essay I examined some of these concerns that surround the contemporary student-athlete. I conclude by noting that there is much work to be done to re-establish trust (with a capital "T")[30] within academe. This is especially true for faculty. The inclusion and participation of commercial athletic programs that have grown on our college and university campuses is a challenge for everyone who forms a part of the college and university system. Overall, much of what I have done in this essay is ask questions, many for which I do not have answers.

But, like the late sociologist Everett C. Hughes, writing in 1945 in the prestigious *American Journal of Sociology*, my overall concern in this essay has been to call attention to the characteristic phenomena I identified as a problem in intercollegiate sports. Like Hughes, I am largely concerned about the heterogeneous and changing character of intercollegiate sports and call on those who are observing special parts of the American social structure to pay more attention to intercollegiate athletics and the relationship between athletics and academics. It is time for college Presidents to really take charge of athletics programs at their institutions, as this action was called for by the Knight Foundation Commission report on college athletics released in 1991 and more recently another report in 2001.[31]

Upward mobility and success for African American student-athletes seems to be out of step on at least two fronts:

1. The student part of the terms is rarely met with equity.
2. The athlete part seems to be more heavily weighed even though only 1 in 3,000 actually make it to the professional ranks.[32] (see Table 5)

By folding the paper under the rubric of Ethics & Honor the plight and conditions of African American Student-Athletes I have been able to demonstrate that there is something less than ethical about the way the majority of African American student athletes are treated in their quest to be athletes as they simultaneously pursuer a higher education at some of our nation's most prestigious colleges and universities.

---

[30]For the larger meaning I give to trust in much of my writing about college athletics see the important work of Professor Francis Fukuyama, 1995, *Trust: The Social Virtues and the Creation of Prosperity*. New York: Free Press.

[31]As Creed Black, then President of the Knight Foundation told a Congressional Committee there is a problem when "rules violations undermines the traditional role of the universities as places where the young people learn ethics and integrity." *Intercollegiate Sports*, Hearings, House of Representatives, p. 9, cited in Zimbalist, p. 210.

[32]See the Table "Making The Pros."

TABLE 5 Making The Pros

	Football	Basketball
High School Participants	265,000	150,000
Making NCAA Teams	16,450	3,800
Playing as seniors	8,930	2,400
Playing in the Pros	215	64
Odds	1 in 1,233	1 in 2,344

Source: NCAA News, October 9, 1989.

To conclude this chapter, I am offering what I term the ten most important things to be considered and implemented when trying to fix the problems of African American student athletes. I am also clear that colleges and the NCAA cannot solve all of these problems facing institutions and their athletes.

Ten Proposals for Reform

1. Coaches who care. Must graduate 75% of all student-athletes regardless of (a) scholarship status or (b) playing ability.

2. Institutions who care: Must deal effectively and swiftly with all coaches who fail to maintain the stated educational mission and goals of the institutions that employ them.

3. Only recruit student-athletes who strive for educational opportunities. Must explain and be vigilant in maintaining quality in the educational lives of all active athletes. These men and women must know that there is a price to pay for not maintaining quality grades (not just eligibility).

4. Only recruit athletes who want an education.

5. Institutional support. The athletic programs that make money off the backs of the student athletes must invest in their education. They must put together effective support programs that are in congruence with the way the educational mission is carved out at their respective institutions. This means going beyond work-study supported tutors for athletes on a given night after they are tired (and full from just having eaten) from a full day in school and on the practice field. Faculty supported mentoring programs, within specific disciplines is one model of support that has been tried and works.

6. Dissolve financially meaningless relationships with sponsoring agencies that do no more than provide uniforms and sneakers for programs (in actuality advertising for the concerns).

7. Prepare for equity in men and women's programs. Hire coaches on the basis of their proven abilities on and off the playing fields.

8. Build in for all student-athletes a stipend for educational needs and personal needs. (This should include at minimum one full fare round-trip for athletes living more than five (5) hours driving time from their homes.)

9. Make sure the curriculum (courses) that student-athletes take can lead to a meaningful career outside of college athletics. Abolish "cake" courses.

10. Be ethical in dealing with student-athletes (male and female) and try harder to be humanistic when they fail in their athletic quest, as many often do.

Finally, all of us in academe have a moral obligation to ensure that female and male student-athletes entering our universities have a chance at succeeding academically.

Robert Bullard
from *Dumping in Dixie*

CHAPTER ONE

Environmentalism and Social Justice

The environmental movement in the United States emerged with agendas that focused on such areas as wilderness and wildlife preservation, resource conservation, pollution abatement, and population control. It was supported primarily by middle- and upper-middle-class whites. Although concern about the environment cut across racial and class lines, environmental activism has been most pronounced among individuals who have above-average education, greater access to economic resources, and a greater sense of personal efficacy.[1]

Mainstream environmental organizations were late in broadening their base of support to include blacks and other minorities, the poor, and working-class persons. The "energy crisis" in the 1970s provided a major impetus for the many environmentalists to embrace equity issues confronting the poor in this country and in the countries of the Third World.[2] Over the years, environmentalism has shifted from a "participatory" to a "power" strategy, where the "core of active environmental movement is focused on litigation, political lobbying, and technical evaluation rather than on mass mobilization for protest marches."[3]

An abundance of documentation shows blacks, lower-income groups, and working-class persons are subjected to a disproportionately large amount of pollution and other environmental stressors in their neighborhoods as well as in their workplaces.[4] However, these groups have only been marginally involved in the nation's environmental movement. Problems facing the black community have been topics of much discussion in recent years. (Here, we use sociologist James Blackwell's definition of the black community, "a highly diversified set of interrelated structures and aggregates of people who are held together by forces of white oppression and racism."[5]) Race has not been eliminated as a factor in the allocation of community amenities.

Research on environmental quality in black communities has been minimal. Attention has been focused on such problems as crime, drugs, poverty, unemployment, and family crisis. Nevertheless, pollution is exacting a heavy toll (in health and environmental costs) on black communities across the nation. There are few studies that document, for example, the way blacks cope with environmental stressors such as municipal solid-waste facilities, hazardous-waste landfills, toxic-waste dumps, chemical emissions from industrial plants, and on-the-job hazards that pose extreme risks to their health. Coping in this case is seen as a response to stress and is defined as "efforts, both action-oriented and intrapsychic, to manage, i.e., master, tolerate, reduce, minimize, environmental and internal demands, conflicts among them, which tax or exceed a person's resources."[6] Coping strategies employed by individuals confronted with a stressor are of two general types: *problem-focused coping* (e.g., individual and/or group efforts to directly address the problem) and *emotion-focused coping* (e.g., efforts to control one's psychological response to the stressor). The decision to take direct action or to tolerate a stressor often depends on how individuals perceive their ability to do something about or have an impact on the stressful situation. Personal efficacy, therefore, is seen as a factor that affects environmental and political activism.[7]

Much research has been devoted to analyzing social movements in the United States. For example, hundreds of volumes have been written in the past several years on the environmental, labor, antiwar, and civil rights movements. Despite this wide coverage, there is a dearth of material on the convergence (and the divergence, for that matter) of environmentalism and social justice advocacy. This appears to be the case in and out of academia. Moreover, few social scientists have studied environmentalism among blacks and other ethnic minorities. This oversight is rooted in historical and ideological factors and in the composition of the core environmental movement and its largely white middle-class profile.

Many of the interactions that emerged among core environmentalists, the poor, and blacks can be traced to distributional equity questions. How are the benefits and burdens of environmental reform distributed? Who gets what, where, and why? Are environmental inequities a result of racism or class barriers or a combination of both? After more than two decades of modern environmentalism, the equity issues have not been resolved. There has been, however, some change in the way environmental problems are presented by mainstream environmental organizations. More important, environmental equity has now become a major item on the local (grassroots) as well as national civil rights agenda.[8]

Much of the leadership in the civil rights movement came from historically black colleges and universities (HBCUs). Black college students were on the "cutting edge" in leading sit-in demonstrations at lunch counters, libraries, parks, and public transit systems that operated under Jim Crow laws. In *The Origins of the Civil Rights Movement*, Aldon D. Morris wrote:

> The tradition of protest is transmitted across generations by older relatives, black institutions, churches, and protest organizations. Blacks interested in social change inevitably gravitate to this "protest community," where they hope to find solutions to a complex problem.
>
> The modern civil rights movement fits solidly into this rich tradition of protest. Like the slave revolts, the Garvey Movement, and the March on Washing-

ton, it was highly organized. Its significant use of the black religious community to accomplish political goals also linked the modern movement to the earlier mass movements which also relied heavily on the church.[9]

Social justice and the elimination of institutionalized discrimination were the major goals of the civil rights movement. Many of the HBCUs are located in some of the most environmentally polluted communities in the nation. These institutions and their students, thus, have a vested interest in seeing that improvements are made in local environmental quality. Unlike their move to challenge other forms of inequity, black student-activists have been conspicuously silent and relatively inactive on environmental problems. Moreover, the resources and talents of the faculties at these institutions have also been underutilized in assisting affected communities in their struggle against polluters, including government and private industries.

The problem of polluted black communities is not a new phenomenon. Historically, toxic dumping and the location of locally unwanted land uses (LULUs) have followed the "path of least resistance," meaning black and poor communities have been disproportionately burdened with these types of externalities. However, organized black resistance to toxic dumping, municipal waste facility siting, and discriminatory environmental and land-use decisions is a relatively recent phenomenon.[10] Black environmental concern has been present but too often has not been followed up with action.

Ecological concern has remained moderately high across nearly all segments of the population. Social equity and concern about distributive impacts, however, have not fared so well over the years. Low-income and minority communities have had few advocates and lobbyists at the national level and within the mainstream environmental movement. Things are changing as environmental problems become more "potent political issues [and] become increasingly viewed as threatening public health."[11]

The environmental movement of the 1960s and 1970s, dominated by the middle class, built an impressive political base for environmental reform and regulatory relief. Many environmental problems of the 1980s and 1990s, however, have social impacts that differ somewhat from earlier ones. Specifically, environmental problems have had serious regressive impacts. These impacts have been widely publicized in the media, as in the case of the hazardous-waste problems at Love Canal and Times Beach. The plight of polluted minority communities is not as well known as the New York and Missouri tragedies. Nevertheless, a disproportionate burden of pollution is carried by the urban poor and minorities.[12]

Few environmentalists realized the sociological implications of the not-in-my-backyard (NIMBY) phenomenon.[13] Given the political climate of the times, the hazardous wastes, garbage dumps, and polluting industries were likely to end up in somebody's backyard. But whose backyard? More often than not, these LULUs ended up in poor, powerless, black communities rather than in affluent suburbs. This pattern has proven to be the rule, even though the bene-fits derived from industrial waste production are directly related to affluence.[14] Public officials and private industry have in many cases responded to the NIMBY phenomenon using the place-in-blacks'-backyard (PIBBY) principle.[15]

Social activists have begun to move environmentalism to the left in an effort to address some of the distributional impact and equity issues.[16] Docu-mentation of civil rights violations has strengthened the move to make envi-ronmental quality a basic right of all individuals. Rising energy costs and a continued erosion of the economy's ability to provide jobs (but not promises) are factors that favor blending the objectives of labor, minorities, and other "underdogs" with those of middle-class environmentalists.[17] Although ecologi-cal sustainability and socioeconomic equality have not been fully achieved, there is clear evidence that the 1980s ushered in a new era of cooperation be-tween environmental and social justice groups. While there is by no means a consensus on complex environmental problems, the converging points of view represent the notion that "environmental problems and...material problems have common roots."[18]

When analyzing the convergence of these groups, it is important to note the relative emphasis that environmental and social justice organizations give to "instrumental" versus "expressive" activities.[19] Environmental organizations have relied heavily on environmentally oriented expressive activities (outdoor recreation, field trips, social functions, etc.), while the social justice move-ments have made greater use of goal-oriented instrumental activities (protest demonstrations, mass rallies, sit-ins, boycotts, etc.) in their effort to produce so-cial change.[20]

The push for environmental equity in the black community has much in common with the development of the modern civil rights movement that began in the South. That is, protest against discrimination has evolved from "organizing efforts of activists functioning through a well-developed indigenous base."[21] Indigenous black institutions, organizations, leaders, and networks are coming together against polluting industries and discriminatory environmental policies. This book addresses this new uniting of backs against institutional bar-riers of racism and classism.

Race Versus Class in Spatial Location

Social scientists agree that a multidimensional web of factors operate in sorting out stratification hierarchies. These factors include occupation, education, value of dwellings, source and amount of income, type of dwelling structures, government and private industry policies and racial and ethnic makeup of resi-dents.[22] Unfortunately, American society has not reached a color-blind state. What role does race play in sorting out land uses? Race continues to be a po-tent variable in explaining the spatial layout of urban areas, including housing patterns, street and highway configurations, commercial development, and in-dustrial facility siting.

Houston, Texas, the nation's fourth largest city, is a classic example of an area where race has played an integral part in land-use outcomes and municipal service delivery.[23] As late as 1982, there were neighborhoods in Houston that still did not have paved streets, gas and sewer connections, running water, regular garbage service, and street markers. Black and Hispanic neighborhoods were far more likely to have service deficiencies than their white counterparts. One of the neighborhoods (Bordersville) was part of the land annexed for the bustling Houston Intercontinental Airport. Another area, Riceville, was a stable black community located in the city's sprawling southwest corridor, a mostly white sector that accounted for nearly one-half of Houston's housing construction in the 1970s.

The city's breakneck annexation policy stretched municipal services thin. Newly annexed unincorporated areas, composed of mostly whites, often gained at the expenses of older minority areas. How does one explain the service disparities in this modern Sunbelt city? After studying the Houston phenomenon for nearly a decade, I have failed to turn up a single case of a white neighborhood (low- or middle-income) in the city that was systematically denied basic municipal services. The significance of race may have declined, but racism has not disappeared when it comes to allocating scarce resources.

Do middle-income blacks have the same mobility options that are available to their white counterparts? The answer to this question is no. Blacks have made tremendous economic and political gains in the past three decades with the passage of equal opportunity initiatives at the federal level. Despite legislation, court orders, and federal mandates, institutional racism and discrimination continue to influence the quality of life in many of the nation's black communities.[24]

The differential residential amenities and land uses assigned to black and white residential areas cannot be explained by class alone. For example, poor whites and poor blacks do not have the same opportunities to "vote with their feet." Racial barriers to education, employment, and housing reduce mobility options available to the black underclass and the black middle class.[25]

Housing is a classic example of this persistent problem. Residential options available to blacks have been shaped largely by (1) federal housing policies, (2) institutional and individual discrimination in housing markets, (3) geographic changes that have taken place in the nation's urban centers, and (4) limited incomes. Federal policies, for example, played a key role in the development of spatially differentiated metropolitan areas where blacks and other visible minorities are segregated from whites, and the poor from the more affluent citizens.[26] Government housing policies fueled the white exodus to the suburbs and accelerated the abandonment of central cities. Federal tax dollars funded the construction of freeway and interstate highway systems. Many of these construction projects cut paths through minority neighborhoods, physically isolated residents from their institutions, and disrupted once-stable communities. The federal government is the "proximate and essential cause of urban apartheid" in the United States.[27] The result of the nation's apartheid-type policies has been limited mobility, reduced housing options and residential packages, and decreased environmental choices for black households.[28]

Environmental degradation takes an especially heavy toll on inner-city neighborhoods because the "poor or nearpoor are the ones most vulnerable to the assaults of air and water pollution, and the stress and tension of noise and squalor."[29] A high correlation has been discovered between characteristics associated with disadvantage (i.e., poverty, occupations below management and professional levels, low rent, and a high concentration of black residents [due to residential segregation and discriminatory housing practices]) and poor air quality.[30] Individuals that are in close proximity to health-threatening problems (i.e., industrial pollution, congestion, and busy freeways) are living in endangered environs. The price that these individuals pay is in the form of higher risks of emphysema, chronic bronchitis, and other chronic pulmonary diseases.[31]

Blacks and other economically disadvantaged groups are often concentrated in areas that expose them to high levels of toxic pollution: namely, urban industrial communities with elevated air and water pollution problems or rural areas with high levels of exposure to farm pesticides. Kruvant described these groups as victims:

> Disadvantaged people are largely victims of middle- and upper-class pollution because they usually live closest to the sources of pollution—power plants, industrial installations, and in central cities where vehicle traffic is heaviest. Usually they have no choice. Discrimination created the situation, and those with wealth and influence have political power to keep polluting facilities away from their homes. Living in poverty areas is bad enough. High pollution makes it worse.[32]

Air pollution in inner-city neighborhoods can be up to five times greater than in suburban areas. Urban areas, in general, have "dirtier air and drinking water, more wastewater and solid-waste problems, and greater exposure to lead and other heavy metals than nonurban areas."[33] The difference between the environmental quality of inner-city and suburban areas was summarized by Blum:

> Suburbanites are exposed to less than half of the environmental health hazards inner-city residents face....The inner-city poor—white, yellow, brown, and black—suffer to an alarming degree from what are euphemistically known as "diseases of adaptation." These are not health adaptations, but diseases and chronic conditions from living with bad air, polluted water, and continued stress.[34]

All Americans, white or black, rich or poor, are entitled to equal protection under the law. Just as this is true for such areas as education, employment, and housing, it also applies to one's physical environment. Environmental discrimination is a fact of life. Here, environmental discrimination is defined as disparate treatment of a group or community based on race, class, or some other distinguishing characteristic. The struggle for social justice by black Americans has been and continues to be rooted in white racism. White racism is a factor in the impoverishment of black communities and has made it easier for black residential areas to become the dumping grounds for all types of health-threatening toxins and industrial pollution.

Government and private industry in general have followed the "path of least resistance" in addressing externalities as pollution discharges, waste disposal, and nonresidential activities that may pose a health threat to nearby communities.[35] Middle- and upper-class households can often shut out the fumes, noise, and odors with their air conditioning, dispose of their garbage to keep out the rats and roaches, and buy bottled water for drinking.[36] Many lower-income households (black or white) cannot afford such "luxury" items; they are subsequently forced to adapt to a lower-quality physical environment.

Minority and low-income residential areas (and their inhabitants) are often adversely affected by unregulated growth, ineffective regulation of industrial toxins, and public policy decisions authorizing locally unwanted land uses that favor those with political and economic clout.[37] Zoning is probably the most widely applied mechanism to regulate land use in the United States. Externalities such as pollution discharges to the air and water, noise, vibrations, and aesthetic problems are often segregated from residential areas for the "public good." Negative effects of nonresidential activities generally decrease with distance from the source. Land-use zoning, thus, is designed as a "protectionist device" to insure a "place for everything and everything in its place."[38] Zoning is ultimately intended to influence and shape land use in accordance with long-range local needs.

Zoning, deed restrictions, and other protectionist land-use mechanisms have failed to effectively protect minority communities, especially low-income minority communities. Logan and Molotch, in their book *Urban Fortunes: The Political Economy of Place*, contend that the various social classes, with or without land-use controls, are "unequally able to protect their environmental interests."[39] In their quest for quality neighborhoods, individuals often find themselves competing for desirable neighborhood amenities (i.e., good schools, police and fire protection, quality health care, and parks and recreational facilities) and resisting negative characteristics (i.e., landfills, polluting industries, freeways, public housing projects, drug-treatment facilities, halfway houses, etc.).

Zoning is not a panacea for land-use planning or for achieving long-range development goals. Implementation of zoning ordinances and land-use plans has a political, economic, and racial dimension. Competition often results between special interest groups (i.e., racial and ethnic minorities, organized civic clubs, neighborhood associations, developers, environmentalists, etc.) for advantageous land use. In many instances, exclusionary zoning, discriminatory housing practices by rental agents, brokers, and lending institutions, and disparate facility siting decisions have contributed to and maintained racially segregated residential areas of unequal quality.[40] These practices persist in spite of years of government intervention.

Why has this happened and what have blacks done to resist these practices? In order to understand the causes of the environmental dilemma that many black and low-income communities find themselves in, the theoretical foundation of environmentalism needs to be explored.

The Theoretical Basis of Environmental Conflict

Environmentalism in the United States grew out of the progressive conservation movement that began in the 1890s. The modern environmental movement, however, has its roots in the civil rights and antiwar movements of the late 1960s.[41] The more radical student activists splintered off from the civil rights and antiwar movements to form the core of the environmental movement in the early 1970s. The student environmental activists affected by the 1970 Earth Day enthusiasm in colleges and universities across the nation had hopes of bringing environmental reforms to the urban poor. They saw their role as environmental advocates for the poor since the poor had not taken action on their own.[42] They were, however, met with resistance and suspicion. Poor and minority residents saw environmentalism as a disguise for oppression and as another "elitist" movement.[43]

Environmental elitism has been grouped into three categories: (1) *compositional elitism* implies that environmentalists come from privileged class strata, (2) *ideological elitism* implies that environmental reforms are a subterfuge for distributing the benefits to environmentalists and costs to nonenvironmentalists, and (3) *impact elitism* implies that environmental reforms have regressive distributional impacts.[44]

Impact elitism has been the major sore point between environmentalists and advocates for social justice who see some reform proposals creating, exacerbating, and sustaining social inequities. Conflict centered largely on the "jobs versus environment" argument. Imbedded in this argument are three competing advocacy groups: (1) *environmentalists* are concerned about leisure and recreation, wildlife and wilderness preservation, resource conservation, pollution abatement, and industry regulation, (2) *social justice advocates'* major concerns include basic civil rights, social equity, expanded opportunity, economic mobility, and institutional discrimination, and (3) *economic boosters* have as their chief concerns maximizing profits, industrial expansion, economic stability, laissez-faire operation, and deregulation.

Economic boosters and pro-growth advocates convinced minority leaders that environmental regulations were bad for business, even when locational decisions had adverse impacts on the less advantaged. Pro-growth advocates used a number of strategies to advance their goals, including public relations campaigns, lobbying public officials, evoking police powers of government, paying off or co-opting dissidents, and granting small concessions when plans could be modified.[45] Environmental reform proposals were presented as prescriptions for plant closures, layoffs, and economic dislocation. Kazis and Grossman referred to this practice as "job blackmail." They insisted that by "threatening their employees with a 'choice' between their jobs and their health, employers seek to make the public believe there are no alternatives to 'business as usual.' "[46]

Pro-growth advocates have claimed the workplace is an arena in which unavoidable trade-offs must be made between jobs and hazards: If workers want to keep their jobs, they must work under conditions that may be hazardous to them, their families, and their community. Black workers are especially vulnerable to job blackmail because of the threat of unemployment and their concentration in certain types of occupations. The black workforce remains overrepresented in low-paying, low-skill, high-risk blue collar and service occupations where there is a more than adequate supply of replacement labor. Black workers are twice as likely to be unemployed as their white counterparts. Fear of unemployment acts as a potent incentive for many blacks to stay in and accept jobs they know are health threatening.

There is inherent conflict between the interest of capital and of labor. Employers have the power to move jobs (and sometimes hazards) as they wish. For example, firms may choose to move their operations from the Northeast and Midwest to the South and Sunbelt, or they may move the jobs to Third World countries where labor is cheaper and there are fewer health and environmental regulations. Moreover, labor unions may feel it necessary to scale down their demands for improved work safety conditions in a depressed economy for fear of layoffs, plant closings, or relocation of industries (e.g., moving to right-to-work states that proliferate in the South). The conflicts, fears, and anxieties manifested by workers are usually built on the false assumption that environmental regulations are automatically linked to job loss.

The offer of a job (any job) to an unemployed worker appears to have served a more immediate need than the promise of a clean environment. There is evidence that new jobs have been created as a direct result of environmental reforms.[47] Who got these new jobs? The newly created jobs are often taken by people who already have jobs or by migrants who possess skills greater than the indigenous workforce. More often than not, "newcomers intervene between the jobs and the local residents, especially the disadvantaged."[48]

Minority residents can point to a steady stream of industrial jobs leaving their communities. Moreover, social justice advocates take note of the miserable track record that environmentalists and preservationists have on improving environmental quality in the nation's racially segregated inner cities and hazardous industrial workplaces, and on providing housing for low-income groups. Decent and affordable housing, for example, is a top environmental problem for inner-city blacks. On the other hand, environmentalists' continued emphasis on wilderness and wildlife preservation appeal to a population that can afford leisure time and travel to these distant locations. This does not mean that poor people and people of color are not interested in leisure or outdoor activities. Many wilderness areas and national parks remain inaccessible to the typical inner-city resident because of inadequate transportation. Physical isolation, thus, serves as a major impediment to black activism in the mainstream conservation and resource management activities.

Translating Concern into Action

A considerable body of literature show that the socioeconomic makeup of environmental activists and the environmentally concerned are markedly different. Activists tend to be drawn disproportionately from the upper middle class, while environmentally concerned individuals tend to come from all socioeconomic strata.[49] Since our focus is on activism rather than concern, social participation models seem most appropriate in explaining the varying levels of environmental activity within the black community. Two of the most prevalent perspectives on social participation rates are expressed in the "social psychological" and "resource mobilization" models.

The basic assumption of the social psychological perspective is that personal characteristics, such as deprivation, status inconsistencies, grievances, and alienation, are useful in explaining motivation for social movement involvement.[50] The resource mobilization perspective, on the other hand, places greater confidence in structural conditions that make individual participation more accessible, including economic resources, organization affiliation, leaders, communication networks, and mastery skills gained through wearing "multiple hats."[51] Given the issues that have drawn minorities into the environmental movement (e.g., social justice and equity issues) and the indigenous black institutions that have initiated and sustained the movement, an integrated model is used to explain the emergence of environmentalism in black communities.[52] That is, both psychological factors (e.g., environmental quality rating, deprivation and sense of inequitable treatment, personal efficacy, and acceptance of trade-offs) as well as structural factors (e.g., social class and organization affiliation) are important predictors of environmental activism that is emerging in black communities.

There is no single agenda or integrated political philosophy in the hundreds of environmental organizations found in the nation. The type of issues that environmental organizations choose can greatly influence the type of constituents they attract.[53] The issues that are most likely to attract the interests of black community residents are those that have been couched in a civil rights or equity framework (see Table 1.1). They include those that (1) focus on inequality and distributional impacts, (2) endorse the "politics of equity" and direct action, (3) appeal to urban mobilized groups, (4) advocate safeguards against environmental blackmail with a strong pro-development stance, and (5) are ideologically aligned with policies that favor social and political "underdogs."

Mainstream environmental organizations, including the "classic" and "mature" groups, have had a great deal of influence in shaping the nation's environmental policy. Classic environmentalism continues to have a heavy emphasis on preservation and outdoor recreation, while mature environmentalism is busy in the area of "tightening regulations, seeking adequate funding for agencies, occasionally focusing on compliance with existing statutes

TABLE 1.1 *Type of Environmental Groups and Issue Characteristics That Appeal to Black Community Residents*

| | Type of Environmental Group | | | |
Issue Characteristic	Mainstream	Grassroots	Social Action	Emergent Coalition
Appeal to urban mobilized groups	−	+	+	+
Concern about inequality and distributional impacts	−/+	−/+	+	+
Endorse the "politics of equity" and direct action	−/+	+	+	−/+
Focus on economic-environment trade-offs	−	−/+	+	+
Champion of the political and economic "underdog"	−	−/+	+	+

−: Group is unlikely to have characteristic.
+: Group is likely to have characteristic.
−/+: Group in some cases may have characteristic.

Source: Adapted from Richard P. Gale, "The Environmental Movement and the Left: Antagonists or Allies?" *Sociological Inquiry* 53 (Spring 1983): Table 1, p. 194.

through court action, and opposing corporate efforts to repeal environmental legislation or weaken standards."[54] These organizations, however, have not had a great deal of success in attracting working-class persons, the large black population in the nation's inner cities, and the rural poor. Many of these individuals do not see the mainstream environmental movement as a vehicle that is championing the causes of the "little man," the "underdog," or the "oppressed."[55]

Recently emerged grassroots environmental groups, some of which are affiliated with mainstream environmental organizations, have begun to bridge the class and ideological gap between core environmentalists (e.g., the Sierra Club) and grassroots organizations (e.g., local activist groups in southeast Louisiana). In some cases, these groups mirror their larger counterparts at the national level in terms of problems and issues selected, membership, ideological alignment, and tactics. Grassroots groups often are organized around area-specific and single-issue problems. They are, however, more inclusive than mainstream environmental organizations in that they focus primarily on local problems. Grassroots environmental organizations, however, may or may not choose to focus on equity, distributional impacts, and economic-environmental trade-off issues. These groups do appeal to some black community residents, especially those who have been active in other confrontational protest activities.

Environmental groups in the black community quite often emerge out of established social action organizations. For example, black leadership has deep roots in the black church and other voluntary associations. These black institutions usually have a track record built on opposition to social injustice and racial discrimination. Many black community residents are affiliated with civic clubs, neighborhood associations, community improvement groups, and an array of antipoverty and antidiscrimination organizations. The infrastructure, thus, is already in place for the emergence of a sustained environmental equity movement in the black community. Black sociologist Aldon Morris contends that the black community "possesses (1) certain basic resources, (2) social activists with strong ties to mass-based indigenous institutions, and (3) tactics and strategies that can be effectively employed against a system of domination."[56]

Social action groups that take on environmental issues as part of their agenda are often on the political Left. They broaden their base of support and sphere of influence by incorporating environmental equity issues as agenda items that favor the disenfranchised. The push for environmental equity is an extension of the civil rights movement, a movement in which direct confrontation and the politics of protest have been real weapons. In short, social action environmental organizations retain much of their civil rights flavor.

Other environmental groups that have appealed to black community residents grew out of coalitions between environmentalists (mainstream and grassroots), social action advocates, and organized labor.[57] These somewhat fragile coalitions operate from the position that social justice and environmental quality are compatible goals. Although these groups are beginning to formulate agendas for action, mistrust still persists as a limiting factor. These groups are often biracial with membership cutting across class and geographic boundaries. There is a down side to these types of coalition groups. For example, compositional factors may engender less group solidarity and sense of "control" among black members, compared to the indigenous social action or grassroots environmental groups where blacks are in the majority and make the decisions. The question of "who is calling the shots" is ever present.

Environmentalists, thus, have had a difficult task convincing blacks and the poor that they are on their side. Mistrust is engendered among economically and politically oppressed groups in this country when they see environmental reforms being used to direct social and economic resources away from problems of the poor toward priorities of the affluent. For example, tighter government regulations and public opposition to disposal facility siting have opened up the Third World as the new dumping ground for this nation's toxic wastes. Few of these poor countries have laws or the infrastructure to handle the wastes from the United States and other Western industrialized nations.[58] Blacks and other ethnic minorities in this country also see their communities being inundated with all types of toxics. This has been especially the case for the southern United States (one of the most underdeveloped regions of the nation) where more than one-half of all blacks live.

Environmentalism and Civil Rights

The civil rights movement has its roots in the southern United States. Southern racism deprived blacks of "political rights, economic opportunity, social justice, and human dignity."[59] The new environmental equity movement also is centered in the South, a region where marked ecological disparities exist between black and white communities.[60] The 1980s have seen the emergence of a small cadre of blacks who see environmental discrimination as a civil rights issue. A fragile alliance has been forged between organized labor, blacks, and environmental groups as exhibited by the 1983 Urban Environment Conference workshops held in New Orleans.[61] Environmental and civil rights issues were presented as compatible agenda items by the conference organizers. Environmental protection and social justice are not necessarily incompatible goals.[62]

The Commission for Racial Justice's 1987 study *Toxic Wastes and Race in the United States* is a clear indication that environmental concerns have reached the civil rights agenda. Reverend Ben Chavis, the commission's executive director, stated:

> Race is a major factor related to the presence of hazardous wastes in residential communities throughout the United States. As a national church-based civil rights agency, we believe that time has come for all church and civil rights organizations to take this issue seriously. We realize that involvement in this type of research is a departure from our traditional protest methodology. However, if we are to advance our struggle in the future, it will depend largely on the availability of timely and reliable information.[63]

A growing number of grassroots organizations and their leaders have begun to incorporate more problem-focused coping strategies (e.g., protests, neighborhood demonstrations, picketing, political pressure, litigation, etc.) to reduce and eliminate environmental stressors. The national black political leadership has demonstrated a willingness to take a strong pro-environment stance. The League of Conservation Voters, for example, assigned the Congressional Black Caucus high marks for having one of the best pro-environment voting records.[64]

Many black communities, however, still do not have the organization, financial resources, or personnel to mount and sustain effective long-term challenges to such unpopular facilities as municipal and hazardous-waste landfills, toxic waste dumps, incinerators, and industrial plants that may pose a threat to their health and safety. Some battles are being waged on "shoestring" budgets. The problem is complicated by the fact that blacks in many cases must go outside their community to find experts on environmental issues. Lawyers, toxicologists, hydrologists, and environmental engineers in today's market are not cheap.

Institutional racism continues to affect policy decisions related to the enforcement of environmental regulations. Slowly, blacks, lower-income groups, and working-class persons are awakening to the dangers of living in a polluted environment. They are beginning to file and win lawsuits challenging governments and private industry that would turn their communities into the dumping grounds for all type of unwanted substances and activities. Whether it is a matter of deciding where a municipal landfill or hazardous-waste facility will be located, or getting a local chemical plant to develop better emergency notification, or trying to secure federal assistance to clean up an area that has already been contaminated by health-threatening chemicals, it is apparent that blacks and other minority groups must become more involved in environmental issues if they want to live healthier lives.

Black communities, mostly in the South, are beginning to initiate action (protests, demonstrations, picketing, political pressure, litigation, and other forms of direct action) against industries and governmental agencies that have targeted their neighborhoods for nonresidential uses including municipal garbage, hazardous wastes, and polluting industries. The environmental "time bombs" that are ticking away in these communities are not high on the agendas of mainstream environmentalists nor have they received much attention from mainstream civil rights advocates. Moreover, polluted black communities have received little national media coverage or remedial action from governmental agencies charged with cleanup of health-threatening pollution problems. The time is long overdue for placing the toxics and minority health concerns (including stress induced from living in contaminated communities) on the agenda of federal and state environmental protection and regulatory agencies. The Commission for Racial Justice's *Toxic Wastes and Race* has at least started government officials, academicians, and grassroots activists talking about environmental problems that disproportionately affect minority communities.

Nevertheless, the "Black Love Canals" exist and many go unnoticed. A case in point is the contamination of Triana, a small, all-black town in northern Alabama. Barbara Reynolds in *National Wildlife* described Triana as the "unhealthiest town in America."[65] Residents of this rural town of about 1,000 people were tested by the Center for Disease Control and were found to be contaminated with the pesticide DDT and the highly toxic industrial chemical PCB (polychlorinated biphenyl). Some of the residents were contaminated with the highest levels of DDT ever recorded. The source of the PCBs was not determined. However, the DDT was produced at nearby Redstone Arsenal Army missile base from 1947 to 1971 by Olin Chemical Company. DDT was banned in the United States in 1971. The manufacturing plant was torn down and over 4,000 tons of DDT residue remained buried in the area and eventually worked its way into Indian Creek, a popular fishing place of the Triana residents. Indian Creek is a tributary of the Tennessee River and is under the jurisdiction of the Tennessee Valley Authority (TVA).

While the elevated level of contamination of these black residents was documented as early as 1978, actions on the part of the U.S. Army or the federal government did not materialize. Clyde Foster, then mayor of Triana, spoke to this lack of concern and inaction on the part of government:

> I did not want a confrontation. I just wanted the scientific investigation to speak for itself. Why did the TVA suggest Triana be studied if DDT was not at all dangerous? How can it kill insects, fish, and birds and not be potentially harmful to people? I knew the stuff was real stable, that it stays in a body for years. Who knows

what effects massive doses could have over a long period of time? The TVA has known about the presence of DDT in the fish of Indian Creek for years, and I found later that the Army checked in 1977 and found a fish with one hundred times the safe DDT level. We received the TVA analysis of the fish from our freezers. Our fish had even higher DDT levels than those they had first tested.... Many of us eat its [Indian Creek's] fish every day. Already there is a hardship among the very poor people who customarily derive sustenance from the river. Our whole community is upset. We needed some help.[66]

It was not until Mayor Foster filed a class-action lawsuit in 1980 against Olin Chemical Company that the problems of these citizens were taken seriously.[67] After many delays and attempts to co-opt the local citizens, the lawsuit was settled out of court in 1983 for $25 million. The settlement agreement had three main points. Olin Chemical Company agreed to (1) clean up residual chemicals, (2) set aside $5 million to pay for long-term medical surveillance and health care of Triana residents, and (3) pay "cash-in-pocket" settlements to each resident. The legal claim against the federal government was withdrawn in order to make the settlement with Olin. The tragedy at Triana is not an isolated incident. There are numerous other cases of poor, black, and powerless communities that are victimized and ignored when it comes to enforcing environmental quality standards equitably. These disparities form the basis for this study and the environmental equity movement.

A Note on the Research Approach

This study examines how community attitudes and socioeconomic characteristics influence activism and mobilization strategies of black residents who are confronted with the threat of environmental stressors. The research on which this study is based was carried out in 1987 and 1988. Initial contact, however, had been made with local opinion leaders in several of the study communities as far back as 1979, after the author had served as a consultant, adviser, workshop lecturer, and guest speaker at a number of community events. A good rapport had been built up over several years with key community actors. This familiarity with the communities greatly enhanced the data-gathering phase of the project. Several data sources were used in order to develop an understanding of the complexities of black environmental mobilization. Three data sources were used: (1) government documents and archival records, (2) in-depth interviews with local opinion leaders, and (3) household surveys.

Notes

1. See Frederick R. Buttel and William L. Flinn, "Social Class and Mass Environmental Beliefs: A Reconsideration," *Environment and Behavior* 10 (September 1978): 433–450; Kenneth M. Bachrach and Alex J. Zautra, "Coping with Community Stress: The Threat of a Hazardous Waste Landfill," *Journal of Health and Social Behavior* 26 (June 1985): 127–141; Paul Mohai, "Public Concern and Elite Involvement in Environmental-Conservation Issues," *Social Science Quarterly* 66 (December 1985): 820–838.

2. Denton E. Morrison, "The Soft Cutting Edge of Environmentalism: Why and How the Appropriate Technology Notion Is Changing the Movement," *Natural Resources Journal* 20 (April 1980): 275–298.

3. Allan Schnaiberg, *The Environment: From Surplus to Scarcity* (New York: Oxford University Press, 1980), pp. 366–377.

4. See Morris E. Davis, "The Impact of Workplace Health and Safety on Black Workers: Assessment and Prognosis," *Labor Studies Journal* 4 (Spring 1981): 29–40; Richard Kazis and Richard Grossman, *Fear at Work: Job Blackmail, Labor, and the Environment* (New York: Pilgrim Press, 1983), Chapter 1; W. J. Kruvant, "People, Energy, and Pollution," in Dorothy K. Newman and Dawn Day, eds., *The American Energy Consumer* (Cambridge, Mass.: Ballinger, 1975), pp. 125–167; Robert D. Bullard, "Solid Waste Sites and the Black Houston Community," *Sociological Inquiry* 53 (Spring 1983): 273–288; Robert D. Bullard, "Endangered Environs: The Price of Unplanned Growth in Boomtown Houston," *California Sociologist* 7 (Summer 1984): 85–101; Robert D. Bullard and Beverly H. Wright, "Dumping Grounds in a Sunbelt City," *Urban Resources* 2 (Winter 1985): 37–39.

5. James E. Blackwell, *The Black Community: Diversity and Unity* (New York: Harper and Row, 1985), p. xiii.

6. Richard E. Lazarus and Raymond Launier, "Stress-Related Transactions Between Persons and Environment," in Lawrence A. Pervin and Michael Lewis, eds., *Perspectives in International Psychology* (New York: Plenum, 1978), pp. 297–327; Bachrach and Zautra, "Coping with Community Stress," pp. 127–129.

7. See Anthony M. Orum, "On Participation in Political Movements," *Journal of Applied Behavioral Science* 10 (April/June 1974): 181–207; Daniel L. Collins, Andrew Baum, and Jerome E. Singer, "Coping with Chronic Stress at Three Mile Island: Psychological and Biological Evidence," *Health Psychology* 2 (1983): 149–166; Mohai, "Public Concern and Elite Involvement," p. 832.

8. Robert D. Bullard and Beverly H. Wright, "Environmentalism and the Politics of Equity: Emergent Trends in the Black Community," *Mid-American Review of Sociology* 12 (Winter 1987): 21–37.

9. Aldon D. Morris, *The Origins of the Civil Rights Movement: Black Communities Organizing for Change* (New York: Free Press, 1984), p. x.

10. See Robert D. Bullard and Beverly H. Wright, "Blacks and the Environment," *Humboldt Journal of Social Relations* 14 (Summer 1987): 165–184; Bullard, "Solid Waste Sites and the Black Houston Community," pp. 273–288; Bullard, "Endangered Environs," pp. 84–102.

11. Riley E. Dunlap, "Public Opinion on the Environment in the Reagan Era: Polls, Pollution, and Politics Revisited," *Environment* 29 (July/August 1987): 6–11, 32–37.

12. Brian J. L. Berry, ed., *The Social Burden of Environmental Pollution: A Comparative Metropolitan Data Source* (Cambridge, Mass.: Ballinger, 1977); Sam Love, "Ecology and Social Justice: Is There a Conflict," *Environmental Action* 4 (1972): 3–6; Julian McCaull, "Discriminatory Air Pollution: If the Poor Don't Breathe," *Environment* 19 (March 1976): 26–32; Vernon Jordan, "Sins of Omission," *Environmental Action* 11 (April 1980): 26–30.

13. Denton E. Morrison, "How and Why Environmental Consciousness Has Trickled Down," in Allan Schnaiberg, Nicholas Watts, and Klaus Zimmermann, eds., *Distributional Conflict in Environmental-Resource Policy* (New York: St. Martin's Press, 1986), pp. 187–220.

14. Robert D. Bullard and Beverly H. Wright, "The Politics of Pollution: Implications for the Black Community," *Phylon* 47 (March 1986): 71–78.

15. Bullard and Wright, "Environmentalism and the Politics of Equity," p. 28.

16. Richard P. Gale, "The Environmental Movement and the Left: Antagonists or Allies?" *Sociological Inquiry* 53 (Spring 1983): 179–199.

17. Craig R. Humphrey and Frederick R. Buttel, *Environment, Energy, and Society* (Belmont, Calif.: Wadsworth Publishing Co., 1982), p. 253.

18. Ibid.

19. Arthur P. Jacoby and Nicholas Babchuk, "Instrumental Versus Expressive Voluntary Associations," *Sociology and Social Research* 47 (1973): 461–471.

20. Gale, "The Environmental Movement and the Left," p. 191.

21. Morris, *The Origins of the Civil Rights Movement*, p. xii.

22. Charles V. Willie, *The Caste and Class Controversy* (Bayside, N.Y.: General Hall, Inc., 1979), pp. 43–44; also Robert D. Bullard, ed., *In Search of the New South: The Black Urban Experience in the 1970s and 1980s* (Tuscaloosa: University of Alabama Press, 1989).

23. See Robert D. Bullard, *Invisible Houston: The Black Experience in Boom and Bust* (College Station: Texas A & M University Press, 1987), pp. 14–31.

24. Robert D. Bullard, "Blacks and the American Dream of Housing," in Jamshid A. Momeni, ed., *Race, Ethnicity, and Minority Housing in the United States* (Westport, Conn.: Greenwood Press, 1986), pp. 53–63; Bullard and Wright, "Environmentalism and the Politics of Equity," pp. 21–37.

25. Robert L. Lineberry, *Equity and Urban Policy: The Distribution of Municipal Public Services* (Beverly Hills: Sage, 1977), pp. 174–175.

26. Karl Taeuber and Alma K. Taeuber, *Negroes in Cities: Residential Segregation and Neighborhood Change* (Chicago: Aldine Publishing Co., 1965); Karl Taeuber, "Racial Segregation: The Persisting Dilemma," *Annals of the American Academy of Political and Social Sciences* 442 (November 1978): 87–96; Karl Taeuber, "Racial Residential Segregation, 28 Cities, 1970–1980," CDE Working Paper, University of Wisconsin, Madison (March 1983), p. 3; Robert D. Bullard, "The Black Family: Housing Alternatives in the 80s," *Journal of Black Studies* 14 (Spring 1984): 341–351.

27. Larry Ford and Ernst Griffin, "The Ghettoization of Paradise," *Geographical Review* 69 (April 1979): 140–158; J. A. Kushner, *Apartheid in America: An Historical and Legal Analysis of Contemporary Racial Segregation in the United States* (Arlington, Va.: Carrolton Press, Inc., 1980), p. 130.

28. Robert P. Burden, "The Forgotten Environment," in Lawrence E. Hinkle and William C. Loring, eds., *The Effects of the Man-Made Environment on Health and Behavior* (Washington, D.C.: U.S. Government Printing Office, 1977), p. 249.

29. Daniel Zwerdling, "Poverty and Pollution," *Progressive* 37 (January 1973): 25–29.

30. Kruvant, "People, Energy, and Pollution," p. 125–167.

31. Douglas Lee and H. K. Lee, "Conclusions and Reservations," in Douglas Lee, ed., *Environmental Factors in Respiratory Disease* (New York: Academic Press, 1972), pp. 250–251; Ronald Brownstein, "The Toxic Tragedy," in Ralph Nader, Ronald Brownstein, and John Richard, eds., *Who's Poisoning America: Corporate Polluters and Their Victims in the Chemical Age* (San Francisco: Sierra Club Books, 1982), pp. 1–52.

32. Kruvant, "People, Energy, and Pollution," p. 166.

33. Kazis and Grossman, *Fear at Work*, p. 48.

34. Barbara Blum, *Cities: An Environmental Wilderness* (Washington, D.C.: Environmental Protection Agency, 1978), p. 3.

35. Bullard and Wright, "Blacks and the Environment," pp. 170–171.

36. Zwerdling, "Poverty and Pollution," p. 27; Bullard and Wright, "The Politics of Pollution," pp. 71–78.

37. Bullard and Wright, "Blacks and the Environment," pp. 168–171; Bullard, "Endangered Environs," pp. 85–86.

38. See Constance Perrin, *Everything in Its Place: Social Order and Land Use in America* (Princeton, N.J.: Princeton University Press, 1977).

39. John R. Logan and Harvey L. Molotch, *Urban Fortunes: The Political Economy of Place* (Berkeley: University of California Press, 1987), p. 158.

40. See Harvey L. Molotch, "The City as a Growth Machine: Toward a Political Economy of Place," *American Journal of Sociology* 82 (1976): 309–330; John R. Logan, "Growth, Politics and Stratification of Places," *American Journal of Sociology* 84 (1978): 404–416; Ann B. Shlay and Peter Rossi, "Keeping up the Neighborhood: Estimating the Effect of Zoning," *American Sociology Review* 46 (December 1981): 703–719; Bullard and Wright, "Blacks and the Environment," pp. 168–171.

41. Humphrey and Buttel, *Environment, Energy, and Society*, pp. 11–136; Gale, "The Environmental Movement and the Left," pp. 179–199.

42. Samuel P. Hays, *Beauty, Health, and Permanence: Environmental Politics in the United States, 1955–1985* (Cambridge, Mass.: Cambridge University Press, 1987), p. 269.

43. David L. Sills, "The Environmental Movement and Its Critics," *Human Ecology* 13 (1975): 1–41; Morrison, "The Soft Cutting Edge of Environmentalism," pp. 275–298; Allan Schnaiberg, "Redistributive Goals Versus Distributive Politics: Social Equity Limits in Environmentalism and Appropriate Technology Movements," *Sociological Inquiry* 53 (Spring 1983): 200–219.

44. Denton E. Morrison and Riley E. Dunlap, "Environmentalism and Elitism: A Conceptual and Empirical Analysis," *Environmental Management* 10 (1986): 581–589.

45. Logan and Molotch, *Urban Fortunes*, pp. 50–98.

46. Kazis and Grossman, *Fear at Work*, p. 37.

47. Alan S. Miller, "Toward an Environment/Labor Coalition," *Environment* 22 (June 1980): 32–39.

48. See Barry Bluestone and Bennett Harrison, *The Deindustrialization of America* (New York: Basic Books, 1982), p. 90.

49. Buttel and Flinn, "Social Class and Mass Environmental Beliefs," pp. 433–450; Robert Cameron Mitchell, "Silent Spring/Solid Majorities," *Public Opinion* 2 (August/September 1979): 16–20; Robert Cameron Mitchell, "Public Opinion and Environmental Politics," in N. J. Vig and M. E. Kraft, eds., *Environmental Policy in the 1980's: Reagan's New Agenda* (Washington, D.C.: Congressional Quarterly Press, 1984), pp. 51–73; Mohai, "Public Concern and Elite Involvement," p. 821; Dorceta E. Taylor, "Blacks and the Environment: Toward an Explanation of the Concern and Action Gap Between Blacks and Whites," *Environment and Behavior* 21 (March 1989): 175–205.

50. See Ron E. Roberts and Robert Marsh Kloss, *Social Movements: Between the Balcony and the Barricade*, 2nd ed. (St. Louis: C. V. Mosby, 1979); James L. Wood and Maurice Jackson, eds., *Social Movements: Development, Participation and Dynamics* (Belmont, Calif.: Wadsworth, 1982).

51. For a detailed discussion of the resource mobilization model, see Anthony Oberschall, *Social Conflict and Social Movement* (Englewood, Cliffs, N.J.: Prentice-Hall, 1973); John D. McCarthy and Mayer Zald, *The Trend of Social Movements in America: Professionalism and Resource Mobilization* (Morristown, N.J.: General Learning Press, 1979); William Gamson, *The Study of Social Protest* (Homewood, Ill.: Dorsey Press, 1975); Charles Tilly, *From Mobilization to Revolution* (Reading, Mass.: Addison-Wesley, 1978); Craig J. Jenkins, "Resource Mobilization Theory and the Study of Social Movements," *Annual Review of Sociology* 9 (1983): 27–53.

52. Edward J. Walsh and Rex Warland, "Social Movement Involvement in the Wake of a Nuclear Accident: Activists and Free-Riders in the TMI Area," *American Sociological Review* 48 (December 1983): 764–780; Mohai, "Public Concern and Elite Involvement," pp. 822–823.

53. The discussion of issues that are likely to attract blacks to the environmental movement was adapted from Gale, "The Environmental Movement and the Left," pp. 182–186.

54. Ibid., p. 184.

55. See Ronald A. Taylor, "Do Environmentalists Care About Poor People?" *U.S. News and World Report* 96 (April 2, 1982): 51–55; Bullard, "Endangered Environs," p. 98; Bullard and Wright, "The Politics of Pollution," pp. 71–78.

56. Morris, *The Origins of the Civil Rights Movement*, p. 282.

57. Miller, "Toward an Environment/Labor Coalition," pp. 32–39; Sue Pollack and JoAnn Grozuczak, *Reagan, Toxics and Minorities* (Washington, D.C.: Urban Environmental Conference, Inc., 1984), Chapter 1; Kazis and Grossman, *Fear at Work*, pp. 3–35.

58. Andrew Porterfield and David Weir, "The Export of Hazardous Waste," *Nation* 245 (October 3, 1987): 340–344; Jim Vallette, *The International Trade in Wastes: A Greenpeace Inventory* (Washington, D.C.: Greenpeace, 1989), pp. 7–16.

59. Jack Bloom, *Class, Race and the Civil Rights Movement* (Bloomington: Indiana University Press, 1987), p. 18.

60. Bullard and Wright, "Environmentalism and the Politics of Equity," p. 32.

61. Urban Environment Conference, Inc., *Taking Back Our Health: An Institute on Surviving the Toxic Threat to Minority Communities* (Washington, D.C.: Urban Environment Conference, Inc., 1985), p. 29.

62. Bullard and Wright, "Environmentalism and the Politics of Equity," pp. 32–33.

63. Commission for Racial Justice, *Toxic Wastes and Race: A National Report on the Racial and Socioeconomic Characteristics of Communities with Hazardous Waste Sites* (New York: United Church of Christ, 1987), p. x.

64. Taylor, "Do Environmentalists Care About Poor People?" pp. 51–52.

65. Barbara Reynolds, "Triana, Alabama: The Unhealthiest Town in America," *National Wildlife* 18 (August 1980): 33; Bullard and Wright, "The Politics of Pollution," p. 75.

66. Michael Haggerty, "Crisis at Indian Creek," *Atlanta Journal and Constitution Magazine* (January 20, 1980): 14–25.

67. Ibid.

Amiri Baraka
A New Reality Is Better Than a New Movie!

How will it go, crumbling earthquake, towering inferno, juggernaut, volcano,
    smashup,
in reality, other than the feverish nearreal fantasy of the capitalist flunky film
    hacks
tho they sense its reality breathing a quake inferno scar on their throat even
    snorts of
100% pure cocaine cant cancel the cold cut of impending death to this society.
    On all the
screens of america, the joint blows up every hour and a half for two dollars an
    fifty cents.
They have taken the niggers out to lunch, for a minute, made us partners (nig-
    ger charlie) or
surrogates (boss nigger) for their horror. But just as superafrikan mobutu can-
    not leop
    ardskinhat his
way out of responsibility for lumumba's death, nor even with his incredible bil-
    lions
    rockefeller
cannot even save his pale ho's titties in the crushing weight of things as they
really are.
How will it go, does it reach you, getting up, sitting on the side of the bed, getting ready to go to work. Hypnotized by the machine, and the cement floor,
the jungle treachery of
    trying
to survive with no money in a money world, of making the boss
100,000 for every 200
    dollars
you get, and then having his brother get you for the rent, and if you want to
buy the car
    you
helped build, your downpayment paid for it, the rest goes to buy his old lady a
foam
    rubber
rhinestone set of boobies for special occasions when kissinger drunkenly fum-
bles with her blouse, forgetting himself.

If you don't like it, what you gonna do about it. That was the question we
asked each
> other, &

still right regularly need to ask. You don't like it? Whatcha gonna do, about it??
The real terror of nature is humanity enraged, the true technicolor spectacle that
> hollywood

cant record. They cant even show you how you look when you go to work, or
when you
> come back.

They cant even show you thinking or demanding the new socialist reality, its
the ultimate
> tidal

wave. When all over the planet, men and women, with heat in their hands,
demand that
> society

be planned to include the lives and self determination of all the people ever to
live. That is the scalding scenario with a cast of just under two billion that they
dare not even whisper. Its called, "We Want It All...The Whole World!"

Black People & Jesse Jackson II

By this time, as well, the center piece of the extravaganza had begun formally.
And people began scurrying to be where they were supposed to be to get their
instructions their inspiration their salaries or whatever the case was.

The big boys are so accommodating of our frustration they had even put
out two sets of tee shirts one with the Dukakis Bentsen regulars and another
with Bentsen's face x'd out and Jesse Jackson's face unmarked and supported. I
thought by now I should try to get to Jesse directly to find out what was on his
mind and what he was going to do. Not just as a reporter for *Essence* magazine,
but for my own and our own edification and self-defense.

But of course getting to Jackson in that maze of indirection and disinforma-
tion was difficult, even though I had been given his suite numbers by people
very close to him. Finally I succeeded in getting an agreement that I could ride
over to the convention with him the night he was to speak. I wanted to hear
what he was going to say, how he summed up life among the Dems rat now!

So that evening my children and I gathered at the appointed place and
waited. And as secret as that point of embarkation was supposed to be there
was a tiny knot of people standing there with us. As it got closer to the time we
were told Jesse would appear, the secret service men in the lobby came over to
me, one bumping me the way they do if they think you have some heat somewhere and are liable to grab for it on sudden surprising impact. We were asked

to move back. A crazy woman danced and made nutty remarks at the edge of the little knot seeming to focus on one gent who left later after conversation with Jesse's aides.

Then one woman I knew to be with the Jackson campaign came over to me and asked me why was I waiting. I told her she shuffled through her papers and told me that there must be some mistake, that my presence was not on the schedule. Of course I protested, I had spoken with the top scheduling person who had talked directly to Jesse—I could hear her doing it—and it was she who had told me what to do.

But now it was not on the schedule. I was wondering was this just the usual criss-cross of bureaucracy, or what, when the crazy woman started dancing just behind me. "Oh, is it my turn?" I told her and in a few seconds she withdrew. At that point C. Delores Tucker, former secretary of state of Pennsylvania, chairperson of the black Democratic caucus, appeared through the door helping Mrs. Rosa Parks. I greeted them, introduced them to the children and chatted while we waited for Jesse.

In a few minutes the main group appeared. The first through the door, leading the way, was Inner City Broadcasting chairman and former Manhattan borough president, Percy Sutton. And then Jesse and his family. When I approached Jesse, "Hey, man what's happening?"

Jesse bent in my direction saying, "I'm sorry, Imamu, but there's no room." As indeed there could not have been. At that point my daughter, Shani, armed with a tiny Polaroid camera I had given her to take pictures of the notables, snapped our picture. Later, the children would tell their mother that Jesse must have known me a long time to call me by the organizational title I held during the '60s, Imamu. History is filled with details.

The kids and I then had to scramble to get over to the convention center in time. Riding on a bus especially set up for carrying delegates and whoever back and forth. I took the kids and several other old friends I'd bumped into who were going over to the viewing rooms equipped with tv monitors. This is where the people close to delegates or officials or whoever watched. Then I took off across the street to the convention center.

But when I got there a few steps away there was a huge crowd of people outside and much weeping and wailing. There was no room in the convention either. Not even for many of the delegates. People waved their delegate badges and the press, including myself and many others, waved their various sets of credentials but the police said the place was overcrowded and no more people would be admitted. Not even the delegates!

Well if the delegates weren't going to be admitted, then who the hell was that inside taking up the space? This argument rumbled around at the tops of many people's voices all around the convention center. There was no room? Well who was there room for?

Thinking about it now such a situation could only be produced by the theatrical atmosphere such conventions produce normally, but now with the addition of the Jackson factor and the question which hung in balance above that convention and city and above us all. What would Jesse say? What would Jesse do? And this question had a celebrity to it and a show business quality that brought out audience, not just delegates, just whoever had the whatever to make it.

At one point I saw Atlanta's mayor, Andy Young, walking behind the glass walls with full entourage a picture of special pleading or was that importance. Enraged I could not get in I began to beat on the glass walls to get Young's attention.

He probably didn't see me but a host of secret service chaps did and a small group came over waving at me to stop banging on the door. I didn't so one pushed the door open and told me to stop. I banged again, Young hadn't left and I was determined to get inside. This brought the fellow half way out the door. He told me if I banged the door again he'd arrest me. It seemed outrageous to me, I wasn't banging at him in the first place. A loose now sparser crowd of the unadmitted looked on, one black radio reporter stepped forward with me. I banged again.

Now the secret service dude stepped forward outside the doors, "I'm gonna arrest you," he was screaming.

"Hey, man, you don't control shit out here…this is Atlanta. You need to take your ass back inside and be important somewhere else."

There were two or three black Atlanta policemen standing a few steps behind me watching. I saw one's hand go up to his mouth and I knew it was cool. They were not going to arrest me for this dude. And when he left they let it all come out in a big roar. "What's your name, man?"

They could appreciate my argument. And they laughed like hell as the ss man went on his way scowling and talking at his wrist radio as he departed to show us we were still savages.

Coming around to the other side of the building still looking to get in the crowds of the left outside milled and trailed around like myself looking for a way in. I came upon a television newsman interviewing Rev. Ralph Abernathy, one time second in command to Dr. King in SCLC. Now he was also standing on the outside. (Martin Luther King, III was also kept outside, it made the next day's papers.)

The newsman was asking about Abernathy's being refused entrance to the convention. "What do you think Rev Jackson would think about you being kept outside the convention tonight?"

"Oh, he wouldn't like it at all. No, he wouldn't like that at all. And I know this was a great speech, one of the most important speeches ever made."

Abernathy went on describing the complete inappropriateness of his being shut out, and as the newsman finished he said. "And what is your name sir?"

I leaped into it, "You don't know Rev Ralph Abernathy? Well how did you even get this job, you're obviously not qualified if you don't know who Ralph Abernathy is. He was Dr. King's second in command in the Civil Rights movement." But I was just covering my own embarrassment and pain at what was happening, that Abernathy could be here standing anonymously in the crowd disconnected from wherever this big top was going.

And as bizarre as this actual indication this had been one materialization of a general perception that the negroes were being asked to be the tail on the donkey or one main negro and the other "necessaries," and for all the swirl and roar, the bravado and even sincere commitment of the rest of whoever..."us" or "them" that the only room on the donkey's tail was for the tiny insects that live there.

I moped up the stairs in the large hall directly opposite the convention center and brooded as the various entertainers and conpersons were introduced. This was the night of the presidential nominations and Jesse would be one of the speakers. I drank Courvoisier and watched the show unfold.

Jesse's whole presence had a magnetism about it that has diminished so rapidly it seems a long time ago already. The campaign, particularly after Super Tuesday, had given him real world statesman status. And as an independent presence, someone representing a specific constituency who had very concrete interests and the will and information to protect them. He had to be recognized and like it or not...like him or not, he must be given the weight of our claim, the respect for the implied power of his position.

Jackson's response to Dukakis missed telephone message racism had done damage to that projection. It had brought a mumble of antipathy from the black masses and turned his image around in a way that made him seem very finite and vulnerable. You don't let nobody insult you (us) like that. Bump Dukakis!, the oath.

But there was still the mystique of the well known, and Jesse had been our hope, even those of us who knew him when and who might even have put him down a decade or so ago for being a petty bourgeois opportunist. All of us had taken hope at the courageous picture Jesse made in opposing and exposing the gunbearers of privilege and imperialism he was running against, besting them at every turn. Our man, big good looking, smart nigger.

But not just the question of the insult, that was just the answer to the question of when the white folks was gonna get to whiting. Where were *our own* priorities? Our own self determined agenda? What was it that we should be doing, armed with the actual dismissal of our humanity as "a problem"? Where was our agenda?

It was the argument that went on in the hotels where the black delegates and political activists and intellectuals were holed up. The line that kept emerging from the sincere and the others not publicly sold, "What are black folks going to get out of this?" The majority of black folks. Not just Sly and the Family Caucus.

The screen I watched the speech on was as big as a four or five story building, in glorious pseudocolor. There was a roaring all around like a sports event. It was not rock concert glitter serrating the edge of the picture but maybe Madison Square Garden one night forty years ago, when The Brown Bomber or Sugar was getting ready to come into the ring. I had my own view of what was going on, based on what I'd run into but also based on a long resident activism in the Black Liberation Movement, including a thorough knowledge of Jesse Jackson. So I was backed away from total submersion in the event. But the whirlwind of this heavyweight bout between fact and mythology, this gaudy class struggle on the big screen, had such a giant roaring rhythm it caught me up in the amazing spectacle.

It is a kind of grandiose arrogance that hits first, the glitter and shine and sparkle and overblown self importance of the importantly manipulated. From the television it seemed a telethon for some new disease, a mass religious conversion or pretension. Circusy and carnival like, but for all that restrained and formal. Everything was fixed and plotted. There was no spontaneity given off just used up labor high polished for resale.

When I focused directly so I could also hear. Jackson was into his speech. What I wanted to know before was what ideas had led to this speech, what real objectives for the African American people, the Rainbow? But now the words were rolling out, the entire space held in breathless tension at our hero's magnetic voice and rhythms.

"We meet at a crossroads," he was saying. The camera panned incessantly getting the white folks' reaction and the few others. There was a rapt attention widespread. These people, for *whatever* reason, were interested in what he was saying.

"Shall we expand, be inclusive, find unity and power, or suffer division and impotence?"

But this question seemed to have been answered. And its answer was now being read to the whole. When the lefts I'd felt closest to had first come upon me it was to assure me that they were passing out literature among the Rainbow folk readying them for the Vice Presidential nomination. Dukakis' nomination of Bentsen, the Democrats' George Bush, was actually a violation of the people's constitutional right to select a vice presidential candidate separately from the presidential candidate. People, according to the U.S. Constitution, voted for people, not parties or party choices.

These lefts' job, they said, would be to circulate the vice presidential nominating instructions and get the necessary petitions signed so they could spearhead the vice presidential nomination. But the rally, and the mounting evidence on all sides seemed to project that not only were black people to be transformed into bugs so they could ride safely in Dukakis' tail, but even the so called anti revisionist (i.e., anti the US Communist Party and Soviet Union) Left was being transformed into a tail pinned to the tail, and they were proud as hell of it for that matter.

But the other shoe had not hit yet, and Jesse was readying to drop it now. "Common Ground," he was saying. "Think of Jerusalem...the birthplace for three great religions" (Do the Israelis know that? ran through my head.)

"Common Ground! That is the challenge to our party tonight. Left wing. Right wing. Progress will come not through boundless liberalism nor static conservatism, but at the critical mass of mutual survival. It takes two wings to fly." (Our preachers excel in metaphor.)

"The bible teaches that when lions and the lambs can lie down together and none will be afraid, there will be peace in the valley. Lions eat lambs;

lambs sensibly flee from lions. Yet, even lions and lambs can find common ground. Why? Neither lions nor lambs want the forest to catch fire. Neither lions nor lambs want acid rain to fall. Neither lions nor lambs can survive nuclear war. If lions and lambs can find common ground, surely we can."

When I heard this it broke my heart. Why? Because he had answered the question. Lions eat lambs. But then went on to unanswer it and make it metaphysical and transparently opportunistic. Though at the end of this speech people hailed it widely, the media hailed it. But even some who were genuinely moved by the speech, if not by its pronouncements, then certainly by the gleaming aesthetic of its form, the deftness of handling of its content had to blanch at *what* Jesse was saying.

"Now we must build a quilt together." He was likening U.S. society to one of his momma's quilts. The one he spoke of now would be a quilt of lions and lambchop bones, of donkey's tail and insects, of the rich and the poor working together to keep both that way.

"Blacks and Hispanics, when we fight for civil rights, we are right—but our patch isn't big enough," suddenly everything was expendable if its expendability, the flexibility of its survival would provide an entrance into that craziness he was publicly aspiring to be accepted into. Even the liberation of the people who had borned him into the world, and upon whose very backs he had ridden into Atlanta for this convention like Jesus came into Galilee riding on another ass on a palm sunday long ago, a few days before his rubout and later triumphant return from the dead. Jesse after the Atlanta debacle can be said to have experienced two thirds of the Jesus trip. Though his return from the dead remains in the mouth of speculation.

"Conservatives and Progressives, when you fight for what you believe, you are right—but your patch isn't big enough." You mean both the slave and the slavemaster are right? Both slavery and freedom are right? Is this what is required to qualify for the nomination as president of the United States, double talk and submission to the will of the mighty?

He would confirm this for us later by quoting a poem that began, "I am tired of sailing my little boat / far inside the harbor bar / I want to go out where the big ships float...." But the living historically valid part of Jesse Jackson his real life ties with black working class life he would also make reference to. At best the living memory of himself necessary for what Du Bois called, "true self consciousness" (as opposed to the "double consciousness" of the negro, who sees nothing directly but only sees himself and the world through the eyes of people who hate him). At worst though this living matter can be used to deceive, grass roots camouflage for anti grass roots ideology.

For instance when Jesse said near the end, "Most poor people are not on welfare. They work hard every day that they can. They sweep the streets. They work. They catch the early bus. They work. They pick up the garbage. They work. They feed our children in school. They work. They take care of other people's children and cannot care for their own..." you could see black people openly weeping and whites too moved to some measure of understanding by this impressive, poetic brother. And yet...and yet...was it all for naught?

I know he broke me down near the end. Only the coldness of my perception and rationale of what all this was prevented some open weeping. The whole was a compendium of many of Jesse's speeches throughout the campaign, and I had heard this part before as well. But it was still cutting, transporting, "Don't give up. Hold on, for the morning comes. How do I know?

"I understand. I am the son of a teenage mother, who was the daughter of a teenage mother. I understand. I was not born with a silver spoon in my mouth. I understand.

"You see Jesse Jackson on television. But you don't know the me that makes me me. Jesse Jackson is my third name. I am adopted. I never spent a night in my daddy's house. I really do understand.

"Born in my mother's bed. She couldn't afford hospital care. I understand.

"Born in a three room house. Bathroom in the back yard. Slop jar by the bed. I understand.

"I am a working person's person. I wasn't born with a silver spoon in my mouth, but a shovel in my hand. My mother was a working mother went to work with runs in her stockings so that I could have new socks and not be embarrassed in school. I really do understand."

It was not just skill he maintained, but it was also feeling, real feeling. And that is Jesse's danger to the Democrats and to white supremacy that he does feel the needs of the people but now in his personal quest for "acceptance" or "significance" or even Jesse-Power (which is not the same as Black Power) he was willing to use the real to cover the deal.

For instance in the very next paragraph of that speech Jesse shows that he knows but also that he is willing to stall to get hold of the ball. But that ball is never coming his way except like those balls fixed to chains that are standard issue for many African Americans inside various joints, the Democratic party included.

Jesse was blowing hard and pretty, like a rhythm blade cut through most of us. "We didn't eat turkey on three o'clock on Thanksgiving day, because Momma was off cooking someone else's turkey. We'd play football to pass the time till momma came home. Around six we would meet her at the bottom of the hill carrying back Du Carcass."

Yes, I swear I heard it, and then in the hotel a black minister had verified it for me. The two of us telling everybody how Jesse had "laid on symbol" as the ancestor jailees used to say. "Lay on symbol." In the transcript of the speech that has now been changed to "leftovers." But he and we who heard know what he said and what he meant. That indeed this merriment was much like a holiday, and yes there were those of us down here who weren't involved in the real business, we were just the marginalia the bubbles rising off the heady brew. We wanted to eat now, but all were gonna get was Du Carcass, some leftovers. The white men and quite a few white women had already et.

It was a weird weird aura that gripped this country just after that speech. In the huge open hall where I sat, and later the media-peoples' bar there was a mixed expression it seemed to me. There had to be simple dismissal by the white majority since that is what their white supremacy instructed them to do, as far as consideration of Jesse's candidacy or even comprehending his stand on the various issues. Jackson had pushed the whole of the electorate to the left, however, made them consider questions and stances that simply would never have been raised without him running in the primaries. So that there was also, along with the automatic dismissal, a stubborn sympathy, at Jackson's courage?, his aggressiveness, his typical nigger problematic maddeningly continuous assertion of his (our) humanity.

Like the quick to snicker cynical media bar types. Forget the fact that I was fixing them in a clearly analytic stare from the beginning of the broadcast, until the end. Still, the quality of their response to what was coming off the tube was easy dismissal crossed with a shadow of fresh consideration perhaps, like blowing pollen every several minutes would blow up their unsuspecting noses and there would be a lean, a curl, a certain coloring to their digging that carried a rumor of something human and common.

Talking to various people during the next few weeks brought that same cross reference, especially from whites. The need to diminish, but at the same time, the need to put that in perspective, to claim after all that Jesse did "Have something."

At the convention however the speech was a blanket air that pinned all of us together in some posture. And those evaluations were paradigms for what I would encounter once I got back home. For the most advanced, the speech was a pastiche of everything Jesse had said during the primaries, except now he was intoning the tragic words, the invitation of public buggery that always prefaced the negro's rise to the bottom.

At the other end of the political spectrum mention of the speech brought religious ecstasy and demonstration of the power of zombification. One would see throughout the rest of the convention the ossification of the Rainbow into a transportable herd of Jessephiles, most who did not understand that Jesse had already given the farm away. The others were the opportunists who benefit from peoples' misinformation and pain.

One of the central topics that began to surface in the cross convention discussions was just who was it negotiating with the Democrats, if indeed negotiations were going on? Since the whole credibility of what Jesse was doing hinged on just what he was gonna get. Since the independent posture the primaries fostered had been generally if not totally dispelled, what Jesse was gonna get, the payoff had taken up much of the conversation since. This was the essence of what Walter Fauntroy, long-time civil rights activist, was saying when I first ran into him. And a host of others, it was obsessional but right on it. What, indeed would be payment for giving up your self-determination? Even in the closed context of black American relationship to the major imperialist parties. You had to get something. So what was it you was getting? In exchange for us, in exchange for these peepas behinds which you done give to the man.

This was the essence of what Farrakhan was asking, and the dissenters at the split rally. The Dukakis negroes' press conference had even broken down into that. And Mayor Hatcher, an old friend since way back in '72 and the National Black Assembly meeting in Gary, had even put the whole discussion in perspective by citing what Dukakis could not do, legally, so we could think more clearly about what he needed to do. In terms of demonstrating to the African American community that our support for him was not just an act of giving up our self determination!

So it was one late night after many meetings that talking to an old political friend might give deeper insight into this whole process. This brother had been with Jesse since before Gary, in fact as far back as Operation Breadbasket, which was the Jesse breakoff Chicago hook-up ostensibly a SCLC chapter but mostly Jesse. Probably even back before that. But certainly when Hatcher became 1st black mayor of a major US city, this brother was there, and so was Jesse. That's when Jesse and Hatcher got tight as well.

But now in a discussion of what we was gonna get, or what Jesse was asking for and what it meant to the rest of us the brother started telling me that Jesse had gotten rid of all his old comrades in arms on his negotiating council with the white folks. He said the campaign structure had not only excised many of the old heads, but replaced them with folks who were almost the antithesis of what Jesse was saying earlier. The apotheosis of which was the white campaign manager, Gerald Austin, who personally fouled up a huge rally we put together at SUNY Stony Brook, in which several thousand students waited at the perimenter of our outside amphitheater while Gerald Austin, a few minutes before Jesse was to appear, and just a few miles away from Stony Brook decided not to bring Jesse in. He put out some garbage about Jesse being ill, but he had spoken at several stops on Long Island before the Stony Brook cancellation and a few stops afterwards.

This is the same manager who a few weeks after the convention was bragging about how much money he had made while he was in the campaign, but how he never believed in the campaign or agreed much with Jackson. But that the money had made it all worthwhile. One wants to know in the first place why was this dude even there? There are black electoral technicians across the country by now, who have been hugely successful. What is the Why? to that one wonders?

And now standing in the half lit rising quiet of last straggler hotel lobbies talking earnestly and quietly to an old friend, there is a sense of grim wonder. Is it a hollowness in us, that we cannot sustain what is required for our own self determination? What is it in a white campaign manager that says so much about the whole process of Jesse Jackson's run for president, once it really got to be that and his own mind was infected with that real fantasy, that he *was* running for president.

But it must be the Double Consciousness Du Bois spoke of, it cannot be anything else. So we must embrace any poisonous confection as "good for us" when actually it's good for somebody else, it's just that we're seeing the world through that somebody else's eyes and not our own. Otherwise the question of

Self Determination would be less misunderstood among us, and there would be less "misdefining" it so it seemed fantastic or oppressive to somebody else, or generally without merit.

So now I was being told that Jesse had stripped his inner circle of those forces who knew him from the Gary/Black Power days. From the days when Jesse had risen in the National Black Convention making a resolution that the assembled pursue the idea of putting together a Black political party.

"Even Mayor Hatcher is gone now," the brother was telling me.

"Hatcher?" I couldn't believe it. There was nobody anywhere who was more of a Jesse supporter than Richard Hatcher of Gary, Indiana. In fact, in the last few years when one mentioned Hatcher, one thought of Jesse Jackson.

"Why?"

"They said he was 'too strident'," the brother was saying.

"Too strident? What the hell you talking about? You know Hatcher, he doesn't even talk loud…"

"Well, that's what they said…He was too strident."

"Who the hell said that?"

"Bentsen," the brother said, and this was someone who certainly would know.

"Bentsen?" I remember there in the darkening hotel lobby I actually started to weep.

Had it gone that far? Was it really, literally about mass denial and opportunism, again? Surely Jesse could not stand up in front of these millions and be seen as the committer of such an outrage. Hatcher?

This is the first time I was given any rundown on Ron Brown, like Dukakis himself, a product of the Special Products Division of Teddy Kennedy, Inc. Any checkout of the RB vita will show that Ron ain't been around too many bloods in his rise to we know now. In Atlanta I simply wondered how he had got so far so fast, but with this fill in it became clearer. And certainly with Brown's helicopter like rise to Democratic party chairman, the plot not only thickened it congealed into something ugly and nasty.

But dig this, Brown is sent into Jesse's camp very late as the connection needed to raise up the Jackson (Negro & Black/Progressive) demands to the level of human understanding. All that grunting about Self Determination and Black Power wouldn't do. We all saw where that stuff leads. Next thing you know, niggers be walking around talking about what they think and shit…!

But then once Brown gets the colored imprimatur, viz the "wit Jesse" then he shows up as leading contender for the Dem party chair's job, whereupon the first thing he says is that he don't represent no niggers in the 1st place, never has and never will! Whew! Slick as a derringer.

Then we see him later speaking at the New Orleans summit a sad reprise of the '72 Gary convention and he is there selling the Democratic party and actually has the mammy tappin temerity to mention Fannie Lou Hamer's name and how he is standing on her shoulders. No, he is defiling her memory and insulting all the rest of us, that's what he doin.

To add insult to injury the Lefts I had been running with sent a person to see me saying they had to talk to me. There was some further bric-a-brac through a phone call, and finally late late at night they, about five, arrived at my room for pow wow. From the outset of the convention I had not been close to them. Their whole stance seemed to me too much of a tail of the tail on the stumbling racist donkey. And this after years of struggling with them to see that electoral politics is relevant in the U.S., that it is a suitable arena for the genuine Left. That this is bourgeois democracy, unlike China or Russia. And that the legal struggle, voting &c., as Mao taught must be carried all the way to the end. For instance all these black mayors and black politicians ought at least to be passing Anti-Klan laws in these cities of black plurality and majority and even where we are the minority. They should be passing Anti-Racism laws, making it a jail offense with a fine, say, for practicing racism. Even the calling of names should be treated like assault, and the Anti-Racism law would see to these folk doing some time. I mean it is absurd to me for people to talk about revolution and can't even elect someone to a local school board!

But climbing into the dirty arena of bourgeois politics, whether electoral politics or trade union work does not mean you are converted to bourgeois politics. But so much like the classic definition of the middle class, these folk were going from one extreme to another, just like an unbalanced middle.

So now fresh from nixing electoral politics altogether for the last eight years they now wanted to worship the sacred behind of political mediocrity. At the '80 convention in San Francisco they were made tail-ready, and now here they sat trying to get me, in the name of "democratic centralism" to turn into the tail's tail, and they themselves had become sad tales of opportunism.

The gist of their jive was that now they would not nominate Jesse as Vice President. Their evaluation of the Dukakis-Bentsen nausea was that the main tails were going to get Bentsen to change his position on some of the key issues. For instance they thought that he would change his position on Contra aid as well as aid for the notorious South African puppet Jonas Savimbi.

As far as tailing the tail the transformation was almost complete. The group sat there trying to convince me that being a tail's tail was revolutionary work.

I caught up to Jesse that next day finally at an SCLC event at one of the hotels, presided over by Rev Lowery, SCLC's current president. The dais bristled with SCLC bigshots, plus Ben Hooks, head of the NAACP.

Waiting for Jesse to enter, I went up to the dais to talk to Hooks and Lowery. I asked about the tv program where Dukakis came to speak after the Bentsen nomination and missed phone message racism. Hooks had maintained his invitation to Dukakis for this major NAACP function and many black people criticized him for it. Many even carried signs at the dinner itself criticizing Dukakis and putting Jesse's name forward. So many that Hooks had to scatter them to save a little face.

But Hooks had made some statement in his introduction that his constituency wanted Jesse but that Bentsen should not fear because they were open minded, &c. That was smooth, I began, how you handled the Dukakis appearance at your dinner. Hooks was acknowledging his smoothness when Lowery piped in, "That's because he's such an expert at Tomming. . . ." Lowery was cracking up.

"But I learned everything I know about Tomming from you, Reverend." And the laughter got bigger. It was all loose and friendly, but at the same time there was a worn out spot of contention lingering easy to spot, from several paces away.

These were rivals, contenders, in a sense. And they both reveled in the fact of their being that, that there was such a field in which to "rival" each other, but at the same time each had a body of real experience and information about the world, and a serious position in human society to show for it.

I suppose also, since I was a licensed militant, this was Lowery keeping his franchise warm at Hooks' expense. Though it should be said now, that given the nature of that gathering, Jesse coming to claim the ex officio throne of SCLC, not any formal position, simply the most worshipful spot, Hooks acquitted himself one of the bunch in a way I hadn't known. After Lowery and Fauntroy singing his standard, "The Impossible Dream" and Rev Willie Barrow, Jesse's associate preacher at PUSH and before that Operation Breadbasket, Hooks came on like Zora Neale's Rev Lovelace. Mean he actually, like they say, low down preached. But then he knew that he was setting the stage for Jesse.

When Jesse came in. I was making all kinds of gestures and sending notes telling him I wanted to talk to him, and finally though I could see he did not seem particularly overjoyed about it he was nodding his head from the stage up and down, yes.

Secret Service folk were collected like they do. And after Jesse's speech getting up through them to the stage was a major piece of work. We shot out the back door, and while photographers were taking his picture, a large group of note employees, kitchen workers, waiters, all gathered in the tiny space just behind the hotel where we stood as Jesse's picture got taken. Jesse was posing and didn't see them at first, but I pointed at the people there and he turned and lit up like a Christmas tree. He began talking to these people, answering questions, the cameramen snapping away. And it was real, 1st that the black masses do or did adore Jesse. I say did because I do not think that adoration is as high today as it was before the Dukakis insult or before the convention. 2nd, Jesse does genuinely feel what he says when he would sing out, "Yes, you domestic workers, truck drivers, cab drivers, waiters, workers on the assembly line, when I get to be president, you'll have a friend in the white house!"

And that is a powerful implication in this land of corporate domination and workers exploitation, for a presidential candidate to say and *mean* that . . . a friend in the white house for working people, particularly black working people. And gradually over the campaign when the zig zag smoke screen of color was occasionally pierced, you could hear the establishment complaining as much about Jesse's "leftist—radical—non-mainstream" position on the issues as about his color. It was Paul Robeson, I think who summed up his position, and the position of black activists in U.S. society in general, saying, "Two things the establishment doesn't like about me are my nationality and my opinions!"

But it was just this legitimate and authentic relationship between the black masses and Jesse Jackson that was his real strength, no matter what the dull candidates or the corporate stooge media had to say. From Super Tuesday on, all the black masses wanted was someone to stand up for them or stand up with them. Someone to speak on their behalf, some leader who genuinely had their interests, all of our interests at heart.

And Jesse has always had the problem of balancing his genuine feeling for black people with his own personal needs and projection. He said elsewhere he wanted to be a workhorse not a showhorse. But how to keep those priorities and principles on top and straight ahead, not compromised into submission and nonexistence. This is one of the abiding contentions about Jesse, that his candidacy this last time had seemed to put to rest. So that even though the "hustler" slander was dropped on Jackson by the legalized dope now in the white house, made you wanna call his momma the real hustler, still to be for real that put down has plagued Jesse since Operation Breadbasket.

And the question now was how did all this get finally to be about the Democratic party? It didn't begin about them. Certainly in the 1972 Gary Convention, calling for a black political party, it wasn't about the Democrats or the Republicans, it was about Self Determination for the African American people. This is the question that was rising through that community now: was there something Jesse was getting to go along with Dukakis and company? Dukakis had been nominated and aside from Jesse's speech, a glittering anthology of Jesse's greatest hits, what had we gotten? Had Jesse gotten something, and the rest of us, as usual (like the Democratic convention in Miami in 1972, or any other time) been left in the dust blown up by our politicians gum bumping?

And now tonight, the vice presidential showdown was roaring towards us. What would Jesse do now, where would all of us be, as a result of this? These things were blowing through my mind as I stood watching Jesse be photographed with the workers exchanging words and banterings in a kind of breathless joy.

In the limousine, with Jesse and Ron Walters, the Howard University political science teacher, and one of Jesse's key advisors as well as an old comrade in struggle from the National Black Assembly, and Walter Fauntroy. I rode in the jump seat facing Jesse, my questions scrawled on a steno notebook. This was going to be the interview, on the way to wherever on Jackson's monstrous schedule.

Nothing was said directly about last night's intro to Mainstream American Mythology via the speech or its fallout. Although the 1st ecstasies were already giving way to a coarser evaluation in terms of the old form vs content saw. As the car sped through downtown Atlanta, people recognizing Jesse and the ss folk in their accompanying cars would smile and wave, or jump up and down and point, or stare relevantly.

I had to talk fast because of the way this was going down. In the car on the way to somewhere else. I came on like a reporter, Essence Magazine, the magazine for Black Women. Although our relationship, all of us in the car, could not be leapfrogged so that the dialogue was completely tactful or completely tactless. "What effect do you think Dukakis' naming of Bentsen as his vice presidential running mate will have on black voters?"

All of us had thrown that question around, and had come up with many answers. Even in the Black Dukakis Democrat press conference I had asked that. That night when Dan Rostenkowski, the Chicago congressman was begging for white Democrats to come back and I had sneaked up behind Moynihan and asked him if he thought that strategy would work? His "We think so", sounded extremely white breadish.

Our opening cross banter had centered directly on What was we gonna get, as a very fat and bottom line question I had relayed to him directly from the folk. So as I whipped out the pad and told him I had about four solid questions I wanted to ask. He began by answering the exchange knowing exactly what was on my mind. "You know the question in the street is what are we gonna get, what is Dukakis gonna give up in exchange for our support?"

"Well, you know it can't all come out, and a lot of people don't understand the process of political negotiations. But we have got something, something real. For instance, Conyers' On site voter registration bill was passed (in the Democratic platform committee) you know that is important, and will put thousands of new voters on the books, bring thousands of new Democrats into the fold."

He talked about this bill as if I didn't know that Conyers had put this together as far back as the 1972 convention. In fact as he cited the legislative pluses black folks were receiving I was struck by how much of it did come right out of that historical 1972 meeting of 8000 black people. It also brought Dick Hatcher back to my mind, and my own tears of the night before.

"The Dellums South African sanctions. This would knock 50 to 100 billion dollars out of that racist economy. That's what we can do.

"The D.C. bill will mean two senators from the District of Columbia, and thousands of jobs, and increase our ability to influence domestic and foreign policy."

"But what effect will Dukakis' choice of Bentsen, someone directly opposed to both these planks, and a whole lot of other things you've talked about have on black people?"

"Dukakis will have to earn black people's vote. I earned it. I convinced them I would represent their interests. But Dukakis will have to go to the areas. Gain a certain comfort level. Learn to speak to black people..."

I wanted to press him on the main question. "But what about the Vice Presidency. A lot of people want you to be nominated, think that's the only way we would a real voice..."

Jesse did not pause, "If I run tonight (for VP nomination) I would win."

So it was not that he didn't think he could win. I thought perhaps it was that...

"But win in July lose in November..."

It sounded now like he had put both feet down in the Democrat party ark.

"You wouldn't run independently? People don't know anything about any Bentsen."

"Bentsen would be able to recover lost Democrats. I have a block of voters, *assured*. He has to revive his."

Yes, now its clear we both know that. And the others riding in the car. And a whole bunch of other folks. So why this direction, this going along with the Donkeys?

"But we have a legislative agenda. Bentsen in the senate supporting D.C. statehood. Things do change. His record does make us uneasy. But we think we can get him to pledge no Contra aid (in Nicaragua) and the support of D.C. statehood. It would mean a net shift of 2 senate votes. That's real power.

"Plus, you don't make Thursday decisions on Sunday. We have to deal with now. The power available now. And we have to use it in a mature way. Zogman raising the Palestinian question. So that becomes a reality on the planks. We can get support on that now. There's a price for winning."

"But talking about Bentsen. Suppose the Democrats lose in November, anyway?"

Without batting an eye, "If the Democrats lose in November, I'm running in 92."

"But don't you think the Vice Presidential nomination would be a means of consolidating some real power?"

"I'm not encouraging the Vice Presidential nomination." This was an absolute reversal of what the preening Lefts had told me previously. I was sure too that they knew it, that they had been told. And in response simply zipped up their tail suits all the way up around the ears and eyes.

Jesse was giving his justification. "That would play directly into Reagan & Bush's hands. I think its a political option we should avoid. We would have no access to Bush."

The question of What? jumped into my mouth again. But Jesse went on. "We have Democratic party leadership within our grasp. Eight at large seats on the Democratic National Committee Friday? Now that's different!" He was laughing and the rest in the car laughed. Different meaning that was real power, that was the great What?.

"Black folks gave the U.S. Senate back to the Democrats. We have to study politics as a science, not emotionally or romantically, or trading our integrity."

It seemed the last statement was aimed at not only the unhip black masses but for militants like your reporter who was still wanting to know what all this had to do with real self determination.

"But there has to be a tension between your platform planks and Bentsen's..."

"South Africa as a terrorist state." He was reciting the Whats? again. Conyers' Voter Registration bill. Make the anti terrorist bill applicable to South Africa. Companies can be ordered out of a terrorist state. We don't trade with a terrorist state. And all the definitions of a terrorist state must now apply to South Africa.

"Our plank about no first use of nuclear weapons. Our plank about fair taxes. Taxing the rich not the middle class and the poor. We're developing the power of negotiation. The tax plank is gaining favor with the convention. Eleven out of fourteen of the minority planks will be accepted. Eighty percent of our delegates have reached the convention. We have to show consistency not schizophrenia. But we have to be Eternally Vigilant," he was putting a heavy emphasis on it because we had reached the hotel. "Otherwise everything could turn into garbage. Any contract is only as good as your ability to enforce it."

There was more, ends and threads, in the main a boastful declaration that Yes, indeed, black people and progressive people were going to get something out of Jesse's decision to go along with the Democrats. It could even be rolled around in your mouth to sound like it had something to do with Black Power. But I felt nothing. I had been talking to a politician. One I had known a long time, one I even loved in many ways, but now what he said was not convincing to me. Also, I had noticed as the convention came up and certainly afterward on the confused trail toward the November election, Jesse talked less and less directly about the issues: Comprehensive Budget, Fair Taxes, Military Spending, The middle east, Central America, Africa, Women, Education, Health Care, and began to compact all of his inspirational platform to the throwaway slogan "Up with Hope, Down with Dope!" As if that was the key to black self determination and equality. As if it was crack that had brought us here on the slave ship. Dope that had stripped us of self determination and put us on plantations and now the big city ghettoes which were just continuations of the plantation slave quarters. As if it was dope that deprived us of education, employment, housing: dope that made us victims of police brutality and white supremacy.

Certainly in a Dukakis Bentsen world Jesse claiming he was the general in charge of the war on drugs was preferable to Jesse talking about the U.S. one sided pro-Israeli policy in the middle east, or U.S. corporate support for fascist South Africa or no contra aid. And Jesse had already begun to comply, at least it seemed that way to me and some of the other kindred sourpusses I held my non-stop discussions with.

Earlier in the year, in Iowa, Jesse had pleaded with me to come with his campaign, to be one of his fighters. I was one of his fighters, but I didn't think then I could be part of the campaign. I wondered what would have happened had I accepted his offer and worked with the campaign, I would suppose in the capacity of a writer and organizer. What would it have been like facing these questions with answers very different from the ones I was getting from Jesse? But that seemed a long time ago now, and our concerns had pushed us apart I thought. Was this same process going on with the large masses of black people? And how would that be registered?

With some more banter and back and forth and a promise to get back together I got out of the car with them at the Marriott and we went our separate ways. Tonight would spell it all out much more clearly.

So "tail" was the name of the game that black folks and the Rainbow were supposed to play. I had heard it from the horse's mouth. However it was described to me, what it still seemed like was like those slaves before they let us fight in the civil war trailing behind Sherman's soldiers. They thought that was the safest place.

Even worse, the so called Left had approached me late that night, even after my weeping fit over Hatcher and in a tiresome and chauvinist display of opportunism demanded allegiance from me to their careerist cavorting. Since the chosen few of these folks had already gotten jobs with the campaign or elsewhere the Rainbow touched and these jobs seemed their goal, their reinforced importance.

At one point I wanted to know why only the nonblack folks had gotten such jobs, but that is the subject of another very serious contemplation. I asked at another point what did they think the Palestinians must think of these so called progressives who openly betrayed them on the floor and agreed not to raise the Palestinian question, so as not to upset the backward racists who ran the Democratic party. "The Palestinians agreed", they shot.

"The Palestinians got a bourgeoisie too." was all I could say. Even as oppressed, even as the African American people were oppressed and still at the same time had a bourgeoisie like as not willing to joyfully cavort with the instruments of their oppression squealing with bought pleasure.

What it all did reveal was that already there was a built in lie for this truth we sought. Just as in every development of black music, there was always a commercial shadow, a paid lie to cover it, to hide the history and meaning, the philosophy of that aesthetic that might help change the whole society, so Jesse's campaign, the rainbow, all of it, already had a coopt factor, a false aspect, a contradiction, that grew up with it, that would try to make us believe that there was nothing possible but nothing and as usual, our enemies owned that, and would give us a taste if we promised to play dead.

At the convention the next night I went from delegation to delegation pushing the line of nominating Jesse for VP and thus overturning the sad line of cooptation and opportunism white supremacy had put together for us to swallow.

I went to those delegations that had the largest concentrations of black people. And from each almost in rote I heard, "Jesse told us not to". Just as he said he had. Urging them to nominate him anyway did no good. From Jersey, New York, Mississippi, South Carolina, Michigan, on and on, came the same answer.

"If you ever see me one night dead drunk and naked walking up the middle of the street babbling out of my mind", I told two ranking folks in the New Jersey delegation and some of the New York folks who were passing anti-UNITA leaflets around, as opposition to Bentsen's pro-UNITA, pro-Savimbi (a South African puppet) position, "Take me inside, off the street, no matter what I tell you, hear?"

But then there are street coaches of drunken naked foolishness, who are slick tonight, who sparkle tonight, whose names are colored names, whose skin is colored, whose teeth are very white though and send signals to their masters on call. Look, they are here amongst us shaking hands, skinning and grinning, clean as new money. There as Wonder Woman tries to sing "...the rocket's red glare" while Donna Felisa Rincon de Gautier, former mayor of San Juan, awaits to be recognized. While George McGovern whiffs and pumps like speech after the medley by the high school bands. The Democrats are using John Philip Sousa so we will not understand at first that these are not picnic band songs but the invitation to the same conflagration "The Reag" urges us to. Picnic Martial.

Negroes named Ron and Willie and Sharon and Charlie and Percy have our lives in their hands amongst the Babbits who look like Donald Sutherland as elegant yuppie of the breadbasket. There's Bill Bradley a jock yup, he's a good guise used to play remember with the nigs. Hey, and there's Superman, I mean Clark Kent, uh, Gore in mufti glowing like an ubermensch.

Then Barbara Jordan in to praise Bentsen and the Democrats her elegant baritone now somewhat shaky, beaming on the 100 foot screen. Two weeks later she almost died from the effort.

"Barbara, Barbara," they're calling. I'm standing among a group of para-plegics in wheelchairs poised at the edge of the huge crowd.

She sounds like Jesse, like what is rhetorically appropriate, "We must take the moral highground. Lloyd Bentsen is sensible, logical, rational...We must temper our emotions"

James Forman talks to me like a distant ghost. He is saying, "Support the party..." I'd wanted a hotdog, and there was a line. But "...the party"? No, he'd said, "...the ticket." But there was no ticket.

Jesse had told me, "Imamu, there's no room..." And it was not just to me he was talking.

Forman was saying, "I support Dukakis because of his firm position on peace in Central America." This was an old comrade in struggle. He was smil-ing like it beat memory away from him, in stiff stubborn geometrical curves. Walking away he was even more shadowy, and I loved him for it, for just being in the lobby fading into the hotdog buyers and not on the starry platform among the Dutch Moriels and Tom Bradleys. There's my old friend Micky Leland, Texas congressman, used to be in the N.B.A. He's introducing...

Maybe it was Senator Glenn who said the separation of church and state was what the people needed not Matthew, Mark, Luke and John as interpreted by Bush, Meese and Reagan...Swaggart and Baker. He said "if they wanted more years maybe they could get ten to twenty"

That was funny, but I forget just how it was said. There were billions of red, white and blue balloons, crepe paper, signs, hats, raps, images, and most of all lies. Swinging, being blown and waved. Covering the truth then being the truth. There was nothing else. That was the truth. The black people mostly grinned and were beat down overwhelmed by the cardboard box and ribbon, the noise makers and their brothers and sisters clean as Ho's teeth in charge of the charge backwards.

And finally that is what it was, by the Democratic party certainly and by those black folks charged by us all with coming away with some direction some indication some clue as to where we move for self determination, without which there is no democracy.

Throughout the night both lifting toward the Bentsen bomb, his appearance, Rostenkowski heralded at least as vulgar as the racism that made it necessary, and all that came after, heading toward the supposed orgasm of Dukakis coming, live, it all seemed a rising tinsel of swelling scream, but on a tin horn. A cheap horn. Maybe because of the endless J. P. Sousa caress that makes all thought cheap.

And I had already seen on the front page of the Atlanta newspaper young black militants crying when Jesse spoke, and I knew if you talked to them about it they would have explanations. A shrug that acknowledged raw emotion and back-handed political clarity and principle. But this was this time and not another. A time when backwardness clogged all entrances and only death was alive and well.

I remember Ted Kennedy and the balloons being released. A stage full of banners and big Jennifer Holliday singing The Battle Hymn of the Republic. Jackie Jackson inside the sea of flags and Jesse next to Mrs. Bentsen. And Mike and Kitty looking at each other. I remember Jesse's family arrayed the night he spoke the deference to the children yet it is not too out of line to suggest that the worst weight of all this long march has been on his wife. You could see it when you talked to her and when you saw her that night on tv, or this night among the white stars of this tacky firmament.

And then Dukakis was speaking. He was laying out his cold curt remedy for paper illness and paper regard. His cold cereal and cold supper. Of high standards and justice of the Ayatollah and Bentsen and Jesse's children being intelligent (unlike most of black ours!) and of his new grandchildren and of Bush and Reagan and of a new era of greatness in America, which now we know is to be drum majored in by Bush and Quayle, when here we thought vaudeville was over a long time ago.

Dukakis was saying, "We will never bring disgrace upon this country, by any act of dishonesty and cowardice…" but hadn't it all been done already? It was dishonest to suggest that Dukakis was a better candidate than Jackson and it was cowardly for the party not to acknowledge Jesse as a legitimate Vice Presidential candidate. And since Jesse insists on valorizing the Dems with his "me too" ism he is implicated as well.

The question of a black presidential candidate and even a black president is not so much at issue as the question of black democracy, self determination and equality in the United States. The ex slave is still displaced after emancipation and without reconstruction The 30,000,000 African Americans still have not even a representative in the Senate, though many now question whether there should even be a senate with two senators for Utah as well as New York, that's hardly one man one vote.

Jesse's decision to go along with the Democratic party's description of him as a non-being means that the will and self determination of the African American people is still being suffocated under the weight of white supremacy.

The peculiar description of Jesse's role during the Dukakis-Bush campaign, problematical and racially polarized is clear indication of this. Jesse's retreat from the issues to just the servant's yodel of "Up with Hope, Down with Dope" is more.

But our push for Jesse is part of our push for ourselves. We do not just want another famous Negro famous for being with white folks. We want democracy in America, we want equality. Jesse represented our desire for Self Determination, the shaping of our own lives with the same opportunity possessed by any other American. But Jesse's great run ended with the ignominious confirmation of our continued slavery. The convention finally, I could understand, was just the big house during a holiday season. And now the house negroes did sing and dance and clap their hands. And were it not for the fact that there was an outside to the house, and the night real and moving away in all directions, in which real people lived and desired, all of those goings on would not seem like utter foolishness. But there is, and they did.

July 1988–June 1989, Atlanta/Newark

Wise 10

So in 1877 the lie grew
we all knew
the heart dead
the lie instead

They talked blood
They put on hoods
They paid for murder
They closed the books

No democracy
No light
primitive times
returned

across the road
the horse men prowled
American guns for African American lives

You'll never vote
you'll never grow
you'll never never never
be free   never
be free

        never

be free
          never
          never
          never
                    Enter Booker T.

Rough Hand Dreamers (Wise 11)

You was a country folk, on the
land. Farmers before farmers
founders of cities, ile ife,
where the world began. Was creator
of university, I trumpet timbuctoo
because I cannot bear to think
you think Banneker was wilder
than the breed. It was the woman
conceived of familiar cows and
architecture. Yon drummers know
how they are hide curers & musicians.
Now they enter the cities to enter future
reality. Now death, now blood, now hooded
criminals, resistance in its human dimension
like electric theories, post all abrahams.

What was it we wanted = Ourselves!
And why? We had been inside others being alive
for nothing
and worked to death
          our murders
          were circuses
          our murderers
          something like
          clowns

A farmer come to the city (Wise 12)

dirt growing in his mind
songs black land come in to
curl your poetry blind.
Banjo

waves and sinking bones
play eyes on sky
blood music

heaven people
say see heaven
they seeing
up side down

now they say we fought for evil
took our guns, the wise ones hid, say you
never was to be here
you never was to be

kept to edge of city
alleys behind the bossman's
house. got a job, you got a space,
you got a bond to heal your face

changed from slave
to convict, gone
from lazy to vagrant
jail lost boy in sleep
jail house/plantation moan
jail, was how they changed it
we
vote among roaches

Wise 13

And now you know
how "ghettoes"
grow

                                                 (you knew
                                                 (how ghettoes)
                                                 grew?   )

                        (Reality
                            for "you"
                    is minstrelsy.)

Acknowledgments

Angelou, Maya. Excerpts from I KNOW WHY THE CAGED BIRD SINGS by Maya Angelou, copyright © 1969 and renewed 1997 by Maya Angelou. Used by permission of Random House, Inc.

Asante, Molefi. Molefi Asante, from AFROCENTRICITY, Africa World Press, 1988, Ch. 2, "The Constituents of Power," pp. 31–43. Reproduced with the permission of Africa World Press, Trenton, New Jersey.

Baldwin, James. Excerpted from "Down at the Cross: Letter from a Region in My Mind," originally published in THE NEW YORKER. Collected in THE FIRE NEXT TIME © 1962, 1963 by James Baldwin. Copyright renewed. Published by Vintage Books. Reprinted by arrangement with the James Baldwin Estate.

Baldwin, James. Excerpted from NO NAME IN THE STREET © 1972 by James Baldwin, copyright renewed. Reprinted by arrangement with the James Baldwin Estate.

Baraka, Amiri. "The Slave" from THE DUTCHMAN AND THE SLAVE by Amiri Baraka. Reprinted by permission of Sterling Lord Literistic, Inc. Copyright 1964 by Amiri Baraka.

Baraka, Amiri. From the book, THE LeROI JONES/AMIRI BARAKA READER by Amiri Baraka. Copyright © 1991, 2000 by Amiri Baraka. Appears by permission of the publisher, Thunder's Mouth Press.

Brooks, Gwendolyn. Gwendolyn Brooks, "Riot" from BLACKS is reprinted by permission of The Estate of Gwendolyn Brooks.

Bullard, Robert. From DUMPING IN DIXIE, 2/E by Robert Bullard. Copyright © 1990 by Westview Press. Reprinted by permission of Westview Press, a member of Perseus Books, L.L.C.

Carmichael, Stokely. From STOKELY SPEAKS by Stokely Carmichael, copyright © 1965, 1971 by Stokely Carmichael. Used by permission of Alfred A. Knopf, a division of Random House, Inc.

Cleaver, Eldridge. Eldridge Cleaver, excerpts from SOUL ON ICE, © 1968. Reproduced with permission of The McGraw-Hill Companies.

Clifton, Lucille. Lucille Clifton, "the lost baby poem" from GOOD WOMAN: POEMS AND A MEMOIR 1969–1980. Copyright © 1987 by Lucille Clifton. Reprinted with the permission of BOA Editions, Ltd.

Clifton, Lucille. Lucille Clifton, "move" from THE BOOK OF LIGHT. Copyright © 1993 by Lucille Clifton. Reprinted with the permission of Copper Canyon Press, P.O. Box 271, Port Townsend, WA 98368-0271.

Cruse, Harold. Pp. 347–73 from THE CRISIS OF THE NEGRO INTELLECTUAL by Harold Cruse. Copyright © 1967 by Harold Cruse. Reprinted by permission of HarperCollins Publishers Inc., William Morrow.

Davis, Angela. "Race and Criminalization: Black Americans and the Punishment Industry" © 1997 by Angela Y. Davis, from THE HOUSE THAT RACE BUILT by Wahneema Lubiano, copyright © 1997 by Wahneema Lubiano. Used by permission of Pantheon Books, a division of Random House, Inc.

Davis, Angela Y. "The Anti-Slavery Movement and the Birth of Women's Rights," from WOMEN, RACE AND CLASS by Angela Davis, copyright © 1981 by Angela Davis. Used by permission of Random House, Inc.

Davis, David Brion. Excerpt from THE PROBLEM OF SLAVERY IN THE AGE OF REVOLUTION by David Brion Davis, copyright © 1999 by David Brion Davis. Used by permission of Oxford University Press, Inc.

Du Bois, W. E. B. "American Negroes and Africa's Rise to Freedom" orig. published 1958, reprinted in W. E. B. DU BOIS READER, Jack B. Moore, ed., MacMillan, 1971, pp. 12–17. Reprinted by permission of The Gale Group.

DuBois, W. E. B. W. E. B. Du Bois, "Trasubstantiation of a Poor White" is reprinted with the permission of Scribner, a Division of Simon & Schuster from BLACK RECONSTRUCTION IN AMERICA, 1860–1880 by W. E. B. Du Bois. Copyright 1935, 1962 by W. E. Burghardt Du Bois.

Evans, Mari. Mari Evans, "I am a Black Woman" from I AM A BLACK WOMAN (New York: William Morrow & Company, 1970). Copyright © 1970 by Mari Evans. Reprinted by permission of the author.

Fisher, Rudolf. Rudolf Fisher, "The Caucasian Storms Harlem," AMERICAN MERCURY, Vol. XI (August 1927).

Garvey, Marcus. Marcus Garvey, "The Future as I See It" is reprinted with the permission of Scribner, a Division of Simon & Schuster from PHILOSOPHY AND OPINIONS OF MARCUS GARVEY edited by Amy Jacques-Garvey. Copyright © 1923, 1925 Amy Jacques-Garvey.

Gayle, Jr., Addison. "Cultural Strangulation: Black Literature and the 'White Aesthetic'" © 1971 by Addison Gayle, Jr. First appeared in THE BLACK AESTHETIC. Reprinted by permission of Marie Brown Associates.

Greenlee, Sam. Sam Greenlee, THE SPOOK WHO SAT BY THE DOOR, Wayne State University Press, 1969, Ch. 12, pp. 134–146. Reprinted by permission of Lawrence Jordan Agency, 345 West 121st Street, New York, NY 10027.

Harding, Vincent. Vincent Harding, pp. 11–14, Ch. 3, "Laying the Foundation in North America," from THE OTHER AMERICAN REVOLUTION, Center for Afro-American Studies, University of California, Los Angeles, and Institute of the Black World, Atlanta, Georgia, 1980. Reprinted by permission.

Himes, Chester. From the book IF HE HOLLERS LET HIM GO by Chester Himes. Copyright © 1986 by Thunder's Mouth Press. Appears by permission of the publisher, Thunder's Mouth Press.

Hughes, Langston. "Goodbye Christ"; "Air Raid Over Harlem"; "The Negro Speaks of Rivers"; "The Weary Blues"; "Come to the Waldorf-Astoria"; "Ballad of Roosevelt"; "Harlem (1)"; "Ballad of the Landlord"; "The Backlash Blues"; "Bombings in Dixie" from THE COLLECTED POEMS OF LANGSTON HUGHES by Langston Hughes, copyright © 1994 by The Estate of Langston Hughes. Used by permission of Alfred A. Knopf, a division of Random House, Inc.

Hurston, Zora Neale. "The Gilded Six-Bits" as taken from THE COMPLETE STORIES by Zora Neale Hurston. Introduction copyright © 1995 by Henry Louis Gates, Jr. and Sieglinde Lemke. Compilation copyright © 1995 by Vivian Bowden, Lois J. Hurston Gaston, Clifford Hurston, Lucy Ann Hurston, Winifred Hurston Clark, Zora Mack Goins, Edgar Hurston, Sr., and Barbara Hurston Lewis. Afterword and Bibliography copyright © 1995 by Henry Louis Gates. Reprinted by permission of HarperCollins Publishers Inc.

James, C.L.R. C.L.R. James, excerpt from pp. 6–18 from THE BLACK JACOBINS. Reproduced with permission of Curtis Brown Ltd, London on behalf of The Estate of C.L.R. James. Copyright © C.L.R. James 1936, 1963, 1980.

Kelley, Robin D. G. From YO' MAMA'S DISFUNKTIONAL by Robin D.G. Kelley. Copyright © 1997 by Robin D.G. Kelley. Reprinted by permission of Beacon Press, Boston.

King, Jr., Martin Luther. Martin Luther King, Jr., "Letter from Birmingham Jail" is reprinted by arrangement with The Heirs to the Estate of Martin Luther King, Jr., c/o Writers House, Inc. as agent for the proprietor. Copyright 1963 by Martin Luther King, Jr., copyright renewed 1991 by Coretta Scott King.

Lorde, Audre. "Power," from THE BLACK UNICORN by Audre Lorde. Copyright © 1978 by Audre Lorde. Used by permission of W. W. Norton & Company, Inc.

Malcolm X. Malcolm X, from MALCOLM X: THE LAST SPEECHES, Pathfinder Press, 1989, "Not just an American problem, but a world problem," pp. 151–181. Copyright © 1989 by Betty Shabazz and Pathfinder Press. Reprinted by permission.

Marable, Manning. Manning Marable, from BEYOND BLACK AND WHITE, Verso 1995, pp. 194–202, 216–229. Reprinted by permission of Verso Books, London.

McKay, Claude. Claude McKay, "If we must die"; "The White House"; "To the white fiends"; "America" from THE SELECTED POEMS OF CLAUDE McKAY. Courtesy of the Literary Representatives for the Works of Claude McKay, Schomburg Center for Research in Black Culture, The New York Public Library, Astor, Lenox and Tilden Foundations.

Morrison, Derrick. Derrick Morrison, "The Combined Character of the Coming American Revolution" from BLACK LIBERATION AND SOCIALISM (Tony Thomas, ed.), Pathfinder Press, 1974, pp. 21–32. Copyright © 1974 by Pathfinder Press. Reprinted by permission.

Persons, Georgia. Ch. 3, "Black Mayoralties and the New Black Politics: From Insurgency to Racial Reconciliation," pp. 38–65 from DILEMMAS OF BLACK POLITICS by Georgia A. Persons. Copyright © 1993 by HarperCollins College Publishers. Reprinted by permission of Pearson Education, Inc.

Reed, Jr., Adolph. Adolph Reed, Jr., "Demobilization in the New Black Political Regime" in Michael Peter Smith and Joe R. Feagin, eds., THE BUBBLING CAULDRON: RACE, ETHNICITY AND THE URBAN CRISIS (University of Minnesota Press 1995), pp. 182–210. Copyright © 1995 by University of Minnesota Press. Reprinted by permission.

Rogers, Carolyn M. "And When the Revolution Came," from HOW I GOT OVAH by Carolyn M. Rodgers, copyright © 1968, 1969, 1970, 1971, 1972, 1973, 1975 by Carolyn M. Rodgers. Used by permission of Doubleday, a division of Random House, Inc.

Rose, Tricia. Tricia Rose, from BLACK NOISE, Wesleyan University Press, 1994, "Voices from the Margins: Rap Music and Contemporary Black Cultural Production," pp. 1–20. Reprinted by permission of Wesleyan University Press.

Sanchez, Sonia. From the book **homegirls and handgrenades** by Sonia Sanchez. Copyright
© 1984 by Sonia Sanchez. Appears by permision of the publisher, Thunder's Mouth
Press.

Seale, Bobby. Bobby Seale, "The Panther Program" and "Why We Are Not Racists" from
SEIZE THE TIME, Random House, 1970, pp. 59–72. Reprinted by permission of
Bobby Seale, founding chairman and National Organizer of the Black Panther Party,
1966–1974. Email: ReachBS@msn.com

Shakur, Sanyika. From MONSTER: THE AUTOBIOGRAPHY OF AN L.A. GANG
MEMBER by Kody Scott (Sanyika Shakur). Copyright © 1993 by Kody Scott. Used by
permission of Grove/Atlantic, Inc.

Smith, Earl. Earl Smith, "African American Intercollegiate Athletes" is reprinted by
permission of the author.

Spero, Sterling D. & Harris, Abram L. From THE BLACK WORKER by Sterling D. Spero
and Abram L. Harris. Copyright 1931 by Columbia University Press. Reprinted by
permission of the publisher.

West, Cornel. Cornel West, KEEPING FAITH, Ch. 5, "The Dilemma of the Black
Intellectual," pp. 67–85, Routledge, 1993. Reprinted by permission.

Wilson, William Julius. William Julius Wilson, excerpt from THE DECLINING
SIGNIFICANCE OF RACE, The University of Chicago Press, 1978, Ch. 6, "Protests,
Politics, and the Changing Black Class Structure," pp. 122–143. Copyright © 1978 by
The University of Chicago Press. Reprinted by permission of The University of
Chicago Press.

Wright, Richard. Richard Wright, Ch. 2, "Tradition and Industrialization" from WHITE
MAN LISTEN!, pp. 74–104, Doubleday 1957. Copyright © 1957 by Richard Wright.
Reprinted by permission of John Hawkins & Associates, Inc.

Zinn, Howard. Pages 167–77 from A PEOPLE'S HISTORY OF THE UNITED STATES by
Howard Zinn. Copyright © 1980 by Howard Zinn. Reprinted by permission of
HarperCollins Publishers, Inc.

Index